ABA·LSAC

OFFICIAL GUIDE

TO ABA-APPROVED LAW SCHOOLS™

2013 EDITION

Produced by the Law School Admission Council and the American Bar Association Section of Legal Education and Admissions to the Bar

The Law School Admission Council (LSAC) is a nonprofit corporation that provides unique, state-of-the-art admission products and services to ease the admission process for law schools and their applicants worldwide. More than 200 law schools in the United States, Canada, and Australia are members of the Council and benefit from LSAC's services.

Library of Congress Catalog Number:

ISBN-13: 978-0-9846360-4-4

ISBN-10: 0-9846360-4-8

ISSN: 1534-3502

LSAC fees, policies, and procedures relating to, but not limited to, test registration, test administration, test score reporting, misconduct and irregularities, Credential Assembly Service (CAS), and other matters may change without notice at any time. Up-to-date LSAC policies and procedures are available at LSAC.org.

Descriptive information about the law schools in this work, including such information and data published in electronic form, is provided by the individual schools. Neither the ABA nor LSAC assumes any responsibility for inaccuracies or for changes in such information that may occur after publication. Questions regarding the accuracy or currency of any such descriptive information should be addressed to the specific law school.

TABLE OF CONTENTS

- Introduction i
- Chapter 1: Being a Lawyer 1
- Chapter 2: Becoming a Lawyer 4
- Chapter 3: The Law School Admission Process 9
- Chapter 4: Applying to Law School 13
- Chapter 5: Choosing a Law School 16
- Chapter 6: Opportunities in Law for Minority Men and Women 21
  - Key Facts for Minority Law School Applicants 22
- Chapter 7: The Accreditation Process 31
- Chapter 8: Pro Bono Legal Services 34
- Chapter 9: Financing Your Legal Education 35
- Chapter 10: Finding a Job 38
- Chapter 11: Geographic Guide to Law Schools in the United States (by region) ... 40
- Chapter 12: Key Facts About ABA-Approved Law Schools 50
  - Admission Data 50
  - Students, Faculty, Tuition 56
- Chapter 13: ABA-Approved Law Schools 63
  (Note: To locate page numbers for individual law schools, refer to the chart on pages 56–62.)
- Appendix A: Legal Education Statistics 864
- Appendix B: Post-JD and Non-JD Programs 867
- Appendix C: Other Organizations 877
- Appendix D: Canadian LSAC-Member Law Schools 879

The school-specific information contained in this edition of the *ABA-LSAC Official Guide to ABA-Approved Law Schools* was collected in 2011. Coverage dates vary within categories:

Bar Passage Data: First-time bar exam takers during the 2010 calendar year.
Academic Attrition: Based on Fall 2010 enrollment.
GPA and LSAT Scores: Fall 2011 entering class.
JD degrees awarded: 2010–2011 academic year.
Tuition and Fees: 2011–2012 academic year.

INTRODUCTION

The *Official Guide to ABA-Approved Law Schools* is a joint effort of the Law School Admission Council (LSAC) and the American Bar Association Section of Legal Education and Admissions to the Bar (ABA).

The Law School Admission Council (LSAC) is a nonprofit corporation whose members are more than 200 law schools in the United States, Canada, and Australia. Headquartered in Newtown, PA, USA, the Council was founded in 1947 to facilitate the law school admission process. The Council has grown to provide unique state-of-the-art admission products and services for law schools and for approximately 85,000 law school applicants each year.

All law schools approved by the American Bar Association (ABA) are LSAC members. Canadian law schools recognized by a provincial or territorial law society or government agency are also members. Accredited law schools outside of the US and Canada are eligible for membership at the discretion of the LSAC Board of Trustees; Melbourne Law School, the University of Melbourne is the first LSAC-member law school outside of North America.

As the largest professional organization in the world, the American Bar Association is the national voice of the legal profession. The Council and the Accreditation Committee of the Section of Legal Education and Admissions to the Bar of the ABA are identified by the US Department of Education as the nationally recognized accrediting agency for professional schools of law. As of March 2012, a total of 201 institutions are approved by the American Bar Association.

The information contained in this book is collected separately by the ABA and LSAC from the ABA-approved law schools that are also members of the Law School Admission Council. One ABA-approved law school, the US Army Judge Advocate General's School, is a specialized law school that is not a member of the Law School Admission Council (see page 31). The two organizations agreed to combine this wealth of information to provide a comprehensive resource for data and descriptions about ABA-approved law schools.

Although no book or website can substitute for direct contact with admission professionals at the law schools, faculty, students, alumni, and prelaw advisors, this guide can inform the process of deciding whether, and where, to attend law school. This guide is designed to provide prospective law school applicants with basic information in a simple format that will facilitate comparisons among schools. In addition to statistics on all ABA-approved law schools, this book contains information intended to help individuals prepare for the rigors and costs associated with attending law school.

The ABA collects quantitative data as part of the accreditation process using questionnaires completed annually during the fall academic semester. Standard 509 of the *Standards and Rules of Procedure for Approval of Law Schools*, as adopted by the ABA House of Delegates in August 1996, states: "A law school shall publish basic consumer information. The information shall be published in a fair and accurate manner reflective of actual practice."

The data collected in the ABA annual questionnaire and published in this guide satisfy a law school's obligation to provide basic consumer information under Standard 509. The data are certified as fair and accurate by the dean of the law school.

The Law School Admission Council collects admission profile data and school descriptions each fall as a service to its member schools and to prospective law school applicants. The information provided by the law schools to LSAC in no way affects the ABA accreditation process and is not meant to satisfy a law school's publication requirements under Standard 509.

Neither LSAC nor ABA condones, approves, or sanctions use of the data contained in this book to rank law schools. Both organizations disapprove of any and all rankings. The deans of 178 law schools have published the following statement regarding rankings:

> The idea that all law schools can be measured by the same yardstick ignores the qualities that make you and law schools unique, and is unworthy of being an important influence on the choice you are about to make. As the deans of schools that range across the spectrum of several rating systems, we strongly urge you to minimize the influence of rankings on your own judgment. In choosing the best school for you, we urge you to get information about all the schools in which you might have some interest. ... Law schools may all have met the same standards of quality to become accredited, but they are quite different from each other. The unique characteristics of each law school will inform you why one school may be best for you and another school best for someone else. We want you to make the best choice for you.

The information contained in this edition of the *ABA-LSAC Official Guide to ABA-Approved Law Schools* was collected in fall 2011. Neither the ABA nor LSAC conducts an audit to verify the accuracy of the information submitted by the law schools. Some of the information, including ABA-accreditation status, may change. The LSAC website, LSAC.org, may contain updated information submitted by a law school. You should check the website of the ABA Section of Legal Education and Admissions to the Bar—americanbar.org/legaled—for updates regarding accreditation status, and the websites of the individual law schools for the most current information available.

CHAPTER 1: BEING A LAWYER

LAWYERS AND THEIR SKILLS

Law practice is so diverse that it is not possible to describe the so-called typical lawyer. Each lawyer works with different clients and different legal problems. Ordinarily, certain basic legal skills are required of all lawyers. They must know:

- how to analyze legal issues in light of the existing state of the law, the direction in which the law is headed, and relevant policy considerations;

- how to synthesize material in light of the fact that many issues are multifaceted and require the combination of diverse elements into a coherent whole;

- how to advocate the views of groups and individuals within the context of the legal system;

- how to give intelligent counsel on the law's requirements;

- how to write and speak clearly; and

- how to negotiate effectively.

Reading and Listening
Lawyers must be able to take in a great deal of information, often on topics about which they are unfamiliar. The ability to digest information from lengthy, dense texts is essential. Equally important is the ability to listen to clients and understand their unique issues and concerns.

Analyzing
Lawyers must be able to determine the fundamental elements of problems. They spend much time discerning the nature and significance of the many issues in a particular problem. In every issue, the lawyer must study the relationship between each element in order to arrive at an answer, result, or solution.

Synthesizing
Lawyers must have the ability to organize large amounts of material in a meaningful, focused, cogent manner. The complexities of many issues and the number of laws either directly or tangentially relevant make this kind of organization crucial.

Advocating
As an advocate, the lawyer's role is to represent his or her client's particular point of view and interests as vigorously as possible. The American judicial system assumes that equitable solutions will emerge from the clash of opposing interests. The success of this adversarial system of American law depends upon the talents and training of the lawyers who work as advocates within it, as speakers and as writers. Lawyers must be able to use their advocacy skills—both written and oral—to marshal evidence and present arguments as to why a particular outcome is desirable.

Counseling
Lawyers also spend a good deal of their time giving clients legal advice. Few ventures in the modern world can be undertaken without some understanding of the law. Through their knowledge of what the law involves, lawyers advise clients about partnerships, decisions, actions, and many other subjects. In many cases, the lawyer's role as a counselor serves as much to prevent litigation as to support it.

Writing and Speaking
Whether in the courtroom or the law office, lawyers must be effective communicators. If lawyers could not translate thoughts and opinions into clear and precise English, it would be difficult for the law to serve society. After all, the law is embodied in words, and many of the disputes that give birth to laws begin with language—its meaning, use, and interpretation. Litigation leads to written judicial opinions; congressional enactments are recorded as printed statutes; and even economic transactions must be expressed as formal, written contracts.

Negotiating
One of the lawyer's primary roles is reconciling divergent interests and opinions. When the parties to a proposed transaction disagree, the lawyer, acting as a facilitator, may be able to help them negotiate to a common ground. Although the client's interests are a lawyer's first priority, often those interests are served best after compromise and conciliation have paved the way to an equitable settlement. Because lawyers are trained to see the implications of alternative courses of action, they are often able to break an impasse.

A legal education is also excellent preparation for many other careers, because the course of study provides a framework for organizing knowledge and teaches an analytical approach to problems. Any or all of the skills described here are useful for those law school graduates who choose not to practice law, but to go into another field. Professions such as banking, insurance, real estate, public relations, human resources, government, education, and international trade are significant areas of employment for law school graduates. The fields of health care, media, and publishing have also attracted law school graduates to their ranks. Law school does not train you for any particular kind of law, but rather acts as a springboard into various professional opportunities. Among the skills learned in law school that are basic to a variety of nonlegal positions are ease in dealing with legal terminology and concepts, ability to analyze facts, and facility in persuading others.

FIELDS OF LAW

Lawyers are central figures in the life of a democratic country. They may deal with major courtroom cases or minor traffic disputes, complex corporate mergers or straightforward real estate transactions. Lawyers may work for giant industries, small businesses, government agencies, international organizations, public interest groups, legal aid offices, and universities—or they may work for themselves. They represent both the impoverished and the wealthy, the helpless and the powerful. Lawyers may work solo, in a small group, or in a large law firm.

According to the American Bar Foundation's *2005 Lawyer Statistical Report* (published in January 2012, pp. 7–8): 75 percent of American lawyers are in private practice (62 percent as solo practitioners or in offices of 5 or fewer lawyers; 18 percent solo or in offices of 6 to 50 lawyers; and 20 percent in firms of more than 50 lawyers); 7.5 percent of the profession work for government agencies; 8.5 percent work for private industries and associations as salaried lawyers or as managers; 1 percent work for legal aid or as public defenders; 1 percent work in legal education; 2.5 percent work in the judiciary; and 4.4 percent are retired or inactive. Many lawyers develop expertise in a particular field of law. Large law firms that provide a full range of legal services tend to employ more specialists. The solo practitioner, who must handle a variety of problems alone, may have greater opportunity to work in several areas. Of course, there are lawyers in large firms who maintain general practices, and lawyers in one-person offices who concentrate on a particular legal issue. Both specialized and general practice can be rewarding. One offers the satisfaction of mastering a particular legal discipline, and the other the challenge of exploring new fields. Following are brief descriptions of selected areas of specialization, though there are many areas of the law that can rightly fall into more than one category.

Civil Rights

Many lawyers entered law school wishing ultimately to work in the field of civil rights—the area of law that is concerned with the balance of governmental power and individual liberties. Although the number of full-time jobs in this field is relatively small, many lawyers whose principal practices are in other fields are able to work in this area by taking cases on a pro bono basis. Full-time civil rights attorneys often work for nonprofit, public interest law firms, or as part of a larger firm with a diverse practice.

Corporate and Securities Law

The corporate lawyer helps clients conduct their business affairs in a manner that is efficient and consistent with the law. The responsibilities of a corporate lawyer can range from preparing the initial articles of incorporation and bylaws for a new enterprise to handling a corporate reorganization under the provisions of federal bankruptcy law. Examples of other areas of corporate law practice include (but are not limited to) contracts, intellectual property, legislative compliance, and liability matters.

Securities law is an extremely complex area that almost always requires the services of a specialist. Lawyers who acquire this specialty are involved with the formation, organization, and financing of corporations through securities such as stock, as well as mergers, acquisitions, and corporate takeovers.

Criminal Law

Criminal defense lawyers represent clients accused of crimes. Their public counterparts are the prosecutors and district attorneys who represent the interests of the state in the prosecution of those accused of crimes. Both types of criminal lawyers deal with fundamental issues of the law and personal liberty. They defend many of the basic rights considered crucial to the preservation of a free and just society.

Education Law

An education law attorney may provide advice, counsel, and representation to a school district or other educational agency in matters pertinent to education law (such as student residency, governance issues, the principal and teacher selection and retention process, student discipline, special-education law, and tuition fraud), and in the development of educational policies. Other education law attorneys may represent parents with special-education or student-expulsion matters against a school district.

Employment and Labor Law

Employment and labor law addresses the legal rights of workers and their employers. Issues might include disputes regarding wages, hours, unlawful termination, child labor, workplace safety, workplace injury and disease, family and related leave, pension and benefit plans, the right to unionize, regulations of and negotiations with union employees, sexual harassment, government civil service systems, and discrimination based upon race, gender, age, and disabilities. Attorneys practicing employment and labor law might represent an individual employee, a group of employees, job applicants, a union, union employees, government workers, a large or small business or organization, a government agency, or interest groups.

Environmental and Natural Resources Law

Environmental law was born out of widespread public and professional concern about the fate of our natural resources. Lawyers in this field may tackle legal and regulatory issues relating to air and water quality, hazardous waste practice, natural gas transportation, oil and gas exploration and development, electric power licensing, water rights, toxic torts, public land use, marine resources, and energy trade regulation. They may work directly for governmental agencies that address environmental problems or represent corporations, public interest groups, and entities concerned about protecting the environment.

Family and Juvenile Law

Family, or domestic relations, law is concerned with relationships between individuals in the context of the family. Many lawyers who practice this kind of law are members of small law firms or are solo practitioners. They specialize in solving problems that arise among family members and in creating or dissolving personal relationships through such means as adoption or divorce.

Health Law

The practice of health law encompasses many different disciplines. Lawyers in this field can be in the private bar or at government agencies. Health lawyers can represent hospitals, physician groups, health maintenance organizations (HMOs), or individual doctors, among many others. Government health lawyers can investigate fraud, deal with Medicare policy and compliance, or oversee public health policy. Many health lawyers are engaged in the business of health care, spending significant time in mergers and acquisitions, tax law, employee benefits, and risk management issues. The impact of technology on health care has been great, with health lawyers helping to guide their clients through intellectual property, biomedicine, and telemedicine issues. Other health lawyers specialize in bioethics and clinical ethics, representing universities and other academic research centers.

Immigration Law

US immigration law deals with legal issues and US policies relating to foreign nationals who come to the United States on a temporary or permanent basis, including the associated legal rights, duties, and obligations of aliens in the United States and the application processes and procedures involved with the naturalization of foreign nationals who wish to become US citizens. US immigration law also deals with legal issues relating to people who are refugees, people who cross US borders by means of fraud or other illegal means, and those who traffic or otherwise illegally transport aliens into the United States. An immigration lawyer may assist clients with all aspects of immigration law, but many choose to specialize in subcategories of immigration law, due to the complexity of the law and the frequency of updates and changes. Specialization areas include asylum/refugee law, business immigration law, and criminal and deportation defense. An attorney practicing in one of the above areas of immigration law may work for the government, a law firm, a community-based organization, or in-house for a company employing foreign nationals.

Intellectual Property Law

Intellectual property law is concerned with the protection of inventors' rights in their discoveries, authors' rights in their creations, and businesses' rights in their identifying marks. Often, an intellectual property lawyer will specialize in a particular area of the law. For example, for those attorneys with a technical background, patent law is a way to combine one's scientific and legal backgrounds into one practice. A copyright attorney counsels authors, composers, and artists on the scope of their rights concerning their creations and personal identities; negotiates contracts; and litigates to enforce these rights. In recent years, copyright law has also focused on technological advances, particularly developments in electronic publishing. Additionally, in today's global economy, intellectual property issues are at the forefront of international trade negotiations.

International Law

International law has grown significantly as a field of practice, reflecting the increasing interdependence of nations and economies. Immigration and refugee law has also assumed increasing importance as more people move more frequently across national boundaries for business, tourism, or permanent resettlement. Public international law provides a limited range of job opportunities, particularly with national governments, international institutions, and public interest bodies. Private international law may offer more extensive employment opportunities, either through law firms or for corporations, banks, or telecommunications firms. Fluency in another language or familiarity with another culture can be a decided advantage for law school graduates who seek to practice in the international arena.

Real Estate Law

Real estate law generally involves anything dealing with real property (land). These laws are designed to determine who owns land and the buildings on it, who has a right to possess and use land or buildings, the sale and purchase of real property, landlord and tenant issues, the development of real property, and compliance with local, state, or national regulations affecting the use of real property. An attorney practicing real estate law may focus on contractual issues by drafting and reviewing contracts; some real estate attorneys may be more focused on litigation issues, such as determining the ownership of land in court, challenging or enforcing easements, seeking to allow the specific development of property, or trying to prevent or alter a planned development of real property. In addition, an attorney practicing real estate law may focus on a specific type of real estate law or a related area of law, such as oil and gas or natural resources law.

Sports and Entertainment Law

Sports law is divided between amateur and professional sports. At the amateur or university level, sports lawyers ensure that athletes and donors are in compliance with National Collegiate Athletic Association (NCAA) rules. They also work with colleges and universities that receive federal aid and are thus subject to Title IX of the Education Amendments of 1972, which prohibits discrimination on the basis of gender in athletic programs. At the professional level, sports lawyers address contract and antitrust issues. They may serve as agents to individual players or represent team owners. Entertainment law generally consists of legal issues affecting television, films, recordings, live performances, and other aspects of the entertainment industry. Entertainment law may involve employment law issues, such as contracts between actors and studios; labor law issues affecting trade unions; and intellectual property law issues, including the protection of creative works such as new songs and the collection of royalties. Entertainment lawyers may assist their clients in negotiating contracts for a record deal or for appearing in a movie, may ensure that their songwriting client obtains the correct amount of royalties for the songs he or she has written, or may go to court to litigate many issues involving the entertainment industry, including disputes over ideas for movies or songs.

Tax Law

In the past 50 years, the importance and complexity of federal, state, and local taxes have necessitated a specialty in this field of law. It is one area of the law where change is constant. The federal Internal Revenue Code and its associated regulations are now several thousand pages in length. New statutes, court decisions, and administrative rulings are issued frequently, and the tax lawyer must be alert to these changes. Economic planning usually includes attention to taxes, and the tax lawyer often assists clients in understanding and minimizing their tax liabilities.

CHAPTER 2: BECOMING A LAWYER

A legal education is both challenging and rewarding. You will develop your analytical, synthesizing, creative, and logical thinking skills, and you will strengthen your reading and debating abilities. A legal education is necessary to become a lawyer in the United States, but it is also excellent preparation for many other careers, both because of the framework it provides for organizing knowledge and the analytical approach it brings to problems. Many teachers, businesspeople, and writers first obtained a legal education before pursuing careers other than law.

PREPARING FOR LAW SCHOOL

Statement on Prelaw Preparation
Prepared by the Pre-Law Committee of the ABA Section of Legal Education and Admissions to the Bar

No Single Path
There is no single path that will prepare you for a legal education. Students who are successful in law school, and who become accomplished professionals, come from many walks of life and educational backgrounds. Some law students enter law school directly from their undergraduate studies without having had any postbaccalaureate work experience. Others begin their legal education significantly later in life, and they bring to their law school education the insights and perspectives gained from their life experiences. Legal education welcomes and values diversity, and you will benefit from the exchange of ideas and different points of view that your colleagues will bring to the classroom.

Undergraduate Education
The ABA does not recommend any undergraduate majors or group of courses to prepare for a legal education. Students are admitted to law school from almost every academic discipline. You may choose to major in subjects that are considered to be traditional preparation for law school, such as history, English, legal studies, philosophy, political science, economics, or business, or you may focus your undergraduate studies in areas as diverse as art, music, science, mathematics, computer science, engineering, nursing, or education. Whatever major you select, you are encouraged to pursue an area of study that interests and challenges you, while taking advantage of opportunities to develop your research and writing skills. Taking a broad range of difficult courses from demanding instructors is excellent preparation for legal education.

A sound legal education will build upon and further refine the skills, values, and knowledge that you already possess. The student who comes to law school lacking a broad range of basic skills and knowledge will face a difficult challenge.

Prelaw Advisor
Undergraduate institutions often assign a person to act as an advisor to current and former students who are interested in pursuing a legal education. That individual can help you with researching and identifying law schools to which you may want to apply. If you are still attending undergraduate school, your prelaw advisor can be helpful in selecting courses that can help you achieve your goal. Many prelaw programs offer interdisciplinary academic programs in legal studies. You may wish to consult your prelaw advisor to find out if such a program exists at your undergraduate institution.

Core Skills and Values*
There are important skills and values, and significant bodies of knowledge that you can acquire prior to law school and that will provide a sound foundation for a legal education. These include analytic and problem-solving skills, critical reading abilities, writing skills, oral communication and listening abilities, general research skills, task organization and management skills, and the values of serving faithfully the interests of others while also promoting justice. If you wish to prepare adequately for a legal education, and for a career in law or for other professional services that involve the use of lawyering skills, you should seek educational, extracurricular, and life experiences that will assist you in developing those attributes. Some brief comments about each of the listed skills and values follow.

Analytic/Problem-Solving Skills
You should seek courses and other experiences that will engage you in critical thinking about important issues, challenge your beliefs, and improve your tolerance for uncertainty. Your legal education will demand that you structure and evaluate arguments for and against propositions that are susceptible to reasoned debate. Good legal education will teach you to "think like a lawyer," but the analytic and problem-solving skills required of lawyers are not fundamentally different from those employed by other professionals. Your law school experience will develop and refine those crucial skills, but you must enter law school with a reasonably well-developed set of analytic and problem-solving abilities.

Critical Reading Abilities
Preparation for legal education should include substantial experience in close reading and critical analysis of complex textual material, for much of what you will do as a law student and lawyer involves careful reading and comprehension of judicial opinions, statutes, documents, and other written materials. As with the other skills discussed in this Statement, you can develop your critical reading ability in a wide range of experiences, including the close reading of complex material in literature, political or economic theory, philosophy, or history. The particular nature of the materials examined is not crucial; what is important is that law school should not be the first time that you are rigorously engaged in the enterprise of carefully reading and understanding, and critically analyzing, complex written material of substantial length.

Writing Skills
As you seek to prepare for a legal education, you should develop a high degree of skill at written communication. Language is the most important tool of a lawyer, and lawyers must learn to express themselves clearly and concisely.

Legal education will provide you with good training in writing, and particularly in the specific techniques and forms of written expression that are common in the law. Fundamental writing skills, however, *must* be acquired and refined before you enter law school. You should seek rigorous and analytical writing opportunities, including preparing original pieces of substantial length and revising written work in response to constructive criticism.

Oral Communication and Listening Abilities
The ability to speak clearly and persuasively is another skill that is essential to your success in law school and the practice of law. You must also have excellent listening skills if you are to understand your clients and others with whom you will

interact daily. As with writing skills, legal education provides excellent opportunities for refining oral communication skills, and particularly for practicing the forms and techniques of oral expression that are most common in the practice of law. Before coming to law school, however, you should seek to develop your basic speaking and listening skills by engaging in debate, making formal presentations in class, or speaking before groups in school, the community, or the workplace.

General Research Skills
Although there are many research sources and techniques that are specific to the law, you do not have to have developed any familiarity with these specific skills or materials before entering law school. However, it would be to your advantage to come to law school having had the experience of undertaking a project that requires significant library research and the analysis of large amounts of information obtained from that research. The ability to use a personal computer is also necessary for law students, both for word processing and for computerized legal research.

Task Organization and Management Skills
To study and practice law, you are going to need to be able to organize large amounts of information, identify objectives, and create a structure for applying that information in an efficient way in order to achieve desired results. Many law school courses, for example, are graded primarily on the basis of one examination at the end of the course, and many projects in the practice of law require the compilation of large amounts of information from a wide variety of sources. You are going to need to be able to prepare and assimilate large amounts of information in an effective and efficient manner. Some of the requisite experience can be obtained through undertaking school projects that require substantial research and writing, or through the preparation of major reports for an employer, a school, or a civic organization.

The Values of Serving Others and Promoting Justice
Each member of the legal profession should be dedicated both to the objectives of serving others honestly, competently, and responsibly, and to the goals of improving fairness and the quality of justice in the legal system. If you are thinking of entering the legal profession, you should seek some significant experience, before coming to law school, in which you may devote substantial effort toward assisting others. Participation in public service projects or similar efforts at achieving objectives established for common purposes can be particularly helpful.

General Knowledge
In addition to the fundamental skills and values listed above, there are some basic areas of knowledge that are helpful to a legal education and to the development of a competent lawyer. Some of the types of knowledge that would maximize your ability to benefit from a legal education include:

- A **broad understanding of history**, including the various factors (social, political, economic, and cultural) that have influenced the development of our society in the United States.

- A **fundamental understanding of political thought** and of the contemporary American political system.

- Some **basic mathematical and financial skills**, such as an understanding of basic precalculus mathematics and an ability to analyze financial data.

- A **basic understanding of human behavior** and social interaction.

- An **understanding of diverse cultures** within and beyond the United States, of international institutions and issues, of world events, and of the increasing interdependence of the nations and communities within our world.

Conclusion
The skills, values, and knowledge discussed in this Statement may be acquired in a wide variety of ways. You may take undergraduate, graduate, or even high school courses that can assist you in acquiring much of this information. You may also gain much of this background through self-learning by reading, in the workplace, or through various other life experiences. Moreover, it is not essential that you come to law school having fully developed all of the skills, values, and knowledge suggested in this Statement. Some of that foundation can be acquired during the initial years of law school. However, if you begin law school having already acquired many of the skills, values, and knowledge listed in this Statement, you will have a significant advantage and will be well prepared to benefit fully from a challenging legal education.

*These core skill and value areas are drawn, in substantial part, from the Statement of Skills and Values contained in the 1992 Report of the American Bar Association Task Force on Law Schools and the Profession, *Legal Education and Professional Development—An Educational Continuum*.

OTHER RESOURCES

For a selected list of books, audiocassettes, and video programs pertaining to legal education and the legal profession, go to LSAC's website, LSAC.org. Search on "Resources for the Prelaw Candidate."

THE JURIS DOCTOR DEGREE

ABA-approved law schools generally require three years of full-time study to earn the Juris Doctor (JD) degree. Most schools with part-time programs require four years of part-time study to earn the JD degree. Most law schools share a common approach to training lawyers. However, they differ in the emphasis they give to certain subjects and teaching methods, such as opportunities for independent study, legal internships, participation in clinical programs, and involvement with governmental affairs.

Law school can be an intense, competitive environment. Students have little time for other interests, especially during the first year of law school. The ABA requires that no full-time student hold an outside job for more than 20 hours a week. Most schools encourage their students to become totally immersed in reading, discussing, and thinking about the law.

The First Year
The newness of the first year of law school is exciting for many and anxiety provoking for almost all. Professors expect you to be prepared in class, but in most courses, grades will be determined primarily from examinations administered at the end of the semester or, at some schools, the end of the year. The professor may give little feedback until the final examination.

The Case Method Approach
The "case method" is what first-year law students are likely to find least familiar. By focusing on the underlying principles that shape the law's approach to different situations, you will learn to distinguish among subtly different legal results and to identify the critical factors that determine a particular outcome. Once these distinctions are mastered, you should be able to apply this knowledge to new situations.

The case method involves the detailed examination of a number of related judicial opinions that describe an area of law. You will also learn to apply the same critical analysis to legislative materials and scholarly articles. The role of the law professor is to provoke and stimulate. For a particular case, he or she may ask questions designed to explore the facts presented, to determine the legal principles applied in reaching a decision, and to analyze the method of reasoning used. In this way, the professor encourages you to relate the case to others and to distinguish it from those with similar but inapplicable precedents. In order to encourage you to learn to defend your reasoning, the professor may adopt a position contrary to the holding of the case.

Because this process places much of the burden of learning on the student, classroom discussions can be exciting. They are also demanding. However uninformed, unprepared, or puzzled you may be, you will be expected to participate in these discussions.

The Ability to Think
The case method reflects the general belief that the primary purpose of law school is not to teach substantive law but to teach you to think like a lawyer. Teachers of law are less concerned about rules and technicalities than are their counterparts in many other disciplines. Although the memorization of specifics may be useful to you, the ability to be analytical and literate is considerably more important than the power of total recall. One reason for this approach to legal education is that in our common-law tradition, the law is constantly evolving and changing; thus, specific rules may quickly lose their relevance.

Law is more an art than a science. The reality lawyers seek in analyzing a case is not always well defined. Legal study, therefore, requires an attentive mind and a tolerance for ambiguity. Because many people believe incorrectly that the study of law involves the memorization of rules in books and principles dictated by learned professors, law schools often attract those people who especially value structure, authority, and order. The study of law does not involve this kind of certainty, however; complex legal questions do not have simple legal solutions.

The Curriculum
As a first-year law student, you will follow a designated course of study that may cover many of the following subjects:

- **Civil procedure**—the process of adjudication in the United States; that is, jurisdiction and standing to sue, motions and pleadings, pretrial procedure, the structure of a lawsuit, and appellate review of trial results.

- **Constitutional law**—the legislative powers of the federal and state governments, and questions of civil liberties and constitutional history, including detailed study of the Bill of Rights and constitutional freedoms.

- **Contracts**—the nature of enforceable promises and rules for determining appropriate remedies in case of nonperformance.

- **Criminal law and criminal procedure**—bases of criminal responsibility, the rules and policies for enforcing sanctions against individuals accused of committing offenses against the public order and well-being, and the rights guaranteed to those charged with criminal violations.

- **Legal method**—introduction to the organization of the American legal system and its processes.

- **Legal writing**—research and writing component of most first-year programs; requires students to research and write memoranda dealing with various legal problems.

- **Property law**—concepts, uses, and historical developments in the treatment of land, buildings, natural resources, and personal objects.

- **Torts**—private wrongs, such as acts of negligence, assault, and defamation, that violate obligations of the law.

In addition to attending classes, you may be required to participate in a moot court exercise in which you take responsibility for arguing a hypothetical court case.

After the first year, you will probably have the opportunity to select from a broad range of courses. Generally, you will take courses in administrative law, civil litigation, commercial law, corporations, evidence, family law, professional responsibility, taxation, and wills and trusts before completing your degree. These universal courses are basic to legal education. Every law school supplements this basic curriculum with additional courses, such as international law, environmental law, conflict of laws, labor law, criminal procedure, and jurisprudence.

Opportunities to Practice What Is Learned
Legal education is primarily academic, in that students devote most of their time to mastering general concepts and principles that shape the law. Most schools offer a variety of

professional skills courses as well. Through clinical programs, law schools offer students direct experience in legal practice. These programs allow second- and third-year students to render counseling, undertake legislative drafting, participate in court trials and appeals, and do other legal work for academic credit. Schools differ in the range and variety of practical education they offer, but the benefits of integrating this experience with theoretical study are well established.

Extracurricular Activities
Student organizations greatly supplement classroom learning. Typically, these organizations are dedicated to advancing the interests of particular groups of law students, such as black, female, Hispanic, or LGBT students; to promoting greater understanding of specific legal fields, such as environmental or international law; or to providing opportunities for involvement in professional, social, and sports activities.

A unique feature of American law schools is that law students manage and edit most of the legal profession's principal scholarly journals. Membership on the editorial staffs of these journals is considered a mark of academic distinction. Selection is ordinarily based on outstanding academic performance, writing ability, or both, as discussed on pages 18–19 of this book.

ADMISSION TO THE BAR

The Bar Examination*
In order to obtain a license to practice law, law school graduates must apply for bar admission through a state board of bar examiners. Most often this board is an agency of the highest state court in the jurisdiction, but occasionally the board is connected more closely to the state's bar association. The criteria for eligibility to take the bar examination or to otherwise qualify for bar admission are set by each jurisdiction.

Licensing involves a demonstration of worthiness in two distinct areas. The first is **competence**. For initial licensure, competence is ordinarily established by showing that the applicant holds an acceptable educational credential (with some exceptions, a JD degree) from an accredited law school that meets educational standards, and by achieving a passing score on the bar examination as set by each jurisdiction. Bar examinations are administered at the end of February and July, with considerably more applicants taking the summer test because it falls just after graduation from law school.

The most common testing configuration consists of a two-day bar examination, one day of which is devoted to the Multistate Bar Examination (MBE), a standardized 200-item test covering six areas (Constitutional Law, Contracts, Criminal Law, Evidence, Real Property, and Torts). The second day of testing is typically drawn from locally crafted essays covering a broad range of subject matter, or two nationally developed tests, the Multistate Essay Examination (MEE) and the Multistate Performance Test (MPT).

In addition, almost all jurisdictions require that the applicant present an acceptable score on the Multistate Professional Responsibility Examination (MPRE), which is separately administered three times a year. Currently, nine jurisdictions have adopted the Uniform Bar Examination (UBE), the score from which will be portable to other UBE jurisdictions. The UBE consists of the MBE, the MEE, and the MPT.

The second area of inquiry by bar examiners involves the **character and fitness** of applicants for a law license. In this regard, bar examiners seek background information concerning each applicant that is relevant to the appropriateness of granting a professional credential. Because law is a public profession, and because the degree of harm a lawyer, once licensed, can inflict is substantial, decisions about who should be admitted to practice law are made carefully by bar examining boards.

Boards of bar examiners in most jurisdictions expect to hear from prospective candidates during the final year of law school. Some boards offer or require law student registration at an earlier point in law school. This preliminary processing, where available, permits the board to review character and fitness issues in advance. As state-specific information is so important (and so variable) in the lawyer-licensing process, law students should contact the board of bar examiners in the jurisdictions in which they are most likely to practice law. Links to state boards are available through the National Conference of Bar Examiners website: ncbex.org.

*This section was written by Erica Moeser, President of the National Conference of Bar Examiners (NCBE).

General Information
Lawyers may practice only in the state or states where they are members of the bar in good standing. However, many states will admit a lawyer to its bar if the lawyer has been admitted to the bar of another state and has practiced law actively for a certain number of years. This is known as "admission by motion." Courts often grant temporary bar admission to out-of-state lawyers for the duration of a specific case.

Many states have student practice rules that, in conjunction with students' academic programs, admit advanced law students who are under the close supervision of an admitted lawyer. A few states require law students to register with the board of bar examiners before graduation or, in some cases, soon after they are enrolled in law school, if they intend to practice in those states. So, if you're planning to attend law school, you should check the bar admission requirements for those states in which you may wish to practice after graduation.

Federal courts set their own standards for admission. It is a common requirement for federal district court admission that the lawyer be admitted to the bar in the state in which the federal district is located or that the applicant have one valid state court admission.

Some state bar associations inquire about the law school admission records of those seeking admission to the bar. You should keep and maintain complete copies of all law school application records throughout the admission cycle and your law school career.

All states accept graduation from an ABA-approved law school as meeting the state's education requirement for eligibility to sit for the bar examination. A number of states have special rules that accept other forms of legal education as sufficient. A good source of information regarding bar admission requirements is the latest edition of the *NCBE/ABA's Comprehensive Guide to Bar Admission Requirements*, which is available online at americanbar.org/groups/legal_education. It should also be available in any law school library or can be ordered through the ABA Service Center at 1.800.285.2221. If you would like additional information relating to bar admissions for a specific state, please contact the appropriate authority in that state. Also, you may want to visit the websites for NCBE (ncbex.org), the ABA (americanbar.org/groups/legal_education), and LSAC (LSAC.org).

Distance Education

The Juris Doctor degree represents a professional education of a most distinct variety. During a law school education, a student is expected to participate in a learning community to develop skills and knowledge that will advance the legal system, society, and the student's career. This law school experience involves interaction with faculty and fellow students outside the classroom as well as in class. Students also learn from each other by inquiry and challenge, review, and study groups.

ABA-approved law schools may not offer a JD degree program that is online or done through correspondence study. ABA-approved law schools may grant credit hours for distance education courses, but no more than 4 credit hours in any term, and no more than 12 credit hours toward the JD degree. Students should be aware that studying law by correspondence or other distance education programs would limit their ability to sit for the bar in many states.

Bar Associations

Bar associations are membership organizations designed to raise the standards of the legal profession and to encourage professionalism. Each state has its own bar association. In the majority of states, membership in the state bar association is mandatory. There are also a variety of national, local, and special-interest bar associations. Many bar associations sponsor programs intended to broaden the availability of legal services and to familiarize the public with the legal profession. They also conduct extensive continuing legal education programs to help members update their skills and their knowledge of the law.

With nearly 400,000 members, the American Bar Association is the largest voluntary professional membership organization in the world. The ABA sponsors a number of programs dealing with legal education, law reform, judicial selection, and professional responsibility. The ABA also promulgates the "Model Rules of Professional Conduct" as an example to the states of the ethics standards that they should enact and enforce in regulating the practice of law in their jurisdiction.

Additionally, there are local and national chapters of bar associations for lawyers from minority groups. Among them are the National Bar Association (nationalbar.org), Hispanic National Bar Association (hnba.com), National Asian Pacific American Bar Association (napaba.org), and National Native American Bar Association (nativeamericanbar.org). You may also find useful information at LSAC.org's Diversity in Law School section (under "Helpful Links").

HOW LAW SCHOOLS DETERMINE WHOM TO ADMIT

Nationally, there are more applicants than spaces available in first-year classes. Schools rely heavily upon selection criteria that bear on expected performance in law school and can be applied objectively to all candidates. Law schools consider a variety of factors in admitting their students. The two factors that all candidates present—prior academic performance and the LSAT score—are fundamental to the admission process.

The most difficult admission decisions are those regarding candidates who are neither so well qualified nor so unsatisfactory as to present a clear-cut case for acceptance or denial. These applicants constitute the majority of the applicant pool at many law schools. However, if you assess your credentials accurately, your likelihood of admission to an ABA-accredited law school is strong.

Criteria That May Be Considered by Law School Admission Committees

- Undergraduate grade-point average

- LSAT score

- Undergraduate course of study

- Graduate work, if any

- College attended

- Improvement in grades and grade distribution

- College curricular and extracurricular activities

- Ethnic/racial background

- Individual character and personality

- Letters of recommendation/evaluations

- Writing skills

- Personal statement or essay

- Work experience or other postundergraduate experiences

- Community activities

- Motivation and reasons for deciding to study law

- State of residency

- Obstacles that have been overcome

- Past accomplishments and leadership

- Conditional admission programs

- Anything else that stands out in an application

THE LAW SCHOOL ADMISSION TEST (LSAT)

The Law School Admission Test (LSAT) is a half-day, standardized test administered four times each year at designated testing centers throughout the world. The test is an integral part of the law school admission process in the United States, Canada, and a growing number of other countries.

The test consists of five 35-minute sections of multiple-choice questions. It provides a standard measure of acquired reading and verbal reasoning skills that law schools can use as one of several factors in assessing applicants. Four of the five sections contribute to the test taker's score. The unscored section, commonly referred to as the variable section, typically is used to pretest new test questions or to preequate new test forms. The placement of this section in the LSAT will vary. A 35-minute writing sample is administered at the end of the test. LSAC does not score the writing sample, but copies of the writing sample are sent to all law schools to which you apply.

The score scale for the LSAT is 120 to 180. Some schools place greater weight than others on the LSAT; most law schools do evaluate your full range of credentials.

What the Test Measures

The LSAT is designed to measure skills that are considered essential for success in law school: the reading and comprehension of complex texts with accuracy and insight, the organization and management of information and the ability to draw reasonable inferences from it, the ability to think critically, and the analysis and evaluation of the reasoning and arguments of others.

The three multiple-choice question types in the LSAT are:

Reading Comprehension Questions

These questions measure the ability to read, with understanding and insight, examples of lengthy and complex materials similar to those commonly encountered in law school. The Reading Comprehension section contains four sets of reading questions, each consisting of a selection of reading material followed by five to eight questions that test reading and reasoning abilities.

Analytical Reasoning Questions

These questions measure the ability to understand a structure of relationships and to draw logical conclusions about that structure. You are asked to reason deductively from a set of statements and rules or principles that describe relationships among persons, things, or events. Analytical Reasoning questions reflect the kinds of complex analyses that a law student performs in the course of legal problem solving.

Logical Reasoning Questions

These questions assess the ability to analyze, critically evaluate, and complete arguments as they occur in ordinary language. Each Logical Reasoning question requires the test taker to read and comprehend a short passage, then answer a question about it. The questions are designed to assess a wide range of skills involved in thinking critically, with an emphasis on skills that are central to legal reasoning. These skills include drawing well-supported conclusions, reasoning by analogy, determining how additional evidence affects an argument, applying principles or rules, and identifying argument flaws.

Your Score as a Predictor of Law School Performance

The LSAT, like any admission test, is not a perfect predictor of law school performance. The predictive power of an admission test is limited by many factors, such as the complexity of the skills the test is designed to measure and the unmeasurable factors that can affect students' performances, such as motivation, physical and mental health, or work and family responsibilities. In spite of these factors, the LSAT compares very favorably with admission tests used in other graduate and professional fields of study. Additional information about scoring can be found on the LSAC website, LSAC.org.

Test Preparation

Most law school applicants familiarize themselves with test directions and question types, practice on sample tests, and study the information available on test-taking techniques and strategies. Although it is difficult to say when examinees are sufficiently prepared, very few people achieve their full potential without some preparation.

You should be so familiar with the instructions and question types that nothing you see on the test can delay or distract you from thinking about how to answer a question. At a minimum, you should review the descriptions of the question types on LSAC's website and simulate the day of the test by taking a practice test that includes a writing sample under actual time constraints. Taking a practice test under timed

conditions helps you to estimate the amount of time you can afford to spend on each question in a section and to determine the question types for which you may need additional practice.

LSAC publishes a variety of materials to help you prepare for the LSAT. See the ad toward the back of this book, or visit LSAC's website—LSAC.org.

Academic Record

Undergraduate performance is generally an important indicator of how someone is likely to perform in law school. Hence, many law schools look closely at college grades when considering individual applications.

Course selection also can make a difference in admission evaluations. Applicants who have taken difficult or advanced courses in their undergraduate study often are evaluated in a more favorable light than students who have concentrated on easier or less advanced subjects.

Many law schools consider undergraduate-performance trends along with a student's numerical average. Thus, they may discount a slow start in a student's undergraduate career if he or she performed exceptionally well in the later school years. Similarly, admission committees may see an undergraduate's strong start followed by a mediocre finish as an indication of less potential to do well in law school. Candidates are advised to comment on irregular grade trends in their applications.

Grade Conversion Table

LSAC Conversion		Grades as Reported on Transcripts			
4.0 Scale	A to F	1 to 5	100–0*	Four Passing Grades	Three Passing Grades
4.33	A+	1+	98–100	Highest Passing Grade (4.0)	Highest Passing Grade (4.0)
4.00	A	1	93–97		
3.67	A–	1–	90–92		
3.50	AB				
3.33	B+	2+	87–89	Second Highest Passing Grade (3.0)	Middle Passing Grade (3.0)
3.00	B	2	83–86		
2.67	B–	2–	80–82		
2.50	BC				
2.33	C+	3+	77–79	Third Highest Passing Grade (2.0)	Lowest Passing Grade (2.0)
2.00	C	3	73–76		
1.67	C–	3–	70–72		
1.50	CD				
1.33	D+	4+	67–69	Lowest Passing Grade (1.0)	
1.00	D	4	63–66		
0.67	D–	4–	60–62		
0.50	DE or DF				
0.00	E and F	5	Below 60	Failure (0.0)	Failure (0.0)

*In some instances, a school's numeric grading scale might be converted differently than shown here.

ADDITIONAL ADMISSION DECISION FACTORS

Law schools consider more than academic records and LSAT scores when evaluating applicants. Some of the most important factors are discussed below.

Letters of Recommendation and Evaluations

The most effective letters of recommendation and evaluations are those from professors who have known you well enough to write with candor, detail, and objectivity about your academic and personal achievements and potential. Letters that compare you to your academic peers are often considered the most useful. Work supervisors also can write in support of your application. Most law schools do not consider general, unreservedly praiseworthy letters helpful. Some schools do not require letters at all and may not read letters of recommendation if they receive them. In addition to or instead of letters of recommendation, many law schools are now using an online tool that allows evaluators to rate a candidate's individual attributes in six categories: intellectual skill, personal qualities,

integrity and honesty, communication, task management, and working with others.

Work Experience

Law schools want diverse, interesting classes, representative of a variety of backgrounds. A candidate who applies to law school several years after completing his or her undergraduate education, and who has demonstrated an ability to succeed in a nonacademic environment, is sometimes more motivated than one who continues his or her education without a break. In fact, only about one-third of law students enter directly from college.

Your Personal Essay

Each candidate to law school has something of interest to present. Maybe you've had some experience, some training, or some dream that sets you apart from others. Law schools want to recruit men and women who are qualified for reasons beyond grades and scores. The essay or personal statement in your application is the place to tell the committee about yourself.

In general, your evaluation of actual experiences and past accomplishments has more value to the committee than speculation about future accomplishments. Also, if you have overcome a serious obstacle in your life to get where you are today, by all means let the admission committee know about it. Any noteworthy personal experience or accomplishment may be an appropriate subject for your essay; however, be sure to do more than just state it. Describe your experience briefly but concretely, and why it had value to you, whether it is a job, your family, a significant accomplishment, or your upbringing. You are simultaneously trying to add information and create structure. Be brief, be factual, be comprehensive, and be organized. You are a storyteller here. You want a living person—you—to emerge. The statement is your opportunity to become vivid and alive to the reader, and it is an opportunity to demonstrate your ability to write and present a prose sample in a professional manner.

Graduate or Professional Study

Prior success or failure in other graduate or professional school work, including other law schools, may also be a factor in the admission committee's decision. In any case, you are required to report such work to any law school to which you apply.

Minority Applicants

Racial and ethnic diversity is essential to the study of law, and greatly benefits the law class, the law school, and the legal profession. All law schools actively seek students who are members of underrepresented racial and ethnic groups and strongly encourage those applicants. (See chapter 6 for further details on minority recruitment and enrollment, and visit DiscoverLaw.org.)

International Applicants

Many students from other countries enroll at US law schools, most frequently in graduate programs (usually called LLM programs) that are designed to meet the needs of people who already hold a recognized law degree from another country but want to learn about the legal system of the United States.

Procedures and requirements for international applicants vary from school to school. You should contact the individual schools that interest you to learn about each school's particular requirements. The Law School Admission Test is an integral part of the law school admission process in the United States, Canada, and a growing number of other countries. Most schools will ask applicants for whom English is not their native language to take a standardized test such as the Test of English as a Foreign Language (TOEFL) or the International English Language Testing System (IELTS). Each school sets its own standard for required minimal scores on the tests.

Many schools require applicants educated outside the US, its territories, and Canada to use either LSAC's Credential Assembly Service or another evaluation service to authenticate and evaluate an applicant's grades and degrees for US admission committees. The applicant is responsible for the cost of this service, and some law schools will require the use of a specific service.

LSAC offers credential assembly services for the collection, authentication, evaluation, and distribution of all transcripts and TOEFL/IELTS scores as appropriate for each law school to which the applicant applies. Detailed information about the services required by each law school is available at LSAC.org.

International students must also demonstrate the ability to pay for schooling in this country in order to apply for a student visa (F-1 form). You may be asked to complete a certification of finances form from the law school; if the school is satisfied that the student can pay, it will issue a form (I-20) to submit to US Citizenship and Immigration Services (USCIS) as part of your application for a student visa. Because of the time required to process entry visas, international applicants are encouraged to apply for admission as early in the process as possible.

International students may be eligible for institutional grants and loans, but are ineligible for federal loans, and (in most schools) are required to have a US cosigner for private loans. Contact the financial aid office at the schools to which you are applying for more details.

Interviews

In general, interviews are not a part of the law school admission process. You are encouraged to visit law schools to gather information, and often an appointment with admission personnel will be a part of the visit. The purpose of your conversation with the admission staff usually will be informational rather than evaluative; the conversation will not become a part of your admission file. An occasional school will grant an interview, and some may even request it, but, in general, you should not count on an interview as a means to state your case for admission; this is best done in the personal statement.

ASSESSING YOURSELF REALISTICALLY

When selecting law schools to which you will apply, the general philosophy is that you should have a threefold plan: dream a little, be realistic, and be safe. Most applicants have no trouble selecting dream schools—those that are almost, but not quite, beyond their grasp—or safe schools—those for which admission is virtually certain. A common strategic error made by applicants is failure to evaluate realistically their chances for admission to a particular law school. The admission data and law school admission profile grids in this book and online at LSAC.org are helpful sources, because the data are provided by the law schools directly to the ABA and LSAC.

Use the Admission Profile Grids in This Book

Check your qualifications against the admission profiles of the law schools that interest you. Most schools publish a grid that indicates the number of applicants with LSAT scores and GPAs like yours who were admitted in the most recent admission year. This gives you a general sense of your competitiveness at that school. These charts will help you determine which schools are your dream schools, your realistic schools, and your safe schools. If your profile meets or exceeds that of a school, it is likely that that school will be as interested in admitting you as you are in being admitted. Other statistics are contained in the school's ABA data, so that material should be read with care as well. A few words of caution: First, law schools consider many other factors beyond the LSAT score and GPA, as described in the previous section ("Additional Admission Decision Factors"), and the grids and data about these credentials only give you part of the story. Second, you should make your final decision about where you will apply only after obtaining additional information from each school. Third, the data in the grids are from a previous application year and may not reflect fluctuations in applicant volume that affect admission decisions.

Research Specific Law Schools That Interest You

Other sources of information include:

- **The school's admission office.** This is a good source for general information about the school and your chances for admission. Do not hesitate to request admission counseling. Be sure to obtain current catalogs and visit the websites for each law school you are considering.

- **Your college or university prelaw advisor.** LSAC provides the name of a prelaw advisor at your degree-granting institution. Your prelaw advisor can often provide you with reliable information about which law schools fit your personal profile. He or she may also be able to tell you which law schools have accepted students from your school in the past and provide you with an overview of the admitted students' credentials. This will help you to determine how law schools have treated applicants from your school in the recent past.

- **Law School Forums.** The Law School Forums, organized by the Law School Admission Council, are excellent opportunities to talk personally with law school representatives from around the country in one central, urban location—usually a hotel exhibit hall. Recent forums have been held in Atlanta, Boston, Chicago, Houston, Los Angeles, Miami, New York City, the San Francisco Bay Area, Toronto, and Washington, DC. In 2011, 209 ABA-approved law schools participated in the forums, and about 9,000 people registered as attendees. Because traveling to a number of law schools can be expensive, many prospective law students find the forums to be the most productive means of gathering information and making school contacts. Forum admission is free; for dates and locations of 2012 Law School Forums, see the ad toward the back of this book, or visit LSAC's website—LSAC.org. Forum preregistration is also available on the LSAC website.

- **School representatives and alumni.** Take advantage of opportunities to talk with law school representatives and alumni. When you talk with alumni, remember that law schools sometimes change fairly quickly. Try to talk to a recent graduate or to one who is active in alumni affairs and therefore knowledgeable about the school as it is today.

- **School visits.** Law schools encourage you to visit. You can learn a great deal about a school from talks with students and faculty members. Many law schools have formal programs in which a currently enrolled student will take you on a tour of the campus and answer your questions. Firsthand experience can be quite valuable in assessing how you would fit into the school.

- **The Internet.** The websites of LSAC (LSAC.org) and the ABA (americanbar.org/groups/legal_education) provide links to the websites of ABA-approved law schools. The various avenues of online social networking are likely to provide many opportunities to link up, electronically at least, with students at law schools you are considering. Do keep in mind that a school may be a right (or wrong) fit for one person but not another. As is always true in online relationships, it's best to keep an open mind when it comes to comments from people you have never met in person. There is no substitution for seeing and experiencing a school for yourself.

Keep Your Options Open

Flexibility is a key word in the law school admission process. Keep your options open. Even during the early stages of the admission process, you should continually reevaluate your prospects and prepare alternative plans. For example, don't set your sights on only one law school and one plan of action. You could severely limit your potential and your chance to practice law.

WORKING WITH LSAC: REGISTERING FOR THE LSAT AND THE CREDENTIAL ASSEMBLY SERVICE (CAS)

The Law School Admission Council (LSAC) administers the LSAT and serves as a liaison for much of the communication between you and the law schools. The LSAC Credential Assembly Service centralizes and standardizes undergraduate academic records to simplify the law school admission process. This service also prepares a report for each law school to which you apply. The registration fee includes law school report preparation, letter of recommendation/ evaluation and transcript processing, and access to electronic applications for all ABA-approved law schools.

Comprehensive information about the LSAT and the Credential Assembly Service can be found at the LSAC website, LSAC.org. The quickest and easiest way to register for both the LSAT and the Credential Assembly Service is online. If you need to obtain a paper registration form, call 215.968.1001.

Planning Ahead for Law School Deadlines

Most law schools have a variety of application requirements and deadlines that you must meet to be considered for admission. If you are applying to a number of schools, the various deadlines and requirements can be confusing. It probably will be helpful if you set up a detailed calendar that will remind you of when, and what you must do, to complete your applications.

In registering for the LSAT, be sure to give yourself enough time to select a convenient testing location and prepare for the test. You also should determine whether each law school in which you are interested will accept scores from the February LSAT administration, which is the last test date in each admission cycle.

BASIC LSAT DATE AND DEADLINE INFORMATION (2012–2013)

All national test dates, both for regular test takers and test takers who are Saturday Sabbath observers, are listed below, along with corresponding regular registration deadlines. Dates shown represent receipt deadlines for mail, telephone, and online registration. The basic fee for the LSAT is $160 (published test centers only). Actual test dates for administrations **outside** the US, Canada, and the Caribbean, which are nondisclosed* tests, will vary. That information, as well as complete details regarding other LSAT information—such as accommodated testing, deadlines and fees for late registrations and nonpublished test centers (domestic and foreign), test date and test center changes, and partial refunds—is available at LSAC.org.

National Test Dates

▪ **Regular**	Monday, June 11, 2012	Saturday, Oct. 6, 2012	Saturday, Dec. 1, 2012	Saturday, Feb. 9, 2013 Nondisclosed*
▪ **Saturday Sabbath Observers**		Wednesday, Oct. 10, 2012 Nondisclosed*	Monday, Dec. 3, 2012 Nondisclosed*	Monday, Feb. 11, 2013 Nondisclosed*
▪ **Score by E-mail**	July 6, 2012	Oct. 31, 2012	Jan. 4, 2013	March 6, 2013
▪ **Score Report Mailed (approx.)**	July 14, 2012	Nov. 8, 2012	Jan. 12, 2013	March 10, 2013

Regular Registration Deadlines (online, mail, and telephone)

▪ **United States, Canada, and the Caribbean**	May 8, 2012	Sept. 4, 2012	Oct. 29, 2012	Jan. 8, 2013

*Persons who take a nondisclosed test receive only their scores. They do not receive their test questions, answer key, or individual responses.

THE CREDENTIAL ASSEMBLY SERVICE

The Credential Assembly Service collects the US and Canadian academic records of law school applicants and summarizes the undergraduate work according to a standard 4.0 system to simplify the admission process. Nearly all American Bar Association-approved law schools (and many non-ABA-approved schools) require that applicants use this service. Applicants who have studied for more than a year outside the US or Canada can use the Credential Assembly Service for transcript evaluation and authentication if required by the law schools to which they are applying.

The Credential Assembly Service prepares a report for each law school to which you apply. There is a registration fee for the service, as well as a fee for each law school report (go to LSAC.org for current fees). Your registration includes law school report preparation, letter of recommendation/evaluation and transcript processing, and access to electronic applications for all ABA-approved law schools.

The Credential Assembly Service creates your law school report by combining:

- LSAT scores and writing sample copies;

- an academic summary report;

- copies of all undergraduate, graduate, and law/professional school transcripts; and

- copies of letters of recommendation and evaluations, if applicable.

Canadian law schools receive an LSAT Law School Report containing LSAT scores and writing sample copies.

Fee Waivers

Fee waivers are available for the LSAT, the Credential Assembly Service (CAS), and *The Official LSAT SuperPrep*. For US citizens, US nationals, or permanent resident aliens of the United States with an Alien Registration Receipt Card (I-151 or I-551), fee waivers can be authorized by LSAC or ABA-approved law schools, which are listed on our website. Canadian citizens must submit their fee waiver request to a Canadian LSAC-member law school even if they plan to apply for admission to a US law school. Fee waivers cannot be granted by financial aid offices of undergraduate institutions, non-ABA-approved law schools, prelaw advisors, or any other individual or organization. Go to LSAC.org or any ABA-approved law school admission office for additional information about fee waivers.

THE ADMISSION PROCESS

Law school applicants can expect that the admission process will be competitive. Nationally, there are more applicants than spaces available in first-year classes; this means that, at some law schools, there will be considerable competition for seats. However, it is probably true that if you assess your credentials accurately, your likelihood of admission to an ABA-accredited law school is strong.

The Importance of Complete Files
Remember that law schools require complete files before making their decisions. A law school will consider your file complete when it has received your application, Credential Assembly Service (CAS) Law School Report (or LSAT Law School Report if the law school does not require the Credential Assembly Service), letters of recommendation or evaluations (if required), personal statement, any requirements unique to the particular school, and application fee.

Rolling Admission
Many law schools operate what is known as a rolling admission process: The school evaluates applications and informs candidates of admission decisions on a continuous basis over several months, usually beginning in late fall and extending to midsummer for wait-listed admission.

Even if you have not yet taken the LSAT, it might be helpful to submit your application early so that your Credential Assembly Service file can be sent to law schools as soon as your test score is available. The earlier you apply, the more seats the school is likely to have available. Most schools try to make comparable decisions throughout the admission season, even those that practice rolling admission. Still, it is disadvantageous to be one of the last applicants to complete a file. Furthermore, the more decisions you receive from law schools early in the process, the better able you will be to make your own decisions, such as whether to apply to more law schools or whether to accept a particular school's offer.

Applying to More Than One School
Last year, 53 percent of all applicants applied to five or fewer law schools. You should be sure to place your applications at schools representing a range of admission standards. Even if you have top qualifications, you should apply to a number of schools where you have an excellent chance of being admitted, based on your review of requirements and admission standards. This is your insurance policy. If you apply to these schools in November, and are accepted to one or more in January or February, you may be disappointed but not panicked if you are later denied admission by your top choices. You should not anticipate that you are assured of acceptance at any particular law school; there are no guarantees. Each year, law schools must choose from among many qualified candidates to create a first-year class.

The Preliminary Review of an Application
Applicants whose qualifications more than fulfill the school's admission standards are usually accepted by an admission committee during the first round of decisions. Candidates whose credentials fall below the school's standards are usually denied admission.

Many applications are not decided upon immediately. They are usually reviewed by a committee that bases its admission decision on many facets of each application (see "How Law Schools Determine Whom to Admit," page 9).

The length of time it takes the committee to review an application varies; consult the individual law schools to which you apply.

Waiting Lists
If you have strong qualifications, but you do not quite match the competition of those currently being admitted at a particular law school, you may be placed on a waiting list for possible admission at a later date. The law school will send you a letter notifying you of its final decision as early as April or as late as July.

Many schools rank students who are on the waiting list. Some law schools will tell you your rank. If a law school doesn't rank its waiting list, you might ask the admission office how many students have been placed on the waiting list.

Seat Deposits
Many law schools use seat deposits to help keep track of their new classes. For example, a typical fee might be $200, which is credited to your first-term tuition if you actually register at the school; if you don't register, the deposit may be forfeited or partially returned. A school may require a larger deposit around July 1, which is also credited to tuition. If you decline the offer of admission after you've paid your deposit, a portion of the money may be refunded, depending on the date you actually decline the offer. At some schools, you may not be refunded any of the deposit.

The official position of the Law School Admission Council is:

> Except under binding early decision plans or for academic terms beginning in the spring or summer, no law school should require an enrollment commitment of any kind to an offer of admission or scholarship prior to April 1. Admitted applicants who have submitted a timely financial aid application should not be required to commit to enroll by having to make a nonrefundable financial commitment until notified of financial aid awards that are within the control of the law school.

Multiple Deposit Notification
Each year, LSAC provides participating law schools with periodic reports detailing the number of applicants who have submitted seat deposits or commitments at other participating schools, along with identification of those other schools. Beginning May 15 each year, these reports also include the names and LSAC account numbers for all candidates who have deposits/commitments at multiple participating schools.

Ethical Conduct in Applying to Law School
The practice of law is an honorable, noble calling. Lawyers play an important role in society by serving both their clients' needs and the public good.

Your submission of an application for admission to law school is your first step in the process of becoming a lawyer. Now is the time, as you take this first important step, to dedicate yourself to a personal standard for your conduct that consists of the highest levels of honesty and ethical behavior.

The legal profession requires its members to behave ethically in the practice of law at all times, in order to protect the interests of clients and the public. You must understand that those who aspire to join the legal profession will be held to the same high standards for truth, full disclosure, and accuracy that are applied to those who practice law. These standards also apply to those aspiring to further their education with a Master of Laws degree (LLM). The legal profession has set standards for ethical conduct by lawyers. Similarly, law schools have set standards for ethical conduct by law school applicants through the Law School Admission Council (LSAC). These standards are known as the *LSAC Rules Governing Misconduct and Irregularities in the Admission Process*. Just as lawyers are required to study, understand, and comply with the ABA's ethical standards, law school applicants are expected to read, understand, and comply with LSAC's ethical standards.

If you fail to comply with LSAC's ethical standards, you may be barred from admission to law school. If you fail to disclose required information on your law school application, or if you engage in misconduct during the admission process that is discovered after you enroll in law school or start to practice law, you may face more serious sanctions. In appropriate cases, state and national bar authorities and other affected persons and institutions may also receive notification. Individual law schools and bar authorities determine what action, if any, they will take in response to a finding of misconduct or irregularity. Such action may include the closing of an admission file, revocation of an offer of admission, dismissal from law school through a school's internal disciplinary channels, or disbarment. Thus, a finding of misconduct or irregularity is a very serious matter.

Take the time, right now, to read LSAC's statement on misconduct and irregularities in the admission process presented below.

Misconduct and Irregularities in the Admission Process

The Law School Admission Council has established procedures for dealing with instances of possible candidate misconduct or irregularities on the LSAT or in the law school admission process. Misconduct or irregularity in the admission process is a serious offense with serious consequences. Intent is not an element of a finding of misconduct or irregularity. This means that an "honest mistake" is not a defense to a charge of misconduct or irregularity. Misconduct or irregularity is defined as the submission, as part of the law school admission process, including, but not limited to, regular, transfer, LLM, and visiting applications, of any information that is false, inconsistent, or misleading, or the omission of information that may result in a false or misleading conclusion, or the violation of any regulation governing the law school admission process, including any violation of LSAT test center regulations.

Examples of misconduct and irregularities include, but are not limited to:

- submission of false, inconsistent, or misleading statements or omission of information requested online or on forms as part of registering for the LSAT or using LSAC's Credential Assembly Service, or on individual law school application forms;

- submission of an altered or a nonauthentic transcript;

- submission of an application containing false, inconsistent, or misleading information;

- submission of an altered, nonauthentic, or unauthorized letter of recommendation;

- falsification of records;

- impersonation of another in taking the LSAT;

- switching of LSAT answer sheets with another;

- taking the LSAT for purposes other than applying to law school;

- copying or sharing information, or any other forms of cheating, on the LSAT;

- obtaining advance access to test materials;

- theft of test materials;

- working on, marking, erasing, reading, or turning pages on sections of the LSAT during unauthorized times;

- bringing prohibited items into the test room;

- falsification of transcript information, school attendance, honors, awards, or employment;

- providing false, inconsistent, or misleading information in the admission and financial aid/scholarship application process; or

- attempt at any of the above.

A charge of misconduct or irregularity may be made prior to a candidate's admission to law school, after matriculation at a law school, or after admission to practice.

When alleged misconduct or irregularity brings into question the validity of the LSAC data about a candidate, the school may be notified of possible data error, and transmission of that data will be withheld until the matter has been resolved by the Law School Admission Council's Misconduct and Irregularities in the Admission Process Subcommittee. The Council will investigate all instances of alleged misconduct or irregularities in the admission process in accordance with the *LSAC Rules Governing Misconduct and Irregularities in the Admission Process*. A subcommittee representative will determine whether misconduct or an irregularity has occurred. If the subcommittee representative determines that a preponderance of the evidence shows misconduct or irregularity, then a report of the determination is sent to all law schools to which the individual has applied, subsequently applies, or has matriculated. Notation that a misconduct or irregularity report is on file is also included on LSAT and LSAC Credential Assembly Service reports to law schools. Such reports are retained indefinitely. More information regarding misconduct and irregularity procedures may be obtained by writing to: LSAC, Misconduct and Irregularities in the Admission Process Subcommittee, 662 Penn Street, Newtown, PA 18940-1802, USA.

CHAPTER 5: CHOOSING A LAW SCHOOL

For some people, the choice of which law school to attend is an easy one. Applicants tend to select the schools they perceive to be the most prestigious or those that offer a program of particular interest or the greatest amount of financial support. Some need to stay in a particular area perhaps because of family or job obligations and will choose nearby schools with part-time programs.

FACTORS TO CONSIDER

The majority of applicants will have to weigh a variety of personal and academic factors to come up with a list of potential schools. Once you have a list, and more than one acceptance letter, you will have to choose a school. Applicants should consider carefully the offerings of each law school before making a decision. The quality of a law school is certainly a major consideration; however, estimations of quality are subjective. You should consider the size, composition, and background of the student body as well as the location, size, and nature of the surrounding community. Remember that the law school is going to be your home for three years. Adjusting to law school and the general attitudes of a professional school is difficult enough without the additional hardship of culture shock. Don't choose a law school in a large city if you can't bear crowds, noise, and a fast pace. And, if you've lived your entire life in an urban environment, can you face the change you will experience in a small town? You also may want to ask yourself if you are already set in an unshakable lifestyle or if you are eager for a new environment.

Other significant factors are the particular strengths or interests of the faculty, the degree to which clinical experience or classroom learning is emphasized, the nature of any special programs offered, the number and type of student organizations, the range of library holdings, and whether a school is public or private. You may wish to consider a school with a strong minority recruitment, retention, and mentoring program, or one with an active student organization for students of your particular ethnic background.

At any rate, you should select more than one law school where you think you could succeed.

Law Schools and Reputation

Many people will tell you to apply to the schools that take students in your GPA and LSAT ranges, and then enroll in the best one that accepts you. However, law school quality can be assessed in a number of ways.

There is a hierarchy of law schools based on reputation, job placement success, strength of faculty, and the prestige of the parent institution (if there is one). In fact, a study done at one university suggests that undergraduate students perceive schools not only in terms of a hierarchy but also in terms of hierarchical clusters. In other words, certain schools are grouped together in terms of equivalent quality and prestige. Also, there are books or magazine articles that assign law schools purported numerical quality rankings.

However, according to the ABA:

> No rating of law schools beyond the simple statement of their accreditation status is attempted or advocated by the official organizations in legal education. Qualities that make one kind of school good for one student may not be as important to another. The American Bar Association and its Section of Legal Education and Admissions to the Bar have issued disclaimers of any law school rating system. Prospective law students should

consider a variety of factors in making their choice among schools.[1]

Since there is no official ranking authority, you should be cautious in using such rankings. The factors that make up a law school's reputation—strength of curriculum, faculty, career services, ability of students, quality of library facilities, and the like—don't lend themselves to quantification. Even if the rankings were more or less accurate, the school's reputation is only one factor among many for you to consider.

What's in a Name?

While going to a "name" school may mean that you will have an easier time finding your first job, it doesn't necessarily mean that you will get a better legal education than if you go to a lesser-known law school. Some schools that were at their peaks years ago are still riding on the wave of that earlier reputation. Others have greatly improved their programs and have recruited talented faculty but have not yet made a name for themselves.

Once admitted, applicants should consider a variety of factors, such as the contacts you may acquire at a school in the area where you hope to practice, the size of the school, and cost. The substantive differences between schools should be your focus when making this important choice rather than the school's reputed ranking.

The Parent University

About 90 percent of ABA-approved law schools are part of a larger university, and there may be some advantages to attending a law school that is part of a university. Such law schools may have more options for joint-degree programs or for taking a nonlaw school course or two. They also may have more academic and social activities, campus theater groups, sports teams, and everything else that comes with university life. Perhaps most important, the university can act as a support system for the law school by providing a wealth of facilities, including student housing and support for career services.

National, Regional, and Local Schools

A national school will generally have an applicant population and a student body that draws almost indistinguishably from the nation as a whole and will have many international students as well. A regional school is likely to have a population that is primarily from the geographic region of its location, though many regional schools have students from all over the country; a number of regional schools draw heavily from a particular geographical area, yet graduates may find jobs all over the country. Generally speaking, a local school is drawing primarily on applicants who either come from or want to practice in the proximate area in which the school is located. Many local law schools have excellent reputations and compete with the national schools in faculty competence, in research-supporting activities, and in resources generally. Check the school's catalog or talk with the admission and placement staff to get a clear breakdown on where their students come from and where they are finding jobs.

[1] *ABA Standards and Rules of Procedure for Approval of Law Schools 2011–2012*, Council Statement 5, p. 149, American Bar Association, Chicago, IL, 2011.

EVALUATION OF LAW SCHOOLS

The best advice on how to select a law school is to choose the school that is best for you. The law schools invest substantial time and effort in evaluating prospective students, and applicants should evaluate law schools with equivalent care. The following are some features to keep in mind as you systematically evaluate law schools. (Costs and other financial criteria are not included below; they are discussed in chapter 9.)

Each listing in this book provides school-specific information in the following categories as well.

Enrollment/Student Body

The academic qualifications of the student body are important to consider. It's a good idea to select a law school where you will be challenged by your classmates. Use the applicant profile grids in this book to check the LSAT scores and GPAs for the previous year's entering class. Try to select a school where your averages will not be significantly different from those of your fellow law students. Because of the important role of student participation in law school classes, your legal education might not be as rewarding as it could be if you are not challenged by your classmates.

You might also inquire about the diversity of the student body. Are a majority of the students the same age, race, gender, and so on? Remember, differences among students will expose you to various points of view; this will be an important aspect of your law school education.

Find out how many students are in a typical class. Much of the learning in law school depends on the quality of class discussion. Small classes provide essential interaction; large classes (and the Socratic method) provide diversity, challenge, and a good mix of reactions, opinions, and criticism.

It is also important to find out the total number of students enrolled at the school. Not surprisingly, the larger law schools tend to offer a larger selection of courses. Of course, more doesn't always mean better, and no one student has time to take all the courses offered at a large school. However, if you think you want to sample a wide range of courses, you are apt to have more opportunity to do so at a law school with a large faculty.

Part of the law school learning experience takes place after class with fellow students and with members of the faculty. Check to see whether faculty and students are on campus for a substantial part of the day.

Larger schools may also offer more extracurricular programs, greater student services, and a larger library. However, faculties and administrators at smaller schools may be able to give students more attention, and students at smaller schools may experience greater camaraderie. The size of a school is a personal consideration. Some students thrive in large schools; others prefer a smaller student community. Ask yourself which kind of student you are.

Faculty

You will undoubtedly want to assess the faculties of the law schools you are considering. School catalogs and websites will give you some idea of the backgrounds of the full-time faculty—what specialties they have, what they have published, and their public service activities. If the catalog tells you only where degrees were earned, ask for more information. You may also want to check the latest edition of the Association of American Law Schools' *Directory of Law Teachers*, which is available at law school libraries. It may help you to know that some members of the faculty have interests similar to your own.

Is the faculty relatively diverse with respect to race, ethnic background, gender, degrees in other fields, and breadth of experience? A faculty with diverse backgrounds will have various points of view and experiences. This diversity will enrich your legal education, broaden your own point of view, and help prepare you for the variety of clients you will work with after law school.

How many full-time professors teach how many students—that is, what is the faculty-to-student ratio?

Although some of the most prestigious law schools are famous for their large sections in the introductory courses, they also provide smaller classes, clinics, simulations, and seminars in advanced subjects. According to the *ABA Standards and Rules of Procedure for Approval of Law Schools*, it is not favorable to have a full-time student-to-full-time faculty ratio of 30 to 1, or greater. Some schools may be especially attractive to some students because of their small faculty-to-student ratio.

Are some of the teachers recognized as authorities in their respective fields through their writings and professional activities? Law school catalogs and websites vary widely regarding information about faculty. Some merely list each faculty member's name along with schools attended and degrees earned. Others may provide details about publications, professional activities, and noteworthy achievements, particularly when an individual is an authority in his or her field.

Are there visiting professors, distinguished lecturers and visitors, symposiums, and the like at the schools you are considering? Law school lectureship programs are a good means of presenting the knowledge and views of academics outside of the particular law school you attend.

The Library and Other Physical Facilities

Chances are you will spend a good deal of time in the law library, so be sure to investigate the library and all that it has to offer. There are several factors to consider when assessing a law school library: the quality of the research resources, ease of access to both print and electronic resources, staff, facilities, and hours of operation. It is also good to determine if the library participates in regional or local networks for information retrieval and interlibrary loan.

Knowing that a library has a volume count of 250,000 or 2.5 million by itself does not provide good information about the quality of the library's collection, so it is vital to look at other factors. All ABA-approved law schools must maintain a library that has the research materials considered essential for the study of law; this includes both primary and secondary sources. Determine how many copies of these essential materials are available and if they are also available in an electronic format. Look to see if the library has any special collections or other important historical materials. If you plan to focus on a particular legal area, be sure to inquire about the library's resources on that topic. Find out all of the electronic resources to which the library subscribes (look beyond Westlaw and LexisNexis) and see if it is possible to access them remotely from off campus. If the law school is affiliated with a university, explore the print and electronic resources of the other campus libraries for possible cross-disciplinary research.

Reference librarians and other professional librarians serve a vital role in the law library. Consider how many professional librarians work in the library and what percentage of librarians have a law degree as well as a library and information science degree. Are there a sufficient number of reference librarians for the number of students and faculty being served? Do the reference librarians offer courses and workshops in legal research techniques, and—if so—how many or how often? Is the library staff helpful? Law schools with evening or part-time programs should make professional reference librarians available in the evenings and on weekends, so be sure to look at the reference desk hours. Also, determine if it is possible to contact the library staff via e-mail or real-time chat.

Since you will need to spend much of your time in the library, make sure its hours will accommodate whatever schedule you might have. While it is not necessary for a library to be open around the clock, it should be open before classes begin each day and remain open well into the night and weekends. Consider if there is a designated area in the library or law school to accommodate 24-hour study after the library closes.

Be sure the library has an adequate number of comfortable seats with at least enough carrels to accommodate a reasonable number of students at any given time. Either in the library or elsewhere in the law building, there should be suitable space for group study and other forms of collaborative work. Does the library have a variety of seating configurations so that students can find a comfortable spot to engage in intense study and research for long periods of time? In addition, consider if there is a food facility within the library, law school, or on campus that maintains generous hours throughout the day, evenings, and weekends.

Access to technology should be available not only in the library, but throughout the law school building and the university. Robust wireless connectivity is essential for efficient research and communication between students and professors, so ask about the quality of the wireless network. Although computer labs are no longer as vital to law students given the proliferation of laptops and netbooks, it may be helpful to determine if there is a computer lab in the library or elsewhere in the law school and whether there is a dedicated information technology department to handle law student technology needs. The information technology department should maintain extensive hours, similar to those of the law library, so that students may conveniently have their technology questions answered.

Curriculum

The range and quality of academic programs is one of the most important factors to consider when choosing a law school.

Almost all law schools follow the traditional first-year core curriculum of civil procedure, criminal law, contracts, legal research and writing, legal methods, torts, constitutional law, and property (see chapter 2). Do not assume that all law schools have programs that suit your personal needs and special interests. If you don't have any specific interests in mind—and many beginning students don't—try to make sure the school offers a wide range of electives so that you will have many options. A thorough grounding in basic legal theory will enable you to apply the principles learned to any area of law to which they pertain.

In fact, you shouldn't overemphasize your search for specialties; most law students are not specialists when they graduate, nor do they need to be. Generally speaking, new lawyers begin to find their specialties only in the second to fifth years of their careers. A well-rounded legal education is the best preparation for almost any career path you take. The schools' individual websites and the descriptions in this book will tell you a good deal about academic programs. You may also wish to ask school representatives questions such as: Does the school offer a variety of courses, or is it especially strong in certain areas; what sizes are the classes; are seminars and small-group classroom experiences available; and are there ample opportunities for developing writing, researching, and drafting skills?

Beyond the content of law school courses, other academic program considerations may be of interest to you as a prospective law student.

Special Programs and Academic Activities

Joint-Degree Programs

Joint-degree programs allow you to pursue law school and graduate degrees simultaneously. Almost every combination is available at some institutions; additionally, many law schools allow you to create your own joint-degree program, even if no such formal program is in place. Among the more popular degrees are the JD/MBA and the JD/MA in areas such as economics or political science. For details, check the individual school listings in this book or check the law school's recruitment materials.

Master of Laws (LLM) and Special-Degree Programs

Many law schools offer advanced degrees that allow students to take graduate-level law courses. The LLM degree is quite common and usually is tailored to individual interests. Some schools offer master of laws degrees with particular concentrations, such as a master of laws in taxation and master of comparative law. Students may enroll in LLM programs only after having received the JD degree.

A few schools also offer very specific, special-degree programs. Some of these specialties include a doctorate in civil law, doctor of juridical science, and doctor of jurisprudence and social policy. Schools also may offer certificate (or otherwise-designated) programs. Finding out what types of advanced degrees a law school offers may help you determine the emphases of the school. (See appendix B for a listing of post-JD programs.)

Part-Time and Evening Programs

Part-time programs may be offered either in the evening or the day. For the last two years, approximately 7 percent of first-year law students have enrolled in law school part time. The conventional wisdom is that if you are financially able to attend law school full time, you ought to do so.

Part-time programs generally take four years to complete instead of three years. While fewer than half of law schools offer part-time programs, if you have economic constraints that make attending a full-time program difficult, then a part-time program offers the opportunity to study law while you are working.

Clinical Programs

Many law schools offer students authentic experiences as lawyers by involving them with clients. The best clinical programs involve students in actual legal situations, simulations of such situations, or a combination of both, either at the school itself or in the community. Clinical programs at some schools offer a team-teaching approach; practical, professional skills are taught along with traditional classroom theory. In this manner, faculty can advise and work closely with students.

Moot Court Competitions

Schools that provide opportunities for students to rehearse trial and appellate advocacy in trial team and moot court competitions help them become adept at using interviewing, counseling, research, advocacy, and negotiation skills.

Student Journals

Most law schools have a law review—a journal of scholarly articles and commentaries on the law—and other student-edited scholarly journals. Writing for the journals of a school can be important to both your legal education and your career in law. Thus, evaluating the journals at a particular law school may be worthwhile when trying to choose the right school to attend.

Traditionally, student journal editors are chosen on the basis of academic standing, but writing ability, regardless of class rank, may also be a criterion. Today, a growing number of schools select journal editors by holding a competition in which students submit a previously assigned writing sample to the current editorial board. If you are on a journal, employers may assume you are either one of the brightest in your class, or an outstanding writer—or both.

If possible, check the journals of the schools you are considering. The character of the journal may be a reflection of the character of the institution that supports it.

Order of the Coif
Many law schools have a chapter of the Order of the Coif, a national honor society for outstanding students. Students are elected to Coif on the basis of scholarship and character. Check to see if the schools you are considering include such a chapter.

Academic Support Programs
Programs for students who need or who are expected to need assistance with legal analysis and writing are offered by most law schools. Students are invited to participate in these programs on the basis of either their entering credentials or their actual law school performance. This assistance may be offered in the summer prior to beginning law school, during the academic year, or both. The aim of academic support programs is to ensure that students have an equal opportunity to compete in law school. For further information about academic assistance programs, consult the admission office at the law school.

Student Organizations
You can also tell something about a law school's intellectual resources and its students by the number and range of student associations and organizations sponsored on campus. Many schools have chapters of the ABA Law Student Division; a student bar association; associations for minority groups, such as the Asian, Black, Hispanic, and Native American law student associations; associations based on religious affiliations; and associations for students with disabilities. Some, but not all, schools sponsor an environmental law society, a gay and lesbian law student society, a legal assistance society, a postconviction assistance project, a civil liberties group, a Federalist Society, a volunteer income-tax assistance program, a law student spouses' club, an international law society, a law and technology society, or a client-counseling society. Through the ABA Commission on Disability Rights (www.americanbar.org/disabilityrights), you can access an online directory that lists resources and student organizations for students with physical or mental disabilities at each ABA-approved law school. Determine which associations are important to you and check individual law school catalogs to see which law schools offer what you need.

Career Services and Employment
One of the tests of a good law school is the effort the institution makes to help its students and graduates understand their career options and find satisfying employment. Planning a career in law requires students to integrate their legal education and personal goals in the context of the employment marketplace. Some students begin law school with a clear idea of how they expect to use their legal education (although they may change their minds along the way). Others are uncertain, or see a number of tempting possibilities. The career services office, faculty, and alumni of the school are valuable resources in the process of understanding and selecting among the many opportunities available to lawyers.

The first role of the career services office is to educate students about career opportunities in all sectors, including government and public service, law firms of all sizes and specialties, corporations, and so forth. To accomplish such a task, a law school may arrange panel presentations, meetings with practicing lawyers in different fields, and a library of career information materials. Career services professionals also collect and distribute vital information and resources; teach students job-search strategies, such as effective interviewing skills and employment research; and discuss students' individual interests, options, and presentation.

In most schools, only a small percentage of the class gets jobs through on-campus interviewing. Therefore, it is important to investigate the additional support provided by the career services staff and the experiences of the school's students and graduates in finding jobs.

Career services offices are concerned about all students, not just those at the top of the class rankings. Most spend a great deal of time and effort working with students individually and marketing the school to potential employers in order to increase students' options. Here are some questions you may want to ask about a school's career services:

• What programs does the school offer to introduce students to career options? Do they seem interesting, relevant, and timely?

• Are the career-counseling professionals accessible, respected, well-qualified, and supportive?

• Are the school's faculty and graduates involved in educating students about their career options?

• What types of employers, and how many, recruit on campus each year? What are the average number of interviews and offers per student? What percentage of students obtain jobs through the on-campus interviewing process?

• What positions have graduates taken in recent years? What jobs do students take during the summers? In what locales do students and graduates work? Are these employment profiles changing?

• What are the average or median salaries for the school's graduates?

• What percentage of students have accepted positions by graduation; within six months of graduation?

• Does the school offer career counseling and information for its graduates?

Pro Bono Programs
Many law schools have programs that offer students the opportunity to put their classroom instruction to work by offering services to the community at no charge. These programs often concentrate on helping indigent and marginalized populations. The programs vary in scope and style, but you should inquire at the law schools to which you are applying about their particular programs.

TRANSFERRING TO ANOTHER LAW SCHOOL

After starting law school, some law students seek to transfer to another law school. This occurs frequently enough to warrant advice and information. There are many reasons that law students seek to transfer, including financial reasons, job relocation of a spouse or partner, or to be closer to family.

Occasionally law students will seek a transfer to another law school that they perceive as having a higher status or ranking.

There are several factors that should be taken into account when considering a decision to transfer to another law school and, frequently, a student contemplating transfer should obtain relevant information concerning the consequences of a transfer. First, many of the strongest and most sustaining relationships between lawyers occur during their first year of law school and these relationships last throughout the law student's career. Students often comment on the loss of community and close friendships they made in their first year when they transfer to another law school. Second, students transferring to another law school are often not eligible for scholarships at the new law school. This factor may be significant for students who are considering forgoing a scholarship award at their home law school when they transfer. Third, many law school law reviews, journals, and moot court programs do not permit transfer students to be considered for membership on the law review and moot court teams until after a year at the new law school. This may preclude transferring law students from being considered for law review at all or for selection for the editorial board of the law review, or for selection to a moot court team. Fourth, in many schools, course selection for the fall will already have been completed by the time the student's transfer application is accepted. As a result, there may be limited access to courses that are desired or perhaps needed as prerequisites for later advanced offerings. Fifth, many law schools do not include the transferring law student's grades earned at the prior law school in the class ranking, and some do not permit transfer students to be eligible for GPA-based graduation honors such as Order of the Coif.

The decision whether to transfer or remain at the law school of original matriculation is a difficult one. Some law students have no or little choice but to transfer for personal or hardship reasons. Other law students considering a transfer do so to game the law school ranking phenomenon. This may be a dangerous gamble because of the negative aspects of law school transfers. Any law student considering transferring should gather as much information as possible concerning the ramifications of the transfer.

A CAREER IN LAW FOR RACIALLY AND ETHNICALLY DIVERSE GROUPS

Despite attempts to encourage the legal profession to reflect the population it serves, members of racial and ethnic groups remain underrepresented in the legal profession. Because lawyers must serve clients from diverse populations in a variety of settings, an increase in the number of lawyers from underrepresented minority groups is crucial. Individual clients, government agencies, and large private or public organizations are all better served by lawyers who offer diverse perspectives and experiences, including those of varied racial and ethnic backgrounds.

In addition, a law career can be a rewarding and fulfilling opportunity for men and women from underrepresented minority groups. Legal training provides career flexibility in a world with global professional opportunities in business, government, education, and other areas.

Support for Diversity
Individual law schools and legal organizations are committed to continued progress toward alleviating the historic shortage of underrepresented minority lawyers. For example, the Law School Admission Council has dedicated resources to numerous projects designed to increase the number of underrepresented minority men and women who attend law schools. Both the American Bar Association Section of Legal Education and Admissions to the Bar (the official accrediting body for law schools) and the Association of American Law Schools (the professional organization of law teachers) require law schools to undertake efforts to ensure diverse faculties and students.

Early Preparation and DiscoverLaw.org
Begin preparation early—that is the best advice for people from racial and ethnic minority groups who are interested in pursuing careers in law. There are a number of programs designed to enhance the skills of underrepresented minority students. Go to DiscoverLaw.org, a primary source of information for racially and ethnically diverse students who wish to explore career opportunities in law during their first and second year of undergraduate school, or even earlier. Discovering law when beginning to explore careers makes it easier to choose a path that will lead to a law degree. High school and first- and second-year undergraduates should visit DiscoverLaw.org for more information.

Admission to Law School
Admission to law school is competitive for all candidates, including members of underrepresented minority groups. The key is to carefully select law schools based on solid research, to pay close attention to guidelines for submitting applications, and to apply early. Law schools often have different admission requirements, so it is important to do sufficient research on specific schools, and apply strategically. Read and reread the information in this book. Also, check school websites or catalogs.

Students may choose to seek advice from prelaw advisors, academic counselors, diversity program directors, and practicing attorneys. Carefully filter advice from others. Remember that every law school is different, and the primary source of information should be the admission office of the school to which the student is interested in applying.

Let the law schools you have selected know that you are interested. Often a school will have a specific outreach program targeted to underrepresented minority students, designated diversity personnel for counseling, or a minority law student organization available to assist applicants. A personal visit is always recommended.

Don't be intimidated by the law school admission process. The schools evaluate every aspect of individual applications, including personal and educational background, undergraduate record, LSAT score, and letters of recommendation and evaluations. It may be advantageous to include information on racial or ethnic identity, especially if it has shaped personal experiences or demonstrated challenges overcome in educational background. Similarly, interesting life experiences and past employment experiences also add to the value of an application.

For information on the number and percentages of specific minority students and specific minority faculty at ABA-approved law schools, consult the individual school data pages and "Key Facts for Minority Law School Applicants" in this publication. Note: New aggregate categories for reporting racial/ethnicity data were adopted in 2011 in accordance with the final guidance issued by the US Department of Education. For more information, see *Federal Register,* Volume 72 (October 19, 2007), "Final Guidance on Maintaining, Collecting, and Reporting Racial and Ethnic Data to the US Department of Education," pages 59266–59279 and The Race and Ethnicity Information Center of the Department of Education's Integrated Postsecondary Education Data System (nces.ed.gov/ipeds; on the home page of this site, go to IPEDS Resources. Scroll down and click on Race/Ethnicity Information Center).

Conditional Admission Programs
Law schools recognize that sometimes the numerical qualifiers and other admission credentials do not adequately assess all candidates for admission. Some law schools have developed conditional admission programs for this purpose. Conditional admission programs typically give students a chance to demonstrate their eligibility for admission to a particular school by taking one or two courses in the summer prior to the start of classes. Students who meet the required performance criteria are offered admission to that school. Guidelines for these programs vary, and candidates should contact the individual law school offering conditional programs to find out program requirements. A list of conditional admission programs can be found in the **Future JD Students** section of LSAC.org (select **Racial/Ethnic Diversity** on the right-hand side of the page, and click on **Helpful Links**).

Being in Law School
Once students are in law school, they will encounter a challenging but manageable academic program. Most law schools offer academic assistance programs to students who may need help during law school. Depending on the individual law school, these services may include additional assistance preparing for the bar examination. Very often a variety of services and programs are in place to ensure student success, including minority law student organizations.

Most students admitted to law school, including underrepresented minority students, perform successfully in law school. They gain admission to the state bar of their choice. Most importantly, they are also able to make effective use of their law degrees, whether practicing law or following other career avenues.

For more information on opportunities in law for underrepresented minority men and women, go to the **Future JD Students** section of LSAC.org, select **Racial/Ethnic Diversity** on the right-hand side of the page, and click on **Helpful Links**.

	Total # Students (Full-Time and Part-Time)	Number and Percentage of Minority Students																			Total Full-Time Faculty, Fall	Total Full-Time Faculty, Spring	Number and Percentage of Minority Faculty					
		All Hispanics		American Indian/Alaska Native		Asian		Black/African American		Native Hawaiian/Pacific Islander		2 or More Races		Nonresident Alien		Unknown		Total # and % Minority Students				Total # and % Full-Time Minority Faculty, Fall		Total # and % Full-Time Minority Faculty, Spring		Total # Part-Time Minority Faculty, Fall	Total # Part-Time Minority Faculty, Spring
	#	#	%	#	%	#	%	#	%	#	%	#	%	#	%	#	%	#	%	#	#	#	%	#	%	#	#
ALABAMA																											
Alabama	509	8	1.6	2	0.4	7	1.4	46	9.0	3	0.6	6	1.2	0	0.0	0	0.0	72	14.1	45	48	5	11.1	6	12.5	1	2
Faulkner	335	5	1.5	4	1.2	5	1.5	26	7.8	2	0.6	0	0.0	0	0.0	9	2.7	42	12.5	20	19	2	10.0	3	15.8	0	0
Samford	489	11	2.2	3	0.6	11	2.2	26	5.3	1	0.2	14	2.9	5	1.0	24	4.9	66	13.5	23	22	4	17.4	4	18.2	2	1
ARIZONA																											
Arizona	440	33	7.5	12	2.7	31	7.0	6	1.4	0	0.0	15	3.4	14	3.2	52	11.8	97	22.0	39	39	7	17.9	8	20.5	2	3
Arizona State	602	64	10.6	28	4.7	21	3.5	10	1.7	0	0.0	16	2.7	5	0.8	27	4.5	139	23.1	52	54	8	15.4	8	14.8	0	1
Phoenix	969	137	14.1	11	1.1	49	5.1	70	7.2	3	0.3	18	1.9	8	0.8	67	6.9	288	29.7	35	30	12	34.3	9	30.0	7	5
ARKANSAS																											
Arkansas	401	19	4.7	7	1.7	10	2.5	33	8.2	1	0.2	1	0.2	1	0.2	1	0.2	71	17.7	28	28	2	7.1	3	10.7	0	0
Arkansas-Little Rock	476	18	3.8	5	1.1	10	2.1	47	9.9	0	0.0	9	1.9	9	1.9	12	2.5	89	18.7	21	21	3	14.3	5	23.8	3	7
CALIFORNIA																											
California-Berkeley	869	122	14.0	14	1.6	168	19.3	47	5.4	0	0.0	0	0.0	36	4.1	86	9.9	351	40.4	86	87	15	17.4	14	16.1	7	9
California-Davis	601	43	7.2	7	1.2	121	20.1	12	2.0	0	0.0	0	0.0	8	1.3	60	10.0	183	30.4	46	47	18	39.1	16	34.0	3	4
California-Hastings	1,244	126	10.1	8	0.6	249	20.0	51	4.1	5	0.4	46	3.7	17	1.4	124	10.0	485	39.0	68	68	12	17.6	13	19.1	9	8
California-Irvine	235	27	11.5	1	0.4	50	21.3	7	3.0	1	0.4	5	2.1	6	2.6	28	11.9	91	38.7	28	23	7	25.0	6	26.1	1	2
California-Los Angeles	987	84	8.5	18	1.8	146	14.8	39	4.0	1	0.1	27	2.7	15	1.5	219	22.2	315	31.9	87	89	15	17.2	13	14.6	1	5
California Western	827	103	12.5	8	1.0	91	11.0	23	2.8	3	0.4	25	3.0	12	1.5	46	5.6	253	30.6	46	42	5	10.9	5	11.9	1	5
Chapman	532	21	3.9	3	0.6	28	5.3	2	0.4	33	6.2	48	9.0	0	0.0	79	14.8	135	25.4	44	49	6	13.6	5	10.2	1	1
Golden Gate	684	62	9.1	3	0.4	117	17.1	14	2.0	5	0.7	15	2.2	12	1.8	72	10.5	216	31.6	39	38	9	23.1	9	23.7	14	11
La Verne	274	56	20.4	2	0.7	36	13.1	5	1.8	5	1.8	3	1.1	6	2.2	0	0.0	107	39.1	19	19	6	31.6	7	36.8	4	5
Loyola Marymount	1,279	163	12.7	8	0.6	259	20.3	51	4.0	4	0.3	4	0.3	0	0.0	73	5.7	489	38.2	69	66	12	17.4	11	16.7	7	5
Pacific, McGeorge	908	63	6.9	19	2.1	150	16.5	18	2.0	0	0.0	0	0.0	13	1.4	0	0.0	250	27.5	49	46	9	18.4	7	15.2	7	9
Pepperdine	629	39	6.2	0	0.0	48	7.6	20	3.2	0	0.0	28	4.5	13	2.1	112	17.8	135	21.5	36	39	5	13.9	6	15.4	2	2
San Diego	982	107	10.9	3	0.3	155	15.8	15	1.5	2	0.2	47	4.8	5	0.5	48	4.9	329	33.5	63	62	5	7.9	4	6.5	7	7
San Francisco	712	88	12.4	5	0.7	92	12.9	55	7.7	2	0.3	41	5.8	0	0.0	66	9.3	283	39.7	38	38	13	34.2	13	34.2	4	5
Santa Clara	967	86	8.9	7	0.7	240	24.8	20	2.1	6	0.6	25	2.6	43	4.4	3	0.3	384	39.7	63	68	12	19.0	13	19.1	6	7
Southern California	648	69	10.6	2	0.3	122	18.8	42	6.5	1	0.2	22	3.4	13	2.0	71	11.0	258	39.8	47	43	5	10.6	6	14.0	7	9

	Total # Students (Full-Time and Part-Time) #	All Hispanics #	All Hispanics %	American Indian/Alaska Native #	American Indian/Alaska Native %	Asian #	Asian %	Black/African American #	Black/African American %	Native Hawaiian/Pacific Islander #	Native Hawaiian/Pacific Islander %	2 or More Races #	2 or More Races %	Nonresident Alien #	Nonresident Alien %	Unknown #	Unknown %	Total # and % Minority Students #	Total # and % Minority Students %	Total Full-Time Faculty, Fall #	Total Full-Time Faculty, Spring #	Total # and % Full-Time Minority Faculty, Fall #	Total # and % Full-Time Minority Faculty, Fall %	Total # and % Full-Time Minority Faculty, Spring #	Total # and % Full-Time Minority Faculty, Spring %	Total # Part-Time Minority Faculty, Fall #	Total # Part-Time Minority Faculty, Spring #
Southwestern	1,121	164	14.6	5	0.4	144	12.8	53	4.7	4	0.4	29	2.6	8	0.7	98	8.7	399	35.6	60	60	14	23.3	15	25.0	5	10
Stanford	571	73	12.8	1	0.2	58	10.2	42	7.4	0	0.0	40	7.0	11	1.9	26	4.6	214	37.5	65	70	10	15.4	12	17.1	3	8
Thomas Jefferson	1,066	150	14.1	11	1.0	40	3.8	63	5.9	89	8.3	0	0.0	15	1.4	0	0.0	353	33.1	42	43	9	21.4	10	23.3	0	2
Western State	511	83	16.2	5	1.0	82	16.0	25	4.9	2	0.4	6	1.2	12	2.3	13	2.5	203	39.7	23	18	7	30.4	4	22.2	1	3
Whittier	700	123	17.6	6	0.9	140	20.0	23	3.3	0	0.0	0	0.0	0	0.0	30	4.3	292	41.7	33	27	3	9.1	1	3.7	3	5
COLORADO																											
Colorado	540	52	9.6	17	3.1	34	6.3	20	3.7	0	0.0	6	1.1	1	0.2	2	0.4	129	23.9	50	48	11	22.0	9	18.8	2	3
Denver	946	73	7.7	9	1.0	30	3.2	22	2.3	0	0.0	23	2.4	0	0.0	32	3.4	157	16.6	68	69	17	25.0	14	20.3	4	4
CONNECTICUT																											
Connecticut	616	49	8.0	4	0.6	58	9.4	24	3.9	1	0.2	0	0.0	10	1.6	54	8.8	136	22.1	47	51	4	8.5	8	15.7	2	4
Quinnipiac	438	20	4.6	2	0.5	23	5.3	8	1.8	0	0.0	6	1.4	1	0.2	45	10.3	59	13.5	35	33	2	5.7	4	12.1	0	0
Yale	638	51	8.0	1	0.2	87	13.6	38	6.0	0	0.0	26	4.1	37	5.8	17	2.7	203	31.8	70	74	9	12.9	7	9.5	4	2
DELAWARE																											
Widener	947	28	3.0	3	0.3	45	4.8	68	7.2	1	0.1	10	1.1	2	0.2	22	2.3	155	16.4	55	51	9	16.4	9	17.6	4	3
DISTRICT OF COLUMBIA																											
American	1,499	229	15.3	14	0.9	125	8.3	137	9.1	5	0.3	16	1.1	45	3.0	121	8.1	526	35.1	117	121	23	19.7	24	19.8	15	16
Catholic	768	34	4.4	3	0.4	64	8.3	68	8.9	3	0.4	5	0.7	26	3.4	199	25.9	177	23.0	56	56	8	14.3	9	16.1	5	7
District of Columbia	359	31	8.6	1	0.3	27	7.5	105	29.2	0	0.0	11	3.1	0	0.0	43	12.0	175	48.7	20	20	10	50.0	10	50.0	15	16
George Washington	1,753	123	7.0	6	0.3	166	9.5	89	5.1	4	0.2	1	0.1	43	2.5	179	10.2	389	22.2	91	94	13	14.3	15	16.0	12	22
Georgetown	1,932	89	4.6	1	0.1	94	4.9	155	8.0	2	0.1	36	1.9	60	3.1	381	19.7	377	19.5	137	130	17	12.4	13	10.0	8	9
Howard	427	18	4.2	2	0.5	7	1.6	351	82.2	9	2.1	1	0.2	12	2.8	7	1.6	388	90.9	25	22	18	72.0	17	77.3	22	24
FLORIDA																											
Ave Maria	489	62	12.7	2	0.4	7	1.4	22	4.5	0	0.0	10	2.0	4	0.8	15	3.1	103	21.1	26	29	2	7.7	1	3.4	1	0
Barry	708	85	12.0	7	1.0	40	5.6	47	6.6	2	0.3	6	0.8	17	2.4	53	7.5	187	26.4	33	34	9	27.3	8	23.5	4	3
Florida A&M	701	79	11.3	6	0.9	24	3.4	383	54.6	0	0.0	8	1.1	0	0.0	3	0.4	500	71.3	34	29	23	67.6	20	69.0	5	4
Florida Coastal	1,753	187	10.7	20	1.1	96	5.5	235	13.4	4	0.2	6	0.3	32	1.8	141	8.0	548	31.3	75	65	7	9.3	9	13.8	3	4
Florida	976	113	11.6	12	1.2	52	5.3	62	6.4	0	0.0	5	0.5	0	0.0	50	5.1	244	25.0	70	69	12	17.1	11	15.9	1	1
Florida International	551	215	39.0	6	1.1	14	2.5	58	10.5	0	0.0	17	3.1	3	0.5	4	0.7	310	56.3	32	31	13	40.6	16	51.6	8	10
Florida State	729	74	10.2	2	0.3	24	3.3	55	7.5	0	0.0	0	0.0	4	0.5	31	4.3	155	21.3	41	44	7	17.1	5	11.4	2	3

Number and Percentage of Minority Students | Number and Percentage of Minority Faculty

	Total # Students (Full-Time and Part-Time)	All Hispanics		American Indian/Alaska Native		Asian		Black/African American		Native Hawaiian/Pacific Islander		2 or More Races		Nonresident Alien		Unknown		Total # and % Minority Students		Total Full-Time Faculty, Fall	Total Full-Time Faculty, Spring	Total # and % Full-Time Minority Faculty, Fall		Total # and % Full-Time Minority Faculty, Spring		Total # Part-Time Minority Faculty, Fall	Total # Part-Time Minority Faculty, Spring
	#	#	%	#	%	#	%	#	%	#	%	#	%	#	%	#	%	#	%	#	#	#	%	#	%	#	#
Miami	1,361	218	16.0	9	0.7	47	3.5	84	6.2	1	0.1	10	0.7	24	1.8	84	6.2	369	27.1	82	82	18	22.0	17	20.7	16	21
Nova Southeastern	1,050	227	21.6	3	0.3	49	4.7	60	5.7	4	0.4	5	0.5	0	0.0	66	6.3	348	33.1	60	59	17	28.3	14	23.7	9	9
St. Thomas	719	268	37.3	6	0.8	21	2.9	46	6.4	0	0.0	32	4.5	9	1.3	0	0.0	373	51.9	39	37	9	23.1	7	18.9	9	10
Stetson	1,080	124	11.5	14	1.3	29	2.7	62	5.7	1	0.1	0	0.0	12	1.1	82	7.6	230	21.3	59	57	9	15.3	8	14.0	8	2
Thomas M. Cooley	3,628	203	5.6	19	0.5	173	4.8	527	14.5	9	0.2	95	2.6	214	5.9	100	2.8	1026	28.3	104	100	13	12.5	13	13.0	20	26
GEORGIA																											
Atlanta's John Marshall	732	39	5.3	11	1.5	9	1.2	177	24.2	46	6.3	0	0.0	3	0.4	12	1.6	282	38.5	42	36	13	31.0	10	27.8	2	3
Emory	810	65	8.0	6	0.7	86	10.6	42	5.2	0	0.0	22	2.7	33	4.1	51	6.3	221	27.3	63	65	6	9.5	6	9.2	0	0
Georgia	691	6	0.9	5	0.7	32	4.6	87	12.6	0	0.0	7	1.0	0	0.0	59	8.5	137	19.8	53	50	6	11.3	6	12.0	0	2
Georgia State	657	11	1.7	2	0.3	51	7.8	65	9.9	0	0.0	4	0.6	0	0.0	47	7.2	133	20.2	61	58	8	13.1	8	13.8	4	3
Mercer	451	10	2.2	6	1.3	26	5.8	39	8.6	0	0.0	0	0.0	1	0.2	48	10.6	81	18.0	26	27	3	11.5	3	11.1	1	1
HAWAI'I																											
Hawai'i	361	27	7.5	3	0.8	115	31.9	5	1.4	27	7.5	89	24.7	6	1.7	21	5.8	266	73.7	32	41	16	50.0	19	46.3	13	15
IDAHO																											
Idaho	358	24	6.7	7	2.0	7	2.0	1	0.3	1	0.3	9	2.5	3	0.8	15	4.2	49	13.7	22	21	3	13.6	2	9.5	0	0
ILLINOIS																											
Chicago	624	46	7.4	1	0.2	55	8.8	39	6.3	0	0.0	33	5.3	16	2.6	85	13.6	174	27.9	77	74	14	18.2	9	12.2	0	0
Chicago-Kent	933	82	8.8	0	0.0	56	6.0	38	4.1	18	1.9	16	1.7	33	3.5	133	14.3	210	22.5	65	66	6	9.2	7	10.6	6	9
DePaul	1,020	92	9.0	7	0.7	65	6.4	68	6.7	1	0.1	0	0.0	18	1.8	112	11.0	233	22.8	54	59	9	16.7	7	11.9	5	4
Illinois	639	45	7.0	3	0.5	64	10.0	48	7.5	0	0.0	22	3.4	24	3.8	39	6.1	182	28.5	51	50	10	19.6	10	20.0	5	5
John Marshall	1,479	103	7.0	11	0.7	99	6.7	120	8.1	2	0.1	2	0.1	9	0.6	79	5.3	337	22.8	75	76	15	20.0	13	17.1	13	9
Loyola-Chicago	869	63	7.2	2	0.2	42	4.8	80	9.2	0	0.0	16	1.8	6	0.7	15	1.7	203	23.4	55	53	10	18.2	7	13.2	10	7
Northern Illinois	321	23	7.2	1	0.3	15	4.7	24	7.5	1	0.3	2	0.6	0	0.0	19	5.9	66	20.6	20	19	6	30.0	7	36.8	1	1
Northwestern	801	54	6.7	5	0.6	143	17.9	59	7.4	0	0.0	34	4.2	40	5.0	0	0.0	295	36.8	94	99	7	7.4	7	7.1	4	10
Southern Illinois	376	5	1.3	4	1.1	11	2.9	5	1.3	1	0.3	0	0.0	0	0.0	30	8.0	26	6.9	26	23	4	15.4	3	13.0	1	1
INDIANA																											
Indiana-Bloomington	692	34	4.9	7	1.0	32	4.6	44	6.4	0	0.0	0	0.0	0	0.0	32	4.6	117	16.9	56	56	6	10.7	8	14.3	0	0
Indiana-Indianapolis	962	25	2.6	6	0.6	56	5.8	63	6.5	0	0.0	0	0.0	26	2.7	0	0.0	150	15.6	44	41	6	13.6	6	14.6	3	2

	Total # Students (Full-Time and Part-Time)	All Hispanics		American Indian/Alaska Native		Asian		Black/African American		Native Hawaiian/Pacific Islander		2 or More Races		Nonresident Alien		Unknown		Total # and % Minority Students		Total Full-Time Faculty, Fall	Total Full-Time Faculty, Spring	Total # and % Full-Time Minority Faculty, Fall		Total # and % Full-Time Minority Faculty, Spring		Total # Part-Time Minority Faculty, Fall	Total # Part-Time Minority Faculty, Spring
	#	#	%	#	%	#	%	#	%	#	%	#	%	#	%	#	%	#	%	#	#	#	%	#	%	#	#
Notre Dame	563	70	12.4	9	1.6	47	8.3	33	5.9	0	0.0	13	2.3	9	1.6	32	5.7	172	30.6	49	44	5	10.2	6	13.6	2	1
Valparaiso	566	50	8.8	5	0.9	27	4.8	65	11.5	3	0.5	13	2.3	4	0.7	11	1.9	163	28.8	29	34	5	17.2	6	17.6	1	2
IOWA																											
Drake	447	21	4.7	0	0.0	8	1.8	18	4.0	0	0.0	3	0.7	3	0.7	14	3.1	50	11.2	27	27	5	18.5	5	18.5	1	3
Iowa	556	30	5.4	6	1.1	39	7.0	16	2.9	1	0.2	0	0.0	8	1.4	0	0.0	92	16.5	42	42	4	9.5	6	14.3	0	0
KANSAS																											
Kansas	463	31	6.7	9	1.9	15	3.2	12	2.6	0	0.0	11	2.4	12	2.6	19	4.1	78	16.8	33	34	4	12.1	3	8.8	0	2
Washburn	413	17	4.1	12	2.9	10	2.4	17	4.1	1	0.2	0	0.0	8	1.9	12	2.9	57	13.8	31	31	6	19.4	6	19.4	0	0
KENTUCKY																											
Kentucky	415	6	1.4	3	0.7	12	2.9	38	9.2	0	0.0	3	0.7	2	0.5	4	1.0	62	14.9	24	23	3	12.5	3	13.0	0	1
Louisville-Brandeis	389	9	2.3	0	0.0	4	1.0	17	4.4	0	0.0	3	0.8	3	0.8	2	0.5	33	8.5	25	24	3	12.0	3	12.5	2	0
Northern Kentucky	569	8	1.4	3	0.5	9	1.6	20	3.5	1	0.2	1	0.2	0	0.0	26	4.6	42	7.4	28	31	4	14.3	4	12.9	2	1
LOUISIANA																											
Louisiana State	687	29	4.2	5	0.7	20	2.9	71	10.3	0	0.0	23	3.3	5	0.7	29	4.2	148	21.5	40	37	5	12.5	5	13.5	1	2
Loyola-New Orleans	813	86	10.6	9	1.1	29	3.6	102	12.5	1	0.1	0	0.0	5	0.6	51	6.3	227	27.9	52	52	13	25.0	11	21.2	2	0
Southern	729	74	10.2	1	0.1	4	0.5	394	54.0	1	0.1	0	0.0	0	0.0	8	1.1	474	65.0	39	36	26	66.7	23	63.9	19	7
Tulane	775	38	4.9	5	0.6	10	1.3	48	6.2	7	0.9	7	0.9	12	1.5	74	9.5	115	14.8	52	56	5	9.6	4	7.1	1	2
MAINE																											
Maine	280	10	3.6	3	1.1	2	0.7	4	1.4	9	3.2	0	0.0	3	1.1	0	0.0	28	10.0	16	17	0	0.0	0	0.0	0	0
MARYLAND																											
Baltimore	1,098	39	3.6	1	0.1	56	5.1	89	8.1	1	0.1	17	1.5	2	0.2	70	6.4	203	18.5	59	49	10	16.9	7	14.3	5	7
Maryland	956	86	9.0	2	0.2	93	9.7	96	10.0	1	0.1	25	2.6	11	1.2	21	2.2	303	31.7	64	65	16	25.0	14	21.5	5	7
MASSACHUSETTS																											
Boston College	784	55	7.0	3	0.4	74	9.4	27	3.4	0	0.0	14	1.8	11	1.4	98	12.5	173	22.1	52	51	9	17.3	10	19.6	1	1
Boston	799	67	8.4	2	0.3	78	9.8	32	4.0	0	0.0	26	3.3	29	3.6	49	6.1	205	25.7	58	58	6	10.3	6	10.3	8	10
Harvard	1,679	135	8.0	10	0.6	180	10.7	177	10.5	0	0.0	30	1.8	108	6.4	165	9.8	532	31.7	137	138	17	12.4	18	13.0	2	4
New England	1,141	31	2.7	1	0.1	41	3.6	19	1.7	0	0.0	28	2.5	9	0.8	176	15.4	120	10.5	38	37	4	10.5	4	10.8	9	5
Northeastern	656	75	11.4	4	0.6	61	9.3	67	10.2	0	0.0	18	2.7	2	0.3	88	13.4	225	34.3	37	35	9	24.3	9	25.7	8	9
Suffolk	1,681	64	3.8	6	0.4	128	7.6	47	2.8	1	0.1	54	3.2	37	2.2	33	2.0	300	17.8	76	80	11	14.5	12	15.0	2	3

	Total # Students (Full-Time and Part-Time)	Number and Percentage of Minority Students																			Total Full-Time Faculty, Fall	Total Full-Time Faculty, Spring	Number and Percentage of Minority Faculty					
		All Hispanics		American Indian/Alaska Native		Asian		Black/African American		Native Hawaiian/Pacific Islander		2 or More Races		Nonresident Alien		Unknown		Total # and % Minority Students				Total # and % Full-Time Minority Faculty, Fall		Total # and % Full-Time Minority Faculty, Spring		Total # Part-Time Minority Faculty, Fall	Total # Part-Time Minority Faculty, Spring
	#	#	%	#	%	#	%	#	%	#	%	#	%	#	%	#	%	#	%	#	#	#	%	#	%	#	#
Western New England	439	12	2.7	7	1.6	17	3.9	15	3.4	0	0.0	0	0.0	1	0.2	29	6.6	51	11.6	28	27	5	17.9	4	14.8	0	1
MICHIGAN																											
Detroit Mercy	669	16	2.4	1	0.1	23	3.4	69	10.3	0	0.0	0	0.0	157	23.5	0	0.0	109	16.3	37	37	4	10.8	3	8.1	2	4
Michigan	1,149	53	4.6	5	0.4	109	9.5	33	2.9	0	0.0	42	3.7	30	2.6	102	8.9	242	21.1	90	92	10	11.1	12	13.0	2	2
Michigan State	915	45	4.9	17	1.9	31	3.4	71	7.8	4	0.4	24	2.6	52	5.7	45	4.9	192	21.0	55	51	8	14.5	8	15.7	1	2
Thomas M. Cooley	3,628	203	5.6	19	0.5	173	4.8	527	14.5	9	0.2	95	2.6	214	5.9	100	2.8	1026	28.3	104	100	13	12.5	13	13.0	20	26
Wayne State	570	17	3.0	3	0.5	38	6.7	34	6.0	0	0.0	0	0.0	14	2.5	40	7.0	92	16.1	38	39	4	10.5	4	10.3	2	1
MINNESOTA																											
Hamline	617	29	4.7	4	0.6	33	5.3	25	4.1	0	0.0	11	1.8	0	0.0	17	2.8	102	16.5	36	35	2	5.6	2	5.7	1	3
Minnesota	752	19	2.5	8	1.1	53	7.0	27	3.6	2	0.3	36	4.8	34	4.5	31	4.1	145	19.3	61	67	7	11.5	7	10.4	3	10
St. Thomas-Minneapolis	483	18	3.7	4	0.8	26	5.4	12	2.5	1	0.2	6	1.2	1	0.2	50	10.4	67	13.9	30	28	5	16.7	6	21.4	7	7
William Mitchell	1,004	28	2.8	7	0.7	37	3.7	23	2.3	18	1.8	18	1.8	9	0.9	139	13.8	131	13.0	41	37	6	14.6	5	13.5	29	25
MISSISSIPPI																											
Mississippi	531	15	2.8	5	0.9	6	1.1	62	11.7	0	0.0	1	0.2	0	0.0	6	1.1	89	16.8	23	27	4	17.4	5	18.5	1	1
Mississippi College	576	7	1.2	3	0.5	5	0.9	48	8.3	0	0.0	0	0.0	0	0.0	24	4.2	63	10.9	26	28	3	11.5	5	17.9	8	6
MISSOURI																											
Missouri	431	13	3.0	1	0.2	9	2.1	31	7.2	0	0.0	13	3.0	2	0.5	16	3.7	67	15.5	28	28	2	7.1	3	10.7	0	0
Missouri-Kansas City	466	15	3.2	3	0.6	13	2.8	20	4.3	0	0.0	1	0.2	4	0.9	29	6.2	52	11.2	37	32	3	8.1	4	12.5	0	0
St. Louis	930	32	3.4	2	0.2	33	3.5	45	4.8	1	0.1	24	2.6	5	0.5	13	1.4	137	14.7	65	64	8	12.3	7	10.9	4	3
Washington University	851	19	2.2	3	0.4	80	9.4	92	10.8	0	0.0	29	3.4	74	8.7	75	8.8	223	26.2	67	63	10	14.9	6	9.5	8	7
MONTANA																											
Montana	252	7	2.8	8	3.2	2	0.8	1	0.4	0	0.0	9	3.6	2	0.8	0	0.0	27	10.7	14	14	2	14.3	4	28.6	0	0
NEBRASKA																											
Creighton	442	17	3.8	0	0.0	17	3.8	13	2.9	0	0.0	2	0.5	5	1.1	16	3.6	49	11.1	24	23	3	12.5	3	13.0	0	1
Nebraska	393	9	2.3	4	1.0	5	1.3	6	1.5	0	0.0	0	0.0	2	0.5	0	0.0	24	6.1	29	26	3	10.3	2	7.7	4	0
NEVADA																											
Nevada	465	52	11.2	8	1.7	50	10.8	26	5.6	3	0.6	0	0.0	0	0.0	23	4.9	139	29.9	33	26	7	21.2	5	19.2	0	0
NEW HAMPSHIRE																											
New Hampshire	394	15	3.8	0	0.0	35	8.9	17	4.3	0	0.0	8	2.0	13	3.3	1	0.3	75	19.0	35	33	1	2.9	1	3.0	2	0

	Total # Students (Full-Time and Part-Time) #	All Hispanics #	All Hispanics %	American Indian/Alaska Native #	American Indian/Alaska Native %	Asian #	Asian %	Black/African American #	Black/African American %	Native Hawaiian/Pacific Islander #	Native Hawaiian/Pacific Islander %	2 or More Races #	2 or More Races %	Nonresident Alien #	Nonresident Alien %	Unknown #	Unknown %	Total # and % Minority Students #	Total # and % Minority Students %	Total Full-Time Faculty, Fall #	Total Full-Time Faculty, Spring #	Total # and % Full-Time Minority Faculty, Fall #	Total # and % Full-Time Minority Faculty, Fall %	Total # and % Full-Time Minority Faculty, Spring #	Total # and % Full-Time Minority Faculty, Spring %	Total # Part-Time Minority Faculty, Fall #	Total # Part-Time Minority Faculty, Spring #
NEW JERSEY																											
Rutgers-Camden	865	60	6.9	1	0.1	56	6.5	49	5.7	1	0.1	9	1.0	4	0.5	47	5.4	176	20.3	49	57	5	10.2	6	10.5	0	3
Rutgers-Newark	800	90	11.3	3	0.4	97	12.1	122	15.3	1	0.1	11	1.4	9	1.1	0	0.0	324	40.5	35	37	10	28.6	11	29.7	2	4
Seton Hall	983	68	6.9	3	0.3	74	7.5	39	4.0	0	0.0	7	0.7	10	1.0	0	0.0	191	19.4	55	57	10	18.2	9	15.8	8	9
NEW MEXICO																											
New Mexico	363	100	27.5	30	8.3	9	2.5	10	2.8	1	0.3	1	0.3	1	0.3	35	9.6	151	41.6	33	34	13	39.4	12	35.3	6	8
NEW YORK																											
Albany	686	18	2.6	1	0.1	33	4.8	20	2.9	0	0.0	20	2.9	11	1.6	117	17.1	92	13.4	44	45	8	18.2	8	17.8	4	4
Brooklyn	1,376	80	5.8	1	0.1	165	12.0	56	4.1	0	0.0	35	2.5	11	0.8	64	4.7	337	24.5	68	68	6	8.8	6	8.8	6	9
Cardozo	1,140	84	7.4	2	0.2	48	4.2	55	4.8	40	3.5	21	1.8	17	1.5	174	15.3	250	21.9	59	65	4	6.8	5	7.7	7	6
CUNY	480	80	16.7	1	0.2	57	11.9	41	8.5	1	0.2	16	3.3	5	1.0	3	0.6	196	40.8	35	35	15	42.9	15	42.9	2	2
Columbia	1,332	92	6.9	8	0.6	205	15.4	105	7.9	0	0.0	25	1.9	129	9.7	35	2.6	435	32.7	129	112	17	13.2	16	14.3	8	12
Cornell	612	65	10.6	12	2.0	88	14.4	45	7.4	0	0.0	19	3.1	45	7.4	0	0.0	229	37.4	53	46	9	17.0	7	15.2	0	0
Fordham	1,496	152	10.2	3	0.2	150	10.0	62	4.1	1	0.1	7	0.5	39	2.6	180	12.0	375	25.1	85	85	16	18.8	17	20.0	20	19
Hofstra	1,074	64	6.0	2	0.2	114	10.6	93	8.7	0	0.0	57	5.3	43	4.0	37	3.4	330	30.7	56	57	9	16.1	9	15.8	2	5
New York Law	1,765	232	13.1	4	0.2	66	3.7	126	7.1	0	0.0	19	1.1	0	0.0	181	10.3	448	25.4	79	64	14	17.7	8	12.5	7	7
New York	1,464	107	7.3	1	0.1	156	10.7	100	6.8	0	0.0	9	0.6	49	3.3	240	16.4	373	25.5	163	143	23	14.1	18	12.6	5	9
Pace	776	40	5.2	3	0.4	56	7.2	27	3.5	0	0.0	26	3.4	5	0.6	66	8.5	152	19.6	48	48	3	6.3	5	10.4	2	1
St. John's	935	91	9.7	0	0.0	72	7.7	42	4.5	0	0.0	24	2.6	12	1.3	18	1.9	229	24.5	56	47	10	17.9	9	19.1	3	9
SUNY	641	18	2.8	4	0.6	24	3.7	30	4.7	0	0.0	17	2.7	22	3.4	36	5.6	93	14.5	54	49	3	5.6	7	14.3	4	7
Syracuse	645	21	3.3	3	0.5	49	7.6	18	2.8	1	0.2	29	4.5	18	2.8	38	5.9	121	18.8	54	56	9	16.7	11	19.6	0	0
Touro	805	74	9.2	2	0.2	50	6.2	87	10.8	1	0.1	0	0.0	8	1.0	39	4.8	214	26.6	40	38	2	5.0	3	7.9	5	5
NORTH CAROLINA																											
Campbell	475	17	3.6	2	0.4	9	1.9	19	4.0	0	0.0	0	0.0	0	0.0	0	0.0	47	9.9	23	23	2	8.7	1	4.3	2	3
Charlotte	1,151	50	4.3	20	1.7	33	2.9	193	16.8	1	0.1	8	0.7	9	0.8	0	0.0	305	26.5	39	36	14	35.9	13	36.1	6	5
Duke	683	37	5.4	1	0.1	74	10.8	44	6.4	0	0.0	4	0.6	14	2.0	29	4.2	160	23.4	66	67	10	15.2	10	14.9	3	8
Elon	365	5	1.4	5	1.4	9	2.5	31	8.5	2	0.5	2	0.5	0	0.0	31	8.5	54	14.8	22	18	3	13.6	3	16.7	1	3
North Carolina	772	73	9.5	9	1.2	46	6.0	58	7.5	3	0.4	27	3.5	12	1.6	59	7.6	216	28.0	44	43	6	13.6	8	18.6	6	4

School	Total # Students (Full-Time and Part-Time) #	All Hispanics #	All Hispanics %	American Indian/Alaska Native #	American Indian/Alaska Native %	Asian #	Asian %	Black/African American #	Black/African American %	Native Hawaiian/Pacific Islander #	Native Hawaiian/Pacific Islander %	2 or More Races #	2 or More Races %	Nonresident Alien #	Nonresident Alien %	Unknown #	Unknown %	Total # and % Minority Students #	Total # and % Minority Students %	Total Full-Time Faculty, Fall #	Total Full-Time Faculty, Spring #	Total # and % Full-Time Minority Faculty, Fall #	Total # and % Full-Time Minority Faculty, Fall %	Total # and % Full-Time Minority Faculty, Spring #	Total # and % Full-Time Minority Faculty, Spring %	Total # Part-Time Minority Faculty, Fall #	Total # Part-Time Minority Faculty, Spring #
North Carolina Central	532	12	2.3	5	0.9	9	1.7	271	50.9	0	0.0	0	0.0	2	0.4	6	1.1	297	55.8	38	38	24	63.2	23	60.5	13	13
Wake Forest	506	30	5.9	8	1.6	14	2.8	46	9.1	1	0.2	6	1.2	1	0.2	53	10.5	105	20.8	48	47	8	16.7	6	12.8	0	0
NORTH DAKOTA																											
North Dakota	251	0	0.0	8	3.2	3	1.2	6	2.4	0	0.0	3	1.2	7	2.8	59	23.5	20	8.0	12	10	1	8.3	1	10.0	0	0
OHIO																											
Akron	536	20	3.7	2	0.4	21	3.9	31	5.8	0	0.0	5	0.9	0	0.0	34	6.3	79	14.7	31	32	3	9.7	3	9.4	0	1
Capital	633	15	2.4	1	0.2	10	1.6	45	7.1	0	0.0	7	1.1	2	0.3	27	4.3	78	12.3	34	33	3	8.8	4	12.1	2	2
Case Western	605	17	2.8	4	0.7	57	9.4	30	5.0	0	0.0	2	0.3	48	7.9	0	0.0	110	18.2	45	46	3	6.7	1	2.2	1	1
Cincinnati	409	12	2.9	0	0.0	25	6.1	28	6.8	0	0.0	0	0.0	2	0.5	0	0.0	65	15.9	32	28	7	21.9	6	21.4	1	5
Cleveland State	557	17	3.1	1	0.2	14	2.5	55	9.9	0	0.0	1	0.2	6	1.1	0	0.0	88	15.8	38	39	6	15.8	6	15.4	4	1
Dayton	488	7	1.4	2	0.4	14	2.9	28	5.7	0	0.0	8	1.6	0	0.0	7	1.4	59	12.1	25	27	5	20.0	5	18.5	1	1
Ohio Northern	311	5	1.6	3	1.0	7	2.3	18	5.8	0	0.0	0	0.0	0	0.0	20	6.4	33	10.6	20	19	4	20.0	4	21.1	0	0
Ohio State	680	28	4.1	8	1.2	54	7.9	45	6.6	2	0.3	0	0.0	9	1.3	42	6.2	137	20.1	46	43	7	15.2	6	14.0	3	4
Toledo	437	14	3.2	3	0.7	11	2.5	16	3.7	0	0.0	0	0.0	6	1.4	96	22.0	44	10.1	28	23	3	10.7	3	13.0	0	0
OKLAHOMA																											
Oklahoma	530	21	4.0	43	8.1	20	3.8	23	4.3	1	0.2	1	0.2	1	0.2	13	2.5	109	20.6	35	32	5	14.3	5	15.6	2	3
Oklahoma City	605	33	5.5	29	4.8	16	2.6	23	3.8	0	0.0	25	4.1	6	1.0	2	0.3	126	20.8	31	31	5	16.1	4	12.9	2	5
Tulsa	361	10	2.8	40	11.1	5	1.4	11	3.0	0	0.0	14	3.9	2	0.6	25	6.9	80	22.2	27	27	4	14.8	4	14.8	1	1
OREGON																											
Lewis & Clark	738	56	7.6	24	3.3	61	8.3	21	2.8	1	0.1	10	1.4	14	1.9	39	5.3	173	23.4	55	57	8	14.5	8	14.0	2	6
Oregon	505	12	2.4	4	0.8	29	5.7	14	2.8	2	0.4	16	3.2	5	1.0	19	3.8	77	15.2	32	32	8	25.0	8	25.0	0	2
Willamette	406	23	5.7	8	2.0	27	6.7	2	0.5	0	0.0	0	0.0	9	2.2	24	5.9	60	14.8	29	31	5	17.2	6	19.4	1	1
PENNSYLVANIA																											
Duquesne	642	6	0.9	3	0.5	17	2.6	15	2.3	0	0.0	0	0.0	3	0.5	0	0.0	41	6.4	24	26	3	12.5	4	15.4	2	4
Earle Mack, Drexel	450	32	7.1	2	0.4	20	4.4	35	7.8	0	0.0	0	0.0	3	0.7	32	7.1	89	19.8	29	29	7	24.1	6	20.7	2	5
Pennsylvania	806	32	4.0	1	0.1	118	14.6	59	7.3	1	0.1	35	4.3	30	3.7	54	6.7	246	30.5	69	72	10	14.5	8	11.1	4	7
Pennsylvania State	596	6	1.0	1	0.2	30	5.0	33	5.5	0	0.0	13	2.2	20	3.4	17	2.9	83	13.9	55	57	7	12.7	8	14.0	1	1
Pennsylvania	806	32	4.0	1	0.1	118	14.6	59	7.3	1	0.1	35	4.3	30	3.7	54	6.7	246	30.5	69	72	10	14.5	8	11.1	4	7
Pittsburgh	701	16	2.3	1	0.1	25	3.6	58	8.3	0	0.0	3	0.4	0	0.0	195	27.8	103	14.7	44	47	5	11.4	4	8.5	3	4

Number and Percentage of Minority Students | Number and Percentage of Minority Faculty

	Total # Students (Full-Time and Part-Time)	All Hispanics		American Indian/Alaska Native		Asian		Black/African American		Native Hawaiian/Pacific Islander		2 or More Races		Nonresident Alien		Unknown		Total # and % Minority Students		Total Full-Time Faculty, Fall	Total Full-Time Faculty, Spring	Total # and % Full-Time Minority Faculty, Fall		Total # and % Full-Time Minority Faculty, Spring		Total # Part-Time Minority Faculty, Fall	Total # Part-Time Minority Faculty, Spring
	#	#	%	#	%	#	%	#	%	#	%	#	%	#	%	#	%	#	%	#	#	#	%	#	%	#	#
Temple	902	77	8.5	9	1.0	73	8.1	68	7.5	0	0.0	13	1.4	9	1.0	11	1.2	240	26.6	58	60	13	22.4	15	25.0	14	18
Villanova	725	54	7.4	2	0.3	42	5.8	19	2.6	0	0.0	13	1.8	3	0.4	31	4.3	130	17.9	40	40	4	10.0	5	12.5	6	8
Widener	419	22	5.3	2	0.5	16	3.8	13	3.1	1	0.2	4	1.0	0	0.0	10	2.4	58	13.8	25	25	2	8.0	4	16.0	0	0
PUERTO RICO																											
Inter American	890	890	100.0	0	0.0	0	0.0	0	0.0	0	0.0	0	0.0	0	0.0	0	0.0	890	100.0	25	25	0	0.0	0	0.0	0	0
Pontifical Catholic	850	850	100.0	0	0.0	0	0.0	0	0.0	0	0.0	0	0.0	0	0.0	0	0.0	850	100.0	26	22	26	100.0	22	100.0	25	28
Puerto Rico	708	708	100.0	0	0.0	0	0.0	0	0.0	0	0.0	0	0.0	0	0.0	0	0.0	708	100.0	27	36	26	96.3	32	88.9	58	52
RHODE ISLAND																											
Roger Williams	555	37	6.7	2	0.4	14	2.5	17	3.1	0	0.0	8	1.4	5	0.9	56	10.1	78	14.1	29	26	4	13.8	3	11.5	2	2
SOUTH CAROLINA																											
Charleston	709	14	2.0	7	1.0	7	1.0	49	6.9	2	0.3	0	0.0	0	0.0	17	2.4	79	11.1	31	30	6	19.4	6	20.0	1	0
South Carolina	666	14	2.1	4	0.6	11	1.7	53	8.0	0	0.0	19	2.9	2	0.3	3	0.5	101	15.2	34	37	3	8.8	4	10.8	2	0
SOUTH DAKOTA																											
South Dakota	237	3	1.3	6	2.5	3	1.3	3	1.3	0	0.0	4	1.7	0	0.0	0	0.0	19	8.0	1	11	0	0.0	0	0.0	1	0
TENNESSEE																											
Memphis	421	7	1.7	3	0.7	10	2.4	40	9.5	0	0.0	0	0.0	0	0.0	0	0.0	60	14.3	18	18	2	11.1	3	16.7	5	5
Tennessee	487	30	6.2	2	0.4	20	4.1	49	10.1	1	0.2	19	3.9	2	0.4	4	0.8	121	24.8	30	31	3	10.0	3	9.7	0	0
Vanderbilt	586	25	4.3	1	0.2	26	4.4	47	8.0	0	0.0	15	2.6	24	4.1	84	14.3	114	19.5	41	32	8	19.5	5	15.6	3	1
TEXAS																											
Baylor	442	25	5.7	1	0.2	20	4.5	8	1.8	0	0.0	24	5.4	6	1.4	2	0.5	78	17.6	28	27	3	10.7	3	11.1	1	3
Houston	830	82	9.9	10	1.2	113	13.6	60	7.2	0	0.0	0	0.0	1	0.1	15	1.8	265	31.9	51	74	8	15.7	8	10.8	11	16
St. Mary's	899	239	26.6	6	0.7	28	3.1	35	3.9	1	0.1	3	0.3	0	0.0	0	0.0	312	34.7	38	35	6	15.8	6	17.1	9	8
SMU Dedman	866	77	8.9	12	1.4	68	7.9	43	5.0	1	0.1	10	1.2	4	0.5	47	5.4	211	24.4	41	44	8	19.5	9	20.5	2	2
South Texas	1,267	196	15.5	5	0.4	111	8.8	48	3.8	2	0.2	35	2.8	3	0.2	109	9.6	397	31.3	44	42	7	15.9	4	9.5	6	3
Texas	1,136	171	15.1	4	0.4	59	5.2	54	4.8	1	0.1	28	2.5	21	1.8	0	0.0	317	27.9	85	93	8	9.4	10	10.8	10	8
Texas Southern	573	162	28.3	3	0.5	44	7.7	262	45.7	0	0.0	0	0.0	2	0.3	0	0.0	471	82.2	33	32	28	84.8	24	75.0	5	16
Texas Tech	690	118	17.1	4	0.6	39	5.7	17	2.5	0	0.0	0	0.0	9	1.3	0	0.0	178	25.8	33	35	6	18.2	6	17.1	2	2
Texas Wesleyan	730	69	9.5	6	0.8	33	4.5	33	4.5	1	0.1	18	2.5	0	0.0	18	2.5	160	21.9	32	28	7	21.9	3	10.7	1	2

	Total # Students (Full-Time and Part-Time)	All Hispanics		American Indian/Alaska Native		Asian		Black/African American		Native Hawaiian/Pacific Islander		2 or More Races		Nonresident Alien		Unknown		Total # and % Minority Students		Total Full-Time Faculty, Fall	Total Full-Time Faculty, Spring	Total # and % Full-Time Minority Faculty, Fall		Total # and % Full-Time Minority Faculty, Spring		Total # Part-Time Minority Faculty, Fall	Total # Part-Time Minority Faculty, Spring
	#	#	%	#	%	#	%	#	%	#	%	#	%	#	%	#	%	#	%	#	#	#	%	#	%	#	#
UTAH																											
Brigham Young	443	31	7.0	5	1.1	18	4.1	5	1.1	14	3.2	0	0.0	5	1.1	0	0.0	73	16.5	25	20	5	20.0	4	20.0	3	2
Utah	398	19	4.8	3	0.8	16	4.0	4	1.0	0	0.0	0	0.0	3	0.8	20	5.0	42	10.6	37	36	7	18.9	6	16.7	0	0
VERMONT																											
Vermont	566	15	2.7	5	0.9	19	3.4	12	2.1	0	0.0	7	1.2	0	0.0	66	11.7	58	10.2	43	40	4	9.3	3	7.5	1	0
VIRGINIA																											
Appalachian	332	14	4.2	0	0.0	8	2.4	17	5.1	0	0.0	7	2.1	0	0.0	15	4.5	46	13.9	16	16	3	18.8	2	12.5	0	0
George Mason	714	23	3.2	8	1.1	66	9.2	7	1.0	0	0.0	3	0.4	13	1.8	8	1.1	107	15.0	36	39	6	16.7	7	17.9	5	11
Liberty	286	10	3.5	2	0.7	8	2.8	14	4.9	1	0.3	6	2.1	4	1.4	18	6.3	41	14.3	21	19	7	33.3	6	31.6	2	3
Regent	434	15	3.5	7	1.6	21	4.8	18	4.1	0	0.0	9	2.1	1	0.2	17	3.9	70	16.1	25	25	5	20.0	5	20.0	2	1
Richmond	454	4	0.9	3	0.7	29	6.4	38	8.4	2	0.4	0	0.0	14	3.1	16	3.5	76	16.7	35	31	3	8.6	2	6.5	3	0
Virginia	1,093	53	4.8	5	0.5	120	11.0	77	7.0	0	0.0	28	2.6	7	0.6	103	9.4	283	25.9	86	81	10	11.6	9	11.1	2	3
Washington and Lee	395	10	2.5	0	0.0	12	3.0	27	6.8	0	0.0	6	1.5	4	1.0	16	4.1	55	13.9	35	35	2	5.7	3	8.6	1	1
William & Mary	637	15	2.4	1	0.2	26	4.1	71	11.1	0	0.0	12	1.9	5	0.8	88	13.8	125	19.6	39	37	4	10.3	6	16.2	4	3
WASHINGTON																											
Gonzaga	506	12	2.4	9	1.8	5	1.0	2	0.4	14	2.8	11	2.2	4	0.8	82	16.2	53	10.5	27	29	3	11.1	4	13.8	0	0
Seattle	1,002	59	5.9	11	1.1	97	9.7	30	3.0	6	0.6	47	4.7	9	0.9	42	4.2	250	25.0	65	66	20	30.8	19	28.8	2	9
Washington	545	35	6.4	12	2.2	56	10.3	9	1.7	3	0.6	0	0.0	14	2.6	20	3.7	115	21.1	56	55	13	23.2	14	25.5	4	10
WEST VIRGINIA																											
West Virginia	418	9	2.2	3	0.7	7	1.7	20	4.8	1	0.2	6	1.4	1	0.2	3	0.7	46	11.0	34	35	6	17.6	5	14.3	0	0
WISCONSIN																											
Marquette	730	50	6.8	8	1.1	31	4.2	44	6.0	3	0.4	0	0.0	2	0.3	0	0.0	136	18.6	38	36	5	13.2	4	11.1	2	2
Wisconsin	792	57	7.2	14	1.8	40	5.1	51	6.4	2	0.3	11	1.4	28	3.5	37	4.7	175	22.1	68	66	11	16.2	13	19.7	5	7
WYOMING																											
Wyoming	226	10	4.4	2	0.9	3	1.3	3	1.3	2	0.9	6	2.7	3	1.3	27	11.9	26	11.5	17	18	2	11.8	2	11.1	0	0

The Role of the ABA Section of Legal Education and Admissions to the Bar

Under Title 34, Chapter VI, §602 of the Code of Federal Regulations, the Council and the Accreditation Committee of the ABA Section of Legal Education and Admissions to the Bar are recognized by the United States Department of Education (DOE) as the accrediting agency for programs that lead to the JD degree. In this function, the Council and the Section are separate and independent from the ABA, as required by DOE regulations.

The Council of the Section promulgates the Standards and Rules of Procedure for Approval of Law Schools with which law schools must comply in order to be ABA-approved. The Standards establish requirements for providing a sound program of legal education. The law school approval process established by the Council is designed to provide a careful and comprehensive evaluation of a law school and its compliance with the Standards.

The Council is comprised of 21 voting members, no more than 10 of whom may be law school deans or faculty members. Other members of the Council include judges, practicing attorneys, one law student, and at least three public members. By tradition, the Chair rotates among a judge, an academic, and a practicing lawyer.

To assist in its accreditation function, the Council has created three Standing Committees, with a similar mix of membership. The Accreditation Committee (19 members) assists the Council in evaluating schools seeking provisional or full approval and monitoring approved schools. It meets five times per year, typically for two-and-a-half days at each meeting. The Standards Review Committee (14 members) assists in reviewing the Standards to assure that they are transparent and that they focus on matters that are central to quality legal education. The Council has established an extensive process to seek comment on current and proposed Standards. The Standards Review Committee meets four times a year, typically for a day-and-a-half. The Questionnaire Committee (10 members) assists in gathering and maintaining the vast information database concerning ABA-approved law schools and their programs. It meets three times each year for a one-day meeting.

The Council and the Accreditation Committee are assisted by the staff of the Office of the Consultant on Legal Education and Admissions to the Bar. As of September 1, 2006, Hulett H. ("Bucky") Askew is the Consultant on Legal Education.

The Standards for Approval of Law Schools, the associated Rules of Procedure, additional information about the accreditation process, and other information about legal education may be found on the website of the Section of Legal Education and Admissions to the Bar: americanbar.org/legaled.

ABA-Approved Schools

As of March 2012, a total of 201 institutions are approved by the Council: 199 confer the first degree in law (the JD degree); the other approved school is the US Army Judge Advocate General's School, which offers an officer's resident graduate course, a specialized program beyond the first degree in law. As of March 2012, two of the 201 approved law schools are provisionally approved: University of California, Irvine School of Law and University of La Verne College of Law.

With an increase in the number of approved law schools, total JD enrollment in approved schools has gone from approximately 98,042 students in 1972 to 146,288 in the fall of 2011. In that same period, enrollment of women increased from 11,878 to 68,262 and minority enrollment increased from 6,730 to 35,859.

The complete list of ABA-approved law schools can be viewed online at americanbar.org/legaled.

The Approval Process

Provisional Approval

A law school may not apply for provisional approval by the ABA until it has been in operation for one year. Schools considering applying for provisional approval are strongly encouraged to contact the Office of the Consultant as early as possible, and well before the year in which the school applies for provisional approval. The Consultant or other senior members of the Consultant's Office staff will meet with representatives of schools seeking provisional approval and provide them with extensive information about the Standards for Approval of Law Schools, the Rules of Procedure, and the accreditation process.

A school must apply for provisional approval after classes have begun in the fall term and before October 15, so that a full site evaluation can be properly scheduled for late in the fall or early in the spring term. The site evaluation process is described on page 32. The school is required to develop an extensive Self-Study, which describes the school in detail, contains a critical evaluation of the school's strengths and weaknesses, establishes goals for the school's future progress, and identifies the means of achieving those goals. The school also completes a Site Evaluation Questionnaire that provides much of the information that a site evaluation team needs to ascertain the basic facts concerning the school and its operation.

The fact-finding report of the initial site evaluation team is sent to the Accreditation Committee, which holds a hearing at which representatives of the school applying for provisional approval appear. After the hearing, the Accreditation Committee makes its recommendation concerning provisional approval to the Council.

A school that applies for provisional approval must establish that it "is in substantial compliance with each of the Standards" and must present "a reliable plan for bringing the school into full compliance with the Standards within three years after receiving provisional approval." The burden is on the school to establish that it fulfills these requirements. If the Accreditation Committee concludes that a school is in substantial compliance with the Standards and that the school has a reliable plan for coming into full compliance, the Committee will recommend that the Council grant provisional approval. If the Committee concludes that either the school is not in substantial compliance or does not have a reliable plan to come into full compliance in three years, it will recommend against provisional approval.

When a school seeks provisional approval, the final decision on the school's application is made by the Council. The Accreditation Committee's findings of fact are binding on the Council unless those findings are not supported by substantial evidence in the record, but the Accreditation Committee's conclusions and recommendations are not binding on the Council.

If the decision of the Council is to grant provisional approval, that decision is final and effective immediately upon notice to the school. If the decision of the Council is to deny provisional approval, the school has the right of appeal to an Appeals Panel appointed annually by the Council.

From an accreditation perspective, a school that is provisionally approved is entitled to all the rights of a fully approved law school. Similarly, from an ABA perspective, graduates of provisionally approved law schools are entitled to the same recognition that is accorded graduates of fully approved schools.

Obtaining Full Approval

Once a school has obtained provisional approval, it remains in provisional status for at least three years. Unless extraordinary circumstances justify an extension, a school may not remain in provisional status for more than five years. In order to be granted full approval, a school must demonstrate that it is in full compliance with each of the Standards; substantial compliance does not suffice. Again, the burden is upon the school to establish full compliance.

During a school's provisional status, the progress of the school is closely monitored. A visit to the school by a full site evaluation team is conducted in years two, four, and five after provisional approval, and a limited site evaluation by one or two site evaluators is conducted during years one and three. After each such site visit, a site evaluation report is submitted to the school and the Accreditation Committee. The Committee reviews the site report and the school's response and sends the school a letter summarizing its findings and indicating any areas where the Committee needs further information or where the school may be out of compliance with one or more Standards.

In the year in which a school is considered for full approval, the process is identical to that undertaken in connection with an application for provisional approval. Decisions on full approval are made only by the Council, by reviewing the findings, conclusions, and recommendations of the Accreditation Committee. If the decision of the Council is to grant full approval, that decision is final and effective immediately upon notice to the school. If the decision of the Council is to deny full approval, the school has the right of appeal to the Appeals Panel.

Oversight of Fully Approved Schools

Schools undergo a full site evaluation in the third year after full approval, and then a full sabbatical site evaluation every seven years.

Each law school is required to complete a comprehensive Annual Questionnaire, which inquires into facts relevant to continued compliance with accrediting Standards. The questionnaire elicits information and data regarding curriculum, faculty, facilities, fiscal and administrative capacity, technology resources, student profiles, bar passage rates, and student placement. Information obtained is reported to the Accreditation Committee on a fact sheet prepared by the Consultant's Office. For schools undergoing a sabbatical review, additional information is reported on a Site Evaluation Questionnaire and both questionnaires are reviewed by the site evaluation team and the Accreditation Committee.

The Accreditation Committee's actions upon review of a site report on a fully approved school are likely to take one of three forms. If the Committee concludes that the school fully complies with all the Standards, it writes the school with that conclusion and indicates that the school remains on the list of approved schools. In the remainder of the cases, the Committee will conclude either that the school does not appear to comply with one or more of the Standards, or that the Committee lacks sufficient information to determine whether or not the school complies. In either case, the Committee's action letter will indicate with specificity the Standard or Standards with which the school does not comply, or for which the Committee lacks sufficient information to determine compliance. The school will then be required, by a specific time, to indicate what steps it has taken to bring itself

into compliance or to provide the information necessary to enable the Committee to determine compliance.

If facts indicating possible noncompliance are presented from any source, the Accreditation Committee may, in its discretion, send a special fact finder to ascertain facts for the Accreditation Committee's consideration on whether the school is in compliance. In addition, major changes in the program or organizational structure of the school may constitute grounds for a special site visit and action by the Accreditation Committee.

Once a finding of noncompliance is made, the school is required to appear at a show cause hearing and demonstrate that it complies with the Standards and that no remedial action is necessary. If the Accreditation Committee finds that the school is, in fact, out of compliance, then it gives the school no more than two years to come into compliance, absent a finding of good cause for extending that time period. If the school fails to come into compliance during that two-year period, the Accreditation Committee initiates action to remove the school from the list of approved law schools.

Site Evaluation Process

Site Evaluation Visits

When a site evaluation is required under the Rules of Procedure, the Office of the Consultant appoints a site evaluation team, typically of six or seven persons, to undertake a site evaluation of the school. The team chairperson is always an experienced site evaluator and frequently a present or former law school dean. The team usually consists of one or two academic law school faculty members, a law librarian, one faculty member with an expertise in professional skills instruction (clinic, simulation skills, or legal writing), one judge or practitioner, and, except on teams visiting a law school that is not affiliated with a university or college, one university administrator who is not a member of a law faculty.

The Site Team is responsible for submitting to the Accreditation Committee a report that addresses the factual information relevant to each of the Standards so that the Accreditation Committee can determine whether a school is in compliance with the Standards. The Section conducts annual workshops to train evaluators and chairs of site evaluation teams. Workshops are also conducted to prepare schools for site evaluation visits.

The site evaluation team carefully reviews the materials the school has provided and visits the school for a three-day period, often from Sunday afternoon through Wednesday morning, following the schedule as outlined in the Section's Conduct Memo (available on the Accreditation page of the Section website: americanbar.org/legaled). During that visit, the team meets with the dean and other leaders of the faculty and law school administration, and with the president and other university administrators (or, in the case of an independent law school, with the leadership of the board of trustees), and tries to have one member of the team meet individually with every member of the faculty. The team also visits as many classes as it can during its site evaluation in order to make judgments concerning the quality of instruction, holds an open meeting with students, and meets with student leaders. In addition, the team meets with alumni and members of the bar and judiciary who are familiar with the school.

At the end of the visit, the team meets with the dean and the president or, in the case of independent law schools, the board chair, to provide an oral report of the team's findings. Shortly after leaving the school, the team drafts and finalizes an extensive written site evaluation report. The report covers all aspects of the school's operation as outlined in the Format Memo (available on the Accreditation page of the Section website: americanbar.org/legaled), including faculty and administration, the academic program, the student body and its success on the bar examination and in job placement, student services, library and information resources, financial resources, and physical facilities and technological capacities. The team's report should be candid in its evaluation of the school and its program and in reporting facts bearing on the school's compliance with the Standards.

The site report and any response by the school, as well as historical information and responses to the Questionnaires, are sent to the Accreditation Committee, and, where appropriate, to the Council to make compliance determinations.

Confidentiality

The Rules of Procedure for the Approval of Law Schools make clear that, in general, all matters relating to the accreditation of a law school are confidential.

CHAPTER 8: PRO BONO LEGAL SERVICES

Written by the ABA Standing Committee on Pro Bono and Public Service

When society confers the privilege to practice law on an individual, he or she accepts the responsibility to promote justice and to make justice equally accessible to all people. Thus, all lawyers should render some legal services without fee or expectation of fee for the good of the public (pro bono publico). Prospective students should be mindful of this responsibility when considering law as a career. The ABA Standards and Rules of Procedure for Approval of Law Schools require schools to provide substantial opportunities for students to participate in pro bono activities. Many schools offer a range of curricular and noncurricular pro bono opportunities and provide career-related public interest law resources, funding, and support. When choosing a law school, it is important to evaluate the law school's public interest and pro bono programs and curricula to find the law school that best matches the student's career-related goals and interests.

What Is Pro Bono?

The term "pro bono" comes from the Latin pro bono publico, which means "for the public good." The American Bar Association has described the parameters of pro bono for practicing lawyers in the *Annotated Model Rules of Professional Conduct*. Nearly every state has an ethical rule that calls upon lawyers to render pro bono services. For those states in which the ABA Model Rules of Professional Conduct have been adopted in whole or part, the pro bono responsibility is usually defined in Rule 6.1. Model Rule 6.1, the full text of which is located on this page, states that lawyers should aspire to render—without fee—at least 50 hours of pro bono publico legal services per year, with an emphasis that these services be provided to people of limited means or nonprofit organizations that serve the poor. The rule recognizes that only lawyers have the special skills and knowledge needed to secure access to justice for low-income people, whose enormous unmet legal needs are well documented.

In the law school setting, pro bono generally refers to student provision of voluntary, law-related services to people of limited means or to community-based nonprofit organizations, for which the student does not receive academic credit or pay. Law students who do pro bono work accomplish more than satisfying much-needed legal needs. They also enhance their career development and make themselves more attractive to potential employers.

Pro Bono Opportunities in Law School

Some schools have formal pro bono programs, staffed by professionals who help match students with outside organizations that do pro bono work. Other schools provide administrative support for student groups engaged in pro bono work while others lack an organized school-wide program, but rely on student groups to form and run projects. Typically, the opportunities cover a wide range of legal needs, such as family law, children's issues, consumer fraud, AIDS-related problems, housing, immigration, taxation, environmental law, criminal defense, elder law, and death penalty appeals. At least 39 law schools require students to engage in pro bono or public service as a condition of graduation. These schools may require a specific number of hours of pro bono legal service as a condition of graduation (e.g., 20–75 hours) or they may require a combination of pro bono legal service, clinical work, and community-based volunteer work. Law schools with voluntary rather than mandatory pro bono service policies encourage students to assist lawyers and legal aid organizations by

offering incentives, such as awards at graduation or special notations on law school transcripts, or by making pro bono an important part of a school's culture.

Benefits of Pro Bono Programs in Law School

Pro bono programs help students develop professionalism and an understanding of a lawyer's responsibility to the community. Participation facilitates student involvement in the community and increases the availability of legal services to needy populations. Students benefit by being able to connect the legal theory learned in their classes with the practical legal issues faced by low-income individuals. They also gain valuable experience and legal skills that can enhance their career development and marketability.

Support for Pro Bono and Public Service in Law School

A number of organizations support pro bono and public service in law school, including the ABA Center for Pro Bono (www.abaprobono.org), the Public Service Law Network Worldwide (www.pslawnet.org), Equal Justice Works (www.equaljusticeworks.org) the Association of American Law Schools (www.aals.org/probono/index.html), and NALP—The Association for Legal Career Professionals (www.nalp.org/publicservice).

For a complete list of law school pro bono-related resources, see the ABA Center for Pro Bono website at www.abaprobono.org.

ABA Model Rules of Professional Conduct Rule 6.1 Voluntary Pro Bono Publico Service

Every lawyer has a professional responsibility to provide legal services to those unable to pay. A lawyer should aspire to render at least (50) hours of pro bono publico legal services per year. In fulfilling this responsibility, the lawyer should:

(a) provide a substantial majority of the (50) hours of legal services without fee or expectation of fee to:

    (1) persons of limited means or

    (2) charitable, religious, civic, community, governmental, and educational organizations in matters that are designed primarily to address the needs of persons of limited means; and

(b) provide any additional services through:

    (1) delivery of legal services at no fee or substantially reduced fee to individuals, groups or organizations seeking to secure or protect civil rights, civil liberties or public rights, or charitable, religious, civic, community, governmental, and educational organizations in matters in furtherance of their organizational purposes, where the payment of standard legal fees would significantly deplete the organization's economic resources or would be otherwise inappropriate;

    (2) delivery of legal services at a substantially reduced fee to persons of limited means; or

    (3) participation in activities for improving the law, the legal system or the legal profession.

In addition, a lawyer should voluntarily contribute financial support to organizations that provide legal services to persons of limited means.

CHAPTER 9: FINANCING YOUR LEGAL EDUCATION

An Overview

Legal education is an investment in your future and is a serious financial investment as well. As with any investment, it is important to consider the pros and cons of entering into such a large expenditure of effort, time, and money. Particularly in uncertain financial times, a realistic assessment of why you are seeking a legal education and how you will pay for it is critical.

The single best source of information about financing a legal education is the financial aid office (or the website) of any LSAC-member law school. LSAC.org provides links to many law schools as well as several good sources of financial aid information.

The cost of a law school education could exceed $150,000. Tuition alone can range from a few thousand dollars to more than $50,000 a year. When calculating the total cost of attending law school, you also have to include the cost of housing, food, books, transportation, and personal expenses. Law schools will set up a "Cost of Attendance" that includes the maximum financial aid you may receive for tuition and living expenses. Today, approximately 80 percent of law school students rely on education loans as their primary, but not exclusive, source of financial aid for law school. These loans must be paid back, and the more a student borrows, the longer the debt will have an impact on a student's life after graduation. Loans from government and private sources at low and moderate interest rates may be available to qualified students. Both federal and private loans are based on the law school's estimate of your need and the overall cost of attendance. Credit history is a factor for private loans and the Federal GradPLUS loan. Students must have excellent credit to be approved for most private loans. Typically, the lowest interest rates are associated with federal loans; private education loans may be available at higher (and often variable) rates. Institutional loans may be available from the school. Scholarships, grants, and fellowships exist, but are limited. Some students are offered part-time employment through the federal work-study program in their second and third years of law school. First-year students are expected to concentrate fully on schoolwork with an ABA-mandated limitation on the number of hours full-time law students are permitted to work.

Changes in financial aid rules and regulations are ongoing, and law school policies vary. Therefore, it is your responsibility to stay current and to educate yourself about financial aid in much the same way that you research law schools when deciding where to apply.

Determining Eligibility

The law school's financial aid office will review your application and calculate your eligibility for the various forms of financial aid from all sources. It is important to carefully review your package and to understand the terms and conditions of all aid offered to you. All applicants for federal student loans must complete the Free Application for Federal Student Aid (FAFSA). If you plan on attending law school on or after July 1, you can apply for federal financial aid through the FAFSA form (FAFSA.gov) after January 1 of the same calendar year.

Your financial need is the difference between your resources and the total cost of attendance. Your unmet financial need is determined by subtracting the amount of your federally calculated Estimated Family Contribution (EFC), as well as any scholarships and/or grants you receive, from the total Cost of Attendance (COA). The budget used for determining need includes tuition, books and supplies, as well as living expenses, transportation, and personal expenses. The Student Expense Budget is set by the law school and will vary by school. Consumer debt is not included in your Student Expense Budget and should be paid before you attend law school.

If your financial circumstances change after you complete and file your financial aid forms, notify the financial aid office so that your need analysis may be revised.

Independent/Dependent Status. All graduate and professional school students are considered independent for the purposes of determining federal aid eligibility. This means that for the purpose of applying for federal aid (including federal loans), submission of parental information is not required. Law schools, however, may require parental income information for institutional grants, loans, and scholarships. You should be aware that the law schools have specific policies and procedures regarding independent status for the allocation of institutional funds. These guidelines will vary by school.

The law school financial aid office will send you a letter explaining your financial aid eligibility. You may be eligible for several different types of aid, which may be available to bring the cost of attending law school within reach. The amount of aid you receive in each category will depend on your own resources and the financial aid policy and resources of each law school.

Credit. Graduate PLUS and private loans are approved on the basis of your credit. Lenders will analyze your credit report before approving a private loan. Most offer prequalification services on the Internet or by phone. If you have a poor credit history, you may be denied a loan. If there is a mistake on your credit report—and there are sometimes mistakes—you will want adequate time to correct the error. It is essential to clear up errors or other discrepancies before you apply for a private or Graduate PLUS loan.

You may want to obtain a copy of your credit report so that you can track and clear up any problems. You can order your free copy from one of the major credit reporting agencies by calling 877.322.8228, or you can go to www.annualcreditreport.com. You may also mail a request to: Annual Credit Report Request Service, PO Box 105283, Atlanta, GA 30348-5283.

Financial Aid Options

Scholarships and Grants

A scholarship or grant is an award that does not have to be repaid. It may be given on the basis of need, or merit, or both. Most scholarships are conferred by individual law schools for attendance at that school. Some organizations may also have scholarships to offer. Among them are local bar associations; fraternities, sororities, and other social clubs; religious or business organizations; and the US Department of Veterans Affairs (gibill.va.gov). The availability of scholarships and grants is limited, but worth researching. Law school admission and financial aid offices can provide information about the resources available. Be aware that many scholarships and grants are merit-based and may require a certain level of academic performance for continuation. Some schools award merit money shortly after admission, while others require separate forms. Some schools award need-based institutional aid. Confirm with each school what their individual school requirements are. Apply early for all institutional aid from law schools. A number of companies offer tuition reimbursement benefits to their employees and to their employees' dependents as well.

Federal Loans

(Unsubsidized) Direct Stafford Loan. A student may borrow a total of $20,500 in Federal Stafford Loans. The interest rate for these loans is 6.8 percent annually and a 1 percent loan fee is deducted at disbursement. Interest starts accruing as soon as the loan is disbursed. These loans have a six-month grace period before repayment begins; they have federal forebearance and deferment options, may be consolidated, and may be repaid under Income-Based Repayment (IBR). These loans may be eligible for inclusion under the federal Public Service Loan Forgiveness (PSLF) program.

Graduate PLUS Loans for Law Students. Students with an absence of bad credit may be eligible to secure a Graduate PLUS loan. The Graduate PLUS is federally guaranteed. Interest accrues while the student is in school, and repayment begins following disbursement. The interest rate is 7.9 percent and a 4 percent loan fee is deducted from the disbursement. The interest rate is fixed for the life of the loan. These loans have federal forebearance and deferment options, may be consolidated, and may be repaid under IBR. These loans may be eligible for inclusion under the federal PSLF program.

Federal Perkins Loan. This loan may be available to students at some schools. Each student's award is determined by the school based on information obtained from the FAFSA. The maximum annual loan is $8,000. These loans may be eligible for inclusion under the federal PSLF program.

For more information about Federal Direct Stafford Loans, the Federal Perkins Loan, Income-Based Repayment, and the Federal Public Service Loan Forgiveness program, go to studentaid.ed.gov.

Private Loans

There are a number of private loan programs available to credit-worthy borrowers. Additionally, some lenders make available postgraduate loans for bar-review study. Eligibility for these bar loans is based on the borrower's credit history and the lending institution's willingness to lend.

The terms and conditions of these programs vary greatly. Pay careful attention to the explanations found in loan application brochures and consumer information. You can also contact the individual programs or visit their websites for further details.

Federal Work-Study

Federal work-study is a program that provides funding for full-time students to work part time during the school year and full time during the summer months. Students sometimes work on campus in a variety of settings or in off-campus nonprofit agencies. ABA standards limit a law student's paid employment to no more than 20 hours per week. Additional information is available from participating law school financial aid offices. Not all schools participate in the federal work-study program.

Veterans Educational Assistance

The US Department of Veterans Affairs administers a number of educational benefit programs for veterans (gibill.va.gov). These include, but are not limited to, the Montgomery GI Bill and the Post-9/11 GI Bill (9/11 GI Bill). The 9/11 GI Bill assists eligible individuals with tuition and fees, a monthly housing allowance, annual books and supplies stipend, and a one-time rural benefit payment for eligible individuals. In addition to the 9/11 GI Bill providing an education benefit for eligible veterans, the education benefit may also be transferred to dependents under certain conditions.

The 9/11 GI Bill also has a provision that established the Yellow Ribbon Program. This program assists with funding tuition and fee expenses not covered by the 9/11 GI Bill. The benefits of this particular program are exclusively for eligible veterans; the Yellow Ribbon benefits cannot be transferred to dependents. For more information on veterans educational assistance, check with the US Department of Veterans Affairs and the Offices of Veterans Affairs on the campuses of the law schools to which you are applying.

Before Law School: Careful Planning

Plan a financial strategy before you enter law school. If possible, pay off any outstanding consumer debt. Save as much money as you can to reduce the amount you will borrow. Have a plan for meeting the expenses of your legal education and anticipate what portion of the plan will be based on borrowing. It is also important that you have a good credit history.

Because most of your financial aid is likely to come from loans, you are likely to graduate from law school with debt to repay. Currently, the average law school debt is about $100,000. Keep accurate records of all loans you receive during your enrollment in law school; this will help you manage your repayments when you complete your education.

Federal loan recipients will be required to attend an entrance interview during the first few weeks of law school and an exit interview before leaving school. During these sessions, your financial aid officer will review with you the terms of your loan, sample repayment schedules, and repayment options.

While in Law School: Living on a Budget

While loans may be available to students with good credit histories, the question of how much to borrow is often asked. The maxim "Live like a student now or you will live like a student later" is a good one to remember. Consult an individual school's Student Expense Budget for estimates of living expenses, and budget accordingly. Track your current spending habits and compare them to the budget at schools of your choice. Share housing; learn to cook. Food expenses are often budget busters. Bring a lunch rather than buying one. While law school may be an excellent long-term investment, paying loans in the short term can be a real burden. Remember, not all lawyers will earn the highest salaries.

Most federal loans allow you to defer payment while you attend law school at least half time. Interest on federal unsubsidized, GradPLUS, and private loans accrues from the date they are disbursed. Be aware that the Student Expense Budget does not allow the use of federal education loan funds to pay for prior consumer debt.

Repayment Options

Your income after law school is an important factor in determining what constitutes manageable payments on your education loans. Although it may be difficult to predict what kind of job you will get (or want) after law school, or exactly what kind of salary you will receive, it is important that you make some assessment of your goals for the purpose of sound debt management. The money you borrow will be paid out of your future earnings and may have a significant effect on that lifestyle. In addition to assessing expected income, you must also create a realistic picture of how much you can afford to pay back on a monthly basis while maintaining the lifestyle that you desire.

You may have to adjust your thinking about how quickly you can pay back your loans, or how much money you can afford to borrow, or just how extravagantly you expect to live in the years following your graduation from law school.

Your education loan debt represents a serious financial commitment which must be repaid. A default on any loan engenders serious consequences, including possible legal action against you by the lender, the government, or both.

Law school graduate debt of $100,000 amounts to almost $1,187 a month on a standard 10-year repayment plan. Federal loans offer graduated and income-sensitive repayment plans that lower monthly payment amounts but increase the number of years of repayment. The Federal Direct Consolidation Loan allows students to repay their Federal Stafford, Ford Federal Direct, and Graduate PLUS loans on an extended repayment schedule, lasting up to 30 years. This repayment allows borrowers to pay a small amount monthly toward their loans, depending on income and the loan amounts. There also may be forgiveness after 25 years, and federal loan forgiveness for government and nonprofit employees after 10 years. The federal government (www.ed.gov) and many lenders have websites with loan repayment and budget calculators.

Graduates Seeking Public Interest Careers. Students who seek to work in public service or the public interest sector of the profession face special challenges in financing their legal educations because salaries for such jobs are comparatively low. Students graduating from law school with the average amount of indebtedness may find that the average entry-level public service or public interest salary ($43,000 for 2009 graduates) will not provide the resources needed to repay their law school loans and cover their basic living expenses.

Students can employ a number of strategies to make it easier (or possible) to pursue a career in the public service or public interest sectors. First, students can borrow less during law school (e.g., attend a lower-tuition institution; follow some of the debt management strategies mentioned in this chapter). Students may also take advantage of programs developed at some law schools to relieve the debt burden for those interested in public interest careers, including

fellowships, scholarships, and loan repayment assistance programs (LRAPs). LRAPs provide financial assistance to law school graduates working in the public interest sector, government, or other lower-paying legal fields. In most cases, this aid is given to graduates in the form of a forgivable loan to help them repay their annual educational debt. Upon completion of the required service obligation, schools will forgive or cancel these loans for program participants. The number of law schools sponsoring LRAPs is limited. Most schools are unable to provide assistance to all applicants.

LRAPs are also administered by state bar foundations, public interest legal employers, and federal and state governments to assist law graduates in pursuing and remaining in public interest jobs. The federal government offers some options to assist graduates seeking legal careers in public service, including the new income-based repayment (IBR) option for federal loan repayment and the Federal Loan Forgiveness Program. The IBR allows any federal education loan borrower the opportunity to make low monthly payments on their federal loans (including, but not limited to, those employed in public service positions), provided that income qualifications are met. The Federal Loan Forgiveness Program allows borrowers who work in government or nonprofits the opportunity to make payments under the IBR, then have their outstanding balances forgiven after 120 eligible payments. Please check with your school or directly with the Department of Education for details on these new programs.

For more information about loan repayment assistance programs or the income-based repayment program, visit ambar.org/studentloans or equaljusticeworks.org.

Note: All figures and calculations are based on current interest rates, loan terms, and fees, and are subject to change.

EMPLOYMENT PROSPECTS

For the past several years, employment of new law school graduates has been negatively affected by the national and regional economic situations. All prospective law students should research and think carefully about prospects after graduation.

Even in times of relative economic weakness, members of each graduating class acquire full- and part-time jobs with an array of public and private, legal and nonlegal organizations. However, future lawyers may have to devote considerable time and energy to secure a first job that they consider acceptable. Opportunities will vary from locality to locality and among legal disciplines, and future demand for people with legal training is almost impossible to predict. Demand for legal services is substantially influenced by the state of the economy. Many parts of the country are underserved by lawyers. Opportunities definitely exist, but the traditional recruiting and hiring models may not apply.

TYPES OF EMPLOYMENT

Law graduates typically obtain legal, nonlegal, and full- and part-time jobs in the following general types of employment settings: private practice, public interest, government and the courts, business and industry, and academia.

Private practice includes all positions within a law firm, including solo practitioner, associate, law clerk, paralegal, and administrative or support staff.

Public interest includes positions funded by the Legal Services Corporation (lsc.gov) and others providing civil, legal, and indigent services. It also includes public defenders as well as positions with unions, nonprofit advocacy groups, and cause-related organizations.

Government jobs include all levels and branches of government, including prosecutor positions and positions with the military and all other agencies, such as the US Small Business Administration, state or local transit authorities, congressional committees, law enforcement, and social services.

Judicial clerkship is a one- or two-year appointment clerking for a judge on the federal, state, or local level. These jobs provide invaluable experience in the court system.

Business and industry jobs may include positions in accounting firms; insurance companies; banking and financial institutions; corporations, companies, and organizations of all sizes, such as private hospitals, retail establishments, and consulting and public relations firms; political campaigns; and trade associations.

Academic jobs might include work in admissions or administration in higher education or other academic settings.

Law-trained individuals also pursue a wide variety of nonlegal careers outside the practice of law itself. Lawyers also work in the media and public relations; as teachers at colleges, graduate schools, and law schools; and in politics and administration.

PLANNING YOUR CAREER

A job-search strategy requires careful self-assessment in much the same way as a school-search strategy does. A legal career should meet the interests, abilities, capacities, and priorities of the individual lawyer. Career satisfaction is a result of doing what one likes to do and being continually challenged by it. It is up to each job seeker to determine the best match of skills and specialties or types of practice.

Networking is an important strategy for finding job leads. Incorporate it into every aspect of your life. Take steps to expand your circle of acquaintances. Consciously seek to make solid contacts and, once you make these contacts, stay in touch. Maintain ties with former professors and former employers. Join your local bar association; volunteer for a committee. Develop reciprocal relationships that will benefit both you and your contact.

All students should take advantage of any programs and workshops offered by the career services office at their law school and should maintain contact with career services staff even after graduation. (See page 19 for more on the role of the career services office.)

RESOURCES FOR JOB SEEKERS

Here is a sampling of the job-seeking and career books that are listed on LSAC.org.

American Bar Association. *Dear Sisters, Dear Daughters: Strategies for Success from Multicultural Women Attorneys.* Chicago: ABA Publishing, 2009.

Bradley, Heather, and **Miriam Bamberger Grogan.** *Judge for Yourself: Clarity, Choice, and Action in Your Legal Career.* Chicago: American Bar Association, produced in cooperation with the Minority Corporate Counsel Association, 2006.

Epstein, Phyllis Horn. *Women-at-Law: Lessons Learned Along the Pathways to Success.* Chicago: American Bar Association, 2004.

Fontaine, Valerie A. *The Right Moves: Job Search and Career Development Strategies for Lawyers.* Washington, DC: NALP, 2006.

Furi-Perry, Ursula. *Fifty Unique Legal Paths: How to Find the Right Job.* Chicago: American Bar Association, 2008.

Gerson, Donna. *Building Career Connections: Networking Tools for Law Students and New Lawyers.* Washington, DC: NALP, 2007.

____. *Choosing Small, Choosing Smart: Job Search Strategies for Lawyers in the Small Firm Market.* Rev. 2nd ed. Washington, DC: NALP, 2005.

Kaplan, Ari L. *The Opportunity Maker: Strategies for Inspiring Your Legal Career Through Creative Networking and Business Development.* St. Paul, MN: Thomson-West, 2008.

Melcher, Michael F. *The Creative Lawyer: A Practical Guide to Authentic Professional Satisfaction.* Chicago: American Bar Association, 2007.

Munneke, Gary A., and **William D. Henslee.** *Nonlegal Careers for Lawyers.* 5th ed. Chicago: American Bar Association, 2006.

Munneke, Gary A., **William D. Henslee**, and **Ellen Wayne.** *The Legal Career Guide: From Law Student to Lawyer.* 5th ed. Chicago: American Bar Association, 2008.

You may also find useful information on the following websites. For up-to-date employment data, go to employmentsummary.abaquestionnaire.org on the American Bar Association's website.

americanbar.org/resources_for_lawyers.html
americanbar.org/lawstudent
nalp.org/nalpdirectoryoflegalemployers
nalp.org/recentgraduates
usajobs.gov
bls.gov/opub/
lsc.gov

(by region)

New England

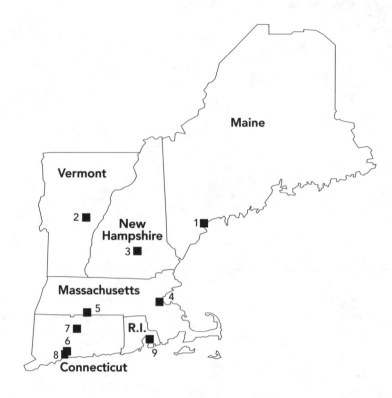

Maine
1. **Portland—Population: 66,194**
   Maine—Enrollment: 270/10

Vermont
2. **South Royalton—Population: 694**
   Vermont—Enrollment: 566/0

New Hampshire
3. **Concord—Population: 42,695**
   New Hampshire—Enrollment: 392/2

Massachusetts
4. **Boston—Population: 617,594**
   Boston College—Enrollment: 782/2
   Boston University—Enrollment: 799/0
   Harvard (Cambridge, MA)—Enrollment: 1,679/0
   New England—Enrollment: 815/326
   Northeastern—Enrollment: 656/0
   Suffolk—Enrollment: 1,101/580

5. **Springfield—Population: 153,060**
   Western New England—Enrollment: 320/119

Connecticut
6. **Hamden—Population: 60,960**
   Quinnipiac—Enrollment: 356/82
7. **Hartford—Population: 124,775**
   Connecticut—Enrollment: 461/155
8. **New Haven—Population: 129,779**
   Yale—Enrollment: 638/0

Rhode Island
9. **Bristol—Population: 22,954**
   Roger Williams—Enrollment: 555/0

"Enrollment" represents the numbers of total full-time/total part-time students unless otherwise indicated.

Population information is derived from the US Bureau of the Census, Population Division, Washington, DC. Data are accurate as of the 2010 Census. City populations reflect the number of people residing in the city proper, not the metropolitan area, which would include outlying suburbs as well.

Northeast

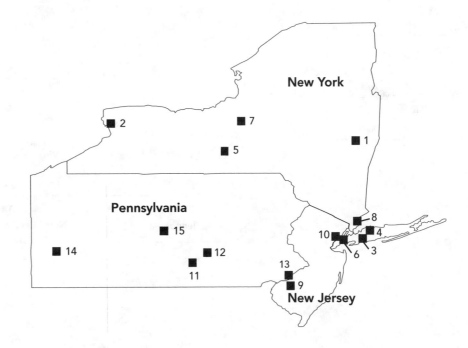

New York

1. **Albany—Population: 97,856**
   Albany—Enrollment: 670/16
2. **Buffalo—Population: 261,310**
   SUNY—Enrollment: 637/4
3. **Hempstead—Population: 53,891**
   Hofstra—Enrollment: 1,004/70
4. **Huntington—Population: 18,046**
   Touro—Enrollment: 580/225
5. **Ithaca—Population: 30,014**
   Cornell—Enrollment: 612/0
6. **New York City—Population: 8,175,133**
   Brooklyn—Enrollment: 1,204/172
   Cardozo, Yeshiva University—Enrollment: 1,038/102
   CUNY—Enrollment: 478/2
   Columbia—Enrollment: 1,331/1
   Fordham—Enrollment: 1,244/252
   New York Law School—Enrollment: 1,365/400
   New York University—Enrollment: 1,464/0
   St. John's (Jamaica, NY)—Enrollment: 787/148
7. **Syracuse—Population: 145,170**
   Syracuse—Enrollment: 640/5
8. **White Plains—Population: 56,853**
   Pace—Enrollment: 644/132

New Jersey

9. **Camden—Population: 77,344**
   Rutgers–Camden—Enrollment: 647/218
10. **Newark—Population: 277,140**
    Rutgers–Newark—Enrollment: 585/215
    Seton Hall—Enrollment: 673/310

Pennsylvania

11. **Carlisle—Population: 18,682**
    Penn State, Dickinson—Enrollment: 596/0
    (Enrollment numbers for Penn State, Dickenson represent the total for the Carlisle and University Park campuses.)
12. **Harrisburg—Population: 49,528**
    Widener—Enrollment: 336/83
13. **Philadelphia—Population: 1,526,006**
    Earl Mack, Drexel—Enrollment: 450/0
    Pennsylvania—Enrollment: 805/1
    Temple—Enrollment: 722/180
    Villanova (Villanova, PA)—Enrollment: 725/0
14. **Pittsburgh—Population: 305,704**
    Duquesne—Enrollment: 448/194
    Pittsburgh—Enrollment: 701/0
15. **University Park (State College)—Population: 42,034**
    Penn State, Dickinson—Enrollment: 596/0
    (Enrollment numbers for Penn State, Dickenson represent the total for the Carlisle and University Park campuses.)

Midsouth

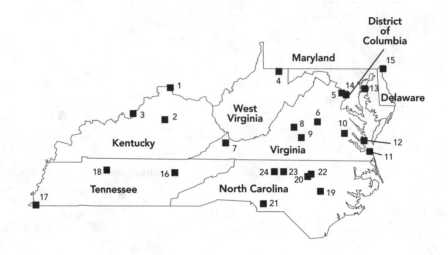

Kentucky
1. **Highland Heights—Population: 6,923**
   Northern Kentucky—Enrollment: 352/217
2. **Lexington—Population: 295,803**
   Kentucky—Enrollment: 415/0
3. **Louisville—Population: 597,337**
   Louisville's Brandeis—Enrollment: 363/26

West Virginia
4. **Morgantown—Population: 29,660**
   West Virginia—Enrollment: 411/7

Virginia
5. **Arlington—Population: 207,627**
   George Mason—Enrollment: 510/204
6. **Charlottesville—Population: 43,475**
   Virginia—Enrollment: 1,093/0
7. **Grundy—Population: 1,021**
   Appalachian—Enrollment: 332/0
8. **Lexington—Population: 7,042**
   Washington and Lee—Enrollment: 395/0
9. **Lynchburg—Population: 75,568**
   Liberty—Enrollment: 286/0
10. **Richmond—Population: 204,214**
    Richmond—Enrollment: 452/2
11. **Virginia Beach—Population: 437,994**
    Regent—Enrollment: 414/20
12. **Williamsburg—Population: 14,068**
    William & Mary—Enrollment: 637/0

Maryland
13. **Baltimore—Population: 620,961**
    Baltimore—Enrollment: 738/360
    Maryland—Enrollment: 735/221

District of Columbia
14. **Washington, DC—Population: 601,723**
    American—Enrollment: 1,239/260
    Catholic—Enrollment: 506/262
    District of Columbia—Enrollment: 252/107
    George Washington—Enrollment: 1,430/323
    Georgetown—Enrollment: 1,671/261
    Howard—Enrollment: 427/0

Delaware
15. **Wilmington—Population: 70,851**
    Widener—Enrollment: 639/308

Tennessee
16. **Knoxville—Population: 178,874**
    Tennessee—Enrollment: 486/1
17. **Memphis—Population: 646,889**
    Memphis—Enrollment: 394/27
18. **Nashville—Population: 601,222**
    Vanderbilt—Enrollment: 586/0

North Carolina
19. **Buies Creek—Population: 2,942**
    Campbell—Enrollment: 475/0
20. **Chapel Hill—Population: 57,233**
    North Carolina—Enrollment: 772/0
21. **Charlotte—Population: 731,424**
    Charlotte—Enrollment: 953/198
22. **Durham—Population: 228,330**
    Duke—Enrollment: 644/39
    North Carolina Central—Enrollment: 437/95
23. **Greensboro—Population: 269,666**
    Elon—Enrollment: 365/0
24. **Winston-Salem—Population: 229,617**
    Wake Forest—Enrollment: 487/19

Southeast

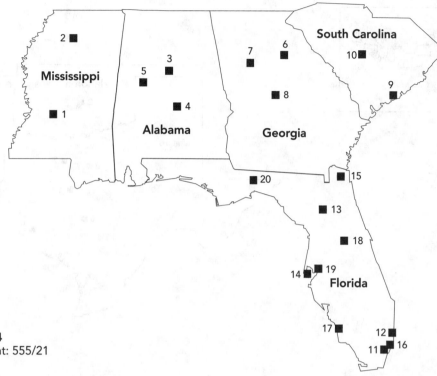

Mississippi

1. **Jackson—Population: 173,514**
   Mississippi College—Enrollment: 555/21
2. **Oxford—Population: 18,916**
   Mississippi—Enrollment: 531/0

Alabama

3. **Birmingham—Population: 212,237**
   Samford—Enrollment: 489/0
4. **Montgomery—Population: 205,764**
   Faulkner—Enrollment: 334/1
5. **Tuscaloosa—Population: 90,468**
   Alabama—Enrollment: 509/0

Georgia

6. **Athens—Population: 115,452**
   Georgia—Enrollment: 691/0
7. **Atlanta—Population: 420,003**
   Atlanta's John Marshall—Enrollment: 528/204
   Emory—Enrollment: 810/0
   Georgia State—Enrollment: 466/191
8. **Macon—Population: 91,351**
   Mercer—Enrollment: 451/0

South Carolina

9. **Charleston—Population: 120,083**
   Charleston—Enrollment: 518/191
10. **Columbia—Population: 129,272**
    South Carolina—Enrollment: 665/1

Florida

11. **Coral Gables—Population: 46,780**
    Miami—Enrollment: 1,290/71
12. **Ft. Lauderdale—Population: 165,521**
    Nova Southeastern—Enrollment: 855/195
13. **Gainesville—Population: 124,354**
    Florida—Enrollment: 976/0

14. **Gulfport—Population: 12,029**
    Stetson—Enrollment: 855/225
15. **Jacksonville—Population: 821,784**
    Florida Coastal—Enrollment: 1,702/51
16. **Miami—Population: 399,457**
    Florida International—Enrollment: 369/182
    St. Thomas—Enrollment: 719/0
17. **Naples—Population: 19,537**
    Ave Maria—Enrollment: 489/0
18. **Orlando—Population: 238,300**
    Barry—Enrollment: 528/180
    Florida A&M—Enrollment: 509/192
19. **Riverview—Population: 71,050**
    Thomas M. Cooley—Enrollment: 737/2,891
    (Enrollment numbers for Thomas Cooley represent the total for the Florida and Michigan campuses.)
20. **Tallahassee—Population: 181,376**
    Florida State—Enrollment: 729/0

Puerto Rico

21. **Ponce—Population: 166,327**
    Pontifical Catholic—Enrollment: 607/243
22. **San Juan—Population: 395,326**
    Inter American—Enrollment: 476/414
    Puerto Rico—Enrollment: 523/185

South Central

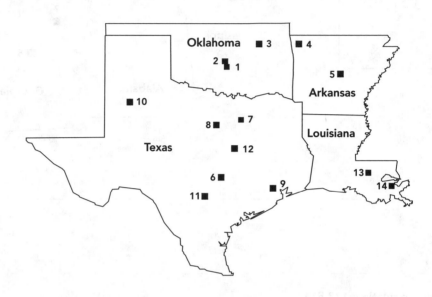

Oklahoma
1. **Norman—Population: 110,925**
   Oklahoma—Enrollment: 530/0
2. **Oklahoma City—Population: 579,999**
   Oklahoma City—Enrollment: 527/78
3. **Tulsa—Population: 391,906**
   Tulsa—Enrollment: 322/39

Arkansas
4. **Fayetteville—Population: 73,580**
   Arkansas–Fayetteville—Enrollment: 401/0
5. **Little Rock—Population: 193,524**
   Arkansas–Little Rock—Enrollment: 325/151

Texas
6. **Austin—Population: 790,390**
   Texas—Enrollment: 1,136/0
7. **Dallas—Population: 1,197,816**
   SMU Dedman—Enrollment: 540/326
8. **Fort Worth—Population: 741,206**
   Texas Wesleyan—Enrollment: 431/299
9. **Houston—Population: 2,099,451**
   Houston—Enrollment: 676/154
   South Texas—Enrollment: 996/271
   Texas Southern—Enrollment: 573/0

10. **Lubbock—Population: 229,573**
    Texas Tech—Enrollment: 690/0
11. **San Antonio—Population: 1,327,407**
    St. Mary's—Enrollment: 664/235
12. **Waco—Population: 124,805**
    Baylor—Enrollment: 435/7

Louisiana
13. **Baton Rouge—Population: 229,493**
    Louisiana State—Enrollment: 663/24
    Southern—Enrollment: 481/248
14. **New Orleans—Population: 343,829**
    Loyola–New Orleans—Enrollment: 685/128
    Tulane—Enrollment: 775/0

Mountain West

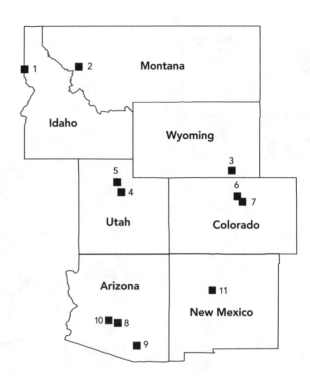

Idaho

1. **Moscow—Population: 23,800**
   Idaho—Enrollment: 358/0

Montana

2. **Missoula—Population: 66,788**
   Montana—Enrollment: 252/0

Wyoming

3. **Laramie—Population: 30,816**
   Wyoming—Enrollment: 226/0

Utah

4. **Provo—Population: 112,488**
   Brigham Young—Enrollment: 430/13
5. **Salt Lake City—Population: 186,440**
   Utah—Enrollment: 398/0

Colorado

6. **Boulder—Population: 97,385**
   Colorado—Enrollment: 540/0
7. **Denver—Population: 600,158**
   Denver—Enrollment: 769/177

Arizona

8. **Tempe—Population: 161,719**
   Arizona State—Enrollment: 602/0
9. **Tucson—Population: 520,116**
   Arizona—Enrollment: 440/0
10. **Phoenix—Population: 1,455,632**
    Phoenix—Enrollment: 697/272

New Mexico

11. **Albuquerque—Population: 545,852**
    New Mexico—Enrollment: 362/1

Far West

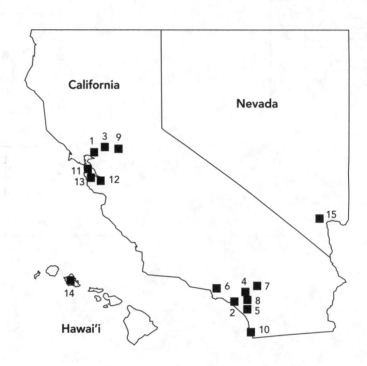

California
1. **Berkeley—Population: 112,580**
   California–Berkeley—Enrollment: 869/0
2. **Costa Mesa—Population: 109,960**
   Whittier—Enrollment: 564/136
3. **Davis—Population: 65,622**
   California–Davis—Enrollment: 601/0
4. **Fullerton—Population: 135,161**
   Western State—Enrollment: 376/135
5. **Irvine—Population: 212,375**
   California–Irvine—235/0
6. **Los Angeles—Population: 3,792,621**
   California–Los Angeles—Enrollment: 987/0
   Loyola Marymount—Enrollment: 1,021/258
   Pepperdine—Enrollment: 629/0
   Southern California—Enrollment: 648/0
   Southwestern—Enrollment: 738/383
7. **Ontario—Population: 163,924**
   La Verne—Enrollment: 181/93
8. **Orange—Population: 136,416**
   Chapman—Enrollment: 506/26
9. **Sacramento—Population: 466,488**
   Pacific, McGeorge—Enrollment: 653/255

10. **San Diego—Population: 1,307,402**
    California Western—Enrollment: 681/146
    San Diego—Enrollment: 840/142
    Thomas Jefferson—Enrollment: 759/307
11. **San Francisco—Population: 805,235**
    California–Hastings—Enrollment: 1,241/3
    Golden Gate—Enrollment: 568/116
    San Francisco—Enrollment: 582/130
12. **Santa Clara—Population: 116,468**
    Santa Clara—Enrollment: 738/229
13. **Stanford—Population: 13,809**
    Stanford—Enrollment: 571/0

Hawai'i
14. **Honolulu—Population: 337,256**
    Hawai'i—Enrollment: 276/85

Nevada
15. **Las Vegas—Population: 583,756**
    Nevada–Las Vegas—Enrollment: 324/141

Northwest

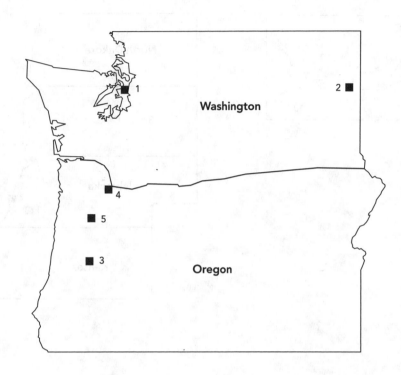

Washington

1. **Seattle—Population: 608,660**
   Seattle—Enrollment: 806/196
   Washington—Enrollment: 545/0
2. **Spokane—Population: 208,916**
   Gonzaga—Enrollment: 506/0

Oregon

3. **Eugene—Population: 156,185**
   Oregon—Enrollment: 505/0
4. **Portland—Population: 583,776**
   Lewis & Clark—Enrollment: 493/245
5. **Salem—Population: 154,637**
   Willamette—Enrollment: 405/1

Midwest

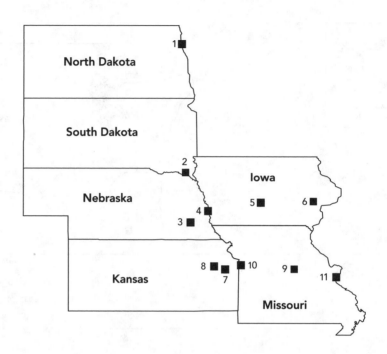

North Dakota
1. **Grand Forks—Population: 52,838**
   North Dakota—Enrollment: 251/0

South Dakota
2. **Vermillion—Population: 10,571**
   South Dakota—Enrollment: 236/1

Nebraska
3. **Lincoln—Population: 258,379**
   Nebraska—Enrollment: 392/1
4. **Omaha—Population: 408,958**
   Creighton—Enrollment: 431/11

Iowa
5. **Des Moines—Population: 203,433**
   Drake—Enrollment: 434/13
6. **Iowa City—Population: 67,862**
   Iowa—Enrollment: 550/6

Kansas
7. **Lawrence—Population: 87,643**
   Kansas—Enrollment: 463/0
8. **Topeka—Population: 127,473**
   Washburn—Enrollment: 413/0

Missouri
9. **Columbia—Population: 108,500**
   Missouri–Columbia—Enrollment: 425/6
10. **Kansas City—Population: 459,787**
    Missouri–Kansas City—Enrollment: 438/28
11. **St. Louis—Population: 319,294**
    St. Louis—Enrollment: 806/124
    Washington University—Enrollment: 847/4

Great Lakes

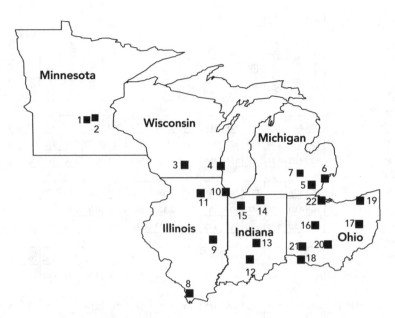

Minnesota

1. **Minneapolis—Population: 382,578**
   Minnesota—Enrollment: 752/0
   St. Thomas—Enrollment: 481/2
2. **St. Paul—Population: 285,068**
   Hamline—Enrollment: 480/137
   William Mitchell—Enrollment: 698/306

Wisconsin

3. **Madison—Population: 233,209**
   Wisconsin—Enrollment: 748/44
4. **Milwaukee—Population: 594,833**
   Marquette—Enrollment: 586/144

Michigan

5. **Ann Arbor—Population: 113,934**
   Michigan—Enrollment: 1,149/0
6. **Detroit—Population: 713,777**
   Detroit Mercy—Enrollment: 556/113
   Wayne State—Enrollment: 462/108
7. **Lansing—Population: 114,297**
   Michigan State—Enrollment: 716/199
   Thomas M. Cooley—Enrollment: 737/2,891
   (Enrollment numbers for Thomas Cooley represent the
   total for the Florida and Michigan campuses.)

Illinois

8. **Carbondale—Population: 25,902**
   Southern Illinois—Enrollment: 373/3
9. **Champaign—Population: 81,055**
   Illinois—Enrollment: 639/0
10. **Chicago—Population: 2,695,598**
    Chicago—Enrollment: 624/0
    Chicago–Kent—Enrollment: 755/178
    DePaul—Enrollment: 828/192
    John Marshall—Enrollment: 1,200/279
    Loyola–Chicago—Enrollment: 731/138
    Northwestern—Enrollment: 801/0
11. **DeKalb—Population: 43,862**
    Northern Illinois—Enrollment: 315/6

Indiana

12. **Bloomington—Population: 80,405**
    Indiana–Bloomington—Enrollment: 692/0
13. **Indianapolis—Population: 820,445**
    Indiana–Indianapolis—Enrollment: 638/324
14. **South Bend—Population: 101,168**
    Notre Dame—Enrollment: 563/0
15. **Valparaiso—Population: 31,730**
    Valparaiso—Enrollment: 541/25

Ohio

16. **Ada—Population: 5,952**
    Ohio Northern—Enrollment: 311/0
17. **Akron—Population: 199,110**
    Akron—Enrollment: 318/218
18. **Cincinnati—Population: 296,943**
    Cincinnati—Enrollment: 409/0
19. **Cleveland—Population: 396,815**
    Case Western Reserve—Enrollment: 600/5
    Cleveland State—Enrollment: 425/132
20. **Columbus—Population: 787,033**
    Capital—Enrollment: 456/177
    Ohio State—Enrollment: 680/0
21. **Dayton—Population: 141,527**
    Dayton—Enrollment: 488/0
22. **Toledo—Population: 287,208**
    Toledo—Enrollment: 357/80

ADMISSION DATA

		Full-Time									Part-Time									Total							
	Application Fee ($)	75% GPA	Median GPA	25% GPA	75% LSAT	Median LSAT	25% LSAT	# of Applicants	# of Offers	# of Matriculants	75% GPA	Median GPA	25% GPA	75% LSAT	Median LSAT	25% LSAT	# of Applicants	# of Offers	# of Matriculants	75% GPA	Median GPA	25% GPA	75% LSAT	Median LSAT	25% LSAT	Total # of Offers	Total # of Matriculants
Alabama																												
Alabama	40	3.94	3.83	3.42	167	165	158	1,872	473	160	0.00	0.00	0.00	0	0	0	0	0	0	3.94	3.83	3.42	167	165	158	473	160
Faulkner	50	3.36	3.04	2.66	152	149	146	717	406	124	0.00	0.00	0.00	0	0	0	0	0	0	3.36	3.04	2.66	152	149	146	406	124
Samford	50	3.53	3.29	2.97	157	155	152	1,405	588	152	0.00	0.00	0.00	0	0	0	0	0	0	3.53	3.29	2.97	157	155	152	588	152
Arizona																												
Arizona	65	3.76	3.54	3.24	163	161	158	1,530	552	137	0.00	0.00	0.00	0	0	0	0	0	0	3.76	3.54	3.24	163	161	158	552	137
Arizona State	60	0.00	0.00	0.00	0	0	0	2,334	664	168	0.00	0.00	0.00	0	0	0	0	0	0	3.77	3.62	3.43	165	162	160	664	168
Phoenix	50	3.32	3.04	2.70	151	148	146	2,039	1,512	371	3.39	3.09	2.53	152	148	146	260	165	79	3.32	3.05	2.70	151	148	146	1,677	450
Arkansas																												
Arkansas	0	3.71	3.47	3.19	158	156	153	1,309	412	136	0.00	0.00	0.00	0	0	0	0	0	0	3.71	3.47	3.19	158	156	153	412	136
Arkansas-Little Rock	0	3.69	3.46	3.08	158	156	153	1,382	432	84	3.46	3.23	2.88	154	152	149	147	43	55	3.63	3.32	2.99	158	154	151	475	139
California																												
California-Berkeley	75	3.88	3.79	3.62	169	167	164	7,253	920	254	0.00	0.00	0.00	0	0	0	0	0	0	3.88	3.79	3.62	169	167	164	920	254
California-Davis	75	3.79	3.63	3.47	165	164	161	3,863	983	192	0.00	0.00	0.00	0	0	0	0	0	0	3.79	3.63	3.47	165	164	161	983	192
California-Hastings	75	3.73	3.60	3.38	165	162	157	5,167	1,491	414	0.00	0.00	0.00	0	0	0	0	0	0	3.73	3.60	3.38	165	162	157	1,491	414
California-Irvine	0	3.69	3.49	3.25	167	165	163	920	219	89	0.00	0.00	0.00	0	0	0	0	0	0	3.69	3.49	3.25	167	165	163	219	89
California-Los Angeles	75	3.88	3.78	3.55	169	168	164	7,328	1,471	319	0.00	0.00	0.00	0	0	0	0	0	0	3.88	3.78	3.55	169	168	164	1,471	319
California Western	55	3.49	3.22	2.94	156	153	150	2,034	1,176	255	3.55	3.15	2.73	154	150	149	174	86	28	3.50	3.21	2.93	156	153	150	1,262	283
Chapman	75	3.71	3.55	3.31	160	158	154	2,592	938	153	3.76	3.44	3.28	168	156	153	230	32	7	3.71	3.56	3.31	160	158	154	970	160
Golden Gate	60	3.41	3.10	2.73	155	153	150	1,957	1,218	182	3.21	2.93	2.72	155	152	150	312	139	47	3.41	3.05	2.73	155	152	150	1,357	229
La Verne	50	3.23	3.02	2.71	155	153	150	978	415	29	3.25	3.05	2.77	157	153	150	204	69	26	3.25	3.05	2.73	156	153	150	484	55
Loyola Marymount	65	3.68	3.55	3.32	163	161	158	4,643	1,507	339	3.63	3.54	3.32	161	159	155	2,138	104	52	3.67	3.55	3.32	163	161	158	1,611	391
Pacific, McGeorge	50	3.56	3.41	3.11	160	158	155	3,282	1,318	176	3.63	3.38	3.01	158	156	152	273	78	49	3.57	3.40	3.09	160	158	155	1,396	225
Pepperdine	60	3.78	3.63	3.33	165	163	158	3,192	1,078	202	0.00	0.00	0.00	0	0	0	0	0	0	3.78	3.63	3.33	165	163	158	1,078	202
San Diego	50	3.60	3.44	3.24	162	160	158	4,009	1,554	273	3.48	3.31	3.07	162	159	156	280	72	27	3.59	3.43	3.24	162	160	158	1,626	300
San Francisco	60	3.60	3.49	3.17	160	158	155	3,719	1,467	189	3.38	3.20	2.88	158	156	153	496	136	57	3.57	3.40	3.08	159	157	155	1,603	246
Santa Clara	75	3.48	3.25	3.07	162	160	158	3,360	1,210	215	3.43	3.22	2.73	160	157	157	329	128	72	3.47	3.24	3.02	161	160	157	1,338	287
Southern California	75	3.77	3.69	3.54	167	167	165	5,987	1,528	199	0.00	0.00	0.00	0	0	0	0	0	0	3.77	3.69	3.54	167	167	165	1,528	199
Southwestern	60	3.50	3.34	3.10	157	155	153	2,879	1,019	285	3.37	3.16	2.95	154	152	150	504	188	119	3.48	3.29	3.04	157	154	152	1,207	404
Stanford	100	3.93	3.85	3.72	172	170	167	3,783	372	180	0.00	0.00	0.00	0	0	0	0	0	0	3.93	3.85	3.72	172	170	167	372	180
Thomas Jefferson	50	3.25	3.00	2.77	153	151	149	2,321	1,280	338	3.30	3.02	2.74	150	148	146	376	198	102	3.26	3.01	2.76	153	151	148	1,478	440
Western State	60	3.35	3.09	2.88	154	151	149	1,501	913	191	3.24	3.14	2.94	156	150	149	381	155	46	3.33	3.09	2.89	155	151	149	1,068	237
Whittier	60	3.22	2.99	2.69	154	152	149	1,947	1,103	222	3.06	2.74	2.58	155	152	150	298	141	52	3.21	2.95	2.66	154	152	149	1,244	274
Colorado																												
Colorado	65	3.80	3.64	3.33	165	164	158	3,175	956	163	0.00	0.00	0.00	0	0	0	0	0	0	3.80	3.64	3.33	165	164	158	956	163
Denver	65	3.64	3.50	3.16	162	160	155	2,161	893	239	3.66	3.48	3.28	159	157	153	264	93	58	3.64	3.49	3.17	161	159	155	986	297
Connecticut																												
Connecticut	60	3.64	3.48	3.21	163	161	158	1,897	589	133	3.63	3.43	3.23	158	157	154	854	222	48	3.64	3.45	3.21	163	159	157	811	181
Quinnipiac	65	3.55	3.29	3.08	158	157	154	1,858	905	104	3.52	3.38	3.22	154	153	150	179	54	19	3.54	3.33	3.09	158	156	154	959	123
Yale		3.96	3.90	3.83	177	173	170	3,173	252	205	0.00	0.00	0.00	0	0	0	0	0	0	3.96	3.90	3.83	177	173	170	252	205

		Admission Fall 2011																									
		Full-Time									Part-Time									Total							
	Application Fee ($)	75% GPA	Median GPA	25% GPA	75% LSAT	Median LSAT	25% LSAT	# of Applicants	# of Offers	# of Matriculants	75% GPA	Median GPA	25% GPA	75% LSAT	Median LSAT	25% LSAT	# of Applicants	# of Offers	# of Matriculants	75% GPA	Median GPA	25% GPA	75% LSAT	Median LSAT	25% LSAT	Total # of Offers	Total # of Matriculants
Delaware																											
Widener	60	3.40	3.14	2.81	154	152	150	1,735	967	227	3.40	3.03	2.67	153	150	148	458	206	86	3.43	3.12	2.81	153	152	149	1,173	313
District of Columbia																											
American	70	3.59	3.45	3.24	163	162	159	6,741	1,900	388	3.59	3.44	3.14	162	160	157	780	175	87	3.59	3.44	3.22	163	162	159	2,075	475
Catholic	65	3.46	3.30	3.11	160	157	151	2,407	817	162	3.44	3.22	3.00	159	156	152	595	167	70	3.45	3.28	3.07	160	157	151	984	232
District of Columbia	35	3.28	3.10	2.78	154	152	150	1,248	332	82	3.34	3.01	2.76	155	153	150	395	95	49	3.28	3.02	2.76	155	153	151	427	131
George Washington	80	3.90	3.82	3.44	168	167	162	7,846	2,255	435	3.91	3.57	3.15	168	167	159	806	100	39	3.90	3.82	3.43	168	167	161	2,355	474
Georgetown	85	3.80	3.71	3.44	171	170	167	9,413	2,542	510	3.80	3.70	3.37	170	167	163	1,781	139	69	3.80	3.71	3.44	171	170	167	2,681	579
Howard	60	3.39	3.13	2.92	155	153	150	1,705	464	137	0.00	0.00	0.00	0	0	0	0	0	0	3.39	3.13	2.92	155	153	150	464	137
Florida																											
Ave Maria	50	3.48	3.04	2.79	153	150	146	1,633	878	151	0.00	0.00	0.00	0	0	0	0	0	0	3.48	3.04	2.79	153	150	146	878	151
Barry		3.27	2.96	2.55	152	149	147	2,066	1,224	218	3.23	2.90	2.59	152	149	147	258	123	49	3.26	2.95	2.55	152	149	147	1,347	267
Florida A&M	33	3.30	3.11	2.80	151	148	145	1,580	600	206	3.42	3.09	2.83	152	149	146	311	111	75	3.34	3.10	2.81	151	148	145	711	281
Florida Coastal	0	3.34	3.09	2.83	151	147	145	4,982	3,362	659	2.96	2.90	2.64	146	145	145	295	131	12	3.33	3.08	2.83	151	147	145	3,493	671
Florida	30	3.82	3.64	3.43	164	162	160	3,024	875	295	0.00	0.00	0.00	0	0	0	0	0	0	3.82	3.64	3.43	164	162	160	875	295
Florida International	20	3.77	3.63	3.26	158	155	152	1,960	427	115	3.79	3.57	3.07	157	152	148	410	58	36	3.77	3.62	3.22	157	155	152	485	151
Florida State	30	3.68	3.47	3.18	163	162	160	2,650	716	200	0.00	0.00	0.00	0	0	0	0	0	0	3.68	3.47	3.18	163	162	160	716	200
Miami	60	3.57	3.38	3.19	160	158	156	4,670	2,195	447	0.00	0.00	0.00	0	0	0	0	0	0	3.57	3.38	3.19	160	158	156	2,195	447
Nova Southeastern	53	3.44	3.25	3.02	152	150	148	1,930	828	297	3.34	3.08	2.77	151	148	147	368	103	57	3.43	3.22	2.98	152	150	148	931	354
St. Thomas	60	3.32	3.03	2.66	153	150	148	2,040	938	251	0.00	0.00	0.00	0	0	0	0	0	0	3.32	3.03	2.66	153	150	148	938	251
Stetson	55	3.58	3.36	3.13	158	155	153	2,814	1,095	277	3.52	3.26	2.98	157	154	152	378	115	67	3.57	3.34	3.11	157	155	153	1,210	344
Thomas M. Cooley	0	3.42	3.07	2.74	154	150	145	3,433	2,795	188	3.35	2.99	2.59	149	145	142	599	435	973	3.35	3.02	2.61	151	146	143	3,230	1,161
Georgia																											
Atlanta's John Marshall	50	3.14	2.79	2.50	152	150	148	1,543	779	191	3.20	2.89	2.53	153	150	148	324	130	73	3.16	2.82	2.52	152	150	148	909	264
Emory	80	3.79	3.70	3.40	166	165	159	3,951	1,287	246	0.00	0.00	0.00	0	0	0	0	0	0	3.79	3.70	3.40	166	165	159	1,287	246
Georgia	50	3.76	3.59	3.30	166	165	162	3,186	814	225	0.00	0.00	0.00	0	0	0	0	0	0	3.76	3.59	3.30	166	165	162	814	225
Georgia State	50	3.62	3.45	3.24	162	160	158	2,234	358	170	3.67	3.36	3.00	161	159	158	331	65	53	3.63	3.43	3.21	162	160	158	423	223
Mercer	50	3.66	3.40	3.07	158	155	151	1,434	634	149	0.00	0.00	0.00	0	0	0	0	0	0	3.66	3.40	3.07	158	155	151	634	149
Hawai'i																											
Hawai'i	75	3.55	3.37	3.15	160	157	154	1,119	218	88	3.53	3.32	3.07	156	153	150	110	39	28	3.55	3.36	3.11	160	156	153	257	116
Idaho																											
Idaho	50	3.57	3.25	2.87	157	154	149	664	371	130	0.00	3.67	0.00	0	159	0	1	1	0	3.57	3.25	2.87	157	154	149	372	130
Illinois																											
Chicago	75	3.94	3.87	3.71	173	171	167	4,783	837	191	0.00	0.00	0.00	0	0	0	0	0	0	3.94	3.87	3.71	173	171	167	837	191
Chicago-Kent	0	3.67	3.53	3.10	162	160	155	3,255	1,331	262	3.64	3.34	3.08	161	158	153	464	110	46	3.66	3.52	3.09	162	160	155	1,441	308
DePaul	60	3.59	3.42	3.13	160	158	155	4,166	1,807	247	3.57	3.44	3.02	158	154	151	577	193	51	3.58	3.42	3.13	160	158	154	2,000	298
Illinois	0	3.85	3.70	3.38	168	163	156	4,219	853	184	0.00	0.00	0.00	0	0	0	0	0	0	3.85	3.70	3.38	168	163	156	853	184
John Marshall	0	3.52	3.29	2.98	156	153	149	3,228	1,675	426	3.43	3.21	2.94	155	151	148	555	211	86	3.51	3.28	2.98	156	153	149	1,886	512
Loyola-Chicago	0	3.57	3.40	3.15	162	160	158	4,590	1,605	244	3.42	3.27	3.11	157	154	150	450	91	30	3.57	3.37	3.13	162	160	156	1,696	274
Northern Illinois	50	3.43	3.19	3.00	155	152	150	998	460	102	3.28	3.28	3.28	155	155	155	60	15	1	3.42	3.20	3.00	155	152	150	475	103
Northwestern	100	3.85	3.75	3.35	171	170	165	4,548	864	264	0.00	0.00	0.00	0	0	0	0	0	0	3.85	3.75	3.35	171	170	165	864	264
Southern Illinois		3.62	3.30	2.96	156	153	151	699	353	120	0.00	0.00	0.00	0	0	0	0	0	0	3.62	3.30	2.96	156	153	151	353	120

	Application Fee ($)	Full-Time									Part-Time									Total							
		75% GPA	Median GPA	25% GPA	75% LSAT	Median LSAT	25% LSAT	# of Applicants	# of Offers	# of Matriculants	75% GPA	Median GPA	25% GPA	75% LSAT	Median LSAT	25% LSAT	# of Applicants	# of Offers	# of Matriculants	75% GPA	Median GPA	25% GPA	75% LSAT	Median LSAT	25% LSAT	Total # of Offers	Total # of Matriculants
Indiana																												
Indiana-Bloomington	50	3.89	3.75	3.38	167	166	158	2,751	925	240	0.00	0.00	0.00	0	0	0	0	0	0	3.89	3.75	3.38	167	166	158	925	240
Indiana-Indianapolis	50	3.72	3.55	3.25	160	157	154	1,381	654	212	3.52	3.30	3.04	156	152	149	259	151	102	3.68	3.44	3.19	159	156	152	805	314
Notre Dame	65	3.74	3.64	3.45	167	166	162	3,059	640	183	0.00	0.00	0.00	0	0	0	0	0	0	3.74	3.64	3.45	167	166	162	640	183
Valparaiso	60	3.48	3.19	2.96	152	149	147	1,313	953	210	3.29	2.96	2.59	148	148	147	78	37	8	3.46	3.19	2.95	151	149	147	990	218
Iowa																												
Drake	50	3.64	3.40	3.06	158	156	153	996	554	142	0.00	0.00	0.00	0	0	0	30	3	0	3.64	3.40	3.06	158	156	153	557	142
Iowa	60	3.81	3.64	3.51	164	161	158	1,872	729	180	0.00	0.00	0.00	0	0	0	0	0	0	3.81	3.64	3.51	164	161	158	729	180
Kansas																												
Kansas	55	3.74	3.51	3.15	159	157	154	819	401	134	0.00	0.00	0.00	0	0	0	0	0	0	3.74	3.51	3.15	159	157	154	401	134
Washburn	40	3.61	3.20	2.86	158	155	152	883	352	124	0.00	0.00	0.00	0	0	0	0	0	0	3.61	3.20	2.86	158	155	152	352	124
Kentucky																												
Kentucky	50	3.80	3.57	3.32	161	159	155	1,114	456	130	0.00	0.00	0.00	0	0	0	0	0	0	3.80	3.57	3.32	161	159	155	456	130
Louisville-Brandeis	50	3.68	3.42	3.20	158	156	152	1,405	443	123	3.61	3.18	2.46	153	151	146	90	23	9	3.68	3.42	3.20	158	156	152	466	132
Northern Kentucky	40	3.56	3.39	3.17	156	154	152	746	389	128	3.58	3.13	2.82	158	153	150	145	74	50	3.56	3.35	3.07	156	154	151	463	178
Louisiana																												
Louisiana State	50	3.66	3.39	3.10	160	158	155	1,418	626	236	0.00	0.00	0.00	0	0	0	0	0	0	3.66	3.39	3.10	160	158	155	626	236
Loyola-New Orleans	45	3.51	3.23	2.98	156	153	151	1,667	1,002	199	3.42	3.15	2.70	155	152	149	127	69	43	3.48	3.22	2.97	156	153	151	1,071	242
Southern	25	3.21	2.91	2.59	149	146	143	738	270	152	3.06	2.79	2.48	146	144	142	311	133	106	3.11	2.85	2.50	148	145	142	403	258
Tulane	60	3.68	3.53	3.31	163	161	158	2,780	1,050	259	0.00	0.00	0.00	0	0	0	0	0	0	3.68	3.53	3.31	163	161	158	1,050	259
Maine																												
Maine	50	3.57	3.36	3.16	158	155	153	988	474	91	0.00	0.00	0.00	0	0	0	0	0	0	3.57	3.36	3.16	158	155	153	474	91
Maryland																												
Baltimore	60	3.51	3.31	3.05	159	156	152	1,619	706	236	3.35	3.15	2.66	157	154	150	486	147	92	3.46	3.25	2.97	158	156	151	853	328
Maryland	70	3.71	3.53	3.31	163	162	156	3,504	712	225	3.83	3.71	3.30	162	157	153	490	76	51	3.75	3.60	3.31	163	162	156	788	276
Massachusetts																												
Boston College	75	3.77	3.66	3.50	166	165	162	5,685	1,366	268	0.00	0.00	0.00	0	0	0	0	0	0	3.77	3.66	3.50	166	165	162	1,366	268
Boston	75	3.78	3.72	3.50	167	167	163	7,073	1,396	242	0.00	0.00	0.00	0	0	0	0	0	0	3.78	3.72	3.50	167	167	163	1,396	242
Harvard	85	3.97	3.89	3.78	176	173	171	6,335	842	559	0.00	0.00	0.00	0	0	0	0	0	0	3.97	3.89	3.78	176	173	171	842	559
New England	65	3.42	3.19	2.96	154	152	149	2,529	1,845	291	3.24	3.02	2.72	152	149	148	635	389	94	3.39	3.15	2.92	153	151	149	2,234	385
Northeastern	75	3.64	3.48	3.24	163	162	154	3,670	1,349	217	0.00	0.00	0.00	0	0	0	0	0	0	3.64	3.48	3.24	163	162	154	1,349	217
Suffolk	60	3.47	3.26	2.92	157	155	152	2,391	1,673	360	3.55	3.26	2.97	155	152	150	543	365	178	3.49	3.26	2.94	157	154	151	2,038	538
Western New England		3.48	3.18	2.92	156	153	151	996	530	84	3.37	3.10	2.77	154	152	150	174	60	22	3.42	3.17	2.85	156	153	151	590	106
Michigan																												
Detroit Mercy	50	3.38	3.13	2.91	156	153	149	1,305	570	189	3.59	3.28	3.01	152	147	145	156	57	34	3.40	3.16	2.92	156	152	147	627	223
Michigan	75	3.87	3.76	3.59	170	169	167	5,424	1,162	359	0.00	0.00	0.00	0	0	0	0	0	0	3.87	3.76	3.59	170	169	167	1,162	359
Michigan State	60	3.74	3.55	3.23	160	157	152	3,551	1,147	306	2.88	2.88	2.88	156	156	156	181	38	1	3.74	3.54	3.22	160	157	152	1,185	307
Thomas M. Cooley	0	3.42	3.07	2.74	154	150	145	3,433	2,795	188	3.35	2.99	2.59	149	145	142	599	435	973	3.35	3.02	2.61	151	146	143	3,230	1,161
Wayne State	50	3.65	3.40	3.12	160	157	155	991	481	164	3.64	3.36	3.10	159	154	152	96	30	17	3.65	3.39	3.11	159	157	155	511	181
Minnesota																												
Hamline	35	3.61	3.40	3.20	156	153	149	1,017	614	141	3.47	3.20	2.81	156	152	146	215	131	64	3.58	3.36	3.13	156	153	148	745	205
Minnesota	75	3.90	3.80	3.41	167	167	157	3,546	880	246	0.00	0.00	0.00	0	0	0	0	0	0	3.90	3.80	3.41	167	167	157	880	246
St. Thomas- Minneapolis	0	3.54	3.30	3.07	161	156	153	1,283	711	171	0.00	0.00	0.00	0	0	0	0	0	0	3.54	3.30	3.07	161	156	153	711	171
William Mitchell	0	3.62	3.41	3.21	159	155	151	1,196	834	260	3.53	3.20	2.92	158	152	148	340	101	49	3.62	3.39	3.16	159	155	150	935	309

		Admission Fall 2011																									
		Full-Time									Part-Time									Total							
	Application Fee ($)	75% GPA	Median GPA	25% GPA	75% LSAT	Median LSAT	25% LSAT	# of Applicants	# of Offers	# of Matriculants	75% GPA	Median GPA	25% GPA	75% LSAT	Median LSAT	25% LSAT	# of Applicants	# of Offers	# of Matriculants	75% GPA	Median GPA	25% GPA	75% LSAT	Median LSAT	25% LSAT	Total # of Offers	Total # of Matriculants
Mississippi																												
Mississippi	40	3.69	3.49	3.24	157	155	151	1,656	534	180	0.00	0.00	0.00	0	0	0	0	0	0	3.69	3.49	3.24	157	155	151	534	180
Mississippi College	0	3.44	3.19	2.78	152	149	147	1,714	987	212	4.00	3.79	3.79	153	152	152	3	3	2	3.44	3.19	2.78	152	149	147	990	214
Missouri																												
Missouri	60	3.70	3.49	3.18	161	158	156	851	348	133	0.00	0.00	0.00	0	0	0	0	0	0	3.70	3.49	3.18	161	158	156	348	133
Missouri-Kansas City	60	3.66	3.35	3.00	157	155	153	846	350	146	3.71	3.53	3.36	164	163	159	46	7	3	3.66	3.35	3.01	157	155	153	357	149
St. Louis	55	3.61	3.39	3.14	158	154	151	1,738	1,023	268	3.49	3.29	2.90	156	153	149	302	93	27	3.58	3.39	3.13	158	154	151	1,116	295
Washington University	70	3.80	3.66	3.22	169	168	162	3,847	979	243	0.00	0.00	0.00	0	0	0	0	0	0	3.80	3.66	3.22	169	168	162	979	243
Montana																												
Montana	60	3.62	3.44	3.23	157	155	152	429	196	85	0.00	0.00	0.00	0	0	0	0	0	0	3.62	3.44	3.23	157	155	152	196	85
Nebraska																												
Creighton	50	3.52	3.19	2.94	155	152	150	1,162	691	131	3.21	3.14	3.03	150	147	145	52	14	4	3.51	3.19	2.94	155	152	150	705	135
Nebraska	50	3.79	3.51	3.33	159	157	153	825	400	128	0.00	0.00	0.00	0	0	0	0	0	0	3.79	3.51	3.33	159	157	153	400	128
Nevada																												
Nevada	50	3.63	3.43	3.18	162	159	157	1,149	246	104	3.66	3.29	2.91	157	156	153	232	48	36	3.64	3.39	3.12	161	159	157	294	140
New Hampshire																												
New Hampshire	55	3.57	3.25	3.00	158	154	151	1,247	627	146	0.00	0.00	0.00	0	0	0	0	0	0	3.57	3.25	3.00	158	154	151	627	146
New Jersey																												
Rutgers-Camden	65	3.70	3.40	3.00	161	161	158	1,663	649	137	3.65	3.24	3.00	161	159	155	0	0	145	3.62	3.32	3.00	161	159	156	649	282
Rutgers-Newark	65	3.61	3.43	3.17	160	158	155	2,218	697	174	3.39	3.04	2.74	159	157	155	579	102	50	3.59	3.36	3.06	160	158	155	799	224
Seton Hall	65	3.67	3.52	3.31	162	160	157	2,779	1,494	203	3.56	3.23	2.96	155	152	149	660	170	63	3.66	3.50	3.22	161	159	155	1,664	266
New Mexico																												
New Mexico	50	3.69	3.33	3.05	161	157	152	921	237	113	0.00	0.00	0.00	0	0	0	0	0	0	3.69	3.33	3.05	161	157	152	237	113
New York																												
Albany	70	3.53	3.31	3.05	157	153	151	2,153	1,113	235	0.00	0.00	0.00	0	0	0	0	0	0	3.53	3.31	3.05	157	153	151	1,113	235
Brooklyn	0	3.55	3.38	3.20	165	163	161	5,174	1,586	316	3.44	3.31	3.14	162	159	157	844	150	74	3.54	3.36	3.19	165	163	160	1,736	390
Cardozo	75	3.73	3.60	3.41	166	164	160	4,241	1,315	269	3.72	3.59	3.38	161	159	157	674	184	110	3.73	3.60	3.40	165	162	158	1,499	379
CUNY	60	3.54	3.29	3.04	158	155	153	1,883	563	171	0.00	0.00	0.00	0	0	0	0	0	0	3.54	3.29	3.04	158	155	153	563	171
Columbia	85	3.82	3.72	3.60	175	172	170	7,459	1,175	406	0.00	0.00	0.00	0	0	0	0	0	0	3.82	3.72	3.60	175	172	170	1,175	406
Cornell	80	3.77	3.63	3.50	169	168	166	5,556	1,152	204	0.00	0.00	0.00	0	0	0	0	0	0	3.77	3.63	3.50	169	168	166	1,152	204
Fordham	70	3.71	3.53	3.35	167	165	163	6,431	1,833	399	3.71	3.52	3.39	165	163	160	1,120	166	80	3.71	3.53	3.36	167	165	163	1,999	479
Hofstra	0	3.56	3.32	2.95	160	159	155	4,154	1,907	364	3.65	3.32	3.06	160	158	156	412	49	6	3.56	3.32	2.95	160	159	155	1,956	370
New York Law	0	3.45	3.25	3.01	157	154	152	5,054	2,294	375	3.39	3.13	2.93	154	152	149	943	310	113	3.44	3.22	2.98	156	154	151	2,604	488
New York	75	3.85	3.71	3.57	174	172	170	7,280	1,759	450	0.00	0.00	0.00	0	0	0	0	0	0	3.85	3.71	3.57	174	172	170	1,759	450
Pace	65	3.65	3.42	3.12	156	154	151	2,439	1,042	226	3.57	3.28	3.05	155	151	149	296	59	16	3.65	3.42	3.12	156	154	151	1,101	242
St. John's	60	3.68	3.48	3.16	162	160	154	3,429	1,496	242	3.75	3.53	3.30	157	154	150	628	143	51	3.69	3.49	3.18	162	160	154	1,639	293
SUNY	75	3.70	3.57	3.36	158	157	154	1,507	583	175	0.00	0.00	0.00	0	0	0	0	0	0	3.70	3.57	3.36	158	157	154	583	175
Syracuse	75	3.56	3.36	3.10	157	155	153	2,484	1,190	255	0.00	0.00	0.00	0	0	0	0	0	0	3.56	3.36	3.10	157	155	153	1,190	255
Touro	60	3.40	3.17	2.93	153	151	149	1,340	706	195	3.47	3.19	2.88	153	149	147	313	145	65	3.42	3.18	2.91	153	151	148	851	260
North Carolina																												
Campbell	50	3.55	3.32	3.10	159	156	153	1,227	517	191	0.00	0.00	0.00	0	0	0	0	0	0	3.55	3.32	3.10	159	156	153	517	191
Charlotte		3.33	3.01	2.61	151	149	146	3,605	2,512	446	3.16	2.92	2.53	150	147	143	350	216	83	3.31	3.00	2.60	151	148	145	2,728	529
Duke	70	3.84	3.75	3.62	171	170	167	6,099	934	211	0.00	0.00	0.00	0	0	0	0	0	0	3.84	3.75	3.62	171	170	167	934	211
Elon	50	3.47	3.20	2.87	156	153	150	854	400	130	0.00	0.00	0.00	0	0	0	0	0	0	3.47	3.20	2.87	156	153	150	400	130

		Admission Fall 2011																								
		Full-Time									Part-Time									Total						
	Application Fee ($)	75% GPA	Median GPA	25% GPA	75% LSAT	Median LSAT	25% LSAT	# of Applicants	# of Offers	# of Matriculants	75% GPA	Median GPA	25% GPA	75% LSAT	Median LSAT	25% LSAT	# of Applicants	# of Offers	# of Matriculants	75% GPA	Median GPA	25% GPA	75% LSAT	Median LSAT	25% LSAT	Total # of Offers	Total # of Matriculants
North Carolina	75	3.69	3.51	3.33	165	163	161	2,576	462	248	0.00	0.00	0.00	0	0	0	0	0	0	3.69	3.51	3.33	165	163	161	462	248
North Carolina Central	50	3.47	3.19	2.91	151	148	145	1,820	366	139	3.62	3.33	3.08	158	151	147	586	79	27	3.49	3.20	2.94	151	148	145	445	166
Wake Forest	60	3.76	3.57	3.20	164	163	160	2,632	948	185	0.00	0.00	0.00	0	0	0	0	0	0	3.76	3.57	3.20	164	163	160	948	185
North Dakota																											
North Dakota	35	3.62	3.33	2.93	154	151	148	457	197	83	0.00	0.00	0.00	0	0	0	0	0	0	3.62	3.33	2.93	154	151	148	197	83
Ohio																											
Akron	0	3.63	3.32	3.12	157	155	152	1,363	685	100	3.63	3.41	3.14	153	151	149	284	198	75	3.63	3.35	3.12	156	153	151	883	175
Capital	40	3.51	3.22	2.99	154	151	148	915	605	162	3.49	3.12	2.89	156	151	146	140	77	44	3.50	3.20	2.95	154	151	148	682	206
Case Western	40	3.67	3.48	3.22	160	158	153	1,651	768	192	0.00	0.00	0.00	0	0	0	0	0	0	3.67	3.48	3.22	160	158	153	768	192
Cincinnati	35	3.80	3.57	3.36	162	160	155	1,572	737	119	0.00	0.00	0.00	0	0	0	0	0	0	3.80	3.57	3.36	162	160	155	737	119
Cleveland State	0	3.52	3.27	3.02	157	155	152	1,332	542	130	3.66	3.38	2.83	157	153	150	225	73	37	3.52	3.28	3.00	157	154	152	615	167
Dayton	50	3.37	3.10	2.78	152	149	148	1,751	1,233	177	0.00	0.00	0.00	0	0	0	0	0	0	3.37	3.10	2.78	152	149	148	1,233	177
Ohio Northern	0	3.66	3.36	3.03	156	154	149	1,228	502	112	0.00	0.00	0.00	0	0	0	0	0	0	3.66	3.36	3.03	156	154	149	502	112
Ohio State	60	3.81	3.63	3.45	165	163	159	2,300	898	211	0.00	0.00	0.00	0	0	0	0	0	0	3.81	3.63	3.45	165	163	159	898	211
Toledo	0	3.57	3.35	3.05	155	153	151	1,301	578	118	3.49	3.25	3.12	156	153	150	139	48	18	3.57	3.33	3.05	155	153	150	626	136
Oklahoma																											
Oklahoma	50	3.75	3.48	3.23	161	158	155	1,105	347	153	0.00	0.00	0.00	0	0	0	0	0	0	3.75	3.48	3.23	161	158	155	347	153
Oklahoma City	50	3.46	3.13	2.86	155	151	149	1,116	607	185	3.38	3.04	2.79	151	149	148	88	35	16	3.45	3.13	2.85	154	151	149	642	201
Tulsa	30	3.58	3.32	3.06	157	155	152	1,466	582	108	0.00	0.00	0.00	0	0	0	0	0	0	3.58	3.32	3.06	157	155	152	582	108
Oregon																											
Lewis & Clark	50	3.70	3.51	3.25	164	162	158	2,706	1,052	187	3.66	3.35	3.12	161	157	153	201	91	39	3.68	3.49	3.20	163	161	157	1,143	226
Oregon	50	3.60	3.39	3.17	160	159	157	2,178	887	183	0.00	0.00	0.00	0	0	0	0	0	0	3.60	3.39	3.17	160	159	157	887	183
Willamette	50	3.42	3.15	2.86	157	155	152	1,092	538	141	0.00	0.00	0.00	0	0	0	0	0	0	3.42	3.15	2.86	157	155	152	538	141
Pennsylvania																											
Duquesne	60	3.67	3.36	3.15	155	153	151	659	391	145	3.53	3.27	3.02	155	153	149	205	85	46	3.62	3.35	3.12	155	153	151	476	191
Earl Mack, Drexel	0	3.66	3.38	3.09	161	159	157	2,464	858	147	0.00	0.00	0.00	0	0	0	0	0	0	3.66	3.38	3.09	161	159	157	858	147
Pennsylvania	80	3.93	3.86	3.58	171	170	166	4,952	863	266	0.00	0.00	0.00	0	0	0	0	0	0	3.93	3.86	3.58	171	170	166	863	266
Pennsylvania State	60	3.77	3.55	3.31	161	159	156	4,820	1,466	185	0.00	0.00	0.00	0	0	0	0	0	0	3.77	3.55	3.31	161	159	156	1,466	185
Pittsburgh	55	3.66	3.45	3.14	161	159	157	2,379	868	230	0.00	0.00	0.00	0	0	0	0	0	0	3.66	3.45	3.14	161	159	157	868	230
Temple	60	3.54	3.39	3.16	163	161	158	3,739	1,465	215	3.62	3.39	3.16	160	158	157	405	109	55	3.56	3.39	3.16	163	160	158	1,574	270
Villanova	75	3.69	3.57	3.36	161	160	157	3,014	1,475	218	0.00	0.00	0.00	0	0	0	0	0	0	3.69	3.57	3.36	161	160	157	1,475	218
Widener	60	3.44	3.15	2.86	152	149	148	1,186	658	130	3.81	3.28	2.99	152	150	148	200	89	25	3.46	3.15	2.85	152	149	148	747	155
Puerto Rico																											
Inter American	63	3.58	3.32	2.98	143	140	135	581	246	139	3.57	3.12	2.93	141	138	134	364	147	107	3.58	3.28	2.95	142	138	135	393	246
Pontifical Catholic		3.57	3.25	2.99	138	136	129	406	260	208	3.54	3.26	2.89	139	134	131	170	114	96	3.57	3.25	2.97	138	135	132	374	304
Puerto Rico	20	3.83	3.59	3.38	151	146	143	377	149	145	3.85	3.58	3.32	149	146	142	174	51	49	3.84	3.59	3.36	151	146	143	200	194
Rhode Island																											
Roger Williams	60	3.55	3.30	3.07	155	151	149	1,388	922	194	0.00	0.00	0.00	0	0	0	0	0	0	3.55	3.30	3.07	155	151	149	922	194
South Carolina																											
Charleston	50	3.42	3.20	2.91	155	153	150	1,784	911	173	3.30	2.84	2.50	151	147	145	270	107	51	3.38	3.13	2.80	154	152	148	1,018	224
South Carolina	60	3.63	3.35	3.08	160	158	155	1,986	725	213	0.00	0.00	0.00	0	0	0	0	0	0	3.63	3.35	3.08	160	158	155	725	213
South Dakota																											
South Dakota	35	3.53	3.27	3.05	148	150	152	400	236	90	0.00	0.00	0.00	0	0	0	0	0	0	3.53	3.27	3.05	148	150	152	236	90

	Application Fee ($)	Full-Time 75% GPA	Median GPA	25% GPA	75% LSAT	Median LSAT	25% LSAT	# of Applicants	# of Offers	# of Matriculants	Part-Time 75% GPA	Median GPA	25% GPA	75% LSAT	Median LSAT	25% LSAT	# of Applicants	# of Offers	# of Matriculants	Total 75% GPA	Median GPA	25% GPA	75% LSAT	Median LSAT	25% LSAT	Total # of Offers	Total # of Matriculants
Tennessee																											
Memphis	25	3.64	3.42	3.10	158	155	153	861	293	136	3.43	3.37	2.92	150	149	145	0	9	8	3.62	3.42	3.09	157	155	153	302	144
Tennessee	15	3.75	3.53	3.24	162	160	156	1,277	435	160	0.00	0.00	0.00	0	0	0	0	0	0	3.75	3.53	3.24	162	160	156	435	160
Vanderbilt	50	3.84	3.73	3.48	170	169	165	3,987	1,054	193	0.00	0.00	0.00	0	0	0	0	0	0	3.84	3.73	3.48	170	169	165	1,054	193
Texas																											
Baylor	40	3.88	3.69	3.37	163	162	159	5,257	807	142	0.00	0.00	0.00	0	0	0	0	0	0	3.88	3.69	3.37	163	162	159	807	142
Houston	70	3.61	3.43	3.22	164	162	159	2,774	807	199	3.53	3.28	2.90	162	160	156	583	96	53	3.60	3.42	3.16	163	161	157	903	252
St. Mary's	55	3.43	3.11	2.82	156	154	152	1,389	654	212	3.32	2.90	2.67	154	152	151	215	70	43	3.42	3.08	2.79	156	154	151	724	255
SMU Dedman	75	3.84	3.72	3.34	166	165	158	2,146	463	157	3.74	3.57	3.16	162	160	152	663	115	75	3.81	3.67	3.31	165	163	157	578	232
South Texas	55	3.49	3.23	2.92	157	154	152	1,972	896	358	3.42	3.26	2.92	153	151	149	335	125	66	3.48	3.24	2.92	157	154	152	1,021	424
Texas	70	3.80	3.69	3.56	170	167	165	4,759	1,303	370	0.00	0.00	0.00	0	0	0	0	0	0	3.80	3.69	3.56	170	167	165	1,303	370
Texas Southern	55	3.37	3.07	2.76	149	147	144	1,911	677	219	0.00	0.00	0.00	0	0	0	0	0	0	3.37	3.07	2.76	149	147	144	677	219
Texas Tech	50	3.66	3.49	3.25	158	155	152	1,420	661	236	0.00	0.00	0.00	0	0	0	0	0	0	3.66	3.49	3.25	158	155	152	661	236
Texas Wesleyan	55	3.51	3.21	2.95	156	153	151	1,506	649	164	3.44	3.23	2.88	154	152	150	317	115	72	3.48	3.22	2.94	155	153	151	764	236
Utah																											
Brigham Young	50	3.87	3.74	3.51	167	163	160	755	207	145	0.00	0.00	0.00	0	0	0	0	0	0	3.87	3.74	3.51	167	163	160	207	145
Utah	60	3.72	3.54	3.41	163	161	157	1,230	378	114	0.00	0.00	0.00	0	0	0	0	0	0	3.72	3.54	3.41	163	161	157	378	114
Vermont																											
Vermont	60	3.54	3.26	3.00	159	154	151	1,020	704	151	0.00	0.00	0.00	0	0	0	0	0	0	3.54	3.26	3.00	159	154	151	704	151
Virginia																											
Appalachian	60	3.32	2.99	2.66	148	144	142	1,177	910	146	0.00	0.00	0.00	0	0	0	0	0	0	3.32	2.99	2.66	148	144	142	910	146
George Mason	35	3.78	3.73	3.27	165	163	157	4,092	996	154	3.76	3.59	3.14	165	164	155	1,262	75	32	3.78	3.72	3.24	165	164	157	1,071	186
Liberty	50	3.53	3.27	2.98	153	150	148	414	200	99	0.00	0.00	0.00	0	0	0	0	0	0	3.53	3.27	2.98	153	150	148	200	99
Regent	50	3.62	3.29	2.99	158	153	150	1,135	435	148	3.15	2.97	2.92	151	149	147	45	10	6	3.60	3.28	2.96	158	153	150	445	154
Richmond	50	3.66	3.50	3.13	164	162	158	2,371	563	154	0.00	0.00	0.00	0	0	0	0	0	0	3.66	3.50	3.13	164	162	158	563	154
Virginia	80	3.94	3.86	3.49	171	170	165	7,379	688	357	0.00	0.00	0.00	0	0	0	0	0	0	3.94	3.86	3.49	171	170	165	688	357
Washington and Lee	0	3.8	3.65	3.5	165	164	159	3,972	964	121	0.00	0.00	0.00	0	0	0	0	0	0	3.80	3.65	3.50	165	164	159	964	121
William & Mary	50	3.82	3.73	3.46	167	165	161	5,937	1,306	217	0.00	0.00	0.00	0	0	0	0	0	0	3.82	3.73	3.46	167	165	161	1,306	217
Washington																											
Gonzaga	50	3.51	3.33	3.15	157	155	153	1,389	739	176	0.00	0.00	0.00	0	0	0	0	0	0	3.51	3.33	3.15	157	155	153	739	176
Seattle	60	3.52	3.33	3.12	160	157	155	2,034	947	263	3.44	3.22	2.90	158	156	153	192	84	59	3.52	3.32	3.10	159	157	154	1,031	322
Washington	60	3.82	3.67	3.44	166	164	161	2,656	586	182	0.00	0.00	0.00	0	0	0	0	0	0	3.82	3.67	3.44	166	164	161	586	182
West Virginia																											
West Virginia	50	3.70	3.41	3.15	157	154	152	1,107	506	141	0.00	0.00	0.00	0	0	0	0	0	0	3.70	3.41	3.15	157	154	152	506	141
Wisconsin																											
Marquette	50	3.54	3.37	3.03	159	157	154	1,803	881	188	3.57	3.29	2.94	157	156	152	202	43	25	3.55	3.35	3.03	159	157	154	924	213
Wisconsin	56	3.78	3.67	3.34	165	163	158	2,864	755	242	3.78	3.67	3.34	165	163	158	0	0	0	3.78	3.67	3.34	165	163	158	755	242
Wyoming																											
Wyoming	50	3.60	3.38	3.13	157	153	150	540	243	69	0.00	0.00	0.00	0	0	0	0	0	0	3.60	3.38	3.13	157	153	150	243	69

| | Admission Fall 2011 | | | | | | | | | | | | | |
| | Student Body | | | | | Faculty | | | | Tuition ($) | | | | Other | |
	# Full-Time	# Part-Time	% Men	% Women	% Minorities	# Full-Time and Other	% Men	% Women	Student/Faculty Ratio	Resident, Full-Time	Nonresident, Full-Time	Resident, Part-Time	Nonresident, Part-Time	Official Guide Page #	Grid Included •
Alabama															
Alabama	509	0	58.7	41.3	14.1	45	60.0	40.0	10.5	$18,030	$30,950			70	•
Faulkner	334	1	60.0	40.0	12.5	20	85.0	15.0	14.6	$32,187	$32,187			278	•
Samford	489	0	58.1	41.9	13.5	23	73.9	26.1	18.0	$34,848	$34,848	$20,714	$20,714	646	•
Arizona															
Arizona	440	0	58.9	41.1	22.0	39	53.8	46.2	10.0	$26,089	$41,051			86	•
Arizona State	602	0	60.5	39.5	23.1	52	69.2	30.8	9.9	$24,471	$38,595			90	•
Phoenix	697	272	52.7	47.3	29.7	35	40.0	60.0	18.3	$37,764		$30,540		586	•
Arkansas															
Arkansas	401	0	57.9	42.1	17.7	28	57.1	42.9	11.9	$11,933	$24,528			94	
Arkansas-Little Rock	325	151	55.7	44.3	18.7	21	57.1	42.9	18.3	$12,176	$24,772	$8,507	$16,904	98	•
California															
California-Berkeley	869	0	43.0	57.0	40.4	86	60.5	39.5	10.9	$50,163	$54,370			138	
California-Davis	601	0	53.1	46.9	30.4	46	56.5	43.5	11.1	$46,485	$54,622			142	•
California-Hastings	1241	3	46.1	53.9	39.0	68	57.4	42.6	15.1	$40,836	$49,336			146	•
California-Irvine	235	0	49.8	50.2	38.7	28	57.1	42.9	6.9	$43,280	$53,125			150	
California-Los Angeles	987	0	53.0	47.0	31.9	87	62.1	37.9	10.9	$44,922	$54,767			154	•
California Western	681	146	47.0	53.0	30.6	46	63.0	37.0	17.0	$42,700	$42,700	$30,020	$30,020	158	•
Chapman	506	26	50.6	49.4	25.4	44	54.5	45.5	9.6	$41,873	$41,873	$33,263	$33,263	182	•
Golden Gate	568	116	46.1	53.9	31.6	39	48.7	51.3	14.1	$40,515	$40,515	$31,135	$31,135	326	•
La Verne	181	93	52.9	47.1	39.1	19	42.1	57.9	13.2	$40,732	$40,732	$32,102	$32,102	394	
Loyola Marymount	1021	258	50.0	50.0	38.2	69	53.6	46.4	15.3	$43,060	$43,060	$28,845	$28,845	414	•
Pacific, McGeorge	653	255	52.9	47.1	27.5	49	57.1	42.9	15.0	$41,393		$27,533		570	•
Pepperdine	629	0	49.4	50.6	21.5	36	69.4	30.6	14.3	$42,840	$42,840			582	•
San Diego	840	142	50.7	49.3	33.5	63	68.3	31.7	14.0	$42,754	$42,754	$30,874	$30,874	650	•
San Francisco	582	130	45.4	54.6	39.7	38	50.0	50.0	14.8	$40,544	$40,544	$28,945	$28,945	654	•
Santa Clara	738	229	52.6	47.4	39.7	63	49.2	50.8	11.9	$41,790	$41,790	$29,254	$29,254	658	•
Southern California	648	0	51.4	48.6	39.8	47	63.8	36.2	12.5	$50,591	$50,591			686	•
Southwestern	738	383	49.2	50.8	35.6	60	55.0	45.0	14.3	$42,200	$42,200	$28,200	$28,200	698	•
Stanford	571	0	57.3	42.7	37.5	65	63.1	36.9	7.8	$49,179	$49,179			702	
Thomas Jefferson	759	307	56.3	43.7	33.1	42	50.0	50.0	19.3	$41,000	$41,000	$30,000	$30,000	750	
Western State	376	135	52.4	47.6	39.7	23	56.5	43.5	22.9	$37,284	$37,284	$25,030	$25,030	826	•
Whittier	564	136	51.9	48.1	41.7	33	45.5	54.5	18.9	$39,140	$39,140	$26,110	$26,110	830	•
Colorado															
Colorado	540	0	51.7	48.3	23.9	50	58.0	42.0	9.8	$31,044	$37,452			214	•
Denver	769	177	50.7	49.3	16.6	68	55.9	44.1	11.7	$38,502	$38,502	$28,382	$28,382	238	•
Connecticut															
Connecticut	461	155	56.7	43.3	22.1	47	59.6	40.4	10.8	$22,052	$45,548	$15,392	$31,812	222	•
Quinnipiac	356	82	51.8	48.2	13.5	35	60.0	40.0	12.6	$45,050	$45,050	$31,780	$31,780	602	•
Yale	638	0	50.6	49.4	31.8	70	75.7	24.3	8.5	$52,525	$52,525			860	•

	Admission Fall 2011														
	Student Body					Faculty				Tuition ($)				Other	
	# Full-Time	# Part-Time	% Men	% Women	% Minorities	# Full-Time and Other	% Men	% Women	Student/Faculty Ratio	Resident, Full-Time	Nonresident, Full-Time	Resident, Part-Time	Nonresident, Part-Time	Official Guide Page #	Grid Included •
Delaware															
Widener	639	308	56.0	44.0	16.4	55	50.9	49.1	14.2	$36,450	$36,450	$26,754	$26,754	834	•
District of Columbia															
American	1239	260	44.6	55.4	35.1	117	52.1	47.9	11.1	$45,096	$45,096	$31,622	$31,622	78	
Catholic	506	262	46.9	53.1	23.0	56	51.8	48.2	11.5	$41,995	$41,995	$31,975	$31,975	178	•
District of Columbia	252	107	41.8	58.2	48.7	20	50.0	50.0	12.9	$9,480	$18,330	$7,230	$13,830	250	
George Washington	1430	323	54.5	45.5	22.2	91	60.4	39.6	15.2	$45,750	$45,750	$35,376	$35,376	310	•
Georgetown	1671	261	53.5	46.5	19.5	137	59.1	40.9	11.9	$46,865	$46,865	$33,500	$33,500	314	
Howard	427	0	40.3	59.7	90.9	25	60.0	40.0	18.7	$29,131	$29,131			354	•
Florida															
Ave Maria	489	0	54.8	45.2	21.1	26	65.4	34.6	19.3	$36,448	$36,448			106	
Barry	528	180	53.1	46.9	26.4	33	54.5	45.5	15.5	$33,630	$33,630	$25,380	$25,380	114	•
Florida A&M	509	192	46.5	53.5	71.3	34	47.1	52.9	20.5	$12,424	$32,327	$8,892	$23,016	282	•
Florida Coastal	1702	51	49.1	50.9	31.3	75	44.0	56.0	21.6	$36,968	$36,968	$29,912	$29,912	286	•
Florida	976	0	56.3	43.8	25.0	70	47.1	52.9	13.7	$18,710	$38,075			290	•
Florida International	369	182	49.9	50.1	56.3	32	46.9	53.1	14.4	$16,585	$30,370	$12,258	$22,367	294	
Florida State	729	0	60.5	39.5	21.3	41	61.0	39.0	14.4	$18,343	$37,905			298	•
Miami	1290	71	57.2	42.8	27.1	82	54.9	45.1	13.2	$39,848	$39,848			446	•
Nova Southeastern	855	195	48.2	51.8	33.1	60	53.3	46.7	16.0	$33,250	$33,250	$25,060	$25,060	542	•
St. Thomas	719	0	50.8	49.2	51.9	39	59.0	41.0	16.1	$34,618	$34,618			642	•
Stetson	855	225	50.4	49.6	21.3	59	52.5	47.5	14.1	$35,466	$35,466	$24,582	$24,582	706	•
Thomas M. Cooley	737	2891	51.3	48.7	28.3	104	59.6	40.4	22.4	$34,340	$34,340	$22,090	$22,090	746	
Georgia															
Atlanta's John Marshall	528	204	49.7	50.3	38.5	42	38.1	61.9	14.0	$34,810	$34,810	$21,074	$21,074	102	•
Emory	810	0	56.8	43.2	27.3	63	54.0	46.0	10.6	$45,098	$45,098			274	•
Georgia	691	0	57.5	42.5	19.8	53	54.7	45.3	12.3	$17,624	$34,732			318	•
Georgia State	466	191	54.5	45.5	20.2	61	52.5	47.5	10.1	$14,770	$34,834	$11,638	$26,686	322	•
Mercer	451	0	56.1	43.9	18.0	26	61.5	38.5	14.0	$36,860	$36,860			442	•
Hawai'i															
Hawai'i	276	85	44.6	55.4	73.7	32	43.8	56.3	8.1	$17,378	$32,522	$1,347	$1,978	342	•
Idaho															
Idaho	358	0	60.3	39.7	13.7	22	54.5	45.5	15.9	$14,040	$26,560			358	•
Illinois															
Chicago	624	0	55.8	44.2	27.9	77	67.5	32.5	8.1	$47,786				194	
Chicago-Kent	755	178	55.2	44.8	22.5	65	61.5	38.5	11.4	$42,030	$42,030	$30,718	$30,718	198	•
DePaul	828	192	53.1	46.9	22.8	54	61.1	38.9	13.9	$41,690	$41,690	$27,250	$27,250	242	•
Illinois	639	0	58.2	41.8	28.5	51	54.9	45.1	12.6	$38,567	$45,567			362	
John Marshall	1200	279	53.6	46.4	22.8	75	65.3	34.7	16.4	$38,180	$38,180	$27,300	$27,300	382	•
Loyola-Chicago	731	138	49.5	50.5	23.4	55	63.6	36.4	13.9	$39,496	$39,496	$29,826	$29,826	418	•
Northern Illinois	315	6	55.8	44.2	20.6	20	50.0	50.0	17.2	$18,688	$33,311			526	•
Northwestern	801	0	53.4	46.6	36.8	94	56.4	43.6	8.4	$51,920	$51,920			534	
Southern Illinois	373	3	62.2	37.8	6.9	26	42.3	57.7	13.0	$15,994	$36,154			690	•

	Student Body					Faculty				Tuition ($)				Other	
	# Full-Time	# Part-Time	% Men	% Women	% Minorities	# Full-Time and Other	% Men	% Women	Student/Faculty Ratio	Resident, Full-Time	Nonresident, Full-Time	Resident, Part-Time	Nonresident, Part-Time	Official Guide Page #	Grid Included •
Indiana															
Indiana-Bloomington	692	0	62.9	37.1	16.9	56	67.9	32.1	10.3	$28,130	$45,602			366	•
Indiana-Indianapolis	638	324	55.3	44.7	15.6	44	59.1	40.9	16.8	$22,323	$43,821	$16,903	$32,854	370	•
Notre Dame	563	0	59.0	41.0	30.6	49	71.4	28.6	9.9	$43,335	$43,335			538	
Valparaiso	541	25	54.2	45.8	28.8	29	69.0	31.0	15.6	$38,086	$38,086	$23,790	$23,790	774	
Iowa															
Drake	434	13	53.2	46.8	11.2	27	70.4	29.6	14.3	$34,006	$34,006			254	•
Iowa	550	6	57.7	42.3	16.5	42	64.3	35.7	11.9	$26,348	$46,056			378	
Kansas															
Kansas	463	0	61.3	38.7	16.8	33	51.5	48.5	13.3	$16,460	$28,648			386	•
Washburn	413	0	62.0	38.0	13.8	31	61.3	38.7	11.9	$17,290	$26,950			798	•
Kentucky															
Kentucky	415	0	57.1	42.9	14.9	24	70.8	29.2	14.6	$18,306	$31,716			390	•
Louisville-Brandeis	363	26	55.8	44.2	8.5	25	60.0	40.0	13.1	$16,716	$32,128	$8,448	$16,154	410	•
Northern Kentucky	352	217	60.8	39.2	7.4	28	64.3	35.7	14.7	$15,886	$33,644	$10,998	$23,292	530	•
Louisiana															
Louisiana State	663	24	56.8	43.2	21.5	40	67.5	32.5	18.6	$17,474	$33,800			406	•
Loyola-New Orleans	685	128	50.1	49.9	27.9	52	53.8	46.2	15.9	$38,266	$38,266	$25,856	$25,856	422	
Southern	481	248	46.5	53.5	65.0	39	43.6	56.4	14.0	$10,014	$16,614	$6,744	$13,344	694	
Tulane	775	0	52.0	48.0	14.8	52	57.7	42.3	14.1	$43,684	$43,684			762	•
Maine															
Maine	270	10	51.8	48.2	10.0	16	75.0	25.0	14.3	$22,986	$33,906			426	
Maryland															
Baltimore	738	360	50.6	49.4	18.5	59	55.9	44.1	17.0	$25,798	$37,900	$19,262	$26,772	110	•
Maryland	735	221	51.6	48.4	31.7	64	48.4	51.6	11.7	$25,405	$36,684	$19,440	$27,899	434	
Massachusetts															
Boston College	782	2	53.4	46.6	22.1	52	59.6	40.4	12.8	$41,818	$41,818			122	
Boston	799	0	50.1	49.9	25.7	58	55.2	44.8	12.2	$42,654	$42,654			126	
Harvard	1679	0	51.8	48.2	31.7	137	74.5	25.5	12.2	$48,786	$48,786			338	
New England	815	326	44.1	55.9	10.5	38	65.8	34.2	23.3	$40,984	$40,984	$30,760	$30,760	490	•
Northeastern	656	0	41.6	58.4	34.3	37	37.8	62.2	15.2	$42,296				522	
Suffolk	1101	580	52.9	47.1	17.8	76	55.3	44.7	17.0	$42,660	$42,660	$31,994	$31,994	710	•
Western New England	320	119	47.4	52.6	11.6	28	46.4	53.6	13.8	$38,240	$38,240	$28,294	$28,294	822	•
Michigan															
Detroit Mercy	556	113	53.2	46.8	16.3	37	48.6	51.4	17.3	$36,050	$36,050	$28,856	$28,856	246	•
Michigan	1149	0	53.5	46.5	21.1	90	64.4	35.6	12.8	$46,830	$49,740			450	
Michigan State	716	199	51.6	48.4	21.0	55	52.7	47.3	14.0	$35,840	$35,840	$28,712	$28,712	454	•
Thomas M. Cooley	737	2891	51.3	48.7	28.3	104	59.6	40.4	22.4	$34,340	$34,340	$22,090	$22,090	746	
Wayne State	462	108	57.9	42.1	16.1	38	60.5	39.5	13.3	$26,118	$28,548	$14,116	$15,412	814	•
Minnesota															
Hamline	480	137	45.5	54.5	16.5	36	58.3	41.7	13.7	$34,555	$34,555	$25,040	$25,040	334	•
Minnesota	752	0	56.0	44.0	19.3	61	60.7	39.3	10.8	$34,817	$43,385			458	•

| | Admission Fall 2011 | | | | | | | | | | | | | | |
| | Student Body | | | | | Faculty | | | | Tuition ($) | | | | Other | |
	# Full-Time	# Part-Time	% Men	% Women	% Minorities	# Full-Time and Other	% Men	% Women	Student/Faculty Ratio	Resident, Full-Time	Nonresident, Full-Time	Resident, Part-Time	Nonresident, Part-Time	Official Guide Page #	Grid Included
St. Thomas- Minneapolis	481	2	56.7	43.3	13.9	30	63.3	36.7	13.6	$34,898	$34,898			638	•
William Mitchell	698	306	51.3	48.7	13.0	41	53.7	46.3	19.2	$35,710	$35,710	$25,840	$25,840	848	•
Mississippi															
Mississippi	531	0	54.4	45.6	16.8	23	73.9	26.1	22.6	$11,293	$24,692			462	•
Mississippi College	555	21	59.9	40.1	10.9	26	50.0	50.0	16.5	$29,150	$29,150			466	•
Missouri															
Missouri	425	6	62.4	37.6	15.5	28	64.3	35.7	12.7	$17,784	$34,000			470	•
Missouri-Kansas City	438	28	64.2	35.8	11.2	37	62.2	37.8	13.3	$16,730	$31,772	$10,199	$19,224	474	•
St. Louis	806	124	54.8	45.2	14.7	65	50.8	49.2	13.7	$36,175	$36,175	$26,325	$26,325	630	•
Washington University	847	4	59.6	40.4	26.2	67	49.3	50.7	11.0	$46,042	$46,042			810	•
Montana															
Montana	252	0	59.1	40.9	10.7	14	57.1	42.9	14.9	$11,578	$27,513			478	•
Nebraska															
Creighton	431	11	62.7	37.3	11.1	24	70.8	29.2	17.1	$32,494	$32,494	$18,302	$18,302	230	•
Nebraska	392	1	60.8	39.2	6.1	29	69.0	31.0	12.9	$13,887	$29,966			482	
Nevada															
Nevada	324	141	57.2	42.8	29.9	33	33.3	66.7	11.9	$24,752	$35,752	$16,126	$23,182	486	
New Hampshire															
New Hampshire	392	2	60.7	39.3	19.0	35	48.6	51.4	15.2	$39,990	$39,990			494	
New Jersey															
Rutgers-Camden	647	218	63.9	36.1	20.3	49	57.1	42.9	13.0	$24,094	$35,358	$19,695	$29,075	618	•
Rutgers-Newark	585	215	56.0	44.0	40.5	35	60.0	40.0	17.0	$25,385	$37,117	$16,558	$24,382	622	•
Seton Hall	673	310	54.2	45.8	19.4	55	60.0	40.0	14.6	$46,840	$46,840	$35,340	$35,340	666	
New Mexico															
New Mexico	362	1	52.6	47.4	41.6	33	48.5	51.5	10.2	$14,532	$32,661			498	
New York															
Albany	670	16	55.0	45.0	13.4	44	40.9	59.1	13.1	$41,845	$41,845	$31,455	$31,455	74	
Brooklyn	1204	172	55.0	45.0	24.5	68	52.9	47.1	17.6	$48,441	$48,441	$36,419	$36,419	134	
Cardozo	1038	102	48.3	51.7	21.9	59	59.3	40.7	15.2	$48,370	$48,370	$48,370	$48,370	170	•
CUNY	478	2	37.5	62.5	40.8	35	34.3	65.7	11.0	$12,207	$19,157	$425	$750	206	•
Columbia	1331	1	52.0	48.0	32.7	129	66.7	33.3	9.2	$52,902	$52,902			218	
Cornell	612	0	51.5	48.5	37.4	53	64.2	35.8	10.0	$53,226	$53,226			226	
Fordham	1244	252	53.2	46.8	25.1	85	63.5	36.5	13.6	$47,986	$47,986	$36,056	$36,056	302	•
Hofstra	1004	70	53.8	46.2	30.7	56	64.3	35.7	15.2	$45,600	$45,600	$34,125	$34,125	346	
New York Law	1365	400	47.7	52.3	25.4	79	64.6	35.4	21.3	$47,800	$47,800	$36,900	$36,900	502	•
New York	1464	0	58.7	41.3	25.5	163	63.8	36.2	9.0	$50,336	$50,336			506	
Pace	644	132	42.8	57.2	19.6	48	58.3	41.7	12.7	$40,978	$40,978	$30,746	$30,746	566	•
St. John's	787	148	57.3	42.7	24.5	56	48.2	51.8	15.4	$46,450	$46,450	$34,840	$34,840	626	•
SUNY	637	4	53.5	46.5	14.5	54	51.9	48.1	12.5	$20,718	$33,718			714	•
Syracuse	640	5	57.4	42.6	18.8	54	59.3	40.7	12.9	$45,647	$45,647			718	•
Touro	580	225	53.7	46.3	26.6	40	57.5	42.5	16.5	$41,890	$41,890	$31,400	$31,400	758	

| | Admission Fall 2011 | | | | | | | | | | | | | | |
| | Student Body | | | | | Faculty | | | Tuition ($) | | | | Other | |
	# Full-Time	# Part-Time	% Men	% Women	% Minorities	# Full-Time and Other	% Men	% Women	Student/Faculty Ratio	Resident, Full-Time	Nonresident, Full-Time	Resident, Part-Time	Nonresident, Part-Time	Official Guide Page #	Grid Included •
North Carolina															
Campbell	475	0	51.4	48.6	9.9	23	73.9	26.1	16.6	$33,910	$33,910			162	•
Charlotte	953	198	46.7	53.3	26.5	39	43.6	56.4	21.5	$36,916	$36,916	$29,850	$29,850	190	
Duke	644	39	59.2	40.8	23.4	66	66.7	33.3	10.0	$49,617				258	
Elon	365	0	54.8	45.2	14.8	22	63.6	36.4	18.4	$34,550	$34,550			270	•
North Carolina	772	0	49.1	50.9	28.0	44	59.1	40.9	14.7	$19,012	$34,119			510	•
North Carolina Central	437	95	41.4	58.6	55.8	38	36.8	63.2	14.7	$10,415	$24,343	$10,415	$24,343	514	•
Wake Forest	487	19	57.9	42.1	20.8	48	60.4	39.6	9.6	$38,756				794	•
North Dakota															
North Dakota	251	0	50.6	49.4	8.0	12	66.7	33.3	18.9	$9,895	$21,580			518	•
Ohio															
Akron	318	218	57.5	42.5	14.7	31	61.3	38.7	13.8	$21,873	$34,428	$17,802	$27,846	66	•
Capital	456	177	55.8	44.2	12.3	34	67.6	32.4	15.1	$32,683	$32,683	$21,413	$21,413	166	•
Case Western	600	5	56.7	43.3	18.2	45	68.9	31.1	12.6	$42,564	$42,564			174	•
Cincinnati	409	0	59.2	40.8	15.9	32	50.0	50.0	11.3	$22,204	$38,720			202	•
Cleveland State	425	132	57.1	42.9	15.8	38	50.0	50.0	11.8	$19,864	$27,204	$15,280	$20,926	210	•
Dayton	488	0	57.8	42.2	12.1	25	52.0	48.0	16.2	$31,598				234	•
Ohio Northern	311	0	59.5	40.5	10.6	20	70.0	30.0	14.0	$32,750	$32,750			546	•
Ohio State	680	0	56.8	43.2	20.1	46	60.9	39.1	15.1	$26,118	$41,068			550	•
Toledo	357	80	60.0	40.0	10.1	28	57.1	42.9	13.2	$20,742	$31,846	$15,569	$23,897	754	•
Oklahoma															
Oklahoma	530	0	56.2	43.8	20.6	35	65.7	34.3	13.9	$19,051	$29,476			554	•
Oklahoma City	527	78	58.5	41.5	20.8	31	58.1	41.9	17.8	$35,470	$35,470	$23,670	$23,670	558	•
Tulsa	322	39	61.5	38.5	22.2	27	59.3	40.7	11.2	$32,056		$17,565		766	•
Oregon															
Lewis & Clark	493	245	47.7	52.3	23.4	55	52.7	47.3	10.1	$36,412	$36,412	$27,320	$27,320	398	•
Oregon	505	0	55.6	44.4	15.2	32	53.1	46.9	14.3	$26,061	$32,505			562	•
Willamette	405	1	57.6	42.4	14.8	29	65.5	34.5	12.9	$32,540	$32,540			840	•
Pennsylvania															
Duquesne	448	194	56.5	43.5	6.4	24	66.7	33.3	20.4	$33,752	$33,752	$26,098	$26,098	262	
Earl Mack, Drexel	450	0	55.8	44.2	19.8	29	41.4	58.6	15.0	$36,051	$36,051			266	•
Pennsylvania	805	1	52.6	47.4	30.5	69	68.1	31.9	10.4	$50,718	$50,718			578	
Pennsylvania State	596	0	56.0	44.0	13.9	55	58.2	41.8	9.2	$38,614	$38,614			574	•
Pittsburgh	701	0	58.5	41.5	14.7	44	56.8	43.2	14.0	$28,734	$35,508			590	•
Temple	722	180	57.1	42.9	26.6	58	58.6	41.4	12.2	$19,788	$32,718	$15,958	$26,308	722	
Villanova	725	0	54.5	45.5	17.9	40	52.5	47.5	19.3	$37,780	$37,780			786	
Widener	336	83	50.8	49.2	13.8	25	52.0	48.0	14.0	$36,450	$36,450	$26,754	$26,754	836	•
Puerto Rico															
Inter American	476	414	45.3	54.7	100.0	25	56.0	44.0	26.0	$14,403	$14,403	$11,204	$11,204	374	
Pontifical Catholic	607	243	49.5	50.5	100.0	26	69.2	30.8	31.9	$14,446		$11,006		594	
Puerto Rico	523	185	43.4	56.6	100.0	27	77.8	22.2	22.9	$7,771	$9,673	$6,451	$11,973	598	•

| | Admission Fall 2011 | | | | | | | | | | | | | |
| | Student Body | | | | Faculty | | | Tuition ($) | | | | Other | |
	# Full-Time	# Part-Time	% Men	% Women	% Minorities	# Full-Time and Other	% Men	% Women	Student/Faculty Ratio	Resident, Full-Time	Nonresident, Full-Time	Resident, Part-Time	Nonresident, Part-Time	Official Guide Page #	Grid Included •
Rhode Island															
Roger Williams	555	0	49.9	50.1	14.1	29	48.3	51.7	17.0	$39,550	$39,550			614	•
South Carolina															
Charleston	518	191	54.2	45.8	11.1	31	51.6	48.4	17.0	$36,774	$36,774	$29,566	$29,566	186	•
South Carolina	665	1	58.9	41.1	15.2	34	64.7	35.3	16.4	$21,026	$42,072			674	•
South Dakota															
South Dakota	236	1	56.1	43.9	8.0	1	100.0	0.0	32.8	$12,340	$24,306	$6,107	$12,090	678	•
Tennessee															
Memphis	394	27	58.7	41.3	14.3	18	66.7	33.3	19.5	$15,690	$37,562	$13,747	$21,699	438	•
Tennessee	486	1	56.5	43.5	24.8	30	60.0	40.0	14.5	$16,456	$35,200			726	•
Vanderbilt	586	0	54.4	45.6	19.5	41	63.4	36.6	13.4	$46,148	$46,148			778	
Texas															
Baylor	435	7	48.0	52.0	17.6	28	71.4	28.6	13.9	$43,573	$43,573			118	•
Houston	676	154	56.9	43.1	31.9	51	68.6	31.4	11.3	$28,130	$38,805	$19,889	$27,006	350	•
St. Mary's	664	235	57.0	43.0	34.7	38	55.3	44.7	22.3	$29,406	$29,406	$17,610	$17,610	634	•
SMU Dedman	540	326	55.3	44.7	24.4	41	58.5	41.5	16.5	$42,057	$42,057	$31,543	$31,543	670	•
South Texas	996	271	54.0	46.0	31.3	44	65.9	34.1	22.6	$26,850	$26,850	$18,100	$18,100	682	•
Texas	1136	0	54.1	45.9	27.9	85	60.0	40.0	10.8	$30,243	$46,028			730	•
Texas Southern	573	0	48.3	51.7	82.2	33	36.4	63.6	14.4	$16,262	$21,212			734	•
Texas Tech	690	0	56.7	43.3	25.8	33	66.7	33.3	17.4	$22,190	$30,680			738	•
Texas Wesleyan	431	299	54.4	45.6	21.9	32	53.1	46.9	19.4	$28,790	$28,790	$20,390	$20,390	742	•
Utah															
Brigham Young	430	13	62.8	37.2	16.5	25	60.0	40.0	16.0	$10,600	$21,200			130	•
Utah	398	0	58.0	42.0	10.6	37	70.3	29.7	9.4	$20,760	$39,410			770	•
Vermont															
Vermont	566	0	50.2	49.8	10.2	43	46.5	53.5	16.9	$43,993	$43,993			782	•
Virginia															
Appalachian	332	0	64.2	35.8	13.9	16	75.0	25.0	17.7	$29,825				82	•
George Mason	510	204	57.6	42.4	15.0	36	77.8	22.2	14.9	$23,720	$38,112	$20,199	$31,331	306	•
Liberty	286	0	64.7	35.3	14.3	21	66.7	33.3	13.4	$30,604				402	
Regent	414	20	53.2	46.8	16.1	25	68.0	32.0	15.4	$32,780	$32,780	$26,420	$26,420	606	•
Richmond	452	2	54.2	45.8	16.7	35	60.0	40.0	12.4	$35,430	$35,430			610	•
Virginia	1093	0	55.3	44.7	25.9	86	73.3	26.7	11.1	$44,600	$49,600			790	
Washington and Lee	395	0	54.2	45.8	13.9	35	65.7	34.3	9.5	$41,947				806	•
William & Mary	637	0	49.8	50.2	19.6	39	64.1	35.9	13.8	$26,200	$36,200			844	•
Washington															
Gonzaga	506	0	56.9	43.1	10.5	27	55.6	44.4	15.3	$34,105	$34,105			330	•
Seattle	806	196	49.1	50.9	25.0	65	52.3	47.7	12.3	$39,282	$39,282	$32,725	$32,725	662	•
Washington	545	0	54.1	45.9	21.1	56	51.8	48.2	9.0	$26,380	$40,450			802	•
West Virginia															
West Virginia	411	7	64.4	35.6	11.0	34	70.6	29.4	10.6	$16,423	$31,367			818	•

| | Admission Fall 2011 | | | | | | | | | | | | | | |
| | Student Body | | | | | Faculty | | | | Tuition ($) | | | | Other | |
	# Full-Time	# Part-Time	% Men	% Women	% Minorities	# Full-Time and Other	% Men	% Women	Student/Faculty Ratio	Resident, Full-Time	Nonresident, Full-Time	Resident, Part-Time	Nonresident, Part-Time	Official Guide Page #	Grid Included •
Wisconsin															
Marquette	586	144	56.3	43.7	18.6	38	55.3	44.7	15.5	$37,570	$37,570	$22,500	$22,500	430	•
Wisconsin	748	44	56.2	43.8	22.1	68	51.5	48.5	11.3	$19,683	$38,811	$1,645	$3,239	852	
Wyoming															
Wyoming	226	0	52.7	47.3	11.5	17	70.6	29.4	11.4	$13,203	$25,533			856	•

CHAPTER 13: ABA-APPROVED LAW SCHOOLS

This chapter is designed to provide consumers with basic information in a simple format that will facilitate the consideration of ABA-approved law schools. Please note that applicants should not use this information as the sole source regarding application and admission. Rather, this book should supplement other avenues of evaluating schools, including making direct contact with admission officers, professors, students, alumni, or prelaw advisors.

The following section includes text and numerical data from 200 ABA-approved law schools that confer the first degree in law (the JD degree). The two pages of numerical data about each school were compiled from questionnaires completed during the fall 2011 academic semester and submitted by ABA-approved law schools to the ABA's Consultant on Legal Education as part of the accreditation process. The completed questionnaires provided to the Consultant's Office are certified by the dean of each law school. Each certification is submitted to the Consultant's Office as an assurance that the information provided accurately reflects prevailing conditions at the law school for which the certification is given. The Consultant's Office, however, does not directly audit the information submitted by the respective institutions on an annual basis.

The information contained in this book is only a small portion of what is collected in the questionnaire for accreditation purposes. Each page is divided into different segments as discussed below. In addition, many of the same data are displayed on the charts in chapters 11 and 12 and in Appendix A to facilitate side-by-side comparisons.

In addition to the two pages of numerical data, each law school provides two pages of descriptive text to LSAC. LSAC edits these text pages for style and formatting, but does not verify the descriptive information provided by the schools. As part of this two-page spread, most schools provide applicant profile grids that illustrate admission prospects based on a combination of LSAT score and GPA. The data in these grids are based on 2010–2011 academic year admission decisions as reported by the schools to LSAC. The grids are intended to be indicative of the applicant profile of last year's entering law school classes; they should not be interpreted as predictors of the likelihood of admission for any applicant.

LSAC collects applicant profile data and school descriptions each fall as a service to its member schools and to prospective law school applicants. The information provided by the law schools to LSAC in no way affects the ABA accreditation process.

SCHOOL NAME

The law schools are arranged in alphabetical order by each institution's primary name. Please note that some schools are known by more than one name. Adjacent to the law school's name and contact information is the date that the school was granted ABA approval. In some cases, that approval may be designated as provisional. A law school that has completed at least one full year of successful operation may apply for provisional approval. A law school is granted provisional approval when it establishes that it substantially complies with each of the Standards and presents a reliable plan for bringing the school into full compliance with all of the Standards within three years after receiving provisional approval. A designation of "Probation" means that the school is in substantial noncompliance with the Standards and is at risk of being removed from the list of approved law schools. It is the ABA's view that students at provisionally

approved law schools or those on probation and persons who graduate while a school is provisionally approved or on probation are entitled to the same recognition as students and graduates of fully approved law schools.

Multiple campuses: Some schools have multiple campuses. Contact the admission office of those schools for more information about curriculum offerings and application processes.

The Basics

The Basics section contains a variety of general information, sorted into the categories listed below.

Type of school: All ABA-approved law schools are either public or private. *Public* means that the school receives money from the state in which the school is located. *Private* indicates the school is not operated by the state.

Term: Indicates whether the school operates on a semester, quarter, or trimester system.

Application deadline: Not all schools have specific deadlines for admission applications. If the item was left blank in the questionnaire completed by the school, it generally means that the school considers applications on a continual basis until the class is filled.

Application fee: Fee charged by most law schools for processing an application for admission.

Financial aid deadline: Indicates the deadline for the school's financial aid form. (The school deadline may not be the same as federal and state deadlines.) If the item was left blank in the questionnaire completed by the school, it generally means that the school considers financial aid applications on a continuing basis.

Can first year start other than fall? Indicates whether the school has an entering class other than in the fall term.

Student-to-faculty ratio: Indicates the number of students relative to the number of instructors for the calendar year. The ratio is calculated by comparing faculty full-time equivalency (FTE) to FTE of JD enrollment. A general definition of faculty FTE is as follows: total full-time faculty plus additional instructional resources. Additional instructional resources include administrators who teach, as well as part-time faculty. Teaching administrators and part-time faculty are included in the faculty FTE at differing weighted factors ranging from .2 to .7. FTE of JD enrollment is calculated as follows: full-time JD enrollment plus two-thirds of part-time JD enrollment less enrollment in semester-abroad programs. For a detailed definition of the ABA's student-to-faculty ratio, please consult the ABA's Standards and Rules of Procedure for Approval of Law Schools at americanbar.org/groups/legal_education.

Student housing: Indicates the number of housing spaces available restricted to law students and number of graduate housing spaces for which law students are eligible.

Faculty and Administrators

This section of the two-page spread contains detailed information on the number, gender, and race of the teachers at the school for both semesters. It should be noted that some schools may have lower part-time numbers in the fall semester because at their school most of the part-time instruction occurs in the spring semester. The five categories of faculty are mutually exclusive. Teachers on leave or sabbatical are not included in the full-time faculty count for the term they are on leave. The *Full-time* row indicates tenured or tenure-track faculty. *Other full-time* indicates nontenured professional skills instructors and nontenured legal writing instructors. *Deans, librarians, & others who teach* are law school administrators who teach at least half-time. Administrators who neither teach nor hold faculty rank are not included in these numbers. Administrators who teach are typically at the school and available to students during the entire year. For this reason, they are counted in fall and spring regardless of their teaching load. *Part-time* during the fall semester includes adjuncts, permanent part time, faculty from another unit, part-time professional skills, and emeritus part time. The *Total* row combines figures from the *Full-time* row through the *Part-time* row.

JD Enrollment and Ethnicity

This section represents the JD enrollment by ethnic category, gender, first-year student, and full-time/part-time status. Students are classified for purposes of enrollment statistics on the basis of whether they are carrying a full load in the division in which they are enrolled. Minority group enrollment is the total enrollment of students who classify themselves as Hispanic, but if not Hispanic, then Black or African American, American Indian or Alaska Native, Asian, Native Hawaiian or Other Pacific Islander, or Two or More Races. Although Puerto Rican law students enrolled in the three approved law schools in Puerto Rico are not classified as minority students in the Total Minority Enrollment chart in Appendix A, they are counted as minorities in all other areas. For more information, see *Federal Register*, Volume 72 (October 19, 2007), "Final Guidance on Maintaining, Collecting, and Reporting Racial and Ethnic Data to the US Department of Education," pp. 59266–59279; and the Race and Ethnicity Information Center of the Department of Education's Integrated Postsecondary Education Data System: nces.ed.gov/ipeds. Nonresident alien students (foreign nationals) and students whose ethnicity is unknown or unspecified are not included as minority students.

JD Degrees Awarded: This indicates the total number of JD degrees awarded during the 2010–2011 academic year.

Curriculum

All information in this category is based on the 12-month period beginning at the close of the prior academic year (e.g., June 2010 through May 2011). In courses where there was enrollment by both full-time and part-time students, schools were asked to classify each of those courses as full time or part time based on time of day and relative enrollment of full-time and part-time students. Some schools that have a part-time program experienced difficulty providing curriculum information that distinguished between full time and part time. In those cases, the part-time column contains zeros. A *small section* means a section of a substantive law course, which may include a legal writing component; small section does not mean a legal writing section standing alone. The *number of classroom course titles beyond first-year curriculum* refers only to classroom courses offered the previous year, not to clinical or field placement possibilities. If a title is offered in both the full-time program and part-time program, the school could count it once in each column. *Seminars* are defined as courses requiring a written work product and having an enrollment limited to no more than 25. A *simulation course* is one in which a substantial portion of the instruction is accomplished through the use of role-playing or drafting exercises (for example, trial advocacy, corporate planning and drafting, negotiations, and estate planning and drafting).

Faculty supervised clinical courses are those courses or placements with other agencies in which full-time faculty have primary professional responsibility for all cases on which students are working. *Field placements* refer to those cases in which someone other than full-time faculty has primary responsibility to the client; these placements are frequently called externships or internships. Schools were also asked not to double count a single course by classifying it both as full time and part time. *Number involved in law journals* and *Number involved in moot court or trial competitions* reflect those students beyond the first year who participated in those activities during the previous year regardless of whether they received credit.

Transfers

This section refers to the number of students who transferred in and transferred out of the law school in the 2010–2011 academic year.

Tuition and Fees

- *Full-time:* Represents the full-time tuition (plus annual fees) for the academic year for a typical first-year student.

- *Part-time:* Represents the part-time tuition (plus annual fees) for the academic year for a typical first-year student. Please note that some schools elected to report part-time tuition on a "per-credit-hour" basis.

- *Tuition Guarantee Program:* Indicates if the law school has a tuition policy that guarantees all entering students the same tuition rate throughout their enrollment.

Living Expenses

This represents the 2011–2012 academic year total living expenses (room, board, etc.) and book expenses for full-time, single, resident students *Living on campus*, *Living off campus*, and *Living at home*. Tuition and fee charges are not included. The figures are used in analyzing law student budgets for loan purposes. Many schools use the same budget amount for all three categories.

GPA and LSAT Scores

This section of the two-page spread contains statistics on the 2011 entering class. All persons in this particular category, regardless of whether they were admitted through any special admission program rather than through the normal admission process, were included. The admission year was calculated from October 1, 2010, through September 30, 2011. Schools that admit in the spring and/or summer were to include those students in the totals. Figures on matriculants include all students who attended at least one class during the first week of the term in which they were admitted. For a small number of schools, applications and admitted applicants are not identified by the school as full time or part time. Therefore, "N/A" appears under the full-time and part-time columns, and the total application and admission offers are entered under the total column.

Percentiles of GPA and LSAT: The GPA and LSAT scores represent the 75th percentile, 25th percentile, and the median scores of the entering class. For example, one quarter (25 percent) of the first-year class has credentials that are *below* the number given for the 25th percentile. Three quarters (75 percent) of the first-year class have credentials that are below the number given for the 75th percentile. One half (50 percent) of the first-year class has credentials that are *below* the number given for the median. For example, if a school reports a 25th percentile/median/75th percentile GPA—3.01/3.25/3.47, then 25 percent of this first-year class had a GPA of *less than* 3.01, 50 percent of this class had a GPA of *less than* 3.25, and 75 percent of this class had a GPA of *less than* 3.47. The same principle holds for the 25th percentile/median/75th percentile LSAT score.

Grants and Scholarships (from prior year)
This indicates the number and percentage of students receiving internal grants or scholarships from law school or university sources. External grants such as state grants are not included. The percentages for full time and part time are based on the total number of full-time and part-time JD students, respectively. The total column percentage is based on total JD enrollment. Zeros are reported in those areas where a school did not provide data. The data represent information from the previous academic year.

Informational and Library Resources
This section of the two-page spread contains basic information about the law library. In addition, it contains brief information about the physical size of the school and the number of networked computers available.

- *Total amount spent on library materials:* Total expenditures for serial subscriptions (print, microforms, and nonprint), monographs (print, microforms, and nonprint), electronic resources purchased during the fiscal year, and electronic resources licensed for the fiscal year.

- *Study seating capacity inside the library:* Number of study seats available for library users.

- *Number of full-time equivalent professional librarians:* The number of full-time equivalent professional librarians who teach or hold faculty rank plus the number of full-time equivalent librarians who do not teach or hold faculty rank.

- *Hours per week library is open:* Number of hours per week that professional staff are on duty in the library.

- *Number of open, wired connections available to students:* Number of open, wired, network connections available to students or, if the library has a wireless network, the number of simultaneous users accommodated within.

- *Number of networked computers available for use by students:* Number of workstations in law school or library computer labs, plus workstations in the library for users that are not in computer labs.

- *Has wireless network:* Indicates whether the school has a wireless network.

- *Requires computer:* Indicates whether the school requires students entering the law school to have a computer.

JD Attrition (from prior year)
Attrition percentages were based on fall 2010 enrollment. *Academic* attrition, for this purpose, refers to those students not continuing their legal studies between October 1, 2010, and October 1, 2011. *Other* attrition may include transfers and students who leave for other reasons.

Employment Summary (9 months after graduation)
For up-to-date employment data, go to employmentsummary.abaquestionnaire.org on the ABA website.

Bar Passage Rates
This section refers to numbers and percentages of law school graduates who took the bar for the first time during calendar year 2010. The pass rates for each jurisdiction were obtained from the National Conference of Bar Examiners. In reporting their first-time bar passage rates, each school must account for at least 70 percent of its first-time takers in the year reported. For some schools, in order to reach this 70 percent threshold, they need to report data for only a single jurisdiction. Other schools may have to report pass rates for multiple jurisdictions in order to account for at least 70 percent of first-time takers in the reporting year. Note that pass rates can vary widely from jurisdiction to jurisdiction; similarly, pass rates among schools can also vary widely. In instances where a school's pass rate is 15 or more points below the states' pass rates, applicants are encouraged to contact the school and obtain data for their ultimate pass rates (i.e., pass rates of repeat takers). Note that Wisconsin permits graduates of the University of Wisconsin Law School and Marquette University Law School to exercise the "diploma privilege" and be admitted to the bar without taking the examination.

APPLICANT PROFILES

Applicant profiles are provided by some schools to give candidates information about the number of applicants and admitted applicants in each cell. For various reasons, the total number of applicants and admitted applicants does not equal the official totals that appear on the ABA data pages in this book.

The purpose of the applicant profiles is to provide information about the LSAT/GPA credentials of applicants and admitted applicants to the schools that provide the profiles. You will note that some schools provide alternatives to the grid format for their profile or no profile at all.

THE UNIVERSITY OF AKRON SCHOOL OF LAW

302 Buchtel Common
Akron, OH 44325-2901
Phone: 800.425.7668; Fax: 330.258.2343
E-mail: lawadmissions@uakron.edu; Website: www.uakron.edu/law

ABA
Approved
Since
1961

The Basics

Type of school	Public
Term	Semester
Application deadline	3/1
Application fee	$0
Financial aid deadline	5/1
Can first year start other than fall?	No
Student to faculty ratio	13.8 to 1
# of housing spaces available restricted to law students	
graduate housing for which law students are eligible	

Faculty and Administrators

	Total		Men		Women		Minorities	
	Spr	Fall	Spr	Fall	Spr	Fall	Spr	Fall
Full-time	27	26	16	18	11	8	3	3
Other full-time	5	5	1	1	4	4	0	0
Deans, librarians, & others who teach	5	6	3	3	2	3	0	0
Part-time	24	17	19	14	5	3	1	0
Total	61	54	39	36	22	18	4	3

Curriculum

	Full-Time	Part-Time
Typical first-year section size	56	63
Is there typically a "small section" of the first-year class, other than Legal Writing, taught by full-time faculty	Yes	Yes
If yes, typical size offered last year	26	22
# of classroom course titles beyond first-year curriculum	87	
# of upper division courses, excluding seminars, with an enrollment: Under 25	80	
25–49	26	
50–74	15	
75–99	1	
100+	0	
# of seminars	36	
# of seminar positions available	788	
# of seminar positions filled	231	145
# of positions available in simulation courses	590	
# of simulation positions filled	253	141
# of positions available in faculty supervised clinical courses	375	
# of faculty supervised clinical positions filled	63	19
# involved in field placements	38	13
# involved in law journals	44	20
# involved in moot court or trial competitions	27	5
# of credit hours required to graduate	88	

JD Enrollment and Ethnicity

	Men		Women		Full-Time		Part-Time		1st-Year		Total		JD Degs. Awd.
	#	%	#	%	#	%	#	%	#	%	#	%	
All Hispanics	11	3.6	9	3.9	15	4.7	5	2.3	4	2.2	20	3.7	5
Am. Ind./AK Nat.	0	0.0	2	0.9	2	0.6	0	0.0	1	0.6	2	0.4	0
Asian	10	3.2	11	4.8	13	4.1	8	3.7	9	5.0	21	3.9	3
Black/Af. Am.	15	4.9	16	7.0	14	4.4	17	7.8	8	4.4	31	5.8	4
Nat. Hl/Pac. Isl.	0	0.0	0	0.0	0	0.0	0	0.0	0	0.0	0	0.0	0
2 or more races	4	1.3	1	0.4	2	0.6	3	1.4	3	1.7	5	0.9	0
Subtotal (minor.)	40	13.0	39	17.1	46	14.5	33	15.1	25	13.8	79	14.7	12
Nonres. Alien	0	0.0	0	0.0	0	0.0	0	0.0	0	0.0	0	0.0	0
White/Cauc.	247	80.2	176	77.2	250	78.6	173	79.4	152	84.0	423	78.9	95
Unknown	21	6.8	13	5.7	22	6.9	12	5.5	4	2.2	34	6.3	9
Total	308	57.5	228	42.5	318	59.3	218	40.7	181	33.8	536		116

Transfers

Transfers in	3
Transfers out	7

Tuition and Fees

	Resident	Nonresident
Full-time	$21,873	$34,428
Part-time	$17,802	$27,846
Tuition Guarantee Program		N

Living Expenses

Estimated living expenses for singles

Living on campus	Living off campus	Living at home
$16,034	$16,034	$16,034

THE UNIVERSITY OF AKRON SCHOOL OF LAW

*ABA
Approved
Since
1961*

GPA and LSAT Scores

	Total	Full-Time	Part-Time
# of apps	1,647	1,363	284
# of offers	883	685	198
# of matrics	175	100	75
75% GPA	3.63	3.63	3.63
Median GPA	3.35	3.32	3.41
25% GPA	3.12	3.12	3.14
75% LSAT	156	157	153
Median LSAT	153	155	151
25% LSAT	151	152	149

Grants and Scholarships (from prior year)

	Total #	Total %	Full-Time #	Full-Time %	Part-Time #	Part-Time %
Total # of students	506		279		227	
Total # receiving grants	247	48.8	177	63.4	70	30.8
Less than 1/2 tuition	90	17.8	55	19.7	35	15.4
Half to full tuition	78	15.4	63	22.6	15	6.6
Full tuition	3	0.6	3	1.1	0	0.0
More than full tuition	76	15.0	56	20.1	20	8.8
Median grant amount			$15,738		$5,744	

Informational and Library Resources

Total amount spent on library materials	$873,286
Study seating capacity inside the library	274
# of full-time equivalent professional librarians	4
Hours per week library is open	105
# of open, wired connections available to students	38
# of networked computers available for use by students	68
Has wireless network?	Y
Requires computer?	N

JD Attrition (from prior year)

	Academic #	Other #	Total #	Total %
1st year	12	17	29	14.4
2nd year	2	4	6	3.2
3rd year	0	1	1	1.3
4th year	0	1	1	2.5

Employment (9 months after graduation)

For up-to-date employment data, go to employmentsummary.abaquestionnaire.org on the ABA website.

Bar Passage Rates

First-time takers	125	Reporting %	72.80
Average school %	94.51	Average state %	86.14
Average pass difference	8.37		

Jurisdiction	Takers	Passers	Pass %	State %	Diff %
Ohio	91	86	94.51	86.14	8.37

THE UNIVERSITY OF AKRON SCHOOL OF LAW

302 Buchtel Common
Akron, OH 44325-2901
Phone: 800.425.7668; Fax: 330.258.2343
E-mail: lawadmissions@uakron.edu; Website: www.uakron.edu/law

Introduction

Located in the heart of downtown Akron and just 45 minutes south of Cleveland, the University of Akron (UA) is one of the 50 largest universities in the country. UA is a comprehensive research and teaching university with degree programs ranging from the associate to the doctoral level. Founded in 1870, UA has celebrated nearly 140 years of academic excellence while forging ahead to meet the complex needs of today's students.

The Akron School of Law was founded in 1921 and merged with UA in 1959. More than 6,000 students have graduated from the law school. Akron Law alumni practice throughout the United States and abroad.

Nearly 180 Akron Law alumni have been or currently are judges in 13 states and the District of Columbia, as well as in the federal court system.

Admission

In order to be considered for admission, the applicant must submit the application form and personal statement. The applicant must also take the LSAT and register for LSAC's Credential Assembly Service before the file may be sent to the Admissions Committee. An applicant may apply during his or her final year of undergraduate studies. The bachelor's degree coursework must be completed prior to law school matriculation. Decisions are made on a rolling basis as soon as the files are complete. The priority deadline is March 1, but applications are accepted throughout the spring and summer months. For more details on admission, please see our website at **www.uakron.edu/law**.

Students enrolled in an American Bar Association (ABA)–accredited law school may apply for transfer or transient status. A law student who has completed neither more nor less than one year (approximately 30 semester credit hours) and is in good academic standing may apply for transfer. A law student who has the dean's permission to visit for one or two semesters may apply for transient status. Consult **www.uakron.edu/law** for details.

Tuition/Fees and Financial Aid (Annual)

Admitted applicants are automatically considered for merit-based scholarships and may apply for need-based scholarships. Upper-division students may apply for merit-based and need-based scholarships. Students also have access to Stafford, Graduate PLUS, and alternative loans, as well as federal work-study funds (summer term only).

Flexible Scheduling

Akron Law offers a traditional full-time JD program, which law students may complete in two and one-half or three years. Akron Law also offers a flexible part-time program, which allows students to attend classes during daytime or evening hours. Part-time students may complete the JD program in as few as three and one-half years or as many as six years. A few upper-division classes are also offered at 7:30 AM to allow students to attend classes before work. Students may transfer from full time to part time (or vice versa) as their needs dictate.

Physical Facilities

The law building includes a 1987 addition to the library and a 1993 addition to the original structure. The university's $200-million New Landscape for Learning campus improvement program includes a new Student Union, Student Recreation and Wellness Center, Student Affairs Building, academic buildings, and parking decks. Approximately 30 acres of new green space were added to the campus to create a more park-like setting. The law school is within one block of the Akron Municipal Court, the court of common pleas, and the Ninth District Court of Appeals. The federal court is a few blocks from campus. Although the law school is in the downtown Akron area, the campus is a green one bordered by grassy areas, decorative plantings, and fountains.

Intellectual Property Center

Akron's JD/LLM in Intellectual Property Law program may be completed in three years on a full-time basis or in four years on a part-time basis, including summer enrollment for both programs. Akron's IP program is one of the most extensive in the nation. Nearly two dozen IP courses are offered either every year or every other year, with additional courses planned.

In addition, Akron offers an LLM degree in Intellectual Property Law. This graduate program, which may be completed on a full-time or part-time basis, provides law graduates with an opportunity to begin or continue a specialization in IP. In addition to the LLM program, Akron Law offers a JD/LLM joint degree program, which allows students to complete both degrees in three years on a full-time basis or four years on a part-time basis.

Curriculum/Special Programs

The first-year curriculum is traditional in content, using traditional and innovative interactive pedagogies. The upper-class curriculum is varied between basic courses and specialty courses, and also focuses on interactive learning pedagogies and development of crucial lawyering skills. All law students are eligible to participate in the programs offered and the services provided by the Academic Success Office. The director of academic success programs counsels students on study techniques, learning styles, time management, and other topics related to academic success. A comprehensive writing program designed to enhance students' skills in research, exposition, drafting, and argumentation is an integral part of the curriculum.

Specialized Studies: Business, Criminal, Intellectual Property, International, Litigation, Public, and Tax.

Joint Degrees: JD/Master in Business Administration, JD/Master in Taxation, JD/Master in Public Administration, JD/Master in Applied Politics, and JD/LLM in Intellectual Property Law.

Certificate Programs: Intellectual Property and Litigation.

LLM Graduate Law Degree: Intellectual Property.

Legal Clinic

Students represent clients in court, at trial, and on appeal. A variety of opportunities for clinical training are offered. Programs offered include Appellate Review; Clinical Seminar; Criminal, Judicial, and Public External Placement clinics; Prisoner Legal Assistance Clinic; Street Law; New Business Legal Clinic; Civil Litigation Clinic; Trial Litigation Clinic; and pro bono opportunities.

Student Activities and Leadership

Our more than 20 law student organizations include the *Akron Law Review*, Black Law Students Association, Asian-Latino Law Students Association, Environmental Law Society, Intellectual Property and Technology Law Association, International Law Society, Law Association for Women, Akron Public Interest Law Society, Student Bar Association, and more. Elections for leadership positions are held each year for day and evening students. Students have many opportunities to sharpen their litigation skills by participating in regional and national mock trial, moot court, and negotiation competitions. Our litigation teams have had tremendous success in competitions throughout the United States.

Library and Technology

UA's campus is wireless, allowing for Internet and network access in any building on campus. The law library contains 287,000 volumes. Students have access to 47.6 million library items, 11 million unique titles that may be delivered through OhioLINK, 3.8 million library items through UA Libraries Catalog, and many full-text resources, including 6,000 journals, more than 7.5 million articles, and 40,000 e-books.

Law students also receive free access to LexisNexis and Westlaw.

Career Planning and Placement

The Career Planning and Placement Office (CPPO) director counsels law students on résumé writing, job searching, interviewing skills, and preparing for entrance into the legal profession. On-campus interviews, a minority clerkship program, an attorney-student mentor program, employment-related seminars, and career fairs are offered. Akron's extensive law alumni database enables the CPPO to assist students with networking opportunities nationwide. The office assists in the placement of students in law-related positions during summer sessions and upper-division years. Graduates receive placement assistance, on request, throughout their careers. Akron's reputation for excellence in legal education and a subsequent high bar passage rate facilitates competitive placements for students and graduates in all areas of practice. Please see our detailed placement stats at **bit.ly/AkronLawCareer**.

Visiting Akron Law

Several programs are offered throughout the year for prospective and admitted students to interact with law students, alumni, faculty, and administration at the School of Law. In addition, guests are welcome to schedule an appointment to visit a class, take a tour, or meet with an admission representative. Prospective students may request additional information at **uakron.edu/law**. For those unable to visit Akron Law, our representatives can also be met on the recruitment road each fall. Consult our website for our national recruitment schedule.

APPLICANT PROFILE

The University of Akron School of Law

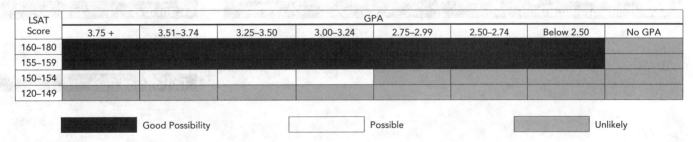

LSAT Score	GPA							
	3.75 +	3.51–3.74	3.25–3.50	3.00–3.24	2.75–2.99	2.50–2.74	Below 2.50	No GPA
160–180								
155–159								
150–154								
120–149								

Good Possibility   Possible   Unlikely

THE UNIVERSITY OF ALABAMA SCHOOL OF LAW

Box 870382
Tuscaloosa, AL 35487
Phone: 205.348.5440; Fax: 205.348.5439
E-mail: admissions@law.ua.edu; Website: www.law.ua.edu

ABA
Approved
Since
1926

The Basics

Type of school	Public
Term	Semester
Application deadline	
Application fee	$40
Financial aid deadline	
Can first year start other than fall?	No
Student to faculty ratio	10.5 to 1
# of housing spaces available restricted to law students	
graduate housing for which law students are eligible	

Faculty and Administrators

	Total		Men		Women		Minorities	
	Spr	Fall	Spr	Fall	Spr	Fall	Spr	Fall
Full-time	42	38	29	25	13	13	6	5
Other full-time	6	7	0	2	6	5	0	0
Deans, librarians, & others who teach	12	12	9	9	3	3	0	0
Part-time	35	35	29	29	6	6	2	1
Total	95	92	67	65	28	27	8	6

Curriculum

	Full-Time	Part-Time
Typical first-year section size	55	0
Is there typically a "small section" of the first-year class, other than Legal Writing, taught by full-time faculty	No	No
If yes, typical size offered last year		
# of classroom course titles beyond first-year curriculum	126	

# of upper division courses, excluding seminars, with an enrollment:		
	Under 25	122
	25–49	29
	50–74	6
	75–99	2
	100+	4

# of seminars	16	
# of seminar positions available	199	
# of seminar positions filled	189	0
# of positions available in simulation courses	487	
# of simulation positions filled	402	0
# of positions available in faculty supervised clinical courses	154	
# of faculty supervised clinical positions filled	146	0
# involved in field placements	93	0
# involved in law journals	128	0
# involved in moot court or trial competitions	116	0
# of credit hours required to graduate	90	

JD Enrollment and Ethnicity

	Men		Women		Full-Time		Part-Time		1st-Year		Total		JD Degs. Awd.
	#	%	#	%	#	%	#	%	#	%	#	%	
All Hispanics	5	1.7	3	1.4	8	1.6	0	0.0	2	1.2	8	1.6	3
Am. Ind./AK Nat.	1	0.3	1	0.5	2	0.4	0	0.0	0	0.0	2	0.4	2
Asian	3	1.0	4	1.9	7	1.4	0	0.0	3	1.8	7	1.4	3
Black/Af. Am.	20	6.7	26	12.4	46	9.0	0	0.0	18	10.9	46	9.0	12
Nat. HI/Pac. Isl.	1	0.3	2	1.0	3	0.6	0	0.0	0	0.0	3	0.6	0
2 or more races	5	1.7	1	0.5	6	1.2	0	0.0	6	3.6	6	1.2	0
Subtotal (minor.)	35	11.7	37	17.6	72	14.1	0	0.0	29	17.6	72	14.1	20
Nonres. Alien	0	0.0	0	0.0	0	0.0	0	0.0	0	0.0	0	0.0	0
White/Cauc.	264	88.3	173	82.4	437	85.9	0	0.0	136	82.4	437	85.9	146
Unknown	0	0.0	0	0.0	0	0.0	0	0.0	0	0.0	0	0.0	0
Total	299	58.7	210	41.3	509	100.0	0	0.0	165	32.4	509		166

Transfers

Transfers in	10
Transfers out	2

Tuition and Fees

	Resident	Nonresident
Full-time	$18,030	$30,950
Part-time		
Tuition Guarantee Program	N	

Living Expenses

Estimated living expenses for singles

Living on campus	Living off campus	Living at home
$16,522	$16,522	$16,522

THE UNIVERSITY OF ALABAMA SCHOOL OF LAW

ABA
Approved
Since
1926

GPA and LSAT Scores

	Total	Full-Time	Part-Time
# of apps	1,872	1,872	0
# of offers	473	473	0
# of matrics	160	160	0
75% GPA	3.94	3.94	0.00
Median GPA	3.83	3.83	0.00
25% GPA	3.42	3.42	0.00
75% LSAT	167	167	0
Median LSAT	165	165	0
25% LSAT	158	158	0

Grants and Scholarships (from prior year)

	Total #	Total %	Full-Time #	Full-Time %	Part-Time #	Part-Time %
Total # of students	509		509		0	
Total # receiving grants	235	46.2	235	46.2	0	0.0
Less than 1/2 tuition	71	13.9	71	13.9	0	0.0
Half to full tuition	83	16.3	83	16.3	0	0.0
Full tuition	13	2.6	13	2.6	0	0.0
More than full tuition	68	13.4	68	13.4	0	0.0
Median grant amount			$14,000		$0	

Informational and Library Resources

Total amount spent on library materials	$1,296,621
Study seating capacity inside the library	506
# of full-time equivalent professional librarians	16
Hours per week library is open	100
# of open, wired connections available to students	73
# of networked computers available for use by students	81
Has wireless network?	Y
Requires computer?	N

JD Attrition (from prior year)

	Academic #	Other #	Total #	Total %
1st year	4	20	24	14.7
2nd year	0	2	2	1.1
3rd year	0	0	0	0.0
4th year	0	0	0	0.0

Employment (9 months after graduation)

For up-to-date employment data, go to employmentsummary.abaquestionnaire.org on the ABA website.

Bar Passage Rates

First-time takers	176	Reporting %	72.73
Average school %	95.31	Average state %	84.91
Average pass difference	10.40		

Jurisdiction	Takers	Passers	Pass %	State %	Diff %
Alabama	128	122	95.31	84.91	10.40

THE UNIVERSITY OF ALABAMA SCHOOL OF LAW

Box 870382
Tuscaloosa, AL 35487
Phone: 205.348.5440; Fax: 205.348.5439
E-mail: admissions@law.ua.edu; Website: www.law.ua.edu

Introduction

The University of Alabama School of Law, the only public law school in Alabama, offers students a nationally recognized, progressive legal education. The law school has served as the training ground for state and national leaders in the legal profession, business, and government. Law students are provided with an abundance of cultural, academic, and athletic opportunities through the university. The curriculum is traditional but diverse. The law school is student-centered; faculty and administration are accessible to students. Although the faculty's first priority is teaching, the professors are actively engaged in scholarly research and writing. Alabama is accredited by the ABA and the AALS.

Library and Physical Facilities

The law school building, which sits on 23 acres of the University of Alabama's campus in Tuscaloosa, was designed by Edward Durell Stone, the architect for the Museum of Modern Art in New York, the US Embassy in New Delhi, and the Kennedy Center for the Performing Arts. Construction on a new wing and renovations to the existing building were completed in 2006. The wing includes new classrooms, the clinical offices, a cafeteria, a career services suite, meeting rooms, and a 24-hour computer lab. The Bounds Law Library provides users with a substantial research collection, student study carrels, the Hugo Black Study, the Howell Heflin Conference Room, and the Payne Special Collections Room. The school is on a wireless network.

Special and Summer Programs

Clinical programs enable law students to gain valuable practical experience in interviewing clients, preparing cases, and participating in courtroom presentations. During the second and third years, students can choose to participate in the Elder Law, Domestic Violence, Civil, Community Development, Capital Defense, Mediation Law, or Criminal Defense clinics. Alabama guarantees every interested student the opportunity to participate in at least one clinic before graduating.

The externship program offers students practical experience while receiving credit. Externships are available during the summers and the second and third academic years. The law school's Public Interest Institute awards grants to encourage students to participate in the area of public interest and honors students who perform public interest work. The institute also has a full-time dean to assist students.

The joint JD/MBA program offers select students an opportunity to earn both an MBA and JD. Students may select from programs designed for them to earn both degrees within three or four years. The graduate program for international students provides international lawyers an opportunity to earn an LLM degree. The law school also offers a part-time LLM in Taxation program for JD degree holders.

The law school's two summer programs at the University of Fribourg in Fribourg, Switzerland, and the Australian National University in Canberra provide a unique international experience. Both programs include a course surveying the host country's national law and a comparative law doctrinal course. In addition, Alabama Law offers current students the opportunity to study abroad for a semester at Tel Aviv University in Israel and the National Law University of New Delhi in India.

Summer school is open to students who have completed the first year.

Admission

A student must obtain a bachelor's degree at an accredited institution before enrolling, but may apply during his or her senior year. Applicants must take the LSAT, preferably in June or October in the year preceding enrollment, and register for the Credential Assembly Service (CAS). Transcripts must show all schools attended. Application materials are available in the late summer each year and accepted in early fall. Applications are processed on a rolling basis. The two most significant factors for admission are the undergraduate GPA and LSAT score. However, the school believes that the law school experience is enriched by a diverse group of students. The Admissions Committee also considers other factors, such as honors, activities, unique work or service experience, difficulty of undergraduate courses, writing ability, trends in academic performance, leadership roles, travel experience, exceptional talents, career achievements, graduate school performance, and history of overcoming adversity. One letter of recommendation or LSAC evaluation is required. The law school recommends that letters be submitted to the Credential Assembly Service. A résumé is also required.

Student Activities

A broad range of student activities adds to the students' law school experience. Student organizations represent diverse interests. These include the Student Bar Association, Black Law Students Association, Public Interest Law Association, Civil Rights Law Students Association, Dorbin Association (women's group), Law Students for Choice, Gay-Straight Alliance, Environmental Law Society, International Law Society, Just Democracy, Labor and Employment Law Society, Law Democrats, Law Republicans, Business Law Society, Criminal Law Association, Defense Lawyers Association, Future Trial Lawyers Association, Christian Legal Society, Sports and Entertainment Law Society, and Latin American Law Association.

The School of Law also offers numerous writing opportunities. The *Alabama Law Review*, a nationally recognized law journal, is edited by students and devotes substantial space to national and state issues. The *Journal of the Legal Profession, Law and Psychology Review*, and *Alabama Civil Rights and Civil Liberties Law Review* are also student-edited law journals. Over 40 percent will graduate with journal experience.

Moot court and trial advocacy teams have enjoyed exceptional success over the years. The law school sponsors teams in several moot court, specialty, and trial advocacy competitions. The moot court and trial advocacy teams have won many team and individual awards in both regional and national competitions.

Expenses and Financial Aid

The majority of students enrolled in the School of Law finance their legal education through loans, savings, earnings, or family contributions. Applicants are considered automatically for first-year scholarships, which are typically based on factors such as GPA and LSAT performance. Scholarships sometimes are renewable during the second and third years—depending upon funding, the student's need, and whether the recipient maintains stated levels of academic achievement. Following acceptance by the law school, each admitted student who applies for federal aid through the Free Application for Federal Student Aid (FAFSA) receives a financial aid packet from the university's Financial Aid Office. Information on loans can be obtained by contacting Student Financial Aid, the University of Alabama, Box 870162, Tuscaloosa, AL 35487-0162; phone: 205.348.6756; website: www.financialaid.ua.edu. Applicants should complete the FAFSA form as soon after January 1 as possible, and may apply online at www.fafsa.ed.gov.

Career Services

The Career Services Office assists students in their efforts to find employment. The office provides individual career counseling, group presentations, speaker programs, and library and database resources. Seminars are presented on résumé writing, interviewing techniques, job-search techniques, judicial clerkships, and nontraditional legal jobs, to name a few. Extensive on-campus interviewing occurs. The law school also participates in job fairs in Atlanta, New York City, Chicago, and Washington, DC. The employment rate within nine months of graduation was 97.4 percent for the class of 2010 with approximately 40 percent practicing outside of Alabama. The national bar passage rate for the same class was 95 percent and the in-state bar passage rate was 95 percent.

Housing

The University of Alabama maintains residence halls and units for students; however, most law students live off campus. The cost of living in Tuscaloosa for a single law student ranges from approximately $500 to $1,100 per month. For information on university housing, students must contact the Office of Residential Life at the University of Alabama at housing@sa.ua.edu.

APPLICANT PROFILE

The University of Alabama School of Law
This grid includes only applicants who earned 120–180 LSAT scores under standard administrations.

LSAT Score	GPA								
	3.75 +	3.50–3.74	3.25–3.49	3.00–3.24	2.75–2.99	2.50–2.74	2.25–2.49	2.00–2.24	Below 2.00
175–180									
170–174									
165–169									
160–164									
155–159									
150–154									
145–149									
140–144									
135–139									
130–134									
125–129									
120–124									

Good Possibility   Possible   Unlikely

Reflects 99% of the total applicant pool; average LSAT data reported.

ALBANY LAW SCHOOL OF UNION UNIVERSITY

80 New Scotland Avenue
Albany, NY 12208-3494
Phone: 518.445.2326; Fax: 518.445.2369
E-mail: admissions@albanylaw.edu; Website: www.albanylaw.edu

The Basics

Type of school	Private
Term	Semester
Application deadline	3/1
Application fee	$70
Financial aid deadline	
Can first year start other than fall?	No
Student to faculty ratio	13.1 to 1
# of housing spaces available restricted to law students	
graduate housing for which law students are eligible	

Faculty and Administrators

	Total		Men		Women		Minorities	
	Spr	Fall	Spr	Fall	Spr	Fall	Spr	Fall
Full-time	45	44	21	18	24	26	8	8
Other full-time	0	0	0	0	0	0	0	0
Deans, librarians, & others who teach	6	5	3	2	3	3	2	2
Part-time	26	28	17	22	9	6	4	4
Total	77	77	41	42	36	35	14	14

Curriculum

		Full-Time	Part-Time
Typical first-year section size		59	0
Is there typically a "small section" of the first-year class, other than Legal Writing, taught by full-time faculty		No	No
If yes, typical size offered last year			
# of classroom course titles beyond first-year curriculum		121	
# of upper division courses, excluding seminars, with an enrollment:	Under 25	68	
	25–49	24	
	50–74	15	
	75–99	7	
	100+	2	
# of seminars		46	
# of seminar positions available		1,012	
# of seminar positions filled		716	0
# of positions available in simulation courses		594	
# of simulation positions filled		426	0
# of positions available in faculty supervised clinical courses		112	
# of faculty supervised clinical positions filled		98	0
# involved in field placements		192	0
# involved in law journals		172	0
# involved in moot court or trial competitions		25	0
# of credit hours required to graduate		87	

JD Enrollment and Ethnicity

	Men		Women		Full-Time		Part-Time		1st-Year		Total		JD Degs. Awd.
	#	%	#	%	#	%	#	%	#	%	#	%	
All Hispanics	13	3.4	5	1.6	18	2.7	0	0.0	3	1.2	18	2.6	11
Am. Ind./AK Nat.	1	0.3	0	0.0	1	0.1	0	0.0	0	0.0	1	0.1	3
Asian	15	4.0	18	5.8	32	4.8	1	6.3	13	5.2	33	4.8	14
Black/Af. Am.	9	2.4	11	3.6	19	2.8	1	6.3	6	2.4	20	2.9	3
Nat. HI/Pac. Isl.	0	0.0	0	0.0	0	0.0	0	0.0	0	0.0	0	0.0	0
2 or more races	8	2.1	12	3.9	20	3.0	0	0.0	14	5.6	20	2.9	0
Subtotal (minor.)	46	12.2	46	14.9	90	13.4	2	12.5	36	14.5	92	13.4	31
Nonres. Alien	4	1.1	7	2.3	11	1.6	0	0.0	5	2.0	11	1.6	5
White/Cauc.	264	70.0	202	65.4	454	67.8	12	75.0	174	70.2	466	67.9	194
Unknown	63	16.7	54	17.5	115	17.2	2	12.5	33	13.3	117	17.1	12
Total	377	55.0	309	45.0	670	97.7	16	2.3	248	36.2	686		242

Transfers

Transfers in	4
Transfers out	15

Tuition and Fees

	Resident	Nonresident
Full-time	$41,845	$41,845
Part-time	$31,455	$31,455
Tuition Guarantee Program		N

Living Expenses

Estimated living expenses for singles

Living on campus	Living off campus	Living at home
N/A	$18,000	$9,100

ALBANY LAW SCHOOL OF UNION UNIVERSITY

ABA
Approved
Since
1930

GPA and LSAT Scores

	Total	Full-Time	Part-Time
# of apps	2,153	2,153	0
# of offers	1,113	1,113	0
# of matrics	235	235	0
75% GPA	3.53	3.53	0.00
Median GPA	3.31	3.31	0.00
25% GPA	3.05	3.05	0.00
75% LSAT	157	157	0
Median LSAT	153	153	0
25% LSAT	151	151	0

Grants and Scholarships (from prior year)

	Total #	Total %	Full-Time #	Full-Time %	Part-Time #	Part-Time %
Total # of students	720		697		23	
Total # receiving grants	244	33.9	236	33.9	8	34.8
Less than 1/2 tuition	113	15.7	111	15.9	2	8.7
Half to full tuition	123	17.1	117	16.8	6	26.1
Full tuition	5	0.7	5	0.7	0	0.0
More than full tuition	3	0.4	3	0.4	0	0.0
Median grant amount			$20,000		$15,000	

Informational and Library Resources

Total amount spent on library materials	$1,804,101
Study seating capacity inside the library	432
# of full-time equivalent professional librarians	7
Hours per week library is open	104
# of open, wired connections available to students	1,142
# of networked computers available for use by students	95
Has wireless network?	Y
Requires computer?	N

JD Attrition (from prior year)

	Academic #	Other #	Total #	Total %
1st year	3	4	7	2.9
2nd year	0	18	18	7.6
3rd year	0	0	0	0.0
4th year	0	0	0	0.0

Employment (9 months after graduation)

For up-to-date employment data, go to employmentsummary.abaquestionnaire.org on the ABA website.

Bar Passage Rates

First-time takers	219	Reporting %	99.09
Average school %	76.04	Average state %	84.92
Average pass difference	–8.88		

Jurisdiction	Takers	Passers	Pass %	State %	Diff %
New York	217	165	76.04	84.92	–8.88

ALBANY LAW SCHOOL OF UNION UNIVERSITY

80 New Scotland Avenue
Albany, NY 12208-3494
Phone: 518.445.2326; Fax: 518.445.2369
E-mail: admissions@albanylaw.edu; Website: www.albanylaw.edu

Introduction

The only law school in the capital of New York State, Albany Law School is the oldest private, independent law school in North America. Our location, in the center of state government, provides unprecedented opportunities for internships, field placements, clinical experience, and career opportunities. Our world-class faculty is dedicated and accessible. Students have access to New York's highest court, federal courts, and the state legislature, as well as to a thriving tech-based economy. The employment rate for our graduates has been well above the national average for law schools for over 25 years.

The Academic Experience

From your first day at Albany Law School, you will be challenged by a rigorous academic curriculum. You will get a firm foundation in fundamental areas of law, plus opportunities to shape your learning to fit your professional interests.

As a first-year student, you begin to acquire the skills that will become the foundation of your legal career. As part of our innovative Introduction to Lawyering course, you will represent a plaintiff or defendant in a simulated case where you conduct legal research, draft motions and memoranda, and participate in client interviews and negotiations. The class culminates with each student presenting an oral argument before some of the state's most notable attorneys.

As a second- and third-year student, you can focus your studies in 1 of 14 concentrations to complement coursework. Opportunities include 7 clinical projects and more than 150 field placement internships in the Albany region, many of them in state and federal government positions as well as in law firms and high-tech companies. Students also participate in real-world work through the Government Law Center, Clinic and Justice Center, and study-abroad programs. Some students pursue a joint-degree program with an area graduate school, earning a master's degree while working toward a Juris Doctor (JD) degree.

Real-Life Experience

Our groundbreaking legal centers and award-winning clinical programs provide the valuable hands-on experience that employers find desirable. You work alongside committed clinical faculty and practicing attorneys to assist low-income clients with real legal issues relating to health law, HIV/AIDS, disabilities, domestic violence, and disputes with the Internal Revenue Service. You will also work with prosecutors, judges, and experienced attorneys through our field placement program.

Because of our unique location, you interact with the leaders in New York state government—countless Albany Law alumni—and visionaries building New York's high-technology base through the programs at the Government Law Center. In the Government Law Center you conduct research, contribute to publications, and participate in conferences and special projects that promote the study of the issues facing government, public policy, and public service.

Your Career

From your first week at school, our Career Center helps you develop a career plan and supports you throughout your job search. Professional career counselors help you define career goals, craft résumés and cover letters, prepare for interviews, and compare employment offers.

The Career Center is a state-of-the-art facility with multiple interview rooms set aside for professionals to conduct on-campus interviews. These rooms are equipped with all the amenities of a law office and are extremely popular with employers.

Job fairs, information sessions, workshops, and panel discussions on a variety of employment-related topics occur almost weekly. The Career Center hosts more than 1,000 interviews each year and conducts off-campus interview programs in metropolitan areas, including New York City; Chicago; Washington, DC; and Boston, exclusively for Albany Law School students. Our alumni are avid supporters of these efforts and participate enthusiastically in center activities.

Our graduates find jobs in law firms, government agencies, public interest organizations, and business and industry throughout the country. About one third of Albany Law School graduates work in the New York City metropolitan area, with large groups of alumni in Boston; Washington, DC; and business centers along the eastern seaboard as far south as Florida.

The employment rate for the class of 2010 was 91 percent—above the national average and consistently above national rates for over 25 years.

Our Community

The Albany Law School community of approximately 700 students, 55 full-time faculty, and 52 part-time faculty is intimate, respectful, and supportive. We welcome students and faculty with diverse backgrounds and talents, and provide an outstanding environment for the pursuit of scholarship, teaching, and public service.

The small size of our student body fosters an environment that encourages camaraderie and frequent contact between students and faculty. We are exclusively a law school. Because we are independent, we are not attached to a larger university.

Nearly 12 percent of our students graduated five or more years before entering law school and had careers in other professions prior to beginning their legal studies. Nearly 50 percent of our students are women, roughly 20 percent are members of a minority group, and they come from all across the United States and several foreign countries.

Our Campus

Albany Law School's facilities honor our 160-year history, while supporting a twenty-first century legal education. The open design of the 53,000 square-foot Schaffer Law Library, a federal depository library, provides an inviting environment with seating for hundreds of students. Book and microfilm collections number more than half a million volumes, and the library supplements its collection with online databases and legal research systems, including LexisNexis and Westlaw.

The library also houses technological devices for the hearing and visually impaired.

The main building of Albany Law School is known as the 1928 Building, acknowledging its year of construction. The building has been recently renovated and houses contemporary lecture halls, seminar-style classrooms, two modern moot courtrooms, and smart classrooms with wireless Internet access and advanced audio, video, computing, and conferencing systems.

A 45,000-square-foot building built in 2000 houses the Law Clinic and Justice Center, Government Law Center, and administrative offices, as well as several classrooms, including a high-tech distance learning classroom. Our new bookstore and student center opened in 2009, along with a new state-of-the-art fitness center.

Student Life

You have dozens of opportunities to participate in student organizations and activities around specific academic, professional, social, cultural, or athletic interests.

Three student-edited journals, the *Albany Law Review*, the *Albany Law Journal of Science and Technology*, and the *Albany Government Law Review* offer cocurricular research and writing opportunities.

Our nationally recognized Moot Court Program enables you to develop skills in trial advocacy, appellate advocacy, client counseling, and negotiating while competing in both intramural and interscholastic competitions.

The Capital Region is home to 16 colleges and universities and boasts museums, galleries, restaurants, shops, theaters, nightclubs for every taste, venues that host professional sporting events, and performing arts centers that attract

national acts. The Adirondack, Berkshire, and Catskill Mountains offer skiing, camping, hiking, and water sports, as well as the Saratoga Race Course for thoroughbred and harness racing. Metropolitan centers in New York City, Boston, and Montreal are all within an easy drive and about 10 trains provide daily service to New York City. All major air carriers operate from the Albany International Airport and provide daily nonstop service to most eastern US cities, with connections worldwide.

Admission and Financial Aid

Albany Law School offers grants based on merit ranging from $5,000 to full-tuition scholarships. Over 30 percent of first-year students receive awards that average $20,000 for each academic year.

When evaluating each individual application, the Admissions Committee takes a highly personalized, holistic approach, reviewing LSAT score, undergraduate grade-point average, strength of the undergraduate program, rigor of the undergraduate curriculum, and life experience. The committee seeks to enroll a student body that enriches the educational experience of all of its members. Albany Law School also seeks to provide future members of the bar who reflect the diversity and sensibilities of our society.

Approximately 90 percent of our students qualify for financial aid, via federal, state, and private loans, or for part-time employment to assist in meeting educational expenses.

We encourage you to visit Albany Law School—meet our faculty, speak with our students, and tour our beautiful facilities. We look forward to meeting you.

APPLICANT PROFILE

Albany Law School attracts talented, diverse students from a wide spectrum of backgrounds and experiences. Applicants come from the highest ranks of their prior graduate and undergraduate institutions. LSAT scores and prior academic performance are important in assisting our Admissions Committee in offering seats to applicants. Those indicators

are, however, not the sole factors weighed when admission decisions are made. Interested applicants are encouraged to explore how their careers can be enhanced by an Albany Law School education. Contact the Admissions Office at 518.445.2326 to discuss your individual qualifications.

AMERICAN UNIVERSITY WASHINGTON COLLEGE OF LAW

4801 Massachusetts Avenue NW, Suite 507
Washington, DC 20016
Phone: 202.274.4101; Fax: 202.274.4107
E-mail: wcladmit@wcl.american.edu; Website: www.wcl.american.edu

ABA
Approved
Since
1940

AMERICAN BAR ASSOCIATION
Section of Legal Education
and Admissions to the Bar

The Basics

Type of school	Private
Term	Semester
Application deadline	3/1
Application fee	$70
Financial aid deadline	3/1
Can first year start other than fall?	No
Student to faculty ratio	11.1 to 1
# of housing spaces available restricted to law students	
graduate housing for which law students are eligible	25

Faculty and Administrators

	Total		Men		Women		Minorities	
	Spr	Fall	Spr	Fall	Spr	Fall	Spr	Fall
Full-time	106	102	60	57	46	45	19	18
Other full-time	15	15	4	4	11	11	5	5
Deans, librarians, & others who teach	1	1	1	1	0	0	1	1
Part-time	148	142	103	93	45	49	16	15
Total	270	260	168	155	102	105	41	39

JD Enrollment and Ethnicity

	Men		Women		Full-Time		Part-Time		1st-Year		Total		JD Degs. Awd.
	#	%	#	%	#	%	#	%	#	%	#	%	
All Hispanics	97	14.5	132	15.9	197	15.9	32	12.3	60	12.6	229	15.3	64
Am. Ind./AK Nat.	8	1.2	6	0.7	10	0.8	4	1.5	5	1.1	14	0.9	4
Asian	59	8.8	66	7.9	101	8.2	24	9.2	40	8.4	125	8.3	51
Black/Af. Am.	43	6.4	94	11.3	108	8.7	29	11.2	28	5.9	137	9.1	44
Nat. HI/Pac. Isl.	0	0.0	5	0.6	4	0.3	1	0.4	1	0.2	5	0.3	0
2 or more races	2	0.3	14	1.7	14	1.1	2	0.8	5	1.1	16	1.1	0
Subtotal (minor.)	209	31.3	317	38.1	434	35.0	92	35.4	139	29.2	526	35.1	163
Nonres. Alien	17	2.5	28	3.4	41	3.3	4	1.5	10	2.1	45	3.0	14
White/Cauc.	391	58.5	416	50.1	661	53.3	146	56.2	302	63.4	807	53.8	278
Unknown	51	7.6	70	8.4	103	8.3	18	6.9	25	5.3	121	8.1	9
Total	668	44.6	831	55.4	1239	82.7	260	17.3	476	31.8	1499		464

Curriculum

	Full-Time	Part-Time
Typical first-year section size	79	91
Is there typically a "small section" of the first-year class, other than Legal Writing, taught by full-time faculty	Yes	No
If yes, typical size offered last year	45	
# of classroom course titles beyond first-year curriculum	297	

# of upper division courses, excluding seminars, with an enrollment:	Under 25	253
	25–49	61
	50–74	45
	75–99	5
	100+	0

# of seminars	144	
# of seminar positions available	2,055	
# of seminar positions filled	1,064	549
# of positions available in simulation courses	1,025	
# of simulation positions filled	381	392
# of positions available in faculty supervised clinical courses	223	
# of faculty supervised clinical positions filled	209	14
# involved in field placements	312	18
# involved in law journals	321	10
# involved in moot court or trial competitions	46	5
# of credit hours required to graduate	86	

Transfers

Transfers in	53
Transfers out	50

Tuition and Fees

	Resident	Nonresident
Full-time	$45,096	$45,096
Part-time	$31,622	$31,622
Tuition Guarantee Program	N	

Living Expenses

Estimated living expenses for singles

Living on campus	Living off campus	Living at home
$22,604	$22,604	$22,604

AMERICAN UNIVERSITY WASHINGTON COLLEGE OF LAW

ABA
Approved
Since
1940

GPA and LSAT Scores

	Total	Full-Time	Part-Time
# of apps	7,521	6,741	780
# of offers	2,075	1,900	175
# of matrics	475	388	87
75% GPA	3.59	3.59	3.59
Median GPA	3.44	3.45	3.44
25% GPA	3.22	3.24	3.14
75% LSAT	163	163	162
Median LSAT	162	162	160
25% LSAT	159	159	157

Grants and Scholarships (from prior year)

	Total		Full-Time		Part-Time	
	#	%	#	%	#	%
Total # of students	1,503		1,243		260	
Total # receiving grants	492	32.7	470	37.8	22	8.5
Less than 1/2 tuition	451	30.0	429	34.5	22	8.5
Half to full tuition	14	0.9	14	1.1	0	0.0
Full tuition	18	1.2	18	1.4	0	0.0
More than full tuition	9	0.6	9	0.7	0	0.0
Median grant amount			$10,000		$5,000	

Informational and Library Resources

Total amount spent on library materials	$2,204,154
Study seating capacity inside the library	596
# of full-time equivalent professional librarians	1.7
Hours per week library is open	119
# of open, wired connections available to students	2,160
# of networked computers available for use by students	166
Has wireless network?	Y
Requires computer?	N

JD Attrition (from prior year)

	Academic	Other	Total	
	#	#	#	%
1st year	0	55	55	10.8
2nd year	0	0	0	0.0
3rd year	0	0	0	0.0
4th year	0	0	0	0.0

Employment (9 months after graduation)

For up-to-date employment data, go to employmentsummary.abaquestionnaire.org on the ABA website.

Bar Passage Rates

First-time takers	445	Reporting %	93.26
Average school %	81.68	Average state %	80.98
Average pass difference	.70		

Jurisdiction	Takers	Passers	Pass %	State %	Diff %
New York	130	107	82.31	84.92	–2.61
Maryland	98	80	81.63	79.96	1.67
Virginia	68	54	79.41	78.15	1.26
California	46	31	67.39	71.24	–3.85
Others (5)	73	67	91.78		

AMERICAN UNIVERSITY WASHINGTON COLLEGE OF LAW

4801 Massachusetts Avenue NW, Suite 507
Washington, DC 20016
Phone: 202.274.4101; Fax: 202.274.4107
E-mail: wcladmit@wcl.american.edu; Website: www.wcl.american.edu

Introduction

American University Washington College of Law (AU WCL) offers an opportunity for the study of law in the center of the nation's legal institutions. The law school is minutes from downtown Washington, yet offers the facilities and ambience of a campus environment in one of the city's most beautiful residential neighborhoods. Founded in 1896 by two women, the law school is national in character. AU WCL offers renowned programs in experiential learning (clinics, externships, trial advocacy), international law, law and government, intellectual property, business, environmental law, health law, and gender. It is committed to the development of the intellectual abilities, professional values, and practical skills required to prepare lawyers to practice in an increasingly complex and transnational world.

Library and Physical Facilities

The John Sherman Myers and Alvina Reckman Myers Law Center houses the Pence Law Library, two courtrooms, classrooms, faculty offices, and administrative offices. The two-story law library is the heart of the complex and seats over 600 students. The entire law school facility has wireless access, and most of the law library seating has wired access as well. The library has more than 600,000 volumes, access to multiple databases, and 14 group-study rooms in addition to individual study carrels and seating. There are a number of research stations and network printing is available to the community. The library collection includes European Community and US government depositories and the Baxter Collection in International Law. Students also have access to the university's library, the Library of Congress, specialized agency libraries, and other area law libraries to which the school is electronically linked. The law school also encompasses more than 12 program offices, several faculty offices, and conference rooms in two neighboring buildings.

Curriculum

The law school offers full- and part-time programs leading to the JD degree, which is awarded after satisfactory completion of 86 credit hours, 32 of which are prescribed. All degree candidates must also fulfill an upper-level writing requirement. While a modified version of the Socratic method is the dominant form of teaching in the first year, faculty increasingly employ such methodologies as role-playing, simulations, and small-group collaborative exercises. The goal is to develop the skills of critical analysis, provide perspectives on the law and lawyering, and deepen understanding of fundamental legal principles. In the Legal Rhetoric Program, basic legal research and writing skills are taught to groups of students by full-time faculty (23 students per section) and practicing attorneys (12 students per section). During the spring semester of the first year, students enroll in an elective first-year course in addition to their required courses. Examples of first-year elective courses are International Law, Introduction to Intellectual Property Law, and Introduction to Public Law. In the second and third years, students elect a course of study drawing from advanced courses, seminars, independent research, externships, and

clinical programs. JD students take upper-level courses with LLM students, learning side by side with more than 180 practicing attorneys from around the world. Students are exposed to a variety of teaching approaches by the law school's distinguished full-time tenured and tenure-track faculty and adjunct professors.

Special Programs

While many of the advanced courses are taught in a traditional classroom setting, a variety of other innovative teaching modes are available to enhance research skills and provide professional training.

- **Clinical Program**—The Washington College of Law was one of the first law schools to develop modern clinical legal education. Typically, more than 200 second- and third-year students participate in one of the 11 law clinics each academic year—making the Clinical Program one of the largest in the nation. All 11 clinics are open to third-year students and 7 are open to second-year students. Full-time faculty and practitioners-in-residence work collaboratively to teach students about client-centered, ethical practices. The Clinical Program serves a diverse clientele, including immigrants and refugees; victims/survivors of domestic violence; juveniles; criminal defendants; low-income taxpayers; individuals seeking help with family law, consumer, disability, and intellectual property issues; community groups; and nonprofit organizations. The 11 clinics include General Practice Clinic, Community and Economic Development Law Clinic, Criminal Justice Clinic, DC Law Students in Court Clinic, Disability Rights Law Clinic, Domestic Violence Law Clinic, Janet R. Spragens Federal Tax Clinic, Glushko-Samuelson Intellectual Property Law Clinic, Immigrant Justice Clinic, International Human Rights Law Clinic, and Women and the Law Clinic.
- **Dual-Degree Programs**—American University offers five domestic dual-degree programs for students seeking to enhance their law degree with additional graduate coursework. These programs are a JD/MA in International Affairs with the School of International Service; JD/MBA with the Kogod School of Business; and JD/MPA, JD/MPP, and JD/MS in Justice, Law, and Society programs with the School of Public Affairs. In addition to our domestic dual-degree programs, the law school offers four international dual-degree programs with law schools in Melbourne, Australia; Ottawa, Canada; Paris, France; and Madrid, Spain. These programs provide students more opportunities to practice law in the international arena.
- **Externship Program**—The program places upper-level students in many governmental, nonprofit, and public interest entities throughout the DC metropolitan area, the US, and abroad. More than 300 students participate in an externship each year.
- **Trial Advocacy Program**—The nationally recognized Stephen S. Weinstein Trial Advocacy Program prepares about 300 students each year to enter the legal community with solid trial litigation skills. The program emphasizes basic skills training, development of case theory and themes, analysis of strategies, and professional ethics.

- **Graduate Study**—Graduate study is available leading to an LLM degree in International Legal Studies, Law and Government, or Trial Advocacy, or an SJD degree in a breadth of legal topics.
- **Summer Programs**—In addition to our summer session courses, the law school offers many intensive summer institutes at our DC location in the areas of international arbitration, human rights, health law, intellectual property, international organizations and diplomacy, government, and environmental law.
- **Study Abroad**—Students have the opportunity to study law for a semester in more than 18 different countries or through one of the law school's five summer abroad programs in Chile, Europe (London/Paris/Geneva), The Hague, Turkey, and Israel. Typically, about 30 percent of the student body studies abroad.

Admission

Applicants to the law school are admitted based on the strength of their entire academic and related record. The Committee on Admissions gives primary emphasis to the undergraduate record, LSAT scores, and major accomplishments and achievements, whether academic, work-related, or extracurricular. The committee considers the benefits from having racial, ethnic, cultural, economic, and geographic diversity among its students. Admission to the law school is highly selective and operates both a binding Early Decision Option and a modified rolling admission process, so early application is strongly encouraged.

Student Activities

The law school has five established journals and several publications edited and published by students. Journals include *Administrative Law Review; American University*

Law Review; American University Business Law Review; American University International Law Review; and *American University Journal of Gender, Social Policy, and the Law.* Other publications include *Criminal Law Brief, Health Law and Policy, Human Rights Brief, Intellectual Property Brief, Labor & Employment Law Forum, Legislation and Policy Brief,* the *Modern American, National Security Law Brief,* and *Sustainable Development Law and Policy.* The Moot Court Honor Society sponsors appellate competitions for first-year and upper-level students and prepares students for a number of national and international interschool appellate competitions. The Mock Trial Honor Society sponsors a closing argument competition for first-year students and prepares student teams for national interschool mock trial competitions. There are more than 50 active student organizations, including the Asian-Pacific American Law Students Association, Black Law Students Association, Latino/a Law Students Association, South Asian Law Students Association, Lambda Law Society, International Trade and Investment Law Society, Intellectual Property Law Society, and Law and Government Society.

Career Services

Staffed by seven attorney counselors, the Office of Career and Professional Development provides individual career and professional development counseling to students and alumni on all aspects of the job search process, and sponsors dozens of educational and job-related programs throughout the year. In addition to supporting students who pursue academic year positions in the Washington metropolitan area to advance their substantive legal skills, the office coordinates both on- and off-campus recruitment for summer and postgraduate opportunities, including regional interview programs in cities such as Boston, New York, and Los Angeles.

APPLICANT PROFILE

The Committee on Admissions considers a number of factors when evaluating a candidate for admission; therefore we elected not to include a grid based on undergraduate GPA and LSAT scores. Many applicants have similar scores, but

each applicant has a unique background of academic, cultural, and professional experiences and achievements. The committee weighs all of these factors when determining a candidate's suitability for admission.

APPALACHIAN SCHOOL OF LAW

1169 Edgewater Drive, PO Box 2825
Grundy, VA 24614
Phone: 800.895.7411 (toll free) or 276.935.4349; Fax: 276.935.8496
E-mail: admissions@asl.edu; Website: www.asl.edu

ABA
Approved
Since
2001

AMERICAN BAR ASSOCIATION
Section of Legal Education
and Admissions to the Bar

The Basics

Type of school	Private
Term	Semester
Application deadline	7/30
Application fee	$60
Financial aid deadline	7/1
Can first year start other than fall?	No
Student to faculty ratio	17.7 to 1
# of housing spaces available restricted to law students	
graduate housing for which law students are eligible	

Faculty and Administrators

	Total		Men		Women		Minorities	
	Spr	Fall	Spr	Fall	Spr	Fall	Spr	Fall
Full-time	16	15	12	11	4	4	2	3
Other full-time	0	1	0	1	0	0	0	0
Deans, librarians, & others who teach	4	4	3	3	1	1	1	1
Part-time	0	1	0	1	0	0	0	0
Total	20	21	15	16	5	5	3	4

Curriculum

	Full-Time	Part-Time
Typical first-year section size	147	0
Is there typically a "small section" of the first-year class, other than Legal Writing, taught by full-time faculty	Yes	No
If yes, typical size offered last year	62	

# of classroom course titles beyond first-year curriculum		44
# of upper division courses, excluding seminars, with an enrollment:	Under 25	18
	25–49	10
	50–74	3
	75–99	10
	100+	0
# of seminars		7
# of seminar positions available		140

	Full-Time	Part-Time
# of seminar positions filled	94	0
# of positions available in simulation courses	533	
# of simulation positions filled	434	0
# of positions available in faculty supervised clinical courses	0	
# of faculty supervised clinical positions filled	0	0
# involved in field placements	124	0
# involved in law journals	48	0
# involved in moot court or trial competitions	35	0
# of credit hours required to graduate	90	

JD Enrollment and Ethnicity

	Men		Women		Full-Time		Part-Time		1st-Year		Total		JD Degs. Awd.
	#	%	#	%	#	%	#	%	#	%	#	%	
All Hispanics	6	2.8	8	6.7	14	4.2	0	0.0	9	6.2	14	4.2	2
Am. Ind./AK Nat.	0	0.0	0	0.0	0	0.0	0	0.0	0	0.0	0	0.0	2
Asian	4	1.9	4	3.4	8	2.4	0	0.0	4	2.8	8	2.4	0
Black/Af. Am.	9	4.2	8	6.7	17	5.1	0	0.0	13	9.0	17	5.1	2
Nat. HI/Pac. Isl.	0	0.0	0	0.0	0	0.0	0	0.0	0	0.0	0	0.0	0
2 or more races	3	1.4	4	3.4	7	2.1	0	0.0	1	0.7	7	2.1	4
Subtotal (minor.)	22	10.3	24	20.2	46	13.9	0	0.0	27	18.6	46	13.9	10
Nonres. Alien	0	0.0	0	0.0	0	0.0	0	0.0	0	0.0	0	0.0	0
White/Cauc.	181	85.0	90	75.6	271	81.6	0	0.0	118	81.4	271	81.6	65
Unknown	10	4.7	5	4.2	15	4.5	0	0.0	0	0.0	15	4.5	18
Total	213	64.2	119	35.8	332	100.0	0	0.0	145	43.7	332		93

Transfers

Transfers in	0
Transfers out	6

Tuition and Fees

	Resident	Nonresident
Full-time	$29,825	
Part-time		
Tuition Guarantee Program		Y

Living Expenses

Estimated living expenses for singles

Living on campus	Living off campus	Living at home
N/A	$28,325	N/A

ABA
Approved
Since
2001

GPA and LSAT Scores

	Total	Full-Time	Part-Time
# of apps	1,177	1,177	0
# of offers	910	910	0
# of matrics	146	146	0
75% GPA	3.32	3.32	0.00
Median GPA	2.99	2.99	0.00
25% GPA	2.66	2.66	0.00
75% LSAT	148	148	0
Median LSAT	144	144	0
25% LSAT	142	142	0

Grants and Scholarships (from prior year)

	Total		Full-Time		Part-Time	
	#	%	#	%	#	%
Total # of students	313		313		0	
Total # receiving grants	50	16.0	50	16.0	0	0.0
Less than 1/2 tuition	14	4.5	14	4.5	0	0.0
Half to full tuition	23	7.3	23	7.3	0	0.0
Full tuition	13	4.2	13	4.2	0	0.0
More than full tuition	0	0.0	0	0.0	0	0.0
Median grant amount			$14,000		$0	

Informational and Library Resources

Total amount spent on library materials	$849,954
Study seating capacity inside the library	232
# of full-time equivalent professional librarians	5
Hours per week library is open	83
# of open, wired connections available to students	772
# of networked computers available for use by students	30
Has wireless network?	Y
Requires computer?	N

JD Attrition (from prior year)

	Academic	Other	Total	
	#	#	#	%
1st year	12	5	17	13.9
2nd year	0	8	8	8.1
3rd year	0	0	0	0.0
4th year	0	0	0	0.0

Employment (9 months after graduation)

For up-to-date employment data, go to employmentsummary.abaquestionnaire.org on the ABA website.

Bar Passage Rates

First-time takers	115	Reporting %	73.04
Average school %	59.51	Average state %	79.30
Average pass difference	−19.79		

Jurisdiction	Takers	Passers	Pass %	State %	Diff %
Virginia	27	17	62.96	78.15	−15.19
North Carolina	18	9	50.00	77.50	−27.50
Kentucky	16	7	43.75	82.03	−38.28
West Virginia	12	9	75.00	76.44	−1.44
Tennessee	11	8	72.73	84.24	−11.51

APPALACHIAN SCHOOL OF LAW

1169 Edgewater Drive, PO Box 2825
Grundy, VA 24614
Phone: 800.895.7411 (toll free) or 276.935.4349; Fax: 276.935.8496
E-mail: admissions@asl.edu; Website: www.asl.edu

Introduction

Founded in 1994, the Appalachian School of Law produces civic-minded lawyers who go on to practice both in the Appalachian region and beyond. As a small, independent law school, ASL offers an intimate environment that is rare among institutions of higher learning. Located in the town of Grundy in southwestern Virginia, ASL provides a quiet setting for the study of law.

Curriculum

While providing a full, traditional legal curriculum, ASL emphasizes practical skills in an effort to help students succeed in real-world practice. Alternative dispute resolution and professional responsibility are infused throughout the curriculum. ASL also offers an Academic Success Program to help students develop and refine the skills necessary to succeed in law school and pass the bar exam.

First-year students are introduced to basics such as civil procedure, contracts, property, and torts, as well as legal research, writing, and other essential skills. The program eases first-year students into the unique requirements of law studies, fosters collegiality and professionalism, and minimizes peer competition. Between their first and second years, students serve an externship with a judge, prosecutor, or legal services organization at sites across the nation.

Second-year students build their knowledge base in subjects such as constitutional law, evidence, secured transactions, business associations, dispute resolution, and more.

Third-year students take additional required courses, a seminar, capstone electives, and practicum courses that emphasize skill-based learning. Topics include negotiation, mediation, interviewing, law office practice, pretrial practice, and trial advocacy.

Community Service

ASL emphasizes community service in an effort to educate responsible civic leaders. Students complete 25 hours of service each semester in a project of their choosing. Although students are able to structure their service to meet their preferences and schedules, ASL assists students by scheduling one afternoon each week that they may devote to service projects. ASL-sponsored projects have included a conflict resolution program taught in public elementary schools; work with Buchanan Neighbors United, a group that provides housing repairs to improve substandard housing; a community recycling project; and a gender-bias study of the Virginia state court system.

Faculty

ASL's expanding faculty offers a depth of private and governmental practice experience as well as teaching experience. Faculty members have been former law clerks to federal and state court judges, government officials, and partners in small and large private law firms. The ASL faculty has published a variety of scholarly works in areas including constitutional law, legal ethics, and business and commercial matters. Small classes enable students to form meaningful relationships with faculty that further enrich their ASL experience.

Students and Student Organizations

ASL's active, enthusiastic student body hails from across the region and the country. The student body elects a Student Bar Association. Students may also participate in numerous student organizations, join the *Appalachian Journal of Law* and the *Appalachian Natural Resources Law Journal*, and compete on the award-winning moot court or trial advocacy teams. ASL has a family resource network for the spouses, partners, and families of law students. A speaker series brings a number of distinguished speakers to campus.

Facilities

ASL's historic classroom and office building was extensively renovated and won an award from the American Institute of Architects. The classroom building is constructed around a courtyard that serves as an informal gathering place. The renovated library provides a modern facility for research and studying. A third building houses student organizations and a coffee shop. The law school also occupies classroom and office space in the adjacent Booth Center for higher education. In 2010, ASL acquired a nearby building that will be renovated to provide classroom, clinic, and office space. Internet connections are available in most classrooms and the library. Wireless Internet access is also available.

Admission and Financial Aid

ASL accepts students who will benefit from a challenging curriculum in a caring environment. Admission decisions are not based on a single criterion; each item is considered in relation to the applicant's total qualifications. Besides undergraduate GPA and the LSAT, other considerations include an applicant's graduate work, character, work history, professional promise, personal commitment, recommendations, life experience, and other nonacademic achievements.

ASL offers a Pre-Admission Summer Opportunity (PASO) program for students who may have the potential to succeed as law students and lawyers, but whose skills and talents may not be reflected fully by their LSAT score and undergraduate performance. PASO provides participants an opportunity to experience law school coursework and allows faculty to evaluate the students' performances to assess their ability to succeed in law school. Participants who demonstrate potential to successfully complete ASL's three-year program are offered admission.

ASL offers both merit- and need-based scholarships. Merit-based scholarships are based on entering LSAT and GPA credentials; the application for admission serves as the application for a merit scholarship.

APPLICANT PROFILE

Appalachian School of Law

LSAT Score	GPA								
	3.75 +	3.50–3.74	3.25–3.49	3.00–3.24	2.75–2.99	2.50–2.74	2.25–2.49	2.00–2.24	Below 2.00
175–180									
170–174									
165–169									
160–164									
155–159									
150–154									
145–149									
140–144									
135–139									
130–134									
120–129									

Good Possibility   Possible   Unlikely

This grid represents data for 100 percent of the applicant pool for fall 2009 admission. It does not reflect the possibility of invitation to participate in the Pre-Admission Summer Opportunity program. This chart is to be used as a general guide only. Nonnumerical factors are strongly considered for all applicants.

THE UNIVERSITY OF ARIZONA JAMES E. ROGERS COLLEGE OF LAW

PO Box 210176, 1201 E. Speedway
Tucson, AZ 85721-0176
Phone: 520.621.7666; Fax: 520.626.3436
E-mail: eric.eden@law.arizona.edu; Website: www.law.arizona.edu

ABA
Approved
Since
1930

The Basics

Type of school	Public
Term	Semester
Application deadline	2/15
Application fee	$65
Financial aid deadline	3/1
Can first year start other than fall?	No
Student to faculty ratio	10.0 to 1
# of housing spaces available restricted to law students	
graduate housing for which law students are eligible	319

Faculty and Administrators

	Total Spr	Total Fall	Men Spr	Men Fall	Women Spr	Women Fall	Minorities Spr	Minorities Fall
Full-time	37	38	21	21	16	17	7	7
Other full-time	2	1	0	0	2	1	1	0
Deans, librarians, & others who teach	15	11	5	5	10	6	2	2
Part-time	43	39	31	23	12	16	3	2
Total	97	89	57	49	40	40	13	11

Curriculum

	Full-Time	Part-Time
Typical first-year section size	73	0
Is there typically a "small section" of the first-year class, other than Legal Writing, taught by full-time faculty	Yes	No
If yes, typical size offered last year	31	
# of classroom course titles beyond first-year curriculum	124	
# of upper division courses, excluding seminars, with an enrollment: Under 25	103	
25–49	19	
50–74	6	
75–99	0	
100+	2	
# of seminars	40	
# of seminar positions available	479	
# of seminar positions filled	320	0
# of positions available in simulation courses	211	
# of simulation positions filled	166	0
# of positions available in faculty supervised clinical courses	100	
# of faculty supervised clinical positions filled	100	0
# involved in field placements	112	0
# involved in law journals	118	0
# involved in moot court or trial competitions	37	0
# of credit hours required to graduate	88	

JD Enrollment and Ethnicity

	Men #	Men %	Women #	Women %	Full-Time #	Full-Time %	Part-Time #	Part-Time %	1st-Year #	1st-Year %	Total #	Total %	JD Degs. Awd.
All Hispanics	18	6.9	15	8.3	33	7.5	0	0.0	15	10.9	33	7.5	17
Am. Ind./AK Nat.	6	2.3	6	3.3	12	2.7	0	0.0	3	2.2	12	2.7	12
Asian	16	6.2	15	8.3	31	7.0	0	0.0	6	4.4	31	7.0	12
Black/Af. Am.	4	1.5	2	1.1	6	1.4	0	0.0	0	0.0	6	1.4	8
Nat. Hl/Pac. Isl.	0	0.0	0	0.0	0	0.0	0	0.0	0	0.0	0	0.0	0
2 or more races	6	2.3	9	5.0	15	3.4	0	0.0	10	7.3	15	3.4	0
Subtotal (minor.)	50	19.3	47	26.0	97	22.0	0	0.0	34	24.8	97	22.0	49
Nonres. Alien	7	2.7	7	3.9	14	3.2	0	0.0	2	1.5	14	3.2	0
White/Cauc.	167	64.5	110	60.8	277	63.0	0	0.0	80	58.4	277	63.0	110
Unknown	35	13.5	17	9.4	52	11.8	0	0.0	21	15.3	52	11.8	0
Total	259	58.9	181	41.1	440	100.0	0	0.0	137	31.1	440		159

Transfers

Transfers in	6
Transfers out	11

Tuition and Fees

	Resident	Nonresident
Full-time	$26,089	$41,051
Part-time		
Tuition Guarantee Program	N	

Living Expenses

Estimated living expenses for singles

Living on campus	Living off campus	Living at home
$21,678	$21,678	$14,678

THE UNIVERSITY OF ARIZONA JAMES E. ROGERS COLLEGE OF LAW

ABA
Approved
Since
1930

GPA and LSAT Scores

	Total	Full-Time	Part-Time
# of apps	1,530	1,530	0
# of offers	552	552	0
# of matrics	137	137	0
75% GPA	3.76	3.76	0.00
Median GPA	3.54	3.54	0.00
25% GPA	3.24	3.24	0.00
75% LSAT	163	163	0
Median LSAT	161	161	0
25% LSAT	158	158	0

Grants and Scholarships (from prior year)

	Total #	Total %	Full-Time #	Full-Time %	Part-Time #	Part-Time %
Total # of students	469		469		0	
Total # receiving grants	355	75.7	355	75.7	0	0.0
Less than 1/2 tuition	225	48.0	225	48.0	0	0.0
Half to full tuition	86	18.3	86	18.3	0	0.0
Full tuition	33	7.0	33	7.0	0	0.0
More than full tuition	11	2.3	11	2.3	0	0.0
Median grant amount			$14,000		$0	

Informational and Library Resources

Total amount spent on library materials	$895,135
Study seating capacity inside the library	379
# of full-time equivalent professional librarians	9
Hours per week library is open	101
# of open, wired connections available to students	0
# of networked computers available for use by students	32
Has wireless network?	Y
Requires computer?	N

JD Attrition (from prior year)

	Academic #	Other #	Total #	Total %
1st year	0	0	0	0.0
2nd year	0	15	15	10.1
3rd year	0	0	0	0.0
4th year	0	0	0	0.0

Employment (9 months after graduation)

For up-to-date employment data, go to
employmentsummary.abaquestionnaire.org on the ABA website.

Bar Passage Rates

First-time takers	136	Reporting %	83.82
Average school %	93.86	Average state %	79.56
Average pass difference	14.30		

Jurisdiction	Takers	Passers	Pass %	State %	Diff %
Arizona	95	89	93.68	80.74	12.94
California	12	11	91.67	71.24	20.43
Nevada	4	4	100.00	72.72	27.28
New York	3	3	100.00	84.92	15.08

THE UNIVERSITY OF ARIZONA JAMES E. ROGERS COLLEGE OF LAW

PO Box 210176, 1201 E. Speedway
Tucson, AZ 85721-0176
Phone: 520.621.7666; Fax: 520.626.3436
E-mail: eric.eden@law.arizona.edu; Website: www.law.arizona.edu

Introduction

Founded in 1915, Arizona Law is the oldest law school in Arizona. During the college's nearly 100 years, many of our country's most distinguished judges and lawyers have pursued their legal educations at Arizona Law. With alumni in 49 states and 40 countries, Arizona Law is prominent around the world. It has a national reputation for providing its students with an exceptional education in a collegial and intellectually challenging atmosphere. Arizona Law is an integral part of the University of Arizona, one of the nation's leading research institutions and most spirited campuses. It is located in Tucson, a vibrant, environmentally unique, and culturally rich city of one million people. It is approved by the ABA, has been a member of the AALS since 1931, and is one of 80 law schools nationwide to have a chapter of the Order of the Coif, the prestigious national law academic honor society.

The College

Arizona Law is a nationally prominent law school with an outstanding academic program that prepares students for leadership and service throughout the state, the country, and internationally. Five core values are the foundation of the college's culture: justice, professional integrity, educational excellence, public leadership, and community service. The environment of the college is further shaped by several key components. First, its size enables students and faculty to learn in a congenial atmosphere. Approximately 150 1L students join upperclassmen, 39 full-time faculty, and many visiting scholars in an intellectually stimulating community. Arizona Law offers a favorable student-to-faculty ratio (11:1). Second, Arizona Law has an outstanding, diverse faculty of gifted teachers and nationally recognized scholars. Twenty-three faculty members hold endowed chairs of professorship, 14 have been elected to the American Law Institute, 3 have been awarded teaching and mentoring awards, 2 are Regents Professors, 1 has been elected to the American Association for the Advancement of Science, and 1 serves as the United Nations Special Rapporteur on the Rights of Indigenous Peoples. Third, Arizona Law takes full advantage of its connection to the University of Arizona by offering a variety of interdisciplinary study opportunities. Finally, the college attracts students of intelligence, energy, and commitment. The JD student body of 470 represents more than 160 undergraduate and graduate schools, many nationalities, diverse ethnic and cultural groups, and unique work, volunteer, and personal achievements. Arizona Law is affiliated with two research and educational centers: The National Law Center for Inter-American Free Trade and the William H. Rehnquist Center on the Constitutional Structures of Government. Both enrich academic life and educational opportunities for Arizona Law students.

Library and Physical Facilities

In the fall of 2008, Arizona Law opened a newly renovated state-of-the-art building and library, the Law Commons, designed to enhance student learning and engagement. The Law Commons is part of the 390-acre campus of the University of Arizona. The Daniel F. Cracchiolo Law Library is one of the foremost legal research facilities in the Southwest. It is a fully networked, technologically sophisticated facility that is constantly evolving to meet research needs. Students also have access to the resources of the Arizona Health Sciences Library and university libraries, with collections exceeding 11 million volumes.

Curriculum

Arizona Law offers an outstanding legal education focusing on traditional areas of legal study as well as cutting-edge and emerging topics of law. In the first year, students are assigned to small sections of 25 students. During their 1L year, students enroll in a year-long Legal Analysis, Writing, and Research class of approximately 12 students. Students may further refine their writing skills by participating in moot court competitions or by enrolling in any of a variety of courses requiring significant writing. Finally, membership on one of the three student-run publications, *Arizona Law Review*, *Arizona Journal of Environmental Law and Policy*, or *Arizona Journal of International and Comparative Law*, provides additional research and writing opportunities.

Arizona Law's first-year curriculum is prescribed, but allows for one elective (Immigration Law, Tax Law, or one of two Administrative Law courses) in the second semester. Students have considerable flexibility in determining upper-division coursework. Arizona Law offers a rich variety of courses and provides opportunities to pursue a general curriculum or to focus studies in specialized areas of concentration, including Indigenous Peoples Law and Policy, Environmental Law, International Trade and Business, Criminal Law, Immigration Law, Tax, Estates and Trusts, and Corporate Law. Arizona Law also offers certificate programs in Criminal Law and Policy, Environmental Law, Science and Policy, Indigenous Peoples Law and Policy, and International Trade and Business Law. Trial Advocacy is also an area of particular strength at Arizona Law with multiple moot court teams and an expansive list of advocacy courses.

Arizona Law believes that experiential learning is an essential ingredient in the educational process. Its extensive clinical education offerings include the Child and Family Law Clinic, Immigration Law Clinic, Indigenous Peoples Clinic, Tribal Courts Clinic, Defense Clinic, Prosecution Clinic, Mortgage Clinic, Bankruptcy Clinic, International Human Rights Advocacy Workshop, UN Special Rapporteur Support Team Project, Arizona Attorney General Clinic, Civil Rights Restoration Clinic, and Veterans Clinic. Students may also participate in student-run advocacy programs. Arizona Law has extensive internship opportunities for which students receive academic credit, including congressional and executive agency internships in Washington, DC; state legislative internships; Arizona governor's office internship; judicial clerkship internships; and internships with several tribal governments.

Arizona Law offers a full-time JD program, which is typically completed in six semesters of study. A total of 88 units and a cumulative grade-point average of 2.0 are required to graduate.

Dual-Degree, LLM, and SJD Programs

Arizona Law is affiliated with one of the strongest research universities in the nation. Students interested in interdisciplinary studies can take advantage of this connection by participating in one of the already established dual-degree programs or may work with the appropriate college to customize their own program. Arizona Law offers the following established dual-degree programs: JD/PhD programs in Philosophy, Psychology, and Economics; JD/MA programs in American Indian Studies, Latin American Studies, Gender and Women's Studies, and Information Resources and Library Science; a JD/MBA; a JD/MPA; a JD/MPH; a JD/MS in Economics, Law, and Environment; and a JD/MMF in Management/Finance. Law students may take six units of coursework in another department for elective credit. Arizona Law offers a JD—Advanced Standing program (for those with an international law degree); LLM programs in International Trade Law and Indigenous Peoples Law and Policy; and a Doctor of Juridical Science (SJD) program.

Admission

Admission to Arizona Law is selective. The following application materials are required: academic record, LSAT score, personal statement, and letters of recommendation. Additional factors considered include the nature and rigor of the undergraduate experience; graduate education; work and travel experience; unique talents or accomplishments; significant extracurricular activities; leadership, strength of character, and integrity; substantial community service; and other circumstances that have influenced the candidate's life or given him or her direction. Arizona Law fosters a dynamic learning community and welcomes students who bring diverse perspectives, ideas, and varied life experiences to the educational process. The deadline for applications is February 15.

Tuition and Financial Aid

Arizona Law's tuition structure and financial aid program afford students the opportunity to pursue a legal education of outstanding quality with less debt burden than is typical of other fine law schools. Tuition and fees for JD students for the 2011–2012 year was $26,089 for Arizona residents and $41,051 for nonresidents. Arizona Law awarded more than $3 million in scholarships to JD students in 2011–2012.

Student Activities

Student organizations play a vital role in the lives of Arizona Law students. From social gatherings to community service opportunities to professional networking events, Arizona Law's more than 30 student groups offer a way to expand social and professional circles. The *Arizona Law Review*, the *Arizona Journal of International and Comparative Law*, and the *Arizona Journal of Environmental Law and Policy* are well-known student-operated and edited scholarly journals. The students in the moot court and trial advocacy programs excel in national and state appellate advocacy competitions.

Career and Professional Development

Arizona Law's Career Office is dedicated to assisting students develop as professionals. It offers individual counseling; programs on résumé, cover letter, and interviewing techniques; and a variety of summer and postgraduate employment opportunities. More than 90 percent of the 1L class engages in real-world summer legal clerkships and internships—one of the highest rates of 1L legal employment in the country. The on-campus Sonoran Desert Public Sector Career Fair provides over 150 summer jobs. Additionally, each year more than 120 law firms, corporations, and government agencies interview Arizona Law students on campus. Students also have the opportunity to be part of the National Off-Campus Interview Program in the following areas: Denver, Albuquerque, Las Vegas, Chicago, New York City, Philadelphia, the District of Columbia, Miami, Houston, and Dallas. Typically, 1L and 2L students are employed in over 20 states and foreign countries each summer. The 2010 postgraduation employment rate was 93 percent (excluding those unknown and not seeking), with 19.5 percent accepting prestigious judicial clerkships (national average is 9.3 percent). Typically, 35 percent of Arizona Law graduates practice outside of Arizona in 15–20 states. The average law firm salary was $92,000 ($122,140 after clerkship year).

APPLICANT PROFILE

The University of Arizona James E. Rogers College of Law
This grid includes only applicants with 120–180 LSAT scores earned under standard administrations.

LSAT Score	3.75 +		3.50–3.74		3.25–3.49		3.00–3.24		2.75–2.99		2.50–2.74		2.25–2.49		2.00–2.24		Below 2.00		No GPA		Total	
	Apps	Adm	Apps	Adm	Apps	Adm	Apps	Adm	Apps	Adm	Apps	Adm	Apps	Adm	Apps	Adm	Apps	Adm	Apps	Adm	Apps	Adm
175–180	0	0	0	0	0	0	0	0	1	1	1	0	0	0	1	0	0	0	1	1	4	2
170–174	11	10	6	6	6	4	2	1	3	3	0	0	1	0	0	0	0	0	0	0	29	24
165–169	40	39	52	49	30	29	24	22	19	8	6	4	5	1	0	0	0	0	3	1	179	153
160–164	72	67	122	91	94	66	55	28	19	4	11	4	14	5	5	1	0	0	7	2	399	268
155–159	69	26	107	29	83	15	66	4	28	1	18	0	8	0	2	0	0	0	9	3	390	78
150–154	40	13	47	5	69	2	53	0	28	1	14	0	7	0	3	0	0	0	3	0	264	21
145–149	9	1	28	2	33	0	41	3	24	0	11	0	6	0	4	0	1	0	3	0	160	6
140–144	2	0	12	1	12	0	14	0	16	0	8	0	3	0	2	0	0	0	3	0	72	1
135–139	2	0	3	0	3	0	10	0	4	0	2	0	3	0	3	0	0	0	3	0	33	0
130–134	0	0	0	0	1	0	2	0	0	0	4	0	0	0	0	0	0	0	2	0	9	0
125–129	0	0	1	0	0	0	0	0	1	0	2	0	0	0	0	0	0	0	0	0	4	0
120–124	0	0	0	0	0	0	0	0	0	0	0	0	0	0	0	0	0	0	0	0	0	0
Total	245	156	378	183	331	116	267	58	143	18	77	8	47	6	20	1	1	0	34	7	1543	553

Apps = Number of Applicants   Adm = Number Admitted   Reflects 100% of the total applicant pool; highest LSAT data reported.

ARIZONA STATE UNIVERSITY—SANDRA DAY O'CONNOR COLLEGE OF LAW

Armstrong Hall, 1100 S. McAllister Avenue, PO Box 877906
Tempe, AZ 85287-7906
Phone: 480.965.1474; Fax: 480.727.7930
E-mail: law.admissions@asu.edu; Website: www.law.asu.edu

ABA Approved Since 1969

The Basics

Type of school	Public
Term	Semester
Application deadline	11/15 2/1
Application fee	$60
Financial aid deadline	3/15
Can first year start other than fall?	No
Student to faculty ratio	9.9 to 1
# of housing spaces available restricted to law students	
graduate housing for which law students are eligible	

Faculty and Administrators

	Total		Men		Women		Minorities	
	Spr	Fall	Spr	Fall	Spr	Fall	Spr	Fall
Full-time	52	49	35	34	17	15	8	8
Other full-time	2	3	2	2	0	1	0	0
Deans, librarians, & others who teach	9	10	3	3	6	7	0	0
Part-time	38	68	24	50	14	18	1	0
Total	101	130	64	89	37	41	9	8

Curriculum

	Full-Time	Part-Time
Typical first-year section size	60	0
Is there typically a "small section" of the first-year class, other than Legal Writing, taught by full-time faculty	Yes	No
If yes, typical size offered last year	33	
# of classroom course titles beyond first-year curriculum	139	

# of upper division courses, excluding seminars, with an enrollment:		
Under 25	86	
25–49	32	
50–74	4	
75–99	8	
100+	0	

# of seminars	66	
# of seminar positions available	900	
# of seminar positions filled	846	0
# of positions available in simulation courses	258	
# of simulation positions filled	235	0
# of positions available in faculty supervised clinical courses	176	
# of faculty supervised clinical positions filled	171	0
# involved in field placements	282	0
# involved in law journals	86	0
# involved in moot court or trial competitions	251	0
# of credit hours required to graduate	89	

JD Enrollment and Ethnicity

	Men		Women		Full-Time		Part-Time		1st-Year		Total		JD Degs. Awd.
	#	%	#	%	#	%	#	%	#	%	#	%	
All Hispanics	31	8.5	33	13.9	64	10.6	0	0.0	14	8.2	64	10.6	14
Am. Ind./AK Nat.	13	3.6	15	6.3	28	4.7	0	0.0	7	4.1	28	4.7	9
Asian	9	2.5	12	5.0	21	3.5	0	0.0	7	4.1	21	3.5	6
Black/Af. Am.	6	1.6	4	1.7	10	1.7	0	0.0	3	1.8	10	1.7	4
Nat. HI/Pac. Isl.	0	0.0	0	0.0	0	0.0	0	0.0	0	0.0	0	0.0	0
2 or more races	10	2.7	6	2.5	16	2.7	0	0.0	6	3.5	16	2.7	0
Subtotal (minor.)	69	19.0	70	29.4	139	23.1	0	0.0	37	21.6	139	23.1	33
Nonres. Alien	2	0.5	3	1.3	5	0.8	0	0.0	1	0.6	5	0.8	3
White/Cauc.	277	76.1	154	64.7	431	71.6	0	0.0	125	73.1	431	71.6	149
Unknown	16	4.4	11	4.6	27	4.5	0	0.0	8	4.7	27	4.5	15
Total	364	60.5	238	39.5	602	100.0	0	0.0	171	28.4	602		200

Transfers

Transfers in	34
Transfers out	3

Tuition and Fees

	Resident	Nonresident
Full-time	$24,471	$38,595
Part-time		
Tuition Guarantee Program		N

Living Expenses

Estimated living expenses for singles

Living on campus	Living off campus	Living at home
$20,906	$20,906	$20,906

ARIZONA STATE UNIVERSITY—SANDRA DAY O'CONNOR COLLEGE OF LAW

ABA Approved Since 1969

GPA and LSAT Scores

	Total	Full-Time	Part-Time
# of apps	2,334	2,334	0
# of offers	664	664	0
# of matrics	168	168	0
75% GPA	3.77	3.77	0.00
Median GPA	3.62	3.62	0.00
25% GPA	3.43	3.43	0.00
75% LSAT	165	165	0
Median LSAT	162	162	0
25% LSAT	160	160	0

Grants and Scholarships (from prior year)

	Total #	Total %	Full-Time #	Full-Time %	Part-Time #	Part-Time %
Total # of students	614		614		0	
Total # receiving grants	322	52.4	322	52.4	0	0.0
Less than 1/2 tuition	194	31.6	194	31.6	0	0.0
Half to full tuition	98	16.0	98	16.0	0	0.0
Full tuition	19	3.1	19	3.1	0	0.0
More than full tuition	11	1.8	11	1.8	0	0.0
Median grant amount			$10,000		$0	

Informational and Library Resources

Total amount spent on library materials	$956,196
Study seating capacity inside the library	584
# of full-time equivalent professional librarians	7
Hours per week library is open	111
# of open, wired connections available to students	187
# of networked computers available for use by students	65
Has wireless network?	Y
Requires computer?	N

JD Attrition (from prior year)

	Academic #	Other #	Total #	Total %
1st year	1	6	7	3.7
2nd year	0	8	8	3.9
3rd year	0	1	1	0.5
4th year	0	0	0	0.0

Employment (9 months after graduation)

For up-to-date employment data, go to employmentsummary.abaquestionnaire.org on the ABA website.

Bar Passage Rates

First-time takers	155	Reporting %	91.61
Average school %	85.92	Average state %	80.74
Average pass difference	5.18		

Jurisdiction	Takers	Passers	Pass %	State %	Diff %
Arizona	142	122	85.92	80.74	5.18

ARIZONA STATE UNIVERSITY—SANDRA DAY O'CONNOR COLLEGE OF LAW

Armstrong Hall, 1100 S. McAllister Avenue, PO Box 877906
Tempe, AZ 85287-7906
Phone: 480.965.1474; Fax: 480.727.7930
E-mail: law.admissions@asu.edu; Website: www.law.asu.edu

Introduction

Founded in 1967, the Arizona State University—Sandra Day O'Connor College of Law combines the best traditions of American legal education with innovative programs supported by strong community partnerships. Our vision includes excellence in all we do, striving to have a meaningful impact on contemporary problems through teaching, research, and collaborative problem-solving. Students are attracted by the quality of the legal education, commitment to innovative teaching and scholarship, reasonable tuition, breadth and depth of the curriculum, numerous opportunities for experiential learning, and excellent student-to-faculty ratio. A busy calendar of conferences, seminars, and speakers enriches the student experience and fosters a strong sense of community. The college has an outstanding faculty, many opportunities for interdisciplinary learning, extensive pro bono opportunities, an exceptional legal writing program, and clinics of significant variety. Our students benefit greatly from the fact that Phoenix is the sixth largest city in the country and a state capital.

Admission

Every completed application receives full review and consideration by the Admissions Committee prior to a decision. Among the factors influencing the admission decision are undergraduate and previous graduate education, LSAT performance, quality and grading patterns of undergraduate institutions, demonstrated commitment to public service, work experience, leadership experience, extracurricular or community activities, history of overcoming economic or other disadvantages, personal experiences with discrimination, overcoming disability, geographic diversity, uniqueness of experience and background, maturity, ability to communicate, foreign language proficiency, honors and awards, service in the armed forces, publications, and exceptional personal talents.

Career Strategy and Professional Development Mentoring Center

Our graduates have proven success in the legal employment market and hold prominent positions and leadership roles throughout the international, national, and Arizona legal communities in business, politics, government, the judiciary, and private firms. A broad range of employers interview our students on campus, at regional interview programs sponsored by the career center, and at job fairs. Through attorney-student mentor programs, speaker series and panels, networking events, career fairs, a large on-campus recruitment program, and individual career counseling, the career center's professional staff serves students in all phases of their professional development and job search.

Curriculum

The College of Law offers one of the best student-to-faculty ratios in the country and a wide variety of courses. Because we have a large, nationally acclaimed faculty with high standards in both teaching and research, we have unusual depth in our course offerings. More than 70 percent of the classes in the second and third year have fewer than 20 students. As part of a premier research institution, the opportunities for interdisciplinary work are extensive. Concurrent degrees are offered with the MBA program, the MSW, the PhD in Psychology, the PhD in Justice and Social Inquiry, and the MD with Mayo Medical School. Further, the college takes full advantage of its unique location in Phoenix by offering about 250 externships and countless opportunities to do pro bono work. Students also have wonderful opportunities to develop their legal writing skills because of our commitment to maintaining an excellent legal writing program.

Clinical Programs

The law school's Clinical Program offers students unparalleled opportunities to practice law in a variety of settings with people who have real legal problems. We offer more than 12 separate clinics and clinical units—civil justice, criminal practice, family violence, healthcare entrepreneurship, immigration, Indian law, innovation advancement, mediation, patent litigation, post-conviction, and public defender—a greater variety of clinics than most law schools of any size. Under the supervision of faculty members who are experts in their subject matter, students manage real cases and represent clients in hearings and trials before courts and administrative agencies, assist in the commercialization and monetization of new technologies, and mediate cases pending in the judicial system. Because of our small student body, we are able to accommodate nearly every student who expresses an interest in the experiential learning offered through the Clinical Program.

Student Activities

To prepare proactive, socially conscious attorneys and leaders, we enhance the traditional classroom experience with many extracurricular and cocurricular activities. We have about 50 active student groups, from the ASU Bar Association and about 30 professional affiliations to 20 pro bono groups. Plus, we grow and change with the interests of our students. On average, about 70 percent of our students participate in pro bono work of some kind, with about one-third of the student body graduating with Pro Bono Distinction. Students are active in ASU student governance and in our communities with public service. Our students are competitive in moot court competitions, both regionally and internationally. Two traditional law journals, the *Arizona State Law Journal* and *Jurimetrics*, and two new online journals, the *Law Journal for Social Justice* and the *Sports and Entertainment Law Journal*, allow additional professional development opportunities for students.

Library and Physical Facilities

The College of Law is composed of Armstrong Hall and the John J. Ross-William C. Blakley Law Library and is set on the eastern edge of the university's beautiful, 700-acre Tempe campus. Armstrong Hall houses the majority of our classrooms, faculty and administrative offices, clinics, and centers, in addition to a café and spacious community areas. The Ross-Blakley Law Library is a stunningly beautiful work of architecture with lots of windows to allow natural light in. Both Armstrong Hall and the Ross-Blakley Law Library are fully equipped with a wireless network.

Center for Law, Science, and Innovation

Founded in 1984, the Center for Law, Science, and Innovation is the oldest, largest, and most comprehensive law and science center in the country. Through the Center, students may receive a certificate in Law, Science, and Technology, specializing in environmental law, genomics and biotechnology law, health law, intellectual property law, or law and psychology. Every year, 10 students from each class are named Center Scholars. Center faculty and students edit and copublish, along with the American Bar Association, the prestigious, peer-refereed *Jurimetrics: The Journal of Law, Science, and Technology*, the oldest and most widely circulated journal in the field of law and science.

The Center for Law and Global Affairs

The Center for Law and Global Affairs supports and inspires research, education, and practice regarding new forms of transnational public-private governance that extend beyond the traditional paradigms of international law. The Center sponsors conferences, colloquia, courses, research, policy initiatives, and publications to study evolving forms of international law, to develop and apply new methodologies to better understand how the rule of law operates in diverse international contexts, to initiate and communicate new policy strategies, and to teach and train students and professionals to work more effectively in the new global regulatory environment. The Center creates an interdisciplinary community of scholars, practitioners, students, and community members interested in better understanding and affecting the relationship between law and an increasingly global world.

The Diane Halle Center for Family Justice

The Diane Halle Center for Family Justice, working with other ASU schools and with community partners, is pursuing direct representation and policy advocacy on core issues of domestic violence, juvenile justice, child abuse, family law, and human rights of children and families through multidisciplinary initiatives in education, advocacy, and scholarship. The Center was established with a $1 million grant from the Bruce T. Halle Family Foundation. The Center houses the Ruth V. McGregor Family Protection Clinic and the Anti-Sex Trafficking Initiative.

Indian Legal Program

The Indian Legal Program enjoys a position of national preeminence. This preeminence is due to the large Native American student population, the Indian Law Certificate program, well-respected faculty, the Indian law curriculum, well-placed alumni, scholarly conferences, and the Indian Legal Clinic. An extraordinary faculty and long-term partnerships with tribal governments contribute to the strength and reputation of the College of Law in this critical area.

LLM Programs

The Master of Laws (LLM) program allows one year of post-JD study tailored to the scholarly and practice interests of participating students. Lawyers may pursue an LLM in Biotechnology and Genomics or an LLM in Tribal Policy, Law, and Government. Some may choose to pursue an LLM focusing on global legal studies, health law and policy, or any of the other areas of strength in the law school's curriculum.

APPLICANT PROFILE

Arizona State University—Sandra Day O'Connor College of Law
This grid includes only applicants with 120–180 LSAT scores earned under standard administrations.

LSAT Score	3.75 +		3.50–3.74		3.25–3.49		3.00–3.24		2.75–2.99		2.50–2.74		2.25–2.49		2.00–2.24		Below 2.00		No GPA		Total	
	Apps	Adm	Apps	Adm	Apps	Adm	Apps	Adm	Apps	Adm	Apps	Adm	Apps	Adm	Apps	Adm	Apps	Adm	Apps	Adm	Apps	Adm
175–180	1	1	1	1	2	2	0	0	1	0	1	1	0	0	0	0	0	0	0	0	6	5
170–174	11	10	10	10	7	7	6	4	4	3	2	1	2	0	0	0	0	0	0	0	42	35
165–169	54	54	70	68	51	46	35	28	24	7	14	1	6	0	0	0	0	0	0	0	254	204
160–164	112	107	167	142	131	63	92	16	27	1	18	1	19	2	6	1	0	0	8	2	580	335
155–159	122	42	173	15	145	2	96	3	47	1	24	0	9	0	3	0	0	0	13	2	632	65
150–154	65	5	79	2	79	3	84	3	39	0	28	0	12	0	9	0	1	0	7	0	403	13
145–149	15	1	43	3	59	0	46	1	30	0	15	0	4	0	3	0	1	0	4	0	220	5
140–144	7	0	16	0	21	0	27	0	18	0	10	0	13	0	2	0	2	0	1	0	117	0
135–139	2	0	3	0	5	0	9	0	9	0	5	0	3	0	4	0	0	0	1	0	41	0
130–134	0	0	1	0	1	0	2	0	1	0	6	0	0	0	0	0	1	0	2	0	14	0
125–129	0	0	0	0	1	0	2	0	1	0	2	0	0	0	1	0	0	0	1	0	8	0
120–124	0	0	0	0	0	0	0	0	1	0	0	0	0	0	0	0	0	0	1	0	2	0
Total	389	220	563	241	502	123	399	55	202	12	125	4	68	2	28	1	5	0	38	4	2319	662

Apps = Number of Applicants
Adm = Number Admitted
Reflects 99% of the total applicant pool; highest LSAT data reported.

UNIVERSITY OF ARKANSAS SCHOOL OF LAW

Robert A. Leflar Law Center
Fayetteville, AR 72701
Phone: 479.575.3102; Fax: 479.575.3937
E-mail: lawadmit@uark.edu; Website: http://law.uark.edu

ABA
Approved
Since
1928

The Basics

Type of school	Public
Term	Semester
Application deadline	4/1
Application fee	$0
Financial aid deadline	3/1
Can first year start other than fall?	No
Student to faculty ratio	11.9 to 1
# of housing spaces available restricted to law students	
graduate housing for which law students are eligible	

Faculty and Administrators

	Total		Men		Women		Minorities	
	Spr	Fall	Spr	Fall	Spr	Fall	Spr	Fall
Full-time	27	27	15	16	12	11	3	2
Other full-time	1	1	0	0	1	1	0	0
Deans, librarians, & others who teach	10	10	5	4	5	6	0	1
Part-time	24	23	17	15	7	8	0	0
Total	62	61	37	35	25	26	3	3

Curriculum

	Full-Time	Part-Time
Typical first-year section size	68	0
Is there typically a "small section" of the first-year class, other than Legal Writing, taught by full-time faculty	No	No
If yes, typical size offered last year		
# of classroom course titles beyond first-year curriculum	97	
# of upper division courses, excluding seminars, with an enrollment: Under 25	98	
25–49	15	
50–74	10	
75–99	3	
100+	0	
# of seminars	10	
# of seminar positions available	150	
# of seminar positions filled	121	0
# of positions available in simulation courses	307	
# of simulation positions filled	245	0
# of positions available in faculty supervised clinical courses	110	
# of faculty supervised clinical positions filled	106	0
# involved in field placements	68	0
# involved in law journals	66	0
# involved in moot court or trial competitions	44	0
# of credit hours required to graduate	90	

JD Enrollment and Ethnicity

	Men		Women		Full-Time		Part-Time		1st-Year		Total		JD Degs. Awd.
	#	%	#	%	#	%	#	%	#	%	#	%	
All Hispanics	10	4.3	9	5.3	19	4.7	0	0.0	5	3.7	19	4.7	2
Am. Ind./AK Nat.	5	2.2	2	1.2	7	1.7	0	0.0	3	2.2	7	1.7	3
Asian	7	3.0	3	1.8	10	2.5	0	0.0	1	0.7	10	2.5	2
Black/Af. Am.	17	7.3	16	9.5	33	8.2	0	0.0	8	5.9	33	8.2	8
Nat. HI/Pac. Isl.	1	0.4	0	0.0	1	0.2	0	0.0	1	0.7	1	0.2	0
2 or more races	0	0.0	1	0.6	1	0.2	0	0.0	0	0.0	1	0.2	0
Subtotal (minor.)	40	17.2	31	18.3	71	17.7	0	0.0	18	13.3	71	17.7	15
Nonres. Alien	1	0.4	0	0.0	1	0.2	0	0.0	1	0.7	1	0.2	0
White/Cauc.	190	81.9	138	81.7	328	81.8	0	0.0	116	85.9	328	81.8	103
Unknown	1	0.4	0	0.0	1	0.2	0	0.0	0	0.0	1	0.2	1
Total	232	57.9	169	42.1	401	100.0	0	0.0	135	33.7	401		119

Transfers

Transfers in	7
Transfers out	2

Tuition and Fees

	Resident	Nonresident
Full-time	$11,933	$24,528
Part-time		
Tuition Guarantee Program		N

Living Expenses

Estimated living expenses for singles

Living on campus	Living off campus	Living at home
$16,766	$16,766	$16,766

UNIVERSITY OF ARKANSAS SCHOOL OF LAW

ABA
Approved
Since
1928

GPA and LSAT Scores

	Total	Full-Time	Part-Time
# of apps	1,309	1,309	0
# of offers	412	412	0
# of matrics	136	136	0
75% GPA	3.71	3.71	0.00
Median GPA	3.47	3.47	0.00
25% GPA	3.19	3.19	0.00
75% LSAT	158	158	0
Median LSAT	156	156	0
25% LSAT	153	153	0

Grants and Scholarships (from prior year)

	Total		Full-Time		Part-Time	
	#	%	#	%	#	%
Total # of students	390		390		0	
Total # receiving grants	169	43.3	169	43.3	0	0.0
Less than 1/2 tuition	82	21.0	82	21.0	0	0.0
Half to full tuition	75	19.2	75	19.2	0	0.0
Full tuition	5	1.3	5	1.3	0	0.0
More than full tuition	7	1.8	7	1.8	0	0.0
Median grant amount			$7,000		$0	

Informational and Library Resources

Total amount spent on library materials	$797,253
Study seating capacity inside the library	402
# of full-time equivalent professional librarians	7
Hours per week library is open	98
# of open, wired connections available to students	73
# of networked computers available for use by students	46
Has wireless network?	Y
Requires computer?	N

JD Attrition (from prior year)

	Academic	Other	Total	
	#	#	#	%
1st year	1	10	11	8.1
2nd year	1	1	2	1.5
3rd year	0	0	0	0.0
4th year	0	0	0	0.0

Employment (9 months after graduation)

For up-to-date employment data, go to
employmentsummary.abaquestionnaire.org on the ABA website.

Bar Passage Rates

First-time takers	128	Reporting %		74.22
Average school %	74.74	Average state %		72.48
Average pass difference	2.26			

Jurisdiction	Takers	Passers	Pass %	State %	Diff %
Arkansas	95	71	74.74	72.48	2.26

UNIVERSITY OF ARKANSAS SCHOOL OF LAW

Robert A. Leflar Law Center
Fayetteville, AR 72701
Phone: 479.575.3102; Fax: 479.575.3937
E-mail: lawadmit@uark.edu; Website: http://law.uark.edu

Introduction

The University of Arkansas School of Law, named one of the top 20 Best Values in legal education, is located on the main university campus at Fayetteville, a vibrant college community with the charm of a small town and the amenities of a much larger city. "One of America's Most Livable Cities," Fayetteville is just a few miles away from the corporate headquarters of such companies as Wal-Mart and Tyson Foods.

The School of Law, established in 1924, offers challenging courses taught by nationally recognized faculty, unique service opportunities, and a close-knit community that puts law students first. In addition to its JD program, the School of Law offers the only advanced legal degree program in agricultural and food law in the United States.

Enrollment/Student Body

Although approximately 75 to 80 percent of the students are Arkansas residents, others are from every part of the United States. Since the school has no undergraduate course prerequisites, the academic backgrounds and nonacademic experiences of the students are varied.

Library and Physical Facilities

The law library has over 331,000 volumes and volume equivalents. Students are trained in the techniques of computer-assisted legal research as well as in traditional research methods. The law library is a federal and state depository for government documents.

Curriculum

The School of Law offers a full-time, three-year program leading to the JD degree. The degree is conferred upon satisfactory completion of 90 semester hours, including 42 hours of required courses. The first year at the School of Law consists of a rigorous course of study that all 1Ls follow and includes courses such as Civil Procedure, Contracts, and Legal Writing. A broad selection of elective second- and third-year courses is available. Students who have completed the first year of law school may earn up to 12 semester hours of credit in summer school, and graduation can be accelerated by one semester of summer coursework.

In addition to the traditional path to the JD, the School of Law offers a joint JD/MBA program with the university's Sam M. Walton College of Business. In addition, the Department of Political Science offers two dual-degree programs with the law school including an MPA/JD path and a JD/MA in international law and politics.

Each year, the LLM program in agricultural and food law prepares a small number of carefully selected attorneys as specialists in the complex legal issues involving agriculture and our food system.

Admission

First-year students are admitted in the fall and only for full-time study. Prior to enrolling in the School of Law,

applicants must have completed all requirements for an undergraduate degree from an accredited four-year college. Admission is based on the applicant's LSAT score and undergraduate GPA. In a small percentage of cases, additional criteria such as age; gender; cultural, ethnic, and racial background; geographic origin; socioeconomic background and status; undergraduate major; graduate studies; career objectives; nonacademic work; and other life experiences are considered by a faculty admission committee. Preference is given to Arkansas residents. For the current status of this preference, contact the school. A nonrefundable tuition deposit is required of all admitted candidates.

The law school's application deadline is April 1 of the year in which admission is sought. Applicants must take the LSAT no later than February. Applications completed after April 1 will be considered only on a space-available basis.

Housing

Housing for single students is available in campus dormitories. For more information about housing, please contact the Housing Office, University of Arkansas, Fayetteville, AR 72701; Phone: 479.575.3951. Information is also available at http://housing.uark.edu. A variety of private off-campus housing options are available in Fayetteville and surrounding communities within easy commuting distance of the law school. For more information, please visit http://offcampushousing.uark.edu/.

Student Activities

The University of Arkansas School of Law is home to an exceptionally strong advocacy skills competition program. The school hosts two intramural appellate advocacy competitions that cumulatively lead to the selection of five appellate moot court interscholastic competition teams through the Board of Advocates and a sixth team selected by the Black Law Students Association. While most team members are third-year students, exceptional second-year students have successfully participated in various competitions.

Students may participate in the writing and publishing of three student-run journals: the *Arkansas Law Review*, the *Journal of Food Law and Policy*, and the *Journal of Islamic Law and Culture*.

The Student Bar Association sponsors a variety of academic and social activities. All students are also eligible for membership in the Law Student Division of the Arkansas Bar Association. Three of the largest national legal fraternities, Delta Theta Phi, Phi Alpha Delta, and Phi Delta Phi, maintain active chapters at the school. The Women's Law Student Association was organized to provide an opportunity for women to discuss and work with common professional interests and problems. Members of the Arkansas Chapter of the Black Law Students Association work as a collective body to inform black students of the availability and advantages of a legal education, to promote the academic success of black law students at Arkansas, and to increase the awareness and commitment of the legal profession to the black community. Other organizations include the Christian Legal Society,

Lambda, the Federalist Society, the Asian Pacific American Law Student Association, and Equal Justice Works.

The law school operates a legal aid clinic providing counseling and representation for university students and indigent persons seeking legal assistance. An Arkansas Supreme Court Rule permits senior law students, upon certification and under supervision, to appear in court on a no-fee basis.

Expenses and Financial Aid

Students are expected to make sufficient financial arrangements for the first year of study without the necessity of seeking employment. All law students are required to be full-time students. All financial aid in the form of Perkins Loans (formerly NDSL), higher education loans, and work-study grants is processed by the University of Arkansas Office of Financial Aid, University of Arkansas, Fayetteville, AR 72701. Merit scholarships are awarded to some entering students. Applications for a limited number of other scholarships are distributed following fall registration in August.

Career Services

The law school maintains an Office of Career Services with a full-time, highly qualified director and staff to assist and advise students and graduates. Services offered by the office include on-campus interviews for permanent and summer employment; individual career counseling sessions; workshops and handbooks regarding résumé preparation, interviewing skills and techniques, and job searches; panels of lawyers who present programs on a variety of topics; a job bulletin; employment outreach; and hosting networking events with local attorneys and judges. The office also maintains employment and bar passage statistics.

Applicant Profile Not Available

UNIVERSITY OF ARKANSAS AT LITTLE ROCK, WILLIAM H. BOWEN SCHOOL OF LAW

1201 McMath Avenue
Little Rock, AR 72202-5142
Phone: 501.324.9903; Fax: 501.324.9909
E-mail: lawadm@ualr.edu; Website: www.ualr.edu/law

ABA
Approved
Since
1969

The Basics

Type of school	Public
Term	Semester
Application deadline	4/15
Application fee	$0
Financial aid deadline	3/1
Can first year start other than fall?	No
Student to faculty ratio	18.3 to 1
# of housing spaces available restricted to law students	
graduate housing for which law students are eligible	

Faculty and Administrators

	Total		Men		Women		Minorities	
	Spr	Fall	Spr	Fall	Spr	Fall	Spr	Fall
Full-time	19	19	10	12	9	7	5	3
Other full-time	2	2	0	0	2	2	0	0
Deans, librarians, & others who teach	8	8	2	1	6	7	4	3
Part-time	36	42	22	29	14	13	7	3
Total	65	71	34	42	31	29	16	9

Curriculum

	Full-Time	Part-Time
Typical first-year section size	88	56
Is there typically a "small section" of the first-year class, other than Legal Writing, taught by full-time faculty	No	No
If yes, typical size offered last year		
# of classroom course titles beyond first-year curriculum	106	

# of upper division courses, excluding seminars, with an enrollment:		
	Under 25	76
	25–49	22
	50–74	9
	75–99	17
	100+	0

# of seminars	16	
# of seminar positions available	257	
# of seminar positions filled	84	130
# of positions available in simulation courses	362	
# of simulation positions filled	261	81
# of positions available in faculty supervised clinical courses	64	
# of faculty supervised clinical positions filled	38	6
# involved in field placements	63	2
# involved in law journals	37	17
# involved in moot court or trial competitions	25	4
# of credit hours required to graduate	90	

JD Enrollment and Ethnicity

	Men		Women		Full-Time		Part-Time		1st-Year		Total		JD Degs. Awd.
	#	%	#	%	#	%	#	%	#	%	#	%	
All Hispanics	14	5.3	4	1.9	13	4.0	5	3.3	3	2.1	18	3.8	7
Am. Ind./AK Nat.	2	0.8	3	1.4	5	1.5	0	0.0	0	0.0	5	1.1	1
Asian	8	3.0	2	0.9	7	2.2	3	2.0	2	1.4	10	2.1	5
Black/Af. Am.	17	6.4	30	14.2	35	10.8	12	7.9	11	7.6	47	9.9	20
Nat. Hl/Pac. Isl.	0	0.0	0	0.0	0	0.0	0	0.0	0	0.0	0	0.0	0
2 or more races	5	1.9	4	1.9	8	2.5	1	0.7	9	6.2	9	1.9	0
Subtotal (minor.)	46	17.4	43	20.4	68	20.9	21	13.9	25	17.2	89	18.7	33
Nonres. Alien	5	1.9	4	1.9	7	2.2	2	1.3	3	2.1	9	1.9	3
White/Cauc.	206	77.7	160	75.8	239	73.5	127	84.1	115	79.3	366	76.9	112
Unknown	8	3.0	4	1.9	11	3.4	1	0.7	4	2.8	12	2.5	2
Total	265	55.7	211	44.3	325	68.3	151	31.7	145	30.5	476		150

Transfers

Transfers in	2
Transfers out	7

Tuition and Fees

	Resident	Nonresident
Full-time	$12,176	$24,772
Part-time	$8,507	$16,904
Tuition Guarantee Program	N	

Living Expenses

Estimated living expenses for singles

Living on campus	Living off campus	Living at home
N/A	$16,217	$11,517

UNIVERSITY OF ARKANSAS AT LITTLE ROCK, WILLIAM H. BOWEN SCHOOL OF LAW

ABA
Approved
Since
1969

GPA and LSAT Scores

	Total	Full-Time	Part-Time
# of apps	1,529	1,382	147
# of offers	475	432	43
# of matrics	139	84	55
75% GPA	3.63	3.69	3.46
Median GPA	3.32	3.46	3.23
25% GPA	2.99	3.08	2.88
75% LSAT	158	158	154
Median LSAT	154	156	152
25% LSAT	151	153	149

Grants and Scholarships (from prior year)

	Total		Full-Time		Part-Time	
	#	%	#	%	#	%
Total # of students	490		338		152	
Total # receiving grants	281	57.3	233	68.9	48	31.6
Less than 1/2 tuition	125	25.5	103	30.5	22	14.5
Half to full tuition	76	15.5	66	19.5	10	6.6
Full tuition	23	4.7	19	5.6	4	2.6
More than full tuition	57	11.6	45	13.3	12	7.9
Median grant amount			$7,000		$3,375	

Informational and Library Resources

Total amount spent on library materials	$929,432
Study seating capacity inside the library	400
# of full-time equivalent professional librarians	6
Hours per week library is open	100
# of open, wired connections available to students	1
# of networked computers available for use by students	67
Has wireless network?	Y
Requires computer?	N

JD Attrition (from prior year)

	Academic	Other	Total	
	#	#	#	%
1st year	1	8	9	5.7
2nd year	2	8	10	6.2
3rd year	0	2	2	1.3
4th year	0	0	0	0.0

Employment (9 months after graduation)

For up-to-date employment data, go to employmentsummary.abaquestionnaire.org on the ABA website.

Bar Passage Rates

First-time takers	119	Reporting %	82.35
Average school %	68.37	Average state %	72.48
Average pass difference	−4.11		

Jurisdiction	Takers	Passers	Pass %	State %	Diff %
Arkansas	98	67	68.37	72.48	−4.11

UNIVERSITY OF ARKANSAS AT LITTLE ROCK, WILLIAM H. BOWEN SCHOOL OF LAW

1201 McMath Avenue
Little Rock, AR 72202-5142
Phone: 501.324.9903; Fax: 501.324.9909
E-mail: lawadm@ualr.edu; Website: www.ualr.edu/law

About the UALR Bowen School of Law

The William H. Bowen School of Law is located in the heart of Little Rock, within a five-minute drive of state and federal courts as well as some of Arkansas's largest law firms and corporations. Established in 1975, the law school is fully accredited by the ABA and is a member of the AALS. In addition to being the seat of state government, Little Rock is Arkansas's legal, business, and financial center. The city's vibrant legal community affords students and alumni many professional opportunities.

Admission

Bowen seeks to enroll approximately 150 students each year. The law school takes a holistic approach to admission, as the Admissions Committee assesses a wide array of applicant factors. The law school values inclusion and is committed to enrolling students of diverse ethnicities and backgrounds. The application deadline is April 15, though candidates are strongly encouraged to apply by January 15. First-year students are admitted for the fall semester only.

Bowen hosts prospective students throughout the year. In addition to attending scheduled events, prospective students may contact the Admissions Office for individual tours, class visits, and meetings with faculty members and current students.

Juris Doctor Curriculum

The Juris Doctor (JD) curriculum seeks to provide students with a strong foundation in core areas of legal study, while providing a diverse selection of electives that embody Bowen's core values of professionalism, public service, and access to justice. Bowen offers one of the best student-to-faculty ratios in the country as well as applied skills courses such as law skills, moot court, legal clinics (litigation, tax, and mediation), and externships. For students who desire to open their own law practice upon graduation, Bowen offers courses and access to resources that support solo practice, such as the Law Office Management course and Solo Practice University®.

To receive the JD, students must complete 90 credit hours, including 44 hours of required courses. Courses are prescribed during the first year of full-time study (or the first two years of part-time study). After that, most of the curriculum is elective, allowing students to explore their interests in many areas of law. Course descriptions and further information about Bowen's curriculum can be found at ualr.edu/law/academics/curriculum/.

Concurrent Degrees

Bowen allows students to pursue law degrees while concurrently pursuing master's degrees in business administration (JD/MBA), public administration (JD/MPA), public health (JD/MPH), public service (JD/MPS), and taxation (JD/MST). Concurrent degrees in law and medicine (JD/MD) and law and pharmacy (JD/PharmD) are also offered. In order to be eligible for one of the concurrent-degree programs, students must be offered admission into both the law school and the school offering the other desired degree.

Enrollment Divisions

Bowen offers both full-time and part-time divisions. Full-time study generally takes three years to complete. Part-time study is generally completed in four years. In both divisions, study may be accelerated by attending summer school.

The environment for full-time students is one of a traditional "academy," where students spend significant portions of their days on campus engaging in various curricular and extracurricular activities.

Bowen is one of the few law schools in the country that is statutorily mandated to offer a part-time division. The division attracts many successful professionals, including state legislators and business executives.

Faculty

The faculty is made up of an outstanding group of scholars, practitioners, and teachers. Full-time professors teach virtually all required courses in both the full-time and part-time divisions. Experienced adjunct professors teach upper-level courses in their areas of specialty. The quality and accessibility of professors are often cited by Bowen students as "favorite things" about the school.

Academic Support

Bowen provides a comprehensive academic support program. This support begins prior to the first class during the week-long orientation program. Once classes begin, the principles taught in orientation are reinforced through a series of relevant workshops and seminars. The assistant dean for academic support also provides advising services to all students, helping them develop study plans, choose courses, and prepare for exams. Finally, Bowen helps ease the transition from law student to lawyer by offering an in-house bar exam prep course.

Clinical Programs

Bowen has three legal clinics that help students bridge the gap between theory learned in the classroom and practice. Through their clinic work, students practice law under the supervision of a faculty member, while at the same time helping to fill unmet legal needs in the community.

Litigation Clinic: Students represent clients involved in many types of cases within the broad areas of juvenile delinquency and family law. Qualified students receive special licenses to practice law in Arkansas.

Mediation Clinic: Students gain valuable experience in the rapidly expanding area of alternative dispute resolution. After extensive training, clinic students act as mediators in disputes relating to child abuse and neglect, juvenile delinquency, custody and visitation, special education, and small claims.

Tax Clinic: Students represent taxpayers involved in disputes with the IRS. Clinic students gain litigation and negotiation experience while acquiring significant knowledge of tax law.

Externships

The Public Service Externship provides students with another opportunity to gain hands-on experience and make significant professional contacts. Externships consist of field placements in government agencies, nonprofit legal services organizations, judiciary offices, and the Arkansas Legislature. Externship students earn academic credit for their participation.

Facilities and Library

Bowen is housed in a historic building originally constructed in the 1930s to house the state's medical school. The spacious facility contains over 150,000 square feet and is compliant with the Americans with Disabilities Act.

The six-story structure has modern classrooms and courtrooms. A renovation was completed recently to install smart technology in the classrooms and courtrooms and wireless Internet throughout the building. The lecture-capture system allows professors to record lectures (video and audio) and make them available to students via the web.

Wrapped around a four-story atrium, the library seats over 300 and houses two computer labs. The library is open seven days a week, and librarians are available on weekdays and Saturdays.

Cost and Financial Aid

With full-time resident tuition around $12,000, Bowen is an exceptional value. In addition, most nonresident students at Bowen earn scholarships that lower their tuition to no more than the resident rate. The law school participates in the Federal Stafford Loan Program, the Federal Graduate PLUS Loan Program, and the Federal Work-Study Program, as well as major private loan programs.

Scholarships

The Bowen School of Law automatically considers all admitted applicants for three scholarships.

Bowen scholarships cover full tuition and fees for up to 90 credit hours. Recipients have exceptional academic credentials, strong LSAT scores, and demonstrated leadership qualities.

Merit scholarships are awarded in amounts up to $21,000. These scholarships are awarded based on an array of factors, including academic achievement, LSAT scores, diversity, and quality of application materials. Personal statements are critical to the selection of merit scholarship recipients.

Nonresident scholarships are awarded in an amount that equals the out-of-state fees required to attend Bowen. All nonresident students are eligible for these scholarships.

Bowen Fellowship Program

Applicants who submit all required materials by January 1 and meet the criteria listed below may be considered for a Bowen Fellowship. Bowen Fellows receive a scholarship of up to full tuition and are given first choice of faculty research assistantships. In addition to the earlier application deadline, Bowen Fellowship applicants must have

- an LSAT score of 159 or higher;
- an undergraduate GPA of 3.3 or higher; and
- a sincere desire to attend Bowen full time.

Student Life

The relatively small student body at Bowen lends itself to a supportive and engaging community. On the curricular side, the *UALR Law Review* and the Moot Court Board are highly sought-after activities. Extracurricular organizations include the ABA, ACLU, Arkansas Bar Association, Arkansas Association of Women Lawyers, Asian Pacific American Law Students Association, Black Law Students Association, Lambda, Christian Legal Society, Hispanic Law Students Association, International Law Society, Part-Time Students Association, Student Animal Defense Fund, and Student Bar Association.

APPLICANT PROFILE

University of Arkansas at Little Rock, William H. Bowen School of Law
This grid includes only applicants who earned 120–180 LSAT scores under standard administrations.

LSAT Score	3.75 +		3.50–3.74		3.25–3.49		3.00–3.24		2.75–2.99		2.50–2.74		2.25–2.49		2.00–2.24		Below 2.00		No GPA		Total	
	Apps	Adm	Apps	Adm	Apps	Adm	Apps	Adm	Apps	Adm	Apps	Adm	Apps	Adm	Apps	Adm	Apps	Adm	Apps	Adm	Apps	Adm
175–180	0	0	0	0	0	0	0	0	0	0	0	0	0	0	1	1	0	0	0	0	1	1
170–174	1	1	1	1	0	0	2	2	1	1	0	0	0	0	0	0	0	0	0	0	5	5
165–169	5	5	5	5	0	0	3	3	2	2	1	1	2	2	0	0	1	0	1	1	20	19
160–164	12	12	14	11	8	6	9	7	6	5	7	7	5	3	2	1	0	0	3	3	66	55
155–159	35	32	48	42	43	39	38	32	28	23	17	11	15	6	6	2	3	0	6	4	239	191
150–154	30	21	49	27	89	42	84	25	53	17	38	12	30	6	13	0	3	0	9	1	398	151
145–149	17	9	56	20	55	7	66	12	54	0	42	0	19	0	11	0	3	0	6	0	329	48
140–144	3	0	23	0	38	0	51	0	51	0	35	0	33	0	15	0	6	0	10	0	265	0
135–139	4	0	9	0	12	0	28	0	16	0	32	0	9	0	2	0	2	0	8	0	122	0
130–134	0	0	4	0	1	0	10	0	8	0	11	0	8	0	2	0	2	0	6	0	52	0
125–129	0	0	0	0	1	0	3	0	2	0	3	0	1	0	1	0	2	0	2	0	15	0
120–124	0	0	1	0	0	0	0	0	0	0	0	0	1	0	0	0	0	0	0	0	2	0
Total	107	80	210	106	247	94	294	81	221	48	186	31	123	17	53	4	22	0	51	9	1514	470

Apps = Number of Applicants
Adm = Number Admitted
Reflects 99% of the total applicant pool; highest LSAT data reported.

ATLANTA'S JOHN MARSHALL LAW SCHOOL

1422 W. Peachtree Street NW
Atlanta, GA 30309
Phone: 404.872.3593; Fax: 404.873.3802
E-mail: admissions@johnmarshall.edu; Website: www.johnmarshall.edu

ABA
Approved
Since
2005

The Basics

Type of school	Private	
Term	Semester	
Application deadline	8/15	
Application fee	$50	
Financial aid deadline	6/30	7/15
Can first year start other than fall?	No	
Student to faculty ratio	14.0 to 1	
# of housing spaces available restricted to law students		
graduate housing for which law students are eligible		

Faculty and Administrators

	Total		Men		Women		Minorities	
	Spr	Fall	Spr	Fall	Spr	Fall	Spr	Fall
Full-time	35	40	15	16	20	24	9	11
Other full-time	1	2	0	0	1	2	1	2
Deans, librarians, & others who teach	3	3	2	2	1	1	1	1
Part-time	22	13	15	8	7	5	3	2
Total	61	58	32	26	29	32	14	16

JD Enrollment and Ethnicity

	Men		Women		Full-Time		Part-Time		1st-Year		Total		JD Degs. Awd.
	#	%	#	%	#	%	#	%	#	%	#	%	
All Hispanics	19	5.2	20	5.4	25	4.7	14	6.9	14	4.9	39	5.3	2
Am. Ind./AK Nat.	2	0.5	9	2.4	8	1.5	3	1.5	6	2.1	11	1.5	1
Asian	8	2.2	1	0.3	6	1.1	3	1.5	0	0.0	9	1.2	2
Black/Af. Am.	56	15.4	121	32.9	115	21.8	62	30.4	81	28.5	177	24.2	22
Nat. HI/Pac. Isl.	22	6.0	24	6.5	39	7.4	7	3.4	24	8.5	46	6.3	0
2 or more races	0	0.0	0	0.0	0	0.0	0	0.0	0	0.0	0	0.0	0
Subtotal (minor.)	107	29.4	175	47.6	193	36.6	89	43.6	125	44.0	282	38.5	27
Nonres. Alien	1	0.3	2	0.5	2	0.4	1	0.5	3	1.1	3	0.4	1
White/Cauc.	253	69.5	182	49.5	322	61.0	113	55.4	156	54.9	435	59.4	102
Unknown	3	0.8	9	2.4	11	2.1	1	0.5	0	0.0	12	1.6	2
Total	364	49.7	368	50.3	528	72.1	204	27.9	284	38.8	732		132

Curriculum

	Full-Time	Part-Time
Typical first-year section size	49	46
Is there typically a "small section" of the first-year class, other than Legal Writing, taught by full-time faculty	No	No
If yes, typical size offered last year		
# of classroom course titles beyond first-year curriculum	101	
# of upper division courses, excluding seminars, with an enrollment: Under 25	61	
25–49	33	
50–74	7	
75–99	0	
100+	0	
# of seminars	9	
# of seminar positions available	138	
# of seminar positions filled	71	17
# of positions available in simulation courses	0	
# of simulation positions filled	0	0
# of positions available in faculty supervised clinical courses	0	
# of faculty supervised clinical positions filled	0	0
# involved in field placements	70	7
# involved in law journals	21	6
# involved in moot court or trial competitions	35	10
# of credit hours required to graduate	88	

Transfers

Transfers in	17
Transfers out	26

Tuition and Fees

	Resident	Nonresident
Full-time	$34,810	$34,810
Part-time	$21,074	$21,074
Tuition Guarantee Program		N

Living Expenses

Estimated living expenses for singles

Living on campus	Living off campus	Living at home
N/A	$23,405	N/A

ABA
Approved
Since
2005

GPA and LSAT Scores

	Total	Full-Time	Part-Time
# of apps	1,867	1,543	324
# of offers	909	779	130
# of matrics	264	191	73
75% GPA	3.16	3.14	3.20
Median GPA	2.82	2.79	2.89
25% GPA	2.52	2.50	2.53
75% LSAT	152	152	153
Median LSAT	150	150	150
25% LSAT	148	148	148

Grants and Scholarships (from prior year)

	Total		Full-Time		Part-Time	
	#	%	#	%	#	%
Total # of students	630		455		175	
Total # receiving grants	38	6.0	29	6.4	9	5.1
Less than 1/2 tuition	23	3.7	21	4.6	2	1.1
Half to full tuition	0	0.0	0	0.0	0	0.0
Full tuition	15	2.4	8	1.8	7	4.0
More than full tuition	0	0.0	0	0.0	0	0.0
Median grant amount			$6,000		$22,325	

Informational and Library Resources

Total amount spent on library materials	$736,240
Study seating capacity inside the library	212
# of full-time equivalent professional librarians	5
Hours per week library is open	86
# of open, wired connections available to students	12
# of networked computers available for use by students	34
Has wireless network?	Y
Requires computer?	N

JD Attrition (from prior year)

	Academic	Other	Total	
	#	#	#	%
1st year	3	13	16	5.9
2nd year	0	17	17	8.5
3rd year	0	1	1	0.7
4th year	0	0	0	0.0

Employment (9 months after graduation)

For up-to-date employment data, go to employmentsummary.abaquestionnaire.org on the ABA website.

Bar Passage Rates

First-time takers	153	Reporting %	100.00
Average school %	63.39	Average state %	83.34

Average pass difference −19.95

Jurisdiction	Takers	Passers	Pass %	State %	Diff %
Georgia	135	80	59.26	83.61	−24.35
Florida	4	4	100.00	77.63	22.37
New Jersey	3	3	100.00	82.34	17.66
North Carolina	2	2	100.00	77.50	22.50
Others (6)	9	8	88.89		

The information on these pages was provided by the law school.

ATLANTA'S JOHN MARSHALL LAW SCHOOL

1422 W. Peachtree Street NW
Atlanta, GA 30309
Phone: 404.872.3593; Fax: 404.873.3802
E-mail: admissions@johnmarshall.edu; Website: www.johnmarshall.edu

The Dean's Introduction

Atlanta's John Marshall Law School (AJMLS) has been educating lawyers and leaders in Georgia since 1933 and now attracts students from around the country. We provide a rigorous, high-quality program of legal education that produces competent and ethical lawyers who are dedicated to helping people, especially in underserved communities. We intentionally instill in our students a sense of obligation to the community and to the legal profession—an obligation to pursue justice, rather than mere personal gain, and to improve society, rather than to solely advance personal ambition. Whether our graduates remain in law practice, become judges, enter politics, or succeed in business, these rich values stay with them.

The Mission

The mission of the law school is to prepare highly competent and professional lawyers who possess a strong social conscience, continually demonstrate high ethical standards, and are committed to the improvement of the legal system and society. The school is dedicated to providing a quality educational opportunity to nontraditional or adult learners, and to other significantly underserved segments of the community. We emphasize the highest standards of ethical and professional conduct. As Supreme Court Justice Thurgood Marshall once said, "There's only one kind of reputation a young lawyer gets in a hurry." Graduates of this law school are trained to do the right thing.

Atlanta Living

The law school campus is centrally located in midtown Atlanta, the social, cultural, and economic hub of the South. It is in close proximity to Atlanta's largest law firms, government offices, state and federal courts, and nonprofit legal organizations. Atlanta also boasts an extensive array of arts, music, sports, and recreational events, making it an exciting place to live.

Facilities, Library, and Modern Technology

The law school is housed in a modern, nine-story building located on one of the major streets in Atlanta. Additional classroom and faculty offices are located in an adjoining building connected by a two-story pedestrian bridge. A new conference center, including a 350-seat auditorium, allows for a constant flow of student programs and symposia.

Our library spreads over three floors, contains more than 200,000 total volumes and equivalents, and provides students and faculty with access to all legal materials necessary to learn the skill of legal research.

The law school has made the inclusion of new technologies throughout the school a priority. All students and faculty enjoy direct and unlimited access to wireless Internet, massive online legal databases, as well as new state-of-the-art technology in multiple classrooms that allows for interactive learning experiences. Students can take both midterm and final exams on their laptops and download them to the school's network.

Prospective students can also apply to AJMLS using a smart phone or tablet at http://m.johnmarshall.edu.

Dedicated Faculty

The AJMLS faculty makes the difference in the student experience and are committed to students' success throughout their legal education and beyond. The faculty is dedicated to providing an intellectually rigorous academic program while instilling the highest sense of professional, ethical, and moral responsibilities that are required of members of the legal profession. All of our faculty members have extensive practical experience in their respective fields of expertise, bringing real-world experience into the classroom. All first-year and required courses are taught in small classes, and professors are easily accessible to their students outside of class. Our small class sizes and low student-to-faculty ratio (one of the best among American law schools) create a supportive environment where students can enjoy learning and express their views.

Commitment to Diversity

Because AJMLS's educational environment focuses on an interactive learning process, a diverse student body is essential to providing a broad range of perspectives in the classroom and the law school community. The Fall 2011 entering class of 264 students includes 53 percent women and 41 percent minorities. The student body is not only ethnically diverse, but it is also varied in life experience and professional backgrounds. Also in the 2011 entering class, the median age of full-time students was 24, and the median age of part-time students was 32.

The Juris Doctor Program

AJMLS's rigorous program of study is designed toward the development of intellectual, analytical, and lawyering skills. From the first-year curriculum, with its predetermined set of core courses, through the third year, with courses that emphasize practical skill development, the Juris Doctor program is designed to promote analytical reasoning, precision in both oral and written communication, and problem-solving skills. Upper-class students can pursue their areas of interest through a broad variety of elective courses.

Full-Time and Part-Time Law Study. AJMLS remains dedicated to providing access to legal education to both traditional and nontraditional students by offering both full-time and part-time law programs. Individuals who are unable to devote themselves to the study of law full time may attend either the part-time evening or part-time day program.

The **JD Honors Program in Criminal Justice** is a unique, innovative curriculum for students planning to be prosecutors, public defenders, or criminal defense lawyers. The Honors Program immerses the student in the criminal justice field from the first day of law school, integrates skills classes with criminal law, and introduces students to the leading prosecutors and defense lawyers in this country. Graduates of this JD program will earn a truly valuable credential.

The **Legal Skills and Professionalism Program** takes a holistic approach to preparing students for success during and after law school. Beginning with writing, the program teaches legal skills and professionalism. The same tools that students use to draft documents in their writing classes are employed to solve legal problems in Negotiations, Mediation, Trial Advocacy, Client Interviewing and Counseling, and other skills courses. In addition, a professionalism component is built into every course in the program, preparing students to confront and resolve real-world professionalism issues as they learn to solve legal problems and meet client goals. The law school faculty comes with diverse law practice backgrounds, including criminal defense and prosecution, administrative law, domestic relations practice, and corporate/transactional work.

Academic Support. Tools for academic growth and professional success are not only fostered through interactive classroom teaching, but also through individual advisement and group workshops. The Office of Academic Achievement (OAA) is dedicated to preparing students to succeed in the classroom, on exams, and ultimately, the bar exam. The OAA works to sharpen academic skills such as critical reading, critical thinking, logic and analysis, and writing. One of the many ways the OAA helps students broaden their understanding of the doctrinal material and achieve academic goals is through the Professional and Academic Success Seminar. First-year students participate in a once-a-week seminar during their first semester to identify and strengthen weaknesses in areas closely related to finding success in law school, on the bar exam, and in practice.

Pro Bono and Externship Programs. The Office of Pro Bono Outreach and Externships provides opportunities for students to develop their legal and professional skills while working in the legal community. Pro Bono Outreach honors the law school's mission of graduating students with a strong social conscience and commitment to improving the legal community. From first-year orientation to graduation, students are given a variety of volunteer opportunities and are honored for their efforts to reach back as they move up. The externship program allows students to earn academic credit while working in legal offices under the supervision of practicing attorneys or judges. Placements include the US Attorney's Office, the Georgia Innocence Project, the Office of Homeland Security, and local prosecutors, public defenders, and judges. The Micronesian externship provides students with the opportunity to work in judicial chambers and a government office in Guam, the Commonwealth of the Northern Marianas, the Federated State of Micronesia, and the Republic of Palau.

Career Development

The Office of Career Development (OCD) offers individualized, professional advice to students about their personal career goals and tailors strategies to assist students in reaching those goals. In addition to providing résumé and interview workshops to facilitate job searches, the OCD also participates in the Georgia Law School Consortium to plan job fairs and other state-wide recruiting efforts, such as judicial clerkships; placement with prosecutors, public interest agencies, and public defenders; and minority recruiting. As a member of the National Association of Law Placement, AJMLS offers its students the opportunity to attend regional hiring consortia that attract private and government recruiters throughout the Southeast.

Admission

The Admissions Committee is dedicated to finding a well-rounded and diverse group of students. In addition to the candidate's academic record and standardized test results, the Admissions Committee will examine with particular care those factors that indicate a high probability for success in law study. Such factors include life experiences, personal or family hardships overcome, demonstrated personal and professional achievements, ability to overcome life's obstacles, the capacity for rigorous intellectual study, the self-discipline demanded by the profession, and a commitment to be of service to the profession and society as a whole.

AJMLS to Open Campus in Savannah, GA

New Savannah Law School Set to Begin Classes August 2012. The American Bar Association's Council on Legal Education and Admissions to the Bar has acquiesced in AJMLS's application to open a branch campus in Savannah, Georgia, for fall 2012. Named the Savannah Law School, the new campus will provide traditional and nontraditional students an opportunity to acquire the skills necessary to enter the profession well-equipped and ready to practice law. Prospective students can apply on their smartphone/tablet at m.savannahlawschool.org or on the Internet at www.savannahlawschool.org/apply. The SLS Office of Admissions can be reached via e-mail at admissions@savannahlawschool.org or by calling 912.346.1657.

APPLICANT PROFILE

Atlanta's John Marshall Law School
This grid includes only applicants who earned 120–180 LSAT scores under standard administrations.

LSAT Score	GPA								
	3.75 +	3.50–3.74	3.25–3.49	3.00–3.24	2.75–2.99	2.50–2.74	2.25–2.49	2.00–2.24	Below 2.00
155–180									
150–154									
145–149									
120–144									

Good Possibility | Possible | Unlikely

AVE MARIA SCHOOL OF LAW

1025 Commons Circle
Naples, FL 34119-1376
Phone: 239.687.5300; Fax: 239.352-2890
E-mail: info@avemarialaw.edu; Website: www.avemarialaw.edu

ABA Approved Since 2002

The Basics

Type of school	Private
Term	Semester
Application deadline	7/1
Application fee	$50
Financial aid deadline	6/1
Can first year start other than fall?	No
Student to faculty ratio	19.3 to 1
# of housing spaces available restricted to law students	113
graduate housing for which law students are eligible	

Faculty and Administrators

	Total		Men		Women		Minorities	
	Spr	Fall	Spr	Fall	Spr	Fall	Spr	Fall
Full-time	22	19	16	14	6	5	1	2
Other full-time	7	7	5	3	2	4	0	0
Deans, librarians, & others who teach	5	6	4	4	1	2	0	0
Part-time	9	13	9	9	0	4	0	1
Total	43	45	34	30	9	15	1	3

Curriculum

	Full-Time	Part-Time
Typical first-year section size	101	0
Is there typically a "small section" of the first-year class, other than Legal Writing, taught by full-time faculty	No	No
If yes, typical size offered last year		

# of classroom course titles beyond first-year curriculum		76
# of upper division courses, excluding seminars, with an enrollment:	Under 25	47
	25–49	15
	50–74	4
	75–99	10
	100+	1
# of seminars		25
# of seminar positions available		411

	Full-Time	Part-Time
# of seminar positions filled	254	0
# of positions available in simulation courses	124	
# of simulation positions filled	90	0
# of positions available in faculty supervised clinical courses	43	
# of faculty supervised clinical positions filled	36	0
# involved in field placements	51	0
# involved in law journals	49	0
# involved in moot court or trial competitions	27	0
# of credit hours required to graduate	90	

JD Enrollment and Ethnicity

	Men		Women		Full-Time		Part-Time		1st-Year		Total		JD Degs. Awd.
	#	%	#	%	#	%	#	%	#	%	#	%	
All Hispanics	28	10.4	34	15.4	62	12.7	0	0.0	22	14.6	62	12.7	10
Am. Ind./AK Nat.	2	0.7	0	0.0	2	0.4	0	0.0	2	1.3	2	0.4	0
Asian	2	0.7	5	2.3	7	1.4	0	0.0	2	1.3	7	1.4	6
Black/Af. Am.	10	3.7	12	5.4	22	4.5	0	0.0	8	5.3	22	4.5	2
Nat. HI/Pac. Isl.	0	0.0	0	0.0	0	0.0	0	0.0	0	0.0	0	0.0	1
2 or more races	3	1.1	7	3.2	10	2.0	0	0.0	3	2.0	10	2.0	3
Subtotal (minor.)	45	16.8	58	26.2	103	21.1	0	0.0	37	24.5	103	21.1	22
Nonres. Alien	3	1.1	1	0.5	4	0.8	0	0.0	2	1.3	4	0.8	2
White/Cauc.	211	78.7	156	70.6	367	75.1	0	0.0	104	68.9	367	75.1	64
Unknown	9	3.4	6	2.7	15	3.1	0	0.0	8	5.3	15	3.1	0
Total	268	54.8	221	45.2	489	100.0	0	0.0	151	30.9	489		88

Transfers

Transfers in	2
Transfers out	18

Tuition and Fees

	Resident	Nonresident
Full-time	$36,448	$36,448
Part-time		
Tuition Guarantee Program		N

Living Expenses

Estimated living expenses for singles

Living on campus	Living off campus	Living at home
$20,999	$20,999	$20,999

AVE MARIA SCHOOL OF LAW

ABA
Approved
Since
2002

GPA and LSAT Scores

	Total	Full-Time	Part-Time
# of apps	1,633	1,633	0
# of offers	878	878	0
# of matrics	151	151	0
75% GPA	3.48	3.48	0.00
Median GPA	3.04	3.04	0.00
25% GPA	2.79	2.79	0.00
75% LSAT	153	153	0
Median LSAT	150	150	0
25% LSAT	146	146	0

Grants and Scholarships (from prior year)

	Total		Full-Time		Part-Time	
	#	%	#	%	#	%
Total # of students	468		468		0	
Total # receiving grants	233	49.8	233	49.8	0	0.0
Less than 1/2 tuition	124	26.5	124	26.5	0	0.0
Half to full tuition	73	15.6	73	15.6	0	0.0
Full tuition	36	7.7	36	7.7	0	0.0
More than full tuition	0	0.0	0	0.0	0	0.0
Median grant amount			$15,000		$0	

Informational and Library Resources

Total amount spent on library materials	$650,340
Study seating capacity inside the library	103
# of full-time equivalent professional librarians	4
Hours per week library is open	105
# of open, wired connections available to students	20
# of networked computers available for use by students	21
Has wireless network?	Y
Requires computer?	N

JD Attrition (from prior year)

	Academic	Other	Total	
	#	#	#	%
1st year	8	27	35	17.4
2nd year	0	4	4	2.2
3rd year	0	0	0	0.0
4th year	0	0	0	0.0

Employment (9 months after graduation)

For up-to-date employment data, go to employmentsummary.abaquestionnaire.org on the ABA website.

Bar Passage Rates

First-time takers	80	Reporting %	70.00
Average school %	53.57	Average state %	80.78
Average pass difference	−27.21		

Jurisdiction	Takers	Passers	Pass %	State %	Diff %
Florida	26	17	65.38	77.63	−12.25
Texas	8	4	50.00	82.68	−32.68
Michigan	6	2	33.33	84.83	−51.50
New York	5	1	20.00	84.92	−64.92
California	4	1	25.00	71.24	−46.24

AVE MARIA SCHOOL OF LAW

1025 Commons Circle
Naples, FL 34119-1376
Phone: 239.687.5300; Fax: 239.352-2890
E-mail: info@avemarialaw.edu; Website: www.avemarialaw.edu

Introduction

Ave Maria School of Law offers students a distinctive legal education that focuses on professional excellence, the moral foundations of the law, and the harmony of faith and reason. As a national Catholic law school, Ave Maria is committed to producing highly competent graduates who are able to reflect critically on the law, the principles that undergird it, and their role within the legal system.

With a student-to-faculty ratio of approximately 19 to 1, Ave Maria students benefit from ready access to experienced faculty members who prepare students to practice at the highest level and to succeed on bar exams throughout the country. The quality of Ave Maria's academic program is recognized by judges throughout the nation who have hired graduates as judicial clerks—with 61 clerkships secured by members of the 2003–2011 graduating classes, most of these federal clerkships.

In the summer of 2009, Ave Maria School of Law relocated to southwest Florida, just seven miles inland of the Gulf of Mexico. The new location has enhanced the school's ability to fulfill its distinctive mission as a Catholic law school dedicated to professional excellence. In the new location, students have found employment and externship opportunities with courts and law firms in nearby Naples and Fort Myers, while the law school's clinical programs have found new opportunities to serve the community.

Ave Maria School of Law encourages applications from students of all faiths who seek a distinctive legal education enriched by the Catholic intellectual tradition.

Curriculum

Ave Maria School of Law awards the Juris Doctor degree after three years (90 credits) of full-time residential study. The required curriculum of 63 credits ensures that all students develop those skills that are fundamental to the effective practice of law—analysis, reasoning, problem solving, research, writing, oral advocacy, and others. Through elective courses, students have the opportunity to focus on specific subject areas of interest, such as commercial law, employment law, international law, and intellectual property law. A central tenet of the educational philosophy at Ave Maria is that law and morality are inherently intertwined.

Faculty

At the core of the Ave Maria School of Law education is the faculty who teach and mentor students. Faculty members bring to the classroom their experience as attorneys in private practice, as judicial clerks, and as teachers and administrators at other law schools. In hiring faculty, the law school administration has sought individuals who would be able to translate the mission of the School of Law in the classroom, in their scholarship, and in their service. Ave Maria faculty members actively contribute to the profession through their legal research, writing, and involvement in professional and civic organizations. Our faculty includes 32 full-time professors. Select upper-level courses are taught by adjunct faculty members drawn from area law firms, corporations, and the judiciary.

Enrollment/Student Body

While many of Ave Maria's students come to the School of Law directly from their undergraduate institutions, others have earned postgraduate degrees and have work experience in fields including business, medicine, engineering, the military, and education. More than 170 different undergraduate colleges are represented at the School of Law, including Brigham Young University, Christendom College, Emory University, Franciscan University of Steubenville, University of Notre Dame, the University of Florida, and many other fine schools.

Career Services/Placement

Ave Maria School of Law graduates accept employment with an array of employers in all regions of the country, including national and regional law firms such as Akin Gump, Sidley Austin, Butzel Long, Reed Smith, Roetzel and Andress, Skadden Arps, and Holland and Hart. Graduates have also been successful in obtaining employment with state and federal governmental agencies, including the US Departments of Justice, Homeland Security, and Defense, as well as multiple prosecutors' offices nationwide. Students gain valuable legal experience throughout the year through volunteer internships, paid clerkships, and the law school's robust externship program. The six-credit Certified Legal Intern Criminal Litigation Externship is a hybrid between a traditional law school clinic and a for-credit externship.

The Career Services Office uses a proactive and individualized approach to assist students during each stage of the career-search process—counseling, strategizing, résumé and cover letter preparation, interviewing, and consideration of employment offers. The full-time staff of four, two of whom are attorneys, is dedicated to expanding employment opportunities for students through the cultivation of relationships with legal employers throughout the region and the nation.

Library/Physical Facilities

The Ave Maria Law Library is housed in an environment that is both welcoming and conducive to research and study. Materials are available in all formats; the collection is particularly strong in digital resources. Apart from a fine compilation of US and international primary and secondary legal materials, the Ave Maria Law Library's collection emphasizes the areas of canon law, bioethics and biotechnology, natural law, and related philosophy, history, political science, and economics titles. Seating in the library includes a variety of carrel, table, group study, and soft seating. Leisure reading in the form of magazines and daily newspapers is provided.

Admission

Ave Maria School of Law enrolls talented individuals from diverse backgrounds who seek a rigorous and distinctive legal education. To this end, Ave Maria evaluates applicants from a whole-person perspective and considers many factors, including work experience, activities, background, obstacles overcome, accomplishments, undergraduate and graduate school records, Law School Admission Test (LSAT) scores, letters of reference, and the applicant's personal statement. Ave Maria recognizes that a diverse student body, drawn from throughout the United States and internationally, enriches the educational experience.

Student Activities

By providing opportunities for interaction among students, faculty, and the legal community, Ave Maria School of Law ensures a vibrant, professional atmosphere and a constructive law school experience. A three-day orientation program, a Distinguished Speaker Series, conferences, and the Board of Visitors Mentor Program, together with a challenging and comprehensive curriculum, provide Ave Maria students with an exceptional law school experience. A multitude of student organizations offer students the opportunity to pursue their specific areas of interest and augment their law school education.

APPLICANT PROFILE

Ave Maria School of Law has chosen not to provide an admission profile grid. This reflects our commitment to consider every applicant from a whole-person perspective. Every component of the application is carefully reviewed,

Housing

Ave Maria School of Law's campus in Naples, Florida, offers on-site housing as well as close-by apartments, condominiums, and single-family homes. The law school provides assistance to students during their search for housing and, if applicable, roommates.

Expenses/Financial Aid

Ave Maria School of Law offers a generous scholarship program that annually provides scholarships ranging from $5,000 up to full tuition to approximately two-thirds of the entering class. Additionally, the School of Law annually awards scholarships ranging from $5,000 to $10,000 to entering students who have a record of service and leadership in select areas. Tuition for members of the fall 2011 entering class is $35,948.

and, while qualifications as measured by LSAT and GPA are important, equal consideration is also given to the applicant's background, letters of recommendation, and personal statement.

UNIVERSITY OF BALTIMORE SCHOOL OF LAW

1420 North Charles Street
Baltimore, MD 21201
Phone: 410.837.4459; Fax: 410.837.4188
E-mail: lwadmiss@ubalt.edu; Website: http://law.ubalt.edu

ABA
Approved
Since
1972

The Basics

Type of school	Public
Term	Semester
Application deadline	7/1
Application fee	$60
Financial aid deadline	3/1
Can first year start other than fall?	No
Student to faculty ratio	17.0 to 1
# of housing spaces available restricted to law students	
graduate housing for which law students are eligible	

Faculty and Administrators

	Total		Men		Women		Minorities	
	Spr	Fall	Spr	Fall	Spr	Fall	Spr	Fall
Full-time	42	50	25	30	17	20	6	7
Other full-time	7	9	4	3	3	6	1	3
Deans, librarians, & others who teach	7	5	3	2	4	3	0	0
Part-time	77	55	51	41	26	14	7	5
Total	133	119	83	76	50	43	14	15

Curriculum

		Full-Time	Part-Time
Typical first-year section size		54	45
Is there typically a "small section" of the first-year class, other than Legal Writing, taught by full-time faculty		No	No
If yes, typical size offered last year			
# of classroom course titles beyond first-year curriculum		132	
# of upper division courses, excluding seminars, with an enrollment:	Under 25	170	
	25–49	31	
	50–74	20	
	75–99	10	
	100+	0	
# of seminars		34	
# of seminar positions available		656	
# of seminar positions filled		300	111
# of positions available in simulation courses		995	
# of simulation positions filled		540	224
# of positions available in faculty supervised clinical courses		191	
# of faculty supervised clinical positions filled		148	21
# involved in field placements		159	18
# involved in law journals		150	14
# involved in moot court or trial competitions		98	9
# of credit hours required to graduate		87	

JD Enrollment and Ethnicity

	Men		Women		Full-Time		Part-Time		1st-Year		Total		JD Degs. Awd.
	#	%	#	%	#	%	#	%	#	%	#	%	
All Hispanics	17	3.1	22	4.1	21	2.8	18	5.0	15	3.6	39	3.6	4
Am. Ind./AK Nat.	0	0.0	1	0.2	1	0.1	0	0.0	0	0.0	1	0.1	0
Asian	20	3.6	36	6.6	44	6.0	12	3.3	23	5.5	56	5.1	16
Black/Af. Am.	28	5.0	61	11.3	44	6.0	45	12.5	49	11.6	89	8.1	23
Nat. Hl/Pac. Isl.	1	0.2	0	0.0	0	0.0	1	0.3	0	0.0	1	0.1	1
2 or more races	8	1.4	9	1.7	14	1.9	3	0.8	10	2.4	17	1.5	0
Subtotal (minor.)	74	13.3	129	23.8	124	16.8	79	21.9	97	23.0	203	18.5	44
Nonres. Alien	2	0.4	0	0.0	2	0.3	0	0.0	2	0.5	2	0.2	0
White/Cauc.	437	78.6	386	71.2	580	78.6	243	67.5	293	69.6	823	75.0	219
Unknown	43	7.7	27	5.0	32	4.3	38	10.6	29	6.9	70	6.4	34
Total	556	50.6	542	49.4	738	67.2	360	32.8	421	38.3	1098		297

Transfers

Transfers in	22
Transfers out	26

Tuition and Fees

	Resident	Nonresident
Full-time	$25,798	$37,900
Part-time	$19,262	$26,772
Tuition Guarantee Program	N	

Living Expenses

Estimated living expenses for singles

Living on campus	Living off campus	Living at home
N/A	$22,800	N/A

UNIVERSITY OF BALTIMORE SCHOOL OF LAW

ABA
Approved
Since
1972

GPA and LSAT Scores

	Total	Full-Time	Part-Time
# of apps	2,105	1,619	486
# of offers	853	706	147
# of matrics	328	236	92
75% GPA	3.46	3.51	3.35
Median GPA	3.25	3.31	3.15
25% GPA	2.97	3.05	2.66
75% LSAT	158	159	157
Median LSAT	156	156	154
25% LSAT	151	152	150

Grants and Scholarships (from prior year)

	Total #	Total %	Full-Time #	Full-Time %	Part-Time #	Part-Time %
Total # of students	1,083		730		353	
Total # receiving grants	184	17.0	143	19.6	41	11.6
Less than 1/2 tuition	78	7.2	47	6.4	31	8.8
Half to full tuition	106	9.8	96	13.2	10	2.8
Full tuition	0	0.0	0	0.0	0	0.0
More than full tuition	0	0.0	0	0.0	0	0.0
Median grant amount			$23,354		$5,250	

Informational and Library Resources

Total amount spent on library materials	$499,185
Study seating capacity inside the library	317
# of full-time equivalent professional librarians	11
Hours per week library is open	94
# of open, wired connections available to students	29
# of networked computers available for use by students	35
Has wireless network?	Y
Requires computer?	N

JD Attrition (from prior year)

	Academic #	Other #	Total #	Total %
1st year	17	29	46	11.0
2nd year	1	3	4	1.2
3rd year	0	0	0	0.0
4th year	0	0	0	0.0

Employment (9 months after graduation)

For up-to-date employment data, go to
employmentsummary.abaquestionnaire.org on the ABA website.

Bar Passage Rates

First-time takers	326	Reporting %	91.41
Average school %	80.20	Average state %	79.96
Average pass difference	.24		

Jurisdiction	Takers	Passers	Pass %	State %	Diff %
Maryland	298	239	80.20	79.96	0.24

UNIVERSITY OF BALTIMORE SCHOOL OF LAW

1420 North Charles Street
Baltimore, MD 21201
Phone: 410.837.4459; Fax: 410.837.4188
E-mail: lwadmiss@ubalt.edu; Website: http://law.ubalt.edu

Introduction

Founded in 1925, the University of Baltimore is one of 13 institutions in the University System of Maryland. Although UB is the sixth largest public law school in the country, with approximately 1,000 JD students, the school prides itself on excellent classroom teaching, small law school sections, and personalized service.

The School of Law remains committed to its traditional values of community involvement, public interest, access, and diversity. Regardless of a graduate's area of practice, the school believes that all of its students should be exposed to the traditional obligation of lawyers to serve the poor and the common good. Finally, the school values a diverse faculty, staff, and student body as an essential part of its pedagogical mission. The School of Law is accredited by the ABA and AALS.

Admission

The School of Law has established an admission policy designed to obtain a diverse and well-qualified student body. In evaluating applicant files, the Admission Committee considers not only the cumulative undergraduate grade-point average and the LSAT score, but also nontraditional factors that may be relevant in determining an applicant's ability to succeed in law school. Applicants are encouraged to discuss fully in a personal statement any such factors they wish the committee to consider in evaluating their application.

Enrollment/Student Body

The School of Law provides three options for pursuing a law degree: a full-time day program, a part-time evening program, and a part-time day program. Approximately a third of the student body is part time, making the part-time division one of the largest in the nation. Over 88 percent of the classes are composed of 50 students or less. The School of Law typically offers between 60 and 65 classes a semester.

Curriculum

The School of Law provides a rich curriculum in both day and evening divisions, offering a wide variety of specialized courses in addition to a solid core curriculum. Our legal skills offerings are especially strong as the School of Law is one of the national leaders in "narrowing the gap" between legal education and the legal profession. Our skills programs begin with the first-year courses in legal analysis, research, and writing and culminate with one of the best legal clinics in the nation. Upper-level courses offer students a range of in-depth concentrations that provide students with a sophisticated understanding of a particular area of law.

Library

The library's permanent collection contains approximately 354,000 books and bound volume equivalents. The collection includes the published reports of federal and state courts, statutes, administrative materials, and secondary materials such as treatises, legal encyclopedias, digests, citators, form books, looseleaf services, and law reviews. The library staff believes that technology should not be considered separate from the study and practice of law: professional reference librarians are available to students seven days a week to show students how to use the computer-assisted legal systems, as well as how to access the library's many web-based resources. The library's two computer labs are open to law students during library hours and, along with the wireless network, provide access to word processing, LexisNexis, Westlaw, the Internet, online catalogs, and other resources.

Joint Degrees

The School of Law offers six joint degrees: JD with MBA, MPA, MS in Criminal Justice, MS in Negotiations and Conflict Management, LLM in Taxation, and the PhD in Policy Science.

Special Programs

Areas of Concentration—The School of Law has an innovative curriculum that allows students the opportunity to develop an in-depth knowledge in a particular area of the law. Students may take courses in one of nine areas of concentration: business law, criminal practice, estate planning, family law, intellectual property, international and comparative law, litigation and advocacy, public service, and real estate practice.

Centers—Students may also gain specialized knowledge in particular areas of the law through participation in the activities of the Law School's centers, including the **Center for Families, Children, and the Courts**, which focuses on the development and implementation of family court planning and reform initiatives throughout the country. The **Center for International and Comparative Law** promotes the study and understanding of international and comparative law and the political and economic institutions that support the international legal order. The center places special emphasis on environmental law, human rights, intellectual property, and international business transactions. The **Center on Applied Feminism** serves as a bridge between feminist legal theory and the law. The center examines how feminist theory can benefit legal practitioners in representing clients, shape legal doctrine, and play a role in policy debates and implementation. The **Stephen L. Snyder Center for Litigation Skills** supports and enhances the acclaimed litigation skills training of the School of Law through a variety of programs and activities, including lectures by prominent lawyers and judges, special conferences, and litigation research. The **Center for Sport and the Law** was established in 2009 with the support of the Baltimore Orioles professional baseball franchise and the Baltimore Ravens professional football franchise to foster academic leadership, community engagement, and student excellence in the theoretical and practical aspects of amateur and professional sports law.

Law Review and Other Periodicals give students an opportunity to hone their skills in research, analysis, and writing. The *University of Baltimore Law Review* offers an in-depth analysis of issues of current concern to practitioners and judges alike. The *Law Forum* specializes in articles that trace developing trends in the law. The *University of Baltimore Journal of Land and Development* is a scholarly, interdisciplinary legal journal that publishes in-depth legal and policy analysis of the range of issues related to land and development.

Clinical, Advocacy, and Internship Programs—Professional development is fostered through clinics in which students represent individuals and organizations in litigation and transactional matters. Clinics include the **Appellate Practice Clinic**, which enables students to brief and argue a case in the Maryland Court of Special Appeals; the **Civil Advocacy Clinic**, which focuses on such issues as consumer protection, public benefits cases, and landlord-tenant disputes; the **Community Development Clinic**, which represents nonprofit community organizations in a variety of housing, economic, social, and cultural development areas; the **Criminal Practice Clinic**, in which students handle misdemeanor and felony matters in the district and circuit courts; the **Disability Law Clinic**, which provides representation to patients in involuntary commitment hearings; the **Family Law Clinic**, where students represent low-income clients seeking child custody, support, divorce, and protection from domestic violence; the **Mediation Clinic for Families**, which permits students to co-mediate family law disputes and engage in projects designed to improve the practice of family mediation; the **Immigrant Rights Clinic**, which enables students to represent low-income immigrants in Immigration Court and in the District Court of Maryland, as well as work with immigrant advocates to develop programs that increase access to justice for immigrant communities; and the **Innocence Project Clinic**, which provides students with the opportunity to review records, interview clients and witnesses, conduct legal research, devise investigative strategies, draft pleadings, and argue motions in cases involving claims of wrongful conviction. **Internship Programs** give students experience clerking for academic credit in the public and private sector,

including positions in the executive, legislative, and judicial branches of state and local governments.

Financial Aid

The university's Financial Aid Office administers federal, state, and institutional loan programs. First-year and transfer applicants are advised to apply for financial aid well in advance of the March 1 deadline. Students are automatically considered for merit-based scholarships. The School of Law awarded more than $1 million in scholarships to students matriculating in 2011.

Career Services

The professional staff of the Law Career Development Office (LCDO) works individually and collectively to establish effective, dynamic relationships with law students and graduates seeking to articulate, develop, and achieve their career goals. By forging cooperative relationships with a host of employers, regionally and nationally, in the public and private sectors, the LCDO and the School of Law have demonstrated significant success in meeting the needs of our law students and alumni who are competing in a challenging and evolving market. Through a host of services, including individual counseling, career workshops, mock interviews, on-campus and off-campus recruitment programs, internship and externship programs, as well as a detailed and extensive library of resources, the LCDO seeks to provide each and every law student and graduate with job-search strategies and the tools to succeed in their professional careers. In addition, through the innovative EXPLOR Program, the LCDO offers first-year students opportunities to gain substantive legal experience their first summer and establish a solid foundation for future success.

APPLICANT PROFILE

University of Baltimore School of Law
This grid includes only applicants who earned 120–180 LSAT scores under standard administrations.

LSAT Score	GPA								
	3.75 +	3.50–3.74	3.25–3.49	3.00–3.24	2.75–2.99	2.50–2.74	2.25–2.49	2.00–2.24	Below 2.00
175–180									
170–174									
165–169									
160–164									
155–159									
150–154									
145–149									
140–144									
Below 140									

◼ Good Possibility   ☐ Possible   ▨ Unlikely

BARRY UNIVERSITY DWAYNE O. ANDREAS SCHOOL OF LAW

6441 East Colonial Drive
Orlando, FL 32807
Phone: 321.206.5600
E-mail: krupert@mail.barry.edu; Website: www.barry.edu/law

ABA
Approved
Since
2002

The Basics

Type of school	Private
Term	Semester
Application deadline	5/1
Application fee	
Financial aid deadline	4/15
Can first year start other than fall?	No
Student to faculty ratio	15.5 to 1
# of housing spaces available restricted to law students	
graduate housing for which law students are eligible	

Faculty and Administrators

	Total		Men		Women		Minorities	
	Spr	Fall	Spr	Fall	Spr	Fall	Spr	Fall
Full-time	34	32	20	18	14	14	8	9
Other full-time	0	1	0	0	0	1	0	0
Deans, librarians, & others who teach	5	6	1	2	4	4	1	2
Part-time	36	30	27	23	9	7	3	4
Total	75	69	48	43	27	26	12	15

Curriculum

	Full-Time	Part-Time
Typical first-year section size	106	50
Is there typically a "small section" of the first-year class, other than Legal Writing, taught by full-time faculty	Yes	Yes
If yes, typical size offered last year	50	50
# of classroom course titles beyond first-year curriculum	94	
# of upper division courses, excluding seminars, with an enrollment: Under 25	80	
25–49	33	
50–74	19	
75–99	5	
100+	0	
# of seminars	17	
# of seminar positions available	340	
# of seminar positions filled	183	54
# of positions available in simulation courses	744	
# of simulation positions filled	515	220
# of positions available in faculty supervised clinical courses	48	
# of faculty supervised clinical positions filled	25	4
# involved in field placements	20	33
# involved in law journals	40	13
# involved in moot court or trial competitions	30	3
# of credit hours required to graduate	90	

JD Enrollment and Ethnicity

	Men #	Men %	Women #	Women %	Full-Time #	Full-Time %	Part-Time #	Part-Time %	1st-Year #	1st-Year %	Total #	Total %	JD Degs. Awd.
All Hispanics	44	11.7	41	12.3	65	12.3	20	11.1	42	15.3	85	12.0	18
Am. Ind./AK Nat.	3	0.8	4	1.2	3	0.6	4	2.2	5	1.8	7	1.0	0
Asian	18	4.8	22	6.6	31	5.9	9	5.0	13	4.7	40	5.6	4
Black/Af. Am.	15	4.0	32	9.6	40	7.6	7	3.9	26	9.5	47	6.6	5
Nat. Hl/Pac. Isl.	1	0.3	1	0.3	2	0.4	0	0.0	2	0.7	2	0.3	1
2 or more races	2	0.5	4	1.2	3	0.6	3	1.7	2	0.7	6	0.8	0
Subtotal (minor.)	83	22.1	104	31.3	144	27.3	43	23.9	90	32.8	187	26.4	28
Nonres. Alien	8	2.1	9	2.7	15	2.8	2	1.1	10	3.6	17	2.4	0
White/Cauc.	251	66.8	200	60.2	330	62.5	121	67.2	153	55.8	451	63.7	140
Unknown	34	9.0	19	5.7	39	7.4	14	7.8	21	7.7	53	7.5	40
Total	376	53.1	332	46.9	528	74.6	180	25.4	274	38.7	708		208

Transfers

Transfers in	6
Transfers out	28

Tuition and Fees

	Resident	Nonresident
Full-time	$33,630	$33,630
Part-time	$25,380	$25,380
Tuition Guarantee Program	N	

Living Expenses

Estimated living expenses for singles

Living on campus	Living off campus	Living at home
N/A	$24,150	$24,150

BARRY UNIVERSITY DWAYNE O. ANDREAS SCHOOL OF LAW

ABA Approved Since 2002

GPA and LSAT Scores

	Total	Full-Time	Part-Time
# of apps	2,324	2,066	258
# of offers	1,347	1,224	123
# of matrics	267	218	49
75% GPA	3.26	3.27	3.23
Median GPA	2.95	2.96	2.90
25% GPA	2.55	2.55	2.59
75% LSAT	152	152	152
Median LSAT	149	149	149
25% LSAT	147	147	147

Grants and Scholarships (from prior year)

	Total #	Total %	Full-Time #	Full-Time %	Part-Time #	Part-Time %
Total # of students	717		553		164	
Total # receiving grants	529	73.8	404	73.1	125	76.2
Less than 1/2 tuition	468	65.3	359	64.9	109	66.5
Half to full tuition	61	8.5	45	8.1	16	9.8
Full tuition	0	0.0	0	0.0	0	0.0
More than full tuition	0	0.0	0	0.0	0	0.0
Median grant amount			$8,000		$6,000	

Informational and Library Resources

Total amount spent on library materials	$1,147,607
Study seating capacity inside the library	336
# of full-time equivalent professional librarians	6
Hours per week library is open	106
# of open, wired connections available to students	0
# of networked computers available for use by students	49
Has wireless network?	Y
Requires computer?	N

JD Attrition (from prior year)

	Academic #	Other #	Total #	Total %
1st year	23	32	55	21.1
2nd year	4	2	6	3.0
3rd year	3	0	3	1.4
4th year	0	0	0	0.0

Employment (9 months after graduation)

For up-to-date employment data, go to employmentsummary.abaquestionnaire.org on the ABA website.

Bar Passage Rates

First-time takers	209	Reporting %	92.34
Average school %	73.58	Average state %	77.63
Average pass difference	−4.05		

Jurisdiction	Takers	Passers	Pass %	State %	Diff %
Florida	193	142	73.58	77.63	−4.05

BARRY UNIVERSITY DWAYNE O. ANDREAS SCHOOL OF LAW

6441 East Colonial Drive
Orlando, FL 32807
Phone: 321.206.5600
E-mail: krupert@mail.barry.edu; Website: www.barry.edu/law

A Growing Presence in Higher Education

Founded in early 1993, the University of Orlando School of Law admitted its first class in 1995. In March of 1999, the School of Law became a part of Barry University, a Catholic international university located in Miami Shores, Florida. The affiliation is an extremely positive one, since both administrations have the same focus—to offer quality academics grounded in a strong ethical foundation with the goal of preparing qualified, competent practicing attorneys.

The School of Law is situated on a charming 20-acre campus in East Orlando, about 15 minutes from downtown. The School of Law facilities include a two-story Law Center building, an Administration and Moot Court building, a classroom and faculty office building, a three-story law library, and a new three-story Legal Advocacy Center.

The Barry Law mission guides everything the law school does, from awarding and maintaining scholarships to arranging mentors to providing career service, academic success guidance, and bar prep programs. The School of Law is proud of the quality education provided, with an emphasis on social justice and a spiritual dimension, all within a caring environment. Candidates who choose to study at Barry Law will enjoy the benefits of a mission-centered university where students get the attention they need to succeed.

The Perfect Venue for Your Legal Education

Central Florida is one of the fastest growing areas in the country. A host of attractions bring millions of visitors to central Florida each year. Just an hour away are the Kennedy Space Center and the beaches of the Atlantic.

Orlando is a major commercial center; many national corporations have headquarters in the city. The area is fast becoming a television and motion picture production center.

Central Florida provides a wealth of first-hand exposure to the practice of corporate and entertainment law, as well as juvenile and criminal law. The Advisory Board is composed of many prominent central Florida attorneys, judges, government officials, and others in the community. Their community affiliations enhance the networking and career opportunities available to Barry's students.

Central Florida enjoys a year-round subtropical climate and offers a wide range of cultural and recreational activities. Accommodations in the immediate area include fully furnished or unfurnished apartments as well as a wide range of single-family dwellings. Orlando has a large number of hotels and executive lodges that offer reduced rates on a weekly or monthly basis.

Orlando is the ideal venue to pursue your legal education.

Mission and Goals of the School of Law

Barry University School of Law seeks to offer a quality legal education in a caring environment that will enable its graduates to apply the skills and knowledge they have acquired to their own personal development, and to the good of society, through the competent and ethical practice of law. The School of Law seeks to provide a learning environment that challenges students to accept intellectual, personal, ethical, spiritual, and social responsibilities. The

school commits itself to assuring a religious dimension in an atmosphere of religious freedom and to providing community service.

An Overview

The School of Law teaches students to become responsible lawyers, trained to assume an active role in the legal community. Students are trained to act in strict accord with the highest ethical standards and to exercise their professional skills competently, with sensitivity to the needs and concerns of their clients.

The School of Law allows students to begin in both the Fall and Spring semesters. The School of Law offers a three-year daytime program structured for full-time students. The School of Law also offers a four-year extended studies program in the evening to accommodate working adults or anyone who is unable to pursue full-time study. The part-time program is available only to those students who begin in the fall semester.

Students at the School of Law have many opportunities to experience the "law-in-action" concept, both in the classroom and through practical application. The law school offers a collegial student/professor relationship indicative of legal education at its best.

Through the in-house Children and Families Clinic, Barry students gain solid practical experience working on actual cases involving disadvantaged children in need of legal services. The School of Law also offers an Immigration Clinic and the Earth Justice Clinic, which focuses on environmental law. Additionally, Barry Law offers a wealth of externship opportunities that allow students to further develop their skills as emerging attorneys while working in various venues. Externship placement currently includes opportunities in the following areas: civil government, civil poverty, judicial, mediation, public defender, and state attorney.

Juris Doctor

The School of Law offers the Juris Doctor (JD) degree. All students in the program must complete 90 semester hours of study in areas that are essential to the understanding and practice of law. Students must complete required courses in subjects that provide a common core of understanding in the law. Students may choose from a wide variety of electives to meet the remaining requirements necessary for graduation.

Scholarship Program

The School of Law proudly offers a merit-based scholarship program. Generally, between 80 and 90 percent of the entering class receives a Barry Law scholarship between $1,000 and $23,000. Admitted candidates are automatically considered for scholarships and do not need to complete any additional forms. If a scholarship is offered to a candidate, notice will be sent with the acceptance letter.

Scholarships are offered for three years for full-time students and four years for part-time students. The law GPA required to maintain an institutional scholarship ranges from 2.6 to 2.8. The majority of enrolled students are able to meet the fair and reasonable renewal requirements; for those who do not meet the law GPA, the scholarship can be prorated in some situations and then adjusted to initial levels once the requisite law GPA is achieved. Contact the financial aid office with more questions in this regard.

Barry Law also offers a Scholarship Bonus Program to second- and third-year students. Students who rank in the top 10 percent and hold at least a 3.2 grade-point average after the first and second year of law school are offered a 75 percent scholarship. What great motivation to rank in the top 10 percent, among other obvious reasons!

Program Objective

The School of Law combines traditional and innovative teaching methods to provide a dynamic, professional program. The JD curriculum is designed to develop students' analytical ability, communication skills, and understanding of the codes of professional responsibility and ethics that are central to the practice of law. The faculty utilizes a variety of teaching methods, including simulations and role-playing.

Seminars and advanced courses in the second and third year of study provide close interaction with faculty.

Barry Law emphasizes research and writing proficiency from the first day of class. Armed with a strong foundation in research and writing, Barry Law students gain an advantage in the legal marketplace.

Graduation Requirements

To be eligible to receive the degree of JD, a student must (1) complete 90 academic credits of instruction with a cumulative grade-point average of 2.0 or above, (2) earn a cumulative grade-point average of 1.8 for all required courses and a passing grade in each of the required courses, (3) successfully complete the writing requirement, (4) complete a minimum of 60 out of 90 academic credits in residence at Barry University School of Law, (5) successfully complete the pro bono requirement, (6) satisfy all financial obligations to Barry University, and (7) be approved by the faculty for graduation.

APPLICANT PROFILE

Barry University Dwayne O. Andreas School of Law

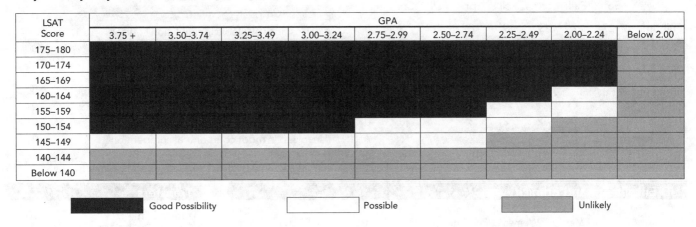

LSAT Score	GPA								
	3.75 +	3.50–3.74	3.25–3.49	3.00–3.24	2.75–2.99	2.50–2.74	2.25–2.49	2.00–2.24	Below 2.00
175–180									
170–174									
165–169									
160–164									
155–159									
150–154									
145–149									
140–144									
Below 140									

■ Good Possibility   □ Possible   ▨ Unlikely

BAYLOR UNIVERSITY SCHOOL OF LAW

1114 South University Parks Drive, One Bear Place #97288
Waco, TX 76798-7288
Phone: 254.710.2529; Fax: 254.710.2316
E-mail: BaylorLaw@baylor.edu; Website: www.baylor.edu/law

ABA
Approved
Since
1931

The Basics

Type of school	Private
Term	Quarter
Application deadline	11/1 2/1 3/1
Application fee	$40
Financial aid deadline	2/1
Can first year start other than fall?	Yes
Student to faculty ratio	13.9 to 1
# of housing spaces available restricted to law students	
graduate housing for which law students are eligible	48

Faculty and Administrators

	Total		Men		Women		Minorities	
	Spr	Fall	Spr	Fall	Spr	Fall	Spr	Fall
Full-time	27	27	19	19	8	8	3	3
Other full-time	0	1	0	1	0	0	0	0
Deans, librarians, & others who teach	5	5	2	2	3	3	0	0
Part-time	37	18	30	15	7	3	3	1
Total	69	51	51	37	18	14	6	4

JD Enrollment and Ethnicity

	Men		Women		Full-Time		Part-Time		1st-Year		Total		JD Degs. Awd.
	#	%	#	%	#	%	#	%	#	%	#	%	
All Hispanics	10	4.7	15	6.5	24	5.5	1	14.3	7	4.7	25	5.7	7
Am. Ind./AK Nat.	0	0.0	1	0.4	1	0.2	0	0.0	0	0.0	1	0.2	2
Asian	9	4.2	11	4.8	20	4.6	0	0.0	4	2.7	20	4.5	18
Black/Af. Am.	5	2.4	3	1.3	7	1.6	1	14.3	2	1.3	8	1.8	4
Nat. HI/Pac. Isl.	0	0.0	0	0.0	0	0.0	0	0.0	0	0.0	0	0.0	3
2 or more races	11	5.2	13	5.7	24	5.5	0	0.0	7	4.7	24	5.4	3
Subtotal (minor.)	35	16.5	43	18.7	76	17.5	2	28.6	20	13.3	78	17.6	37
Nonres. Alien	3	1.4	3	1.3	6	1.4	0	0.0	2	1.3	6	1.4	2
White/Cauc.	172	81.1	184	80.0	351	80.7	5	71.4	127	84.7	356	80.5	119
Unknown	2	0.9	0	0.0	2	0.5	0	0.0	1	0.7	2	0.5	0
Total	212	48.0	230	52.0	435	98.4	7	1.6	150	33.9	442		158

Curriculum

	Full-Time	Part-Time
Typical first-year section size	55	0
Is there typically a "small section" of the first-year class, other than Legal Writing, taught by full-time faculty	Yes	No
If yes, typical size offered last year	46	
# of classroom course titles beyond first-year curriculum	90	

# of upper division courses, excluding seminars, with an enrollment:		
	Under 25	93
	25–49	36
	50–74	24
	75–99	8
	100+	0

# of seminars		9
# of seminar positions available		103
# of seminar positions filled	103	0
# of positions available in simulation courses		1,194
# of simulation positions filled	1,194	0
# of positions available in faculty supervised clinical courses		5
# of faculty supervised clinical positions filled	5	0
# involved in field placements	129	0
# involved in law journals	83	0
# involved in moot court or trial competitions	71	0
# of credit hours required to graduate		126

Transfers

Transfers in	0
Transfers out	3

Tuition and Fees

	Resident	Nonresident
Full-time	$43,573	$43,573
Part-time		
Tuition Guarantee Program		N

Living Expenses

Estimated living expenses for singles

Living on campus	Living off campus	Living at home
$20,544	$17,460	$5,550

BAYLOR UNIVERSITY SCHOOL OF LAW

ABA Approved Since 1931

GPA and LSAT Scores

	Total	Full-Time	Part-Time
# of apps	5,257	5,257	0
# of offers	807	807	0
# of matrics	142	142	0
75% GPA	3.88	3.88	0.00
Median GPA	3.69	3.69	0.00
25% GPA	3.37	3.37	0.00
75% LSAT	163	163	0
Median LSAT	162	162	0
25% LSAT	159	159	0

Grants and Scholarships (from prior year)

	Total #	Total %	Full-Time #	Full-Time %	Part-Time #	Part-Time %
Total # of students	476		466		10	
Total # receiving grants	352	73.9	352	75.5	0	0.0
Less than 1/2 tuition	147	30.9	147	31.5	0	0.0
Half to full tuition	143	30.0	143	30.7	0	0.0
Full tuition	9	1.9	9	1.9	0	0.0
More than full tuition	53	11.1	53	11.4	0	0.0
Median grant amount			$22,185		$0	

Informational and Library Resources

Total amount spent on library materials	$1,350,739
Study seating capacity inside the library	279
# of full-time equivalent professional librarians	3
Hours per week library is open	108
# of open, wired connections available to students	783
# of networked computers available for use by students	44
Has wireless network?	Y
Requires computer?	N

JD Attrition (from prior year)

	Academic #	Other #	Total #	Total %
1st year	0	5	5	2.7
2nd year	0	9	9	5.6
3rd year	0	0	0	0.0
4th year	0	0	0	0.0

Employment (9 months after graduation)

For up-to-date employment data, go to employmentsummary.abaquestionnaire.org on the ABA website.

Bar Passage Rates

First-time takers	156	Reporting %	98.72
Average school %	94.16	Average state %	82.68
Average pass difference	11.48		

Jurisdiction	Takers	Passers	Pass %	State %	Diff %
Texas	154	145	94.16	82.68	11.48

BAYLOR UNIVERSITY SCHOOL OF LAW

1114 South University Parks Drive, One Bear Place #97288
Waco, TX 76798-7288
Phone: 254.710.2529; Fax: 254.710.2316
E-mail: BaylorLaw@baylor.edu; Website: www.baylor.edu/law

Introduction

Baylor University School of Law is a private, ABA-approved law school and is a member of the Association of American Law Schools. Formally organized in 1857, Baylor Law School is the oldest law school in Texas and is located on the campus of Baylor University in Waco, Texas. Waco is located in central Texas, has a total area population of over 220,000, and offers a diverse and rich array of cultural and recreational opportunities, as well as very moderate living costs.

Baylor Law School stands at the forefront of practice-oriented law schools nationally. Baylor is clear about its mission—to equip students upon graduation to practice law effectively and ethically. Students are trained and mentored in all facets of law, including theoretical analysis, practical application, legal writing, advocacy, professional responsibility, and negotiation and counseling skills.

Enrollment/Diversity

Baylor Law School is small by choice, with entering classes of approximately 60 students in the spring, 30 in the summer, and 75 in the fall. Baylor Law School has a target total student population of 420. We keep our program small because we are interested in producing quality, not quantity.

Baylor Law School is deeply committed to enrolling classes that are rich in diversity. Indeed, diversity is an important element of our educational mission. The total minority enrollment in the law school for the fall 2011 term was nearly 20 percent and the total female population was over 50 percent. The student body represents over 35 states among its population. While the Law School Admission Test (LSAT) score and undergraduate grade-point average are strong indicators for academic ability, Baylor is committed to considering carefully all factors of every applicant's application file, including socioeconomic disadvantage, bilingual language skills, work experience, community involvement, leadership roles, and communication skills. These factors enable us to enroll classes that are well qualified and especially distinctive.

Faculty

Baylor Law School is committed to providing its students with a classroom and courtroom experience that will prepare them fully for practice. Faculty members, committed to the equally important missions of teaching and scholarship, hold degrees from law schools and universities throughout the nation and include former law clerks for various appellate courts throughout the nation.

Faculty members are experts in their areas and have substantial practical experience. They produce a significant amount of legal scholarship, which results in their demand as speakers at legal institutes and civic functions. One of the distinctive features of the faculty is that professors maintain unrestricted hours for student consultation. Every professor is available for lending advice and guidance in all academic, professional, and other matters of concern to students.

Facilities and Technology

The Sheila and Walter Umphrey Law Center, home to Baylor Law School, is one of the finest law school facilities in the nation. At every stage of the design of the Law Center, the most important goal was to put teaching first. The building houses every facility a modern law school requires: classrooms that are unsurpassed as teaching facilities; an advocacy suite, including state-of-the-art courtrooms that provide the optimum environment for advocacy training—Baylor's centerpiece of excellence; a large, two-story appellate advocacy courtroom/classroom; a library with comfortable study and seating space in several impressive reading rooms; a student lounge and patio overlooking the Brazos River; and faculty offices that support faculty mentoring, which is the hallmark of our program.

The Law Center is ready for the twenty-first century, with wireless connectivity throughout, data ports at every seat, access to the library's online database, and full access to LexisNexis and Westlaw databases. The law school uses a sophisticated course-management system that allows the faculty to post assignments, syllabi, and course announcements, and provides discussion boards.

Trial Advocacy Program

Procedure is the tool of the trial lawyer, and the bedrock of Baylor Law School's nationally ranked advocacy program is Practice Court—an ultra-intensive study of civil procedure. In addition to procedural law, students will learn the art of trial advocacy in a rigorous required six-month program of skills training during the third year of law school. In Practice Court, students try lawsuits from beginning to end. Most importantly, students learn how to be self-assured, poised, and confident in any practice area.

Baylor Law School has a long record of successfully competing at the national and regional levels in both moot court and mock trial interscholastic competitions. In fact, because of its standing as one of the top advocacy programs in the nation, Baylor Law School is consistently invited to the prestigious Tournament of Champions. Baylor Law School is also proud to host its own elite invitational trial advocacy competition, the National Top Gun Mock Trial Competition, which includes the top student advocates from other nationally recognized programs.

Curriculum and Special Programs

The required curriculum is structured to provide a logical progression for legal study from fundamental legal doctrine in first-year courses to increasingly more sophisticated and complex second- and third-year courses. The challenging curriculum, along with providing students the opportunity to perform specialized lawyering tasks under the direct supervision of accomplished lawyers, also prepares them for the rigors of any type of modern legal practice. Additionally, students have the opportunity to complete a more concentrated course of study and training in eight areas of interest: general civil litigation, business litigation, business transactions, criminal practice, estate planning, real estate and natural resources, administrative practice, and intellectual property. There are also three joint degrees: JD/MBA, JD/MTax, and JD/MPPA.

Baylor Law School views the legal profession as a service endeavor. As such, Baylor Law School was honored to receive the 2010 Commitment to Service Award from the Texas Access to Justice Commission in recognition of the school's commitment to service.

Scholarships and Financial Aid

Baylor Law School has an extraordinarily generous scholarship program. Scholarships are awarded to entering students based primarily on undergraduate GPA and LSAT scores. These scholarships are automatically awarded to students who qualify. Scholarship awards generally range from partial to full tuition. The law school also participates in all nationally recognized financial aid programs.

Admission

Baylor Law School has three entering classes—spring (February), summer (May), and fall (August)—with completely separate application processes. Each class has far more applications than seats available; however, admission to the spring or summer classes is slightly less competitive than admission to the fall class.

The admissions process considers each application in its entirety and considers many factors beyond test scores and undergraduate GPA. Such factors include employment experience, demonstrated leadership potential, cocurricular and extracurricular activities, ethnicity, academic performance trends, undergraduate major, caliber of undergraduate school, life experience, circumstances of particular disadvantage, and any other relevant information submitted by the applicant. Any factors the applicant would like to be taken into consideration should be addressed in a personal statement.

Student Life

Students will find a stimulating variety of enjoyable student activities and organizations that will enhance their legal education. Students can compete interscholastically on Baylor Law School's nationally recognized mock trial and moot court teams. Students can hone their writing and legal scholarship abilities by being a member of the *Baylor Law Review*, which is a legal periodical published quarterly by the students under the supervision of faculty. Baylor Law School also offers a wide array of special-interest student organizations focused on particular areas of law.

Career Development and Bar Passage

The Career Development Office is committed year-round to providing students with the support and resources they need in pursuing their chosen career paths. Shortly after graduation, approximately 90 percent of our 2011 graduates seeking employment were employed or enrolled in graduate-degree programs. Baylor Law School graduates find positions throughout the nation in private practice in large and small firms, government agencies, judicial clerkships, public interest organizations, and public and private corporations.

The Career Development Office provides extensive one-on-one training on job-search techniques, interview skills, job strategies, and résumé- and cover-letter-writing techniques. The office coordinates an on-campus interview program and posts job listings from employers around the country. The office also hosts regular seminars to foster professional development for students.

Our record of success on the Texas Bar exam is unsurpassed by any other Texas law school. Fourteen out of the last twenty-two times, Baylor Law School has had the highest bar passage rate on the Texas Bar exam. In July 2011, 95.88 percent of Baylor graduates passed the Texas Bar exam the first time. The overall state pass rate was 88.36 percent. Graduates taking other state bar exams have been exceptionally successful as well.

APPLICANT PROFILE

Baylor University School of Law
This grid includes only fall 2011 applicants who earned 120–180 LSAT scores under standard administrations.

LSAT Score	GPA 3.75 +		3.50–3.74		3.25–3.49		3.00–3.24		2.75–2.99		2.50–2.74		2.25–2.49		2.00–2.24		Below 2.00		No GPA		Total	
	Apps	Adm	Apps	Adm	Apps	Adm	Apps	Adm	Apps	Adm	Apps	Adm	Apps	Adm	Apps	Adm	Apps	Adm	Apps	Adm	Apps	Adm
175–180	1	1	0	0	1	1	1	1	3	0	2	0	0	0	0	0	0	0	0	0	8	3
170–174	17	17	9	9	11	8	17	3	4	0	1	0	3	0	2	0	0	0	1	1	65	38
165–169	62	62	75	72	57	49	55	10	27	3	14	0	4	0	2	0	0	0	4	0	300	196
160–164	142	97	171	90	150	67	114	27	53	8	30	0	13	0	7	0	0	0	6	1	686	290
155–159	173	6	246	4	252	0	184	0	126	0	49	0	19	0	11	0	1	0	9	0	1070	10
150–154	59	0	93	0	118	0	110	0	68	0	33	0	23	0	6	0	2	0	7	0	519	0
145–149	14	0	54	0	44	0	47	0	42	0	22	0	12	0	2	0	1	0	8	0	246	0
140–144	7	0	20	0	22	0	36	0	24	0	22	0	12	0	5	0	2	0	6	0	156	0
135–139	1	0	2	0	2	0	10	0	15	0	8	0	6	0	1	0	1	0	2	0	48	0
130–134	2	0	1	0	1	0	4	0	4	0	3	0	1	0	4	0	1	0	2	0	23	0
125–129	0	0	0	0	0	0	1	0	2	0	2	0	1	0	0	0	1	0	0	0	7	0
120–124	0	0	0	0	1	0	0	0	0	0	0	0	0	0	0	0	0	0	0	0	1	0
Total	478	183	671	175	659	125	579	41	368	11	186	0	94	0	40	0	9	0	45	2	3129	537

Apps = Number of Applicants
Adm = Number Admitted
Reflects 100% of the total fall 2011 applicant pool; highest LSAT data reported.

BOSTON COLLEGE LAW SCHOOL

Office of Admissions, 885 Centre Street
Newton, MA 02459
Phone: 617.552.4351; Fax: 617.552.2917
E-mail: bclawadm@bc.edu; Website: www.bc.edu/law

The Basics

Type of school	Private
Term	Semester
Application deadline	3/1
Application fee	$75
Financial aid deadline	3/15
Can first year start other than fall?	No
Student to faculty ratio	12.8 to 1
# of housing spaces available restricted to law students	
graduate housing for which law students are eligible	32

Faculty and Administrators

	Total		Men		Women		Minorities	
	Spr	Fall	Spr	Fall	Spr	Fall	Spr	Fall
Full-time	50	52	29	31	21	21	10	9
Other full-time	1	0	1	0	0	0	0	0
Deans, librarians, & others who teach	13	12	4	4	9	8	2	3
Part-time	37	38	27	32	10	6	1	1
Total	101	102	61	67	40	35	13	13

JD Enrollment and Ethnicity

	Men		Women		Full-Time		Part-Time		1st-Year		Total		JD Degs. Awd.
	#	%	#	%	#	%	#	%	#	%	#	%	
All Hispanics	30	7.2	25	6.8	55	7.0	0	0.0	18	6.7	55	7.0	11
Am. Ind./AK Nat.	2	0.5	1	0.3	3	0.4	0	0.0	0	0.0	3	0.4	1
Asian	29	6.9	45	12.3	74	9.5	0	0.0	23	8.6	74	9.4	36
Black/Af. Am.	10	2.4	17	4.7	27	3.5	0	0.0	6	2.2	27	3.4	12
Nat. HI/Pac. Isl.	0	0.0	0	0.0	0	0.0	0	0.0	0	0.0	0	0.0	0
2 or more races	7	1.7	7	1.9	14	1.8	0	0.0	8	3.0	14	1.8	1
Subtotal (minor.)	78	18.6	95	26.0	173	22.1	0	0.0	55	20.4	173	22.1	61
Nonres. Alien	6	1.4	5	1.4	11	1.4	0	0.0	5	1.9	11	1.4	6
White/Cauc.	292	69.7	210	57.5	500	63.9	2	100.0	170	63.2	502	64.0	201
Unknown	43	10.3	55	15.1	98	12.5	0	0.0	40	14.9	98	12.5	17
Total	419	53.4	365	46.6	782	99.7	2	0.3	269	34.3	784		285

Curriculum

	Full-Time	Part-Time
Typical first-year section size	88	0
Is there typically a "small section" of the first-year class, other than Legal Writing, taught by full-time faculty	Yes	No
If yes, typical size offered last year	30	
# of classroom course titles beyond first-year curriculum	162	

# of upper division courses, excluding seminars, with an enrollment:	Under 25	39
	25–49	32
	50–74	8
	75–99	10
	100+	2

# of seminars	79	
# of seminar positions available	1,172	
# of seminar positions filled	633	0
# of positions available in simulation courses	632	
# of simulation positions filled	501	0
# of positions available in faculty supervised clinical courses	135	
# of faculty supervised clinical positions filled	117	0
# involved in field placements	87	0
# involved in law journals	150	0
# involved in moot court or trial competitions	47	0
# of credit hours required to graduate	85	

Transfers

Transfers in	15
Transfers out	8

Tuition and Fees

	Resident	Nonresident
Full-time	$41,818	$41,818
Part-time		
Tuition Guarantee Program		N

Living Expenses

Estimated living expenses for singles

Living on campus	Living off campus	Living at home
N/A	$18,690	N/A

BOSTON COLLEGE LAW SCHOOL

ABA Approved Since 1932

GPA and LSAT Scores

	Total	Full-Time	Part-Time
# of apps	5,685	5,685	0
# of offers	1,366	1,366	0
# of matrics	268	268	0
75% GPA	3.77	3.77	0.00
Median GPA	3.66	3.66	0.00
25% GPA	3.50	3.50	0.00
75% LSAT	166	166	0
Median LSAT	165	165	0
25% LSAT	162	162	0

Grants and Scholarships (from prior year)

	Total #	Total %	Full-Time #	Full-Time %	Part-Time #	Part-Time %
Total # of students	797		796		1	
Total # receiving grants	417	52.3	417	52.4	0	0.0
Less than 1/2 tuition	275	34.5	275	34.5	0	0.0
Half to full tuition	133	16.7	133	16.7	0	0.0
Full tuition	7	0.9	7	0.9	0	0.0
More than full tuition	2	0.3	2	0.3	0	0.0
Median grant amount			$18,000		$0	

Informational and Library Resources

Total amount spent on library materials	$1,519,890
Study seating capacity inside the library	673
# of full-time equivalent professional librarians	10
Hours per week library is open	106
# of open, wired connections available to students	1,084
# of networked computers available for use by students	139
Has wireless network?	Y
Requires computer?	N

JD Attrition (from prior year)

	Academic #	Other #	Total #	Total %
1st year	0	15	15	5.7
2nd year	0	1	1	0.4
3rd year	0	0	0	0.0
4th year	0	0	0	0.0

Employment (9 months after graduation)

For up-to-date employment data, go to employmentsummary.abaquestionnaire.org on the ABA website.

Bar Passage Rates

First-time takers	257	Reporting %	75.88
Average school %	95.89	Average state %	88.48
Average pass difference	7.41		

Jurisdiction	Takers	Passers	Pass %	State %	Diff %
Massachusetts	146	140	95.89	89.67	6.22
New York	49	47	95.92	84.92	11.00

BOSTON COLLEGE LAW SCHOOL

Office of Admissions, 885 Centre Street
Newton, MA 02459
Phone: 617.552.4351; Fax: 617.552.2917
E-mail: bclawadm@bc.edu; Website: www.bc.edu/law

Introduction

Since its founding in 1929, Boston College Law School has earned a national reputation for educational excellence and the highest standards of professionalism while fostering a unique spirit of community among its students, faculty, and staff. The school's Jesuit heritage means it has a special focus on justice and the ethical practice of law, while supporting the development of the whole person. The faculty is highly focused on both teaching and mentoring, building upon a student's core strengths in the classroom and beyond.

The school works hard to provide the building blocks of any successful legal career with a mixture of theory and skills-based learning opportunities. The diverse curriculum is designed to help students develop the framework needed to adapt successfully to changes in society and the legal profession, and the school's nationally recognized research and writing, advocacy, and clinical programs, as well as unique externships and dual-degree programs, help prepare new lawyers for the actual, real-world practice of law. During their job search, they have access to one of the strongest and most loyal alumni associations in the country for networking and mentoring. BC Law graduates often refer to their time in law school as some of the best years of their lives, and their fondness for the school shows in their enthusiasm and support.

Boston College Law School is located on an attractive 40-acre campus in Newton, Massachusetts, just minutes from downtown Boston. It is fully accredited and has a chapter of the Order of the Coif, the prestigious national law school honorary society.

Library and Physical Facilities

The BC Law campus is an intriguing mix of old-style elegance and new-world innovation—a testament to the power of technology, engineering, and design. Students can connect to the network from anywhere. Data ports are available from every library carrel, as well as every classroom seat in the East Wing; wireless technology is also available anywhere in the library and in every classroom. The library encourages individual or group study, with its desk and lounge areas, computer centers, audiovisual resource rooms, and private study rooms. With its soaring atrium entry and light-filled spaces, the East Wing includes classrooms and faculty offices, administrative offices for a career services center and a career resources library, two conference rooms, and the John J. and Mary Daly Curtin Public Interest Center (a suite of offices for student groups working on public service projects). The East Wing's brick exterior complements the law library and the Stuart House administration building, as well as the Barat House alumni and development building. The three buildings form an attractive courtyard for outdoor use by the Law School community. All academic, administrative, library, and service facilities are accessible to physically challenged persons.

Curriculum

The faculty of Boston College Law School strongly believe in the importance of a general legal education designed to enable graduates to adapt to the changing demands of law practice, supported by a strong skills-based approach that gives students real-world experience in the practice of law.

Areas of particular focus include international law, constitutional law, business law, dispute resolution, immigration law, environmental law, criminal law, family law, tax law, intellectual property law, and clinical programs.

In the first year, all students take traditional courses, including Civil Procedure, Constitutional Law, Contracts, Property Law, Criminal Law, and Torts. In addition, an intensive, two-semester Legal Reasoning, Research, and Writing course is required. In the spring semester, students are allowed to take one three-credit elective. Over 200 courses are offered in the second and third years.

Externships

The Semester in Practice program offers individually designed placement with judges, government agencies, public interest organizations, and law firms in the greater Boston area. The International Human Rights semester in practice offers a unique opportunity to work at an international human rights organization such as the International Criminal Court, the Special Tribunal for Cambodia, the Inter-American Court of Human Rights, the Jesuit Refugee Service, and internationally oriented NGOs in the US. The course is designed to provide students with real-world experience and critical insight into international legal institutions, and to prepare them for international legal practice, with special emphasis on human rights. The Attorney General Program provides an intensive full-year clinical experience in the Government Bureau of the Massachusetts Office of the Attorney General. The Judicial Process course includes placement with a specific superior court justice. The London Program has both academic and experiential components. The program provides students with a critical insight into comparative legal institutions with special emphasis on international regulatory process, whether in environmental or securities regulation, antitrust, intellectual property, or human rights.

Clinical Programs

The Law School is committed to making clinical experiences available to all students who desire them. The Boston College Legal Assistance Bureau (LAB) was one of the first of its kind in the country when it was founded in 1968 and remains a model for many others across the country. At LAB, students assume responsibility for representation of indigent clients through the Civil Litigation, Housing, and Community Enterprise clinics.

Students in the Criminal Justice Clinic prosecute or defend criminal cases in state court. The Judge and Community Courts class examines the interaction between the local court and the community it serves. In Juvenile Rights Advocacy, students advocate for troubled youth and work toward juvenile justice policy reform. In the Immigration Law Clinic, students advise clients and work on administrative and appellate litigation under the supervision of practicing attorneys.

Extracurricular and Cocurricular Activities

Selected students may participate in the following writing programs: *Boston College Law Review, Boston College Environmental Affairs Law Review, Boston College International and Comparative Law Review, Boston College Journal of Law and Social Justice*, and the *Uniform Commercial Code Reporter-Digest.*

Boston College Law School supports over a dozen different internal competitions, including negotiation, client counseling, moot court, and mock trial. In addition, selected students may compete in national and international moot court competitions, which are judged by faculty, state and federal judges, and practicing attorneys. These competitions allow students to enhance negotiation, counseling, and oral advocacy skills. BC Law students consistently outperform their peers. Teams have won a number of national competitions in recent years, including the Frederick Douglass, Immigration Law, European Law, and National Religious Freedom competitions.

Expenses and Financial Aid

The Financial Aid Office administers the Law School's scholarship and grant programs, federal and private loan programs, and the Federal Work-Study Program. Scholarship funds are awarded based on both need and merit. Approximately 82 percent of the students currently enrolled are awarded financial aid, and 54 percent of these students receive scholarship assistance as part of their financial aid awards. Scholarships awarded for the first year will be automatically renewed for the second and third years provided that students make satisfactory academic progress. Each year, three entering students are awarded full-tuition Public Service Scholarships because of their demonstrated commitment to public interest law. The Law School also offers a generous Loan Repayment Assistance Program for graduates who pursue careers in legal services, government, and not-for-profit organizations.

Housing

Boston College Law School does not offer on-campus housing for law students. However, the dedicated staff at the Office of Residential Life's Off-Campus Housing Office provide services and resources to all graduate students in their housing search. Each year, the Office of Residential Life hosts a housing fair to help you in your search for housing in the local neighborhoods. The Roommate Finder is an online database for students seeking roommates to occupy a current or new apartment. For more information about housing for law students, please contact the Off-Campus Housing Office at 617.552.3075 or visit their website at www.bc.edu/offcampus.

Career Services

The Office of Career Services is dedicated to helping students make the transition from law student to employed professional.

APPLICANT PROFILE

The Law School considers many factors during the admission process. The admissions committee is one of the largest at the school, and works hard to ensure the acceptance of a well-rounded, diverse group of students, looking beyond test scores and GPA. Academic achievement and LSAT scores are extremely significant, but work and professional experience, college and volunteer activities, the quality of recommendations, and the personal statement also play an important role in this decision-making process. BC Law has no minimum cutoff either

The range of opportunities for graduates spans virtually the entire spectrum of legal practice. Each year more than 1,000 prospective employers solicit applications from Boston College law students. During the 2010–2011 recruitment season, approximately 270 law firms, government agencies, corporations, and public interest organizations from 19 states interviewed Boston College law students as part of on- and off-campus recruiting programs, and an additional 150 employers requested résumé collections. More than 12,000 alumni are presently practicing in 50 states and around the globe.

Student Life

BC Law is a unique community focused upon the development of the whole person, nurturing students not just academically, but socially and spiritually. The school has a vibrant social life with over 40 active student groups, a welcome reception in the fall, dean's office hosted events such as Oktoberfest and Harvest Desserts, dean town meetings, and mentoring programs with faculty and alumni. BC Law has an extensive Academic Support Program. Student groups host many events during the year that bring in outside speakers, including lectures, film screenings, and discussion panels. The Law Students Association and other groups host jointly sponsored events such as Culture Shock, which examines the role of privilege in society, and Diversity Month. The school has an established pro bono program that centralizes activities and encourages students to explore pro bono opportunities, with student participants acknowledged during graduation ceremonies.

Public Interest

BC Law has a long, celebrated tradition of public service. The Office of Career Services has a dedicated director of public interest programs who helps coordinate the school's various efforts (including the Pro Bono Program, Spring Break Trips to Navajo Nation, immigration-focused projects, and areas of need such as New Orleans after Hurricane Katrina), as well as advising students pursuing a career in public service and helping with placement. The school is home to the John and Mary Curtin Center for Public Interest Programs. BC Law's Public Interest Scholarships assist students with tuition, and the school's Francis X. Bellotti Loan Repayment Program (LRAP) assists with debt relief for graduates working in public interest related positions. The Public Interest Law Foundation (PILF) at BC Law also funds a number of summer stipends each year.

for GPA or LSAT. In evaluating the undergraduate record, class rank as well as courses taken are considered. If the LSAT has been taken more than once, all scores are considered in the review process. Boston College Law School strongly encourages applications from qualified minority, disabled, or other students who have been socially, economically, or culturally disadvantaged. Each applicant is evaluated in an effort to ensure that all relevant credentials are considered.

BOSTON UNIVERSITY SCHOOL OF LAW

765 Commonwealth Avenue
Boston, MA 02215
Phone: 617.353.3100; Fax: 617.353.0578
E-mail: bulawadm@bu.edu; Website: www.bu.edu/law

ABA
Approved
Since
1925

The Basics

Type of school	Private
Term	Semester
Application deadline	11/15 3/1
Application fee	$75
Financial aid deadline	3/1
Can first year start other than fall?	No
Student to faculty ratio	12.2 to 1
# of housing spaces available restricted to law students	
graduate housing for which law students are eligible	810

Faculty and Administrators

	Total		Men		Women		Minorities	
	Spr	Fall	Spr	Fall	Spr	Fall	Spr	Fall
Full-time	54	55	31	29	23	26	6	6
Other full-time	4	3	3	3	1	0	0	0
Deans, librarians, & others who teach	7	2	4	1	3	1	0	0
Part-time	97	88	67	63	30	25	10	8
Total	162	148	105	96	57	52	16	14

JD Enrollment and Ethnicity

	Men #	Men %	Women #	Women %	Full-Time #	Full-Time %	Part-Time #	Part-Time %	1st-Year #	1st-Year %	Total #	Total %	JD Degs. Awd.
All Hispanics	33	8.3	34	8.5	67	8.4	0	0.0	19	7.9	67	8.4	27
Am. Ind./AK Nat.	0	0.0	2	0.5	2	0.3	0	0.0	0	0.0	2	0.3	2
Asian	29	7.3	49	12.3	78	9.8	0	0.0	27	11.2	78	9.8	28
Black/Af. Am.	9	2.3	23	5.8	32	4.0	0	0.0	6	2.5	32	4.0	13
Nat. HI/Pac. Isl.	0	0.0	0	0.0	0	0.0	0	0.0	0	0.0	0	0.0	1
2 or more races	8	2.0	18	4.5	26	3.3	0	0.0	11	4.5	26	3.3	3
Subtotal (minor.)	79	19.8	126	31.6	205	25.7	0	0.0	63	26.0	205	25.7	74
Nonres. Alien	13	3.3	16	4.0	29	3.6	0	0.0	8	3.3	29	3.6	7
White/Cauc.	283	70.8	233	58.4	516	64.6	0	0.0	152	62.8	516	64.6	179
Unknown	25	6.3	24	6.0	49	6.1	0	0.0	19	7.9	49	6.1	13
Total	400	50.1	399	49.9	799	100.0	0	0.0	242	30.3	799		273

Curriculum

	Full-Time	Part-Time
Typical first-year section size	89	0
Is there typically a "small section" of the first-year class, other than Legal Writing, taught by full-time faculty	Yes	No
If yes, typical size offered last year	45	
# of classroom course titles beyond first-year curriculum	192	

# of upper division courses, excluding seminars, with an enrollment:	Under 25	105
	25–49	51
	50–74	11
	75–99	4
	100+	2

# of seminars	74	
# of seminar positions available	1,373	
# of seminar positions filled	1,077	0
# of positions available in simulation courses	492	
# of simulation positions filled	424	0
# of positions available in faculty supervised clinical courses	192	
# of faculty supervised clinical positions filled	140	0
# involved in field placements	113	0
# involved in law journals	319	0
# involved in moot court or trial competitions	46	0
# of credit hours required to graduate	84	

Transfers

Transfers in	27
Transfers out	13

Tuition and Fees

	Resident	Nonresident
Full-time	$42,654	$42,654
Part-time		
Tuition Guarantee Program	N	

Living Expenses

Estimated living expenses for singles

Living on campus	Living off campus	Living at home
$17,618	$17,618	$12,430

BOSTON UNIVERSITY SCHOOL OF LAW

ABA Approved Since 1925

GPA and LSAT Scores

	Total	Full-Time	Part-Time
# of apps	7,073	7,073	0
# of offers	1,396	1,396	0
# of matrics	242	242	0
75% GPA	3.78	3.78	0.00
Median GPA	3.72	3.72	0.00
25% GPA	3.50	3.50	0.00
75% LSAT	167	167	0
Median LSAT	167	167	0
25% LSAT	163	163	0

Grants and Scholarships (from prior year)

	Total #	Total %	Full-Time #	Full-Time %	Part-Time #	Part-Time %
Total # of students	822		821		1	
Total # receiving grants	550	66.9	550	67.0	0	0.0
Less than 1/2 tuition	317	38.6	317	38.6	0	0.0
Half to full tuition	216	26.3	216	26.3	0	0.0
Full tuition	6	0.7	6	0.7	0	0.0
More than full tuition	11	1.3	11	1.3	0	0.0
Median grant amount			$15,000		$0	

Informational and Library Resources

Total amount spent on library materials	$1,913,864
Study seating capacity inside the library	600
# of full-time equivalent professional librarians	12
Hours per week library is open	102
# of open, wired connections available to students	0
# of networked computers available for use by students	94
Has wireless network?	Y
Requires computer?	N

JD Attrition (from prior year)

	Academic #	Other #	Total #	Total %
1st year	0	16	16	6.0
2nd year	0	0	0	0.0
3rd year	2	0	2	0.7
4th year	0	0	0	0.0

Employment (9 months after graduation)

For up-to-date employment data, go to employmentsummary.abaquestionnaire.org on the ABA website.

Bar Passage Rates

First-time takers	250	Reporting %	95.60
Average school %	97.08	Average state %	87.46
Average pass difference	9.62		

Jurisdiction	Takers	Passers	Pass %	State %	Diff %
Massachusetts	128	124	96.88	89.67	7.21
New York	111	108	97.30	84.92	12.38

BOSTON UNIVERSITY SCHOOL OF LAW

765 Commonwealth Avenue
Boston, MA 02215
Phone: 617.353.3100; Fax: 617.353.0578
E-mail: bulawadm@bu.edu; Website: www.bu.edu/law

Introduction

Boston University School of Law offers one of the finest legal educations in the nation, attracting students from all over the country and abroad. A pioneer in American legal education, the school was founded in 1872 on the principles that legal education should be open to all men and women of ability without regard to background or beliefs, and that it should balance theory and analysis with practical training. Today, the school's innovative curriculum combines theoretical courses, clinical training, and specialized offerings—including concentrations, dual degrees, and semesters abroad. The full-time faculty of distinguished scholars and teachers ranks among the most productive of the nation's law schools and is known for its superb teaching. The students represent a range of educational backgrounds, ethnicities, races, age groups, and employment histories.

The city of Boston is an exciting place to study law and launch a career. BU Law's location presents students with enormous opportunities. They can gain invaluable experience through the myriad job and internship opportunities that flow from Boston's status as a major business, financial, and legal center. Boston is home to many high-tech and start-up companies, as well as leading institutions in health care, finance, and many other fields. In addition, Boston is a major government center. It is both the state capital and the home of numerous federal institutions such as the Federal Reserve Bank of Boston, making the city a laboratory for clinics, pro bono volunteering, and externships.

Faculty

At BU Law, our faculty members make the difference—to our students, as teachers; to the law, as scholars; and to the local and global community, as advocates. Our students routinely cite the faculty's excellence in teaching as one of the chief virtues of the school. BU Law faculty members come from a range of backgrounds, and include six US Supreme Court clerks and representatives of such diverse intellectual movements as law and economics and feminist legal theory. Twelve faculty members have doctoral degrees in various disciplines, and dozens have extensive experience shaping public policy and representing clients. They have authored texts in key fields, such as securitization, labor and employment, federal courts, contracts, copyright, and administrative law, among others. Impassioned advocates who frequently lend their expertise to pro bono causes—locally, nationally, and internationally—BU Law faculty members take pride in sharing these experiences inside and outside of the classroom.

Curriculum

BU Law offers one of the widest ranges of academic opportunities available at any American law school. At BU Law, students can explore virtually any area of law from among the school's 190 classes and seminars. They can concentrate and focus their studies, if they choose, in any of five important fields—international law, health law, intellectual property law, business organizations and finance law, or litigation and dispute resolution—and thus design a curriculum around courses that prepare them for exciting work in specific areas of interest.

Dual-Degree Programs

Students can pursue any of 14 dual-degree programs, combining law study with graduate coursework in a program that leads to a JD and a master's degree. Those dual degrees include a JD/MA in International Relations, JD/MS in Mass Communications, JD/MA in English, JD/MA in History, JD/MBA, JD/MBA in Health Sector Management, JD/MA in Preservation Studies, JD/MA in Philosophy, and JD/MPH in Public Health. Students interested in tax or banking can earn a combined JD/Master of Laws (LLM) degree in these fields on an accelerated basis. BU Law offers 3 three-year, international dual-degree programs, leading to a JD from Boston University simultaneously with an LLM in European Law from the Université Panthéon-Assas (Paris), an LLM in International and European Business Law from Universidad Pontificia Comillas (Madrid), or an LLM in Asian Legal Studies from the National University of Singapore.

Study Abroad

Students at BU Law can immerse themselves in a foreign legal culture for a semester, studying international and comparative law in one of BU Law's 14 semester-long study-abroad programs. Programs offered in 2012–2013 include Oxford University (United Kingdom); Université Jean Moulin, Lyon III (France); Universidad Pontificia Comillas de Madrid (Spain); Leiden University (the Netherlands); Bucerius Law School, Hamburg (Germany); Université Panthéon-Assas, Paris II (France); University of Florence (Italy); University of Hong Kong (China); Tsinghua University (China); University of Buenos Aires (Argentina); Tel Aviv University (Israel); National University of Singapore (Singapore); University College London (United Kingdom); and the Graduate Institute of International and Development Studies, Geneva (Switzerland).

Clinical Programs

For hands-on practical training, BU Law has long been recognized as having some of the finest clinical offerings in the country, enhanced by an ever-growing collection of externships. Students can gain valuable experience through the Criminal Clinical Program (Prosecution, Adult and Juvenile Defense); the Civil Litigation Program (Housing, Employment, Family, and Disability Clinic; the Asylum and Human Rights Clinic; and the Employment Rights Clinic); various legislative clinics (the Africa i-Parliaments Clinic, and the clinic in American Legislative Practice); the Immigration Detention Clinic; the Human Trafficking Clinic; and the Wrongful Convictions Clinic. For experience beyond the clinics, students can take advantage of BU Law's many Boston-based Externship Programs, or they can go even further afield in the Semester in Practice Program, with established programs in Government Lawyering in Washington, DC; death penalty litigation in Atlanta, Georgia; human rights work in Geneva, Switzerland; and independent placements designed by students and faculty.

Transactional Program

A new transactional training program provides BU Law students with knowledge of substantive business and financial law, as well as the practice skills to deliver informed services to clients. The program provides an integrated skills curriculum, in a sequence of three courses, to train commercial lawyers and corporate dealmakers in drafting, structuring, and negotiating agreements. BU Law students finish their education with a sophisticated understanding of the work of deal lawyers and with skills that make them valuable team members from day one.

Public Interest Programs

BU Law has a long tradition of training public service leaders. The BU Law Career Development and Public Service Office runs an in-house Pro Bono Program and helps provide pathways to public interest employment. While still in school, students have participated in any number of pro bono projects. In 2012, students participated in eight spring break pro bono trips to such locations as New Orleans, Louisiana, to provide necessary civil and criminal legal services as the city continues to rebuild; Harlingen, Texas, to assist with the South Texas Pro Bono Asylum Representation Project; Kansas City, Missouri, to work with the Death Penalty Litigation Clinic; Detroit, Michigan, to provide legal services to the country's poorest urban residents; and Oklahoma City to provide assistance to low-income Native Americans through Oklahoma Indian Legal Services. The Public Interest Project (PIP) provides grants through fundraising efforts to support students working in summer public interest jobs.

Student Life

Students are encouraged to engage in student organizations, extracurricular activities, and community service. BU Law supports six nationally recognized law journals run by students. The Dean hosts lunches and town hall meetings with students to provide updates and solicit feedback. The school frequently organizes brown bag lunches for students with faculty speakers. The Student Government Association (SGA) and the numerous active student organizations work on projects initiated by students. The Live Well, Learn Well program helps law students find ways to maintain healthy lifestyles consistent with their busy lives. The Academic Enhancement Program features workshops on issues such as work/family balance, law school exam-taking strategies, and time and stress management. A comprehensive diversity program features varied cultural events and numerous

speakers on topics of particular interest to diverse communities. Events take place throughout the year and culminate in a multifaceted Diversity Week each spring.

Career Development

The BU Law Office of Career Development and Public Service Office (CDO) is committed to helping each law student see all the possibilities that a BU Law degree affords them. The CDO offers a comprehensive program of services to students and alumni, including personal advising, instructional workshops and events, and print and online resources. Students benefit from the expertise of a diverse range of attorney career advisers, participate in numerous workshops to hone job search skills, and learn strategies for choosing a career that fits the student's interests and talents. Alumni assist students in the Mock Interview Program and the First-Year Mentoring Program, and participate in panel discussions, receptions, and individual advising sessions. BU Law offers an extensive on- and off-campus recruiting program. Our graduates pursue careers throughout the US and around the world in large, midsize, and small law firms; federal, state, and local government; nonprofit organizations; business; and academia. BU Law remains committed to preparing all of its graduates with the substantive knowledge, practical legal skills, networking opportunities, and job search strategies to meet today's challenges in the legal employment market.

Financial Aid

A top-quality legal education is a significant investment, and Boston University School of Law is committed to making the expense manageable. We support our students both through direct and indirect financial assistance and through professional financial aid counseling before, during, and even after your three years of law school. BU Law invests more than three million dollars of scholarship aid in each entering class. Typically, more than 65 percent of our students receive institutional scholarships, averaging about $17,000 per year and ranging from $5,000 to full tuition. Scholarship awards come in categories of merit-based and need-based aid, as well as aid reserved for students with a demonstrated commitment to public service. All scholarships are automatically renewed for the full three years. Our graduates who are employed in government or nonprofit organizations can qualify for up to $10,000 per year through our Loan Repayment Assistance Program.

APPLICANT PROFILE

Each year Boston University School of Law enrolls a class of students characterized by extraordinary academic achievements and diverse life experiences. LSAT scores and undergraduate GPAs are important components of an application, but numbers alone never determine an admissions decision. The Admissions Committee carefully evaluates each applicant's essays, transcripts, letters of

recommendation, and any other information that helps us to understand the applicant's potential. BU Law's founding commitment to diversity, starting in 1872, continues to inform our admissions decisions today. We encourage each applicant to share with us how they might contribute to BU Law's vibrant learning community.

BRIGHAM YOUNG UNIVERSITY—J. REUBEN CLARK LAW SCHOOL

340 JRCB
Provo, UT 84602-8000
Phone: 801.422.4277; Fax: 801.422.0389
E-mail: admissions@law.byu.edu; Website: www.law.byu.edu

ABA
Approved
Since
1974

The Basics

Type of school	Private
Term	Semester
Application deadline	3/1
Application fee	$50
Financial aid deadline	5/1
Can first year start other than fall?	No
Student to faculty ratio	16.0 to 1
# of housing spaces available restricted to law students	
graduate housing for which law students are eligible	

Faculty and Administrators

	Total		Men		Women		Minorities	
	Spr	Fall	Spr	Fall	Spr	Fall	Spr	Fall
Full-time	20	25	12	15	8	10	4	5
Other full-time	0	0	0	0	0	0	0	0
Deans, librarians, & others who teach	18	18	14	14	4	4	1	1
Part-time	40	40	29	29	11	11	2	3
Total	78	83	55	58	23	25	7	9

Curriculum

	Full-Time	Part-Time
Typical first-year section size	75	0
Is there typically a "small section" of the first-year class, other than Legal Writing, taught by full-time faculty	Yes	No
If yes, typical size offered last year	50	
# of classroom course titles beyond first-year curriculum	128	

# of upper division courses, excluding seminars, with an enrollment:	Under 25	69
	25–49	27
	50–74	13
	75–99	5
	100+	1

# of seminars	27	
# of seminar positions available	494	
# of seminar positions filled	253	0
# of positions available in simulation courses	710	
# of simulation positions filled	533	0
# of positions available in faculty supervised clinical courses	0	
# of faculty supervised clinical positions filled	0	0
# involved in field placements	245	0
# involved in law journals	175	0
# involved in moot court or trial competitions	127	0
# of credit hours required to graduate	90	

JD Enrollment and Ethnicity

	Men		Women		Full-Time		Part-Time		1st-Year		Total		JD Degs. Awd.
	#	%	#	%	#	%	#	%	#	%	#	%	
All Hispanics	17	6.1	14	8.5	31	7.2	0	0.0	16	11.0	31	7.0	8
Am. Ind./AK Nat.	5	1.8	0	0.0	5	1.2	0	0.0	3	2.1	5	1.1	1
Asian	5	1.8	13	7.9	15	3.5	3	23.1	6	4.1	18	4.1	10
Black/Af. Am.	2	0.7	3	1.8	4	0.9	1	7.7	3	2.1	5	1.1	4
Nat. Hl/Pac. Isl.	9	3.2	5	3.0	12	2.8	2	15.4	2	1.4	14	3.2	5
2 or more races	0	0.0	0	0.0	0	0.0	0	0.0	0	0.0	0	0.0	0
Subtotal (minor.)	38	13.7	35	21.2	67	15.6	6	46.2	30	20.7	73	16.5	28
Nonres. Alien	2	0.7	3	1.8	5	1.2	0	0.0	3	2.1	5	1.1	1
White/Cauc.	238	85.6	127	77.0	358	83.3	7	53.8	112	77.2	365	82.4	122
Unknown	0	0.0	0	0.0	0	0.0	0	0.0	0	0.0	0	0.0	0
Total	278	62.8	165	37.2	430	97.1	13	2.9	145	32.7	443		151

Transfers

Transfers in	2
Transfers out	1

Tuition and Fees

	Resident	Nonresident
Full-time	$10,600	$21,200
Part-time		
Tuition Guarantee Program		N

Living Expenses

Estimated living expenses for singles

Living on campus	Living off campus	Living at home
$18,752	$18,752	$8,620

BRIGHAM YOUNG UNIVERSITY—J. REUBEN CLARK LAW SCHOOL

ABA
Approved
Since
1974

GPA and LSAT Scores

	Total	Full-Time	Part-Time
# of apps	755	755	0
# of offers	207	207	0
# of matrics	145	145	0
75% GPA	3.87	3.87	0.00
Median GPA	3.74	3.74	0.00
25% GPA	3.51	3.51	0.00
75% LSAT	167	167	0
Median LSAT	163	163	0
25% LSAT	160	160	0

Grants and Scholarships (from prior year)

	Total #	Total %	Full-Time #	Full-Time %	Part-Time #	Part-Time %
Total # of students	444		443		1	
Total # receiving grants	163	36.7	163	36.8	0	0.0
Less than 1/2 tuition	85	19.1	85	19.2	0	0.0
Half to full tuition	25	5.6	25	5.6	0	0.0
Full tuition	49	11.0	49	11.1	0	0.0
More than full tuition	4	0.9	4	0.9	0	0.0
Median grant amount			$5,140		$0	

Informational and Library Resources

Total amount spent on library materials	$1,207,385
Study seating capacity inside the library	906
# of full-time equivalent professional librarians	11
Hours per week library is open	105
# of open, wired connections available to students	535
# of networked computers available for use by students	36
Has wireless network?	Y
Requires computer?	Y

JD Attrition (from prior year)

	Academic #	Other #	Total #	Total %
1st year	1	1	2	1.3
2nd year	0	1	1	0.7
3rd year	0	0	0	0.0
4th year	0	0	0	0.0

Employment (9 months after graduation)

For up-to-date employment data, go to
employmentsummary.abaquestionnaire.org on the ABA website.

Bar Passage Rates

First-time takers	137	Reporting %	70.80
Average school %	91.74	Average state %	85.11
Average pass difference	6.63		

Jurisdiction	Takers	Passers	Pass %	State %	Diff %
Utah	74	70	94.59	89.35	5.24
California	19	15	78.95	71.24	7.71
Nevada	4	4	100.00	72.72	27.28

BRIGHAM YOUNG UNIVERSITY—J. REUBEN CLARK LAW SCHOOL

340 JRCB
Provo, UT 84602-8000
Phone: 801.422.4277; Fax: 801.422.0389
E-mail: admissions@law.byu.edu; Website: www.law.byu.edu

Introduction

Since its founding less than 40 years ago, the J. Reuben Clark Law School at Brigham Young University has been distinguished by the strength of its program and the accomplishments of its graduates. The Law School has produced 13 United States Supreme Court clerkships and has an enviable placement record throughout the country in all branches of the legal profession. The Law School's relatively small entering class size of 150 lends itself to individualized instruction, while the university, with its 30,000 students, provides all the athletic, cultural, and social opportunities that a student may expect from a larger school. The Law School is fully accredited by the American Bar Association, is a member of the Association of American Law Schools, and has a chapter of the Order of the Coif.

Library and Physical Facilities

The Howard W. Hunter Law Library is one of the most technologically advanced law libraries in the world. It houses 475 individual study carrels with full Internet and LAN computer connectivity (hardwired and wireless). Thus, each student in his or her private study space has access to electronic resources that include Westlaw, LexisNexis, and the growing Hunter Law Library Electronic Reserve, which contains archives of past examinations. In convenient locations, printers and scanners are available for students on all library floors. The law library also contains 18 group-study rooms (4 of which are family-support rooms to assist law students who are parents and need to view closed-circuit broadcasts of classes) and spacious casual seating in open areas. Office and research space, along with a conference room for the Law School's four scholarly journals, two advocacy groups, and the Student Bar Association, are also conveniently located. Specialized rooms are dedicated to video viewing, interactive video, microforms, and television hookups. The Rex E. Lee Reading Room and the Law School Conference Center Room provide ample space for special seminars and receptions. The library houses a collection of over 500,000 volumes or volume equivalents. Via interlibrary loan, students have access to many more titles found in the catalogs and collections of over 9,100 other worldwide institutions that, like Hunter Library, subscribe to the Online Computer Library Center (OCLC). A mock trial courtroom with state-of-the-art technology provides a superb training ground for learning trial advocacy skills. An open and spacious student commons area provides students with comfortable seating and a place to dine and have conversations with colleagues.

Faculty and Curriculum

The combination of the small entering class size and our internationally renowned faculty creates unique opportunities for learning. Together, our faculty seek to meet the challenge of making a difference worldwide as they engage in research, publishing, and advocacy. The objective of the Law School's curriculum is to maximize the students' mastery of legal reasoning and other legal skills while teaching the basic substantive rules of law. Approximately 140 courses and seminars are offered each year by a faculty of 28 full-time members and over 50 adjunct faculty members. In addition, the Law School provides opportunities for students to develop practical skills through international and US externships with private law firms, corporations, and agencies, as well as public defenders, legal services, city and county attorneys, judges, attorneys general, and guardians ad litem. Students receive one credit for every 50 hours of work.

The Rex E. Lee Advocacy Program

In addition to knowing the law, lawyers must synthesize complex information, analyze and formulate strategy, predict outcomes, and present information persuasively. The Rex E. Lee Advocacy Program administers a two-semester required course for first-year law students in the essential skills of legal writing, research, analysis, and oral advocacy. Students receive individualized attention during one-on-one conferences with instructors and teaching assistants and in small classes. In the Advocacy Program, students learn and practice the critical skills that bring success in both law school and the profession.

International Center for Law and Religion Studies

The BYU International Center for Law and Religion Studies promotes religious freedom by studying and disseminating the laws, principles, and institutions affecting the interaction of state and religion throughout the world. The center sponsors and participates in symposia and conferences with scholars, government leaders, nongovernment groups, and religious organizations from numerous countries and faith traditions, in an ongoing effort to promote religious liberty for individuals and cooperative relationships between governments and religious organizations. Additionally, the center produces US and internationally based scholarship on law and religion topics. Finally, the center sponsors three important websites (www.iclrs.org, www.religlaw.org, and www.strasbourg consortium.org) dedicated to disseminating in-depth knowledge on law and religion in every country on earth.

The Externship Program

The Law School offers an academic externship program as a capstone experience to students following their first year of law school. This program allows students to work with judges, law firms, corporations, public interest groups, and government organizations throughout the world. During the summer of 2011, over 200 students completed an externship, earning an average of four units of law school credit. Forty-seven of those placements were international, with externships in 25 different countries.

The Academic Success Program

The Academic Success Program (ASP) is designed to help students adjust to and meet the rigorous demands of a legal education. The ASP offers legal skills workshops with personal feedback, individual tutoring, and one-on-one legal writing instruction to all students upon request and by dean's referral.

Cocurricular Programs

The objective of the cocurricular program at the Law School is to make a law review-quality experience available to larger numbers of students. Comparable standards of excellence in research, writing, and editing are offered in six programs: the *Brigham Young University Law Review*, the Board of Advocates Moot Court, Trial Advocacy, the *BYU Journal of Public Law*, the *Brigham Young University Education and Law Journal*, and *International Law and Management Review*.

Career Services

The Career Services Office (CSO) is available to all students and graduates seeking employment. The CSO offers two legal career-planning courses featuring skills training and presentations by practicing attorneys who participate as guest lecturers. The office also publishes a *Professional Development Handbook, Job Hunt Book, Public Service Handbook, Alternative Careers Handbook*, and *Judicial Clerkship Handbook* and maintains a webpage with links for both students and employers. About 98 percent of the graduates who are seeking work accept employment within nine months after graduation, and graduates are placed in all 50 states and a number of foreign countries. The CSO brings firms to campus every year for on-campus interviews and has interviewing events and job fairs in Washington, DC; New York; Southern California; and Nevada.

APPLICANT PROFILE

Brigham Young University—J. Reuben Clark Law School
This grid includes only applicants who earned 120–180 LSAT scores under standard administrations.

LSAT Score	3.75 +		3.50–3.74		3.25–3.49		3.00–3.24		2.75–2.99		2.50–2.74		2.25–2.49		2.00–2.24		Below 2.00		No GPA		Total	
	Apps	Adm	Apps	Adm	Apps	Adm	Apps	Adm	Apps	Adm	Apps	Adm	Apps	Adm	Apps	Adm	Apps	Adm	Apps	Adm	Apps	Adm
175–180	4	3	3	3	1	0	0	0	0	0	0	0	0	0	0	0	0	0	0	0	8	6
170–174	19	16	13	8	0	0	3	2	1	0	2	0	0	0	0	0	0	0	0	0	38	26
165–169	35	32	25	20	21	11	10	5	7	1	3	0	0	0	2	0	0	0	2	0	105	69
160–164	47	37	66	17	40	7	11	2	9	2	3	0	3	0	0	0	0	0	8	1	187	66
155–159	28	12	61	6	53	5	18	0	9	1	3	0	1	0	1	0	0	0	5	1	179	25
150–154	23	4	26	1	29	1	22	1	16	1	6	1	2	0	0	0	0	0	2	0	126	9
145–149	7	1	10	1	19	1	14	1	11	1	8	0	2	0	0	0	0	0	2	0	73	5
140–144	1	0	5	0	5	0	7	0	6	0	3	0	1	0	0	0	1	0	0	0	29	0
135–139	1	0	1	0	2	0	0	0	0	0	1	0	2	0	0	0	0	0	3	0	10	0
130–134	0	0	0	0	0	0	0	0	2	0	2	0	0	0	0	0	0	0	1	0	5	0
125–129	0	0	0	0	0	0	0	0	0	0	1	0	0	0	0	0	0	0	0	0	1	0
120–124	0	0	0	0	0	0	0	0	0	0	0	0	0	0	0	0	0	0	0	0	0	0
Total	165	105	210	56	170	25	85	11	61	6	32	1	11	0	3	0	1	0	23	2	761	206

Apps = Number of Applicants
Adm = Number Admitted
Reflects 100% of the total applicant pool; highest LSAT data reported.

BROOKLYN LAW SCHOOL

250 Joralemon Street
Brooklyn, NY 11201-9846
Phone: 718.780.7906; Fax: 718.780.0395
E-mail: admitq@brooklaw.edu; Website: www.brooklaw.edu

ABA
Approved
Since
1937

The Basics

Type of school	Private
Term	Semester
Application deadline	4/1
Application fee	$0
Financial aid deadline	
Can first year start other than fall?	No
Student to faculty ratio	17.6 to 1
# of housing spaces available restricted to law students	558
graduate housing for which law students are eligible	

Faculty and Administrators

	Total		Men		Women		Minorities	
	Spr	Fall	Spr	Fall	Spr	Fall	Spr	Fall
Full-time	63	66	33	34	30	32	5	6
Other full-time	5	2	2	2	3	0	1	0
Deans, librarians, & others who teach	8	9	2	3	6	6	1	1
Part-time	95	80	67	59	28	21	9	6
Total	171	157	104	98	67	59	16	13

Curriculum

	Full-Time	Part-Time
Typical first-year section size	48	27
Is there typically a "small section" of the first-year class, other than Legal Writing, taught by full-time faculty	Yes	No
If yes, typical size offered last year	41	
# of classroom course titles beyond first-year curriculum	207	

# of upper division courses, excluding seminars, with an enrollment:		
	Under 25	139
	25–49	42
	50–74	19
	75–99	17
	100+	10

# of seminars	86	
# of seminar positions available	1,377	
# of seminar positions filled	1,215	53
# of positions available in simulation courses	1,373	
# of simulation positions filled	981	122
# of positions available in faculty supervised clinical courses	407	
# of faculty supervised clinical positions filled	393	14
# involved in field placements	688	23
# involved in law journals	287	12
# involved in moot court or trial competitions	110	7
# of credit hours required to graduate	86	

JD Enrollment and Ethnicity

	Men		Women		Full-Time		Part-Time		1st-Year		Total		JD Degs. Awd.
	#	%	#	%	#	%	#	%	#	%	#	%	
All Hispanics	37	4.9	43	6.9	73	6.1	7	4.1	26	6.7	80	5.8	31
Am. Ind./AK Nat.	0	0.0	1	0.2	1	0.1	0	0.0	1	0.3	1	0.1	1
Asian	75	9.9	90	14.5	147	12.2	18	10.5	45	11.7	165	12.0	70
Black/Af. Am.	24	3.2	32	5.2	45	3.7	11	6.4	17	4.4	56	4.1	17
Nat. HI/Pac. Isl.	0	0.0	0	0.0	0	0.0	0	0.0	0	0.0	0	0.0	0
2 or more races	16	2.1	19	3.1	30	2.5	5	2.9	12	3.1	35	2.5	10
Subtotal (minor.)	152	20.1	185	29.9	296	24.6	41	23.8	101	26.2	337	24.5	129
Nonres. Alien	4	0.5	7	1.1	10	0.8	1	0.6	7	1.8	11	0.8	2
White/Cauc.	562	74.2	402	64.9	844	70.1	120	69.8	236	61.1	964	70.1	319
Unknown	39	5.2	25	4.0	54	4.5	10	5.8	42	10.9	64	4.7	4
Total	757	55.0	619	45.0	1204	87.5	172	12.5	386	28.1	1376		454

Transfers

Transfers in	33
Transfers out	20

Tuition and Fees

	Resident	Nonresident
Full-time	$48,441	$48,441
Part-time	$36,419	$36,419
Tuition Guarantee Program		N

Living Expenses

Estimated living expenses for singles

Living on campus	Living off campus	Living at home
$24,343	$24,343	$9,428

BROOKLYN LAW SCHOOL

*ABA
Approved
Since
1937*

GPA and LSAT Scores

	Total	Full-Time	Part-Time
# of apps	6,018	5,174	844
# of offers	1,736	1,586	150
# of matrics	390	316	74
75% GPA	3.54	3.55	3.44
Median GPA	3.36	3.38	3.31
25% GPA	3.19	3.20	3.14
75% LSAT	165	165	162
Median LSAT	163	163	159
25% LSAT	160	161	157

Grants and Scholarships (from prior year)

	Total		Full-Time		Part-Time	
	#	%	#	%	#	%
Total # of students	1,461		1,293		168	
Total # receiving grants	1115	76.3	1052	81.4	63	37.5
Less than 1/2 tuition	501	34.3	462	35.7	39	23.2
Half to full tuition	531	36.3	510	39.4	21	12.5
Full tuition	0	0.0	0	0.0	0	0.0
More than full tuition	83	5.7	80	6.2	3	1.8
Median grant amount			$25,432		$11,475	

Informational and Library Resources

Total amount spent on library materials	$1,302,002
Study seating capacity inside the library	665
# of full-time equivalent professional librarians	11
Hours per week library is open	108
# of open, wired connections available to students	1,984
# of networked computers available for use by students	142
Has wireless network?	Y
Requires computer?	N

JD Attrition (from prior year)

	Academic	Other	Total	
	#	#	#	%
1st year	8	30	38	7.9
2nd year	1	0	1	0.2
3rd year	0	0	0	0.0
4th year	0	0	0	0.0

Employment (9 months after graduation)

For up-to-date employment data, go to
employmentsummary.abaquestionnaire.org on the ABA website.

Bar Passage Rates

First-time takers	461	Reporting %	94.36
Average school %	89.20	Average state %	84.92
Average pass difference	4.28		

Jurisdiction	Takers	Passers	Pass %	State %	Diff %
New York	435	388	89.20	84.92	4.28

BROOKLYN LAW SCHOOL

250 Joralemon Street
Brooklyn, NY 11201-9846
Phone: 718.780.7906; Fax: 718.780.0395
E-mail: admitq@brooklaw.edu; Website: www.brooklaw.edu

The Law Campus

Situated at the junction of the Brooklyn Heights Historic District, the Brooklyn Civic Center, and downtown Brooklyn, our school boasts a location unrivaled for its legal, cultural, and historical character. Students share their environs with federal and state judges, government officials, and lawyers in private practice, many of them alumni. Within a few-block radius are the US District Court; US Bankruptcy Court; US Attorney's Office; the New York State Supreme Court, Appellate Division; Family Court; the Brooklyn District Attorney; the Kings County Surrogate's Court; the New York City Civil and Criminal Courts; the Legal Aid Society; and numerous law firms. These are our laboratories, a backdrop for learning few schools can replicate.

Our Neighborhood

Overlooking New York Harbor and lower Manhattan lies Brooklyn's most charming neighborhood, Brooklyn Heights, the first New York City neighborhood to be designated as a historic district and where you will find much of our campus. Many of our students and faculty live here in residence halls or in private apartments and homes located on graceful, tree-lined streets, where many original townhouses, brownstone mansions, carriage houses, churches, and public buildings recall old-world urban elegance.

Multibillion-dollar construction projects continue to recast Brooklyn as the new center of New York City's energy. Nearby neighborhoods—Carroll Gardens, Cobble Hill, Park Slope, Williamsburg, and DUMBO (Down Under the Manhattan Bridge Overpass)—offer trendy, affordable housing and a profusion of bistros, boutiques, galleries, and clubs, all contributing to GQ magazine citing Brooklyn as the "Coolest City on the Planet." Clearly, Brooklyn possesses the attributes to support its growing reputation as the hippest part of New York City.

Manhattan at Our Doorstep

Minutes away is the financial, legal, business, and cultural crossroads of the world: Manhattan. Proximity to Wall Street gives students easy access to school-year externships and summer jobs with major law firms and financial institutions. Students enjoy a great campus in a dynamic urban environment, softened by a small-neighborhood feel. This is New York City on a human scale—Manhattan without the hassle.

Building for Your Future

In recent years, BLS has made significant investments in capital improvements to serve its needs well into the twenty-first century. Nine residences—including our largest, the 21-story high-rise, Feil Hall—allow us to **guarantee housing** to all first-year students, engendering a strong sense of campus community. The library offers more than 589,000 multiformat volumes, numerous periodicals, and close to 300 databases accessible on and off campus. As one of the largest and most modern in the city, the 78,000-square-foot facility boasts 27 group-study rooms, seating for nearly 700,

and 5 PC/Mac labs hosting nearly 100 workstations. We offer 2,400 other student-accessible wired network connections, and wireless network connections throughout our academic and residential buildings.

Our Faculty: Diverse, Brilliant, and User-Friendly

Our 73 full-time faculty members, joined by over 130 adjuncts (including many distinguished judges, practitioners, and corporate counsel), comprise one of the largest faculties in New York. They are extraordinarily talented and, above all, superb teachers. Shaping public policy and making law in the community at large, they are also prolific authors. They are recognized nationally and globally for their scholarship in such areas as Capital Defender and Criminal Law, Commercial and Bankruptcy Law, Corporate and Securities Law, Evidence, Family Law, Gender Discrimination, Human Rights, Information Privacy and Internet Law, Intellectual Property, International Business Law, Tax, and Torts. BLS offers a congenial community. Its learning environment, while rigorous and challenging, remains supportive and nurturing. Faculty members are accessible to students in a way that few faculties are. There is a strong correlation between the priority we assign to teaching and mentoring and student success on the bar examination. Our 2011 graduates who took the New York State Bar Examination for the first time had an 89.1 percent passing rate, well ahead of the 78.5 percent statewide rate for first-time takers.

Our Alumni: Accomplished and Accessible

One of our great strengths is the size, stature, and loyalty of our approximately 19,300 graduates in 49 states and Washington, DC; 3 US territories; and 35 foreign countries—among the largest alumni families of any law school.

Our Students: The Best and the Brightest

The 2011 entering class included students from 27 states, plus Washington, DC; Puerto Rico; and 5 foreign countries. More than half of the class are graduates of many of the nation's most prestigious colleges and universities. Seventy-two percent of them completed undergraduate work at least one year before enrolling here. More than half achieved LSAT scores of 163 or higher. Minorities represented approximately 28 percent of the class, while some 41 percent of the students were women.

The Career Center

Our Career Center team consists of experienced attorneys, including a director who brings over 20 years of multifaceted experience to the position, seven counselors, two employer relations specialists, and four dedicated career assistants. Through early outreach, an individualized approach to counseling, and comprehensive career development programs, the Center is committed to providing candidates with the building blocks necessary for a rewarding legal career. Students are helped to discover the practice of law and to determine individual interests, and are guided towards their careers from the first semester, through graduation and beyond. Through this rigorous approach to career development, graduates continue to find employment with a wide range of employers in the public and private sector. For our current employment statistics, please visit the school's website at www.brooklaw.edu/careers/employmentstatistics/bypractice.aspx.

First-Year Program of Study

Day students take one core course in a seminar section of about 40 students, allowing for significant individualized skills training. Our goal is to help students cultivate the ability to think clearly, analyze problems thoroughly and carefully, and recognize that no legal issue exists in a social, philosophical, economic, or political vacuum. Students participate in **Fundamentals of Law Practice**, a program structured to fully develop writing, analytic and research abilities, as well as the art of written and oral persuasion. An **Academic Success Program**, combining an early-start summer course with a series of support workshops, helps students reach their potential. This contributes to our exceptionally high retention rate between the first and second year.

Upper-Class Program of Study: The Art and Craft of Lawyering

Our **upper-class curriculum** bridges the gap between law school and law practice, making law school something students enjoy, not merely endure. Students create individualized programs, choosing from approximately 240 electives in 19 concentrations and areas of interest. Five **Certificate Programs** (in Business, Criminal, Intellectual Property, International, and Real Estate Law) recognize a student's depth of study and proficiency in these practice areas. Nearly 60 percent of all students and 75 percent of full-time students participate in one or more of our **28 clinics and externships**. This includes over 400 students enrolled this year in one of our in-house clinics, and over 700 students participating in externships in legal departments and judicial chambers, experiencing the law in real time. Simulation courses enrolled nearly 1,100 students this past year.

Beyond the Core Curriculum

Consistently recognized as among the country's top law schools in supporting public interest law, Brooklyn's **Edward V. Sparer Public Interest Law Fellowship Program** has placed some 475 students in a wide array of summer internships at leading public interest organizations nationwide and abroad. **Public Service Grants** support public service employment. The **Dennis J. Block Center for the Study of International Business Law**, and its Fellowship Program, provide a rewarding educational experience for those pursuing careers in that field. A **Trade Secrets Initiative** provides coverage of key trade secrets cases and related legislative/regulatory developments world-wide. Two Fellows, selected annually, research, update, and maintain the database. An **International Human Rights Fellowship Program** awards stipends for summer internships allowing students to work with prestigious human rights organizations overseas. **Global Justice Fellowships** are funded by the student-run International Law Society. We sponsor four student-edited journals: the *Brooklyn Law Review*, the *Journal of Law and Policy*, the *Brooklyn Journal of International Law*, and the *Brooklyn Journal of Corporate, Financial, and Commercial Law*. **Zaretsky Bankruptcy and Commercial Law Fellowships** are awarded to students based on demonstrated academic achievement and commitment to those areas of law. Over the past decade, our **Moot Court** teams have garnered 20 national championships and 39 other first-place prizes. Our **Center for the Study of Law, Language, and Cognition** explores how developments in the cognitive sciences—including neuroscience, psychology, and linguistics—have dramatic implications for the theory and practice of law. Our **Center for Health, Science, and Public Policy** engages students in the legal issues and public policy concerns confronting health care organizations. **Joint-degree** options allow students to concurrently earn master's degrees in business administration, city and regional planning, urban planning, political science, or library and information science. Finally, we offer **exchange programs** in Argentina, England, Germany, Hong Kong, Ireland, and Israel, as well as summer **study-abroad programs** in China and Italy.

APPLICANT PROFILE

Admission to Brooklyn Law School is based on an appraisal of each applicant's character and fitness, commitment to legal education, academic achievement, aptitude for successful law study, life experience, and other pertinent indications of professional promise. BLS does not offer an LSAT/GPA admission profile; numbers alone cannot provide a comprehensive assessment of a candidate's potential for law school success. While matrices may be helpful, too often they discourage those with profiles slightly below published numerical benchmarks who may still be competitive for admission. Moreover, such profiles reduce the selection process to a two-dimensional matrix, which fails to portray accurately our admission practices. To be sure, candidates with high test scores and commensurate grades are more likely to gain admission than those with lower grades and scores. Nevertheless, no combination of grades and scores guarantees admission. Nonquantifiable factors also significantly influence our decisions. A partial list includes quality of schools attended, strength of the program of study, grade trends, content of faculty recommendations, cogency of the candidate's writing, campus leadership, significant service to the community, nature and quality of any work experience or foreign study/travel, awards and honors, and military service. We have a century-long tradition of offering opportunities to members of underrepresented groups.

UNIVERSITY OF CALIFORNIA, BERKELEY, SCHOOL OF LAW

2850 Telegraph Avenue, Suite 500
Berkeley, CA 94705-7220
Phone: 510.642.2274; Fax: 510.643.6222
E-mail: admissions@law.berkeley.edu; Website: www.law.berkeley.edu

ABA
Approved
Since
1923

The Basics

Type of school	Public
Term	Semester
Application deadline	2/1
Application fee	$75
Financial aid deadline	3/2
Can first year start other than fall?	No
Student to faculty ratio	10.9 to 1
# of housing spaces available restricted to law students	
graduate housing for which law students are eligible	1,300

Faculty and Administrators

	Total		Men		Women		Minorities	
	Spr	Fall	Spr	Fall	Spr	Fall	Spr	Fall
Full-time	67	65	46	42	21	23	14	15
Other full-time	20	21	8	10	12	11	0	0
Deans, librarians, & others who teach	6	5	2	2	4	3	1	1
Part-time	86	55	57	37	29	18	9	7
Total	179	146	113	91	66	55	24	23

JD Enrollment and Ethnicity

	Men		Women		Full-Time		Part-Time		1st-Year		Total		JD Degs. Awd.
	#	%	#	%	#	%	#	%	#	%	#	%	
All Hispanics	59	15.8	63	12.7	122	14.0	0	0.0	33	13.0	122	14.0	24
Am. Ind./AK Nat.	5	1.3	9	1.8	14	1.6	0	0.0	2	0.8	14	1.6	3
Asian	62	16.6	106	21.4	168	19.3	0	0.0	47	18.6	168	19.3	50
Black/Af. Am.	22	5.9	25	5.1	47	5.4	0	0.0	19	7.5	47	5.4	12
Nat. HI/Pac. Isl.	0	0.0	0	0.0	0	0.0	0	0.0	0	0.0	0	0.0	0
2 or more races	0	0.0	0	0.0	0	0.0	0	0.0	0	0.0	0	0.0	0
Subtotal (minor.)	148	39.6	203	41.0	351	40.4	0	0.0	101	39.9	351	40.4	89
Nonres. Alien	15	4.0	21	4.2	36	4.1	0	0.0	8	3.2	36	4.1	12
White/Cauc.	177	47.3	219	44.2	396	45.6	0	0.0	127	50.2	396	45.6	153
Unknown	34	9.1	52	10.5	86	9.9	0	0.0	17	6.7	86	9.9	55
Total	374	43.0	495	57.0	869	100.0	0	0.0	253	29.1	869		309

Curriculum

	Full-Time	Part-Time
Typical first-year section size	96	0
Is there typically a "small section" of the first-year class, other than Legal Writing, taught by full-time faculty	Yes	No
If yes, typical size offered last year	27	

# of classroom course titles beyond first-year curriculum		238
# of upper division courses, excluding seminars, with an enrollment:	Under 25	114
	25–49	56
	50–74	10
	75–99	22
	100+	9
# of seminars		129
# of seminar positions available		2,892
# of seminar positions filled	2,039	0
# of positions available in simulation courses		2,335
# of simulation positions filled	1,078	0
# of positions available in faculty supervised clinical courses		677
# of faculty supervised clinical positions filled	274	0
# involved in field placements	148	0
# involved in law journals	171	0
# involved in moot court or trial competitions	69	0
# of credit hours required to graduate		85

Transfers

Transfers in	19
Transfers out	7

Tuition and Fees

	Resident	Nonresident
Full-time	$50,163	$54,370
Part-time		
Tuition Guarantee Program		N

Living Expenses

Estimated living expenses for singles

Living on campus	Living off campus	Living at home
$21,722	$21,722	$21,722

UNIVERSITY OF CALIFORNIA, BERKELEY, SCHOOL OF LAW

ABA
Approved
Since
1923

GPA and LSAT Scores

	Total	Full-Time	Part-Time
# of apps	7,253	7,253	0
# of offers	920	920	0
# of matrics	254	254	0
75% GPA	3.88	3.88	0.00
Median GPA	3.79	3.79	0.00
25% GPA	3.62	3.62	0.00
75% LSAT	169	169	0
Median LSAT	167	167	0
25% LSAT	164	164	0

Grants and Scholarships (from prior year)

	Total		Full-Time		Part-Time	
	#	%	#	%	#	%
Total # of students	916		916		0	
Total # receiving grants	595	65.0	595	65.0	0	0.0
Less than 1/2 tuition	476	52.0	476	52.0	0	0.0
Half to full tuition	92	10.0	92	10.0	0	0.0
Full tuition	6	0.7	6	0.7	0	0.0
More than full tuition	21	2.3	21	2.3	0	0.0
Median grant amount		$14,259			$0	

Informational and Library Resources

Total amount spent on library materials	$3,043,759
Study seating capacity inside the library	338
# of full-time equivalent professional librarians	15
Hours per week library is open	100
# of open, wired connections available to students	175
# of networked computers available for use by students	92
Has wireless network?	Y
Requires computer?	N

JD Attrition (from prior year)

	Academic	Other	Total	
	#	#	#	%
1st year	0	2	2	0.7
2nd year	1	7	8	2.5
3rd year	0	2	2	0.6
4th year	0	0	0	0.0

Employment (9 months after graduation)

For up-to-date employment data, go to employmentsummary.abaquestionnaire.org on the ABA website.

Bar Passage Rates

First-time takers	258	Reporting %	82.56
Average school %	92.02	Average state %	71.24
Average pass difference	20.78		

Jurisdiction	Takers	Passers	Pass %	State %	Diff %
California	213	196	92.02	71.24	20.78

UNIVERSITY OF CALIFORNIA, BERKELEY, SCHOOL OF LAW

2850 Telegraph Avenue, Suite 500
Berkeley, CA 94705-7220
Phone: 510.642.2274; Fax: 510.643.6222
E-mail: admissions@law.berkeley.edu; Website: www.law.berkeley.edu

Introduction

Learning at Berkeley Law means joining a stimulating intellectual community that is part of a tradition of academic excellence, professional leadership, and public service. Berkeley's location in the San Francisco Bay Area, with influences from Silicon Valley and the Pacific Rim, provides an unparalleled opportunity to study at one of the world's leading institutions of legal education, policy, and research. Its academic program includes specialized study in business, law, and economics; environmental law; law and technology; international and comparative legal studies; and social justice and public interest. The curriculum is complemented by research centers and clinical programs that provide real client work. Berkeley Law offers a broad three-year curriculum leading to the JD degree and postgraduate programs leading to LLM and JSD degrees. The interdisciplinary Jurisprudence and Social Policy (JSP) program leads to MA and PhD degrees. The school is a member of AALS and is ABA approved.

Location

UC Berkeley occupies a beautiful 1,232-acre campus bordered by wooded rolling hills. Berkeley is known for its intellectual, social, and political engagement. With its multinational population, rich diversity of arts, and sense of political adventure, Berkeley reflects and affects the rest of the country. Yet, it is an intimate city of friendly neighborhoods, renowned restaurants, coffeehouses, bookstores, parks, and open spaces. Across the bay lies San Francisco, home to internationally recognized museums, the opera, ballet, symphony, and restaurants. The mild climate makes outdoor activities possible year-round.

Students

Berkeley Law seeks a student body with a broad set of interests, life experiences, and perspectives. The intellectual excellence, varied skill sets, and backgrounds of the students are among its great strengths. Students received undergraduate degrees from more than 100 universities, about half at schools outside California.

Faculty

Berkeley's faculty members are internationally recognized experts in fields ranging from law and technology, to youth violence and juvenile justice, to environmental law. They include recipients of Fulbright and Guggenheim fellowships and a MacArthur "genius" grant, as well as authors of casebooks used worldwide. Lecturers are drawn from prominent law firms and institutions.

Library and Physical Facilities

The law library is one of the finest law collections in the world. Its extensive holdings include the Robbins Religious and Civil Law Collection of titles in ecclesiastical, civil, comparative, and international law, and extensive collections of foreign, comparative, human rights, and environmental law. The law library is also a depository for United States, United Nations, and European Union documents and is linked to the university system's holdings of more than seven million volumes.

The law library provides online databases, three computer labs with Internet access, spacious reading rooms, and a photocopying service. Multimedia capabilities are available. Wireless access is available throughout the law school complex and much of the Berkeley campus.

The school is composed of four adjoining buildings with classrooms, seminar rooms, auditoriums, the law library, lounges, reception rooms, a café, dining and study areas, and offices.

Housing

The campus Housing Office offers apartments, rental listings, residence halls, and student family apartments. One of the residence halls, Manville Hall, is a studio apartment complex reserved for law students. Across the street from the school, International House accommodates students from the United States and abroad.

Admission

Requirements: bachelor's degree, LSAT, and registration with LSAC's Credential Assembly Service; application fee: $75; deadline: February 1 (early application strongly preferred).

Applicants' LSAT scores and undergraduate grade-point averages (GPAs) are important criteria for evaluating academic ability. Applicants may use the mean LSAT percentile and undergraduate GPAs of the previous year's admitted applicant pool as a guide for assessing their chances of admission. Because Berkeley Law takes other factors into account in making admission decisions, higher or lower scores and grades neither ensure nor preclude admission.

Student Activities

Students edit and publish 13 legal periodicals: *Asian American Law Journal; Berkeley Business Law Journal; Berkeley Journal of African American Law and Policy; Berkeley Journal of Criminal Law; Berkeley Journal of Employment and Labor Law; Berkeley Journal of Gender, Law and Justice; Berkeley Journal of International Law; Berkeley La Raza Law Journal; Berkeley Journal of Middle Eastern and Islamic Law; Berkeley Technology Law Journal; California Law Review; Ecology Law Quarterly;* and *Berkeley Journal of Entertainment and Sports Law.*

More than 50 student groups focus on a variety of interests, including animal law, disability law, sports and entertainment law, and workers' rights.

JD Curriculum

Berkeley Law's broad and innovative curriculum is one of the most dynamic among law schools. Opportunities for study in specific areas of the law connect students to our renowned faculty members. The first-year curriculum includes Civil Procedure, Contracts, Criminal Law, Legal Research and Writing, Property, Torts, Written and Oral Advocacy, and two elective courses. The flexible second- and third-year curricula offer a variety of legal topics and course styles, including seminars, individual and group research projects, clinical work, and judicial externships. Students may work on clinical projects providing direct legal services to clients or work with lawyers on large cases or legal matters. The Center for Clinical Education, Berkeley Law's in-house clinical facility, offers the Death Penalty Clinic; the International Human Rights Law Clinic; and the Samuelson Law, Technology, and Public Policy Clinic. The East Bay Community Law Center is the community-based component of the program. Other clinical opportunities include the Domestic Violence Practicum and field placements.

Centers and Institutes

Berkeley Law's centers and institutes act as incubators for cutting-edge legal research, where students collaborate with leading scholars and practitioners working on complex issues. Projects are often centered on specific cases or legislation, and can have broad influence on law and policy in such areas as business, philosophy, public policy, sociology, and technology. The centers also sponsor conferences, roundtables, and other presentations on pertinent issues. They push the frontiers of legal scholarship and make Berkeley one of the most exciting places in the world to study law. They include:

- Berkeley Center for Law, Business, and the Economy
- Berkeley Center for Law and Technology
- Center for Law, Energy, and the Environment
- Center for the Study of Law and Society
- Chief Justice Earl Warren Institute on Law and Social Policy
- Human Rights Center
- Institute for Legal Research
- Miller Institute for Global Challenges and Law
- Kadish Center for Morality, Law, and Public Affairs
- Robert D. Burch Center for Tax Policy and Public Finance
- Thelton E. Henderson Center for Social Justice
- Berkeley Institute for Jewish Law and Israeli Law, Economy, and Society

Financial Aid

Requirements: FAFSA need analysis form; Need Access Application; the deadline for priority consideration is March 2.

The law school seeks to provide need-based financial aid sufficient to permit any admitted student to attend. A majority of the students receive some form of financial aid.

The financial aid awarded by UC Berkeley's Financial Aid Office is need-based and includes mostly federal student loans. The financial aid awarded by Berkeley Law includes federal student loans and other campus-based awards such as work-study. Additionally, the law school administers a variety of grants and scholarships based on financial need and/or need and academic merit.

Career Development

The Office of Career Development is a resource for students, alumni, and prospective employers. It operates one of the largest on-campus recruitment programs in the country, provides opportunities for legal employment, and maintains an online job database of positions available throughout the nation. The staff conducts career counseling, résumé workshops, and programs on traditional and nontraditional law careers in the private and public sectors.

Applicant Profile Not Available

UNIVERSITY OF CALIFORNIA, DAVIS SCHOOL OF LAW (KING HALL)

Admission Office, 400 Mrak Hall Drive
Davis, CA 95616-5201
Phone: 530.752.6477
E-mail: admissions@law.ucdavis.edu; Website: www.law.ucdavis.edu

ABA
Approved
Since
1968

The Basics

Type of school	Public
Term	Semester
Application deadline	2/1
Application fee	$75
Financial aid deadline	3/2
Can first year start other than fall?	No
Student to faculty ratio	11.1 to 1
# of housing spaces available restricted to law students	
graduate housing for which law students are eligible	844

Faculty and Administrators

	Total		Men		Women		Minorities	
	Spr	Fall	Spr	Fall	Spr	Fall	Spr	Fall
Full-time	46	46	27	26	19	20	16	18
Other full-time	1	0	0	0	1	0	0	0
Deans, librarians, & others who teach	8	9	3	3	5	6	4	5
Part-time	25	17	18	12	7	5	4	3
Total	80	72	48	41	32	31	24	26

Curriculum

	Full-Time	Part-Time
Typical first-year section size	67	0
Is there typically a "small section" of the first-year class, other than Legal Writing, taught by full-time faculty	Yes	No
If yes, typical size offered last year	32	
# of classroom course titles beyond first-year curriculum	100	

# of upper division courses, excluding seminars, with an enrollment:		
	Under 25	74
	25–49	18
	50–74	9
	75–99	7
	100+	6

# of seminars	13	
# of seminar positions available	271	
# of seminar positions filled	223	0
# of positions available in simulation courses	467	
# of simulation positions filled	395	0
# of positions available in faculty supervised clinical courses	172	
# of faculty supervised clinical positions filled	139	0
# involved in field placements	126	0
# involved in law journals	392	0
# involved in moot court or trial competitions	175	0
# of credit hours required to graduate	88	

JD Enrollment and Ethnicity

	Men #	Men %	Women #	Women %	Full-Time #	Full-Time %	Part-Time #	Part-Time %	1st-Year #	1st-Year %	Total #	Total %	JD Degs. Awd.
All Hispanics	21	6.6	22	7.8	43	7.2	0	0.0	11	5.7	43	7.2	19
Am. Ind./AK Nat.	4	1.3	3	1.1	7	1.2	0	0.0	2	1.0	7	1.2	1
Asian	60	18.8	61	21.6	121	20.1	0	0.0	41	21.4	121	20.1	51
Black/Af. Am.	8	2.5	4	1.4	12	2.0	0	0.0	2	1.0	12	2.0	3
Nat. Hi/Pac. Isl.	0	0.0	0	0.0	0	0.0	0	0.0	0	0.0	0	0.0	2
2 or more races	0	0.0	0	0.0	0	0.0	0	0.0	0	0.0	0	0.0	0
Subtotal (minor.)	93	29.2	90	31.9	183	30.4	0	0.0	56	29.2	183	30.4	76
Nonres. Alien	4	1.3	4	1.4	8	1.3	0	0.0	2	1.0	8	1.3	3
White/Cauc.	189	59.2	161	57.1	350	58.2	0	0.0	124	64.6	350	58.2	84
Unknown	33	10.3	27	9.6	60	10.0	0	0.0	13	6.8	60	10.0	32
Total	319	53.1	282	46.9	601	100.0	0	0.0	192	31.9	601		195

Transfers

Transfers in	25
Transfers out	12

Tuition and Fees

	Resident	Nonresident
Full-time	$46,485	$54,622
Part-time		
Tuition Guarantee Program		N

Living Expenses

Estimated living expenses for singles

Living on campus	Living off campus	Living at home
N/A	$16,866	N/A

UNIVERSITY OF CALIFORNIA, DAVIS SCHOOL OF LAW (KING HALL)

ABA Approved Since 1968

GPA and LSAT Scores

	Total	Full-Time	Part-Time
# of apps	3,863	3,863	0
# of offers	983	983	0
# of matrics	192	192	0
75% GPA	3.79	3.79	0.00
Median GPA	3.63	3.63	0.00
25% GPA	3.47	3.47	0.00
75% LSAT	165	165	0
Median LSAT	164	164	0
25% LSAT	161	161	0

Grants and Scholarships (from prior year)

	Total #	Total %	Full-Time #	Full-Time %	Part-Time #	Part-Time %
Total # of students	589		589		0	
Total # receiving grants	432	73.3	432	73.3	0	0.0
Less than 1/2 tuition	238	40.4	238	40.4	0	0.0
Half to full tuition	188	31.9	188	31.9	0	0.0
Full tuition	0	0.0	0	0.0	0	0.0
More than full tuition	6	1.0	6	1.0	0	0.0
Median grant amount			$22,000		$0	

Informational and Library Resources

Total amount spent on library materials	$979,951
Study seating capacity inside the library	311
# of full-time equivalent professional librarians	8
Hours per week library is open	67
# of open, wired connections available to students	0
# of networked computers available for use by students	47
Has wireless network?	Y
Requires computer?	N

JD Attrition (from prior year)

	Academic #	Other #	Total #	Total %
1st year	1	15	16	8.3
2nd year	0	0	0	0.0
3rd year	0	1	1	0.5
4th year	0	0	0	0.0

Employment (9 months after graduation)

For up-to-date employment data, go to employmentsummary.abaquestionnaire.org on the ABA website.

Bar Passage Rates

First-time takers	192	Reporting %	93.23
Average school %	80.45	Average state %	71.24
Average pass difference	9.21		

Jurisdiction	Takers	Passers	Pass %	State %	Diff %
California	179	144	80.45	71.24	9.21

UNIVERSITY OF CALIFORNIA, DAVIS SCHOOL OF LAW (KING HALL)

Admission Office, 400 Mrak Hall Drive
Davis, CA 95616-5201
Phone: 530.752.6477
E-mail: admissions@law.ucdavis.edu; Website: www.law.ucdavis.edu

Introduction

The School of Law at the University of California, Davis, is one of the nation's premier institutions of legal learning. The school is characterized by the scholarly excellence and ambition of its faculty and student body, as well as its commitment to the creation of a diverse community serving the welfare of its constituents and the world around it. It is fully accredited by the American Bar Association and is a member of the Association of American Law Schools. The school is housed in a newly expanded and renovated state-of-the-art building, King Hall, named for Dr. Martin Luther King Jr. in honor of his efforts to promote social and political justice.

The Davis campus, a major research university consistently among the country's top 20 in research funding, is a little over an hour from San Francisco, and 15 minutes from Sacramento, within easy reach of major recreational areas such as Napa, Carmel, and Lake Tahoe. The campus occupies 3,600 acres within the bike-friendly and charming college town of Davis.

The law school's idyllic surroundings and close proximity to the Bay Area and the state capital create abundant opportunities for a well-rounded educational and professional experience. The campus offers a full range of excellent graduate and professional programs.

Library and Physical Facilities

Faculty offices, classrooms, and the Mabie Law Library are housed in King Hall, which has just undergone a major expansion and renovation that makes it one of the most beautiful and functional facilities in the country. It has two moot courtrooms, a pretrial skills laboratory, a large computer lab, study carrels, student journal offices, lounges, an infant care co-op, and offices for student organizations, all easily accessible to disabled students. Each law student has 24-hour access to the building.

Study carrels are assigned to first-year students, and librarians assist students with legal research needs. Students enjoy access to numerous legal print and online resources via the library and California Digital Library.

Classrooms have the latest in audiovisual and multimedia technology. Wireless Internet access is available throughout the law school.

Curriculum

The School of Law offers a three-year, full-time program in law leading to the Juris Doctor degree, and a postgraduate program leading to an LLM. A faculty with a national reputation for cutting-edge scholarship and devoted teaching works hand-in-hand with an outstanding and diverse student body. The faculty includes worldwide leaders in many fields, including Constitutional Law; Intellectual Property; Environmental Law; Civil Rights; Critical Race Theory; Trusts, Wills, and Estates; Property; Contracts; Corporate Law and Securities; Evidence; Criminal Law and Procedure; Civil Procedure; Complex Litigation; Latinos and the Law; and Immigration Law. Each first-year section typically has about 65 students, and each student is taught at least one of the required first-year courses in a small group of 30–35 students.

A distinctive feature of the school is a weeklong introductory course preceding the formal first-year curriculum. Upper-division courses may be selected within broad areas of concentration such as criminal justice, business and taxation, civil litigation, estate planning and taxation, labor and employment law, environmental law, human rights and social justice law, immigration law, intellectual property, international law, and constitutional and other public law. Students may also combine JD studies with another graduate or professional program such as an MBA.

Special Programs

The school is known for its superb clinical programs in which students work under the supervision of practicing lawyers in many different substantive areas. Students also participate in externships in trial and appellate courts as well as in federal, state, and local government offices and nonprofit organizations throughout California and in Washington, DC.

The law school has four in-house clinics: Immigration, Civil Rights, Prison Law, and Family Protection.

The Immigration Law Clinic, in which students work with one of the best immigration faculties in the United States, allows students to assist immigrants facing deportation.

Students participating in the Civil Rights Clinic appear in federal court in constitutional litigation, representing people who might otherwise have no counsel.

The Family Protection Clinic represents many low-income people who are not native English speakers and who need family law and domestic violence assistance.

First-year students perform an oral argument as a part of the required legal research and writing program, and can later participate in the formal Moot Court Program, which emphasizes appellate advocacy. Skills courses cover the major elements of both litigation and nonlitigation practice. These include pretrial skills (interviewing, counseling, and document drafting); negotiation, mediation, and alternative dispute resolution; business planning; and trial practice. The school has enjoyed excellent success in state, national, and international competitions in moot court and negotiations.

Students in the Public Interest Law Program receive a certificate based on required coursework, practical experience, and community service. This program culminates each year in a public service graduation ceremony, at which a graduating student is presented with the Martin Luther King Jr. Community Service Award. Students in the Environmental Law Program receive a certificate for completion of an environmental curriculum. King Hall students can also participate in a Pro Bono Program designed to both help address the unmet legal service needs of disadvantaged persons and nonprofit organizations and impress upon students the professional responsibility of lawyers to perform public service.

Admission

While the admission process is highly selective, it is by no means mechanical. The Admission Committee seeks excellent students of diverse backgrounds and interests. Each application is carefully reviewed with consideration given to many factors, including undergraduate grades and trends, LSAT scores, economic and other disadvantages, advanced studies, work experience, extracurricular and community activities, maturity, and commitment to the study of law. Residency is not a factor in the admission process. Open houses and information sessions for prospective applicants occur throughout the year. Guided tours can be arranged.

Student Life

King Hall is unusual among the nation's leading law schools because of its wonderful sense of community. The student body is small compared to that of most schools, which lessens competition among a highly qualified student cohort. Students work extraordinarily well with each other, faculty, administrators, and staff. Faculty and administrators have an open-door policy for students. Cooperation and collegiality are the hallmarks of intellectual life at King Hall, and alumni look back fondly on their law school years.

An academic support program, including a bar preparation component during the third year, is available to all students. Students run five journals: the UC Davis Law Review and specialized journals in international law, environmental law, juvenile justice law, and business law.

Students sit on the student/faculty Educational Policy, Faculty Appointments, and Admission Committees. There are about 30 active student organizations encompassing a wide variety of interests. The La Raza Law Students Association's Lorenzo Patiño banquet honoring an alumnus and the King Hall Legal Foundation auction to raise funds for public interest are two of many student-sponsored events that highlight each academic year. The extremely positive attitude of King Hall students was noted and commented upon in our most recent ABA inspection report.

Expenses and Financial Aid

The School of Law Financial Aid Office is available for the exclusive use of law students who desire school-related financial aid counseling and advice. All financial aid services, from entrance through graduation, are administered at the law school. The school participates in all nationally recognized aid programs, such as the Federal Direct Loan Program and Federal Work-Study. Over 75 percent of King Hall students receive scholarships and/or need-based grants as part of their financial aid awards. Each year, two entering students are selected to receive the prestigious Martin Luther King Jr. Scholarships based on demonstrated commitment to public interest. University student loan and grant funds are available for child care. FAFSA and Need Access forms are required for aid consideration.

Housing

A wide variety of reasonably priced housing is available in the local community. The university maintains on-campus apartments for students and student families.

Career Services

The Career Services Office consists of four counselors, all with JDs, who had significant and diverse legal careers prior to joining the office. The counselors assist students in securing summer and post-JD positions, and also provide detailed review of résumés, cover letters, and other application materials. All services, including mock interviews, speakers, and training workshops, are geared to serve the needs of students and alumni seeking all types of legal employment.

Approximately 100 employers visit the campus to interview students. Many others advertise using the school's online database. Off-campus interviewing opportunities are also provided. The Career Services staff conducts significant outreach to potential employers in all legal sectors.

APPLICANT PROFILE

University of California, Davis School of Law (King Hall)
This grid includes only applicants who earned 120–180 LSAT scores under standard administrations.

LSAT Score	3.75 + Apps	Adm	3.50–3.74 Apps	Adm	3.25–3.49 Apps	Adm	3.00–3.24 Apps	Adm	2.75–2.99 Apps	Adm	2.50–2.74 Apps	Adm	2.25–2.49 Apps	Adm	2.00–2.24 Apps	Adm	Below 2.00 Apps	Adm	No GPA Apps	Adm	Total Apps	Adm
175–180	2	2	5	5	12	11	6	2	0	0	3	0	0	0	2	1	0	0	0	0	30	21
170–174	36	33	48	44	28	19	24	12	11	2	9	1	4	0	0	0	0	0	3	1	163	112
165–169	145	137	227	201	184	91	114	25	49	3	31	1	8	0	1	0	1	1	18	6	778	465
160–164	238	170	397	113	324	32	177	6	58	1	29	0	14	0	3	0	0	0	39	7	1279	329
155–159	144	36	224	15	197	1	131	1	76	0	25	0	10	0	5	0	1	0	20	1	833	54
150–154	48	1	98	0	100	1	90	0	57	0	24	0	10	0	4	0	0	0	7	0	438	2
145–149	16	0	33	1	52	0	43	0	36	0	11	0	13	0	2	0	0	0	5	0	211	1
140–144	2	0	18	0	10	0	25	0	17	0	11	0	9	0	1	0	0	0	3	0	96	0
135–139	3	0	4	0	3	0	6	0	5	0	5	0	2	0	2	0	0	0	1	0	31	0
130–134	0	0	2	0	4	0	2	0	1	0	4	0	1	0	1	0	0	0	1	0	16	0
125–129	0	0	1	0	1	0	0	0	0	0	2	0	1	0	0	0	0	0	0	0	5	0
120–124	0	0	0	0	0	0	0	0	0	0	0	0	0	0	0	0	0	0	0	0	0	0
Total	634	379	1057	379	915	155	618	46	310	6	154	2	72	0	21	1	2	1	97	15	3880	984

Apps = Number of Applicants
Adm = Number Admitted
Reflects 100% of the total applicant pool; highest LSAT data reported.

UNIVERSITY OF CALIFORNIA, HASTINGS COLLEGE OF THE LAW

200 McAllister Street
San Francisco, CA 94102
Phone: 415.565.4623; Fax: 415.581.8946
E-mail: admiss@uchastings.edu; Website: www.uchastings.edu

ABA
Approved
Since
1939

The Basics

Type of school	Public
Term	Semester
Application deadline	3/1
Application fee	$75
Financial aid deadline	3/1
Can first year start other than fall?	No
Student to faculty ratio	15.1 to 1
# of housing spaces available restricted to law students	280
graduate housing for which law students are eligible	280

Faculty and Administrators

	Total		Men		Women		Minorities	
	Spr	Fall	Spr	Fall	Spr	Fall	Spr	Fall
Full-time	67	67	42	39	25	28	13	12
Other full-time	1	1	0	0	1	1	0	0
Deans, librarians, & others who teach	4	5	0	1	4	4	1	2
Part-time	85	62	55	40	30	22	8	9
Total	157	135	97	80	60	55	22	23

Curriculum

	Full-Time	Part-Time
Typical first-year section size	77	0
Is there typically a "small section" of the first-year class, other than Legal Writing, taught by full-time faculty	No	No
If yes, typical size offered last year		
# of classroom course titles beyond first-year curriculum	188	
# of upper division courses, excluding seminars, with an enrollment: Under 25	136	
25–49	62	
50–74	13	
75–99	19	
100+	1	
# of seminars	69	
# of seminar positions available	1,348	
# of seminar positions filled	855	0
# of positions available in simulation courses	1,730	
# of simulation positions filled	1,394	0
# of positions available in faculty supervised clinical courses	246	
# of faculty supervised clinical positions filled	204	0
# involved in field placements	197	0
# involved in law journals	479	0
# involved in moot court or trial competitions	137	0
# of credit hours required to graduate	86	

JD Enrollment and Ethnicity

	Men		Women		Full-Time		Part-Time		1st-Year		Total		JD Degs. Awd.
	#	%	#	%	#	%	#	%	#	%	#	%	
All Hispanics	60	10.5	66	9.9	125	10.1	1	33.3	41	9.8	126	10.1	34
Am. Ind./AK Nat.	5	0.9	3	0.4	8	0.6	0	0.0	3	0.7	8	0.6	3
Asian	99	17.2	150	22.4	249	20.1	0	0.0	86	20.5	249	20.0	78
Black/Af. Am.	17	3.0	34	5.1	51	4.1	0	0.0	30	7.2	51	4.1	9
Nat. HI/Pac. Isl.	0	0.0	5	0.7	5	0.4	0	0.0	3	0.7	5	0.4	0
2 or more races	21	3.7	25	3.7	46	3.7	0	0.0	21	5.0	46	3.7	0
Subtotal (minor.)	202	35.2	283	42.2	484	39.0	1	33.3	184	43.9	485	39.0	124
Nonres. Alien	4	0.7	13	1.9	17	1.4	0	0.0	4	1.0	17	1.4	7
White/Cauc.	307	53.5	311	46.4	616	49.6	2	66.7	205	48.9	618	49.7	214
Unknown	61	10.6	63	9.4	124	10.0	0	0.0	26	6.2	124	10.0	66
Total	574	46.1	670	53.9	1241	99.8	3	0.2	419	33.7	1244		411

Transfers

Transfers in	32
Transfers out	20

Tuition and Fees

	Resident	Nonresident
Full-time	$40,836	$49,336
Part-time		
Tuition Guarantee Program	N	

Living Expenses

Estimated living expenses for singles

Living on campus	Living off campus	Living at home
$19,930	$19,930	$19,930

UNIVERSITY OF CALIFORNIA, HASTINGS COLLEGE OF THE LAW

*ABA
Approved
Since
1939*

GPA and LSAT Scores

	Total	Full-Time	Part-Time
# of apps	5,167	5,167	0
# of offers	1,491	1,491	0
# of matrics	414	414	0
75% GPA	3.73	3.73	0.00
Median GPA	3.60	3.60	0.00
25% GPA	3.38	3.38	0.00
75% LSAT	165	165	0
Median LSAT	162	162	0
25% LSAT	157	157	0

Grants and Scholarships (from prior year)

	Total #	Total %	Full-Time #	Full-Time %	Part-Time #	Part-Time %
Total # of students	1,248		1,247		1	
Total # receiving grants	976	78.2	976	78.3	0	0.0
Less than 1/2 tuition	867	69.5	867	69.5	0	0.0
Half to full tuition	109	8.7	109	8.7	0	0.0
Full tuition	0	0.0	0	0.0	0	0.0
More than full tuition	0	0.0	0	0.0	0	0.0
Median grant amount			$11,800		$0	

Informational and Library Resources

Total amount spent on library materials	$1,367,347
Study seating capacity inside the library	793
# of full-time equivalent professional librarians	10
Hours per week library is open	102
# of open, wired connections available to students	514
# of networked computers available for use by students	149
Has wireless network?	Y
Requires computer?	N

JD Attrition (from prior year)

	Academic #	Other #	Total #	Total %
1st year	2	4	6	1.6
2nd year	0	23	23	5.1
3rd year	0	0	0	0.0
4th year	0	0	0	0.0

Employment (9 months after graduation)

For up-to-date employment data, go to employmentsummary.abaquestionnaire.org on the ABA website.

Bar Passage Rates

First-time takers	404	Reporting %	100.00
Average school %	80.21	Average state %	71.83
Average pass difference	8.38		

Jurisdiction	Takers	Passers	Pass %	State %	Diff %
California	386	310	80.31	71.24	9.07
New York	12	9	75.00	84.92	−9.92
Kansas	1	1	100.00	90.00	10.00
Massachusetts	1	1	100.00	89.67	10.33
Others (4)	4	3	75.00		

UNIVERSITY OF CALIFORNIA, HASTINGS COLLEGE OF THE LAW

200 McAllister Street
San Francisco, CA 94102
Phone: 415.565.4623; Fax: 415.581.8946
E-mail: admiss@uchastings.edu; Website: www.uchastings.edu

Introduction

UC Hastings College of the Law offers a superb legal education in San Francisco, one of the world's great cities. Hastings was the first public law school in California, founded in 1878 as the law department of the University of California. The faculty at Hastings is composed of exceptional teachers who are also nationally known scholars. They are accessible to students and encourage a collaborative learning environment. Hastings has produced more judges than any other law school in the state, and its graduates can be found practicing law throughout California and the nation, in every kind of setting. Hastings graduates also have a significant presence in business and government.

The law school is situated in the heart of the city, near City Hall, state and federal courts, the arts district, the financial district, and the downtown shopping area. This central location provides access for students to pursue internships and externships with judges, city and state agencies, and nearby nonprofit research and advocacy groups. The location also provides unparalleled opportunities for recreation: theater, music, restaurants, professional and amateur sports, and a world-class transportation system.

Library, Technology, and Housing

Hastings is an urban campus with three buildings, all having wireless Internet access. The classroom building was renovated in 2000, and renovation of the library/administration building was completed in the fall of 2007. The new library is designed to be both comfortable and functional, with small-group study rooms, both open areas and individual carrels, and access to traditional and online research tools. McAllister Tower is a splendid, remodeled art deco building with 250 apartments, many with stunning views of the city. The building also features a comfortable lounge and a gym, including a basketball court often frequented by local attorneys and judges as well as Hastings students.

Curriculum

The UC Hastings curriculum offers a broad spectrum of foundational and specialized courses. The law school's curricular strengths mirror the strengths of San Francisco. Students can focus on international human rights and business law, public interest law, intellectual property law, business and tax law, or litigation and its alternatives. San Francisco is a global city that draws on experts from Silicon Valley and the greater Bay Area to enrich course offerings.

Special Programs

- **Concentrations:** Students may earn a certificate of concentration in any of the following areas: Civil Litigation and Dispute Resolution, Criminal Law, Law and Health Sciences, Intellectual Property, International Law, Social Justice Lawyering, or Tax Law.
- **Clinics and Judicial Externships:** Hastings provides an exciting and diverse array of opportunities for students to gain practical experience. Under clinical faculty supervision, students represent real clients in in-house and out-placement clinics specializing in community development, environmental law, labor and employment, housing and disability rights, law reform, international human rights, immigrants' rights, and legislation. In these clinics, students learn a variety of lawyering techniques, including counseling and planning, litigation, alternative dispute resolution, and legislation. Simulation courses teach trial and appellate advocacy, negotiation, mediation, contract drafting, problem solving, and professional ethics. More than 100 students a year spend a semester serving as externs in the state and federal courts, including the Supreme Court of California.
- **International Programs:** Hastings offers an exceptionally strong curriculum focusing on international human rights, as well as international business and trade law. In addition, students may participate in the work of the Center for Gender and Refugee Studies, the Immigrants' Rights Clinic, and the Hastings-to-Haiti Partnership. Hastings also offers over 17 study-abroad programs in Argentina, Australia, Spain, China, Denmark, England, France, Germany, Hungary, Italy, and the Netherlands and supports students who wish to study abroad in other locations.
- **Joint-Degree Programs:** Hastings students may participate in a joint-degree program with any accredited graduate program throughout the country. Hastings students have simultaneously earned degrees in public policy, public health, and business administration, among others.
- **Legal Education Opportunity Program (LEOP):** Hastings recognizes that the traditional numeric criteria used to determine admission may not be the best indicators of academic potential for students from adverse backgrounds. Applicants admitted through LEOP are offered resources designed to assist them to excel academically throughout their entire course of study. Twenty percent of each year's entering class at Hastings is comprised of LEOP participants.
- **Centers and Institutes:** Students have opportunities to work in the law school's highly acclaimed research and advocacy centers: the Center for Gender and Refugee Studies, the Center for Negotiation and Dispute Resolution, the Center for State and Local Government Law, the Center for WorkLife Law, and the Public Law Research Institute.
- **Intercollegiate Moot Court Team:** Hastings has one of the most successful and most well-respected Moot Court programs in the United States. Each year Hastings participates in numerous intercollegiate Moot Court competitions covering a wide range of current legal issues, and is among the top programs in the country.
- **LLM Program:** Graduates of non-US law schools may earn a master of laws degree in US Legal Studies.
- **MSL Program:** Health and science professionals who do not seek to practice law, but who instead want to equip themselves with a more sophisticated understanding of legal reasoning and doctrine may pursue a one-year master of studies in law degree.

Cocurricular and Student Activities

The strength and diversity of the Hastings student body are reflected in more than 60 student organizations that sponsor intellectual, social, and political events. Hastings publishes nine student-edited law reviews. The *Hastings Law Journal* is a general-interest publication. In addition, eight specialty law reviews focus on a variety of issues, including business law, constitutional law, communication and entertainment law, international and comparative law, environmental law, science and technology, and the law relating to race or gender. Students may also join the college's award-winning moot court, negotiation, client counseling, and trial practice teams, which compete in state, national, and international competitions. Students also engage in a variety of legal and nonlegal community service activities in and around the Hastings neighborhood.

Financial Aid

The majority of UC Hastings students receive need-based and merit-based financial assistance from college-administered sources. Scholarships and grants recognize and encourage the achievement, service, and professional promise of students. Students who pursue qualifying public interest and government sector employment may receive loan repayment assistance after graduation through the Public Interest Career Assistance Program (PICAP).

Career Services

UC Hastings offers one of the most comprehensive law career services offices in the West. The office assists students and alumni in clarifying their goals, acquiring job-search strategies, and honing interviewing techniques. It provides access to full-time, part-time, and summer job listings. Every year, more than 200 employers visit the campus to interview students for both summer associate positions and permanent postgraduation employment. Several hundred additional employers from throughout the nation participate in the recruit-by-mail program.

APPLICANT PROFILE

University of California, Hastings College of the Law
This grid includes only applicants who earned 120–180 LSAT scores under standard administrations.

LSAT Score	GPA																				
	3.75 +		3.50–3.74		3.25–3.49		3.00–3.24		2.75–2.99		2.50–2.74		2.25–2.49		2.00–2.24		Below 2.00		No GPA		Total	
	Apps	Adm	Apps	Adm	Apps	Adm	Apps	Adm	Apps	Adm	Apps	Adm	Apps	Adm	Apps	Adm	Apps	Adm	Apps	Adm	Apps	Adm
175–180	4	3	8	6	10	7	10	5	0	0	2	0	0	0	3	1	0	0	0	0	37	22
170–174	47	37	60	46	45	25	33	12	17	5	11	3	4	0	0	0	0	0	2	1	219	129
165–169	186	167	254	209	200	102	127	39	63	11	33	5	9	0	4	0	0	0	22	14	898	547
160–164	255	207	445	206	378	73	210	18	73	4	37	2	23	2	5	0	0	0	39	9	1465	521
155–159	151	90	295	62	308	18	183	15	109	5	42	0	18	1	4	0	0	0	26	0	1136	191
150–154	68	11	140	25	163	14	152	7	96	0	47	1	25	0	5	0	2	0	15	1	713	59
145–149	25	3	58	11	102	1	76	0	54	0	34	0	27	0	4	0	0	0	10	0	390	15
140–144	7	1	22	1	23	0	50	0	34	0	28	0	19	0	5	0	0	0	5	0	193	2
135–139	0	0	8	0	5	0	15	0	12	0	11	0	7	0	5	0	3	0	2	0	68	0
130–134	0	0	1	0	4	0	3	0	3	0	6	0	2	0	7	0	0	0	2	0	28	0
125–129	0	0	1	0	0	0	1	0	1	0	2	0	2	0	0	0	0	0	0	0	7	0
120–124	0	0	0	0	0	0	0	0	0	0	0	0	0	0	0	0	0	0	0	0	0	0
Total	743	519	1292	566	1238	240	860	96	462	25	253	11	136	3	42	1	5	0	123	25	5154	1486

Apps = Number of Applicants
Adm = Number Admitted
Reflects 99% of the total applicant pool; highest LSAT data reported.

UNIVERSITY OF CALIFORNIA, IRVINE SCHOOL OF LAW

401 East Peltason Drive, Suite 1000
Irvine, CA 92697-8000
Phone: 949.824.4545
E-mail: lawadmit@lawuci.edu; Website: www.law.uci.edu

Provisional ABA Approved Since 2011

The Basics

Type of school	Public
Term	Semester
Application deadline	3/1
Application fee	$0
Financial aid deadline	3/2
Can first year start other than fall?	No
Student to faculty ratio	6.9 to 1
# of housing spaces available restricted to law students	
graduate housing for which law students are eligible	250

Faculty and Administrators

	Total Spr	Total Fall	Men Spr	Men Fall	Women Spr	Women Fall	Minorities Spr	Minorities Fall
Full-time	21	28	12	16	9	12	5	7
Other full-time	2	0	2	0	0	0	1	0
Deans, librarians, & others who teach	0	2	0	0	0	2	0	0
Part-time	8	13	6	10	2	3	2	1
Total	31	43	20	26	11	17	8	8

Curriculum

	Full-Time	Part-Time
Typical first-year section size	42	0
Is there typically a "small section" of the first-year class, other than Legal Writing, taught by full-time faculty	Yes	No
If yes, typical size offered last year	21	

# of classroom course titles beyond first-year curriculum		34
# of upper division courses, excluding seminars with an enrollment:	Under 25	26
	25–49	5
	50–74	0
	75–99	0
	100+	0

	Full-Time	Part-Time
# of seminars	3	
# of seminar positions available	72	
# of seminar positions filled	27	0
# of positions available in simulation courses	60	
# of simulation positions filled	43	0
# of positions available in faculty supervised clinical courses	0	
# of faculty supervised clinical positions filled	0	0
# involved in field placements	33	0
# involved in law journals	53	0
# involved in moot court or trial competitions	18	0
# of credit hours required to graduate	86	

JD Enrollment and Ethnicity

	Men #	Men %	Women #	Women %	Full-Time #	Full-Time %	Part-Time #	Part-Time %	1st-Year #	1st-Year %	Total #	Total %	JD Degs. Awd.
All Hispanics	10	8.5	17	14.4	27	11.5	0	0.0	8	9.0	27	11.5	0
Am. Ind./AK Nat.	0	0.0	1	0.8	1	0.4	0	0.0	0	0.0	1	0.4	0
Asian	22	18.8	28	23.7	50	21.3	0	0.0	23	25.8	50	21.3	0
Black/Af. Am.	2	1.7	5	4.2	7	3.0	0	0.0	3	3.4	7	3.0	0
Nat. HI/Pac. Isl.	1	0.9	0	0.0	1	0.4	0	0.0	1	1.1	1	0.4	0
2 or more races	1	0.9	4	3.4	5	2.1	0	0.0	3	3.4	5	2.1	0
Subtotal (minor.)	36	30.8	55	46.6	91	38.7	0	0.0	38	42.7	91	38.7	0
Nonres. Alien	3	2.6	3	2.5	6	2.6	0	0.0	2	2.2	6	2.6	0
White/Cauc.	66	56.4	44	37.3	110	46.8	0	0.0	45	50.6	110	46.8	0
Unknown	12	10.3	16	13.6	28	11.9	0	0.0	4	4.5	28	11.9	0
Total	117	49.8	118	50.2	235	100.0	0	0.0	89	37.9	235		0

Transfers

Transfers in	6
Transfers out	1

Tuition and Fees

	Resident	Nonresident
Full-time	$43,280	$53,125
Part-time		
Tuition Guarantee Program	N	

Living Expenses

Estimated living expenses for singles

Living on campus	Living off campus	Living at home
$17,625	$24,004	$17,625

UNIVERSITY OF CALIFORNIA, IRVINE SCHOOL OF LAW

ABA
Approved
Since
2011

GPA and LSAT Scores

	Total	Full-Time	Part-Time
# of apps	920	920	0
# of offers	219	219	0
# of matrics	89	89	0
75% GPA	3.69	3.69	0.00
Median GPA	3.49	3.49	0.00
25% GPA	3.25	3.25	0.00
75% LSAT	167	167	0
Median LSAT	165	165	0
25% LSAT	163	163	0

Grants and Scholarships (from prior year)

	Total		Full-Time		Part-Time	
	#	%	#	%	#	%
Total # of students	142		142		0	
Total # receiving grants	143	100.7	143	100.7	0	0.0
Less than 1/2 tuition	0	0.0	0	0.0	0	0.0
Half to full tuition	75	52.8	75	52.8	0	0.0
Full tuition	67	47.2	67	47.2	0	0.0
More than full tuition	1	0.7	1	0.7	0	0.0
Median grant amount			$0		$0	

Informational and Library Resources

Total amount spent on library materials	$1,611,627
Study seating capacity inside the library	300
# of full-time equivalent professional librarians	5
Hours per week library is open	84
# of open, wired connections available to students	0
# of networked computers available for use by students	61
Has wireless network?	Y
Requires computer?	N

JD Attrition (from prior year)

	Academic	Other	Total	
	#	#	#	%
1st year	0	1	1	1.2
2nd year	0	1	1	1.7
3rd year	0	0	0	0.0
4th year	0	0	0	0.0

Employment (9 months after graduation)

For up-to-date employment data, go to employmentsummary.abaquestionnaire.org on the ABA website.

Bar Passage Rates

First-time takers	0	Reporting %	
Average school %		Average state %	
Average pass difference			

Jurisdiction	Takers	Passers	Pass %	State %	Diff %

UNIVERSITY OF CALIFORNIA, IRVINE SCHOOL OF LAW

401 East Peltason Drive, Suite 1000
Irvine, CA 92697-8000
Phone: 949.824.4545
E-mail: lawadmit@lawuci.edu; Website: www.law.uci.edu

Introduction

UC Irvine School of Law, the first new public law school in California in more than 40 years, opened its doors to its first class in August 2009. Shortly thereafter, in June 2011, UC Irvine School of Law was granted provisional accreditation by the American Bar Association. Provisional accreditation means that graduating students can take the bar exam in California without taking a qualifying "baby bar" exam.

"We are extremely pleased to have fielded such a high-caliber student body," said Dean Erwin Chemerinsky, who is also one of the top constitutional scholars in the nation. "Along with a highly rated faculty, this allows us to be considered among the best law schools in the country from the very start," he said.

UCI Law seeks to create the ideal law school for the twenty-first century by doing the best job in the country of training lawyers for the practice of law at the highest levels of the profession. The Law School's innovative curriculum stresses hands-on learning, interdisciplinary study, and public service. Interdisciplinary study is also at the heart of UCI, and there are several concurrent-degree programs that students may wish to consider.

Information for Prospective Students

Prospective students are encouraged to contact the Admissions Office to learn more about UC Irvine School of Law and to have their questions answered. The Admissions Office also attends recruiting events across the country and hosts information sessions, class visits, and tours on a regular basis. Prospective students should visit www.law.uci.edu/prospective/index.html for more information or call 949.824.4545.

The Area

UC Irvine School of Law boasts modern facilities on a beautiful and expansive campus in suburban Southern California accessible to both Los Angeles and San Diego. UC Irvine is as beautiful as its surrounding Southern California location. The campus itself is centered around tranquil Aldrich Park—a 19-acre botanical garden with more than 11,000 trees and shrubs.

The campus also is home to a vibrant performing arts program, a wide range of athletic facilities and teams, the Arts Plaza (a unique, outdoor gallery and performance space), the Anteater Recreation Center, and the Irvine Barclay Theatre. The Bren Events Center provides an exciting and prestigious array of music, performance, exhibition, sporting, and other public events.

With UC Irvine's ideal Southern California location—between Los Angeles and San Diego and surrounded by coastline, mountains, and desert—students have a wealth of recreational and cultural options and venues. The Irvine Ranch land reserve includes 37,000 acres designated by the US Secretary of the Department of the Interior as a National Natural Landmark. From nearby Disneyland, and other theme parks, to the Segerstrom Center for the Arts and the South Coast Repertory theater company, there's always something to do.

Admission

The School of Law admits first-year JD students and transfer students only in the fall semester; visiting students are accepted in both fall and spring. The basic requirements for admission to the School of Law are a bachelor's degree earned prior to the beginning of the first law school semester from an accredited institution of higher education and a valid LSAT score. Please refer to the online application instructions for more information about the specific components of the application process.

All applicants must submit a completed application form, official transcripts, at least two letters of recommendation, and a valid LSAT score not more than five years old. There is no application fee. Applicants must also register with the Law School Admission Council's (LSAC) Credential Assembly Service (CAS).

The School of Law seeks to create a community of law students from a broad spectrum of society, with strong qualifications and the greatest potential to contribute to the diversity and intellectual vibrancy of UCI School of Law.

Faculty

The faculty at UC Irvine School of Law are some of the nation's leading scholars and teachers, representing a broad range of expertise, including biotechnology, business law, civil procedure, civil rights, constitutional law, criminal law, equality and discrimination, international dispute resolution, diversity, education and law, environmental law, gender and law, government regulation and policy, intellectual property, labor and employment law, law and pop culture, law and psychology, legal ethics and professional responsibility, and urban planning.

The School of Law now has 29 full-time and 6 joint appointments. The School of Law also has 5 teaching law librarians and 12 adjunct faculty members. The student-to-faculty ratio is very low, about 7 to 1. The faculty, recruited from prestigious law schools from around the country, has a high level of scholarly impact.

Enrollment/Student Body

Since its inaugural year, the law school has drawn students with high median grade-point averages and LSAT scores. Students enjoy a student-to-faculty ratio of 7 to 1, which ensures small classes and easy access to professors outside the classroom.

UCI School of Law is proud to have some of the nation's most qualified, diverse, and highly motivated law students. UCI School of Law students have come from the best institutions in the country and with myriad experiences in academia and the professional arena.

Library and Physical Facilities

The University of California, Irvine School of Law Library serves as the intellectual heart of the Law School community. Located on the lower two floors of the Law Building, the Law Library is open 80 hours a week and comfortably seats 300. The Law Library provides access to an array of primary and secondary materials selected to support the developing curriculum and scholarship of the newly founded school. Wireless access throughout the library and a 30-seat computer lab facilitate access to the growing collection of electronic resources.

The Law School occupies space in three buildings, which face each other across a shared courtyard and open parking lot—the Law building, Education building, and Multipurpose Academic and Administrative (MPAA) building. The **Law** building houses faculty offices, classrooms, and the Law Library. The first floor of the **Education** building is where the Law School's administrative office suite is located, along with the large, tiered classrooms and moot court classroom. The **MPAA** building contains additional classrooms, clinic space, the Career Development Office, a student lounge, student organization offices, locker rooms, and several faculty offices. (Two other academic units also occupy space in the MPAA building: the Paul Merage School of Business and the Department of Education.)

The school's space plan was developed around two important principles: the school had to be on campus in order to support integration and interdisciplinary collaboration with other departments and schools, and, it would have to have enough space to support the school's growth to a student body of 600 students and 55 full-time faculty members. The dean's vision placed a priority on creating spaces where faculty and students could serendipitously interact and providing superior technological support, including strong wireless capacity in classrooms and throughout the school.

Curriculum

UCI Law has an innovative curriculum designed to prepare students for the practice of law at the highest levels of the profession. The first-year JD curriculum teaches students areas of legal doctrine traditionally taught in the first year, but in an innovative way that focuses on teaching methods of legal analysis and skills that all lawyers use.

Students thus receive an education that includes the traditional areas of legal doctrine, but in an innovative context designed to prepare them for practice in the twenty-first century. Many other features of the first year are designed to prepare students for the practice of law. All first-year students are assigned a lawyer mentor and are required to spend a specified number of hours observing that lawyer at work.

There is an active pro bono program in which students have the opportunity to do volunteer work in many different contexts beginning in their first year. Also, students are actively engaged in helping to create the institutions of the new law school.

Student Life and Organizations

The atmosphere of the school is warm and collegial. Everyone—faculty, staff, and students—has the chance to play a key role in shaping the school. The students have created numerous organizations, many of which don't exist at other law schools. Student organizations are a vital part of student life at UCI Law. There are a variety of student organizations that continually produce activities and events for the campus community. As a relatively new law school, the number of student organizations continues to grow.

Expenses and Financial Aid

The Office of Financial Aid determines eligibility for institutional financial aid and ensures that eligible students are appropriately awarded federal student aid. The School of Law offers merit-based and need-based aid, as well as other types of scholarships. Students are encouraged to submit their FAFSA application on time to ensure delivery of funds, both scholarships and loans.

In addition to managing the delivery of all types of financial aid funds, we offer law students financial services in the form of loan counseling, advice on maintaining financial aid eligibility, specialty information workshops, and web-based tools to manage an education loan portfolio.

Career Services

The Career Development Office promotes and coordinates employment opportunities in public service, the private sector, and alternative careers, as well as providing professional career services and acting as a liaison between students and employers. Our mission is to provide students with the tools to make informed decisions about employment opportunities and career paths through one-on-one counseling, panel presentations, job fairs, workshops, recruitment programs, job postings, and networking opportunities.

Our inaugural class members each obtained legal jobs in the summer of 2010, including internships with federal and state judges and public interest organizations and positions in government agencies, private law firms, and international human rights offices. And despite a continued weak economy, all of the inaugural class and the second class found law-related employment in the summer of 2011.

Applicant Profile Not Available

UNIVERSITY OF CALIFORNIA AT LOS ANGELES (UCLA) SCHOOL OF LAW

Law Admissions Office, 71 Dodd Hall, Box 951445
Los Angeles, CA 90095-1445
Phone: 310.825.2080
E-mail: admissions@law.ucla.edu; Website: www.law.ucla.edu

ABA Approved Since 1950

The Basics

Type of school	Public
Term	Semester
Application deadline	2/1
Application fee	$75
Financial aid deadline	3/2
Can first year start other than fall?	No
Student to faculty ratio	10.9 to 1
# of housing spaces available restricted to law students	
graduate housing for which law students are eligible	260

Faculty and Administrators

	Total Spr	Total Fall	Men Spr	Men Fall	Women Spr	Women Fall	Minorities Spr	Minorities Fall
Full-time	78	72	51	45	27	27	12	11
Other full-time	11	15	7	9	4	6	1	4
Deans, librarians, & others who teach	10	10	7	6	3	4	2	2
Part-time	33	24	20	18	13	6	5	1
Total	132	121	85	78	47	43	20	18

JD Enrollment and Ethnicity

	Men #	Men %	Women #	Women %	Full-Time #	Full-Time %	Part-Time #	Part-Time %	1st-Year #	1st-Year %	Total #	Total %	JD Degs. Awd.
All Hispanics	36	6.9	48	10.3	84	8.5	0	0.0	31	9.7	84	8.5	30
Am. Ind./AK Nat.	8	1.5	10	2.2	18	1.8	0	0.0	4	1.3	18	1.8	4
Asian	63	12.0	83	17.9	146	14.8	0	0.0	47	14.7	146	14.8	53
Black/Af. Am.	16	3.1	23	5.0	39	4.0	0	0.0	7	2.2	39	4.0	13
Nat. HI/Pac. Isl.	0	0.0	1	0.2	1	0.1	0	0.0	0	0.0	1	0.1	2
2 or more races	15	2.9	12	2.6	27	2.7	0	0.0	8	2.5	27	2.7	0
Subtotal (minor.)	138	26.4	177	38.1	315	31.9	0	0.0	97	30.3	315	31.9	102
Nonres. Alien	8	1.5	7	1.5	15	1.5	0	0.0	4	1.3	15	1.5	7
White/Cauc.	240	45.9	198	42.7	438	44.4	0	0.0	155	48.4	438	44.4	146
Unknown	137	26.2	82	17.7	219	22.2	0	0.0	64	20.0	219	22.2	87
Total	523	53.0	464	47.0	987	100.0	0	0.0	320	32.4	987		342

Curriculum

	Full-Time	Part-Time
Typical first-year section size	80	0
Is there typically a "small section" of the first-year class, other than Legal Writing, taught by full-time faculty	Yes	No
If yes, typical size offered last year	40	
# of classroom course titles beyond first-year curriculum	166	
# of upper division courses, excluding seminars, with an enrollment: Under 25	73	
25–49	26	
50–74	17	
75–99	14	
100+	9	
# of seminars	51	
# of seminar positions available	822	
# of seminar positions filled	761	0
# of positions available in simulation courses	221	
# of simulation positions filled	211	0
# of positions available in faculty supervised clinical courses	185	
# of faculty supervised clinical positions filled	159	0
# involved in field placements	146	0
# involved in law journals	368	0
# involved in moot court or trial competitions	14	0
# of credit hours required to graduate	87	

Transfers

Transfers in	40
Transfers out	5

Tuition and Fees

	Resident	Nonresident
Full-time	$44,922	$54,767
Part-time		
Tuition Guarantee Program	N	

Living Expenses

Estimated living expenses for singles

Living on campus	Living off campus	Living at home
$20,965	$20,226	$12,624

UNIVERSITY OF CALIFORNIA AT LOS ANGELES (UCLA) SCHOOL OF LAW

ABA
Approved
Since
1950

GPA and LSAT Scores

	Total	Full-Time	Part-Time
# of apps	7,328	7,328	0
# of offers	1,471	1,471	0
# of matrics	319	319	0
75% GPA	3.88	3.88	0.00
Median GPA	3.78	3.78	0.00
25% GPA	3.55	3.55	0.00
75% LSAT	169	169	0
Median LSAT	168	168	0
25% LSAT	164	164	0

Grants and Scholarships (from prior year)

	Total #	Total %	Full-Time #	Full-Time %	Part-Time #	Part-Time %
Total # of students	999		999		0	
Total # receiving grants	739	74.0	739	74.0	0	0.0
Less than 1/2 tuition	567	56.8	567	56.8	0	0.0
Half to full tuition	144	14.4	144	14.4	0	0.0
Full tuition	3	0.3	3	0.3	0	0.0
More than full tuition	25	2.5	25	2.5	0	0.0
Median grant amount				$13,450		$0

Informational and Library Resources

Total amount spent on library materials	$1,786,000
Study seating capacity inside the library	783
# of full-time equivalent professional librarians	14
Hours per week library is open	121
# of open, wired connections available to students	1,430
# of networked computers available for use by students	115
Has wireless network?	Y
Requires computer?	N

JD Attrition (from prior year)

	Academic #	Other #	Total #	Total %
1st year	0	11	11	3.6
2nd year	0	2	2	0.6
3rd year	0	1	1	0.3
4th year	0	0	0	0.0

Employment (9 months after graduation)

For up-to-date employment data, go to employmentsummary.abaquestionnaire.org on the ABA website.

Bar Passage Rates

First-time takers	346	Reporting %	84.97
Average school %	83.33	Average state %	71.24
Average pass difference	12.09		

Jurisdiction	Takers	Passers	Pass %	State %	Diff %
California	294	245	83.33	71.24	12.09

UNIVERSITY OF CALIFORNIA AT LOS ANGELES (UCLA) SCHOOL OF LAW

Law Admissions Office, 71 Dodd Hall, Box 951445
Los Angeles, CA 90095-1445
Phone: 310.825.2080
E-mail: admissions@law.ucla.edu; Website: www.law.ucla.edu

Introduction

Located in the heart of Southern California and nestled in a beautiful and safe residential neighborhood, UCLA School of Law is less than seven miles from the Pacific Ocean, and is housed on the UCLA campus. UCLA Law acquired and maintains its strong standing by creating pioneering academic programs, cultivating top legal scholars, and educating students who go on to be leaders in our society.

Los Angeles offers unparalleled access to numerous recreational opportunities and activities, such as sporting events, theaters, museums, and live performances. UCLA Law is close enough to the thriving metropolis of Los Angeles for students to partake in the vibrant social and cultural scene, yet secluded enough for students to focus on their legal studies. The incredible weather, the international reach of the city, and the intellectually stimulating environment all contribute to a student's law school experience.

Curriculum

The law school offers a three-year, full-time course of study leading to a Juris Doctor degree. UCLA differs from many other institutions in that it invests major resources in its first-year Lawyering Skills program. This program combines the beginning of skills training, such as client interviewing and counseling, with traditional legal research and writing. The law school also provides students with a small, intimate learning environment that includes three small classes for the first-year and upper-level courses that meet off campus (including at faculty members' homes).

Faculty

The UCLA School of Law faculty is a treasured asset. Faculty members are leaders in their respective fields and are the mainstay of UCLA Law's high-quality legal education programs. They are some of the finest teachers in the academy, expanding the frontiers of interdisciplinary legal scholarship. Each year, the UCLA Law faculty demonstrates the caliber of its intellectual abilities by publishing groundbreaking scholarship in leading academic journals and law reviews, and the work is widely cited.

Special Programs

Academic Programs and Specializations: UCLA Law boasts numerous diverse programs and centers, each enabling students to study significant areas of the law. They include the Lowell Milken Institute for Business Law and Policy; Critical Race Studies Program; David J. Epstein Program in Public Interest Law and Policy; Entertainment, Media, and Intellectual Property Law Program; Environmental Law Program; International and Comparative Law Program; International Human Rights Law Program; and the Law and Philosophy Program.

Research Centers and Programs: UCLA School of Law has always emphasized progressive research on relevant topics. Research centers and programs include the Center for Law and Economics; Emmett Center on Climate Change and the Environment; Empirical Legal Scholars Program; Empirical Research Group; Globalization and Labor Standards; Health and Human Rights Law Project; Native Nations Law and Policy Center; Negotiation and Conflict Resolution Program; Program on Understanding Law, Science, and Evidence (PULSE); Sanela Diana Jenkins Human Rights Project; UCLA-RAND Center for Law and Public Policy; Williams Institute on Sexual Orientation Law and Public Policy; and UCLA Ziman Center for Real Estate.

Study-Abroad and Externship Programs: Law students may spend one semester abroad through student exchange agreements with universities in Argentina, Australia, France, Israel, Japan, Norway, Spain, and Switzerland. Some students also obtain approval for an individualized study-abroad program. UCLA Law has an extensive national and international student externship program. The law school has developed a core group of judicial and agency externships that include externships with federal judges, government agencies, public interest law firms, and nonprofit organizations. In addition, the UCDC Program is a uniquely collaborative full-time externship program in Washington, DC. Both full-time and part-time externships are available. Students can also propose new agency externships tailored to their academic goals.

Clinical Law Program: Since pioneering clinical legal education in the early 1970s, UCLA Law's Clinical Law Program has blazed a path of innovation and excellence. Typically, there are more than 30 clinical offerings each year with more than 300 clinical spots available for students. Some examples include the Civil Rights Litigation Clinic; Criminal Defense Clinic; Environmental Law Clinic; Immigration Clinic; Intellectual Property Clinic: Counseling Emerging Technologies and Enterprises; International Justice Clinic; and Supreme Court Clinic.

Joint Degrees

A number of students find it advantageous to pursue formal training in another field of study concurrently with their legal training. Typically, such concurrent-degree programs lead, after four years of study, to the simultaneous award of a Juris Doctor and an advanced degree from another school or department. Formal joint-degree programs are offered in the following areas: JD/MA (Afro-American Studies), JD/MA (American Indian Studies), JD/MBA (Anderson School of Management), JD/PhD (Philosophy), JD/MPH (Public Health), JD/MPP (Public Policy), JD/MSW (Social Welfare), and JD/MA (Urban and Regional Planning).

Student Life and Student Activities

A collegial environment at UCLA Law also affords students many opportunities for participation and leadership in numerous student organizations and student-edited journals. UCLA School of Law has 13 student journals on a wide range of topics that are managed and edited by students.

UCLA Law's student body is composed of a diverse group of future lawyers reflecting a broad range of backgrounds and experiences. We are immensely proud of our racial diversity and long-standing commitment to diversity in legal education. Our law school celebrates a multiracial community that helps all groups bridge racial lines and is a reflection of Los Angeles, where UCLA Law is located, one of the world's most vibrant and dynamic cities.

Diverse student interests are represented in approximately 40 student organizations. The Moot Court Honors Program is open to all second- and third-year students and offers a large and effective program of mock appellate advocacy. The program also hosts a first-year competition, as well as the prestigious Roscoe Pound competition.

Housing

There are many housing options open to UCLA Law students, and the law school hosts a web-based service to help students with their roommate search. There are both university-owned and privately owned apartments from which to choose. For more information, please visit www.law.ucla.edu/housing.

Admission and Financial Aid

All applicants must have a baccalaureate degree from an accredited university or college of approved standing and must take the LSAT no later than the February administration. Admission is based primarily on proven outstanding academic and intellectual ability, taking into consideration the LSAT and factors such as the breadth, depth, and rigor of the undergraduate educational program. The Admissions Committee may also consider whether economic, physical, or other hardships and challenges have been overcome. Distinctive programmatic contributions, community or public service, letters of recommendation, work experience, career achievement, language ability, and career goals (with particular attention paid to the likelihood of the applicant representing underrepresented communities) are also factors taken into consideration.

Both need- and merit-based aid are available. All admitted students are automatically considered for merit scholarships. To apply for need-based aid, the FAFSA (www.fafsa.ed.gov) and the Need Access application (www.needaccess.org) should be filed no later than March 2. Applicants admitted to the law school as nonresident students (for tuition purposes)

are eligible to be considered for resident classification if certain eligibility requirements are met. Most nonresident law students are able to achieve residency status during the second year of law school.

Career Services

The Office of Career Services provides students and alumni with professional career services and acts as a liaison between students and employers. Each first-year student is assigned to a counselor who will assist him or her through all the phases of career preparation, from the first-year summer job to postgraduate employment. The office is also dedicated to advising and assisting students interested in pursuing postgraduate judicial clerkships. The office has one counselor dedicated to judicial clerkships and one dedicated to helping 3Ls and alumni secure employment.

The office coordinates on-campus interviews and off-campus career fairs with approximately 350 interviewers from law firms, corporations, government agencies, and public interest organizations visiting the school annually. The office also hosts numerous panels, programs, and events, including an annual Small/Mid-Sized Law Firm Reception, an annual Government Reception and Information Fair, and an Alumni Mentor Program.

UCLA Law graduates are in high demand among employers from all major sectors of the country, with California, New York, and Washington, DC, representing the largest employment markets for our students.

Students and graduates seeking to pursue public interest employment can take advantage of the opportunities offered by our Office of Public Interest Programs. There is a loan repayment assistance program to increase the ability of JD graduates to pursue public service legal careers. For more information on our loan repayment assistance program, please visit http://www.law.ucla.edu/lrap. For more on our office of career services, please visit our blog at http://bruinbriefs.blogspot.com/ or our website at http://www.law.ucla.edu/career-services.

APPLICANT PROFILE

University of California at Los Angeles (UCLA) School of Law
This grid includes only applicants who earned 120–180 LSAT scores under standard administrations.

LSAT Score	3.75 +		3.50–3.74		3.25–3.49		3.00–3.24		2.75–2.99		2.50–2.74		2.25–2.49		2.00–2.24		Below 2.00		No GPA		Total	
	Apps	Adm	Apps	Adm	Apps	Adm	Apps	Adm	Apps	Adm	Apps	Adm	Apps	Adm	Apps	Adm	Apps	Adm	Apps	Adm	Apps	Adm
175–180	76	51	66	33	44	8	27	3	3	0	5	0	0	0	2	0	0	0	2	0	225	95
170–174	451	333	388	209	210	46	102	9	25	1	11	0	3	1	0	0	0	0	25	5	1215	604
165–169	798	420	741	178	388	37	167	8	48	2	16	0	10	0	2	0	1	0	58	0	2229	645
160–164	406	72	475	24	326	21	157	8	47	1	33	1	19	1	4	0	0	0	53	1	1520	129
155–159	192	11	271	13	227	10	140	1	75	0	36	0	12	0	4	0	2	0	23	0	982	35
150–154	93	5	137	2	136	0	116	0	62	0	32	0	14	0	6	0	0	0	21	0	617	7
145–149	31	0	59	0	72	0	76	0	57	0	24	0	18	0	7	0	1	0	12	0	357	0
140–144	4	0	24	0	30	0	43	0	29	0	19	0	12	0	2	0	1	0	11	0	175	0
135–139	3	0	9	0	5	0	10	0	12	0	14	0	7	0	2	0	1	0	6	0	69	0
130–134	1	0	2	0	5	0	5	0	6	0	10	0	5	0	5	0	1	0	1	0	41	0
125–129	0	0	2	0	1	0	0	0	0	0	2	0	2	0	2	0	0	0	2	0	11	0
120–124	0	0	0	0	0	0	1	0	0	0	1	0	0	0	0	0	0	0	0	0	2	0
Total	2055	892	2174	459	1444	122	844	29	364	4	203	1	102	2	36	0	7	0	214	6	7443	1515

Apps = Number of Applicants
Adm = Number Admitted
Reflects 99% of the total applicant pool; highest LSAT data reported.

CALIFORNIA WESTERN SCHOOL OF LAW

225 Cedar Street
San Diego, CA 92101
Phone: 800.255.4252, ext. 1401 or 619.525.1401
E-mail: admissions@cwsl.edu; Website: www.CaliforniaWestern.edu

The Basics

Type of school	Private
Term	Semester
Application deadline	4/2 11/1
Application fee	$55
Financial aid deadline	4/2 10/15
Can first year start other than fall?	Yes
Student to faculty ratio	17.0 to 1
# of housing spaces available restricted to law students	
graduate housing for which law students are eligible	

Faculty and Administrators

	Total		Men		Women		Minorities	
	Spr	Fall	Spr	Fall	Spr	Fall	Spr	Fall
Full-time	37	42	24	27	13	15	3	4
Other full-time	5	4	3	2	2	2	2	1
Deans, librarians, & others who teach	13	13	5	5	8	8	3	3
Part-time	40	49	24	24	16	25	5	9
Total	95	108	56	58	39	50	13	17

JD Enrollment and Ethnicity

	Men		Women		Full-Time		Part-Time		1st-Year		Total		JD Degs. Awd.
	#	%	#	%	#	%	#	%	#	%	#	%	
All Hispanics	41	10.5	62	14.2	85	12.5	18	12.3	38	15.6	103	12.5	31
Am. Ind./AK Nat.	4	1.0	4	0.9	5	0.7	3	2.1	0	0.0	8	1.0	1
Asian	35	9.0	56	12.8	77	11.3	14	9.6	27	11.1	91	11.0	36
Black/Af. Am.	9	2.3	14	3.2	18	2.6	5	3.4	9	3.7	23	2.8	9
Nat. HI/Pac. Isl.	1	0.3	2	0.5	3	0.4	0	0.0	1	0.4	3	0.4	1
2 or more races	9	2.3	16	3.7	23	3.4	2	1.4	15	6.2	25	3.0	8
Subtotal (minor.)	99	25.4	154	35.2	211	31.0	42	28.8	90	37.0	253	30.6	86
Nonres. Alien	7	1.8	5	1.1	12	1.8	0	0.0	4	1.6	12	1.5	5
White/Cauc.	262	67.4	254	58.0	427	62.7	89	61.0	139	57.2	516	62.4	171
Unknown	21	5.4	25	5.7	31	4.6	15	10.3	10	4.1	46	5.6	29
Total	389	47.0	438	53.0	681	82.3	146	17.7	243	29.4	827		291

Curriculum

	Full-Time	Part-Time
Typical first-year section size	80	0
Is there typically a "small section" of the first-year class, other than Legal Writing, taught by full-time faculty	No	No
If yes, typical size offered last year		
# of classroom course titles beyond first-year curriculum	118	

# of upper division courses, excluding seminars, with an enrollment:		
	Under 25	130
	25–49	28
	50–74	12
	75–99	20
	100+	2

# of seminars	34	
# of seminar positions available	792	
# of seminar positions filled	493	62
# of positions available in simulation courses	1,794	
# of simulation positions filled	1,156	159
# of positions available in faculty supervised clinical courses	74	
# of faculty supervised clinical positions filled	60	7
# involved in field placements	183	13
# involved in law journals	72	8
# involved in moot court or trial competitions	37	3
# of credit hours required to graduate	89	

Transfers

Transfers in	6
Transfers out	10

Tuition and Fees

	Resident	Nonresident
Full-time	$42,700	$42,700
Part-time	$30,020	$30,020
Tuition Guarantee Program		N

Living Expenses

Estimated living expenses for singles

Living on campus	Living off campus	Living at home
N/A	$23,160	$14,970

CALIFORNIA WESTERN SCHOOL OF LAW

ABA Approved Since 1962

GPA and LSAT Scores

	Total	Full-Time	Part-Time
# of apps	2,208	2,034	174
# of offers	1,262	1,176	86
# of matrics	283	255	28
75% GPA	3.50	3.49	3.55
Median GPA	3.21	3.22	3.15
25% GPA	2.93	2.94	2.73
75% LSAT	156	156	154
Median LSAT	153	153	150
25% LSAT	150	150	149

Grants and Scholarships (from prior year)

	Total #	Total %	Full-Time #	Full-Time %	Part-Time #	Part-Time %
Total # of students	919		786		133	
Total # receiving grants	451	49.1	411	52.3	40	30.1
Less than 1/2 tuition	198	21.5	182	23.2	16	12.0
Half to full tuition	174	18.9	162	20.6	12	9.0
Full tuition	8	0.9	7	0.9	1	0.8
More than full tuition	71	7.7	60	7.6	11	8.3
Median grant amount			$20,340		$18,975	

Informational and Library Resources

Total amount spent on library materials	$1,284,726
Study seating capacity inside the library	510
# of full-time equivalent professional librarians	10
Hours per week library is open	110
# of open, wired connections available to students	540
# of networked computers available for use by students	88
Has wireless network?	Y
Requires computer?	N

JD Attrition (from prior year)

	Academic #	Other #	Total #	Total %
1st year	27	30	57	17.4
2nd year	0	1	1	0.3
3rd year	2	1	3	1.0
4th year	0	0	0	0.0

Employment (9 months after graduation)

For up-to-date employment data, go to employmentsummary.abaquestionnaire.org on the ABA website.

Bar Passage Rates

First-time takers	280	Reporting %	97.14
Average school %	70.61	Average state %	71.63
Average pass difference	−1.02		

Jurisdiction	Takers	Passers	Pass %	State %	Diff %
California	257	179	69.65	71.24	−1.59
Nevada	4	3	75.00	72.72	2.28
Washington	3	2	66.67	71.22	−4.55
Utah	2	2	100.00	89.35	10.65
Virginia	2	2	100.00	78.15	21.85

CALIFORNIA WESTERN SCHOOL OF LAW

225 Cedar Street
San Diego, CA 92101
Phone: 800.255.4252, ext. 1401 or 619.525.1401
E-mail: admissions@cwsl.edu; Website: www.CaliforniaWestern.edu

Introduction

California Western School of Law is the independent San Diego law school that educates lawyers as creative problem solvers and principled advocates—lawyers who frame the practice of law as a helping, collaborative profession. The law school's centers and institutes offer students many opportunities to explore the full scope of the law in real-life situations. California Western, accredited by the ABA (1962) and AALS (1967), emphasizes both theory and practice—rigorous academics and renowned real-world clinical programs—and invites students to explore the wide expanse of the law while preparing for practice.

Library and Physical Facilities

The award-winning, four-story, 50,000-square-foot law library was dedicated in 2000 by US Supreme Court Justice Anthony Kennedy. The library holds more than 350,000 volumes, including approximately 5,600 serial subscriptions, microforms equivalent to 162,000 volumes, audio- and videotapes, and access to a large number of online databases. The library also offers an excellent computer lab and is wired with high-speed digital lines supporting over 250 data ports in addition to wireless access. Renovations to the historic classroom building at California Western have provided several large lecture halls, office space for 30 on-campus student organizations, a 1,840-square-foot student lounge, individual study rooms, and a computer lab. Students enjoy additional access to the student network and Internet via campus-wide wireless technology.

Curriculum

The California Western curriculum offers a broad and diverse selection of courses. The law school provides a rigorous, traditional legal education with an emphasis on developing problem-solving, communication, writing, and analytical skills. Areas of concentration are also offered in eight fields of study: business law; international law; labor and employment law; child, family, and elder law; criminal law; creative problem solving; intellectual property, telecommunications, and technology-regulations law; and health law and policy. Numerous academic programs, including clinical placements and skills-based learning, supplement the course curriculum.

In addition to the traditional three-year curriculum, California Western offers a trimester academic calendar that allows students to study law year-round to complete their legal education in two years. California Western also offers a part-time day program.

Interdisciplinary Programs

California Western offers several dual-degree programs, allowing students to study two disciplines concurrently. The dual-degree program with the University of California, San Diego, offers degrees in political science (JD/PhD) and history (JD/PhD). California Western and the University of California, San Diego, also offer a joint degree in health law studies (MAS). In addition, California Western offers a dual-degree program with San Diego State University in both business (JD/MBA) and social work (JD/MSW).

University of California, San Diego Affiliation

California Western and the University of California, San Diego have an Agreement of Association that provides broad interdisciplinary opportunities for the faculty and students of both institutions. These opportunities include joint academic degrees, joint research efforts, a vibrant speaker series, sharing of facilities, and community outreach programs.

Study-Abroad Programs

Students have the opportunity to study in academic programs throughout the world, including in Chile, England, Ireland, Malta, and the Czech Republic. Additionally, semester-abroad opportunities are available at Victoria University of Wellington in New Zealand, the University of Aarhus in Denmark, the University of Paris X-Nanterre in France, and Leiden University School of Law in the Netherlands. Students may also choose to do an academic internship with the International Criminal Process Clinic at The Hague, the Netherlands.

Special Programs

The Center for Creative Problem Solving investigates collaborative approaches to communication, conflict resolution, and problem solving. The Center develops curriculum, research, and projects to educate students and lawyers on methods for preventing problems and creatively solving those problems that already exist. It also houses *Proyecto ACCESO*, a Latin American center for training lawyers, judges, law students, government officials, and community leaders in the skills of oral advocacy, problem solving, and other forms of conflict resolution.

Through the California Innocence Project, law students work alongside practicing criminal defense lawyers to seek the release of wrongfully convicted prisoners. Law students assist in the investigation, write briefs, and advocate for the release of clients.

The Institute of Health Law Studies is a health law center that focuses on "improving health care today for all our tomorrows." It performs research, participates in advocacy activities, engages in community service, and provides education to advance its mission.

The law school offers the LLM in Trial Advocacy specializing in Federal Criminal Law. International lawyers who are interested in studying comparative law or the US legal system may pursue the Master of Laws in Comparative Law (LLM) and the Master of Comparative Law (MCL).

Clinical Internship Program

California Western's Clinical Internship Program provides opportunities for students to gain practical lawyering experience in law offices, corporations, government agencies, and courts. Nearly 70 percent of California Western students participate in this popular program. Students have the opportunity to intern in almost any area of law. Out-of-town internships are available for students interested in developing these skills outside of San Diego. Our students have worked in many countries, including Argentina, Brazil, Chile, China, England, the Philippines, Poland, Singapore, Spain, Sweden, and Switzerland. Students have arranged internships at the United Nations, the Asian Development Bank, the International Criminal Tribunal for Rwanda, Paramount Studios, the Federal Communications Commission, and the US Department of State.

Student Activities

The *Law Review* and the *International Law Journal* publish articles by academic scholars and practitioners as well as by California Western students. Students edit and manage these publications under supervision from faculty advisors and a professional staff.

The Moot Court Honors Board allows students interested in trial and appellate advocacy skills to practice and compete against other students. Under the supervision and guidance of faculty coaches, students also participate in advocacy competitions around the country. California Western advocacy teams are nationally recognized, and our students have won many regional and national awards in these competitions.

California Western has a vibrant student government. Nearly 30 student organizations reflect a broad range of interests and diversity.

Career Services

Career Services offers individualized, professional advice to students about their personal career goals and tailors strategies to assist students in reaching those goals. The department coordinates the on-campus recruitment program, career development programming, practice-area panel discussions, national alumni mentor network, Pro Bono Honors and Public Service Programs, and access to technological resources for career development. Prospective employers and alumni regularly visit the campus to meet with interested students.

Alumni

California Western's nearly 9,000 alumni work in large firms, domestic and foreign governments, large corporations, private practice, the judiciary, and academia. The law school's Alumni Admissions Recruiter program matches alumni with prospective students in the areas in which they reside. The

Admissions Office can provide prospective students with a list of alumni in their area who are available to talk with them about employment opportunities and career advice.

Diversity

California Western's belief is that a richly diversified student body enhances the academic and interpersonal experiences of the law school. Half of the student body is female and approximately one-third is of an ethnic minority. California Western does not discriminate on the basis of race, color, creed, religion, sex, national origin, disability, sexual orientation, or veteran status.

Admission

Admission decisions are made on a rolling basis. Applicants are admitted based on an evaluation of the LSAT score, undergraduate academic record, personal statement, letters of recommendation, and other criteria, including work experience, campus and community activities, life/personal experiences, and evidence of leadership promise. Students are admitted to California Western to begin in August and January. A bachelor's degree and registration with LSAC's Credential Assembly Service are required. Application deadlines: fall—April 1; spring—November 1.

Financial Aid and Scholarships

More than 90 percent of California Western's students receive some form of financial assistance to fund their legal education. Need-based financial aid includes loans and work study. Numerous scholarships are awarded based on academic criteria and LSAT scores. Scholarships include the prestigious Kennedy Scholarship, the Robert J. Grey Jr. Scholarship, and the Trustees' Scholarship which, among other benefits, provides full tuition for three years. Other merit-based full and partial scholarships are awarded to incoming students, including diversity, career transition, and creative problem-solving scholarships. Academic achievement scholarships are available to continuing students. Scholarships are awarded by the Admissions Office after reviewing student admission applications.

APPLICANT PROFILE

California Western School of Law
This grid includes only applicants who earned 120–180 LSAT scores under standard administrations.

LSAT Score	3.75 +		3.50–3.74		3.25–3.49		3.00–3.24		2.75–2.99		2.50–2.74		Below 2.50		No GPA		Total	
	Apps	Adm	Apps	Adm	Apps	Adm	Apps	Adm	Apps	Adm	Apps	Adm	Apps	Adm	Apps	Adm	Apps	Adm
170–180	0	0	0	0	0	0	0	0	1	1	0	0	1	1	0	0	2	2
165–169	1	1	2	2	4	4	3	3	4	4	4	4	1	0	0	0	19	18
160–164	10	10	15	15	29	28	30	27	15	14	11	11	10	7	4	2	124	114
155–159	29	27	51	50	85	82	98	89	83	72	48	36	32	15	3	3	429	374
150–154	36	35	93	88	165	153	165	129	119	78	68	24	50	8	13	11	709	526
145–149	11	11	78	57	102	42	136	30	101	13	54	0	43	1	8	4	533	158
140–144	7	2	23	2	29	0	46	1	40	0	22	1	26	0	2	0	195	6
Below 140	3	0	2	0	6	0	8	0	18	0	13	0	10	0	1	0	61	0
Total	97	86	264	214	420	309	486	279	381	182	220	76	173	32	31	20	2072	1198

Apps = Number of Applicants   Adm = Number Admitted   Reflects 99% of the total applicant pool; highest LSAT data reported.

Miscellaneous applicants with no LSAT (i.e., MCL/LLM program) and nonstandard administration not in grid.

CAMPBELL UNIVERSITY, NORMAN ADRIAN WIGGINS SCHOOL OF LAW

225 Hillsborough Street
Raleigh, NC 27603
Phone: 919.865.5988; Fax: 919.865.5992
E-mail: admissions@law.campbell.edu; Website: www.law.campbell.edu

ABA Approved Since 1979

The Basics

Type of school	Private
Term	Semester
Application deadline	5/1
Application fee	$50
Financial aid deadline	5/1
Can first year start other than fall?	No
Student to faculty ratio	16.6 to 1
# of housing spaces available restricted to law students	
graduate housing for which law students are eligible	

Faculty and Administrators

	Total		Men		Women		Minorities	
	Spr	Fall	Spr	Fall	Spr	Fall	Spr	Fall
Full-time	23	23	17	17	6	6	1	2
Other full-time	0	0	0	0	0	0	0	0
Deans, librarians, & others who teach	4	4	2	2	2	2	0	0
Part-time	35	29	25	22	10	7	3	2
Total	62	56	44	41	18	15	4	4

Curriculum

	Full-Time	Part-Time
Typical first-year section size	42	0
Is there typically a "small section" of the first-year class, other than Legal Writing, taught by full-time faculty	No	No
If yes, typical size offered last year		
# of classroom course titles beyond first-year curriculum	106	
# of upper division courses, excluding seminars, with an enrollment: Under 25	63	
25–49	29	
50–74	8	
75–99	3	
100+	0	
# of seminars	31	
# of seminar positions available	600	
# of seminar positions filled	530	0
# of positions available in simulation courses	675	
# of simulation positions filled	624	0
# of positions available in faculty supervised clinical courses	36	
# of faculty supervised clinical positions filled	36	0
# involved in field placements	194	0
# involved in law journals	63	0
# involved in moot court or trial competitions	132	0
# of credit hours required to graduate	90	

JD Enrollment and Ethnicity

	Men #	Men %	Women #	Women %	Full-Time #	Full-Time %	Part-Time #	Part-Time %	1st-Year #	1st-Year %	Total #	Total %	JD Degs. Awd.
All Hispanics	5	2.0	12	5.2	17	3.6	0	0.0	8	4.2	17	3.6	6
Am. Ind./AK Nat.	1	0.4	1	0.4	2	0.4	0	0.0	2	1.1	2	0.4	0
Asian	6	2.5	3	1.3	9	1.9	0	0.0	3	1.6	9	1.9	3
Black/Af. Am.	5	2.0	14	6.1	19	4.0	0	0.0	11	5.8	19	4.0	5
Nat. Hl/Pac. Isl.	0	0.0	0	0.0	0	0.0	0	0.0	0	0.0	0	0.0	0
2 or more races	0	0.0	0	0.0	0	0.0	0	0.0	0	0.0	0	0.0	0
Subtotal (minor.)	17	7.0	30	13.0	47	9.9	0	0.0	24	12.6	47	9.9	14
Nonres. Alien	0	0.0	0	0.0	0	0.0	0	0.0	0	0.0	0	0.0	0
White/Cauc.	227	93.0	201	87.0	428	90.1	0	0.0	166	87.4	428	90.1	120
Unknown	0	0.0	0	0.0	0	0.0	0	0.0	0	0.0	0	0.0	0
Total	244	51.4	231	48.6	475	100.0	0	0.0	190	40.0	475		134

Transfers

Transfers in	1
Transfers out	3

Tuition and Fees

	Resident	Nonresident
Full-time	$33,910	$33,910
Part-time		
Tuition Guarantee Program	N	

Living Expenses

Estimated living expenses for singles

Living on campus	Living off campus	Living at home
N/A	$26,700	N/A

CAMPBELL UNIVERSITY, NORMAN ADRIAN WIGGINS SCHOOL OF LAW

ABA
Approved
Since
1979

GPA and LSAT Scores

	Total	Full-Time	Part-Time
# of apps	1,227	1,227	0
# of offers	517	517	0
# of matrics	191	191	0
75% GPA	3.55	3.55	0.00
Median GPA	3.32	3.32	0.00
25% GPA	3.10	3.10	0.00
75% LSAT	159	159	0
Median LSAT	156	156	0
25% LSAT	153	153	0

Grants and Scholarships (from prior year)

	Total #	Total %	Full-Time #	Full-Time %	Part-Time #	Part-Time %
Total # of students	450		450		0	
Total # receiving grants	173	38.4	173	38.4	0	0.0
Less than 1/2 tuition	108	24.0	108	24.0	0	0.0
Half to full tuition	62	13.8	62	13.8	0	0.0
Full tuition	3	0.7	3	0.7	0	0.0
More than full tuition	0	0.0	0	0.0	0	0.0
Median grant amount			$10,700		$0	

Informational and Library Resources

Total amount spent on library materials	$1,014,015
Study seating capacity inside the library	266
# of full-time equivalent professional librarians	5
Hours per week library is open	102
# of open, wired connections available to students	0
# of networked computers available for use by students	45
Has wireless network?	Y
Requires computer?	N

JD Attrition (from prior year)

	Academic #	Other #	Total #	Total %
1st year	9	12	21	12.8
2nd year	1	0	1	0.7
3rd year	0	1	1	0.7
4th year	0	0	0	0.0

Employment (9 months after graduation)

For up-to-date employment data, go to
employmentsummary.abaquestionnaire.org on the ABA website.

Bar Passage Rates

First-time takers	109	Reporting %	95.41
Average school %	85.57	Average state %	77.78
Average pass difference	7.79		

Jurisdiction	Takers	Passers	Pass %	State %	Diff %
North Carolina	93	78	83.87	77.50	6.37
South Carolina	5	5	100.00	79.69	20.31
Virginia	3	3	100.00	78.15	21.85
Colorado	1	1	100.00	82.79	17.21
Texas	1	1	100.00	82.68	17.32

CAMPBELL UNIVERSITY, NORMAN ADRIAN WIGGINS SCHOOL OF LAW

225 Hillsborough Street
Raleigh, NC 27603
Phone: 919.865.5988; Fax: 919.865.5992
E-mail: admissions@law.campbell.edu; Website: www.law.campbell.edu

Introduction

The Norman Adrian Wiggins School of Law at Campbell University is a highly demanding, purposely small, and intensely personal community of faculty and students. Campbell Law's aim, guided by transcendent values, is to develop lawyers who possess moral conviction, social compassion, and professional competence; who view the law as a calling to serve others and to create a more just society.

Campbell Law School is a private law school that is fully accredited by the American Bar Association, boasting more than three decades of excellence in legal education. Located within walking distance of the North Carolina state legislature; federal and state courts; federal, state, and local government agencies; and the region's top law firms, corporations, and nonprofits, Campbell Law provides a living legal laboratory to its students.

Campbell Law School encourages students to examine the relationship between spiritual and legal issues, to explore the theological foundations for law, to think differently about justice and the legal system, and to consider how they can help achieve a more just and merciful society. While embracing an intellectual perspective rooted in Christian tradition, Campbell Law School is committed to free and open discussion of ideas. Students are under no obligation to embrace any particular way of thinking.

For the past 25 years, Campbell Law's record of success on the North Carolina Bar exam is unsurpassed by any other North Carolina law school.

Raleigh was recently labeled the number 1 "Best American City" and the number 1 "Best Place for Business and Careers." Raleigh offers a rich cultural history in a progressive setting and is located just a few hours from legendary beaches in one direction and the scenic Blue Ridge Mountains in the other.

Enrollment

Campbell Law School is one of the smallest ABA-accredited private law schools in the country. With a limited first-year enrollment, students enjoy the many advantages of a law school that remains purposely small. Our community of students and faculty is intensely personal—students build a network of relationships that supports them during their legal studies and extends far beyond graduation.

Currently, our student body is comprised of 475 students from 23 different states, holding degrees from 109 colleges and universities with 57 different majors represented. Campbell Law School is committed to enrolling a diverse student body and has an overall minority enrollment of 10 percent.

Faculty

Campbell Law School's faculty is a community of scholars who make teaching their priority. They are readily accessible and serve students as mentors, coaches, and professional role models. All faculty have open-door office policies and are available to consult regularly with students on an individual basis. Our professors are deeply committed to the search for knowledge through meaningful legal scholarship, but never at the expense of their devotion to the academic success and professional development of each student.

Facilities and Technology

Campbell Law School is located in the heart of downtown Raleigh. Each of the Law School's classrooms and courtrooms has video cameras to record lectures that most professors post via Blackboard for student review and use. In addition, the entire Law School is wireless, including student access to printers.

Curriculum

Campbell Law School holds students to the highest standards of thinking, speaking, and writing logically. To accomplish this goal, the course of instruction is exceptionally rigorous.

In a national survey, Campbell Law School's Trial Advocacy Program has been called one of the most rigorous in the nation. Every second-year student is required to plan and participate in a mock trial. Because of this, our graduates are exceptionally well prepared to advocate for their clients, whether in the boardroom or the courtroom.

Campbell Law School offers a joint Juris Doctor/Master of Business Administration degree, and has pioneered a joint Juris Doctor/Master of Trust and Wealth Management degree, which is the only program of its kind in the country. Both of these programs can be completed within three years. Campbell also offers two dual-degree programs with North Carolina State University, a Juris Doctor/Master of Public Administration and a Juris Doctor/Master of Business Administration. The dual-degree programs can be completed in four years.

Special Programs

The Juvenile Justice Project is a collaboration between Campbell Law School and the North Carolina Governor's Crime Commission. Students are trained in the application of mediation and other alternative dispute-resolution processes and have the opportunity to assist in the mediation of juvenile law disputes.

Prisoner Assistance and Legal Services (PALS) provides our students with an opportunity to serve older prisoners by addressing the unique problems of aging in prison.

Externship programs provide students with a meaningful education experience in a public service environment. Students receive up to two hours of academic credit for uncompensated, substantive legal work through externship placements.

The Senior Law Clinic serves the legal needs of low-income senior citizens in the greater Raleigh region.

Student Publications and Organizations

One of the primary motivations for keeping enrollment limited at Campbell Law School is to offer all students outstanding opportunities to gain valuable experiences in activities and organizations.

The *Campbell Law Review* is a student publication of scholarly writings on current legal topics. It is a valued research tool for judges, attorneys, legislatures, educators, and students. Writers and editors for the *Campbell Law Review* are students who demonstrate the highest degree of academic excellence. Participation is by invitation only.

The *Campbell Law Observer* is a monthly student publication that features reports on recent state and federal court opinions, scholarly articles on current legal topics, and subjects of general interest to members of the legal community.

Campbell Law School is also the official international headquarters for the Delta Theta Phi Law Fraternity, one of the leading professional law fraternities in the world.

Admission

Campbell Law School's Admissions Committee takes seriously its responsibility for admitting qualified applicants. Campbell Law believes each applicant we accept has the potential to succeed in our program and pursue a legal education and professional career consistent with Campbell Law School's vision and tradition of excellence. The Admissions Committee bases its selection on the applicant's academic credentials, including LSAT score, undergraduate grade-point average (UGPA), level of writing skills, breadth of studies, and other criteria including, but not limited to, work, life, and leadership experience; depth of particular interest; and any other aspect of an applicant's background suggesting suitability for the study and practice of law.

Expenses and Financial Aid

Campbell Law School recognizes the high cost of a quality education. Every effort is made to ensure that no qualified applicant is denied the opportunity to study law for financial reasons. Assistance may be provided in the form of institutional scholarships, endowed scholarships, loans, and work-study programs. Approximately 60 percent of students receive scholarship assistance. Approximately 95 percent of students receive financial aid.

In and Around Raleigh

The Raleigh area offers students many housing options in a mix of urban, suburban, and rural areas. The Raleigh community combines the charm of small town roots with easy access to urban amenities. The region offers housing for every taste and budget.

The city offers a variety of museums, performance centers, and other cultural scenes. The area also offers a full schedule of collegiate and professional spectator sports, including Atlantic Coast Conference (ACC) basketball and football and the Carolina Hurricanes of the National Hockey League (NHL).

Career Services

The Career and Professional Development Center helps students chart a course toward securing summer and permanent employment from their first semester at Campbell Law School.

Employers of Campbell Law School graduates include small and large firms, courts, all branches of the military, judges, government agencies and offices, public service organizations, and corporations.

While 80 percent of Campbell Law graduates remain in North Carolina to practice law, 20 percent choose to practice across the nation and around the world. Currently, Campbell Law alumni live and practice in 40 states and 6 countries.

APPLICANT PROFILE

Campbell University, Norman Adrian Wiggins School of Law
This grid includes only applicants who earned 120–180 LSAT scores under standard administrations.

LSAT Score	3.75 +		3.50–3.74		3.25–3.49		3.00–3.24		2.75–2.99		2.50–2.74		Below 2.50		No GPA		Total	
	Apps	Adm	Apps	Adm	Apps	Adm	Apps	Adm	Apps	Adm	Apps	Adm	Apps	Adm	Apps	Adm	Apps	Adm
170–180	2	2	1	1	3	3	1	1	1	1	0	0	0	0	0	0	8	8
165–169	3	3	4	4	3	3	3	3	3	2	0	0	1	1	1	1	18	17
160–164	16	15	25	24	19	18	27	27	12	10	10	5	11	7	1	1	121	107
155–159	30	29	54	52	82	77	61	55	38	25	17	8	16	2	1	1	299	249
150–154	34	21	79	47	87	35	76	24	43	5	26	4	20	0	3	2	368	138
145–149	15	1	28	2	38	0	58	2	36	1	23	0	19	0	1	0	218	6
140–144	2	0	7	0	15	0	26	0	22	0	12	0	18	0	4	0	106	0
Below 140	1	0	5	0	6	0	14	0	9	0	15	0	16	0	2	0	68	0
Total	103	71	203	130	253	136	266	112	164	44	103	17	101	10	13	5	1206	525

Apps = Number of Applicants
Adm = Number Admitted
Reflects 100% of the total applicant pool; highest LSAT data reported.

CAPITAL UNIVERSITY LAW SCHOOL

303 E. Broad Street
Columbus, OH 43215-3200
Phone: 614.236.6310; Fax: 614.236.6972
E-mail: admissions@law.capital.edu; Website: www.law.capital.edu

ABA Approved Since 1950

The Basics

Type of school	Private
Term	Semester
Application deadline	5/1
Application fee	$40
Financial aid deadline	7/15
Can first year start other than fall?	No
Student to faculty ratio	15.1 to 1
# of housing spaces available restricted to law students	
graduate housing for which law students are eligible	

Faculty and Administrators

	Total		Men		Women		Minorities	
	Spr	Fall	Spr	Fall	Spr	Fall	Spr	Fall
Full-time	30	32	21	23	9	9	4	3
Other full-time	3	2	0	0	3	2	0	0
Deans, librarians, & others who teach	6	6	2	1	4	5	1	1
Part-time	28	25	22	19	6	6	2	2
Total	67	65	45	43	22	22	7	6

Curriculum

	Full-Time	Part-Time
Typical first-year section size	89	50
Is there typically a "small section" of the first-year class, other than Legal Writing, taught by full-time faculty	Yes	Yes
If yes, typical size offered last year	37	25
# of classroom course titles beyond first-year curriculum	194	
# of upper division courses, excluding seminars, with an enrollment: Under 25	131	
25–49	32	
50–74	16	
75–99	10	
100+	1	
# of seminars	11	
# of seminar positions available	165	
# of seminar positions filled	82	25
# of positions available in simulation courses	1,414	
# of simulation positions filled	566	152
# of positions available in faculty supervised clinical courses	96	
# of faculty supervised clinical positions filled	65	8
# involved in field placements	174	17
# involved in law journals	152	9
# involved in moot court or trial competitions	26	2
# of credit hours required to graduate	89	

JD Enrollment and Ethnicity

	Men		Women		Full-Time		Part-Time		1st-Year		Total		JD Degs. Awd.
	#	%	#	%	#	%	#	%	#	%	#	%	
All Hispanics	4	1.1	11	3.9	14	3.1	1	0.6	11	5.3	15	2.4	2
Am. Ind./AK Nat.	1	0.3	0	0.0	1	0.2	0	0.0	1	0.5	1	0.2	0
Asian	5	1.4	5	1.8	3	0.7	7	4.0	2	1.0	10	1.6	3
Black/Af. Am.	14	4.0	31	11.1	27	5.9	18	10.2	13	6.3	45	7.1	8
Nat. HI/Pac. Isl.	0	0.0	0	0.0	0	0.0	0	0.0	0	0.0	0	0.0	0
2 or more races	3	0.8	4	1.4	5	1.1	2	1.1	4	1.9	7	1.1	10
Subtotal (minor.)	27	7.6	51	18.2	50	11.0	28	15.8	31	14.9	78	12.3	23
Nonres. Alien	1	0.3	1	0.4	1	0.2	1	0.6	0	0.0	2	0.3	0
White/Cauc.	310	87.8	216	77.1	388	85.1	138	78.0	170	81.7	526	83.1	132
Unknown	15	4.2	12	4.3	17	3.7	10	5.6	7	3.4	27	4.3	18
Total	353	55.8	280	44.2	456	72.0	177	28.0	208	32.9	633		173

Transfers

Transfers in	6
Transfers out	10

Tuition and Fees

	Resident	Nonresident
Full-time	$32,683	$32,683
Part-time	$21,413	$21,413
Tuition Guarantee Program		N

Living Expenses

Estimated living expenses for singles

Living on campus	Living off campus	Living at home
N/A	$13,785	$13,785

CAPITAL UNIVERSITY LAW SCHOOL

ABA Approved Since 1950

GPA and LSAT Scores

	Total	Full-Time	Part-Time
# of apps	1,055	915	140
# of offers	682	605	77
# of matrics	206	162	44
75% GPA	3.50	3.51	3.49
Median GPA	3.20	3.22	3.12
25% GPA	2.95	2.99	2.89
75% LSAT	154	154	156
Median LSAT	151	151	151
25% LSAT	148	148	146

Grants and Scholarships (from prior year)

	Total		Full-Time		Part-Time	
	#	%	#	%	#	%
Total # of students	656		486		170	
Total # receiving grants	330	50.3	264	54.3	66	38.8
Less than 1/2 tuition	263	40.1	209	43.0	54	31.8
Half to full tuition	66	10.1	54	11.1	12	7.1
Full tuition	1	0.2	1	0.2	0	0.0
More than full tuition	0	0.0	0	0.0	0	0.0
Median grant amount			$12,000		$5,000	

Informational and Library Resources

Total amount spent on library materials	$1,264,517
Study seating capacity inside the library	460
# of full-time equivalent professional librarians	5
Hours per week library is open	92
# of open, wired connections available to students	113
# of networked computers available for use by students	26
Has wireless network?	Y
Requires computer?	N

JD Attrition (from prior year)

	Academic	Other	Total	
	#	#	#	%
1st year	26	31	57	23.7
2nd year	3	1	4	1.9
3rd year	0	2	2	1.2
4th year	0	3	3	8.6

Employment (9 months after graduation)

For up-to-date employment data, go to employmentsummary.abaquestionnaire.org on the ABA website.

Bar Passage Rates

First-time takers	169	Reporting %	93.49
Average school %	90.51	Average state %	86.14
Average pass difference	4.37		

Jurisdiction	Takers	Passers	Pass %	State %	Diff %
Ohio	158	143	90.51	86.14	4.37

CAPITAL UNIVERSITY LAW SCHOOL

303 E. Broad Street
Columbus, OH 43215-3200
Phone: 614.236.6310; Fax: 614.236.6972
E-mail: admissions@law.capital.edu; Website: www.law.capital.edu

Introduction

Capital University Law School, located in downtown Columbus, is at the epicenter of Ohio's legal, business, and government community. Our location provides students with an ideal environment to study law and a wealth of opportunities to gain practical legal experience, meet future employers, and establish a network of contacts within the legal arena. The Law School is within walking distance of the Ohio Supreme Court, the Ohio Court of Appeals, the Ohio Attorney General's Office, the state legislature, major law firms, numerous state agencies, and Fortune 500 corporations.

Innovation and leadership are intrinsic traits of our heritage. For more than a century, Capital Law School has produced some of the finest judges, partners, and associates of respected law firms; officials at all levels of government; business professionals; and influential community leaders. We invite you to closely examine all of the factors that distinguish this law school:

- Outstanding faculty
- Superior bar passage and employment rates
- Innovative curriculum
- Extensive and diverse externship opportunities
- Remarkable alumni
- Commitment to serving diverse communities

Curriculum

Capital University Law School is committed to providing our full- and part-time students with a first-rate education. The Law School's comprehensive curriculum balances theoretical knowledge and practical applications of the law. Courses are both intellectually challenging and cutting edge, equipping our students with essential lawyering skills necessary for effective, creative, and ethical legal counseling and advocacy. By graduation, our alumni have made the transition from law student to legal practitioner—prepared to meet the challenges and demands of the evolving practice of law.

Teaching is a core value at Capital University Law School. Capital Law students describe the faculty as knowledgeable, accessible, collegial, cooperative, and true mentors. Outside of the classroom, our faculty are accomplished scholars who distinguish themselves through their research, scholarship, and authorship of books and journal publications. In a recent study, Capital Law School's faculty is noted for scholarly productivity.

To learn more about Capital Law's rich curriculum and distinguished faculty, visit www.law.capital.edu.

Multicultural Affairs

Capital University Law School takes pride in its history of providing a legal education for groups who historically have been excluded from or underrepresented in law schools. Capital University Law School is committed to supporting and embracing diversity in all of its forms. The Law School actively recruits students of all races and sexual orientations.

Students come to Capital with diverse educational, cultural, social, and professional backgrounds. Capital University Law School embraces and values the varied perspectives our students bring to the school.

Capital has many programs and benefits that support students of color. The presence of minority faculty, a director of multicultural affairs, availability of financial aid, academic as well as nonacademic support, and participation in the Columbus Bar Association Minority Clerkship Program are some of the things available to our students. In addition to the services at the Law School, Columbus also presents a diverse and supportive community in which our law students can live, learn, play, and explore.

Special Programs

Diversity of opportunity is a trademark of Capital University Law School. Capital students have the unique opportunity to create their own academic path and pursue their personal passions through our specialized and innovative academic programs.

Concentrations

The Law School's concentration certificates allow students to focus their electives in specific areas of the law by combining theoretical and practical classroom experience with faculty expertise. Capital offers concentrations in eight specialty areas:

- Children and Family Law
- Civil Litigation
- Criminal Litigation
- Dispute Resolution
- Environmental Law
- Governmental Affairs
- Labor and Employment Law
- Small Business Entities and Publicly Held Companies

Joint-Degree Programs

The Law School's joint-degree programs allow students to advance their education without delaying their career plans. These accelerated programs enable students to complete two degrees with a substantial reduction in total credit hours and in less time than it would take to obtain them separately. Capital offers a Juris Doctor with any of the following degrees:

- Master of Business Administration
- Master of Sports Administration
- Master of Science in Nursing
- Master of Theology
- Master of Laws in Business
- Master of Laws in Business and Taxation
- Master of Laws in Taxation

Centers and Legal Clinics

Our commitment to immersing you in the real-world environment of law is best exemplified by our diverse externship program, along with our centers and legal clinics. Students enrich their academic environment by working closely with clinical attorneys and experiencing the challenges and rewards of practicing law and giving back to the community-at-large. The Law School's centers and clinics include:

- The Center for Dispute Resolution
- The National Center for Adoption Law and Policy
- The General Litigation Clinic
- The Mediation Clinic
- The Family Advocacy Clinic
- The Small Business Clinic

Admission

Capital University Law School seeks to attract a diverse pool of applicants who are motivated, committed, and possess the requisite skills and abilities to study law. Admission to the Law School is based on a thorough review of each individual's application file in its entirety. Rarely does any single factor, either LSAT score or undergraduate grade-point average, determine a candidate's status.

The Law School's Admission Committee thoughtfully and thoroughly evaluates the competitiveness and difficulty of each candidate's undergraduate and graduate coursework, personal statement, letters of recommendation, employment history, writing ability, leadership experience, extracurricular activities, general background, and any additional information the candidate feels is important to the admission decision. All of these factors, along with the LSAT score and grade-point average, are weighed during the admission process.

Student Activities

Capital Law School offers many organizations and activities to help you round out your education. Extra- and cocurricular activities range from more than 20 student groups and at least 10 competition teams to the *Capital University Law Review*. Clubs are educational, professional, and social while encouraging the legal community's collaboration and engagement. Student organizations at Capital University Law School offer many opportunities for leadership development, networking, and interaction with professionals in various specialties.

The Law School supports associations for students with common values and backgrounds, as well as groups focused on specific areas of law such as sports and entertainment, environmental issues, and intellectual property. The *Capital University Law Review* provides the legal community scholarly analysis of contemporary legal issues. Students may expand their writing and editing skills through membership on the *Law Review*. Those wishing to hone their skills and test them in competition will want to investigate Capital's highly successful moot court teams. Students may participate in national competitions, such as the Philip C. Jessup International Law and the Frederick Douglass Moot Court competitions. Teams also are selected in the areas of environmental law, sports law, labor law, and tax.

Professional Development

The Capital Law School Office of Professional Development provides individual career counseling for students and alumni and a wide variety of career-related programs, including Continuing Legal Education programs for alumni. The office provides an online job-posting board, coordinates employer recruiting programs, and maintains an extensive library of books and other relevant resources. It also houses the Law School's Public Interest Center and administers the Pro Bono Recognition Program.

Capital Law School graduates pursue a variety of legal and nonlegal employment opportunities. For the class of 2010, 85 percent of those graduates seeking employment were employed within nine months of graduation, based upon data reported by 140 of the 177 students who graduated in 2010. Private practice is the largest of these areas, with approximately 55 percent of the graduating class entering this field. Many Capital graduates enter public service (19.5 percent), which includes government, public interest, and judicial clerkship positions, while others find employment in corporations and academia. For detailed employment information about Capital, visit our website at law.capital.edu/Employment_Data.aspx.

APPLICANT PROFILE

Capital University Law School

LSAT Score	GPA								
	3.75 +	3.50–3.74	3.25–3.49	3.00–3.24	2.75–2.99	2.50–2.74	2.25–2.49	2.00–2.24	Below 2.00
175–180									
170–174									
165–169									
160–164									
155–159									
150–154									
145–149									
140–144									
135–139									
130–134									
125–129									
120–124									

■ Good Possibility □ Possible ▨ Unlikely

BENJAMIN N. CARDOZO SCHOOL OF LAW, YESHIVA UNIVERSITY

55 Fifth Avenue
New York, NY 10003
Phone: 212.790.0274; Fax: 212.790.0482
E-mail: lawinfo@yu.edu; Website: www.cardozo.yu.edu

ABA
Approved
Since
1978

The Basics

Type of school	Private
Term	Semester
Application deadline	4/1
Application fee	$75
Financial aid deadline	4/1
Can first year start other than fall?	Yes
Student to faculty ratio	15.2 to 1
# of housing spaces available restricted to law students	120
graduate housing for which law students are eligible	

Faculty and Administrators

	Total		Men		Women		Minorities	
	Spr	Fall	Spr	Fall	Spr	Fall	Spr	Fall
Full-time	64	58	41	35	23	23	5	4
Other full-time	1	1	0	0	1	1	0	0
Deans, librarians, & others who teach	5	5	3	3	2	2	1	1
Part-time	99	107	63	66	36	41	6	7
Total	169	171	107	104	62	67	12	12

Curriculum

		Full-Time	Part-Time
Typical first-year section size		50	50
Is there typically a "small section" of the first-year class, other than Legal Writing, taught by full-time faculty		No	No
If yes, typical size offered last year			
# of classroom course titles beyond first-year curriculum		159	
# of upper division courses, excluding seminars, with an enrollment:	Under 25	39	
	25–49	41	
	50–74	22	
	75–99	10	
	100+	14	
# of seminars		78	
# of seminar positions available		1,515	
# of seminar positions filled		1,042	0
# of positions available in simulation courses		722	
# of simulation positions filled		558	0
# of positions available in faculty supervised clinical courses		171	
# of faculty supervised clinical positions filled		166	0
# involved in field placements		267	0
# involved in law journals		352	0
# involved in moot court or trial competitions		63	0
# of credit hours required to graduate		84	

JD Enrollment and Ethnicity

	Men		Women		Full-Time		Part-Time		1st-Year		Total		JD Degs. Awd.
	#	%	#	%	#	%	#	%	#	%	#	%	
All Hispanics	32	5.8	52	8.8	77	7.4	7	6.9	31	8.9	84	7.4	19
Am. Ind./AK Nat.	1	0.2	1	0.2	2	0.2	0	0.0	0	0.0	2	0.2	2
Asian	13	2.4	35	5.9	40	3.9	8	7.8	26	7.4	48	4.2	40
Black/Af. Am.	22	4.0	33	5.6	54	5.2	1	1.0	20	5.7	55	4.8	19
Nat. HI/Pac. Isl.	17	3.1	23	3.9	40	3.9	0	0.0	0	0.0	40	3.5	0
2 or more races	10	1.8	11	1.9	18	1.7	3	2.9	12	3.4	21	1.8	0
Subtotal (minor.)	95	17.2	155	26.3	231	22.3	19	18.6	89	25.5	250	21.9	80
Nonres. Alien	7	1.3	10	1.7	16	1.5	1	1.0	3	0.9	17	1.5	11
White/Cauc.	361	65.5	338	57.4	651	62.7	48	47.1	150	43.0	699	61.3	153
Unknown	88	16.0	86	14.6	140	13.5	34	33.3	107	30.7	174	15.3	136
Total	551	48.3	589	51.7	1038	91.1	102	8.9	349	30.6	1140		380

Transfers

Transfers in	45
Transfers out	13

Tuition and Fees

	Resident	Nonresident
Full-time	$48,370	$48,370
Part-time	$48,370	$48,370
Tuition Guarantee Program		N

Living Expenses

Estimated living expenses for singles

Living on campus	Living off campus	Living at home
$24,568	$24,568	N/A

BENJAMIN N. CARDOZO SCHOOL OF LAW, YESHIVA UNIVERSITY

ABA
Approved
Since
1978

GPA and LSAT Scores

	Total	Full-Time	Part-Time
# of apps	4,915	4,241	674
# of offers	1,499	1,315	184
# of matrics	379	269	110
75% GPA	3.73	3.73	3.72
Median GPA	3.60	3.60	3.59
25% GPA	3.40	3.41	3.38
75% LSAT	165	166	161
Median LSAT	162	164	159
25% LSAT	158	160	157

Grants and Scholarships (from prior year)

	Total #	Total %	Full-Time #	Full-Time %	Part-Time #	Part-Time %
Total # of students	1,124		1,025		99	
Total # receiving grants	624	55.5	611	59.6	13	13.1
Less than 1/2 tuition	264	23.5	254	24.8	10	10.1
Half to full tuition	206	18.3	203	19.8	3	3.0
Full tuition	133	11.8	133	13.0	0	0.0
More than full tuition	21	1.9	21	2.0	0	0.0
Median grant amount			$25,000		$10,000	

Informational and Library Resources

Total amount spent on library materials	$1,779,817
Study seating capacity inside the library	446
# of full-time equivalent professional librarians	7
Hours per week library is open	88
# of open, wired connections available to students	30
# of networked computers available for use by students	137
Has wireless network?	Y
Requires computer?	N

JD Attrition (from prior year)

	Academic #	Other #	Total #	Total %
1st year	0	29	29	8.3
2nd year	1	5	6	1.5
3rd year	0	0	0	0.0
4th year	0	0	0	0.0

Employment (9 months after graduation)

For up-to-date employment data, go to employmentsummary.abaquestionnaire.org on the ABA website.

Bar Passage Rates

First-time takers	373	Reporting %	93.83
Average school %	85.14	Average state %	84.92
Average pass difference	.22		

Jurisdiction	Takers	Passers	Pass %	State %	Diff %
New York	350	298	85.14	84.92	0.22

BENJAMIN N. CARDOZO SCHOOL OF LAW, YESHIVA UNIVERSITY

55 Fifth Avenue
New York, NY 10003
Phone: 212.790.0274; Fax: 212.790.0482
E-mail: lawinfo@yu.edu; Website: www.cardozo.yu.edu

Introduction

Cardozo Law offers students a stimulating intellectual educational experience, rooted in the values of ethics, public service, and scholarship. Known for providing high intellectual standards and pioneering hands-on experiences, Cardozo Law also provides students with a deep understanding of how law relates to other expressions of the human spirit, including philosophy, economics, politics, history, art, and literature. Cardozo offers superb programs in intellectual property law, criminal law, alternative dispute resolution, international and human rights law, public interest law, and legal theory. A highly energetic and supportive faculty engages students from 43 countries and all regions of the United States. Extensive clinical and externship opportunities draw on the resources available in New York City, and programs, centers, and clinics, such as the Innocence Project and the Heyman Center for Corporate Governance, are well known for innovation and leadership. Unique hands-on clinical opportunities are offered, including the Holocaust Claims Restitution Clinic, the Indie Film Clinic, and the Kathryn O. Greenberg Immigration Justice Clinic. These clinics train students in connecting theory with practical application of the law. Field clinics designed to help students become practice-ready are offered in partnership with legal institutions in the metropolitan area, including the New York Attorney General's office, city government departments, and nonprofits in fields such as consumer rights, health law, and art law. A Cardozo legal education emphasizes the pursuit of intellectual excellence while providing a wealth of lawyering opportunities.

Faculty

Professors at Cardozo are accessible and engaged in all aspects of students' professional development. They are committed to making the classroom experience vital and engaging, as well as pursuing serious scholarship, with more than half holding advanced degrees, such as PhDs, in addition to their law degrees. Cultivating an atmosphere of intellectual dialogue and curiosity, faculty members work closely with students on conferences that attract world-class guest speakers in all legal specialties. Cardozo Law professors have extensive connections within the New York City legal community and elsewhere. Many who teach here are prolific writers. They are frequently cited among academics worldwide and write publications that serve as required reading in law schools throughout the nation. Cardozo's clinical faculty is known for its innovative leadership. From the renowned Innocence Project to the pioneering Indie Film Clinic, our faculty members help students to develop hands-on skills in courtrooms, negotiations, transactional law experience, public policy advocacy, and mediation practice. Cardozo faculty members see it as their job to prepare students to be ready to practice law as leaders in a new age, and to hold fast to the core values of justice, equality, and ethics.

A Campus in New York City

Cardozo is located in a vibrant neighborhood in Greenwich Village, just blocks from Union Square. It is easily accessible to all points in New York City, including the courts, Wall Street, Midtown, and the art and music centers on the East and West Sides of Manhattan. The law school's state-of-the-art facility includes a moot courtroom, additional library space, a center for student life, student and faculty offices, and fully wired classrooms and seminar rooms.

The Cardozo residence hall is located on a residential, tree-lined street just one block south of the main building. Studio, one-bedroom, and two-bedroom apartments—all of which are air-conditioned, fully furnished, and equipped with kitchens—are available for incoming students.

Students/Student Activities

The student body at Cardozo is a diverse and impressive group. A typical entering class includes graduates from more than 145 colleges, and from 32 states and 12 foreign countries. Roughly 26 percent of the class are members of minority groups and 48 percent have been out of college between one and five years. Approximately 10 percent hold advanced degrees.

More than half of the second- and third-year students participate on one of six student-edited journals or in the Moot Court Honor Society. Scholarly journals include the *Cardozo Law Review, Cardozo Arts and Entertainment Law Journal, Cardozo Journal of International and Comparative Law, Cardozo Journal of Law and Gender, Cardozo Journal of Conflict Resolution,* and *Cardozo Public Law, Policy, and Ethics Journal.*

Career Services

Cardozo students benefit from a large network of working alumni and a career services office staffed by six professional counselors, all of whom have JD degrees. Students are offered individual assistance with interviewing techniques, résumé writing, and job-search strategies, as well as workshops and opportunities for learning about a variety of legal careers from attorneys in the field.

Ninety-three percent of those reporting from the class of 2010 were employed within several months of graduation. Approximately 48 percent of these graduates went into private practice at average starting salaries ranging from $59,000 to $120,000. Over 30 percent of the class entered the public sector in a broad range of positions, including jobs in judges' chambers, governmental agencies, and public interest organizations.

Clinical Opportunities/Special Programs

Cardozo has a commitment to a particular style of education that seeks to blend theory and practice—to expose students to the abstractions, intellectual and ethical conundrums, and overarching theories of the American legal system, as well as to the concrete skills and values they need to be first-rate attorneys. A wealth of clinical programs combines professional work experience with academic supervision, yielding students uniquely qualified to apply what they have studied. Nearly 400 students each year take advantage of one of these opportunities to represent real clients (under the supervision of expert attorneys), gaining invaluable skills while performing important community service representing the poor, the elderly, and the indigent.

In the **Innocence Project**, students represent prisoners whose innocence may be proved through DNA testing; in the

Prosecutor Practicum, students work in the Manhattan District Attorney's Office; the **Bet Tzedek Legal Services Clinic** provides legal assistance to the elderly and disabled; the **Mediation Clinic** provides training and certification in alternative dispute resolution; the **Human Rights and Genocide Clinic** provides students with the opportunity to design and implement creative solutions to improve the lives of victims of human rights abuses throughout the world; Cardozo's simulation-based **Intensive Trial Advocacy Program** sharpens students' trial skills; and students in the **Criminal Defense Clinic** represent defendants in Manhattan Criminal Court. Other clinics include the **Family Court Clinic**, **Tax Clinic**, **Criminal Appeals Clinic**, **Divorce Mediation Clinic**, **Housing Rights Clinic**, **Immigration Justice Clinic**, **Indie Film Clinic**, **Labor and Employment Law Clinic**, **Guardianship Clinic**, and **Securities Arbitration Clinic**.

Externships offer students the opportunity to work in a legal position, thereby developing important skills and gaining significant real-world experience. Through externships and internships, students can obtain credit for substantive legal work under the direct supervision of an attorney or judge at the work site. The **Intellectual Property Law Program** combines a specialized curriculum with related externships in this burgeoning area of practice; the **Alexander Judicial Fellows Program** places outstanding third-year students in clerkships with prominent federal judges; the **Entertainment Law Experience** enables students to complete legal internships during the school year or the summer with entertainment law employers; the **Heyman/ACCA In-House Counsel Internship** introduces second- and third-year students to the practice of law in a corporate law department; in the **Holocaust Claims Restitution Practicum**, students pursue claims made by Holocaust survivors and their heirs; the **Immigration Law Externship** places students in law offices and agencies handling immigration matters; and the **Corporation Counsel's Appellate Externship** places students in the Appeals Division of the New York City Law Department (Corporation Counsel).

Cardozo's Center for Public Service Law emphasizes the school's commitment to serving the greater public good and helping students find meaningful ways to engage in public service. In the summer of 2011, more than 250 first- and second-year students received summer funding to allow them to work either domestically or abroad in the public sector at legal services providers, public interest organizations, government agencies, district attorneys' offices, the US Attorney's Office, and federal and state judicial chambers. The Public Service Scholars Program provides a community within the Law School that supports and encourages students to develop skills as public interest advocates and leaders. The Postgraduate Public Service Fellowship provides new graduates with funding to work in the public sector prior to entering full-time employment. The Laurie M. Tisch Loan Repayment Assistance Program (LRAP) benefits graduates who choose to pursue careers in public interest/public service law by assisting with some of the burden of large educational debts. Intellectual life at Cardozo extends beyond the classroom. The school sponsors numerous conferences, panels, and symposia that provoke dialogue and critical thought on wide-ranging topics in constitutional law, communications law and policy, human rights, corporate governance, and legal ethics.

Curriculum

Cardozo offers a rich curriculum that has been especially recognized for its offerings in intellectual property law (students may receive both the JD and master of laws [LLM] degrees in seven semesters), alternative dispute resolution (students may receive both the JD and master of laws [LLM] degrees in seven semesters), criminal law, corporate law, and international law. Upper-level courses are elective except for a course in professional responsibility, completion of advanced legal research, an upper-level writing requirement, and fulfillment of minimal distribution requirements.

Cardozo offers LLM degrees in dispute resolution and advocacy, intellectual property law, comparative legal thought, and general studies. A joint-degree program between Cardozo and the Wurzweiler School of Social Work allows students to earn both the JD and MSW degrees in four years of study. Students may also pursue a JD/MPH (Master of Public Health) and a JD/MBE (Master of Science in Bioethics) offered with the Albert Einstein College of Medicine.

Admission/Alternative Entry/Financial Aid

Students may enter Cardozo in the fall, in January, or in May. Those entering in January complete six semesters of law school in two-and-a-half years. Those entering in May complete the first-year curriculum in three part-time semesters, while the second and third years are completed on a full-time basis (students will graduate in three years). These alternative entry programs can be particularly appealing to midyear graduates and returning students.

Both need- and merit-based scholarships are available. Approximately 84 percent of the students receive some financial aid. Instructions on applying for aid can be found at www.cardozo.yu.edu/studentfinance.

APPLICANT PROFILE

Benjamin N. Cardozo School of Law, Yeshiva University
This grid includes only applicants who earned 120–180 LSAT scores under standard administrations.

LSAT Score	GPA																
	3.75 +		3.50–3.74		3.25–3.49		3.00–3.24		2.75–2.99		2.50–2.74		Below 2.50		No GPA		Total
	Apps	Adm	Apps	Adm	Apps	Adm	Apps	Adm	Apps	Adm	Apps	Adm	Apps	Adm	Apps	Adm	Apps	Adm
170–180	96	81	59	47	46	26	17	7	11	2	13	0	6	0	9	4	257	167
165–169	167	151	256	231	179	99	99	18	52	5	28	1	18	1	25	13	824	519
160–164	252	185	372	176	299	58	175	23	58	5	32	0	22	0	36	12	1246	459
155–159	118	47	185	41	197	27	147	18	64	3	38	0	17	0	21	3	787	139
150–154	59	15	103	15	132	8	113	0	65	0	24	0	24	0	7	0	527	38
Below 150	33	0	44	0	77	0	100	0	72	0	45	0	44	0	18	0	433	0
Total	725	479	1019	510	930	218	651	66	322	15	180	1	131	1	116	32	4074	1322

Apps = Number of Applicants   Adm = Number Admitted   Reflects 99% of the total applicant pool; highest LSAT data reported.

CASE WESTERN RESERVE UNIVERSITY SCHOOL OF LAW

11075 East Boulevard
Cleveland, OH 44106
Phone: 216.368.3600, 800.756.0036; Fax: 216.368.0185
E-mail: lawadmissions@case.edu, lawmoney@case.edu; Website: http://law.case.edu

ABA
Approved
Since
1923

The Basics

Type of school	Private
Term	Semester
Application deadline	11/30 2/1 4/1
Application fee	$40
Financial aid deadline	5/1
Can first year start other than fall?	No
Student to faculty ratio	12.6 to 1
# of housing spaces available restricted to law students	
graduate housing for which law students are eligible	110

Faculty and Administrators

	Total		Men		Women		Minorities	
	Spr	Fall	Spr	Fall	Spr	Fall	Spr	Fall
Full-time	39	41	26	28	13	13	1	3
Other full-time	7	4	6	3	1	1	0	0
Deans, librarians, & others who teach	2	3	1	2	1	1	0	0
Part-time	54	28	38	18	16	10	1	1
Total	102	76	71	51	31	25	2	4

Curriculum

	Full-Time	Part-Time
Typical first-year section size	80	0
Is there typically a "small section" of the first-year class, other than Legal Writing, taught by full-time faculty	No	No
If yes, typical size offered last year		
# of classroom course titles beyond first-year curriculum	136	

# of upper division courses, excluding seminars, with an enrollment:		
	Under 25	96
	25–49	29
	50–74	9
	75–99	4
	100+	0

# of seminars	15	
# of seminar positions available	169	
# of seminar positions filled	114	0
# of positions available in simulation courses	670	
# of simulation positions filled	580	0
# of positions available in faculty supervised clinical courses	58	
# of faculty supervised clinical positions filled	58	0
# involved in field placements	111	0
# involved in law journals	144	0
# involved in moot court or trial competitions	47	0
# of credit hours required to graduate	88	

JD Enrollment and Ethnicity

	Men		Women		Full-Time		Part-Time		1st-Year		Total		JD Degs. Awd.
	#	%	#	%	#	%	#	%	#	%	#	%	
All Hispanics	8	2.3	9	3.4	16	2.7	1	20.0	10	5.1	17	2.8	5
Am. Ind./AK Nat.	3	0.9	1	0.4	4	0.7	0	0.0	3	1.5	4	0.7	1
Asian	24	7.0	33	12.6	57	9.5	0	0.0	21	10.8	57	9.4	11
Black/Af. Am.	11	3.2	19	7.3	30	5.0	0	0.0	16	8.2	30	5.0	6
Nat. Hi/Pac. Isl.	0	0.0	0	0.0	0	0.0	0	0.0	0	0.0	0	0.0	0
2 or more races	0	0.0	2	0.8	2	0.3	0	0.0	0	0.0	2	0.3	3
Subtotal (minor.)	46	13.4	64	24.4	109	18.2	1	20.0	50	25.6	110	18.2	26
Nonres. Alien	22	6.4	26	9.9	47	7.8	1	20.0	19	9.7	48	7.9	2
White/Cauc.	275	80.2	172	65.6	444	74.0	3	60.0	126	64.6	447	73.9	175
Unknown	0	0.0	0	0.0	0	0.0	0	0.0	0	0.0	0	0.0	0
Total	343	56.7	262	43.3	600	99.2	5	0.8	195	32.2	605		203

Transfers

Transfers in	19
Transfers out	21

Tuition and Fees

	Resident	Nonresident
Full-time	$42,564	$42,564
Part-time		
Tuition Guarantee Program		N

Living Expenses

Estimated living expenses for singles

Living on campus	Living off campus	Living at home
$20,067	$20,067	$20,067

CASE WESTERN RESERVE UNIVERSITY SCHOOL OF LAW

ABA Approved Since 1923

GPA and LSAT Scores

	Total	Full-Time	Part-Time
# of apps	1,651	1,651	0
# of offers	768	768	0
# of matrics	192	192	0
75% GPA	3.67	3.67	0.00
Median GPA	3.48	3.48	0.00
25% GPA	3.22	3.22	0.00
75% LSAT	160	160	0
Median LSAT	158	158	0
25% LSAT	153	153	0

Grants and Scholarships (from prior year)

	Total		Full-Time		Part-Time	
	#	%	#	%	#	%
Total # of students	627		624		3	
Total # receiving grants	441	70.3	441	70.7	0	0.0
Less than 1/2 tuition	379	60.4	379	60.7	0	0.0
Half to full tuition	53	8.5	53	8.5	0	0.0
Full tuition	9	1.4	9	1.4	0	0.0
More than full tuition	0	0.0	0	0.0	0	0.0
Median grant amount			$9,333		$0	

Informational and Library Resources

Total amount spent on library materials	$1,438,756
Study seating capacity inside the library	352
# of full-time equivalent professional librarians	11
Hours per week library is open	104
# of open, wired connections available to students	100
# of networked computers available for use by students	57
Has wireless network?	Y
Requires computer?	N

JD Attrition (from prior year)

	Academic	Other	Total	
	#	#	#	%
1st year	1	2	3	1.3
2nd year	2	23	25	13.4
3rd year	0	1	1	0.5
4th year	0	0	0	0.0

Employment (9 months after graduation)

For up-to-date employment data, go to employmentsummary.abaquestionnaire.org on the ABA website.

Bar Passage Rates

First-time takers	201	Reporting %	71.14
Average school %	89.51	Average state %	85.66
Average pass difference	3.85		

Jurisdiction	Takers	Passers	Pass %	State %	Diff %
Ohio	108	97	89.81	86.14	3.67
New York	21	18	85.71	84.92	0.79
Pennsylvania	14	13	92.86	83.06	9.80

CASE WESTERN RESERVE UNIVERSITY SCHOOL OF LAW

11075 East Boulevard
Cleveland, OH 44106
Phone: 216.368.3600, 800.756.0036; Fax: 216.368.0185
E-mail: lawadmissions@case.edu, lawmoney@case.edu; Website: http://law.case.edu

Welcome

At Case Western Reserve University School of Law our innovative and visionary curriculum combines the best of classical legal education with cutting-edge experiential opportunities. Our rapidly expanding experiential program and our semester-long foreign study programs and externships prepare our students to be ready at graduation to hit the ground running. Our courses are taught by accomplished and nationally known scholars who are always available to our students. We are part of a world-class university where many of our schools and programs are at the top of their respective fields. We encourage our students to take advantage of all of these opportunities. Finally, while our reach is global, our home is Cleveland, an affordable and enjoyable setting to study law.

The Curriculum and Concentrations

Our students participate in CaseArc, our four-semester integrated lawyering skills program that coordinates experientially based instruction in fundamental lawyering skills with traditional classroom methods for teaching legal analysis. In this program, our students research and write memos and briefs, interview and counsel clients, draft and negotiate contracts, and experience how lawyers make deals happen, solve legal problems, make presentations to courts, and negotiate criminal or civil settlements.

Because we are part of a world-class research university, we offer our students 10 dual-degree options, including Management, Art History and Museum Studies, Legal History, Bioethics, Political Science, Social Work, Nonprofit Management, Public Health, Medicine, and Biochemistry. For students who wish to focus on a particular area of law, we offer 10 concentrations, including Law and Technology, Law and the Arts, Criminal Law, Business Organizations, Litigation and Dispute Resolution, Health Law, International Law, National Security Law, Individual Rights and Social Reform, and Public and Regulatory Institutions.

In addition, our 200-plus courses and unique opportunities to participate in practice laboratories, clinics, externships at home and abroad, and semester-long study abroad almost anywhere in the world give our graduates the skills, judgment, experience, and confidence to practice twenty-first-century law and to deal with the challenges of an ever-changing world.

Academic Centers

The Academic Centers provide rich opportunities that stimulate learning, networking, and career development, and include first-year electives, special seminars and symposia, clinical opportunities, internships, and work and study-abroad opportunities. Our Law-Medicine Center was the first health law program in the country, offering a broad variety of courses and extracurricular opportunities to prepare our students for the rapidly evolving world of health care law. In addition to extensive international law course offerings, the Frederick K. Cox International Law Center helps students gain employment in the field of international law by providing summer, semester-long (for academic credit), and postgraduation international internship grants. The Cox Center also sponsors the highly successful Jessup Moot Court Team. The Center for Law, Technology, and the Arts teaches our students to counsel all types of creative clients, including inventors, musicians, visual artists, and athletes and then helps the students gain experience in cultural and technological organizations and law firms. Our Center for Business Law and Regulation offers a dynamic and comprehensive combination of curricular offerings and extracurricular programs in business law and regulation. Finally, our Milton A. Kramer Law Clinic provides our third-year students the opportunity to put their lawyering skills to work representing real clients in civil, criminal, and business matters.

Commitment to Career Success

We believe that the type and quality of services provided by a career services office are important to consider in choosing which school to attend. We pride ourselves on offering comprehensive general programming to the entire student body as well as personal attention to each student's individual career ambitions. Our Career Services Office programming provides our students with real job opportunities with leading employers coast to coast. Our aggressive approach to employer development and outreach has resulted in great job success for our graduates: a 91.6 percent employment rate for our class of 2010 (national average: 90.5 percent). More than 300 employers participate in our fall recruitment programs, which include on-campus interviews as well as interview programs in New York, Chicago, Los Angeles, Boston, and Washington, DC.

The University and Cleveland

We are part of a world-class university. Case Western Reserve University stands among the nation's foremost independent research institutions with an endowment of well over $1 billion. The law school is located on the university's campus in the heart of University Circle—a unique park-like setting that includes the Cleveland Art Museum, Cleveland Botanical Garden, Cleveland Orchestra, Cleveland Museum of Natural History, University Hospitals, the Cleveland Clinic, and the new home of the Cleveland Museum of Contemporary Art.

Unique neighborhoods are within walking distance of campus and offer students and young professionals modern and safe places to live, shop, dine, and socialize. Accommodations vary from hip and modern lofts and condos to fun college town apartments. Housing is also very affordable.

Cleveland is a world corporate center for leading national and multinational companies that specialize in transportation, insurance, retail, commercial banking, and finance. It is the headquarters for several of the nation's largest law firms and home to a number of foreign consulates. It is also a city of medicine with dozens of hospitals and medical centers with international reputations for outstanding patient care and contributions to medical research. Plus, opportunities for fun abound in Cleveland with our nationally recognized restaurant scene, the country's second-largest theater district, the Rock and Roll Hall of Fame, three professional sports teams, and the extensive and beautiful Cleveland Metroparks system.

Student Activities and Leadership

There are more than 30 student organizations reflecting the wide range of our students' interests, including the Black Law Students Association, Asian Pacific American Law Students Association, Federalist Society, National Lawyers Guild, Lambda Law Students Association, and Student Animal Legal Defense Fund. Our students contribute to the community through organizations such as Cultivating Connections, Street Law, and Big Buddies, in cooperation with Big Brothers/Big Sisters. Our student organizations not only allow students the opportunity to explore legal interests with peers, but also provide a valuable proving ground for leadership skill development. Our student organization leaders have also taken leadership roles in their groups' national and regional organizations, and have the opportunity to represent Case Western at national and regional conferences. Our scholarly journals are the *Case Western Reserve Law Review*, the *Journal of International Law*, *Health Matrix: Journal of Law-Medicine*, and the *Journal of Law, Technology, and the Internet*. There is also ample opportunity for participation in moot court and mock trial competitions.

Admission and Financial Aid

The Admission Process—Our admission process is selective. Each applicant receives full-file review. The Early Decision program application deadline is November 30; applicants are notified by December 15. The regular admission process begins in December and concludes by May 15, at which time a summer waiting list is established. The application fee is waived for candidates who apply electronically.

Financial Aid and Scholarships—Each year, we offer academic scholarships ranging from partial to full tuition; leadership grants, awarded to students with unique backgrounds whose records demonstrate leadership qualities and who will enrich the diversity of the student body; interest area scholarships; and up to two Law-Medicine Fellowships, which provide a combination of scholarship aid and summer research fellowship.

Loan Repayment Assistance Program—We provide financial assistance for selected graduates who use their legal training to provide services that are in the public interest.

Visiting Case Western Reserve University School of Law

We offer many opportunities for prospective students to visit the law school. Just check our website to watch our video, check the schedule for the annual Open House, or schedule an individual visit (or all three of the above).

APPLICANT PROFILE

Case Western Reserve University School of Law
This grid includes only applicants who earned 120–180 LSAT scores.

LSAT Score	GPA						
	3.75 +	3.50–3.74	3.25–3.49	3.00–3.24	2.75–2.99	2.50–2.74	Below 2.50
165–180	Good Possibility	Good Possibility	Good Possibility	Good Possibility	Good Possibility	Possible	Possible
163–164	Good Possibility	Good Possibility	Good Possibility	Good Possibility	Good Possibility	Possible	Unlikely
161–162	Good Possibility	Good Possibility	Good Possibility	Good Possibility	Possible	Possible	Unlikely
159–160	Good Possibility	Good Possibility	Good Possibility	Good Possibility	Possible	Possible	Unlikely
157–158	Good Possibility	Good Possibility	Good Possibility	Possible	Possible	Possible	Unlikely
154–156	Possible	Possible	Unlikely	Unlikely	Unlikely	Unlikely	Unlikely
150–153	Unlikely	Unlikely	Unlikely	Unlikely	Unlikely	Unlikely	Unlikely
Below 150	Unlikely	Unlikely	Unlikely	Unlikely	Unlikely	Unlikely	Unlikely

Legend: Good Possibility | Possible | Unlikely

THE CATHOLIC UNIVERSITY OF AMERICA, COLUMBUS SCHOOL OF LAW

Cardinal Station
Washington, DC 20064
Phone: 202.319.5151; Fax: 202.319.6285
E-mail: admissions@law.edu; Website: www.law.edu

ABA
Approved
Since
1925

The Basics

Type of school	Private
Term	Semester
Application deadline	3/12
Application fee	$65
Financial aid deadline	7/1
Can first year start other than fall?	No
Student to faculty ratio	11.5 to 1
# of housing spaces available restricted to law students	
graduate housing for which law students are eligible	

Faculty and Administrators

	Total		Men		Women		Minorities	
	Spr	Fall	Spr	Fall	Spr	Fall	Spr	Fall
Full-time	50	52	26	27	24	25	8	7
Other full-time	6	4	2	2	4	2	1	1
Deans, librarians, & others who teach	2	3	1	2	1	1	1	1
Part-time	73	51	59	35	14	16	7	5
Total	131	110	88	66	43	44	17	14

JD Enrollment and Ethnicity

	Men		Women		Full-Time		Part-Time		1st-Year		Total		JD Degs. Awd.
	#	%	#	%	#	%	#	%	#	%	#	%	
All Hispanics	17	4.7	17	4.2	23	4.5	11	4.2	17	7.4	34	4.4	9
Am. Ind./AK Nat.	1	0.3	2	0.5	2	0.4	1	0.4	2	0.9	3	0.4	0
Asian	23	6.4	41	10.0	35	6.9	29	11.1	15	6.6	64	8.3	26
Black/Af. Am.	24	6.7	44	10.8	34	6.7	34	13.0	36	15.7	68	8.9	7
Nat. HI/Pac. Isl.	3	0.8	0	0.0	1	0.2	2	0.8	0	0.0	3	0.4	0
2 or more races	2	0.6	3	0.7	2	0.4	3	1.1	0	0.0	5	0.7	2
Subtotal (minor.)	70	19.4	107	26.2	97	19.2	80	30.5	70	30.6	177	23.0	44
Nonres. Alien	12	3.3	14	3.4	19	3.8	7	2.7	7	3.1	26	3.4	11
White/Cauc.	175	48.6	191	46.8	255	50.4	111	42.4	84	36.7	366	47.7	142
Unknown	103	28.6	96	23.5	135	26.7	64	24.4	68	29.7	199	25.9	64
Total	360	46.9	408	53.1	506	65.9	262	34.1	229	29.8	768		261

Curriculum

	Full-Time	Part-Time
Typical first-year section size	52	70
Is there typically a "small section" of the first-year class, other than Legal Writing, taught by full-time faculty	Yes	Yes
If yes, typical size offered last year	26	35

# of classroom course titles beyond first-year curriculum		135
# of upper division courses, excluding seminars, with an enrollment:	Under 25	121
	25–49	32
	50–74	13
	75–99	2
	100+	0
# of seminars		43
# of seminar positions available		678
# of seminar positions filled	325	138
# of positions available in simulation courses		382
# of simulation positions filled	187	125
# of positions available in faculty supervised clinical courses		145
# of faculty supervised clinical positions filled	100	36
# involved in field placements	186	25
# involved in law journals	224	34
# involved in moot court or trial competitions	45	9
# of credit hours required to graduate		84

Transfers

Transfers in	5
Transfers out	33

Tuition and Fees

	Resident	Nonresident
Full-time	$41,995	$41,995
Part-time	$31,975	$31,975
Tuition Guarantee Program		N

Living Expenses

Estimated living expenses for singles

Living on campus	Living off campus	Living at home
$27,202	$27,202	$27,202

THE CATHOLIC UNIVERSITY OF AMERICA, COLUMBUS SCHOOL OF LAW

ABA Approved Since 1925

GPA and LSAT Scores

	Total	Full-Time	Part-Time
# of apps	3,002	2,407	595
# of offers	984	817	167
# of matrics	232	162	70
75% GPA	3.45	3.46	3.44
Median GPA	3.28	3.30	3.22
25% GPA	3.07	3.11	3.00
75% LSAT	160	160	159
Median LSAT	157	157	156
25% LSAT	151	151	152

Grants and Scholarships (from prior year)

	Total #	Total %	Full-Time #	Full-Time %	Part-Time #	Part-Time %
Total # of students	858		562		296	
Total # receiving grants	364	42.4	258	45.9	106	35.8
Less than 1/2 tuition	308	35.9	208	37.0	100	33.8
Half to full tuition	51	5.9	46	8.2	5	1.7
Full tuition	5	0.6	4	0.7	1	0.3
More than full tuition	0	0.0	0	0.0	0	0.0
Median grant amount			$12,500		$10,000	

Informational and Library Resources

Total amount spent on library materials	$1,457,503
Study seating capacity inside the library	502
# of full-time equivalent professional librarians	11
Hours per week library is open	115
# of open, wired connections available to students	243
# of networked computers available for use by students	107
Has wireless network?	Y
Requires computer?	N

JD Attrition (from prior year)

	Academic #	Other #	Total #	Total %
1st year	5	40	45	16.4
2nd year	1	3	4	1.7
3rd year	0	0	0	0.0
4th year	0	0	0	0.0

Employment (9 months after graduation)

For up-to-date employment data, go to employmentsummary.abaquestionnaire.org on the ABA website.

Bar Passage Rates

First-time takers	259	Reporting %	80.69
Average school %	77.51	Average state %	80.20
Average pass difference	–2.69		

Jurisdiction	Takers	Passers	Pass %	State %	Diff %
Maryland	113	91	80.53	79.96	0.57
Virginia	63	44	69.84	78.15	–8.31
New York	33	27	81.82	84.92	–3.10

THE CATHOLIC UNIVERSITY OF AMERICA, COLUMBUS SCHOOL OF LAW

Cardinal Station
Washington, DC 20064
Phone: 202.319.5151; Fax: 202.319.6285
E-mail: admissions@law.edu; Website: www.law.edu

Introduction

Founded in 1897, the Catholic University of America, Columbus School of Law is located on the 193-acre campus of the university. Students and faculty have easy access to nearly limitless legal resources: the Supreme Court, Congress, the United States and District of Columbia courts, and other federal, executive, and administrative agencies and branches of government. For a campus so close to a center of world power, it is peaceful, pleasant, and scenic, offering a sense of neighborhood and community. Classes are small and personal.

The law school is proud of its vibrant intellectual tradition and extends it to exploring new intersections of issues of law and morality. Students are trained and encouraged to use their hearts and minds, in concert with their skills, to practice effectively in the complex world of the twenty-first century. The school welcomes students of all religious, racial, and ethnic backgrounds to a program that is renowned for its consistently high number of graduates entering public and community service. The Columbus School of Law has been a member of the AALS since 1921 and was approved by the ABA in 1925.

Enrollment/Student Body

Total enrollment is typically more than 900 students. Law students come from nearly every state and a dozen foreign countries. More than 30 percent of the school's enrollment is part time, making its evening program one of the most flexible and accommodating available anywhere. First-year classes typically have 32 to 70 students. Upper-class courses range from 10 to 70 students. Faculty members keep posted office hours and are accessible for informal sessions, making for a more personalized education.

Faculty

The 70-member full-time faculty bring a wealth of experience and expertise to the classroom. The majority have practiced in the private sector. Adjunct faculty members are primarily active legal practitioners and complement the real-world flavor of course offerings. Classroom instruction is supplemented by many distinguished guest speakers, such as federal appellate judges, justices of the US Supreme Court, and leading academicians and theologians from around the world.

Library and Physical Facilities

The Library of Congress and specialized law collections throughout the city complement the law school's legal collections of over 425,000 volumes and numerous research databases. The law school facility, completed in 1994, houses all components of the law school. Law students have full access to other campus facilities, including a 40-acre athletic complex.

Curriculum

The prescribed first-year curriculum and method of teaching are designed to develop the analytical skills that characterize the able lawyer and to give the student familiarity with the major substantive areas of law. They are also designed as an introduction to jurisprudence and the Catholic intellectual tradition as it relates to the larger questions of social justice. While lawyers traditionally have been heavily involved with the commercial interests of private or corporate clients, law is becoming increasingly responsive to problems that affect the public interest. The CUA law school curriculum is designed to provide students with the basic knowledge to become effective lawyers in a changing legal environment.

Special Programs

CUA Law's institutes and special programs offer certification of a student's developed expertise in his or her chosen legal specialty. Each program provides invaluable externship opportunities, offering for-credit placements that are available nowhere else but in Washington, DC.

The Institute for Communications Law Studies offers unique specialized training in communications law, ranging from First Amendment law to FCC practices and procedures. Students are trained to think critically about the broader impact that mass media has upon society and human behavior.

The Comparative and International Law Institute provides superb background training to students who intend to specialize in international law. The institute offers a six-week summer-abroad program at the Jagiellonian University in Cracow, Poland.

The Law and Public Policy Program is designed for students who desire to make a difference through legislative change. The program combines classroom study in legislative and administrative processes with externships in government agencies and advocacy organizations that affect national public policy.

The Securities Law Program integrates a broad concentration of securities and corporate law courses with a required externship program. Adjunct instructors and program faculty bring vast knowledge to the classroom, as many have practiced with the Securities and Exchange Commission (SEC), the National Association of Securities Dealers (NASD), and private firms.

The Interdisciplinary Program on Law and Religion was created to provide a forum for study, research, and public discussion of the questions that arise from the nexus of law and religion. These include many of society's most challenging issues, such as bioethics, international human rights, and marriage law.

The Program of Studies in Jurisprudence exists to promote inquiry into the role of law in relation to culture and culture's orientation to the human good. The scope of its inquiry is both theoretical and practical. In its theoretical aspect, the program aims to contribute to the academic fields of jurisprudence, the philosophy of law, and Christian political and social ethics. In its practical dimension, it seeks to foster the renewal and transformation of culture, under contemporary circumstances, through law and law reform.

Clinical Programs

Columbus Community Legal Services recently observed its 40th year of assisting the underserved population of the nation's capital. The law school offers eight clinical programs, including five that emphasize client representation, case planning, and trial and administrative advocacy. Nine simulation courses are also offered that closely approximate real-life lawyering through simulated courtroom, mediation, and arbitration exercises. The two other clinical offerings are the SEC Observer Program and the Legal Externship Program.

Admission

While considerable weight is given to an applicant's grade-point average and LSAT score, admission decisions are also influenced by such factors as leadership potential, class rank, substantial involvement in volunteer community service activities, potential for contributing to diversity, and relevant work experience. Close attention is also paid to a candidate's personal statement and reasons for wanting to study at CUA.

Student Activities

The *Catholic University Law Review*, the *Journal of Contemporary Health Law and Policy*, and *CommLaw Conspectus: Journal of Communications Law and Policy* are scholarly law journals staffed and published by outstanding students. The Moot Court Board, in addition to facilitating at least eight intraschool competitions each year, also hosts two major contests at CUA: the National Telecommunications Competition and the Sutherland Cup. There are over 40 voluntary student organizations at the Columbus School of Law, encompassing a broad range of professional interests, ethnic and racial affiliations, political and religious perspectives, and recreational activities.

Financial Aid

Following the offer of admission, all prospective students are automatically evaluated for merit-based scholarships. Approximately 25–30 percent of each year's entering class has been awarded a scholarship. Given the significant financial investment of a law degree, the Office of Financial Aid is committed to providing all students with timely information and guidance.

Career Services

The Office of Career and Professional Development actively supports students and graduates in their search for employment by providing counseling as well as workshops, panel discussions, and access to a national alumni network. A comprehensive on-campus interviewing program is conducted annually. The school's small size makes it possible for all students to secure guidance with individualized career strategy and planning.

Housing

The Washington, DC, metropolitan area boasts many off-campus housing opportunities for prospective law students. Each summer, the Office of Admissions assists incoming students with the housing search by coordinating a roommate name exchange and an online housing forum. The law school is convenient to public transportation, including Washington's Metrorail system.

APPLICANT PROFILE

The Catholic University of America, Columbus School of Law
This grid includes only applicants who earned 120–180 LSAT scores under standard administrations.

LSAT Score	GPA																
	3.75 +		3.50–3.74		3.25–3.49		3.00–3.24		2.75–2.99		2.50–2.74		Below 2.50		No GPA		Total	
	Apps	Adm	Apps	Adm	Apps	Adm	Apps	Adm	Apps	Adm	Apps	Adm	Apps	Adm	Apps	Adm	Apps	Adm
170–180	4	4	5	4	5	4	4	4	2	2	0	0	1	0	0	0	21	18
165–169	17	17	30	29	25	18	14	11	12	10	7	4	4	1	0	0	109	90
160–164	47	45	115	107	114	107	75	66	47	36	19	4	24	7	11	7	452	379
155–159	82	63	213	121	231	77	172	59	82	14	44	8	29	0	17	5	870	347
150–154	75	10	128	16	196	33	166	24	96	5	57	2	43	1	16	0	777	91
145–149	27	4	56	4	91	12	119	19	76	8	41	0	32	0	6	0	448	47
140–144	5	0	18	0	38	0	46	0	34	0	28	0	24	0	3	0	196	0
Below 140	2	0	5	0	11	0	24	0	23	0	23	0	36	0	7	0	131	0
Total	259	143	570	281	711	251	620	183	372	75	219	18	193	9	60	12	3004	972

Apps = Number of Applicants
Adm = Number Admitted
Reflects 99% of the total applicant pool; highest LSAT data reported.

CHAPMAN UNIVERSITY SCHOOL OF LAW

One University Drive
Orange, CA 92866
Phone: 877.CHAPLAW or 714.628.2500; Fax: 714.628.2501
E-mail: lawadm@chapman.edu; Website: www.chapman.edu/law

ABA
Approved
Since
1998

The Basics

Type of school	Private
Term	Semester
Application deadline	4/15
Application fee	$75
Financial aid deadline	3/1
Can first year start other than fall?	No
Student to faculty ratio	9.6 to 1
# of housing spaces available restricted to law students	
graduate housing for which law students are eligible	20

Faculty and Administrators

	Total		Men		Women		Minorities	
	Spr	Fall	Spr	Fall	Spr	Fall	Spr	Fall
Full-time	49	44	26	24	23	20	5	6
Other full-time	0	0	0	0	0	0	0	0
Deans, librarians, & others who teach	5	5	3	3	2	2	0	0
Part-time	40	29	35	25	5	4	1	1
Total	94	78	64	52	30	26	6	7

Curriculum

	Full-Time	Part-Time
Typical first-year section size	53	53
Is there typically a "small section" of the first-year class, other than Legal Writing, taught by full-time faculty	No	No
If yes, typical size offered last year		
# of classroom course titles beyond first-year curriculum	163	

# of upper division courses, excluding seminars, with an enrollment:		
	Under 25	101
	25–49	32
	50–74	15
	75–99	1
	100+	0

# of seminars	12	
# of seminar positions available	203	
# of seminar positions filled	90	42
# of positions available in simulation courses	501	
# of simulation positions filled	467	29
# of positions available in faculty supervised clinical courses	233	
# of faculty supervised clinical positions filled	122	15
# involved in field placements	141	5
# involved in law journals	175	2
# involved in moot court or trial competitions	59	2
# of credit hours required to graduate	88	

JD Enrollment and Ethnicity

	Men		Women		Full-Time		Part-Time		1st-Year		Total		JD Degs. Awd.
	#	%	#	%	#	%	#	%	#	%	#	%	
All Hispanics	13	4.8	8	3.0	20	4.0	1	3.8	1	0.6	21	3.9	7
Am. Ind./AK Nat.	2	0.7	1	0.4	3	0.6	0	0.0	1	0.6	3	0.6	0
Asian	15	5.6	13	4.9	26	5.1	2	7.7	21	13.3	28	5.3	0
Black/Af. Am.	0	0.0	2	0.8	2	0.4	0	0.0	0	0.0	2	0.4	0
Nat. HI/Pac. Isl.	13	4.8	20	7.6	33	6.5	0	0.0	1	0.6	33	6.2	27
2 or more races	22	8.2	26	9.9	46	9.1	2	7.7	29	18.4	48	9.0	7
Subtotal (minor.)	65	24.2	70	26.6	130	25.7	5	19.2	53	33.5	135	25.4	41
Nonres. Alien	0	0.0	0	0.0	0	0.0	0	0.0	0	0.0	0	0.0	4
White/Cauc.	169	62.8	149	56.7	301	59.5	17	65.4	95	60.1	318	59.8	96
Unknown	35	13.0	44	16.7	75	14.8	4	15.4	10	6.3	79	14.8	36
Total	269	50.6	263	49.4	506	95.1	26	4.9	158	29.7	532		177

Transfers

Transfers in	9
Transfers out	10

Tuition and Fees

	Resident	Nonresident
Full-time	$41,873	$41,873
Part-time	$33,263	$33,263
Tuition Guarantee Program	N	

Living Expenses

Estimated living expenses for singles

Living on campus	Living off campus	Living at home
$27,509	$27,509	$15,719

CHAPMAN UNIVERSITY SCHOOL OF LAW

ABA Approved Since 1998

GPA and LSAT Scores

	Total	Full-Time	Part-Time
# of apps	2,822	2,592	230
# of offers	970	938	32
# of matrics	160	153	7
75% GPA	3.71	3.71	3.76
Median GPA	3.56	3.55	3.44
25% GPA	3.31	3.31	3.28
75% LSAT	160	160	168
Median LSAT	158	158	156
25% LSAT	154	154	153

Grants and Scholarships (from prior year)

	Total		Full-Time		Part-Time	
	#	%	#	%	#	%
Total # of students	574		546		28	
Total # receiving grants	213	37.1	213	39.0	0	0.0
Less than 1/2 tuition	69	12.0	69	12.6	0	0.0
Half to full tuition	43	7.5	43	7.9	0	0.0
Full tuition	67	11.7	67	12.3	0	0.0
More than full tuition	34	5.9	34	6.2	0	0.0
Median grant amount			$35,794		$0	

Informational and Library Resources

Total amount spent on library materials	$1,045,784
Study seating capacity inside the library	305
# of full-time equivalent professional librarians	6
Hours per week library is open	106
# of open, wired connections available to students	587
# of networked computers available for use by students	69
Has wireless network?	Y
Requires computer?	N

JD Attrition (from prior year)

	Academic #	Other #	Total #	Total %
1st year	11	19	30	14.4
2nd year	2	3	5	2.9
3rd year	0	0	0	0.0
4th year	0	0	0	0.0

Employment (9 months after graduation)

For up-to-date employment data, go to employmentsummary.abaquestionnaire.org on the ABA website.

Bar Passage Rates

First-time takers	158	Reporting %	95.57
Average school %	68.21	Average state %	71.24

Average pass difference   –3.03

Jurisdiction	Takers	Passers	Pass %	State %	Diff %
California	151	103	68.21	71.24	–3.03

CHAPMAN UNIVERSITY SCHOOL OF LAW

One University Drive
Orange, CA 92866
Phone: 877.CHAPLAW or 714.628.2500; Fax: 714.628.2501
E-mail: lawadm@chapman.edu; Website: www.chapman.edu/law

Introduction

Chapman University School of Law is located in the historic Old Towne district of Orange, California. We are part of a university that is 144 years old. The law school, established in 1995, received its accreditation in 2006.

The law school has gained a national reputation for its high-quality faculty, students, and facilities. The law school has focus areas in entertainment law, business law, international law, taxation, environmental/real estate/land use, and advocacy and dispute resolution; a joint JD/MBA degree, joint JD/MFA degree in film producing, and a joint JD/MFA degree in Creative Writing; and LLM degrees in taxation and prosecutorial science. We also offer clinical opportunities in the areas of family violence, immigration law, elder law, constitutional law, and mediation and alternative dispute resolution. Our students have obtained rewarding externship and internship opportunities. The law school's successes have been aided by its location in vibrant and dynamic Orange County.

Affiliation with a well-established university allows for cross-disciplinary engagement, joint degrees, and a lively and engaging intellectual environment beyond the classroom. Chapman University offers an impressive selection of artistic and cultural opportunities for its students.

Enrollment/Student Body

Chapman Law has committed itself to building a small, talented, and diverse student body. Total student enrollment in 2011–2012 was approximately 600 law students.

The 2011 entering class consisted of 160 law students. The students were divided into three first-year sections. The Legal Research and Writing course has a maximum of 20 students in each of nine sections. Currently, about 19 percent of the entering class comes from outside California, and the minority enrollment is 34 percent.

Competition for seats is keen. Approximately 34 percent of applicants in the 2011 applicant pool were admitted.

Faculty

Chapman has assembled an impressive law faculty (including four former US Supreme Court clerks) who are excellent teachers, accomplished scholars, and outstanding mentors. Chapman Law's environment is conducive to learning. Students have access to the faculty and frequent opportunities to engage them in both formal and informal settings. Our student-to-faculty ratio is 9.61 to 1.

Library and Physical Facilities

The beautiful Donald P. Kennedy Hall opened in 1999 with state-of-the-art learning facilities in its classrooms, law library, and trial and appellate courtrooms.

Library holdings now exceed 348,000 volumes and volume equivalents. The collection is fully accessible to students both in hard copy and through the computer network.

Library carrels and desktops are generous in number, and wireless connectivity is available throughout the building.

Several group-study rooms are available for student use and extended research.

Two state-of-the-art courtrooms provide computers, cameras, and electronic blackboards for trial advocacy exercises, competitions, and formal hearings by visiting courts.

Special Programs/Clinics/Externships

The law school offers the JD/MBA and JD/MFA programs, affording students the opportunity to earn the equivalent of two accredited professional degrees in four years instead of the typical five. Chapman's George L. Argyros School of Business and Economics is AACSB accredited. Our Dodge College of Film and Media Arts is housed in a state-of-the-art building with the latest digital technology.

About 10 percent of the students choose to focus their electives in one of six certificate areas: entertainment law, international law, tax law, environmental/real estate/land use, alternative dispute resolution, and business law. The Tax-Law Emphasis Program affords students the opportunity to represent claimants against the IRS in the US Tax Court Clinic. The Center for Land Resources allows students to network with practicing professionals. In the Externship Program, students work with appellate judges, trial judges, district attorneys, public defenders, and (just starting) corporate legal departments and law firms, where they gain hands-on experience and academic credit.

Clinic offerings include family violence/immigration law, elder law, entertainment law, constitutional litigation, mediation, and tax law. Clinics allow students opportunities to represent actual clients in an array of legal settings.

Admission

The Admissions Office reviews your academic record and LSAT score, but also considers additional indicators of potential success in law school.

Student Curricular and Cocurricular Activities

The law school offers many activities that enrich the academic program and provide important training in leadership. Two scholarly journals offer valuable experience in research, writing, and editing. The Student Bar Association administers a full range of programs. Other organizations include, but are not limited to, the Minority Law Students Association, the Asian Pacific American Law Students Association, the Public Interest Law Foundation, the Federalist Society, and the student-run Honor Council.

Externships allow students to earn academic credit while working in a variety of government agencies, judges' chambers, and public interest organizations, entertainment companies, and (just starting) corporate legal departments and law firms, to develop the practical skills and confidence they will need after graduation.

Chapman offers a range of advocacy experiences, including participation in mock trial, moot court, client counseling, international law, mediation, and negotiation competitions.

Scholarships and Financial Aid

Chapman Law offers a generous merit- and need-based scholarship program. For the 2011 entering class, more than 64 percent of new students received scholarships. After the first year, law students are eligible to renew their merit scholarships provided they maintain a GPA of 3.0 or above in their classes after the first-year grades are posted. For 2011, approximately $6 million in scholarship funds were distributed among a student body of approximately 600. This included merit- and need-based scholarships.

Chapman also offers a full range of loan programs to supplement students' financial resources, including Direct loans, Graduate PLUS loans, Perkins loans, and private loans.

Career Services

Helping our students find jobs is our top priority. Chapman Law provides students and alumni with comprehensive career services and resources that aid them in selecting their career direction and in reaching their goals. The office is staffed by an assistant dean, associate, assistant director, alumni counselor, recruitment coordinator, and an administrative assistant. The Career Services Office facilitates interviews for our students with legal employers during our On-Campus Interview and Résumé Collection Program in both the fall and spring. The office also provides students the opportunity to meet with prominent members of the legal community through frequent panels, a highly successful Attorney Mentor Program, and an extensive Mock Interview Program. In keeping with the Chapman mission of personalized education, the counselors meet with individual students to review résumés and cover letters, to aid in self-assessment and goal orientation, to discuss specific opportunities unique to the student's needs, and to provide training, support, and feedback in all aspects of exploring career options.

APPLICANT PROFILE

Chapman University School of Law
This grid includes only applicants who earned 120–180 LSAT scores under standard administrations.

LSAT Score	GPA																			
	3.75 +		3.50–3.74		3.25–3.49		3.00–3.24		2.75–2.99		2.50–2.74		2.25–2.49		2.00–2.24		Below 2.00		No GPA		Total	
	Apps	Adm	Apps	Adm	Apps	Adm	Apps	Adm	Apps	Adm	Apps	Adm	Apps	Adm	Apps	Adm	Apps	Adm	Apps	Adm	Apps	Adm
175–180	0	0	0	0	0	0	1	1	0	0	1	0	0	0	1	0	0	0	0	0	3	1
170–174	4	4	3	2	1	1	2	2	3	2	0	0	0	0	0	0	0	0	0	0	13	11
165–169	15	15	20	20	13	13	9	9	11	9	13	5	4	1	1	0	0	0	2	1	88	73
160–164	49	48	78	77	78	72	62	61	49	24	28	7	20	3	6	1	0	0	1	1	371	294
155–159	86	84	160	158	208	107	176	48	114	22	56	3	16	0	7	0	3	0	3	1	829	423
150–154	49	39	98	78	222	30	189	4	117	1	65	0	29	0	13	0	4	0	14	2	800	154
145–149	20	9	53	5	94	0	96	1	73	0	53	0	32	1	10	0	0	0	8	0	439	16
140–144	2	0	18	0	28	0	53	0	37	0	24	0	14	0	3	0	1	0	1	0	181	0
135–139	4	0	4	0	6	0	14	0	13	0	11	0	6	0	2	0	2	0	2	0	64	0
130–134	0	0	1	0	2	0	2	0	2	0	4	0	5	0	1	0	0	0	0	0	17	0
125–129	0	0	0	0	1	0	0	0	0	0	0	0	1	0	1	0	0	0	0	0	3	0
120–124	0	0	0	0	0	0	0	0	0	0	1	0	0	0	0	0	0	0	0	0	1	0
Total	229	199	435	340	653	223	604	126	419	58	256	15	127	5	45	1	10	0	31	5	2809	972

Apps = Number of Applicants
Adm = Number Admitted
Reflects 99% of the total applicant pool; highest LSAT data reported.

CHARLESTON SCHOOL OF LAW

81 Mary Street, PO Box 535
Charleston, SC 29402
Phone: 843.377.2143; Fax: 843.329.0491
E-mail: info@charlestonlaw.edu; Website: www.charlestonlaw.edu

The Basics

Type of school	Private
Term	Semester
Application deadline	3/1 4/1
Application fee	$50
Financial aid deadline	4/1 5/15
Can first year start other than fall?	No
Student to faculty ratio	17.0 to 1
# of housing spaces available restricted to law students	
graduate housing for which law students are eligible	

Faculty and Administrators

	Total		Men		Women		Minorities	
	Spr	Fall	Spr	Fall	Spr	Fall	Spr	Fall
Full-time	30	31	16	16	14	15	6	6
Other full-time	0	0	0	0	0	0	0	0
Deans, librarians, & others who teach	9	9	4	4	5	5	0	0
Part-time	29	35	21	21	8	14	0	1
Total	68	75	41	41	27	34	6	7

Curriculum

	Full-Time	Part-Time
Typical first-year section size	63	50
Is there typically a "small section" of the first-year class, other than Legal Writing, taught by full-time faculty	No	No
If yes, typical size offered last year		
# of classroom course titles beyond first-year curriculum	114	

# of upper division courses, excluding seminars, with an enrollment:		
	Under 25	111
	25–49	34
	50–74	34
	75–99	1
	100+	0

# of seminars	21	
# of seminar positions available	498	
# of seminar positions filled	238	86
# of positions available in simulation courses	614	
# of simulation positions filled	340	94
# of positions available in faculty supervised clinical courses	0	
# of faculty supervised clinical positions filled	0	0
# involved in field placements	92	67
# involved in law journals	96	7
# involved in moot court or trial competitions	29	6
# of credit hours required to graduate	88	

JD Enrollment and Ethnicity

	Men #	Men %	Women #	Women %	Full-Time #	Full-Time %	Part-Time #	Part-Time %	1st-Year #	1st-Year %	Total #	Total %	JD Degs. Awd.
All Hispanics	6	1.6	8	2.5	11	2.1	3	1.6	5	2.2	14	2.0	1
Am. Ind./AK Nat.	2	0.5	5	1.5	4	0.8	3	1.6	3	1.3	7	1.0	0
Asian	4	1.0	3	0.9	6	1.2	1	0.5	3	1.3	7	1.0	4
Black/Af. Am.	17	4.4	32	9.8	29	5.6	20	10.5	17	7.6	49	6.9	16
Nat. HI/Pac. Isl.	1	0.3	1	0.3	2	0.4	0	0.0	1	0.4	2	0.3	0
2 or more races	0	0.0	0	0.0	0	0.0	0	0.0	0	0.0	0	0.0	0
Subtotal (minor.)	30	7.8	49	15.1	52	10.0	27	14.1	29	13.0	79	11.1	21
Nonres. Alien	0	0.0	0	0.0	0	0.0	0	0.0	0	0.0	0	0.0	0
White/Cauc.	344	89.6	269	82.8	453	87.5	160	83.8	188	84.3	613	86.5	174
Unknown	10	2.6	7	2.2	13	2.5	4	2.1	6	2.7	17	2.4	1
Total	384	54.2	325	45.8	518	73.1	191	26.9	223	31.5	709		196

Transfers

Transfers in	5
Transfers out	13

Tuition and Fees

	Resident	Nonresident
Full-time	$36,774	$36,774
Part-time	$29,566	$29,566
Tuition Guarantee Program	N	

Living Expenses

Estimated living expenses for singles

Living on campus	Living off campus	Living at home
N/A	$19,250	$19,250

ABA
Approved
Since
2006

GPA and LSAT Scores

	Total	Full-Time	Part-Time
# of apps	2,054	1,784	270
# of offers	1,018	911	107
# of matrics	224	173	51
75% GPA	3.38	3.42	3.30
Median GPA	3.13	3.20	2.84
25% GPA	2.80	2.91	2.50
75% LSAT	154	155	151
Median LSAT	152	153	147
25% LSAT	148	150	145

Grants and Scholarships (from prior year)

	Total		Full-Time		Part-Time	
	#	%	#	%	#	%
Total # of students	702		520		182	
Total # receiving grants	233	33.2	216	41.5	17	9.3
Less than 1/2 tuition	230	32.8	213	41.0	17	9.3
Half to full tuition	3	0.4	3	0.6	0	0.0
Full tuition	0	0.0	0	0.0	0	0.0
More than full tuition	0	0.0	0	0.0	0	0.0
Median grant amount			$7,500		$5,000	

Informational and Library Resources

Total amount spent on library materials	$905,503
Study seating capacity inside the library	438
# of full-time equivalent professional librarians	7
Hours per week library is open	104
# of open, wired connections available to students	0
# of networked computers available for use by students	7
Has wireless network?	Y
Requires computer?	Y

JD Attrition (from prior year)

	Academic	Other	Total	
	#	#	#	%
1st year	3	21	24	10.1
2nd year	1	2	3	1.3
3rd year	0	2	2	1.0
4th year	0	1	1	2.6

Employment (9 months after graduation)

For up-to-date employment data, go to employmentsummary.abaquestionnaire.org on the ABA website.

Bar Passage Rates

First-time takers	172	Reporting %	82.56
Average school %	77.46	Average state %	79.69
Average pass difference	−2.23		

Jurisdiction	Takers	Passers	Pass %	State %	Diff %
South Carolina	142	110	77.46	79.69	−2.23

CHARLESTON SCHOOL OF LAW

81 Mary Street, PO Box 535
Charleston, SC 29402
Phone: 843.377.2143; Fax: 843.329.0491
E-mail: info@charlestonlaw.edu; Website: www.charlestonlaw.edu

Introduction

The Charleston School of Law (CSOL) offers students the unique opportunity to study the time-honored practice of law amid the beauty and grace of one of the South's oldest and most prestigious cities, Charleston, South Carolina. Founded in 2003, CSOL is a freestanding school. The School of Law received full accreditation from the ABA on August 4, 2011.

Located in beautiful downtown Charleston, South Carolina, the school is conveniently situated near the historic "four corners of the law" as well as a thriving legal community and the federal and county courthouses. The open intellectual environment at CSOL complements the progressive nature of the city of Charleston. With its diverse economy, rich cultural heritage, thriving tourist industry, and natural amenities, the city—home to one of the nation's busiest ports—is a hub of activity. Charleston is attractive, fun, and consistently named one of the best places in the country to live, work, and learn. The city is home to other institutions of higher education, including the Medical University of South Carolina, the Citadel, and the College of Charleston. The 580,000-person metropolitan area is served by a strong program of cultural activities. Spoleto Festival USA, an internationally renowned arts festival of opera, dance, music, and theater, draws more than 85,000 people to the city each summer. Visitors and residents delight in Charleston's nationally recognized restaurants, vibrant nightlife, walks along the historic Battery, tours of historic homes, boating, sailing, golf, and beachcombing on nearby Sullivan's Island, Isle of Palms, Folly Beach, or Kiawah Island.

Library

The Sol Blatt Jr. Law Library, located in a historic 1857 railroad building, offers the feel of Charleston while housing a wireless network that provides access to an ever-growing digital collection. In just seven years, the library has built a digital and print collection that includes over 600,000 titles.

Students have access to the full text of primary and secondary sources of American law 24 hours a day, 7 days a week from anywhere in the world via the Internet. In addition to the traditional legal databases of Westlaw and LexisNexis, students also have electronic access to the full text of materials from Eighteenth Century Collections Online, BNA, CCH, CIAO, Environmental Law Reporter, HeinOnline, LLMC, LexisNexis Congressional, LexisNexis State Capital, The Making of Modern Law, Primary Sources on the Web, Treatises & Trials, the Making of the Modern World, Matthew Bender, Pro Quest Legislative Insight, RIA Checkpoint, and US Supreme Court Records and Briefs, Tax Analysts, Inc., and vLex. For cost-effective training to become twenty-first century lawyers, students learn to integrate print and electronic research in a study space that manages to combine the historical charm of Charleston with the functionality of twenty-first century access to digital information.

Expenses and Financial Aid

Tuition for the 2011–2012 academic year was as follows: full time—$36,674; part time—$29,466; estimated living expenses—$18,000. The school offers both need-based and academic merit-based scholarships. Applicants that want to be considered for merit scholarships must have a completed file on or before February 1. Merit-based scholarship decisions are made in early March. Need-based scholarship applications must be received no later than May 15. Applicants should be eligible for federal student loans and are encouraged to complete the FAFSA no later than April 15. For the 2012–2013 academic year, CSOL plans to participate in the Post-9/11 GI Bill: Yellow Ribbon Program.

Admission

CSOL requires applicants to have earned a bachelor's degree from an accredited institution prior to enrolling in the school. CSOL offers both a full- and part-time program of study leading to the Juris Doctor degree. Beginning students are accepted for the fall semester only. All applicants are required to take the LSAT and register with LSAC's Credential Assembly Service. Applicants should submit a completed application, a personal statement, a résumé, two letters of recommendation, and a $50 application fee. Applicants who are accepted will be required to submit a dean's certification form from all colleges or universities attended for 12 or more credit hours. Applications for the full-time program must be submitted on or before March 1; the deadline for those applying to the part-time program is April 1.

Many factors are considered; however, the two most important factors in reviewing an application are the cumulative undergraduate GPA and the LSAT. If an applicant has multiple LSAT scores, the highest score will be considered. A score is valid for three years. Other factors taken into consideration are graduate work, military or significant work experience, letters of recommendation, the personal statement, and community service.

Curriculum

Students at CSOL study law in a collegial learning environment. The low student-to-faculty ratio, 17:1, is a testament to the student-centered focus. The goals of CSOL include teaching the practice of law as a profession serving the public and instituting and coordinating legal outreach programs for the South Carolina and American Bars; local, state, and federal governments; and the general population.

Courses in torts, property, contracts, civil procedure, and legal research, analysis, and writing comprise the first-year curriculum. Required upper-level courses include business associations, commercial law, constitutional law, criminal law, criminal procedure, evidence, trusts and estates, and professional responsibility, as well as an advanced writing requirement and a skills course.

All students are required to perform a minimum of 30 hours of public service prior to graduation and to participate in the professionalism program during each year of law school.

Special Programs

The school offers a dynamic externship program that provides students the opportunity to gain practical work experience in legal business environments while earning course credit. Students have the opportunity to work under the direct supervision of members of the judiciary and attorneys in private practice, as well as in the public sector or in public interest jobs. In 2011, more than 110 organizations, including county public defenders' offices, state agencies, state and federal courts, and nonprofit agencies in South Carolina and beyond, offered more than 122 externship opportunities to students.

Housing

The school does not offer on-campus housing. Charleston offers many options for off-campus living. Whether students opt to live in the downtown historic district, at one of the nearby beaches, or in one of the many convenient neighborhoods and communities, they will find that carriage houses, apartments, or rental houses are available. The office of admission works with incoming and continuing students to find housing in the Charleston area.

Student Activities

Students have the opportunity to work on the publication of two law reviews. A student board publishes the *Charleston Law Review* on a quarterly basis. Students may also work with federal magistrate judges to publish the printed edition of the *Federal Courts Law Review*. There are other writing opportunities with *MALABU, the Maritime Law Bulletin*, and *Resolved, Journal of Alternative Dispute Resolution*.

Students participate in various Advocacy Programs ... Moot Court, Mock Trial, Alternative Dispute Resolution, as well as many others. CSOL students have won or placed in several competitions.

The school has more than 30 student organizations, including, but not limited to, the Student Bar Association,

Black Law Students Association, International Law Society, Environmental Law Society, Criminal Law Society, Children's Advocacy and Family Law Society, and Women in Law.

CSOL students also have the opportunity to become members of the Charleston County Bar Association.

Career Services

The Career Services Department provides a wide range of career development services for CSOL students and creates opportunities to connect students with employers in an efficient and supportive manner. The department serves as a liaison between students and legal employers. The staff provides individual career counseling and assistance with job application materials as well as programming on career-related issues. They also coordinate the on-campus interview program, forward job application materials to employers, post positions, and participate in national and regional career fairs.

The department is available to assist students in finding part-time employment while enrolled in law school, as well as summer employment and full-time permanent employment upon graduation. The Charleston area provides myriad opportunities for part-time employment while students are enrolled in their second and third years of law school.

CSOL prepares students for careers in all areas of legal practice. Regardless of a student's path after graduation, CSOL strives to instill in students the value of public service. All students must complete 30 hours of pro bono legal service under the supervision of a licensed attorney before they graduate. The Director of Public Service and Pro Bono within the Career Services Department develops and supports pro bono opportunities and provides guidance to students in their selection of pro bono work.

APPLICANT PROFILE

Charleston School of Law

LSAT Score	GPA								
	3.75 +	3.50–3.74	3.25–3.49	3.00–3.24	2.75–2.99	2.50–2.74	2.25–2.49	2.00–2.24	Below 2.00
175–180									
170–174									
165–169									
160–164									
155–159									
150–154									
145–149									
140–144									
135–139									
130–134									
125–129									
120–124									

■ Good Possibility   □ Possible   ▨ Unlikely

CHARLOTTE SCHOOL OF LAW

2145 Suttle Avenue
Charlotte, NC 28208
Phone: 704.971.8500; Fax: 704.971.8599
E-mail: admissions@charlottelaw.edu; Website: www.charlottelaw.edu

ABA
Approved
Since
2008

Section of Legal Education
and Admissions to the Bar

The Basics

Type of school	Private	
Term	Semester	
Application deadline	1/25	8/15
Application fee		
Financial aid deadline		
Can first year start other than fall?	Yes	
Student to faculty ratio	21.5 to 1	
# of housing spaces available restricted to law students		
graduate housing for which law students are eligible		

Faculty and Administrators

	Total		Men		Women		Minorities	
	Spr	Fall	Spr	Fall	Spr	Fall	Spr	Fall
Full-time	33	39	12	17	21	22	13	14
Other full-time	3	0	3	0	0	0	0	0
Deans, librarians, & others who teach	5	3	1	2	4	1	2	1
Part-time	31	40	19	21	12	19	5	6
Total	72	82	35	40	37	42	20	21

Curriculum

	Full-Time	Part-Time
Typical first-year section size	75	60
Is there typically a "small section" of the first-year class, other than Legal Writing, taught by full-time faculty	No	No
If yes, typical size offered last year		
# of classroom course titles beyond first-year curriculum	96	

# of upper division courses, excluding seminars, with an enrollment:		
	Under 25	72
	25–49	32
	50–74	10
	75–99	11
	100+	2

# of seminars	19	
# of seminar positions available	375	
# of seminar positions filled	195	63
# of positions available in simulation courses	92	
# of simulation positions filled	63	21
# of positions available in faculty supervised clinical courses	204	
# of faculty supervised clinical positions filled	63	17
# involved in field placements	43	13
# involved in law journals	38	5
# involved in moot court or trial competitions	18	5
# of credit hours required to graduate	90	

Transfers

Transfers in	10
Transfers out	22

Tuition and Fees

	Resident	Nonresident
Full-time	$36,916	$36,916
Part-time	$29,850	$29,850
Tuition Guarantee Program	N	

Living Expenses

Estimated living expenses for singles

Living on campus	Living off campus	Living at home
N/A	$21,305	$21,305

JD Enrollment and Ethnicity

	Men		Women		Full-Time		Part-Time		1st-Year		Total		JD Degs. Awd.
	#	%	#	%	#	%	#	%	#	%	#	%	
All Hispanics	19	3.5	31	5.1	38	4.0	12	6.1	24	4.3	50	4.3	4
Am. Ind./AK Nat.	8	1.5	12	2.0	18	1.9	2	1.0	15	2.7	20	1.7	3
Asian	19	3.5	14	2.3	27	2.8	6	3.0	22	3.9	33	2.9	3
Black/Af. Am.	68	12.6	125	20.4	147	15.4	46	23.2	117	20.9	193	16.8	1
Nat. HI/Pac. Isl.	1	0.2	0	0.0	1	0.1	0	0.0	1	0.2	1	0.1	0
2 or more races	2	0.4	6	1.0	6	0.6	2	1.0	7	1.3	8	0.7	0
Subtotal (minor.)	117	21.7	188	30.7	237	24.9	68	34.3	186	33.2	305	26.5	11
Nonres. Alien	3	0.6	6	1.0	9	0.9	0	0.0	5	0.9	9	0.8	0
White/Cauc.	418	77.7	419	68.4	707	74.2	130	65.7	369	65.9	837	72.7	87
Unknown	0	0.0	0	0.0	0	0.0	0	0.0	0	0.0	0	0.0	0
Total	538	46.7	613	53.3	953	82.8	198	17.2	560	48.7	1151		98

*ABA
Approved
Since
2008*

GPA and LSAT Scores

	Total	Full-Time	Part-Time
# of apps	3,955	3,605	350
# of offers	2,728	2,512	216
# of matrics	529	446	83
75% GPA	3.31	3.33	3.16
Median GPA	3.00	3.01	2.92
25% GPA	2.60	2.61	2.53
75% LSAT	151	151	150
Median LSAT	148	149	147
25% LSAT	145	146	143

Grants and Scholarships (from prior year)

	Total #	Total %	Full-Time #	Full-Time %	Part-Time #	Part-Time %
Total # of students	812		669		143	
Total # receiving grants	598	73.6	547	81.8	51	35.7
Less than 1/2 tuition	562	69.2	512	76.5	50	35.0
Half to full tuition	35	4.3	34	5.1	1	0.7
Full tuition	1	0.1	1	0.1	0	0.0
More than full tuition	0	0.0	0	0.0	0	0.0
Median grant amount			$9,500		$7,500	

Informational and Library Resources

Total amount spent on library materials	$834,758
Study seating capacity inside the library	435
# of full-time equivalent professional librarians	8
Hours per week library is open	105
# of open, wired connections available to students	0
# of networked computers available for use by students	56
Has wireless network?	Y
Requires computer?	Y

JD Attrition (from prior year)

	Academic #	Other #	Total #	Total %
1st year	47	48	95	19.3
2nd year	4	3	7	3.1
3rd year	0	0	0	0.0
4th year	0	0	0	0.0

Employment (9 months after graduation)

For up-to-date employment data, go to employmentsummary.abaquestionnaire.org on the ABA website.

Bar Passage Rates

First-time takers	77	Reporting %	90.91
Average school %	84.28	Average state %	77.62
Average pass difference	6.66		

Jurisdiction	Takers	Passers	Pass %	State %	Diff %
North Carolina	66	55	83.33	77.50	5.83
South Carolina	4	4	100.00	79.69	20.31

CHARLOTTE SCHOOL OF LAW

2145 Suttle Avenue
Charlotte, NC 28208
Phone: 704.971.8500; Fax: 704.971.8599
E-mail: admissions@charlottelaw.edu; Website: www.charlottelaw.edu

Introduction

Welcome to Charlotte School of Law and the city of Charlotte, commercial center for one of the fastest-growing, most vibrant areas in the southeast. One glance at a news website, newspaper, or news magazine will reveal the importance of law in a changing environment. Few economic, social, or political issues get explored very long without some reference to law or legal process. Pursuing a law degree is thus a rewarding and satisfying experience. This is particularly true at CharlotteLaw, which combines a traditional curriculum with a focus on professional preparedness. This approach, combined with a strong connection with the legal community, provides students with opportunities to develop important skills and to be prepared for the rigors of law practice upon graduation.

In the past several years, the CharlotteLaw student body has grown both in size and diversity. Our students come from over 46 states. Our faculty has grown to include both scholars and practitioners—all dedicated to the school's mission to maintain a student-centered focus that promotes professional preparedness and serves underrepresented communities. In August of 2008, the school moved to a new state-of-the-art facility in West Charlotte that focuses on the student experience by incorporating the latest in technology and an emphasis on a collaborative learning environment. CharlotteLaw received full accreditation from the American Bar Association on June 10, 2011.

CharlotteLaw is committed to student success, ensuring that its traditional curriculum includes skills training and thorough preparation for the bar examination. Students also have access to externships and internships in the area's legal system, experiences that greatly enhance career growth and success.

An important part of the CharlotteLaw "magic" has to do with our location in Charlotte, North Carolina. Charlotte is a dynamic, rapidly growing, international city, which offers a rich array of family, educational, sports/recreational, cultural, and other opportunities. Our pleasant weather and close proximity to the sea and mountains provide a wonderful venue in which to study and pursue a career afterward. Indeed, North and South Carolina have one of the lowest proportions of lawyers in the United States and collectively is one of the fastest growing regions in the country.

We welcome you to learn more about our school. We encourage you to visit our campus, observe a class, and talk with our faculty and current students to discover for yourself the CharlotteLaw difference.

Mission

Our entire academic mission is structured around three core concepts that we strongly believe make the CharlotteLaw experience a unique and powerful one. These three ideals drive decision making as well as our academic approach; together they form a keen vision for the school.

- Practical preparation is critical. A rigorous curriculum has been created to ensure that our students are equipped with practical skills that will allow them to thrive in a professional setting. Students are taught not only the traditions and theory of law, but also how to apply this learning through critical thinking and analytical skill sets. We address what using a law degree in real life can mean to an individual both personally and professionally.
- Our students are our focus. Our faculty is driven by a desire to motivate and energize the student community in every aspect of the Charlotte School of Law experience. Professors are accessible mentors who take an active role in the development of students and help them to embrace their legal education and capitalize on the opportunities within the school's and community's network of resources. Student success is of the utmost importance to everyone at the institution, on every level.
- It is essential to reflect our community. The Charlotte School of Law believes strongly that tomorrow's leaders must reflect and interact effectively with an eclectic collective of people and cultures. Consequently, our inclusive environment fosters a demanding, yet supportive, educational setting for a richly diverse community.

Faculty and Administration

The Charlotte School of Law faculty and administration have come together from various backgrounds and achievements to design a practice-ready curriculum and a supportive environment where students are inspired to learn, prepared to serve, and qualified to lead with excellence. Every member of our team is deeply committed to making sure our students have the skills to bridge each area of legal practice and are better equipped for professional life no matter what path they choose for themselves upon graduation.

Program Options

The need for legal literacy has become a reality of complex contemporary business and government. A law degree adds value to almost any career one can imagine, and an increasing number of professionals are finding in the JD degree an experience that equips them well with the analytical, writing, counseling, and advocacy skills that are invaluable, no matter what one's calling.

Charlotte School of Law offers a full-time day program and a part-time program. In order to accommodate the varied needs of our students, the part-time program can be completed during the day or in the evening. Charlotte School of Law is one of few law schools to offer a spring program that starts in January. Both programs require the completion of 90 credit hours for graduation.

Admission

The Charlotte School of Law attracts applicants from not only North and South Carolina, but also from all over the United States. The process to gain admission is competitive; however, those who have scored well on the Law School Admission Test (LSAT) and have a good undergraduate grade-point average (in addition to other indicators of success) are good candidates to study law in our student-centered program.

CharlotteLaw offers a full-time program (completed in three years) and a flexible part-time program (completed in four years, summers included). Applications are accepted and reviewed throughout the academic year for entrance into either our fall or spring class. We do not have an application deadline; however, in order to have the best chance of being selected to join the CharlotteLaw family, you are encouraged to get your application in early and to complete the application process early (have all required materials on file). Early applicants with competitive numbers have the **best** chance of receiving a merit-based scholarship award.

The CharlotteLaw admission office staff will attempt to notify an applicant if a required item is missing from the application file. However, the applicant remains ultimately responsible for ensuring that the application file is completed in a timely fashion. Applicants are strongly encouraged to retain copies of all application information submitted.

File Review Process: Fall semester applications are reviewed after October 1 of each year. The file review process continues until the class-size goal is met.

January semester applications are reviewed after September 15 of each year. The file review process continues until the class-size goal is met.

Deferred Admission: Charlotte School of Law does not defer admission from one year to the following year. However, an applicant may be granted a deferral based on extreme circumstances after submitting a request in writing to the Admissions Department. Otherwise, applicants who are offered admission, but do not enroll must reapply.

Transfer/Visiting Students: Applications to transfer to Charlotte School of Law or to attend as a visiting student are evaluated by the Admissions Committee and the academic dean on a case-by-case basis. **Transfer or visiting status is granted only to applicants who are currently in law school.** If such an applicant is accepted, further details, instructions, and forms will be sent to the accepted applicant. Contact the Admissions Office with questions: 704.971.8540 or admissions@charlottelaw.edu.

Financial Aid

The cost to attend law school may make your dream seem out of reach. Before you move to plan B, stop and think about the cost associated with anything worth doing. Law school is an investment in you and an investment in your future.

To offset the cost of tuition, CharlotteLaw offers federal loans and merit-based scholarship awards to applicants who qualify. We also have a performance-based scholarship program for continuing students.

Visit the financial aid page of the Charlotte School of Law website for more information: www.charlottelaw.org/ admissions/admissionscontent.aspx?id=70.

APPLICANT PROFILE

Charlotte School of Law has elected not to publish an admission profile based on LSAT score and UGPA. While both numerical indicators are very important in understanding an applicant's potential for success in law school, those two factors are not the only ones taken into consideration.

Charlotte Law currently uses no form of indexing system in reaching its admission decisions. Each completed application file is thoroughly reviewed in its entirety by a team of faculty and admission professionals.

THE UNIVERSITY OF CHICAGO LAW SCHOOL

Admissions Office, 1111 E. 60th Street
Chicago, IL 60637
Phone: 773.702.9494; Fax: 773.834.0942
E-mail: admissions@law.uchicago.edu; Website: www.law.uchicago.edu

ABA
Approved
Since
1923

The Basics

Type of school	Private
Term	Quarter
Application deadline	12/1 2/1
Application fee	$75
Financial aid deadline	2/1
Can first year start other than fall?	No
Student to faculty ratio	8.1 to 1
# of housing spaces available restricted to law students	
graduate housing for which law students are eligible	659

Faculty and Administrators

	Total		Men		Women		Minorities	
	Spr	Fall	Spr	Fall	Spr	Fall	Spr	Fall
Full-time	61	67	39	46	22	21	7	12
Other full-time	13	10	10	6	3	4	2	2
Deans, librarians, & others who teach	3	3	1	1	2	2	0	0
Part-time	66	31	57	26	9	5	0	0
Total	143	111	107	79	36	32	9	14

Curriculum

	Full-Time	Part-Time
Typical first-year section size	104	0
Is there typically a "small section" of the first-year class, other than Legal Writing, taught by full-time faculty	No	No
If yes, typical size offered last year		
# of classroom course titles beyond first-year curriculum		181

# of upper division courses, excluding seminars, with an enrollment:		
Under 25		26
25–49		43
50–74		21
75–99		11
100+		1

# of seminars		75
# of seminar positions available		1,482
# of seminar positions filled	991	0
# of positions available in simulation courses		154
# of simulation positions filled	146	0
# of positions available in faculty supervised clinical courses		132
# of faculty supervised clinical positions filled	132	0
# involved in field placements	6	0
# involved in law journals	122	0
# involved in moot court or trial competitions	12	0
# of credit hours required to graduate		105

JD Enrollment and Ethnicity

	Men		Women		Full-Time		Part-Time		1st-Year		Total		JD Degs. Awd.
	#	%	#	%	#	%	#	%	#	%	#	%	
All Hispanics	26	7.5	20	7.2	46	7.4	0	0.0	18	9.4	46	7.4	17
Am. Ind./AK Nat.	0	0.0	1	0.4	1	0.2	0	0.0	0	0.0	1	0.2	0
Asian	25	7.2	30	10.9	55	8.8	0	0.0	17	8.9	55	8.8	20
Black/Af. Am.	21	6.0	18	6.5	39	6.3	0	0.0	13	6.8	39	6.3	13
Nat. HI/Pac. Isl.	0	0.0	0	0.0	0	0.0	0	0.0	0	0.0	0	0.0	0
2 or more races	19	5.5	14	5.1	33	5.3	0	0.0	6	3.1	33	5.3	10
Subtotal (minor.)	91	26.1	83	30.1	174	27.9	0	0.0	54	28.3	174	27.9	60
Nonres. Alien	7	2.0	9	3.3	16	2.6	0	0.0	8	4.2	16	2.6	4
White/Cauc.	201	57.8	148	53.6	349	55.9	0	0.0	100	52.4	349	55.9	115
Unknown	49	14.1	36	13.0	85	13.6	0	0.0	29	15.2	85	13.6	25
Total	348	55.8	276	44.2	624	100.0	0	0.0	191	30.6	624		204

Transfers

Transfers in	16
Transfers out	1

Tuition and Fees

	Resident	Nonresident
Full-time	$47,786	
Part-time		
Tuition Guarantee Program	N	

Living Expenses

Estimated living expenses for singles

Living on campus	Living off campus	Living at home
$22,536	$22,536	$22,536

THE UNIVERSITY OF CHICAGO LAW SCHOOL

ABA Approved Since 1923

GPA and LSAT Scores

	Total	Full-Time	Part-Time
# of apps	4,783	4,783	0
# of offers	837	837	0
# of matrics	191	191	0
75% GPA	3.94	3.94	0.00
Median GPA	3.87	3.87	0.00
25% GPA	3.71	3.71	0.00
75% LSAT	173	173	0
Median LSAT	171	171	0
25% LSAT	167	167	0

Grants and Scholarships (from prior year)

	Total		Full-Time		Part-Time	
	#	%	#	%	#	%
Total # of students	634		634		0	
Total # receiving grants	356	56.2	356	56.2	0	0.0
Less than 1/2 tuition	312	49.2	312	49.2	0	0.0
Half to full tuition	36	5.7	36	5.7	0	0.0
Full tuition	4	0.6	4	0.6	0	0.0
More than full tuition	4	0.6	4	0.6	0	0.0
Median grant amount			$10,000		$0	

Informational and Library Resources

Total amount spent on library materials	$2,085,390
Study seating capacity inside the library	483
# of full-time equivalent professional librarians	10
Hours per week library is open	82
# of open, wired connections available to students	1,115
# of networked computers available for use by students	26
Has wireless network?	Y
Requires computer?	Y

JD Attrition (from prior year)

	Academic	Other	Total	
	#	#	#	%
1st year	0	1	1	0.5
2nd year	0	1	1	0.5
3rd year	0	0	0	0.0
4th year	0	0	0	0.0

Employment (9 months after graduation)

For up-to-date employment data, go to employmentsummary.abaquestionnaire.org on the ABA website.

Bar Passage Rates

First-time takers	199	Reporting %	70.85
Average school %	94.33	Average state %	87.49
Average pass difference	6.84		

Jurisdiction	Takers	Passers	Pass %	State %	Diff %
Illinois	81	78	96.30	89.38	6.92
New York	60	55	91.67	84.92	6.75

THE UNIVERSITY OF CHICAGO LAW SCHOOL

Admissions Office, 1111 E. 60th Street
Chicago, IL 60637
Phone: 773.702.9494; Fax: 773.834.0942
E-mail: admissions@law.uchicago.edu; Website: www.law.uchicago.edu

Introduction

Chicago graduates lead and innovate in government, public interest, academia, and business, as well as in law. For this reason, Chicago aims not to certify lawyers, but to train well-rounded, critical, and socially conscious thinkers and doers. Three cornerstones provide the foundation for Chicago's educational mission: the marketplace of ideas, participatory learning, and interdisciplinary inquiry.

Enrollment/Student Body

Our students' chief passions are ideas. They have shown this passion through their academic success, and they exhibit signs of great professional promise. Typically, 5,000 applicants seek approximately 190 seats in each incoming class. Chicago students come from more than 100 undergraduate institutions with degrees in nearly every discipline, and one in ten have graduate degrees. Many of our students have also had interesting and successful careers before law school.

Faculty

What distinguishes Chicago faculty is their devotion to both teaching and scholarship. This might seem a contradiction at first, but at Chicago, teaching and scholarship complement each other. Chicago professors blaze trails in legal thought, and their revolutionary ideas infuse classroom discussion with immediacy and excitement. Our professors write the books, draft the statutes, and decide the cases that students read at law schools across America. During the 2011–2012 academic year, our faculty will teach more than 170 courses and seminars at the Law School.

Curriculum

As a first-year student, you will take a core sequence covering five principal areas of the law: contracts, torts, property, criminal law, and civil procedure; a required interdisciplinary course called Elements of the Law; an elective; and a yearlong course on research and writing. This curriculum familiarizes you with the basic principles of Anglo-American law, cultivates legal reasoning, develops writing ability, and introduces students to interdisciplinary approaches to the law.

In the second and third years, you can choose courses from the full range of Chicago's more than 170 classes. Generally, classes are small; more than 60 percent have fewer than 25 students in them. Additionally, in an average year, about one-third of the second- and third-year students take classes in other divisions of the university. We do not ask our students to choose a concentration, but rather let them put together a personalized education based on their individual interests.

Special Programs

The Law School encourages interdisciplinary work. All students may take 12 hours of coursework anywhere in the university. Students may also apply for four formal joint-degree programs either at the same time they apply to the Law School or in their first year. They may also work with Law School and university staff to arrange concurrent degrees. Formal joint-degree programs are with the Booth School of Business (MBA, PhD), the Economics Department (PhD), the Harris School of Public Policy (MPP), and the Committee on International Relations (MA).

The Law School is home to a wide variety of research programs. These programs provide excellent outlets for both the theoretical and empirical work of both faculty and students. In addition, these programs host conferences, publish working papers, and support journals. Centers currently at the Law School include the Center for Civil Justice, the Center for Comparative Constitutionalism, the Center for Studies in Criminal Justice, the Institute for Law and Economics, and the Center for Law, Philosophy, and Human Values.

Clinical Opportunities

Housed in the Arthur Kane Center, our clinics involve more than 120 students each year in representing clients with real-world problems. The Mandel Legal Aid Clinic handles matters involving appellate advocacy, criminal and juvenile justice, employment discrimination, environmental law, civil rights, housing, immigration, mental health, and federal criminal law. The Institute for Justice Clinic on Entrepreneurship assists aspiring entry-level entrepreneurs from low- and moderate-income neighborhoods. We also have the Immigrant Children's Advocacy Project, which provides a unique opportunity for our students to draw on immigration law, international law, family, and children's rights law. Recently added are the Exoneration Project, which provides representation to clients who are asserting their actual innocence in state and federal court, the Prosecution and Defense Clinic, where students combine in-class intensive criminal law study with a clinical placement in a prosecutor's or public defender's office, and the Gendered Violence and the Law Clinic, where students assist with representation of domestic and sexual violence survivors. The Law School also partners with outside agencies to provide additional clinical opportunities to our students.

Student Activities

About 40 percent of upper-class students serve on one of the three student-edited journals, which include the *University of Chicago Law Review*, the *University of Chicago Legal Forum*, and the *Chicago Journal of International Law*. The Hinton Moot Court Board conducts a program in appellate advocacy for upper-class students, and first-year students participate in a moot court as part of the Bigelow Legal Research and Writing Program. More than 60 student organizations provide opportunities for the exploration of legal specialties, affiliation with like-minded students, or networking within identity groups.

Career Services

Our career services office assists students with permanent and summer employment. Seven professional career advisors counsel students in one-on-one planning sessions. Programs on types of practices and nontraditional careers are organized throughout the year for students. The office focuses on individualized counseling and coaching based on each student's career and life goals. The top five destinations our graduates choose for employment are Chicago, Los Angeles, New York, San Francisco, and Washington, DC.

Location

Hyde Park provides Chicago students with the best of all possible worlds—a campus with a college-town atmosphere just a few miles from the downtown area of a vibrant city. Hyde Park is a dynamic community with parks, museums, and multiple bookstores. The Law School is located at the southern end of campus, facing an expansive "front lawn" known as the Midway Plaisance. Surrounding the Law School is a tree-lined, diverse residential neighborhood, a sandy Lake Michigan beach, and two sprawling parks. The campus itself is a Gothic masterpiece where limestone buildings built around tree-shaded quadrangles sport gargoyles, ivy, and turrets. The Law School's modern building promotes interaction among faculty and students, while the recently remodeled library and classroom wing enhance the learning experience.

Housing

A graduate residence hall, located two blocks from the Law School, is available to law students. Most rooms are singles with private baths. In addition, the university has plenty of single- and married-student neighborhood housing available. Many students choose to rent housing from private landlords. Housing in Chicago is very affordable compared to most major cities. Buses run frequently throughout the surrounding neighborhood, providing transportation to and from residences and the Law School. Public transportation is easily accessible to other neighborhoods in Chicago.

Admission

Each year we seek to create a community from among the best and brightest law school applicants. We want students who are intellectually curious, lively, and collegial in their academic approach. We want students who will take their legal education seriously, but not take themselves too seriously. And because we are preparing students to enter a multifaceted profession, we want multidimensional students with a wide range of talents, backgrounds, experiences, and accomplishments. We do not use indices, formulas, or cutoffs.

Financial Aid

Your Chicago legal education is an investment in your future. Because many students will not have sufficient personal resources to make this investment, Chicago provides generous financial aid. Twenty students in the class of 2015 will receive Rubenstein Scholarships, covering full tuition for all three years. Approximately 50 percent of Chicago Law students receive scholarships. The Law School also provides funding for students who work in public interest positions during their summers. After graduation, the Law School provides financial assistance to graduates who enter careers in public interest legal work through our generous Loan Repayment Assistance Program. Graduates earning $80,000 or less in a government, nonprofit, or public interest job can receive benefits.

APPLICANT PROFILE

We seek to create a community from among the best, the brightest, and the most interesting law school applicants. We do not believe that the LSAT and GPA alone provide us with sufficient information to evaluate an applicant's likely contributions to our community; therefore, we do not use any formulas, indices, or numerical cutoffs. We do not provide an applicant profile here because it would be based solely on the LSAT and GPA.

CHICAGO-KENT COLLEGE OF LAW, ILLINOIS INSTITUTE OF TECHNOLOGY

Office of Admissions, 565 West Adams Street
Chicago, IL 60661
Phone: 312.906.5020; Fax: 312.906.5274
E-mail: admissions@kentlaw.edu; Website: www.kentlaw.edu

ABA Approved Since 1936

The Basics

Type of school	Private
Term	Semester
Application deadline	3/1
Application fee	$0
Financial aid deadline	4/1
Can first year start other than fall?	Yes
Student to faculty ratio	11.4 to 1
# of housing spaces available restricted to law students	
graduate housing for which law students are eligible	

Faculty and Administrators

	Total		Men		Women		Minorities	
	Spr	Fall	Spr	Fall	Spr	Fall	Spr	Fall
Full-time	65	64	42	40	23	24	7	5
Other full-time	1	1	1	0	0	1	0	1
Deans, librarians, & others who teach	3	3	1	1	2	2	1	1
Part-time	105	86	75	69	30	17	9	6
Total	174	154	119	110	55	44	17	13

Curriculum

	Full-Time	Part-Time
Typical first-year section size	53	34
Is there typically a "small section" of the first-year class, other than Legal Writing, taught by full-time faculty	No	No
If yes, typical size offered last year		

# of classroom course titles beyond first-year curriculum		149
# of upper division courses, excluding seminars, with an enrollment:	Under 25	220
	25–49	46
	50–74	21
	75–99	10
	100+	3
# of seminars		45
# of seminar positions available		570

	Full-Time	Part-Time
# of seminar positions filled	344	59
# of positions available in simulation courses	601	
# of simulation positions filled	277	274
# of positions available in faculty supervised clinical courses	238	
# of faculty supervised clinical positions filled	222	7
# involved in field placements	205	11
# involved in law journals	58	3
# involved in moot court or trial competitions	86	3
# of credit hours required to graduate	87	

JD Enrollment and Ethnicity

	Men		Women		Full-Time		Part-Time		1st-Year		Total		JD Degs. Awd.
	#	%	#	%	#	%	#	%	#	%	#	%	
All Hispanics	44	8.5	38	9.1	65	8.6	17	9.6	30	9.6	82	8.8	15
Am. Ind./AK Nat.	0	0.0	0	0.0	0	0.0	0	0.0	0	0.0	0	0.0	0
Asian	23	4.5	33	7.9	42	5.6	14	7.9	22	7.0	56	6.0	24
Black/Af. Am.	19	3.7	19	4.5	27	3.6	11	6.2	13	4.1	38	4.1	12
Nat. HI/Pac. Isl.	9	1.7	9	2.2	12	1.6	6	3.4	0	0.0	18	1.9	6
2 or more races	8	1.6	8	1.9	15	2.0	1	0.6	5	1.6	16	1.7	5
Subtotal (minor.)	103	20.0	107	25.6	161	21.3	49	27.5	70	22.3	210	22.5	62
Nonres. Alien	16	3.1	17	4.1	27	3.6	6	3.4	14	4.5	33	3.5	9
White/Cauc.	318	61.7	239	57.2	458	60.7	99	55.6	186	59.2	557	59.7	244
Unknown	78	15.1	55	13.2	109	14.4	24	13.5	44	14.0	133	14.3	24
Total	515	55.2	418	44.8	755	80.9	178	19.1	314	33.7	933		339

Transfers

Transfers in	24
Transfers out	7

Tuition and Fees

	Resident	Nonresident
Full-time	$42,030	$42,030
Part-time	$30,718	$30,718
Tuition Guarantee Program	N	

Living Expenses

Estimated living expenses for singles

Living on campus	Living off campus	Living at home
$21,098	$21,098	$21,098

CHICAGO-KENT COLLEGE OF LAW, ILLINOIS INSTITUTE OF TECHNOLOGY

ABA
Approved
Since
1936

GPA and LSAT Scores

	Total	Full-Time	Part-Time
# of apps	3,719	3,255	464
# of offers	1,441	1,331	110
# of matrics	308	262	46
75% GPA	3.66	3.67	3.64
Median GPA	3.52	3.53	3.34
25% GPA	3.09	3.10	3.08
75% LSAT	162	162	161
Median LSAT	160	160	158
25% LSAT	155	155	153

Grants and Scholarships (from prior year)

	Total #	Total %	Full-Time #	Full-Time %	Part-Time #	Part-Time %
Total # of students	970		785		185	
Total # receiving grants	576	59.4	488	62.2	88	47.6
Less than 1/2 tuition	287	29.6	230	29.3	57	30.8
Half to full tuition	200	20.6	182	23.2	18	9.7
Full tuition	67	6.9	56	7.1	11	5.9
More than full tuition	22	2.3	20	2.5	2	1.1
Median grant amount			$20,000		$10,000	

Informational and Library Resources

Total amount spent on library materials	$581,962
Study seating capacity inside the library	440
# of full-time equivalent professional librarians	12
Hours per week library is open	93
# of open, wired connections available to students	1,770
# of networked computers available for use by students	32
Has wireless network?	Y
Requires computer?	Y

JD Attrition (from prior year)

	Academic #	Other #	Total #	Total %
1st year	10	26	36	11.6
2nd year	0	1	1	0.3
3rd year	0	0	0	0.0
4th year	0	0	0	0.0

Employment (9 months after graduation)

For up-to-date employment data, go to
employmentsummary.abaquestionnaire.org on the ABA website.

Bar Passage Rates

First-time takers	252	Reporting %	95.63
Average school %	93.78	Average state %	89.38
Average pass difference	4.40		

Jurisdiction	Takers	Passers	Pass %	State %	Diff %
Illinois	241	226	93.78	89.38	4.40

CHICAGO-KENT COLLEGE OF LAW, ILLINOIS INSTITUTE OF TECHNOLOGY

Office of Admissions, 565 West Adams Street
Chicago, IL 60661
Phone: 312.906.5020; Fax: 312.906.5274
E-mail: admissions@kentlaw.edu; Website: www.kentlaw.iit.edu

Introduction

Chicago-Kent College of Law, Illinois Institute of Technology, is a national leader in legal education, recognized for the strength of its faculty and for its innovative approaches to traditional legal education. The second oldest law school in Illinois, Chicago-Kent was founded in 1888 by two judges who believed that legal education should be available to working men and women. The law school's first female student graduated in 1891, and the first African American woman admitted to the bar in Illinois (and the second admitted to practice law in the United States) was a graduate of the class of 1894. Today, Chicago-Kent students come from 40 states and 16 countries. Forty-five percent of the students are women, and 23 percent are students of color. The law school is also proud to count among its students and graduates the 2007 and 2008 National Trial Competition champions, the 2008 and 2009 National Moot Court Competition champions, and the winners of the 2010 National Institute for Trial Advocacy Tournament of Champions.

Drawing on its distinctive affiliation with Illinois Institute of Technology, Chicago-Kent is at the vanguard of exploring new frontiers in the law raised by biotechnology, cyberspace, environmental regulation, intellectual property, international business transactions and trade, and much more. Chicago-Kent is located in downtown Chicago, the heart of the city's commercial and legal communities. The law school is accredited by the American Bar Association and is a member of the Association of American Law Schools and the Order of the Coif.

Faculty

The foundation for academic excellence at Chicago-Kent is derived from its faculty, who engage in broad-ranging legal scholarship and research. As advisors frequently approached for their expertise, faculty members help shape policy and thinking on a variety of issues, and make it a point to involve students in their particular areas of influence.

Library and Facilities

Chicago-Kent's modern, ten-story building features a three-story atrium, five-level library, technologically advanced classrooms and courtroom, auditorium, computer labs, student lounges, and cafeteria. Chicago-Kent's library is one of the largest law school libraries in the country. The collection includes the Library of International Relations and a wealth of material on environmental and energy law, intellectual property law, international trade law, and labor law.

The law school houses a robust computer network infrastructure. The wireless network is accessible throughout the building and supports the latest protocols. In addition, there are over 1,900 wired network connections located in key areas, including the library, individual seats in the majority of classrooms, and student lounge areas.

Affordable housing is available in nearby urban and suburban neighborhoods. Furnished apartments are available for Chicago-Kent students at Tailor Lofts, a new loft-style development located within walking distance of the law school in student-friendly Greektown. Dormitory housing is available on the university's main campus, approximately five miles south of the law school. A free shuttle runs between the two campuses. The law school is close to all public transportation downtown.

Curriculum

Both full-time and part-time programs are available. Full-time students usually complete the JD degree in three years. Part-time students usually finish in four years. Students may apply to transfer between divisions after completing the first year. First-year class sizes typically range from 30 to 90 students.

Degrees available include JD, JD/MBA, JD/MPA, JD/MPH, JD/LLM in Taxation, JD/LLM in Financial Services Law, JD/LLM in Family Law, JD/MS in Finance, JD/MS in Environmental Management and Sustainability, LLM in Taxation, LLM in Financial Services Law, LLM in Family Law, LLM in International Intellectual Property Law, and LLM in International and Comparative Law.

Practical Skills Training

Legal Research and Writing—Chicago-Kent's acclaimed legal research and writing program is one of the most comprehensive in the nation. The three-year, five-course curriculum teaches students to research, analyze, and communicate effectively about a wide range of legal problems.

Clinical Education—The Law Offices of Chicago-Kent, one of the largest in-house clinical education programs in the country, offers 11 in-house clinical practice areas and externship programs with placements in law firms, corporate legal departments, government agencies, not-for-profit organizations, and federal and state court judges.

Trial Advocacy—The law school offers a two-semester sequence in trial advocacy and an intensive course taught by veteran judges and experienced practitioners.

Certificate Programs

Business Law—The program prepares students for careers involving business law by requiring a broad range of business courses, a specialized writing course, and a business-related experience.

Criminal Litigation—The program emphasizes both theory and practical skills development to provide comprehensive and balanced preparation for a career in criminal prosecution or defense.

Environmental and Energy Law—The program's interdisciplinary approach to the problems of environmental regulation and natural resources allocation prepares students for practice through a series of courses in law, economic and public policy analysis, and the scientific aspects of environmental problems.

Intellectual Property Law—The program focuses on issues relating to patent, trademark, copyright, trade secrets, and unfair competition, both in the United States and abroad.

International and Comparative Law—The program encompasses study in international business and trade, international and comparative law, and international human rights.

Labor and Employment Law—The program provides students with theoretical and practical training in the law governing the workplace.

Litigation and Alternative Dispute Resolution—The program stresses the connection between legal doctrine, skills and values, and the art of lawyering. It is designed to educate students to become reflective practitioners with a lawyering identity that incorporates high standards of competence, ethics, and social responsibility.

Public Interest Law—The program provides students with a background in public interest law and policy, in addition to individualized curriculum and career planning. The law school also supports a number of public interest resources and activities, including the Center for Access to Justice and Technology, which aims to make justice more accessible to the public through the use of the Internet.

Institutes and Centers

Chicago-Kent is home to 10 institutes and centers with missions that range from conducting scholarly and practical research on legal and social issues to providing topical programming to developing public interest services. Through these initiatives, many of which involve cross-disciplinary projects, students learn to appreciate and adapt to major social and global influences that can change the legal profession and its practice.

- Center for Access to Justice and Technology
- Center for Information, Society, and Policy
- Center for Open Government
- Global Law and Policy Initiative
- IIT Center for Diabetes Research and Policy
- Institute for Law and the Humanities
- Institute for Law and the Workplace
- Institute for Science, Law, and Technology
- Institute on the Supreme Court of the United States (ISCOTUS)
- Jury Center

Admission

Admission is highly selective. Each application is individually reviewed and decisions are based on a range of factors, including quantitative and qualitative criteria. Although the GPA and LSAT are important criteria, consideration also is given to nonnumerical factors such as the nature and rigor of the undergraduate curriculum, writing ability, graduate work and professional experience, extracurricular activities, diversity, and the personal statement. The admission requirements for the full- and part-time divisions are the same. The law school is committed to attracting and retaining students from a variety of racial, ethnic, economic, geographic, and educational backgrounds.

Student Activities

Student editors and staff, in association with a faculty editor, publish the *Chicago-Kent Law Review* in symposium format. Moot Court and Trial Advocacy teams successfully compete in local, regional, and national competitions each year, providing numerous opportunities to develop litigation expertise. Diverse student interests are represented in a wide variety of social, political, and professional student groups.

Scholarship Support

Substantial scholarship assistance is offered to entering and continuing students based on factors that include merit, financial need, and contribution to the law school community. The Honors Scholars Program provides renewable scholarships of full tuition and living expenses, research assistantships, and special seminars to a select group of students who demonstrate exceptional academic and leadership ability.

Career Services

The Office of Career Services, with six full-time staff, offers individual counseling on résumé writing, interview techniques, and job-search strategies and sponsors both on- and off-campus interview programs.

APPLICANT PROFILE

Chicago-Kent College of Law, Illinois Institute of Technology
This grid includes only applicants who earned 120–180 LSAT scores under standard administrations.

LSAT Score	3.75 + Apps	Adm	3.50–3.74 Apps	Adm	3.25–3.49 Apps	Adm	3.00–3.24 Apps	Adm	2.75–2.99 Apps	Adm	2.50–2.74 Apps	Adm	2.25–2.49 Apps	Adm	2.00–2.24 Apps	Adm	Below 2.00 Apps	Adm	No GPA Apps	Adm	Total Apps	Adm
170–180	15	10	12	10	11	8	5	4	8	6	1	0	2	2	2	2	0	0	1	1	57	43
165–169	56	32	69	49	52	43	34	31	32	26	18	13	8	7	1	1	1	0	3	2	274	204
160–164	96	91	145	135	160	141	118	93	55	49	35	33	24	18	7	6	0	0	30	24	670	590
155–159	115	103	221	160	247	29	221	30	132	9	69	4	29	1	12	0	0	0	32	4	1078	340
150–154	88	74	145	103	188	14	184	13	123	2	73	3	26	0	12	0	1	0	33	1	873	210
Below 150	43	9	90	17	138	1	144	1	128	0	110	0	69	0	37	0	15	0	33	0	807	28
Total	413	319	682	474	796	236	706	172	478	92	306	53	158	28	71	9	17	0	132	32	3759	1415

Apps = Number of Applicants
Adm = Number Admitted
Reflects 99% of the total applicant pool; highest LSAT data reported.

This grid represents admission data for applicants to both the full- and part-time programs. The information in this grid is to be used only as an approximate gauge of the likelihood of admission and not as a guarantee. Individual accomplishments and other nonnumerical factors are also of importance to the Admissions Committee.

UNIVERSITY OF CINCINNATI COLLEGE OF LAW

PO Box 210040, Office of Admission and Financial Aid
Cincinnati, OH 45221-0040
Phone: 513.556.0078; Fax: 513.556.2391
E-mail: admissions@law.uc.edu; Website: www.law.uc.edu

ABA
Approved
Since
1923

AMERICAN BAR ASSOCIATION
Section of Legal Education
and Admissions to the Bar

The Basics

Type of school	Public
Term	Semester
Application deadline	3/1
Application fee	$35
Financial aid deadline	3/1
Can first year start other than fall?	No
Student to faculty ratio	11.3 to 1
# of housing spaces available restricted to law students	
graduate housing for which law students are eligible	409

Faculty and Administrators

	Total		Men		Women		Minorities	
	Spr	Fall	Spr	Fall	Spr	Fall	Spr	Fall
Full-time	28	32	11	16	17	16	6	7
Other full-time	0	0	0	0	0	0	0	0
Deans, librarians, & others who teach	8	8	5	4	3	4	1	2
Part-time	36	34	28	23	8	11	5	1
Total	72	74	44	43	28	31	12	10

Curriculum

		Full-Time	Part-Time
Typical first-year section size		72	0
Is there typically a "small section" of the first-year class, other than Legal Writing, taught by full-time faculty		Yes	No
If yes, typical size offered last year		24	
# of classroom course titles beyond first-year curriculum		97	
# of upper division courses, excluding seminars, with an enrollment:	Under 25	61	
	25–49	26	
	50–74	3	
	75–99	4	
	100+	1	
# of seminars		18	
# of seminar positions available		255	
# of seminar positions filled		216	0
# of positions available in simulation courses		242	
# of simulation positions filled		242	0
# of positions available in faculty supervised clinical courses		56	
# of faculty supervised clinical positions filled		56	0
# involved in field placements		157	0
# involved in law journals		131	0
# involved in moot court or trial competitions		86	0
# of credit hours required to graduate		90	

JD Enrollment and Ethnicity

	Men		Women		Full-Time		Part-Time		1st-Year		Total		JD Degs. Awd.
	#	%	#	%	#	%	#	%	#	%	#	%	
All Hispanics	5	2.1	7	4.2	12	2.9	0	0.0	5	4.2	12	2.9	3
Am. Ind./AK Nat.	0	0.0	0	0.0	0	0.0	0	0.0	0	0.0	0	0.0	0
Asian	12	5.0	13	7.8	25	6.1	0	0.0	5	4.2	25	6.1	8
Black/Af. Am.	9	3.7	19	11.4	28	6.8	0	0.0	9	7.6	28	6.8	6
Nat. HI/Pac. Isl.	0	0.0	0	0.0	0	0.0	0	0.0	0	0.0	0	0.0	0
2 or more races	0	0.0	0	0.0	0	0.0	0	0.0	0	0.0	0	0.0	0
Subtotal (minor.)	26	10.7	39	23.4	65	15.9	0	0.0	19	16.0	65	15.9	17
Nonres. Alien	0	0.0	2	1.2	2	0.5	0	0.0	0	0.0	2	0.5	1
White/Cauc.	216	89.3	126	75.4	342	83.6	0	0.0	100	84.0	342	83.6	102
Unknown	0	0.0	0	0.0	0	0.0	0	0.0	0	0.0	0	0.0	0
Total	242	59.2	167	40.8	409	100.0	0	0.0	119	29.1	409		120

Transfers

Transfers in	9
Transfers out	3

Tuition and Fees

	Resident	Nonresident
Full-time	$22,204	$38,720
Part-time		
Tuition Guarantee Program		N

Living Expenses

Estimated living expenses for singles

Living on campus	Living off campus	Living at home
$18,336	$18,336	$18,336

ABA
Approved
Since
1923

GPA and LSAT Scores

	Total	Full-Time	Part-Time
# of apps	1,572	1,572	0
# of offers	737	737	0
# of matrics	119	119	0
75% GPA	3.80	3.80	0.00
Median GPA	3.57	3.57	0.00
25% GPA	3.36	3.36	0.00
75% LSAT	162	162	0
Median LSAT	160	160	0
25% LSAT	155	155	0

Grants and Scholarships (from prior year)

	Total #	Total %	Full-Time #	Full-Time %	Part-Time #	Part-Time %
Total # of students	408		408		0	
Total # receiving grants	288	70.6	288	70.6	0	0.0
Less than 1/2 tuition	257	63.0	257	63.0	0	0.0
Half to full tuition	28	6.9	28	6.9	0	0.0
Full tuition	3	0.7	3	0.7	0	0.0
More than full tuition	0	0.0	0	0.0	0	0.0
Median grant amount			$6,500		$0	

Informational and Library Resources

Total amount spent on library materials	$917,040
Study seating capacity inside the library	334
# of full-time equivalent professional librarians	8
Hours per week library is open	95
# of open, wired connections available to students	6
# of networked computers available for use by students	62
Has wireless network?	Y
Requires computer?	N

JD Attrition (from prior year)

	Academic #	Other #	Total #	Total %
1st year	0	6	6	4.2
2nd year	0	0	0	0.0
3rd year	0	0	0	0.0
4th year	0	0	0	0.0

Employment (9 months after graduation)

For up-to-date employment data, go to employmentsummary.abaquestionnaire.org on the ABA website.

Bar Passage Rates

First-time takers	119	Reporting %	100.00
Average school %	93.27	Average state %	85.25
Average pass difference	8.02		

Jurisdiction	Takers	Passers	Pass %	State %	Diff %
Ohio	100	92	92.00	86.14	5.86
California	4	4	100.00	71.24	28.76
Kentucky	3	3	100.00	82.03	17.97
Alaska	1	1	100.00	80.55	19.45
Others (11)	11	11	100.00		

UNIVERSITY OF CINCINNATI COLLEGE OF LAW

PO Box 210040, Office of Admission and Financial Aid
Cincinnati, OH 45221-0040
Phone: 513.556.0078; Fax: 513.556.2391
E-mail: admissions@law.uc.edu; Website: www.law.uc.edu

Introduction

The University of Cincinnati College of Law is the nation's premier small, urban, public law school. As the fourth oldest continuously operating law school in the country, students benefit from an intimate collegial environment and personal attention from faculty, while having access to groundbreaking centers and institutes like the Center for Race, Gender, and Social Justice; the Corporate Law Center; the Urban Morgan Institute for Human Rights; the Ohio Innocence Project (OIP); and the Entrepreneurship and Community Development Clinic. Located on a campus recently noted by *Forbes* magazine as one of the most beautiful in the world, the College of Law provides easy access to downtown Cincinnati, which includes over 650 law firms; headquarters to Fortune 500 corporations; and state, county, and federal courts, including the US Court of Appeals for the Sixth Circuit. While the university is one of America's top 20 public research institutions and boasts a total student population of over 42,000, the College of Law remains one of the smallest law schools in the nation with approximately 135 students per incoming class.

Student Body

The 409 students in the College of Law come from an amazingly wide variety of backgrounds, experiences, and perspectives. The student body is also talented academically, as the 75th/25th LSAT and UGPA percentiles for fall 2011 were 162/155 and 3.80/3.36, respectively. The College of Law is committed to enrolling a diverse class, as 16 percent of our students are from minority backgrounds, about 40 percent are female, and 39 percent enroll from states other than Ohio. The average age of the entering class is 25; however, 21 percent of the class is 27 or older.

Faculty

The college employs a full-time faculty of 28 who pride themselves on their teaching, scholarship, and accessibility to students. As the core of the academic program, faculty members bring areas of expertise into the classroom that add depth, perspective, and professionalism to the law students' studies. The student-to-faculty ratio of 11 to 1 provides ample opportunities for individual discussions with faculty and in-depth research in areas of interest.

Library and Physical Facilities

The Robert S. Marx Law Library has a seasoned staff that is able to assist students with research and technical questions. Two computer labs and a wireless network throughout the law building enable students to maximize online research capabilities, and our skilled IT staff members are readily available to assist law students. The law library, which can seat the entire law student body at one time, manages collections carefully to support faculty and student research and the college curriculum.

Curriculum

First-year students are divided into six individual sections, creating an unusual advantage of very small first-year sections (typically no larger than 25). The small-section modules allow for further inquiry beyond the typical first-year curriculum. First-year students take three courses in small sections during the academic year with opportunities to study with all members of their class over the entire year. The upper level is well balanced between theory and skills-related courses. Institutes and research centers exist in the areas of international human rights, criminal law (Ohio Innocence Project), corporate law, law and psychiatry, the Center for Practice, and a newly established Center for Race, Gender, and Social Justice. In addition, the college offers joint programs with women's studies, business, political science, community planning, and social work. In addition to OIP, the law school also offers clinical opportunities via the Appellate Law Clinic (Sixth Circuit Court of Appeals), the Indigent Defense Clinic, the Domestic Violence and Civil Protection Order Clinic housed downtown at the Cincinnati Legal Aid offices, and the Entrepreneurship and Community Development Clinic, which focuses on small businesses.

Special Programs

The College of Law recognizes that a lawyer needs both a firm grasp on subject matter and expertise in professional skills. The college, therefore, has developed an extensive legal research and writing program that not only encompasses first-year courses, but upper-level courses as well. The Center for Professional Development provides students with extern experiences, which are opportunities to work with practicing attorneys and public clinics. The Rosenthal Institute for Justice has been endowed to ensure that popular programs like the Ohio Innocence Project are available to students now and in the future. Each institute and research center offers a fellowship program, research opportunities, and in-depth study in their respective areas. The college was the first to offer a joint degree in law and women's studies, and has the oldest endowed international human rights program at an American law school, the Urban Morgan Institute for Human Rights.

Admission Standards

Admission to the college is based upon a selective review of each applicant's file by the Admissions Committee. Although the Admissions Committee relies on the grade-point average and LSAT score to determine the applicant's academic potential, other nonquantitative factors believed to be relevant to success in law school are considered; that is, the quality of the applicant's education, participation in community service, employment experience, graduate work, and letters of recommendation. The educational philosophy of the college reflects a belief that a quality legal education is enhanced through having a heterogeneous student body. The committee, therefore, also considers race, cultural background, unusual personal circumstances, and age. Admission decisions are made on a rolling basis. The College of Law also offers a binding Early Decision Program. Students interested in applying through the Early Decision Program must have a completed application on file by December 1. The college is committed to enrolling a diverse and engaging class each year.

Student Activities

The College of Law offers numerous opportunities for students to sharpen their legal writing, advocacy, and leadership skills. The *University of Cincinnati Law Review,* founded in 1927, was the first law review published by an Ohio law school. The Urban Morgan Institute for Human Rights edits the *Human Rights Quarterly,* the leading international human rights journal in the world. The *Immigration and Nationality Law Review* is an annual publication of papers on the subjects of immigration and citizenship. The *Freedom Center Journal,* a collaboration between the law school and the National Underground Railroad Freedom Center, offers opportunities to publish scholarly works about cutting-edge issues of today, informed by the legacy of historic struggles for freedom. The College of Law also offers a well-respected Moot Court Program with teams participating in many national competitions. The college hosts the Rendigs National Products Liability Moot Court Competition each spring.

Expenses and Financial Aid

For the 2011–2012 academic year, resident and nonresident tuition and fees are $22,204 and $38,720, respectively. The Graduate Metro Rate (for those residing in approved

northern Kentucky counties) is $22,444. Nonresidents can reclassify as state residents by becoming independent and self-sustaining for their first year in law school. Cincinnati is a cosmopolitan yet affordable Midwestern city with living expenses estimated at $18,000 for the nine-month academic year. Cincinnati was recently ranked the fifth least expensive city in the nation in which to live. Scholarships are awarded to approximately 65 percent of the student body in order to attract an academically talented and diverse student body. The FAFSA should be filed by March 1 as a priority deadline in order to qualify for student loan packages by spring. A large percentage of second- and third-year students work with law firms, companies, and agencies in the Greater Cincinnati area to offset living expenses or student loan debt.

Placement

Annually, about half of our graduates enter private practice while others accept positions with public interest organizations, government agencies, businesses, and academia. Members of the class of 2010 were selected for the Presidential Management Fellowship Program and the Equal Justice Works Fellowship Program and obtained clerkships among the nation's highest courts. Since 2001, Ohio has been one of the top 10 states for entry-level legal employment opportunities. While many of our graduates obtain positions within the state of Ohio, our 2010 graduates also secured employment in 15 other states, the District of Columbia, and one foreign country.

APPLICANT PROFILE

University of Cincinnati College of Law
This grid includes only applicants who earned 120–180 LSAT scores under standard administrations.

LSAT Score	GPA 3.75 + Apps	Adm	3.50–3.74 Apps	Adm	3.25–3.49 Apps	Adm	3.00–3.24 Apps	Adm	2.75–2.99 Apps	Adm	2.50–2.74 Apps	Adm	2.25–2.49 Apps	Adm	2.00–2.24 Apps	Adm	Below 2.00 Apps	Adm	No GPA Apps	Adm	Total Apps	Adm
175–180	2	2	1	1	1	1	0	0	1	1	0	0	0	0	1	0	0	0	0	0	6	5
170–174	8	8	7	7	6	5	9	8	6	4	3	3	1	1	0	0	0	0	1	1	41	37
165–169	39	37	43	39	27	22	23	17	22	13	7	2	3	1	0	0	0	0	1	0	165	131
160–164	94	88	115	103	107	92	88	57	49	26	31	10	8	1	3	0	0	0	7	6	502	383
155–159	73	56	118	51	92	17	65	2	22	1	12	1	7	0	2	0	0	0	7	2	398	130
150–154	38	15	59	15	74	9	47	4	20	1	15	0	5	0	2	0	0	0	6	0	266	44
145–149	7	3	22	2	21	1	15	0	19	0	14	0	7	0	3	0	0	0	1	0	109	6
140–144	1	0	7	0	10	0	10	0	7	0	8	0	3	0	3	0	1	0	1	0	51	0
135–139	1	0	2	0	4	0	3	0	3	0	4	0	1	0	0	0	1	0	0	0	19	0
130–134	0	0	0	0	0	0	1	0	1	0	3	0	0	0	2	0	0	0	0	0	7	0
125–129	0	0	0	0	0	0	0	0	1	0	1	0	0	0	0	0	0	0	0	0	2	0
120–124	0	0	0	0	0	0	0	0	0	0	0	0	0	0	0	0	0	0	0	0	0	0
Total	263	209	374	218	342	147	261	88	151	46	98	16	35	3	16	0	2	0	24	9	1566	736

Apps = Number of Applicants
Adm = Number Admitted
Reflects 100% of the total applicant pool; highest LSAT data reported.

CITY UNIVERSITY OF NEW YORK SCHOOL OF LAW

2 Court Square
Long Island City, NY 11101
Phone: 718.340.4210; Fax: 718.340.4435
E-mail: admissions@mail.law.cuny.edu; Website: www.law.cuny.edu

ABA
Approved
Since
1985

The Basics

Type of school	Public
Term	Semester
Application deadline	3/15
Application fee	$60
Financial aid deadline	5/1
Can first year start other than fall?	No
Student to faculty ratio	11.0 to 1
# of housing spaces available restricted to law students	
graduate housing for which law students are eligible	

Faculty and Administrators

	Total		Men		Women		Minorities	
	Spr	Fall	Spr	Fall	Spr	Fall	Spr	Fall
Full-time	34	34	13	12	21	22	14	14
Other full-time	1	1	0	0	1	1	1	1
Deans, librarians, & others who teach	14	14	4	3	10	11	5	6
Part-time	15	10	6	5	9	5	2	2
Total	64	59	23	20	41	39	22	23

Curriculum

	Full-Time	Part-Time
Typical first-year section size	80	0
Is there typically a "small section" of the first-year class, other than Legal Writing, taught by full-time faculty	Yes	No
If yes, typical size offered last year	20	

# of classroom course titles beyond first-year curriculum		52
# of upper division courses, excluding seminars, with an enrollment:	Under 25	48
	25–49	24
	50–74	9
	75–99	4
	100+	7
# of seminars		28
# of seminar positions available		567

	Full-Time	Part-Time
# of seminar positions filled	454	0
# of positions available in simulation courses	624	
# of simulation positions filled	580	0
# of positions available in faculty supervised clinical courses	220	
# of faculty supervised clinical positions filled	234	0
# involved in field placements	46	0
# involved in law journals	51	0
# involved in moot court or trial competitions	40	0
# of credit hours required to graduate		91

JD Enrollment and Ethnicity

	Men		Women		Full-Time		Part-Time		1st-Year		Total		JD Degs. Awd.
	#	%	#	%	#	%	#	%	#	%	#	%	
All Hispanics	25	13.9	55	18.3	80	16.7	0	0.0	34	19.3	80	16.7	11
Am. Ind./AK Nat.	0	0.0	1	0.3	1	0.2	0	0.0	0	0.0	1	0.2	0
Asian	20	11.1	37	12.3	56	11.7	1	50.0	26	14.8	57	11.9	14
Black/Af. Am.	20	11.1	21	7.0	41	8.6	0	0.0	12	6.8	41	8.5	7
Nat. HI/Pac. Isl.	0	0.0	1	0.3	1	0.2	0	0.0	1	0.6	1	0.2	0
2 or more races	6	3.3	10	3.3	16	3.3	0	0.0	7	4.0	16	3.3	3
Subtotal (minor.)	71	39.4	125	41.7	195	40.8	1	50.0	80	45.5	196	40.8	35
Nonres. Alien	1	0.6	4	1.3	5	1.0	0	0.0	3	1.7	5	1.0	3
White/Cauc.	107	59.4	169	56.3	276	57.7	0	0.0	92	52.3	276	57.5	72
Unknown	1	0.6	2	0.7	2	0.4	1	50.0	1	0.6	3	0.6	1
Total	180	37.5	300	62.5	478	99.6	2	0.4	176	36.7	480		111

Transfers

Transfers in	3
Transfers out	2

Tuition and Fees

	Resident	Nonresident
Full-time	$12,207	$19,157
Part-time	$425	$750
Tuition Guarantee Program		N

Living Expenses

Estimated living expenses for singles

Living on campus	Living off campus	Living at home
N/A	$15,743	$6,072

CITY UNIVERSITY OF NEW YORK SCHOOL OF LAW

ABA Approved Since 1985

GPA and LSAT Scores

	Total	Full-Time	Part-Time
# of apps	1,883	1,883	0
# of offers	563	563	0
# of matrics	171	171	0
75% GPA	3.54	3.54	0.00
Median GPA	3.29	3.29	0.00
25% GPA	3.04	3.04	0.00
75% LSAT	158	158	0
Median LSAT	155	155	0
25% LSAT	153	153	0

Grants and Scholarships (from prior year)

	Total #	Total %	Full-Time #	Full-Time %	Part-Time #	Part-Time %
Total # of students	440		438		2	
Total # receiving grants	126	28.6	126	28.8	0	0.0
Less than 1/2 tuition	80	18.2	80	18.3	0	0.0
Half to full tuition	10	2.3	10	2.3	0	0.0
Full tuition	36	8.2	36	8.2	0	0.0
More than full tuition	0	0.0	0	0.0	0	0.0
Median grant amount			$940		$0	

Informational and Library Resources

Total amount spent on library materials	$597,271
Study seating capacity inside the library	223
# of full-time equivalent professional librarians	10
Hours per week library is open	61
# of open, wired connections available to students	62
# of networked computers available for use by students	113
Has wireless network?	Y
Requires computer?	N

JD Attrition (from prior year)

	Academic #	Other #	Total #	Total %
1st year	7	9	16	9.6
2nd year	4	2	6	4.0
3rd year	1	0	1	0.8
4th year	0	0	0	0.0

Employment (9 months after graduation)

For up-to-date employment data, go to employmentsummary.abaquestionnaire.org on the ABA website.

Bar Passage Rates

First-time takers	126	Reporting %	86.51
Average school %	72.48	Average state %	84.92
Average pass difference	−12.44		

Jurisdiction	Takers	Passers	Pass %	State %	Diff %
New York	109	79	72.48	84.92	−12.44

CITY UNIVERSITY OF NEW YORK SCHOOL OF LAW

2 Court Square
Long Island City, NY 11101
Phone: 718.340.4210; Fax: 718.340.4435
E-mail: admissions@mail.law.cuny.edu; Website: www.law.cuny.edu

Mission

Following its motto of "Law in the Service of Human Needs," the mission of the City University of New York (CUNY) School of Law is to train excellent public interest lawyers through a curriculum that integrates doctrine, legal theory, clinical education, and professional responsibility.

New Location

In 2012 CUNY Law will move from its current location in Flushing, Queens, to 2 Court Square in Long Island City. This central location will allow for an easier commute from all five boroughs and from around the region. Moreover, the move will enable the school to realize its long-held ambition to establish a part-time program, an innovation that would help make the law school accessible to a more diverse range of students. With its greater centrality, its mission will be enhanced by the closer proximity to the public interest community and to its clients.

Academic Program

CUNY Law's unique and integrated curriculum has made it a national leader in progressive legal education heralded by the Carnegie Foundation for the Advancement of Teaching. The curriculum engages students in a thoughtful combination of rigorous coursework in traditional substantive areas and a lawyering program that teaches the skills recognized by the American Bar Association as necessary for competent practice (problem solving, legal analysis and reasoning, legal research, factual investigation, and communication—including legal writing and oral argument, counseling, negotiation, litigation and alternative dispute resolution procedures, organization and management of legal work, and recognition and resolution of ethical dilemmas). All first-year students take a required two-semester Lawyering Seminar where they focus on the fundamental skills of legal analysis and legal writing and engage in simulations requiring a wide range of lawyering tasks. They draft documents, interview and counsel clients, engage in negotiations, and make arguments before trial and appellate courts. Faculty guidance, supervision, and feedback permeate the process. In the second year, each student elects a four-credit Lawyering Seminar focused on developing more advanced lawyering skills in a subject matter area of choice, including trial practice, mediation, labor, and appellate advocacy. Fifteen CUNY law students were offered Revson Fellowships in the summer of 2011. Excellent and comprehensive academic support is provided by the Irene Diamond Professional Skills Center.

Diversity

The diversity of New York City is reflected in our dynamic student body and faculty. Women constitute 63 percent of the student body; minorities, 41 percent. Faculty percentages are similar: 65 percent are women and 42 percent are people of color. The concern for diversity is also threaded through the curriculum, for example, a required course for all first-year students is Liberty, Equality, and Due Process, which examines issues of racial and gender equality and sexual orientation in the context of legal and historical analysis.

Clinical Programs

Clinical Programs include Community Economic Development, Criminal Defense, Elder Law, Equality, Health Law, Immigrant and Refugee Rights, International Women's Human Rights, and Mediation. Following Lawyering Seminars in the first two years, all students have opportunities to participate in 12 to 16 credit clinical courses in their third year. Students engage in individual representation of clients and work on projects in collaboration with community groups, organizers, and international organizations to address issues of social justice. Recent work includes legal victories in low-wage labor campaigns, amicus briefs to international tribunals, community education projects throughout New York, and interdisciplinary representation of clients who have suffered trauma from torture and domestic abuse.

Student Life

Despite the relatively small size of the law school, numerous student organizations thrive on campus. Students also have a major role in the law school's governance, recognizing and preparing them for their future as professionals and community leaders. One exemplary student program is the Mississippi Project; since 1992, this program has sent a delegation of law students to Mississippi over midyear break to work with lawyers in civil rights organizations across the state. CUNY students work and learn together in an exceptionally collaborative, noncompetitive atmosphere and interact on a first-name basis with the faculty. The student experience is further enriched by New York City's cultural offerings and by the exceptional resources of the third-largest university system in the country, City University of New York.

Faculty

Most of this diverse faculty have themselves been public interest practitioners, with experience in a wide area of issues, including employment discrimination, immigration, racial justice, environmental law, women's rights, labor, and international law. They have worked in China, Haiti, South Africa, Mongolia, Costa Rica, the Middle East, Russia, Papua New Guinea, Australia, Central America, the Philippines, and many other countries. Their prestigious awards include Fulbright, Ford, MacArthur, Revson, Rockefeller, and National Endowment for the Humanities fellowships. Their scholarship reflects their interest in, among other areas, international human rights and access to justice for underserved communities.

Career Opportunities

CUNY law graduates are employed in the full range of public interest jobs—legal services and public defender organizations, government agencies, international human rights organizations, not-for-profits, and the judiciary. Approximately 80–90 percent of alumni/ae secure positions within nine months of graduation. Historically, 55–65 percent of graduates enter the public interest/public service profession each year, while 25–30 percent are employed at private firms from large to small and solo community-based practices. CUNY law graduates are consistently awarded judicial clerkships and prestigious public interest postgraduate fellowships that include the Equal Justice Works, Skadden, Echoing Green, Yale Public Interest Initiative grants, and the Georgetown University Law Center fellowships, as well as the Fulbright. Although the vast majority are employed in the mid-Atlantic states, CUNY graduates can be found throughout the United States and abroad where they are engaged in international human rights work.

Child Care

CUNY Law School offers its students an on-site Early Childhood Program, the first and still one of the few on-site child care centers in legal education in the nation. The Children's Center provides reasonably priced, high-quality, nurturing care for children, with a quality program of education and recreational activities in a caring, multicultural environment. At our new location at 2 Court Square in Long Island City, in addition to a beautiful new classroom, the children will have an alternate indoor space located on the ground floor of the law school known as "The Beacon." This space is sunny and has floor to ceiling windows. A regularly reserved time will be scheduled exclusively for toddlers. In addition, the children will be able to either walk or ride in our buggy to nearby John F. Murray Park. Enrollment spaces are limited and the age range of children may vary from 3 months up to 3 years.

Special Opportunities

The law school offers a number of unique programs and initiatives that enrich the experience of students and provide

continuing support for graduates. The Community Legal Resource Network (CLRN) of alumni provides resources and supports graduates working in solo or small-firm practices in underserved communities. The LaunchPad for Justice, through a special practice order in conjunction with the New York State Courts, provides an opportunity for recent grads to argue in court on behalf of individuals facing housing legal issues, while waiting for admission to the NY State Bar. CLRN also established the Incubator for Justice in Manhattan. The Incubator houses and trains eight CUNY grads at a time, over an 18-month period, in basic business issues such as billing, record-keeping, technology, bookkeeping, and taxes while, at the same time, facilitating Incubator participants' involvement in larger justice initiatives and in subject-based training in immigration law, labor and employment, and other topics that will arise continually as these attorneys build their practices. CUNY Law's nationally ranked clinical program provides students with direct legal representation to underserved communities. Finally, the law school is part of a rich university, the City University of New York, and law students may take some interdisciplinary graduate courses with the approval of the Academic Dean.

Nontraditional Students

The law school's student profile includes many individuals returning to school after careers, and many who possess advanced degrees. The average age of the student body is 27; some students enter directly from undergraduate school while others are older, making the law school a comfortable environment.

Affordable Tuition

CUNY offers an excellent legal education at substantially less than half the cost of most private law schools.

APPLICANT PROFILE

City University of New York School of Law
This grid includes only applicants who earned 120–180 LSAT scores under standard administrations.

LSAT Score	GPA																				
	3.75 +		3.50–3.74		3.25–3.49		3.00–3.24		2.75–2.99		2.50–2.74		2.25–2.49		2.00–2.24		Below 2.00		No GPA		Total
	Apps	Adm	Apps	Adm	Apps	Adm	Apps	Adm	Apps	Adm	Apps	Adm	Apps	Adm	Apps	Adm	Apps	Adm	Apps	Adm	Apps	Adm
175–180	0	0	0	0	0	0	0	0	0	0	0	0	0	0	0	0	0	0	0	0	0	0
170–174	2	2	2	2	2	1	2	2	1	0	1	1	0	0	0	0	0	0	0	0	10	8
165–169	8	7	5	4	14	14	7	6	4	3	4	1	2	0	0	0	0	0	3	3	47	38
160–164	22	19	25	22	26	22	25	18	14	8	16	4	7	3	3	0	0	0	3	3	141	99
155–159	38	32	55	49	82	64	66	41	53	30	25	8	18	2	5	0	1	1	8	6	351	233
150–154	47	26	102	38	120	59	132	35	88	15	46	5	21	1	4	1	3	0	19	3	582	183
145–149	24	0	61	0	93	0	96	0	58	0	52	0	27	0	6	0	2	0	22	0	441	0
140–144	14	0	42	0	29	0	50	0	39	0	23	0	19	0	4	0	2	0	5	0	227	0
135–139	1	0	11	0	9	0	15	0	18	0	10	0	13	0	2	0	5	0	2	0	86	0
130–134	0	0	0	0	3	0	4	0	3	0	8	0	4	0	1	0	1	0	2	0	26	0
125–129	0	0	0	0	0	0	0	0	1	0	3	0	1	0	0	0	1	0	1	0	7	0
120–124	0	0	0	0	0	0	0	0	1	0	1	0	0	0	0	0	0	0	0	0	2	0
Total	156	86	303	115	378	160	397	102	280	56	189	19	112	6	25	1	15	1	65	15	1920	561

Apps = Number of Applicants
Adm = Number Admitted
Reflects 99% of the total applicant pool; highest LSAT data reported.

CLEVELAND STATE UNIVERSITY—CLEVELAND-MARSHALL COLLEGE OF LAW

Office of Admission, 1801 Euclid Avenue, LB 138
Cleveland, OH 44115-2214
Phone: 216.687.2304, toll-free 866.687.2304; Fax: 216.687.6881
E-mail: admissions@law.csuohio.edu; Website: www.law.csuohio.edu

ABA
Approved
Since
1957

The Basics

Type of school	Public
Term	Semester
Application deadline	5/1
Application fee	$0
Financial aid deadline	5/1
Can first year start other than fall?	No
Student to faculty ratio	11.8 to 1
# of housing spaces available restricted to law students	
graduate housing for which law students are eligible	25

Faculty and Administrators

	Total		Men		Women		Minorities	
	Spr	Fall	Spr	Fall	Spr	Fall	Spr	Fall
Full-time	37	36	21	18	16	18	6	6
Other full-time	2	2	1	1	1	1	0	0
Deans, librarians, & others who teach	5	6	0	2	5	4	0	1
Part-time	35	37	24	26	11	11	1	4
Total	79	81	46	47	33	34	7	11

Curriculum

	Full-Time	Part-Time
Typical first-year section size	52	36
Is there typically a "small section" of the first-year class, other than Legal Writing, taught by full-time faculty	No	No
If yes, typical size offered last year		
# of classroom course titles beyond first-year curriculum	93	

# of upper division courses, excluding seminars, with an enrollment:		
	Under 25	92
	25–49	32
	50–74	11
	75–99	0
	100+	0

	Full-Time	Part-Time
# of seminars	20	
# of seminar positions available	293	
# of seminar positions filled	138	49
# of positions available in simulation courses	240	
# of simulation positions filled	165	52
# of positions available in faculty supervised clinical courses	106	
# of faculty supervised clinical positions filled	73	9
# involved in field placements	87	9
# involved in law journals	84	11
# involved in moot court or trial competitions	37	10
# of credit hours required to graduate	90	

JD Enrollment and Ethnicity

	Men		Women		Full-Time		Part-Time		1st-Year		Total		JD Degs. Awd.
	#	%	#	%	#	%	#	%	#	%	#	%	
All Hispanics	6	1.9	11	4.6	13	3.1	4	3.0	8	4.8	17	3.1	3
Am. Ind./AK Nat.	1	0.3	0	0.0	1	0.2	0	0.0	0	0.0	1	0.2	0
Asian	5	1.6	9	3.8	13	3.1	1	0.8	9	5.5	14	2.5	5
Black/Af. Am.	27	8.5	28	11.7	40	9.4	15	11.4	16	9.7	55	9.9	11
Nat. HI/Pac. Isl.	0	0.0	0	0.0	0	0.0	0	0.0	0	0.0	0	0.0	0
2 or more races	0	0.0	1	0.4	0	0.0	1	0.8	0	0.0	1	0.2	0
Subtotal (minor.)	39	12.3	49	20.5	67	15.8	21	15.9	33	20.0	88	15.8	19
Nonres. Alien	4	1.3	2	0.8	3	0.7	3	2.3	2	1.2	6	1.1	7
White/Cauc.	275	86.5	188	78.7	355	83.5	108	81.8	130	78.8	463	83.1	158
Unknown	0	0.0	0	0.0	0	0.0	0	0.0	0	0.0	0	0.0	1
Total	318	57.1	239	42.9	425	76.3	132	23.7	165	29.6	557		185

Transfers

Transfers in	4
Transfers out	3

Tuition and Fees

	Resident	Nonresident
Full-time	$19,864	$27,204
Part-time	$15,280	$20,926
Tuition Guarantee Program		N

Living Expenses

Estimated living expenses for singles

Living on campus	Living off campus	Living at home
$18,800	$18,800	$18,800

CLEVELAND STATE UNIVERSITY—CLEVELAND-MARSHALL COLLEGE OF LAW

ABA
Approved
Since
1957

GPA and LSAT Scores

	Total	Full-Time	Part-Time
# of apps	1,557	1,332	225
# of offers	615	542	73
# of matrics	167	130	37
75% GPA	3.52	3.52	3.66
Median GPA	3.28	3.27	3.38
25% GPA	3.00	3.02	2.83
75% LSAT	157	157	157
Median LSAT	154	155	153
25% LSAT	152	152	150

Grants and Scholarships (from prior year)

	Total		Full-Time		Part-Time	
	#	%	#	%	#	%
Total # of students	610		453		157	
Total # receiving grants	199	32.6	165	36.4	34	21.7
Less than 1/2 tuition	91	14.9	85	18.8	6	3.8
Half to full tuition	49	8.0	31	6.8	18	11.5
Full tuition	59	9.7	49	10.8	10	6.4
More than full tuition	0	0.0	0	0.0	0	0.0
Median grant amount			$9,232		$3,150	

Informational and Library Resources

Total amount spent on library materials	$959,720
Study seating capacity inside the library	493
# of full-time equivalent professional librarians	8
Hours per week library is open	95
# of open, wired connections available to students	207
# of networked computers available for use by students	84
Has wireless network?	Y
Requires computer?	N

JD Attrition (from prior year)

	Academic	Other	Total	
	#	#	#	%
1st year	12	22	34	17.5
2nd year	1	1	2	1.1
3rd year	1	0	1	0.5
4th year	0	0	0	0.0

Employment (9 months after graduation)

For up-to-date employment data, go to employmentsummary.abaquestionnaire.org on the ABA website.

Bar Passage Rates

First-time takers	174	Reporting %	87.36
Average school %	85.53	Average state %	86.14

Average pass difference −0.61

Jurisdiction	Takers	Passers	Pass %	State %	Diff %
Ohio	152	130	85.53	86.14	−0.61

CLEVELAND STATE UNIVERSITY—CLEVELAND-MARSHALL COLLEGE OF LAW

Office of Admission, 1801 Euclid Avenue, LB 138
Cleveland, OH 44115-2214
Phone: 216.687.2304, toll-free 866.687.2304; Fax: 216.687.6881
E-mail: admissions@law.csuohio.edu; Website: www.law.csuohio.edu

Who We Are

Since 1897, C|M|LAW has provided an excellent legal education to a strong and diverse student body. Our law school has a proud heritage: it was the first law school in Ohio to admit women; it was one of the first law schools in Ohio to admit students of color; and our graduates have served for decades in prominent positions in law firms, the judiciary, government, and business. Today, our graduates are practicing law with distinction around the world. C|M|LAW offers a distinctive legal education that is flexible and affordable with full- and part-time (day and evening) options and reasonable tuition that allows our students to graduate with minimal debt.

Points of Pride

C|M|LAW just opened its state-of-the-art, digitally integrated trial courtroom providing simulation-based learning for law students and legal professionals. Designed to look and function exactly like a federal courtroom, this facility enables C|M|LAW students to prepare to be outstanding trial lawyers. We lead all Ohio public law schools in the percentage of graduates working in full-time jobs that require a law degree (according to NALP data). C|M|LAW was the recipient of the Law School Admission Council's first Diversity Matters Award in recognition of our commitment to diversity in the law school and the legal profession.

Where We Are

C|M|LAW is located on Cleveland State University's modern, urban campus in downtown Cleveland. The University is a dynamic, growing, and engaged campus that has built a new student center and a new education building, created on-campus restaurants, expanded parking facilities, and established new green spaces. Our students enjoy all Cleveland has to offer, including the Cleveland Museum of Art, the world-renowned Cleveland Orchestra, Botanical Gardens, Playhouse Square, the House of Blues, four professional sports teams, and a fantastic foodie scene. On North Coast Harbor sit the Great Lakes Science Center and the Rock and Roll Hall of Fame and Museum. The law school is proximate to federal, state, and county courthouses. Cleveland is also the headquarters for many large corporations and law firms.

Learn Law: Our Curriculum

The C|M|LAW curriculum is designed to ensure that graduates are well positioned to meet the challenges of transitioning from the study of law to practicing it. C|M|LAW offers concentrations in Business Law, Civil Litigation and Dispute Resolution, Criminal Law, Employment and Labor Law, and International and Comparative Law. The Center for Health Law and Policy provides focused study in the areas of health law regulation, health law policy and ethics, and health law business and litigation. The first year includes a required course on Legislation and Regulation, an area of growing importance in contemporary law practice, while continuing to provide students with a firm foundation in traditional first-year subjects that are grounded primarily in case and common law. Our new "Problem of the Semester" seeks to infuse our curriculum with concepts of ethics and professionalism by presenting the same problem into classes and lectures across the curriculum. Students see the same issue approached from multiple perspectives to understand the broader implications of the problem.

Joint-Degree Programs and Graduate Programs

Five joint-degree programs are offered: the JD/MPA (Master of Public Administration); the JD/MUPDD (Master of Urban Planning, Design, and Development); the JD/MBA (Master of Business Administration); the JD/MAES (Master of Arts in Environmental Studies); and the JD/MSES (Master of Science in Environmental Science). The law school also offers a graduate LLM degree and Master of Legal Studies.

Live Justice: From Classroom to Practice

To ensure our students have the necessary lawyering skills, C|M|LAW now requires all students to complete an externship, clinic, or skills-based course. Clinical programs offer students academic credit for serving clients in the areas of law and public policy, employment law, urban development, fair housing, environmental law, and community health advocacy. Externship programs include the Judicial Externship Program in which students work with state, appellate, and federal court judges; the Public Interest Externship Program, which focuses on governmental work with the county prosecutor and public defender, a bankruptcy trustee, the Office of Immigration and Customs Enforcement, and the US Attorney (civil and criminal); and the Independent Externship Program where students may propose a placement in a public service office. The Pro Bono Program at C|M|LAW offers a variety of community service opportunities, including teaching practical law in public high schools, assisting with the legal needs of women recently released from incarceration, and addressing the concerns of the poor by delivering legal assistance in cooperation with local attorneys and community agencies.

Getting In

While admission to C|M|LAW is competitive, it need not be intimidating. The admission committee reviews all applications with care and sensitivity, taking into consideration academic performance, LSAT scores, work and life experience, and readiness for the rigors of legal education. We are committed to enrolling academically talented and diverse students. In doing so, we recognize and embrace that academic talent and diversity can be identified in many interesting and exciting ways. Undergraduate grades and LSAT results are the most significant factors in our admission decision; however, an applicant's personal statement, letters of recommendation, and overall strength of the file are factors also strongly considered in the admission process. Criteria for admission are identical for full- and part-time applicants.

Alternate Admission Program: The Legal Career Opportunities Program

The Legal Career Opportunities Program (LCOP) invites applications from individuals who demonstrate the ability to succeed in law school but have encountered life circumstances or other adversities that have affected their traditional academic indicators, such as LSAT scores and/or undergraduate grades. In most cases, applicants to the LCOP have academic indicators that are a bit lower than those of regularly admitted applicants; however, LCOP applicants demonstrate through their career and professional accomplishments, personal statements, letters of recommendation, graduate work, and/or significantly improved academic performance over a period of time, their likelihood for success in law school. LCOP is not a provisional program. Being admitted through the program is acceptance to the law school.

Finances

Applicants are considered for scholarships at the time of admission. Our financial aid program utilizes merit-based scholarships and federal loan programs. C|M|LAW has a loan repayment assistance program (LRAP) to help support students choosing to work in public service jobs upon graduation.

Library and Technology

The C|M|LAW library is one of the 15 largest academic law libraries in the country. The law library is a superior research and learning facility where our students prepare for legal practice in the twenty-first century with access to electronic research services, a computer lab, group study rooms, and a research instruction room. The library even includes a Professional and Study Skills room dedicated to helping students study smarter and succeed in law school. Our students study in a four-story, light-filled space that includes over 200 carrels with built-in power and wireless access for laptop computers. Cutting-edge technology is used in classrooms, our moot courtroom, and our new electronic trial courtroom. The technology staff assists students with installing software, providing laptops for examinations, and even helping students pick the right computer for law school. C|M|LAW has been recognized for our use and support of technology by the American Association of Law Libraries and *National Jurist* magazine.

Career Planning

From day one, we help you build your future. Employers have confidence in the education our students receive and value C|M|LAW graduates. When it's time for you to begin your job search, we will be ready to help you, be it in Northeast Ohio or any region across the country. Our professional staff are members of the bar and have experience and relationships within the legal community, providing them with valuable resources in the job-search process. Individual counseling is at the core of our services, but counseling is only one of the many resources we make available to you. At C|M|LAW, numerous opportunities exist for you to gain exposure to potential employers in large and small law firms, government, public interest organizations, and in-house settings. We have alumni in all 50 states working as attorneys, judges, in-house counsel, professors and university administrators, government employees, human resource professionals, and more. Your possibilities are endless and our generous network of alumni and friends continue to open doors for generations of our graduates.

Student Life

C|M|LAW works hard to provide all students with the necessary academic and professional support to learn law and live justice. C|M|LAW offers the Academic Excellence Program (academic support), the Ohio Bar Examination Strategies and Tactics course, first-year peer advising, a long-standing alumni mentoring program, over 30 student organizations, and award-winning Moot Court and Trial teams. Our students live in convenient and affordable housing in downtown Cleveland and surrounding suburbs. Tuition includes free public transportation and two blocks away is a brand-new transit center.

APPLICANT PROFILE

Cleveland State University—Cleveland-Marshall College of Law
This grid includes only applicants who earned 120–180 LSAT scores under standard administrations.

LSAT Score	GPA																
	3.75 +		3.50–3.74		3.25–3.49		3.00–3.24		2.75–2.99		2.50–2.74		Below 2.50		No GPA		Total
	Apps	Adm	Apps	Adm	Apps	Adm	Apps	Adm	Apps	Adm	Apps	Adm	Apps	Adm	Apps	Adm	Apps	Adm
170–180	2	2	1	1	1	1	2	2	0	0	0	0	1	1	0	0	7	7
165–169	6	6	4	4	4	4	0	0	1	1	0	0	0	0	0	0	15	15
160–164	22	20	15	15	19	18	11	11	17	13	7	5	5	4	3	2	99	88
155–159	34	32	59	58	54	53	52	50	39	35	19	15	11	4	7	3	275	250
150–154	30	22	64	49	82	57	96	52	59	22	31	6	28	5	15	4	405	217
145–149	27	3	46	3	72	7	77	8	57	1	41	0	42	1	13	0	375	23
140–144	10	0	21	1	33	4	63	1	55	0	41	0	46	1	11	0	280	7
Below 140	4	0	10	0	18	0	27	0	20	0	24	0	31	0	10	0	144	0
Total	135	85	220	131	283	144	328	124	248	72	163	26	164	16	59	9	1600	607

Apps = Number of Applicants
Adm = Number Admitted
Reflects 99% of the total applicant pool; highest LSAT data reported.

UNIVERSITY OF COLORADO LAW SCHOOL

Office of Admissions, UCB 403, Wolf Law Building
Boulder, CO 80309-0403
Phone: 303.492.7203; Fax: 303.492.2542
E-mail: lawadmin@colorado.edu; Website: www.colorado.edu/law

ABA
Approved
Since
1923

The Basics

Type of school	Public
Term	Semester
Application deadline	11/15 3/15
Application fee	$65
Financial aid deadline	4/1
Can first year start other than fall?	No
Student to faculty ratio	9.8 to 1
# of housing spaces available restricted to law students	
graduate housing for which law students are eligible	547

Faculty and Administrators

	Total		Men		Women		Minorities	
	Spr	Fall	Spr	Fall	Spr	Fall	Spr	Fall
Full-time	46	48	27	27	19	21	9	11
Other full-time	2	2	2	2	0	0	0	0
Deans, librarians, & others who teach	1	3	1	2	0	1	0	0
Part-time	29	31	18	26	11	5	3	2
Total	78	84	48	57	30	27	12	13

JD Enrollment and Ethnicity

	Men		Women		Full-Time		Part-Time		1st-Year		Total		JD Degs. Awd.
	#	%	#	%	#	%	#	%	#	%	#	%	
All Hispanics	25	9.0	27	10.3	52	9.6	0	0.0	15	9.3	52	9.6	5
Am. Ind./AK Nat.	9	3.2	8	3.1	17	3.1	0	0.0	3	1.9	17	3.1	7
Asian	14	5.0	20	7.7	34	6.3	0	0.0	12	7.4	34	6.3	7
Black/Af. Am.	12	4.3	8	3.1	20	3.7	0	0.0	6	3.7	20	3.7	3
Nat. HI/Pac. Isl.	0	0.0	0	0.0	0	0.0	0	0.0	0	0.0	0	0.0	0
2 or more races	3	1.1	3	1.1	6	1.1	0	0.0	5	3.1	6	1.1	0
Subtotal (minor.)	63	22.6	66	25.3	129	23.9	0	0.0	41	25.3	129	23.9	22
Nonres. Alien	0	0.0	1	0.4	1	0.2	0	0.0	0	0.0	1	0.2	0
White/Cauc.	216	77.4	192	73.6	408	75.6	0	0.0	119	73.5	408	75.6	153
Unknown	0	0.0	2	0.8	2	0.4	0	0.0	2	1.2	2	0.4	0
Total	279	51.7	261	48.3	540	100.0	0	0.0	162	30.0	540		175

Curriculum

	Full-Time	Part-Time
Typical first-year section size	75	0
Is there typically a "small section" of the first-year class, other than Legal Writing, taught by full-time faculty	Yes	No
If yes, typical size offered last year	34	
# of classroom course titles beyond first-year curriculum	108	

# of upper division courses, excluding seminars, with an enrollment:	Under 25	80
	25–49	33
	50–74	12
	75–99	5
	100+	1

# of seminars	18	
# of seminar positions available	247	
# of seminar positions filled	205	0
# of positions available in simulation courses	518	
# of simulation positions filled	401	0
# of positions available in faculty supervised clinical courses	119	
# of faculty supervised clinical positions filled	94	0
# involved in field placements	213	0
# involved in law journals	144	0
# involved in moot court or trial competitions	101	0
# of credit hours required to graduate	89	

Transfers

Transfers in	14
Transfers out	2

Tuition and Fees

	Resident	Nonresident
Full-time	$31,044	$37,452
Part-time		
Tuition Guarantee Program		N

Living Expenses

Estimated living expenses for singles

Living on campus	Living off campus	Living at home
$18,092	$18,386	$10,996

UNIVERSITY OF COLORADO LAW SCHOOL

ABA
Approved
Since
1923

GPA and LSAT Scores

	Total	Full-Time	Part-Time
# of apps	3,175	3,175	0
# of offers	956	956	0
# of matrics	163	163	0
75% GPA	3.80	3.80	0.00
Median GPA	3.64	3.64	0.00
25% GPA	3.33	3.33	0.00
75% LSAT	165	165	0
Median LSAT	164	164	0
25% LSAT	158	158	0

Grants and Scholarships (from prior year)

	Total		Full-Time		Part-Time	
	#	%	#	%	#	%
Total # of students	546		546		0	
Total # receiving grants	292	53.5	292	53.5	0	0.0
Less than 1/2 tuition	240	44.0	240	44.0	0	0.0
Half to full tuition	28	5.1	28	5.1	0	0.0
Full tuition	9	1.6	9	1.6	0	0.0
More than full tuition	15	2.7	15	2.7	0	0.0
Median grant amount			$7,998		$0	

Informational and Library Resources

Total amount spent on library materials	$1,282,406
Study seating capacity inside the library	444
# of full-time equivalent professional librarians	9
Hours per week library is open	102
# of open, wired connections available to students	81
# of networked computers available for use by students	78
Has wireless network?	Y
Requires computer?	N

JD Attrition (from prior year)

	Academic	Other	Total	
	#	#	#	%
1st year	0	2	2	1.1
2nd year	0	4	4	2.2
3rd year	0	0	0	0.0
4th year	0	0	0	0.0

Employment (9 months after graduation)

For up-to-date employment data, go to employmentsummary.abaquestionnaire.org on the ABA website.

Bar Passage Rates

First-time takers	168	Reporting %	87.50
Average school %	95.24	Average state %	82.79
Average pass difference	12.45		

Jurisdiction	Takers	Passers	Pass %	State %	Diff %
Colorado	147	140	95.24	82.79	12.45

UNIVERSITY OF COLORADO LAW SCHOOL

Office of Admissions, UCB 403, Wolf Law Building
Boulder, CO 80309-0403
Phone: 303.492.7203; Fax: 303.492.2542
E-mail: lawadmin@colorado.edu; Website: www.colorado.edu/law

Introduction

Colorado Law, established in 1892, is located on the Boulder campus of the University of Colorado and lies at the foot of the Rocky Mountains. High admission standards, a relatively small student body, and a favorable student-to-faculty ratio of 9.8 to 1 assure a stimulating and challenging academic environment that encourages class participation and interaction with faculty. The school is a charter member of the AALS and is ABA approved.

Faculty

Faculty members have a demonstrated record of excellence in teaching, research, and public service. They include some of the nation's leading scholars; particular strengths evidenced by faculty publications are constitutional law, natural resources and environmental law, Indian law, energy, business, dispute resolution, and technology law.

Physical Facilities and Library

The law school is housed in the 180,000-square-foot Wolf Law Building, located on the edge of the CU Boulder campus. The Wolf Law Building features state-of-the-art classrooms, two high-tech courtrooms, and the largest resource collection and most technologically advanced law library in the 12-state Rocky Mountain region. The Wolf Law Building is the first LEED Gold-certified public law school building in the country under the standards of the US Green Building Council's certification program.

The William A. Wise Law Library serves the students, staff, and faculty of Colorado Law, as well as the bench and bar. Students can connect laptops to the school's wireless network or use one of the 65 computers available in the library to perform online legal research.

Special Programs

Clinics—In the **Criminal Defense Clinic**, students learn basic criminal practice skills and represent clients in actual cases, from beginning to end, in municipal and county courts in Boulder County.

In the **Civil Practice Clinic**, students represent low-income clients in a variety of civil law settings, including family court and in front of administrative law judges.

The **Appellate Advocacy Clinic** alternates annually between cases from the public defender's office and from the attorney general's office. Each student is responsible for completing an appellate brief and attending the oral argument in the Colorado Supreme Court or the Colorado Court of Appeals.

In the **Juvenile Law Clinic**, students represent children and youth who are abused, neglected, or accused of a crime, addressing all of the legal needs of the child client. They also represent school districts as the petitioner in truancy matters.

In the **Family Law Clinic**, students provide legal services to low-income Coloradans who need help with family law matters such as divorces, issues related to parenting time, and child support.

The **American Indian Law Clinic** provides students with faculty-supervised experience giving legal assistance in matters including tribal sovereignty, child welfare, preservation of tribal identity, employment discrimination, public benefits, preservation of Native lands, and more.

In the **Entrepreneurial Law Clinic**, students work with local entrepreneurs, providing transactional legal services for the formation and development of small businesses.

The **Technology Law and Policy Clinic** gives students the opportunity to advocate in the public interest concerning technology issues before regulatory entities, courts, legislatures, and standard-setting bodies.

The **Natural Resources Litigation Clinic** involves students in representing public interest clients in environmental cases related to federal public lands, wildlife, and other issues. The Natural Resources Law Center has three major areas of activity: research and publication, legal education, and the distinguished visitors and fellows program.

Research Centers—The Byron R. White Center for the Study of American Constitutional Law; the Silicon Flatirons Center for Law, Technology, and Entrepreneurship; the Natural Resources Law Center; and the Center for Energy and Environmental Security provide opportunities for students to assist in conducting specialized research, promoting publication, and hosting conferences.

Curriculum

In addition to strong and varied course offerings, students can earn a certificate in tax, American Indian law, intellectual property and technology law, juvenile and family law, or environmental law.

The first-year curriculum is required of all students. During the second and third years, students may emphasize such areas of the law as natural resources, environmental law, criminal law, business, constitutional law, tax, public interest, American Indian law, litigation, intellectual property law, and jurisprudence. Established joint-degree programs are the JD/MBA, JD/MD, JD/MPA, JD/MST, JD/MURP, and a JD/MS or PhD in Environmental Science.

Students can broaden their international perspectives and understanding of law and law practice by participating in the JD/LLB dual-degree program with the University of Alberta Faculty of Law (Canada). Colorado Law has a partnership with the University of San Diego (USD) School of Law to give our students access to an extensive Summer Law Study Abroad program, offering courses in four locations: Barcelona, Florence, London, and Paris. Students also have the opportunity to attend Bucerius Law School in Germany and Bar Ilan University in Israel through international exchange programs.

Colorado Law offers Master of Laws (LLM) degrees in three areas of study in which the strength of our faculty, curriculum, and programs are recognized nationally and internationally. The areas of study are entrepreneurial law, information technology and intellectual property, and natural resources law.

Admission

Admission to Colorado Law is competitive. At a minimum, a bachelor's degree from an institution that is accredited by an agency recognized by the US Department of Education is required. The LSAT and registration with LSAC's Credential Assembly Service are required. Offers of admission are influenced heavily by GPA and LSAT score, but they are considered in the context of the entire application. Substantial weight is accorded to special qualities such as leadership, character, diversity, and commitment to service. The school seeks to increase the ethnic, cultural, and other diversity of its student body. The binding Early Decision application deadline is November 15; the regular application deadline is March 15. The earliest admission letters go out in December, and the class is filled on a rolling basis. Admission is sometimes possible from a waiting list. Colorado Law accepts a small number of transfer students for the fall semester. Law students may seek visiting status in the fall or spring semester. Transfer and visitor admission criteria include law school performance.

Financial Aid

Scholarships for incoming students are based on merit. Nonresident students qualify for lower resident tuition rates by maintaining domicile in Colorado for 12 consecutive months. Current students may apply for additional scholarships and awards for their second and third years. Students applying for financial aid should file the FAFSA as soon as possible after January 1 and before the priority deadline of April 1.

Student Activities

Over 35 student organizations invite participation in projects, programs, and social activities. The *University of Colorado Law Review*, *Journal on Telecommunications and High Technology Law*, and *Colorado Journal of International Environmental Law and Policy* are scholarly journals edited entirely by students. Students also participate in a number of moot court competitions and have won regional, national, and international recognition in these events.

Housing

For information about the university's family housing, call 303.492.6384. Most students live in apartments and houses in the surrounding community.

Career Development

Colorado Law prepares students for a wide variety of careers and encourages students to take an intentional and creative approach to planning their careers. Starting with 1L orientation where career development is a theme, we bring in speakers and have programming to support students' career exploration. The Career Development Office (CDO) has four career advisors with JDs and experience helping students and alumni succeed in the current job market. Specifically, the office directly assists students in finding summer and postgraduate jobs, internships, externships, clerkships, and other opportunities, by offering programming such as on-campus interviews, résumé collections, brown-bag speakers, mock interviews, and career fairs, and through employer outreach and matching efforts. In addition, Colorado Law has an Assistant Dean who focuses entirely on outreach to employers and a Senior Director who was instrumental in developing the Colorado Pledge to Diversity 1L Summer Clerkship Program.

APPLICANT PROFILE

University of Colorado Law School
This grid includes only applicants who earned 120–180 LSAT scores under standard administrations.

LSAT Score	3.75 +		3.50–3.74		3.25–3.49		3.00–3.24		2.75–2.99		2.50–2.74		2.25–2.49		2.00–2.24		Below 2.00		No GPA		Total	
	Apps	Adm	Apps	Adm	Apps	Adm	Apps	Adm	Apps	Adm	Apps	Adm	Apps	Adm	Apps	Adm	Apps	Adm	Apps	Adm	Apps	Adm
175–180	2	1	3	2	4	3	0	0	3	2	3	2	0	0	1	0	0	0	0	0	16	10
170–174	40	39	29	26	22	18	16	10	11	5	4	3	2	0	0	0	0	0	0	0	124	101
165–169	122	116	174	151	122	94	58	31	33	16	12	5	9	2	0	0	0	0	8	2	538	417
160–164	231	151	258	71	215	37	140	17	46	3	27	1	9	2	2	0	0	0	11	1	939	283
155–159	152	42	227	32	189	11	136	7	57	2	19	0	6	0	5	0	0	0	7	0	798	94
150–154	60	11	71	7	98	2	101	3	58	3	21	0	8	0	4	0	1	0	2	0	424	26
145–149	8	0	27	0	48	0	41	0	29	0	20	0	9	0	2	0	3	0	4	0	191	0
140–144	3	0	11	0	18	0	15	0	18	0	6	0	8	0	0	0	0	0	1	0	80	0
135–139	3	0	3	0	3	0	4	0	5	0	6	0	3	0	1	0	1	0	1	0	30	0
130–134	0	0	0	0	2	0	4	0	0	0	5	0	2	0	1	0	1	0	1	0	16	0
125–129	0	0	0	0	0	0	1	0	0	0	0	0	0	0	0	0	0	0	1	0	2	0
120–124	0	0	0	0	0	0	0	0	0	0	0	0	0	0	0	0	0	0	0	0	0	0
Total	621	360	803	289	721	165	516	68	260	31	123	11	56	4	16	0	6	0	36	3	3158	931

Apps = Number of Applicants   Adm = Number Admitted   Reflects 99% of the total applicant pool; highest LSAT data reported.

COLUMBIA UNIVERSITY SCHOOL OF LAW

435 West 116th Street
New York, NY 10027
Phone: 212.854.2670; Fax: 212.854.1109
E-mail: admissions@law.columbia.edu; Website: www.law.columbia.edu/admissions

ABA
Approved
Since
1923

The Basics

Type of school	Private
Term	Semester
Application deadline	11/15 2/15
Application fee	$85
Financial aid deadline	3/1
Can first year start other than fall?	No
Student to faculty ratio	9.2 to 1
# of housing spaces available restricted to law students	489
graduate housing for which law students are eligible	631

Faculty and Administrators

	Total		Men		Women		Minorities	
	Spr	Fall	Spr	Fall	Spr	Fall	Spr	Fall
Full-time	110	127	75	85	35	42	16	17
Other full-time	2	2	1	1	1	1	0	0
Deans, librarians, & others who teach	14	14	5	5	9	9	2	2
Part-time	126	93	94	64	32	29	12	8
Total	252	236	175	155	77	81	30	27

Curriculum

	Full-Time	Part-Time
Typical first-year section size	103	0

Is there typically a "small section" of the first-year class, other than Legal Writing, taught by full-time faculty	Yes	No
If yes, typical size offered last year	36	

# of classroom course titles beyond first-year curriculum		235

# of upper division courses, excluding seminars, with an enrollment:		
	Under 25	93
	25–49	36
	50–74	23
	75–99	15
	100+	19

# of seminars		137
# of seminar positions available	2,592	
# of seminar positions filled	2,080	0
# of positions available in simulation courses	444	
# of simulation positions filled	434	0
# of positions available in faculty supervised clinical courses	155	
# of faculty supervised clinical positions filled	155	0
# involved in field placements	207	0
# involved in law journals	732	0
# involved in moot court or trial competitions	48	0
# of credit hours required to graduate	83	

JD Enrollment and Ethnicity

	Men		Women		Full-Time		Part-Time		1st-Year		Total		JD Degs. Awd.
	#	%	#	%	#	%	#	%	#	%	#	%	
All Hispanics	41	5.9	51	8.0	92	6.9	0	0.0	35	8.6	92	6.9	22
Am. Ind./AK Nat.	3	0.4	5	0.8	8	0.6	0	0.0	2	0.5	8	0.6	1
Asian	90	13.0	115	18.0	205	15.4	0	0.0	63	15.5	205	15.4	74
Black/Af. Am.	33	4.8	72	11.3	105	7.9	0	0.0	37	9.1	105	7.9	38
Nat. HI/Pac. Isl.	0	0.0	0	0.0	0	0.0	0	0.0	0	0.0	0	0.0	1
2 or more races	10	1.4	15	2.3	24	1.8	1	100.0	10	2.5	25	1.9	11
Subtotal (minor.)	177	25.5	258	40.4	434	32.6	1	100.0	147	36.2	435	32.7	147
Nonres. Alien	50	7.2	79	12.4	129	9.7	0	0.0	35	8.6	129	9.7	27
White/Cauc.	441	63.6	292	45.7	733	55.1	0	0.0	197	48.5	733	55.0	282
Unknown	25	3.6	10	1.6	35	2.6	0	0.0	27	6.7	35	2.6	0
Total	693	52.0	639	48.0	1331	99.9	1	0.1	406	30.5	1332		456

Transfers

Transfers in	46
Transfers out	2

Tuition and Fees

	Resident	Nonresident
Full-time	$52,902	$52,902
Part-time		
Tuition Guarantee Program	N	

Living Expenses

Estimated living expenses for singles

Living on campus	Living off campus	Living at home
$22,070	$22,070	$6,060

COLUMBIA UNIVERSITY SCHOOL OF LAW

ABA Approved Since 1923

GPA and LSAT Scores

	Total	Full-Time	Part-Time
# of apps	7,459	7,459	0
# of offers	1,175	1,175	0
# of matrics	406	406	0
75% GPA	3.82	3.82	0.00
Median GPA	3.72	3.72	0.00
25% GPA	3.60	3.60	0.00
75% LSAT	175	175	0
Median LSAT	172	172	0
25% LSAT	170	170	0

Grants and Scholarships (from prior year)

	Total		Full-Time		Part-Time	
	#	%	#	%	#	%
Total # of students	1,344		1,343		1	
Total # receiving grants	658	49.0	658	49.0	0	0.0
Less than 1/2 tuition	498	37.1	498	37.1	0	0.0
Half to full tuition	128	9.5	128	9.5	0	0.0
Full tuition	22	1.6	22	1.6	0	0.0
More than full tuition	10	0.7	10	0.7	0	0.0
Median grant amount			$13,200		$0	

Informational and Library Resources

Total amount spent on library materials	$2,368,944
Study seating capacity inside the library	369
# of full-time equivalent professional librarians	19
Hours per week library is open	104
# of open, wired connections available to students	3,028
# of networked computers available for use by students	135
Has wireless network?	Y
Requires computer?	N

JD Attrition (from prior year)

	Academic	Other	Total	
	#	#	#	%
1st year	0	3	3	0.7
2nd year	0	5	5	1.1
3rd year	0	1	1	0.2
4th year	0	0	0	0.0

Employment (9 months after graduation)

For up-to-date employment data, go to employmentsummary.abaquestionnaire.org on the ABA website.

Bar Passage Rates

First-time takers	424	Reporting %	81.60
Average school %	97.69	Average state %	84.92
Average pass difference	12.77		

Jurisdiction	Takers	Passers	Pass %	State %	Diff %
New York	346	338	97.69	84.92	12.77

COLUMBIA UNIVERSITY SCHOOL OF LAW

435 West 116th Street
New York, NY 10027
Phone: 212.854.2670; Fax: 212.854.1109
E-mail: admissions@law.columbia.edu; Website: www.law.columbia.edu/admissions

Introduction

Columbia Law School is distinguished, perhaps uniquely among leading US law schools, as an international center of legal education that stimulates its students to consider the full dimensions of the possibility of the law—as an intellectual pursuit, as a career, and as an instrument of human progress. The character of academic and social life at Columbia is fiercely democratic, dynamic, creative, and innovative. The Law School is especially committed to educating students of differing perspectives, from diverse backgrounds, and with varied life experiences.

Professional prospects for Columbia Law School graduates are quite extraordinary. Our graduates proceed to productive careers in every conceivable arena of practice, business, and advocacy. While Columbia-trained attorneys are especially well-regarded for their work in corporate law and finance, an unusually high number also serve as state and federal judges, prosecutors, civil rights and human rights advocates, legal scholars, public defenders, entrepreneurs, business executives, elected government officials, and national and international leaders. Many alumni contribute significantly to the shaping of US culture at large. Currently, our graduates serve in leadership roles across the fields of government, art, music, film, publishing, science, professional athletics, philanthropy, and higher education.

With an exceptionally talented student body and faculty and a strong tradition of encouraging students with specialized interests to develop those interests in depth, Columbia Law School provides a legal education that gives our students a singular capacity for imagination, originality, and high responsibility in their professional lives.

JD Student Body Profile

Columbia continues to place among the handful of the most highly selective JD programs in our nation—as evaluated by the principal criteria used to measure admission selectivity (application volume, acceptance rates, LSAT scores, and academic performance). Indeed, in recent years, the demand for a Columbia legal education has never been greater, and the academic credentials of our entering classes are stronger than ever. Columbia's JD student body is further distinguished by standing as one of the most culturally diverse among America's leading law schools. Men and women choosing to study law at Columbia hail from the small towns, farms, and suburbs of the West, Midwest, and South; the industrial corridors and ivy halls of the Northeast; the inner cities of every major US metropolis; and the international centers of Europe, Asia, Africa, and Latin America.

Each entering class reflects the broad range of economic, ethnic, and cultural backgrounds found in the United States. And from around the world, we welcome students who will enrich learning at Columbia and thereafter advance the developing legal cultures of their homelands.

With one of the largest percentages of international students in its JD program of any leading law school; with one of the very highest percentages of students of color; with its students hailing from 48 states, roughly 43 foreign countries, and more than 200 different colleges and universities; and with 15 percent of its JD students having earned at least one graduate or professional degree before studying law, Columbia's student body abounds with a diversity of life experiences, cultural backgrounds, and intellectual perspectives.

The Law School Campus

Columbia Law School's main building, Jerome Greene Hall, has undergone significant expansion and improvements devoted primarily to our students, including library renovations and the creation of a student commons that includes a student lounge and café. New seminar rooms and state-of-the-art multimedia classrooms have also been designed to provide students with full Internet and other legal research access. Across the street from Greene Hall is William C. Warren Hall, home to the *Columbia Law Review*, Morningside Heights Legal Services (a law school clinic serving our community), and the Center for Public Interest Law.

William and June Warren Hall includes amphitheater-style classrooms equipped with modern teaching resources, a center for the law school's international programs, and conference facilities. It is also home to the offices of Admissions, Financial Aid, Registration Services, Student Services, Graduate Legal Studies, and International Programs.

The expansion of the law school's facilities has greatly enhanced the quality of life and learning at Columbia. Students have a superb learning environment that is conducive to community building and social and intellectual engagement, and reflects the changing nature of legal education in the twenty-first century.

Library Resources and Research Facilities

Columbia's library is one of the largest and most comprehensive law collections in the world. It is especially rich in US law and legal history, international law, comparative law, Roman law, and the legal literature of the major European countries, China, and Japan. Access to the Internet and electronic documents provide additional resources, with materials from Germany, South Africa, and a wide range of international organizations. In addition, the many libraries of the university, containing more than seven million volumes, are available to law students.

The law library's online catalog provides complete access to the library's collection, acts as an index to the major legal serials, and provides access to the online catalogs of other major law school libraries. Columbia provides its law students with some of the most sophisticated technologies of any law school in the nation.

Curriculum

The foundation of the JD program consists of Legal Methods (an intensive three-week introductory course), Legal Practice Workshop (a two-semester course that provides training in legal research, writing, and analysis), Contracts, Torts, Constitutional Law, Civil Procedure, Property, Criminal Law, Foundation Year Moot Court, and one elective focusing on the law's engagement with public policy, the intellectual and historical foundations of the rule of law, or the law's transnational and comparative expression. Recent elective offerings have included Art of Legal Persuasion; Critical Legal Thought; Foundations of the Regulatory State; Law and Contemporary Society; Law and Economics; Law and Social Science; Lawyering Across Multiple Legal Orders; Legislation; Principles of Intellectual Property; Regulation: Decentralization and Globalization; the Regulatory and Administrative State; the Rule of Law: Perspectives and Philosophy; and Terror and Consent.

Columbia has a special commitment to clinical education, which places the student in the role of a lawyer doing a lawyer's actual work under intensive faculty supervision. Some examples of clinical opportunities are Lawyering in the Digital Age, Nonprofit Organizations/Small Business, Child Advocacy, Mediation, Environmental Law, Human Rights, and a clinic in Sexuality and Gender Law, the first clinic of its type in the nation. Unique to Columbia is a summer program that places more than 150 students in civil and human rights internships in law firms and organizations throughout this country and around the world. Especially distinguished are Columbia's offerings in international, foreign, and comparative law; constitutional law and theory; corporate and securities law; intellectual property; critical race theory; human rights; and public interest law.

Research Centers and Special Programs

Research centers and special programs include the Kernochan Center for Law, Media, and the Arts; Julius Silver Program in Law, Science, and Technology; Center for Climate Change Law; Center for Law and Philosophy; Center for Law and Economic Studies; Center for the Study of Law and Culture; Center for Public Interest Law; Program on Careers in Law and Teaching; Human Rights Institute; Parker School of Foreign and Comparative Law; Center for Chinese Legal Studies; Center for Japanese Legal Studies; Center for Korean Legal Studies; European Legal Studies Center; Center for Contract and Economic Organization; Center on Corporate Governance; Center on Crime, Community, and the Law; Center on Global Legal Problems; Center for Institutional and Social Change; Vale Columbia Center on Sustainable International Investment; Social Justice Initiatives; and the Charles Evans Gerber Transactional Studies Program.

Admission

All first-year students enter in mid-August. Candidates applying for regular admission should apply after September 1 of the year preceding their desired matriculation, but before February 15, the application deadline. Early Decision candidates must complete their applications by November 15 and are notified in December. All other applications are generally reviewed in the order in which they are completed, and decisions are made and sent out on a rolling basis.

Applicant Profile Not Available

UNIVERSITY OF CONNECTICUT SCHOOL OF LAW

45 Elizabeth Street
Hartford, CT 06105
Phone: 860.570.5100; Fax: 860.570.5153
E-mail: admissions@law.uconn.edu; Website: www.law.uconn.edu

ABA
Approved
Since
1933

The Basics

Type of school	Public
Term	Semester
Application deadline	3/15
Application fee	$60
Financial aid deadline	3/15
Can first year start other than fall?	No
Student to faculty ratio	10.8 to 1
# of housing spaces available restricted to law students	
graduate housing for which law students are eligible	

Faculty and Administrators

	Total		Men		Women		Minorities	
	Spr	Fall	Spr	Fall	Spr	Fall	Spr	Fall
Full-time	44	41	24	26	20	15	8	4
Other full-time	7	6	2	2	5	4	0	0
Deans, librarians, & others who teach	8	4	2	1	6	3	2	2
Part-time	75	48	58	38	17	10	4	2
Total	134	99	86	67	48	32	14	8

Curriculum

	Full-Time	Part-Time
Typical first-year section size	67	50
Is there typically a "small section" of the first-year class, other than Legal Writing, taught by full-time faculty	Yes	Yes
If yes, typical size offered last year	25	27
# of classroom course titles beyond first-year curriculum	164	

# of upper division courses, excluding seminars, with an enrollment:		
	Under 25	101
	25–49	25
	50–74	9
	75–99	0
	100+	0

# of seminars	71	
# of seminar positions available	1,311	
# of seminar positions filled	753	233
# of positions available in simulation courses	710	
# of simulation positions filled	537	162
# of positions available in faculty supervised clinical courses	158	
# of faculty supervised clinical positions filled	147	6
# involved in field placements	109	40
# involved in law journals	154	23
# involved in moot court or trial competitions	42	2
# of credit hours required to graduate	86	

JD Enrollment and Ethnicity

	Men		Women		Full-Time		Part-Time		1st-Year		Total		JD Degs. Awd.
	#	%	#	%	#	%	#	%	#	%	#	%	
All Hispanics	26	7.4	23	8.6	36	7.8	13	8.4	11	6.1	49	8.0	11
Am. Ind./AK Nat.	3	0.9	1	0.4	2	0.4	2	1.3	2	1.1	4	0.6	1
Asian	22	6.3	36	13.5	47	10.2	11	7.1	27	14.9	58	9.4	17
Black/Af. Am.	11	3.2	13	4.9	19	4.1	5	3.2	8	4.4	24	3.9	15
Nat. Hl/Pac. Isl.	0	0.0	1	0.4	1	0.2	0	0.0	1	0.6	1	0.2	0
2 or more races	0	0.0	0	0.0	0	0.0	0	0.0	0	0.0	0	0.0	0
Subtotal (minor.)	62	17.8	74	27.7	105	22.8	31	20.0	49	27.1	136	22.1	44
Nonres. Alien	4	1.1	6	2.2	7	1.5	3	1.9	2	1.1	10	1.6	1
White/Cauc.	251	71.9	165	61.8	308	66.8	108	69.7	113	62.4	416	67.5	117
Unknown	32	9.2	22	8.2	41	8.9	13	8.4	17	9.4	54	8.8	15
Total	349	56.7	267	43.3	461	74.8	155	25.2	181	29.4	616		177

Transfers

Transfers in	12
Transfers out	5

Tuition and Fees

	Resident	Nonresident
Full-time	$22,052	$45,548
Part-time	$15,392	$31,812
Tuition Guarantee Program	N	

Living Expenses

Estimated living expenses for singles		
Living on campus	Living off campus	Living at home
N/A	$15,050	$5,800

UNIVERSITY OF CONNECTICUT SCHOOL OF LAW

*ABA
Approved
Since
1933*

GPA and LSAT Scores

	Total	Full-Time	Part-Time
# of apps	2,751	1,897	854
# of offers	811	589	222
# of matrics	181	133	48
75% GPA	3.64	3.64	3.63
Median GPA	3.45	3.48	3.43
25% GPA	3.21	3.21	3.23
75% LSAT	163	163	158
Median LSAT	159	161	157
25% LSAT	157	158	154

Grants and Scholarships (from prior year)

	Total #	Total %	Full-Time #	Full-Time %	Part-Time #	Part-Time %
Total # of students	620		440		180	
Total # receiving grants	353	56.9	297	67.5	56	31.1
Less than 1/2 tuition	191	30.8	144	32.7	47	26.1
Half to full tuition	146	23.5	139	31.6	7	3.9
Full tuition	3	0.5	3	0.7	0	0.0
More than full tuition	13	2.1	11	2.5	2	1.1
Median grant amount			$10,200		$5,000	

Informational and Library Resources

Total amount spent on library materials	$1,586,132
Study seating capacity inside the library	904
# of full-time equivalent professional librarians	8
Hours per week library is open	89
# of open, wired connections available to students	778
# of networked computers available for use by students	137
Has wireless network?	Y
Requires computer?	N

JD Attrition (from prior year)

	Academic #	Other #	Total #	Total %
1st year	0	6	6	3.2
2nd year	1	4	5	2.6
3rd year	0	2	2	1.0
4th year	0	1	1	2.9

Employment (9 months after graduation)

For up-to-date employment data, go to employmentsummary.abaquestionnaire.org on the ABA website.

Bar Passage Rates

First-time takers	232	Reporting %	75.43
Average school %	94.28	Average state %	85.69
Average pass difference	8.59		

Jurisdiction	Takers	Passers	Pass %	State %	Diff %
Connecticut	142	135	95.07	84.76	10.31
Massachusetts	33	30	90.91	89.67	1.24

UNIVERSITY OF CONNECTICUT SCHOOL OF LAW

45 Elizabeth Street
Hartford, CT 06105
Phone: 860.570.5100; Fax: 860.570.5153
E-mail: admissions@law.uconn.edu; Website: www.law.uconn.edu

Introduction

As a result of several decades of sustained intellectual and foundational growth, the University of Connecticut School of Law has emerged as one of the leading public law schools in the United States. Because of Connecticut's extraordinary ratio of full-time students to full-time faculty, 75 percent of the advanced courses have 25 or fewer students. An outstanding and accessible faculty; an intensive first-year skills program; a rich and varied curriculum, including more than a dozen legal clinics; four student-edited journals; student organizations active across the spectrum of legal and social concerns; a regular flow of visiting lecturers; and a committed body of graduates throughout the country, combine to make the University of Connecticut a law school of exceptional strength.

Library and Physical Facilities

The campus, listed on the National Register of Historic Places, is arguably the most beautiful in the United States. The library, completed in 1996, is one of the largest legal research and technology centers in the world, with more than 500,000 volumes housed in the 120,000-square-foot facility.

With its immediate neighbors—the Hartford Seminary, the University of Hartford, the Connecticut Historical Society, and the Connecticut Attorney General's Office—the school is part of an academic enclave in a turn-of-the-century residential neighborhood.

Experiential Learning

Connecticut was a pioneer in clinical legal education, and our experiential learning opportunities continue to be a distinguishing strength of the school. The law school provides a broad range of experiential learning opportunities in which students can integrate practical experience with the theory learned in the classroom. These programs enable students to develop crucial lawyering skills, deepen their understanding of how the law and legal institutions operate on the ground, and explore possible career options.

Connecticut has a generous student practice rule enabling second- and third-year students, under the supervision of faculty attorneys, to represent clients in any court in our jurisdiction. This experience allows students to gain the practical lawyering skills involved in client intake, case strategy and development, motion practice and oral advocacy, as well as alternate dispute resolution.

Students may participate in our in-house legal clinics or our externship clinics. Clinical offerings include the following areas: asylum and human rights, criminal law (trial and appellate), environmental law, intellectual property, judicial clerkship, legislative clerkship, LGBT civil rights, mediation, poverty law, state's attorney, street law, and taxation. Students can also gain invaluable experience with our two affiliated nonprofit organizations. The **Center for Children's Advocacy, Inc.**, works on behalf of the legal rights of underprivileged children. **The Connecticut Urban Legal Initiative, Inc.**, identifies neighborhood problems that typify urban blight and devises strategies to revitalize communities.

The Individual Externship Program offers students an opportunity for experiential learning that is tailored to the students' own interests and their educational and career goals. Hundreds of organizations participate in our externship program.

The **Semester in Washington, DC**, places selected students in selected federal agencies, legislative offices, or nonprofit groups for one semester of service.

Specialized Programs: Centers, Certificates, and Dual Degrees

The **Intellectual Property Certificate Program** exposes participants to a broad curriculum of courses, from classes on patent, trademark, and copyright law to specialized seminars, including those in art law, cyberlaw, and European Union IP law. In addition, our Intellectual Property and Entrepreneurship Clinic was selected by the US Patent and Trademark Office (USPTO) to participate in a special clinical program. The **Tax Studies Certificate Program** affords an opportunity to participate in a supervised writing project, externship, or clinic in the area of tax law. Participants in the certificate program may begin their tax studies in Federal Income Tax in their first year and continue the study of taxation in a variety of courses during the last four semesters of law school. A **Human Rights Certificate Program** offers students the opportunity to work with world-renowned experts at the law school and the College of Liberal Arts and Sciences in a demanding and varied interdisciplinary study of global affairs and social justice. The law school has also created a **Law and Public Policy Certificate Program**, a flexible program in which students may enroll in a diverse collection of courses with faculty at the law school and within the University of Connecticut's Department of Public Policy.

The **Insurance Law Center** offers a specialized insurance curriculum with its LLM program, innovative research initiatives on the role of insurance in law and society, conferences and workshops, and the student-edited *Connecticut Insurance Law Journal*. The **Center for Energy and Environmental Law** brings together experts from many disciplines to tackle the urgent task of offering and analyzing better ways to meet the world's energy needs and preparing the leaders of tomorrow for the difficult choices that lie ahead.

The law school offers several interdisciplinary programs: JD/LLM in Insurance Law, JD/Master of Business Administration, JD/Master of Public Administration, JD/Master of Public Health, and JD/Master of Social Work.

Law school offerings in environmental law are supplemented by a semester exchange program with **Vermont Law School**.

International Study

The economic and political realities of globalization place new demands on the graduates of the law school. International law occupies an increasingly prominent place in the curriculum, reinforced by the student-edited *Connecticut Journal of International Law*. The law school has formal and informal study-abroad programs with universities in Aix-en-Provence, Barcelona, Berlin, Dublin, Exeter, Haifa, Leiden, London, Mannheim, Nottingham, Siena, and Tilburg. These relationships bring a wealth of international visitors to the school. Legal scholars have visited and lectured from Albania, Argentina, Bulgaria, China, the Czech Republic, France, Germany, Great Britain, Hungary, Israel, Korea, Kyrgyzstan, Latvia, the Netherlands, Poland, Romania, Russia, South Africa, Taiwan, and Ukraine. The LLM in United States Legal Studies for graduates of foreign law schools provides further opportunity for our students to learn from and study with peers trained in different legal systems.

Career Planning Center

Connecticut operates a comprehensive career planning office for the benefit of students and alumni. The Career Planning Office is staffed by four attorneys and although all can act as generalists, each has a focused expertise in private sector, public interest, nontraditional, clerkships, and other areas of interest to our students. The school offers a geographically diverse on-campus interview program, extensive individual and group counseling, a resource library, job listings, employment information sessions, and newsletters.

The school holds three off-campus interview programs each fall in Washington, DC; Boston; and New York City, and schedules on-campus interviews throughout the year. In addition, the school participates in several off-site job fairs.

Within six months of graduation, 83.1 percent of the class of 2011 were employed, including 11.6 percent in judicial clerkships.

Student Activities

Selected students may participate in one of four student-edited journals: the Connecticut Law Review, the Connecticut Journal of International Law, the Connecticut Insurance Law Journal, and the Connecticut Public Interest Law Journal.

The Connecticut Moot Court Board and the Mock Trial Association provide students with the opportunity to practice oral advocacy in intramural and interscholastic competitions.

Participants have placed extremely well in regional, national, and international competitions.

The Student Bar Association is the representative student government of the school. It manages an annual budget consisting of funds derived from the student activities fee and university tuition to support the various student organizations and to generally enhance the quality of student life. Under the governance of the Student Bar, a large number of student-run organizations, reflecting the diversity of our students, have active chapters on campus.

Services for Students With Disabilities

The Director of Student Services, Dr. Jane Thierfeld Brown, works with students with disabilities in the development and implementation of reasonable accommodations to allow access to the school's physical facilities as well as its educational and extracurricular programs.

Students with disabilities who are considering applying or who have been admitted to the School of Law are invited to tour the campus. Students may contact Dr. Brown (860.570.5130) regarding accommodations.

Character and Fitness

In accordance with Section 504(a) of the American Bar Association's Standards for Approval of Law Schools, applicants to the law school should understand that there are character, fitness, and other qualifications for admission to the bar. Applicants are therefore encouraged, prior to matriculation, to determine what those requirements are in the states in which the applicant intends to practice. Additional information is available at the website of the National Conference of Bar Examiners. Please also review the Admission to the Bar section of the University of Connecticut School of Law Student Handbook.

APPLICANT PROFILE

University of Connecticut School of Law
This grid includes only full-time applicants with LSAT scores earned under standard administrations.

LSAT Score	GPA 3.75 +		3.50–3.74		3.25–3.49		3.00–3.24		2.75–2.99		2.50–2.74		2.25–2.49		2.00–2.24		Below 2.00		No GPA		Total	
	Apps	Adm	Apps	Adm	Apps	Adm	Apps	Adm	Apps	Adm	Apps	Adm	Apps	Adm	Apps	Adm	Apps	Adm	Apps	Adm	Apps	Adm
175–180	2	2	3	3	0	0	0	0	0	0	1	0	0	0	0	0	0	0	0	0	6	5
170–174	11	10	9	9	4	4	4	2	4	1	3	1	0	0	0	0	0	0	1	0	36	27
165–169	30	29	58	54	35	33	31	25	14	3	8	1	7	0	0	0	0	0	2	0	185	145
160–164	74	57	136	105	129	85	82	47	29	6	15	4	8	0	0	0	0	0	6	2	479	306
155–159	74	25	148	43	158	44	100	15	46	4	21	1	4	1	2	0	2	0	19	4	574	137
150–154	44	11	59	7	103	10	85	7	36	2	33	0	9	0	3	0	0	0	8	0	380	37
145–149	14	4	26	1	29	1	49	0	23	0	19	0	5	0	4	0	0	0	10	0	179	6
140–144	5	0	15	1	19	0	27	0	12	0	16	0	4	0	2	0	0	0	3	0	103	1
135–139	2	0	6	0	11	0	5	0	10	0	5	0	7	0	1	0	0	0	3	0	50	0
130–134	0	0	1	0	2	0	8	0	0	0	3	0	1	0	0	0	0	0	2	0	17	0
125–129	1	0	0	0	0	0	2	0	1	0	2	0	0	0	0	0	1	0	0	0	7	0
120–124	0	0	0	0	0	0	0	0	0	0	0	0	0	0	0	0	0	0	0	0	0	0
Total	257	138	461	223	490	177	393	96	175	16	126	7	45	1	12	0	3	0	54	6	2016	664

Apps = Number of Applicants
Adm = Number Admitted
Reflects 99% of total applicant pool; highest LSAT data reported.

CORNELL LAW SCHOOL

Myron Taylor Hall
Ithaca, NY 14853-4901
Phone: 607.255.5141
E-mail: lawadmit@lawschool.cornell.edu; Website: www.lawschool.cornell.edu

The Basics

Type of school	Private
Term	Semester
Application deadline	2/1
Application fee	$80
Financial aid deadline	3/15
Can first year start other than fall?	No
Student to faculty ratio	10.0 to 1
# of housing spaces available restricted to law students	48
graduate housing for which law students are eligible	150

Faculty and Administrators

	Total		Men		Women		Minorities	
	Spr	Fall	Spr	Fall	Spr	Fall	Spr	Fall
Full-time	46	53	31	34	15	19	7	9
Other full-time	0	0	0	0	0	0	0	0
Deans, librarians, & others who teach	10	8	4	3	6	5	1	1
Part-time	15	29	13	21	2	8	0	0
Total	71	90	48	58	23	32	8	10

Curriculum

	Full-Time	Part-Time
Typical first-year section size	103	0
Is there typically a "small section" of the first-year class, other than Legal Writing, taught by full-time faculty	Yes	No
If yes, typical size offered last year	34	
# of classroom course titles beyond first-year curriculum	140	

# of upper division courses, excluding seminars, with an enrollment:	Under 25	41
	25–49	21
	50–74	11
	75–99	3
	100+	4

# of seminars	46	
# of seminar positions available	736	
# of seminar positions filled	590	0
# of positions available in simulation courses	238	
# of simulation positions filled	162	0
# of positions available in faculty supervised clinical courses	172	
# of faculty supervised clinical positions filled	166	0
# involved in field placements	42	0
# involved in law journals	308	0
# involved in moot court or trial competitions	92	0
# of credit hours required to graduate	84	

JD Enrollment and Ethnicity

	Men		Women		Full-Time		Part-Time		1st-Year		Total		JD Degs. Awd.
	#	%	#	%	#	%	#	%	#	%	#	%	
All Hispanics	29	9.2	36	12.1	65	10.6	0	0.0	17	8.4	65	10.6	18
Am. Ind./AK Nat.	5	1.6	7	2.4	12	2.0	0	0.0	6	3.0	12	2.0	2
Asian	33	10.5	55	18.5	88	14.4	0	0.0	33	16.3	88	14.4	36
Black/Af. Am.	15	4.8	30	10.1	45	7.4	0	0.0	13	6.4	45	7.4	11
Nat. HI/Pac. Isl.	0	0.0	0	0.0	0	0.0	0	0.0	0	0.0	0	0.0	0
2 or more races	5	1.6	14	4.7	19	3.1	0	0.0	11	5.4	19	3.1	0
Subtotal (minor.)	87	27.6	142	47.8	229	37.4	0	0.0	80	39.6	229	37.4	67
Nonres. Alien	16	5.1	29	9.8	45	7.4	0	0.0	23	11.4	45	7.4	11
White/Cauc.	212	67.3	126	42.4	338	55.2	0	0.0	99	49.0	338	55.2	122
Unknown	0	0.0	0	0.0	0	0.0	0	0.0	0	0.0	0	0.0	0
Total	315	51.5	297	48.5	612	100.0	0	0.0	202	33.0	612		200

Transfers

Transfers in	6
Transfers out	10

Tuition and Fees

	Resident	Nonresident
Full-time	$53,226	$53,226
Part-time		
Tuition Guarantee Program	N	

Living Expenses

Estimated living expenses for singles

Living on campus	Living off campus	Living at home
$19,230	$19,230	$19,230

ABA Approved Since 1923

GPA and LSAT Scores

	Total	Full-Time	Part-Time
# of apps	5,556	5,556	0
# of offers	1,152	1,152	0
# of matrics	204	204	0
75% GPA	3.77	3.77	0.00
Median GPA	3.63	3.63	0.00
25% GPA	3.50	3.50	0.00
75% LSAT	169	169	0
Median LSAT	168	168	0
25% LSAT	166	166	0

Grants and Scholarships (from prior year)

	Total #	Total %	Full-Time #	Full-Time %	Part-Time #	Part-Time %
Total # of students	615		615		0	
Total # receiving grants	278	45.2	278	45.2	0	0.0
Less than 1/2 tuition	226	36.7	226	36.7	0	0.0
Half to full tuition	52	8.5	52	8.5	0	0.0
Full tuition	0	0.0	0	0.0	0	0.0
More than full tuition	0	0.0	0	0.0	0	0.0
Median grant amount			$15,000		$0	

Informational and Library Resources

Total amount spent on library materials	$1,485,074
Study seating capacity inside the library	416
# of full-time equivalent professional librarians	8
Hours per week library is open	132
# of open, wired connections available to students	32
# of networked computers available for use by students	71
Has wireless network?	Y
Requires computer?	N

JD Attrition (from prior year)

	Academic #	Other #	Total #	Total %
1st year	0	14	14	6.8
2nd year	0	0	0	0.0
3rd year	0	1	1	0.5
4th year	0	0	0	0.0

Employment (9 months after graduation)

For up-to-date employment data, go to employmentsummary.abaquestionnaire.org on the ABA website.

Bar Passage Rates

First-time takers	192	Reporting %	80.21
Average school %	90.26	Average state %	83.59
Average pass difference	6.67		

Jurisdiction	Takers	Passers	Pass %	State %	Diff %
New York	139	129	92.81	84.92	7.89
California	15	10	66.67	71.24	−4.57

CORNELL LAW SCHOOL

Myron Taylor Hall
Ithaca, NY 14853-4901
Phone: 607.255.5141
E-mail: lawadmit@lawschool.cornell.edu; Website: www.lawschool.cornell.edu

Lawyers in the Best Sense

When Cornell University's founding president, Andrew Dickson White, began to lay plans for a law department at Cornell University, he wrote that he wanted to educate "not swarms of hastily prepared pettifoggers, but a fair number of well-trained, large-minded, morally based *lawyers in the best sense . . .*" He hoped graduates of the school would become "a blessing to the country, at the bar, on the bench, and in various public bodies." More than a century since President White's vision, this ideal still holds true. A small, top-tier law school located in beautiful surroundings, Cornell draws on, and contributes to, the resources of a great university, consistently producing well-rounded lawyers and accomplished practitioners cut from a different cloth. Cornell is a national center of learning located in Ithaca, New York, the heart of the Finger Lakes region of New York State. The law school's small classes, broad curriculum, and distinguished faculty, combined with the advantages of being part of one of the world's leading research universities, make it ideal for those who value both depth and breadth in their legal studies. Students find Ithaca to be a safe and nonstressful, yet culturally rich, environment in which to pursue legal studies.

Enrollment/Student Body

Sixty percent of Cornell's entering students have taken one or more years between completion of their undergraduate degree and enrollment in law school. Selective admission standards, combined with an emphasis on applicants' unique records and achievements, ensure that the student body is made up of people with wide-ranging interests, skills, concerns, and backgrounds.

Library, Physical Facilities, and Computing

The law school is located in the renovated and expanded Myron Taylor Hall, at the heart of the scenic 745-acre Cornell University campus. Hughes Hall, the law school dormitory, is adjacent to the main law school building and contains single rooms for about 45 students and a dining facility.

Cornell is one of the nation's leaders in the development and support of electronic legal research. It combines outstanding collections with professional expertise and access to worldwide electronic information sources for Anglo-American, as well as foreign and international law. Students have access to the full array of Internet services. The law school's multiple-node network, wireless network, and computer terminals are available to students for word processing, legal research, statistical analysis, and database management. Students also have access to the many satellite computer clusters and mainframe facilities located on the university campus.

Faculty

Cornell's faculty are known not only as prolific scholars but also as great teachers. Tenured and tenure-track faculty teach and produce scholarship in their area of law; clinical faculty run client-focused and simulation courses centered around legal aid and several specialty clinics; and a large number of visitors, associated faculty from other university divisions, and adjunct faculty teach at the school each year. Many of the latter group are legal scholars and professors from other countries who teach in the law school's significant international program.

Curriculum/Clinical Studies

Cornell offers a national law curriculum leading to the JD degree. First-year students take a group of required courses and an intensive lawyering course stressing a variety of legal research, writing, and advocacy techniques. After the first year, students may choose from a wide range of elective courses, including many seminars and problem courses.

The Cornell Legal Aid Clinic, offering legal services to individuals financially unable to employ an attorney, provides students with the chance to engage in the supervised practice of law under the direction of experienced attorneys. Clinical faculty also conduct a variety of other specialized clinics and skills courses within the regular curriculum. Students can select from a bevy of clinical courses, such as the Advanced Human Rights Clinic; Advanced Labor Law; Attorneys for Children; Capital Punishment Clinic 1 and 2; Criminal Defense Trial Clinic; Cross-national Human Rights Clinic; e-Government Clinic 1 and 2; Immigration Appellate Law and Advocacy Clinic; Innocence Clinic; International Human Rights Clinic; Labor Law Clinic; Land Use, Development, and Natural Resource Protection Clinic; Prosecution Trial Clinic; Securities Law Clinics 1, 2, and 3; US Attorney's Office Clinics 1 and 2; and Water Law in Theory and Practice 1.

Joint Dual-Degrees

Being part of a world-renowned university, and the interdisciplinary environment it provides, is of great benefit. Cornell Law School and Cornell University offer many opportunities for combined-degree programs, including both three- and four-year programs for the JD/MBA (business degree from the Johnson School of Graduate Management); JD/MPA (public affairs degree from the Cornell Institute of Public Affairs); JD/MILR (labor relations degree from the School of Industrial and Labor Relations); JD/MRP (regional planning degree from the College of Architecture, Art, and Planning); and a JD/MA or PhD in a variety of fields (master's or PhD degree from the graduate school). Law students can also take as many as 12 credits outside of the law school for law school credit.

International Legal Studies

The Berger International Legal Studies Program is one of the country's oldest and most distinguished programs in international legal education. The Clarke Program in East Asian Law and Culture brings an exciting interdisciplinary and humanistic focus to the study of law in East Asia. Cornell's comprehensive program features a unique JD specialization opportunity; a three-year JD/LLM degree in international and comparative law; a four-year JD/Master en Droit (French law degree) program; a three-year JD/MLLP (German law degree) program; a Paris summer institute with the Sorbonne Law School at the Université Paris 1 (Panthéon-Sorbonne); a comprehensive speaker series; Mori, Hamada, and Matsumoto (Tokyo law firm) Faculty Exchange; Conseil d'Etat Clerkship (French Supreme Court Clerkship); a founding member of the Turin Interuniversity Centre; a large number of visiting foreign professors and scholars; a weekly luncheon discussion series; international moot court competitions; law clinics; internships; and a leading journal of international and comparative law edited by students. Students have the option to spend one semester abroad at a partner law school (we have agreements with 22 partner schools in 16 different countries), or to design an individual "term away" at a foreign law facility with which Cornell is not partnered.

In addition, the Clarke Initiative for Law and Development in the Middle East sponsors seminars, colloquia, and lectures and supports student and faculty exchanges with institutions in the region.

Programs and Projects

Cornell Law School is the home for several unique programs and projects of interest to students. These programs and projects include the following: Avon Global Center for Women and Justice (improve access to justice in an effort to eliminate violence against women and girls); Death Penalty Project (clinics and symposia related to capital punishment); e-Rulemaking Initiative (technology and practice of e-rulemaking); Clarke Scholars Program (visiting scholars); ILR-Law School Program on Conflict Resolution (raising the standards of arbitration, mediation, and other methods of alternative dispute resolution); Institute for Social Sciences; *Journal of Empirical Legal Studies* (only legal journal dedicated exclusively to empirical legal scholarship); Lay Participation in Law International Research Collaborative (transnational collaborative team dedicated to research on lay participation in court systems); Legal Information Institute (world's leading investigator of new ways to perform electronic legal research); Clarke Business Law Institute (classes, more faculty, seminars, conferences, and other programming); BR Legal (represent start-up companies); and Empirical Studies Project (empirical study of court cases).

Student Activities

Student-edited law journals include the *Cornell Law Review*, the *Cornell International Law Journal*, and the *Cornell Journal*

of Law and Public Policy. Student organizations and activities include American Constitution Society, Asian Pacific American Law Students Association, Black Law Students Association, Briggs Society of International Law, Business Law Society, Christian Legal Society, Cornell Advocates for Human Rights, Cornell Animal Legal Defense Fund, Cornell Sports and Entertainment Law Consortium, Cornell Law Student Association, Cornell Law United, Cornell Law Democrats, Cornell Law Republicans, Environmental Law Society, Federalist Society, J. Reuben Clark Law Society, Jewish Law Student Association, LAMBDA, Latino American Law Students Association, Law Students for Reproductive Justice, MS JD Board, Moot Court Board, National Lawyers Guild, Native American Law Students Association, Phi Alpha Delta, Phi Delta Phi, Public Interest Law Union, South Asian Law Students Association, Students for Marriage Equality, Transfer Network Association, and the Women's Law Coalition.

Expenses and Financial Aid

Cornell offers an institutional-based financial aid program. About 50 percent of students receive scholarship aid (awards averaging more than $15,000 per year), with a higher percentage receiving government-backed loans.

Our Public Interest Low Income Protection Plan, one of the most generous of such programs, assists those choosing qualifying public interest law jobs through the use of a moderated loan repayment plan and loan forgiveness.

Career Services

Cornell's students continue to be among the most recruited in the country. Every fall, hundreds of employers from across the country recruit Cornell students on campus and at job fairs in Boston, Los Angeles, New York, and Washington, DC. A professionally staffed Career Services Office provides employment counseling to students and serves as a liaison to legal employers. In addition, Cornell has two full-time professional staff members (assistant dean and director for public service) dedicated to public interest job opportunities and counseling.

APPLICANT PROFILE

Admission to Cornell Law is very competitive. Members of the most recent entering class had an aggregate 3.63 undergraduate grade-point average and median LSAT scores that placed them in the 97th percentile nationwide (168). But Cornell Law does not evaluate candidates by the numbers alone. The admission committee carefully considers such nonquantifiable factors as extracurricular and community activities, life experience and work background, and

recommendations. Cornell Law subscribes to the university's long-standing tradition of affirmative action, and members of traditionally underrepresented minority groups are encouraged to mention their status where they think it is relevant. The decision to offer admission ultimately rests on whether the committee is convinced that the applicant will be an energetic, productive, and successful member of the Cornell Law community and eventually, the legal profession.

CREIGHTON UNIVERSITY SCHOOL OF LAW

2500 California Plaza
Omaha, NE 68178
Phone: 402.280.2586; Fax: 402.280.3161
E-mail: lawadmit@creighton.edu; Website: www.creighton.edu/law

The Basics

Type of school	Private
Term	Semester
Application deadline	5/1
Application fee	$50
Financial aid deadline	7/1
Can first year start other than fall?	No
Student to faculty ratio	17.1 to 1
# of housing spaces available restricted to law students	
graduate housing for which law students are eligible	

Faculty and Administrators

	Total Spr	Total Fall	Men Spr	Men Fall	Women Spr	Women Fall	Minorities Spr	Minorities Fall
Full-time	21	23	14	16	7	7	3	3
Other full-time	2	1	2	1	0	0	0	0
Deans, librarians, & others who teach	11	11	8	8	3	3	1	1
Part-time	24	23	16	12	8	11	1	0
Total	58	58	40	37	18	21	5	4

Curriculum

	Full-Time	Part-Time
Typical first-year section size	70	0
Is there typically a "small section" of the first-year class, other than Legal Writing, taught by full-time faculty	Yes	No
If yes, typical size offered last year	36	
# of classroom course titles beyond first-year curriculum	83	
# of upper division courses, excluding seminars, with an enrollment: Under 25	68	
25–49	27	
50–74	8	
75–99	5	
100+	0	
# of seminars	15	
# of seminar positions available	289	
# of seminar positions filled	241	0
# of positions available in simulation courses	547	
# of simulation positions filled	503	0
# of positions available in faculty supervised clinical courses	32	
# of faculty supervised clinical positions filled	29	0
# involved in field placements	71	0
# involved in law journals	44	0
# involved in moot court or trial competitions	57	0
# of credit hours required to graduate	94	

JD Enrollment and Ethnicity

	Men #	Men %	Women #	Women %	Full-Time #	Full-Time %	Part-Time #	Part-Time %	1st-Year #	1st-Year %	Total #	Total %	JD Degs. Awd.
All Hispanics	11	4.0	6	3.6	17	3.9	0	0.0	7	5.0	17	3.8	3
Am. Ind./AK Nat.	0	0.0	0	0.0	0	0.0	0	0.0	0	0.0	0	0.0	1
Asian	11	4.0	6	3.6	17	3.9	0	0.0	6	4.3	17	3.8	7
Black/Af. Am.	7	2.5	6	3.6	9	2.1	4	36.4	6	4.3	13	2.9	3
Nat. HI/Pac. Isl.	0	0.0	0	0.0	0	0.0	0	0.0	0	0.0	0	0.0	0
2 or more races	2	0.7	0	0.0	2	0.5	0	0.0	2	1.4	2	0.5	0
Subtotal (minor.)	31	11.2	18	10.9	45	10.4	4	36.4	21	15.0	49	11.1	14
Nonres. Alien	3	1.1	2	1.2	5	1.2	0	0.0	2	1.4	5	1.1	0
White/Cauc.	233	84.1	139	84.2	365	84.7	7	63.6	109	77.9	372	84.2	139
Unknown	10	3.6	6	3.6	16	3.7	0	0.0	8	5.7	16	3.6	0
Total	277	62.7	165	37.3	431	97.5	11	2.5	140	31.7	442		153

Transfers

Transfers in	4
Transfers out	7

Tuition and Fees

	Resident	Nonresident
Full-time	$32,494	$32,494
Part-time	$18,302	$18,302
Tuition Guarantee Program	N	

Living Expenses

Estimated living expenses for singles

Living on campus	Living off campus	Living at home
$16,755	$16,755	$6,855

ABA Approved Since 1924

GPA and LSAT Scores

	Total	Full-Time	Part-Time
# of apps	1,214	1,162	52
# of offers	705	691	14
# of matrics	135	131	4
75% GPA	3.51	3.52	3.21
Median GPA	3.19	3.19	3.14
25% GPA	2.94	2.94	3.03
75% LSAT	155	155	150
Median LSAT	152	152	147
25% LSAT	150	150	145

Grants and Scholarships (from prior year)

	Total #	Total %	Full-Time #	Full-Time %	Part-Time #	Part-Time %
Total # of students	471		459		12	
Total # receiving grants	222	47.1	222	48.4	0	0.0
Less than 1/2 tuition	164	34.8	164	35.7	0	0.0
Half to full tuition	41	8.7	41	8.9	0	0.0
Full tuition	16	3.4	16	3.5	0	0.0
More than full tuition	1	0.2	1	0.2	0	0.0
Median grant amount			$8,000		$0	

Informational and Library Resources

Total amount spent on library materials	$1,490,649
Study seating capacity inside the library	371
# of full-time equivalent professional librarians	6
Hours per week library is open	106
# of open, wired connections available to students	190
# of networked computers available for use by students	28
Has wireless network?	Y
Requires computer?	N

JD Attrition (from prior year)

	Academic #	Other #	Total #	Total %
1st year	3	11	14	9.4
2nd year	0	1	1	0.6
3rd year	0	0	0	0.0
4th year	0	0	0	0.0

Employment (9 months after graduation)

For up-to-date employment data, go to employmentsummary.abaquestionnaire.org on the ABA website.

Bar Passage Rates

First-time takers	137	Reporting %	100.00
Average school %	86.13	Average state %	89.06
Average pass difference	−2.93		

Jurisdiction	Takers	Passers	Pass %	State %	Diff %
Iowa	60	53	88.33	91.09	−2.76
Nebraska	29	26	89.66	89.83	−0.17
Colorado	11	7	63.64	82.79	−19.15
Utah	6	5	83.33	89.35	−6.02
Others (14)	31	27	87.10		

CREIGHTON UNIVERSITY SCHOOL OF LAW

2500 California Plaza
Omaha, NE 68178
Phone: 402.280.2586; Fax: 402.280.3161
E-mail: lawadmit@creighton.edu; Website: www.creighton.edu/law

The School of Law

The School of Law, established in 1904, has been a member of the Association of American Law Schools (AALS) since 1907 and was approved by the American Bar Association (ABA) in 1924. Alumni from the law school are practicing in all 50 states and in several foreign countries. The law school's current enrollment is 442. Students come from 35 states, 3 foreign countries, and 159 undergraduate institutions.

Introduction

Creighton University, a privately endowed and supported Jesuit university, was founded in 1878. Creighton is the most diverse educational institution of its size in the nation. In addition to the School of Law, Creighton has a School of Medicine, School of Dentistry, School of Pharmacy and Health Professions, School of Nursing, College of Business Administration, College of Arts and Sciences, and a Graduate School, making it the center of professional education in the Midwest. The university is located just blocks from downtown Omaha, a metropolitan area with a population of approximately 800,000. Known as the River City, Omaha is the heart of the Midlands and the largest metroplex between Chicago and Denver.

Faculty

The faculty is composed of 28 full-time professors and a group of part-time specialists chosen from the bench and bar. Creighton's full-time faculty members have earned reputations as outstanding classroom teachers. In addition, faculty scholarship brings to the classroom insights gained through the publication of leading texts and thought-provoking articles. A distinguished adjunct faculty of judges and practicing attorneys teach courses in specialty areas. Faculty offices surround the Law School Commons, making them easily accessible to students. Faculty members maintain an open-door policy that encourages students to drop in to discuss the latest case, current events, or the newest restaurant in town.

Library and Physical Facilities

The School of Law is entirely contained in the Ahmanson Law Center. The attractive Klutznick Law Library/McGrath North Mullin and Kratz Legal Research Center encompasses 45,480 assignable square feet and is located on both levels of the Law Center. Wireless network coverage is campus-wide. Many tables and carrels are also wired with both power and data connections. A variety of comfortable individual, group study, reading room, and computer-use seating options are available in a pleasant, service-oriented setting. In addition to other legal information specialists, the Law Library employs four lawyer-librarians (JD/MLS librarians) who each deliver reference service and teach. The Law Library provides access to one of the finest legal collections in the region. It houses a large, carefully selected array of print and electronic Anglo-American, comparative, and international law resources. Other features of the library include two computer labs, two reading rooms, and an inspiring rare book collection comprised primarily of British legal texts and treatises from the sixteenth to the nineteenth centuries.

Areas of Concentration

Students may earn a certificate indicating that they focused their studies in a particular area of concentration. Areas of concentration are (a) Business Law, (b) Criminal Law and Procedure, (c) International and Comparative Law, and (d) Litigation. The curriculum prepares students for the practice of law in any state.

Combined-Degree Programs

Creighton's School of Law, College of Business Administration, and Graduate School offer a JD/MBA, a JD/MS in Information Technology Management, a JD/MS in Negotiation and Dispute Resolution, a JD/MA in International Relations, and a JD/MS in Government Organization and Leadership.

Clinics and Internships

The Milton R. Abrahams Legal Clinic provides third-year students with the opportunity to learn the lawyering process in a way that is not provided in most law school courses. Clinic students represent low-income clients on a variety of civil matters that vary in complexity. Students conduct interviews, prepare pleadings, conduct legal research and writing, and appear in court for hearings and trials. Clinic students are certified to practice law under the supervision of clinic faculty and licensed attorneys.

The Community Economic Development (CED) Law Clinic provides third-year students with an opportunity to work on a broad range of transactional and business law issues affecting community development. Students in the CED Clinic represent a client base of small business owners and nonprofit and community-based organizations that serve low-income communities across the state of Nebraska and Western Iowa. Students will get valuable hands-on experience while helping entrepreneurs create and maintain jobs.

Students may also participate in a broad variety of internships with city, county, and federal legal offices in the Omaha area.

The Werner Institute

The Werner Institute, the most richly endowed program of its kind in the country, is a national leader in the field of conflict resolution with an interdisciplinary curriculum leading to graduate certificates and master's degrees in the field. The institute places a strong emphasis on a systems approach to conflict resolution and focuses on the preparation of leaders in the field with specialized applications in areas of greatest need, such as conflict within and among organizations, businesses, health care, and communities.

Student Activities

The Student Bar Association (SBA) is the student government of the law school. The purpose of the organization is to make law students aware of the obligations and opportunities existing for lawyers through SBA activities, promote a consciousness of professional responsibility, and provide a forum for student activities. The *Creighton Law Review*, edited and managed by students, is a scholarly legal journal that is circulated nationally and internationally. The School of Law also has an online, student-managed journal, the *Creighton International and Comparative Law Journal*, which is available electronically. The school has over 20 different active student organizations.

Financial Aid and Scholarships

Creighton University School of Law offers two types of financial aid: merit-based scholarships and federal government loans. Students seeking financial aid and scholarships must complete the Free Application for Federal Student Aid (FAFSA). Creighton University participates in the US Department of Education's Direct Loan Program. All first-year scholarships have merit requirements, including, but not limited to, LSAT score and undergraduate grade-point average. Admitted applicants with an LSAT score and undergraduate grade-point average above Creighton's medians for the previous year will receive strong consideration for scholarship assistance. Applicants who qualify for a scholarship will be notified at the time of acceptance.

Frances M. Ryan Diversity Scholarship Program

The School of Law actively recruits minority students and has a substantial diversity scholarship program. Applicants who wish to be considered for a Ryan Diversity Scholarship must make note of it on their admission application.

Career Development Office

The Career Development Office provides a full array of services to Creighton Law students, including individual career counseling, a law alumni network stretching from coast to coast, on-campus and off-campus interview programs, alumni networking events in a variety of cities nationwide, and a dynamic website that allows students to explore career opportunities throughout the world. Nine months after graduation, 90.3 percent of the class of 2010 was employed, enrolled in a full-time degree program, or not seeking employment. Of those employed, 92.3 percent were employed in positions requiring or preferring a Juris Doctor degree. Graduates from the class of 2010 are working in the areas of business, government, private practice, public interest, and as judicial clerks in 18 states and the District of Columbia.

APPLICANT PROFILE

Creighton University School of Law
This grid includes only applicants who earned 120–180 LSAT scores under standard administrations.

LSAT Score	3.75 +		3.50–3.74		3.25–3.49		3.00–3.24		2.75–2.99		2.50–2.74		2.25–2.49		2.00–2.24		Below 2.00		No GPA		Total	
	Apps	Adm	Apps	Adm	Apps	Adm	Apps	Adm	Apps	Adm	Apps	Adm	Apps	Adm	Apps	Adm	Apps	Adm	Apps	Adm	Apps	Adm
175–180	0	0	0	0	0	0	0	0	0	0	0	0	0	0	0	0	0	0	0	0	0	0
170–174	1	1	0	0	0	0	0	0	3	3	0	0	1	1	0	0	0	0	0	0	5	5
165–169	5	5	5	5	3	3	3	3	0	0	3	3	0	0	0	0	0	0	0	0	19	19
160–164	21	21	19	19	22	22	14	14	10	10	3	3	6	6	3	0	0	0	0	0	98	95
155–159	38	37	61	58	58	57	42	42	28	26	14	12	8	5	8	7	0	0	3	3	260	247
150–154	46	37	81	66	90	73	83	56	51	30	33	15	14	4	4	1	0	0	6	4	408	286
145–149	21	6	47	15	40	5	61	15	45	7	28	3	11	0	4	0	0	0	4	0	261	51
140–144	3	0	20	0	26	0	22	0	18	1	17	0	9	0	3	0	2	0	2	1	122	2
135–139	3	0	4	0	6	0	6	0	8	0	5	0	2	0	4	0	0	0	0	0	38	0
130–134	0	0	0	0	0	0	3	0	2	0	6	0	0	0	0	0	0	0	3	0	14	0
125–129	0	0	0	0	0	0	0	0	0	0	1	0	0	0	1	0	0	0	0	0	2	0
120–124	0	0	0	0	0	0	0	0	0	0	0	0	0	0	0	0	0	0	0	0	0	0
Total	138	107	237	163	245	160	234	130	165	77	110	36	51	16	27	8	2	0	18	8	1227	705

Apps = Number of Applicants
Adm = Number Admitted
Reflects 100% of the total applicant pool; highest LSAT data reported.

UNIVERSITY OF DAYTON SCHOOL OF LAW

300 College Park, 112 Keller Hall
Dayton, OH 45469-2760
Phone: 937.229.3555; Fax: 937.229.4194
E-mail: lawinfo@udayton.edu; Website: www.udayton.edu/law

ABA Approved Since 1975

The Basics

Type of school	Private
Term	Semester
Application deadline	3/1 5/1
Application fee	$50
Financial aid deadline	3/1 5/1
Can first year start other than fall?	Yes
Student to faculty ratio	16.2 to 1
# of housing spaces available restricted to law students graduate housing for which law students are eligible	107

Faculty and Administrators

	Total		Men		Women		Minorities	
	Spr	Fall	Spr	Fall	Spr	Fall	Spr	Fall
Full-time	25	24	15	13	10	11	5	5
Other full-time	2	1	0	0	2	1	0	0
Deans, librarians, & others who teach	10	5	3	1	7	4	1	1
Part-time	21	14	18	9	3	5	1	1
Total	58	44	36	23	22	21	7	7

Curriculum

	Full-Time	Part-Time
Typical first-year section size	87	0
Is there typically a "small section" of the first-year class, other than Legal Writing, taught by full-time faculty	No	No
If yes, typical size offered last year		
# of classroom course titles beyond first-year curriculum	70	

# of upper division courses, excluding seminars, with an enrollment:		
	Under 25	77
	25–49	18
	50–74	17
	75–99	6
	100+	0

# of seminars	13	
# of seminar positions available	240	
# of seminar positions filled	186	0
# of positions available in simulation courses	420	
# of simulation positions filled	246	0
# of positions available in faculty supervised clinical courses	24	
# of faculty supervised clinical positions filled	24	0
# involved in field placements	135	0
# involved in law journals	73	0
# involved in moot court or trial competitions	20	0
# of credit hours required to graduate	90	

JD Enrollment and Ethnicity

	Men		Women		Full-Time		Part-Time		1st-Year		Total		JD Degs. Awd.
	#	%	#	%	#	%	#	%	#	%	#	%	
All Hispanics	3	1.1	4	1.9	7	1.4	0	0.0	1	0.6	7	1.4	4
Am. Ind./AK Nat.	1	0.4	1	0.5	2	0.4	0	0.0	2	1.2	2	0.4	1
Asian	6	2.1	8	3.9	14	2.9	0	0.0	2	1.2	14	2.9	5
Black/Af. Am.	11	3.9	17	8.3	28	5.7	0	0.0	9	5.3	28	5.7	11
Nat. HI/Pac. Isl.	0	0.0	0	0.0	0	0.0	0	0.0	0	0.0	0	0.0	0
2 or more races	4	1.4	4	1.9	8	1.6	0	0.0	6	3.5	8	1.6	0
Subtotal (minor.)	25	8.9	34	16.5	59	12.1	0	0.0	20	11.7	59	12.1	21
Nonres. Alien	0	0.0	0	0.0	0	0.0	0	0.0	0	0.0	0	0.0	0
White/Cauc.	254	90.1	168	81.6	422	86.5	0	0.0	144	84.2	422	86.5	149
Unknown	3	1.1	4	1.9	7	1.4	0	0.0	7	4.1	7	1.4	1
Total	282	57.8	206	42.2	488	100.0	0	0.0	171	35.0	488		171

Transfers

Transfers in	2
Transfers out	48

Tuition and Fees

	Resident	Nonresident
Full-time	$31,598	
Part-time		
Tuition Guarantee Program	N	

Living Expenses

Estimated living expenses for singles

Living on campus	Living off campus	Living at home
$16,500	$16,500	$16,500

UNIVERSITY OF DAYTON SCHOOL OF LAW

ABA
Approved
Since
1975

GPA and LSAT Scores

	Total	Full-Time	Part-Time
# of apps	1,751	1,751	0
# of offers	1,233	1,233	0
# of matrics	177	177	0
75% GPA	3.37	3.37	0.00
Median GPA	3.10	3.10	0.00
25% GPA	2.78	2.78	0.00
75% LSAT	152	152	0
Median LSAT	149	149	0
25% LSAT	148	148	0

Grants and Scholarships (from prior year)

	Total		Full-Time		Part-Time	
	#	%	#	%	#	%
Total # of students	524		524		0	
Total # receiving grants	296	56.5	296	56.5	0	0.0
Less than 1/2 tuition	268	51.1	268	51.1	0	0.0
Half to full tuition	28	5.3	28	5.3	0	0.0
Full tuition	0	0.0	0	0.0	0	0.0
More than full tuition	0	0.0	0	0.0	0	0.0
Median grant amount			$7,000		$0	

Informational and Library Resources

Total amount spent on library materials	$793,239
Study seating capacity inside the library	489
# of full-time equivalent professional librarians	4
Hours per week library is open	102
# of open, wired connections available to students	0
# of networked computers available for use by students	34
Has wireless network?	Y
Requires computer?	N

JD Attrition (from prior year)

	Academic	Other	Total	
	#	#	#	%
1st year	7	24	31	15.3
2nd year	0	33	33	23.4
3rd year	0	1	1	0.6
4th year	0	0	0	0.0

Employment (9 months after graduation)

For up-to-date employment data, go to
employmentsummary.abaquestionnaire.org on the ABA website.

Bar Passage Rates

First-time takers	140	Reporting %	81.43
Average school %	80.71	Average state %	86.07
Average pass difference	-5.36		

Jurisdiction	Takers	Passers	Pass %	State %	Diff %
Ohio	74	57	77.03	86.14	-9.11
Illinois	13	11	84.62	89.38	-4.76
Indiana	10	7	70.00	80.93	-10.93
Missouri	8	8	100.00	90.24	9.76
Pennsylvania	5	5	100.00	83.06	16.94

UNIVERSITY OF DAYTON SCHOOL OF LAW

300 College Park, 112 Keller Hall
Dayton, OH 45469-2760
Phone: 937.229.3555; Fax: 937.229.4194
E-mail: lawinfo@udayton.edu; Website: www.udayton.edu/law

Introduction and Mission

Our mission is to enroll a diverse group of intellectually curious, self-disciplined, and well-motivated men and women, and to educate them in the substantive and procedural principles of public and private law. We seek to graduate highly qualified attorneys who will uphold the highest professional standards and recognize that service to others is the chief measure of professional competence.

We offer a full-time JD program providing a distinguished tradition of concern for the individual student in a supportive and professional environment. Our curriculum gives students a foundation in traditional courses but also helps them develop their skills with innovative programs like our legal skills courses and curricular concentrations. Our diverse student body of 480 promotes ample opportunity for one-on-one interaction with faculty, staff, and fellow students, creating an atmosphere of collegiality. Our student body actively participates in a myriad of law school organizations and community service opportunities. The University of Dayton School of Law is accredited by the ABA and is a member of the AALS.

Facilities and Campus

Joseph E. Keller Hall is a 122,500-square-foot complex featuring a dramatic atrium, a variety of classroom and meeting spaces, and an expansive law library. Internet access is readily available via our wireless network from virtually any location in the law building. Every seat in the 325,000-volume **Zimmerman Law Library** has access to a power outlet as well as the wireless network. The library contains a computer training center where students learn to conduct online and computer-based research as well as study rooms that allow students to meet in groups of up to 20.

Founded in 1850, the **University of Dayton** enrolls more than 10,000 undergraduate and graduate students. The campus of nearly 400 scenic acres is located minutes from the city's center and has a fitness center, a student health center, child care, meal plans, and banking services. On-campus housing located within three blocks of the law school is available for over half of the entering class.

The Dayton Community

With a population of approximately 840,000, the Dayton Metro Area offers many amenities of larger urban areas while retaining its scenic, lush, and green open spaces. As the birthplace of the Wright Brothers, the city has a variety of flight-related museums and events, as well as many other cultural and recreational activities. You will find housing, shopping, restaurants, and entertainment districts that are varied and affordable. Cheer for the UD Flyers, Cincinnati Reds, or the Dayton Dragons, who have the longest active sold-out streak in all of US pro sports. For the outdoor enthusiast, Dayton's beautiful river bikeways, recreation trails, and parks provide miles and acres of exhilaration. If students want to explore beyond Dayton, they can reach Cincinnati or Columbus in an hour or visit the quaint towns of Yellow Springs, Waynesville, or Lebanon in less than 30 minutes.

Curriculum and Programs

We offer a traditional education that blends theory and practice with a focus on attaining essential lawyering and problem-solving skills. The emphasis on acquiring legal skills through real-world practical experience, capstone and clinic courses, and a required externship prepares students for a successful legal career. Students may choose from various curricular concentrations focused on particular areas of the law.

Entering students may choose to begin their first year in **May** or **August**. By starting in May in our Accelerated Program, students may complete their JD in two calendar years instead of the traditional three years.

Legal Profession Course Sequence—This comprehensive two-semester, six-credit-hour sequence helps students build legal research, analytical, and writing skills in the context of the evolving technology used in law practice. Small groups meet with experienced full-time faculty for training in such important skills as accessing and understanding legal authority and effectively communicating legal analysis within specific practice areas. These courses stress the practical application of research and writing skills necessary to produce clear, effective legal documents.

Academic Success Program—This program provides academic assistance to all students from the time they enter law school until the transition to the Road to Bar Pass Program. Workshops are offered throughout the year on class preparation, case synthesis, outlining/flowcharting, and exam writing.

The Academic Excellence Program is a learning community for first-year students that is designed to help participants make the transition to law school through structured study groups and skill-building workshops.

Externships—This semester-long legal apprenticeship in a legal setting, such as a governmental agency, law firm, corporation, court, or legal aid office, provides students the opportunity to practice their craft, to observe highly respected attorneys and judges at work, and to network with the legal community.

Capstone Courses—These courses are designed as a synthesis and completion of previously studied material. During their last semester, each student takes a capstone course specially designed to provide closure to their legal education. Students are asked to demonstrate their ability to apply to real and simulated legal problems the substantive knowledge and practical skills acquired during their time at the University of Dayton School of Law.

Road to Bar Pass—The School of Law encourages bar exam success during law school by offering a bar preparation course. It also supports bar exam success after graduation by providing services that offer support ranging from planning a schedule, to reviewing practice questions, and sponsoring simulated exams.

Graduate Programs

Our **Master of Laws (LLM) in Intellectual Property and Technology Law** is for students who already possess a JD and desire to further their legal expertise in the area of intellectual property. The **Master of Study of Law (MSL) in Intellectual Property and Technology Law** is for students who do not possess a JD but desire an in-depth understanding of intellectual property.

Faculty

With backgrounds spanning a spectrum of legal endeavors, many of our faculty members are known nationally for their expertise and scholarship. As prominent scholars and leaders, our professors transfer their expertise to students both inside and outside of the classroom. Students consistently praise our faculty, not only for their outstanding teaching skills, but also for their constant involvement in, concern for, and support of students' lives.

Student Life

Collegiality, support, and a welcoming atmosphere distinguish our diverse student body. Students may participate in organizations that help develop writing, research, and oral advocacy skills; those that speak to their mutual professional interests; or those that provide support of a student's personal and biographical background and interests. Our Student Bar Association is made up of officers and representatives from each class who oversee all student organizations and it is the voice of student governance at the law school.

Career Services

Whether providing online networking for recent alumni, or working one-on-one with students to hone their job search, career services is a priority at the School of Law. Our Career Services Office has outpaced many of its peers in placing graduates in full-time law jobs. The assistant dean and his staff are committed to providing comprehensive career

planning and placement services to assist students and alumni with identifying and securing positions commensurate with each individual's interests and career goals.

Admission

The Admissions Committee looks for a well-rounded and diverse group of students for each entering class. Undergraduate GPA and LSAT score are seriously considered, but commitment, motivation, leadership, and a breadth and depth of experiences are also a large part of the applicant review. Decisions are made on a rolling basis, beginning November 1 and continuing through late spring.

Financial Aid

Approximately half of the entering class receives scholarships. The majority of our scholarships are merit based, with the goal of diversifying the class also taken into consideration. Renewal of merit scholarships is dependent upon academic performance at the end of the preceding two semesters.

Federal Direct loans up to $20,500 are also available to our students. Alternative loans may also be used to cover the cost of a legal education, should scholarships and federal loans not do so. Federal and alternative loans are available pending a student's citizenship status and credit rating.

Prospective Students

Prospective students are encouraged to contact the Office of Admissions for questions or to schedule informational visits. Office hours are 8:30 AM to 4:30 PM, Monday through Friday.

APPLICANT PROFILE

University of Dayton School of Law
This grid includes only applicants who earned 120–180 LSAT scores under standard administrations.

LSAT Score	3.75 + Apps	Adm	3.50–3.74 Apps	Adm	3.25–3.49 Apps	Adm	3.00–3.24 Apps	Adm	2.75–2.99 Apps	Adm	2.50–2.74 Apps	Adm	2.25–2.49 Apps	Adm	2.00–2.24 Apps	Adm	Below 2.00 Apps	Adm	No GPA Apps	Adm	Total Apps	Adm
175–180	0	0	0	0	0	0	0	0	0	0	0	0	0	0	0	0	0	0	0	0	0	0
170–174	1	1	3	3	0	0	0	0	0	0	0	0	0	0	0	0	0	0	0	0	4	4
165–169	9	9	3	3	3	3	2	2	1	1	0	0	0	0	0	0	0	0	0	0	18	18
160–164	13	13	13	13	14	14	16	16	14	13	6	6	3	3	2	0	0	0	1	0	82	78
155–159	33	33	34	32	53	53	51	48	33	32	30	26	9	8	7	2	0	0	1	1	251	235
150–154	40	39	83	82	111	109	114	108	87	80	54	45	30	24	6	2	3	1	10	5	538	495
145–149	28	26	77	68	102	85	108	88	84	61	59	39	25	14	12	1	1	0	7	0	503	382
140–144	5	1	28	4	44	4	44	4	40	1	29	3	15	0	11	0	2	0	7	0	225	17
135–139	0	0	7	0	17	0	18	0	19	0	14	0	6	0	5	0	1	0	0	0	87	0
130–134	0	0	0	0	2	0	4	0	7	0	9	0	3	0	1	0	1	0	1	0	28	0
125–129	0	0	1	0	1	0	2	0	0	0	1	0	1	0	1	0	0	0	0	0	7	0
120–124	0	0	0	0	0	0	0	0	0	0	1	0	0	0	0	0	0	0	0	0	1	0
Total	129	122	249	205	347	268	359	266	285	188	203	119	92	49	45	5	8	1	27	6	1744	1229

Apps = Number of Applicants
Adm = Number Admitted
Reflects 99% of the total applicant pool; highest LSAT data reported.

UNIVERSITY OF DENVER STURM COLLEGE OF LAW

2255 E. Evans Avenue, Suite 115
Denver, CO 80208
Phone: 303.871.6135; Fax: 303.871.6992
E-mail: admissions@law.du.edu; Website: www.law.du.edu

ABA Approved Since 1923

The Basics

Type of school	Private
Term	Semester
Application deadline	6/1
Application fee	$65
Financial aid deadline	2/15 3/1
Can first year start other than fall?	No
Student to faculty ratio	11.7 to 1
# of housing spaces available restricted to law students	
graduate housing for which law students are eligible	46

Faculty and Administrators

	Total		Men		Women		Minorities	
	Spr	Fall	Spr	Fall	Spr	Fall	Spr	Fall
Full-time	62	62	35	34	27	28	14	16
Other full-time	7	6	4	4	3	2	0	1
Deans, librarians, & others who teach	7	6	4	3	3	3	0	0
Part-time	60	57	48	44	12	13	4	4
Total	136	131	91	85	45	46	18	21

Curriculum

	Full-Time	Part-Time
Typical first-year section size	80	60
Is there typically a "small section" of the first-year class, other than Legal Writing, taught by full-time faculty	Yes	Yes
If yes, typical size offered last year	40	40
# of classroom course titles beyond first-year curriculum	208	

# of upper division courses, excluding seminars, with an enrollment:		
	Under 25	241
	25–49	57
	50–74	15
	75–99	3
	100+	2

# of seminars	20	
# of seminar positions available	373	
# of seminar positions filled	323	50
# of positions available in simulation courses	403	
# of simulation positions filled	348	55
# of positions available in faculty supervised clinical courses	135	
# of faculty supervised clinical positions filled	127	8
# involved in field placements	397	34
# involved in law journals	176	18
# involved in moot court or trial competitions	66	7
# of credit hours required to graduate	90	

JD Enrollment and Ethnicity

	Men #	Men %	Women #	Women %	Full-Time #	Full-Time %	Part-Time #	Part-Time %	1st-Year #	1st-Year %	Total #	Total %	JD Degs. Awd.
All Hispanics	35	7.3	38	8.2	54	7.0	19	10.7	28	9.5	73	7.7	29
Am. Ind./AK Nat.	5	1.0	4	0.9	7	0.9	2	1.1	2	0.7	9	1.0	6
Asian	16	3.3	14	3.0	26	3.4	4	2.3	5	1.7	30	3.2	17
Black/Af. Am.	8	1.7	14	3.0	17	2.2	5	2.8	4	1.4	22	2.3	6
Nat. Hl/Pac. Isl.	0	0.0	0	0.0	0	0.0	0	0.0	0	0.0	0	0.0	1
2 or more races	7	1.5	16	3.4	20	2.6	3	1.7	11	3.7	23	2.4	2
Subtotal (minor.)	71	14.8	86	18.5	124	16.1	33	18.6	50	16.9	157	16.6	61
Nonres. Alien	0	0.0	0	0.0	0	0.0	0	0.0	0	0.0	0	0.0	0
White/Cauc.	393	81.9	364	78.1	617	80.2	140	79.1	238	80.7	757	80.0	211
Unknown	16	3.3	16	3.4	28	3.6	4	2.3	7	2.4	32	3.4	15
Total	480	50.7	466	49.3	769	81.3	177	18.7	295	31.2	946		287

Transfers

Transfers in	16
Transfers out	11

Tuition and Fees

	Resident	Nonresident
Full-time	$38,502	$38,502
Part-time	$28,382	$28,382
Tuition Guarantee Program	N	

Living Expenses

Estimated living expenses for singles

Living on campus	Living off campus	Living at home
$16,707	$16,707	$16,707

UNIVERSITY OF DENVER STURM COLLEGE OF LAW

ABA Approved Since 1923

GPA and LSAT Scores

	Total	Full-Time	Part-Time
# of apps	2,425	2,161	264
# of offers	986	893	93
# of matrics	297	239	58
75% GPA	3.64	3.64	3.66
Median GPA	3.49	3.50	3.48
25% GPA	3.17	3.16	3.28
75% LSAT	161	162	159
Median LSAT	159	160	157
25% LSAT	155	155	153

Grants and Scholarships (from prior year)

	Total		Full-Time		Part-Time	
	#	%	#	%	#	%
Total # of students	960		768		192	
Total # receiving grants	419	43.6	372	48.4	47	24.5
Less than 1/2 tuition	253	26.4	220	28.6	33	17.2
Half to full tuition	114	11.9	102	13.3	12	6.3
Full tuition	50	5.2	48	6.2	2	1.0
More than full tuition	2	0.2	2	0.3	0	0.0
Median grant amount			$17,000		$10,000	

Informational and Library Resources

Total amount spent on library materials	$1,024,061
Study seating capacity inside the library	333
# of full-time equivalent professional librarians	5
Hours per week library is open	108
# of open, wired connections available to students	1,535
# of networked computers available for use by students	26
Has wireless network?	Y
Requires computer?	Y

JD Attrition (from prior year)

	Academic	Other	Total	
	#	#	#	%
1st year	7	7	14	4.7
2nd year	3	14	17	4.5
3rd year	0	1	1	0.4
4th year	0	0	0	0.0

Employment (9 months after graduation)

For up-to-date employment data, go to employmentsummary.abaquestionnaire.org on the ABA website.

Bar Passage Rates

First-time takers	366	Reporting %	78.96
Average school %	86.16	Average state %	82.79
Average pass difference	3.37		

Jurisdiction	Takers	Passers	Pass %	State %	Diff %
Colorado	289	249	86.16	82.79	3.37

UNIVERSITY OF DENVER STURM COLLEGE OF LAW

2255 E. Evans Avenue, Suite 115
Denver, CO 80208
Phone: 303.871.6135; Fax: 303.871.6992
E-mail: admissions@law.du.edu; Website: www.law.du.edu

Introduction

The University of Denver Sturm College of Law opened its doors in 1892 and has been breaking ground in legal education ever since. Our faculty pride themselves in training students for successful careers as legal practitioners by offering a variety of challenging and exciting courses in addition to experiential learning opportunities through our Student Law Office, externships with law firms, and clerkships with judges. Our new building, with over 181,000 square feet spanning four stories, is the first law building to be awarded the Gold Leadership in Energy and Environmental Design (LEED) certification by the US Green Building Council. Downtown Denver—where the state legislature, courthouses, regional federal agencies, state agencies, and law firms are found—is 10 minutes away by Light Rail, and the Rocky Mountains are just a short drive to the west.

Curriculum/Special Programs

Denver Law provides a solid foundation of core classes on which to build your career in law. In addition, we offer a wide range of specialized classes that permit our faculty to bring their scholarship into the classroom.

Lawyering Process Program—The first-year curriculum includes an innovative Lawyering Process program, which provides first-year students an introduction to the law and the legal system, and teaches students how to research legal questions and write about them in several formats.

Environmental and Natural Resources Law—Drawing upon its location in one of the nation's natural resource and energy capitals, Denver Law offers a rich program in environmental and natural resources law. Extensive course offerings are supplemented with abundant opportunities for externships at local natural resource companies, environmental advocacy and protection groups, and government enforcement agencies. Students may also participate in our Environmental Law Clinic, student organizations, the *Water Law Review*, writing competitions, and natural resources moot court competitions.

International Legal Studies—The International Legal Studies program is designed for students interested in international comparative law, international organizations, or transnational business. Students in the program may work on the *Denver Journal of International Law and Policy* as staff members and editors. The International Law Society and Ved Nanda Center for International Law sponsor a rich schedule of outside speakers and an annual conference focused on a current issue in international law.

Corporate and Commercial Law—As one of the nation's biggest tourism magnets, Denver provides a practical backdrop for students interested in business and commercial law. In addition to foundation courses and specialized seminars, corporate internships and highly prized one-semester assignments with large local corporations are available for interested students to pursue.

Lawyering in Spanish—This program celebrates the globalization of Spanish culture by providing an opportunity to learn the specialized vocabulary and counseling techniques required to represent Spanish-speaking clients in the United States and abroad.

Clinics—In 1904 Denver Law launched the first Student Law Office (SLO) in the United States. The SLO offers the following clinics: Civil Litigation, Civil Rights, Community Law, Criminal Defense, Environmental, and Mediation/Arbitration. Students represent indigent clients at all levels of the dispute resolution process. If the case reaches the litigation phase, the student handles all aspects of pretrial, trial preparation, and the trial itself under faculty supervision.

Student Activities

Trial Advocacy—The Advocacy Department at Denver Law provides its students with the highest quality preparation for success in their professional careers by providing education and simulation in the four areas of advocacy—Client Advocacy, Pre-Trial Advocacy, Trial Advocacy, and Appellate Advocacy. The department achieves this through innovative professional skills courses, simulated courtroom situations, and competitive tournaments. The department's three national trial teams and eight moot court teams consistently garner awards and recognition at both regional and nationally ranked tournaments, and the school's Moot Court Board produces six competitions per academic year.

Journals—Five scholarly journals are edited at Denver Law, allowing students to participate in research in varied fields. Academic credit is awarded for work on the *Denver University Law Review, Denver Journal of International Law and Policy, Sports and Entertainment Law Journal, Transportation Law Journal,* and *University of Denver Water Law Review.*

Student Organizations—A wide range of student organizations contribute to the vibrant environment of the Sturm College of Law. Among those groups are the Animal Legal Defense Fund, Asian Pacific American Law Students' Association, Black Law Students' Association, Business Law Society, Christian Legal Society, Federalist Society, International Law Society, Intellectual Property Law Society, J. Reuben Clarke Law Society, Jewish Law Students Association, Latino Law Students Association, Native American Law Students Association, Natural Resources and Environmental Law Society, Phi Alpha Delta, Public Interest Law Group, and Sports and Entertainment Law Society.

Admission

All applications should be submitted online and reach the Sturm College of Law between September and February to receive maximum consideration for admission for the following August. Students may only begin law study in the fall semester. Applicants must take the LSAT and register with LSAC's Credential Assembly Service. LSAT scores and records of academic performance are individually evaluated in the admission process. The applicant's personal statement, résumé, and letters of recommendation are thoroughly reviewed as well as work experience, significant personal accomplishments, leadership roles, a commitment to community service, and other activities that show initiative, growth, and maturity.

Expenses and Financial Aid

All admitted students are considered for scholarships. No additional application is required, except for the Chancellor Scholarship. Scholarships offered to entering first-year students may be renewed each year based on satisfactory academic performance.

The Chancellor Scholar program is offered to students with a demonstrated history of excellence in scholarship and public service. The program awards full-tuition scholarships to a limited number of qualified students committed to public interest issues. The scholarships are available to entering first-year day-division and evening-division students.

Additional one-year scholarships may be offered to continuing students based on law school performance. Students may also apply for federal loans, up to the cost of attendance.

Career Services

The Career Development Center (CDC) assists students and alumni in the formulation of career plans and connects potential employers with qualified applicants. Their services include educating students and alumni in developing necessary skills to locate and obtain satisfying and meaningful employment, connecting students and alumni to the world of work, and facilitating employers' connections with students and alumni.

Housing

On-campus graduate housing is available at the University of Denver. However, the majority of law students choose to live off campus.

APPLICANT PROFILE

University of Denver Sturm College of Law
This grid includes only applicants who earned 120–180 LSAT scores under standard administrations.

LSAT Score	3.75 +		3.50–3.74		3.25–3.49		3.00–3.24		2.75–2.99		2.50–2.74		2.25–2.49		2.00–2.24		Below 2.00		No GPA		Total	
	Apps	Adm	Apps	Adm	Apps	Adm	Apps	Adm	Apps	Adm	Apps	Adm	Apps	Adm	Apps	Adm	Apps	Adm	Apps	Adm	Apps	Adm
175–180	0	0	0	0	0	0	0	0	1	0	1	1	0	0	0	0	0	0	0	0	2	1
170–174	4	4	2	2	1	1	3	3	7	7	2	2	1	0	0	0	0	0	0	0	20	19
165–169	20	20	47	45	41	38	25	24	10	10	5	4	4	1	1	0	0	0	4	2	157	144
160–164	80	78	103	98	106	97	115	112	57	54	24	15	14	6	3	0	0	0	5	4	507	464
155–159	102	67	191	99	207	33	153	15	83	8	37	2	12	0	6	0	0	0	6	1	797	225
150–154	61	33	97	52	135	18	137	9	76	1	43	1	19	1	10	0	0	0	13	1	591	116
145–149	6	1	27	1	55	1	41	1	41	0	19	0	15	0	2	0	0	0	8	4	214	8
140–144	3	0	10	1	19	0	17	0	20	0	4	0	7	0	3	0	0	0	3	0	86	1
135–139	3	0	2	0	4	0	5	0	7	0	4	0	5	0	0	0	0	0	2	0	32	0
130–134	1	0	1	0	2	0	4	0	1	0	1	0	2	0	1	0	0	0	3	0	16	0
125–129	0	0	0	0	0	0	0	0	0	0	2	0	0	0	0	0	0	0	1	0	3	0
120–124	0	0	0	0	0	0	1	0	0	0	0	0	0	0	0	0	0	0	0	0	1	0
Total	280	203	480	298	570	188	501	164	303	80	142	25	79	8	26	0	0	0	45	12	2426	978

Apps = Number of Applicants
Adm = Number Admitted
Reflects 99% of the total applicant pool; highest LSAT data reported.

DEPAUL UNIVERSITY COLLEGE OF LAW

25 East Jackson Boulevard
Chicago, IL 60604-2219
Phone: 312.362.6831 or 800.428.7453; Fax: 312.362.5280
E-mail: lawinfo@depaul.edu; Website: www.law.depaul.edu

ABA
Approved
Since
1925

The Basics

Type of school	Private
Term	Semester
Application deadline	3/1
Application fee	$60
Financial aid deadline	4/1
Can first year start other than fall?	No
Student to faculty ratio	13.9 to 1
# of housing spaces available restricted to law students	
graduate housing for which law students are eligible	254

Faculty and Administrators

	Total		Men		Women		Minorities	
	Spr	Fall	Spr	Fall	Spr	Fall	Spr	Fall
Full-time	59	54	34	33	25	21	7	9
Other full-time	0	0	0	0	0	0	0	0
Deans, librarians, & others who teach	3	5	2	4	1	1	1	1
Part-time	69	60	43	40	26	20	4	5
Total	131	119	79	77	52	42	12	15

Curriculum

	Full-Time	Part-Time
Typical first-year section size	82	48
Is there typically a "small section" of the first-year class, other than Legal Writing, taught by full-time faculty	No	No
If yes, typical size offered last year		

# of classroom course titles beyond first-year curriculum		152
# of upper division courses, excluding seminars, with an enrollment:	Under 25	175
	25–49	43
	50–74	13
	75–99	14
	100+	3

	Full-Time	Part-Time
# of seminars	17	
# of seminar positions available	340	
# of seminar positions filled	165	33
# of positions available in simulation courses	652	
# of simulation positions filled	46	524
# of positions available in faculty supervised clinical courses	202	
# of faculty supervised clinical positions filled	195	7
# involved in field placements	244	0
# involved in law journals	72	0
# involved in moot court or trial competitions	12	0
# of credit hours required to graduate	86	

JD Enrollment and Ethnicity

	Men		Women		Full-Time		Part-Time		1st-Year		Total		JD Degs. Awd.
	#	%	#	%	#	%	#	%	#	%	#	%	
All Hispanics	39	7.2	53	11.1	73	8.8	19	9.9	36	12.0	92	9.0	32
Am. Ind./AK Nat.	3	0.6	4	0.8	5	0.6	2	1.0	1	0.3	7	0.7	0
Asian	26	4.8	39	8.2	53	6.4	12	6.3	15	5.0	65	6.4	22
Black/Af. Am.	25	4.6	43	9.0	52	6.3	16	8.3	20	6.7	68	6.7	15
Nat. HI/Pac. Isl.	0	0.0	1	0.2	1	0.1	0	0.0	0	0.0	1	0.1	1
2 or more races	0	0.0	0	0.0	0	0.0	0	0.0	0	0.0	0	0.0	0
Subtotal (minor.)	93	17.2	140	29.3	184	22.2	49	25.5	72	24.1	233	22.8	70
Nonres. Alien	6	1.1	12	2.5	17	2.1	1	0.5	2	0.7	18	1.8	3
White/Cauc.	367	67.7	290	60.7	536	64.7	121	63.0	201	67.2	657	64.4	216
Unknown	76	14.0	36	7.5	91	11.0	21	10.9	24	8.0	112	11.0	30
Total	542	53.1	478	46.9	828	81.2	192	18.8	299	29.3	1020		319

Transfers

Transfers in	18
Transfers out	17

Tuition and Fees

	Resident	Nonresident
Full-time	$41,690	$41,690
Part-time	$27,250	$27,250
Tuition Guarantee Program		Y

Living Expenses

Estimated living expenses for singles

Living on campus	Living off campus	Living at home
$24,500	$24,500	$24,500

DEPAUL UNIVERSITY COLLEGE OF LAW

*ABA
Approved
Since
1925*

GPA and LSAT Scores

	Total	Full-Time	Part-Time
# of apps	4,743	4,166	577
# of offers	2,000	1,807	193
# of matrics	298	247	51
75% GPA	3.58	3.59	3.57
Median GPA	3.42	3.42	3.44
25% GPA	3.13	3.13	3.02
75% LSAT	160	160	158
Median LSAT	158	158	154
25% LSAT	154	155	151

Grants and Scholarships (from prior year)

	Total		Full-Time		Part-Time	
	#	%	#	%	#	%
Total # of students	1,056		853		203	
Total # receiving grants	961	91.0	799	93.7	162	79.8
Less than 1/2 tuition	833	78.9	673	78.9	160	78.8
Half to full tuition	128	12.1	126	14.8	2	1.0
Full tuition	0	0.0	0	0.0	0	0.0
More than full tuition	0	0.0	0	0.0	0	0.0
Median grant amount			$15,000		$4,000	

Informational and Library Resources

Total amount spent on library materials	$1,189,572
Study seating capacity inside the library	510
# of full-time equivalent professional librarians	8
Hours per week library is open	94
# of open, wired connections available to students	20
# of networked computers available for use by students	180
Has wireless network?	Y
Requires computer?	N

JD Attrition (from prior year)

	Academic	Other	Total	
	#	#	#	%
1st year	13	20	33	10.6
2nd year	0	1	1	0.3
3rd year	0	0	0	0.0
4th year	0	0	0	0.0

Employment (9 months after graduation)

For up-to-date employment data, go to
employmentsummary.abaquestionnaire.org on the ABA website.

Bar Passage Rates

First-time takers	288	Reporting %	92.01
Average school %	89.81	Average state %	89.38
Average pass difference	.43		

Jurisdiction	Takers	Passers	Pass %	State %	Diff %
Illinois	265	238	89.81	89.38	0.43

DEPAUL UNIVERSITY COLLEGE OF LAW

25 East Jackson Boulevard
Chicago, IL 60604-2219
Phone: 312.362.6831 or 800.428.7453; Fax: 312.362.5280
E-mail: lawinfo@depaul.edu; Website: www.law.depaul.edu

Introduction

DePaul University College of Law is centered in the heart of downtown Chicago, providing its students with a rich and dynamic urban setting. DePaul University is the nation's largest Catholic University and the ninth largest private university, as well as Illinois' largest private university. The College of Law is fully accredited by the ABA, is a member of AALS and Order of the Coif, and offers full-time, part-time, and summer programs. Its location—centered within the city's business and legal communities—provides students with extensive contact with Chicago's legal community, and students gain access to a national law alumni network of more than 14,000 strong. The law school is within walking distance of the state and federal courts, a variety of government offices, and numerous corporations and law firms. DePaul law graduates reside in all 50 states and in more than 20 countries, and among them are three former mayors of Chicago, more than 350 state and federal judges, and numerous CEOs, CFOs, executives, and partners at corporations and law firms worldwide.

Students

DePaul University was founded in 1898 by the Vincentian Fathers as a school for children of immigrants. Its students represent a rich diversity in age, ethnicity, education, and career experiences. This broad diversity of backgrounds and knowledge provides a connectedness within the institution, creating a genuine sense of community among the students, faculty, and staff. The average age of the entering class is 24 and is comprised of 50 percent women and 24 percent minorities. Forty-five percent of the full-time class is from out of state.

Faculty

DePaul faculty members are recognized scholars who represent a variety of professional backgrounds and specialties. Consistent with the university's Vincentian mission of service to the community, they work tirelessly in service to the legal profession and to the community and have achieved national recognition in teaching, research, scholarly activities, and professional service. They are extremely accessible, approachable, and deeply committed to the success of their students.

Library, Publications, Research Centers, and Institutes

The College of Law's three-story law library offers extensive resources for study and research. Its staff includes 7 professional librarians and 12 full-time support staff, and it is open year-round.

DePaul offers writing, publishing, and editing opportunities through seven student-edited law journals and a traditional law review that explore issues in nearly every area and specialization of the law, including business and commercial law; art, technology, and intellectual property law; health care law; social justice; sports law; women, gender, and the law; and rule of law.

The College of Law also maintains 15 research centers and institutes dedicated to teaching, research, advocacy, student placement, and public education and engagement across a wide range of disciplines:

- Health Law Institute
- International Aviation Law Institute
- International Human Rights Law Institute
- International Weapons Control Center
- Asian Legal Studies Institute
- Schiller DuCanto and Fleck Family Law Center
- Center for Intellectual Property Law and Information Technology
- Center for Justice in Capital Cases
- Center for Animal Law
- Center for Public Interest Law
- Center for Dispute Resolution
- Center for Advocacy and Dispute Resolution
- Center for Art, Museum, and Cultural Heritage Law
- Center for Jewish Law and Judaic Studies
- Center for Church-State Studies

Special Programs

Academic Support Program: DePaul considers the success of every student paramount to its success as a law school. For more than a decade, the law school's Academic Support Program has helped first-year students develop the critical thinking and analytical skills that law school demands.

Bar Passage Program: Through a series of workshops, DePaul's Bar Passage Program ensures that graduating students are aware of the rigors of this all-encompassing exam and learn how to prepare for it academically, financially, and emotionally.

Clinical Programs: Since 1977, students have gained valuable hands-on experience through the college's now 10 clinical concentrations: Advanced Immigrant Detainee, Asylum/Immigration, Civil Rights Law, Criminal Appeals, Death Penalty, Family Law, Misdemeanor, Poverty Law, Special Education Advocacy, Technology/Intellectual Property, and starting spring 2012, a new concentration in Housing Law.

Field Placement Program: With more than 3,500 placements in the past 36 years, DePaul's Field Placement Program provides academic credit through supervised fieldwork with federal and state judges, various municipal agencies, and a number of nonprofit and for-profit organizations.

Certificate Programs: DePaul recognizes the growing integration of legal issues in nearly every professional field and offers 11 comprehensive certificate programs to help students develop specific professional and legal expertise in Business Law, Child and Family Law, Criminal Law, Health Law, International and Comparative Law, Public Interest Law, Taxation, and four in Intellectual Property Law (General, Arts and Museum, Information Technology, and Patents).

Study Abroad: DePaul offers unique immersion experiences that focus on international legal issues ranging from financial transactions to employment law to human rights, while providing students with an opportunity to learn about the history and culture of another country:

- Beijing, China: International Transactions in the Asia-Pacific Region

- Buenos Aires, Argentina: Legal Dimensions of Doing Business in Latin America
- Chiapas, Mexico: Human Rights Practicum
- Heredia, Costa Rica: Human Rights Law in the Americas
- Madrid, Spain: European Business and Commercial Law and Human Rights Law
- Prague, Czech Republic, and Vienna, Austria: Global Employment Law and Business Organizations
- Sorrento, Italy: Comparative Constitutional Law, International Law, and International Dispute Resolution

Joint-Degree and Master of Laws (LLM) Programs:
DePaul offers four joint-degree and four master of laws (LLM) programs:

- JD/MBA with DePaul's nationally recognized Kellstadt Graduate School of Business
- JD/MS in Public Service Management promotes effective management of government and nonprofit organizations
- JD/MA in International Studies offers concentrations in International Political Economy and Global Culture and complements DePaul's strong international law offerings
- JD/MS in Computer Science explores the intersections of law, computer science, telecommunications, and information systems
- DePaul's master of laws (LLM) programs include Health Law, Intellectual Property Law, International Law, and Taxation
- Specialized First-Year Legal Writing Sections: Applicants may apply for a seat in one of three specialized sections of Legal Analysis, Research, and Communication, which focus on child and family law, intellectual property law, or public interest law.

Housing

Located in Chicago's Loop just two blocks south of the law school, University Center is a recently developed residence hall offering furnished apartments and suites. Amenities include a rooftop garden, multimedia rooms, a fitness center, food court, laundry facilities, shops on the lower level, 24-hour security, and keycard access to the building and elevators.

Admission

DePaul adheres to a policy of nondiscrimination and encourages applications from traditionally underrepresented groups. Admission decisions are based on a variety of factors, and each file is reviewed thoroughly. Undergraduate GPA and LSAT scores are significant admission criteria. For the 2011–2012 academic year, 4,228 candidates applied for admission to the full-time program, and 589 applied to the part-time program. Admitted students are automatically considered for available merit-based scholarships.

Career Services

DePaul's Law Career Services Office is dedicated to the needs of law students and offers valuable assets such as one-on-one career counseling, job fairs, résumé and cover letter reviews, and exhaustive online job postings for students and alumni.

APPLICANT PROFILE

DePaul University College of Law
This grid includes only applicants who earned 120–180 LSAT scores under standard administrations.

LSAT Score	3.75 +		3.50–3.74		3.25–3.49		3.00–3.24		2.75–2.99		2.50–2.74		2.25–2.49		2.00–2.24		Below 2.00		No GPA		Total	
	Apps	Adm	Apps	Adm	Apps	Adm	Apps	Adm	Apps	Adm	Apps	Adm	Apps	Adm	Apps	Adm	Apps	Adm	Apps	Adm	Apps	Adm
175–180	0	0	2	1	1	1	1	1	0	0	2	1	0	0	1	0	0	0	0	0	7	4
170–174	5	5	10	9	13	11	9	9	8	8	4	3	4	3	1	1	0	0	0	0	54	49
165–169	48	46	62	62	63	60	33	32	29	27	12	10	10	9	0	0	1	0	1	1	259	247
160–164	148	146	194	192	209	203	143	136	82	79	48	44	27	23	11	8	0	0	10	8	872	839
155–159	167	143	300	242	326	114	273	54	139	22	68	4	34	0	16	1	2	0	17	5	1342	585
150–154	104	52	208	94	290	54	256	18	145	3	82	0	37	0	8	0	0	0	22	3	1152	224
145–149	44	13	101	16	149	7	144	2	87	4	74	0	30	0	15	0	4	0	14	1	662	43
120–144	14	0	27	0	59	0	92	1	80	0	67	0	46	0	24	0	7	0	24	0	440	1
Total	530	405	904	616	1110	450	951	253	570	143	357	62	188	35	76	10	14	0	88	18	4788	1992

Apps = Number of Applicants
Adm = Number Admitted
Reflects 99% of the total applicant pool; highest LSAT data reported.

UNIVERSITY OF DETROIT MERCY SCHOOL OF LAW

Admissions Office, 651 East Jefferson Avenue
Detroit, MI 48226
Phone: 313.596.0264
E-mail: udmlawao@udmercy.edu; Website: www.law.udmercy.edu

ABA
Approved
Since
1933

The Basics

Type of school	Private
Term	Semester
Application deadline	4/15
Application fee	$50
Financial aid deadline	4/1
Can first year start other than fall?	No
Student to faculty ratio	17.3 to 1
# of housing spaces available restricted to law students	
graduate housing for which law students are eligible	

Faculty and Administrators

	Total		Men		Women		Minorities	
	Spr	Fall	Spr	Fall	Spr	Fall	Spr	Fall
Full-time	31	31	14	13	17	18	3	4
Other full-time	6	6	5	5	1	1	0	0
Deans, librarians, & others who teach	11	10	7	7	4	3	0	0
Part-time	39	38	27	24	12	14	4	2
Total	87	85	53	49	34	36	7	6

JD Enrollment and Ethnicity

	Men		Women		Full-Time		Part-Time		1st-Year		Total		JD Degs. Awd.
	#	%	#	%	#	%	#	%	#	%	#	%	
All Hispanics	2	0.6	14	4.5	13	2.3	3	2.7	3	1.4	16	2.4	8
Am. Ind./AK Nat.	0	0.0	1	0.3	1	0.2	0	0.0	0	0.0	1	0.1	2
Asian	10	2.8	13	4.2	17	3.1	6	5.3	6	2.7	23	3.4	5
Black/Af. Am.	31	8.7	38	12.1	45	8.1	24	21.2	14	6.4	69	10.3	22
Nat. HI/Pac. Isl.	0	0.0	0	0.0	0	0.0	0	0.0	0	0.0	0	0.0	0
2 or more races	0	0.0	0	0.0	0	0.0	0	0.0	0	0.0	0	0.0	0
Subtotal (minor.)	43	12.1	66	21.1	76	13.7	33	29.2	23	10.5	109	16.3	37
Nonres. Alien	85	23.9	72	23.0	157	28.2	0	0.0	70	32.0	157	23.5	41
White/Cauc.	228	64.0	175	55.9	323	58.1	80	70.8	126	57.5	403	60.2	132
Unknown	0	0.0	0	0.0	0	0.0	0	0.0	0	0.0	0	0.0	0
Total	356	53.2	313	46.8	556	83.1	113	16.9	219	32.7	669		210

Curriculum

	Full-Time	Part-Time
Typical first-year section size	72	51
Is there typically a "small section" of the first-year class, other than Legal Writing, taught by full-time faculty	No	No
If yes, typical size offered last year		
# of classroom course titles beyond first-year curriculum	203	

# of upper division courses, excluding seminars, with an enrollment:		
Under 25	119	
25–49	56	
50–74	12	
75–99	0	
100+	0	

# of seminars	13	
# of seminar positions available	208	
# of seminar positions filled	119	35
# of positions available in simulation courses	828	
# of simulation positions filled	536	139
# of positions available in faculty supervised clinical courses	238	
# of faculty supervised clinical positions filled	170	45
# involved in field placements	89	19
# involved in law journals	50	4
# involved in moot court or trial competitions	67	7
# of credit hours required to graduate	90	

Transfers

Transfers in	0
Transfers out	25

Tuition and Fees

	Resident	Nonresident
Full-time	$36,050	$36,050
Part-time	$28,856	$28,856
Tuition Guarantee Program	N	

Living Expenses

Estimated living expenses for singles

Living on campus	Living off campus	Living at home
N/A	$21,606	$13,762

UNIVERSITY OF DETROIT MERCY SCHOOL OF LAW

ABA Approved Since 1933

GPA and LSAT Scores

	Total	Full-Time	Part-Time
# of apps	1,461	1,305	156
# of offers	627	570	57
# of matrics	223	189	34
75% GPA	3.40	3.38	3.59
Median GPA	3.16	3.13	3.28
25% GPA	2.92	2.91	3.01
75% LSAT	156	156	152
Median LSAT	152	153	147
25% LSAT	147	149	145

Grants and Scholarships (from prior year)

	Total		Full-Time		Part-Time	
	#	%	#	%	#	%
Total # of students	727		572		155	
Total # receiving grants	184	25.3	153	26.7	31	20.0
Less than 1/2 tuition	160	22.0	133	23.3	27	17.4
Half to full tuition	23	3.2	19	3.3	4	2.6
Full tuition	0	0.0	0	0.0	0	0.0
More than full tuition	1	0.1	1	0.2	0	0.0
Median grant amount			$8,000		$3,000	

Informational and Library Resources

Total amount spent on library materials	$1,548,156
Study seating capacity inside the library	265
# of full-time equivalent professional librarians	5
Hours per week library is open	92
# of open, wired connections available to students	15
# of networked computers available for use by students	28
Has wireless network?	Y
Requires computer?	N

JD Attrition (from prior year)

	Academic	Other	Total	
	#	#	#	%
1st year	13	45	58	21.2
2nd year	0	1	1	0.5
3rd year	0	0	0	0.0
4th year	0	0	0	0.0

Employment (9 months after graduation)

For up-to-date employment data, go to employmentsummary.abaquestionnaire.org on the ABA website.

Bar Passage Rates

First-time takers	155	Reporting %	74.84
Average school %	77.59	Average state %	84.83
Average pass difference	–7.24		

Jurisdiction	Takers	Passers	Pass %	State %	Diff %
Michigan	116	90	77.59	84.83	–7.24

UNIVERSITY OF DETROIT MERCY SCHOOL OF LAW

Admissions Office, 651 East Jefferson Avenue
Detroit, MI 48226
Phone: 313.596.0264
E-mail: udmlawao@udmercy.edu; Website: www.law.udmercy.edu

Introduction

Founded in 1912, the University of Detroit Mercy School of Law (UDM Law) is a private law school in downtown Detroit sponsored by the Society of Jesus (Jesuits) and the Sisters of Mercy of the Americas. Located opposite the General Motors headquarters in the Renaissance Center, the School is within walking distance of federal and state courts, downtown law firms, and Detroit's municipal center. Windsor, Ontario, Canada, is a five-minute drive by tunnel or bridge across the Detroit River. Metropolitan Detroit not only offers renowned cultural institutions like the Detroit Institute of Art and the Detroit Opera House, but provides a distinctive setting for the study of contemporary legal issues such as energy and the environment, immigration, global transactions, and complex corporate transactions.

UDM Law offers a comprehensive legal education through day and evening programs that incorporate a broad array of required and elective courses to prepare practice-ready graduates. The School is approved by the ABA and is a member of the AALS.

Law School Campus

UDM Law's historic campus features completely renovated classrooms and common areas with wireless access, administrative and student service offices, a bookstore, a cafeteria, and student organization offices, all located within the law school complex. The School's Kresge Law Library contains comfortable individual and group study, reading, and computer areas. The library houses more than 340,000 volumes and serves as a federal depository.

Curriculum

UDM Law offers a three-year, full-time program and day and evening part-time programs leading to the JD degree. Required courses include Applied Legal Theory and Analysis, Basic Federal Tax, Civil Procedure, Constitutional Law, Contracts, Criminal Law, Evidence, Professional Responsibility, Property, Torts, Law Firm Program courses, an international or comparative law course, a clinic, and a seminar.

Applied Legal Theory and Analysis immerses first-year students in the fundamental lawyering skills of communication, research, legal analysis and reasoning, and problem-solving. In its Law Firm Program courses, third-year students receive work assignments, feedback, and professional skills development as if they were first-year lawyers in law firms, government agencies, and other legal settings. Law Firm Program courses focus on a substantive area of the law or a type of practice. The School's Law Firm Program includes more than 20 courses in areas such as Bankruptcy, Environmental Law, Floor Financing, Health Law, Immigration Law, International Arbitration, Software Licensing, and Toxic Torts.

UDM Law's legal education program offers several clinical opportunities: Appellate Advocacy Clinic through the State Appellate Defender Office, Consumer Defense Clinic, Criminal Trial Clinic, Immigration Law Clinic, Juvenile Law Appellate Clinic, Mediation Training and Mediation Clinic,

Mortgage Foreclosure Defense Clinic, Urban Law Clinic, US Court of Appeals for Veterans Claims Practice and Procedure Clinic, Veterans Clinic, Youth Justice Clinic, and a wide array of externships. UDM's Mobile Law Offices have taken the clinic's immigration, veterans, and other services beyond the campus and into the community.

Special Programs

- **Dual Canadian and American JD**—The School of Law and the University of Windsor Faculty of Law offer a unique Dual JD program designed to educate students to understand the legal doctrines and cultures of the United States and Canada. Students complete 60 credits at UDM and 44 credits at Windsor. Most required courses taken at both law schools cover US and Canadian law relevant to the subject areas. The program enables the successful student to obtain an American Bar Association-approved Juris Doctor (JD) from UDM Law and the Canadian JD from Windsor.
- **JD/LED**—The University of Detroit Mercy School of Law (UDM) and the Instituto Tecnológico y de Estudios Superiores de Monterrey (ITESM), Mexico's leading private law school, have partnered to offer the Degree of the Americas program, a multiple-degree program that allows students bilingual in Spanish and English to earn law degrees in three countries: the United States, Mexico, and Canada. Students enrolled in this program can earn two (JD/LED) or three (Dual Canadian and American JD/LED) degrees in less time than would be required for each degree pursued independently.
- **Joint JD/MBA**—The School of Law and the College of Business Administration collaborate to offer an integrated degree program leading to the JD and MBA degrees. Students enrolled in the joint-degree program can earn both degrees in significantly less time than would be required for degrees pursued independently. Students are first admitted to and attend law school. At the end of the first year of law school, students apply to the joint-degree program.
- **Intellectual Property Law Institute**—Through a consortium with other law schools, UDM Law offers a wide variety of courses in intellectual property such as Copyright Law, Patent Law, Computer Law, Entertainment Law, and others.
- **French Scholar Program**—The School of Law participates in a professional exchange program with the Universite d'Auvergne Clermont-Ferrand. French scholars visiting the law school each spring teach a comparative law course in English while UDM Law alumni teach at Clermont-Ferrand.
- **Special Summer Program (SSP)**—UDM Law offers this conditional admission program for applicants who do not meet the minimum standards for admission, but who show potential for the study of law. This seven-week program, beginning in late May, requires students to demonstrate ability in the study of substantive law, legal writing, and research in order to be eligible for admission as a regular student in the fall semester.

Student Organizations and Activities

The School of Law's students edit and publish the *Law Review*, a quarterly publication of scholarly articles.

A student **Moot Court Board of Advocacy** administers the School of Law's Keenan and Professional Responsibility competitions; participates in state, regional, and national competitions in first amendment law, ethics, and other areas; and helps to administer the G. Mennen Williams mandatory moot court competition for first-year students. In 2009, UDM Law's Moot Court team won the first national invitational moot court competition.

The **Student Bar Association (SBA)**, affiliated with the Law Student Division of the American Bar Association, plays a significant role in student affairs. As the student government of the school, the SBA authorizes other student organizations, including the Black Law Student Association, the Environmental Law Society, Phi Alpha Delta, St. Thomas More Society, the Women's Law Caucus, the Arab and Chaldean Law Student Association, the Sports and Entertainment Law Society, and many others. Students also regularly publish a student newsletter, *In Brief*.

Career Services

The School's Career Services Office provides students with a wide range of opportunities through which they may explore career paths in law. The Office sponsors a Preparing to Practice series for upper-class students that introduces them to a variety of practice areas and issues. The Career Services staff provide career counseling services, including résumé and cover letter review. The Office administers the school's annual on-campus interview programs, maintains multiple job information resources, sponsors a mock interview program for first-year students, and hosts numerous networking events to acquaint students with practitioners.

Admission

UDM Law encourages applicants to submit an application for admission by April 15. The Admission Committee considers all elements of an application, including undergraduate grade-point average, Law School Admission Test scores, writing skills, leadership and maturity as evidenced by work and service experiences, graduate work, letters of recommendation, and the personal statement. The Committee reviews applications as they become complete on a continuous basis and communicates decisions as early as possible. The Scholarship Committee considers all admitted applicants for scholarship eligibility. The School awards a significant number of renewable and nonrenewable scholarships to incoming first-year students.

The University of Detroit Mercy and the School of Law adhere to nondiscrimination policies.

APPLICANT PROFILE

University of Detroit Mercy School of Law
This grid includes only applicants who earned 120–180 LSAT scores under standard administrations.

LSAT Score	3.75 +		3.50–3.74		3.25–3.49		3.00–3.24		2.75–2.99		2.50–2.74		2.25–2.49		2.00–2.24		Below 2.00		No GPA		Total	
	Apps	Adm	Apps	Adm	Apps	Adm	Apps	Adm	Apps	Adm	Apps	Adm	Apps	Adm	Apps	Adm	Apps	Adm	Apps	Adm	Apps	Adm
175–180	0	0	0	0	0	0	0	0	0	0	0	0	0	0	0	0	0	0	0	0	0	0
170–174	0	0	0	0	0	0	0	0	0	0	0	0	0	0	0	0	0	0	1	1	1	1
165–169	2	0	3	1	2	1	1	0	1	1	0	0	4	3	0	0	0	0	15	10	28	16
160–164	5	3	4	3	3	3	7	7	7	4	3	2	3	2	1	1	0	0	47	33	80	58
155–159	7	6	15	13	43	40	35	26	23	19	19	12	3	2	2	1	0	0	95	60	242	179
150–154	11	9	34	28	39	34	42	33	40	30	26	19	9	7	6	2	2	0	73	11	282	173
145–149	9	8	24	20	56	43	57	41	50	23	38	12	29	3	10	1	1	0	47	0	321	151
140–144	4	3	24	11	38	12	44	9	45	6	32	0	20	0	11	0	8	0	33	2	259	43
135–139	4	0	9	0	15	0	17	0	26	0	13	0	11	0	11	0	1	0	20	0	127	0
130–134	0	0	2	0	2	0	3	0	4	0	7	0	7	0	4	0	1	0	8	0	38	0
125–129	0	0	0	0	0	0	1	0	1	0	2	0	1	0	3	0	0	0	1	0	9	0
120–124	0	0	0	0	0	0	0	0	1	0	0	0	1	0	0	0	0	0	1	0	3	0
Total	42	29	115	76	198	133	207	116	198	83	140	45	88	17	48	5	13	0	341	117	1390	621

Apps = Number of Applicants
Adm = Number Admitted
Reflects 99% of the total applicant pool; highest LSAT data reported.

UNIVERSITY OF THE DISTRICT OF COLUMBIA—DAVID A. CLARKE SCHOOL OF LAW

4200 Connecticut Avenue NW, Building 52
Washington, DC 20008
Phone: 202.274.7341; Fax: 202.274.5583
E-mail: lawadmission@udc.edu; Website: www.law.udc.edu

ABA
Approved
Since
1991

The Basics

Type of school	Public
Term	Semester
Application deadline	3/15
Application fee	$35
Financial aid deadline	3/31
Can first year start other than fall?	No
Student to faculty ratio	12.9 to 1
# of housing spaces available restricted to law students	
graduate housing for which law students are eligible	

Faculty and Administrators

	Total		Men		Women		Minorities	
	Spr	Fall	Spr	Fall	Spr	Fall	Spr	Fall
Full-time	20	20	11	10	9	10	10	10
Other full-time	0	0	0	0	0	0	0	0
Deans, librarians, & others who teach	3	3	1	1	2	2	1	1
Part-time	22	23	10	9	12	14	16	15
Total	45	46	22	20	23	26	27	26

Curriculum

	Full-Time	Part-Time
Typical first-year section size	90	40
Is there typically a "small section" of the first-year class, other than Legal Writing, taught by full-time faculty	Yes	No
If yes, typical size offered last year	45	

# of classroom course titles beyond first-year curriculum		54
# of upper division courses, excluding seminars, with an enrollment:	Under 25	31
	25–49	16
	50–74	3
	75–99	4
	100+	0
# of seminars		12
# of seminar positions available		238
# of seminar positions filled	238	0
# of positions available in simulation courses		40
# of simulation positions filled	40	0
# of positions available in faculty supervised clinical courses		181
# of faculty supervised clinical positions filled	173	8
# involved in field placements	11	0
# involved in law journals	42	0
# involved in moot court or trial competitions	2	0
# of credit hours required to graduate		90

JD Enrollment and Ethnicity

	Men		Women		Full-Time		Part-Time		1st-Year		Total		JD Degs. Awd.
	#	%	#	%	#	%	#	%	#	%	#	%	
All Hispanics	12	8.0	19	9.1	28	11.1	3	2.8	10	7.8	31	8.6	10
Am. Ind./AK Nat.	1	0.7	0	0.0	0	0.0	1	0.9	1	0.8	1	0.3	1
Asian	10	6.7	17	8.1	18	7.1	9	8.4	9	7.0	27	7.5	4
Black/Af. Am.	46	30.7	59	28.2	68	27.0	37	34.6	34	26.4	105	29.2	21
Nat. HI/Pac. Isl.	0	0.0	0	0.0	0	0.0	0	0.0	0	0.0	0	0.0	0
2 or more races	3	2.0	8	3.8	7	2.8	4	3.7	5	3.9	11	3.1	0
Subtotal (minor.)	72	48.0	103	49.3	121	48.0	54	50.5	59	45.7	175	48.7	36
Nonres. Alien	0	0.0	0	0.0	0	0.0	0	0.0	0	0.0	0	0.0	0
White/Cauc.	60	40.0	81	38.8	105	41.7	36	33.6	42	32.6	141	39.3	40
Unknown	18	12.0	25	12.0	26	10.3	17	15.9	28	21.7	43	12.0	2
Total	150	41.8	209	58.2	252	70.2	107	29.8	129	35.9	359		78

Transfers

Transfers in	8
Transfers out	15

Tuition and Fees

	Resident	Nonresident
Full-time	$9,480	$18,330
Part-time	$7,230	$13,830
Tuition Guarantee Program	N	

Living Expenses

Estimated living expenses for singles

Living on campus	Living off campus	Living at home
N/A	$31,059	$15,075

UNIVERSITY OF THE DISTRICT OF COLUMBIA—DAVID A. CLARKE SCHOOL OF LAW

ABA
Approved
Since
1991

GPA and LSAT Scores

	Total	Full-Time	Part-Time
# of apps	1,643	1,248	395
# of offers	427	332	95
# of matrics	131	82	49
75% GPA	3.28	3.28	3.34
Median GPA	3.02	3.10	3.01
25% GPA	2.76	2.78	2.76
75% LSAT	155	154	155
Median LSAT	153	152	153
25% LSAT	151	150	150

Grants and Scholarships (from prior year)

	Total #	Total %	Full-Time #	Full-Time %	Part-Time #	Part-Time %
Total # of students	316		256		60	
Total # receiving grants	165	52.2	131	51.2	34	56.7
Less than 1/2 tuition	69	21.8	53	20.7	16	26.7
Half to full tuition	66	20.9	54	21.1	12	20.0
Full tuition	30	9.5	24	9.4	6	10.0
More than full tuition	0	0.0	0	0.0	0	0.0
Median grant amount			$3,000		$2,500	

Informational and Library Resources

Total amount spent on library materials	$725,851
Study seating capacity inside the library	230
# of full-time equivalent professional librarians	8
Hours per week library is open	102
# of open, wired connections available to students	14
# of networked computers available for use by students	17
Has wireless network?	Y
Requires computer?	Y

JD Attrition (from prior year)

	Academic #	Other #	Total #	Total %
1st year	5	21	26	20.6
2nd year	0	0	0	0.0
3rd year	0	0	0	0.0
4th year	0	0	0	0.0

Employment (9 months after graduation)

For up-to-date employment data, go to
employmentsummary.abaquestionnaire.org on the ABA website.

Bar Passage Rates

First-time takers	78	Reporting %	76.92
Average school %	50.00	Average state %	77.21

Average pass difference −27.21

Jurisdiction	Takers	Passers	Pass %	State %	Diff %
Maryland	30	12	40.00	79.96	−39.96
District of Columbia	12	9	75.00	64.93	10.07
Virginia	11	6	54.55	78.15	−23.60
New York	7	3	42.86	84.92	−42.06

UNIVERSITY OF THE DISTRICT OF COLUMBIA—DAVID A. CLARKE SCHOOL OF LAW

4200 Connecticut Avenue NW, Building 52
Washington, DC 20008
Phone: 202.274.7341; Fax: 202.274.5583
E-mail: lawadmission@udc.edu; Website: www.law.udc.edu

Introduction

In 1986, the District of Columbia Council authorized the establishment of the District of Columbia School of Law. The council created a dual mission for the School of Law and charged its Board of Governors with a mandate to recruit and enroll, to the degree feasible, students from ethnic, racial, or other population groups that in the past had been underrepresented among persons admitted to the bar. It also charged the board with representing the legal needs of low-income persons, particularly those who reside in the District of Columbia.

The DC School of Law, the only publicly funded law school in Washington, DC, merged with the University of the District of Columbia (UDC) in 1996 and became the University of the District of Columbia School of Law. In April 1998, the UDC School of Law was named the UDC David A. Clarke School of Law (UDC-DCSL). The law school operates full-time day and part-time evening divisions leading to the JD degree as well as an LLM program.

Physical Facilities and Library

In 2011, the School of Law moved to a new spacious 100,000-square-foot five-story building, located about a block from the UDC's Van Ness campus in the upper northwest section of Washington, DC. The School of Law is in a neighborhood known for its harmonious blend of residences, businesses, embassies, and the Rock Creek Park.

The law library is a teaching-, research-, and practice-oriented library. It contains more than 257,000 volumes and volume equivalents. The law library expands its collection on an ongoing basis, with an emphasis on reference and scholarly materials that support legal education and the clinical programs. The library's online catalog is available at http://catalog.law.udc.edu/search.

The Charles N. and Hilda H. M. Mason Law Library is a beautiful and modern facility that provides the traditional and high-tech resources required for today's study of the law. In addition, the Internet and law library resources are accessible via the law library's wireless LAN throughout the law library and the School of Law.

The university and law school campuses are conveniently located on the Metro's Red Line at the UDC/Van Ness subway stop.

Curriculum

Consistent with UDC School of Law's mission, the basic program is designed to provide a well-rounded theoretical and practical legal education that will enable students to be effective and ethical advocates, and to represent the legal needs of low-income residents through the school's legal clinics.

Full-time and part-time first-year students participate in New Student Orientation, which introduces them to the study of law and to the School of Law community. During orientation, students take Law and Justice, a course which introduces legal, political, social, and philosophical aspects of poverty and inequality in American society. They also take Lawyering Process I. Students participate in the Dean's

Reception and in other events planned by the Dean of Students and student organizations.

In the first year, students must complete 40 hours of community service and take a prescribed program consisting of required courses and one elective course. After the first year, students must also take courses in Evidence, Constitutional Law I and II, Professional Responsibility, and Moot Court. Each UDC-DCSL student is required to produce significant pieces of writing each of the three or four years of study. The School of Law offers summer courses, mandatory clinics, and an internship program; it does not allow early graduation.

While the emphasis of the school is on public interest law, the overall curriculum—clinic and classroom—provides the skills necessary to pursue any field of law.

Clinical Program

Students are required to complete two, seven-credit clinics during their second and third years. The clinics offered in the 2011–2012 academic year were Housing and Consumer Law, HIV/AIDS Law, Juvenile and Special Education Law, Legislation, Government Accountability Project, Community Development Law and Small Business, Low-Income Taxpayers, and Immigration and Human Rights.

Academic Support and Summer Program

UDC-DCSL considers academic support to be an integral part of its course of study. Students in academic difficulty at the end of their first semester may apply to the enhanced program, which may involve adjusting courseloads, taking a legal reasoning course, counseling, and group and individual tutoring. In addition, faculty members hold extra review sessions during the semester in required courses and provide sample examination questions with model answers.

The School of Law offers the Mason Enhancement Program for Academic Success, a four-week conditional-admission summer program, to selected entering students.

Internship Program

Students in the second and third year may elect to do a four- or ten-credit internship, where they may work in federal or local government agencies; judicial, legislative, or congressional offices; or in public interest legal organizations. Students are required to attend a weekly internship seminar at the school. The School of Law emphasizes the importance of supervision, educational merit, and public service in each internship. Students may also participate in the Summer Public Interest Fellowship program.

Admission

Admission is based upon academic and nonacademic achievements and professional promise. UDC-DCSL considers the applicant's LSAT score and grades in tandem with other criteria that it believes may provide a more accurate measure of a candidate's determination, commitment, and potential for success in the study of law. The Admission Committee also considers other submitted application materials, such as the personal statement and essays, recommendations, community service, and employment experience. Applicants are encouraged to contact the Admission Office or to visit www.law.udc.edu for information about visiting the School of Law, sitting in on a class, and attending one of the Law Day-Open House programs or Information Sessions.

Financial Assistance and Scholarships

The financial aid policy provides students with financial assistance to support full-time and part-time study. This is usually accomplished through a combination of scholarships, grants, and loans. These include merit- and need-based scholarships, the Federal Direct unsubsidized and GradPLUS loan programs, and federal and other work-study employment. About 70 percent of UDC-DCSL students receive scholarship assistance, and 96 percent receive some form of financial aid. Detailed information about financial aid application policies and procedures is available on the School of Law's website.

Student Activities

The first issue of the annual *District of Columbia Law Review* was published in 1992. Active student organizations include the Student Bar Association, Black Law Students Association, International Law Students Association, Voces Juridicas, OutLaw, Women's Law Society, Sports and Entertainment Student Lawyers Association, Christian Law Society, Phi Alpha Delta, Innocence Project, and the National Lawyers Guild.

Career Services

The Career Services Office provides employment information, individual career counseling, and résumé assistance to the School of Law's student body and graduates. The office maintains listings of permanent job openings, fellowships, summer clerkships, and part-time opportunities. The office also coordinates potential internship sites and invites employers to conduct on-campus interviews. The office provides resources for career planning, counseling sessions to assist students in developing their career goals, résumé workshops, and other relevant seminars.

APPLICANT PROFILE

The David A. Clarke School of Law prides itself on its admission philosophy, comprehensive and competitive admission process, and student diversity. While the applicant profile grids can be helpful to students, they may also discourage some students whose numerical profiles are slightly below the school's LSAT and GPA medians, but whose life experiences, for example, may be compelling. Numbers do not always provide an accurate picture of an applicant's potential for law study or motivation to succeed. The School of Law, therefore, does not provide an applicant profile grid, but rather a brief description of its student body. The student body is a diverse and accomplished group. The age range of students is 20 to 61 years. The average age is

28 years. People of color comprise about half of the student body, and women comprise more than half of the students. More than 34 states and over 120 undergraduate schools are represented in the student body. The School of Law seeks to admit about 150 students to its full- and part-time divisions. Smaller class sizes provide students with an ideal student-to-faculty ratio and a rich theoretical and practical learning environment. The LSAT mean for the fall 2011 entering class was 153, and the 25th and 75th LSAT percentiles were 150 and 155, respectively. The GPA mean was 3.10. The student body represents strong contribution potential and competency for the study of law.

DRAKE UNIVERSITY LAW SCHOOL

2507 University Avenue
Des Moines, IA 50311-4505
Phone: 800.44.DRAKE, ext. 2782 or 515.271.2782; Fax: 515.271.1990
E-mail: lawadmit@drake.edu; Website: www.law.drake.edu

ABA
Approved
Since
1923

The Basics

Type of school	Private
Term	Semester
Application deadline	4/1
Application fee	$50
Financial aid deadline	3/1
Can first year start other than fall?	Yes
Student to faculty ratio	14.3 to 1
# of housing spaces available restricted to law students	
graduate housing for which law students are eligible	82

Faculty and Administrators

	Total		Men		Women		Minorities	
	Spr	Fall	Spr	Fall	Spr	Fall	Spr	Fall
Full-time	26	26	15	18	11	8	5	5
Other full-time	1	1	1	1	0	0	0	0
Deans, librarians, & others who teach	9	9	4	4	5	5	0	0
Part-time	23	21	13	13	10	8	3	1
Total	59	57	33	36	26	21	8	6

Curriculum

	Full-Time	Part-Time
Typical first-year section size	79	0
Is there typically a "small section" of the first-year class, other than Legal Writing, taught by full-time faculty	Yes	No
If yes, typical size offered last year	46	
# of classroom course titles beyond first-year curriculum	102	

# of upper division courses, excluding seminars, with an enrollment:		
	Under 25	76
	25–49	20
	50–74	9
	75–99	4
	100+	0

# of seminars	12	
# of seminar positions available	227	
# of seminar positions filled	169	0
# of positions available in simulation courses	484	
# of simulation positions filled	307	0
# of positions available in faculty supervised clinical courses	106	
# of faculty supervised clinical positions filled	106	0
# involved in field placements	138	0
# involved in law journals	77	0
# involved in moot court or trial competitions	70	0
# of credit hours required to graduate	90	

JD Enrollment and Ethnicity

	Men		Women		Full-Time		Part-Time		1st-Year		Total		JD Degs. Awd.
	#	%	#	%	#	%	#	%	#	%	#	%	
All Hispanics	9	3.8	12	5.7	21	4.8	0	0.0	9	6.1	21	4.7	3
Am. Ind./AK Nat.	0	0.0	0	0.0	0	0.0	0	0.0	0	0.0	0	0.0	0
Asian	5	2.1	3	1.4	8	1.8	0	0.0	1	0.7	8	1.8	1
Black/Af. Am.	8	3.4	10	4.8	18	4.1	0	0.0	4	2.7	18	4.0	13
Nat. HI/Pac. Isl.	0	0.0	0	0.0	0	0.0	0	0.0	0	0.0	0	0.0	0
2 or more races	2	0.8	1	0.5	3	0.7	0	0.0	1	0.7	3	0.7	0
Subtotal (minor.)	24	10.1	26	12.4	50	11.5	0	0.0	15	10.2	50	11.2	17
Nonres. Alien	0	0.0	3	1.4	0	0.0	3	23.1	3	2.0	3	0.7	0
White/Cauc.	208	87.4	172	82.3	370	85.3	10	76.9	123	83.7	380	85.0	119
Unknown	6	2.5	8	3.8	14	3.2	0	0.0	6	4.1	14	3.1	23
Total	238	53.2	209	46.8	434	97.1	13	2.9	147	32.9	447		159

Transfers

Transfers in	1
Transfers out	8

Tuition and Fees

	Resident	Nonresident
Full-time	$34,006	$34,006
Part-time		
Tuition Guarantee Program		N

Living Expenses

Estimated living expenses for singles

Living on campus	Living off campus	Living at home
N/A	$17,910	$5,205

DRAKE UNIVERSITY LAW SCHOOL

*ABA
Approved
Since
1923*

GPA and LSAT Scores

	Total	Full-Time	Part-Time
# of apps	1,000	996	30
# of offers	557	554	3
# of matrics	142	142	0
75% GPA	3.64	3.64	0.00
Median GPA	3.40	3.40	0.00
25% GPA	3.06	3.06	0.00
75% LSAT	158	158	0
Median LSAT	156	156	0
25% LSAT	153	153	0

Grants and Scholarships (from prior year)

	Total		Full-Time		Part-Time	
	#	%	#	%	#	%
Total # of students	463		451		12	
Total # receiving grants	274	59.2	274	60.8	0	0.0
Less than 1/2 tuition	148	32.0	148	32.8	0	0.0
Half to full tuition	89	19.2	89	19.7	0	0.0
Full tuition	23	5.0	23	5.1	0	0.0
More than full tuition	14	3.0	14	3.1	0	0.0
Median grant amount			$15,000		$0	

Informational and Library Resources

Total amount spent on library materials	$1,085,297
Study seating capacity inside the library	705
# of full-time equivalent professional librarians	7
Hours per week library is open	110
# of open, wired connections available to students	192
# of networked computers available for use by students	130
Has wireless network?	Y
Requires computer?	N

JD Attrition (from prior year)

	Academic	Other	Total	
	#	#	#	%
1st year	2	10	12	7.5
2nd year	0	1	1	0.7
3rd year	0	0	0	0.0
4th year	0	0	0	0.0

Employment (9 months after graduation)

For up-to-date employment data, go to
employmentsummary.abaquestionnaire.org on the ABA website.

Bar Passage Rates

First-time takers	137	Reporting %	74.45
Average school %	91.17	Average state %	90.18
Average pass difference	.99		

Jurisdiction	Takers	Passers	Pass %	State %	Diff %
Iowa	97	88	90.72	91.09	–0.37
Nevada	5	5	100.00	72.72	27.28

DRAKE UNIVERSITY LAW SCHOOL

2507 University Avenue
Des Moines, IA 50311-4505
Phone: 800.44.DRAKE, ext. 2782 or 515.271.2782; Fax: 515.271.1990
E-mail: lawadmit@drake.edu; Website: www.law.drake.edu

Introduction

Drake University Law School can trace its history back to 1865, making it one of the nation's 25 oldest law schools. Accredited by the ABA, the Law School provides a personal education with a low (14:1) student-to-faculty ratio. Our commitment to an education that balances theory and practice has earned the Law School a reputation for training proven practitioners.

Drake Law School is the only law school in Iowa's capital city. The close relationship between Drake Law School and the greater Des Moines area legal community provides students with the opportunity to get hands-on experience with the executive, judicial, and legislative branches of state government; the federal courts; federal and state administrative agencies; and a wide array of law firms and businesses.

Legal Clinic

The Drake Legal Clinic, housed in the beautiful Neal and Bea Smith Law Center, is one of the best training facilities in the country. The center operates much like a real law firm providing incomparable hands-on experience to students who participate. This state-of-the-art facility includes a technologically enhanced courtroom, office space for students, a library, and seminar rooms.

First-Year Trial Practicum

The only program of its kind in the country, the Trial Practicum adds an important experiential learning dimension to the first-year curriculum. During the spring semester, students observe an actual state court trial—from jury selection to verdict—in the courtroom of the Neal and Bea Smith Law Center. Breakout discussion groups and post-trial debriefings of the attorneys, judges, and jurors poignantly illustrate how law on the books becomes law in action.

Centers of Excellence and Certificate Programs

Agricultural Law Center—Our internationally recognized agricultural law program addresses the important issues in American and international law and policy regarding food production. Students conduct research, publish an agricultural law journal, and write articles on a wide range of topics. The center frequently hosts international agricultural law scholars who teach courses on international issues and topics such as farmland preservation, legal issues in biotechnology, and tax planning for agricultural businesses. The center also offers a series of one-week courses for students and attorneys in the Summer Agricultural Law Institute. The center offers a **Food and Agricultural Law Certificate** program, the first of its kind at an American law school.

Business Law Certificate Program—The Business Law Certificate Program is designed to guide and further the interests of students in a business or transactional practice and prepare them for careers in business law, including private practice, with state or federal agencies, or as inside counsel for private and public companies. The certificate provides formal recognition of the knowledge, experience, and skills achieved by students who complete coursework and activities related to business, commercial, and transactional practice.

Constitutional Law Center—Drake is one of only four schools selected to receive a congressional endowment for the establishment of a Constitutional Law Resource Center. The center sponsors a lecture series and annual symposia featuring nationally recognized constitutional scholars. The nationally renowned Dwight D. Opperman Lecture in Constitutional Law has been delivered by 11 current and former justices of the United States Supreme Court. The center also offers a **Constitutional Law and Civil Rights Certificate** program and conducts the Summer Institute in Constitutional Law, a program designed for first-year students interested in getting their law school careers off to an early start. Students beginning in the Summer Institute who elect to take additional summer courses may accelerate their studies and graduate in December of their third year.

Intellectual Property Law Center—Our dynamic center offers an innovative curriculum, providing students with a solid foundation in both the theoretical and practical aspects of intellectual property law. The center serves as an international research hub, fostering partnerships with leading research institutions from around the world. Every year, the center sponsors groundbreaking symposia and distinguished lectures, hosts eminent speakers and internationally recognized experts, publishes books and an occasional paper series, and develops international research and outreach programs.

Center for Legislative Practice—Drake is one of only a few schools in the country that offers a **Legislative Practice Certificate**. Classroom study and a wide range of internships expose students to the underpinnings of legislative and rule-making processes. Students who complete the program are uniquely prepared to work for administrative or government agencies, to research and draft legislation, to represent businesses and organizations with government interests, or to work in a variety of other public policy making positions. Drake's close proximity to the State Capitol and other state and federal offices, trade associations, union headquarters, and public interest group agencies provides students with numerous opportunities to learn firsthand how these institutions operate.

The **Middleton Center for Children's Rights** pursues a broad agenda, advancing children's rights through the legal process, training, public information, and public policy formation. Drake Law students learn the interdisciplinary process essential to addressing the complex issues involved in child welfare and children's rights.

The **International and Comparative Law and Human Rights Certificate** program combines coursework in Drake's international and comparative law and related course offerings with a required study-abroad experience.

Litigation and Dispute Resolution Certification—Drake Law School has achieved a well-deserved reputation for its education and training of future litigators, mediators, negotiators, and judges. Our alumni are well represented among the nation's leading trial and appellate lawyers and on both the federal and state courts. The Litigation and Dispute Resolution Certificate program capitalizes on the school's traditional strengths in advocacy and dispute resolution.

Summer in France

Add an international element to your legal education by participating in our summer program at the University of Nantes Law School in France. Classes in comparative and international law and on-site visits to European legal institutions allow you to absorb and experience another country's legal system and be better prepared to practice law in a global society.

Joint-Degree Programs

Students may combine their Juris Doctor degree with the Master of Business Administration, Master of Public Administration, or Doctor of Pharmacy degree from Drake University. Students may also combine the JD degree with a Master of Arts in Political Science or Master of Science in Agricultural Economics (in cooperation with Iowa State University); a Master of Social Work (in cooperation with the University of Iowa); a Master of Health Care Administration; or a Master of Public Health (in cooperation with Des Moines University).

Student Activities

Drake Law students participate in many student organizations and cocurricular activities. Drake students publish two journals, the *Drake Law Review* and the *Journal of Agricultural Law*. *Drake Law Review* was named among the nation's 35 most-cited legal periodicals by the courts from 2003 to 2010. Drake moot court teams consistently win regional competitions and finish strongly in national competitions. The award-winning Student Bar Association and honorary societies provide students with leadership, public service, and learning opportunities. Drake students have also formed approximately 30 organizations around their special interests, including Drake Law Women, Black Law Students Association, Asian Pacific American Law Student Association, Hispanic Latino Law Student Association, LGBT Student Association, International Law Society, Christian Legal Society, Environmental Law Society, Federalist Society, American Constitution Society, Intellectual Property Law Society, Agricultural Law Society, Alternative Dispute Resolution Society, and Business Law Society.

Networking

Drake Law School alumni practice in all 50 states and several foreign countries. The Career Development Office has a comprehensive, national alumni network set up to assist students with their career plans no matter where they want to go. Attorneys who participate in the alumni career network help students learn about the job market in their state and help ensure a smooth transition for students from law school to practice. Many area alumni also participate in our Partner's Program, which pairs first-year law students with practicing attorneys.

Career Development

The Career Development Office offers career planning and counseling services, assistance with résumés and cover letter preparation, salary and geographical employment statistics, nationwide job postings, and state bar examination information. The office also arranges interviews—both on and off campus—and exchanges job listings with over 100 other law schools around the country.

APPLICANT PROFILE

Drake University Law School
This grid includes only applicants who earned 120–180 LSAT scores under standard administrations.

LSAT Score	3.75 +		3.50–3.74		3.25–3.49		3.00–3.24		2.75–2.99		2.50–2.74		2.25–2.49		2.00–2.24		Below 2.00		No GPA		Total	
	Apps	Adm	Apps	Adm	Apps	Adm	Apps	Adm	Apps	Adm	Apps	Adm	Apps	Adm	Apps	Adm	Apps	Adm	Apps	Adm	Apps	Adm
175–180	0	0	0	0	0	0	0	0	0	0	0	0	0	0	0	0	0	0	0	0	0	0
170–174	1	1	4	4	0	0	0	0	1	1	0	0	0	0	0	0	0	0	0	0	6	6
165–169	9	8	5	5	0	0	1	1	1	1	0	0	2	2	0	0	0	0	0	0	18	17
160–164	34	33	17	17	20	19	15	14	5	5	3	2	3	2	2	1	1	1	0	0	100	94
155–159	33	32	67	65	69	65	38	36	28	26	15	10	7	1	9	3	0	0	0	0	266	238
150–154	37	25	66	51	67	42	68	32	49	14	21	5	8	0	4	0	1	0	4	3	325	172
145–149	19	5	31	8	35	7	39	1	26	1	21	0	5	0	3	0	0	0	3	2	182	24
140–144	4	0	7	0	13	0	11	1	17	1	7	0	7	0	3	0	2	0	1	0	72	2
135–139	1	1	2	0	2	0	3	0	4	0	1	0	2	0	3	0	0	0	1	0	19	1
130–134	0	0	1	0	0	0	2	0	2	0	1	0	1	0	2	0	0	0	2	0	11	0
125–129	0	0	0	0	0	0	1	0	0	0	1	0	0	0	1	0	0	0	0	0	3	0
120–124	0	0	0	0	0	0	0	0	0	0	0	0	0	0	1	0	0	0	0	0	1	0
Total	138	105	200	150	206	133	178	85	133	49	70	17	35	5	28	4	4	1	11	5	1003	554

Apps = Number of Applicants
Adm = Number Admitted
Reflects 99% of the total applicant pool; highest LSAT data reported.

DUKE UNIVERSITY SCHOOL OF LAW

210 Science Drive, Box 90393
Durham, NC 27708-0393
Phone: 919.613.7020; Fax: 919.613.7257
E-mail: admissions@law.duke.edu; Website: www.law.duke.edu/admis/

ABA
Approved
Since
1931

The Basics

Type of school	Private
Term	Semester
Application deadline	2/15
Application fee	$70
Financial aid deadline	3/15
Can first year start other than fall?	Yes
Student to faculty ratio	10.0 to 1
# of housing spaces available restricted to law students	
graduate housing for which law students are eligible	

Faculty and Administrators

	Total		Men		Women		Minorities	
	Spr	Fall	Spr	Fall	Spr	Fall	Spr	Fall
Full-time	57	55	42	40	15	15	9	9
Other full-time	10	11	4	4	6	7	1	1
Deans, librarians, & others who teach	12	11	5	5	7	6	1	1
Part-time	68	35	45	21	23	14	8	3
Total	147	112	96	70	51	42	19	14

Curriculum

	Full-Time	Part-Time
Typical first-year section size	80	0
Is there typically a "small section" of the first-year class, other than Legal Writing, taught by full-time faculty	Yes	No
If yes, typical size offered last year	43	
# of classroom course titles beyond first-year curriculum	201	

# of upper division courses, excluding seminars, with an enrollment:		
	Under 25	94
	25–49	39
	50–74	9
	75–99	7
	100+	3

# of seminars	99	
# of seminar positions available	1,499	
# of seminar positions filled	1,019	0
# of positions available in simulation courses	738	
# of simulation positions filled	695	0
# of positions available in faculty supervised clinical courses	174	
# of faculty supervised clinical positions filled	163	0
# involved in field placements	83	0
# involved in law journals	310	0
# involved in moot court or trial competitions	87	0
# of credit hours required to graduate	84	

JD Enrollment and Ethnicity

	Men		Women		Full-Time		Part-Time		1st-Year		Total		JD Degs. Awd.
	#	%	#	%	#	%	#	%	#	%	#	%	
All Hispanics	22	5.4	15	5.4	35	5.4	2	5.1	14	6.6	37	5.4	16
Am. Ind./AK Nat.	1	0.2	0	0.0	1	0.2	0	0.0	0	0.0	1	0.1	1
Asian	37	9.2	37	13.3	69	10.7	5	12.8	28	13.3	74	10.8	17
Black/Af. Am.	19	4.7	25	9.0	44	6.8	0	0.0	17	8.1	44	6.4	20
Nat. HI/Pac. Isl.	0	0.0	0	0.0	0	0.0	0	0.0	0	0.0	0	0.0	0
2 or more races	2	0.5	2	0.7	3	0.5	1	2.6	1	0.5	4	0.6	1
Subtotal (minor.)	81	20.0	79	28.3	152	23.6	8	20.5	60	28.4	160	23.4	55
Nonres. Alien	7	1.7	7	2.5	14	2.2	0	0.0	7	3.3	14	2.0	5
White/Cauc.	299	74.0	181	64.9	450	69.9	30	76.9	141	66.8	480	70.3	117
Unknown	17	4.2	12	4.3	28	4.3	1	2.6	3	1.4	29	4.2	30
Total	404	59.2	279	40.8	644	94.3	39	5.7	211	30.9	683		207

Transfers

Transfers in	7
Transfers out	1

Tuition and Fees

	Resident	Nonresident
Full-time	$49,617	
Part-time		
Tuition Guarantee Program	N	

Living Expenses

Estimated living expenses for singles

Living on campus	Living off campus	Living at home
N/A	$17,708	N/A

DUKE UNIVERSITY SCHOOL OF LAW

*ABA
Approved
Since
1931*

GPA and LSAT Scores

	Total	Full-Time	Part-Time
# of apps	6,099	6,099	0
# of offers	934	934	0
# of matrics	211	211	0
75% GPA	3.84	3.84	0.00
Median GPA	3.75	3.75	0.00
25% GPA	3.62	3.62	0.00
75% LSAT	171	171	0
Median LSAT	170	170	0
25% LSAT	167	167	0

Grants and Scholarships (from prior year)

	Total #	Total %	Full-Time #	Full-Time %	Part-Time #	Part-Time %
Total # of students	681		644		37	
Total # receiving grants	535	78.6	535	83.1	0	0.0
Less than 1/2 tuition	454	66.7	454	70.5	0	0.0
Half to full tuition	64	9.4	64	9.9	0	0.0
Full tuition	16	2.3	16	2.5	0	0.0
More than full tuition	1	0.1	1	0.2	0	0.0
Median grant amount			$16,000		$0	

Informational and Library Resources

Total amount spent on library materials	$1,786,026
Study seating capacity inside the library	585
# of full-time equivalent professional librarians	10
Hours per week library is open	168
# of open, wired connections available to students	894
# of networked computers available for use by students	111
Has wireless network?	Y
Requires computer?	N

JD Attrition (from prior year)

	Academic #	Other #	Total #	Total %
1st year	0	2	2	0.8
2nd year	0	0	0	0.0
3rd year	0	0	0	0.0
4th year	0	0	0	0.0

Employment (9 months after graduation)

For up-to-date employment data, go to employmentsummary.abaquestionnaire.org on the ABA website.

Bar Passage Rates

First-time takers	216	Reporting %	84.26
Average school %	95.60	Average state %	81.33
Average pass difference	14.27		

Jurisdiction	Takers	Passers	Pass %	State %	Diff %
New York	67	65	97.01	84.92	12.09
California	27	24	88.89	71.24	17.65
North Carolina	27	24	88.89	77.50	11.39
Texas	12	12	100.00	82.68	17.32
Others (8)	49	49	100.00		

DUKE UNIVERSITY SCHOOL OF LAW

210 Science Drive, Box 90393
Durham, NC 27708-0393
Phone: 919.613.7020; Fax: 919.613.7257
E-mail: admissions@law.duke.edu; Website: www.law.duke.edu/admis/

Introduction

Duke Law School is one of the nation's leading law schools, known for its emphasis on leadership, ethics, scholarly research, professional development, and programs that serve the profession and the community. Students come to Duke Law from every state and, as alumni, work in top law firms and companies around the country and world.

One of the reasons students choose Duke Law is its collaborative environment, where growth is encouraged not only through rigorous scholarship, but also through cooperation and support. Because the school is small, students enjoy uniquely close interactions with faculty and fellow students. Duke Law's faculty members are among the nation's most respected experts in fields ranging from constitutional law and national security to intellectual property and international business. In addition, professors are deeply dedicated to teaching and are accessible and responsive to students. Their open-door policy encourages students to ask questions, continue discussions, and seek advice on specialized interests. Faculty-student interaction extends beyond the classroom to committee work, research, pro bono opportunities, career counseling, and mentoring. Ultimately, students experience a supportive environment where the focus is on training and developing the whole person in an atmosphere that values different perspectives, backgrounds, and orientations.

Enrollment/Student Body

Duke Law admits a select group of students with diverse backgrounds who have in common a record of academic excellence. In 2011, JD students came to Duke from 37 states and 10 foreign countries. These students represented 97 different undergraduate institutions and had a wealth of different experiences. Approximately 34 percent of the students entering Duke Law in 2011 came directly from college, while the other 66 percent entered law school after gaining experience for a year or more in another profession or graduate school.

Faculty

Central to Duke Law's success is its faculty. Well respected in the legal field, Duke Law professors are known for groundbreaking legal scholarship that impacts public policy and the legal profession. A large number of faculty are also practitioners in both the public and private sectors in the United States and abroad. Their backgrounds are as varied as they are distinguished: they are former Fulbright Scholars, Rhodes Scholars, and Marshall Scholars. A number of faculty members have served as Supreme Court clerks; several serve in leadership and advisory roles for government agencies. Faculty members hold joint appointments in departments throughout the university and have obtained PhDs in a wide variety of disciplines. Several visiting professors from abroad teach at Duke Law each year, and many full-time faculty members have extensive international connections.

Dual Degrees

Duke Law faculty believe that society is best served by lawyers with diverse education and training. The law school jointly sponsors numerous academic and professional programs in conjunction with other schools or departments at Duke University. In addition, students may pursue a three-year JD/DESS (Diplôme d'études supérieures spécialisées) in global business law in partnership with Université Paris I and Sciences Po in Paris.

The law school and the graduate school jointly sponsor programs of study in law and several other disciplines, including (at the master's level) Art History, Biomedical Engineering, Classical Studies, Cultural Anthropology, East Asian Studies, Economics, Electrical and Computer Engineering, English, Environmental Science and Policy, Global Health, History, Humanities, Literature, Mechanical Engineering, Philosophy, Political Science, Psychology, Religion, Romance Studies, and Sociology. The only additional time necessary to obtain both degrees is the summer prior to the first year of school. At the doctoral level, dual programs in Philosophy and Political Science are available.

The law school offers dual-professional degrees with the Fuqua School of Business, the Divinity School, the Nicholas School of the Environment, the School of Medicine, and the Sanford School of Public Policy. A special option is available to complete the JD/MBA in seven semesters.

Duke Law students may also earn graduate certificates in Slavic, Eurasian, and East European Legal Studies; Health Care Policy; Health System Management; or Women's Studies.

Special Programs

JD/LLM in International and Comparative Law—Duke Law has pioneered a unique joint-degree program that makes it possible for students to earn a JD and a Master of Laws in International and Comparative Law concurrently in three years. The only additional time needed is the summer prior to the first year of law school and the first half of the following summer, during which students attend one of Duke's Institutes in Transnational Law, either in Switzerland or Hong Kong.

JD/LLM in Law and Entrepreneurship—Duke Law has established a new program offering a concurrent JD and Master of Laws in Law and Entrepreneurship. The JD/LLMLE requires additional coursework and participation in an internship during the first and second summers of law school. Curricular opportunities include participation in the Startup Ventures Clinic, internships in local entrepreneurial businesses, and specialized coursework devoted to understanding the unique funding, business, and legal needs of startup companies.

International Study Abroad and Externships—Duke Law has arrangements with 21 top international universities, which give all interested Duke students an opportunity to study abroad. Duke Law also offers international externship opportunities at public sector institutions that engage in international work. Duke has preapproved externships, but students are also encouraged to submit their own proposals.

Legal Clinics—Duke Law School's clinical program has grown exponentially and houses a variety of clinics that offer a wide range of hands-on opportunities. A newly constructed clinical office suite brings a number of the programs together, allowing them to function as a public interest law firm. Clinical opportunities include AIDS Legal Project, Animal Law Clinic, Appellate Litigation Clinic, Children's Law Clinic, Community Enterprise Clinic, Environmental Law and Policy Clinic, Guantanamo Defense Clinic, Startup Ventures Clinic, and Wrongful Convictions Clinic. The school is also launching a pilot clinic in International Human Rights.

Centers—Interdisciplinary collaboration at Duke is fostered by a number of centers and programs, including the Arts Project; Center for Criminal Justice and Professional Responsibility; Center for Genome Ethics, Law, and Policy; Center for International and Comparative Law; Center for Judicial Studies; Center on Law, Race and Politics; Center for Sports and the Law; Center for the Study of the Public Domain; Center on Law, Ethics, and National Security; Global Capital Markets Center; Nicholas Institute for Environmental Policy Solutions; and Program in Public Law.

Duke in DC—Duke Law offers students with an interest in public policy at the federal level the opportunity to spend a semester in Washington, DC. They will pursue an externship that may include positions on Capitol Hill, on the personal staff of house members and senators, with congressional committees, with NGOs and lobbying groups, and in the executive branch.

Wintersession—Wintersession provides students with a number of practical, professional skills development opportunities. Short, unique, hands-on courses are offered for a half-credit during a four-day period over winter break; programs focus on critical professional skills such as contract drafting, taking a deposition, creating a business entity, and more. Wintersession also provides students with an extraordinary opportunity to interact with and learn from the accomplished Duke Law alumni and other lawyers who teach the courses.

Writing Program—Duke Law has an excellent and comprehensive writing program taught by nine full-time faculty who teach a mandatory first-year writing and research course as well as a range of upper-level courses that focus on specific writing skills such as judicial writing, writing in civil practice, writing for electronic discovery, and more. The writing faculty support Duke Law students in all of their writing endeavors, helping them to develop and perfect the skills necessary to produce top-quality legal writing.

Admission and Financial Aid

Admission to Duke Law School is highly competitive. In addition to the academic criteria, other factors may help to distinguish some applicants. These include capacity for leadership, dedication to community service, excellence in a particular field, motivation, graduate study, work experience, extracurricular activities, and character.

Duke Law tries to achieve broad diversity in terms of general background, geography, and undergraduate institutions represented. Students are chosen not only for their potential for academic success, but also because of qualities that will enhance the overall character of the class.

Admitted applicants are eligible for consideration for merit- and need-based scholarship awards. A select group of outstanding entering students are chosen each year as Mordecai Scholars and receive a full-tuition scholarship. Mordecai Scholars possess a record of extraordinary leadership and scholarly achievement prior to law school, and the personal qualities that are likely to result in community involvement and leadership.

Cocurricular Activities

Scholarship in the classroom is reinforced through a variety of opportunities for hands-on leadership training and professional experience. Through pro bono work, legal clinics, public interest projects, moot court, and opportunities for scholarly writing and editing on eight different legal journals, Duke prepares students for the real-world practice of law.

Professional Development

The award-winning Duke Blueprint provides structure to students' legal education and professional development by challenging them to engage intellectually, embody integrity, build relationships, serve the community, and become effective leaders.

Duke Law graduates find employment in all sectors of the legal profession and in all parts of the United States and the world. Many begin their careers in law firms. Top law firms from across the country interview on campus each year, and the number of interviews available and offers made far exceeds the number of students interviewing. Others pursue judicial clerkships—about 15 to 20 percent of each class—or work for government agencies or business enterprises. The school is dedicated to assisting every student in successfully launching his or her career, and typically 95 percent of each class is employed within nine months of graduation.

Duke places special emphasis on support for students interested in a career in public service. Staff from both the Career Center and the Office of Pro Bono and Public Interest help students find opportunities both during and after law school. The law school provides financial support for these goals with grants to subsidize summer employment and a Loan Repayment Assistance Program for graduates who enter a life of public service.

APPLICANT PROFILE

Duke University School of Law has elected not to provide an applicant profile based only on GPA and LSAT score, since these are not the only criteria used in admission decisions. As we assemble a talented and diverse student body, we take into account the individual circumstances of each applicant and consider a wide range of factors, including significant

extracurricular or community involvement, work experience, advanced degrees, and other notable achievements. A hallmark of Duke Law is a close-knit group of students and faculty, and we seek candidates who will be enthusiastic and active members of our community.

DUQUESNE UNIVERSITY SCHOOL OF LAW

201 Edward J. Hanley Hall, 900 Locust Street
Pittsburgh, PA 15282-0700
Phone: 412.396.6296; Fax: 412.396.1073
E-mail: campion@duq.edu; Website: www.duq.edu/law

ABA
Approved
Since
1960

The Basics

Type of school	Private		
Term	Semester		
Application deadline	4/1	5/1	6/1
Application fee	$60		
Financial aid deadline	5/31		
Can first year start other than fall?	No		
Student to faculty ratio	20.4 to 1		
# of housing spaces available restricted to law students			
graduate housing for which law students are eligible			

Faculty and Administrators

	Total		Men		Women		Minorities	
	Spr	Fall	Spr	Fall	Spr	Fall	Spr	Fall
Full-time	25	23	18	16	7	7	4	3
Other full-time	1	1	0	0	1	1	0	0
Deans, librarians, & others who teach	8	8	5	4	3	4	2	2
Part-time	49	45	32	33	17	12	4	2
Total	83	77	55	53	28	24	10	7

JD Enrollment and Ethnicity

	Men		Women		Full-Time		Part-Time		1st-Year		Total		JD Degs. Awd.
	#	%	#	%	#	%	#	%	#	%	#	%	
All Hispanics	2	0.6	4	1.4	5	1.1	1	0.5	0	0.0	6	0.9	3
Am. Ind./AK Nat.	2	0.6	1	0.4	2	0.4	1	0.5	0	0.0	3	0.5	0
Asian	10	2.8	7	2.5	10	2.2	7	3.6	7	3.7	17	2.6	1
Black/Af. Am.	7	1.9	8	2.9	10	2.2	5	2.6	3	1.6	15	2.3	6
Nat. HI/Pac. Isl.	0	0.0	0	0.0	0	0.0	0	0.0	0	0.0	0	0.0	0
2 or more races	0	0.0	0	0.0	0	0.0	0	0.0	0	0.0	0	0.0	0
Subtotal (minor.)	21	5.8	20	7.2	27	6.0	14	7.2	10	5.3	41	6.4	10
Nonres. Alien	2	0.6	1	0.4	3	0.7	0	0.0	3	1.6	3	0.5	0
White/Cauc.	340	93.7	258	92.5	418	93.3	180	92.8	179	94.7	598	93.1	199
Unknown	0	0.0	0	0.0	0	0.0	0	0.0	0	0.0	0	0.0	0
Total	363	56.5	279	43.5	448	69.8	194	30.2	189	29.4	642		209

Curriculum

	Full-Time	Part-Time
Typical first-year section size	80	50
Is there typically a "small section" of the first-year class, other than Legal Writing, taught by full-time faculty	No	No
If yes, typical size offered last year		
# of classroom course titles beyond first-year curriculum	128	
# of upper division courses, excluding seminars, with an enrollment: Under 25	43	
25–49	28	
50–74	10	
75–99	7	
100+	0	
# of seminars	29	
# of seminar positions available	691	
# of seminar positions filled	384	145
# of positions available in simulation courses	107	
# of simulation positions filled	72	35
# of positions available in faculty supervised clinical courses	68	
# of faculty supervised clinical positions filled	51	8
# involved in field placements	47	20
# involved in law journals	24	13
# involved in moot court or trial competitions	19	1
# of credit hours required to graduate	86	

Transfers

Transfers in	0
Transfers out	14

Tuition and Fees

	Resident	Nonresident
Full-time	$33,752	$33,752
Part-time	$26,098	$26,098
Tuition Guarantee Program	N	

Living Expenses

Estimated living expenses for singles

Living on campus	Living off campus	Living at home
$13,560	$13,560	$4,550

DUQUESNE UNIVERSITY SCHOOL OF LAW

ABA
Approved
Since
1960

GPA and LSAT Scores

	Total	Full-Time	Part-Time
# of apps	864	659	205
# of offers	476	391	85
# of matrics	191	145	46
75% GPA	3.62	3.67	3.53
Median GPA	3.35	3.36	3.27
25% GPA	3.12	3.15	3.02
75% LSAT	155	155	155
Median LSAT	153	153	153
25% LSAT	151	151	149

Grants and Scholarships (from prior year)

	Total #	Total %	Full-Time #	Full-Time %	Part-Time #	Part-Time %
Total # of students	688		454		234	
Total # receiving grants	208	30.2	163	35.9	45	19.2
Less than 1/2 tuition	116	16.9	89	19.6	27	11.5
Half to full tuition	35	5.1	25	5.5	10	4.3
Full tuition	49	7.1	44	9.7	5	2.1
More than full tuition	8	1.2	5	1.1	3	1.3
Median grant amount			$15,000		$5,880	

Informational and Library Resources

Total amount spent on library materials	$797,886
Study seating capacity inside the library	411
# of full-time equivalent professional librarians	7
Hours per week library is open	102
# of open, wired connections available to students	20
# of networked computers available for use by students	79
Has wireless network?	Y
Requires computer?	N

JD Attrition (from prior year)

	Academic #	Other #	Total #	Total %
1st year	2	14	16	7.4
2nd year	3	0	3	1.4
3rd year	0	0	0	0.0
4th year	0	0	0	0.0

Employment (9 months after graduation)

For up-to-date employment data, go to employmentsummary.abaquestionnaire.org on the ABA website.

Bar Passage Rates

First-time takers	204	Reporting %	86.76
Average school %	86.44	Average state %	83.06
Average pass difference	3.38		

Jurisdiction	Takers	Passers	Pass %	State %	Diff %
Pennsylvania	177	153	86.44	83.06	3.38

DUQUESNE UNIVERSITY SCHOOL OF LAW

201 Edward J. Hanley Hall, 900 Locust Street
Pittsburgh, PA 15282-0700
Phone: 412.396.6296; Fax: 412.396.1073
E-mail: campion@duq.edu; Website: www.duq.edu/law

Introduction

The Duquesne University School of Law is a Catholic law
school that has been in existence since 1911 and is the only
multiple-division law school in western Pennsylvania.
Admission requirements, instruction, and the nature and
scope of the work required of students are identical for both
the full-time day division and the part-time evening and
part-time day divisions. The School of Law is approved by the
ABA and is a member of the AALS.

Situated on the attractive 43-acre Duquesne University
campus, the law school is within walking distance to the
vibrant Pittsburgh downtown legal, corporate, and
government communities.

Recognized as one of the best cities in which to practice
law and a center for corporate and legal headquarters,
Pittsburgh is a leading metropolis for high technology
ventures and a thriving arts and cultural community, with
major-league sports entertainment.

Library and Physical Facilities

Duquesne's proximity to the Pittsburgh region's legal center
makes the law school library a major source for legal research
and information services. The Duquesne law library has
assumed management responsibility of the Allegheny County
Law Library, resulting in one of the largest collections of legal
materials in Pennsylvania.

The law school recently completed a $12 million renovation
and expansion, adding 33,000 square feet to Hanley Hall. The
four new floors of space include a state-of-the-art moot
courtroom (giving us three), three new technology-aided
classrooms with ports and power sources at every seat, an
upgraded lounge area with a cafeteria, new faculty and
administrative offices, student locker areas, a conference
room, and a wireless computer lab.

Curriculum

The course of study offered at the School of Law is sufficiently
broad to prepare students for practice in all states. Three
years are required for completion of the course of study in
the day division, four years in the evening division and the
part-time day division. Eighty-six credits are required
for graduation.

While emphasis is placed upon skills such as legal research
and writing and trial advocacy, the required courses are
sufficiently broad to provide all students with the requisite
skills to become competent lawyers in any field of practice. A
wide selection of elective courses, seminars, and student
in-house and internal clinics allows students to focus on
specialized legal fields and explore the contemporary
problems of law and society.

Admission

*Bachelor's degree required. Application deadlines: day, April
1; evening, May 1; part-time day, June 1; rolling admission.
LSAT and registration with LSAC's Credential Assembly
Service (CAS) required.*

All candidates for admission must take the LSAT, register
for the Credential Assembly Service (CAS), and be graduates
of an accredited college or university before enrolling in the
law school. Personal interviews are not granted, but
applicants are encouraged to schedule an appointment to
visit the school for an information session or a tour of
the facilities.

The admission process is selective. Most applicants apply
well in advance of the deadlines. Students are admitted only
for the fall semester.

In evaluating applications, the complete academic record is
reviewed with consideration given to the competitiveness of
the undergraduate institution, the college major, rank in class,
and the overall academic performance. The LSAT is
considered an important factor. Graduate study,
extracurricular activities, and recommendations also
contribute to the committee's assessment. Work experience
is considered when an applicant has been employed full time
for a significant length of time.

Joint-Degree Programs

The School of Law offers the following joint-degree
programs: JD/MBA, JD/MS-Environmental Science and
Management, JD/MA-Healthcare Ethics, and JD/MDiv.

Clinical Opportunities

The School of Law operates six in-house live client clinics and
a simulation course. The **Bill of Rights Clinic** offers students
an opportunity to work with clients before the Human
Relations Commission, the US Equal Employment
Opportunity Commission (EEOC), the US District Court for
Western Pennsylvania, and the Third Circuit Court of Appeals.
In the **Civil and Family Justice Law Clinic** students assist
clients while working at one of five placements on civil cases
related to matters involving family law issues. The **Community
Enterprise Clinic** provides legal assistance, counseling, and
representation to nonprofit groups and organizations
committed to effecting change in Greater Pittsburgh
communities. In the **Criminal Advocacy Clinic** students assist
in the representation of criminal defendants at the Allegheny
County Office of Conflict Counsel. The award-winning
Unemployment Compensation Clinic provides
representation to clients before unemployment compensation
referees in hearings, and on appeals, to the Board of Review.
The **Urban Development Clinic** provides a range of legal
services associated with real estate development occurring in
several distressed communities in Greater Pittsburgh. The
E-Discovery Simulation Course offers an intense, practical
introduction to electronic discovery through a simulated
litigation exercise.

International Programs

The Law School has established a summer program and
faculty exchange with the China University of Political Science
and Law (CUPL). Located in Beijing, CUPL, with official ties to
China's Ministry of Justice, is the most prestigious center for
legal study in all of China. Duquesne has an outstanding
ABA-approved summer program of study on comparative law

and the European Union at the American College Dublin. The Summer Study of European Law program was newly launched in the summer of 2011 with students having the opportunity to study at the University of Cologne and experience different cultures in Cologne, Paris, and Brussels while spending three weeks of summer in Europe.

Student Activities

The Student Bar Association maintains a liaison between students and faculty and sponsors social and professional activities for the student body.

Membership in the *Duquesne Law Review* is based on the demonstrated academic ability of the student as well as his or her interest in becoming active in this publication. *Juris*, the law school news magazine, is an ABA award-winning publication containing articles of current interest to the entire legal community. Students also publish the *Duquesne Business Law Journal*.

Financial Aid

Duquesne consistently strives to ensure that the outstanding private legal education provided by the law school is within the reach of all qualified students. Merit scholarships are awarded to outstanding day-division applicants, grants-in-aid are awarded primarily on the basis of need, and state and federal government-sponsored loans are available.

Housing

Law students have access to an array of housing options throughout the neighborhoods of Pittsburgh and the surrounding communities. The Office of Commuter Affairs will assist law students in their search for housing by providing a list of available locations. For further information, please write to the Office of Commuter Affairs, Duquesne University, Pittsburgh, PA 15282, or call 412.396.6660.

Career Services

The Career Services Office staff offers assistance to students and alumni who are interested in obtaining full-time, part-time, and summer employment. The office offers a fall and spring on-campus interview program in which law firms, government agencies, corporations, and accounting firms conduct individual interviews.

The School of Law is a member of the National Association for Law Placement, the National Association for Public Interest Law Publication Network, and the Allegheny County Bar Association Minority Job Fair.

Graduates have consistently been placed at a rate at or above 90 percent within six months of graduation. The law school has nearly 5,000 alumni throughout the United States and in several foreign countries.

APPLICANT PROFILE

The law school recognizes the different strengths presented by our day division, evening division, and part-time day students and acknowledges that the diversity in the groups cannot be accurately or completely represented in a single grid of average undergraduate GPA and LSAT scores. Graduate degrees, personal and professional accomplishments, and extensive employment experience predominate in the evening, part-time, and day divisions.

These factors are considered crucial to an individual assessment of admissibility. Applications are reviewed individually, and factors such as leadership experience, community service, and other nonacademic experiences are considered. Applicants should contact the Admissions Office for specific information on the current year's class; phone: 412.396.6296. Applicants are encouraged to visit the law school.

EARLE MACK SCHOOL OF LAW, DREXEL UNIVERSITY

3320 Market Street, Suite 100
Philadelphia, PA 19104
Phone: 215.895.1529
E-mail: LawAdmissions@drexel.edu; Website: www.earlemacklaw.drexel.edu

ABA
Approved
Since
2008

The Basics

Type of school	Private
Term	Semester
Application deadline	8/1
Application fee	$0
Financial aid deadline	5/1
Can first year start other than fall?	No
Student to faculty ratio	15.0 to 1
# of housing spaces available restricted to law students	
graduate housing for which law students are eligible	356

Faculty and Administrators

	Total		Men		Women		Minorities	
	Spr	Fall	Spr	Fall	Spr	Fall	Spr	Fall
Full-time	25	24	14	12	11	12	5	6
Other full-time	4	5	0	0	4	5	1	1
Deans, librarians, & others who teach	6	8	4	6	2	2	1	1
Part-time	44	28	30	17	14	11	5	2
Total	79	65	48	35	31	30	12	10

Curriculum

	Full-Time	Part-Time
Typical first-year section size	76	0
Is there typically a "small section" of the first-year class, other than Legal Writing, taught by full-time faculty	No	No
If yes, typical size offered last year		

# of classroom course titles beyond first-year curriculum		113
# of upper division courses, excluding seminars, with an enrollment:	Under 25	86
	25–49	26
	50–74	4
	75–99	0
	100+	0
# of seminars		15
# of seminar positions available		248
# of seminar positions filled	162	0
# of positions available in simulation courses	392	
# of simulation positions filled	333	0
# of positions available in faculty supervised clinical courses	8	
# of faculty supervised clinical positions filled	8	0
# involved in field placements	136	0
# involved in law journals	50	0
# involved in moot court or trial competitions	46	0
# of credit hours required to graduate		85

JD Enrollment and Ethnicity

	Men		Women		Full-Time		Part-Time		1st-Year		Total		JD Degs. Awd.
	#	%	#	%	#	%	#	%	#	%	#	%	
All Hispanics	18	7.2	14	7.0	32	7.1	0	0.0	14	9.3	32	7.1	8
Am. Ind./AK Nat.	1	0.4	1	0.5	2	0.4	0	0.0	1	0.7	2	0.4	1
Asian	9	3.6	11	5.5	20	4.4	0	0.0	4	2.7	20	4.4	6
Black/Af. Am.	19	7.6	16	8.0	35	7.8	0	0.0	12	8.0	35	7.8	9
Nat. HI/Pac. Isl.	0	0.0	0	0.0	0	0.0	0	0.0	0	0.0	0	0.0	0
2 or more races	0	0.0	0	0.0	0	0.0	0	0.0	0	0.0	0	0.0	0
Subtotal (minor.)	47	18.7	42	21.1	89	19.8	0	0.0	31	20.7	89	19.8	24
Nonres. Alien	3	1.2	0	0.0	3	0.7	0	0.0	0	0.0	3	0.7	0
White/Cauc.	183	72.9	143	71.9	326	72.4	0	0.0	110	73.3	326	72.4	100
Unknown	18	7.2	14	7.0	32	7.1	0	0.0	9	6.0	32	7.1	7
Total	251	55.8	199	44.2	450	100.0	0	0.0	150	33.3	450		131

Transfers

Transfers in	0
Transfers out	5

Tuition and Fees

	Resident	Nonresident
Full-time	$36,051	$36,051
Part-time		
Tuition Guarantee Program		N

Living Expenses

Estimated living expenses for singles

Living on campus	Living off campus	Living at home
$23,789	$23,356	$22,286

EARLE MACK SCHOOL OF LAW, DREXEL UNIVERSITY

ABA Approved Since 2008

GPA and LSAT Scores

	Total	Full-Time	Part-Time
# of apps	2,464	2,464	0
# of offers	858	858	0
# of matrics	147	147	0
75% GPA	3.66	3.66	0.00
Median GPA	3.38	3.38	0.00
25% GPA	3.09	3.09	0.00
75% LSAT	161	161	0
Median LSAT	159	159	0
25% LSAT	157	157	0

Grants and Scholarships (from prior year)

	Total #	Total %	Full-Time #	Full-Time %	Part-Time #	Part-Time %
Total # of students	440		440		0	
Total # receiving grants	376	85.5	376	85.5	0	0.0
Less than 1/2 tuition	171	38.9	171	38.9	0	0.0
Half to full tuition	202	45.9	202	45.9	0	0.0
Full tuition	1	0.2	1	0.2	0	0.0
More than full tuition	2	0.5	2	0.5	0	0.0
Median grant amount			$20,000		$0	

Informational and Library Resources

Total amount spent on library materials	$999,093
Study seating capacity inside the library	347
# of full-time equivalent professional librarians	12
Hours per week library is open	93
# of open, wired connections available to students	741
# of networked computers available for use by students	15
Has wireless network?	Y
Requires computer?	Y

JD Attrition (from prior year)

	Academic #	Other #	Total #	Total %
1st year	3	0	3	2.0
2nd year	0	7	7	4.4
3rd year	0	0	0	0.0
4th year	0	0	0	0.0

Employment (9 months after graduation)

For up-to-date employment data, go to employmentsummary.abaquestionnaire.org on the ABA website.

Bar Passage Rates

First-time takers	110	Reporting %	80.91
Average school %	82.02	Average state %	83.06

Average pass difference −1.04

Jurisdiction	Takers	Passers	Pass %	State %	Diff %
Pennsylvania	89	73	82.02	83.06	−1.04

EARLE MACK SCHOOL OF LAW, DREXEL UNIVERSITY

3320 Market Street, Suite 100
Philadelphia, PA 19104
Phone: 215.895.1529
E-mail: LawAdmissions@drexel.edu; Website: www.earlemacklaw.drexel.edu

Introduction

The Earle Mack School of Law at Drexel University offers a curriculum and programs built upon the principle that students learn best when hands-on experience is part of their education. Philadelphia, which boasts one of America's largest legal communities and a host of cultural attractions, has a lot to offer law students and young lawyers. Because Drexel University is located in the thriving University City neighborhood, the Earle Mack School of Law is the perfect place to learn by doing. The Earle Mack School of Law is one of just two law schools in the nation offering co-op education—an approach that employers recognize produces outstanding, practice-ready lawyers. The co-op program is combined with an extensive menu of experiential offerings ranging from live-client clinics to high-quality simulation courses. The curriculum has been designed to ensure that students engage in active learning of the law. This practical experience pays off in different ways.

Our law students master legal principles and the real-world skills needed to apply them. Students gain confidence and savvy as they meet with clients, argue before judges, and engage in the many other tasks that define the legal profession. Along the way, students also launch lasting professional networks with many lawyers who become mentors, advisors, and even future employers. Even within the four walls of the law school, we infuse the traditional law school experience with practical skills. Thus, our curriculum features all the traditional courses tested on the bar mixed with innovative new offerings such as Transactional Lawyering, Regulating Patient Safety, E-Commerce Law, and Crime and Community. Professors incorporate experiential education into many courses, allowing students to simulate appellate arguments in Constitutional Law or to play the parts of prosecutors and defenders in Criminal Law. Every 1L completes an immersive week in Interviewing, Negotiation, and Counseling.

We have intentionally limited the size of our student body, which allows every student to play an important part in the law school. Students can get involved in myriad existing groups or develop their own.

Location

Located in the University City neighborhood just adjacent to downtown Philadelphia, the law school is mere blocks from the heart of one of the nation's largest and most dynamic legal communities. University City is so named because of the 40,000 students from Drexel University and the University of Pennsylvania who combine to create an exciting, vibrant community. Thanks to our location, affordable student housing is located a short walk or trolley ride away, and students are able to meet after class at many of the nearby restaurants, shops, and bars.

Faculty

Our faculty are nationally recognized scholars and experienced practitioners who share a commitment to innovative teaching and the integration of theory and practice. And they are widely recognized as experts in their fields.

Our faculty publish in respected journals, collaborate with other leading scholars, and present their work nationally and internationally. They are also widely respected outside of legal education, and professors at the Earle Mack School of Law appear on CNN and NPR, are quoted in the *New York Times*, and testify before Congress. On issues ranging from national health-care policy to the future of Social Security, or from race and the criminal justice system to the importance of having cameras in the courthouse, our faculty are opinion leaders.

Curriculum

From the first week of law school, students are immersed in questions about professionalism and the proper role of an attorney in our society. We help students master the critical skills of legal argumentation and writing with a nationally recognized year-long Legal Methods program. Our core curriculum covers material that every graduate will need to succeed on the bar and beyond. In the spring, 1Ls can begin to direct their own education, selecting a first-year elective.

Upper-level students choose from a menu of electives that help deepen their understanding of the legal system and expand this knowledge in particular areas of expertise. In addition to three concentrations—Intellectual Property, Health Law, and Business and Entrepreneurship Law—the law school offers course sequences in many areas of interest, including International Law, Employment Law, Criminal Law, Civil Litigation, Property and Real Estate, and Trial Advocacy. The law school offers specialty courses such as Animal Law, Sports Law, and Law and Mind Sciences. We also offer several joint-degree opportunities, including a JD-PhD in clinical psychology, a JD-MBA with the Drexel's LeBow College of Business, a JD-MPH with Drexel School of Public Health, and the JD-MSPP through Drexel's Center for Public Policy.

Admission and Financial Aid

We seek out and aggressively recruit students who will be exceptional practitioners and leaders. We consider an applicant's entire application, including both objective factors like the LSAT and GPA, and characteristics like leadership skills, work experience, and commitment to service. We utilize rolling admissions, but encourage students to apply as early as possible, since scholarship and admission decisions are weighted favorably toward early applicants. We provide very attractive scholarships to students who are well-matched to our program, and we offer financial aid counseling that is attentive to our students' needs.

Experiential Learning

The **Co-op Program** provides a unique opportunity for law students to synthesize the legal theory learned in the classroom with the critical knowledge and professional skills learned in the field under the close supervision of experienced practitioners. Our commitment to integrating the Co-op Program into the curriculum and the singular focus students give to their placements distinguish it from experiential programs offered by other law schools. The Co-op Program is a semester-long field placement during the second or third year of study that allows a student to work in a law firm, corporation, judicial office, public interest organization, or government agency. Each placement is chosen for the quality experience that it can provide law students as part of their overall academic experience. Students learn the law relevant to the practice area and the skills needed to succeed there. They also get acquainted with the host institution and the industries to which it belongs while building professional networks with the practitioners who work there.

In the year-long **Clinical Program**, students gain firsthand experience representing clients while earning academic credit. The Civil Litigation Field Clinic, which operates in tandem with Philadelphia Legal Assistance, allows students to represent clients in cases involving domestic violence. The Criminal Litigation Field Clinic, which operates in partnership with the Defender Association of Philadelphia, allows students to represent clients in preliminary hearings on felonies and to argue legal motions and try misdemeanor cases in Philadelphia's municipal court. Our in-house Appellate Litigation Clinic offers students the opportunity to argue cases involving criminal law, immigration, and the rights of the indigent in state and federal appellate courts. Our in-house Entrepreneurial Law Clinic allows students to help entrepreneurs get their new businesses off the ground. Providing legal services to start-up businesses enables students to develop critical skills for work with clients while helping to fuel economic vitality in the city.

The law school's innovative **Trial Advocacy Program** trains students in the essential practical skills of litigation. In Pretrial Advocacy, students learn how to interview a client, plan pretrial investigation, identify and retain experts, and draft pleadings and motions. During the trial preparation phase, students also learn how to develop a theory of the case as well as deposition strategies and other discovery techniques. In Trial Advocacy, experienced trial lawyers and judges provide live demonstrations relating to jury selection, opening and closing statements, and direct- and cross-examination of lay and expert witnesses. Students also learn how to use computer technology to create state-of-the-art trial exhibits that will enhance the presentation of evidence at trial. Trial Advocacy ends with a capstone experience in which each student

litigates a mock trial in a courtroom before real judges and veteran attorneys. Assisting individuals or groups traditionally underserved by the private bar is the goal of our mandatory 50-hour **Pro Bono Service Requirement**. Working with supervising attorneys, students gain practical, hands-on experience in a real legal setting. Pro Bono Service is a vital part of our curriculum that demonstrates the commitment of faculty and administrators to developing our students' professionalism.

Student Activities

The law school is a lively community that celebrates diversity and encourages students to pursue their passions. Our students have accrued an exemplary record of performance in competition, with the **Trial Team Moot Court Board** and **Alternative Dispute Resolution Team** winning regional and national contests. In one year alone, our teams won a national legislation competition, reached the national semi-finals in both mock trial competition and negotiation and mediation competition, and the national quarter-finals in moot court competition. The *Drexel Law Review* has published work from America's leading jurists and scholars and has been cited by the American Bar Association House of Delegates. Other student organizations include the American Constitution Society, the Black Law Students Association, the Federalist Society, the International Law and Human Rights Society, the Latin American Law Student Association, the Middle Eastern Law Students Association, OUTLAW, and the Women's Law Society.

Career Strategies and Transition to Practice

Our Career Strategies Office features three full-time attorney advisors, including a specialist in government and public interest law. Services range from individual counseling, mock interviews, and résumé and cover-letter writing to a host of recruiting events, mentoring programs, and networking opportunities. Students receive support and guidance for developing career strategies from advisors and faculty starting with the first year. Employers are regular visitors for receptions and events in addition to On-Campus Interviewing.

APPLICANT PROFILE

Earle Mack School of Law, Drexel University

LSAT Score	GPA								
	3.75 +	3.50–3.74	3.25–3.49	3.00–3.24	2.75–2.99	2.50–2.74	2.25–2.49	2.00–2.24	Below 2.00
175–180									
170–174									
165–169									
160–164									
155–159									
150–154									
145–149									
140–144									
120–139									

■ Good Possibility □ Possible ▨ Unlikely

ELON UNIVERSITY SCHOOL OF LAW

201 North Greene Street
Greensboro, NC 27401
Phone: 336.279.9200; Fax: 336.279.8199
E-mail: law@elon.edu; Website: www.law.elon.edu

ABA Approved Since 2008

The Basics

Type of school	Private
Term	Semester
Application deadline	6/30
Application fee	$50
Financial aid deadline	
Can first year start other than fall?	No
Student to faculty ratio	18.4 to 1
# of housing spaces available restricted to law students	
graduate housing for which law students are eligible	

Faculty and Administrators

	Total		Men		Women		Minorities	
	Spr	Fall	Spr	Fall	Spr	Fall	Spr	Fall
Full-time	15	17	10	12	5	5	3	3
Other full-time	3	5	0	2	3	3	0	0
Deans, librarians, & others who teach	6	6	3	3	3	3	1	1
Part-time	23	12	18	9	5	3	3	1
Total	47	40	31	26	16	14	7	5

JD Enrollment and Ethnicity

	Men		Women		Full-Time		Part-Time		1st-Year		Total		JD Degs. Awd.
	#	%	#	%	#	%	#	%	#	%	#	%	
All Hispanics	4	2.0	1	0.6	5	1.4	0	0.0	3	2.3	5	1.4	3
Am. Ind./AK Nat.	2	1.0	3	1.8	5	1.4	0	0.0	4	3.1	5	1.4	0
Asian	6	3.0	3	1.8	9	2.5	0	0.0	6	4.7	9	2.5	2
Black/Af. Am.	10	5.0	21	12.7	31	8.5	0	0.0	14	10.9	31	8.5	5
Nat. HI/Pac. Isl.	2	1.0	0	0.0	2	0.5	0	0.0	1	0.8	2	0.5	0
2 or more races	1	0.5	1	0.6	2	0.5	0	0.0	0	0.0	2	0.5	2
Subtotal (minor.)	25	12.5	29	17.6	54	14.8	0	0.0	28	21.7	54	14.8	12
Nonres. Alien	0	0.0	0	0.0	0	0.0	0	0.0	0	0.0	0	0.0	0
White/Cauc.	155	77.5	125	75.8	280	76.7	0	0.0	93	72.1	280	76.7	87
Unknown	20	10.0	11	6.7	31	8.5	0	0.0	8	6.2	31	8.5	0
Total	200	54.8	165	45.2	365	100.0	0	0.0	129	35.3	365		99

Curriculum

	Full-Time	Part-Time
Typical first-year section size	30	0
Is there typically a "small section" of the first-year class, other than Legal Writing, taught by full-time faculty	Yes	No
If yes, typical size offered last year	30	
# of classroom course titles beyond first-year curriculum	76	
# of upper division courses, excluding seminars, with an enrollment: Under 25	20	
25–49	16	
50–74	6	
75–99	3	
100+	0	
# of seminars	7	
# of seminar positions available	133	
# of seminar positions filled	109	0
# of positions available in simulation courses	193	
# of simulation positions filled	163	0
# of positions available in faculty supervised clinical courses	38	
# of faculty supervised clinical positions filled	38	0
# involved in field placements	55	0
# involved in law journals	25	0
# involved in moot court or trial competitions	31	0
# of credit hours required to graduate	90	

Transfers

Transfers in	4
Transfers out	4

Tuition and Fees

	Resident	Nonresident
Full-time	$34,550	$34,550
Part-time		
Tuition Guarantee Program	N	

Living Expenses

Estimated living expenses for singles

Living on campus	Living off campus	Living at home
$23,243	$23,243	$23,243

ELON UNIVERSITY SCHOOL OF LAW

ABA
Approved
Since
2008

GPA and LSAT Scores

	Total	Full-Time	Part-Time
# of apps	854	854	0
# of offers	400	400	0
# of matrics	130	130	0
75% GPA	3.47	3.47	0.00
Median GPA	3.20	3.20	0.00
25% GPA	2.87	2.87	0.00
75% LSAT	156	156	0
Median LSAT	153	153	0
25% LSAT	150	150	0

Grants and Scholarships (from prior year)

	Total #	Total %	Full-Time #	Full-Time %	Part-Time #	Part-Time %
Total # of students	342		342		0	
Total # receiving grants	280	81.9	280	81.9	0	0.0
Less than 1/2 tuition	227	66.4	227	66.4	0	0.0
Half to full tuition	31	9.1	31	9.1	0	0.0
Full tuition	22	6.4	22	6.4	0	0.0
More than full tuition	0	0.0	0	0.0	0	0.0
Median grant amount			$10,000		$0	

Informational and Library Resources

Total amount spent on library materials	$702,096
Study seating capacity inside the library	333
# of full-time equivalent professional librarians	4
Hours per week library is open	102
# of open, wired connections available to students	102
# of networked computers available for use by students	35
Has wireless network?	Y
Requires computer?	N

JD Attrition (from prior year)

	Academic #	Other #	Total #	Total %
1st year	2	9	11	8.4
2nd year	0	1	1	0.9
3rd year	0	0	0	0.0
4th year	0	0	0	0.0

Employment (9 months after graduation)

For up-to-date employment data, go to employmentsummary.abaquestionnaire.org on the ABA website.

Bar Passage Rates

First-time takers	96	Reporting %	85.42
Average school %	79.27	Average state %	77.50
Average pass difference	1.77		

Jurisdiction	Takers	Passers	Pass %	State %	Diff %
North Carolina	82	65	79.27	77.50	1.77

ELON UNIVERSITY SCHOOL OF LAW

201 North Greene Street
Greensboro, NC 27401
Phone: 336.279.9200; Fax: 336.279.8199
E-mail: law@elon.edu; Website: www.law.elon.edu

Introduction

Elon University School of Law was established in 2006 at a dedication ceremony led by retired US Supreme Court Justice Sandra Day O'Connor. Excellence in the law through engaged learning and leadership development forms the center of the school's mission and purpose. The program of legal education at Elon Law prepares students to be not only successful lawyers who excel at the highest levels of the profession, but also global citizens who lead in solving challenges facing their communities, nation, and world.

Location

Elon University School of Law is located in downtown Greensboro, North Carolina, the third largest city in North Carolina, with a regional population of about 1.5 million. The law school is located at the center of the area's legal community, including major law firms, government offices, and district and federal courts. The downtown area also provides a rich cultural environment, with restaurants, music venues, museums and theaters, a new minor league baseball stadium, and recreational facilities. All law students are provided free memberships to a new YMCA just a few blocks from the law school.

Advisory Board

The law school's advisory board includes prominent judges, attorneys, and business leaders who advise the university in shaping the vision for the school and its future development. The board is chaired by David Gergen, who held positions in the administrations of Presidents Nixon, Ford, Reagan, and Clinton. The board also includes two former North Carolina governors, three former North Carolina Supreme Court chief justices, a former president of the American Bar Association, and a former US ambassador.

Curriculum

The law school operates on a three-term model, with fall and spring semesters of 13 weeks and a winter term offering courses and practical experiences in leadership and the law. While at Elon, students take a wide array of required courses and electives, and each student selects at least one of four concentrations in their second year: Business, Litigation, Public Interest, and General Practice.

Leadership Emphasis

Over the course of the three-year program, Elon Law incorporates the best of leadership education through courses, community activities, and capstone experiences. Elon lawyers will begin their careers as knowledgeable, self-aware, skillful, and innovative professionals. Elon Law prepares its graduates to be not only successful lawyers who can excel at the highest levels of the profession, but also leading contributors to the well-being of the region, nation, and world. In addition to a rigorous core curriculum that allows students to develop extensive legal knowledge, taught by a faculty with a passion for innovative teaching, the school also provides students with in-depth skills training, teamwork experiences, opportunities for direct client engagement, and an innovative Preceptor Program through which experienced lawyers from a broad range of practice settings mentor law students. The Joseph M. Bryan Distinguished Leadership Lecture Series brings accomplished leaders from a variety of disciplines to Elon to share their experiences and perspectives.

Preceptor Program

More than 50 volunteer attorneys serve annually as preceptors to Elon's first-year law students. As professional advisors, they observe and provide feedback to students about their classroom performances and invite students to accompany them to observe trials, initial client interviews, depositions, and/or mediations. Through these experiences, students are mentored and guided in their professional development and entry to the legal profession.

Clinics

Two clinical programs at Elon Law put legal theory into practice, providing students with essential lawyering skills through casework management, research, writing, client interaction, and courtroom advocacy, while also helping individuals in need. Current clinical offerings include the Juvenile Justice Intervention and Mediation Clinic and a Wills Clinic. The Legal Aid Housing and Domestic Relations field placement program and externships in governmental, judicial, and public interest law offices provide students with additional opportunities to gain practical legal experience.

Engaged Learning and CELL

In addition to offering students extensive field-based experiences with practicing attorneys, judges, and business leaders, Elon law professors employ various methods of instruction, including Socratic, group presentations, projects, and problem method, actively engaging students in their studies. To facilitate the faculty's development as excellent teachers and their ability to tap students' potential for learning, the law school has established the Center for Engaged Learning in the Law (CELL).

Law Library

The depth and breadth of the Elon Law library collection compares favorably with other law schools and is considerably larger than typical academic law libraries at their earliest stage of development. Students may access a wide variety of digital and online databases from both on- and off-campus locations. The collection is designed specifically to support the four practice-area concentrations with additional emphasis in the areas of leadership and professional ethics. The library, like the rest of the law school building, is served by a wireless network with full, high-speed Internet access.

Facilities

The School of Law is located in the four-floor, 84,000-square-foot H. Michael Weaver Building, specially designed to support Elon's engaged approach to legal education. Elon Law is one of only a few schools in the nation to house a working court. The North Carolina Business Court uses the school's high-tech courtroom, and the court's offices are also located within the building, giving students the opportunity to observe and interact with judges and attorneys. The law school's facilities also include a clinical law center, tiered classrooms with extensive multimedia capabilities, a spacious and comfortable library, full wireless network access, and a coffee bar and welcoming common area for students.

Career Services

The Career Services Office provides professional development workshops and networking opportunities for students and alumni, coordinates on-campus interview sessions and résumé requests for employers, builds relationships with prospective employers of students and alumni, and schedules job fair participation nationwide. Ninety-five percent of the class of 2009 has secured legal employment, and students at Elon Law continue to have significant success in securing employment after graduation and in internship placements with judges, law firms, and other legal employers across the nation.

Admission

Each year, the law school seeks to enroll a talented and diverse class of approximately 130 students. The law school offers two decision cycles: early decision and regular decision. Early-decision applicants agree that, if offered admission, they will enroll at Elon Law. Early-decision candidates receive decisions by December 31. Regular-decision applications are accepted throughout the admission cycle and decisions on these applications are made on a rolling basis throughout this period, with most decisions made by the middle of April. Prospective students are encouraged to visit the school to speak with an admission professional, tour the law school with a student ambassador, and visit a class.

Financial Planning

Financial aid is available to law students in the form of scholarships and loans. Scholarships are awarded on the basis of academic merit and financial need. Merit scholarships are awarded based on applicants' potential for outstanding contributions to the law school, the legal profession, and society. Admitted applicants are automatically considered for merit-based scholarships. Need-based scholarships are based on the FAFSA information. Many law students participate in federal loan programs such as unsubsidized Federal Stafford Loans and GradPLUS Loans.

Student Activities

A rich variety of student activities, organizations, and leadership opportunities make extracurricular life at Elon an excellent complement to classroom learning. Student activities at Elon Law cover a wide spectrum of academic interest areas, identity groups, political affiliations, sports, moot court activities, and service organizations.

In addition to the *Elon Law Review*, Moot Court Program, and Student Bar Association, there are over 20 active student organizations, including the Black Law Students Association, Federalist Society, Latin American Law Students Association, and Women's Law Association. The Moot Court Program is student run and coordinates intramural and national competitions, as well as participates in regional, national, and international competitions. The Student Bar Association, along with the student organizations, sponsor a range of professional, service, athletic, and social events.

APPLICANT PROFILE

Elon University School of Law

LSAT Score	GPA								
	3.75 +	3.50–3.74	3.25–3.49	3.00–3.24	2.75–2.99	2.50–2.74	2.25–2.49	2.00–2.24	Below 2.00
175–180	■	■	■	■			▨	▨	▨
170–174	■	■	■	■			▨	▨	▨
165–169	■	■	■	■			▨	▨	▨
160–164	■	■	■	■			▨	▨	▨
155–159	■	■	■	■			▨	▨	▨
150–154	■	■	■	■		▨	▨	▨	▨
145–149					▨	▨	▨	▨	▨
140–144	▨			▨	▨	▨	▨	▨	▨
135–139	▨	▨	▨	▨	▨	▨	▨	▨	▨
130–134	▨	▨	▨	▨	▨	▨	▨	▨	▨
125–129	▨	▨	▨	▨	▨	▨	▨	▨	▨
120–124	▨	▨	▨	▨	▨	▨	▨	▨	▨

■ Good Possibility   ☐ Possible   ▨ Unlikely

EMORY UNIVERSITY SCHOOL OF LAW

Gambrell Hall, 1301 Clifton Road
Atlanta, GA 30322-2770
Phone: 404.727.6802; Fax: 404.727.2477
E-mail: lawinfo@law.emory.edu; Website: www.law.emory.edu

ABA
Approved
Since
1923

The Basics

Type of school	Private
Term	Semester
Application deadline	3/1
Application fee	$80
Financial aid deadline	3/1
Can first year start other than fall?	No
Student to faculty ratio	10.6 to 1
# of housing spaces available restricted to law students	
graduate housing for which law students are eligible	826

Faculty and Administrators

	Total		Men		Women		Minorities	
	Spr	Fall	Spr	Fall	Spr	Fall	Spr	Fall
Full-time	65	63	34	34	31	29	6	6
Other full-time	0	0	0	0	0	0	0	0
Deans, librarians, & others who teach	4	4	3	3	1	1	1	1
Part-time	43	49	32	42	11	7	0	0
Total	112	116	69	79	43	37	7	7

Curriculum

	Full-Time	Part-Time
Typical first-year section size	98	0
Is there typically a "small section" of the first-year class, other than Legal Writing, taught by full-time faculty	Yes	No
If yes, typical size offered last year	49	
# of classroom course titles beyond first-year curriculum	125	

# of upper division courses, excluding seminars, with an enrollment:		
	Under 25	91
	25–49	24
	50–74	16
	75–99	8
	100+	5

# of seminars	15	
# of seminar positions available	231	
# of seminar positions filled	183	0
# of positions available in simulation courses	1,186	
# of simulation positions filled	947	0
# of positions available in faculty supervised clinical courses	190	
# of faculty supervised clinical positions filled	112	0
# involved in field placements	269	0
# involved in law journals	172	0
# involved in moot court or trial competitions	86	0
# of credit hours required to graduate	90	

JD Enrollment and Ethnicity

	Men		Women		Full-Time		Part-Time		1st-Year		Total		JD Degs. Awd.
	#	%	#	%	#	%	#	%	#	%	#	%	
All Hispanics	36	7.8	29	8.3	65	8.0	0	0.0	15	6.0	65	8.0	23
Am. Ind./AK Nat.	2	0.4	4	1.1	6	0.7	0	0.0	1	0.4	6	0.7	1
Asian	50	10.9	36	10.3	86	10.6	0	0.0	24	9.7	86	10.6	23
Black/Af. Am.	14	3.0	28	8.0	42	5.2	0	0.0	8	3.2	42	5.2	24
Nat. HI/Pac. Isl.	0	0.0	0	0.0	0	0.0	0	0.0	0	0.0	0	0.0	0
2 or more races	7	1.5	15	4.3	22	2.7	0	0.0	7	2.8	22	2.7	0
Subtotal (minor.)	109	23.7	112	32.0	221	27.3	0	0.0	55	22.2	221	27.3	71
Nonres. Alien	16	3.5	17	4.9	33	4.1	0	0.0	19	7.7	33	4.1	6
White/Cauc.	303	65.9	202	57.7	505	62.3	0	0.0	158	63.7	505	62.3	120
Unknown	32	7.0	19	5.4	51	6.3	0	0.0	16	6.5	51	6.3	28
Total	460	56.8	350	43.2	810	100.0	0	0.0	248	30.6	810		225

Transfers

Transfers in	19
Transfers out	11

Tuition and Fees

	Resident	Nonresident
Full-time	$45,098	$45,098
Part-time		
Tuition Guarantee Program		N

Living Expenses

Estimated living expenses for singles

Living on campus	Living off campus	Living at home
$26,282	$26,282	$26,282

EMORY UNIVERSITY SCHOOL OF LAW

ABA Approved Since 1923

GPA and LSAT Scores

	Total	Full-Time	Part-Time
# of apps	3,951	3,951	0
# of offers	1,287	1,287	0
# of matrics	246	246	0
75% GPA	3.79	3.79	0.00
Median GPA	3.70	3.70	0.00
25% GPA	3.40	3.40	0.00
75% LSAT	166	166	0
Median LSAT	165	165	0
25% LSAT	159	159	0

Grants and Scholarships (from prior year)

	Total #	Total %	Full-Time #	Full-Time %	Part-Time #	Part-Time %
Total # of students	792		792		0	
Total # receiving grants	553	69.8	553	69.8	0	0.0
Less than 1/2 tuition	275	34.7	275	34.7	0	0.0
Half to full tuition	261	33.0	261	33.0	0	0.0
Full tuition	2	0.3	2	0.3	0	0.0
More than full tuition	15	1.9	15	1.9	0	0.0
Median grant amount			$22,000		$0	

Informational and Library Resources

Total amount spent on library materials	$1,131,019
Study seating capacity inside the library	516
# of full-time equivalent professional librarians	13
Hours per week library is open	96
# of open, wired connections available to students	64
# of networked computers available for use by students	72
Has wireless network?	Y
Requires computer?	N

JD Attrition (from prior year)

	Academic #	Other #	Total #	Total %
1st year	0	4	4	1.4
2nd year	0	11	11	4.1
3rd year	0	0	0	0.0
4th year	0	0	0	0.0

Employment (9 months after graduation)

For up-to-date employment data, go to employmentsummary.abaquestionnaire.org on the ABA website.

Bar Passage Rates

First-time takers	153	Reporting %	76.47
Average school %	94.87	Average state %	83.61
Average pass difference	11.26		

Jurisdiction	Takers	Passers	Pass %	State %	Diff %
Georgia	117	111	94.87	83.61	11.26

EMORY UNIVERSITY SCHOOL OF LAW

Gambrell Hall, 1301 Clifton Road
Atlanta, GA 30322-2770
Phone: 404.727.6802; Fax: 404.727.2477
E-mail: lawinfo@law.emory.edu; Website: www.law.emory.edu

Introduction

Emory's location in Atlanta, a national business and legal center, gives law students the opportunity to take advanced classes from, and work with, some of the leading judges and lawyers in the United States. Atlanta also is one of America's most beautiful and culturally diverse cities.

The law school also benefits from being located on the campus of Emory University, which was founded in 1836. Emory University School of Law is accredited by the American Bar Association, is a member of the Association of American Law Schools, and has a chapter of the Order of the Coif.

Curriculum

The basic program of study involves three years of full-time study leading to the JD degree. The fall semester runs from late August to mid-December; the spring semester begins in early January and ends in mid-May.

The program of courses for the first year is generally prescribed, though beginning with the spring 2011 semester, first-year students may choose one elective. The program of courses for the second and third years primarily is elective. Students can sample a broad spectrum of courses or concentrate on a particular area of law.

All first-year courses and the basic second- and third-year courses are taught by full-time faculty members. A distinguished group of judges and practicing attorneys offer specialized courses.

Library and Physical Facilities

Emory School of Law is located in Gambrell Hall, part of Emory's 630-acre campus in Druid Hills, six miles southeast of downtown Atlanta.

Gambrell Hall contains classrooms, faculty offices, administrative offices, student-organization offices, and a 325-seat auditorium. The school provides wireless Internet access throughout its facilities. Gambrell Hall also houses a state-of-the-art courtroom with computer connections for judge, counsel, and jury; a document camera; a DVD player; videoconferencing; and a four-camera operation with feeds to remote locations.

The Hugh F. MacMillan Law Library sits adjacent to Gambrell Hall and is designed for easy student access. Students are trained on LexisNexis and Westlaw terminals and learn both the techniques of computer-assisted legal research and traditional research methods. Students also may use the library's computer labs that offer Apple and PC computers.

Special Programs

Emory Law combines a practical and disciplined approach toward the study of law with a commitment to providing students with experiential learning opportunities that engage them in the many roles the law plays in our society. Our students engage with the law through learning opportunities that create graduates who are ready to apply their knowledge to make an impact in real and significant ways, as lawyers and as citizens of the world. We teach the practice of law through our outstanding programs in trial techniques, intellectual property, child advocacy, and environmental law, as well as through expanded emphasis on transactional skills. Our centers of excellence in law and religion, world law, feminism and legal theory, and transactional law are interdisciplinary, integrative, and international in approach.

Emory's Trial Techniques Program affords our students exposure to the challenges of conducting direct and cross-examination, developing a case theory and approach, and conducting opening and closing arguments. More than half of the students participate in Emory's field placement program, where students may earn academic credit while clerking for a federal judge, researching intellectual property issues for major corporations such as the Coca-Cola Company, and representing clients on behalf of Atlanta Legal Aid.

Emory Law's Center for Transactional Law and Practice is at the forefront of educating students and professionals on topics related to business transactions. Students participate through Emory's Transactional Law Certificate Program, while the center offers a number of workshops and seminars designed specifically for practicing attorneys. The center also regularly hosts a conference for educators in the area of teaching transactional skills.

Students also may gain practical experience in intellectual property and corporate/commercial law by participating in TI:GER (Technological Innovation: Generating Economic Results), a program of technology and business law cosponsored by Emory's School of Law and Economics Department and Georgia Institute of Technology's Dupree School of Management. Students may participate in one of Emory's own clinics: the Barton Child Law and Policy Center, working to promote and protect the well-being of neglected and abused children; the Barton Juvenile Defender Clinic, representing children charged with delinquent acts; the Turner Environmental Law Clinic, offering a practical clinical education to the aspiring environmental attorney; or the International Humanitarian Law Clinic, focusing on upholding the rule of law on behalf of detainees and on educating and training officials on humanitarian law in war-torn countries.

Emory offers a comprehensive international law program and is home to the World Law Institute. Emory Law capitalizes on the presence of other strong campus programs by combining coursework and programs to create unique and synergistic programs of study. The law school offers joint-degree programs with Emory's Goizueta Business School, Candler School of Theology, School of Public Health, and the Graduate School of Arts and Sciences.

Admission

The law school accepts beginning students for the fall term only. Prior to enrollment, a student must have earned a bachelor's degree from an approved institution. Applications for admission must be received by Emory no later than March 1. Early applications are encouraged. Many factors are considered in making admission decisions. Of particular importance are academic accomplishments and LSAT scores. Extracurricular activities, work experience, level of quality and difficulty of undergraduate courses, performance in graduate school, and letters of recommendation are also considered. We encourage applications from members of underrepresented groups, and such applicants should provide the Dean of Admission with specific information about their background or accomplishments that would be of particular interest. Applicants are encouraged to visit the law school. Upon acceptance, applicants are required to submit a nonrefundable $750 tuition deposit to reserve a space in the entering class.

Student Activities

A wide variety of organizations and activities are available to students. There are three law reviews at Emory—*Emory Law Journal, Emory Bankruptcy Developments Journal,* and *Emory International Law Review*—and more than 30 percent of the second- and third-year students are involved in law review research, writing, and editing.

Students also participate in moot court and mock trial. Each first-year student prepares a brief and presents an oral argument. In addition, many second- and third-year students compete in intramural and national moot court competitions.

There are approximately 40 student organizations reflecting a broad range of special interest and social groups as well as a very active Student Bar Association.

Career Services

A full-time career services office assists students in obtaining permanent, summer, and part-time employment. It arranges interviews with employers from many parts of the country and maintains extensive files on a wide variety of professional opportunities across the United States. Many Emory graduates join private law firms after graduation. Others work as judicial clerks, enter government service, or work for banks, corporations, or legal aid agencies.

The majority of Emory's students stay in the Southeast. Approximately 25 percent work in the Northeast and Mid-Atlantic. Smaller percentages work in the Midwest, Southwest, and West.

The career services office provides extensive training on résumé writing, interview skills, and job-search techniques, as well as numerous opportunities to network with attorneys in a variety of practice areas and settings.

APPLICANT PROFILE

Emory University School of Law

LSAT Score	GPA								
	3.75 +	3.50–3.74	3.25–3.49	3.00–3.24	2.75–2.99	2.50–2.74	2.25–2.49	2.00–2.24	Below 2.00
175–180									
170–174									
165–169									
160–164									
155–159									
150–154									
145–149									
140–144									
135–139									
130–134									
125–129									
120–124									

■ Good Possibility □ Possible ▨ Unlikely

Note: This graph reflects admission decisions for fall 2011 and is to be used only as a general guide to determining chances for admittance.

FAULKNER UNIVERSITY, THOMAS GOODE JONES SCHOOL OF LAW

5345 Atlanta Highway
Montgomery, AL 36109
Phone: 334.386.7210
E-mail: law@faulkner.edu; Website: www.faulkner.edu/law

The Basics

Type of school	Private
Term	Semester
Application deadline	6/15
Application fee	$50
Financial aid deadline	7/1
Can first year start other than fall?	No
Student to faculty ratio	14.6 to 1
# of housing spaces available restricted to law students	
graduate housing for which law students are eligible	

Faculty and Administrators

	Total		Men		Women		Minorities	
	Spr	Fall	Spr	Fall	Spr	Fall	Spr	Fall
Full-time	18	19	15	16	3	3	3	2
Other full-time	1	1	1	1	0	0	0	0
Deans, librarians, & others who teach	12	12	6	6	6	6	0	0
Part-time	4	7	2	5	2	2	0	0
Total	35	39	24	28	11	11	3	2

JD Enrollment and Ethnicity

	Men		Women		Full-Time		Part-Time		1st-Year		Total		JD Degs. Awd.
	#	%	#	%	#	%	#	%	#	%	#	%	
All Hispanics	3	1.5	2	1.5	5	1.5	0	0.0	2	1.6	5	1.5	3
Am. Ind./AK Nat.	2	1.0	2	1.5	4	1.2	0	0.0	4	3.2	4	1.2	1
Asian	3	1.5	2	1.5	4	1.2	1	100.0	3	2.4	5	1.5	1
Black/Af. Am.	13	6.5	13	9.7	26	7.8	0	0.0	12	9.7	26	7.8	8
Nat. HI/Pac. Isl.	0	0.0	2	1.5	2	0.6	0	0.0	0	0.0	2	0.6	0
2 or more races	0	0.0	0	0.0	0	0.0	0	0.0	0	0.0	0	0.0	0
Subtotal (minor.)	21	10.4	21	15.7	41	12.3	1	100.0	21	16.9	42	12.5	13
Nonres. Alien	0	0.0	0	0.0	0	0.0	0	0.0	0	0.0	0	0.0	0
White/Cauc.	175	87.1	109	81.3	284	85.0	0	0.0	96	77.4	284	84.8	89
Unknown	5	2.5	4	3.0	9	2.7	0	0.0	7	5.6	9	2.7	0
Total	201	60.0	134	40.0	334	99.7	1	0.3	124	37.0	335		102

Curriculum

	Full-Time	Part-Time
Typical first-year section size	75	0
Is there typically a "small section" of the first-year class, other than Legal Writing, taught by full-time faculty	No	No
If yes, typical size offered last year		
# of classroom course titles beyond first-year curriculum	51	
# of upper division courses, excluding seminars, with an enrollment: Under 25	41	
25–49	15	
50–74	9	
75–99	0	
100+	0	
# of seminars	8	
# of seminar positions available	96	
# of seminar positions filled	71	5
# of positions available in simulation courses	226	
# of simulation positions filled	187	11
# of positions available in faculty supervised clinical courses	80	
# of faculty supervised clinical positions filled	75	1
# involved in field placements	73	2
# involved in law journals	42	3
# involved in moot court or trial competitions	49	0
# of credit hours required to graduate	90	

Transfers

Transfers in	0
Transfers out	9

Tuition and Fees

	Resident	Nonresident
Full-time	$32,187	$32,187
Part-time		
Tuition Guarantee Program		N

Living Expenses

Estimated living expenses for singles

Living on campus	Living off campus	Living at home
N/A	$22,400	N/A

FAULKNER UNIVERSITY, THOMAS GOODE JONES SCHOOL OF LAW

ABA
Approved
Since
2006

GPA and LSAT Scores

	Total	Full-Time	Part-Time
# of apps	717	717	0
# of offers	406	406	0
# of matrics	124	124	0
75% GPA	3.36	3.36	0.00
Median GPA	3.04	3.04	0.00
25% GPA	2.66	2.66	0.00
75% LSAT	152	152	0
Median LSAT	149	149	0
25% LSAT	146	146	0

Grants and Scholarships (from prior year)

	Total		Full-Time		Part-Time	
	#	%	#	%	#	%
Total # of students	354		341		13	
Total # receiving grants	110	31.1	110	32.3	0	0.0
Less than 1/2 tuition	43	12.1	43	12.6	0	0.0
Half to full tuition	51	14.4	51	15.0	0	0.0
Full tuition	16	4.5	16	4.7	0	0.0
More than full tuition	0	0.0	0	0.0	0	0.0
Median grant amount			$15,500		$0	

Informational and Library Resources

Total amount spent on library materials	$611,730
Study seating capacity inside the library	213
# of full-time equivalent professional librarians	6
Hours per week library is open	94
# of open, wired connections available to students	205
# of networked computers available for use by students	40
Has wireless network?	Y
Requires computer?	N

JD Attrition (from prior year)

	Academic	Other	Total	
	#	#	#	%
1st year	20	18	38	26.0
2nd year	0	0	0	0.0
3rd year	0	0	0	0.0
4th year	0	0	0	0.0

Employment (9 months after graduation)

For up-to-date employment data, go to employmentsummary.abaquestionnaire.org on the ABA website.

Bar Passage Rates

First-time takers	83	Reporting %	89.16
Average school %	91.90	Average state %	84.48
Average pass difference	7.42		

Jurisdiction	Takers	Passers	Pass %	State %	Diff %
Alabama	60	55	91.67	84.91	6.76
Georgia	8	7	87.50	83.61	3.89
South Carolina	4	4	100.00	79.69	20.31
Tennessee	2	2	100.00	84.24	15.76

FAULKNER UNIVERSITY, THOMAS GOODE JONES SCHOOL OF LAW

5345 Atlanta Highway
Montgomery, AL 36109
Phone: 334.386.7210
E-mail: law@faulkner.edu; Website: www.faulkner.edu/law

Faulkner University, Thomas Goode Jones School of Law

Thomas Goode Jones School of Law has a rich tradition of educating law students. In keeping with its mission, the school seeks excellence in all things and promotes learning with integrity in a caring Christian environment that sustains and nurtures faith. The School of Law encourages and prepares students for lives of service and purpose.

The School of Law became part of Faulkner University in 1983. Faulkner University, Thomas Goode Jones School of Law ("Faulkner Law") received provisional accreditation by the American Bar Association in 2006 and full approval in 2009. Faulkner Law continues its rise with an innovative curriculum, an energetic faculty, a diverse student body, rigorous professional education, and a rich commitment to justice and service to the bench and bar.

Montgomery and the River Region

The School of Law is located in the capital of Alabama. Montgomery is widely known as the birthplace of the Confederacy and the American Civil Rights Movement. It is home to some of the nation's most historically significant landmarks and monuments. One can visit the First White House of the Confederacy and the steps of the state capitol building where Jefferson Davis was sworn in as President of the Confederate States of America. On these same steps, Dr. Martin Luther King Jr. completed the freedom march from Selma to Montgomery. Here Dr. King advocated for equality of all people, regardless of race.

Along with its rich history, Montgomery is known for its contribution to the arts. One notable contribution is the Wynton M. Blount Cultural Park, which includes the Montgomery Museum of Fine Arts, the acclaimed Alabama Shakespeare Festival, and the beautiful Shakespeare Gardens.

Montgomery offers a small-town atmosphere with big-city amenities. Montgomery also boasts excellent access to the legal community as it is home to the Supreme Court of Alabama, the Alabama legislature, and more than 200 law firms or other organizations that employ lawyers within a short driving distance of campus.

Library and Physical Facilities

In 2011, the School of Law completed construction of the Allen Law Center, adding additional classrooms, a new courtroom, clinical law offices, and student space. Classrooms are outfitted for laptop computers, and wireless Internet is available throughout the building and library. Students have access to the student lounge, a new coffee shop, and conference rooms for student organization meetings.

The George H. Jones Jr. Law Library supports the School of Law's curriculum and the legal research requirements of its students and faculty. Computers on both floors of the library enable free access to the Internet, word processing packages, and legal research databases. A spacious computer lab facilitates computer-assisted legal instruction and research.

Alternative Dispute Resolution Program

The Alternative Dispute Resolution (ADR) Program enables law students to integrate their knowledge of conflict management principles and dispute resolution processes with professional skills. This program allows students to receive training normally available only through on-the-job experience after graduation.

Students can earn a certificate in ADR, which is not a supplemental degree but an opportunity for Juris Doctor candidates to enrich their skills training while still in law school. The certificate in ADR requires completion of the following courses: Arbitration, Dispute Resolution Processes, Interviewing/Counseling and Negotiation, Mediation Clinic, and an elective skills course. All of the certificate courses contain both an academic component and a skills component.

Advocacy Program

The School of Law's Advocacy Programs prepare students for the rigors of litigation and the practice of law through national and intraschool competitions. Student advocates travel throughout the United States to participate in numerous moot court, mock trial, negotiation, and mediation competitions. The School of Law's record of regional and national championships is a testament to its cocurricular advocacy program's emphasis on excellence in trial and appellate skills. Recent team successes, to name a few, include the 2012 August A. Rendigs National Products Liability Moot Court Competition Champion, 2012 National Trial Competition (NTC) Regional Semi-Finalist, 2012 ABA-National Appellate Advocacy Competition (NAAC) Regional Finalist and Regional Semi-Finalist, 2011 Lone Star Classic trial competition National Finalist, 2011 Mercer Legal Ethics and Professionalism Moot Court Competition Best Brief, 2010 August A. Rendigs Moot Court Competition National Champion, 2010 Frederick Douglass Moot Court Southern Regional Champion, and 2010 National Moot Court Competition (ACTL) National Quarterfinalist. In addition to national competitions, the Faulkner Law Student Board of Advocates host three intramural competitions each year that provide all students with an opportunity to participate in moot court and mock trial competition.

Clinical Opportunities and Externships

Clinics and externships provide students with demanding, real-life experiences. The clinics immerse students in an ethical, creative practice environment designed to serve clients with excellence and to empower students to practice with independence, confidence, and integrity. In conjunction with our many community partners, students participating in our legal clinics and externships are able to serve the most vulnerable of our neighbors while preparing for sophisticated, meaningful work.

The School of Law operates three clinical programs: the Mediation Clinic, the Family Violence Clinic, and the Elder Law Clinic. Each clinic includes rigorous doctrinal learning and skills training.

In the Mediation Clinic, students mediate cases for litigants in area small claims courts. The Mediation Clinic is an integral component of the School of Law's certificate program in Alternative Dispute Resolution, and students receive recognition from the Alabama Center for Dispute Resolution upon completing their work in that clinic.

In the Family Violence Clinic, students represent victims of domestic violence and child abuse in area courts to receive protective orders and provide services to vulnerable clients in need. The School of Law and Legal Services of Alabama are the recipients of the Family Sunshine Center's President's Special Service Award in recognition of outstanding service and support through the Family Violence Clinic.

In the Elder Law Clinic, students provide pro bono legal advice to clients over 60. Clinic students prepare estate planning documents, powers of attorney, and advance medical directives, and they provide advice and counsel on government benefits, consumer protection, and financial exploitation. Students also present community education programs to groups of local seniors to promote self-reliance and advocacy.

The School of Law's Externship Program affords students the opportunity to supplement their classroom experience by working in a variety of legal settings. Students receive academic credit for their supervised legal work in judicial, governmental, military, public service, and public interest law offices. Students work in federal and state courts with prosecutors, defenders, policy makers, and issue advocates. Students routinely count their externship work as among their best moments in law school.

Foundations Course

Reflecting the School of Law's commitment to prepare competent and ethical lawyers for the practice of law, a centerpiece of the first-year curriculum is Foundations of Law, a course that introduces students to the foundational ideas of our legal institutions. The Foundations course emphasizes the basics of legal reasoning: the doctrine of precedent, the distinction between rules and principles, standards of decision-making, and most importantly for new law students, the rudiments of logic, including a heavy focus on syllogistic reasoning and inferences.

Public Interest Program

The School of Law's commitment to serve those who otherwise could not afford such assistance complements the legal profession's rich tradition of service.

The Public Interest Program provides opportunities for students to begin their career of service while utilizing the practical skills obtained in their legal education. This program is voluntary and provides students with opportunities to provide community service or work for nonprofit organizations, government agencies, and/or private attorneys or firms conducting pro bono legal work. To be recognized as a fellow in this program, students are challenged to perform at least 50 hours of voluntary service during their law school career.

Student Organizations

The Student Bar Association (SBA) serves the student body and every student is a member. The SBA fosters relationships with members of the legal community and sponsors social functions and fundraising events. The judicial branch of the SBA is the Honor Court.

Other student organizations at the law school include the American Association for Justice, American Constitution Society, Black Law Students Association, Board of Advocates, Christian Legal Society, Law School Democrats, Federalist Society, Jones Law Republicans, Jones Public Interest Law Foundation, Phi Alpha Delta, Student Animal Legal Defense Fund, and Women's Legal Society. The Alabama Defense Lawyers Association and the Alabama Criminal Defense Lawyers Association will allow law students from the School of Law to participate as student members.

The *Faulkner Law Review* is a scholarly legal journal published by student editors and members. Membership is considered an honor and provides students an opportunity to hone their research and writing skills.

Scholarships, Tuition, and Fees

The School of Law offers merit-based scholarships to qualified entering students. Admitted applicants are automatically considered for scholarship awards. Awards range from 10 percent tuition forgiveness to 100 percent tuition forgiveness. Scholarships are also available to upper-level students who perform well academically during their first year or two years of law school.

Please consult the law school's website for current tuition rates. Students pay a Student Activities Fee of $350, which is charged only once at the outset of a student's law school career, and an Emergency Notification Fee of $10, which is charged per semester.

APPLICANT PROFILE

Faulkner University, Thomas Goode Jones School of Law

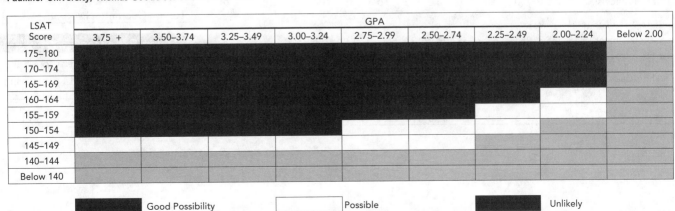

LSAT Score	GPA								
	3.75 +	3.50–3.74	3.25–3.49	3.00–3.24	2.75–2.99	2.50–2.74	2.25–2.49	2.00–2.24	Below 2.00
175–180									
170–174									
165–169									
160–164									
155–159									
150–154									
145–149									
140–144									
Below 140									

Good Possibility   Possible   Unlikely

FLORIDA A&M UNIVERSITY COLLEGE OF LAW

201 Beggs Avenue
Orlando, FL 32801
Phone: 407.254.3268; Fax: 407.254.2450
E-mail: famulaw.admissions@famu.edu; Website: www.law.famu.edu

ABA
Approved
Since
2004

The Basics

Type of school	Public
Term	Semester
Application deadline	5/31
Application fee	$33
Financial aid deadline	3/1
Can first year start other than fall?	No
Student to faculty ratio	20.5 to 1
# of housing spaces available restricted to law students	
graduate housing for which law students are eligible	

Faculty and Administrators

	Total		Men		Women		Minorities	
	Spr	Fall	Spr	Fall	Spr	Fall	Spr	Fall
Full-time	24	25	11	12	13	13	17	18
Other full-time	5	9	4	4	1	5	3	5
Deans, librarians, & others who teach	9	8	3	3	6	5	8	6
Part-time	20	15	14	13	6	2	4	5
Total	58	57	32	32	26	25	32	34

Curriculum

		Full-Time	Part-Time
Typical first-year section size		75	60
Is there typically a "small section" of the first-year class, other than Legal Writing, taught by full-time faculty		No	No
If yes, typical size offered last year			
# of classroom course titles beyond first-year curriculum		156	
# of upper division courses, excluding seminars, with an enrollment:	Under 25	98	
	25–49	41	
	50–74	17	
	75–99	0	
	100+	0	
# of seminars		19	
# of seminar positions available		309	
# of seminar positions filled		168	67
# of positions available in simulation courses		314	
# of simulation positions filled		183	108
# of positions available in faculty supervised clinical courses		120	
# of faculty supervised clinical positions filled		51	18
# involved in field placements		34	6
# involved in law journals		44	7
# involved in moot court or trial competitions		27	6
# of credit hours required to graduate		90	

JD Enrollment and Ethnicity

	Men		Women		Full-Time		Part-Time		1st-Year		Total		JD Degs. Awd.
	#	%	#	%	#	%	#	%	#	%	#	%	
All Hispanics	33	10.1	46	12.3	57	11.2	22	11.5	34	13.4	79	11.3	21
Am. Ind./AK Nat.	5	1.5	1	0.3	2	0.4	4	2.1	2	0.8	6	0.9	1
Asian	13	4.0	11	2.9	20	3.9	4	2.1	5	2.0	24	3.4	2
Black/Af. Am.	159	48.8	224	59.7	287	56.4	96	50.0	164	64.6	383	54.6	72
Nat. HI/Pac. Isl.	0	0.0	0	0.0	0	0.0	0	0.0	0	0.0	0	0.0	2
2 or more races	3	0.9	5	1.3	7	1.4	1	0.5	8	3.1	8	1.1	0
Subtotal (minor.)	213	65.3	287	76.5	373	73.3	127	66.1	213	83.9	500	71.3	98
Nonres. Alien	0	0.0	0	0.0	0	0.0	0	0.0	0	0.0	0	0.0	0
White/Cauc.	112	34.4	86	22.9	133	26.1	65	33.9	38	15.0	198	28.2	53
Unknown	1	0.3	2	0.5	3	0.6	0	0.0	3	1.2	3	0.4	2
Total	326	46.5	375	53.5	509	72.6	192	27.4	254	36.2	701		153

Transfers

Transfers in	0
Transfers out	9

Tuition and Fees

	Resident	Nonresident
Full-time	$12,424	$32,327
Part-time	$8,892	$23,016
Tuition Guarantee Program		N

Living Expenses

Estimated living expenses for singles

Living on campus	Living off campus	Living at home
N/A	$26,086	$14,648

FLORIDA A&M UNIVERSITY COLLEGE OF LAW

ABA
Approved
Since
2004

GPA and LSAT Scores

	Total	Full-Time	Part-Time
# of apps	1,891	1,580	311
# of offers	711	600	111
# of matrics	281	206	75
75% GPA	3.34	3.30	3.42
Median GPA	3.10	3.11	3.09
25% GPA	2.81	2.80	2.83
75% LSAT	151	151	152
Median LSAT	148	148	149
25% LSAT	145	145	146

Grants and Scholarships (from prior year)

	Total		Full-Time		Part-Time	
	#	%	#	%	#	%
Total # of students	669		458		211	
Total # receiving grants	39	5.8	31	6.8	8	3.8
Less than 1/2 tuition	20	3.0	19	4.1	1	0.5
Half to full tuition	2	0.3	2	0.4	0	0.0
Full tuition	17	2.5	10	2.2	7	3.3
More than full tuition	0	0.0	0	0.0	0	0.0
Median grant amount			$4,500		$7,562	

Informational and Library Resources

Total amount spent on library materials	$791,621
Study seating capacity inside the library	416
# of full-time equivalent professional librarians	7
Hours per week library is open	100
# of open, wired connections available to students	60
# of networked computers available for use by students	63
Has wireless network?	Y
Requires computer?	N

JD Attrition (from prior year)

	Academic	Other	Total	
	#	#	#	%
1st year	37	37	74	25.7
2nd year	4	4	8	4.4
3rd year	0	1	1	0.6
4th year	0	0	0	0.0

Employment (9 months after graduation)

For up-to-date employment data, go to
employmentsummary.abaquestionnaire.org on the ABA website.

Bar Passage Rates

First-time takers	145	Reporting %	74.48
Average school %	61.11	Average state %	77.63
Average pass difference	−16.52		

Jurisdiction	Takers	Passers	Pass %	State %	Diff %
Florida	108	66	61.11	77.63	−16.52

FLORIDA A&M UNIVERSITY COLLEGE OF LAW

201 Beggs Avenue
Orlando, FL 32801
Phone: 407.254.3268; Fax: 407.254.2450
E-mail: famulaw.admissions@famu.edu; Website: www.law.famu.edu

A Unique History

The College of Law is proud to be a part of Florida A&M University (FAMU), the largest single-campus historically black university in the United States in terms of enrollment and in terms of the number of baccalaureate degrees granted. Founded in 1887, FAMU is a comprehensive, public, coeducational, and fully accredited land-grant university offering a broad range of instruction, research, and service programs at the undergraduate, graduate, and professional levels. Located on the highest of seven hills in the capital city of Tallahassee, FAMU is the third oldest of the nine institutions in Florida's State University System. The College of Law's rich tradition of excellence dates back to its original founding in 1949. Between 1949 and 1968, the College of Law graduated 57 students. In 2002, the FAMU College of Law reopened in downtown Orlando, Florida, as the only public law school in Central Florida. In 2006, the College of Law moved into its brand-new permanent building at 201 Beggs Avenue. The College of Law offers a quality legal education at an affordable price in state-of-the-art facilities and has been nationally recognized for its diverse student body and its clinical programs. The College of Law received full accreditation from the American Bar Association in July 2009.

The College of Law is located in Orlando, considered to be one of the most beautiful and dynamic cities in Florida. A racially and culturally diverse community, Orlando is considered not only one of the fastest growing metropolitan areas in Florida, but also one of the fastest major employment markets in the nation. Orlando offers affordable housing, great weather year-round, and easy access to cultural and recreational activities such as Disney World, Universal Studios, and various professional athletic teams. Located in the heart of downtown, the College of Law is within walking distance of government buildings, courthouses, and a wide variety of cultural, educational, and recreational opportunities.

An Active and Multicultural Student Body

Since opening in the fall of 2002, FAMU College of Law has admitted nine entering classes and has a current student enrollment exceeding 600 students. The College of Law has consistently received national recognition as one of the most diverse law schools in the nation, making for a classroom experience unduplicated elsewhere. The College of Law is committed to helping its students further develop their talents, professional skills, and goals. To that end, we offer cocurricular and extracurricular activities, including our award-winning competition teams. These cocurricular and extracurricular programs enhance not only the study of the law, but students' leadership and professional abilities and oral and written communication skills. FAMU College of Law students are very active within the law school and in the Central Florida community. As students at a recently reestablished law school, they have taken on the challenge of establishing organizations that will serve current and future students for years to come. The FAMU College of Law Student Bar Association supports and governs all student activities and organizations at the College of Law. Since 2002, students have founded the Jesse J. McCrary Jr. Chapter of the National Black Law Students Association; the Association

of Trial Lawyers of America; the Women's Law Caucus; the Entertainment, Arts, and Sports Law Society; the Hispanic Law Students; the Federalist Society; Phi Alpha Delta; and many other student organizations.

Programs of Study

The FAMU College of Law offers both a full-time day program and a part-time evening program of study. Full-time day program students must successfully complete six semesters or three academic years in order to fulfill their degree requirements. Enrollment in the day program represents a commitment to the full-time study of law. Part-time evening program students must successfully complete their degree requirements in four years consisting of eight semesters and three summers. Part-time evening classes typically meet Monday through Thursday beginning at 6:00 PM. The part-time evening program is designed for students who are unable to attend school on a full-time basis and want to earn a law degree while working full time. Courses in both programs demand the same standards of performance by students and are taught by full-time faculty members who are assisted by adjunct faculty.

Curriculum

The law school offers a rigorous traditional curriculum of required and elective courses that are complemented by extensive skills training that includes an intensive three-year writing program and a strong clinical program. The College of Law's curriculum is designed to provide students with both the intellectual and practical skills necessary to meet the demands of the modern practice of law by combining theoretical coursework with clinical and practical experiences. Through the use of elective courses and leading practitioners as adjunct faculty, students are introduced to emerging trends and developments in the law.

The Center for International Law and Justice

The Center for International Law and Justice was created to cultivate student interest in human rights and freedom, providing students with a substantive background in international law and foreign affairs as well as the application of policy in the developing world—specifically, Africa, Asia, the Caribbean, and Latin America. Beginning in the first year of study, students may opt into the international law track. The center offers a new certificate of study in **International Human Rights Law and Global Justice Studies**. In addition, the center annually awards an International Human Rights Fellowship, which provides scholarship and summer internship support to a student with a track record of public service and a keen interest or experience in international human rights law and international affairs.

A Commitment to Public Service

At the core of the College of Law mission is a commitment to public service. As such, all students are required to engage in public service by participating in and satisfactorily completing one of several available clinical offerings or by completing at least 20 hours in a pro bono experience. *National Jurist* magazine recently cited the College of Law as among the top in the nation for providing students with clinical opportunities. The Clinical Program educates students in the practical art of lawyering, while providing quality legal representation to underserved individuals and organizations. Additionally, the Clinical Program helps students explore career potential by exposing them to a broad spectrum of legal opportunities. Via a combination of in-house clinics and externships, the Clinical Program includes the following practice areas: Guardian Ad Litem, Community Economic Development, Housing, Homelessness and Legal Advocacy, Criminal Defense, Criminal Prosecution, Death Penalty, and Volunteer Income Tax Assistance.

Amazing Affordability

Tuition rates at FAMU College of Law are consistently the most affordable among Florida law schools, and nationally, FAMU Law tuition rates offer a tremendous value. For the 2011–2012 academic year, tuition for Florida residents was $392.46 per credit hour, and tuition for non-Florida residents was $1,034.49 per credit hour. Approximately 90 percent of law students are receiving some form of financial aid, including federal loans and merit-based scholarships. Merit-based scholarships are awarded to a select number of entering full-time and part-time students who have excelled academically and who possess other outstanding qualifications for the study of law. All admitted students are automatically considered for these awards, which vary from $1,000 to full tuition.

The Admission Process

Admission to the College of Law has become increasingly competitive. Accordingly, applicants are strongly encouraged to apply early in the process to maximize chances for admission. The law school seeks diligent, hardworking students with a broad array of talents and experiences who demonstrate both an exceptional aptitude for the study of law and a strong history of, or commitment to, public service. Selection for admission is based on a thorough evaluation of all factors in an applicant's file. While an applicant's academic record and LSAT performance are weighted heavily in the evaluation process, the Admissions Committee considers other factors, including writing ability, as evidenced by the LSAT writing sample and the personal statement; community and public service; academic honors and awards; work experience; leadership ability; extracurricular activities; letters of recommendation; and character and motivation.

Applicant Profile

While an applicant's undergraduate record and LSAT score are important, they are not the sole determinants for admission to law school. There are no combinations of grades or scores that assure admission or denial. An applicant's transcripts are analyzed for breadth and depth of coursework, trends in grades, and rank. The competitiveness of an applicant's school and major are taken into consideration as are special activities, honors, and awards received by the applicant. Other aspects of the application significantly influence the decision, such as work experience and evidence of a commitment to, or interest in, public service. In making its decision, the faculty Admissions Committee aims to enroll an entering class of students with the strongest combination of qualifications and the greatest potential to contribute to FAMU College of Law and to the legal profession.

APPLICANT PROFILE

Florida A&M University College of Law
This grid includes only applicants who earned 120–180 LSAT scores under standard administrations.

LSAT Score	3.75 +		3.50–3.74		3.25–3.49		3.00–3.24		2.75–2.99		2.50–2.74		2.25–2.49		2.00–2.24		Below 2.00		No GPA		Total	
	Apps	Adm	Apps	Adm	Apps	Adm	Apps	Adm	Apps	Adm	Apps	Adm	Apps	Adm	Apps	Adm	Apps	Adm	Apps	Adm	Apps	Adm
175–180	0	0	0	0	0	0	0	0	0	0	0	0	0	0	0	0	0	0	0	0	0	0
170–174	0	0	0	0	0	0	0	0	0	0	0	0	0	0	0	0	0	0	0	0	0	0
165–169	0	0	0	0	1	1	0	0	0	0	2	2	1	1	0	0	0	0	0	0	4	4
160–164	1	1	3	3	9	7	4	4	5	5	2	2	0	0	0	0	1	0	0	0	25	22
155–159	7	7	10	8	12	11	15	14	11	8	8	5	6	5	4	2	0	0	0	0	73	60
150–154	7	6	44	38	39	34	52	42	46	41	37	30	29	17	12	4	3	0	2	2	271	214
145–149	23	16	51	41	79	53	128	92	104	55	94	54	44	18	23	4	6	0	13	5	565	338
140–144	13	6	55	16	87	18	110	27	117	10	75	6	59	0	35	0	14	0	12	0	577	83
135–139	6	0	17	0	27	0	36	0	57	0	47	0	23	0	17	0	4	0	13	0	247	0
130–134	0	0	4	0	6	0	17	0	16	0	16	0	10	0	11	0	2	0	6	0	88	0
125–129	1	0	1	0	2	0	6	0	1	0	5	0	5	0	3	0	1	0	1	0	26	0
120–124	0	0	0	0	0	0	0	0	0	0	2	0	0	0	0	0	0	0	0	0	2	0
Total	58	36	185	106	262	124	368	179	357	119	288	99	177	41	105	10	31	0	47	7	1878	721

Apps = Number of Applicants
Adm = Number Admitted
Reflects 99% of the total applicant pool; highest LSAT data reported.

FLORIDA COASTAL SCHOOL OF LAW

8787 Baypine Road
Jacksonville, FL 32256
Phone: 904.680.7710, toll-free: 877.210.2591; Fax: 904.680.7692
E-mail: admissions@fcsl.edu; Website: www.fcsl.edu

ABA
Approved
Since
2002

The Basics

Type of school	Private
Term	Semester
Application deadline	8/15 1/23
Application fee	$0
Financial aid deadline	
Can first year start other than fall?	Yes
Student to faculty ratio	21.6 to 1
# of housing spaces available restricted to law students	
graduate housing for which law students are eligible	

Faculty and Administrators

	Total		Men		Women		Minorities	
	Spr	Fall	Spr	Fall	Spr	Fall	Spr	Fall
Full-time	61	69	28	32	33	37	9	7
Other full-time	4	6	0	1	4	5	0	0
Deans, librarians, & others who teach	10	10	2	2	8	8	1	1
Part-time	62	61	41	41	21	20	4	3
Total	137	146	71	76	66	70	14	11

Curriculum

		Full-Time	Part-Time
Typical first-year section size		75	0
Is there typically a "small section" of the first-year class, other than Legal Writing, taught by full-time faculty		No	No
If yes, typical size offered last year			
# of classroom course titles beyond first-year curriculum		125	
# of upper division courses, excluding seminars, with an enrollment:	Under 25	158	
	25–49	82	
	50–74	51	
	75–99	12	
	100+	1	
# of seminars		24	
# of seminar positions available		537	
# of seminar positions filled		372	0
# of positions available in simulation courses		2,434	
# of simulation positions filled		2,112	0
# of positions available in faculty supervised clinical courses		150	
# of faculty supervised clinical positions filled		150	0
# involved in field placements		273	0
# involved in law journals		64	0
# involved in moot court or trial competitions		145	0
# of credit hours required to graduate		90	

JD Enrollment and Ethnicity

	Men		Women		Full-Time		Part-Time		1st-Year		Total		JD Degs. Awd.
	#	%	#	%	#	%	#	%	#	%	#	%	
All Hispanics	91	10.6	96	10.8	179	10.5	8	15.7	68	10.0	187	10.7	40
Am. Ind./AK Nat.	9	1.0	11	1.2	18	1.1	2	3.9	12	1.8	20	1.1	4
Asian	42	4.9	54	6.1	93	5.5	3	5.9	35	5.2	96	5.5	27
Black/Af. Am.	59	6.9	176	19.7	230	13.5	5	9.8	110	16.2	235	13.4	41
Nat. HI/Pac. Isl.	2	0.2	2	0.2	4	0.2	0	0.0	1	0.1	4	0.2	0
2 or more races	2	0.2	4	0.4	6	0.4	0	0.0	3	0.4	6	0.3	2
Subtotal (minor.)	205	23.8	343	38.5	530	31.1	18	35.3	229	33.7	548	31.3	114
Nonres. Alien	14	1.6	18	2.0	32	1.9	0	0.0	12	1.8	32	1.8	6
White/Cauc.	551	64.0	481	53.9	1007	59.2	25	49.0	382	56.3	1032	58.9	296
Unknown	91	10.6	50	5.6	133	7.8	8	15.7	56	8.2	141	8.0	37
Total	861	49.1	892	50.9	1702	97.1	51	2.9	679	38.7	1753		453

Transfers

Transfers in	3
Transfers out	90

Tuition and Fees

	Resident	Nonresident
Full-time	$36,968	$36,968
Part-time	$29,912	$29,912
Tuition Guarantee Program	N	

Living Expenses

Estimated living expenses for singles

Living on campus	Living off campus	Living at home
N/A	$20,380	$20,380

FLORIDA COASTAL SCHOOL OF LAW

ABA
Approved
Since
2002

GPA and LSAT Scores

	Total	Full-Time	Part-Time
# of apps	5,277	4,982	295
# of offers	3,493	3,362	131
# of matrics	671	659	12
75% GPA	3.33	3.34	2.96
Median GPA	3.08	3.09	2.90
25% GPA	2.83	2.83	2.64
75% LSAT	151	151	146
Median LSAT	147	147	145
25% LSAT	145	145	145

Grants and Scholarships (from prior year)

	Total		Full-Time		Part-Time	
	#	%	#	%	#	%
Total # of students	1,742		1,683		59	
Total # receiving grants	798	45.8	741	44.0	57	96.6
Less than 1/2 tuition	717	41.2	669	39.8	48	81.4
Half to full tuition	79	4.5	71	4.2	8	13.6
Full tuition	2	0.1	1	0.1	1	1.7
More than full tuition	0	0.0	0	0.0	0	0.0
Median grant amount			$7,500		$8,100	

Informational and Library Resources

Total amount spent on library materials	$1,192,959
Study seating capacity inside the library	618
# of full-time equivalent professional librarians	15
Hours per week library is open	105
# of open, wired connections available to students	3,780
# of networked computers available for use by students	126
Has wireless network?	Y
Requires computer?	N

JD Attrition (from prior year)

	Academic	Other	Total	
	#	#	#	%
1st year	86	114	200	25.5
2nd year	7	4	11	2.3
3rd year	1	1	2	0.4
4th year	0	0	0	0.0

Employment (9 months after graduation)

For up-to-date employment data, go to
employmentsummary.abaquestionnaire.org on the ABA website.

Bar Passage Rates

First-time takers	426	Reporting %	71.83
Average school %	74.84	Average state %	77.89
Average pass difference	−3.05		

Jurisdiction	Takers	Passers	Pass %	State %	Diff %
Florida	291	216	74.23	77.63	−3.40
Pennsylvania	15	13	86.67	83.06	3.61

FLORIDA COASTAL SCHOOL OF LAW

8787 Baypine Road
Jacksonville, FL 32256
Phone: 904.680.7710, toll-free: 877.210.2591; Fax: 904.680.7692
E-mail: admissions@fcsl.edu; Website: www.fcsl.edu

Introduction

Fully accredited by the ABA, Florida Coastal School of Law offers the finest legal education, coupling traditional approaches with student/faculty partnerships and practical, real-world perspectives. Led by exceptional internationally accomplished faculty, Coastal Law creates an innovative educational experience that produces first-rate lawyers with uncompromised ethics and professional responsibility, as well as sharp legal skills.

Our Students

Coastal Law students represent more than 320 undergraduate colleges and universities from nearly every state in the United States, as well as Puerto Rico, the Virgin Islands, Canada, Germany, and China. While enrolled, students work closely with faculty members who not only share their legal expertise, but also their experiences, perspectives, and expansive networks. We believe our supportive learning environment makes a difference in students' educational experiences and personal growth, ultimately giving them an edge in professional preparation.

Our Faculty

Coastal Law's full-time faculty members represent approximately 50 ABA-accredited law schools from across the country, including Harvard University, George Washington University, Duke University, Georgetown University, Columbia University, New York University, and the University of Florida. Together, they boast international legal and academic accomplishments, from authoring dozens of case books and articles to counseling the Iraqi Constitutional Commission and advising the United Nations' war crimes tribunal in The Hague. Further, as former judges, government officials, general and in-house counsel, corporate executives, and attorneys practicing in law firms, they offer realistic legal perspectives.

Our City

Coastal Law is located in Jacksonville, a metropolitan center of more than one million people, including one of the youngest populations in Florida. Boasting 68 miles of ocean coastline, 300 miles of riverfront, and one of the largest park systems in the country, it offers an outstanding array of outdoor activities of all types. In addition, the city is dotted with unique neighborhoods, exceptional arts, entertainment, culture, and a variety of professional sports, including the NFL, PGA Tour, LPGA, ATP World Tour, and baseball. Jacksonville provides the idyllic setting for a legal education during warm winters and beach-filled summers.

Our Facilities

Meticulously designed by one of the top firms of its kind worldwide, to reflect both our traditional and realistic approaches to legal education, Florida Coastal School of Law's lakefront campus boasts 220,000 square feet of state-of-the-art learning technologies. From our interactive trial and appellate courtrooms, to our computer labs, podcasting capabilities, and wireless technology, the tools at Coastal Law make us one of the most sophisticated legal facilities nationwide.

Curriculum and Certificate Programs

Among the many advantages that set Coastal Law apart from our comparative schools is the curriculum, which allows our students to align career choices with specialized areas of expertise. Successful completion of a certificate program not only represents significant learning, but can also exhibit to potential employers a student's dedication to the corresponding practice area. Coastal Law offers five certificate programs: **Sports Law**, **Family Law**, **International and Comparative Law**, **Environmental Law**, and **Advanced Legal Research**, **Writing**, **and Drafting**.

Live Client Clinics

Under the supervision of full-time faculty members, Coastal Law students can gain experience representing indigent clients and play a part in each phase of legal representation, including the initial client interview, case planning and development, drafting letters and pleadings, discovery and negotiation, and even representing their clinic clients in court and administrative hearings. Clinical programs include: the **Family Law Clinic**, the **Consumer Law Clinic**, the **Immigrant Rights Clinic**, the **Disability and Benefits Clinic**, and the **Housing Rights Clinic**.

Moot Court

Coastal Law has a deep tradition of advocacy excellence, with our moot court program consistently ranking among the nation's best. Since 2005, our teams have won 18 championships and more than 80 total best oral advocate and best brief awards. While our team's incredible successes are rewarding, the true benefit exists in the skills our students develop. In preparing for moot court competitions, Coastal Law students learn the very best techniques in legal research and writing, analyzing case law, developing arguments, and sharpening critical thinking. These are precisely the skills that prove essential in legal practice after graduation.

Joint-Degree Programs

The Davis College of Business at Jacksonville University, a first-tier program, and Florida Coastal School of Law have created a joint-degree program through which qualified students may pursue a Juris Doctor (JD) and a Master's Degree in Business Administration (MBA) from both schools simultaneously. Graduates with a joint JD/MBA degree can develop the skills needed to pursue careers in the business and legal professions, especially where those areas overlap, such as investment and commercial banking, management consulting, government regulation, and business policy analysis. In addition to concurrently participating in the academic and social life of both schools, students will be able to obtain both diplomas in four years, as compared to the five years required to earn both degrees when pursued separately.

Bar Preparation and Success

Coastal Law graduates taking the bar exam in Florida and in other states often excel. To ensure our graduates are well prepared for the exam, we work with students to identify personal learning styles and customize time management skills. Coastal Law students also have open access to our academic success counselors and to bar preparation classes and study groups. Coastal Law provides every student with the resources required to succeed academically, on the bar exam, and as they transition into practice.

Career Services

Coastal Law's Career Services Department (CSD) is committed to empowering students and alumni to pursue the careers of their choice. From individual counseling, résumé critiques, and job-search strategies to attorney panels and on-campus interviewing programs, the CSD offers

comprehensive services and resources that can guide students along individual career paths. In addition, the CSD offers our alumni assistance in making changes in practice, career direction, or geographic area.

Closing Invitation From the Dean

The basic curriculum and the traditional three-year time period required for legal education have remained very constant for more than a century. However, it is more important than ever that a law school take maximum advantage of this limited time to prepare its graduates to enter the profession well equipped. At Florida Coastal School of Law, the study of law blends acquiring a comprehensive knowledge of the law with developing the critical thinking and practical skills essential to its practice. Ensuring the careful balance of each of these components is an integral part of the educational process we deliver. To determine whether Florida Coastal School of Law is right for you, feel free to contact any member of our law school community and ask about their experiences here. We also welcome visitors and encourage campus tours.

APPLICANT PROFILE

Florida Coastal School of Law
This grid includes only applicants who earned 120–180 LSAT scores under standard administrations.

LSAT Score	3.75 +		3.50–3.74		3.25–3.49		3.00–3.24		2.75–2.99		2.50–2.74		2.25–2.49		2.00–2.24		Below 2.00		No GPA		Total	
	Apps	Adm	Apps	Adm	Apps	Adm	Apps	Adm	Apps	Adm	Apps	Adm	Apps	Adm	Apps	Adm	Apps	Adm	Apps	Adm	Apps	Adm
175–180	0	0	0	0	0	0	0	0	0	0	0	0	0	0	0	0	0	0	0	0	0	0
170–174	0	0	0	0	0	0	0	0	0	0	0	0	0	0	0	0	0	0	0	0	0	0
165–169	2	2	1	1	3	3	2	2	2	0	4	4	1	1	0	0	0	0	0	0	15	13
160–164	15	15	20	18	19	17	19	18	20	17	15	14	3	2	3	2	1	0	0	0	115	103
155–159	38	37	82	77	84	81	109	102	77	63	66	58	21	14	11	1	2	0	1	1	491	434
150–154	80	76	182	171	250	234	269	251	200	178	144	124	62	33	27	9	6	0	8	4	1228	1080
145–149	70	65	190	179	308	292	417	374	285	252	224	148	98	25	33	1	6	0	17	7	1648	1343
140–144	30	21	104	61	169	93	222	93	217	62	161	20	107	4	59	0	10	0	14	3	1093	357
135–139	10	1	27	2	75	3	60	4	93	1	75	0	37	0	26	0	4	0	11	0	418	11
130–134	0	0	8	0	13	0	19	0	19	1	20	1	13	0	13	0	8	0	5	0	118	2
125–129	1	0	2	0	0	0	3	0	3	0	4	1	4	0	2	0	2	0	2	0	23	1
120–124	0	0	0	0	0	0	1	0	0	0	3	0	1	0	0	0	0	0	1	0	6	0
Total	246	217	616	509	921	723	1121	844	916	574	716	370	347	79	174	13	39	0	59	15	5155	3344

Apps = Number of Applicants
Adm = Number Admitted
Reflects 99% of the total applicant pool; highest LSAT data reported.

UNIVERSITY OF FLORIDA, FREDRIC G. LEVIN COLLEGE OF LAW

141 Bruton-Geer Hall, PO Box 117622
Gainesville, FL 32611-7622
Phone: 352.273.0890, Toll-free: 877.429.1297; Fax: 352.392.4087
E-mail: admissions@law.ufl.edu; Website: www.law.ufl.edu

ABA
Approved
Since
1925

The Basics

Type of school	Public
Term	Semester
Application deadline	3/15
Application fee	$30
Financial aid deadline	4/15
Can first year start other than fall?	No
Student to faculty ratio	13.7 to 1
# of housing spaces available restricted to law students	
graduate housing for which law students are eligible	

Faculty and Administrators

	Total		Men		Women		Minorities	
	Spr	Fall	Spr	Fall	Spr	Fall	Spr	Fall
Full-time	61	61	31	27	30	34	11	12
Other full-time	8	9	5	6	3	3	0	0
Deans, librarians, & others who teach	17	19	9	10	8	9	2	3
Part-time	33	32	28	22	5	10	1	1
Total	119	121	73	65	46	56	14	16

JD Enrollment and Ethnicity

	Men		Women		Full-Time		Part-Time		1st-Year		Total		JD Degs. Awd.
	#	%	#	%	#	%	#	%	#	%	#	%	
All Hispanics	63	11.5	50	11.7	113	11.6	0	0.0	36	12.4	113	11.6	42
Am. Ind./AK Nat.	5	0.9	7	1.6	12	1.2	0	0.0	5	1.7	12	1.2	4
Asian	26	4.7	26	6.1	52	5.3	0	0.0	17	5.8	52	5.3	34
Black/Af. Am.	22	4.0	40	9.4	62	6.4	0	0.0	12	4.1	62	6.4	23
Nat. HI/Pac. Isl.	0	0.0	0	0.0	0	0.0	0	0.0	0	0.0	0	0.0	0
2 or more races	4	0.7	1	0.2	5	0.5	0	0.0	2	0.7	5	0.5	4
Subtotal (minor.)	120	21.9	124	29.0	244	25.0	0	0.0	72	24.7	244	25.0	107
Nonres. Alien	0	0.0	0	0.0	0	0.0	0	0.0	0	0.0	0	0.0	0
White/Cauc.	396	72.1	286	67.0	682	69.9	0	0.0	201	69.1	682	69.9	290
Unknown	33	6.0	17	4.0	50	5.1	0	0.0	18	6.2	50	5.1	14
Total	549	56.3	427	43.8	976	100.0	0	0.0	291	29.8	976		411

Curriculum

	Full-Time	Part-Time
Typical first-year section size	100	0
Is there typically a "small section" of the first-year class, other than Legal Writing, taught by full-time faculty	Yes	No
If yes, typical size offered last year	50	
# of classroom course titles beyond first-year curriculum	178	

# of upper division courses, excluding seminars, with an enrollment:	Under 25	92
	25–49	53
	50–74	25
	75–99	12
	100+	11

# of seminars	41	
# of seminar positions available	602	
# of seminar positions filled	481	0
# of positions available in simulation courses	594	
# of simulation positions filled	560	0
# of positions available in faculty supervised clinical courses	138	
# of faculty supervised clinical positions filled	102	0
# involved in field placements	281	0
# involved in law journals	353	0
# involved in moot court or trial competitions	109	0
# of credit hours required to graduate	88	

Transfers

Transfers in	52
Transfers out	4

Tuition and Fees

	Resident	Nonresident
Full-time	$18,710	$38,075
Part-time		
Tuition Guarantee Program		N

Living Expenses

Estimated living expenses for singles

Living on campus	Living off campus	Living at home
$14,710	$15,750	$6,990

UNIVERSITY OF FLORIDA, FREDRIC G. LEVIN COLLEGE OF LAW

ABA
Approved
Since
1925

GPA and LSAT Scores

	Total	Full-Time	Part-Time
# of apps	3,024	3,024	0
# of offers	875	875	0
# of matrics	295	295	0
75% GPA	3.82	3.82	0.00
Median GPA	3.64	3.64	0.00
25% GPA	3.43	3.43	0.00
75% LSAT	164	164	0
Median LSAT	162	162	0
25% LSAT	160	160	0

Grants and Scholarships (from prior year)

	Total #	Total %	Full-Time #	Full-Time %	Part-Time #	Part-Time %
Total # of students	1,044		1,044		0	
Total # receiving grants	257	24.6	257	24.6	0	0.0
Less than 1/2 tuition	186	17.8	186	17.8	0	0.0
Half to full tuition	69	6.6	69	6.6	0	0.0
Full tuition	0	0.0	0	0.0	0	0.0
More than full tuition	2	0.2	2	0.2	0	0.0
Median grant amount			$5,000		$0	

Informational and Library Resources

Total amount spent on library materials	$1,204,193
Study seating capacity inside the library	765
# of full-time equivalent professional librarians	7
Hours per week library is open	98
# of open, wired connections available to students	0
# of networked computers available for use by students	47
Has wireless network?	Y
Requires computer?	Y

JD Attrition (from prior year)

	Academic #	Other #	Total #	Total %
1st year	0	10	10	3.2
2nd year	0	6	6	1.8
3rd year	0	0	0	0.0
4th year	0	0	0	0.0

Employment (9 months after graduation)

For up-to-date employment data, go to employmentsummary.abaquestionnaire.org on the ABA website.

Bar Passage Rates

First-time takers	377	Reporting %	83.55
Average school %	87.94	Average state %	77.63
Average pass difference	10.31		

Jurisdiction	Takers	Passers	Pass %	State %	Diff %
Florida	315	277	87.94	77.63	10.31

UNIVERSITY OF FLORIDA, FREDRIC G. LEVIN COLLEGE OF LAW

141 Bruton-Geer Hall, PO Box 117622
Gainesville, FL 32611-7622
Phone: 352.273.0890, Toll-free: 877.429.1297; Fax: 352.392.4087
E-mail: admissions@law.ufl.edu; Website: www.law.ufl.edu

Introduction

The University of Florida Levin College of Law is one of the nation's most comprehensive and widely respected law schools. It was founded in 1909, has been a member of the Association of American Law Schools since 1920, and was approved by the American Bar Association in 1925. It boasts an impressive list of distinguished visitors to campus, including six visits by Supreme Court Justices in the past six years. Its beautiful campus features expansive, state-of-the-art facilities thanks to efforts such as a $25-million expansion and renovation project completed in 2005 and a trial advocacy center completed in November 2009.

The college's faculty are highly accomplished scholars, educators, and practitioners whose broad knowledge base and strong teaching skills are highly praised in student evaluations. Many are authors of treatises, casebooks, or major books used by law schools and practitioners throughout the nation, as well as hundreds of articles in law reviews and specialty journals.

The law school is known for graduating state and national legal, political, business, government, and educational leaders, and for nurturing a strong alumni network, the UF Law "Gator Nation." UF Law graduates include five ABA presidents—including 2010–2011 President Stephen Zack—numerous federal and state judges, partners in major national and international law firms, members of Congress and the Cabinet, governors, and state legislators. Alumni support has built the endowment into one of the largest in the country for public law schools. This, combined with the state's financial assistance, allows the college to remain affordable while its academic quality rivals many of the best-known private colleges.

The University of Florida is one of the nation's largest and most comprehensive universities, is a member of the prestigious Association of American Universities, and is recognized as one of the nation's leading research universities by the Carnegie Commission on Higher Education. The campus occupies 2,000 acres, mostly within the city of Gainesville's 131,000-population area in North Central Florida. The area is consistently ranked among the best places to live in America, with extensive educational, cultural, and recreational offerings.

Programs and Curriculum

The Levin College of Law offers students strong fundamentals and a diverse range of specializations and interdisciplinary options. The activities and scholarship of its unusually large faculty allow for numerous interesting programs and curricular concentrations. More than 70 courses and 15 to 20 seminars are offered each semester. Students can earn a certificate in Environmental and Land Use Law, Criminal Law, Estates and Trusts Practice, Family Law, Intellectual Property Law, or International and Comparative Law. The Levin College of Law also offers one of the most extensive joint-degree programs of any US law school, including popular joint degrees in Business, Public Health/Medicine, Education, and Engineering, among many other areas. Students can gain hands-on experience in litigation, negotiation, mediation, client relations, and government service at the highest levels

through a broad array of courses, study-abroad opportunities, externships, pro bono work, and clinical programs. The first-year curriculum is required, as is a second-year drafting course and Professional Responsibility in the third year. JD candidates must produce—under close faculty supervision—a major, written, finished product that shows evidence of original systematic scholarship based on individual research. Students often satisfy this requirement through a "senior paper" produced while enrolled in a seminar.

The richness and diversity of the school's faculty, student body, and course offerings are strengthened by the presence of its top-ranked Graduate Tax Program—leading to an LLM in Taxation, LLM in International Taxation, or SJD in Taxation. The school also offers an LLM in Environmental and Land Use Law, as well as an LLM in Comparative Law for foreign lawyers. In addition, UF Law is a major hub for international legal programs and has decades of experience and relationships in Latin America and Europe. The college's innovative centers and institutes include the Center for Governmental Responsibility, Center on Children and Families, Criminal Justice Center, Center for the Study of Race and Race Relations, Camp Center for Estate and Elder Law Planning, and Institute for Dispute Resolution.

Student/Extracurricular Activities

More than 65 active extracurricular organizations at the law school help students develop valuable skills and professional contacts as well as make a positive difference in the community. Students can earn credits and polish their legal skills through cocurricular organizations such as the *Florida Law Review*, *Florida Journal of International Law*, *University of Florida Journal of Law and Public Policy*, *Journal of Technology Law and Policy*, and trophy-winning US and international moot court and trial teams.

Library and Facilities

Following completion in 2005 of a major expansion and renovation project, the Lawton Chiles Legal Information Center is now one of the largest academic law libraries in the Southeast and among the top 20 in the nation in terms of space. The expanded library offers comfortable study areas, reading rooms, computer training labs, multimedia workstations, and reference rooms for use by students and faculty. Two new three-story education buildings feature spacious, state-of-the-art classrooms equipped to offer the latest in teaching technology, including desktop outlets for laptop use, wireless Internet access, and "smart podia."

The most recent addition to the law school is the sophisticated, high-tech, two-and-a-half story Martin H. Levin Advocacy Center, which features a fully functional trial and appellate courtroom, audience gallery, and bench for seven judges.

Career Development

Professional counselors in the college's Center for Career Development offer a wide variety of services and programs to help students plan a self-directed career search and develop marketing skills that will serve them for many years to come.

Staff members help students develop legal credentials; capitalize on their diverse strengths and experiences; explore legal and nontraditional career paths; and find summer internships, externships, and clerkships, as well as permanent postgraduation employment. They also help link students with alumni, practitioners, and the community, and host large on-campus recruiting events that bring numerous employers to campus each year. Other resources include workshops and seminars on practical career skills, individual career and job-search counseling, on- and off-campus networking events, and an online job bank with downloadable handouts, samples, and forms.

Admission

Through its admissions process, the Levin College of Law seeks to admit and enroll students who will excel academically, attain the highest standards of professional excellence and integrity, and bring vision, creativity, and commitment to the legal profession. The LSAT, LSAC Credential Assembly Service, admissions statement, and résumé are required. Recommendation letters are not required, but up to four will be accepted. A bachelor's degree from an accredited college or university is required prior to enrollment.

The admissions staff and the faculty admissions committee base their decisions on the applicant's academic credentials, including LSAT score, UGPA, level of writing skills, and breadth of studies, as well as on other information including, but not limited to, the applicant's work and other life experience, leadership experience, depth of particular interest, and any other aspect of an applicant's background suggesting suitability for the study and practice of law.

Students may transfer in August, January, or May from ABA-approved law schools, but only applicants who have completed the required first-year, full-time curriculum before enrolling at UF and who are in the upper one-third of their class will be considered. A transfer certification form from the dean is required, and no more than 29 semester hours will be transferred.

The law school seeks to enroll approximately 300 (full-time only) students each fall. The college places great importance on obtaining a diverse class and actively recruits minority students. To arrange an appointment or a tour of the law school, contact the Admissions Office.

Expenses and Financial Aid

The 2011–2012 tuition is $18,709.80 for Florida residents and $38,074.50 for nonresidents. Additional expenses total approximately $15,890 for books, supplies, computer (required), clothing, room, food, transportation, student orientation fee (entering students only), and personal/insurance.

Merit-based and merit/need-based scholarships and grants, and short- and long-term loans (FAFSA required) are available to qualified students. Merit awards are based on information collected in the application for admission. To be considered for merit/need-based scholarships and need-based grants, admitted students must submit a FAFSA and a UF Law Financial Aid Application for need-based scholarships and grants.

Housing

Housing is available for single students in dormitories and for families in university apartments. Plentiful off-campus housing is available. New and current UF law students may access the UF College of Law Roommate Referral System online.

APPLICANT PROFILE

University of Florida, Fredric G. Levin College of Law
This grid includes only applicants who earned 120–180 LSAT scores under standard administrations.

LSAT Score	3.75 + Apps	Adm	3.50–3.74 Apps	Adm	3.25–3.49 Apps	Adm	3.00–3.24 Apps	Adm	2.75–2.99 Apps	Adm	2.50–2.74 Apps	Adm	2.25–2.49 Apps	Adm	2.00–2.24 Apps	Adm	Below 2.00 Apps	Adm	No GPA Apps	Adm	Total Apps	Adm
175–180	5	4	0	0	1	1	0	0	0	0	0	0	0	0	0	0	0	0	0	0	6	5
170–174	20	16	18	18	17	14	6	4	5	5	0	0	0	0	0	0	0	0	0	0	66	57
165–169	77	72	79	77	56	53	37	34	23	13	16	5	5	1	1	0	1	0	12	10	307	265
160–164	152	143	241	173	193	61	103	28	48	7	21	2	4	0	3	0	0	0	22	5	787	419
155–159	167	76	247	22	200	5	110	4	73	5	38	0	17	0	2	0	0	0	21	0	875	112
150–154	74	4	112	6	133	1	99	2	62	0	31	0	13	0	6	0	0	0	14	1	544	14
145–149	41	1	60	0	59	0	80	0	41	0	29	0	12	0	12	0	3	0	4	0	341	1
140–144	8	0	29	0	40	0	32	0	30	0	17	0	15	0	6	0	1	0	2	0	180	0
135–139	1	0	3	0	10	0	12	0	14	0	16	0	2	0	1	0	1	0	4	0	64	0
130–134	0	0	2	0	3	0	3	0	3	0	6	0	0	0	4	0	1	0	2	0	24	0
125–129	0	0	0	0	0	0	1	0	0	0	0	0	0	0	0	0	1	0	0	0	2	0
120–124	0	0	0	0	0	0	0	0	0	0	0	0	0	0	0	0	0	0	0	0	0	0
Total	545	316	791	296	712	135	483	72	299	30	174	7	68	1	35	0	8	0	81	16	3196	873

Apps = Number of Applicants
Adm = Number Admitted
Reflects 99% of the total applicant pool; highest LSAT data reported.

FLORIDA INTERNATIONAL UNIVERSITY COLLEGE OF LAW

RDB 1055
Miami, FL 33186
Phone: 305.348.8006; Fax: 305.348.2965
E-mail: lawadmit@fiu.edu; Website: http://law.fiu.edu/

The Basics

Type of school	Public
Term	Semester
Application deadline	5/1
Application fee	$20
Financial aid deadline	2/15
Can first year start other than fall?	No
Student to faculty ratio	14.4 to 1
# of housing spaces available restricted to law students	
graduate housing for which law students are eligible	43

Faculty and Administrators

	Total		Men		Women		Minorities	
	Spr	Fall	Spr	Fall	Spr	Fall	Spr	Fall
Full-time	28	29	16	14	12	15	14	12
Other full-time	3	3	2	1	1	2	2	1
Deans, librarians, & others who teach	7	6	5	3	2	3	4	3
Part-time	20	19	13	12	7	7	10	8
Total	58	57	36	30	22	27	30	24

JD Enrollment and Ethnicity

	Men		Women		Full-Time		Part-Time		1st-Year		Total		JD Degs. Awd.
	#	%	#	%	#	%	#	%	#	%	#	%	
All Hispanics	100	36.4	115	41.7	141	38.2	74	40.7	60	39.5	215	39.0	60
Am. Ind./AK Nat.	1	0.4	5	1.8	3	0.8	3	1.6	0	0.0	6	1.1	0
Asian	5	1.8	9	3.3	9	2.4	5	2.7	1	0.7	14	2.5	4
Black/Af. Am.	21	7.6	37	13.4	36	9.8	22	12.1	16	10.5	58	10.5	12
Nat. HI/Pac. Isl.	0	0.0	0	0.0	0	0.0	0	0.0	0	0.0	0	0.0	0
2 or more races	10	3.6	7	2.5	8	2.2	9	4.9	6	3.9	17	3.1	20
Subtotal (minor.)	137	49.8	173	62.7	197	53.4	113	62.1	83	54.6	310	56.3	96
Nonres. Alien	0	0.0	3	1.1	3	0.8	0	0.0	2	1.3	3	0.5	0
White/Cauc.	136	49.5	98	35.5	166	45.0	68	37.4	66	43.4	234	42.5	74
Unknown	2	0.7	2	0.7	3	0.8	1	0.5	1	0.7	4	0.7	5
Total	275	49.9	276	50.1	369	67.0	182	33.0	152	27.6	551		175

Curriculum

	Full-Time	Part-Time
Typical first-year section size	57	38
Is there typically a "small section" of the first-year class, other than Legal Writing, taught by full-time faculty	No	No
If yes, typical size offered last year		
# of classroom course titles beyond first-year curriculum	81	

# of upper division courses, excluding seminars, with an enrollment:	Under 25	122
	25–49	31
	50–74	18
	75–99	5
	100+	0

# of seminars	9	
# of seminar positions available	145	
# of seminar positions filled	115	28
# of positions available in simulation courses	402	
# of simulation positions filled	333	63
# of positions available in faculty supervised clinical courses	148	
# of faculty supervised clinical positions filled	97	28
# involved in field placements	93	20
# involved in law journals	34	5
# involved in moot court or trial competitions	73	13
# of credit hours required to graduate	90	

Transfers

Transfers in	10
Transfers out	4

Tuition and Fees

	Resident	Nonresident
Full-time	$16,585	$30,370
Part-time	$12,258	$22,367
Tuition Guarantee Program	N	

Living Expenses

Estimated living expenses for singles

Living on campus	Living off campus	Living at home
$18,466	$24,776	$12,596

FLORIDA INTERNATIONAL UNIVERSITY COLLEGE OF LAW

*ABA
Approved
Since
2004*

GPA and LSAT Scores

	Total	Full-Time	Part-Time
# of apps	2,370	1,960	410
# of offers	485	427	58
# of matrics	151	115	36
75% GPA	3.77	3.77	3.79
Median GPA	3.62	3.63	3.57
25% GPA	3.22	3.26	3.07
75% LSAT	157	158	157
Median LSAT	155	155	152
25% LSAT	152	152	148

Grants and Scholarships (from prior year)

	Total #	Total %	Full-Time #	Full-Time %	Part-Time #	Part-Time %
Total # of students	588		395		193	
Total # receiving grants	260	44.2	207	52.4	53	27.5
Less than 1/2 tuition	185	31.5	177	44.8	8	4.1
Half to full tuition	69	11.7	25	6.3	44	22.8
Full tuition	1	0.2	1	0.3	0	0.0
More than full tuition	5	0.9	4	1.0	1	0.5
Median grant amount			$5,000		$5,000	

Informational and Library Resources

Total amount spent on library materials	$827,692
Study seating capacity inside the library	322
# of full-time equivalent professional librarians	7
Hours per week library is open	95
# of open, wired connections available to students	35
# of networked computers available for use by students	63
Has wireless network?	Y
Requires computer?	N

JD Attrition (from prior year)

	Academic #	Other #	Total #	Total %
1st year	7	4	11	6.6
2nd year	1	2	3	1.5
3rd year	2	0	2	1.1
4th year	0	0	0	0.0

Employment (9 months after graduation)

For up-to-date employment data, go to
employmentsummary.abaquestionnaire.org on the ABA website.

Bar Passage Rates

First-time takers	136	Reporting %	100.00
Average school %	80.88	Average state %	77.63
Average pass difference	3.25		

Jurisdiction	Takers	Passers	Pass %	State %	Diff %
Florida	136	110	80.88	77.63	3.25

FLORIDA INTERNATIONAL UNIVERSITY COLLEGE OF LAW

RDB 1055
Miami, FL 33186
Phone: 305.348.8006; Fax: 305.348.2965
E-mail: lawadmit@fiu.edu; Website: http://law.fiu.edu/

Introduction

The Florida International University College of Law is South Florida's only publicly supported law school. Established in 2000, FIU College of Law is a member of the AALS. The international allure of the city of Miami and the diverse character of the institution is reflected in the curriculum which integrates important developments in the globalization of both public and private law.

The FIU College of Law academic program takes a unique approach to both international and comparative law by incorporating these perspectives into all domestic law classes and boasts of an impressive faculty of experts in various fields of law. FIU College of Law focuses in the preparation of high-caliber, ethical, and effective attorneys for the general practice of law while also encouraging a strong commitment to public service and community relations.

Curriculum and Special Programs

The FIU College of Law's academic program, while devoted to all the traditional components of an excellent American legal education, also emphasizes international and comparative law. To this end, the required curriculum includes a three-hour, first-year course titled Introduction to International and Comparative Law. Further, all domestic law courses include an international or comparative law dimension. This pervasive approach to international and comparative law encourages students to analyze legal systemic, political, economic, social, and other cultural differences that may contribute to different legal treatment of comparable problems in different countries. The College of Law also offers a foreign summer program in Sevilla, Spain.

As Miami's premier public research university, FIU offers a broad range of high quality, graduate-level degree programs. Law students interested in interdisciplinary study may take advantage of several joint-degree programs, including the following: JD/Master of Business Administration, JD/Master of International Business, JD/Master of Latin American and Caribbean Studies, JD/Master of Public Administration, JD/MS in Psychology, JD/Master of Social Work, JD/MS in Criminal Justice, and JD/Master of Science in Environmental Sciences.

In addition to a strong doctrinal program, the College of Law's Clinical Program advances the law school's goals of educating lawyers for the ethical and effective practice of law and of promoting community service through the representation of real clients. Presently, there are eight clinics available—the Carlos A. Costa Immigration and Human Rights Clinic; the Community Development Clinic; the Investor Advocacy Clinic; the Consumer Bankruptcy Clinic; the Education Advocacy Clinic; the Environmental Clinic; the Health, Ethics, Law and Policy Clinic; and the Immigrant Children's Justice Clinic—as well as externships in Criminal/Civil Law and the Florida Judiciary. The curriculum also emphasizes instruction in the legal skills and values of the profession. The Legal Skills and Values Program combines demanding traditional instruction in legal research and writing with an introduction to other lawyering skills, like interviewing and counseling, and issues of professionalism.

Moreover, as a public, urban law school, the College of Law is committed to serving the community of which it is a part by educating future lawyers who will understand the value—to the community and to themselves personally—of helping those in need. In recognition of this important mission, students must satisfy a community service requirement.

Admission

The FIU College of Law offers both a full-time day and part-time evening program. The review of applications is done on a rolling basis. An LSAC Credential Assembly Service report, three letters of recommendation, and a personal statement are required.

While a prospective student's academic record and LSAT performance are weighted heavily in the evaluative process, the Admissions Committee considers other factors, including leadership ability, commitment to public service, command of global issues, work history, military service, any history of criminality or academic misconduct, and evidence of obstacles that an applicant may have overcome (for example, English is not the applicant's native language, discrimination, economic or family hardship, and severe medical conditions, etc.). The Admissions Committee encourages each applicant to answer all questions with candor, detail, and, where appropriate, to give specific examples of relevant background experiences.

Transfer students from other ABA-approved law schools may apply if they are in good standing at their current institutions. Visit our website at http://law.fiu.edu/ for additional information.

Financial Aid

The primary financial aid resources available to students are loans and need- or merit-based scholarships. Students must apply for financial aid (FAFSA) to be considered for any type of loan or need-based scholarship. No separate application is needed for merit-based scholarships. Eligible students will be considered based on the information provided in their admission application. Financial aid is granted on an annual basis, and awards are subject to student eligibility and availability of funds. Tuition is comparable to other Florida state-supported law schools at $473 per credit for Florida residents and $932 per credit for nonresidents. An additional $24,776 (approximate) can be expected to cover room and board, books, transportation, and personal expenses. Please call 305.348.8006 for further information.

Library

The Law Library supports the law school curriculum, the research needs of its students and faculty, and the public's interest in access to critical legal materials. It contains over 220,000 volumes in book and microform format, over 4,000 digitized books, and an electronic archive of 1.6 million pages of historic codes, statutes, and regulations. The Law Library provides law students with a full range of electronic legal information resources, including Westlaw, LexisNexis, HeinOnline, BNA, CCH, and other web-based databases.

When performing background, factual, and/or interdisciplinary research, law students draw upon the Green Library on FIU's Maidique campus, which offers access to more than 1.5 million volumes and extensive electronic resources. The Law Library is staffed by six full-time and two part-time professional librarians, two of whom have law degrees. In addition to a comprehensive collection of core US materials, the library has an extensive collection of international, comparative, and foreign law materials, with a particular focus on Latin America and the Caribbean, international trade, and the workings of international tribunals and multilateral institutions.

Career Planning and Placement Office

The Career Development Office (CDO) provides a multitude of expert services and professional resources to assist students and alumni in finding employment and launching careers in the legal profession. The CDO continues to cultivate outstanding relationships with many leading employers, in Florida and nationwide, including a host of public service employers, federal agencies, and the Courts.

Professional and personal satisfaction is critical to any successful legal or law-related career. The CDO dedicates its considerable energies and resources to assisting students with developing individualized short- and long-term career strategies that allow students to successfully navigate through a broad spectrum of career options. The CDO serves as a resource for students and informational bridge between students and employers based in the South Florida community, regionally, and throughout the nation.

CDO Services include the following:

- Personalized career counseling
- Application material review
- Skills workshops and programming
- Panel discussions on career choices in the private, public, government, and alternative sectors
- Professional development programs
- Interview programs
- Career Resource Library
- Job Postings—FIU Law Symplicity Job Bank

The CDO is committed to providing students with the tools necessary to pursue a wide range of career opportunities and to make informed career-related decisions.

Student Activities

Success in law school involves more than just intellectual curiosity and a sense of purpose. It involves the refining of time management skills, handling stress proactively, and forging relationships with faculty and peers. It also involves making the best possible use of available services and opportunities. Students bring a wealth of distinctive educational and professional experiences to the College of Law. However, they all share a common interest and goal: service to the law school, the local community, and the profession. Together with the support of the faculty and the administration, students have created a number of organizations and cocurricular activities reflective of this commitment. In its brief but productive history, the College of Law has established a thriving clinical and externship program, award-winning moot court and trial advocacy programs competing locally and nationally against teams throughout the country, and 23 student organizations, including the Student Bar Association.

APPLICANT PROFILE

The Florida International University College of Law Admissions Committee seeks to enroll a diverse group of students who have demonstrated academic and personal achievement. While a prospective student's academic record and LSAT performance are weighted heavily in the evaluative process, the Admissions Committee considers other factors, including leadership ability, commitment to public service, command of global issues, work history, military service, any history of criminality or academic misconduct, and evidence of obstacles that an applicant may have overcome (for example, English is not the applicant's native language, discrimination, economic or family hardship, severe medical condition, disability, etc.).

THE FLORIDA STATE UNIVERSITY COLLEGE OF LAW

425 West Jefferson Street
Tallahassee, FL 32306-1601
Phone: 850.644.3787; Fax: 850.644.7284
E-mail: admissions@law.fsu.edu; Website: www.law.fsu.edu

ABA
Approved
Since
1968

The Basics

Type of school	Public
Term	Semester
Application deadline	3/15
Application fee	$30
Financial aid deadline	3/1
Can first year start other than fall?	No
Student to faculty ratio	14.4 to 1
# of housing spaces available restricted to law students	
graduate housing for which law students are eligible	1,000

Faculty and Administrators

	Total		Men		Women		Minorities	
	Spr	Fall	Spr	Fall	Spr	Fall	Spr	Fall
Full-time	44	41	27	25	17	16	5	7
Other full-time	0	0	0	0	0	0	0	0
Deans, librarians, & others who teach	15	10	3	2	12	8	3	3
Part-time	30	33	25	25	5	8	3	2
Total	89	84	55	52	34	32	11	12

Curriculum

	Full-Time	Part-Time
Typical first-year section size	67	0
Is there typically a "small section" of the first-year class, other than Legal Writing, taught by full-time faculty	No	No
If yes, typical size offered last year		
# of classroom course titles beyond first-year curriculum	130	

# of upper division courses, excluding seminars, with an enrollment:	Under 25	93
	25–49	43
	50–74	20
	75–99	5
	100+	4

# of seminars	16	
# of seminar positions available	288	
# of seminar positions filled	241	0
# of positions available in simulation courses	1,001	
# of simulation positions filled	626	0
# of positions available in faculty supervised clinical courses	49	
# of faculty supervised clinical positions filled	49	0
# involved in field placements	136	0
# involved in law journals	183	0
# involved in moot court or trial competitions	57	0
# of credit hours required to graduate	88	

JD Enrollment and Ethnicity

	Men		Women		Full-Time		Part-Time		1st-Year		Total		JD Degs. Awd.
	#	%	#	%	#	%	#	%	#	%	#	%	
All Hispanics	48	10.9	26	9.0	74	10.2	0	0.0	17	8.5	74	10.2	18
Am. Ind./AK Nat.	1	0.2	1	0.3	2	0.3	0	0.0	0	0.0	2	0.3	1
Asian	13	2.9	11	3.8	24	3.3	0	0.0	8	4.0	24	3.3	7
Black/Af. Am.	21	4.8	34	11.8	55	7.5	0	0.0	15	7.5	55	7.5	22
Nat. HI/Pac. Isl.	0	0.0	0	0.0	0	0.0	0	0.0	0	0.0	0	0.0	0
2 or more races	0	0.0	0	0.0	0	0.0	0	0.0	0	0.0	0	0.0	0
Subtotal (minor.)	83	18.8	72	25.0	155	21.3	0	0.0	40	20.0	155	21.3	48
Nonres. Alien	2	0.5	2	0.7	4	0.5	0	0.0	3	1.5	4	0.5	0
White/Cauc.	338	76.6	201	69.8	539	73.9	0	0.0	148	74.0	539	73.9	224
Unknown	18	4.1	13	4.5	31	4.3	0	0.0	9	4.5	31	4.3	8
Total	441	60.5	288	39.5	729	100.0	0	0.0	200	27.4	729		280

Transfers

Transfers in	57
Transfers out	8

Tuition and Fees

	Resident	Nonresident
Full-time	$18,343	$37,905
Part-time		
Tuition Guarantee Program	N	

Living Expenses

Estimated living expenses for singles

Living on campus	Living off campus	Living at home
$17,700	$17,700	$17,700

THE FLORIDA STATE UNIVERSITY COLLEGE OF LAW

ABA
Approved
Since
1968

GPA and LSAT Scores

	Total	Full-Time	Part-Time
# of apps	2,650	2,650	0
# of offers	716	716	0
# of matrics	200	200	0
75% GPA	3.68	3.68	0.00
Median GPA	3.47	3.47	0.00
25% GPA	3.18	3.18	0.00
75% LSAT	163	163	0
Median LSAT	162	162	0
25% LSAT	160	160	0

Grants and Scholarships (from prior year)

	Total #	Total %	Full-Time #	Full-Time %	Part-Time #	Part-Time %
Total # of students	779		779		0	
Total # receiving grants	322	41.3	322	41.3	0	0.0
Less than 1/2 tuition	218	28.0	218	28.0	0	0.0
Half to full tuition	88	11.3	88	11.3	0	0.0
Full tuition	3	0.4	3	0.4	0	0.0
More than full tuition	13	1.7	13	1.7	0	0.0
Median grant amount			$3,500		$0	

Informational and Library Resources

Total amount spent on library materials	$941,966
Study seating capacity inside the library	444
# of full-time equivalent professional librarians	11
Hours per week library is open	168
# of open, wired connections available to students	0
# of networked computers available for use by students	41
Has wireless network?	Y
Requires computer?	Y

JD Attrition (from prior year)

	Academic #	Other #	Total #	Total %
1st year	1	19	20	10.0
2nd year	4	0	4	1.4
3rd year	0	0	0	0.0
4th year	0	0	0	0.0

Employment (9 months after graduation)

For up-to-date employment data, go to employmentsummary.abaquestionnaire.org on the ABA website.

Bar Passage Rates

First-time takers	244	Reporting %	86.07
Average school %	86.19	Average state %	77.63
Average pass difference	8.56		

Jurisdiction	Takers	Passers	Pass %	State %	Diff %
Florida	210	181	86.19	77.63	8.56

THE FLORIDA STATE UNIVERSITY COLLEGE OF LAW

425 West Jefferson Street
Tallahassee, FL 32306-1601
Phone: 850.644.3787; Fax: 850.644.7284
E-mail: admissions@law.fsu.edu; Website: www.law.fsu.edu

Introduction

The Florida State University College of Law is recognized as one of the nation's top 50 law schools. The school encourages close working relationships among students and faculty of the sort that characterize the best liberal arts colleges. Cutting-edge faculty members make it a priority to be available to students outside and inside the classroom. The attentive faculty greatly value the insights of other disciplines that can be brought to bear upon the study of law, integrating insights from such varied disciplines as history, philosophy, psychology, sociology, economics, and finance. The faculty is rated among the nation's best in terms of per capita scholarly impact and includes nationally and internationally recognized experts.

Florida State Law offers law students a wealth of legal employment opportunities. Located in Tallahassee, a city with more than 500 law firms and numerous government agencies, the law school is just steps away from the state capitol, the Florida Supreme Court, and the United States District Court for the Northern District of Florida.

One of the greatest strengths of Florida State Law is its over 8,000 highly engaged alumni. Graduates work in 49 states and 19 countries. Alumni are prominent in all Florida cities and are in major US markets, including Atlanta, Chicago, New York, Los Angeles, and Washington, DC. They practice in large and small law firms, are leaders in business, are lawmakers and policy advisors at the state and national levels, serve as judges, and teach at law schools around the nation.

Enrollment/Student Body

Florida State University College of Law receives 13 applications for every seat in its entering class. The fall 2011 entering class had a median LSAT score of 162 and a median GPA of 3.47. Accepting students from a wide variety of backgrounds enriches the law school experience. Currently, the talented student body represents 32 states, 15 countries, and 191 colleges and universities. Florida State has been recognized nationally as one of the best law schools for Hispanic students.

Curriculum

Florida State University College of Law's three-year curriculum begins with traditional courses and expands to include the latest in theoretical and interdisciplinary analyses. The first-year curriculum is rigorous, traditional, and prescribed. It provides a foundation in history, doctrine, process, and analysis that students need to fully appreciate more specialized elective courses offered in the second and third years of law school.

The law school has five cocurricular academic organizations, including three student-edited journals and trial and appellate advocacy teams. The journals include the *Florida State University Law Review*, the *Journal of Land Use and Environmental Law*, and the *Journal of Transnational Law and Policy*. The law school's advocacy teams are highly successful. Since 2010, the moot court team has won first place in one international competition and in nine national competitions. For two consecutive years, the mock trial team has won first place in the Florida Justice Association's E. Earle Zehmer Mock Trial Competition.

Special Programs

Florida State University College of Law has especially strong programs in environmental law, international law, business, and criminal law, with certificate programs in environmental law, international law, and business law. Florida State's program in environmental law is recognized as one of the best in the country.

Building on its highly ranked environmental law program, Florida State offers an LLM in Environmental Law and Policy. The law school's newest degree offering gives JD holders the opportunity to concentrate in, or enhance their knowledge of, environmental law, land use law, natural resources law, and energy law. The law school also offers an LLM in American Law for Foreign Lawyers, which provides foreign graduate students trained in law the opportunity to develop an understanding of the American legal system and the role of law in the United States.

The College of Law offers nine joint-degree programs in cooperation with other colleges, schools, and departments at Florida State. The joint degrees bring together law with business, economics, information studies, international affairs, public administration, social work, child and family sciences, sport management, and urban and regional planning.

Florida State Law has one of the most extensive externship programs in the United States. The clinical externship program places students at more than 100 externship sites throughout Florida and elsewhere. Students may even select international externships in locations around the world, including with the International Bar Association in London, the International Criminal Tribunal for the former Yugoslavia (The Hague), and the Court of Appeal in the Republic of Botswana.

The law school's internationally recognized Public Interest Law Center provides on-campus clinical legal training for second- and third-year students. Students are certified by the Florida Supreme Court to practice law as interns and, under the supervision of licensed attorneys, are responsible for all facets of cases to which they are assigned. The center has three clinics: the Children's Advocacy Clinic, the Family Law Clinic, and the Medical-Legal Partnership—an innovative collaboration between Florida State's law and medical schools that partners law students with medical students, social work students, lawyers, and physicians to examine patients' social determinants of health.

Florida State Law also sponsors a summer program at Oxford University in England. As the oldest ongoing summer program in Oxford sponsored by a US law school, it provides students with a unique opportunity to study comparative law and the history of the common law and its institutions in their original setting.

Physical Facilities and Research Center

The physical facilities of Florida State University College of Law consist of B.K. Roberts Hall, the connected Research Center, and the Village Green, which is composed of four restored houses. In January 2012, the law school expanded into a 50,000-square-foot Advocacy Center, which is directly across the street from the school's other facilities. The building has five courtrooms—four with jury boxes—and is the nation's finest advocacy training facility. In addition, it includes offices for our Public Interest Law Center and its three clinics, faculty offices for our top-rated Environmental Law Program and for our Business Law Program, offices and dedicated interview rooms for the Placement Office, and additional classrooms—including a video-conference room—and study spaces. All of the law school's classrooms are either new or recently remodeled. Classrooms are equipped with technology podiums that allow professors to present multimedia lectures. A strong wireless infrastructure allows students to utilize the Internet during class, throughout the building, and outdoors.

Florida State University College of Law students have 24/7 access to the Research Center. The distinctive feature of the Research Center is that its faculty proactively train students and other faculty members to produce highly sophisticated, cost-effective legal research. For example, it offers specialized courses in efficient research relating to environmental law, economics, business and tax law, and international law. In 2011, it started offering a Certificate in Florida Legal Research, which helps students develop the legal research skills most useful to new lawyers in Florida. The law school's Research Center has been significantly remodeled during the past few years to be more user-friendly.

Student Activities

Students have the opportunity to participate in many extracurricular organizations. More than 35 student and service organizations allow students to become leaders at the law school and active participants in the legal community. The Phi Alpha Delta legal fraternity maintains a chapter on campus. In addition, Florida State University College of Law was granted a chapter of the Order of the Coif in 1979. Twice in the past four years, our Student Bar Association has been selected SBA of the Year by the Law Student Division of the American Bar Association. In 2010, the SBA received the Public Interest National Achievement Award from the Law Student Division. This group serves an active student government role and coordinates many law school-sponsored social activities, community projects, and programs. In 2006, 2011, and 2012, the Black Law Students Association was named National Chapter of the Year by the National Black Law Students Association.

Career Services and Bar Exam

The law school provides assistance to law students, graduates, and legal employers through its Placement Office. Florida State University College of Law students have access to a list of more than 600 alumni who have volunteered to serve them as Career Placement Mentors. Students are encouraged to take advantage of the law school's on-campus interviewing programs and individual career counseling services. A variety of seminars and workshops on career options, résumé writing, and interviewing skills are also available.

Within nine months of graduation, 90.7 percent of the graduating class of 2011 found employment. For 8 of the last 13 administrations of the Florida Bar examination, Florida State's bar passage rate was either first or second among Florida's 11 law schools. Graduates who take the exam in jurisdictions outside of Florida do equally well.

APPLICANT PROFILE

The Florida State University College of Law
This grid includes only applicants who earned 120–180 LSAT scores under standard administrations.

LSAT Score	3.75 + Apps	Adm	3.50–3.74 Apps	Adm	3.25–3.49 Apps	Adm	3.00–3.24 Apps	Adm	2.75–2.99 Apps	Adm	2.50–2.74 Apps	Adm	2.25–2.49 Apps	Adm	2.00–2.24 Apps	Adm	Below 2.00 Apps	Adm	No GPA Apps	Adm	Total Apps	Adm
175–180	0	0	0	0	0	0	0	0	0	0	0	0	0	0	0	0	0	0	0	0	0	0
170–174	8	7	5	5	4	4	2	2	2	2	1	1	0	0	0	0	0	0	0	0	22	21
165–169	35	35	41	41	21	21	21	21	15	15	9	8	4	4	1	1	0	0	2	2	149	148
160–164	88	88	143	136	130	100	104	77	51	29	27	20	5	1	4	2	0	0	9	6	561	459
155–159	125	42	180	28	190	7	122	2	68	1	40	0	14	0	1	0	0	0	10	0	750	80
150–154	70	4	118	2	118	2	79	0	70	0	35	0	11	0	7	0	1	0	8	0	517	8
145–149	33	0	63	0	63	0	78	0	44	0	38	0	16	0	9	0	1	0	4	0	349	0
140–144	7	0	24	0	50	0	29	0	32	0	24	0	16	0	9	0	0	0	0	0	191	0
135–139	2	0	2	0	8	0	4	0	18	0	13	0	6	0	3	0	1	0	2	0	59	0
130–134	0	0	1	0	5	0	3	0	2	0	5	0	0	0	2	0	0	0	2	0	20	0
125–129	1	0	0	0	0	0	2	0	0	0	2	0	1	0	1	0	0	0	0	0	7	0
120–124	0	0	0	0	0	0	1	0	0	0	2	0	1	0	0	0	0	0	0	0	4	0
Total	369	176	577	212	589	134	445	102	302	47	196	29	74	5	37	3	3	0	37	8	2629	716

Apps = Number of Applicants
Adm = Number Admitted
Reflects 99% of the total applicant pool; highest LSAT data reported.

FORDHAM UNIVERSITY SCHOOL OF LAW

140 West 62nd Street
New York, NY 10023
Phone: 212.636.6810; Fax: 212.636.7984
E-mail: lawadmissions@law.fordham.edu; Website: http://law.fordham.edu

ABA
Approved
Since
1936

The Basics

Type of school	Private
Term	Semester
Application deadline	3/15
Application fee	$70
Financial aid deadline	4/1
Can first year start other than fall?	No
Student to faculty ratio	13.6 to 1
# of housing spaces available restricted to law students	130
graduate housing for which law students are eligible	69

Faculty and Administrators

	Total		Men		Women		Minorities	
	Spr	Fall	Spr	Fall	Spr	Fall	Spr	Fall
Full-time	85	85	54	54	31	31	17	16
Other full-time	0	0	0	0	0	0	0	0
Deans, librarians, & others who teach	22	20	8	8	14	12	3	3
Part-time	194	162	115	99	79	63	19	20
Total	301	267	177	161	124	106	39	39

Curriculum

	Full-Time	Part-Time
Typical first-year section size	80	80
Is there typically a "small section" of the first-year class, other than Legal Writing, taught by full-time faculty	Yes	Yes
If yes, typical size offered last year	40	40

# of classroom course titles beyond first-year curriculum		242
# of upper division courses, excluding seminars, with an enrollment:	Under 25	45
	25–49	54
	50–74	21
	75–99	10
	100+	8
# of seminars		150
# of seminar positions available		2,984
# of seminar positions filled	1,464	522
# of positions available in simulation courses		959
# of simulation positions filled	439	408
# of positions available in faculty supervised clinical courses		770
# of faculty supervised clinical positions filled	506	62
# involved in field placements	100	71
# involved in law journals	454	43
# involved in moot court or trial competitions	224	13
# of credit hours required to graduate		83

JD Enrollment and Ethnicity

	Men		Women		Full-Time		Part-Time		1st-Year		Total		JD Degs. Awd.
	#	%	#	%	#	%	#	%	#	%	#	%	
All Hispanics	80	10.1	72	10.3	130	10.5	22	8.7	44	9.2	152	10.2	44
Am. Ind./AK Nat.	1	0.1	2	0.3	2	0.2	1	0.4	2	0.4	3	0.2	1
Asian	64	8.0	86	12.3	108	8.7	42	16.7	63	13.2	150	10.0	30
Black/Af. Am.	30	3.8	32	4.6	52	4.2	10	4.0	19	4.0	62	4.1	23
Nat. HI/Pac. Isl.	1	0.1	0	0.0	1	0.1	0	0.0	1	0.2	1	0.1	0
2 or more races	4	0.5	3	0.4	5	0.4	2	0.8	0	0.0	7	0.5	7
Subtotal (minor.)	180	22.6	195	27.9	298	24.0	77	30.6	129	27.1	375	25.1	105
Nonres. Alien	14	1.8	25	3.6	37	3.0	2	0.8	23	4.8	39	2.6	6
White/Cauc.	504	63.3	398	56.9	765	61.5	137	54.4	300	63.0	902	60.3	248
Unknown	98	12.3	82	11.7	144	11.6	36	14.3	24	5.0	180	12.0	69
Total	796	53.2	700	46.8	1244	83.2	252	16.8	476	31.8	1496		428

Transfers

Transfers in	17
Transfers out	10

Tuition and Fees

	Resident	Nonresident
Full-time	$47,986	$47,986
Part-time	$36,056	$36,056
Tuition Guarantee Program	N	

Living Expenses

Estimated living expenses for singles

Living on campus	Living off campus	Living at home
$25,583	$25,583	$25,583

ABA Approved Since 1936

GPA and LSAT Scores

	Total	Full-Time	Part-Time
# of apps	7,551	6,431	1,120
# of offers	1,999	1,833	166
# of matrics	479	399	80
75% GPA	3.71	3.71	3.71
Median GPA	3.53	3.53	3.52
25% GPA	3.36	3.35	3.39
75% LSAT	167	167	165
Median LSAT	165	165	163
25% LSAT	163	163	160

Grants and Scholarships (from prior year)

	Total #	Total %	Full-Time #	Full-Time %	Part-Time #	Part-Time %
Total # of students	1,481		1,217		264	
Total # receiving grants	523	35.3	471	38.7	52	19.7
Less than 1/2 tuition	480	32.4	432	35.5	48	18.2
Half to full tuition	37	2.5	33	2.7	4	1.5
Full tuition	6	0.4	6	0.5	0	0.0
More than full tuition	0	0.0	0	0.0	0	0.0
Median grant amount			$10,000		$7,500	

Informational and Library Resources

Total amount spent on library materials	$1,901,599
Study seating capacity inside the library	454
# of full-time equivalent professional librarians	14
Hours per week library is open	119
# of open, wired connections available to students	601
# of networked computers available for use by students	225
Has wireless network?	Y
Requires computer?	N

JD Attrition (from prior year)

	Academic #	Other #	Total #	Total %
1st year	0	5	5	1.0
2nd year	1	13	14	2.9
3rd year	0	0	0	0.0
4th year	0	0	0	0.0

Employment (9 months after graduation)

For up-to-date employment data, go to employmentsummary.abaquestionnaire.org on the ABA website.

Bar Passage Rates

First-time takers	464	Reporting %	96.12
Average school %	88.12	Average state %	84.92
Average pass difference	3.20		

Jurisdiction	Takers	Passers	Pass %	State %	Diff %
New York	446	393	88.12	84.92	3.20

FORDHAM UNIVERSITY SCHOOL OF LAW

140 West 62nd Street
New York, NY 10023
Phone: 212.636.6810; Fax: 212.636.7984
E-mail: lawadmissions@law.fordham.edu; Website: http://law.fordham.edu

Introduction

Fordham Law has been dedicated to preparing great leaders in the legal profession for over a century. The school is proud of its unique and compelling mission: to provide a complete legal education that stresses equally academic excellence, the craft of lawyering, a focus on ethics, and a spirit of public service. The unwavering commitment to these values—combined with the school's dynamic New York City location—offers Fordham Law graduates an unparalleled opportunity to pursue a broad spectrum of careers. The school's signature public service and human rights programs encourage lawyers to pursue the lives of responsible and noble legal practice. A faculty distinguished by its commitment both to teaching and to scholarship creates an atmosphere in which students learn creatively and think critically.

Fordham Law's prime location in Manhattan provides convenient access to all New York City has to offer, enabling students to begin their careers at the center of the world's legal, financial, and cultural capital. The school's campus is adjacent to Lincoln Center for the Performing Arts, a mere two blocks from Central Park, and steps away from the transportation and shopping hub of Columbus Circle. Fordham Law puts a strong focus on the importance of experiential education, and the school's location puts students close to a broad range of professional opportunities at some of the largest law firms in the world, the busiest federal and state courts, the US Attorney General's Offices, the United Nations, Wall Street, and a myriad of state and federal agencies. Fordham lawyers practice in all 50 states, the District of Columbia, and 73 nations around the world. Among our more than 19,000 alumni are partners and associates of leading law firms, CEOs of major corporations, academics, and individuals engaged in public service.

Curriculum

Fordham's innovative and challenging curriculum balances substantive theory with ample hands-on lawyering opportunities. The school offers a remarkable depth of courses in fundamental areas such as contracts, criminal law, legal ethics, and civil procedure. Additionally, traditional and emerging areas of legal practice—including intellectual property, international human rights, and corporate and finance law—are well represented by professors who are specialists in their fields. Most importantly, these professors are passionate teachers who recognize the significance of welcoming students and being accessible.

Fordham also promotes the art and science of legal analysis and the cultivation of a vigorous ongoing dialogue between students and professor through the following nationally renowned academic centers:

Brendan Moore Advocacy Center fosters the teaching and study of lawyers as advocates, with special emphasis on client representation at the trial level.

The Center for Corporate, Securities, and Financial Law serves as the focal point for the school's business law programs and includes roundtable discussions with business leaders, corporate law practitioners, and state and federal regulators.

The Leitner Center for International Law and Justice contributes to the promotion of social justice by encouraging knowledge of, and respect for, international law and human rights standards. The center oversees an annual fact-finding mission, providing law students the opportunity to participate in human rights work overseas.

Louis Stein Center for Law and Ethics promotes the integration of ethical perspectives in legal practice, legal institutions, and the development of the law generally. The center also oversees the Stein Scholars Program, a program for students who demonstrate commitment to public service and who undertake specialized academic work in legal ethics.

The Feerick Center for Social Justice works with students, alumni, lawyers, and community volunteers to connect low-income New Yorkers to the legal resources they need and cannot afford.

The Forum on Law, Culture, and Society is a public humanities program that invites the general public to satisfy its intellectual curiosity on matters of law, justice, and civil society in a dynamic and engaging town hall setting.

The Center on Law and Information Policy (CLIP) supports and conducts research, organizes workshops and conferences, and hosts and facilitates high-level public discourse on topics such as data privacy and security, peer-to-peer technologies and intellectual property protection of information assets, and the liability of Internet intermediaries.

The Intellectual Property Institute fosters awareness of and encourages interest in cutting-edge issues in US, European, and Asian IP law as well as in multinational treaties and intergovernmental organizations.

The Fashion Law Institute provides legal assistance to design students and designers and offers assistance on issues facing the fashion industry.

The Center on National Security engages in research, policy work, and public programming on cutting-edge national and global security issues, including cybersecurity.

Cocurricular Activities

There are six student-edited law journals at Fordham, as well as two intramural moot court competitions.

The school also participates in interschool competitions, fielding award-winning appellate moot court teams, trial advocacy teams, and alternative dispute resolution teams.

Worldwide Significance

Fordham Law cultivates in its students a critical global perspective through an array of international programs, including

- the nation's preeminent Center on European Union Law;
- the school's Stein Center for Law and Ethics;
- an International Antitrust Law and Policy Conference, now in its 39th year;
- an annual International Intellectual Property Law Conference, now in its 20th year;
- the Leitner Center for International Law and Justice;
- a Belfast/Dublin summer program, which offers two weeks of study in each city with a special emphasis on international alternative dispute resolution;

- a summer program in Seoul, Korea, at Sungkyunkwan University College of Law (SKKU) that offers courses in international and comparative law as well as internships at local law firms, companies, and governmental offices;
- a Ghana summer law program, building on our long and successful history of partnership with Ghanaian legal institutions, that offers students the opportunity to study Ghanaian and international law, as well as internships in Ghana;
- semester study-abroad programs offered in Italy, the Netherlands, Germany, Spain, Japan, Brazil, Korea, and the People's Republic of China;
- five graduate degree programs—the LLM in International Business and Trade Law; the LLM in Banking, Corporate, and Finance Law; the LLM in Intellectual Property and Information Technology Law; the LLM in International Law and Justice; and the LLM in US and Comparative Law—that have created a network of Fordham alumni in more than 70 countries; and
- the first Fashion Law Institute at any US law school.

Experiential Programs

Fordham's clinical program encourages students to integrate legal analysis with lawyering theory and skills by assuming lawyering roles or performing lawyering functions in problem-solving settings. Fordham Law's clinical program—one of the largest in the nation—engages more than 550 students in live-client clinics and simulation courses in 15 practice areas. Fordham also offers one of the widest ranges of externship placements in American legal education—more than 250 opportunities at nonprofit and nongovernmental organizations and in state and federal courts.

Career Development

Fordhams Law's Career Planning Center has developed a comprehensive and focused approach to assisting students and alumni with their career development in both the public and private sectors.
- The CPC and Public Interest Resource Center work collaboratively on the extensive 1L Career Development Curriculum.
- Each spring and fall, the CPC organizes an extensive On-Campus Interview Program, attracting hundreds of employers. Please visit law.fordham.edu/employmentstats to view a PDF of the employers who participated.

Public Service

Fordham believes that the development of a lifelong commitment to public service is an integral part of a legal education. Last year, Fordham law students volunteered over 158,000 hours of public service. More than half of the graduating class devoted 50 or more hours of their time through the school's nationally recognized Public Interest Resource Center (PIRC). The PIRC's 25 student-run organizations address issues concerning the environment, housing for the poor, domestic violence, unemployment, police brutality, the death penalty, immigration, and community service. Fordham also has a Loan Repayment Assistance Program (LRAP) to assist those who pursue public service careers. Today, Fordham continues to set the standard for law schools nationwide by assisting and inspiring those students who, regardless of their ultimate career choice, are committed to the spirit of pro bono publico—work for the public good.

Living at Lincoln Center

Approximately 80 spaces are set aside for entering students in McMahon Hall, the university's Lincoln Center residence. Students live in two- or three-bedroom apartments, each of which contains private bedrooms, a living room, full kitchen, and bath. Preference is given to those students who live beyond a commutable distance from the law school. Inquiries regarding housing should be directed to the law school Office of Admissions.

Applicant Profile

Fordham's Admissions Committee—comprised of full-time faculty members and administrators—evaluates each complete application received. While the best available evidence suggests that LSAT scores and undergraduate GPAs should be accorded significant weight in evaluating most applicants, the Admissions Committee believes that securing the most interesting, diverse, and exciting class involves the evaluation of other qualitative factors as well. The combination of academic excellence and experiences is considered in evaluating applicants' potential contributions to their success at Fordham and beyond.

APPLICANT PROFILE

Fordham University School of Law
This grid includes only applicants who earned 120–180 LSAT scores under standard administrations.

LSAT Score	GPA													
	3.75 +		3.50–3.74		3.25–3.49		3.00–3.24		Below 3.00		No GPA		Totals	
	Apps	Adm	Apps	Adm	Apps	Adm	Apps	Adm	Apps	Adm	Apps	Adm	Apps	Adm
170–180	146	125	155	140	116	90	64	30	52	5	13	8	546	398
165–169	360	318	534	440	358	189	184	56	122	8	61	34	1619	1045
160–164	412	142	636	150	523	85	273	34	169	5	71	6	2084	422
155–159	204	23	356	29	372	31	225	19	179	4	40	1	1376	107
120–154	167	7	315	7	445	6	376	4	547	2	76	1	1926	27
Total	1289	615	1996	766	1814	401	1122	143	1069	24	261	50	7551	1999

Apps = Number of Applicants
Adm = Number Admitted
Highest LSAT data reported.

GEORGE MASON UNIVERSITY SCHOOL OF LAW

3301 Fairfax Drive, MS 1G3
Arlington, VA 22201
Phone: 703.993.8010; Fax: 703.993.8088
E-mail: lawadmit@gmu.edu; Website: www.law.gmu.edu

ABA
Approved
Since
1980

The Basics

Type of school	Public
Term	Semester
Application deadline	4/1
Application fee	$35
Financial aid deadline	3/1
Can first year start other than fall?	No
Student to faculty ratio	14.9 to 1
# of housing spaces available restricted to law students	
graduate housing for which law students are eligible	

Faculty and Administrators

	Total		Men		Women		Minorities	
	Spr	Fall	Spr	Fall	Spr	Fall	Spr	Fall
Full-time	37	34	32	28	5	6	6	5
Other full-time	2	2	0	0	2	2	1	1
Deans, librarians, & others who teach	4	3	3	2	1	1	0	0
Part-time	117	81	81	59	36	22	11	5
Total	160	120	116	89	44	31	18	11

Curriculum

	Full-Time	Part-Time
Typical first-year section size	77	67
Is there typically a "small section" of the first-year class, other than Legal Writing, taught by full-time faculty	No	No
If yes, typical size offered last year		
# of classroom course titles beyond first-year curriculum	136	

# of upper division courses, excluding seminars, with an enrollment:	Under 25	231
	25–49	22
	50–74	14
	75–99	0
	100+	0

# of seminars	28	
# of seminar positions available	420	
# of seminar positions filled	185	105
# of positions available in simulation courses	428	
# of simulation positions filled	253	98
# of positions available in faculty supervised clinical courses	114	
# of faculty supervised clinical positions filled	41	19
# involved in field placements	110	9
# involved in law journals	154	22
# involved in moot court or trial competitions	17	17
# of credit hours required to graduate	89	

JD Enrollment and Ethnicity

	Men		Women		Full-Time		Part-Time		1st-Year		Total		JD Degs. Awd.
	#	%	#	%	#	%	#	%	#	%	#	%	
All Hispanics	15	3.6	8	2.6	20	3.9	3	1.5	8	4.3	23	3.2	6
Am. Ind./AK Nat.	6	1.5	2	0.7	4	0.8	4	2.0	2	1.1	8	1.1	0
Asian	32	7.8	34	11.2	46	9.0	20	9.8	13	6.9	66	9.2	19
Black/Af. Am.	0	0.0	7	2.3	5	1.0	2	1.0	4	2.1	7	1.0	5
Nat. HI/Pac. Isl.	0	0.0	0	0.0	0	0.0	0	0.0	0	0.0	0	0.0	0
2 or more races	1	0.2	2	0.7	2	0.4	1	0.5	2	1.1	3	0.4	2
Subtotal (minor.)	54	13.1	53	17.5	77	15.1	30	14.7	29	15.4	107	15.0	32
Nonres. Alien	7	1.7	6	2.0	11	2.2	2	1.0	2	1.1	13	1.8	2
White/Cauc.	348	84.7	238	78.5	414	81.2	172	84.3	155	82.4	586	82.1	136
Unknown	2	0.5	6	2.0	8	1.6	0	0.0	2	1.1	8	1.1	0
Total	411	57.6	303	42.4	510	71.4	204	28.6	188	26.3	714		170

Transfers

Transfers in	5
Transfers out	16

Tuition and Fees

	Resident	Nonresident
Full-time	$23,720	$38,112
Part-time	$20,199	$31,331
Tuition Guarantee Program	N	

Living Expenses

Estimated living expenses for singles

Living on campus	Living off campus	Living at home
$16,800	$23,210	$10,500

GEORGE MASON UNIVERSITY SCHOOL OF LAW

*ABA
Approved
Since
1980*

GPA and LSAT Scores

	Total	Full-Time	Part-Time
# of apps	4,514	4,092	1,262
# of offers	1,071	996	75
# of matrics	186	154	32
75% GPA	3.78	3.78	3.76
Median GPA	3.72	3.73	3.59
25% GPA	3.24	3.27	3.14
75% LSAT	165	165	165
Median LSAT	164	163	164
25% LSAT	157	157	155

Grants and Scholarships (from prior year)

	Total #	Total %	Full-Time #	Full-Time %	Part-Time #	Part-Time %
Total # of students	731		505		226	
Total # receiving grants	95	13.0	68	13.5	27	11.9
Less than 1/2 tuition	76	10.4	61	12.1	15	6.6
Half to full tuition	13	1.8	5	1.0	8	3.5
Full tuition	0	0.0	0	0.0	0	0.0
More than full tuition	6	0.8	2	0.4	4	1.8
Median grant amount			$8,000		$8,000	

Informational and Library Resources

Total amount spent on library materials	$1,078,974
Study seating capacity inside the library	370
# of full-time equivalent professional librarians	6
Hours per week library is open	98
# of open, wired connections available to students	961
# of networked computers available for use by students	28
Has wireless network?	Y
Requires computer?	N

JD Attrition (from prior year)

	Academic #	Other #	Total #	Total %
1st year	1	23	24	8.1
2nd year	1	7	8	3.7
3rd year	0	1	1	0.7
4th year	0	0	0	0.0

Employment (9 months after graduation)

For up-to-date employment data, go to
employmentsummary.abaquestionnaire.org on the ABA website.

Bar Passage Rates

First-time takers	232	Reporting %	76.72
Average school %	84.27	Average state %	78.48
Average pass difference	5.79		

Jurisdiction	Takers	Passers	Pass %	State %	Diff %
Virginia	145	121	83.45	78.15	5.30
Maryland	33	29	87.88	79.96	7.92

GEORGE MASON UNIVERSITY SCHOOL OF LAW

3301 Fairfax Drive, MS 1G3
Arlington, VA 22201
Phone: 703.993.8010; Fax: 703.993.8088
E-mail: lawadmit@gmu.edu; Website: www.law.gmu.edu

Introduction

George Mason University School of Law sits on the doorstep of the nation's capital. One of Virginia's public law schools, it was established by authority of the Virginia General Assembly in 1979. By virtue of its unparalleled location, George Mason is able to offer its students numerous opportunities for practical experiences during their law school career.

Library and Physical Facilities

In 1999, the law school relocated to a state-of-the-art facility, Hazel Hall, equipped with electrical and data connections at every classroom and library seat, and two ultramodern moot courtrooms. The opening of a large plaza and new building in January 2011 expanded the facilities available to law students.

The school is a member of the library network of the Consortium for Continuing Higher Education in Northern Virginia, affording access to general university and public library collections.

Enrollment/Student Body

George Mason University is an equal opportunity/affirmative action institution.

Curriculum

George Mason University School of Law offers both full- and part-time divisions. The full-time division operates during the day and takes three years to complete. Students who elect the part-time division study at night during the first year and generally take four years to complete the requirements for the Juris Doctor degree.

George Mason offers an interdisciplinary approach to legal study. A grounding in economics and basic mathematical and financial skills is important to a sophisticated legal education and to the development of a competent attorney. To ensure that George Mason graduates have this grounding, all students take a first-year course in Economic Foundations.

George Mason law students complete a three-year legal writing program, which emphasizes the use of technology and continual practice of skills in the development of actual transactions and cases.

The curriculum begins with exposure to the courses fundamental to a well-rounded legal education. Students at George Mason may also elect to enroll in one of our specialty programs, thus demonstrating depth as well as breadth in their training. All specialties are offered in both the full-time and part-time divisions.

George Mason has a number of programs offering students practical experience: Immigration Law, Domestic Relations, Law and Mental Illness, Regulatory Law, Patent Law, Virginia Practice, the Clinic for Legal Assistance to Service Members and Veterans, and a Supreme Court Clinic. As a leader in technology and law, George Mason is the headquarters for the Information Economy Project. George Mason is also home to the Center for Infrastructure Protection (CIP), a program that fully integrates the disciplines of law, policy, and technology for enhancing the security of cyber networks and economic processes supporting the nation's critical infrastructure.

Special Programs

- **Homeland and National Security Law**—enables students interested in specializing in this field to present potential employers (both in government and in the private sector) with a credential that reflects a solid foundation in homeland and national security law.
- **Corporate and Securities Law**—prepares students to work in a variety of fields related to corporate law and financial markets. By developing a thorough understanding of both law and underlying theory, students are prepared to deal with rapidly changing business and legal environments.
- **Regulatory Law**—prepares students for practice in, and before, the numerous agencies that regulate business and other activities. Students are taught economics, the economic analysis of law, administrative law, legislation, lobbying, and negotiation, as well as several substantive areas of regulatory law.
- **International Business Law**—prepares students for practice in the rapidly changing global business community and provides them with a well-rounded legal education emphasizing analytical and writing skills.
- **Litigation Law**—provides an academic program for students interested in litigation and other dispute resolution processes. This is not a clinical training program. The track courses focus on the processes of dispute resolution and lawyers' roles from an analytical perspective.
- **Intellectual Property Law**—is designed for students having a degree in engineering or one of the physical or biological sciences who intend to practice within the field of intellectual property.
- **Technology Law Program**—combines coursework in the fields of technology law, intellectual property law, and business law. The program prepares students for work in law firms that serve high-technology clients, as in-house counsel for Internet start-up companies, and as attorneys for state and federal regulatory agencies with jurisdiction over technology industries.
- **LLM Programs**—for students wishing to pursue specialized study beyond the JD, George Mason offers two LLM programs: (1) the **LLM in Law and Economics**, and (2) the **LLM in Intellectual Property Law**. Detailed information about these programs is available at www.law.gmu.edu/academics/llm.html.
- Additionally, George Mason offers programs in Criminal Law, Legal and Economic Theory, Personal Law, and Tax Law.

Admission

Two of the primary factors considered in the admission process are performance on the LSAT and undergraduate grade-point average. Other factors that are considered include difficulty of undergraduate major, undergraduate institution attended, possession of advanced degrees, writing ability, recommendations, extracurricular activities, employment experience, demonstrated commitment to public and community service, leadership skills and experience, history of overcoming personal or professional challenges, and other academic, personal, and professional achievements.

Student Activities

George Mason University provides many services to enhance the law school experience and enable students to take full advantage of the university's educational and personal enrichment opportunities.

Student activities include the *George Mason Law Review*; *Civil Rights Law Journal*; the *Journal of Law, Economics, and Policy*; the *Journal of International Commercial Law*; a prestigious moot court program; an active trial advocacy program; a newspaper; and numerous law-related organizations. Students have an unparalleled opportunity to gain experience in such varied settings as the Office of the US Attorney for both the District of Columbia and the Eastern District of Virginia, as well as federal courts and agencies, local governments, and private firms. Information about George Mason's various student organizations and externship opportunities can be found at www.law.gmu.edu/students/orgs and www.law.gmu.edu/academics/clinics.

Diversity Student Services, Academic Support Services, Disability Support Services, and the Office of Veterans

Services provide specialized assistance, as does the Counseling Center, where a staff of professionals help students to reach personal, social, and academic goals.

Expenses and Financial Aid

George Mason University participates in the Direct Lending Program. There is no deadline for applying for financial aid, but applicants should complete the FAFSA as soon as possible in order to assure the timely award of aid.

In addition to loans available through the Direct Lending Program, George Mason students are eligible for a number of merit-based fellowships.

Career Services

The Office of Career, Academic, and Alumni Services aids students and alumni in finding permanent, part-time, and summer jobs, as well as school year externships and internships, by serving as a clearinghouse for information on available positions. It also advises on résumé and interview preparation and coordinates on-campus interviews. More than 150 firms, businesses, and government agencies come to campus each year. Graduates find employment in the legal profession throughout the country.

APPLICANT PROFILE

George Mason University School of Law
This grid includes only applicants who earned 120–180 LSAT scores under standard administrations.

LSAT Score	GPA 3.75+ Apps	Adm	3.50–3.74 Apps	Adm	3.25–3.49 Apps	Adm	3.00–3.24 Apps	Adm	2.75–2.99 Apps	Adm	2.50–2.74 Apps	Adm	2.25–2.49 Apps	Adm	2.00–2.24 Apps	Adm	Below 2.00 Apps	Adm	No GPA Apps	Adm	Total Apps	Adm
175–180	2	1	0	0	2	1	0	0	2	1	1	1	0	0	0	0	0	0	0	0	7	4
170–174	20	15	18	13	19	13	13	9	8	1	6	5	3	2	1	0	0	0	1	1	89	59
165–169	92	74	163	138	117	98	86	71	47	29	29	13	11	4	1	0	3	2	12	11	561	440
160–164	209	197	325	78	287	37	207	28	82	13	29	3	23	3	6	0	0	0	39	1	1207	360
155–159	188	139	326	22	299	6	196	2	88	1	47	0	14	0	12	1	2	0	32	0	1204	171
150–154	95	24	148	4	169	0	158	0	84	0	46	0	19	0	12	0	1	0	20	0	752	28
145–149	25	2	65	0	71	0	97	0	64	0	40	0	18	0	9	0	3	0	10	0	402	2
140–144	12	0	23	0	36	0	42	0	40	0	23	0	13	0	14	0	7	0	4	0	214	0
135–139	7	0	8	0	12	0	17	0	14	0	9	0	14	0	4	0	1	0	6	0	92	0
130–134	2	0	0	0	3	0	8	0	4	0	3	0	3	0	4	0	3	0	1	0	31	0
125–129	0	0	1	0	0	0	1	0	0	0	5	0	1	0	1	0	0	0	1	0	10	0
120–124	0	0	0	0	0	0	0	0	0	0	0	0	0	0	0	0	0	0	0	0	0	0
Total	652	452	1077	255	1015	155	825	110	433	45	238	22	119	9	64	1	20	2	126	13	4569	1064

Apps = Number of Applicants
Adm = Number Admitted
Reflects 100% of the total applicant pool; highest LSAT data reported.

THE GEORGE WASHINGTON UNIVERSITY LAW SCHOOL

2000 H Street NW
Washington, DC 20052
Phone: 202.994.7230; Fax: 202.994.3597
E-mail: jdadmit@law.gwu.edu; Website: www.law.gwu.edu

The Basics

Type of school	Private
Term	Semester
Application deadline	12/15 3/31
Application fee	$80
Financial aid deadline	3/1 6/1
Can first year start other than fall?	No
Student to faculty ratio	15.2 to 1
# of housing spaces available restricted to law students	538
graduate housing for which law students are eligible	390

Faculty and Administrators

	Total		Men		Women		Minorities	
	Spr	Fall	Spr	Fall	Spr	Fall	Spr	Fall
Full-time	90	87	57	53	33	34	14	13
Other full-time	4	4	0	2	4	2	1	0
Deans, librarians, & others who teach	21	21	9	10	12	11	5	5
Part-time	199	155	146	120	53	35	22	12
Total	314	267	212	185	102	82	42	30

Curriculum

	Full-Time	Part-Time
Typical first-year section size	96	35
Is there typically a "small section" of the first-year class, other than Legal Writing, taught by full-time faculty	Yes	No
If yes, typical size offered last year	36	
# of classroom course titles beyond first-year curriculum	226	

# of upper division courses, excluding seminars, with an enrollment:		
	Under 25	320
	25–49	109
	50–74	41
	75–99	14
	100+	22

# of seminars	49	
# of seminar positions available	784	
# of seminar positions filled	429	190
# of positions available in simulation courses	1,322	
# of simulation positions filled	363	846
# of positions available in faculty supervised clinical courses	139	
# of faculty supervised clinical positions filled	126	13
# involved in field placements	343	52
# involved in law journals	488	49
# involved in moot court or trial competitions	368	50
# of credit hours required to graduate	84	

JD Enrollment and Ethnicity

	Men		Women		Full-Time		Part-Time		1st-Year		Total		JD Degs. Awd.
	#	%	#	%	#	%	#	%	#	%	#	%	
All Hispanics	57	6.0	66	8.3	113	7.9	10	3.1	42	8.3	123	7.0	21
Am. Ind./AK Nat.	3	0.3	3	0.4	5	0.3	1	0.3	1	0.2	6	0.3	2
Asian	84	8.8	82	10.3	121	8.5	45	13.9	52	10.3	166	9.5	48
Black/Af. Am.	41	4.3	48	6.0	63	4.4	26	8.0	26	5.2	89	5.1	29
Nat. HI/Pac. Isl.	1	0.1	3	0.4	4	0.3	0	0.0	0	0.0	4	0.2	0
2 or more races	0	0.0	1	0.1	1	0.1	0	0.0	0	0.0	1	0.1	3
Subtotal (minor.)	186	19.5	203	25.5	307	21.5	82	25.4	121	24.0	389	22.2	103
Nonres. Alien	23	2.4	20	2.5	39	2.7	4	1.2	18	3.6	43	2.5	12
White/Cauc.	645	67.5	497	62.4	944	66.0	198	61.3	327	64.9	1142	65.1	322
Unknown	102	10.7	77	9.7	140	9.8	39	12.1	38	7.5	179	10.2	74
Total	956	54.5	797	45.5	1430	81.6	323	18.4	504	28.8	1753		511

Transfers

Transfers in	104
Transfers out	10

Tuition and Fees

	Resident	Nonresident
Full-time	$45,750	$45,750
Part-time	$35,376	$35,376
Tuition Guarantee Program	Y	

Living Expenses

Estimated living expenses for singles

Living on campus	Living off campus	Living at home
$28,650	$28,650	$28,650

THE GEORGE WASHINGTON UNIVERSITY LAW SCHOOL

ABA Approved Since 1923

GPA and LSAT Scores

	Total	Full-Time	Part-Time
# of apps	8,652	7,846	806
# of offers	2,355	2,255	100
# of matrics	474	435	39
75% GPA	3.90	3.90	3.91
Median GPA	3.82	3.82	3.57
25% GPA	3.43	3.44	3.15
75% LSAT	168	168	168
Median LSAT	167	167	167
25% LSAT	161	162	159

Grants and Scholarships (from prior year)

	Total #	Total %	Full-Time #	Full-Time %	Part-Time #	Part-Time %
Total # of students	1,709		1,410		299	
Total # receiving grants	814	47.6	774	54.9	40	13.4
Less than 1/2 tuition	503	29.4	468	33.2	35	11.7
Half to full tuition	136	8.0	134	9.5	2	0.7
Full tuition	79	4.6	78	5.5	1	0.3
More than full tuition	96	5.6	94	6.7	2	0.7
Median grant amount			$13,000		$6,000	

Informational and Library Resources

Total amount spent on library materials	$2,908,725
Study seating capacity inside the library	637
# of full-time equivalent professional librarians	24
Hours per week library is open	110
# of open, wired connections available to students	54
# of networked computers available for use by students	71
Has wireless network?	Y
Requires computer?	Y

JD Attrition (from prior year)

	Academic #	Other #	Total #	Total %
1st year	1	31	32	5.9
2nd year	2	1	3	0.5
3rd year	1	1	2	0.4
4th year	0	0	0	0.0

Employment (9 months after graduation)

For up-to-date employment data, go to employmentsummary.abaquestionnaire.org on the ABA website.

Bar Passage Rates

First-time takers	488	Reporting %	95.70
Average school %	93.56	Average state %	81.02
Average pass difference	12.54		

Jurisdiction	Takers	Passers	Pass %	State %	Diff %
New York	144	139	96.53	84.92	11.61
Virginia	116	106	91.38	78.15	13.23
Maryland	83	77	92.77	79.96	12.81
California	40	33	82.50	71.24	11.26
Others (18)	84	82	97.62		

THE GEORGE WASHINGTON UNIVERSITY LAW SCHOOL

2000 H Street NW
Washington, DC 20052
Phone: 202.994.7230; Fax: 202.994.3597
E-mail: admissions@law.gwu.edu; Website: www.law.gwu.edu

Introduction

GW Law provides a legal education that literally cannot be found anywhere else—an education premised on law in action:

- At GW Law, constitutional law is not just a course; it is current events.
- At GW Law, we offer unparalleled opportunities to take part in the real world of law and policy practice.
- At GW Law, helping students build a successful career is a top priority from day one.
- At GW Law, faculty members and students work daily on the key global challenges of our day.

This is a legal education to change the world, an opportunity to dynamically engage in law and policy that no other school can match.

We are a distinctive school with a distinctive mission and set of opportunities for students. And, as the legal market experiences radical change, the education we offer will come to be seen as increasingly important.

A Law School for the 21st Century

In this era of dynamic transformation, our vision of what a law school can be offers the following distinctive features:

Personalized Pathways: With over 500 course offerings each year, GW provides focused paths of study in nearly every area of law imaginable. These pathways go far beyond course selection, however. At GW Law, students can combine coursework; unparalleled interaction with leading lawyers, judges, and policymakers in the field; high-level externships; and unique capstone experiences to learn both theory and practice and to develop an integrated series of skills, experiences, and contacts that cannot be found anywhere else.

Engagement in the Real World: GW Law refuses to sit in an ivory tower, divorced from the real world of law and policy practice. Our full-time faculty members routinely testify in Congress, litigate leading cases, collaborate with think-tanks, serve on international courts and commissions, and work at the highest levels of government. Our adjunct faculty includes the leading lawyers in the legal capital of the world. And our students get to take part in all of it: interacting with Supreme Court justices, World Bank officials, financial regulators, military leaders, and State Department lawyers; working on actual public policy projects tackling the most important challenges of our time; taking an active role in real-world legal matters and studying abroad.

Externships: No other law school can match the externship opportunities we provide, with over 500 students per year receiving extensive course credit to get hands-on training at the highest levels of government, public interest, and the judiciary. Whatever your area of interest, we have a leading lawyer willing to mentor you, supervise your work, and provide you with the practical experience that will jump-start your career.

Professional Development Training: At GW, we believe legal training is not only about substantive knowledge; lawyers also need to know how to work in teams to solve problems, how to understand the changing economics of law practice, how to develop clients, how to construct effective networks, and how to think creatively about building a lifetime of career options. Our new integrated professional development training program gives our students a sophisticated understanding of these crucial skills.

Clinics and Pro Bono Activities: GW was one of the first law schools in the nation to embrace clinical education, and today our clinics provide intensive training and practical experience working with real clients across many areas of criminal and civil litigation, administrative adjudication, appellate practice, and business planning and entrepreneurship. In addition, our pro bono program—headed by Alan Morrison, one of the legendary public interest lawyers in US history—builds even more opportunities for engagement, with programs ranging from helping the wrongly convicted to writing legal documents for cancer patients to working with the Special Master in charge of assessing damages after the BP oil spill. As a result, our students have almost limitless opportunities to become engaged in the real-world practice of law and policy. In addition, the school awards nearly one hundred summer public interest fellowships annually and provides loan repayment assistance to graduates embarking on public interest careers.

Mentoring, Counseling, and Networking for Careers: With some 20,000 alumni all over the world and in every area of practice, GW Law can connect students with a vast network of mentors, advisors, and career contacts. But merely having a network is not enough. At GW, we also have dedicated staff devoted to helping students make those connections. And with one of the largest career development offices in the country, our focus is on one-to-one counseling from day one, to ensure that students effectively bridge the gap from law school to law practice.

A Welcoming, Nurturing Community: While we offer the unlimited opportunities of a large school in our nation's capital, we also prioritize student well-being, offering personalized attention and numerous resources designed to build a nurturing and supportive environment. And the Dean holds drop-in hours once a week starting at 4:30 PM; students can come without an appointment, and office hours continue as long as there are students who want to chat. That's our commitment to students, as they develop their own pathways through law school.

In short, all top law schools are not alike. GW offers a legal education for students both in the classroom and beyond to tackle the world. And we do so in a nurturing environment with opportunities that simply cannot be found anywhere else.

Joint-Degree and Study-Abroad Programs

Joint degrees are offered in the areas of business, public administration, public health, public policy, international affairs, history/US legal history, and women's studies. Summer study-abroad opportunities include the GW-Oxford Program in International Human Rights Law, the GW-Munich Intellectual Property Law Program, the GW-Augsburg (Germany) Student Exchange Program, and the University of Groningen in the Netherlands and Universita-Commerciale "Luigi Bocconi" in Milan, Italy. GW also is a member of the North American Consortium on Legal Education, which allows students to study at member Canadian and Mexican law schools.

Student Activities

Membership is available on nine publications—the *George Washington Law Review*, the *George Washington International Law Review* and its new *National Security Law Digest*, the *Journal of Energy and Environmental Law*, the *Public Contract Law Journal* (cosponsored by the ABA Section of Public Contract Law), the *Federal Circuit Bar Journal*, the *American Intellectual Property Law Quarterly Journal* (published by AIPLA and housed at GW), the *Federal Communications Bar Journal* (in collaboration with the Federal Communication Bar Association), and the *International Law in Domestic Courts Journal*.

Three skills boards—the Moot Court Board, Mock Trial Board, and Alternative Dispute Resolution Board—provide numerous opportunities for participation in competitions around the world. In addition, approximately 50 student groups are active at the law school, sponsoring social, educational, career, and public interest-related programs.

Finally, over 400 events take place on the law school campus each year, an average of three per day during the school year. During 2011–2012, these events ranged from a two-day summit meeting of the US Supreme Court justices and judges from the European Court of Human Rights, to a cybersecurity working group featuring high-ranking officials from the US Military's Cybercommand, to public events with SEC Commissioners, members of Congress, the State Department Legal Adviser, and leading scholars. The opportunities for engagement are truly limitless.

Office of Professional Development and Career Strategy

At GW Law, the traditional career services model has been transformed into a dynamic, proactive operation that works to help every single student bridge the gap from law school to law practice. We have instituted a professional development training program for all 1Ls, and every student will be assigned a career counselor beginning in the first semester who will meet with that student each semester thereafter and engage intimately in the job search process. An alumni mentoring program allows each incoming student to be assigned as they arrive at school to an attorney from practice who will meet with the student at least twice in the first year and provide a shadowing/networking experience. In addition, an associate dean for academic development works with each student to help construct a career path that combines courses, externships, mentors, and job networking. And with approximately 20,000 graduates, GW Law has among the most extensive alumni networks in the country. Finally, our innovative Pathways to Practice Program provides financial assistance to graduating students to perform volunteer legal work for up to a full year after graduation.

Financial Assistance

The GW Law Financial Aid Office counsels and assists applicants and current students in applying for various sources of financial aid: loans at negotiated, competitive terms; need-based tuition grants; and outside scholarships. All applicants are considered for merit-based aid, including general merit awards, as well as public interest, environmental, and Teach for America merit scholarships. An estimated 85 percent of GW law students receive some sort of financial aid.

APPLICANT PROFILE

The George Washington University Law School
This grid includes only applicants who earned 120–180 LSAT scores under standard administrations.

LSAT Score	3.75 +		3.50–3.74		3.25–3.49		3.00–3.24		2.75–2.99		2.50–2.74		2.25–2.49		2.00–2.24		Below 2.00		No GPA		Total	
	Apps	Adm	Apps	Adm	Apps	Adm	Apps	Adm	Apps	Adm	Apps	Adm	Apps	Adm	Apps	Adm	Apps	Adm	Apps	Adm	Apps	Adm
175–180	20	20	31	29	27	19	13	8	3	1	4	0	0	0	3	1	0	0	0	0	101	78
170–174	245	228	224	194	159	115	92	52	32	14	18	9	7	2	1	0	0	0	15	12	793	626
165–169	648	496	825	367	513	144	244	76	71	17	38	9	19	1	1	0	2	0	81	17	2442	1127
160–164	666	316	767	12	554	17	259	12	83	7	49	2	21	2	6	0	0	0	86	7	2491	375
155–159	285	98	389	4	314	8	179	5	98	3	43	0	15	1	11	0	2	0	42	1	1378	120
150–154	104	14	173	3	178	0	140	0	67	0	49	0	19	0	8	0	3	0	27	0	768	17
145–149	34	0	65	0	69	0	77	1	51	0	28	0	20	0	5	0	2	0	14	0	365	1
140–144	8	0	24	0	34	0	41	0	18	0	24	0	4	0	10	0	3	0	4	0	170	0
135–139	4	0	6	0	10	0	10	0	18	0	9	0	10	0	4	0	0	0	6	0	77	0
130–134	0	0	2	0	2	0	6	0	3	0	6	0	1	0	3	0	1	0	1	0	25	0
125–129	0	0	1	0	1	0	0	0	0	0	1	0	1	0	0	0	1	0	3	0	8	0
120–124	0	0	0	0	0	0	0	0	0	0	0	0	0	0	1	0	0	0	0	0	1	0
Total	2014	1172	2507	609	1861	303	1061	154	444	42	269	20	117	6	53	1	14	0	279	37	8619	2344

Apps = Number of Applicants
Adm = Number Admitted
Reflects 99% of the total applicant pool; highest LSAT data reported.

GEORGETOWN UNIVERSITY LAW CENTER

600 New Jersey Avenue, NW, Room 589
Washington, DC 20001
Phone: 202.662.9010; Fax: 202.662.9439
E-mail: admis@law.georgetown.edu; Website: www.law.georgetown.edu

The Basics

Type of school	Private
Term	Semester
Application deadline	3/1
Application fee	$85
Financial aid deadline	3/1
Can first year start other than fall?	No
Student to faculty ratio	11.9 to 1
# of housing spaces available restricted to law students	291
graduate housing for which law students are eligible	

Faculty and Administrators

	Total		Men		Women		Minorities	
	Spr	Fall	Spr	Fall	Spr	Fall	Spr	Fall
Full-time	124	130	76	79	48	51	12	16
Other full-time	6	7	2	2	4	5	1	1
Deans, librarians, & others who teach	22	17	6	8	16	9	4	4
Part-time	145	122	115	95	30	27	9	8
Total	297	276	199	184	98	92	26	29

Curriculum

	Full-Time	Part-Time
Typical first-year section size	99	69
Is there typically a "small section" of the first-year class, other than Legal Writing, taught by full-time faculty	Yes	Yes
If yes, typical size offered last year	34	22
# of classroom course titles beyond first-year curriculum	461	
# of upper division courses, excluding seminars, with an enrollment: Under 25	236	
25–49	76	
50–74	30	
75–99	13	
100+	11	
# of seminars	290	
# of seminar positions available	4,003	
# of seminar positions filled	1,879	963
# of positions available in simulation courses	2,111	
# of simulation positions filled	1,109	653
# of positions available in faculty supervised clinical courses	283	
# of faculty supervised clinical positions filled	278	5
# involved in field placements	259	17
# involved in law journals	708	54
# involved in moot court or trial competitions	580	94
# of credit hours required to graduate	85	

JD Enrollment and Ethnicity

	Men		Women		Full-Time		Part-Time		1st-Year		Total		JD Degs. Awd.
	#	%	#	%	#	%	#	%	#	%	#	%	
All Hispanics	49	4.7	40	4.4	78	4.7	11	4.2	28	4.8	89	4.6	35
Am. Ind./AK Nat.	0	0.0	1	0.1	1	0.1	0	0.0	1	0.2	1	0.1	1
Asian	39	3.8	55	6.1	81	4.8	13	5.0	4	0.7	94	4.9	55
Black/Af. Am.	56	5.4	99	11.0	144	8.6	11	4.2	50	8.7	155	8.0	43
Nat. HI/Pac. Isl.	1	0.1	1	0.1	2	0.1	0	0.0	0	0.0	2	0.1	2
2 or more races	12	1.2	24	2.7	32	1.9	4	1.5	3	0.5	36	1.9	17
Subtotal (minor.)	157	15.2	220	24.5	338	20.2	39	14.9	86	14.9	377	19.5	153
Nonres. Alien	32	3.1	28	3.1	55	3.3	5	1.9	22	3.8	60	3.1	19
White/Cauc.	631	61.1	483	53.7	955	57.2	159	60.9	239	41.3	1114	57.7	426
Unknown	213	20.6	168	18.7	323	19.3	58	22.2	231	40.0	381	19.7	47
Total	1033	53.5	899	46.5	1671	86.5	261	13.5	578	29.9	1932		645

Transfers

Transfers in	71
Transfers out	8

Tuition and Fees

	Resident	Nonresident
Full-time	$46,865	$46,865
Part-time	$33,500	$33,500
Tuition Guarantee Program	N	

Living Expenses

Estimated living expenses for singles

Living on campus	Living off campus	Living at home
$23,635	$23,635	$17,180

GEORGETOWN UNIVERSITY LAW CENTER

*ABA
Approved
Since
1924*

GPA and LSAT Scores

	Total	Full-Time	Part-Time
# of apps	11,194	9,413	1,781
# of offers	2,681	2,542	139
# of matrics	579	510	69
75% GPA	3.80	3.80	3.80
Median GPA	3.71	3.71	3.70
25% GPA	3.44	3.44	3.37
75% LSAT	171	171	170
Median LSAT	170	170	167
25% LSAT	167	167	163

Grants and Scholarships (from prior year)

	Total		Full-Time		Part-Time	
	#	%	#	%	#	%
Total # of students	1,960		1,626		334	
Total # receiving grants	657	33.5	648	39.9	9	2.7
Less than 1/2 tuition	430	21.9	421	25.9	9	2.7
Half to full tuition	225	11.5	225	13.8	0	0.0
Full tuition	2	0.1	2	0.1	0	0.0
More than full tuition	0	0.0	0	0.0	0	0.0
Median grant amount			$17,900		$5,000	

Informational and Library Resources

Total amount spent on library materials	$2,924,468
Study seating capacity inside the library	1,060
# of full-time equivalent professional librarians	26
Hours per week library is open	107
# of open, wired connections available to students	840
# of networked computers available for use by students	218
Has wireless network?	Y
Requires computer?	Y

JD Attrition (from prior year)

	Academic	Other	Total	
	#	#	#	%
1st year	0	12	12	2.0
2nd year	0	4	4	0.6
3rd year	0	0	0	0.0
4th year	0	1	1	1.4

Employment (9 months after graduation)

For up-to-date employment data, go to employmentsummary.abaquestionnaire.org on the ABA website.

Bar Passage Rates

First-time takers	645	Reporting %	78.91
Average school %	89.39	Average state %	80.45
Average pass difference	8.94		

Jurisdiction	Takers	Passers	Pass %	State %	Diff %
New York	233	221	94.85	84.92	9.93
Maryland	107	98	91.59	79.96	11.63
California	87	65	74.71	71.24	3.47
Virginia	82	71	86.59	78.15	8.44

GEORGETOWN UNIVERSITY LAW CENTER

600 New Jersey Avenue, NW, Room 589
Washington, DC 20001
Phone: 202.662.9010; Fax: 202.662.9439
E-mail: admis@law.georgetown.edu; Website: www.law.georgetown.edu

Introduction

Georgetown Law, founded in 1870, is a dynamic and diverse intellectual community in which to study law. Not only does its curriculum include a staggering number of courses and seminars, but its distinguished full-time faculty is one of the nation's largest and is augmented by the experience and perspective of outstanding members of the bench and bar. The goal is education in its fullest sense—not only mastery of law, but a sense of the philosophical, political, and ethical dimensions of law. Preeminent in the fields of constitutional, international, and tax law, as well as clinical legal education, Georgetown Law's faculty is also known for its expertise in civil rights, corporate law, environmental law, family law, feminist jurisprudence, health law, human rights, immigration and refugee law, intellectual property law, legal history, and securities law. The Supreme Court, the Congress of the United States, and the Library of Congress are within walking distance of the campus, forming a unique environment for creative legal thought and learning.

The Law Center Campus

Georgetown Law's campus is the culmination of a longtime goal to create a campus that will nurture students in mind, body, and spirit. McDonough Hall, with its lecture halls, seminar rooms, faculty offices, bookstore, student dining area, and lounges, is the academic center of the campus.

The Hotung Building brings all the major components of Georgetown Law's international programs under one roof and includes the John Wolff International and Comparative Law Library. The Sport and Fitness Center features a four-lane lap pool, basketball and racquetball courts, and a café and lounge with wireless network connectivity.

The Law Center's Edward Bennett Williams Law Library houses the fourth largest academic law library collection in the nation. The library also provides students with access to web-based services providing the most advanced research support available.

The campus features a vibrant residential program, with housing for approximately 300 students in the Gewirz Student Center. The building offers a variety of apartment styles with one, two, and three bedrooms with full kitchens and baths in each suite. Apartments designed for students with disabilities are also available. Resident Fellows offer programming to the 1L residents throughout the academic year ranging from fireside chats with faculty members, to talent shows, to informal seminars on course outlining and exam-taking.

Curriculum

Georgetown Law offers full-time and part-time programs leading to the JD degree. Entry to both programs is in the fall. First-year students in the full-time program choose either the A or B curriculum. Curriculum A is the traditional first-year curriculum, which parallels those at all other major law schools, and includes one elective course in the spring semester. Curriculum B includes courses that emphasize the sources of law in history, philosophy, political theory, and economics. It also seeks to reflect the increasingly public nature of contemporary law. Rather than an elective,

Curriculum B students take a fall seminar in legal theory. Full-time students are required to be in residence for six semesters; part-time students must be in residence for eight semesters or its equivalent.

The curriculum includes an innovative program for first-year students titled "Week One: Law in a Global Context." Involving an intensive week of study of complex problems of international and transnational law, the purpose is to deepen students' understanding of how legal problems increasingly transcend national boundaries and involve more than one legal system. The skills-based format of Week One also introduces students to Georgetown Law's extensive experiential curriculum, where students may choose from problem-solving, simulation, externship, and other experiential learning courses, up to and including our nationally and internationally recognized clinics.

Georgetown Law offers a large and wide-ranging upper-level curriculum. Of the more than 350 courses offered to upper-class students, more than 150 have enrollments under 25 students. The only upper-class course requirements are a course in professional responsibility and a seminar or approved supervised research project meeting the upper-class legal writing requirement.

Joint Degrees

Georgetown Law offers 15 joint-degree programs: JD/Master of Public Policy; JD/Master of Science in Foreign Service; JD/Master of Arts in Arab Studies; JD/Master of Arts in German and European Studies; JD/Master of Arts in Latin American Studies; JD/Master of Arts in Russian, Eurasian, and East European Studies; JD/Master of Arts in Security Studies; JD/Master of Business Administration; JD/Master of Public Health (with Johns Hopkins School of Public Health); JD/Master of Arts or Doctorate in Philosophy; JD/Doctorate in Government (Master of Arts En Passant); JD/LLM in Taxation; JD/LLM in Securities and Financial Regulation; JD/LLM in International Business and Economic Law; and the JD/LLM in National Security Law.

Transnational, International, and Comparative Law Programs

Georgetown Law has many highly regarded programs dealing with different aspects of cross-border law.

Students have the unique opportunity to study for a semester in London at the Center for Transnational Legal studies, a Georgetown-led partnership of over 20 leading schools from five continents. Distinguished faculty, drawn from around the world, teach a transnational curriculum to a global student body in a context where there is no host school, majority nationality, or domestic legal system.

The Global Law Scholars Program, which combines language skills with directed legal training, provides an opportunity for a limited number of full-time JD students to prepare for a law practice involving more than one legal system.

Georgetown Law also offers a summer law program in London with distinguished professors from Europe and the US, as well as the opportunity to study abroad for a semester at prestigious institutions in Europe, Asia, India, Israel, Latin America, and Australia.

The Law Center's International Summer Internship Program offers opportunities to work abroad in law firms, corporations, and government organizations. Georgetown Law's Institute of International Economic Law awards a certificate in World Trade Organization studies to students who fulfill special course requirements.

Clinical Programs and Public Interest Law

Georgetown Law, a pioneer in clinical legal education, offers an unmatched clinical program. Our 14 clinics offer approximately 300 students per year an opportunity to enroll in clinics where (1) they represent clients in court or in administrative hearings, or (2) they work in a nontrial context in federal and local agencies, schools, and other institutions.

Georgetown Law's unparalleled public interest offerings include a Loan Repayment Assistance Program, a stand-alone public interest career office, guaranteed summer funding for public interest and government internships, a comprehensive student pro bono program, an extensive and diverse public interest curriculum, and public interest scholarships and a public interest fellowship program. The Office of Public Interest and Community Service (OPICS) houses a public interest resource library, provides specialist career advising on government and nonprofit internships and employment, oversees student and student group volunteer activities, and serves as the student liaison to the faculty and administration.

Admission

Georgetown Law evaluates candidates on two scales: academic or objective criteria and personal criteria. Academic information includes undergraduate and graduate records and LSAT scores. Personal factors include extracurricular activities, recommendations, work experience, and diversity of background. Georgetown Law does not use numerical cutoffs. Early application is encouraged since Georgetown Law employs a rolling admission process.

Student Activities

Cocurricular life at the Law Center centers around the more than 75 law student organizations that support students' personal, social, spiritual, political, and professional interests. The largest of these organizations, the student-led Barristers' Council, fields dozens of teams in appellate advocacy, mock trial, and alternative dispute resolution divisions, and competes successfully in national and international competitions. Students also share in the governance of the Law Center through the Student Bar Association and more than a dozen student/faculty committees, and supplement their academic pursuits by editing and publishing 11 scholarly journals and the *Law Weekly*, the award-winning school newspaper.

Financial Aid

Georgetown Law offers need-based, three-year financial aid grants to approximately one-third of the entering full-time class. Federal and commercial loans, along with on- and off-campus work-study opportunities, are also available. Approximately 90 percent of Georgetown Law's JD students obtain financial aid.

Acknowledged as one of the nation's top programs by Equal Justice Works, Georgetown Law's Loan Repayment Assistance Program assists JD graduates in pursuing careers in public service.

Career Services

The Office of Career Services (OCS) offers a wide range of career counseling and related programming. First-year students work closely with advisors who counsel them individually throughout law school. The fall recruiting program is one of the largest in the country, and OCS sponsors a robust judicial clerkship application process.

APPLICANT PROFILE

Since the Georgetown Law Admissions Committee takes into consideration a number of factors in evaluating whether a candidate would be suitable for admission, we cannot provide an applicant profile based solely on GPA and LSAT scores. In making such determinations, the Committee focuses on various aspects of a candidate's background and experience that, in combination with a candidate's academic record and LSAT score, give insight into a candidate's suitability for admission.

UNIVERSITY OF GEORGIA SCHOOL OF LAW

Harold Hirsch Hall, 225 Herty Drive
Athens, GA 30602-6012
Phone: 706.542.7060; Fax: 706.542.5556
E-mail: ugajd@uga.edu; Website: www.law.uga.edu

ABA
Approved
Since
1930

The Basics

Type of school	Public
Term	Semester
Application deadline	3/1
Application fee	$50
Financial aid deadline	3/1
Can first year start other than fall?	No
Student to faculty ratio	12.3 to 1
# of housing spaces available restricted to law students	
graduate housing for which law students are eligible	732

Faculty and Administrators

	Total		Men		Women		Minorities	
	Spr	Fall	Spr	Fall	Spr	Fall	Spr	Fall
Full-time	46	50	29	28	17	22	6	6
Other full-time	4	3	1	1	3	2	0	0
Deans, librarians, & others who teach	7	7	3	3	4	4	0	0
Part-time	22	14	18	12	4	2	2	0
Total	79	74	51	44	28	30	8	6

Curriculum

	Full-Time	Part-Time
Typical first-year section size	83	0
Is there typically a "small section" of the first-year class, other than Legal Writing, taught by full-time faculty	No	No
If yes, typical size offered last year		
# of classroom course titles beyond first-year curriculum	121	

# of upper division courses, excluding seminars, with an enrollment:		
	Under 25	93
	25–49	31
	50–74	19
	75–99	7
	100+	0

# of seminars	35	
# of seminar positions available	630	
# of seminar positions filled	553	0
# of positions available in simulation courses	375	
# of simulation positions filled	346	0
# of positions available in faculty supervised clinical courses	599	
# of faculty supervised clinical positions filled	590	0
# involved in field placements	115	0
# involved in law journals	198	0
# involved in moot court or trial competitions	398	0
# of credit hours required to graduate	88	

JD Enrollment and Ethnicity

	Men		Women		Full-Time		Part-Time		1st-Year		Total		JD Degs. Awd.
	#	%	#	%	#	%	#	%	#	%	#	%	
All Hispanics	2	0.5	4	1.4	6	0.9	0	0.0	0	0.0	6	0.9	4
Am. Ind./AK Nat.	1	0.3	4	1.4	5	0.7	0	0.0	2	0.9	5	0.7	0
Asian	18	4.5	14	4.8	32	4.6	0	0.0	12	5.3	32	4.6	11
Black/Af. Am.	32	8.1	55	18.7	87	12.6	0	0.0	40	17.6	87	12.6	26
Nat. HI/Pac. Isl.	0	0.0	0	0.0	0	0.0	0	0.0	0	0.0	0	0.0	0
2 or more races	2	0.5	5	1.7	7	1.0	0	0.0	0	0.0	7	1.0	6
Subtotal (minor.)	55	13.9	82	27.9	137	19.8	0	0.0	54	23.8	137	19.8	47
Nonres. Alien	0	0.0	0	0.0	0	0.0	0	0.0	0	0.0	0	0.0	2
White/Cauc.	307	77.3	188	63.9	495	71.6	0	0.0	156	68.7	495	71.6	150
Unknown	35	8.8	24	8.2	59	8.5	0	0.0	17	7.5	59	8.5	23
Total	397	57.5	294	42.5	691	100.0	0	0.0	227	32.9	691		222

Transfers

Transfers in	6
Transfers out	4

Tuition and Fees

	Resident	Nonresident
Full-time	$17,624	$34,732
Part-time		
Tuition Guarantee Program	N	

Living Expenses

Estimated living expenses for singles

Living on campus	Living off campus	Living at home
$13,096	$16,520	$9,198

UNIVERSITY OF GEORGIA SCHOOL OF LAW

*ABA
Approved
Since
1930*

GPA and LSAT Scores

	Total	Full-Time	Part-Time
# of apps	3,186	3,186	0
# of offers	814	814	0
# of matrics	225	225	0
75% GPA	3.76	3.76	0.00
Median GPA	3.59	3.59	0.00
25% GPA	3.30	3.30	0.00
75% LSAT	166	166	0
Median LSAT	165	165	0
25% LSAT	162	162	0

Grants and Scholarships (from prior year)

	Total #	Total %	Full-Time #	Full-Time %	Part-Time #	Part-Time %
Total # of students	703		703		0	
Total # receiving grants	434	61.7	434	61.7	0	0.0
Less than 1/2 tuition	195	27.7	195	27.7	0	0.0
Half to full tuition	229	32.6	229	32.6	0	0.0
Full tuition	6	0.9	6	0.9	0	0.0
More than full tuition	4	0.6	4	0.6	0	0.0
Median grant amount			$9,000		$0	

Informational and Library Resources

Total amount spent on library materials	$1,104,104
Study seating capacity inside the library	455
# of full-time equivalent professional librarians	8
Hours per week library is open	121
# of open, wired connections available to students	0
# of networked computers available for use by students	32
Has wireless network?	Y
Requires computer?	N

JD Attrition (from prior year)

	Academic #	Other #	Total #	Total %
1st year	1	4	5	2.0
2nd year	0	1	1	0.4
3rd year	0	0	0	0.0
4th year	0	0	0	0.0

Employment (9 months after graduation)

For up-to-date employment data, go to employmentsummary.abaquestionnaire.org on the ABA website.

Bar Passage Rates

First-time takers	215	Reporting %	94.42
Average school %	97.03	Average state %	83.34
Average pass difference	13.69		

Jurisdiction	Takers	Passers	Pass %	State %	Diff %
Georgia	181	175	96.69	83.61	13.08
North Carolina	6	6	100.00	77.50	22.50
New York	5	5	100.00	84.92	15.08
Florida	4	4	100.00	77.63	22.37
Others (7)	7	7	100.00		

The information on these pages was provided by the law school.

UNIVERSITY OF GEORGIA SCHOOL OF LAW

Harold Hirsch Hall, 225 Herty Drive
Athens, GA 30602-6012
Phone: 706.542.7060; Fax: 706.542.5556
E-mail: ugajd@uga.edu; Website: www.law.uga.edu

Introduction

The University of Georgia School of Law (Georgia Law), founded in 1859, is on the campus of the University of Georgia in Athens, Georgia. The university provides an excellent setting for the study of law with superb libraries and outstanding academic, cultural, recreational, and social opportunities. Athens, a town of 100,000, is the commercial and legal center for northeast Georgia and is approximately one hour from downtown Atlanta. Athens also features a cultural richness ranging from local restaurants and quirky shops to the latest in the alternative music scene.

The School of Law is approved by the ABA, is a member of the AALS, and has a chapter of the Order of the Coif.

The Student Body

The law school student body shares a strong sense of community, and the school prides itself on the collegiality among students, faculty, and staff. The entering class usually numbers in the low 200s, and the entire student body, including LLM students, averages 650 students. The law school is also a vital part of the university community, which supports a cosmopolitan mix of over 33,000 undergraduate, graduate, and professional students. Many law students take advantage of these assets by taking courses in other schools and colleges of the university and by participating in the intellectual and social life of the campus.

Curriculum

The law curriculum is rich and diverse. The first year of study consists of required core courses; after its completion, students may choose from a wealth of classes, seminars, and clinical programs to suit their interests.

Clinical program opportunities, both criminal and civil, abound. Clinical education expands upon the classroom knowledge by providing essential experiential learning. Students interested in criminal law can participate in the Prosecutorial Clinic, the Criminal Defense Clinic, or the Capital Assistance Project. Students interested in environmental law, family law, public interest law, and any of a number of other areas of study will find that the Civil Externship Clinic, Family Violence Clinic, Mediation Practicum, Public Interest Practicum, Environmental Law Practicum, Special Education Practicum, and Appellate Litigation Clinic add to their understanding and preparedness. Students also have the opportunity to spend a semester working in the nation's capitol through the Washington, DC, Semester in Practice program launched in Spring 2012.

Faculty

While some law schools choose to emphasize either scholarship or teaching, the University of Georgia seeks a balance of the two, firmly believing that classroom teaching is enhanced by scholarly expertise. The college town setting fosters student-faculty interaction by increasing faculty availability and promoting a conducive atmosphere for dialogue.

The faculty includes authors of some of our country's leading legal scholarship, recipients of the university's highest honors for teaching excellence, Fulbright Scholars, and former law clerks for the US Supreme Court and appellate courts. Most bring practical experience to the classroom as well; they have been trial and corporate attorneys, and many continue to accept pro bono cases or serve as consultants.

Faculty expertise is expanded by the addition of outstanding adjuncts, attorneys from the region's most powerful firms, international attorneys, government leaders, and prominent practitioners. In addition, the law school's Dean Rusk Center annually is host to several international scholars who may teach mini-courses in their areas of interest. Recent courses include international human rights, dispute settlement in the World Trade Organization, and EC competition law.

Educational Enrichment Programs

University of Georgia law students have several opportunities to expand their educational horizons. First, joint programs with other schools and colleges in the university enable students to complete two degrees in less time than it would take to pursue them separately. Existing joint programs include JD/MBA (business administration), JD/MPA (public administration), JD/MHP (historic preservation), JD/MSW (social work), and JD/MEd in Sports Studies.

Students may also take graduate coursework in other schools and colleges of the university and have it count as elective credit toward the 88 semester hours required for graduation. For example, students interested in tax law might take courses in the school of accounting, and students interested in public policy might take courses in the School of Public and International Affairs. Finally, those who are not interested in the joint-degree programs, but want more coursework than can be satisfied by elective credit, may pursue other advanced degrees at the same time they are fulfilling the requirements for the law degree.

Study Abroad

Nothing helps one to better understand the culture of another country than actually studying and living in a foreign land. At Georgia Law, this concept is fully embraced. Several opportunities for legal study and work experience in other parts of the world are provided on an annual basis. They include:

Georgia Law at Oxford—This exciting 15-week program runs from January through April and is one of the few semester-long study-abroad programs offered by an American law school. Selected second- and third-year law students take four courses and receive 12 semester hours of credit.

Global Internship Program—Established in 2001, this initiative provides students with 6 to 10 weeks of study or work experience in one of more than 30 countries spanning the world. Each participant receives funding from the law school to help offset travel and living costs.

Georgia Law Summer Program in Brussels and Geneva—Hosted by two highly prestigious European institutions of higher learning: L'Institut d'Études

Européennes, Facultés universitaires Saint-Louis (IEE) in Brussels and the Graduate Institute of International and Development Studies (Graduate Institute) in Geneva, this three-week course is designed to provide an introduction to the legal system of the European Union, with an emphasis on EU business law, as well as a concentrated study of international trade law practice under the WTO.

Georgia Law Summer Program in China—Partnering with Tsinghua University in Beijing and Fudan University in Shanghai, this three-week study-abroad program in China's two largest cities offers an introduction to the Chinese legal system with an emphasis on commercial and trade law. There is the potential for Georgia Law students to remain in the country at the end of the program for a four- to six-week internship in one of several law firms. Georgia Law students received partial tuition scholarships in the summer of 2010.

Equal Justice Foundation Fellowships—These awards provide grants to law students who engage in public interest legal work in positions that otherwise would not be funded. Recently, EJF fellowship recipients have used their funds to gain international experience and aid foreign causes.

Library and Physical Facilities

The law library's vast collection makes it among the largest in legal education. While it has extensive holdings in international law, it focuses on being a functional library serving the needs of students. The university's main library is adjacent to the law school and is one of the largest research libraries in the nation.

The law school is headquartered in Hirsch Hall on the northern edge of the campus, the most scenic and historic section of the university. Dean Rusk Hall, adjacent to Hirsch Hall, provides additional classroom and office space. The majority of clinical settings are just a short walk away in the downtown area.

Career Services

The law school offers a fully staffed career services office that assists law students and graduates. Graduates typically get jobs in private practice, government, public interest, and in federal judicial clerkships. The career services website is a comprehensive source of information.

Alumni practice in 39 states and over 49 countries. Employers from all 50 states and 25 countries have utilized the Legal Career Services Office to target Georgia Law students for summer and full-time employment.

Advocacy Programs

Georgia Law's accomplished Moot Court and Mock Trial programs focus on developing critical oral and written advocacy skills. Team members learn how to write persuasively and how to make convincing oral presentations that will withstand intense scrutiny by the court. Through this incredible practical learning experience, Georgia Law students become powerful advocates.

Georgia Law's Moot Court and Mock Trial programs have won several national titles, regional crowns, and state trophies.

Student Publications

Students at Georgia Law publish three highly regarded legal journals: the *Georgia Law Review*, the *Georgia Journal of International and Comparative Law*, and the *Journal of Intellectual Property Law*, a nationally recognized IP specialty journal. The journals, which are frequently cited by federal and state courts, textbooks, treatises, and other law reviews, follow the customary format, with articles from leading scholars and practitioners comprising the bulk of the content and another section consisting of student notes.

APPLICANT PROFILE

University of Georgia School of Law
This grid includes only applicants who earned 120–180 LSAT scores under standard administrations.

LSAT Score	3.75 +		3.50–3.74		3.25–3.49		3.00–3.24		2.75–2.99		2.50–2.74		Below 2.50		No GPA		Total	
	Apps	Adm	Apps	Adm	Apps	Adm	Apps	Adm	Apps	Adm	Apps	Adm	Apps	Adm	Apps	Adm	Apps	Adm
170–180	38	37	34	33	23	20	19	18	10	7	3	2	2	1	1	1	130	119
165–169	140	134	174	164	98	96	93	87	36	28	13	10	5	4	16	15	575	538
160–164	216	53	235	20	208	7	92	3	28	0	25	0	13	0	25	0	842	83
155–159	179	14	166	8	141	6	88	2	40	0	23	0	10	0	8	0	655	30
150–154	101	11	91	10	95	4	79	4	49	0	29	0	16	0	7	0	467	29
145–149	54	3	57	6	50	1	45	0	29	0	22	0	16	0	9	0	282	10
140–144	11	1	22	0	24	0	26	0	19	0	17	0	18	0	3	0	140	1
Below 140	0	0	7	0	11	0	15	0	8	0	15	0	22	0	3	0	81	0
Total	739	253	786	241	650	134	457	114	219	35	147	12	102	5	72	16	3172	810

Apps = Number of Applicants
Adm = Number Admitted
Reflects 100% of the total applicant pool; highest LSAT data reported.

GEORGIA STATE UNIVERSITY COLLEGE OF LAW

PO Box 4037
Atlanta, GA 30302-4037
Phone: 404.413.9000; Fax: 404.413.9225
E-mail: admissions@law.gsu.edu; Website: http://law.gsu.edu

ABA
Approved
Since
1984

The Basics

Type of school	Public
Term	Semester
Application deadline	3/15
Application fee	$50
Financial aid deadline	11/1
Can first year start other than fall?	No
Student to faculty ratio	10.1 to 1
# of housing spaces available restricted to law students	
graduate housing for which law students are eligible	650

Faculty and Administrators

	Total		Men		Women		Minorities	
	Spr	Fall	Spr	Fall	Spr	Fall	Spr	Fall
Full-time	47	50	25	28	22	22	7	7
Other full-time	11	11	4	4	7	7	1	1
Deans, librarians, & others who teach	10	10	4	4	6	6	2	2
Part-time	38	13	25	6	13	7	3	4
Total	106	84	58	42	48	42	13	14

Curriculum

		Full-Time	Part-Time
Typical first-year section size		70	0
Is there typically a "small section" of the first-year class, other than Legal Writing, taught by full-time faculty		No	No
If yes, typical size offered last year			
# of classroom course titles beyond first-year curriculum		112	
# of upper division courses, excluding seminars, with an enrollment:	Under 25	84	
	25–49	41	
	50–74	14	
	75–99	1	
	100+	0	
# of seminars		33	
# of seminar positions available		441	
# of seminar positions filled		381	0
# of positions available in simulation courses		228	
# of simulation positions filled		225	0
# of positions available in faculty supervised clinical courses		119	
# of faculty supervised clinical positions filled		90	0
# involved in field placements		149	0
# involved in law journals		65	0
# involved in moot court or trial competitions		89	0
# of credit hours required to graduate		90	

Transfers

Transfers in	4
Transfers out	4

JD Enrollment and Ethnicity

	Men #	Men %	Women #	Women %	Full-Time #	Full-Time %	Part-Time #	Part-Time %	1st-Year #	1st-Year %	Total #	Total %	JD Degs. Awd.
All Hispanics	4	1.1	7	2.3	5	1.1	6	3.1	8	3.7	11	1.7	7
Am. Ind./AK Nat.	1	0.3	1	0.3	2	0.4	0	0.0	0	0.0	2	0.3	1
Asian	21	5.9	30	10.0	40	8.6	11	5.8	12	5.5	51	7.8	14
Black/Af. Am.	24	6.7	41	13.7	39	8.4	26	13.6	21	9.7	65	9.9	11
Nat. HI/Pac. Isl.	0	0.0	0	0.0	0	0.0	0	0.0	0	0.0	0	0.0	0
2 or more races	2	0.6	2	0.7	2	0.4	2	1.0	1	0.5	4	0.6	3
Subtotal (minor.)	52	14.5	81	27.1	88	18.9	45	23.6	42	19.4	133	20.2	36
Nonres. Alien	0	0.0	0	0.0	0	0.0	0	0.0	0	0.0	0	0.0	0
White/Cauc.	277	77.4	200	66.9	344	73.8	133	69.6	159	73.3	477	72.6	130
Unknown	29	8.1	18	6.0	34	7.3	13	6.8	16	7.4	47	7.2	20
Total	358	54.5	299	45.5	466	70.9	191	29.1	217	33.0	657		186

Tuition and Fees

	Resident	Nonresident
Full-time	$14,770	$34,834
Part-time	$11,638	$26,686
Tuition Guarantee Program		N

Living Expenses

Estimated living expenses for singles

Living on campus	Living off campus	Living at home
$15,958	$15,061	$7,810

ABA
Approved
Since
1984

GPA and LSAT Scores

	Total	Full-Time	Part-Time
# of apps	2,565	2,234	331
# of offers	423	358	65
# of matrics	223	170	53
75% GPA	3.63	3.62	3.67
Median GPA	3.43	3.45	3.36
25% GPA	3.21	3.24	3.00
75% LSAT	162	162	161
Median LSAT	160	160	159
25% LSAT	158	158	158

Grants and Scholarships (from prior year)

	Total		Full-Time		Part-Time	
	#	%	#	%	#	%
Total # of students	660		457		203	
Total # receiving grants	152	23.0	108	23.6	44	21.7
Less than 1/2 tuition	52	7.9	32	7.0	20	9.9
Half to full tuition	26	3.9	12	2.6	14	6.9
Full tuition	74	11.2	64	14.0	10	4.9
More than full tuition	0	0.0	0	0.0	0	0.0
Median grant amount			$2,500		$2,000	

Informational and Library Resources

Total amount spent on library materials	$992,451
Study seating capacity inside the library	376
# of full-time equivalent professional librarians	10
Hours per week library is open	103
# of open, wired connections available to students	955
# of networked computers available for use by students	133
Has wireless network?	Y
Requires computer?	N

JD Attrition (from prior year)

	Academic	Other	Total	
	#	#	#	%
1st year	4	15	19	8.5
2nd year	1	0	1	0.5
3rd year	0	0	0	0.0
4th year	0	0	0	0.0

Employment (9 months after graduation)

For up-to-date employment data, go to employmentsummary.abaquestionnaire.org on the ABA website.

Bar Passage Rates

First-time takers	167	Reporting %	100.00
Average school %	92.81	Average state %	83.61
Average pass difference	9.20		

Jurisdiction	Takers	Passers	Pass %	State %	Diff %
Georgia	167	155	92.81	83.61	9.20

GEORGIA STATE UNIVERSITY COLLEGE OF LAW

PO Box 4037
Atlanta, GA 30302-4037
Phone: 404.413.9000; Fax: 404.413.9225
E-mail: admissions@law.gsu.edu; Website: http://law.gsu.edu

Introduction

Georgia State University College of Law is located in downtown Atlanta, the center for legal, financial, and governmental activities in the Southeast. This location provides easy access to federal, state, and local courts and agencies; the state capitol and legislature; corporations; major law firms in the metropolitan area; and the library and other facilities of Georgia State University.

The College of Law began operation in 1982. The College of Law is accredited by the ABA and is a member of the AALS.

Library and Physical Facilities

The College of Law library is designed and equipped to meet the demanding research needs of today's students, faculty members, staff, and members of the legal community. With a collection of more than 171,276 hard-copy volumes, more than 228,117 microform-equivalent volumes, and almost 60,000 electronic titles, the library provides research materials in American, British, Canadian, and international law. Students find a host of computer applications available in the law library computer lab, which is staffed by computer consultants. The college dedicates state-of-the-art computer equipment for training purposes only in our computer training room. The classrooms and study carrels accommodate laptop computers.

The College of Law is one of the leading law schools in the Southeast. Located on a 39-acre campus in the heart of downtown Atlanta, the Urban Life building houses a moot courtroom equipped with state-of-the-art video technology and provides activities directed toward trial and appellate advocacy. Students have access to many other campus facilities, including the athletic complex, which offers a variety of individual fitness opportunities and team sports.

Curriculum

The college offers students the opportunity to study full or part time and provides a traditional yet innovative curriculum. It offers extensive coverage of the foundational areas of the law to first-year students while providing an array of elective opportunities in public and private law. Opportunities range from the study of legal philosophy and jurisprudence to vital skills training through courses in litigation, counseling, negotiation, legal drafting, and alternative dispute resolution.

The growth of technology in our lives is reflected in courses in Intellectual Property and Computers and the Law; in our innovative course, Law and the Internet; and in the increasing use of computer programs and online discussion groups. Opportunities exist for in-depth study in international and comparative law, environmental law, health law, tax law, employment law, commercial law, and bankruptcy.

Admission

The College of Law actively seeks to enroll a student body with diversity in educational, cultural, and racial backgrounds that will enrich the educational experience of the entire group.

Applicants are encouraged to visit. Please make arrangements through the Office of Admissions to tour the campus; talk with students, faculty, and admissions staff; or attend a class.

Special Programs

Dual-Degree Programs—Seven dual JD and master's degree programs are available with Georgia State University's J. Mack Robinson College of Business, the Andrew Young School of Policy Studies, the Department of Philosophy in the College of Arts and Sciences, and the College of Architecture at the Georgia Institute of Technology.

International Programs—Students have the opportunity to participate in two summer-abroad programs. These are the Transnational Comparative Dispute Resolution Program in Europe and the Summer Legal and Policy Study Program in comparative and international law in Brazil.

Clinics—The Low-Income Taxpayer Clinic and the Health Law Partnership (HeLP) Clinic provide a live-client component to the college's Lawyer Skills Externship Development Program. Both clinics give students hands-on, real-life experience in client representation and handling cases. Work in the Tax Clinic teaches case management, evidence gathering, document preparation, interviewing, counseling, and effective negotiation. The Health Law Partnership Clinic offers a community service clinic that provides students with opportunities to work on cases related to children's health and welfare, including clinics on site at three Atlanta-area children's hospitals where low-income children and their families are eligible for these services aimed at eliminating socioeconomic barriers to optimum health.

Externships—Externships are designed to tie theoretical knowledge to a practical base of experience in the profession. Externships involve actual participation in rendering legal services. Students interested in the externship program should contact the Lawyer Skills Development Externship Office.

Trial Advocacy—The College of Law offers students an extensive variety of opportunities in the area of trial advocacy. Our litigation workshop, offered each spring semester, provides second-year students with an intensive skills training experience. Working in small seminar groups, students are asked to conduct drafting and simulation exercises on all phases of the pretrial and trial process, including a full jury trial. In addition to the workshop, the college offers several advanced litigation courses in which students can further enhance their advocacy skills in civil and criminal areas.

Moot Court—Each year, students compete in several of the most challenging and prestigious moot court competitions throughout the country. The Moot Court Program has achieved substantial renown and success in its 28-year history. The National Moot Court Competition, sponsored by the Association of the Bar of the City of New York, is the oldest and most recognized national competition, and the College of Law became the first law school in Georgia to place first in that competition. Teams from the college have since won numerous other competitions.

Centers—The College of Law has two centers: the Center for Law, Health, and Society and the Center for the Comparative Study of Metropolitan Growth. The Center for Law, Health, and Society promotes the integration of health law and ethics into (1) health policy and research, (2) the health sciences, (3) the provision of health services, and (4) the interdisciplinary education of law students. The Center for the Comparative Study of Metropolitan Growth produces research, teaching, and academic exchange on the range of issues relating to metropolitan growth.

Student Activities

The *Georgia State University Law Review* is published four times a year by students who have demonstrated outstanding writing and academic skills.

The college also boasts a nationally renowned student mock trial program in which our students compete annually in numerous mock trial competitions held at locations throughout the country. Our student teams have amassed an incredible record of success at the national, regional, and state levels. The College of Law has won numerous national, regional, and state championships.

The College of Law regards student organizations as an important part of a legal education experience and encourages participation in our wide variety of organizations, some traditionally found in law schools, some less common. The college recognizes over 30 organizations, most of which are affiliated with national professional associations. We are proud of the accomplishments of these groups.

Career Services

The Career Services Office offers a broad range of services. Students may begin using the office in November of the first year of law school and may continue utilizing career planning services throughout their careers. Specific programs geared toward minority students are the Atlanta Bar Association Minority Clerkship Program and the Southeastern Minority Job Fair. Typically, over 93 percent of each graduating class accepts employment within six months of graduation.

APPLICANT PROFILE

Georgia State University College of Law
This grid includes only applicants who earned 120–180 LSAT scores under standard administrations.

LSAT Score	GPA								
	3.75 +	3.50–3.74	3.25–3.49	3.00–3.24	2.75–2.99	2.50–2.74	2.25–2.49	2.00–2.24	Below 2.00
175–180									
170–174									
165–169									
160–164									
155–159									
150–154									
145–149									
140–144									
135–139									
130–134									
125–129									
120–124									

■ Good Possibility   □ Possible   ▨ Unlikely

GOLDEN GATE UNIVERSITY SCHOOL OF LAW

536 Mission Street, Office of Admissions
San Francisco, CA 94105-2968
Phone: 415.442.6630 or 800.GGU.4YOU; Fax: 415.442.6631
E-mail: lawadmit@ggu.edu; Website: www.law.ggu.edu

ABA
Approved
Since
1956

The Basics

Type of school	Private
Term	Semester
Application deadline	4/1
Application fee	$60
Financial aid deadline	
Can first year start other than fall?	No
Student to faculty ratio	14.1 to 1
# of housing spaces available restricted to law students	
graduate housing for which law students are eligible	

Faculty and Administrators

	Total		Men		Women		Minorities	
	Spr	Fall	Spr	Fall	Spr	Fall	Spr	Fall
Full-time	36	36	20	19	16	17	9	9
Other full-time	2	3	0	0	2	3	0	0
Deans, librarians, & others who teach	8	7	2	3	6	4	0	1
Part-time	95	73	53	35	42	38	11	14
Total	141	119	75	57	66	62	20	24

Curriculum

	Full-Time	Part-Time
Typical first-year section size	66	50
Is there typically a "small section" of the first-year class, other than Legal Writing, taught by full-time faculty	Yes	Yes
If yes, typical size offered last year	24	20
# of classroom course titles beyond first-year curriculum	173	

# of upper division courses, excluding seminars, with an enrollment:		
	Under 25	203
	25–49	49
	50–74	10
	75–99	2
	100+	0

# of seminars	41	
# of seminar positions available	399	
# of seminar positions filled	337	30
# of positions available in simulation courses	440	
# of simulation positions filled	390	41
# of positions available in faculty supervised clinical courses	107	
# of faculty supervised clinical positions filled	101	2
# involved in field placements	190	14
# involved in law journals	129	7
# involved in moot court or trial competitions	79	5
# of credit hours required to graduate	88	

JD Enrollment and Ethnicity

	Men		Women		Full-Time		Part-Time		1st-Year		Total		JD Degs. Awd.
	#	%	#	%	#	%	#	%	#	%	#	%	
All Hispanics	29	9.2	33	8.9	54	9.5	8	6.9	29	12.7	62	9.1	10
Am. Ind./AK Nat.	1	0.3	2	0.5	3	0.5	0	0.0	1	0.4	3	0.4	2
Asian	45	14.3	72	19.5	94	16.5	23	19.8	43	18.8	117	17.1	36
Black/Af. Am.	7	2.2	7	1.9	13	2.3	1	0.9	4	1.7	14	2.0	4
Nat. Hl/Pac. Isl.	4	1.3	1	0.3	4	0.7	1	0.9	0	0.0	5	0.7	2
2 or more races	6	1.9	9	2.4	13	2.3	2	1.7	11	4.8	15	2.2	0
Subtotal (minor.)	92	29.2	124	33.6	181	31.9	35	30.2	88	38.4	216	31.6	54
Nonres. Alien	7	2.2	5	1.4	12	2.1	0	0.0	8	3.5	12	1.8	5
White/Cauc.	189	60.0	195	52.8	315	55.5	69	59.5	118	51.5	384	56.1	107
Unknown	27	8.6	45	12.2	60	10.6	12	10.3	15	6.6	72	10.5	26
Total	315	46.1	369	53.9	568	83.0	116	17.0	229	33.5	684		192

Transfers

Transfers in	2
Transfers out	36

Tuition and Fees

	Resident	Nonresident
Full-time	$40,515	$40,515
Part-time	$31,135	$31,135
Tuition Guarantee Program	N	

Living Expenses

Estimated living expenses for singles

Living on campus	Living off campus	Living at home
N/A	$24,641	N/A

GOLDEN GATE UNIVERSITY SCHOOL OF LAW

ABA
Approved
Since
1956

GPA and LSAT Scores

	Total	Full-Time	Part-Time
# of apps	2,269	1,957	312
# of offers	1,357	1,218	139
# of matrics	229	182	47
75% GPA	3.41	3.41	3.21
Median GPA	3.05	3.10	2.93
25% GPA	2.73	2.73	2.72
75% LSAT	155	155	155
Median LSAT	152	153	152
25% LSAT	150	150	150

Grants and Scholarships (from prior year)

	Total		Full-Time		Part-Time	
	#	%	#	%	#	%
Total # of students	732		616		116	
Total # receiving grants	343	46.9	301	48.9	42	36.2
Less than 1/2 tuition	199	27.2	175	28.4	24	20.7
Half to full tuition	113	15.4	99	16.1	14	12.1
Full tuition	31	4.2	27	4.4	4	3.4
More than full tuition	0	0.0	0	0.0	0	0.0
Median grant amount			$15,000		$10,000	

Informational and Library Resources

Total amount spent on library materials	$1,218,591
Study seating capacity inside the library	460
# of full-time equivalent professional librarians	8
Hours per week library is open	95
# of open, wired connections available to students	572
# of networked computers available for use by students	120
Has wireless network?	Y
Requires computer?	N

JD Attrition (from prior year)

	Academic	Other	Total	
	#	#	#	%
1st year	24	50	74	23.2
2nd year	8	4	12	6.5
3rd year	0	0	0	0.0
4th year	0	0	0	0.0

Employment (9 months after graduation)

For up-to-date employment data, go to employmentsummary.abaquestionnaire.org on the ABA website.

Bar Passage Rates

First-time takers	174	Reporting %	97.13
Average school %	57.99	Average state %	71.24
Average pass difference	−13.25		

Jurisdiction	Takers	Passers	Pass %	State %	Diff %
California	169	98	57.99	71.24	−13.25

GOLDEN GATE UNIVERSITY SCHOOL OF LAW

536 Mission Street, Office of Admissions
San Francisco, CA 94105-2968
Phone: 415.442.6630 or 800.GGU.4YOU; Fax: 415.442.6631
E-mail: lawadmit@ggu.edu; Website: www.law.ggu.edu

Introduction

Founded in 1901, Golden Gate University School of Law is located in the heart of San Francisco's legal and financial district. The law school is noted for integrating legal theory with practice-based skills training. Golden Gate Law relies on a distinguished faculty who share a strong commitment to both excellence in teaching and accessibility to students. The law school is fully ABA-accredited and is a member in good standing of the AALS.

Program Options

Golden Gate Law offers both a three-year full-time day program and a four-year part-time evening program. The law school also offers an enhanced JD program under the Honors Lawyering Program. Two formal joint-degree programs, the JD/MBA and JD/PhD, are also available.

Honors Lawyering Program

The Honors Lawyering Program (HLP) takes a unique approach to legal education, integrating the theory, skills, and values learned in the classroom with actual work in the legal community—a modern version of the traditional apprenticeship. HLP students attend a regular first-year curriculum, participate in an intensive skills-focused summer session, and then transition to a full-time fall apprenticeship. In the spring, students return to full-time classes with a new appreciation for the practice of law. During their third year, students complete a second apprenticeship and have the option to enroll in additional practice-based courses. HLP courses meet in small sections that combine lawyering skills training with the substantive law curriculum. By the third week of the summer session, students begin representing real clients under the guidance and supervision of the professors, who are themselves practicing attorneys. Students may apprentice in private law firms, companies, courts, government agencies, and public interest organizations anywhere in the Bay Area or around the world.

Public Interest Law

Golden Gate Law is considered one of the best public interest law schools in the country. Golden Gate Law owes its reputation to several factors, including the law school's curriculum, which extends to all areas of public interest law. Golden Gate Law also supports a formidable externship program, which offers myriad opportunities to engage in public interest work. Golden Gate Law offers a Certificate of Specialization in Public Interest Law, and students with prior public and community service experience may apply to the Public Interest Scholars Program, which provides selected students with special scholarships and eligibility for a summer employment stipend. Numerous student organizations support public interest work, including the Public Interest Law Foundation (PILF), which raises funds for students working in unpaid public interest internships.

Joint Degrees and Certificates of Specialization

Students may earn a joint JD/MBA through the law school and the Ageno School of Business at Golden Gate University or a joint JD/PhD in Clinical Psychology in conjunction with Palo Alto University.

Golden Gate Law also offers JD students the opportunity to earn **Certificates of Specialization** in Business Law, Criminal Law, Environmental Law, Family Law, Intellectual Property Law, International Legal Studies, Labor and Employment Law, Litigation, Public Interest Law, Real Estate Law, Taxation, and Youth Law. Requirements for the areas of specialization vary, but students generally complete required coursework, writing assignments, and clinical experience to earn a Certificate of Specialization.

Clinical Programs

Golden Gate Law has one of the most extensive clinical programs in the country, offering students opportunities to earn academic credit while working closely with practicing attorneys and real clients in the community.

The law school has three on-site clinics. In the **Women's Employment Rights Clinic**, students represent low-income workers facing unfair labor practices. Through the **Environmental Law and Justice Clinic**, students assist low-income communities and communities of color in protecting their environmental interests and reducing their exposure to environmental hazards. The **Pro Bono Tax Clinic** provides assistance to low-income individuals in tax disputes before the California State Board of Equalization.

Through Golden Gate Law's extensive field placement externships, students work under the supervision of faculty, judges, and attorneys in government agencies, law offices, and judges' chambers. These externships include Criminal Litigation, Consumer Rights, Environmental Law, Family Law, Homeless Advocacy, Judicial Externship Program, Real Estate Law, and Youth Law.

Centers

The Center on Urban Environmental Law takes the city as a natural starting point in assessing how the law shapes environmental conditions. The Center's research efforts produce white papers focusing on regulatory strategies to improve urban environments.

The Intellectual Property Law Center brings together students, faculty, and practitioners to explore developments in the ever-changing area of IP law and policy.

The Litigation Center provides students with a clear path to the specific skills necessary to become successful courtroom advocates. The Center immerses students in an integrated litigation curriculum augmented by the school's participation in regional and national advocacy and mock trial competitions.

The Sompong Sucharitkul Center for Advanced International Legal Studies serves as a hub for international law studies, hosting an annual conference and publishing the *Annual Survey of International and Comparative Law*.

The Paris Program

Students selected for Golden Gate Law's Paris Summer Comparative Law Program travel to France for the summer and take courses covering a number of current issues in international law. The curriculum combines introductory courses on France's legal system and comparative law courses. Legal luminaries from Europe and North America are also featured. Students also benefit from instruction from both Golden Gate Law faculty and French faculty and practitioners. Those students fluent in French also have the opportunity to remain in France for additional internships with French law firms after the end of the regular summer term.

Graduate Law Programs

Golden Gate Law offers five highly regarded LLM (Master of Laws) programs in Environmental Law, Intellectual Property Law, International Legal Studies, Taxation, and US Legal Studies. The law school also offers an advanced SJD program in International Legal Studies.

Law Library

The Law Library houses the largest law collection in the San Francisco financial district—more than 350,000 volumes. Its holdings include a comprehensive series of case law reporters, statutes, digests, encyclopedias, periodicals, and treatises dealing with American law; a strong tax law collection; an extensive microforms collection; and a growing body of work in environmental law and international law. The international law holdings target selected Pacific Rim countries and English, Canadian, and other Commonwealth materials. Current students have full access to a variety of Internet-based legal databases and resources.

Law Reviews, Journals, and Student Life

Golden Gate Law publishes the *Golden Gate University Law Review*, the *Environmental Law Journal*, and the *Annual Survey of International and Comparative Law*. The *Law Review* and journals provide students with the opportunity to showcase their research, writing, and editing skills.

The law school also has more than 30 student organizations ranging from groups representing specific political or cultural interests to groups focusing on specific areas of law. The very active student government represents the law school student body on important issues facing individuals, student organizations, and the law school. Through these groups, students have many opportunities to participate in programs and attend lectures hosted by a variety of organizations. These opportunities not only enrich the law school learning experience, but also hone students' networking skills. Students are encouraged to participate at all levels.

Career Services and Placement

The Law Career Services (LCS) office helps students prepare for a successful legal career by providing myriad services throughout law school and beyond. LCS assists students in researching the legal market, developing contacts, and building practical and networking skills through jobs and internships. For first-year students, LCS provides an online *Job Search Guide* and workshops on writing résumés and cover letters. For upper-division students, LCS offers print and online job listings; meetings with recent graduates who speak with students about their career experiences; individual and small-group career counseling; job-search workshops, panels, and events highlighting the career paths of Golden Gate alumni and other attorneys; special recruitment programs; and more. Many of these services remain available to students after graduation.

Admission and Scholarships

Golden Gate Law strives to admit students who seek a rigorous and holistic legal education that integrates experiential learning with a solid foundation in current legal theory. The application process is designed to identify applicants who possess the ability to succeed in the classroom and contribute to the legal community at large.

Golden Gate Law awards merit scholarships to both entering and continuing students. All students are reviewed for merit scholarships as part of the admission process. The law school also offers a Public Interest Scholars Program (PISP) scholarship and an Environmental Law Scholars Program (ELSP) scholarship. Both the PISP and the ELSP scholarships require a separate statement of interest and a list of prior commitment/activities from the student as part of the regular law school application.

APPLICANT PROFILE

Golden Gate University School of Law
This grid includes only applicants who earned 120–180 LSAT scores under standard administrations.

LSAT Score	3.75 +		3.50–3.74		3.25–3.49		3.00–3.24		2.75–2.99		2.50–2.74		2.25–2.49		2.00–2.24		Below 2.00		No GPA		Total	
	Apps	Adm	Apps	Adm	Apps	Adm	Apps	Adm	Apps	Adm	Apps	Adm	Apps	Adm	Apps	Adm	Apps	Adm	Apps	Adm	Apps	Adm
175–180	0	0	1	0	0	0	0	0	0	0	0	0	0	0	0	0	0	0	0	0	1	0
170–174	1	1	0	0	0	0	0	0	1	0	0	0	0	0	0	0	0	0	0	0	2	1
165–169	5	5	10	10	7	7	8	8	4	4	5	5	0	0	1	1	0	0	1	1	41	41
160–164	14	13	25	22	35	29	32	30	19	15	14	13	8	8	6	5	1	0	2	2	156	137
155–159	38	35	79	73	118	112	126	117	79	71	53	43	20	18	9	4	1	1	6	6	529	480
150–154	42	39	106	96	166	147	155	127	118	90	78	51	42	25	12	7	6	1	15	9	740	592
145–149	15	12	53	32	114	28	105	12	91	9	66	1	42	1	19	0	0	0	6	3	511	98
140–144	5	0	16	5	28	0	71	1	38	1	37	0	24	0	8	0	2	0	8	0	237	7
135–139	1	1	4	0	6	0	9	0	11	0	10	0	11	0	10	0	3	0	1	0	66	1
130–134	0	0	1	0	1	0	8	0	0	0	4	0	3	0	3	0	0	0	2	0	22	0
125–129	0	0	1	0	0	0	2	0	0	0	1	0	0	0	0	0	0	0	0	0	4	0
120–124	0	0	0	0	0	0	0	0	0	0	0	0	0	0	0	0	0	0	0	0	0	0
Total	121	106	296	238	475	323	516	295	361	190	268	113	150	52	68	17	13	2	41	21	2309	1357

Apps = Number of Applicants   Adm = Number Admitted   Reflects 99% of the total applicant pool; highest LSAT data reported.

GONZAGA UNIVERSITY SCHOOL OF LAW

PO Box 3528
Spokane, WA 99220-3528
Phone: 800.793.1710 or 509.313.5532; Fax: 509.313.3697
E-mail: admissions@lawschool.gonzaga.edu; Website: www.law.gonzaga.edu

ABA
Approved
Since
1951

The Basics

Type of school	Private
Term	Semester
Application deadline	4/15
Application fee	$50
Financial aid deadline	2/1
Can first year start other than fall?	No
Student to faculty ratio	15.3 to 1
# of housing spaces available restricted to law students	
graduate housing for which law students are eligible	506

Faculty and Administrators

	Total		Men		Women		Minorities	
	Spr	Fall	Spr	Fall	Spr	Fall	Spr	Fall
Full-time	28	26	17	15	11	11	4	3
Other full-time	1	1	0	0	1	1	0	0
Deans, librarians, & others who teach	5	5	3	2	2	3	1	1
Part-time	30	27	22	19	8	8	0	0
Total	64	59	42	36	22	23	5	4

Curriculum

	Full-Time	Part-Time
Typical first-year section size	85	0
Is there typically a "small section" of the first-year class, other than Legal Writing, taught by full-time faculty	Yes	No
If yes, typical size offered last year	34	
# of classroom course titles beyond first-year curriculum	78	

# of upper division courses, excluding seminars, with an enrollment:		
Under 25	88	
25–49	26	
50–74	12	
75–99	4	
100+	0	

# of seminars	28	
# of seminar positions available	565	
# of seminar positions filled	436	0
# of positions available in simulation courses	574	
# of simulation positions filled	455	0
# of positions available in faculty supervised clinical courses	169	
# of faculty supervised clinical positions filled	138	0
# involved in field placements	139	0
# involved in law journals	107	0
# involved in moot court or trial competitions	57	0
# of credit hours required to graduate	90	

JD Enrollment and Ethnicity

	Men #	Men %	Women #	Women %	Full-Time #	Full-Time %	Part-Time #	Part-Time %	1st-Year #	1st-Year %	Total #	Total %	JD Degs. Awd.
All Hispanics	8	2.8	4	1.8	12	2.4	0	0.0	0	0.0	12	2.4	3
Am. Ind./AK Nat.	6	2.1	3	1.4	9	1.8	0	0.0	2	1.1	9	1.8	2
Asian	2	0.7	3	1.4	5	1.0	0	0.0	4	2.3	5	1.0	4
Black/Af. Am.	0	0.0	2	0.9	2	0.4	0	0.0	1	0.6	2	0.4	0
Nat. HI/Pac. Isl.	8	2.8	6	2.8	14	2.8	0	0.0	0	0.0	14	2.8	3
2 or more races	6	2.1	5	2.3	11	2.2	0	0.0	6	3.4	11	2.2	2
Subtotal (minor.)	30	10.4	23	10.6	53	10.5	0	0.0	13	7.3	53	10.5	14
Nonres. Alien	1	0.3	3	1.4	4	0.8	0	0.0	2	1.1	4	0.8	0
White/Cauc.	211	73.3	156	71.6	367	72.5	0	0.0	150	84.7	367	72.5	137
Unknown	46	16.0	36	16.5	82	16.2	0	0.0	12	6.8	82	16.2	9
Total	288	56.9	218	43.1	506	100.0	0	0.0	177	35.0	506		160

Transfers

Transfers in	7
Transfers out	8

Tuition and Fees

	Resident	Nonresident
Full-time	$34,105	$34,105
Part-time		
Tuition Guarantee Program	N	

Living Expenses

Estimated living expenses for singles

Living on campus	Living off campus	Living at home
$14,365	$14,365	$14,365

ABA Approved Since 1951

GPA and LSAT Scores

	Total	Full-Time	Part-Time
# of apps	1,389	1,389	0
# of offers	739	739	0
# of matrics	176	176	0
75% GPA	3.51	3.51	0.00
Median GPA	3.33	3.33	0.00
25% GPA	3.15	3.15	0.00
75% LSAT	157	157	0
Median LSAT	155	155	0
25% LSAT	153	153	0

Grants and Scholarships (from prior year)

	Total #	Total %	Full-Time #	Full-Time %	Part-Time #	Part-Time %
Total # of students	507		503		4	
Total # receiving grants	350	69.0	350	69.6	0	0.0
Less than 1/2 tuition	308	60.7	308	61.2	0	0.0
Half to full tuition	24	4.7	24	4.8	0	0.0
Full tuition	18	3.6	18	3.6	0	0.0
More than full tuition	0	0.0	0	0.0	0	0.0
Median grant amount			$13,500		$0	

Informational and Library Resources

Total amount spent on library materials	$941,728
Study seating capacity inside the library	507
# of full-time equivalent professional librarians	6
Hours per week library is open	110
# of open, wired connections available to students	140
# of networked computers available for use by students	83
Has wireless network?	Y
Requires computer?	N

JD Attrition (from prior year)

	Academic #	Other #	Total #	Total %
1st year	6	18	24	13.4
2nd year	0	1	1	0.6
3rd year	0	0	0	0.0
4th year	0	0	0	0.0

Employment (9 months after graduation)

For up-to-date employment data, go to employmentsummary.abaquestionnaire.org on the ABA website.

Bar Passage Rates

First-time takers	181	Reporting %	72.93
Average school %	78.79	Average state %	74.56
Average pass difference	4.23		

Jurisdiction	Takers	Passers	Pass %	State %	Diff %
Washington	85	70	82.35	71.22	11.13
Oregon	14	8	57.14	75.22	–18.08
Idaho	13	11	84.62	82.69	1.93
Utah	13	10	76.92	89.35	–12.43
California	7	5	71.43	71.24	0.19

GONZAGA UNIVERSITY SCHOOL OF LAW

PO Box 3528
Spokane, WA 99220-3528
Phone: 800.793.1710 or 509.313.5532; Fax: 509.313.3697
E-mail: admissions@lawschool.gonzaga.edu; Website: www.law.gonzaga.edu

Introduction

Gonzaga University School of Law is dedicated to providing students with an excellent legal education and promoting the intellectual life of the university. To fulfill this dedication, the law school fosters a vibrant culture of scholarly inquiry; delivers rich and diverse learning experiences; teaches broad knowledge of legal doctrine, theory, and policy; and nurtures professional skills and social consciousness, all consistent with the law school's mission as Jesuit, Catholic, and humanistic. Gonzaga is committed to educating a diverse student community, including students of all backgrounds and beliefs.

The campus is located in Spokane, Washington, a four-season city with the Spokane River flowing through its center. Step outside the School of Law onto the Centennial Trail to enjoy the picturesque walk into beautiful downtown Spokane. The metropolitan area of approximately 500,000 people serves as the hub of the Inland Northwest, a large area running from the Cascade Mountains in the west to the Rockies in the east. The Spokane International Airport is conveniently located 10 miles from the Gonzaga University campus.

Spokane is a cultural center for the area, with professional and amateur theater groups, a symphony, numerous art galleries, and other cultural offerings. Spokane also serves as the region's hub for health care, higher education, agriculture, and light industry and is a recreational sports area abundant with lakes, mountains, and forests.

Physical Facilities and Library

On the banks of the Spokane River, Gonzaga University School of Law provides a stunning setting for research and learning. Beautiful outdoor spaces, roof plazas, balconies, and comfortable lounges encourage student and faculty interaction. The law school offers a variety of classroom and library spaces to accommodate traditional courses, smaller skills-based courses, collaborative work, and individual study. Two large computer labs, wireless network access, and advanced classroom technology throughout the building facilitate today's mobile work environment. The Chastek Library is the largest legal research facility between Seattle and Minneapolis with a collection of over 300,000 volumes and an extensive array of electronic resources. The library offers many services to support the instructional, research, and scholarly endeavors of the law school and university community. Librarians provide reference support and play an active role in legal research instruction using both traditional and electronic resources.

Curriculum and Faculty

Gonzaga has a rigorous curriculum that focuses on legal doctrine, analysis, problem solving, values, and ethics. Equally as important is the emphasis on practical experience to develop real-world lawyering skills.

The term "teaching faculty" applies in a very special way to the School of Law faculty. The Jesuit tradition demands a high degree of student-professor interaction inside and outside the classroom, and this emphasis attracts exceptional faculty. Gonzaga's focus on the individual student, a favorable student-to-faculty ratio, and the promotion of positive rather than negative competition provides an atmosphere of success in which to study.

Special Programs

The unique first-year program at Gonzaga pairs two doctrinal courses each semester with a skills and professionalism lab that immediately begins the process of turning law students into lawyers. In the fall semester, Civil Procedure and Torts are paired with a lab that emphasizes the development of litigation skills. In the spring, Contracts and Property are paired with a lab that exposes the students to the transactional law side of the profession. Both labs also include instruction and exercises that are designed to help our students begin to identify and develop the professional values and habits that will be a part of their lives as attorneys.

Gonzaga's skills training continues into the second year through our two-year Legal Research and Writing program. In addition, all students are required to engage in experiential learning, either through working in a professional externship or in Gonzaga's legal clinic, during their upper-class years. Students can earn up to 15 credits in externship or clinic placements, during which they learn real-world lawyering skills under the supervision of lawyers in the field.

The Center for Law in Public Service supports the aspirations of students who study law in order to use their knowledge and skills for public service, whether they wish to make a full-time practice of public service law or to promote the public good through part-time pro bono legal work or other means. The center provides curricular and extracurricular avenues for students to acquire the skills and substantive knowledge applicable to practicing public service law.

Gonzaga offers dual-degree programs leading to the JD/MBA, the JD/MAcc, and the JD/MSW degrees.

Admission

The School of Law endeavors to attract students with ambitious minds, professional motivation, commitment to the highest ethics and values of the legal profession, and an interest in public service. Consideration of applicants is not restricted to impersonal statistics, but includes recognition and review of the enriching qualities of applicants reflected in their personal statements, résumés, and letters of recommendation. Gonzaga seeks to enroll a diverse student body.

Student Activities

Gonzaga's educational philosophy is based on the centuries-old Ignatian model of educating the whole person—mind, body, and spirit. Students, therefore, find it easy to become involved in a broad range of activities at the School of Law. Gonzaga competes regionally and nationally in various moot court competitions. The student-run *Gonzaga Law Review* is circulated throughout the country, and the *Gonzaga Journal of International Law*, an online international law journal, receives submissions from around the world. The Student Bar Association is a strong, active organization that encourages student involvement, and there is ample opportunity to participate in intraschool moot court competitions, and other legal organizations and activities. Whatever your interests or career goals, there are activities available that will enhance your knowledge and abilities, while contributing to the community.

Housing

The Gonzaga campus is in a residential area in close proximity to downtown Spokane. Even within walking distance of the law school, rental rates are reasonably priced. For further information, please review the Gonzaga University Housing and Residence Office website: www.gonzaga.edu/Student-Life/Off-Campus-Living/GU-Owned.asp.

Financial Aid

Law school is a career investment. For students who need financial assistance to help fund this investment, we encourage filing the Free Application for Federal Student Aid (FAFSA). Gonzaga also provides more than $2 million in scholarship aid to entering law students, and your admission application will serve as your scholarship application. All law school applicants are automatically considered for scholarships. However, students who are interested in

applying for the Thomas More Scholarship need to apply separately. The Thomas More Scholarship Program provides a unique opportunity for talented individuals to realize their commitment to serving the public interest through law. For more information, please review the Thomas More Program website: www.law.gonzaga.edu/Admissions/financial_aid_and_scholarships/default.asp. Gonzaga awards up to five Thomas More Scholarships a year, covering 100 percent of tuition.

Professional Development

The Center for Professional Development is committed to serving the needs of students, employers, and alumni. The Center helps students integrate into the professional world of law practice from the first day of classes by providing up-to-date job listings, library resources, interview tools, and workshops. Recognizing that career development is a lifelong process, the office provides graduates access to services throughout their professional lives. Prospective employers are encouraged to utilize our recruitment services, including online job postings, job fairs, customized recruiting, and interviewing programs. We encourage prospective students to meet with our career counselors to learn more about legal opportunities.

APPLICANT PROFILE

Gonzaga University School of Law
This grid includes only applicants who earned 120–180 LSAT scores under standard administrations.

LSAT Score	3.75 +		3.50–3.74		3.25–3.49		3.00–3.24		2.75–2.99		2.50–2.74		2.25–2.49		2.00–2.24		Below 2.00		No GPA		Total	
	Apps	Adm	Apps	Adm	Apps	Adm	Apps	Adm	Apps	Adm	Apps	Adm	Apps	Adm	Apps	Adm	Apps	Adm	Apps	Adm	Apps	Adm
170–180	1	1	1	1	1	1	0	0	2	2	0	0	0	0	0	0	0	0	0	0	5	5
165–169	4	4	8	8	5	5	5	5	1	1	3	2	0	0	0	0	0	0	0	0	26	25
160–164	18	18	35	35	25	23	31	31	19	14	8	3	5	0	1	0	1	0	0	0	143	124
155–159	41	40	75	70	99	98	94	85	39	30	32	10	15	1	5	0	0	0	1	1	401	335
150–154	40	28	71	47	132	92	113	65	80	19	37	3	16	1	4	0	1	0	4	0	498	255
145–149	4	0	40	0	44	0	36	0	28	0	22	0	5	0	2	0	1	0	2	0	184	0
140–144	5	0	8	0	13	0	20	0	16	0	13	0	4	0	1	0	1	0	2	0	83	0
Below 140	0	0	2	0	7	0	10	0	6	0	8	0	3	0	1	0	1	0	2	0	40	0
Total	113	91	240	161	326	219	309	186	191	66	123	18	48	2	14	0	5	0	11	1	1388*	744

Apps = Number of Applicants
Adm = Number Admitted
Reflects 100% of the total applicant pool; highest LSAT data reported.
*Includes 8 applicants without an LSAT score.

HAMLINE UNIVERSITY SCHOOL OF LAW

1536 Hewitt Avenue
Saint Paul, MN 55104
Phone: 651.523.2461, 800.388.3688; Fax: 651.523.3064
E-mail: lawadm@hamline.edu; Website: www.hamline.edu/law

ABA
Approved
Since
1975

The Basics

Type of school	Private
Term	Semester
Application deadline	4/1
Application fee	$35
Financial aid deadline	4/10
Can first year start other than fall?	No
Student to faculty ratio	13.7 to 1
# of housing spaces available restricted to law students	
graduate housing for which law students are eligible	60

Faculty and Administrators

	Total		Men		Women		Minorities	
	Spr	Fall	Spr	Fall	Spr	Fall	Spr	Fall
Full-time	35	34	21	19	14	15	2	2
Other full-time	0	2	0	2	0	0	0	0
Deans, librarians, & others who teach	7	7	2	2	5	5	3	3
Part-time	52	43	25	23	27	20	3	1
Total	94	86	48	46	46	40	8	6

Curriculum

		Full-Time	Part-Time
Typical first-year section size		60	45
Is there typically a "small section" of the first-year class, other than Legal Writing, taught by full-time faculty		No	No
If yes, typical size offered last year			
# of classroom course titles beyond first-year curriculum		192	
# of upper division courses, excluding seminars, with an enrollment:	Under 25	132	
	25–49	45	
	50–74	14	
	75–99	1	
	100+	0	
# of seminars		15	
# of seminar positions available		248	
# of seminar positions filled		158	34
# of positions available in simulation courses		182	
# of simulation positions filled		127	17
# of positions available in faculty supervised clinical courses		104	
# of faculty supervised clinical positions filled		86	0
# involved in field placements		83	9
# involved in law journals		78	12
# involved in moot court or trial competitions		62	8
# of credit hours required to graduate		88	

JD Enrollment and Ethnicity

	Men		Women		Full-Time		Part-Time		1st-Year		Total		JD Degs. Awd.
	#	%	#	%	#	%	#	%	#	%	#	%	
All Hispanics	7	2.5	22	6.5	21	4.4	8	5.8	12	5.9	29	4.7	13
Am. Ind./AK Nat.	2	0.7	2	0.6	2	0.4	2	1.5	1	0.5	4	0.6	1
Asian	12	4.3	21	6.3	26	5.4	7	5.1	12	5.9	33	5.3	15
Black/Af. Am.	7	2.5	18	5.4	20	4.2	5	3.6	8	4.0	25	4.1	3
Nat. HI/Pac. Isl.	0	0.0	0	0.0	0	0.0	0	0.0	0	0.0	0	0.0	0
2 or more races	5	1.8	6	1.8	9	1.9	2	1.5	4	2.0	11	1.8	0
Subtotal (minor.)	33	11.7	69	20.5	78	16.3	24	17.5	37	18.3	102	16.5	32
Nonres. Alien	0	0.0	0	0.0	0	0.0	0	0.0	0	0.0	0	0.0	0
White/Cauc.	241	85.8	257	76.5	389	81.0	109	79.6	161	79.7	498	80.7	149
Unknown	7	2.5	10	3.0	13	2.7	4	2.9	4	2.0	17	2.8	31
Total	281	45.5	336	54.5	480	77.8	137	22.2	202	32.7	617		212

Transfers

Transfers in	3
Transfers out	8

Tuition and Fees

	Resident	Nonresident
Full-time	$34,555	$34,555
Part-time	$25,040	$25,040
Tuition Guarantee Program		N

Living Expenses

Estimated living expenses for singles

Living on campus	Living off campus	Living at home
$12,551	$18,799	$18,799

HAMLINE UNIVERSITY SCHOOL OF LAW

ABA
Approved
Since
1975

GPA and LSAT Scores

	Total	Full-Time	Part-Time
# of apps	1,232	1,017	215
# of offers	745	614	131
# of matrics	205	141	64
75% GPA	3.58	3.61	3.47
Median GPA	3.36	3.40	3.20
25% GPA	3.13	3.20	2.81
75% LSAT	156	156	156
Median LSAT	153	153	152
25% LSAT	148	149	146

Grants and Scholarships (from prior year)

	Total		Full-Time		Part-Time	
	#	%	#	%	#	%
Total # of students	652		456		196	
Total # receiving grants	363	55.7	279	61.2	84	42.9
Less than 1/2 tuition	145	22.2	106	23.2	39	19.9
Half to full tuition	140	21.5	103	22.6	37	18.9
Full tuition	65	10.0	60	13.2	5	2.6
More than full tuition	13	2.0	10	2.2	3	1.5
Median grant amount			$19,813		$11,888	

Informational and Library Resources

Total amount spent on library materials	$860,760
Study seating capacity inside the library	355
# of full-time equivalent professional librarians	7
Hours per week library is open	116
# of open, wired connections available to students	506
# of networked computers available for use by students	48
Has wireless network?	Y
Requires computer?	Y

JD Attrition (from prior year)

	Academic	Other	Total	
	#	#	#	%
1st year	0	3	3	1.3
2nd year	0	12	12	6.8
3rd year	0	0	0	0.0
4th year	0	0	0	0.0

Employment (9 months after graduation)

For up-to-date employment data, go to
employmentsummary.abaquestionnaire.org on the ABA website.

Bar Passage Rates

First-time takers	236	Reporting %	70.34
Average school %	92.77	Average state %	92.29
Average pass difference	.48		

Jurisdiction	Takers	Passers	Pass %	State %	Diff %
Minnesota	148	137	92.57	92.21	0.36
Wisconsin	18	17	94.44	92.93	1.51

HAMLINE UNIVERSITY SCHOOL OF LAW

1536 Hewitt Avenue
Saint Paul, MN 55104
Phone: 651.523.2461, 800.388.3688; Fax: 651.523.3064
E-mail: lawadm@hamline.edu; Website: www.hamline.edu/law

Introduction

Hamline University School of Law is a collaborative community where students work together to best serve clients and society. Hamline offers a full-time weekday and part-time weekend program, both of which provide a challenging curriculum, excellent faculty, and diverse experiential learning opportunities. Our expert faculty members challenge students to realize their full potential through innovative educational experiences—both inside and outside the classroom. Hamline students graduate ready to practice law and inspired to use their legal education to solve problems and make a difference in the world. And, our outstanding career services professionals are well-connected advocates for every Hamline Law graduate.

Hamline Law also serves as a catalyst for reframing the legal landscape through distinguished guest speakers, thought-provoking symposia, and nationally recognized centers of excellence, such as Hamline's renowned Dispute Resolution Institute, and the Health Law Institute, which is considered among the nation's top 20. Our new Business Law Institute is built on the foundation of strong business law courses that have long been a bedrock of the Hamline legal education.

Hamline alumni are employed in all aspects of the law, including private practice, government agencies, and public and private corporate environments. They also work in the court system as prosecutors, public defenders, and members of the judiciary at the state and federal level. Some alumni use their legal education as a backdrop for nontraditional legal employment outside the justice system. Hamline graduates are active and involved with the School of Law by serving as moot court and competition judges, adjunct faculty, practicum supervisors, program and classroom speakers, and mentors for individual students.

At the Heart of It All

Hamline's School of Law is set in the heart of a safe, energetic, comprehensive, tree-lined campus, offering amenities that include on-campus housing and a variety of dining options. Hamline's health and fitness center contains a full range of exercise equipment, a running track, and a swimming pool. Our location in the Midway neighborhood of Saint Paul means we're in the middle of everything that Saint Paul and Minneapolis have to offer—from renowned theater and world-class museums to great dining and a broad range of recreational activities and major league sports. Nearly two dozen Fortune 500 companies are headquartered in the Twin Cities as well.

Inside the law school building, students will find all of the resources they need to succeed. The Law Library staff is readily available to provide supportive services, along with nearly 300,000 volumes and electronic databases—giving students access to the libraries of seven other colleges and universities through a consortium agreement. Hamline's Annette K. Levine Moot Court Room provides a technologically relevant setting for holding moot court competitions and observing actual court proceedings.

Rigorous and Supportive Learning Environment

Hamline's core curriculum provides the analytical grounding necessary for success. In addition to a rich full-time program, Hamline offers a unique part-time weekend program that is taught by the same respected faculty members who teach in the weekday program. The law school also offers dual-degree and course exchange options, which allow students to combine their legal education with a second disciplinary focus in the areas of business administration, public administration, nonprofit management, creative writing, and organizational leadership. Hamline's curriculum in negotiation, arbitration, and mediation is second to none.

Hamline's rigorous offerings reflect considerable depth and innovation. Our recently reconfigured first-year curriculum includes International Law as well as Practice, Problem-Solving and Professionalism (P3), a course designed to provide students with the context of legal practice and to frame lawyering as a broad profession grounded in problem-solving and dispute resolution. Hamline students may concentrate their studies in a variety of substantive areas: alternative dispute resolution, corporate/commercial law, child advocacy, criminal law, government and regulatory affairs, health law, intellectual property, international law, labor and employment, litigation and trial practice, property law, and public law and human rights.

At Hamline, professors move beyond traditional lectures to offer truly collaborative, student-centered classroom experiences while simultaneously conducting cutting-edge scholarship. Our accessible professors are dedicated to an open-door policy. An emphasis on seminars allows students to learn in small classes, make presentations, and create original research on topics of personal interest, ensuring that students work closely with Hamline's dedicated faculty throughout their law school experience. The Constance Bakken Fellows program provides funding for collaborative research between faculty and students.

Experiential Learning: At Home and Abroad

Hamline students further expand their skills by competing in appellate advocacy and negotiation competitions throughout the country and around the world. Hamline's 10 legal clinics give students real-world experience in the practice of health law, immigration law, small business planning, criminal law, child advocacy, alternative dispute resolution, education law, and trial practice. Each clinic operates as a small law office with students handling their own caseload and representing clients under the supervision of experienced in-house or adjunct faculty members.

Likewise, Hamline's externship program enables students to work directly with mentor attorneys and judges, and places students in private law firms, corporations, judges' chambers, public agencies, legislative offices, and businesses. In addition, all Hamline students must complete 24 hours of pro bono service as a graduation requirement.

Through experiential learning opportunities, Hamline students absorb real-world legal lessons, gain a wealth of knowledge in case management and other lawyering skills, and establish valuable contacts in the professional legal community.

Hamline encourages international study for the development of a truly global perspective. Many students participate in an international exchange program with Hamline's European law school partners. Others compete in the Vienna International Moot Court Competition. Hamline provides conferences, classes, and training in London, Oslo, Budapest, and Jerusalem, among other international locations. With international lawyers from around the world in our Master in Law (LLM) program and our academic programs abroad, Hamline offers a truly global learning environment.

A Dynamic Student Community

Hamline attracts a dynamic and diverse student population. Students in our fall 2011 incoming class represented 30 states and 99 undergraduate institutions, and 17 percent were students of color. Hamline also offers a graduate program leading to a Master in Law (LLM) degree for lawyers holding an LLB or equivalent degree from outside the United States. These students contribute to the cultural richness of the Hamline learning communities.

Opportunities for student involvement abound at Hamline University School of Law. The Hamline Law Review and the Hamline Journal of Public Law and Policy are entirely staffed by law students. Hamline students also provide editorial assistance for the internationally respected Journal of Law and Religion. Hamline students can participate in more than 15 moot court teams, and with 35 active student organizations, students easily find professional, cultural, and social connections to match their interests.

Hamline law students believe they can make a difference in their community and frequently this passion can be seen through the innovative programs and initiatives they develop on campus. In recent years, for example, members of the Hamline Latino Law Student Association launched an annual event, Juris Fiesta, which raises funds for the Latino Law Student Scholarship and attracts national Latino legal leaders

as keynote speakers. Another student organization, the Hamline Law Veterans' Association, has established an endowed annual scholarship for an eligible veteran.

Career Assistance

The Career Services Office is committed to assisting all Hamline law students in career planning and job searches. Dedicated and experienced counselors provide informational programs, mock interviews, one-on-one career counseling, résumé assistance, and networking opportunities through an established mentoring program. They also organize on-campus interviews and work extensively with employers to advance Hamline law students and to solicit postings and information for the online job bank. Students are strongly encouraged to participate in the programs offered by the Career Services Office and to build professional networks with alumni and other legal professionals.

Admission and Financial Aid

The School of Law maintains a selection process that emphasizes a rigorous but fair examination of each person as an individual, not merely as a set of credentials. In addition to the LSAT and undergraduate GPA, the admission committee gives significant weight to motivation, personal experiences, employment history, graduate education, maturity, letters of recommendation, and the ability to articulate one's interest in, and suitability for, the study of law. Hamline's admission policy is designed to enhance the academic rigor, professional dedication, social concern, and diversity of the student body, including cultural, economic, racial, ethnic composition, as well as sexual orientation. Hamline also provides a comprehensive financial aid program, which includes merit-based scholarships. At Hamline, 95 percent of law students qualify for need-based loans.

APPLICANT PROFILE

Hamline University School of Law
This grid includes only applicants with 120–180 LSAT scores earned under standard administrations.

LSAT Score	GPA																
	3.75 +		3.50–3.74		3.25–3.49		3.00–3.24		2.75–2.99		2.50–2.74		Below 2.50		No GPA		Totals
	Apps	Adm	Apps	Adm	Apps	Adm	Apps	Adm	Apps	Adm	Apps	Adm	Apps	Adm	Apps	Adm	Apps	Adm
170–180	1	1	3	3	0	0	0	0	0	0	0	0	0	0	0	0	4	4
165–169	9	9	6	6	4	4	3	2	4	3	1	1	0	0	1	0	28	25
160–164	17	17	22	20	18	18	18	15	8	7	3	3	3	2	0	0	89	82
155–159	33	32	45	43	51	49	41	38	20	14	15	10	7	1	2	1	214	188
150–154	31	30	56	55	72	64	75	61	45	28	23	14	19	1	4	3	325	256
145–149	19	17	51	39	66	51	72	34	40	10	25	5	27	2	4	1	304	159
140–144	9	4	23	8	30	8	26	3	25	0	19	0	19	0	6	1	157	24
Below 140	3	0	9	0	15	0	13	0	19	0	19	0	15	0	7	0	100	0
Total	122	110	215	174	256	194	248	153	161	62	105	33	90	6	24	6	1221	738

Apps = Number of Applicants
Adm = Number Admitted
Reflects 99% of the total applicant pool; highest LSAT data reported.

HARVARD LAW SCHOOL

1563 Massachusetts Avenue, Austin Hall
Cambridge, MA 02138
Phone: 617.495.3109
E-mail: jdadmiss@law.harvard.edu; Website: www.law.harvard.edu

The Basics

Type of school	Private
Term	Semester
Application deadline	2/1
Application fee	$85
Financial aid deadline	4/1
Can first year start other than fall?	No
Student to faculty ratio	12.2 to 1
# of housing spaces available restricted to law students	603
graduate housing for which law students are eligible	3,211

Faculty and Administrators

	Total		Men		Women		Minorities	
	Spr	Fall	Spr	Fall	Spr	Fall	Spr	Fall
Full-time	118	116	91	91	27	25	17	15
Other full-time	20	21	9	11	11	10	1	2
Deans, librarians, & others who teach	8	8	6	6	2	2	2	2
Part-time	50	31	34	23	16	8	4	2
Total	196	176	140	131	56	45	24	21

JD Enrollment and Ethnicity

	Men		Women		Full-Time		Part-Time		1st-Year		Total		JD Degs. Awd.
	#	%	#	%	#	%	#	%	#	%	#	%	
All Hispanics	57	6.6	78	9.6	135	8.0	0	0.0	50	8.9	135	8.0	45
Am. Ind./AK Nat.	6	0.7	4	0.5	10	0.6	0	0.0	2	0.4	10	0.6	2
Asian	74	8.5	106	13.1	180	10.7	0	0.0	56	9.9	180	10.7	66
Black/Af. Am.	80	9.2	97	12.0	177	10.5	0	0.0	53	9.4	177	10.5	61
Nat. HI/Pac. Isl.	0	0.0	0	0.0	0	0.0	0	0.0	0	0.0	0	0.0	0
2 or more races	11	1.3	19	2.3	30	1.8	0	0.0	19	3.4	30	1.8	0
Subtotal (minor.)	228	26.2	304	37.6	532	31.7	0	0.0	180	31.9	532	31.7	174
Nonres. Alien	53	6.1	55	6.8	108	6.4	0	0.0	49	8.7	108	6.4	8
White/Cauc.	484	55.6	390	48.2	874	52.1	0	0.0	282	50.0	874	52.1	317
Unknown	105	12.1	60	7.4	165	9.8	0	0.0	48	8.5	165	9.8	86
Total	870	51.8	809	48.2	1679	100.0	0	0.0	564	33.6	1679		585

Curriculum

	Full-Time	Part-Time
Typical first-year section size	80	0
Is there typically a "small section" of the first-year class, other than Legal Writing, taught by full-time faculty	No	No
If yes, typical size offered last year		
# of classroom course titles beyond first-year curriculum	320	

# of upper division courses, excluding seminars, with an enrollment:	Under 25	112
	25–49	66
	50–74	32
	75–99	12
	100+	27

# of seminars	74	
# of seminar positions available	1,102	
# of seminar positions filled	1,058	0
# of positions available in simulation courses	1,064	
# of simulation positions filled	1,001	0
# of positions available in faculty supervised clinical courses	586	
# of faculty supervised clinical positions filled	527	0
# involved in field placements	187	0
# involved in law journals	1,100	0
# involved in moot court or trial competitions	375	0
# of credit hours required to graduate	88	

Transfers

Transfers in	30
Transfers out	0

Tuition and Fees

	Resident	Nonresident
Full-time	$48,786	$48,786
Part-time		
Tuition Guarantee Program	N	

Living Expenses

Estimated living expenses for singles

Living on campus	Living off campus	Living at home
$23,814	$23,814	$23,814

HARVARD LAW SCHOOL

ABA
Approved
Since
1923

GPA and LSAT Scores

	Total	Full-Time	Part-Time
# of apps	6,335	6,335	0
# of offers	842	842	0
# of matrics	559	559	0
75% GPA	3.97	3.97	0.00
Median GPA	3.89	3.89	0.00
25% GPA	3.78	3.78	0.00
75% LSAT	176	176	0
Median LSAT	173	173	0
25% LSAT	171	171	0

Grants and Scholarships (from prior year)

	Total		Full-Time		Part-Time	
	#	%	#	%	#	%
Total # of students	1,762		1,762		0	
Total # receiving grants	864	49.9	864	49.9	0	0.0
Less than 1/2 tuition	508	28.8	508	28.8	0	0.0
Half to full tuition	243	14.0	243	14.0	0	0.0
Full tuition	87	5.0	87	5.0	0	0.0
More than full tuition	26	1.5	26	1.5	0	0.0
Median grant amount			$19,705		$0	

Informational and Library Resources

Total amount spent on library materials	$3,507,076
Study seating capacity inside the library	749
# of full-time equivalent professional librarians	38
Hours per week library is open	106
# of open, wired connections available to students	1,650
# of networked computers available for use by students	166
Has wireless network?	Y
Requires computer?	N

JD Attrition (from prior year)

	Academic	Other	Total	
	#	#	#	%
1st year	0	2	2	0.4
2nd year	0	1	1	0.2
3rd year	0	0	0	0.0
4th year	0	0	0	0.0

Employment (9 months after graduation)

For up-to-date employment data, go to
employmentsummary.abaquestionnaire.org on the ABA website.

Bar Passage Rates

First-time takers	558	Reporting %	96.06
Average school %	95.34	Average state %	83.94
Average pass difference	11.40		

Jurisdiction	Takers	Passers	Pass %	State %	Diff %
New York	315	298	94.60	84.92	9.68
Massachusetts	98	96	97.96	89.67	8.29
California	85	80	94.12	71.24	22.88
Illinois	38	37	97.37	89.38	7.99

HARVARD LAW SCHOOL

1563 Massachusetts Avenue, Austin Hall
Cambridge, MA 02138
Phone: 617.495.3109
E-mail: jdadmiss@law.harvard.edu; Website: www.law.harvard.edu

A Legal Metropolis

Harvard Law School combines the resources of the world's premier center for legal education and research with educational settings designed to enrich individual and interactive learning. The result is a uniquely vibrant and collaborative environment. Harvard's scope generates enormous vitality through its depth of academic options, a wide array of research programs, a diverse student body drawn from across the nation and around the world, and a global network of distinguished alumni. Harvard Law School offers students a curriculum of unparalleled breadth: more than 350 courses, seminars, and reading groups that together reflect the remarkable range of the faculty's expertise and interests. Within this dynamic environment, law students have broad opportunities for intellectual engagement with faculty and classmates. Over 100 of our courses have fewer than 25 students enrolled; additionally, there are nearly 80 seminars in which small groups of students work closely with faculty. First-year sections have 80 students, and opportunities to work directly with faculty members abound. For example, all first-year students may join intimate (fewer than 15 students), faculty-led reading groups on topics ranging from cyberlaw to climate change to terrorism. Harvard's extensive resources and collaborative approach create unmatched opportunities to prepare for leadership in public service, private practice, the judiciary, academia, business, or government.

Public Service

HLS strongly promotes public service. The school guarantees funding for summer public interest work, and over 500 JD students received funds to work in 39 countries and 34 states plus Washington, DC, in 2011. The Office of Public Interest Advising provides comprehensive services to students pursuing public service careers. The Low Income Protection Plan allows graduates substantial financial flexibility to pursue lower-paying employment, and a variety of fellowship programs provide additional support to graduates entering public service. Reflecting its public service commitment, HLS has a 40-hour minimum pro bono work requirement, with students actually completing an average of more than 600 hours of pro bono work during law school.

Faculty

The centerpiece of the HLS experience is working directly with scholars who shape the landscape of American and international law. The faculty includes leading specialists in every subject area. Beyond the classroom, students provide critical support to faculty producing cutting-edge research and influencing the development of the law and of societies around the world.

Programs of Study

To guide students as they move through the three years of law school and to create a tool for better coordination and collaboration between faculty members, the faculty has developed "programs of study." Students do not sign up for any program; nor should any student feel compelled to adhere to one. Instead, the programs of study reflect the best advice from faculty about how to approach particular subjects and potential careers. The six programs of study offer suggestions about how students can navigate our extensive course offerings with a sense of their relationship to different avenues of study and opportunities to move progressively through more advanced work before graduation. The programs of study can give students a picture of how different courses and seminars can relate to the work of practicing lawyers and academics, and how clinical work, summer opportunities, and fellowships also enhance your learning and development.

The six programs of study are:
- Criminal Justice
- International and Comparative Law
- Law and Business
- Law and Government
- Law and Social Change
- Law, Science, and Technology

International Scope

Harvard Law School presents students with tremendous opportunities to engage in the world. With students coming from more than 70 countries to study here and with hundreds of current students going abroad each year to work, study, engage in research, or advocate for change, HLS is truly a global crossroads. Each year, the Law School offers more than 90 courses, seminars, and reading groups taught with an international, foreign, or comparative law component. Research centers, such as the East Asian Legal Studies Program or the Program on International Financial Systems, offer students access to visiting scholars and cutting-edge ideas through colloquia, conferences, and research opportunities. Harvard's 4,500 alumni living outside the United States provide an unparalleled network of opportunity for potential collaboration and camaraderie for members of the community. In addition, scholars come to HLS from all over the world to make use of the incredible international collections housed in the law library.

Student Life

At HLS, a wide variety of extracurricular activities complement and enrich the classroom and clinical experiences. Whether exploring professional interests, serving the public, or merely socializing, students engage in an enormous range of activity on the HLS campus beyond the classroom. At present, there are more than 100 student organizations and journals at HLS. Student organizations based on social, political, service, or professional interests plan workshops, panels, concerts, networking opportunities, and conferences for almost every day of the academic year. Other activities planned by first-year social chairs, the second-year social committee, the third-year class marshals, as well as the Dean of Students Office, create a collegial and community-oriented environment on campus. Students are given a wide range of opportunities to create and implement ideas for activities and are encouraged to pursue their interests by forming new student organizations or planning one-time events.

Clinical Programs

The Clinical Legal Education Program is one of the most important and valued aspects of a Harvard Law School education, confirming our commitment to public service and to providing our students with the best possible educational experience. With dozens of in-house clinics and hundreds of externships, Harvard Law School has more clinical opportunities than any law school in the world. Some of the clinics include Mediation and Negotiation, Supreme Court Advocacy, Immigration, Human Rights, CyberLaw, Child Advocacy, Criminal Justice, Criminal Prosecution, Death Penalty, Disability Law, Domestic Violence, Education Law, Employment Civil Rights, Environmental Law, Estate Planning, Family Law, GLBT Law, Gender Violence, Government Lawyer, Health Law, Post-Foreclosure Eviction Defense, Predatory Lending/Consumer Protection, and Sports Law.

Clinical education at HLS helps to introduce and explore the roles and responsibilities of a lawyer. Taking a clinical course may aid students in thinking about what sort of law practice or lawyering work they like most. Mentored practice, in an educational setting, also helps students begin to understand their learning styles while getting a head start on learning the skills they will need when they begin their careers.

The Clinical Legal Education Program at Harvard Law School has three basic components:

- direct student responsibility for clients in a realistic practice setting;
- supervision and mentoring by an experienced practitioner; and
- companion classroom sessions in which clinical experience supports and contributes to further discussion and thought.

Seventy-two percent of stud   ipated in clinical work during the 2011 academi   nical courses get enthusiastic reviews from stuc   pants, most of whom find them challenging and ed   Many students find that this practical lawyering   sense of personal accomplishment as well as p   l development because, in most cases, the   increasing access to justice for the most marginalize   nbers of society. HLS also offers externship placements at various government agencies, nonprofits, and small firms. Students can also design independent clinical work projects that are tailored to unique interests. Finally, many students take advantage of the winter term, spending three to four weeks off campus in a clinical setting and then coming back to campus and continuing the work remotely for the following semester.

Employment After Graduation

More than 700 employers recruit on campus at HLS each year. Upon graduation, roughly 65 percent of HLS graduates enter private practice, about 20 percent enter judicial clerkships, and about 15 percent enter public interest or government work, business and industry, academia, or other unique pursuits. Virtually every year, the number of HLS graduates clerking for the US Supreme Court surpasses the number from any other law school. In fact, approximately one-fourth of all Supreme Court clerks over the last decade graduated from HLS. After clerkships, many HLS graduates pursue careers in public interest, government, and academia.

APPLICANT PROFILE

HLS does not provide a profile chart because it would be based solely upon undergraduate GPA and LSAT scores. Admission decisions are based on many factors beyond the GPA and LSAT. Each application is read thoroughly by our team of admissions professionals and faculty admissions committee members. Although most admitted candidates graduated near the top of their college classes and present LSAT scores in the top few percentiles, a significant proportion of candidates who meet these characterizations may not be offered admission. At the same time, some admitted candidates apply with lower GPA and LSAT credentials but offer combined academic and other achievements that impress the admissions committee. Candidates with higher grades and scores tend to be admitted at higher rates than candidates with lower grades and scores, but at no point on the GPA or LSAT scales are the chances for admission to Harvard Law School zero or 100 percent.

UNIVERSITY OF HAWAI'I AT MĀNOA | WILLIAM S. RICHARDSON SCHOOL OF LAW

2515 Dole Street
Honolulu, HI 96822-2350
Phone: 808.956.5557; Fax: 808.956.3813
E-mail: lawadm@hawaii.edu; Website: www.law.hawaii.edu

ABA
Approved
Since
1974

The Basics

Type of school	Public
Term	Semester
Application deadline	2/1
Application fee	$75
Financial aid deadline	3/1
Can first year start other than fall?	No
Student to faculty ratio	8.1 to 1
# of housing spaces available restricted to law students	
graduate housing for which law students are eligible	36

Faculty and Administrators

	Total		Men		Women		Minorities	
	Spr	Fall	Spr	Fall	Spr	Fall	Spr	Fall
Full-time	39	29	17	12	22	17	17	13
Other full-time	2	3	2	2	0	1	2	3
Deans, librarians, & others who teach	16	16	3	3	13	13	9	8
Part-time	43	23	28	12	15	11	15	13
Total	100	71	50	29	50	42	43	37

Curriculum

	Full-Time	Part-Time
Typical first-year section size	99	53
Is there typically a "small section" of the first-year class, other than Legal Writing, taught by full-time faculty	No	No
If yes, typical size offered last year		
# of classroom course titles beyond first-year curriculum	93	

# of upper division courses, excluding seminars, with an enrollment:	Under 25	55
	25–49	8
	50–74	2
	75–99	2
	100+	0

	Full-Time	Part-Time
# of seminars	79	
# of seminar positions available	989	
# of seminar positions filled	821	91
# of positions available in simulation courses	222	
# of simulation positions filled	163	0
# of positions available in faculty supervised clinical courses	158	
# of faculty supervised clinical positions filled	154	1
# involved in field placements	109	2
# involved in law journals	58	0
# involved in moot court or trial competitions	41	0
# of credit hours required to graduate	89	

JD Enrollment and Ethnicity

	Men		Women		Full-Time		Part-Time		1st-Year		Total		JD Degs. Awd.
	#	%	#	%	#	%	#	%	#	%	#	%	
All Hispanics	9	5.6	18	9.0	23	8.3	4	4.7	17	11.3	27	7.5	2
Am. Ind./AK Nat.	0	0.0	3	1.5	3	1.1	0	0.0	2	1.3	3	0.8	1
Asian	40	24.8	75	37.5	90	32.6	25	29.4	49	32.5	115	31.9	26
Black/Af. Am.	1	0.6	4	2.0	3	1.1	2	2.4	3	2.0	5	1.4	2
Nat. HI/Pac. Isl.	17	10.6	10	5.0	25	9.1	2	2.4	9	6.0	27	7.5	15
2 or more races	36	22.4	53	26.5	67	24.3	22	25.9	40	26.5	89	24.7	23
Subtotal (minor.)	103	64.0	163	81.5	211	76.4	55	64.7	120	79.5	266	73.7	69
Nonres. Alien	4	2.5	2	1.0	5	1.8	1	1.2	1	0.7	6	1.7	1
White/Cauc.	40	24.8	28	14.0	44	15.9	24	28.2	26	17.2	68	18.8	21
Unknown	14	8.7	7	3.5	16	5.8	5	5.9	4	2.6	21	5.8	10
Total	161	44.6	200	55.4	276	76.5	85	23.5	151	41.8	361		101

Transfers

Transfers in	1
Transfers out	7

Tuition and Fees

	Resident	Nonresident
Full-time	$17,378	$32,522
Part-time	$1,347	$1,978
Tuition Guarantee Program		N

Living Expenses

Estimated living expenses for singles

Living on campus	Living off campus	Living at home
$13,221	$15,485	$6,166

UNIVERSITY OF HAWAI'I AT MĀNOA | WILLIAM S. RICHARDSON SCHOOL OF LAW

ABA
Approved
Since
1974

GPA and LSAT Scores

	Total	Full-Time	Part-Time
# of apps	1,229	1,119	110
# of offers	257	218	39
# of matrics	116	88	28
75% GPA	3.55	3.55	3.53
Median GPA	3.36	3.37	3.32
25% GPA	3.11	3.15	3.07
75% LSAT	160	160	156
Median LSAT	156	157	153
25% LSAT	153	154	150

Grants and Scholarships (from prior year)

	Total #	Total %	Full-Time #	Full-Time %	Part-Time #	Part-Time %
Total # of students	353		295		58	
Total # receiving grants	242	68.6	223	75.6	19	32.8
Less than 1/2 tuition	229	64.9	212	71.9	17	29.3
Half to full tuition	13	3.7	11	3.7	2	3.4
Full tuition	0	0.0	0	0.0	0	0.0
More than full tuition	0	0.0	0	0.0	0	0.0
Median grant amount			$5,000		$2,500	

Informational and Library Resources

Total amount spent on library materials	$630,357
Study seating capacity inside the library	355
# of full-time equivalent professional librarians	13
Hours per week library is open	96
# of open, wired connections available to students	246
# of networked computers available for use by students	28
Has wireless network?	Y
Requires computer?	Y

JD Attrition (from prior year)

	Academic #	Other #	Total #	Total %
1st year	1	6	7	4.9
2nd year	0	4	4	3.1
3rd year	0	1	1	1.2
4th year	0	0	0	0.0

Employment (9 months after graduation)

For up-to-date employment data, go to employmentsummary.abaquestionnaire.org on the ABA website.

Bar Passage Rates

First-time takers	74	Reporting %	93.24
Average school %	75.36	Average state %	77.04
Average pass difference	−1.68		

Jurisdiction	Takers	Passers	Pass %	State %	Diff %
Hawaii	69	52	75.36	77.04	−1.68

UNIVERSITY OF HAWAI'I AT MĀNOA | WILLIAM S. RICHARDSON SCHOOL OF LAW

2515 Dole Street
Honolulu, HI 96822-2350
Phone: 808.956.5557; Fax: 808.956.3813
E-mail: lawadm@hawaii.edu; Website: www.law.hawaii.edu

Introduction

The William S. Richardson School of Law at the University of Hawai'i is located at the foot of beautiful Mānoa Valley, minutes from sandy beaches and lush rain forests, as well as from the economic and legal center of urban Honolulu. We offer an excellent academic program with professors committed to outstanding teaching, scholarship, and community service. Our school is particularly noted for its collegial atmosphere, accessible faculty, and extraordinary cultural and ethnic diversity.

Placement after graduation is consistently very high. Our distinguished alumni serve as leaders in Hawai'i, as well as in national and international arenas. We are recognized particularly for our programs in environmental law, Native Hawaiian law, and international law with an Asian and Pacific focus. The William S. Richardson School of Law is fully accredited by the American Bar Association and is a member of the American Association of Law Schools.

Programs of Study

We offer a three-year, full-time JD program and an evening, part-time JD program. Law students may earn certificates in Environmental Law, Pacific-Asian Legal Studies, and Native Hawaiian Law. Summer courses are available as well as specialized short courses with distinguished visiting faculty in January (J Term). We also offer a one-year LLM program for international lawyers studying American law.

Environmental Law Program

The Law School's Environmental Law Program (ELP) was established in 1988 in recognition of the special challenges in developing an environmentally sustainable economy within a unique and fragile island environment. It has grown into a comprehensive program with a regional, national, and international reputation for excellence in teaching, scholarship, and public service. Thanks to its dedicated faculty, alumni, and friends throughout Hawai'i and the Pacific region, ELP offers unparalleled opportunities for students interested in focusing their studies in the environmental law field. The ELP has several components: (1) Certificate in Environmental Law; (2) faculty and student scholarship; (3) community outreach and education; (4) moot court; (5) colloquia series; (6) off-campus learning; (7) student-led Environmental Law Society; (8) career counseling and placement; and (9) professional service.

Pacific-Asian Legal Studies

Enhanced by Hawai'i's location, population, culture, and economic relationships, we offer an exceptional program in Pacific-Asian Legal Studies (PALS). The program has the twofold purpose of conducting research and enriching the JD curriculum. Many faculty members have expertise in Pacific/Asian scholarship, teaching, and law reform. Recent course offerings in PALS have included, for example, Chinese Business Law, Chinese Law and Society, Pacific Island Legal Systems, Korean Law, Philippine Law, Japanese Law and Society, and US-Japan Business Transactions. The Certificate in Pacific-Asian Legal Studies allows students to focus their coursework and to earn recognition of their specialization in addition to the JD.

Selected students may do a full semester externship in an agency or entity for academic credit with approval in certain Pacific Island nations, Asia, or elsewhere. Students may also arrange a semester of study with law faculties in Asia.

Ka Huli Ao Center for Excellence in Native Hawaiian Law

Ka Huli Ao Center for Excellence in Native Hawaiian Law was established in 2005 by a federal grant. The center focuses on education, research, community outreach, and the preservation of invaluable historical, legal, traditional, and customary materials. It offers new courses and supports Native Hawaiian law students as they pursue legal careers and leadership roles. Students may earn a certificate in Native Hawaiian Law.

Clinical Opportunities

All students are required to take at least one clinical course, and most students will take many such practical courses. We offer an extensive array of clinical and professional skills opportunities. Clinical courses teach and model excellent practice skills and stress a reflective method of looking at lawyering behavior. These courses are taught by full-time faculty as well as by some of Hawai'i's finest judges and lawyers who evaluate and mentor student efforts in presenting oral arguments, handling depositions, and negotiating for their clients in simulated sessions as well as with real clients. Skills taught in the various clinical courses include interviewing, counseling, drafting, fact investigation, negotiation, alternative dispute resolution, motion practice, trial practice, appellate practice, and legal writing. Our Clinical Program also directly addresses the legal problems faced by some of Hawai'i's most vulnerable people.

Community Service and Pro Bono

Our Pro Bono Program introduces students to public interest voluntary service and encourages them to respond directly to unmet needs in the community. Each student must do at least 60 hours of law-related work in one or more agencies or projects approved by the Law School pro bono advisor. In the past, students have worked for a wide variety of public service groups such as the Legal Aid Society of Hawai'i, Volunteer Legal Services, Native Hawaiian Legal Corporation, and the Earthjustice Legal Defense Fund.

JD Admission

Admission to both our full- and part-time JD programs is determined by an applicant's academic achievement, aptitude for the study of law, and professional promise. Preference is given to residents of Hawai'i and to nonresidents with strong ties to, or special interest in, Hawai'i, the Asia/Pacific region, environmental law, or other programs in the Law School. Approximately 20 percent of our students are nonresidents.

In addition to the LSAT and undergraduate GPA, factors considered for admission include academic work beyond the bachelor's degree, work experience, writing ability, community service, diversity, overcoming adversity, and unusual accomplishments.

Applications from students wishing to transfer or wishing to visit for a semester or two are considered for both August and January admission.

LLM Admission

Our Master of Laws (LLM) Program is restricted to applicants who have earned a bachelor's degree in law, or its equivalent, from an institution outside the United States. Admission decisions are based upon a candidate's previous law study, work experience, English writing ability, letters of recommendation, and TOEFL or IELTS scores. There is no LSAT requirement.

Student Activities

Student editorial boards publish the *University of Hawai'i Law Review* and the online *Asian-Pacific Law and Policy Journal*. Students also organize and participate in many aspects of our extensive moot court program, including competing in many national competitions. Student teams regularly perform well, bringing home national and international titles and awards.

Most students are active in a variety of organizations within the Law School and in the Honolulu community. A sampling includes Advocates for Public Interest Law (APIL), student divisions of the American Bar Association, American Inns of Court, Phi Delta Phi and Delta Theta Phi, Hawai'i Women Lawyers, and the Environmental Law Society. Student affinity groups include the Filipino Law Students Association, Black Law Students Association, La Alianza, LAMBDA, and the 'Ahahui o Hawai'i, an organization primarily for Native Hawaiian law students.

Library and Physical Facilities

The classroom building features a moot courtroom and an open courtyard that facilitate informal conversations and activities. Law students have full access to all facilities of the university, including the health, counseling, and computing centers, as well as extensive athletic facilities. The Law School buildings have wireless Internet access throughout for students, faculty, and staff.

Career Services

We assist students and alumni to obtain part-time, summer, and associate positions in the public interest and private sectors through our Career Development Office. Most students choose to remain in Hawai'i and the Asia/Pacific region, so that about 85 percent of our graduates work in Hawai'i after graduation. Many firms in Honolulu, government employers, and public interest organizations participate in on-campus interviews for second- and third-year students. Our students also are unusually successful in obtaining judicial clerkships upon graduation. Recent graduating classes have had an employment rate nine months after graduation generally varying from 80 to 100 percent.

APPLICANT PROFILE

University of Hawai'i at Mānoa | William S. Richardson School of Law
This grid includes only applicants who earned 120–180 LSAT scores under standard administrations.

LSAT Score	3.75 +		3.50–3.74		3.25–3.49		3.00–3.24		2.75–2.99		2.50–2.74		2.25–2.49		2.00–2.24		Below 2.00		No GPA		Totals	
	Apps	Adm	Apps	Adm	Apps	Adm	Apps	Adm	Apps	Adm	Apps	Adm	Apps	Adm	Apps	Adm	Apps	Adm	Apps	Adm	Apps	Adm
175–180	0	0	0	0	1	1	0	0	0	0	0	0	0	0	1	0	0	0	0	0	2	1
170–174	4	3	3	1	3	1	1	0	2	1	1	0	2	0	0	0	0	0	0	0	16	6
165–169	10	7	14	13	16	10	15	5	8	1	8	1	2	0	0	0	0	0	0	0	73	37
160–164	15	7	45	27	45	26	34	11	16	4	20	3	10	0	3	0	1	0	4	1	193	79
155–159	45	14	62	17	83	29	69	16	54	4	17	0	13	1	3	0	0	0	5	3	351	84
150–154	24	5	49	6	76	5	70	12	35	2	36	2	12	0	3	0	2	0	9	2	316	34
145–149	13	1	25	0	35	1	42	2	30	2	14	0	12	0	5	0	2	0	6	0	184	6
140–144	6	1	12	3	17	2	20	0	21	2	9	0	12	2	5	0	1	0	5	0	108	10
135–139	2	0	5	0	1	0	10	0	10	0	9	0	3	0	1	0	2	0	1	0	44	0
130–134	1	0	0	0	2	0	3	0	1	0	5	0	1	0	0	0	1	0	0	0	14	0
125–129	0	0	0	0	0	0	0	0	0	0	2	0	0	0	0	0	0	0	0	0	2	0
120–124	0	0	0	0	0	0	0	0	0	0	0	0	0	0	0	0	0	0	0	0	0	0
Total	120	38	215	67	279	75	264	46	177	16	121	6	67	3	21	0	9	0	30	6	1303	257

Apps = Number of Applicants
Adm = Number Admitted
Reflects 99% of the total applicant pool; highest LSAT data reported.

HOFSTRA UNIVERSITY—MAURICE A. DEANE SCHOOL OF LAW

121 Hofstra University
Hempstead, NY 11549
Phone: 516.463.5916; Fax: 516.463.6264
E-mail: lawadmissions@hofstra.edu; Website: http://law.hofstra.edu

The Basics

Type of school	Private
Term	Semester
Application deadline	4/15
Application fee	$0
Financial aid deadline	4/1
Can first year start other than fall?	No
Student to faculty ratio	15.2 to 1
# of housing spaces available restricted to law students	
graduate housing for which law students are eligible	225

Faculty and Administrators

	Total		Men		Women		Minorities	
	Spr	Fall	Spr	Fall	Spr	Fall	Spr	Fall
Full-time	57	56	35	36	22	20	9	9
Other full-time	0	0	0	0	0	0	0	0
Deans, librarians, & others who teach	2	4	1	1	1	3	1	1
Part-time	53	37	37	33	16	4	5	2
Total	112	97	73	70	39	27	15	12

Curriculum

	Full-Time	Part-Time
Typical first-year section size	116	116
Is there typically a "small section" of the first-year class, other than Legal Writing, taught by full-time faculty	Yes	Yes
If yes, typical size offered last year	33	33

# of classroom course titles beyond first-year curriculum		150
# of upper division courses, excluding seminars, with an enrollment:	Under 25	115
	25–49	38
	50–74	12
	75–99	21
	100+	4

	Full-Time	Part-Time
# of seminars	64	
# of seminar positions available	1,218	
# of seminar positions filled	847	136
# of positions available in simulation courses	1,143	
# of simulation positions filled	772	173
# of positions available in faculty supervised clinical courses	136	
# of faculty supervised clinical positions filled	108	14
# involved in field placements	176	9
# involved in law journals	198	7
# involved in moot court or trial competitions	71	1
# of credit hours required to graduate	87	

JD Enrollment and Ethnicity

	Men		Women		Full-Time		Part-Time		1st-Year		Total		JD Degs. Awd.
	#	%	#	%	#	%	#	%	#	%	#	%	
All Hispanics	34	5.9	30	6.0	53	5.3	11	15.7	18	5.0	64	6.0	15
Am. Ind./AK Nat.	1	0.2	1	0.2	2	0.2	0	0.0	0	0.0	2	0.2	1
Asian	52	9.0	62	12.5	105	10.5	9	12.9	33	9.1	114	10.6	36
Black/Af. Am.	35	6.1	58	11.7	81	8.1	12	17.1	35	9.7	93	8.7	23
Nat. HI/Pac. Isl.	0	0.0	0	0.0	0	0.0	0	0.0	0	0.0	0	0.0	0
2 or more races	28	4.8	29	5.8	57	5.7	0	0.0	33	9.1	57	5.3	0
Subtotal (minor.)	150	26.0	180	36.3	298	29.7	32	45.7	119	32.9	330	30.7	75
Nonres. Alien	25	4.3	18	3.6	42	4.2	1	1.4	15	4.1	43	4.0	11
White/Cauc.	380	65.7	284	57.3	628	62.5	36	51.4	215	59.4	664	61.8	193
Unknown	23	4.0	14	2.8	36	3.6	1	1.4	13	3.6	37	3.4	18
Total	578	53.8	496	46.2	1004	93.5	70	6.5	362	33.7	1074		297

Transfers

Transfers in	11
Transfers out	24

Tuition and Fees

	Resident	Nonresident
Full-time	$45,600	$45,600
Part-time	$34,125	$34,125
Tuition Guarantee Program		N

Living Expenses

Estimated living expenses for singles

Living on campus	Living off campus	Living at home
$23,481	$22,823	$9,259

HOFSTRA UNIVERSITY—MAURICE A. DEANE SCHOOL OF LAW

*ABA
Approved
Since
1971*

GPA and LSAT Scores

	Total	Full-Time	Part-Time
# of apps	4,566	4,154	412
# of offers	1,956	1,907	49
# of matrics	370	364	6
75% GPA	3.56	3.56	3.65
Median GPA	3.32	3.32	3.32
25% GPA	2.95	2.95	3.06
75% LSAT	160	160	160
Median LSAT	159	159	158
25% LSAT	155	155	156

Grants and Scholarships (from prior year)

	Total #	Total %	Full-Time #	Full-Time %	Part-Time #	Part-Time %
Total # of students	1,061		945		116	
Total # receiving grants	541	51.0	502	53.1	39	33.6
Less than 1/2 tuition	301	28.4	275	29.1	26	22.4
Half to full tuition	192	18.1	183	19.4	9	7.8
Full tuition	48	4.5	44	4.7	4	3.4
More than full tuition	0	0.0	0	0.0	0	0.0
Median grant amount			$20,000		$8,726	

Informational and Library Resources

Total amount spent on library materials	$1,410,148
Study seating capacity inside the library	484
# of full-time equivalent professional librarians	9
Hours per week library is open	168
# of open, wired connections available to students	164
# of networked computers available for use by students	116
Has wireless network?	Y
Requires computer?	N

JD Attrition (from prior year)

	Academic #	Other #	Total #	Total %
1st year	13	31	44	12.1
2nd year	3	5	8	2.3
3rd year	0	2	2	0.6
4th year	2	1	3	7.1

Employment (9 months after graduation)

For up-to-date employment data, go to employmentsummary.abaquestionnaire.org on the ABA website.

Bar Passage Rates

First-time takers	355	Reporting %	88.45
Average school %	77.39	Average state %	84.92
Average pass difference	−7.53		

Jurisdiction	Takers	Passers	Pass %	State %	Diff %
New York	314	243	77.39	84.92	−7.53

HOFSTRA UNIVERSITY—MAURICE A. DEANE SCHOOL OF LAW

121 Hofstra University
Hempstead, NY 11549
Phone: 516.463.5916; Fax: 516.463.6264
E-mail: lawadmissions@hofstra.edu; Website: http://law.hofstra.edu

Introduction

The Maurice A. Deane School of Law at Hofstra University prepares passionate students to have an impact in the legal community and beyond. For 41 years, Hofstra Law has provided an education rich in both the theory and skills needed to produce outstanding lawyers, business executives, and community leaders. Located on the campus of Hofstra University in Hempstead, New York, Hofstra Law is 20 miles outside New York City in suburban Long Island. Hofstra Law offers a JD program, as well as LLM graduate degrees in American Legal Studies (for foreign law graduates) and Family Law. A JD/MBA joint-degree program is available in conjunction with the University's Frank G. Zarb School of Business.

Vibrant Campus Life

Hofstra Law, situated on the 240-acre Hofstra University main campus, provides a vibrant community for students studying the law. Few, if any, law schools can match the combination of Hofstra Law's green campus and its easy access to New York City, the hub of the nation's legal profession. Students living on campus in graduate housing enjoy a parklike setting that is home to one of the country's great arboretums. Yet, they can also take a free Hofstra shuttle bus to train stations that provide service to Manhattan in less than 40 minutes or drive just a few miles to world-class beaches.

Cutting-Edge Curriculum

As one of only a few US law schools to require Transnational Law as a first-year course, Hofstra Law is at the forefront of the changing realities of legal practice. This innovative course allows students to put their studies into a broader context by exploring the relationship between international law, foreign legal systems, and the US legal system. With the school offering more than 200 upper-level courses, students can explore practically any area of law and choose from concentrations in alternative dispute resolution, business law (honors concentration), criminal law and procedure, energy and environmental law, family law, and health law. Hofstra Law's advanced curriculum helps develop well-trained and practice-ready professionals. A survey of law firms conducted by the Hanover Research Council revealed that Hofstra Law graduates rate highly in a majority of competencies, including business knowledge, communication skills, advocacy skills, and general workplace skills.

Internationally Renowned Faculty

Hofstra Law's full-time faculty is composed of outstanding scholars, talented clinicians, and dedicated legal writing, academic support, and skills instructors. Faculty members have clerked for US Supreme Court justices, chaired major American Bar Association and law reform committees, received awards for scholarship and leadership in legal education and community affairs, and are recognized leaders in clinical and skills training. Their publications reflect a wide range of interests and expertise, ongoing participation in important scholarly debates, and significant contributions to the study and teaching of law. The faculty's open-door policy creates an accessible and collegial environment and reflects professors' engagement with their students.

Student Life

Hofstra Law students publish five journals: *Hofstra Law Review*, *Hofstra Labor and Employment Law Journal*, and *Journal of International Business and Law* are student-run; *ACTEC Law Journal* and *Family Court Review* are peer-reviewed and published under the auspices of the American College of Trust and Estate Counsel and the Association of Family and Conciliation Courts, respectively. There are more than 40 student organizations, ranging from Hofstra Law Women and the Black Law Students Association to the Public Justice Foundation and the International Law Society.

Professional Career Services

Hofstra Law provides a range of services to promote the career and professional growth of students. The Office of Career Services offers individual career and professional development counseling, educational programming, mock interviews, an extensive online employer database, and comprehensive on-campus interviewing. Hofstra Law also prepares students to succeed in a shifting legal marketplace by ensuring that they possess practice-ready skills and knowledge to meet the needs of employers and the expectations they have of new lawyers. These include interpersonal communication, client relations, and business cultivation—critical areas that influence the important yet subtle dynamics of legal practice. Through such events as the annual two-day Success Strategies Boot Camp, accomplished lawyers, academics, consultants, and law school administrators help students acquire knowledge and develop abilities that will differentiate them and help them transition smoothly into the workplace.

Innovative Clinical Program

Hofstra Law is widely recognized as a pioneer in fully integrating clinical education into a traditional law school curriculum. By the late 1970s, the school had one of the largest clinical programs in the nation. Over the years, its clinics have become well known in legal circles in the metropolitan area. As students represent individuals facing real legal challenges, they gain valuable hands-on experience: they advocate in court, counsel clients, conduct fact investigations, and mediate disputes. Hofstra Law's current clinical opportunities are in Political Asylum, Child Advocacy, Community and Economic Development, Criminal Justice, Criminal Prosecution (Practicum), Juvenile Justice (Practicum), Law Reform Advocacy, Mediation, and Securities Arbitration.

Training for Legal Practice

Recognizing that the well-rounded graduate needs to apply classroom theory to real-world situations, Hofstra Law offers extensive skills and simulation-based training. The Externship Program provides an opportunity to gain substantive legal experience under the direct supervision and guidance of an experienced attorney. Other training tools include moot court competitions, conferences, workshops with accomplished attorneys, intensive pretrial and mediation courses, and a trial techniques program based on the curriculum of the National Institute for Trial Advocacy.

International Legal Education

Hofstra Law offers study-abroad programs in Pisa, Italy (summer); Curaçao (winter intersession); and Cuba and Otavalo, Ecuador (spring). The school recently launched several new initiatives, including the Global Legal Practice Externship Program and a language-development partnership with Rosetta Stone, and became a participant in the Public-Private Partnership for Justice Reform in Afghanistan. Hofstra Law is also a founding member of the European-American Consortium for Legal Education (EACLE), offering semester-long exchange programs with the East China University of Political Science and Law (Shanghai), Erasmus University Rotterdam, the University of Erlangen-Nuremberg, Ghent University, the University of Helsinki, and the University of Parma.

Engaging Centers and Institutes

Both nationally and internationally recognized, Hofstra Law's centers and institutes attract thought leaders for research, debate, and the exchange of knowledge.

Center for Applied Legal Reasoning: This multidisciplinary center focuses on the study of theories of legal reasoning and the development of pedagogies to train students for the practice of law.

Center for Children, Families, and the Law: An interdisciplinary organization, this center is dedicated to education, research, and public service focused on children and families involved in the legal system.

Center for Legal Advocacy: This center features innovative programs aimed at improving client representation skills and enhancing the level of advocacy in the profession.

Institute for Health Law and Policy: Designed to train attorneys in the field of health law, this institute concentrates on the study and formulation of health care policy.

Institute for the Study of Conflict Transformation: This institute promotes the understanding of conflict processes and intervention from the transformative mediation framework.

Institute for the Study of Gender, Law, and Public Policy: The mission of this institute is to facilitate teaching, research, and scholarship concerning gender as it relates to law and public policy.

Institute for the Study of Legal Ethics: As a research center, this institute explores critical issues concerning lawyers' ethics and the legal profession.

Law, Logic, and Technology Research Laboratory: The LLT Lab conducts empirical research on legal reasoning in substantive areas of law, using a logic-based analytical framework and state-of-the-art technology, to create knowledge, skills, and tools that enhance legal practice and legal education.

Perry Weitz Institute for the Study of Mass Torts: This institute is dedicated to researching the issues and dynamics that arise in mass torts, class actions, and aggregate litigation, as well as processes for the adjudication of such claims and alternatives to litigation.

Rewarding Fellowships and Scholarships

Each year, Hofstra Law awards fellowships to entering JD students based on their demonstrated commitment to advocacy in several areas. Fellowship recipients receive tuition assistance, gain valuable internship experience, and pursue a course of study that provides the knowledge and skills needed to make an impact in their chosen field. The **Child and Family Advocacy Fellowship** is awarded to individuals who plan to use their legal education to advocate for the interests of children and families. The **Health Law and Policy Fellowship** is awarded to individuals who want to represent medical providers, patients, and pharmaceutical companies and advance health law policy. The **Lesbian, Gay, Bisexual, and Transgender Rights Fellowship** is awarded to individuals who plan to use their legal education to advocate for the interests of the LGBT community. The **Dwight L. Greene Memorial Scholarship** is awarded to individuals who have a commitment to advocacy on behalf of minority groups. Information about these opportunities is available at http://law.hofstra.edu/Fellowships. Other endowed scholarships are available for entering and continuing law students.

APPLICANT PROFILE

The Admissions Committee reviews not only an applicant's academic record and LSAT performance, but the entire application to determine whether the applicant is likely to be successful at Hofstra Law. Hofstra Law seeks a diverse student body made up of individuals who will thrive in the school's experiential-learning program, which trains them to make an impact in the legal profession, the business world, and society.

UNIVERSITY OF HOUSTON LAW CENTER

100 Law Center
Houston, TX 77204-6060
Phone: 713.743.2280; Fax: 713.743.2194
E-mail: lawadmissions@uh.edu; Website: www.law.uh.edu

ABA
Approved
Since
1950

The Basics

Type of school	Public
Term	Semester
Application deadline	11/15 2/15 5/15
Application fee	$70
Financial aid deadline	4/1
Can first year start other than fall?	No
Student to faculty ratio	11.3 to 1
# of housing spaces available restricted to law students	
graduate housing for which law students are eligible	935

Faculty and Administrators

	Total		Men		Women		Minorities	
	Spr	Fall	Spr	Fall	Spr	Fall	Spr	Fall
Full-time	63	51	46	35	17	16	8	8
Other full-time	11	0	4	0	7	0	0	0
Deans, librarians, & others who teach	4	3	4	3	0	0	0	0
Part-time	91	68	67	50	24	18	16	11
Total	169	122	121	88	48	34	24	19

JD Enrollment and Ethnicity

	Men		Women		Full-Time		Part-Time		1st-Year		Total		JD Degs. Awd.
	#	%	#	%	#	%	#	%	#	%	#	%	
All Hispanics	38	8.1	44	12.3	70	10.4	12	7.8	29	11.6	82	9.9	31
Am. Ind./AK Nat.	6	1.3	4	1.1	9	1.3	1	0.6	2	0.8	10	1.2	0
Asian	63	13.3	50	14.0	91	13.5	22	14.3	41	16.3	113	13.6	27
Black/Af. Am.	16	3.4	44	12.3	45	6.7	15	9.7	18	7.2	60	7.2	20
Nat. Hl/Pac. Isl.	0	0.0	0	0.0	0	0.0	0	0.0	0	0.0	0	0.0	0
2 or more races	0	0.0	0	0.0	0	0.0	0	0.0	0	0.0	0	0.0	0
Subtotal (minor.)	123	26.1	142	39.7	215	31.8	50	32.5	90	35.9	265	31.9	78
Nonres. Alien	0	0.0	1	0.3	1	0.1	0	0.0	0	0.0	1	0.1	6
White/Cauc.	339	71.8	210	58.7	450	66.6	99	64.3	160	63.7	549	66.1	196
Unknown	10	2.1	5	1.4	10	1.5	5	3.2	0	0.0	15	1.8	1
Total	472	56.9	358	43.1	676	81.4	154	18.6	251	30.2	830		281

Curriculum

	Full-Time	Part-Time
Typical first-year section size	70	50
Is there typically a "small section" of the first-year class, other than Legal Writing, taught by full-time faculty	Yes	Yes
If yes, typical size offered last year	35	25

# of classroom course titles beyond first-year curriculum		219
# of upper division courses, excluding seminars, with an enrollment:	Under 25	131
	25–49	41
	50–74	20
	75–99	7
	100+	0
# of seminars		20
# of seminar positions available		284
# of seminar positions filled	199	37
# of positions available in simulation courses		750
# of simulation positions filled	534	75
# of positions available in faculty supervised clinical courses		235
# of faculty supervised clinical positions filled	92	12
# involved in field placements	258	12
# involved in law journals	125	14
# involved in moot court or trial competitions	80	13
# of credit hours required to graduate		90

Transfers

Transfers in	24
Transfers out	3

Tuition and Fees

	Resident	Nonresident
Full-time	$28,130	$38,805
Part-time	$19,889	$27,006
Tuition Guarantee Program		N

Living Expenses

Estimated living expenses for singles

Living on campus	Living off campus	Living at home
$12,974	$16,122	$9,822

UNIVERSITY OF HOUSTON LAW CENTER

ABA
Approved
Since
1950

GPA and LSAT Scores

	Total	Full-Time	Part-Time
# of apps	3,357	2,774	583
# of offers	903	807	96
# of matrics	252	199	53
75% GPA	3.60	3.61	3.53
Median GPA	3.42	3.43	3.28
25% GPA	3.16	3.22	2.90
75% LSAT	163	164	162
Median LSAT	161	162	160
25% LSAT	157	159	156

Grants and Scholarships (from prior year)

	Total #	Total %	Full-Time #	Full-Time %	Part-Time #	Part-Time %
Total # of students	877		701		176	
Total # receiving grants	498	56.8	498	71.0	0	0.0
Less than 1/2 tuition	458	52.2	458	65.3	0	0.0
Half to full tuition	38	4.3	38	5.4	0	0.0
Full tuition	1	0.1	1	0.1	0	0.0
More than full tuition	1	0.1	1	0.1	0	0.0
Median grant amount			$2,200		$0	

Informational and Library Resources

Total amount spent on library materials	$1,395,760
Study seating capacity inside the library	550
# of full-time equivalent professional librarians	11
Hours per week library is open	168
# of open, wired connections available to students	0
# of networked computers available for use by students	10
Has wireless network?	Y
Requires computer?	N

JD Attrition (from prior year)

	Academic #	Other #	Total #	Total %
1st year	0	1	1	0.4
2nd year	2	9	11	4.2
3rd year	0	4	4	1.3
4th year	0	0	0	0.0

Employment (9 months after graduation)

For up-to-date employment data, go to employmentsummary.abaquestionnaire.org on the ABA website.

Bar Passage Rates

First-time takers	277	Reporting %	95.67
Average school %	89.43	Average state %	82.68
Average pass difference	6.75		

Jurisdiction	Takers	Passers	Pass %	State %	Diff %
Texas	265	237	89.43	82.68	6.75

UNIVERSITY OF HOUSTON LAW CENTER

100 Law Center
Houston, TX 77204-6060
Phone: 713.743.2280; Fax: 713.743.2194
E-mail: lawadmissions@uh.edu; Website: www.law.uh.edu

Introduction

The University of Houston (UH) Law Center is located at the University of Houston, three miles south of downtown. The state-assisted UH Law Center, located in one of the nation's top 10 largest legal markets, is noted throughout the South and Southwest not only for its excellence, but also for its progressive and innovative approach to the teaching of law. The College of Law, the academic branch of the UH Law Center, is fully accredited by the American Bar Association and the American Association of Law Schools and has a chapter of the Order of the Coif, the national legal honorary scholastic society. The Law Center confers a Juris Doctor (JD) degree as a first degree in law and a Master of Laws (LLM) degree to students pursuing work beyond the JD degree.

Curriculum/Basic Program of Study

The first-year curriculum at the UH Law Center is prescribed. Students are also required to complete a course in professional responsibility, a practice-skills course, and one major piece of legal research and writing before graduation. While emphasis is placed on legal theory and the varying approaches to the law, there are many opportunities for hands-on learning.

Special Programs

The University of Houston Law Center emphasizes current legal and administrative problems confronting the region and nation, including intellectual property law, environmental law, energy law, tax law, health law, and international law. The UH Law Center is home to the Health Law and Policy Institute, a research and instruction center on interdisciplinary issues. The UH Law Center is also host to the Criminal Justice Institute; the Institute for Higher Education Law and Governance; the Institute for Intellectual Property and Information Law; the Environment, Energy and Natural Resource Center; the Center for Children, Law, and Policy; the Blakely Advocacy Institute; the Center for Consumer Law; and the Program on Law and Computation.

Clinical Programs and Trial Advocacy

The UH Law Center offers a wide variety of opportunities to gain hands-on experience. The UH Law Center houses several clinics, which gives students practice opportunities in providing legal services to indigent clients. The available clinics include the civil practice clinic, consumer law clinic, criminal practice clinic, immigration clinic, mediation clinic, and transactional clinic. Students can also choose from among different areas of concentration, such as externships focusing on health or environmental law, or select an internship with a government agency or a court.

Practice skills courses, coordinated through the Blakely Advocacy Institute, are an integral part of the curriculum. Students can enhance their skills in trial, negotiation, pretrial, and appellate work through hands-on courses that simulate real-life situations. Several levels of courses are offered in civil and criminal advocacy. Intramural mock trial and moot court competitions are sponsored by the Advocates, an affiliated student organization. The institute also sponsors teams for criminal and civil interscholastic moot court and mock trial competitions, with UH Law Center students earning top honors in national and international competitions.

Activities

Extracurricular activities give voice to the diversity of the campus. Student groups represent special interests and provide important avenues to help law students succeed. Many arrange mentoring programs and match first-year students with second- or third-year students or working professionals. Others coordinate résumé-writing workshops, guest speaker forums, preregistration discussions of specific course offerings, or law-related charitable efforts that benefit the community.

The Student Bar Association (SBA) has input into every facet of student life at the UH Law Center. The SBA participates in the first-year orientation, organizes the annual charity Fun Run, aids in the selection of student representatives to sit on various faculty committees, and represents student attitudes and views both within and outside the UH Law Center.

Students are encouraged to become involved in one or more student organizations; to participate in the scholarly *Houston Law Review, Houston Journal of International Law, Houston Journal of Health Law and Policy, Houston Business and Tax Law Journal, Environmental and Energy Law and Policy Journal,* and the *Journal of Consumer and Commercial Law;* and to compete in tournaments ranging from moot court to mock trial, from mediation to negotiation.

UH Law Center students are active in a large number of student organizations, including the Association of Women in Law, Black Law Students Association, Hispanic Law Students Association, Asian Law Students Association, Outlaw (GLBT student organization), Lex Judaica (Jewish students), Muslim Law Students Association, J. Reuben Clark Law Society, Christian Legal Society, Public Interest Law Organization, Health Law Organization, Intellectual Property Student Organization, Energy and Environmental Law Society, Federalist Society, International Law Society, American Constitution Society for Law and Policy, Phi Delta Phi, Phi Alpha Delta, Delta Theta Phi, and Sports and Entertainment Law Organization.

Career Development

The Office of Career Development strives for a creative approach in its job search partnership with students. The First Year Initiative exposes first-year students to a comprehensive career education series that surveys dozens of career opportunities. Students in small groups actively gather the information they need to make informed decisions on their career plans.

The Office of Career Development also presents a variety of panel discussions, receptions, and seminars with members of the Houston legal community to assist students in understanding law career options. Topics covered include duties and responsibilities of a law clerk, judicial clerkship opportunities, solo practice, and nontraditional uses of a law degree.

The office provides individual assistance in résumé preparation and interviewing techniques for all students and alumni. The annual On Campus Interview Program for second- and third-year students seeking summer clerkships and permanent positions to commence upon graduation attracts approximately 100 prospective employers to the campus.

Admission

The UH Law Center enrolls full-time (day) students and part-time (evening) students beginning in the fall semester, which starts in August. There is no spring or summer admission.

Demonstrated academic ability and strong LSAT scores are not the only criteria for admission. Consideration is also given to background, achievements, honors, extracurricular activities, service to others, unique abilities, hardships overcome, advanced degrees, employment, and leadership. The UH Law Center is also committed to diversity, and the UH System Board of Regents recognizes and endorses the benefits of diversity in the university setting. The Admissions Committee will consider the following additional factors: cultural history, ethnic origin, and race. These and other elements may be addressed in a personal statement of up to three pages, double-spaced.

APPLICANT PROFILE

University of Houston Law Center
This grid includes only applicants who earned 120–180 LSAT scores under standard administrations.

LSAT Score	GPA 3.75 +		3.50–3.74		3.25–3.49		3.00–3.24		2.75–2.99		2.50–2.74		Below 2.50		No GPA		Total	
	Apps	Adm	Apps	Adm	Apps	Adm	Apps	Adm	Apps	Adm	Apps	Adm	Apps	Adm	Apps	Adm	Apps	Adm
170–180	11	11	11	11	21	19	21	19	6	6	5	2	4	2	0	0	79	70
165–169	45	44	81	80	65	62	44	43	32	22	16	9	4	1	0	0	287	261
160–164	112	97	147	109	162	105	99	48	45	17	23	7	21	2	11	7	620	392
155–159	113	41	174	24	183	27	165	15	96	4	40	0	29	0	13	1	813	112
150–154	57	9	115	12	167	13	159	9	107	2	50	1	35	0	8	3	698	49
145–149	29	5	63	4	78	2	86	2	75	0	41	0	45	0	14	5	431	18
140–144	5	0	17	0	51	0	61	0	52	0	41	0	41	0	17	0	285	0
Below 140	4	0	8	0	17	0	25	0	30	0	26	0	27	0	7	0	144	0
Total	376	207	616	240	744	228	660	136	443	51	242	19	206	5	70	16	3357	902

Apps = Number of Applicants
Adm = Number Admitted
Reflects 100% of the total applicant pool; highest LSAT data reported.

HOWARD UNIVERSITY SCHOOL OF LAW

Office of Admissions, 2900 Van Ness Street NW
Washington, DC 20008
Phone: 202.806.8008/8009; Fax: 202.806.8162
E-mail: admissions@law.howard.edu; Website: www.law.howard.edu

ABA
Approved
Since
1931

AMERICAN BAR ASSOCIATION
Section of Legal Education
and Admissions to the Bar

The Basics

Type of school	Private
Term	Semester
Application deadline	3/15
Application fee	$60
Financial aid deadline	2/1
Can first year start other than fall?	No
Student to faculty ratio	18.7 to 1
# of housing spaces available restricted to law students	
graduate housing for which law students are eligible	15

Faculty and Administrators

	Total		Men		Women		Minorities	
	Spr	Fall	Spr	Fall	Spr	Fall	Spr	Fall
Full-time	19	21	12	13	7	8	15	16
Other full-time	3	4	1	2	2	2	2	2
Deans, librarians, & others who teach	7	8	3	3	4	5	7	8
Part-time	35	33	24	21	11	12	24	22
Total	64	66	40	39	24	27	48	48

Curriculum

	Full-Time	Part-Time
Typical first-year section size	50	0
Is there typically a "small section" of the first-year class, other than Legal Writing, taught by full-time faculty	No	No
If yes, typical size offered last year		

# of classroom course titles beyond first-year curriculum		131
# of upper division courses, excluding seminars, with an enrollment:	Under 25	78
	25–49	19
	50–74	12
	75–99	0
	100+	0
# of seminars		32
# of seminar positions available		481
# of seminar positions filled	474	0
# of positions available in simulation courses		223
# of simulation positions filled	223	0
# of positions available in faculty supervised clinical courses		146
# of faculty supervised clinical positions filled	123	0
# involved in field placements	66	0
# involved in law journals	45	0
# involved in moot court or trial competitions	53	0
# of credit hours required to graduate		88

JD Enrollment and Ethnicity

	Men		Women		Full-Time		Part-Time		1st-Year		Total		JD Degs. Awd.
	#	%	#	%	#	%	#	%	#	%	#	%	
All Hispanics	7	4.1	11	4.3	18	4.2	0	0.0	6	4.3	18	4.2	7
Am. Ind./AK Nat.	1	0.6	1	0.4	2	0.5	0	0.0	2	1.4	2	0.5	0
Asian	2	1.2	5	2.0	7	1.6	0	0.0	1	0.7	7	1.6	4
Black/Af. Am.	138	80.2	213	83.5	351	82.2	0	0.0	116	84.1	351	82.2	131
Nat. HI/Pac. Isl.	6	3.5	3	1.2	9	2.1	0	0.0	4	2.9	9	2.1	3
2 or more races	1	0.6	0	0.0	1	0.2	0	0.0	0	0.0	1	0.2	0
Subtotal (minor.)	155	90.1	233	91.4	388	90.9	0	0.0	129	93.5	388	90.9	145
Nonres. Alien	3	1.7	9	3.5	12	2.8	0	0.0	3	2.2	12	2.8	1
White/Cauc.	10	5.8	10	3.9	20	4.7	0	0.0	6	4.3	20	4.7	10
Unknown	4	2.3	3	1.2	7	1.6	0	0.0	0	0.0	7	1.6	1
Total	172	40.3	255	59.7	427	100.0	0	0.0	138	32.3	427		157

Transfers

Transfers in	1
Transfers out	7

Tuition and Fees

	Resident	Nonresident
Full-time	$29,131	$29,131
Part-time		
Tuition Guarantee Program	N	

Living Expenses

Estimated living expenses for singles

Living on campus	Living off campus	Living at home
N/A	$23,612	N/A

HOWARD UNIVERSITY SCHOOL OF LAW

ABA Approved Since 1931

GPA and LSAT Scores

	Total	Full-Time	Part-Time
# of apps	1,705	1,705	0
# of offers	464	464	0
# of matrics	137	137	0
75% GPA	3.39	3.39	0.00
Median GPA	3.13	3.13	0.00
25% GPA	2.92	2.92	0.00
75% LSAT	155	155	0
Median LSAT	153	153	0
25% LSAT	150	150	0

Grants and Scholarships (from prior year)

	Total #	Total %	Full-Time #	Full-Time %	Part-Time #	Part-Time %
Total # of students	473		473		0	
Total # receiving grants	208	44.0	208	44.0	0	0.0
Less than 1/2 tuition	53	11.2	53	11.2	0	0.0
Half to full tuition	118	24.9	118	24.9	0	0.0
Full tuition	5	1.1	5	1.1	0	0.0
More than full tuition	32	6.8	32	6.8	0	0.0
Median grant amount			$12,500		$0	

Informational and Library Resources

Total amount spent on library materials	$727,156
Study seating capacity inside the library	457
# of full-time equivalent professional librarians	12
Hours per week library is open	105
# of open, wired connections available to students	578
# of networked computers available for use by students	214
Has wireless network?	Y
Requires computer?	Y

JD Attrition (from prior year)

	Academic #	Other #	Total #	Total %
1st year	6	14	20	12.4
2nd year	1	5	6	3.9
3rd year	0	0	0	0.0
4th year	0	0	0	0.0

Employment (9 months after graduation)

For up-to-date employment data, go to employmentsummary.abaquestionnaire.org on the ABA website.

Bar Passage Rates

First-time takers	127	Reporting %	70.08
Average school %	68.54	Average state %	81.39
Average pass difference	−12.85		

Jurisdiction	Takers	Passers	Pass %	State %	Diff %
New York	41	30	73.17	84.92	−11.75
Maryland	27	20	74.07	79.96	−5.89
Virginia	9	5	55.56	78.15	−22.59
California	6	2	33.33	71.24	−37.91
Others (2)	6	4	66.67		

HOWARD UNIVERSITY SCHOOL OF LAW

Office of Admissions, 2900 Van Ness Street NW
Washington, DC 20008
Phone: 202.806.8008/8009; Fax: 202.806.8162
E-mail: admissions@law.howard.edu; Website: www.law.howard.edu

Introduction

Howard University, a coeducational, private institution in Washington, DC, was chartered by the US Congress in 1867. Howard is historically (and continues to be) a majority African American institution that offers an educational experience of exceptional quality and value to students with high academic potential. Particular emphasis is placed on providing educational opportunities for promising African Americans and other persons of color who are underrepresented in the legal profession, as well as for nonminority persons with a strong interest in civil and human rights and public service. The main campus of Howard is located in northwest Washington, DC, on Georgia Avenue, and the law school is located on a separate 22-acre campus on Van Ness Street NW, adjacent to Connecticut Avenue, approximately three miles from the main campus.

The School of Law opened its doors in 1869. Originally, there was a great need to train lawyers with a strong commitment to helping black Americans secure and protect their newly established rights. Today, as a national law school, Howard is dedicated to protecting the rights of all Americans and understands that its place in the annals of legal history demands that it maintains and exemplifies truth, equality, and excellence in the pursuit of justice. The law school has a diverse student body and faculty. Howard University School of Law is fully accredited by the American Bar Association and the Association of American Law Schools, and certifies its graduates for bar examination in all jurisdictions of the United States.

Special Programs

The School of Law has a strong commitment to public service and to human and civil rights. Many programs and activities of the school reflect that fact. The school also provides an opportunity for clinical experience in civil and criminal litigation. Howard law school also offers a summer study-abroad program in comparative and international law at the University of the Western Cape in South Africa. The six-week program is approved by the ABA and offers constitutional, business, and trade law courses for credit. A student-exchange program has been established with Vermont Law School, University of New Mexico School of Law, and Maine School of Law. Through the exchange program, a limited number of third-year JD students may spend a semester at one of these law schools to take advantage of curricular offerings that may be of specific interest to them. The Institute for Intellectual Property and Social Justice (IIPSJ) is concerned with disparity of access to, and exploitation of, intellectual property as it relates to racial and economic inequities. IIPSJ's focus is on examining and utilizing intellectual property to advance social justice in this country and globally. IIPSJ sponsors numerous programs for students, attorneys, and judges; publishes papers; and supports externships for students.

Curriculum

The curriculum leading to the first degree in law covers three academic years of two semesters each. During the first two years, emphasis is on the fundamental analytical concepts and skills of the law and the system by which it is administered—the functions required of a lawyer within a legal system based upon the common law. The curriculum in the third year provides diversified experiences, especially for students in the clinical programs. Students are encouraged to participate in one of the seven clinics or externships that are in nonprofits, governmental agencies, and other public interest settings.

Degree Programs

The School of Law offers programs leading to the Juris Doctor (JD), Master of Laws (LLM) for foreign law graduates, and Juris Doctor/Master of Business Administration (JD/MBA) degrees.

An applicant to the JD program must have a baccalaureate degree from an accredited college or university before enrolling in the Howard University School of Law. Competitive numerical predictors for admission to Howard University include a Law School Admission Test (LSAT) score of 153 and above and an undergraduate grade-point average (UGPA) of 3.4. In addition to the LSAT score and UGPA, we consider the rigor of an applicant's undergraduate course of study, letters of recommendation (particularly from faculty members who have taught the applicant), any graduate study, employment, extracurricular activities, and other indicators of potential for success in law school and excellence in the profession.

Applicants to the JD/MBA program must apply and meet the independent admission requirements of both schools, including completion of the GMAT.

The LLM program offers foreign law graduates an opportunity to further their legal studies through advanced study and research. To be admitted as a candidate for the LLM degree, applicants must be in high academic standing; have a degree in law from an accredited foreign university or its equivalent (as determined by the faculty of law); and have some experience in the judiciary, administrative establishment, bar, or law faculty.

Research Facilities

Howard University School of Law has a state-of-the-art, four-story, 76,000-square-foot law library. This facility provides space for a book collection of up to 215,000 volumes; seating for over 295 students (more than 70 percent of the student population), including 90 open carrels, with all locations wired for computer use; enlarged microfilm and audiovisual facilities; and distinctive rooms of wood and brick for special collections, newspaper and periodical reading, and the rare book collection.

The law library is both a working collection for law students and lawyers and a research institution for legal scholars. The civil rights archive contains briefs, working papers, and materials of the NAACP and other civil rights organizations. The library has a collection that emphasizes civil and political rights and literature to support study of the legal problems of the poor. Its collection has been expanded to also include considerable CD-ROM resources. The law library has an online catalog system, e-mail capabilities, and Internet access.

Student Activities

The *Howard Law Journal* publishes scholarly articles for academic and professional interest. The national, international, and trial advocacy moot court teams, which sponsor intramural competition and participate in competitions nationwide, have won numerous honors. The Student Bar Association is the general student governing organization. The *Barrister*, the student newspaper, publishes several issues a year. Other organizations represent students from diverse ethnic backgrounds, including African Americans, Latinos, Africans, Caribbean Islanders, and Asian Pacific Islanders.

Career Services

The Office of Career Services is an integral part of the law school. To assist students, the office offers workshops on job-search techniques and résumé writing, as well as seminars on career development and practice specialties. The office also maintains an extensive resource library with online employer research systems, newsletters, and updated listings of career opportunities. Each year, the Office of Career Services sponsors two on-campus interview programs, and more than 220 recruiters from law firms, government agencies, and corporations interview promising students and graduates for a broad array of employment opportunities. Approximately 1,670 interviews are scheduled annually. Graduates receive highly competitive and prestigious judicial clerkships and work for large, medium, and small private firms; federal, state, and local government agencies; public interest organizations; and public and private corporations throughout the United States.

APPLICANT PROFILE

Howard University School of Law
This grid includes only applicants who earned 120–180 LSAT scores under standard administrations.

LSAT Score	GPA																		
	3.75 +		3.50–3.74		3.25–3.49		3.00–3.24		2.75–2.99		2.50–2.74		2.25–2.49		2.00–2.24		Below 2.00		No GPA		Totals	
	Apps	Adm	Apps	Adm	Apps	Adm	Apps	Adm	Apps	Adm	Apps	Adm	Apps	Adm	Apps	Adm	Apps	Adm	Apps	Adm	Apps	Adm
175–180	0	0	0	0	0	0	0	0	0	0	0	0	0	0	0	0	0	0	0	0	0	0
170–174	1	1	1	1	0	0	1	1	0	0	0	0	1	0	0	0	0	0	0	0	4	3
165–169	0	0	2	2	1	1	2	1	2	1	3	2	0	0	0	0	0	0	0	0	10	7
160–164	2	2	12	11	16	11	11	6	9	6	10	4	7	3	2	0	0	0	0	0	69	43
155–159	18	15	25	20	51	38	46	32	32	24	23	13	10	0	2	1	1	0	3	2	211	145
150–154	25	16	56	38	109	61	96	49	81	27	44	8	30	0	4	0	7	0	5	0	457	199
145–149	26	12	79	24	104	10	131	11	85	1	61	0	31	0	13	0	4	0	12	1	546	59
140–144	15	2	38	0	54	0	77	1	62	0	57	0	37	0	16	0	5	0	7	1	368	4
135–139	8	0	9	0	10	0	26	0	33	0	21	0	11	0	4	0	5	0	4	0	131	0
130–134	0	0	4	0	3	0	9	0	9	0	10	0	7	0	3	0	0	0	0	0	45	0
125–129	0	0	0	0	0	0	2	0	0	0	5	0	0	0	1	0	1	0	0	0	9	0
120–124	0	0	0	0	0	0	0	0	0	0	0	0	0	0	1	0	0	0	0	0	1	0
Total	95	48	226	96	348	121	401	101	313	59	234	27	134	3	46	1	23	0	31	4	1851	460

Apps = Number of Applicants
Adm = Number Admitted
Reflects 99% of the total applicant pool; highest LSAT data reported.

UNIVERSITY OF IDAHO COLLEGE OF LAW

PO Box 442321
Moscow, ID 83844-2321
Phone: 208.885.2300; Fax: 208.885.5709
E-mail: lawadmit@uidaho.edu; Website: www.law.uidaho.edu

ABA
Approved
Since
1925

The Basics

Type of school	Public
Term	Semester
Application deadline	2/15
Application fee	$50
Financial aid deadline	3/15
Can first year start other than fall?	No
Student to faculty ratio	15.9 to 1
# of housing spaces available restricted to law students	
graduate housing for which law students are eligible	300

Faculty and Administrators

	Total		Men		Women		Minorities	
	Spr	Fall	Spr	Fall	Spr	Fall	Spr	Fall
Full-time	17	19	10	12	7	7	2	3
Other full-time	4	3	0	0	4	3	0	0
Deans, librarians, & others who teach	8	9	3	3	5	6	1	1
Part-time	21	19	11	11	10	8	0	0
Total	50	50	24	26	26	24	3	4

Curriculum

	Full-Time	Part-Time
Typical first-year section size	65	0
Is there typically a "small section" of the first-year class, other than Legal Writing, taught by full-time faculty	No	No
If yes, typical size offered last year		

# of classroom course titles beyond first-year curriculum		85
# of upper division courses, excluding seminars, with an enrollment:	Under 25	60
	25–49	14
	50–74	3
	75–99	3
	100+	3
# of seminars		17
# of seminar positions available		273
# of seminar positions filled	197	0
# of positions available in simulation courses		230
# of simulation positions filled	200	0
# of positions available in faculty supervised clinical courses		166
# of faculty supervised clinical positions filled	102	0
# involved in field placements	88	0
# involved in law journals	43	0
# involved in moot court or trial competitions	16	0
# of credit hours required to graduate		90

JD Enrollment and Ethnicity

	Men		Women		Full-Time		Part-Time		1st-Year		Total		JD Degs. Awd.
	#	%	#	%	#	%	#	%	#	%	#	%	
All Hispanics	12	5.6	12	8.5	24	6.7	0	0.0	5	3.9	24	6.7	5
Am. Ind./AK Nat.	2	0.9	5	3.5	7	2.0	0	0.0	4	3.1	7	2.0	1
Asian	5	2.3	2	1.4	7	2.0	0	0.0	2	1.6	7	2.0	3
Black/Af. Am.	1	0.5	0	0.0	1	0.3	0	0.0	1	0.8	1	0.3	1
Nat. HI/Pac. Isl.	1	0.5	0	0.0	1	0.3	0	0.0	1	0.8	1	0.3	1
2 or more races	8	3.7	1	0.7	9	2.5	0	0.0	3	2.3	9	2.5	3
Subtotal (minor.)	29	13.4	20	14.1	49	13.7	0	0.0	16	12.5	49	13.7	14
Nonres. Alien	1	0.5	2	1.4	3	0.8	0	0.0	1	0.8	3	0.8	0
White/Cauc.	176	81.5	115	81.0	291	81.3	0	0.0	109	85.2	291	81.3	87
Unknown	10	4.6	5	3.5	15	4.2	0	0.0	2	1.6	15	4.2	3
Total	216	60.3	142	39.7	358	100.0	0	0.0	128	35.8	358		104

Transfers

Transfers in	4
Transfers out	5

Tuition and Fees

	Resident	Nonresident
Full-time	$14,040	$26,560
Part-time		
Tuition Guarantee Program		N

Living Expenses

Estimated living expenses for singles

Living on campus	Living off campus	Living at home
$16,340	$16,340	$16,340

UNIVERSITY OF IDAHO COLLEGE OF LAW

ABA Approved Since 1925

GPA and LSAT Scores

	Total	Full-Time	Part-Time
# of apps	665	664	1
# of offers	372	371	1
# of matrics	130	130	0
75% GPA	3.57	3.57	0.00
Median GPA	3.25	3.25	3.67
25% GPA	2.87	2.87	0.00
75% LSAT	157	157	0
Median LSAT	154	154	159
25% LSAT	149	149	0

Grants and Scholarships (from prior year)

	Total #	Total %	Full-Time #	Full-Time %	Part-Time #	Part-Time %
Total # of students	349		349		0	
Total # receiving grants	120	34.4	115	33.0	5	0.0
Less than 1/2 tuition	95	27.2	93	26.6	2	0.0
Half to full tuition	18	5.2	16	4.6	2	0.0
Full tuition	6	1.7	6	1.7	0	0.0
More than full tuition	1	0.3	0	0.0	1	0.0
Median grant amount			$1,820		$0	

Informational and Library Resources

Total amount spent on library materials	$984,721
Study seating capacity inside the library	330
# of full-time equivalent professional librarians	5
Hours per week library is open	82
# of open, wired connections available to students	300
# of networked computers available for use by students	49
Has wireless network?	Y
Requires computer?	N

JD Attrition (from prior year)

	Academic #	Other #	Total #	Total %
1st year	3	6	9	6.9
2nd year	1	0	1	0.9
3rd year	0	0	0	0.0
4th year	0	0	0	0.0

Employment (9 months after graduation)

For up-to-date employment data, go to employmentsummary.abaquestionnaire.org on the ABA website.

Bar Passage Rates

First-time takers	85	Reporting %	100.00
Average school %	69.44	Average state %	79.94

Average pass difference –10.50

Jurisdiction	Takers	Passers	Pass %	State %	Diff %
Idaho	53	41	77.36	82.69	–5.33
Washington	22	8	36.36	71.22	–34.86
Utah	3	3	100.00	89.35	10.65
Alaska	1	1	100.00	80.55	19.45
Others (6)	6	6	100.00		

UNIVERSITY OF IDAHO COLLEGE OF LAW

PO Box 442321
Moscow, ID 83844-2321
Phone: 208.885.2300; Fax: 208.885.5709
E-mail: lawadmit@uidaho.edu; Website: www.law.uidaho.edu

Introduction

The College of Law, established in 1909, has been a member of the AALS since 1914 and has been accredited by the ABA since 1925. As Idaho's leader in legal education, the College of Law emphasizes quality over quantity and is founded on collegiality and a dedication to the highest ideals of a noble profession.

College of Law students benefit from an attentive, dedicated, and accessible faculty as well as the unique opportunity to combine residential university community and metropolitan living and learning. The primary location of the College of Law is the Menard Law Building on the main campus of the University of Idaho in Moscow, Idaho. However, through the Semester in Practice and Third Year in Boise programs, third-year students may elect to engage in classroom and experiential learning in Boise, Idaho, one of America's fastest growing metropolitan areas.

Enrollment/Student Body

With an overall enrollment around 350, students at the College of Law have a wide variety of backgrounds and life experiences. Students come mostly from the West, representing almost 100 colleges and universities, 24 different states, and several foreign countries. Approximately 60 percent of our students are Idaho residents. The College of Law welcomes and actively seeks diversity, with particular attention to students of color and those who have overcome socioeconomic disadvantage. Due to our highly selective admission process and positive learning environment, including an academic support program run by a licensed attorney, academic attrition is less than 3 percent.

Technology, Library, and Physical Facilities

The College of Law occupies a building with full wireless Internet access and a newly renovated, state-of-the-art courtroom. The law library houses a collection of more than 240,000 volumes and volume-equivalents and more than 4,800 serial titles. The law library also provides a computer lab; LexisNexis, Westlaw, Dialog, and HeinOnline services; and the US Congressional Serial Set. Membership in the Western Library Network and the Inland Northwest Library Automation Network allows users to access holdings of libraries across the nation. Law students also have access to the other libraries of the University of Idaho and those at Washington State University, located 8 miles away in Pullman, Washington.

Curriculum

All first-year students are required to take courses in Legal Research and Writing, Contracts, Criminal Law, Torts, Statutory Reading and Interpretation, Property, Civil Procedure and Introduction to Law, and Constitutional Law. After the first year, students must take Professional Responsibility and Constitutional Law II. Afterward, they may choose to pursue an area of emphasis. The College of Law provides emphases in natural resources and environmental law, business law and entrepreneurship, advocacy and dispute resolution, and Native American law.

Practical Skills

The College of Law places great importance on public service and the development of practical skills. Our distinctive Pro Bono Program, which requires all students to complete at least 40 hours of approved pro bono service before graduation, engages students in substantial, law-related public service and provides a learning experience outside the classroom.

There are eight live-client clinics available at the College of Law: (1) general practice clinic, (2) appellate clinic, (3) immigration clinic, (4) small business legal clinic, (5) tax clinic, (6) domestic violence and sexual assault clinic, (7) economic development clinic, and (8) mediation clinic.

Students may also sharpen their practical skills by participating in our externship program, completing a semester in practice, and/or participating in a wide variety of faculty- and lawyer-supervised skills competitions.

Dual Degrees

Dual JD/MS/PhD degrees in water resources are offered as part of the one-of-a-kind Waters of the West initiative offered in cooperation with the University of Idaho College of Natural Resources. There are three options for emphasis: engineering and science, science and management, and law, management, and policy.

Dual JD/MS Environmental Science degrees are available in cooperation with the University of Idaho College of Graduate Studies Environmental Science Program.

Dual JD/MS degrees are offered in Bioregional Planning and Community Design.

Dual JD/Master of Accounting degrees in cooperation with the University of Idaho College of Business and Economics and dual JD/Master of Accounting, Taxation Emphasis degrees in cooperation with Boise State University are also available. These programs are particularly valuable for students interested in practicing tax law.

Admission

Applications are accepted beginning in October preceding the year in which enrollment is desired. Our law program is full time. Although students have the option of spending all or part of their third year in Boise, Idaho, students must spend their first and second years in Moscow, Idaho. Applicants must submit college transcripts and letters of recommendation through LSAC's Credential Assembly Service (CAS). The application priority deadline is February 15, but we recommend late-fall application. Applications submitted after February 15 will be reviewed, but timely applications will receive priority consideration. The Admission Committee looks at each applicant holistically, including, but not limited to, LSAT score, academic record and background, writing ability, personal statement, work and life experiences, and recommendations.

Student Activities

Students belong to more than 30 active student organizations. The Student Bar Association represents student interests, both educational and social. The *Idaho Law Review*, which covers topics ranging from state and regional problems to national and international issues, and *The Crit* (an electronic journal of critical legal studies), give students valuable writing and editing experience. The Board of Student Advocates and the Law Students for Appropriate Dispute Resolution coordinate intramural competitions and provide opportunities for students to participate in national competitions that build professional skills. Other groups include the American Civil Liberties Union, Latino Law Caucus, Federalist Society, Multicultural Law Caucus, Native American Law Students Association, OUTLaw, J. Reuben Clark Law Society, and the Women's Law Caucus.

Career Development

The Career Development Office, run by a licensed attorney, facilitates students' career planning and their search for summer and permanent employment. The office actively promotes job opportunities, including arranging on-campus interview and recruit-by-mail programs. Historically, over 90 percent of graduates find employment within nine months of graduation or go on to advanced graduate study. The college has exceptional success placing students in federal and state judicial clerkships as the first step in their careers. A majority of students find employment in Idaho, although Utah, Washington, and Oregon are also popular. Idaho graduates are employed throughout the United States and several foreign countries.

APPLICANT PROFILE

University of Idaho College of Law
This grid includes only applicants who earned 120–180 LSAT scores under standard administrations.

LSAT Score	3.75 +		3.50–3.74		3.25–3.49		3.00–3.24		2.75–2.99		2.50–2.74		2.25–2.49		2.00–2.24		Below 2.00		No GPA		Total	
	Apps	Adm	Apps	Adm	Apps	Adm	Apps	Adm	Apps	Adm	Apps	Adm	Apps	Adm	Apps	Adm	Apps	Adm	Apps	Adm	Apps	Adm
175–180	0	0	0	0	0	0	0	0	0	0	0	0	0	0	0	0	0	0	0	0	0	0
170–174	0	0	1	1	0	0	0	0	1	1	0	0	0	0	0	0	0	0	0	0	2	2
165–169	7	7	5	5	2	2	0	0	0	0	0	0	2	2	0	0	0	0	2	2	18	18
160–164	10	10	14	14	14	13	6	6	4	3	6	6	4	3	1	1	0	0	0	0	59	56
155–159	20	20	32	31	33	33	34	34	19	18	12	8	7	6	5	5	0	0	3	3	165	158
150–154	16	12	32	24	42	23	40	16	44	16	16	6	11	3	3	1	1	0	3	2	208	103
145–149	8	3	18	6	33	7	26	5	12	2	9	1	8	0	1	0	1	0	3	0	119	24
140–144	3	0	10	2	9	1	10	2	12	2	6	0	5	0	2	1	0	0	2	0	59	8
135–139	1	0	3	1	6	0	3	1	2	0	2	0	2	0	0	0	0	0	0	0	19	2
130–134	0	0	0	0	1	0	1	0	1	0	2	0	0	0	0	0	0	0	1	0	6	0
125–129	0	0	0	0	0	0	0	0	0	0	0	0	0	0	2	0	0	0	1	0	3	0
120–124	0	0	0	0	0	0	0	0	0	0	0	0	0	0	0	0	0	0	0	0	0	0
Total	65	52	115	84	140	79	120	64	95	42	53	21	39	14	14	8	2	0	15	7	658	371

Apps = Number of Applicants
Adm = Number Admitted
Reflects 99% of the total applicant pool; highest LSAT data reported.

UNIVERSITY OF ILLINOIS COLLEGE OF LAW

504 East Pennsylvania Avenue
Champaign, IL 61820
Phone: 217.244.6415
E-mail: admissions@law.illinois.edu; Website: www.law.illinois.edu

The Basics

Type of school	Public
Term	Semester
Application deadline	3/15
Application fee	$0
Financial aid deadline	3/15
Can first year start other than fall?	No
Student to faculty ratio	12.6 to 1
# of housing spaces available restricted to law students	
graduate housing for which law students are eligible	639

Faculty and Administrators

	Total		Men		Women		Minorities	
	Spr	Fall	Spr	Fall	Spr	Fall	Spr	Fall
Full-time	41	43	25	26	16	17	9	9
Other full-time	9	8	3	2	6	6	1	1
Deans, librarians, & others who teach	11	12	5	7	6	5	1	2
Part-time	53	53	41	39	12	14	5	5
Total	114	116	74	74	40	42	16	17

Curriculum

	Full-Time	Part-Time
Typical first-year section size	56	0
Is there typically a "small section" of the first-year class, other than Legal Writing, taught by full-time faculty	Yes	No
If yes, typical size offered last year	38	
# of classroom course titles beyond first-year curriculum	141	

# of upper division courses, excluding seminars, with an enrollment:		
	Under 25	125
	25–49	36
	50–74	14
	75–99	3
	100+	4

# of seminars	46	
# of seminar positions available	858	
# of seminar positions filled	561	0
# of positions available in simulation courses	1,264	
# of simulation positions filled	1,139	0
# of positions available in faculty supervised clinical courses	114	
# of faculty supervised clinical positions filled	111	0
# involved in field placements	233	0
# involved in law journals	174	0
# involved in moot court or trial competitions	66	0
# of credit hours required to graduate	90	

JD Enrollment and Ethnicity

	Men		Women		Full-Time		Part-Time		1st-Year		Total		JD Degs. Awd.
	#	%	#	%	#	%	#	%	#	%	#	%	
All Hispanics	23	6.2	22	8.2	45	7.0	0	0.0	23	12.5	45	7.0	14
Am. Ind./AK Nat.	1	0.3	2	0.7	3	0.5	0	0.0	0	0.0	3	0.5	3
Asian	37	9.9	27	10.1	64	10.0	0	0.0	14	7.6	64	10.0	12
Black/Af. Am.	18	4.8	30	11.2	48	7.5	0	0.0	22	12.0	48	7.5	20
Nat. HI/Pac. Isl.	0	0.0	0	0.0	0	0.0	0	0.0	0	0.0	0	0.0	0
2 or more races	14	3.8	8	3.0	22	3.4	0	0.0	15	8.2	22	3.4	0
Subtotal (minor.)	93	25.0	89	33.3	182	28.5	0	0.0	74	40.2	182	28.5	49
Nonres. Alien	11	3.0	13	4.9	24	3.8	0	0.0	9	4.9	24	3.8	9
White/Cauc.	246	66.1	148	55.4	394	61.7	0	0.0	92	50.0	394	61.7	112
Unknown	22	5.9	17	6.4	39	6.1	0	0.0	9	4.9	39	6.1	20
Total	372	58.2	267	41.8	639	100.0	0	0.0	184	28.8	639		190

Transfers

Transfers in	16
Transfers out	6

Tuition and Fees

	Resident	Nonresident
Full-time	$38,567	$45,567
Part-time		
Tuition Guarantee Program		N

Living Expenses

Estimated living expenses for singles

Living on campus	Living off campus	Living at home
$16,618	$16,618	$16,618

UNIVERSITY OF ILLINOIS COLLEGE OF LAW

ABA Approved Since 1923

GPA and LSAT Scores

	Total	Full-Time	Part-Time
# of apps	4,219	4,219	0
# of offers	853	853	0
# of matrics	184	184	0
75% GPA	3.85	3.85	0.00
Median GPA	3.70	3.70	0.00
25% GPA	3.38	3.38	0.00
75% LSAT	168	168	0
Median LSAT	163	163	0
25% LSAT	156	156	0

Grants and Scholarships (from prior year)

	Total #	Total %	Full-Time #	Full-Time %	Part-Time #	Part-Time %
Total # of students	640		640		0	
Total # receiving grants	636	99.4	636	99.4	0	0.0
Less than 1/2 tuition	369	57.7	369	57.7	0	0.0
Half to full tuition	236	36.9	236	36.9	0	0.0
Full tuition	0	0.0	0	0.0	0	0.0
More than full tuition	31	4.8	31	4.8	0	0.0
Median grant amount			$19,542		$0	

Informational and Library Resources

Total amount spent on library materials	$1,409,645
Study seating capacity inside the library	387
# of full-time equivalent professional librarians	9
Hours per week library is open	102
# of open, wired connections available to students	824
# of networked computers available for use by students	39
Has wireless network?	Y
Requires computer?	N

JD Attrition (from prior year)

	Academic #	Other #	Total #	Total %
1st year	0	10	10	4.4
2nd year	0	3	3	1.4
3rd year	0	1	1	0.5
4th year	0	0	0	0.0

Employment (9 months after graduation)

For up-to-date employment data, go to employmentsummary.abaquestionnaire.org on the ABA website.

Bar Passage Rates

First-time takers	184	Reporting %	81.52
Average school %	92.67	Average state %	89.38
Average pass difference	3.29		

Jurisdiction	Takers	Passers	Pass %	State %	Diff %
Illinois	150	139	92.67	89.38	3.29

UNIVERSITY OF ILLINOIS COLLEGE OF LAW

504 East Pennsylvania Avenue
Champaign, IL 61820
Phone: 217.244.6415
E-mail: admissions@law.illinois.edu; Website: www.law.illinois.edu

Introduction

Established in 1897, the University of Illinois College of Law is consistently regarded as one of the nation's top public law schools. An American Bar Association-approved law school since 1923, a charter member of the Association of American Law Schools, and the home of the founding chapter of the law honor society now known as the Order of the Coif, Illinois Law is a leader in interdisciplinary legal education.

The University of Illinois has earned a reputation of international stature. Its distinguished faculty, outstanding resources, breadth of academic programs and research disciplines, and large, diverse student body constitute an educational community ideally suited for scholarship and research. Since its founding in 1867, the University of Illinois has been committed to excellence in research, teaching, and public engagement.

Specialty Programs

The Program in Business Law and Policy highlights various areas of the college's expertise, including empirical work, law and economics, unincorporated and closely held firms, securities markets, entrepreneurship, the role of social norms, and corporate social responsibility.

The Program in Comparative Labor and Employment Law and Policy explores matters of comparative and transnational law, including comparative constitutional law, comparative criminal procedure, and comparative labor and employment law.

The Program in Constitutional Theory, History, and Law fosters scholarship, discussion, and debate on subjects relating to constitutional interpretation and history through workshops, lectures, and conferences.

The Program in Criminal Law and Procedure builds on a century-long tradition of criminal law and procedure at Illinois, promoting scholarship and discussion, funding conferences and other programs, and promoting teaching and service related to criminal law.

The Program in Health Law and Policy promotes cutting-edge research, policy analysis, and public service on critical issues in health care and facilitates collaboration among government leaders, practitioners, and academic researchers on issues of increasing complexity.

The Program in Intellectual Property and Technology Law fosters scholarship and analysis at the intersection of law, supercomputing, agricultural biotechnology, information science, engineering, and numerous other areas.

The Program in Law, Behavior, and Social Science promotes interdisciplinary research and teaching at the intersection of law and the social sciences, sponsoring a working-paper series, faculty workshops, and internal faculty seminars on cutting-edge books and scholarship.

The Law and Philosophy Program advances knowledge on legal topics of philosophical significance, particularly those that implicate moral and political issues.

The Legal History Program seeks to further knowledge and appreciation of legal history, with a particular emphasis on American, British, and comparative legal-historical scholarship.

Clinics and Field Placements

The College of Law offers six in-house clinics and seven field placement programs (including externships) where students have the opportunity to work with and solve problems for real clients. The clinics and field placements provide opportunities for students to experience law practice in a supportive, reflective setting that is focused on their learning. Students experiment with different styles of lawyering and explore a variety of legal work that may assist them in choosing a career path.

Joint-Degree Programs

The College of Law administers 12 formal joint JD and master's or doctoral degree programs. The combined degrees available are JD-MBA; JD-MS in Chemistry; JD-MCS; JD-MHRIR; JD-MS in Journalism; JD-MD; JD-MS in Natural Resources and Environmental Sciences; JD-PhD in Philosophy; JD-PhD or JD-MA in Political Science; JD-MUP; and JD-DVM.

Student Activities

The small size and tight-knit community of Illinois Law allow students to directly participate in an extensive variety of activities. Students run and write for the college's journals: the *University of Illinois Law Review*; *Elder Law Journal*; *University of Illinois Journal of Law, Technology, and Policy*; and *Illinois Law Update*. In addition, students may participate in moot court competitions, which feature internal, external, and national contests; live-client legal clinics; negotiation and client counseling competitions; and faculty-student committees.

Most students participate in at least one of the almost 40 student organizations. These organizations plan countless lectures, debates, charitable activities, sporting events, law firm visits, and social receptions.

Library and Physical Facilities

A hallmark of a great university and a great law school is its library. The University Library has one of the largest public university collections in the world. The Albert E. Jenner, Jr. Memorial Law Library offers students top-notch legal academic resources. Our reference librarians are experts in legal research, with graduate degrees in law and in information science. And the library's various seating areas provide comfortable space for research and scholarship, offering a variety of options for both quiet and group study. Wireless access to the Internet is available to the law school community.

Directly across the street from the law school is one of the country's largest athletic recreation centers, with indoor and outdoor swimming pools, tennis courts, four gyms, weight and exercise equipment, archery, and ball courts of all kinds. The facility is free for students.

Scholarships

The College of Law awards a number of scholarships, ranging from $1,000 to full tuition, based upon previous academic success, promise in the study of law, and other relevant factors. Once awarded, the scholarship is guaranteed to remain in effect provided the student remains enrolled as a full-time student at the College of Law. There are no minimum grade point average or other academic performance requirements for continuation of a scholarship.

Champaign-Urbana Community

A micro-urban community known for its big-city amenities yet small-town accessibility, safety, and friendliness, Champaign-Urbana is a vibrant and affordable college town with a lively cultural scene, a variety of restaurants, and numerous recreational opportunities. Public transportation via the Champaign-Urbana mass transit system is free for all University of Illinois students.

Champaign-Urbana was named one of the world's 10 "Hot New Tech Cities" by *Newsweek* magazine and boasts an assortment of restaurants, shopping, coffee houses, nightlife (including plenty of clubs and live music venues), movie theaters, athletic facilities, museums, galleries, and bookstores. Weekend getaways to Chicago, St. Louis, and Indianapolis are within a three-hour interstate drive, and Chicago is also easily reached by train, bus, or plane.

An average rental cost for a one-bedroom apartment is $600, and the average for a two-bedroom apartment is $700. The median home price is $125,000. The majority of College of Law students live in off-campus housing; however, the University of Illinois has a limited number of graduate and family housing units available.

APPLICANT PROFILE

Our admission process takes into consideration many factors beyond the undergraduate GPA and the LSAT score. A statistical grid, as is typically provided here, only takes into consideration these two factors. Admission decisions at the University of Illinois College of Law are based on the

Admission Committee's experienced judgment applied to individual cases. Consequently, we have chosen not to provide applicants with a grid that does not accurately portray our admission process.

INDIANA UNIVERSITY MAURER SCHOOL OF LAW—BLOOMINGTON

211 S. Indiana Avenue
Bloomington, IN 47405-7001
Phone: 812.855.4765; Fax: 812.855.1967
E-mail: lawadmis@indiana.edu; Website: www.law.indiana.edu

ABA
Approved
Since
1937

The Basics

Type of school	Public
Term	Semester
Application deadline	3/1
Application fee	$50
Financial aid deadline	3/10
Can first year start other than fall?	No
Student to faculty ratio	10.3 to 1
# of housing spaces available restricted to law students graduate housing for which law students are eligible	800

Faculty and Administrators

	Total		Men		Women		Minorities	
	Spr	Fall	Spr	Fall	Spr	Fall	Spr	Fall
Full-time	52	55	32	38	20	17	8	6
Other full-time	4	1	3	0	1	1	0	0
Deans, librarians, & others who teach	17	16	9	9	8	7	0	0
Part-time	20	16	15	13	5	3	0	0
Total	93	88	59	60	34	28	8	6

Curriculum

	Full-Time	Part-Time
Typical first-year section size	78	0
Is there typically a "small section" of the first-year class, other than Legal Writing, taught by full-time faculty	No	
If yes, typical size offered last year		
# of classroom course titles beyond first-year curriculum	110	

# of upper division courses, excluding seminars, with an enrollment:		
	Under 25	69
	25–49	31
	50–74	6
	75–99	6
	100+	3

# of seminars	19	
# of seminar positions available	357	
# of seminar positions filled	303	0
# of positions available in simulation courses	650	
# of simulation positions filled	398	0
# of positions available in faculty supervised clinical courses	98	
# of faculty supervised clinical positions filled	91	0
# involved in field placements	279	0
# involved in law journals	162	0
# involved in moot court or trial competitions	57	0
# of credit hours required to graduate	88	

JD Enrollment and Ethnicity

	Men		Women		Full-Time		Part-Time		1st-Year		Total		JD Degs. Awd.
	#	%	#	%	#	%	#	%	#	%	#	%	
All Hispanics	15	3.4	19	7.4	34	4.9	0	0.0	13	5.4	34	4.9	7
Am. Ind./AK Nat.	5	1.1	2	0.8	7	1.0	0	0.0	1	0.4	7	1.0	2
Asian	16	3.7	16	6.2	32	4.6	0	0.0	18	7.5	32	4.6	14
Black/Af. Am.	26	6.0	18	7.0	44	6.4	0	0.0	13	5.4	44	6.4	19
Nat. Hl/Pac. Isl.	0	0.0	0	0.0	0	0.0	0	0.0	0	0.0	0	0.0	0
2 or more races	0	0.0	0	0.0	0	0.0	0	0.0	0	0.0	0	0.0	0
Subtotal (minor.)	62	14.3	55	21.4	117	16.9	0	0.0	45	18.7	117	16.9	42
Nonres. Alien	0	0.0	0	0.0	0	0.0	0	0.0	0	0.0	0	0.0	0
White/Cauc.	349	80.2	194	75.5	543	78.5	0	0.0	181	75.1	543	78.5	154
Unknown	24	5.5	8	3.1	32	4.6	0	0.0	15	6.2	32	4.6	1
Total	435	62.9	257	37.1	692	100.0	0	0.0	241	34.8	692		197

Transfers

Transfers in	0
Transfers out	9

Tuition and Fees

	Resident	Nonresident
Full-time	$28,130	$45,602
Part-time		
Tuition Guarantee Program	N	

Living Expenses

Estimated living expenses for singles

Living on campus	Living off campus	Living at home
$22,882	$22,882	$22,882

INDIANA UNIVERSITY MAURER SCHOOL OF LAW—BLOOMINGTON

ABA Approved Since 1937

GPA and LSAT Scores

	Total	Full-Time	Part-Time
# of apps	2,751	2,751	0
# of offers	925	925	0
# of matrics	240	240	0
75% GPA	3.89	3.89	0.00
Median GPA	3.75	3.75	0.00
25% GPA	3.38	3.38	0.00
75% LSAT	167	167	0
Median LSAT	166	166	0
25% LSAT	158	158	0

Grants and Scholarships (from prior year)

	Total #	Total %	Full-Time #	Full-Time %	Part-Time #	Part-Time %
Total # of students	646		646		0	
Total # receiving grants	608	94.1	608	94.1	0	0.0
Less than 1/2 tuition	339	52.5	339	52.5	0	0.0
Half to full tuition	104	16.1	104	16.1	0	0.0
Full tuition	67	10.4	67	10.4	0	0.0
More than full tuition	98	15.2	98	15.2	0	0.0
Median grant amount			$15,883		$0	

Informational and Library Resources

Total amount spent on library materials	$1,645,119
Study seating capacity inside the library	670
# of full-time equivalent professional librarians	10
Hours per week library is open	115
# of open, wired connections available to students	147
# of networked computers available for use by students	82
Has wireless network?	Y
Requires computer?	Y

JD Attrition (from prior year)

	Academic #	Other #	Total #	Total %
1st year	0	8	8	3.3
2nd year	0	9	9	4.3
3rd year	0	0	0	0.0
4th year	0	0	0	0.0

Employment (9 months after graduation)

For up-to-date employment data, go to employmentsummary.abaquestionnaire.org on the ABA website.

Bar Passage Rates

First-time takers	202	Reporting %	72.77
Average school %	82.99	Average state %	83.53

Average pass difference –0.54

Jurisdiction	Takers	Passers	Pass %	State %	Diff %
Indiana	89	75	84.27	80.93	3.34
Illinois	34	30	88.24	89.38	–1.14
New York	24	17	70.83	84.92	–14.09

INDIANA UNIVERSITY MAURER SCHOOL OF LAW—BLOOMINGTON

211 S. Indiana Avenue
Bloomington, IN 47405-7001
Phone: 812.855.4765; Fax: 812.855.1967
E-mail: lawadmis@indiana.edu; Website: www.law.indiana.edu

Introduction

The Indiana University Maurer School of Law—Bloomington provides the highest quality legal education in a relaxed, collegial setting. Founded in 1842, the law school is located on the beautifully wooded campus of one of the nation's largest teaching and research universities. The presence of the university, including the world-famous Jacobs School of Music, offers students cultural opportunities available in few urban areas, while retaining the advantages of a small university town. With a student body of fewer than 675 students, drawn from more than 200 undergraduate schools in the United States and abroad, the law school is small enough to retain its distinctive sense of community and collegiality, while large enough to facilitate a stimulating, cosmopolitan environment. The school is a charter member of the Association of American Law Schools (AALS) and is approved by the American Bar Association (ABA).

Library and Physical Facilities

With nearly 450,000 bound volumes, over 1.6 million microfilm pieces, and more than 34,000 electronic titles, the law library is one of the premier law libraries in the United States, the largest in the state of Indiana, and was named one of the top law school libraries in the nation by a national law school magazine. Law-trained librarians give instruction in research techniques and provide reference assistance. While continuing its commitment to a high-quality print collection, the library is a national leader in computer applications in legal education. Through Internet access (from the School of Law or their homes), students can utilize systems specific to law, such as LexisNexis and Westlaw, or access the rapidly expanding array of global information sources. All students are required to possess a laptop computer. Students may write their examinations using their laptops, but are not required to do so. The law school building features wireless access throughout, laptop-ready classrooms, and an outstanding law library where students can enjoy spectacular views of the wooded campus as they study. Recent renovations added three new classrooms to the second floor, new technology and seating in all classrooms, and several faculty offices. Across the street, a brand-new professional skills building houses additional classrooms and clinical space, including offices, student workspace, interview rooms, and more.

Curriculum

Indiana Law has an innovative course on the legal profession. In the four-credit, first-year, spring course, students explore the economic and sociolegal structure and substance of the modern legal profession through in-depth ethnographic studies of—among others—solo and large firm practice, in-house counsel, government agencies, judges, and public interest practice. With this integrated first-year foundation as a guide, decisions regarding areas of study and career goals become more meaningful. Upper-level courses support a formative education that develops skills alongside traditional scholarship, culminating in a meaningful capstone course.

The school also offers traditional specialized courses, such as intellectual property, communications and Internet law, law and biomedical advances, immigration law, international business transactions, and environmental law. The school offers intensive training in litigation and dispute resolution. Students may participate in clinics that enable them to deal with client problems and, in some cases, represent clients in local courts, all under close faculty supervision.

Joint-Degree Programs

Formal joint-degree programs combine the award of a JD degree with a master's degree in business, accounting, public affairs, environmental science, journalism, telecommunications, or library science. The duration of most joint-degree programs is four years. However, the School of Law and the Kelley School of Business have recently established an intensive three-year JD/MBA program. Informal concurrent-degree programs with other disciplines (pursuing a JD and a master's or doctoral degree) are frequently designed to meet students' learning and career goals.

Opportunities to Study Abroad

The School of Law provides students with a wide variety of opportunities to study abroad. A limited number of second- and third-year students can take advantage of the unique opportunity to study in and immerse themselves in the legal education system and culture of another country. Semester-long opportunities are available through exchange programs with Université Panthéon-Assas (Paris II), France; ESADE Law School in Barcelona, Spain; Bucerius Law School in Hamburg, Germany; China University of Political Science and Law in Beijing (CUPL); Friedrich-Schiller University of Jena, Germany; University of Warsaw in Warsaw, Poland; the University of Auckland in Auckland, New Zealand; University of Hong Kong, Hong Kong; Zhejiang University in Hangzhou, China; and Peking University School of Transnational Law in Shenzhen, China. All classes, with the exception of those taken at Bucerius, Hong Kong, Auckland, and Zhejiang, are taught in the school's respective native language. Finally, the law school offers all students the opportunity to participate in summer study-abroad programs hosted by the Institute on International and Comparative Law in England, France, Italy, and Spain. All courses are taught in English.

Summer-Start Program

A summer-start program is offered for students who wish to begin their legal studies in the summer session. This program allows students to take one four-credit class in the summer in a small, intimate environment as they make the transition into the law school.

Admission

Generally, the quality and size of the applicant pool forces the Admissions Committee to rely heavily on the undergraduate grade-point average and the LSAT score. However, numerical indicators are not the only considerations used in evaluating applications. The committee considers the quality of the applicant's undergraduate institution, level and rigor of coursework, letters of recommendation (particularly those from faculty), graduate work, employment during and after college, extracurricular activities, potential for service to the profession, educational/geographic/socioeconomic diversity, and personal statement. Applicants are encouraged to explain matters that may have adversely affected their undergraduate performance. Applicants who feel they have been disadvantaged because of economic, educational, racial, or cultural factors are urged to bring this to the attention of the Admissions Committee.

Housing

The Bloomington area offers a variety of housing options for students. There are numerous apartments and houses available as off-campus rentals as well as on-campus housing. Information regarding off-campus housing options is provided to admitted students throughout the spring and summer.

Student Activities

A variety of student organizations present opportunities for involvement in groups focused on specialized areas of the law and public service. Some of the most active groups include the Black Law Student Association, Women's Law Caucus, Public Interest Law Foundation, Latino Law Student Association, and the Environmental Law Society. Students may also obtain practical experience through a number of clinical opportunities, including the Community Legal Clinic;

Conservation Law Clinic; Criminal Law Externship; Disability Law Clinic; Elmore Entrepreneurship Law Clinic; Viola J. Taliaferro Children and Mediation Clinic; Inmate Legal Assistance Project; Tenant Assistance Project; Public Interest Internship Program; Federal Courts Clinic; Immigration Law Practicum; Indiana Legal Services Externship; Intellectual Property Practicum; Student Legal Services Externship, Washington, DC; Public Interest Program; and the Protective Order Project. Second- and third-year students are offered the opportunity to gain valuable writing, editing, and advocacy skills through participation in the moot court competition or on one of our three journals. The *Indiana Law Journal* publishes articles by legal scholars, practitioners, jurists, and Indiana University law students. The *Federal Communications Law Journal* is the nation's oldest and largest-circulation communications law journal. The *Indiana Journal of Global Legal Studies* is a multidisciplinary journal that specializes in international and comparative law articles.

Career Placement

The Office of Career and Professional Development actively provides career planning and employment assistance to law students and alumni. Both on- and off-campus interviews are coordinated to facilitate contact between students and employers. In recent years, more than 96 percent of graduates have secured employment within nine months of graduation. More than half are located outside the state of Indiana. Graduates are found in all 50 states and in 31 foreign countries.

APPLICANT PROFILE

Indiana University Maurer School of Law—Bloomington
This grid includes only applicants who earned 120–180 LSAT scores under standard administrations.

LSAT Score	3.75 +		3.50–3.74		3.25–3.49		3.00–3.24		2.75–2.99		2.50–2.74		Below 2.50		No GPA		Total	
	Apps	Adm	Apps	Adm	Apps	Adm	Apps	Adm	Apps	Adm	Apps	Adm	Apps	Adm	Apps	Adm	Apps	Adm
175–180	5	5	4	2	7	6	7	2	3	3	4	3	3	0	0	0	33	21
170–174	46	41	46	31	31	26	24	15	13	7	10	4	3	1	3	1	176	126
165–169	179	166	172	106	131	73	82	45	54	31	22	10	17	8	13	4	670	443
160–164	197	110	154	7	115	8	87	2	24	0	16	0	9	0	34	0	636	127
155–159	151	114	156	5	151	4	84	1	38	0	12	0	4	0	22	1	618	125
150–154	57	45	81	5	92	2	83	2	28	0	13	1	7	0	12	1	373	56
145–149	17	13	24	0	23	0	22	0	16	0	10	0	10	0	6	0	128	13
140–144	1	1	9	1	10	0	7	0	7	0	6	0	10	0	3	0	53	2
Below 140	1	1	0	0	4	0	1	0	9	0	9	0	6	0	1	0	31	1
Total	654	496	646	157	564	119	397	67	192	41	102	18	69	9	94	7	2718	914

Apps = Number of Applicants
Adm = Number Admitted
Reflects 99% of the total applicant pool; highest LSAT data reported.

INDIANA UNIVERSITY ROBERT H. MCKINNEY SCHOOL OF LAW

530 West New York Street
Indianapolis, IN 46202-3225
Phone: 317.274.2459; Fax: 317.278.4780
E-mail: lawadmit@iupui.edu; Website: indylaw.indiana.edu

ABA
Approved
Since
1944

The Basics

Type of school	Public
Term	Semester
Application deadline	11/15 3/1
Application fee	$50
Financial aid deadline	3/10
Can first year start other than fall?	No
Student to faculty ratio	16.8 to 1
# of housing spaces available restricted to law students	
graduate housing for which law students are eligible	288

Faculty and Administrators

	Total		Men		Women		Minorities	
	Spr	Fall	Spr	Fall	Spr	Fall	Spr	Fall
Full-time	38	42	21	24	17	18	6	6
Other full-time	3	2	3	2	0	0	0	0
Deans, librarians, & others who teach	14	14	7	7	7	7	2	2
Part-time	48	38	30	26	18	12	2	3
Total	103	96	61	59	42	37	10	11

Curriculum

	Full-Time	Part-Time
Typical first-year section size	92	98
Is there typically a "small section" of the first-year class, other than Legal Writing, taught by full-time faculty	No	No
If yes, typical size offered last year		
# of classroom course titles beyond first-year curriculum	122	

# of upper division courses, excluding seminars, with an enrollment:		
Under 25	105	
25–49	49	
50–74	25	
75–99	12	
100+	4	

# of seminars	11	
# of seminar positions available	205	
# of seminar positions filled	135	32
# of positions available in simulation courses	648	
# of simulation positions filled	423	159
# of positions available in faculty supervised clinical courses	68	
# of faculty supervised clinical positions filled	41	22
# involved in field placements	138	25
# involved in law journals	103	25
# involved in moot court or trial competitions	136	40
# of credit hours required to graduate	90	

JD Enrollment and Ethnicity

	Men		Women		Full-Time		Part-Time		1st-Year		Total		JD Degs. Awd.
	#	%	#	%	#	%	#	%	#	%	#	%	
All Hispanics	14	2.6	11	2.6	17	2.7	8	2.5	13	3.2	25	2.6	5
Am. Ind./AK Nat.	2	0.4	4	0.9	3	0.5	3	0.9	3	0.7	6	0.6	1
Asian	24	4.5	32	7.4	41	6.4	15	4.6	21	5.2	56	5.8	10
Black/Af. Am.	23	4.3	40	9.3	25	3.9	38	11.7	27	6.7	63	6.5	15
Nat. Hi/Pac. Isl.	0	0.0	0	0.0	0	0.0	0	0.0	0	0.0	0	0.0	0
2 or more races	0	0.0	0	0.0	0	0.0	0	0.0	0	0.0	0	0.0	0
Subtotal (minor.)	63	11.8	87	20.2	86	13.5	64	19.8	64	15.8	150	15.6	31
Nonres. Alien	14	2.6	12	2.8	19	3.0	7	2.2	7	1.7	26	2.7	6
White/Cauc.	455	85.5	331	77.0	533	83.5	253	78.1	335	82.5	786	81.7	214
Unknown	0	0.0	0	0.0	0	0.0	0	0.0	0	0.0	0	0.0	0
Total	532	55.3	430	44.7	638	66.3	324	33.7	406	42.2	962		251

Transfers

Transfers in	17
Transfers out	7

Tuition and Fees

	Resident	Nonresident
Full-time	$22,323	$43,821
Part-time	$16,903	$32,854
Tuition Guarantee Program	N	

Living Expenses

Estimated living expenses for singles

Living on campus	Living off campus	Living at home
N/A	$21,124	N/A

INDIANA UNIVERSITY ROBERT H. MCKINNEY SCHOOL OF LAW

*ABA
Approved
Since
1944*

GPA and LSAT Scores

	Total	Full-Time	Part-Time
# of apps	1,640	1,381	259
# of offers	805	654	151
# of matrics	314	212	102
75% GPA	3.68	3.72	3.52
Median GPA	3.44	3.55	3.30
25% GPA	3.19	3.25	3.04
75% LSAT	159	160	156
Median LSAT	156	157	152
25% LSAT	152	154	149

Grants and Scholarships (from prior year)

	Total #	Total %	Full-Time #	Full-Time %	Part-Time #	Part-Time %
Total # of students	918		595		323	
Total # receiving grants	369	40.2	283	47.6	86	26.6
Less than 1/2 tuition	312	34.0	249	41.8	63	19.5
Half to full tuition	29	3.2	26	4.4	3	0.9
Full tuition	19	2.1	0	0.0	19	5.9
More than full tuition	9	1.0	8	1.3	1	0.3
Median grant amount			$6,000		$2,200	

Informational and Library Resources

Total amount spent on library materials	$1,115,810
Study seating capacity inside the library	499
# of full-time equivalent professional librarians	10
Hours per week library is open	105
# of open, wired connections available to students	1,144
# of networked computers available for use by students	139
Has wireless network?	Y
Requires computer?	N

JD Attrition (from prior year)

	Academic #	Other #	Total #	Total %
1st year	0	14	14	3.8
2nd year	2	7	9	2.9
3rd year	2	0	2	0.9
4th year	0	0	0	0.0

Employment (9 months after graduation)

For up-to-date employment data, go to employmentsummary.abaquestionnaire.org on the ABA website.

Bar Passage Rates

First-time takers	283	Reporting %	91.17
Average school %	82.95	Average state %	80.93
Average pass difference	2.02		

Jurisdiction	Takers	Passers	Pass %	State %	Diff %
Indiana	258	214	82.95	80.93	2.02

INDIANA UNIVERSITY ROBERT H. MCKINNEY SCHOOL OF LAW

530 West New York Street
Indianapolis, IN 46202-3225
Phone: 317.274.2459; Fax: 317.278.4780
E-mail: lawadmit@iupui.edu; Website: indylaw.indiana.edu

Introduction

Founded in 1894 as the Indiana Law School, the IU Robert H. McKinney School of Law has emerged as a premier educational institution, located in the dynamic heart of Indiana on the Indianapolis campus of Indiana University—Purdue University. This campus is also home to the IU Schools of Medicine, Dentistry, Nursing, and Social Work. The law school building, Lawrence W. Inlow Hall, is a state-of-the-art facility, enabling the faculty to employ the latest technology and teaching methods. The building houses modern classrooms, private study areas, and an unparalleled law library. The school is just steps away from the state's courts, the legislature, and major law firms, giving students opportunities to observe the legal process in action and to participate in that process as law clerks, judicial externs, and legislative staff assistants. The school is the largest in the state of Indiana and one of the few Big Ten law schools to offer the cultural, recreational, and professional advantages of an urban educational environment.

Clinical Experiences

The law school offers several clinical programs. The Civil Practice Clinic allows students the opportunity to represent clients in a variety of cases, including housing, divorce, child support, consumer, and administrative matters. In the Disability Clinic, students represent school-age children with special needs, as well as persons who are afflicted with HIV, Alzheimer's disease, and AIDS. In the Criminal Defense Clinic, students represent clients in criminal cases involving a variety of misdemeanor or class D felony charges. Additional clinical opportunities include the Immigration Law Clinic, the Appellate Practice Clinic, the Health and Human Rights Clinic, and the Wrongful Conviction Clinic, which involves claims of innocence in postconviction proceedings.

Externships and Special Programs

The school's research centers and programs make significant contributions to the profession, both locally and nationally. The William S. and Christine S. Hall Center for Law and Health is considered one of the top health law programs in the nation. The center serves as a preeminent information resource on health law issues for the bar, government, and health care community. Through the center, students may pursue a concentration in law and health and participate in the *Indiana Health Law Review*.

The Program on Law and State Government enriches the dialogue between the academic legal community and state government policymakers. The program offers externships with more than 40 government offices and also sponsors a mediation course that qualifies students to become registered civil mediators. Additionally, the program sponsors a fellowship that allows students to host an academic event and write a publishable academic paper on critical legal or regulatory issues pertinent to state government.

The Program in Environmental and Natural Resources Law offers training in this dynamic area of law that addresses issues such as resource development and conservation, pollution control, energy and transportation policy, and environmental justice and equity.

The Global Crisis Leadership Forum is a joint initiative of the IU Robert H. McKinney School of Law and IU School of Public and Environmental Affairs that organizes workshops, forum discussions, and training programs in the field of global crisis management. The forum also performs a biennial counter-terrorism simulation exercise in which students work with experts in the field to respond to a series of simulated crises.

The Center for Intellectual Property Law and Innovation provides experience for students in the fast-growing area of intellectual property.

The Court Externship Program provides externships with federal, state, and local courts. Externs work closely with judges and law clerks, learning about the legal process by experiencing it firsthand.

International Law Program

Because the school recognizes that international considerations touch all areas of the law from human rights to economic issues, it established the Center for International and Comparative Law. A wide variety of international courses, combined with opportunities for overseas experiences, demonstrate our commitment to a legal education with a world view.

Our Program in International Human Rights Law has placed students in internships with human rights organizations in locations from Argentina to Zimbabwe.

The law school sponsors a summer program in China. Established in 1987, the Chinese Law Summer Program is hosted by Renmin (People's) University of China School of Law and introduces students to the Chinese legal and lawyering systems, its dispute resolution mechanisms, and Chinese constitutional law.

In addition to offering several courses and seminars in the area of international law, the school sponsors the *Indiana International and Comparative Law Review* and a student organization, the International Law Society. It is also home to the editorial offices of the *European Journal of Law Reform*.

Joint-Degree Programs

The school offers eight joint-degree options in cooperation with IU's School of Medicine, School of Business, School of Public and Environmental Affairs, School of Library and information Science, School of Liberal Arts, and the School of Social Work. Available degrees are the Doctor of Jurisprudence and Doctor of Medicine (JD/MD), Master of Business Administration (JD/MBA), Master of Health Administration (JD/MHA), Master of Public Affairs (JD/MPA), Master of Public Health (JD/MPH), Master of Library Science (JD/MLS), Master of Arts in Philosophy (JD/MPhil), and Master of Social Work (JD/MSW).

Special Summer Program

Summer admission is offered to a select group of applicants who can benefit from a rigorous, individualized summer course. Applicants who have either an LSAT score or a GPA that is outside of the median range of accepted students, persons who are returning to school after several years outside of the classroom, and students for whom English is a second language may be considered for the summer program. Summer admittees earn two credits toward their JD degrees. Continuation in the fall is not contingent upon performance in the summer program. There is no special application procedure. Applicants who are not presumptively admitted and whose files are completed by February 1, may be considered for this program.

ICLEO

Additionally, the school strongly supports the Indiana Conference for Legal Education Opportunity program, which provides those who are currently underrepresented in the legal profession or underrepresented in practice areas with assistance in preparing for law school through a six-week summer institute.

Admission

The LSAT and LSAC's Credential Assembly Service are required.

The law school seeks to attain a culturally rich and diverse student body. To this end, admission decisions are based on a variety of factors in addition to the LSAT score and undergraduate GPA.

Indiana University Robert H. McKinney School of Law offers an early decision program. Early decision candidates must have their applications completed, with their Credential Assembly Service Law School Report, by November 15, and will be notified of the admission committee's decision by late December.

Academic Support Programs

The Student Affairs Office designs, manages, and implements academic support services, strategies, and outreach programs for students. Academic support programs currently offered include workshops on study skills, time management, exam preparation, bar exam advising, bar exam preparation, and sessions on academic advising topics and resources.

Students are offered assistance through the Dean's Tutorial Society. Supervised by a tenured faculty member, the tutorial society is staffed by academically distinguished students who offer individual tutoring as well as assistance in case briefing and exam preparation.

Student Activities

Students can participate in any of 30 different interest groups and organizations, ranging from Amnesty International to the Sports and Entertainment Law Society. The school also offers an extensive moot court program, a client counseling program, and three law reviews. The law reviews are *Indiana Law Review*, *Indiana International and Comparative Law Review*, and *Indiana Health Law Review*.

Office of Professional Development

The Office of Professional Development provides career counseling and job-search assistance to students and alumni. Services include an on-campus interview program, a résumé review service, a mock interview program, and a variety of workshops and seminars.

APPLICANT PROFILE

Indiana University Robert H. McKinney School of Law
This grid includes only applicants who earned 120–180 LSAT scores under standard administrations.

LSAT Score	3.75 +		3.50–3.74		3.25–3.49		3.00–3.24		2.75–2.99		2.50–2.74		2.25–2.49		2.00–2.24		Below 2.00		No GPA		Total	
	Apps	Adm	Apps	Adm	Apps	Adm	Apps	Adm	Apps	Adm	Apps	Adm	Apps	Adm	Apps	Adm	Apps	Adm	Apps	Adm	Apps	Adm
170–180	5	5	4	4	0	0	6	6	0	0	0	0	0	0	0	0	0	0	0	0	15	15
165–169	12	12	14	14	8	8	7	7	6	6	3	1	3	3	1	1	1	0	1	1	56	53
160–164	29	29	35	35	35	34	35	34	18	15	11	6	2	2	5	2	0	0	2	2	172	159
155–159	56	52	84	76	106	81	68	49	55	38	20	9	6	2	3	1	0	0	12	10	410	318
150–154	48	46	86	70	112	40	106	26	68	14	24	2	15	0	8	0	0	0	18	5	485	203
145–149	24	12	48	14	77	19	60	3	40	3	27	0	15	0	10	0	0	0	14	2	315	53
140–144	4	2	18	4	22	2	23	4	20	0	16	1	12	0	8	0	2	0	6	0	131	13
Below 140	0	0	3	0	6	0	10	0	13	0	17	0	5	0	3	0	1	0	7	0	65	0
Total	178	158	292	217	366	184	315	129	220	76	118	19	58	7	38	4	4	0	60	20	1649	814

Apps = Number of Applicants
Adm = Number Admitted
Reflects 99% of the total applicant pool; highest LSAT data reported.

INTER AMERICAN UNIVERSITY SCHOOL OF LAW

PO Box 70351
San Juan, PR 00936-8351
Phone: 787.751.1912, exts. 2011, 2012
Website: www.derecho.inter.edu

The Basics

Type of school	Private
Term	Semester
Application deadline	
Application fee	$63
Financial aid deadline	6/30
Can first year start other than fall?	No
Student to faculty ratio	26.0 to 1
# of housing spaces available restricted to law students	
graduate housing for which law students are eligible	

Faculty and Administrators

	Total		Men		Women		Minorities	
	Spr	Fall	Spr	Fall	Spr	Fall	Spr	Fall
Full-time	24	24	14	14	10	10	0	0
Other full-time	1	1	0	0	1	1	0	0
Deans, librarians, & others who teach	4	4	2	2	2	2	0	0
Part-time	50	47	36	32	14	15	0	0
Total	79	76	52	48	27	28	0	0

Curriculum

		Full-Time	Part-Time
Typical first-year section size		45	60
Is there typically a "small section" of the first-year class, other than Legal Writing, taught by full-time faculty		Yes	Yes
If yes, typical size offered last year		8	6
# of classroom course titles beyond first-year curriculum		28	
# of upper division courses, excluding seminars, with an enrollment:	Under 25	52	
	25–49	44	
	50–74	18	
	75–99	0	
	100+	0	
# of seminars		10	
# of seminar positions available		200	
# of seminar positions filled		80	120
# of positions available in simulation courses		100	
# of simulation positions filled		60	40
# of positions available in faculty supervised clinical courses		31	
# of faculty supervised clinical positions filled		26	5
# involved in field placements		0	0
# involved in law journals		16	2
# involved in moot court or trial competitions		19	3
# of credit hours required to graduate		92	

JD Enrollment and Ethnicity

	Men		Women		Full-Time		Part-Time		1st-Year		Total		JD Degs. Awd.
	#	%	#	%	#	%	#	%	#	%	#	%	
All Hispanics	403	100.0	487	100.0	476	100.0	414	100.0	271	100.0	890	100.0	248
Am. Ind./AK Nat.	0	0.0	0	0.0	0	0.0	0	0.0	0	0.0	0	0.0	0
Asian	0	0.0	0	0.0	0	0.0	0	0.0	0	0.0	0	0.0	0
Black/Af. Am.	0	0.0	0	0.0	0	0.0	0	0.0	0	0.0	0	0.0	0
Nat. HI/Pac. Isl.	0	0.0	0	0.0	0	0.0	0	0.0	0	0.0	0	0.0	0
2 or more races	0	0.0	0	0.0	0	0.0	0	0.0	0	0.0	0	0.0	0
Subtotal (minor.)	403	100.0	487	100.0	476	100.0	414	100.0	271	100.0	890	100.0	248
Nonres. Alien	0	0.0	0	0.0	0	0.0	0	0.0	0	0.0	0	0.0	0
White/Cauc.	0	0.0	0	0.0	0	0.0	0	0.0	0	0.0	0	0.0	0
Unknown	0	0.0	0	0.0	0	0.0	0	0.0	0	0.0	0	0.0	0
Total	403	45.3	487	54.7	476	53.5	414	46.5	271	30.4	890		248

Transfers

Transfers in	31
Transfers out	20

Tuition and Fees

	Resident	Nonresident
Full-time	$14,403	$14,403
Part-time	$11,204	$11,204
Tuition Guarantee Program		Y

Living Expenses

Estimated living expenses for singles

Living on campus	Living off campus	Living at home
N/A	$19,868	$15,136

INTER AMERICAN UNIVERSITY SCHOOL OF LAW

ABA Approved Since 1969

GPA and LSAT Scores

	Total	Full-Time	Part-Time
# of apps	945	581	364
# of offers	393	246	147
# of matrics	246	139	107
75% GPA	3.58	3.58	3.57
Median GPA	3.28	3.32	3.12
25% GPA	2.95	2.98	2.93
75% LSAT	142	143	141
Median LSAT	138	140	138
25% LSAT	135	135	134

Grants and Scholarships (from prior year)

	Total #	Total %	Full-Time #	Full-Time %	Part-Time #	Part-Time %
Total # of students	866		474		392	
Total # receiving grants	48	5.5	30	6.3	18	4.6
Less than 1/2 tuition	2	0.2	2	0.4	0	0.0
Half to full tuition	5	0.6	1	0.2	4	1.0
Full tuition	41	4.7	27	5.7	14	3.6
More than full tuition	0	0.0	0	0.0	0	0.0
Median grant amount			$3,854		$4,404	

Informational and Library Resources

Total amount spent on library materials	$533,756
Study seating capacity inside the library	302
# of full-time equivalent professional librarians	8
Hours per week library is open	100
# of open, wired connections available to students	24
# of networked computers available for use by students	41
Has wireless network?	Y
Requires computer?	N

JD Attrition (from prior year)

	Academic #	Other #	Total #	Total %
1st year	0	9	9	3.5
2nd year	10	11	21	8.1
3rd year	2	1	3	1.2
4th year	0	0	0	0.0

Employment (9 months after graduation)

For up-to-date employment data, go to employmentsummary.abaquestionnaire.org on the ABA website.

Bar Passage Rates

First-time takers	259	Reporting %	191.89
Average school %	48.89	Average state %	51.61

Average pass difference –2.72

Jurisdiction	Takers	Passers	Pass %	State %	Diff %
Puerto Rico	497	243	48.89	51.61	–2.72

INTER AMERICAN UNIVERSITY SCHOOL OF LAW

PO Box 70351
San Juan, PR 00936-8351
Phone: 787.751.1912, exts. 2011, 2012
Website: www.derecho.inter.edu

Introduction

The Inter American University School of Law is one of the 11 units of the Inter American University of Puerto Rico, a private nonprofit educational corporation accredited by the Middle States Association of Colleges and Schools (Commission on Higher Education), the Puerto Rico Council of Higher Education, and the Commonwealth of Puerto Rico Department of Education. The School of Law is approved by the ABA and is located in San Juan, the capital city of Puerto Rico. Since its founding, the School of Law has succeeded in meeting the needs of the legal profession, in particular, and Puerto Rico's society in general.

Enrollment/Student Body

The incoming class for academic year 2011–2012 was composed of 246 students. The student body comes mainly from Puerto Rico, although applicants from the mainland are encouraged to apply.

Library and Physical Facilities

The law school has developed its library into a center of access to traditional library services as well as computerized legal research services.

In 1993, the school was relocated to a new building that features seven classrooms equipped with air conditioning, accessibility for students with disabilities, state-of-the-art audiovisual equipment, seminar rooms, a library, a legal clinic, faculty offices, a conference room, a lounge, a Continuing Legal Education Program office, *Inter American School of Law Review* offices, student organization offices, administrative offices, a chapel, a student center, a cafeteria, a bookstore, an auditorium with a seating capacity of 310, parking, and more. The site has been landscaped to achieve a sense of serenity and beauty compatible with the building's functions.

In January 1990, the library signed a collaboration agreement to establish a consortium with the law school library of the Catholic University of Puerto Rico and the library of the Supreme Court of Puerto Rico, with the purpose of coordinating collection development and sharing its resources through an automated bibliographic network, interlibrary loans, and telecommunication services.

Curriculum

The JD program covers three years in the day division and four years in the evening division. Candidates must complete a minimum of 92 credit hours with a GPA of at least 2.5 to qualify for graduation.

Inter American University School of Law offers a three-week preparation course to be taken during the summer on a compulsory basis by students admitted to the school. Students who enter law school must be willing to make a heavy commitment.

For its part, Inter American University is willing to provide the best possible professional educational experience through the careful recruitment of a first-rate faculty, the development of a progressive curriculum, and a willingness to create new and exciting programs of clinical studies and research.

Admission

Proficiency in Spanish is essential to the program. Applicants must have a minimum grade-point average of 2.5, an immunization certificate (for students ages 21 and below), and a police department certificate of good conduct; those seeking admission may also be required to appear for a personal interview.

Candidates are required to take the Examen de Admisión a Estudios de Posgrado (EXADEP), the Aptitude Test for Graduate Education, and the Law School Admission Test (LSAT). Students should attain a 575 minimum score on the EXADEP and a minimum score of 130 on the LSAT. Application forms and other relevant information concerning the EXADEP may be obtained from Educational Testing Service, American International Plaza, 250 Muñoz Rivera Avenue, Suite 315, Hato Rey, PR 00918.

Housing

The university does not provide housing for law students. However, the areas surrounding the School of Law contain many private houses, apartments, and condominiums for rent.

Student Activities

Student organizations include the student council, an organization that represents the student body and participates in matters of administrative policy related to students' interests. Council representatives serve on various faculty committees as well as the university senate and the board of trustees.

Other student organizations are the Law Student Division of the American Bar Association; the Phi Alpha Delta legal fraternity (composed not only of law students, but also of distinguished honorary members who are supreme court justices, federal district court judges, and prominent attorneys); the National Association of Law Students; the Women Law Students Association; United Students Forging an Environmental Consciousness; the Law Student Division of the Inter-American Federation of Lawyers; the Association of Trial Lawyers of America; the Hispanic National Bar Association; the Federal Bar Association; the Student's Cooperative Bookstore; and the Hispanic Notarial Bar Association.

The *Inter American School of Law Review* is the official publication of the School of Law. Its members work under the supervision of an editorial board of four students chosen on the basis of merit and dedication to the *Law Review* and an academic advisor who is a faculty member appointed by the dean.

Clinical Programs

The faculty's Legal Aid Clinical Program is integrated with the Community Law Office through a combined effort of the US Legal Services Corporation and Inter American University. Law students are provided with the opportunity to learn skills such as interviewing, negotiation, counseling, fact gathering and analysis, legal research and drafting, decision making about alternative strategies, and preparation for trial and field practice. They also represent clients before administrative agencies and courts under the close supervision of the program's staff attorney-professors, pursuant to the rules of the Supreme Court of Puerto Rico. Students also gain practical experience by serving with Puerto Rico Legal Services, Inc.; the San Juan Community Law Office, Inc.; the Legal Aid Society of Puerto Rico; the district attorney's offices; and the Environmental Quality Board.

Career Services

The mission of the Career Placement Office is to prepare students and alumni for the legal job market by encouraging them to conduct self-assessments in an effort to focus their job searches, as well as to educate students and alumni on their legal and nonlegal options in today's competitive legal market. This is accomplished through a variety of services including, but not limited to, individual counseling, group seminars, self-assessment materials, interviewing programs, a career resource library, and the alumni network.

Continuing Legal Education Program

The Continuing Legal Education (CLE) program offers advanced courses and seminars concerning different fields of law that may be of interest to practicing lawyers as well as to the community in general.

The CLE program enjoys a good reputation and has been able to develop a consistent course offering, primarily in the following categories: courses designed for specialists; refresher courses for experienced lawyers; courses designed to provide information in nontraditional areas or stimulated by recent legislation, decisions, or agency rulings; and courses designed to develop lawyering skills.

Cost and Financial Aid

As of the date this report was published, the cost per credit is $457. Once admitted, the student pays $125 to reserve a place in the class and $435 for the preparatory course that takes place in July.

There is a deferred payment plan and financial aid options that include the Federal Direct Loan Program, Stafford loans, the Commonwealth Education Fund, the State Student Incentive Grants program, the Federal Work-Study program, and alternative loans for the regular academic program as well as for bar study (Alternative Bar Loans). The university also has an Honor Scholarship program for law students based on academic accomplishment and financial need.

Applicant Profile Not Available

THE UNIVERSITY OF IOWA COLLEGE OF LAW

320 Melrose Avenue
Iowa City, IA 52242
Phone: 800.553.4692, ext. 9095; 319.335.9095; Fax: 319.335.9646
E-mail: law-admissions@uiowa.edu; Website: www.law.uiowa.edu

ABA
Approved
Since
1923

The Basics

Type of school	Public
Term	Semester
Application deadline	3/1
Application fee	$60
Financial aid deadline	
Can first year start other than fall?	No
Student to faculty ratio	11.9 to 1
# of housing spaces available restricted to law students	
graduate housing for which law students are eligible	

Faculty and Administrators

	Total Spr	Total Fall	Men Spr	Men Fall	Women Spr	Women Fall	Minorities Spr	Minorities Fall
Full-time	39	39	25	25	14	14	6	4
Other full-time	3	3	3	2	0	1	0	0
Deans, librarians, & others who teach	11	11	5	6	6	5	2	2
Part-time	23	10	15	6	8	4	0	0
Total	76	63	48	39	28	24	8	6

Curriculum

	Full-Time	Part-Time
Typical first-year section size	70	0

	Yes	No
Is there typically a "small section" of the first-year class, other than Legal Writing, taught by full-time faculty		
If yes, typical size offered last year	40	

# of classroom course titles beyond first-year curriculum		65
# of upper division courses, excluding seminars, with an enrollment:	Under 25	53
	25–49	21
	50–74	14
	75–99	6
	100+	0
# of seminars		27
# of seminar positions available		331
# of seminar positions filled	302	0
# of positions available in simulation courses	273	
# of simulation positions filled	256	0
# of positions available in faculty supervised clinical courses	81	
# of faculty supervised clinical positions filled	81	0
# involved in field placements	91	0
# involved in law journals	200	0
# involved in moot court or trial competitions	43	0
# of credit hours required to graduate	84	

JD Enrollment and Ethnicity

	Men #	Men %	Women #	Women %	Full-Time #	Full-Time %	Part-Time #	Part-Time %	1st-Year #	1st-Year %	Total #	Total %	JD Degs. Awd.
All Hispanics	18	5.6	12	5.1	30	5.5	0	0.0	10	5.6	30	5.4	11
Am. Ind./AK Nat.	3	0.9	3	1.3	6	1.1	0	0.0	1	0.6	6	1.1	0
Asian	24	7.5	15	6.4	39	7.1	0	0.0	15	8.3	39	7.0	14
Black/Af. Am.	8	2.5	8	3.4	15	2.7	1	16.7	6	3.3	16	2.9	7
Nat. HI/Pac. Isl.	0	0.0	1	0.4	1	0.2	0	0.0	1	0.6	1	0.2	0
2 or more races	0	0.0	0	0.0	0	0.0	0	0.0	0	0.0	0	0.0	0
Subtotal (minor.)	53	16.5	39	16.6	91	16.5	1	16.7	33	18.3	92	16.5	32
Nonres. Alien	5	1.6	3	1.3	8	1.5	0	0.0	3	1.7	8	1.4	4
White/Cauc.	263	81.9	193	82.1	451	82.0	5	83.3	144	80.0	456	82.0	147
Unknown	0	0.0	0	0.0	0	0.0	0	0.0	0	0.0	0	0.0	0
Total	321	57.7	235	42.3	550	98.9	6	1.1	180	32.4	556		183

Transfers

Transfers in	4
Transfers out	4

Tuition and Fees

	Resident	Nonresident
Full-time	$26,348	$46,056
Part-time		
Tuition Guarantee Program	N	

Living Expenses

Estimated living expenses for singles

Living on campus	Living off campus	Living at home
$16,633	$16,633	$8,623

THE UNIVERSITY OF IOWA COLLEGE OF LAW

ABA Approved Since 1923

GPA and LSAT Scores

	Total	Full-Time	Part-Time
# of apps	1,872	1,872	0
# of offers	729	729	0
# of matrics	180	180	0
75% GPA	3.81	3.81	0.00
Median GPA	3.64	3.64	0.00
25% GPA	3.51	3.51	0.00
75% LSAT	164	164	0
Median LSAT	161	161	0
25% LSAT	158	158	0

Grants and Scholarships (from prior year)

	Total #	Total %	Full-Time #	Full-Time %	Part-Time #	Part-Time %
Total # of students	574		574		0	
Total # receiving grants	284	49.5	284	49.5	0	0.0
Less than 1/2 tuition	130	22.6	130	22.6	0	0.0
Half to full tuition	13	2.3	13	2.3	0	0.0
Full tuition	112	19.5	112	19.5	0	0.0
More than full tuition	29	5.1	29	5.1	0	0.0
Median grant amount			$22,554		$0	

Informational and Library Resources

Total amount spent on library materials	$3,406,593
Study seating capacity inside the library	705
# of full-time equivalent professional librarians	14
Hours per week library is open	106
# of open, wired connections available to students	517
# of networked computers available for use by students	105
Has wireless network?	Y
Requires computer?	N

JD Attrition (from prior year)

	Academic #	Other #	Total #	Total %
1st year	0	8	8	4.0
2nd year	0	4	4	2.2
3rd year	0	2	2	1.1
4th year	0	0	0	0.0

Employment (9 months after graduation)

For up-to-date employment data, go to employmentsummary.abaquestionnaire.org on the ABA website.

Bar Passage Rates

First-time takers	194	Reporting %	72.68
Average school %	91.49	Average state %	88.60
Average pass difference	2.89		

Jurisdiction	Takers	Passers	Pass %	State %	Diff %
Iowa	70	65	92.86	91.09	1.77
Illinois	32	30	93.75	89.38	4.37
Minnesota	15	15	100.00	92.21	7.79
California	12	10	83.33	71.24	12.09
New York	12	9	75.00	84.92	–9.92

THE UNIVERSITY OF IOWA COLLEGE OF LAW

320 Melrose Avenue
Iowa City, IA 52242
Phone: 800.553.4692, ext. 9095; 319.335.9095; Fax: 319.335.9646
E-mail: law-admissions@uiowa.edu; Website: www.law.uiowa.edu

Introduction

The University of Iowa College of Law, founded in 1865, is the oldest law school in continuous operation west of the Mississippi River. Iowa enjoys a top national reputation, and its faculty is renowned for its outstanding scholarship and teaching.

The college is located in Iowa City, a cosmopolitan college town that is home to a dynamic teaching and research university and over 60,000 people. Students from all 50 states and roughly 100 countries attend the university. Iowa City offers a rich cultural life, Big Ten athletic events, and the world-famous Iowa Writers' Workshop.

The Boyd Law Building's central campus location on a bluff overlooking the Iowa River provides a professional enclave well-suited to the college's intensive style of education as well as easy access to the academic, cultural, social, and recreational resources of a major research university.

Admission

Iowa strives to enroll a student body that reflects the academic quality and diversity expected of a leading national law school. The college's numbers-plus policy looks beyond numerical indicators and utilizes a full file review to evaluate an applicant's potential contribution to enhancing classroom discussion. Factors such as maturity, work experience, ability to overcome adversity, and cultural background are considered.

Enrollment Date

Iowa offers only one starting date for entering students: August. All students may "accelerate" their course of study toward the JD degree by taking summer and intersession classes. The minimum time of study is no fewer than 27 months after the student has started law study at this law school or at a law school from which transfer credit has been accepted.

Curriculum

The students are the heart of our institution. A broad and wide-ranging curriculum, small classes, accessible professors, and caring administrators are just a few examples of Iowa's student-centered orientation.

Iowa's curriculum establishes a solid foundation for a lifetime of professional growth and personal development. Students take an active role in their professional training. We go the extra measure to ensure that our students have the proper resources and learning environment to maximize their individual development as professionals.

First-year students have at least one class each semester with approximately 40 students; courses taught in this small-section format allow extensive class participation and interaction with a faculty member. After completing the set of required first-year courses exploring fundamental legal concepts, students plan their own course of study from a rich menu of mainstream, specialized, and clinical offerings. Second- and third-year courses cover the range of specialties within the legal profession, allowing students to sample liberally and follow professional interests.

At Iowa, students benefit from the serious emphasis the college places on both interdisciplinary study and the study of international and comparative law. Interdisciplinary courses and research programs are actively encouraged; nearly one-third of the college's faculty members offer courses or conduct research in the international and comparative law fields.

Legal Analysis, Writing, and Research Program

The Legal Analysis, Writing, and Research (LAWR) program at the College of Law is a two-semester, first-year course (two credits each semester), with classes of 20 students, and is designed to equip participants with effective skills in legal analysis, writing, and research.

Iowa Law Library

The University of Iowa College of Law Library is consistently recognized as one of the finest and largest law libraries in the nation. The library's international holdings are impressive; it includes a complete collection of United Nations documents since the UN's founding in 1945. The Law Library received significant and high praise in the 2010 *National Jurist* survey of law libraries that are located in the United States. Additionally, wireless Internet is available throughout the library.

Special Programs

The first writing center in the country established specifically for a law school community, Iowa's Writing Resource Center serves as an extension of the classroom and supplements the college's Legal Analysis, Writing, and Research program. Members of the writing center's staff help law students with a broad range of writing, including class assignments, law journal articles, and résumés and cover letters. The center's staff teaches strategies for overcoming writer's block, adapting materials for various audiences, and generally improving the quality of students' writing.

The Academic Achievement Program (AAP) helps students achieve their full academic potential as they move from successful undergraduate careers to face the new challenges of law study. AAP presents a variety of programs, including a first-semester lecture series for new students. Individual study-skills counseling is also available for all students.

Clinical Law Programs

The Clinical Law programs give students opportunities to gain experience in many different areas of substantive law including criminal defense, disability rights, domestic violence, employment law, family law, general civil law, immigration law, international project law, law and public policy, and public benefits. Externship opportunities are available with federal trial courts, the Iowa Attorney General, legal services offices, US Attorneys' offices, Federal Public Defenders' offices, and the Iowa City City Attorney, among others. Through the representation of real clients, students are able to develop and hone a diverse complement of lawyering skills from interviewing, counseling, and drafting court papers to trial practice, appellate advocacy, legislative lobbying, and policy development.

International Law

Iowa offers one of the nation's strongest programs for the study of international and comparative law. The school offers five study-abroad programs. Iowa is the stateside home of the London Law Consortium through which seven US law schools conduct a study-abroad program for a spring semester in London. The Iowa/Bordeaux summer program offers one month of intensive coursework in Arcachon, France. Students also have the opportunity to participate in an exchange program with Bucerius Law School in Germany as well as to study at Católica University in Lisbon, Portugal, and in Nijmegen, the Netherlands. In addition, students may receive credit for participating in study-abroad programs offered by other ABA-approved law schools.

Student Activities

Student activities at the law school include the American Constitution Society; the Asian American Law Students Association; the Black Law Students Association; the Christian Legal Society; Client Counseling; the Environmental Law Society; the Equal Justice Foundation; the Federalist Society; the Intellectual Property Law Society; the International Law Society; the Iowa Campaign for Human Rights; the *Iowa Law Review*; the Iowa Student Bar Association; the J. Reuben Clark Law Society; the Jewish Law Students Association; the *Journal of Corporation Law*; the *Journal of Gender, Race and Justice*; the *Journal of Transnational Law and Contemporary Problems*; the Latino Law Student Association; Law Students for Reproductive Justice; the Middle Eastern Law Students Association; Moot Court; the National Lawyers Guild; the Native American Law Students Association; the Order of the Coif; the Organization for Women Law Students and Staff; the Outlaws; Parents/Partners Weekend; Phi Alpha Delta; Phi Delta Phi; the *Pro Bono* Society; the Stephenson Competition; Supreme Court Day; and Trial Advocacy.

Expenses and Financial Aid

All admitted students are automatically considered for merit scholarships and fellowships based on their academic achievements. A separate application is not required. The college administers its substantial financial aid program to advance the goals of its selective admission policy. More than 90 percent of our students receive some form of financial aid. Grants, scholarships, work-study funds, and loans are awarded on a need or merit basis for the purpose of providing access to legal education for the talented and diverse students admitted to the college. A number of part-time employment opportunities are also available to second- and third-year students; nonresident students with a quarter-time research assistant position (10 hours per week) are classified as residents for tuition purposes. Eligibility for financial aid based on need is established by completion of the FAFSA, available at www.fafsa.ed.gov.

Career Services

Admitted students are strongly encouraged to pursue career counseling, which helps them clarify and articulate career and life plans with the JD or LLM; enables participation in internships, externships, summer associate positions, and other experiential legal opportunities; and aids in the development of strategic job-search plans for a wide range of legal careers. Each year, many 1Ls participate in the Partner for a Day program with alumni and employers, which helps them make career decisions and develop professional networks. To facilitate interviewing for summer and full-time employment, the Career Services Office provides students with access to national job fairs, résumé collections, video interviews, and on-campus interviews. The law school's participation in interview consortia on the East Coast and West Coast provides students with many interview opportunities outside of the Midwest. Finally, the Career Services Office offers continued services to alumni seeking career advice.

Applicant Profile Not Available

THE JOHN MARSHALL LAW SCHOOL

315 South Plymouth Court
Chicago, IL 60604
Phone: 800.537.4280; 312.987.1406; Fax: 312.427.5136
E-mail: admission@jmls.edu; Website: www.jmls.edu

ABA
Approved
Since
1951

The Basics

Type of school	Private
Term	Semester
Application deadline	4/1 11/1
Application fee	$0
Financial aid deadline	4/1
Can first year start other than fall?	Yes
Student to faculty ratio	16.4 to 1
# of housing spaces available restricted to law students	
graduate housing for which law students are eligible	

Faculty and Administrators

	Total		Men		Women		Minorities	
	Spr	Fall	Spr	Fall	Spr	Fall	Spr	Fall
Full-time	70	69	49	47	21	22	13	15
Other full-time	6	6	1	2	5	4	0	0
Deans, librarians, & others who teach	10	10	6	6	4	4	2	2
Part-time	110	133	73	93	37	40	9	13
Total	196	218	129	148	67	70	24	30

JD Enrollment and Ethnicity

	Men		Women		Full-Time		Part-Time		1st-Year		Total		JD Degs. Awd.
	#	%	#	%	#	%	#	%	#	%	#	%	
All Hispanics	51	6.4	52	7.6	75	6.3	28	10.0	39	7.4	103	7.0	31
Am. Ind./AK Nat.	4	0.5	7	1.0	10	0.8	1	0.4	10	1.9	11	0.7	3
Asian	53	6.7	46	6.7	85	7.1	14	5.0	40	7.6	99	6.7	19
Black/Af. Am.	42	5.3	78	11.4	79	6.6	41	14.7	41	7.8	120	8.1	26
Nat. HI/Pac. Isl.	1	0.1	1	0.1	1	0.1	1	0.4	2	0.4	2	0.1	0
2 or more races	0	0.0	2	0.3	1	0.1	1	0.4	2	0.4	2	0.1	0
Subtotal (minor.)	151	19.0	186	27.1	251	20.9	86	30.8	134	25.5	337	22.8	79
Nonres. Alien	5	0.6	4	0.6	8	0.7	1	0.4	4	0.8	9	0.6	7
White/Cauc.	595	75.0	459	66.9	876	73.0	178	63.8	363	69.0	1054	71.3	276
Unknown	42	5.3	37	5.4	65	5.4	14	5.0	25	4.8	79	5.3	27
Total	793	53.6	686	46.4	1200	81.1	279	18.9	526	35.6	1479		389

Curriculum

		Full-Time	Part-Time
Typical first-year section size		80	50
Is there typically a "small section" of the first-year class, other than Legal Writing, taught by full-time faculty		No	No
If yes, typical size offered last year			
# of classroom course titles beyond first-year curriculum		281	
# of upper division courses, excluding seminars, with an enrollment:	Under 25	236	
	25–49	74	
	50–74	33	
	75–99	22	
	100+	0	
# of seminars		40	
# of seminar positions available		1,000	
# of seminar positions filled		730	124
# of positions available in simulation courses		1,858	
# of simulation positions filled		1,048	262
# of positions available in faculty supervised clinical courses		90	
# of faculty supervised clinical positions filled		72	9
# involved in field placements		315	5
# involved in law journals		316	19
# involved in moot court or trial competitions		102	6
# of credit hours required to graduate		90	

Transfers

Transfers in	12
Transfers out	40

Tuition and Fees

	Resident	Nonresident
Full-time	$38,180	$38,180
Part-time	$27,300	$27,300
Tuition Guarantee Program	N	

Living Expenses

Estimated living expenses for singles

Living on campus	Living off campus	Living at home
$23,849	$23,849	$23,849

THE JOHN MARSHALL LAW SCHOOL

ABA Approved Since 1951

GPA and LSAT Scores

	Total	Full-Time	Part-Time
# of apps	3,783	3,228	555
# of offers	1,886	1,675	211
# of matrics	512	426	86
75% GPA	3.51	3.52	3.43
Median GPA	3.28	3.29	3.21
25% GPA	2.98	2.98	2.94
75% LSAT	156	156	155
Median LSAT	153	153	151
25% LSAT	149	149	148

Grants and Scholarships (from prior year)

	Total #	Total %	Full-Time #	Full-Time %	Part-Time #	Part-Time %
Total # of students	1,442		1,125		317	
Total # receiving grants	703	48.8	542	48.2	161	50.8
Less than 1/2 tuition	516	35.8	419	37.2	97	30.6
Half to full tuition	91	6.3	54	4.8	37	11.7
Full tuition	38	2.6	26	2.3	12	3.8
More than full tuition	58	4.0	43	3.8	15	4.7
Median grant amount			$10,000		$6,000	

Informational and Library Resources

Total amount spent on library materials	$1,135,137
Study seating capacity inside the library	754
# of full-time equivalent professional librarians	11
Hours per week library is open	96
# of open, wired connections available to students	0
# of networked computers available for use by students	64
Has wireless network?	Y
Requires computer?	N

JD Attrition (from prior year)

	Academic #	Other #	Total #	Total %
1st year	44	63	107	21.0
2nd year	0	0	0	0.0
3rd year	0	0	0	0.0
4th year	0	0	0	0.0

Employment (9 months after graduation)

For up-to-date employment data, go to employmentsummary.abaquestionnaire.org on the ABA website.

Bar Passage Rates

First-time takers	378	Reporting %	93.92
Average school %	88.73	Average state %	89.38

Average pass difference −0.65

Jurisdiction	Takers	Passers	Pass %	State %	Diff %
Illinois	355	315	88.73	89.38	−0.65

THE JOHN MARSHALL LAW SCHOOL

315 South Plymouth Court
Chicago, IL 60604
Phone: 800.537.4280; 312.987.1406; Fax: 312.427.5136
E-mail: admission@jmls.edu; Website: www.jmls.edu

Introduction

Since its founding in 1899, The John Marshall Law School has become one of the nation's largest freestanding institutions dedicated to the teaching of law. The school offers a curriculum, writing courses, and a trial advocacy program that prepare students in the theory and practice of law. Students attend both day and evening classes at the 315 South Plymouth Court location in Chicago's Loop.

The law school's reputation has been built by alumni who work as attorneys in private practice, government, industry, and the judiciary. Among its graduates are President Obama's former Chief of Staff and former US Secretary of Commerce, a member of the Illinois Supreme Court, and the chief judge of the Circuit Court of Cook County, the largest unified court system in the United States.

Students learn in rigorous classes taught by a highly regarded faculty and adjunct faculty. Coursework is supplemented with practical experience through clinical and externship programs. Located in the heart of Chicago's legal, financial, and commercial districts, The John Marshall Law School offers a location that is steps from the federal courthouse and blocks from the central offices of the Circuit Court of Cook County. Its students clerk or find positions with Chicago's top law firms, as well as with boutique firms.

The law school holds accreditations from the American Bar Association, the American Association of Law Schools, and the North Central Association of Colleges and Schools. The ethnically and racially diverse student population reflects the law school's founding principles of access and opportunity.

Curriculum

The law school offers both day and evening programs for JD, MS, and LLM students. Students can be admitted into a joint JD/LLM curriculum after their second year. Students are admitted in both January and August. The law school's JD curriculum places major emphasis on legal foundation classes with required Lawyering Skills writing courses. Students have the option of earning a JD degree with a concentration in advocacy/dispute resolution, business, elder law, employee benefits, estate planning, general practice, information technology and privacy law, intellectual property law, international law, public interest law, or real estate law. Students also can earn a JD degree with a certificate of specialization in alternative dispute resolution, elder law, health law, intellectual property law, international human rights law, sustainability, or trial advocacy.

John Marshall offers students the option of earning a JD/MPA, JD/MA, or JD/MBA degree through relationships with area institutions. The law school also offers MS degrees for the nonlawyer in the areas of employee benefits, information technology and privacy law, intellectual property law, real estate law, and tax law.

John Marshall offers the largest selection of LLM degrees in the Midwest. Lawyers interested in specializing in an area of law for an LLM degree can select from employee benefits, estate planning, information technology and privacy law, intellectual property law, international business and trade law, real estate law, tax law, and trial advocacy and dispute resolution.

Clinics, Externships, and Special Programs

Clinical experience is one of the best hands-on learning techniques. John Marshall's Fair Housing Legal Clinic offers assistance to persons who have been discriminated against in their housing choices. Students learn interview techniques, claims investigation, pleadings, motions, and trial preparation.

The Patent Law Clinic gives students the opportunity to assist needy inventors in preparing and securing patents.

The Immigration Clinic gives students training through the Midwest Immigrant and Human Rights Center where they assist immigrants with asylum claims.

The Veterans Legal Support Center & Clinic gives students the opportunity to assist veterans filing medical and education claims with the United States Department of Veterans Affairs, as well as the opportunity to provide representation for veterans during the appeals process through a statewide network of pro bono attorneys.

The Post-Conviction and Innocence Claims Clinic, in conjunction with the Cook County Public Defender's Office, offers students the opportunity to assist public defenders as they review communications, past transcripts, and records; conduct legal research; and conduct field investigations in cases of appeal.

Students also can gain hands-on experience through externships. Students are paired with attorneys and judges through Judicial Externships, the Defenders Clinic, the Local Government Clinic, and the Prosecution Clinic.

Library

The recently renovated Louis L. Biro Law Library occupies the sixth through tenth floors of the law school's State Street building. A team of over 20 professional librarians and staff members work to serve the students during the 96 hours per week that the library is open. The library holds over 410,000 volumes and microform equivalents and provides on-campus and remote access to over 4,000 titles via our specialty electronic databases. Students have wireless access throughout the law school, and the library offers seating for 750, including eight group-study rooms. In addition to supporting the research and instructional needs of the students, faculty, and staff of the law school, the library is also open to members of the Chicago Bar Association.

Admission

Students are admitted in August and January. Applications for August entrance may be filed between October 1 and March 1; for January entrance, between May 1 and October 15. The LSAT score is evaluated together with the cumulative grade-point average and other relevant factors, including difficulty of undergraduate program, postgraduate experience, leadership potential, business and professional background, and letters of recommendation. Applicants from disadvantaged groups will be given special consideration in cases where their overall records are competitive with other applicants. Minority representation in the class enrolled in 2011 was 33 percent. Applicants with a B+ average overall and an LSAT score in the 67th percentile may be presumed to be within the range for favorable consideration.

Student Activities

There are five honors programs: the *John Marshall Law Review*, the *Journal of Computer and Information Law*, the *Review of Intellectual Property Law* (an online journal), the Moot Court Honors Program, and the Trial Advocacy and Dispute Resolution Honors Program. John Marshall has a long-standing tradition of success in interscholastic competitions and sends teams to more than 30 moot court and mock trial competitions annually.

The student community at John Marshall includes more than 40 student organizations engaging in social awareness, community service, legal discussions, and social activities. Every student group at the law school reflects the diversity, highlights the talents, and enhances the opportunities of our total student body.

John Marshall welcomes numerous well-known visitors and scholars each year. In addition to giving lectures and presentations, our distinguished guests can be found meeting with individual classes or holding roundtable discussions with interested students and faculty.

Career Opportunities

The Career Services Office (CSO) offers personal assistance to help students assess and refine their career goals. The CSO sponsors more than 60 career-related programs each year, many featuring alumni as panelists and speakers. A robust Alumni Mentor Program has mentors meeting with students one-on-one to provide real-world advice on practice areas, law school courses, and the day-to-day practice of law. The CSO also aggressively promotes John Marshall students to employers. John Marshall graduates are employed at 34 of Chicago's 35 largest firms. Public service is another favored career path, with graduates serving as attorneys in the courts and government. Nearly one-fifth of all Illinois judges (circuit, appellate, and state supreme court) are John Marshall alumni.

Correspondence

We encourage you to visit our website at www.jmls.edu and to visit the law school. Tour arrangements can be made through our Office of Admission and visitors are welcome to sit in on a class and talk with students and faculty. An admission counselor can explain the admission process and a representative from our Financial Aid Office can help you understand what loans and scholarships are available.

APPLICANT PROFILE

The John Marshall Law School
This grid includes only applicants who earned 120–180 LSAT scores under standard administrations.

LSAT Score	GPA						
	3.75 +	3.50–3.74	3.25–3.49	3.00–3.24	2.75–2.99	2.50–2.74	Below 2.50
175–180	Good Possibility	Good Possibility	Good Possibility	Good Possibility	Good Possibility	Good Possibility	Good Possibility
170–174	Good Possibility	Good Possibility	Good Possibility	Good Possibility	Good Possibility	Good Possibility	Good Possibility
165–169	Good Possibility	Good Possibility	Good Possibility	Good Possibility	Good Possibility	Good Possibility	Good Possibility
160–164	Good Possibility	Good Possibility	Good Possibility	Good Possibility	Good Possibility	Good Possibility	Good Possibility
155–159	Good Possibility	Good Possibility	Good Possibility	Good Possibility	Good Possibility	Possible	Possible
150–154	Good Possibility	Good Possibility	Possible	Possible	Possible	Unlikely	Unlikely
145–149	Unlikely	Unlikely	Possible	Possible	Possible	Unlikely	Unlikely
140–144	Unlikely	Unlikely	Unlikely	Unlikely	Unlikely	Unlikely	Unlikely
135–139	Unlikely	Unlikely	Unlikely	Unlikely	Unlikely	Unlikely	Unlikely
130–134	Unlikely	Unlikely	Unlikely	Unlikely	Unlikely	Unlikely	Unlikely
125–129	Unlikely	Unlikely	Unlikely	Unlikely	Unlikely	Unlikely	Unlikely
120–124	Unlikely	Unlikely	Unlikely	Unlikely	Unlikely	Unlikely	Unlikely

Legend: ■ Good Possibility   □ Possible   ▨ Unlikely

THE UNIVERSITY OF KANSAS SCHOOL OF LAW

1535 West 15th Street
Lawrence, KS 66045-7608
Phone: 866.220.3654 (toll free), 785.864.4378; Fax: 785.864.5054
E-mail: admitlaw@ku.edu; Website: www.law.ku.edu

ABA
Approved
Since
1923

The Basics

Type of school	Public
Term	Semester
Application deadline	5/1
Application fee	$55
Financial aid deadline	2/15
Can first year start other than fall?	Yes
Student to faculty ratio	13.3 to 1
# of housing spaces available restricted to law students	
graduate housing for which law students are eligible	500

Faculty and Administrators

	Total		Men		Women		Minorities	
	Spr	Fall	Spr	Fall	Spr	Fall	Spr	Fall
Full-time	31	28	19	17	12	11	3	3
Other full-time	3	5	0	0	3	5	0	1
Deans, librarians, & others who teach	6	6	4	5	2	1	2	2
Part-time	25	19	16	14	9	5	2	0
Total	65	58	39	36	26	22	7	6

JD Enrollment and Ethnicity

	Men		Women		Full-Time		Part-Time		1st-Year		Total		JD Degs. Awd.
	#	%	#	%	#	%	#	%	#	%	#	%	
All Hispanics	18	6.3	13	7.3	31	6.7	0	0.0	6	4.5	31	6.7	4
Am. Ind./AK Nat.	6	2.1	3	1.7	9	1.9	0	0.0	2	1.5	9	1.9	7
Asian	9	3.2	6	3.4	15	3.2	0	0.0	3	2.3	15	3.2	12
Black/Af. Am.	7	2.5	5	2.8	12	2.6	0	0.0	4	3.0	12	2.6	8
Nat. HI/Pac. Isl.	0	0.0	0	0.0	0	0.0	0	0.0	0	0.0	0	0.0	0
2 or more races	7	2.5	4	2.2	11	2.4	0	0.0	4	3.0	11	2.4	0
Subtotal (minor.)	47	16.5	31	17.3	78	16.8	0	0.0	19	14.4	78	16.8	31
Nonres. Alien	6	2.1	6	3.4	12	2.6	0	0.0	1	0.8	12	2.6	8
White/Cauc.	218	76.8	136	76.0	354	76.5	0	0.0	103	78.0	354	76.5	125
Unknown	13	4.6	6	3.4	19	4.1	0	0.0	9	6.8	19	4.1	3
Total	284	61.3	179	38.7	463	100.0	0	0.0	132	28.5	463		167

Curriculum

	Full-Time	Part-Time
Typical first-year section size	63	0
Is there typically a "small section" of the first-year class, other than Legal Writing, taught by full-time faculty	Yes	No
If yes, typical size offered last year	21	
# of classroom course titles beyond first-year curriculum	105	

# of upper division courses, excluding seminars, with an enrollment:		
	Under 25	90
	25–49	41
	50–74	12
	75–99	3
	100+	1

# of seminars	15	
# of seminar positions available	336	
# of seminar positions filled	215	0
# of positions available in simulation courses	285	
# of simulation positions filled	253	0
# of positions available in faculty supervised clinical courses	207	
# of faculty supervised clinical positions filled	157	0
# involved in field placements	138	0
# involved in law journals	91	0
# involved in moot court or trial competitions	108	0
# of credit hours required to graduate	90	

Transfers

Transfers in	17
Transfers out	1

Tuition and Fees

	Resident	Nonresident
Full-time	$16,460	$28,648
Part-time		
Tuition Guarantee Program	N	

Living Expenses

Estimated living expenses for singles

Living on campus	Living off campus	Living at home
$17,218	$17,218	$17,218

THE UNIVERSITY OF KANSAS SCHOOL OF LAW

ABA Approved Since 1923

GPA and LSAT Scores

	Total	Full-Time	Part-Time
# of apps	819	819	0
# of offers	401	401	0
# of matrics	134	134	0
75% GPA	3.74	3.74	0.00
Median GPA	3.51	3.51	0.00
25% GPA	3.15	3.15	0.00
75% LSAT	159	159	0
Median LSAT	157	157	0
25% LSAT	154	154	0

Grants and Scholarships (from prior year)

	Total #	Total %	Full-Time #	Full-Time %	Part-Time #	Part-Time %
Total # of students	497		497		0	
Total # receiving grants	365	73.4	365	73.4	0	0.0
Less than 1/2 tuition	293	59.0	293	59.0	0	0.0
Half to full tuition	56	11.3	56	11.3	0	0.0
Full tuition	8	1.6	8	1.6	0	0.0
More than full tuition	8	1.6	8	1.6	0	0.0
Median grant amount			$2,270		$0	

Informational and Library Resources

Total amount spent on library materials	$702,150
Study seating capacity inside the library	481
# of full-time equivalent professional librarians	6
Hours per week library is open	93
# of open, wired connections available to students	0
# of networked computers available for use by students	51
Has wireless network?	Y
Requires computer?	N

JD Attrition (from prior year)

	Academic #	Other #	Total #	Total %
1st year	0	7	7	4.2
2nd year	0	4	4	2.4
3rd year	0	0	0	0.0
4th year	0	0	0	0.0

Employment (9 months after graduation)

For up-to-date employment data, go to employmentsummary.abaquestionnaire.org on the ABA website.

Bar Passage Rates

First-time takers	139	Reporting %	75.54
Average school %	91.43	Average state %	90.08
Average pass difference	1.35		

Jurisdiction	Takers	Passers	Pass %	State %	Diff %
Kansas	70	66	94.29	90.00	4.29
Missouri	35	30	85.71	90.24	-4.53

THE UNIVERSITY OF KANSAS SCHOOL OF LAW

1535 West 15th Street
Lawrence, KS 66045-7608
Phone: 866.220.3654 (toll free), 785.864.4378; Fax: 785.864.5054
E-mail: admitlaw@ku.edu; Website: www.law.ku.edu

KU Law

Three years at KU Law will transform you. You will work extraordinarily hard. You will study theory, policy, the law on the books, and the law in practice. And you will walk away ready to confront the world's legal challenges. A rich curriculum, topflight faculty, collegial environment—all in a vibrant university town brimming with intellectual and cultural abundance. KU Law—a great place to be.

Lawrence, Kansas

Championship basketball and the legendary Phog Allen Fieldhouse are what many people think of when visiting Lawrence, Kansas. While Lawrence and KU are the home of a great basketball tradition, living in Lawrence encompasses so much more. Routinely ranked as one of the top college towns in America, Lawrence prides itself on its thriving music scene, dynamic arts community, and a host of outdoor activities. Historic Massachusetts Street ("Mass Street") is the heart of downtown Lawrence. With its diverse restaurants, clubs, and shops, Mass Street is the community center and a gathering place for students, professors, and locals. Lawrence's weekly farmers' markets feature organic and locally grown food from farms in the Kaw Valley. And students seeking golf, biking, running, or sailing can enjoy all these activities in and around Lawrence.

Where Teaching Matters

KU Law faculty care about teaching. They are committed to excellence in the classroom and to serving as mentors for law students. This is the KU Law tradition. Students are encouraged to consult regularly with their professors about their progress in the study of law as well as career plans, job opportunities, and the professional responsibilities of lawyers. Law faculty offices are located throughout Green Hall, and doors are open to students.

Faculty members enrich their teaching by researching and writing about the areas of law they teach. They regularly participate in symposia, publish widely in legal journals, and enjoy national and international recognition for the quality of their scholarship. Notably, many of the textbooks used at KU Law and at law schools across the country are authored by our faculty.

Learning the Law—Academics and Practice

Our philosophy at KU Law is to teach our students the foundations of the law, then provide them with the hands-on experience necessary to begin their careers ready for practice. We offer 13 clinical programs with more than 200 available clinical openings for students. KU Law clinical students work directly with partner legal organizations to serve their clients. Students with an interest in becoming prosecutors work directly with county and states' attorneys in the courtroom as part of our Criminal Prosecution Clinic. For students inclined toward representing defendants, the Paul E. Wilson Project for Innocence allows them the chance to advocate on behalf of wrongly convicted defendants. Starting this year, students in our Supreme Court clinic will work with

the Kansas Supreme Court researching topics vital to the future of jurisprudence in our home state. These are just a few of the opportunities available for students to experience law as it happens.

The school's setting at the heart of a major university also makes possible the 12 joint-degree programs open to law students. The most popular joint-degree programs are business, health services administration, and social welfare, but joint degrees are also available in East Asian languages and cultures, economics, indigenous studies, journalism, philosophy, political science, public administration, urban planning, and East European, Eurasian, and Russian Studies.

Summer Start Program

The law school's unique summer start program is fully integrated with the curriculum of the fall and spring semesters. Students who enroll as summer starters have the option of either using the credits earned during the summer to lighten their courseload during their first year, or accelerating their graduation by a semester through additional summer coursework between their first and second years. Such students will graduate at the end of their third year fall semester.

Small Class Sizes, Extensive Course Selection

Small classes are instrumental in fostering the closely knit and supportive environment found in Green Hall. More than two-thirds of our upper-level classes feature class sizes of 25 (or fewer) students. These seminar-sized classes allow students and professors to engage in extended discussion and discourse. Students also have a rich course selection to choose from, with more than 100 upper-level courses offered. KU Law students can focus on a number of core strengths, including intellectual property, corporate, media, tax, public interest, tribal, natural resources environment, and advocacy. Certificate programs in each of these areas ensure students will have ample opportunities to study in these fields.

Jayhawk Lawyers

KU Law is a national law school with a strong regional presence. Over the past four years our graduating students—Jayhawk Lawyers—have found employment in more than 35 states across the nation. Recent graduates have found positions clerking for the US Supreme Court and working for the nation's top law firms in New York, Dallas, and Chicago, and even overseas. Closer to home, many students stay in Kansas and benefit from the diverse and local Kansas economy. Our location in the I-70 technology corridor directs many of our students toward a practice in intellectual property law. Others practice sophisticated corporate law in both the litigation and transactional departments of major law firms. Still others venture to rural counties to serve the needs of communities across the state. Our graduates also excel as prosecutors, defenders, and judges in local, state, and federal courts.

A History of Diversity

Since its founding in 1878, KU Law has been open to all qualified applicants—regardless of gender or ethnicity. We are proud of this history, and we remain committed to providing access to a legal education for men and women of all religions, ethnicities, sexual orientations, and physical abilities. Attracting students from diverse backgrounds ensures that all points of view will be heard in our classrooms and in the legal community.

International and Comparative Law

KU Law has one of the leading International and Comparative Law programs in the region. Students studying international law are taught by leading academics in the fields of international trade and finance. The school also hosts the Center for International Trade and Agriculture, which promotes research and outreach for students, scholars, and policymakers throughout the region and the world. KU Law

students can add to their experience by taking part in our study-abroad programs in England, Ireland, and Turkey. Past teachers have included US Supreme Court Justices Antonin Scalia and Ruth Bader Ginsburg.

International students can enroll in either the LLM or two-year JD program, which enables them to practice law in the United States or take what they have learned back to their home countries. Students who complete a KU Law LLM are eligible to apply for transfer to the two-year program. KU Law also offers an SJD program for international scholars.

Affordability

Finally, KU Law takes prides in its ability to offer a world-class legal education at a reasonable rate of tuition. Our students graduate with an average debt burden far below the amounts found at other law schools. Affordability means choice for our graduates—they can choose to start their careers serving the public, clerking for the judicial system, or pursuing entrepreneurial opportunities in law and business.

APPLICANT PROFILE

The University of Kansas School of Law
This grid includes only applicants who earned 120–180 LSAT scores under standard administrations.

LSAT Score	GPA								
	3.75 +	3.50–3.74	3.25–3.49	3.00–3.24	2.75–2.99	2.50–2.74	2.25–2.49	2.00–2.24	Below 2.00
175–180	■	■	■	■	■				▒
170–174	■	■	■	■	■				
165–169	■	■	■	■	■			▒	▒
160–164	■	■	■	■	■			▒	▒
155–159	■	■	■	■			▒	▒	▒
150–154	■	■	■	■	▒	▒	▒	▒	▒
145–149				▒	▒	▒	▒	▒	▒
140–144	▒		▒	▒	▒	▒	▒	▒	▒
135–139	▒	▒	▒	▒	▒	▒	▒	▒	▒
130–134	▒	▒	▒	▒	▒	▒	▒	▒	▒
125–129	▒	▒	▒	▒	▒	▒	▒	▒	▒
120–124	▒	▒	▒	▒	▒	▒	▒	▒	▒

■ Good Possibility   ☐ Possible   ▒ Unlikely

UNIVERSITY OF KENTUCKY COLLEGE OF LAW

209 Law Building, 620 South Limestone Street
Lexington, KY 40506-0048
Phone: 859.257.1678; Fax: 859.257.3950
E-mail: lawadmissions@email.uky.edu; Website: www.law.uky.edu

ABA
Approved
Since
1925

The Basics

Type of school	Public
Term	Semester
Application deadline	3/1
Application fee	$50
Financial aid deadline	3/15
Can first year start other than fall?	No
Student to faculty ratio	14.6 to 1
# of housing spaces available restricted to law students	
graduate housing for which law students are eligible	419

Faculty and Administrators

	Total		Men		Women		Minorities	
	Spr	Fall	Spr	Fall	Spr	Fall	Spr	Fall
Full-time	23	24	16	17	7	7	3	3
Other full-time	0	0	0	0	0	0	0	0
Deans, librarians, & others who teach	9	13	4	6	5	7	2	2
Part-time	20	19	13	14	7	5	1	0
Total	52	56	33	37	19	19	6	5

Curriculum

	Full-Time	Part-Time
Typical first-year section size	65	0
Is there typically a "small section" of the first-year class, other than Legal Writing, taught by full-time faculty	Yes	No
If yes, typical size offered last year	45	
# of classroom course titles beyond first-year curriculum	107	

# of upper division courses, excluding seminars, with an enrollment:		
	Under 25	64
	25–49	29
	50–74	11
	75–99	0
	100+	0

# of seminars	10	
# of seminar positions available	160	
# of seminar positions filled	153	0
# of positions available in simulation courses	150	
# of simulation positions filled	70	0
# of positions available in faculty supervised clinical courses	32	
# of faculty supervised clinical positions filled	31	0
# involved in field placements	78	0
# involved in law journals	54	0
# involved in moot court or trial competitions	53	0
# of credit hours required to graduate	90	

JD Enrollment and Ethnicity

	Men #	Men %	Women #	Women %	Full-Time #	Full-Time %	Part-Time #	Part-Time %	1st-Year #	1st-Year %	Total #	Total %	JD Degs. Awd.
All Hispanics	4	1.7	2	1.1	6	1.4	0	0.0	2	1.5	6	1.4	2
Am. Ind./AK Nat.	3	1.3	0	0.0	3	0.7	0	0.0	1	0.8	3	0.7	0
Asian	8	3.4	4	2.2	12	2.9	0	0.0	3	2.3	12	2.9	3
Black/Af. Am.	18	7.6	20	11.2	38	9.2	0	0.0	10	7.7	38	9.2	11
Nat. HI/Pac. Isl.	0	0.0	0	0.0	0	0.0	0	0.0	0	0.0	0	0.0	1
2 or more races	0	0.0	3	1.7	3	0.7	0	0.0	1	0.8	3	0.7	0
Subtotal (minor.)	33	13.9	29	16.3	62	14.9	0	0.0	17	13.1	62	14.9	17
Nonres. Alien	1	0.4	1	0.6	2	0.5	0	0.0	2	1.5	2	0.5	0
White/Cauc.	200	84.4	147	82.6	347	83.6	0	0.0	107	82.3	347	83.6	119
Unknown	3	1.3	1	0.6	4	1.0	0	0.0	4	3.1	4	1.0	0
Total	237	57.1	178	42.9	415	100.0	0	0.0	130	31.3	415		136

Transfers

Transfers in	9
Transfers out	3

Tuition and Fees

	Resident	Nonresident
Full-time	$18,306	$31,716
Part-time		
Tuition Guarantee Program	N	

Living Expenses

Estimated living expenses for singles

Living on campus	Living off campus	Living at home
$15,694	$15,694	$5,994

UNIVERSITY OF KENTUCKY COLLEGE OF LAW

ABA Approved Since 1925

GPA and LSAT Scores

	Total	Full-Time	Part-Time
# of apps	1,114	1,114	0
# of offers	456	456	0
# of matrics	130	130	0
75% GPA	3.80	3.80	0.00
Median GPA	3.57	3.57	0.00
25% GPA	3.32	3.32	0.00
75% LSAT	161	161	0
Median LSAT	159	159	0
25% LSAT	155	155	0

Grants and Scholarships (from prior year)

	Total #	Total %	Full-Time #	Full-Time %	Part-Time #	Part-Time %
Total # of students	419		419		0	
Total # receiving grants	285	68.0	285	68.0	0	0.0
Less than 1/2 tuition	171	40.8	171	40.8	0	0.0
Half to full tuition	106	25.3	106	25.3	0	0.0
Full tuition	2	0.5	2	0.5	0	0.0
More than full tuition	6	1.4	6	1.4	0	0.0
Median grant amount			$5,000		$0	

Informational and Library Resources

Total amount spent on library materials	$1,181,743
Study seating capacity inside the library	313
# of full-time equivalent professional librarians	7
Hours per week library is open	100
# of open, wired connections available to students	9
# of networked computers available for use by students	40
Has wireless network?	Y
Requires computer?	N

JD Attrition (from prior year)

	Academic #	Other #	Total #	Total %
1st year	1	3	4	3.0
2nd year	0	0	0	0.0
3rd year	0	0	0	0.0
4th year	0	0	0	0.0

Employment (9 months after graduation)

For up-to-date employment data, go to employmentsummary.abaquestionnaire.org on the ABA website.

Bar Passage Rates

First-time takers	133	Reporting %	77.44
Average school %	84.47	Average state %	82.03
Average pass difference	2.44		

Jurisdiction	Takers	Passers	Pass %	State %	Diff %
Kentucky	103	87	84.47	82.03	2.44

UNIVERSITY OF KENTUCKY COLLEGE OF LAW

209 Law Building, 620 South Limestone Street
Lexington, KY 40506-0048
Phone: 859.257.1678; Fax: 859.257.3950
E-mail: lawadmissions@email.uky.edu; Website: www.law.uky.edu

Introduction

The University of Kentucky College of Law is a small, state-supported law school on the main campus of the university in scenic Lexington, Kentucky, a city of approximately 250,000 in the center of the Bluegrass horse farm region. Founded in 1908, the college has been a member of the AALS since 1912 and has been accredited by the ABA since 1925. The faculty has wide experience in law practice and government service, as well as teaching and research. UK Law has a strong tradition of faculty concern about their students' progress and success. The curriculum offers broad training in the law and legal methods, drawing upon sources from all jurisdictions. Accordingly, UK Law graduates are prepared to practice in any of the 50 states.

Library and Physical Facilities

The college is self-contained in a contemporary building that provides all facilities for a complete program of legal education. All classrooms have been renovated with the addition of state-of-the-art teaching technology. Classrooms provide for student use of laptop computers with wired and wireless Internet access. The law library is on the college's wireless network with a number of attractive study areas, and laptops are available for you to check out and use in the library.

Curriculum

UK Law offers a full-time program only, designed to be completed over three academic years or two and one-half years if you take classes during both summer sessions. Some first-year classes are divided into three sections to give you more individual attention, and you will be in a small legal writing section. As an upper-level student, you can select from a full range of elective courses in both traditional and newly developing legal fields. After the first year, the only specific requirements are that you take a course in professional ethics, take at least one professional skills course, and complete a seminar involving substantial writing.

Legal Clinic

UK Law's Legal Clinic is located in its own building near the college. As a third-year student in the clinic course, you would represent low-income clients in a variety of civil legal matters. The clinic is supervised by a faculty member who was a very successful trial attorney for 10 years.

Externships

UK Law offers 10 externships for course credit. The Judicial Clerkship Externship enables you to serve as a law clerk for a local state or federal judge. The Fayette Commonwealth Attorney's Office Externship enables you to participate in criminal prosecutions. The Federal Correctional Institute Externship permits you to counsel federal inmates in civil and criminal matters. In the externship with the Kentucky Innocence Project, you work on selected criminal appeals where a claim of factual innocence is made. The externship with the US Attorney's Office gives you the opportunity to work on federal appellate briefs in both criminal and civil cases. The Children's Law Center Externship allows you to work on high-conflict custody cases representing children, while the Child Advocacy Today Externship gives you the opportunity to help at-risk children where their legal and medical issues intersect. The Department of Public Advocacy Externship enables you to work with the defense in criminal trials. The externship with the UK HealthCare Risk Management Office gives you firsthand experience with hospital risk management issues and procedures. The Energy and Environment Cabinet Externship gives you insight into the legal and policy issues arising from energy development and environmental protection.

Joint Degrees

If you are interested in a career in international law, public or private law, international business, or in government service in the international sector, you should consider the four-year **JD/MA** dual-degree program with UK's Patterson School of Diplomacy and International Commerce. You must apply and be admitted to both programs.

The **JD/MBA** joint degree can be obtained in as little time as four years. You must apply and be admitted to both the UK College of Law and UK's Gatton College of Business and Economics.

If you are interested in a career in public administration, public service, or politics, you should consider the four-year **JD/MPA** joint-degree program with UK's Martin School of Public Policy. You must apply and be admitted to both programs.

Student Activities

There are a variety of cocurricular activities in which you may earn course credit. The *Kentucky Law Journal* is the 10th oldest American law review and is edited entirely by students, as is the *Kentucky Journal for Equine, Agricultural, and Natural Resources Law*. The college fields several moot court teams that participate in both national and international competitions. UK Law's Trial Advocacy Team advanced to national title competitions in six of the last seven years, placing second nationally in 2009. The Mock Trial Team for UK's Black Law Students Association won the Southeast Region of the Thurgood Marshall Moot Court Competition in both 2006 and 2008, placing second in the nation in 2006.

UK Law's Student Bar Association (SBA) serves as the law student governing body and student activities board. The SBA publishes a weekly online student newspaper and sponsors regular student social events and community service activities. UK's SBA was recognized by the ABA as the best student bar association in the nation in 2002.

The Student Public Interest Law Foundation, through grants and fundraising, sponsors 15 to 20 summer internships with public interest and public service organizations selected by the students who apply. Other active student groups include the Black Law Students Association, the Latino/a Law Student Association, the Asian-Pacific Islander Law Student Association, OUTLaw, the Women's Law Caucus, the Federalist Society, the American Constitutional Society, the

Criminal Law Society, the International Law Society, the Environmental Law Society, the Equine Law Society, the Health Law Society, the Intellectual Property Law Society, the Tax Law Society, the Libertarian Law Society, and the Student Animal Legal Defense Fund.

Admission

Admission is considered and granted by the faculty Admissions Committee. Each file is reviewed completely and is voted on by the full committee. While your undergraduate academic record and LSAT score(s) are the primary indicators for potential success in law school, all other factors you present will be considered. You are urged to read the full description of the admission process on our website and to provide full information about your intellectual and nonacademic achievements. The February LSAT is the last examination accepted by the Admissions Committee for that year. In almost all cases, your highest LSAT score will be used by the committee in making the admission decision. Admission as a first-year student is for the fall term only.

Scholarships and Financial Aid

Over 60 percent of UK Law's 2011 entering class received some form of scholarship award. UK Law offers a number of three-year scholarships based on merit and/or contributions to diversity, for which you will be considered automatically after admission. For the largest and most prestigious award, the Bert Combs Scholarship, you must be selected for an interview. UK Law also offers three-year merit and diversity

tuition-reduction fellowships for nonresidents of Kentucky. You have the option of including a brief statement about your eligibility for merit and/or diversity awards with your admission application, but a separate scholarship application is not required. UK Law students are eligible for loan assistance through the Federal Direct Student Loan Program and federal graduate PLUS loan program, as well as through national private loan programs. Admitted candidates are mailed complete information on financial aid. To receive forms and information prior to admission, contact UK's Student Financial Aid Office, 128 Funkhouser Building, University of Kentucky, Lexington, KY 40506-0054.

Career Services

UK Law students have the benefit of a large on-campus job interview program for regional employers, as well as national placement through the college's participation in numerous off-campus interviewing conferences. The Career Services Office also uses alumni contacts to connect students with employers nationwide. Two UK Law graduates who are former practicing attorneys are on staff to offer advice and guidance to UK Law students and alumni.

UK Law's job placement rate consistently exceeds national averages. For the 2010 graduating class, 95 percent were employed or in advanced-degree programs within nine months after graduation. A majority of UK Law graduates choose private practice, with 15 to 25 percent of each graduating class selected for prestigious state and federal judicial clerkships.

APPLICANT PROFILE

University of Kentucky College of Law
This grid includes only applicants who earned 120–180 LSAT scores under standard administrations.

LSAT Score	GPA								
	3.75 +	3.50–3.74	3.25–3.49	3.00–3.24	2.75–2.99	2.50–2.74	2.25–2.49	2.00–2.24	Below 2.00
175–180									
170–174									
165–169									
160–164									
155–159									
150–154									
145–149									
140–144									
135–139									
130–134									
125–129									
120–124									

Good Possibility   Possible   Unlikely

UNIVERSITY OF LA VERNE COLLEGE OF LAW

320 East D Street
Ontario, CA 91764
Phone: 877.858.4529; Fax: 909.460.2082
E-mail: lawadm@laverne.edu; Website: http://law.laverne.edu

Provisional ABA Approved Since 2006

The Basics

Type of school	Private
Term	Semester
Application deadline	7/1
Application fee	$50
Financial aid deadline	3/2
Can first year start other than fall?	Yes
Student to faculty ratio	13.2 to 1
# of housing spaces available restricted to law students	
graduate housing for which law students are eligible	

Faculty and Administrators

	Total		Men		Women		Minorities	
	Spr	Fall	Spr	Fall	Spr	Fall	Spr	Fall
Full-time	19	19	9	8	10	11	7	6
Other full-time	0	0	0	0	0	0	0	0
Deans, librarians, & others who teach	8	5	5	5	3	0	3	2
Part-time	39	30	23	23	16	7	5	4
Total	66	54	37	36	29	18	15	12

Curriculum

	Full-Time	Part-Time
Typical first-year section size	30	15
Is there typically a "small section" of the first-year class, other than Legal Writing, taught by full-time faculty	No	No
If yes, typical size offered last year		
# of classroom course titles beyond first-year curriculum	75	

# of upper division courses, excluding seminars, with an enrollment:		
	Under 25	83
	25–49	37
	50–74	2
	75–99	0
	100+	0

# of seminars	8	
# of seminar positions available	120	
# of seminar positions filled	69	15
# of positions available in simulation courses	505	
# of simulation positions filled	348	129
# of positions available in faculty supervised clinical courses	24	
# of faculty supervised clinical positions filled	13	3
# involved in field placements	102	12
# involved in law journals	34	5
# involved in moot court or trial competitions	27	4
# of credit hours required to graduate	88	

JD Enrollment and Ethnicity

	Men		Women		Full-Time		Part-Time		1st-Year		Total		JD Degs. Awd.
	#	%	#	%	#	%	#	%	#	%	#	%	
All Hispanics	28	19.3	28	21.7	44	24.3	12	12.9	16	32.0	56	20.4	20
Am. Ind./AK Nat.	2	1.4	0	0.0	2	1.1	0	0.0	0	0.0	2	0.7	0
Asian	15	10.3	21	16.3	23	12.7	13	14.0	6	12.0	36	13.1	11
Black/Af. Am.	3	2.1	2	1.6	2	1.1	3	3.2	0	0.0	5	1.8	1
Nat. HI/Pac. Isl.	0	0.0	5	3.9	4	2.2	1	1.1	2	4.0	5	1.8	2
2 or more races	1	0.7	2	1.6	3	1.7	0	0.0	0	0.0	3	1.1	0
Subtotal (minor.)	49	33.8	58	45.0	78	43.1	29	31.2	24	48.0	107	39.1	34
Nonres. Alien	2	1.4	4	3.1	6	3.3	0	0.0	0	0.0	6	2.2	2
White/Cauc.	94	64.8	67	51.9	97	53.6	64	68.8	26	52.0	161	58.8	80
Unknown	0	0.0	0	0.0	0	0.0	0	0.0	0	0.0	0	0.0	0
Total	145	52.9	129	47.1	181	66.1	93	33.9	50	18.2	274		116

Transfers

Transfers in	1
Transfers out	34

Tuition and Fees

	Resident	Nonresident
Full-time	$40,732	$40,732
Part-time	$32,102	$32,102
Tuition Guarantee Program		N

Living Expenses

Estimated living expenses for singles

Living on campus	Living off campus	Living at home
$24,310	$24,310	$24,310

UNIVERSITY OF LA VERNE COLLEGE OF LAW

ABA
Approved
Since
2006

GPA and LSAT Scores

	Total	Full-Time	Part-Time
# of apps	1,182	978	204
# of offers	484	415	69
# of matrics	55	29	26
75% GPA	3.25	3.23	3.25
Median GPA	3.05	3.02	3.05
25% GPA	2.73	2.71	2.77
75% LSAT	156	155	157
Median LSAT	153	153	153
25% LSAT	150	150	150

Grants and Scholarships (from prior year)

	Total		Full-Time		Part-Time	
	#	%	#	%	#	%
Total # of students	426		312		114	
Total # receiving grants	377	88.5	276	88.5	101	88.6
Less than 1/2 tuition	230	54.0	156	50.0	74	64.9
Half to full tuition	136	31.9	113	36.2	23	20.2
Full tuition	11	2.6	7	2.2	4	3.5
More than full tuition	0	0.0	0	0.0	0	0.0
Median grant amount			$16,500		$8,250	

Informational and Library Resources

Total amount spent on library materials	$966,957
Study seating capacity inside the library	209
# of full-time equivalent professional librarians	9
Hours per week library is open	96
# of open, wired connections available to students	100
# of networked computers available for use by students	35
Has wireless network?	Y
Requires computer?	N

JD Attrition (from prior year)

	Academic	Other	Total	
	#	#	#	%
1st year	21	51	72	43.6
2nd year	8	6	14	12.7
3rd year	0	0	0	0.0
4th year	0	0	0	0.0

Employment (9 months after graduation)

For up-to-date employment data, go to
employmentsummary.abaquestionnaire.org on the ABA website.

Bar Passage Rates

First-time takers	95	Reporting %	100.00
Average school %	52.63	Average state %	72.28

Average pass difference –19.65

Jurisdiction	Takers	Passers	Pass %	State %	Diff %
California	87	42	48.28	71.24	–22.96
Nevada	2	2	100.00	72.72	27.28
Utah	2	2	100.00	89.35	10.65
Connecticut	1	1	100.00	84.76	15.24
Others (3)	3	3	100.00		

UNIVERSITY OF LA VERNE COLLEGE OF LAW

320 East D Street
Ontario, CA 91764
Phone: 877.858.4529; Fax: 909.460.2082
E-mail: lawadm@laverne.edu; Website: http://law.laverne.edu

Introduction

The University of La Verne College of Law, located just east of Los Angeles in inland Southern California, is situated in a growing metropolitan region of more than 6 million people. Founded in 1970, La Verne Law is a part of the University of La Verne, which enjoys a 121-year reputation for providing a sound learning experience built on values, diversity, lifelong learning, and community service. Distinguished faculty, personalized attention, and a supportive campus community provide the foundation for enhanced academic and professional success.

Faculty

La Verne Law's faculty members are leading experts in their fields. Many have experience in either the public or private sectors and boast backgrounds as diverse and highly regarded as they are. In the classroom, they infuse instruction with practical knowledge to provide a firm understanding of both legal theory and application. Outside of class, they remain accessible to students to provide guidance and assistance as needed.

Curriculum

La Verne Law provides a rigorous legal education rooted in the foundational elements of law and its practical applications. The law school offers both full-time and part-time programs leading to the Juris Doctor degree.

Both programs are designed to provide grounding in legal theory, lawyering skills, and ethics: areas critical to the modern practice of law. Successful completion of the JD degree at the University of La Verne College of Law requires completion of a total of 88 units.

Students interested in a career in business or public administration can take advantage of La Verne Law's Juris Doctor/Master of Business Administration (JD/MBA) and Juris Doctor/Master of Public Administration (JD/MPA) dual-degree programs with the University of La Verne's College of Business and Public Management. Applicants must meet the admission standards of each degree program and should consult with each college for specific entrance requirements.

La Verne Law also offers students the opportunity to participate in cocurricular activities including the *University of La Verne Law Review*, as well as Moot Court, Trial Team, and Alternative Dispute Resolution competition teams.

Practical Skills and Clinics

La Verne Law requires all students to take part in a Lawyering Skills Practicum course that offers the chance to simulate the practice of law. The law school also houses two campus-based clinics that allow students to work directly on legal issues with real clients, under the guidance of accomplished attorneys. The Disability Rights Legal Center focuses on disability civil rights litigation and special-education issues for low-income and minority families. The Justice and Immigration Clinic allows students to represent asylum applicants who cannot return to their home countries because of persecution based on race, religion, nationality, political opinion, or membership in a particular social group.

Outside of class, La Verne Law students are given the opportunity to do externships with government agencies including the District Attorney's Office and the Public Defender's Office, judges, public interest organizations, and legal nonprofits.

Campus and Library

La Verne Law is ideally situated with easy access to freeways and airports, and within reach to the many dining, shopping, entertainment, social, and outdoor activities intrinsic to the culture of Southern California. A 64,000-square-foot campus center is designed to give students ready access to technology, and it includes a state-of-the-art computer lab and on-campus Internet access via a combination of hardwired and wireless connections. Classrooms are equipped with the latest audiovisual technologies, and La Verne Law's moot courtroom includes a custom-designed audio-video system used for trial and appellate exercises. A large, grassy park provides shade trees and picnic areas.

La Verne Law's library boasts more than 300,000 print and microform resources, including federal and California statutory law, court opinions, administrative rules and regulations, major treatises on a variety of legal topics, form and practice books, numerous legal periodicals, and access to a huge variety of electronic databases. The Law Library also serves as a selective depository for federal and California government documents, including legislative materials. Reference librarians, expert legal researchers who hold both JD and MLS degrees, are available for consultation Monday through Friday. The Law Library also hosts a free series of short courses allowing law students the opportunity to obtain a Certificate in Legal Research.

Admission

La Verne Law seeks out students who demonstrate a desire and ability to apply themselves to the rigors of law school and to embrace the professional standards inherent in the practice of law. To fit the needs of every student, the law school offers both part-time and full-time programs.

The law school's commitment to personalized assistance extends to its admission process. The Admissions Committee considers a variety of criteria in the selection of applicants, including LSAT performance, academic ability, educational and professional achievements, motivation for entering the legal profession, work ethic, diversity, leadership skills, and moral character.

Career Services

La Verne Law's Career Services and Professional Development Office provides students with resources and opportunities to make the most of their legal education and career goals. Services available to both students and alumni include

- individualized career counseling and résumé, cover-letter, and writing-sample review;

- career and professional development workshops on topics ranging from interviewing skills to negotiating a job offer;
- on-campus interview and networking opportunities with representatives from law firms, corporations, government agencies, and public interest organizations;
- a continually updated database of job postings featuring opportunities for law clerk positions, externships, judicial clerkships, and postgraduate positions;
- the opportunity, through the law school's Mentor Program and Mock Interview Program, for students to connect with practicing attorneys for career advice, or for alumni and other practitioners to help students transition smoothly into inland Southern California's legal community;
- the opportunity to obtain paid law clerk positions with a law firm;
- panels and receptions where students hear from and mingle with attorneys and potential employers from a variety of practice areas; and
- career fairs and consortium events with other Southern California ABA-approved law schools.

La Verne Law alumni have been successful in obtaining positions with law firms, corporations, government agencies, and public interest organizations. Many have started their own thriving practices; some have earned the honor of serving on the bench.

Student Activities

La Verne Law students have the opportunity to participate in a wide variety of extracurricular activities. They may take part in a number of student organizations, or in some cases establish their own per school policy. Most student activity is both social and career focused, reflecting a broad array of interests, cultures, and lifestyles. The organizations on campus include the Alternative Dispute Resolution Association, the American Constitution Society, the Armenian Law Society, the Asian Pacific American Law Student Association, the Black Law Students Association, the Criminal Law Society, Delta Theta Phi Law Fraternity, the Family Law Society, the Federalist Society, the Hispanic National Bar Association, the International Law Students Association, the J. Reuben Clark Law Society, Phi Alpha Delta Law Fraternity, Pride Law Alliance, the Public Interest Law Foundation, the Society of Legal Studies and Business, the Sports and Entertainment Law Society, the Women's Legal Society, and the Student Bar Association.

Scholarships and Financial Aid

A vast majority of students at La Verne Law receive some kind of financial assistance to pay for their law school education. The Office of Financial Aid works closely with students to walk them through the process of applying for student loans, grants, and work-study programs. One-on-one financial counseling is provided to all students to ensure that they complete law school with the least amount of debt possible. Applying for assistance will not jeopardize a student's chance for admission. Generous merit- and need-based scholarships are also available to qualified students.

APPLICANT PROFILE

The University of La Verne College of Law, located just east of Los Angeles in inland Southern California, is situated in a growing metropolitan region of more than six million people. Founded in 1970, La Verne Law is a part of the University of La Verne, which enjoys a 121-year reputation for providing a sound learning experience built on values, diversity, lifelong learning, and community service. Distinguished faculty, personalized attention, and a supportive campus community provide the foundation for enhanced academic and professional success.

LEWIS & CLARK LAW SCHOOL

10015 SW Terwilliger Boulevard
Portland, OR 97219-7799
Phone: 800.303.4860 or 503.768.6613; Fax: 503.768.6793
E-mail: lawadmss@lclark.edu; Website: law.lclark.edu

ABA Approved Since 1970

The Basics

Type of school	Private
Term	Semester
Application deadline	3/1
Application fee	$50
Financial aid deadline	3/1
Can first year start other than fall?	No
Student to faculty ratio	10.1 to 1
# of housing spaces available restricted to law students graduate housing for which law students are eligible	22

Faculty and Administrators

	Total		Men		Women		Minorities	
	Spr	Fall	Spr	Fall	Spr	Fall	Spr	Fall
Full-time	55	52	31	29	24	23	8	7
Other full-time	2	3	0	0	2	3	0	1
Deans, librarians, & others who teach	14	12	6	5	8	7	1	1
Part-time	41	43	27	28	14	15	6	2
Total	112	110	64	62	48	48	15	11

Curriculum

		Full-Time	Part-Time
Typical first-year section size		82	62
Is there typically a "small section" of the first-year class, other than Legal Writing, taught by full-time faculty		Yes	Yes
If yes, typical size offered last year		44	31
# of classroom course titles beyond first-year curriculum		145	
# of upper division courses, excluding seminars, with an enrollment:	Under 25	130	
	25–49	38	
	50–74	12	
	75–99	6	
	100+	1	
# of seminars		28	
# of seminar positions available		515	
# of seminar positions filled		241	123
# of positions available in simulation courses		722	
# of simulation positions filled		372	169
# of positions available in faculty supervised clinical courses		201	
# of faculty supervised clinical positions filled		120	57
# involved in field placements		102	18
# involved in law journals		108	32
# involved in moot court or trial competitions		98	36
# of credit hours required to graduate		89	

JD Enrollment and Ethnicity

	Men		Women		Full-Time		Part-Time		1st-Year		Total		JD Degs. Awd.
	#	%	#	%	#	%	#	%	#	%	#	%	
All Hispanics	27	7.7	29	7.5	34	6.9	22	9.0	18	8.1	56	7.6	8
Am. Ind./AK Nat.	7	2.0	17	4.4	12	2.4	12	4.9	5	2.3	24	3.3	4
Asian	19	5.4	42	10.9	43	8.7	18	7.3	16	7.2	61	8.3	25
Black/Af. Am.	8	2.3	13	3.4	7	1.4	14	5.7	5	2.3	21	2.8	10
Nat. HI/Pac. Isl.	0	0.0	1	0.3	1	0.2	0	0.0	0	0.0	1	0.1	0
2 or more races	5	1.4	5	1.3	8	1.6	2	0.8	9	4.1	10	1.4	0
Subtotal (minor.)	66	18.8	107	27.7	105	21.3	68	27.8	53	23.9	173	23.4	47
Nonres. Alien	9	2.6	5	1.3	9	1.8	5	2.0	4	1.8	14	1.9	7
White/Cauc.	252	71.6	260	67.4	353	71.6	159	64.9	150	67.6	512	69.4	162
Unknown	25	7.1	14	3.6	26	5.3	13	5.3	15	6.8	39	5.3	17
Total	352	47.7	386	52.3	493	66.8	245	33.2	222	30.1	738		233

Transfers

Transfers in	30
Transfers out	6

Tuition and Fees

	Resident	Nonresident
Full-time	$36,412	$36,412
Part-time	$27,320	$27,320
Tuition Guarantee Program		N

Living Expenses

Estimated living expenses for singles

Living on campus	Living off campus	Living at home
N/A	$21,400	$21,400

LEWIS & CLARK LAW SCHOOL

ABA
Approved
Since
1970

GPA and LSAT Scores

	Total	Full-Time	Part-Time
# of apps	2,907	2,706	201
# of offers	1,143	1,052	91
# of matrics	226	187	39
75% GPA	3.68	3.70	3.66
Median GPA	3.49	3.51	3.35
25% GPA	3.20	3.25	3.12
75% LSAT	163	164	161
Median LSAT	161	162	157
25% LSAT	157	158	153

Grants and Scholarships (from prior year)

	Total #	Total %	Full-Time #	Full-Time %	Part-Time #	Part-Time %
Total # of students	741		529		212	
Total # receiving grants	312	42.1	265	50.1	47	22.2
Less than 1/2 tuition	231	31.2	197	37.2	34	16.0
Half to full tuition	77	10.4	64	12.1	13	6.1
Full tuition	3	0.4	3	0.6	0	0.0
More than full tuition	1	0.1	1	0.2	0	0.0
Median grant amount			$12,500		$10,000	

Informational and Library Resources

Total amount spent on library materials	$1,378,374
Study seating capacity inside the library	385
# of full-time equivalent professional librarians	8
Hours per week library is open	113
# of open, wired connections available to students	908
# of networked computers available for use by students	87
Has wireless network?	Y
Requires computer?	N

JD Attrition (from prior year)

	Academic #	Other #	Total #	Total %
1st year	2	15	17	6.9
2nd year	0	5	5	2.2
3rd year	0	0	0	0.0
4th year	0	0	0	0.0

Employment (9 months after graduation)

For up-to-date employment data, go to employmentsummary.abaquestionnaire.org on the ABA website.

Bar Passage Rates

First-time takers	164	Reporting %	81.71
Average school %	79.10	Average state %	75.22
Average pass difference	3.88		

Jurisdiction	Takers	Passers	Pass %	State %	Diff %
Oregon	134	106	79.10	75.22	3.88

LEWIS & CLARK LAW SCHOOL

10015 SW Terwilliger Boulevard
Portland, OR 97219-7799
Phone: 800.303.4860 or 503.768.6613; Fax: 503.768.6793
E-mail: lawadmss@lclark.edu; Website: law.lclark.edu

Introduction

Lewis & Clark Law School believes in a balanced approach to legal education that ensures a solid theoretical foundation along with hands-on experience in practice. Situated next to a state park, the campus is one of the most beautiful in the nation. Students are only a moment away from an extensive trail system used by joggers, walkers, and bicyclists.

Enrollment/Student Body

The approximately 750 students attending the Law School represent a spectrum of ages, experiences, and priorities. Business executives, scientists, students of politics, musicians, and school teachers—people from many disciplines—meet at the Law School in a common pursuit. The atmosphere is one of mutual support during a time of academic challenge. Students and faculty can often be found discussing questions long after class has ended.

Faculty

The full-time faculty were educated at the nation's most distinguished law schools. They reflect a breadth of experience and interests that give depth and creative energy to their teaching. A number of faculty members have spent sabbaticals in recent years teaching in other countries; several have been Fulbright professors in such places as China, Greece, Germany, and Venezuela.

Library and Physical Facilities

The resources and staff of the Paul L. Boley Law Library, the largest law library in the state and the second largest in the Northwest, well exceed the standards set by the Association of American Law Schools.

Our collection includes extensive materials in environmental law, federal legislative history, tax law, commercial law, intellectual property, and legal history. We are also the only academic law library in the country to be a Patent and Trademark Depository Library. Supporting our collection is a sophisticated computer infrastructure of instruction labs and local area networks.

The Law School library is an exquisite study space with computer labs equipped with the latest technology. Wireless access is available on the entire campus.

Framed by majestic fir trees, the campus is composed of contemporary buildings with classrooms and a large state park within a moment's walk from the library. Traditional student needs and those of individuals with disabilities are met through a variety of facilities.

Curriculum

The Law School confers the JD degree and specialized LLM degrees in Environmental and Natural Resources Law and Animal Law. Students may also apply for a joint JD/LLM program in Environmental and Natural Resources Law. To earn a JD, a student must take a prescribed first-year set of courses. In the upper division, students must take a seminar, Constitutional Law II, and Professionalism, and fulfill two writing requirements. Students choose between a three-year day program and a four-year evening program. Admission criteria, faculty, academic opportunities, and graduation requirements are the same for each.

Because the Law School offers both a full-time and a part-time program, students have great flexibility in scheduling courses and in determining the pace at which they want to pursue law school. Classes are offered both during the day and in the evening. Many students transfer between divisions and use the summer school program to accelerate progress toward graduation. Regardless of the division in which a student is enrolled, students may select courses from either the day or evening schedule as they find appropriate.

Specific Special Programs

Certificates: By taking a group of upper-division courses approved by the faculty, and by maintaining a superior grade-point average in those courses, a student may earn a certificate showing a concentration in environmental and natural resources law, public interest law, global law, business law, tax law, intellectual property law, or criminal law.

The Law School has nationally recognized natural resources/environmental law and public interest law programs. The school is also home to an incredibly strong business and commercial law program. The intellectual property law program and global law program are particularly dynamic, and our criminal law program houses the first national organization in the United States to study and enhance the effectiveness of victim's rights law. Lewis & Clark is also a national leader of animal law programs and curriculums. All the traditional areas of legal study are fully covered. Students who do not wish to pursue a certificate may choose to study another area of particular interest.

Clinical Opportunities, Externships, and Simulations: A student may create a schedule with precisely the mix of practical skills courses that fit that student's interests and needs. Students may choose among live client clinical experience, externships and internships, or simulation courses. The legal clinic located in downtown Portland offers students the opportunity to interview and counsel real clients, prepare documents, conduct trials, negotiate settlements, and prepare appeals. Other established clinics at Lewis & Clark are the small business legal clinic, an environmental law clinic, an international environmental law clinic, a low-income taxpayer clinic, an animal law clinic, a crime victim advocacy clinic, and a business law practicum. Externships place a student in full-time work for a semester or for a summer. Requirements for an externship vary as students have part-time, full-time, and different credit externship options. Externs are placed throughout the United States and in foreign countries. Clinical internship seminars are similar to externships but the student works only part-time, attending other classes during the semester. Clinical internship seminars include placements with in-house counsel, government agencies, law firms, and public interest, nonprofit organizations. Other courses, such as moot courts, advanced advocacy, trial advocacy, criminal law seminar, estate planning seminar, corporate transactions seminar, and family mediation seminar, involve extensive simulations.

Admission

Lewis & Clark affirmatively seeks a diverse student body. The Admissions Committee makes a serious effort to consider each applicant as an individual. Factors such as college, program of study, length of time since the degree was obtained, experience, writing ability, and community activities are taken into consideration. Only those candidates with excellent professional promise are admitted. Academic attrition is low, averaging two to four percent.

Student Activities

Activities include three law reviews, *Environmental Law*, *Animal Law*, and *Lewis & Clark Law Review*; nine distinct moot court teams; numerous speakers on campus; programs that bring outstanding legal scholars to campus for lectures and seminars; and many student organizations reflecting the diverse makeup of the student body.

Expenses and Financial Aid

Approximately 40 percent of the students at Lewis & Clark receive some scholarship support during their law school career. The school annually awards renewable merit-based Dean's Scholarships to incoming students. In addition, loan money and work-study funds are available. There is no separate application procedure for scholarship funds. Scholarship consideration is part of the admission process. Students are reviewed on the basis of undergraduate record, LSAT score, writing ability, and activities.

Students interested in loans need to apply for financial aid as early as possible and should not wait for an admission decision to begin the financial aid application. Applicants should submit the FAFSA (Free Application for Federal Student Aid) at www.fafsa.ed.gov.

Career Services

The Career Services Office maintains and runs an extraordinary number and variety of programs. In addition to posting clerk positions for law students and running the on-campus interviews, the office maintains an extensive mentoring program, runs dozens of panels each year on various areas of practice, and counsels individual students from the first year onward. The Career Services staff consists of experienced administrators, counselors, and professionals, including a full-time coordinator to assist public interest-minded students.

APPLICANT PROFILE

Lewis & Clark Law School
This grid includes only applicants who earned 120–180 LSAT scores under standard administrations.

LSAT Score	3.75 +		3.50–3.74		3.25–3.49		3.00–3.24		2.75–2.99		2.50–2.74		Below 2.50		No GPA		Total	
	Apps	Adm	Apps	Adm	Apps	Adm	Apps	Adm	Apps	Adm	Apps	Adm	Apps	Adm	Apps	Adm	Apps	Adm
170–180	34	31	21	21	21	18	13	13	3	3	5	4	8	3	1	1	106	94
165–169	59	55	90	79	71	63	50	34	36	25	15	7	13	4	3	2	337	269
160–164	155	124	215	144	183	107	143	68	57	23	23	8	19	2	9	3	804	479
155–159	107	47	225	80	202	41	128	19	70	8	42	5	23	2	17	9	814	211
150–154	42	6	89	12	114	21	111	16	69	4	29	1	13	0	13	4	480	64
145–149	6	0	40	10	58	5	39	5	38	0	16	0	11	1	5	0	213	21
140–144	5	0	14	0	9	0	19	0	19	0	16	0	12	0	2	0	96	0
Below 140	2	0	5	0	6	0	9	0	8	0	9	0	4	0	4	0	47	0
Total	410	263	699	346	664	255	512	155	300	63	155	25	103	12	54	19	2897	1138

Apps = Number of Applicants
Adm = Number Admitted
Reflects 100% of the total applicant pool; highest LSAT data reported.

LIBERTY UNIVERSITY SCHOOL OF LAW

1971 University Boulevard
Lynchburg, VA 24502
Phone: 434.592.5300; Fax: 434.592.5400
E-mail: lawadmissions@liberty.edu; Website: www.law.liberty.edu

ABA
Approved
Since
2006

The Basics

Type of school	Private
Term	Semester
Application deadline	9/1 6/1
Application fee	$50
Financial aid deadline	
Can first year start other than fall?	No
Student to faculty ratio	13.4 to 1
# of housing spaces available restricted to law students	
graduate housing for which law students are eligible	

Faculty and Administrators

	Total		Men		Women		Minorities	
	Spr	Fall	Spr	Fall	Spr	Fall	Spr	Fall
Full-time	18	19	12	12	6	7	6	7
Other full-time	1	2	1	2	0	0	0	0
Deans, librarians, & others who teach	9	8	6	5	3	3	2	2
Part-time	14	9	10	8	4	1	3	2
Total	42	38	29	27	13	11	11	11

JD Enrollment and Ethnicity

	Men		Women		Full-Time		Part-Time		1st-Year		Total		JD Degs. Awd.
	#	%	#	%	#	%	#	%	#	%	#	%	
All Hispanics	8	4.3	2	2.0	10	3.5	0	0.0	5	5.4	10	3.5	2
Am. Ind./AK Nat.	2	1.1	0	0.0	2	0.7	0	0.0	0	0.0	2	0.7	0
Asian	4	2.2	4	4.0	8	2.8	0	0.0	0	0.0	8	2.8	1
Black/Af. Am.	7	3.8	7	6.9	14	4.9	0	0.0	5	5.4	14	4.9	9
Nat. HI/Pac. Isl.	1	0.5	0	0.0	1	0.3	0	0.0	1	1.1	1	0.3	0
2 or more races	4	2.2	2	2.0	6	2.1	0	0.0	1	1.1	6	2.1	3
Subtotal (minor.)	26	14.1	15	14.9	41	14.3	0	0.0	12	12.9	41	14.3	15
Nonres. Alien	4	2.2	0	0.0	4	1.4	0	0.0	3	3.2	4	1.4	0
White/Cauc.	144	77.8	79	78.2	223	78.0	0	0.0	70	75.3	223	78.0	75
Unknown	11	5.9	7	6.9	18	6.3	0	0.0	8	8.6	18	6.3	0
Total	185	64.7	101	35.3	286	100.0	0	0.0	93	32.5	286		90

Curriculum

	Full-Time	Part-Time
Typical first-year section size	60	0
Is there typically a "small section" of the first-year class, other than Legal Writing, taught by full-time faculty	Yes	No
If yes, typical size offered last year	17	
# of classroom course titles beyond first-year curriculum	53	

# of upper division courses, excluding seminars, with an enrollment:		
Under 25	40	
25–49	28	
50–74	6	
75–99	2	
100+	0	

# of seminars	3	
# of seminar positions available	45	
# of seminar positions filled	45	0
# of positions available in simulation courses	535	
# of simulation positions filled	535	0
# of positions available in faculty supervised clinical courses	22	
# of faculty supervised clinical positions filled	11	0
# involved in field placements	84	0
# involved in law journals	32	0
# involved in moot court or trial competitions	29	0
# of credit hours required to graduate	90	

Transfers

Transfers in	2
Transfers out	4

Tuition and Fees

	Resident	Nonresident
Full-time	$30,604	
Part-time		
Tuition Guarantee Program	N	

Living Expenses

Estimated living expenses for singles

Living on campus	Living off campus	Living at home
$17,534	$17,534	$17,534

LIBERTY UNIVERSITY SCHOOL OF LAW

ABA Approved Since 2006

GPA and LSAT Scores

	Total	Full-Time	Part-Time
# of apps	414	414	0
# of offers	200	200	0
# of matrics	99	99	0
75% GPA	3.53	3.53	0.00
Median GPA	3.27	3.27	0.00
25% GPA	2.98	2.98	0.00
75% LSAT	153	153	0
Median LSAT	150	150	0
25% LSAT	148	148	0

Grants and Scholarships (from prior year)

	Total #	Total %	Full-Time #	Full-Time %	Part-Time #	Part-Time %
Total # of students	313		313		0	
Total # receiving grants	306	97.8	306	97.8	0	0.0
Less than 1/2 tuition	158	50.5	158	50.5	0	0.0
Half to full tuition	115	36.7	115	36.7	0	0.0
Full tuition	33	10.5	33	10.5	0	0.0
More than full tuition	0	0.0	0	0.0	0	0.0
Median grant amount			$12,527		$0	

Informational and Library Resources

Total amount spent on library materials	$1,016,201
Study seating capacity inside the library	277
# of full-time equivalent professional librarians	10
Hours per week library is open	95
# of open, wired connections available to students	0
# of networked computers available for use by students	38
Has wireless network?	Y
Requires computer?	N

JD Attrition (from prior year)

	Academic #	Other #	Total #	Total %
1st year	19	15	34	25.8
2nd year	3	0	3	3.3
3rd year	0	0	0	0.0
4th year	0	0	0	0.0

Employment (9 months after graduation)

For up-to-date employment data, go to employmentsummary.abaquestionnaire.org on the ABA website.

Bar Passage Rates

First-time takers	52	Reporting %	100.00
Average school %	71.13	Average state %	79.74

Average pass difference −8.61

Jurisdiction	Takers	Passers	Pass %	State %	Diff %
Virginia	20	14	70.00	78.15	−8.15
North Carolina	4	1	25.00	77.50	−52.50
Texas	3	3	100.00	82.68	17.32
Georgia	3	2	66.67	83.61	−16.94
Florida	3	3	100.00	77.63	22.37

LIBERTY UNIVERSITY SCHOOL OF LAW

1971 University Boulevard
Lynchburg, VA 24502
Phone: 434.592.5300; Fax: 434.592.5400
E-mail: lawadmissions@liberty.edu; Website: www.law.liberty.edu

Introduction

Distinctively Christian, Liberty University School of Law has attracted national attention for its innovative program of legal education, competitive teams, and practice opportunities for its students. The student body will cap at approximately 450 to maintain the small classes and collegiality that students and faculty now enjoy. The law school and adjoining law library are advantageously located on one level in Liberty's million-square-foot Campus North complex. The 330-seat ceremonial courtroom features a nine-seat bench, which replicates the US Supreme Court bench. Two other mock trial courtrooms, all classrooms, and the law library feature the latest technologies. Liberty's 802.11n wireless network currently hosts approximately 950 wireless access points (WAPs) and distributes 16 streaming multichannels through a wireless connection known as Internet Protocol Television (IPTV). The 6,500-acre campus rests in the eastern foothills of the Blue Ridge Mountains in Central Virginia, within easy driving distance of Washington, DC.

Program of Legal Education

Liberty's groundbreaking law program has three distinct but related components: foundations of law, substantive law courses, and lawyering skills. In keeping with the law school's mission "to equip future leaders in law with a superior legal education in fidelity to the Christian faith expressed through the Holy Scriptures," the foundations courses explore the thoughts and writings of those who shaped the American legal system. The Christian worldview permeates the curriculum. The six-semester skills program has two threads: a litigation thread and a planning thread. Each student moves a simulated case from the initial client interview to the court verdict and develops the practice skills essential to planning client affairs. While the core courses look much the same as at other law schools—same course names, same subject matter coverage, same casebooks—Liberty's distinction is in the linkage of the substantive law courses to the foundations and lawyering skills courses. The law faculty is highly accessible to students throughout each day. In addition to academic advising and support from faculty, many Liberty law students take advantage of the academic support program.

Academic Support

The Academic Support Program begins with an intensive four-day Barristers' Orientation for entering students. During the academic year, the program staff assists law students in achieving their full academic potential, helping them with class preparation, class participation, and examination strategies. Support includes post-class reviews prior to taking law school examinations and practice-exam workshops. The program director holds workshops on case briefing, note taking, time and stress management, outlining, exam preparation, and legal writing. All students may take advantage of one-on-one tutorials to help them assimilate course materials and apply classroom knowledge to law school examinations. The Academic Support Program also assists students with bar examination preparation.

Clinics, Externships, and Centers

The law school places a high priority on equipping students with the skills necessary to practice law, as evidenced in its Lawyering Skills Program. Its externship and clinical programs provide the next step in the continuum of classroom learning, from simulation to client- and real-life practice experience. The Constitutional Litigation Clinic works in conjunction with Liberty Counsel, a nonprofit legal organization specializing in constitutional law, which has offices on the Liberty University campus. Students work on live, real-time legal issues through current cases that address constitutional law challenges. The School of Law has formed a partnership with Liberty Counsel in founding the Liberty Center for Law and Policy. The center trains law students who have career plans and interests in public policy law with a focus on the legislative process, constitutional law, and religious liberty advocacy.

The law school engages in traditional externship placements through its Criminal Law Externship Program. This program places law students as externs in county and federal prosecutors' offices and in public defenders' offices, under the supervision of experienced practitioners. Students are placed in a variety of field-study venues, including offices of US attorneys, commonwealth attorneys, district attorneys, and attorneys general; judicial clerkships at local, state, and federal courts; courts of appeal and state supreme courts; and in public interest organizations. The public service externship component gives students a wide variety of individualized experiences in public service law and pro bono legal assistance. In addition, Liberty law students obtain externships and summer positions in venues ranging from the White House and the Department of Homeland Security, to private law firms and corporations.

Cocurricular and Student Activities

In addition to the Student Bar Association (SBA) and many student organizations, the law school has nationally competitive teams in moot court, negotiation, and alternative dispute resolution, along with a developing transactional competition program. Students produce the *Liberty University Law Review* and the *Liberty Legal Journal*. Many law students volunteer their time in pro bono activities. The law school also matches students with private practitioners engaged in pro bono work and provides them opportunities to intern in legal aid offices, public defender offices, and prosecutorial offices. Student life includes attending the wide range of events on the campus of Liberty University and enjoying the sociability of the law school community. Law students have access to the university's many recreational facilities, which include the year-round Snowflex synthetic ski slope (the first of its kind in North America), ice rink, 112-acre lake, and equestrian center. Off campus, law students enjoy the rich history and natural beauty of Central Virginia.

Career Services

The Center for Career and Professional Development serves law students and alumni by providing tools to develop skills essential for career development, by cultivating a lifelong commitment to professionalism and community service, and by promoting regional and national awareness of the law school's distinctive program of legal study. The center cultivates internship and pro bono opportunities and works cooperatively with the school's clinical and externship programs to foster relationships with members of the bench and bar to the benefit of students and alumni. Alumni are working in all sectors of law practice. Placement statistics are available at the center.

Information Resources and Technologies

With many comfortable seating areas and close proximity to the classrooms, Ehrhorn Law Library provides an environment conducive to research, study, and writing. To its growing collection of nearly 300,000 volumes and volume equivalents, the law library is continually adding titles that support the curriculum and undergird the law school's mission. Along with its extensive microform archives, the law library provides access to law-related and general databases via the Internet through any web browser. These electronic databases are available to law students on or off campus. Reliable wired and wireless access to the Internet is provided throughout the law school facility. Every classroom has SMART technology. The law school community benefits from a high level of university support for its state-of-the-art computing, instructional, informational, and audiovisual technologies.

Admission and Financial Aid

Many law schools have developed courses of study that give expression to a particular jurisprudential perspective, be it law and economics, legal realism, or policy-oriented jurisprudence. Liberty University School of Law has chosen to do the same, developing its curriculum and standards of conduct consistent with the Christian worldview. Its admission process is designed to identify those who desire to receive a legal education from this perspective. Each completed applicant file is reviewed by a law faculty committee. That committee gives careful attention to a full range of factors that indicate the applicant's likelihood of success in law school and the legal profession. It attempts to identify strengths and indicators of success that may not show up in test scores and to ensure that students make fully informed decisions in deciding to attend Liberty University School of Law. Written applications and letters of recommendation are used to identify applicants with strong communication skills, levels of interest, personal traits, and life experiences that exhibit a calling to law and potential for success in legal education and the practice of law. The personal statement, which addresses prescribed discussion points noted in the application for admission, is of particular importance in the admission decision.

Institutional scholarships are awarded on the basis of prior academic excellence and indicators of law school success, and for demonstrated leadership and service in keeping with the law school's mission. Committed to debt management, the law school assists each student with a financial aid package to meet individual needs.

The Office of Admissions and Financial Aid assists prospective students and law students with the law school admission process, financial aid, and other matters related to relocation and matriculation. To schedule a visit, call 434.592.5300 or e-mail lawadmissions@liberty.edu.

APPLICANT PROFILE

Liberty University School of Law recognizes that LSAT scores and undergraduate GPAs are important indicators of academic success, but that a number of other factors must be considered in making admission decisions. An important purpose of interviews and written applications is to identify applicants with particular communications skills, levels of interest, personal traits, and life experiences that evince a calling to law and potential for success in legal education. Factors providing predictors of success in law school may include: demonstrated leadership, highly motivated and successful employment history, proficiency in written and oral communication skills, and a detailed explanation of personal reading and study habits, including the books having the greatest impact on the applicant's intellectual life. Breadth of intellectual interest and ability is an indicator of interest in, and appreciation for, the kind of education offered at the law school.

The law school looks at more than numbers. Questions asked on the application and during the interview process are designed to identify strengths that do not show up in test scores and to ensure that students are fully informed of the kind of legal education provided at Liberty.

LOUISIANA STATE UNIVERSITY, PAUL M. HEBERT LAW CENTER

202 Law Center
Baton Rouge, LA 70803
Phone: 225.578.8646; Fax: 225.578.8647
E-mail: admissions@law.lsu.edu; Website: www.law.lsu.edu

ABA
Approved
Since
1926

The Basics

Type of school	Public
Term	Semester
Application deadline	3/1
Application fee	$50
Financial aid deadline	7/1
Can first year start other than fall?	No
Student to faculty ratio	18.6 to 1
# of housing spaces available restricted to law students	
graduate housing for which law students are eligible	

Faculty and Administrators

	Total		Men		Women		Minorities	
	Spr	Fall	Spr	Fall	Spr	Fall	Spr	Fall
Full-time	29	29	21	20	8	9	3	3
Other full-time	8	11	4	7	4	4	2	2
Deans, librarians, & others who teach	7	8	6	6	1	2	0	0
Part-time	31	27	30	24	1	3	2	1
Total	75	75	61	57	14	18	7	6

Curriculum

	Full-Time	Part-Time
Typical first-year section size	79	0
Is there typically a "small section" of the first-year class, other than Legal Writing, taught by full-time faculty	Yes	No
If yes, typical size offered last year	20	
# of classroom course titles beyond first-year curriculum	165	

# of upper division courses, excluding seminars, with an enrollment:		
	Under 25	134
	25–49	42
	50–74	20
	75–99	7
	100+	2

# of seminars	22	
# of seminar positions available	440	
# of seminar positions filled	227	0
# of positions available in simulation courses	516	
# of simulation positions filled	457	0
# of positions available in faculty supervised clinical courses	58	
# of faculty supervised clinical positions filled	49	0
# involved in field placements	100	0
# involved in law journals	51	0
# involved in moot court or trial competitions	74	0
# of credit hours required to graduate	94	

JD Enrollment and Ethnicity

	Men #	Men %	Women #	Women %	Full-Time #	Full-Time %	Part-Time #	Part-Time %	1st-Year #	1st-Year %	Total #	Total %	JD Degs. Awd.
All Hispanics	12	3.1	17	5.7	28	4.2	1	4.2	8	3.4	29	4.2	10
Am. Ind./AK Nat.	3	0.8	2	0.7	3	0.5	2	8.3	0	0.0	5	0.7	2
Asian	13	3.3	7	2.4	20	3.0	0	0.0	5	2.1	20	2.9	1
Black/Af. Am.	33	8.5	38	12.8	71	10.7	0	0.0	34	14.3	71	10.3	8
Nat. HI/Pac. Isl.	0	0.0	0	0.0	0	0.0	0	0.0	0	0.0	0	0.0	0
2 or more races	8	2.1	15	5.1	23	3.5	0	0.0	15	6.3	23	3.3	0
Subtotal (minor.)	69	17.7	79	26.6	145	21.9	3	12.5	62	26.1	148	21.5	21
Nonres. Alien	1	0.3	4	1.3	5	0.8	0	0.0	1	0.4	5	0.7	0
White/Cauc.	300	76.9	205	69.0	485	73.2	20	83.3	166	69.7	505	73.5	141
Unknown	20	5.1	9	3.0	28	4.2	1	4.2	9	3.8	29	4.2	12
Total	390	56.8	297	43.2	663	96.5	24	3.5	238	34.6	687		174

Transfers

Transfers in	2
Transfers out	6

Tuition and Fees

	Resident	Nonresident
Full-time	$17,474	$33,800
Part-time		
Tuition Guarantee Program	N	

Living Expenses

Estimated living expenses for singles

Living on campus	Living off campus	Living at home
$16,018	$18,458	$9,890

LOUISIANA STATE UNIVERSITY, PAUL M. HEBERT LAW CENTER

ABA
Approved
Since
1926

GPA and LSAT Scores

	Total	Full-Time	Part-Time
# of apps	1,418	1,418	0
# of offers	626	626	0
# of matrics	236	236	0
75% GPA	3.66	3.66	0.00
Median GPA	3.39	3.39	0.00
25% GPA	3.10	3.10	0.00
75% LSAT	160	160	0
Median LSAT	158	158	0
25% LSAT	155	155	0

Grants and Scholarships (from prior year)

	Total		Full-Time		Part-Time	
	#	%	#	%	#	%
Total # of students	633		616		17	
Total # receiving grants	443	70.0	443	71.9	0	0.0
Less than 1/2 tuition	205	32.4	205	33.3	0	0.0
Half to full tuition	121	19.1	121	19.6	0	0.0
Full tuition	59	9.3	59	9.6	0	0.0
More than full tuition	58	9.2	58	9.4	0	0.0
Median grant amount			$6,824		$0	

Informational and Library Resources

Total amount spent on library materials	$1,001,953
Study seating capacity inside the library	471
# of full-time equivalent professional librarians	9
Hours per week library is open	104
# of open, wired connections available to students	60
# of networked computers available for use by students	40
Has wireless network?	Y
Requires computer?	N

JD Attrition (from prior year)

	Academic	Other	Total	
	#	#	#	%
1st year	5	8	13	5.8
2nd year	0	0	0	0.0
3rd year	0	0	0	0.0
4th year	0	0	0	0.0

Employment (9 months after graduation)

For up-to-date employment data, go to employmentsummary.abaquestionnaire.org on the ABA website.

Bar Passage Rates

First-time takers	177	Reporting %	84.18
Average school %	75.17	Average state %	66.26
Average pass difference	8.91		

Jurisdiction	Takers	Passers	Pass %	State %	Diff %
Louisiana	149	112	75.17	66.26	8.91

LOUISIANA STATE UNIVERSITY, PAUL M. HEBERT LAW CENTER

202 Law Center
Baton Rouge, LA 70803
Phone: 225.578.8646; Fax: 225.578.8647
E-mail: admissions@law.lsu.edu; Website: www.law.lsu.edu

Introduction

The Louisiana State University (LSU) Law Center was originally established as the Louisiana State University Law School in 1906, pursuant to an authorization contained in the university charter. In 1979, the Law Center was renamed the Paul M. Hebert Law Center of Louisiana State University. The Law Center holds membership in the Association of American Law Schools (AALS) and is on the approved list of the American Bar Association (ABA).

Library and Physical Facilities

The Law Center, constructed in 1936 and dedicated in 1938, has added extensive facilities since its original construction. Both buildings were vastly renovated over several years at a cost in excess of $17 million and were completed in 2004. The renovated complex provides classroom areas, seminar and discussion rooms, meeting areas, and a courtroom and Law Clinic. The Law Clinic is a self-contained legal services office located in the Law Center where students are certified to practice law pursuant to Louisiana Supreme Court Rule XX. Separate offices for student research and student activities, such as the *Louisiana Law Review*, Moot Court Board, and Student Bar Association, are included in the facility. The law library, housed in the complex, provides one of the most complete collections of Roman and modern civil law reports and materials in the country. Library resources include reading and discussion rooms, study carrels, computer labs, and audiovisual facilities. Students also have access to other campus facilities, including the LSU Student Health Center, residential housing, and the Student Recreation Complex. The Law Center is located on the main campus of LSU in close proximity to the undergraduate campus and other units with which the Law Center has joint-degree or cocurricular programs.

Curriculum

The LSU Law Center has established a JD/CL program through which all graduates receive the Juris Doctor (JD) degree and a Graduate Diploma in Comparative Law (CL). First-year students follow a prescribed curriculum and, thereafter, may choose from a wide variety of courses to complete their degrees, including skills training courses and a newly expanded clinical program designed to take full advantage of the Law Center's location in Louisiana's capital city. The Law Center's dedication to the study of both civil and common law prepares its graduates to practice in any state and in many foreign countries. Six semesters of resident study are required for the degree. In addition to its full-time law faculty, the LSU Law Center invites a number of distinguished lecturers, including practicing attorneys and legal scholars, to teach courses in their areas of specialty each semester. A number of faculty members have law degrees from foreign countries.

Summer Session Abroad

The Law Center conducts a summer program in Lyon, France, and, when student interest warrants, in Buenos Aires,

Argentina. All classes are conducted in English and are designed to meet the requirements of the ABA and AALS.

Special Programs

A wide variety of courses afford each student the opportunity to participate in the preparation and trial of mock cases, both civil and criminal, and also to develop skills in legal negotiation and counseling. LSU sponsors and encourages student participation in national trial and appellate competitions throughout the school year.

In cooperation with the Center for Continuing Professional Development, the Law Center presents seminars, institutes, and conferences for practicing lawyers.

The LSU Law Center admits candidates for the Master of Laws (LLM) degree. This program is highly selective and admits students with exceptional ability.

Admission

The Admissions Committee considers many factors in reaching admission decisions. While the quantitative predictors of success in law school (performance on the LSAT and the undergraduate GPA of applicants) are heavily weighed factors in the admission decision, the Admissions Committee considers many other factors, such as the ability to analyze and write well, as demonstrated by the personal statement and the written portion of the LSAT; two letters of recommendation from teachers or others who can express an opinion on the applicant's aptitude for the study of law; the rigor of the undergraduate program of study and grade trends; extracurricular activities; work experience or military service; social and economic background; and other evidence of an applicant's aptitude for the study of law and likely contribution to academic and community life. A baccalaureate degree from an accredited college or university is required for admission.

Applicants are advised to take the LSAT in June, and not later than December, prior to the year in which they seek admission to the Law Center. The Law Center admits students only in the fall and only for full-time study. There are no night courses offered. Transfer applications are considered.

Louisiana State University assures equal opportunity for all qualified persons without regard to race, color, religion, sexual orientation, national origin, age, disability, marital status, or veteran's status in the admission to, participation in, or employment in the programs and activities that the university operates.

Joint Programs

In addition to earning a JD/CL, LSU Law students may also earn a Master of Mass Communication (MMC) degree through the LSU Manship School of Mass Communication, or a Master of Business Administration (MBA), Master of Public Administration (MPA), or MS in Finance, through the LSU E.J. Ourso College of Business. The combined-degree programs are typically completed in four years. Applicants must apply to each institution separately.

Student Activities

The *Louisiana Law Review* was established to encourage high quality legal scholarship in the student body, to contribute to the development of the law through scholarly criticism and analysis, and to serve the bar of Louisiana through comments and discussion of current cases and legal problems. It is edited by a board of student editors with faculty cooperation. The Law Center is also making preparations for another journal that will focus on Energy Law.

The Louisiana Chapter of the Order of the Coif, a national honorary law fraternity, was established at the Law Center in 1942. Election to the Order of the Coif is recognized as the highest honor a law student may receive.

Because a large number of graduates of the Law Center go directly into practice, the LSU Law Center has an extensive Trial Advocacy Program in which moot court training is offered both for trial work and in appellate argument.

Students have an opportunity to be a part of more than 30 student organizations representing a variety of interests, including, but not limited to, the Public Interest Law Society (PILS), the International Law Society, the Federalist Society, the Black Law Students Association, the American Constitution Society, the Environmental Law Society, and the Tax Club.

All students at the Law Center are members of the Student Bar Association. This association promotes and coordinates student activities within the Law Center and serves as an instructional medium for postgraduate bar association activities.

Expenses and Financial Aid

The Scholarship Committee automatically considers all admitted students for scholarship support. Scholarships range from $2,000 to full-tuition awards. Awards are offered to applicants whom the committee believes will best contribute to the academic and community life of the Law Center.

Student loans are available to help qualified students who need financial assistance to continue their education. Detailed information on all loan funds may be secured by contacting the LSU Office of Undergraduate Admissions and Student Aid, 1146 Pleasant Hall, Baton Rouge, LA 70803.

Career Services

The Career Services Office is dedicated to enhancing the personal growth and professional opportunities for law students and alumni through individual counseling, workshops, and events. Employers from across the United States, including private law firms, governmental agencies, state and federal judges, nonprofit organizations, and corporations recruit students yearly from the LSU Law Center through visits to the campus, consortiums, and job fairs. More than 150 legal employers visit the school each year to recruit LSU Law Center students.

APPLICANT PROFILE

Louisiana State University, Paul M. Hebert Law Center
This grid includes only applicants who earned 120–180 LSAT scores under standard administrations.

LSAT Score	GPA																					
	3.75 +		3.50–3.74		3.25–3.49		3.00–3.24		2.75–2.99		2.50–2.74		2.25–2.49		2.00–2.24		Below 2.00		No GPA		Total	
	Apps	Adm	Apps	Adm	Apps	Adm	Apps	Adm	Apps	Adm	Apps	Adm	Apps	Adm	Apps	Adm	Apps	Adm	Apps	Adm	Apps	Adm
175–180	0	0	0	0	0	0	0	0	0	0	0	0	0	0	0	0	0	0	0	0	0	0
170–174	1	1	6	6	2	2	1	1	0	0	1	1	0	0	0	0	0	0	0	0	11	11
165–169	9	9	11	11	11	11	10	9	6	6	4	4	0	0	0	0	0	0	0	0	51	50
160–164	34	33	38	38	51	48	31	30	24	20	14	13	8	4	3	1	0	0	2	2	205	189
155–159	53	43	119	84	119	69	94	49	64	19	15	4	11	3	3	0	1	0	3	0	482	271
150–154	47	22	72	15	88	10	72	13	41	8	27	7	7	0	2	0	0	0	6	2	362	77
145–149	21	5	28	7	41	9	47	8	27	1	18	0	7	0	1	0	2	0	2	0	194	30
140–144	4	0	13	0	14	0	21	0	16	0	13	0	5	0	1	0	2	0	1	0	90	0
135–139	2	0	2	0	4	0	8	0	6	0	8	0	0	0	0	0	1	0	0	0	31	0
130–134	0	0	1	0	2	0	0	0	1	0	2	0	3	0	0	0	0	0	0	0	9	0
125–129	0	0	0	0	0	0	0	0	1	0	2	0	0	0	0	0	0	0	0	0	3	0
120–124	0	0	0	0	0	0	0	0	0	0	0	0	0	0	0	0	0	0	0	0	0	0
Total	171	113	290	161	332	149	284	110	186	54	104	29	41	7	10	1	6	0	14	4	1438	628

Apps = Number of Applicants
Adm = Number Admitted
Reflects 100% of the total applicant pool; highest LSAT data reported.

UNIVERSITY OF LOUISVILLE'S BRANDEIS SCHOOL OF LAW

University of Louisville
Louisville, KY 40292
Phone: 502.852.6364; Fax: 502.852.8971
E-mail: lawadmissions@louisville.edu; Website: www.law.louisville.edu

ABA Approved Since 1931

ABA
Section of Legal Education and Admissions to the Bar

The Basics

Type of school	Public
Term	Semester
Application deadline	3/15
Application fee	$50
Financial aid deadline	5/15
Can first year start other than fall?	No
Student to faculty ratio	13.1 to 1
# of housing spaces available restricted to law students	
graduate housing for which law students are eligible	102

Faculty and Administrators

	Total		Men		Women		Minorities	
	Spr	Fall	Spr	Fall	Spr	Fall	Spr	Fall
Full-time	24	25	13	15	11	10	3	3
Other full-time	0	0	0	0	0	0	0	0
Deans, librarians, & others who teach	10	10	7	7	3	3	1	1
Part-time	16	11	10	5	6	6	0	2
Total	50	46	30	27	20	19	4	6

JD Enrollment and Ethnicity

	Men		Women		Full-Time		Part-Time		1st-Year		Total		JD Degs. Awd.
	#	%	#	%	#	%	#	%	#	%	#	%	
All Hispanics	5	2.3	4	2.3	9	2.5	0	0.0	4	2.9	9	2.3	6
Am. Ind./AK Nat.	0	0.0	0	0.0	0	0.0	0	0.0	0	0.0	0	0.0	0
Asian	1	0.5	3	1.7	3	0.8	1	3.8	0	0.0	4	1.0	3
Black/Af. Am.	7	3.2	10	5.8	15	4.1	2	7.7	10	7.2	17	4.4	4
Nat. HI/Pac. Isl.	0	0.0	0	0.0	0	0.0	0	0.0	0	0.0	0	0.0	0
2 or more races	0	0.0	3	1.7	3	0.8	0	0.0	2	1.4	3	0.8	3
Subtotal (minor.)	13	6.0	20	11.6	30	8.3	3	11.5	16	11.6	33	8.5	16
Nonres. Alien	2	0.9	1	0.6	3	0.8	0	0.0	1	0.7	3	0.8	0
White/Cauc.	200	92.2	151	87.8	328	90.4	23	88.5	120	87.0	351	90.2	121
Unknown	2	0.9	0	0.0	2	0.6	0	0.0	1	0.7	2	0.5	1
Total	217	55.8	172	44.2	363	93.3	26	6.7	138	35.5	389		138

Curriculum

	Full-Time	Part-Time
Typical first-year section size	68	0
Is there typically a "small section" of the first-year class, other than Legal Writing, taught by full-time faculty	No	No
If yes, typical size offered last year		
# of classroom course titles beyond first-year curriculum	70	
# of upper division courses, excluding seminars, with an enrollment: Under 25	28	
25–49	25	
50–74	40	
75–99	2	
100+	0	
# of seminars	21	
# of seminar positions available	342	
# of seminar positions filled	187	63
# of positions available in simulation courses	451	
# of simulation positions filled	236	44
# of positions available in faculty supervised clinical courses	19	
# of faculty supervised clinical positions filled	16	0
# involved in field placements	142	25
# involved in law journals	82	5
# involved in moot court or trial competitions	45	2
# of credit hours required to graduate	90	

Transfers

Transfers in	8
Transfers out	4

Tuition and Fees

	Resident	Nonresident
Full-time	$16,716	$32,128
Part-time	$8,448	$16,154
Tuition Guarantee Program		N

Living Expenses

Estimated living expenses for singles

Living on campus	Living off campus	Living at home
$18,802	$18,802	$10,432

UNIVERSITY OF LOUISVILLE'S BRANDEIS SCHOOL OF LAW

ABA
Approved
Since
1931

GPA and LSAT Scores

	Total	Full-Time	Part-Time
# of apps	1,495	1,405	90
# of offers	466	443	23
# of matrics	132	123	9
75% GPA	3.68	3.68	3.61
Median GPA	3.42	3.42	3.18
25% GPA	3.20	3.20	2.46
75% LSAT	158	158	153
Median LSAT	156	156	151
25% LSAT	152	152	146

Grants and Scholarships (from prior year)

	Total #	Total %	Full-Time #	Full-Time %	Part-Time #	Part-Time %
Total # of students	426		379		47	
Total # receiving grants	146	34.3	134	35.4	12	25.5
Less than 1/2 tuition	111	26.1	105	27.7	6	12.8
Half to full tuition	35	8.2	29	7.7	6	12.8
Full tuition	0	0.0	0	0.0	0	0.0
More than full tuition	0	0.0	0	0.0	0	0.0
Median grant amount			$6,000		$4,500	

Informational and Library Resources

Total amount spent on library materials	$1,432,544
Study seating capacity inside the library	370
# of full-time equivalent professional librarians	6
Hours per week library is open	89
# of open, wired connections available to students	0
# of networked computers available for use by students	37
Has wireless network?	Y
Requires computer?	N

JD Attrition (from prior year)

	Academic #	Other #	Total #	Total %
1st year	14	6	20	13.2
2nd year	3	10	13	10.5
3rd year	1	0	1	0.8
4th year	1	0	1	5.6

Employment (9 months after graduation)

For up-to-date employment data, go to employmentsummary.abaquestionnaire.org on the ABA website.

Bar Passage Rates

First-time takers	125	Reporting %	84.80
Average school %	90.57	Average state %	82.03
Average pass difference	8.54		

Jurisdiction	Takers	Passers	Pass %	State %	Diff %
Kentucky	106	96	90.57	82.03	8.54

UNIVERSITY OF LOUISVILLE'S BRANDEIS SCHOOL OF LAW

University of Louisville
Louisville, KY 40292
Phone: 502.852.6364; Fax: 502.852.8971
E-mail: lawadmissions@louisville.edu; Website: www.law.louisville.edu

Introduction

Founded in 1846, the University of Louisville's Brandeis School of Law is Kentucky's oldest law school and America's fifth oldest law school in continuous operation. Heir to the legacy of Justice Louis D. Brandeis, the school is distinguished by a rich history, national outreach, and profound dedication to public service. UofL Law is an integral part of the University of Louisville, a premier research institution founded in 1798.

UofL Law is exceptional in many ways. We boast a strong core curriculum, enhanced by specialized and interdisciplinary studies. We offer a full-time program (three years) and a part-time program (four or five years). Faculty members dedicated to both teaching and research guide students with strong academic skills and diverse backgrounds. From a supportive legal community, we draw in job opportunities and adjuncts who bring their real-world expertise to the classroom. International exchanges, for faculty and for students, expose our school to global opportunities.

The metropolitan area, with a population of approximately one million, combines a gracious ambience of southern hospitality with cultural, aesthetic, and recreational attractions, including historic Churchill Downs, the Actors Theatre of Louisville, the Speed Art Museum, the brand new state-of-the-art KFC Yum! Center, and the Muhammad Ali Institute for Peace and Justice. UofL Law is located minutes away from the largest legal community in the region. Our expansive alumni network spanning 49 states and six countries is invaluable to your success.

Enrollment/Student Body

The School of Law enrolls first-year students beginning in the fall semester, which starts in August. Candidates may apply for admission to either the full-time (three-year) division or the part-time (four-to-five-year) division.

Candidates must have completed a bachelor's degree at an accredited college or university prior to enrollment. All undergraduate majors are acceptable, with courses that emphasize critical reasoning, writing, and communication skills recognized as good preparation for the study of law. With an entering class of 140 each fall, first-year class sizes seldom exceed 70 students. Basic Legal Skills (the first-year writing course) is broken down into smaller class sizes of around 22 students.

The entire student body, composed of almost as many women as men, numbers around 400, allowing every student the opportunity to develop close relationships with his or her professors.

Faculty

Professors at UofL Law are masters of the intellectual and practical skills central to success in the legal profession. Many UofL Law professors have practiced law, worked in government, or clerked for federal judges. Our faculty excels in teaching, scholarship, and service to the community. They collaborate with colleagues at other law schools and in other departments at the University of Louisville. Public officials throughout the United States often rely on their expertise.

With 35 full-time faculty members (including 13 women and 4 faculty members of color) and numerous part-time or adjunct teachers, the faculty-to-student ratio is 1 to 13. Students have the opportunity to explore issues important to them through close cooperation with individual members of the faculty.

Curriculum

The law school's full-time and part-time divisions are both daytime programs, with all classes occurring between the hours of 8:00 AM and 5:00 PM. Both divisions share the same curriculum, faculty, and academic standards. The foundational classes during the first year are standardized for students. After completing the first-year curriculum, students choose from core courses in doctrinal subjects, advanced research and writing, and professional responsibility. Students may also take advantage of a rich variety of specialized and interdisciplinary electives.

A highly successful Academic Success Program directed by Kimberly Ballard, a magna cum laude graduate of UofL Law, offers structured study groups, academic success seminars, a library with study aids, and individual academic counseling. The Academic Success Office at UofL Law is committed to helping every student achieve his or her full potential.

Samuel L. Greenebaum Public Service Program

Reflecting the spirit of Justice Louis D. Brandeis, UofL Law was one of America's first five law schools to adopt public service as part of the prescribed course of study. Through this public service work, students develop practical skills, serve their communities, and establish professional values. All students are required to complete 30 hours of pro bono service as a condition of graduation.

During the 2010–2011 academic year, over 100 placements were maintained, 11 of which were new to the program. Within these 100 placements existed over 200 service opportunities, which allowed each student to be matched to a public service choice that was of the most interest to them.

Library and Physical Facilities

The law school is housed in Wilson W. Wyatt Hall, a gracious colonial-style building overlooking the formal entrance to the University of Louisville's Belknap Campus—a traditional college campus located in an urban setting.

The school's law library houses a collection of more than 400,000 volumes and microform volume equivalents, carefully selected to aid student instruction and promote research. The library still receives original briefs of the US Supreme Court—a rare distinction for a law school and a practice originated by Justice Brandeis that continues today.

State-of-the-art instructional and research technologies; two computer labs; the Allen Courtroom's contemporary litigation environment; wireless access in the library, classrooms, and common areas; and a full-time technology staff provide a wealth of services to every law student. The school's website serves as our community bulletin board. Students can download course syllabi, assignments, handouts, old exams, and other materials; browse job listings from the Office of

Professional Development; review the Academic Support Program's catalog of study aids; and get news, calendars, schedules, and more. Technology is increasingly part of legal teaching and learning as the faculty continue to incorporate presentations and Internet resources into the classroom experience.

Special Programs

The School of Law offers seven dual-degree programs designed to enhance the students' understanding, skills, and career opportunities in both areas of study. Each program requires application and admission to both participating schools. Programs include the Juris Doctor/Master of Business Administration (JD/MBA); Juris Doctor/Master of Arts in Political Science (JD/MAPS); Juris Doctor/Master of Arts in Bioethics and Medical Humanities (JD/MA); Juris Doctor/Master of Arts in Humanities (JD/MAH); Juris Doctor/Master of Divinity (JD/MDiv) at the Louisville Presbyterian Theological Seminary; Juris Doctor/Master of Science in Social Work (JD/MSSW); and Juris Doctor/Master of Urban Planning (JD/MUP).

The school also operates clinical externship programs in which upper-class students, with supervision, represent clients and appear in court. A third-year student may receive credit by working in the criminal arena (DA or PD), the tax arena (IRS), the judicial branch (various judges), family law (Center for Women and Families or Legal Aid Society), or technology (University of Louisville Office of Technology Transfer).

The law school operates a live-client clinic, housed in the same building as the Legal Aid Society. Under the direction and supervision of faculty, students in the clinic gain experience interacting with and representing clients.

International experience is another unique opportunity. The Brandeis School offers faculty or student exchanges with law schools in France, England, Germany, Finland, Australia, and South Africa.

Practical Success

Participating annually in about a dozen moot court and professional skills competitions, the law school has won several regional and national championships, including, most recently, the New York University Immigration Law Moot Court Competition and the National Saul Lefkowitz Trademark Competition.

Real clients, real cases, real problems, and real solutions are what you'll find at the UofL Law Clinic. Law students gain practical experience applying their newly acquired legal skills to public housing and domestic violence cases. Students act as primary attorneys under the supervision of the clinic's director.

Students are also actively involved in writing for and publishing the University of Louisville Law Review, the Journal of Law and Education, and the Journal of Animal and Environmental Law.

Graduates of the University of Louisville's Brandeis School of Law consistently achieve high employment rates.

Admission

Applicants may apply beginning October 1 through March 15. Both full-time and part-time first-year students must start classes in the fall semester.

For the best chance of consideration, it is recommended that the LSAT be taken no later than December. Scores from LSATs taken in June, prior to the first semester of enrollment, will be considered only under extraordinary circumstances.

APPLICANT PROFILE

University of Louisville's Brandeis School of Law
This grid includes only applicants who earned 120–180 LSAT scores under standard administrations.

LSAT Score	3.75 +		3.50–3.74		3.25–3.49		3.00–3.24		2.75–2.99		2.50–2.74		2.25–2.49		2.00–2.24		Below 2.00		No GPA		Total	
	Apps	Adm	Apps	Adm	Apps	Adm	Apps	Adm	Apps	Adm	Apps	Adm	Apps	Adm	Apps	Adm	Apps	Adm	Apps	Adm	Apps	Adm
175–180	0	0	0	0	0	0	0	0	0	0	0	0	0	0	0	0	0	0	0	0	0	0
170–174	0	0	2	2	2	2	2	2	0	0	0	0	0	0	0	0	0	0	0	0	6	6
165–169	5	5	5	5	3	3	4	3	3	3	2	0	1	1	1	0	0	0	0	0	24	20
160–164	23	23	18	17	19	19	23	21	11	5	6	5	4	2	3	1	1	0	1	1	109	94
155–159	51	47	58	46	78	58	94	43	35	9	32	11	16	1	8	0	0	0	2	1	374	216
150–154	45	24	77	24	111	23	111	12	70	3	53	3	18	1	4	1	2	0	1	1	492	92
145–149	13	6	52	13	49	5	48	4	40	1	40	2	20	0	10	0	0	0	1	0	273	31
140–144	2	1	16	2	26	0	32	2	24	0	32	0	11	0	8	0	0	0	6	0	157	5
135–139	0	0	5	0	6	0	5	0	5	0	7	0	3	0	0	0	1	0	0	0	32	0
130–134	1	0	1	0	1	0	3	0	1	0	1	0	0	0	0	0	0	0	1	0	9	0
125–129	0	0	0	0	1	0	0	0	0	0	1	0	0	0	1	0	0	0	0	0	3	0
120–124	0	0	0	0	0	0	0	0	0	0	0	0	0	0	0	0	0	0	0	0	0	0
Total	140	106	234	109	296	110	322	87	189	21	174	21	73	5	35	2	4	0	12	3	1479	464

Apps = Number of Applicants
Adm = Number Admitted
Reflects 100% of the total applicant pool; highest LSAT data reported.

LOYOLA LAW SCHOOL, LOYOLA MARYMOUNT UNIVERSITY

919 Albany Street
Los Angeles, CA 90015
Phone: 213.736.1074; Fax: 213.736.6523
E-mail: admissions@lls.edu; Website: www.lls.edu

ABA
Approved
Since
1935

The Basics

Type of school	Private
Term	Semester
Application deadline	2/1
Application fee	$65
Financial aid deadline	3/11
Can first year start other than fall?	No
Student to faculty ratio	15.3 to 1
# of housing spaces available restricted to law students	
graduate housing for which law students are eligible	

Faculty and Administrators

	Total		Men		Women		Minorities	
	Spr	Fall	Spr	Fall	Spr	Fall	Spr	Fall
Full-time	64	67	34	36	30	31	11	12
Other full-time	2	2	2	1	0	1	0	0
Deans, librarians, & others who teach	16	16	8	8	8	8	4	4
Part-time	76	63	53	46	23	17	5	7
Total	158	148	97	91	61	57	20	23

Curriculum

		Full-Time	Part-Time
Typical first-year section size		86	58
Is there typically a "small section" of the first-year class, other than Legal Writing, taught by full-time faculty		No	No
If yes, typical size offered last year			
# of classroom course titles beyond first-year curriculum		143	
# of upper division courses, excluding seminars, with an enrollment:	Under 25	180	
	25–49	46	
	50–74	12	
	75–99	10	
	100+	9	
# of seminars		51	
# of seminar positions available		877	
# of seminar positions filled		304	267
# of positions available in simulation courses		1,780	
# of simulation positions filled		730	516
# of positions available in faculty supervised clinical courses		286	
# of faculty supervised clinical positions filled		206	54
# involved in field placements		226	49
# involved in law journals		207	25
# involved in moot court or trial competitions		61	4
# of credit hours required to graduate		87	

JD Enrollment and Ethnicity

	Men		Women		Full-Time		Part-Time		1st-Year		Total		JD Degs. Awd.
	#	%	#	%	#	%	#	%	#	%	#	%	
All Hispanics	61	9.5	102	16.0	127	12.4	36	14.0	60	15.3	163	12.7	53
Am. Ind./AK Nat.	5	0.8	3	0.5	6	0.6	2	0.8	2	0.5	8	0.6	3
Asian	116	18.1	143	22.4	203	19.9	56	21.7	82	20.9	259	20.3	89
Black/Af. Am.	28	4.4	23	3.6	38	3.7	13	5.0	18	4.6	51	4.0	18
Nat. HI/Pac. Isl.	0	0.0	4	0.6	4	0.4	0	0.0	1	0.3	4	0.3	2
2 or more races	4	0.6	0	0.0	1	0.1	3	1.2	0	0.0	4	0.3	4
Subtotal (minor.)	214	33.4	275	43.0	379	37.1	110	42.6	163	41.6	489	38.2	169
Nonres. Alien	0	0.0	0	0.0	0	0.0	0	0.0	0	0.0	0	0.0	0
White/Cauc.	386	60.3	331	51.8	576	56.4	141	54.7	216	55.1	717	56.1	208
Unknown	40	6.3	33	5.2	66	6.5	7	2.7	13	3.3	73	5.7	26
Total	640	50.0	639	50.0	1021	79.8	258	20.2	392	30.6	1279		403

Transfers

Transfers in	44
Transfers out	13

Tuition and Fees

	Resident	Nonresident
Full-time	$43,060	$43,060
Part-time	$28,845	$28,845
Tuition Guarantee Program	N	

Living Expenses

Estimated living expenses for singles

Living on campus	Living off campus	Living at home
N/A	$26,042	$13,894

LOYOLA LAW SCHOOL, LOYOLA MARYMOUNT UNIVERSITY

ABA
Approved
Since
1935

GPA and LSAT Scores

	Total	Full-Time	Part-Time
# of apps	6,781	4,643	2,138
# of offers	1,611	1,507	104
# of matrics	391	339	52
75% GPA	3.67	3.68	3.63
Median GPA	3.55	3.55	3.54
25% GPA	3.32	3.32	3.32
75% LSAT	163	163	161
Median LSAT	161	161	159
25% LSAT	158	158	155

Grants and Scholarships (from prior year)

	Total #	Total %	Full-Time #	Full-Time %	Part-Time #	Part-Time %
Total # of students	1,289		1,013		276	
Total # receiving grants	434	33.7	386	38.1	48	17.4
Less than 1/2 tuition	176	13.7	151	14.9	25	9.1
Half to full tuition	236	18.3	219	21.6	17	6.2
Full tuition	0	0.0	0	0.0	0	0.0
More than full tuition	22	1.7	16	1.6	6	2.2
Median grant amount			$22,000		$12,500	

Informational and Library Resources

Total amount spent on library materials	$2,461,512
Study seating capacity inside the library	585
# of full-time equivalent professional librarians	12
Hours per week library is open	108
# of open, wired connections available to students	320
# of networked computers available for use by students	85
Has wireless network?	Y
Requires computer?	N

JD Attrition (from prior year)

	Academic #	Other #	Total #	Total %
1st year	13	29	42	10.3
2nd year	1	1	2	0.5
3rd year	0	0	0	0.0
4th year	0	0	0	0.0

Employment (9 months after graduation)

For up-to-date employment data, go to employmentsummary.abaquestionnaire.org on the ABA website.

Bar Passage Rates

First-time takers	393	Reporting %	97.46
Average school %	80.94	Average state %	71.24
Average pass difference	9.70		

Jurisdiction	Takers	Passers	Pass %	State %	Diff %
California	383	310	80.94	71.24	9.70

LOYOLA LAW SCHOOL, LOYOLA MARYMOUNT UNIVERSITY

919 Albany Street
Los Angeles, CA 90015
Phone: 213.736.1074; Fax: 213.736.6523
E-mail: admissions@lls.edu; Website: www.lls.edu

Law School and Campus

Loyola Law School was founded in 1920 and is one of California's largest law schools. Having graduated more than 16,000 men and women, Loyola has had a profound effect on the legal profession and on American history. Known best for producing many of our nation's most exciting and influential attorneys, Loyola instills in its graduates a deep commitment to public service and ethical practice while emphasizing the philosophical, analytical, and professional skills essential to the lawyering process.

The Law School, a division of Loyola Marymount University (LMU), includes nearly 1,300 full-time day and part-time evening students, nearly 140 full-time and adjunct faculty, and 110 administrative and technical staff. Housed on a modern, innovative campus, including eight buildings, a spacious parking facility, green lawns, and athletic courts, Loyola encompasses an entire city block in downtown Los Angeles. The academic and social spaces are dedicated solely to the law school community—the environment is warm and welcoming. World-renowned architect Frank Gehry has received national and international recognition for the campus design.

The cornerstone of the campus, the William M. Rains Law Library, is one of the largest private law libraries in the western United States, providing extensive research capabilities with a collection of over 600,000 volumes and the latest advances in information technology.

Our central location, just minutes away from many courts, major law firms, and public interest agencies, provides excellent opportunities for our students. Students also have easy access to LA Live, an entertainment and sports venue that includes the Staples Center, Nokia Theatre, Grammy Museum, a movie theater, and restaurants.

JD—Juris Doctor

The Juris Doctor prepares students to be effective lawyers and judges in any jurisdiction in the United States. Loyola recognizes that a quality education must do more than simply prepare a student to file a lawsuit or draft a contract. The program is designed to teach students to think and reason critically. The faculty strives to instill in students a respect and appreciation for the law and a desire to improve the society in which we live.

The Juris Doctor is offered in both a **full-time, three-year day division** and a **part-time, four-year evening division**.

Other Programs

- **JD/MBA**—Loyola Law School and the Graduate Program of the College of Business Administration of Loyola Marymount University offer a dual-degree program in law and business. **Graduates of the program receive the Juris Doctor (JD) and the Master of Business Administration (MBA).** A graduate certificate in International Business can also be earned with the MBA. The dual-degree program allows students to earn both degrees in four years instead of the five normally required to complete the degree programs separately. The program is only open to full-time day students. Students may receive up to 12 units of business classes toward the 87 units required to earn a JD, and may be allowed to count up to 12 units of law classes toward the 54 units required to earn an MBA. Applicants must apply and be accepted separately to the Law School and the MBA program. Applicants must also apply and be accepted to the JD/MBA program. Applications for the JD/MBA program may be submitted after the first year of law school. Interested applicants should contact the LMU College of Business Administration to request an application for the MBA program and the Law School Office of Admissions to request an application for the JD/MBA program.

- **Tax LLM and JD/LLM in Tax—Loyola also offers the Master of Laws (LLM) degree in Taxation.** This degree distinguishes tax specialists by its advanced legal theory, tax policy, and scholarship. **Students may earn both the JD degree and the LLM in Taxation in three years** (rather than the four years typically required to complete the degree programs separately) by completing an intensive summer tax session and by taking advanced tax courses that count for double credit toward both the Juris Doctor and the LLM in Taxation.

Faculty

The Loyola faculty are exceptional teachers who maintain an open-door policy to encourage free and continuous interaction with their students. They are scholars who publish innovative theories, influencing the development and direction of the legal profession. They also draft hundreds of scholarly articles and books, advise law firms and agencies on recent developments, and lecture at universities around the world. Our faculty include seasoned attorneys with extensive and varied practice experience as United States Supreme Court clerks, public interest lawyers, agency chiefs, and law firm partners.

Curriculum

The Law School's new Concentration Programs combine rigorous intellectual training with clinical and experiential programs and are guided by our faculty and alumni advisors. Concentrations are available in Civil Litigation and Advocacy, Corporate Law, Criminal Justice, Entertainment/Media Law, Environmental Law, Intellectual Property, International and Comparative Law, Law and Entrepreneurship, Public Interest, and Tax Law. Students can earn recognition on their transcript for completing these intensive programs. This program signals to employers that Loyola students will provide immediate value and perform effectively as soon as they enter the legal profession.

Other areas of study available at Loyola include Disability Law, Health Care Law, and Patent and Technology Law.

Innovative Programs, Centers, and Clinics

Loyola demonstrates its commitment to public service by requiring all students to donate 40 hours to working in the public interest sector. The **Public Interest Law Department** coordinates public interest activities, counsels students about law practice and fellowships, and administers five public service programs. Loyola's downtown Public Interest Law Center houses two of our premier clinical programs, the **Disability Rights Legal Center** and the **Center for Conflict Resolution**. On campus, students can participate with the **Center for Juvenile Law and Policy**, work with faculty as research assistants, or participate in our faculty-led conferences and symposia. Students have many opportunities through these programs to work with clients, practice their skills, and receive individualized feedback from faculty members and directors.

Our excellent **trial advocacy programs** also allow upper-division students to compete in noted trial competitions. Loyola students have won numerous awards at international and national trial advocacy and moot court competitions in recent years. Students interested in spending the summer abroad may attend one of our **international programs** in Costa Rica, China, Cyprus, or Italy.

Other opportunities include the **Entertainment Law Practicum**, which allows students to get hands-on experience through field placements at television networks, major movie studios, record companies, talent agencies, and entertainment law firms. Loyola's **Business Law Practicum** offers an innovative approach to educating business lawyers with practical, real-world training. Through the **Immigration Justice Practicum** students cover substantive immigration law issues in a fall semester class and work in the spring semester for an organization that handles immigration issues. Finally, our **externship program** exposes students to **many other areas of practice** as they work for government offices, public interest organizations, or private corporations.

Admission and Financial Aid/Scholarships

Admission to the law school is based on a comprehensive evaluation that includes LSAT performance, undergraduate academic record, the personal statement, and letters of recommendation. Professional experience, extracurricular activities, community involvement, and qualities such as motivation, maturity, and focus are also closely evaluated. A prospective student may also submit a résumé.

Applications for admission are accepted on a rolling basis. The committee begins reading complete files in December. Deadlines are **February 1** for the day program and **April 16** for the evening program. Early applicants have greater prospects for gaining admission and receiving scholarship awards.

All admitted students are considered for our scholarship programs. The committee uses the merits of the file to evaluate the admitted student's potential to contribute to our community. In addition to the general scholarship program, Loyola offers the **Public Interest Scholars Program** for students interested in having a career in public service. For graduates working at public interest organizations or with government agencies, a **Loan Repayment Assistance Program** is also available. Entering students can work with our dedicated financial aid staff to find other sources (primarily loans) to help fund their educational and personal expenses.

Career Services

The Office of Career Services (OCS) offers a wealth of services, programs, and resources to students and alumni. A large professional staff counsels and assists students and graduates in the job development process. Hundreds of national, international, and regional employers recruit from Loyola annually. Graduates are employed by the nation's most prestigious private and public legal organizations. Overall placement figures are consistently strong, and our alumni are a critical source of support through participation in recruitment and hiring and their involvement with campus programs.

APPLICANT PROFILE

Loyola Law School, Loyola Marymount University
This grid includes only applicants who earned 120–180 LSAT scores under standard administrations.

LSAT Score	3.75 +		3.50–3.74		3.25–3.49		3.00–3.24		2.75–2.99		2.50–2.74		2.25–2.49		2.00–2.24		Below 2.00		No GPA		Total	
	Apps	Adm	Apps	Adm	Apps	Adm	Apps	Adm	Apps	Adm	Apps	Adm	Apps	Adm	Apps	Adm	Apps	Adm	Apps	Adm	Apps	Adm
175–180	2	1	3	2	1	1	0	0	1	0	1	0	0	0	1	0	0	0	0	0	9	4
170–174	24	23	28	24	26	19	15	9	7	2	4	0	2	0	1	0	0	0	3	0	110	77
165–169	103	93	139	127	114	96	79	50	45	17	25	4	7	1	1	0	0	0	6	1	519	389
160–164	180	158	305	253	271	170	189	75	77	17	46	7	24	3	6	1	1	0	25	7	1124	691
155–159	196	128	346	161	358	57	221	17	129	10	58	2	25	0	3	0	0	0	19	0	1355	375
150–154	91	20	165	35	236	11	215	2	114	2	69	1	17	0	13	0	0	0	18	1	938	72
145–149	29	1	76	0	114	0	96	0	72	0	43	1	17	0	7	0	0	0	15	0	469	2
140–144	3	0	22	0	35	0	62	0	38	0	30	0	16	0	4	0	0	0	7	0	217	0
135–139	3	0	10	0	7	0	13	0	21	0	14	0	7	0	4	0	2	0	4	0	85	0
130–134	1	0	3	0	4	0	2	0	7	0	8	0	5	0	4	0	0	0	1	0	35	0
125–129	0	0	1	0	0	0	0	0	1	0	1	0	2	0	1	0	0	0	0	0	6	0
120–124	0	0	0	0	0	0	0	0	0	0	1	0	0	0	0	0	0	0	0	0	2	0
Total	632	424	1098	602	1166	354	892	153	512	48	300	15	122	4	45	1	3	0	99	9	4869	1610

Apps = Number of Applicants
Adm = Number Admitted
Represents 99% of applicant pool; highest LSAT data reported.

LOYOLA UNIVERSITY CHICAGO SCHOOL OF LAW

25 East Pearson Street, Suite 1208
Chicago, IL 60611
Phone: 312.915.7170; Fax: 312.915.7906
E-mail: law-admissions@luc.edu; Website: www.luc.edu/law

ABA
Approved
Since
1925

The Basics

Type of school	Private
Term	Semester
Application deadline	3/1
Application fee	$0
Financial aid deadline	3/1
Can first year start other than fall?	No
Student to faculty ratio	13.9 to 1
# of housing spaces available	
restricted to law students	96
graduate housing for which law students are eligible	106

Faculty and Administrators

	Total		Men		Women		Minorities	
	Spr	Fall	Spr	Fall	Spr	Fall	Spr	Fall
Full-time	49	48	31	31	18	17	6	8
Other full-time	4	7	2	4	2	3	1	2
Deans, librarians, & others who teach	15	16	5	5	10	11	2	2
Part-time	96	129	45	69	51	60	7	10
Total	164	200	83	109	81	91	16	22

Curriculum

		Full-Time	Part-Time
Typical first-year section size		82	31
Is there typically a "small section" of the first-year class, other than Legal Writing, taught by full-time faculty		Yes	No
If yes, typical size offered last year		20	
# of classroom course titles beyond first-year curriculum		218	
# of upper division courses, excluding seminars, with an enrollment:	Under 25	196	
	25–49	37	
	50–74	14	
	75–99	3	
	100+	0	
# of seminars		55	
# of seminar positions available		1,210	
# of seminar positions filled		507	211
# of positions available in simulation courses		1,260	
# of simulation positions filled		777	218
# of positions available in faculty supervised clinical courses		168	
# of faculty supervised clinical positions filled		114	21
# involved in field placements		113	28
# involved in law journals		173	43
# involved in moot court or trial competitions		63	14
# of credit hours required to graduate		86	

JD Enrollment and Ethnicity

	Men		Women		Full-Time		Part-Time		1st-Year		Total		JD Degs. Awd.
	#	%	#	%	#	%	#	%	#	%	#	%	
All Hispanics	25	5.8	38	8.7	51	7.0	12	8.7	24	8.7	63	7.2	14
Am. Ind./AK Nat.	0	0.0	2	0.5	1	0.1	1	0.7	0	0.0	2	0.2	0
Asian	17	4.0	25	5.7	32	4.4	10	7.2	14	5.1	42	4.8	11
Black/Af. Am.	27	6.3	53	12.1	63	8.6	17	12.3	34	12.4	80	9.2	13
Nat. HI/Pac. Isl.	0	0.0	0	0.0	0	0.0	0	0.0	0	0.0	0	0.0	0
2 or more races	5	1.2	11	2.5	16	2.2	0	0.0	8	2.9	16	1.8	0
Subtotal (minor.)	74	17.2	129	29.4	163	22.3	40	29.0	80	29.1	203	23.4	38
Nonres. Alien	4	0.9	2	0.5	5	0.7	1	0.7	3	1.1	6	0.7	2
White/Cauc.	342	79.5	303	69.0	551	75.4	94	68.1	190	69.1	645	74.2	193
Unknown	10	2.3	5	1.1	12	1.6	3	2.2	2	0.7	15	1.7	16
Total	430	49.5	439	50.5	731	84.1	138	15.9	275	31.6	869		249

Transfers

Transfers in	13
Transfers out	23

Tuition and Fees

	Resident	Nonresident
Full-time	$39,496	$39,496
Part-time	$29,826	$29,826
Tuition Guarantee Program		N

Living Expenses

Estimated living expenses for singles

Living on campus	Living off campus	Living at home
$20,584	$20,584	$20,584

LOYOLA UNIVERSITY CHICAGO SCHOOL OF LAW

*ABA
Approved
Since
1925*

GPA and LSAT Scores

	Total	Full-Time	Part-Time
# of apps	5,040	4,590	450
# of offers	1,696	1,605	91
# of matrics	274	244	30
75% GPA	3.57	3.57	3.42
Median GPA	3.37	3.40	3.27
25% GPA	3.13	3.15	3.11
75% LSAT	162	162	157
Median LSAT	160	160	154
25% LSAT	156	158	150

Grants and Scholarships (from prior year)

	Total #	Total %	Full-Time #	Full-Time %	Part-Time #	Part-Time %
Total # of students	851		692		159	
Total # receiving grants	608	71.4	544	78.6	64	40.3
Less than 1/2 tuition	477	56.1	416	60.1	61	38.4
Half to full tuition	106	12.5	103	14.9	3	1.9
Full tuition	25	2.9	25	3.6	0	0.0
More than full tuition	0	0.0	0	0.0	0	0.0
Median grant amount			$10,600		$6,000	

Informational and Library Resources

Total amount spent on library materials	$819,374
Study seating capacity inside the library	457
# of full-time equivalent professional librarians	8
Hours per week library is open	101
# of open, wired connections available to students	328
# of networked computers available for use by students	64
Has wireless network?	Y
Requires computer?	N

JD Attrition (from prior year)

	Academic #	Other #	Total #	Total %
1st year	0	1	1	0.3
2nd year	1	23	24	9.2
3rd year	0	0	0	0.0
4th year	0	0	0	0.0

Employment (9 months after graduation)

For up-to-date employment data, go to employmentsummary.abaquestionnaire.org on the ABA website.

Bar Passage Rates

First-time takers	241	Reporting %	98.76
Average school %	88.66	Average state %	89.41
Average pass difference	−0.75		

Jurisdiction	Takers	Passers	Pass %	State %	Diff %
Illinois	236	209	88.56	89.38	−0.82
Wisconsin	2	2	100.00	92.93	7.07

LOYOLA UNIVERSITY CHICAGO SCHOOL OF LAW

25 East Pearson Street, Suite 1208
Chicago, IL 60611
Phone: 312.915.7170; Fax: 312.915.7906
E-mail: law-admissions@luc.edu; Website: www.luc.edu/law

Introduction

The School of Law is located on the Water Tower Campus of the university, a few blocks north of the Chicago Loop. This campus adjoins Michigan Avenue at the historical Water Tower, a Chicago landmark, in approximately the center of the renowned Magnificent Mile, a commercial center over which the John Hancock Center towers. This location provides ready access to the state and federal courts and to the offices of most other institutions of federal, state, and local government, as well as the cultural centers of Chicago. The school is a member of the AALS and is approved by the ABA. The School of Law celebrated its 100th anniversary in 2008.

Library and Facilities

The Philip H. Corboy Law Center, at 25 East Pearson Street, provides Loyola's law students with a modern and enhanced learning environment. The School of Law library is located on floors 3–5 of the Law Center. More than 400,000 volumes enhance Loyola's broad-based law curriculum and support the varied research needs of students and faculty. Offering custom-designed furnishings and custom carrels, the 43,900-square-foot facility creates a comfortable and accommodating atmosphere for users. The library is open 100 hours each week, with expanded hours during examination periods. The law library is fully staffed with professional librarians and paraprofessionals to assist students and faculty.

Across the street from the Law Center is a 25-story, 600-bed residence hall, Baumhart Hall, which opened in fall 2006. This structure enables graduate, professional, and undergraduate student residents to experience contemporary living in fully furnished apartments. Amenities include a 24-hour security staff, a food court and late-night café, a state-of-the-art fitness center, wireless access in apartment bedrooms and public areas, and a laundry room equipped with "smart system" washers and dryers. Rent includes all utilities, heat and air-conditioning, cable, and high-speed Internet access.

Foreign Study Programs

Since 1983, the School of Law has offered a program of international and comparative law courses at the John Felice Rome Center, the university's campus in Rome, Italy. Each summer, for approximately four weeks, law students can take one or more of the courses offered in Rome by members of Loyola's law faculty. In 1997, the law school added a program in Strasbourg, France. This one-week optional field study follows the summer program in Rome.

In summer 2008, Loyola inaugurated a three-week program in China. In addition to time in the classroom, students hear from guest lecturers and experience guided excursions to sites in Beijing and the surrounding areas.

In 1989, Loyola inaugurated its London Comparative Advocacy Program in which students travel to London between semesters for approximately 15 days to become immersed in the world of the British barrister.

In spring 2003, Loyola inaugurated an immersion program at Universidad Alberto Hurtado, a Jesuit law school in Santiago, Chile.

Clinical Legal Education

For students, faculty, and alumni, Loyola's four legal clinics represent a valuable bridge between theory and practice, classroom and career. Through the clinics, the School of Law offers service to others in a way that gives them dignity while providing students with practical legal experience. In spring 2003, the law school celebrated the 20th anniversary of its clinical program that began with the founding of its Community Law Center Clinic, followed later by the Federal Tax Clinic, Child and Family Law Clinic, the Business Law Clinic, the Life After Innocence Project, and the Health Justice Project.

Special Opportunities

The School of Law has dual-degree programs with the School of Social Work, the Department of Political Science, the School of Education, and the Graduate School of Business. Automatic acceptance into the master's of political science program is granted to candidates admitted to the law school. Provisional admission to the MBA program is granted based upon LSAT score and law school grades. The multidegree programs are structured to allow completion after four years. Loyola offers accelerated LLM programs in health law, child and family law, and taxation to JD students who fulfill program requirements. Recognizing the increasing need for specialization in legal education and practice, the school offers specialized curricula in five key areas: International Law and Practice, Health Law, Child and Family Law, Advocacy, and Tax Law.

Child and Family Law Center

The Loyola ChildLaw Center was created in 1993 to prepare law students to represent abused and neglected children. The center is the first of its kind at any American law school; it was the recipient of the National Association of Counsel for Children 1996 Outstanding Legal Advocacy Award, and it draws on the full resources of Loyola University, including the schools of medicine, social work, and education. The program includes an LLM degree and a master's degree program for nonlawyers.

The center houses our renowned ChildLaw and Education Institute, offering students an integrated curriculum in education law, interdisciplinary research, and outreach experiences, with the opportunity to represent children confronting barriers to educational equality. Law students also may obtain a unique dual degree with the School of Education, which will result in a JD and MA in Comparative Education.

The law school and Teach for America (TFA) have entered into a partnership. TFA corps members who are interested in using their legal education to advocate for children's legal interests and well-being may receive matching AmeriCorps Awards.

Annually, child and family law fellows are selected from the entering law class. One fellowship is reserved for a TFA corps member. Each fellow receives financial support.

LOYOLA UNIVERSITY CHICAGO SCHOOL OF LAW

Institute for Health Law

The Beazley Institute for Health Law was created in 1984 in recognition of the need for an academic forum to study the field of health law and to act as a vehicle to foster dialogue between the law and the health sciences. Through the institute, the law school offers an SJD in Health Law and Policy and an LLM in Health Law. In addition, it offers the first Master of Jurisprudence (MJ) in Health Law and Doctor of Law (DLaw) in Health Law and Policy, providing health care professionals with an intensive overview in health law. More than two dozen health law classes are offered at the law school.

Institute for Consumer Antitrust Studies

The Institute for Consumer Antitrust Studies is an independent, academically based institute designed to explore the effect of antitrust and consumer law enforcement on the individual consumer and the general public. The institute was founded by a grant from the US District Court for the Northern District of Illinois and is supported by Loyola and private donors.

Advocacy

Loyola prepares its students for careers of leadership at the bar and on the bench. For over 100 years, Loyola's tradition of educating and training top litigators has produced some of the country's most accomplished and recognized trial attorneys and judges. The Dan K. Webb Center for Advocacy is composed of a second-year required course in advocacy, courses in beginning and advanced trial advocacy, numerous moot court competitions, the Corboy Fellowship Program in Trial Advocacy for mock trial competitions, and a wide variety of litigation-related courses and an extensive curriculum in alternative dispute resolution. A certificate in advocacy is available for students who complete a menu of advocacy courses.

Symbolic of our advocacy success is our selection by the National Institute for Trial Advocacy as the site for two of its largest advocacy training programs, the Midwest Regional Trial Advocacy Program and the Midwest Regional Deposition Training Program.

Admission

Factors other than LSAT scores and college grades are considered. Such factors include work experience, personal goals, specialized education, and other evidence of the ability to contribute invaluable insight to law classes.

Career Services

The Career Resources Office assists students and alumni with career planning and employment selection. Seminars by practicing attorneys and alumni, résumé preparation, interviewing techniques, individual counseling, and job-search strategies are just some of the programs administered by the Career Resources Office.

A year-round, on-campus employer interview and recruitment program provides employment opportunities.

The School of Law is a member of NALP.

Cocurricular Activities

Students are encouraged to participate in cocurricular activities. There are six student-edited publications, including the *Annals of Health Law, Children's Legal Rights Journal, Consumer Law Review, International Law Review, Loyola University Chicago Law Journal,* and *Public Interest Law Reporter.* Students compete in more than 20 moot court and mock trial national and international competitions. All students are members of the Loyola Student Bar Association, the principal instrument of student government. There are over 30 student organizations devoted to legal practice, ethnic groups, or law student chapters of professional bar associations.

APPLICANT PROFILE

Loyola University Chicago School of Law
This grid includes only applicants who earned 120–180 LSAT scores under standard administrations.

LSAT Score	3.75 +		3.50–3.74		3.25–3.49		3.00–3.24		2.50–2.99		2.00–2.49		Below 2.00		No GPA		Total	
	Apps	Adm	Apps	Adm	Apps	Adm	Apps	Adm	Apps	Adm	Apps	Adm	Apps	Adm	Apps	Adm	Apps	Adm
165–180	74	71	113	107	90	88	42	39	50	31	10	4	2	0	1	1	382	341
160–164	179	172	241	233	219	198	164	137	119	49	33	10	0	0	12	7	967	806
155–159	181	89	332	156	344	67	270	40	213	27	40	6	0	0	18	1	1398	386
145–154	162	20	272	39	426	42	389	33	405	17	95	3	5	0	31	2	1785	156
120–144	20	0	40	0	71	0	94	1	163	1	73	0	7	0	19	0	487	2
Total	616	352	998	535	1150	395	959	250	950	125	251	23	14	0	81	11	5019	1691

Apps = Number of Applicants
Adm = Number Admitted
Reflects 99% of the total applicant pool; highest LSAT data reported.

LOYOLA UNIVERSITY NEW ORLEANS COLLEGE OF LAW

7214 St. Charles Avenue, Box 904
New Orleans, LA 70118
Phone: 504.861.5575; Fax: 504.861.5772
E-mail: ladmit@loyno.edu; Website: http://law.loyno.edu/

ABA Approved Since 1931

The Basics

Type of school	Private
Term	Semester
Application deadline	
Application fee	$45
Financial aid deadline	
Can first year start other than fall?	No
Student to faculty ratio	15.9 to 1
# of housing spaces available restricted to law students	55
graduate housing for which law students are eligible	55

Faculty and Administrators

	Total Spr	Total Fall	Men Spr	Men Fall	Women Spr	Women Fall	Minorities Spr	Minorities Fall
Full-time	40	40	23	22	17	18	11	11
Other full-time	12	12	7	6	5	6	0	2
Deans, librarians, & others who teach	3	5	2	3	1	2	0	1
Part-time	27	25	21	21	6	4	0	2
Total	82	82	53	52	29	30	11	16

Curriculum

	Full-Time	Part-Time
Typical first-year section size	44	42
Is there typically a "small section" of the first-year class, other than Legal Writing, taught by full-time faculty	No	No
If yes, typical size offered last year		
# of classroom course titles beyond first-year curriculum	213	

# of upper division courses, excluding seminars, with an enrollment:		
Under 25	43	
25–49	36	
50–74	35	
75–99	4	
100+	0	

# of seminars	44	
# of seminar positions available	876	
# of seminar positions filled	514	183
# of positions available in simulation courses	0	
# of simulation positions filled	0	0
# of positions available in faculty supervised clinical courses	185	
# of faculty supervised clinical positions filled	110	0
# involved in field placements	87	0
# involved in law journals	18	0
# involved in moot court or trial competitions	40	0
# of credit hours required to graduate	90	

JD Enrollment and Ethnicity

	Men #	Men %	Women #	Women %	Full-Time #	Full-Time %	Part-Time #	Part-Time %	1st-Year #	1st-Year %	Total #	Total %	JD Degs. Awd.
All Hispanics	41	10.1	45	11.1	79	11.5	7	5.5	30	12.4	86	10.6	20
Am. Ind./AK Nat.	6	1.5	3	0.7	4	0.6	5	3.9	4	1.7	9	1.1	0
Asian	17	4.2	12	3.0	27	3.9	2	1.6	4	1.7	29	3.6	9
Black/Af. Am.	32	7.9	70	17.2	87	12.7	15	11.7	22	9.1	102	12.5	33
Nat. HI/Pac. Isl.	0	0.0	1	0.2	1	0.1	0	0.0	1	0.4	1	0.1	1
2 or more races	0	0.0	0	0.0	0	0.0	0	0.0	0	0.0	0	0.0	0
Subtotal (minor.)	96	23.6	131	32.3	198	28.9	29	22.7	61	25.2	227	27.9	63
Nonres. Alien	4	1.0	1	0.2	4	0.6	1	0.8	3	1.2	5	0.6	1
White/Cauc.	276	67.8	254	62.6	444	64.8	86	67.2	165	68.2	530	65.2	153
Unknown	31	7.6	20	4.9	39	5.7	12	9.4	13	5.4	51	6.3	14
Total	407	50.1	406	49.9	685	84.3	128	15.7	242	29.8	813		231

Transfers

Transfers in	4
Transfers out	4

Tuition and Fees

	Resident	Nonresident
Full-time	$38,266	$38,266
Part-time	$25,856	$25,856
Tuition Guarantee Program	N	

Living Expenses

Estimated living expenses for singles

Living on campus	Living off campus	Living at home
$20,300	$20,300	$15,000

LOYOLA UNIVERSITY NEW ORLEANS COLLEGE OF LAW

ABA Approved Since 1931

GPA and LSAT Scores

	Total	Full-Time	Part-Time
# of apps	1,794	1,667	127
# of offers	1,071	1,002	69
# of matrics	242	199	43
75% GPA	3.48	3.51	3.42
Median GPA	3.22	3.23	3.15
25% GPA	2.97	2.98	2.70
75% LSAT	156	156	155
Median LSAT	153	153	152
25% LSAT	151	151	149

Grants and Scholarships (from prior year)

	Total #	Total %	Full-Time #	Full-Time %	Part-Time #	Part-Time %
Total # of students	834		681		153	
Total # receiving grants	286	34.3	277	40.7	9	5.9
Less than 1/2 tuition	120	14.4	114	16.7	6	3.9
Half to full tuition	134	16.1	133	19.5	1	0.7
Full tuition	14	1.7	12	1.8	2	1.3
More than full tuition	18	2.2	18	2.6	0	0.0
Median grant amount			$20,531		$11,170	

Informational and Library Resources

Total amount spent on library materials	$1,313,327
Study seating capacity inside the library	366
# of full-time equivalent professional librarians	1
Hours per week library is open	106
# of open, wired connections available to students	40
# of networked computers available for use by students	74
Has wireless network?	Y
Requires computer?	N

JD Attrition (from prior year)

	Academic #	Other #	Total #	Total %
1st year	4	11	15	5.6
2nd year	3	1	4	1.3
3rd year	0	1	1	0.4
4th year	0	0	0	0.0

Employment (9 months after graduation)

For up-to-date employment data, go to employmentsummary.abaquestionnaire.org on the ABA website.

Bar Passage Rates

First-time takers	296	Reporting %	71.62
Average school %	66.98	Average state %	67.28

Average pass difference –0.30

Jurisdiction	Takers	Passers	Pass %	State %	Diff %
Louisiana	193	133	68.91	66.26	2.65
Florida	19	9	47.37	77.63	–30.26

LOYOLA UNIVERSITY NEW ORLEANS COLLEGE OF LAW

7214 St. Charles Avenue, Box 904
New Orleans, LA 70118
Phone: 504.861.5575; Fax: 504.861.5772
E-mail: ladmit@loyno.edu; Website: http://law.loyno.edu/

Introduction

It is a rare combination of wide-ranging programs of study, real-life opportunities, and a commitment to the community that makes Loyola University New Orleans College of Law stand apart. It is an institution that trains lawyers to think critically and be advocates for social justice. The entire Loyola law school community provides an atmosphere for our students to excel, succeed, and become productive members of legal communities across the country. It is a school where students have the opportunity to learn from a prestigious faculty, participate in many activities to hone their practical lawyering skills, and serve the New Orleans community through our many clinical offerings.

Loyola New Orleans is a Catholic institution of higher learning in the Jesuit tradition. The College of Law was established in 1914, approved by the ABA in 1931, and has been a member of the AALS since 1934. The College of Law is committed to excellence in legal education in the tradition of its spiritual heritage, with the goal being wisdom, not mere technical competence. The law school welcomes all persons who strive for the truth and who are prepared to challenge all assumptions in light of this commitment.

Physical Facilities and Library

Loyola University has two campuses, both located approximately five miles from the historic French Quarter. The 20-acre main campus, in the heart of the uptown residential community, faces the nationally recognized Audubon Park and Zoo. The 4.2-acre Broadway campus is the home of the College of Law, including the newly renovated Broadway Building (completed in 2011), which is the new home of our Stuart H. Smith Law Clinic and Center for Social Justice and Career Development and Law Practice Center.

The law library's collection of over 371,000 volumes and microform equivalents supports the curriculum and research needs of the students. The library has extensive computer facilities in place to access information outside its confines. The Online Catalog Library Center service permits the library to access a national bibliographic database of over 10 million publications. The law library houses two computer labs equipped with 59 personal computers on a network with access to the Internet, LexisNexis, Westlaw, e-mail, and other computer resources; remote-controlled viewing/listening rooms; and a computerized legal research room.

Curriculum and Special Programs

The curricula at Loyola New Orleans have been shaped by Louisiana's unique role as the only state in the union that has a legal system based on significant elements of both the civil law and common law traditions. The civil law was imported into Louisiana during the 18th century, when it was first a colony of France, and later, Spain. As a result of Louisiana's unique legal heritage, Loyola New Orleans has developed separate curricula: civil law and common law, both full-time and part-time. It is important to note that the Loyola New Orleans JD degree will allow a graduate to sit for the bar in any of the 50 states, without regard for the curriculum chosen. Loyola offers a Certificate in Common Law Studies

and a Certificate in Civil Law Studies for students who wish to acquire a foundation in both disciplines. Full-time students are required to be in residence for a minimum of six full semesters. The normal time frame for part-time students is eight semesters and one summer session. At the graduate level, the law school offers an LLM for International Students for graduates of non-US law schools.

Law Skills and Experiential Learning Program—Loyola has one of the most unique and far-reaching professional lawyering skills programs in the country. Recognizing hands-on, learn-by-doing opportunities that develop the future practitioner's skills to be as important as traditional academic studies, the curriculum incorporates specialized courses and the expertise of attorneys and judges. Currently, over 100 members of the bench and bar teach in the skills curriculum. Skills courses are offered tuition free, and students are required to complete eight skills credits but may complete as many above those required as they choose. Practical experiences will also be incorporated into the traditional law classes starting in the first year.

International Law—Loyola has summer sessions on four continents and in six countries, established ties with a number of important foreign law schools, sent its professors to teach or lecture at law schools in more than a dozen foreign countries, and hosted lectures by a number of professors from non-US law schools. Summer courses are taught in special five-week, summer-abroad sessions in Mexico and Eastern Europe (Russia, Hungary, and Austria). There are two- and three-week sessions offered each summer in Brazil or Costa Rica. Students may obtain a Certificate in International Legal Studies. There are seminar courses that have short trips abroad to Austria, Italy, and Turkey.

Public Interest Law—As part of Loyola's Jesuit commitment to social justice, the law school provides many courses and activities as part of this specialty, including the very active Law Clinic and Center for Social Justice. Most of the public interest focus falls under the umbrella of the Gillis Long Poverty Law Center. A loan forgiveness program is available for graduates working in eligible public interest employment.

Environmental Law—Loyola received a $2 million grant to establish a faculty chair for environmental law. A nationally renowned scholar heads the Loyola Center for Environmental Law and Land Use, which was created to address legal issues relative to economic development, environmental protection, and the public's role in environmental policy issues. A certificate in environmental law is available.

Tax Law—Loyola recently established a certificate program designed to certify students in this area of law and assist those students who may choose to pursue an LLM in Tax upon graduation.

Other Areas of Significant Emphasis—Other areas of significant emphasis include corporate law and maritime law.

Clinical Education—The law clinic is a vital component of the law school. Students chosen to participate in the senior-year program will be assigned cases, both civil and criminal, and will be expected to prepare them for trial prior to actually participating in the trial process. The areas of law practiced in the clinic are criminal (both prosecution and defense), immigration, family law, workplace justice, mediation, and community justice. Upper-division students also have an opportunity to serve as judicial clerks in the federal extern program.

Joint-Degree Programs—Loyola offers three combined degrees: JD/Master of Business Administration, JD/Master of Public Administration, and JD/Master of Urban and Regional Planning.

Scholarly Publications and Student Activities

The *Loyola Law Review* is published by a student editorial board and includes student work and articles written by specialists from the practicing bar and academic community. Staff membership is based on scholarship and interest in legal writing.

The *Loyola University New Orleans Journal of Public Interest Law* is devoted to issues faced by the poor, children, the elderly, and all others who are unable to afford legal representation.

The *Loyola Intellectual Property and High Technology Law Annual* is a scholarly publication focusing on current legal issues in patents, copyrights, trademarks, and technology law.

The *Loyola Maritime Law Journal* provides an avenue for research and writing in the field of maritime law. Staff membership is based on scholarship.

The Moot Court Board, selected from prior years' competitions, is responsible for the Moot Court Program. Teams are entered each year in competitions. Loyola teams have an impressive winning record in a wide variety of local, regional, national, and international competitions.

There are a number of student organizations, including, but not limited to, three legal fraternities as well as the Intellectual Property Law Society, Sports and Entertainment Law Society, and Health Care Law Society.

Admission

The law school begins processing applications for admission on September 1 each year. The first decision letters are generally released in December. The admission decision is based on an initial evaluation of a combination of the LSAT score and the undergraduate cumulative grade-point average. Additionally, the undergraduate institution attended, the undergraduate major, and any grade trends will be taken into consideration. Also included in the evaluation will be the required personal statement, letters of recommendation, and résumés, all of which may present a more illuminating portrait of the applicant's skills and accomplishments. Competition for acceptance to the law school is high, thus all information provided is used to make the final admission decision.

Career Services

The Career Development and Law Practice Center offers a variety of services to both students and alumni. The office maintains and operates a career-planning center, assists students in preparing résumés, videotapes mock interviews, and conducts seminars on career planning, employment opportunities, and interviewing techniques. The office actively solicits job opportunities for summer and school-term clerkships, as well as employment options for each year's graduating class.

APPLICANT PROFILE

Loyola University New Orleans College of Law
This grid includes only applicants who earned 120–180 LSAT scores under standard administrations.

LSAT Score	GPA								
	3.75 +	3.50–3.74	3.25–3.49	3.00–3.24	2.75–2.99	2.50–2.74	2.25–2.49	2.00–2.24	Below 2.00
175–180									
170–174									
165–169									
160–164									
155–159									
150–154									
145–149									
140–144									
135–139									
130–134									
125–129									
120–124									

Good Possibility   Possible   Unlikely

The College of Law considers many factors beyond LSAT score and GPA. This chart should be used only as a general guide.

UNIVERSITY OF MAINE SCHOOL OF LAW

246 Deering Avenue
Portland, ME 04102
Phone: 207.780.4341; Fax: 207.780.4018
E-mail: mainelaw@usm.maine.edu; Website: http://mainelaw.maine.edu

ABA
Approved
Since
1962

The Basics

Type of school	Public
Term	Semester
Application deadline	3/1
Application fee	$50
Financial aid deadline	2/15
Can first year start other than fall?	No
Student to faculty ratio	14.3 to 1
# of housing spaces available restricted to law students	
graduate housing for which law students are eligible	275

Faculty and Administrators

	Total		Men		Women		Minorities	
	Spr	Fall	Spr	Fall	Spr	Fall	Spr	Fall
Full-time	16	16	12	12	4	4	0	0
Other full-time	1	0	1	0	0	0	0	0
Deans, librarians, & others who teach	7	7	3	3	4	4	0	0
Part-time	15	13	11	9	4	4	0	0
Total	39	36	27	24	12	12	0	0

Curriculum

	Full-Time	Part-Time
Typical first-year section size	96	0
Is there typically a "small section" of the first-year class, other than Legal Writing, taught by full-time faculty	Yes	No
If yes, typical size offered last year	51	
# of classroom course titles beyond first-year curriculum	69	

# of upper division courses, excluding seminars, with an enrollment:		
	Under 25	49
	25–49	15
	50–74	2
	75–99	0
	100+	0

# of seminars	29	
# of seminar positions available	442	
# of seminar positions filled	351	0
# of positions available in simulation courses	142	
# of simulation positions filled	136	0
# of positions available in faculty supervised clinical courses	60	
# of faculty supervised clinical positions filled	57	0
# involved in field placements	61	0
# involved in law journals	50	0
# involved in moot court or trial competitions	22	0
# of credit hours required to graduate	90	

JD Enrollment and Ethnicity

	Men		Women		Full-Time		Part-Time		1st-Year		Total		JD Degs. Awd.
	#	%	#	%	#	%	#	%	#	%	#	%	
All Hispanics	5	3.4	5	3.7	10	3.7	0	0.0	3	3.3	10	3.6	3
Am. Ind./AK Nat.	2	1.4	1	0.7	3	1.1	0	0.0	0	0.0	3	1.1	1
Asian	2	1.4	0	0.0	2	0.7	0	0.0	2	2.2	2	0.7	0
Black/Af. Am.	0	0.0	4	3.0	3	1.1	1	10.0	0	0.0	4	1.4	2
Nat. HI/Pac. Isl.	1	0.7	8	5.9	8	3.0	1	10.0	3	3.3	9	3.2	2
2 or more races	0	0.0	0	0.0	0	0.0	0	0.0	0	0.0	0	0.0	0
Subtotal (minor.)	10	6.9	18	13.3	26	9.6	2	20.0	8	8.7	28	10.0	8
Nonres. Alien	2	1.4	1	0.7	3	1.1	0	0.0	3	3.3	3	1.1	2
White/Cauc.	133	91.7	116	85.9	241	89.3	8	80.0	81	88.0	249	88.9	80
Unknown	0	0.0	0	0.0	0	0.0	0	0.0	0	0.0	0	0.0	0
Total	145	51.8	135	48.2	270	96.4	10	3.6	92	32.9	280		90

Transfers

Transfers in	5
Transfers out	0

Tuition and Fees

	Resident	Nonresident
Full-time	$22,986	$33,906
Part-time		
Tuition Guarantee Program		N

Living Expenses

Estimated living expenses for singles

Living on campus	Living off campus	Living at home
$16,622	$16,622	$8,228

UNIVERSITY OF MAINE SCHOOL OF LAW

ABA
Approved
Since
1962

GPA and LSAT Scores

	Total	Full-Time	Part-Time
# of apps	988	988	0
# of offers	474	474	0
# of matrics	91	91	0
75% GPA	3.57	3.57	0.00
Median GPA	3.36	3.36	0.00
25% GPA	3.16	3.16	0.00
75% LSAT	158	158	0
Median LSAT	155	155	0
25% LSAT	153	153	0

Grants and Scholarships (from prior year)

	Total #	Total %	Full-Time #	Full-Time %	Part-Time #	Part-Time %
Total # of students	278		278		0	
Total # receiving grants	87	31.3	87	31.3	0	0.0
Less than 1/2 tuition	82	29.5	82	29.5	0	0.0
Half to full tuition	0	0.0	0	0.0	0	0.0
Full tuition	1	0.4	1	0.4	0	0.0
More than full tuition	4	1.4	4	1.4	0	0.0
Median grant amount			$4,000		$0	

Informational and Library Resources

Total amount spent on library materials	$680,673
Study seating capacity inside the library	226
# of full-time equivalent professional librarians	5
Hours per week library is open	97
# of open, wired connections available to students	0
# of networked computers available for use by students	10
Has wireless network?	Y
Requires computer?	N

JD Attrition (from prior year)

	Academic #	Other #	Total #	Total %
1st year	0	5	5	5.3
2nd year	0	1	1	1.1
3rd year	0	0	0	0.0
4th year	0	0	0	0.0

Employment (9 months after graduation)

For up-to-date employment data, go to employmentsummary.abaquestionnaire.org on the ABA website.

Bar Passage Rates

First-time takers	89	Reporting %	93.26
Average school %	86.75	Average state %	88.73
Average pass difference	−1.98		

Jurisdiction	Takers	Passers	Pass %	State %	Diff %
Maine	60	51	85.00	88.37	−3.37
Massachusetts	23	21	91.30	89.67	1.63

UNIVERSITY OF MAINE SCHOOL OF LAW

246 Deering Avenue
Portland, ME 04102
Phone: 207.780.4341; Fax: 207.780.4018
E-mail: mainelaw@usm.maine.edu; Website: http://mainelaw.maine.edu

Introduction

Maine Law is a vibrant and distinctive place to study law. Students study law in a supportive and personalized environment and are prepared for success in today's global economy.

Maine Law holds a pivotal place in state and regional affairs and is a destination point for students, scholars, and civic leaders from near and far. The state's only law school, and one of the smallest in the nation, Maine Law fosters educational and scholarly excellence, professionalism, and public service through a close community of faculty members and students. Our location in the vibrant coastal city of Portland, Maine—the largest city in the state and two hours north of Boston—allows students to benefit from a multitude of hands-on training opportunities offered through clinical programs, externships, community service projects, and employment. We have a tradition of training remarkably distinguished graduates—governors, federal and state judges, prominent lawyers, and civic leaders—who remain close to the law school. We are the law school of the University of Maine System and an administrative unit of the University of Southern Maine (USM).

Location

The law school is located in Portland, one of the most livable cities in the United States, and the largest city in Maine. It has the charm of a small town with the cultural activities of a large city. Opportunities to participate in year-round outdoor activities are abundant.

Faculty

Faculty members are well-regarded for their commitment to teaching, for their accessibility to students, and for their cutting-edge scholarship. They come from a variety of backgrounds and have extensive experience in private practice and public service. They make significant contributions to legislative, judicial, and professional institutions; community organizations; and policy and economic development initiatives. Their research spans matters of state, national, and international interest and examines topics as varied as international treaty practice, Maine tort law, coastal zone management, federal tax elections, constitutional controls over the military, intellectual property, and commercial practice.

Curriculum

Maine Law offers a broad-based curriculum that helps prepare students for practice in all states. The school's strengths are in business and commercial law, environmental and marine law, international law, intellectual property, clinical training, and trial advocacy. Ninety credit hours are required for graduation.

The first-year curriculum is a prescribed program consisting of courses that allow students to develop legal analytical skills as well as the ability to read and understand cases and statutory material. The program provides the foundation course in legal research and writing, including a moot court experience. Most courses after the first year are elective. All students are required to complete Professional Responsibility, Constitutional Law II, and a perspective course—one that places the law in a broader philosophical, historical, or comparative context. Each student must fulfill an upper-level writing requirement through a substantial research paper under the direction of a member of the faculty, through a seminar or independent study, or through membership on the *Maine Law Review* or *Ocean and Coastal Law Journal*. Maine Law's practical skills program includes courses in trial practice, negotiation, and alternative dispute resolution. The course in advanced trial advocacy has fielded award-winning teams.

Special Programs

Cumberland Legal Aid Clinic—Third-year students represent clients under faculty supervision in this approved legal assistance office. Students work on family law and domestic matters, juvenile justice, and criminal, consumer, housing, employment, and probate issues at both the trial and appellate levels. The clinic also provides representation for prisoners in a variety of civil matters. All clinical courses work with the state's domestic violence project.

Intellectual Property Law Clinic—Students have the rare opportunity to work with clients involved with developing new products and businesses. Under the supervision of intellectual property lawyers at the Center for Law and Innovation, students work directly with independent inventors, entrepreneurs, and research scientists engaged in technology transfer.

Externships—Students have access to numerous clinical externship opportunities, for academic credit, in many areas. Externships are available with government agencies and nonprofit organizations.

Center for Law and Innovation—The Center for Law and Innovation provides students with courses, conferences, and hands-on experiences to enhance their understanding of the role of law in the development of technological progress and innovation. In addition to offering courses in intellectual property and Internet law, the center provides summer-session technology law courses that bring distinguished scholars and practitioners to the school. Externship opportunities are available with the Maine Patent Program, a unique service program established by the Maine legislature to provide education and legal assistance regarding the patent process to Maine inventors, entrepreneurs, and businesses.

Marine Law Institute (MLI)—The MLI is an ocean and coastal law program that conducts research on laws and policies affecting ocean and coastal resources. The program also supports a student-edited journal and offers courses and seminars in coastal zone law, marine resources law, port security, law of the sea, and admiralty.

Pro Bono Program—The faculty has established a voluntary standard of 80 hours of pro bono legal service for each student during his or her three years of law school and has instituted a means of encouraging students to fulfill that standard while recognizing those who follow through with it.

Joint-Degree Programs—Maine Law and the University of Southern Maine offer the following joint-degree programs: JD/MCP in Community Planning and Development, JD/MS in

Health Policy and Management, JD/MA in Public Policy and Management with the Edmund S. Muskie School of Public Service, and a JD/MBA with the School of Business.

International-Exchange Programs—Semester-exchange programs are available with Dalhousie University Schulich School of Law, University of New Brunswick Faculty of Law, National University of Ireland, Université du Maine, and University of Buckingham.

Student Activities

The Student Bar Association performs the varied functions of student government and acts as an umbrella organization of other student organizations, such as the American Constitution Society, Animal Legal Defense Fund, Black Law Students Association, Business Law Association, Environmental Law Society, Federalist Society, Health Law Association, International Law Society, Latino/Latina Law Students Association, Lesbian/Gay/Bisexual/Transgender Law Caucus, Maine Association for Public Interest Law, Maine Association for Law and Innovation, National Lawyers Guild, Native American Law Association, Prisoner Justice Project, Sports and Entertainment Law Society, and the Women's Law Association.

The *Maine Law Review* and the *Ocean and Coastal Law Journal* are scholarly journals managed, edited, and published by students. Students interested in developing written and oral advocacy skills participate in Moot Court and/or the Trial Advocacy Team.

Career Services

The Career Services Office provides a full range of services, including counseling; career resource materials; specific summer, full-time, part-time, and work-study job listings; and extensive on-campus recruiting. The small size of the law school ensures services tailored to meet the specific needs of its students. A number of workshops, speakers, and panel discussions throughout the year assist students in learning about the diverse opportunities available to them.

Expenses, Financial Aid, and Housing

Maine Law offers a reasonable tuition charge to both residents and nonresidents. The FAFSA priority deadline is February 15. A number of scholarships are available for entering students. Candidates for admission will automatically be considered for all scholarships for which they are eligible. There are no dorms for law students, however, there are plenty of rental properties situated around the law school. There is also a privately owned and operated student housing complex located less than five minutes from the law school. For tuition rates for the current year, please visit our website, www.mainelaw.maine.edu.

APPLICANT PROFILE

University of Maine School of Law
This grid includes only applicants who earned 120–180 LSAT scores under standard administrations.

LSAT Score	3.75 +		3.50–3.74		3.25–3.49		3.00–3.24		2.75–2.99		2.50–2.74		2.25–2.49		2.00–2.24		Below 2.00		No GPA		Total	
	Apps	Adm	Apps	Adm	Apps	Adm	Apps	Adm	Apps	Adm	Apps	Adm	Apps	Adm	Apps	Adm	Apps	Adm	Apps	Adm	Apps	Adm
175–180	2	1	0	0	0	0	0	0	0	0	0	0	0	0	0	0	0	0	0	0	2	1
170–174	2	2	2	2	0	0	1	1	0	0	2	2	0	0	0	0	0	0	0	0	7	7
165–169	7	7	9	9	6	6	6	6	4	4	2	2	1	0	0	0	0	0	2	2	37	36
160–164	12	12	21	21	28	27	30	27	8	7	4	1	4	1	2	0	1	0	0	0	110	96
155–159	25	23	49	48	70	68	47	43	37	25	17	4	10	1	8	1	0	0	5	3	268	216
150–154	21	18	42	20	77	38	76	15	50	12	26	5	17	0	5	0	0	0	4	2	318	110
145–149	12	4	24	4	27	5	43	5	29	2	20	0	7	0	3	0	0	0	7	3	172	23
140–144	2	0	13	1	11	2	12	0	15	2	8	0	4	0	1	0	0	0	0	0	66	5
135–139	0	0	2	0	2	0	3	0	3	0	2	0	1	0	1	0	0	0	3	0	17	0
130–134	0	0	1	0	1	0	0	0	0	0	1	0	2	0	1	0	0	0	0	0	6	0
125–129	0	0	0	0	0	0	0	0	0	0	2	0	0	0	0	0	0	0	0	0	2	0
120–124	0	0	0	0	0	0	0	0	0	0	0	0	0	0	0	0	0	0	0	0	0	0
Total	83	67	163	105	222	146	218	97	146	52	84	14	46	2	21	1	1	0	21	10	1005	494

Apps = Number of Applicants
Adm = Number Admitted
Reflects 100% of the total applicant pool; highest LSAT data reported.

MARQUETTE UNIVERSITY LAW SCHOOL

Office of Admissions, PO Box 1881, 1215 West Michigan Street
Milwaukee, WI 53201-1881
Phone: 414.288.6767; Fax: 414.288.0676
E-mail: law.admission@marquette.edu; Website: http://law.marquette.edu

ABA
Approved
Since
1925

The Basics

Type of school	Private
Term	Semester
Application deadline	4/1 6/1
Application fee	$50
Financial aid deadline	3/1
Can first year start other than fall?	No
Student to faculty ratio	15.5 to 1
# of housing spaces available restricted to law students	
graduate housing for which law students are eligible	

Faculty and Administrators

	Total		Men		Women		Minorities	
	Spr	Fall	Spr	Fall	Spr	Fall	Spr	Fall
Full-time	36	37	20	20	16	17	4	5
Other full-time	0	1	0	1	0	0	0	0
Deans, librarians, & others who teach	10	4	3	3	7	1	1	0
Part-time	39	37	24	23	15	14	2	2
Total	85	79	47	47	38	32	7	7

JD Enrollment and Ethnicity

	Men		Women		Full-Time		Part-Time		1st-Year		Total		JD Degs. Awd.
	#	%	#	%	#	%	#	%	#	%	#	%	
All Hispanics	29	7.1	21	6.6	43	7.3	7	4.9	15	6.8	50	6.8	10
Am. Ind./AK Nat.	6	1.5	2	0.6	7	1.2	1	0.7	4	1.8	8	1.1	2
Asian	15	3.6	16	5.0	22	3.8	9	6.3	14	6.3	31	4.2	6
Black/Af. Am.	19	4.6	25	7.8	37	6.3	7	4.9	19	8.6	44	6.0	13
Nat. HI/Pac. Isl.	1	0.2	2	0.6	3	0.5	0	0.0	3	1.4	3	0.4	0
2 or more races	0	0.0	0	0.0	0	0.0	0	0.0	0	0.0	0	0.0	0
Subtotal (minor.)	70	17.0	66	20.7	112	19.1	24	16.7	55	24.9	136	18.6	31
Nonres. Alien	0	0.0	2	0.6	1	0.2	1	0.7	0	0.0	2	0.3	0
White/Cauc.	341	83.0	251	78.7	473	80.7	119	82.6	166	75.1	592	81.1	199
Unknown	0	0.0	0	0.0	0	0.0	0	0.0	0	0.0	0	0.0	0
Total	411	56.3	319	43.7	586	80.3	144	19.7	221	30.3	730		230

Curriculum

	Full-Time	Part-Time
Typical first-year section size	69	35
Is there typically a "small section" of the first-year class, other than Legal Writing, taught by full-time faculty	Yes	No
If yes, typical size offered last year	53	

# of classroom course titles beyond first-year curriculum		145
# of upper division courses, excluding seminars, with an enrollment:	Under 25	91
	25–49	45
	50–74	13
	75–99	4
	100+	0
# of seminars		27
# of seminar positions available		405
# of seminar positions filled	244	61
# of positions available in simulation courses		624
# of simulation positions filled	440	110
# of positions available in faculty supervised clinical courses		76
# of faculty supervised clinical positions filled	52	13
# involved in field placements	204	51
# involved in law journals	105	26
# involved in moot court or trial competitions	43	13
# of credit hours required to graduate		90

Transfers

Transfers in	13
Transfers out	10

Tuition and Fees

	Resident	Nonresident
Full-time	$37,570	$37,570
Part-time	$22,500	$22,500
Tuition Guarantee Program		N

Living Expenses

Estimated living expenses for singles

Living on campus	Living off campus	Living at home
$19,230	$19,230	$19,230

MARQUETTE UNIVERSITY LAW SCHOOL

*ABA
Approved
Since
1925*

GPA and LSAT Scores

	Total	Full-Time	Part-Time
# of apps	2,005	1,803	202
# of offers	924	881	43
# of matrics	213	188	25
75% GPA	3.55	3.54	3.57
Median GPA	3.35	3.37	3.29
25% GPA	3.03	3.03	2.94
75% LSAT	159	159	157
Median LSAT	157	157	156
25% LSAT	154	154	152

Grants and Scholarships (from prior year)

	Total #	Total %	Full-Time #	Full-Time %	Part-Time #	Part-Time %
Total # of students	758		585		173	
Total # receiving grants	353	46.6	300	51.3	53	30.6
Less than 1/2 tuition	280	36.9	228	39.0	52	30.1
Half to full tuition	68	9.0	67	11.5	1	0.6
Full tuition	5	0.7	5	0.9	0	0.0
More than full tuition	0	0.0	0	0.0	0	0.0
Median grant amount			$7,750		$4,000	

Informational and Library Resources

Total amount spent on library materials	$1,815,233
Study seating capacity inside the library	445
# of full-time equivalent professional librarians	9
Hours per week library is open	82
# of open, wired connections available to students	107
# of networked computers available for use by students	64
Has wireless network?	Y
Requires computer?	N

JD Attrition (from prior year)

	Academic #	Other #	Total #	Total %
1st year	2	12	14	5.5
2nd year	0	2	2	0.9
3rd year	0	0	0	0.0
4th year	0	0	0	0.0

Employment (9 months after graduation)

For up-to-date employment data, go to
employmentsummary.abaquestionnaire.org on the ABA website.

Bar Passage Rates

First-time takers	257	Reporting %	109.34
Average school %	97.21	Average state %	91.40
Average pass difference	5.81		

Jurisdiction	Takers	Passers	Pass %	State %	Diff %
Wisconsin	229	229	100.00	92.93	7.07
Illinois	19	17	89.47	89.38	0.09
New York	5	4	80.00	84.92	–4.92
Colorado	3	3	100.00	82.79	17.21
Others (20)	25	20	80.00		

MARQUETTE UNIVERSITY LAW SCHOOL

Office of Admissions, PO Box 1881, 1215 West Michigan Street
Milwaukee, WI 53201-1881
Phone: 414.288.6767; Fax: 414.288.0676
E-mail: law.admission@marquette.edu; Website: http://law.marquette.edu

Introduction

For more than a century, Marquette University Law School has been committed to training men and women to serve the public interest by becoming highly skilled and ethical attorneys. Traditionally, the curriculum has emphasized the practical aspects of legal education. In recent years, that emphasis has expanded to include particular excellence in the areas of intellectual property, dispute resolution, sports law, labor and employment law, criminal law, family law, and litigation-related courses. The National Sports Law Institute, the premier sports law program in the United States, is a part of the Law School. Our nearly 7,000 alumni serve in a broad range of legal, public, and corporate positions throughout the US.

The Law School is located on the university campus—two blocks from the Milwaukee County Courthouse and a short walk from the federal courthouse and downtown Milwaukee. Marquette is the only law school in southeast Wisconsin. Marquette—a Catholic, Jesuit, and urban university—is the largest private university in the state. The Catholic and Jesuit nature of the school manifests itself in a specific concern for the well-being of each individual, whether he or she is a student, a legal client, or the victim of a crime. Persons of all religious and cultural backgrounds attend Marquette, serve on our faculty, and are valued in our community. The Law School is committed to academic freedom, the broadest possible scope of inquiry, and the examination of any subject.

Milwaukee is a lively city on Lake Michigan, 90 miles north of Chicago. Wisconsin's largest city, with a metropolitan-area population of about 1.5 million, Milwaukee retains the appeal of a small town. Clean and well run, it is known for its many cultural and entertainment festivals and the variety of its cuisine.

Enrollment/Student Body

Within the Marquette Law School community, people know and care about one another. Our students come together from more than 200 different colleges and universities, and hail from 40 different states, as well as from a handful of foreign countries. Our faculty includes 40 full-time professors in addition to prominent practicing attorneys and judges who serve as adjunct professors.

Law students at Marquette represent a broad range of backgrounds, beliefs, and life experiences. Our minority enrollment is about 18 percent of the student body. We respect our different traditions and believe diversity enriches the legal education we offer.

Library and Physical Facilities

In summer 2010, the Law School moved into an entirely new structure, Eckstein Hall. This state-of-the-art building—LEED certified and award winning—features the latest technology and houses a full-service café, a conference center, a fitness center, two courtrooms, underground parking, and more. The path-breaking four-level "library without borders" offers ample study and work space while meeting the goals for a law library in this era of digital legal research. More details regarding Eckstein Hall may be found on the Law School's website.

Curriculum

The Law School offers full-time and part-time programs leading to the JD degree. The Law School's curriculum is rooted in core courses that include consideration of the theoretical underpinnings of the law as well as the practical application of substantive legal concepts. The curriculum is national in focus and scope and emphasizes the skills and values necessary to be a competent and ethical lawyer as well as a contributing citizen and community leader. Our adjunct faculty includes many of the state's outstanding practitioners who supplement required and core courses by teaching a broad range of electives.

Students may earn a JD/MBA through the Law School and the College of Business Administration; of special note is the JD/MBA with a sports business concentration. Joint programs with the graduate school allow students to earn a JD/MA in international affairs, the history of philosophy, social and applied philosophy, or political science. In conjunction with the Medical College of Wisconsin, we offer the JD/MA in bioethics. Each joint-degree program requires meeting all requirements of both the Law School and the other degree-granting institution; typically, each program can be completed in four years. As an alternative to a joint degree, law students may take up to six hours of coursework in a related graduate program at Marquette, such as public policy, sociology, philosophy, or history.

Special Programs

The Law School's comprehensive trial practice courses provide an exceptional opportunity for students to develop trial skills. Distinctive clinics include the prosecutor and defender clinics, judicial internships, and numerous supervised field work opportunities.

Marquette Law School's sports law program provides a comprehensive offering of sports law courses and student internships with sports organizations, as well as opportunities for membership on the *Marquette Sports Law Review* and the sports law moot court team. Our broad, well-rounded curriculum is designed to provide students with both theoretical and practical education concerning legal regulation of the amateur and professional sports industries. Law students who fulfill certain requirements are eligible to earn a sports law certificate in addition to the JD. More information on the program and the certificate may be found at http://law.marquette.edu, then click **Sports Law**.

In 2011, the Law School added two more certificate programs, in dispute resolution and litigation. Like the sports law certificate, these new certificate programs entail substantive curricular and experiential learning requirements. A student who fulfills these requirements is eligible to earn a certificate in addition to the JD. More information about these certificate programs may be found on the Law School's website.

The Law School's Restorative Justice Initiative (RJI) gives law students the opportunity to work with victims of crime, offenders, and community members toward repairing the harm that crime has caused. More information on the RJI may be found at http://law.marquette.edu/rji.

Admission and Financial Aid

Evaluation of completed applications begins after October 1 and continues through the spring. Although the applicant's LSAT score and academic record are important considerations in the selection process, the Admissions Committee also considers qualitative factors, such as letters of recommendation, essays, work experience, extracurricular activities, and personal accomplishments and characteristics that contribute to the diversity of the school, the legal community, and the profession. Admitted applicants are required to submit nonrefundable tuition deposits in April and June. These deposits are applied to the student's fall semester tuition. Interviews are not part of the application process.

Although most students finance their educations through a combination of loan programs, all applicants offered admission each cycle are considered for merit scholarship awards as long as funds remain available. Additionally, the Law School has established a Loan Repayment Assistance Program (LRAP) to help graduates in government service or public interest practice repay their educational loans. More information on LRAP may be found at http://go.mu.edu/HXO9gn.

Diploma Privilege

Since 1933, graduates of the Law School who qualify have been admitted to the practice of law in Wisconsin without having to take the Wisconsin Bar Examination. Marquette graduates are entitled to sit for bar examinations in any US jurisdiction.

Student Activities

The Law School publishes the *Marquette Law Review*, the *Marquette Sports Law Review*, the *Marquette Intellectual Property Law Review*, and the *Marquette Elder's Advisor* (elder law journal); each journal is student-edited. Students may develop advocacy skills in moot court competitions. Marquette moot court teams have won regional titles and championships in national competitions. Nearly 50 student organizations are active at the Law School. A list of student groups and descriptions of their activities may be found on the Law School's website under **Current Students**.

Career Services

The Career Planning Center (CPC) processes hundreds of listings of employment opportunities, coordinates campus interviews, and provides counseling assistance to students—helping them to assess career options, tailor job search strategies, and navigate the competitive job market in a personal way. The CPC will help students network with Marquette alumni and other potential resource persons. The Law School's employment rate consistently exceeds the national average. Our goals are to keep our placement rate high and to ensure a good fit and job satisfaction for all our graduates.

Housing

Ample, affordable housing is available throughout Milwaukee and its suburbs. Information and assistance on securing housing may be obtained from the Office of University Apartments and Off-Campus Student Services; telephone: 414.288.7281, web: www.marquette.edu/offcampus.

APPLICANT PROFILE

Marquette University Law School
This grid includes only applicants who earned 120–180 LSAT scores under standard administrations.

LSAT Score	GPA 3.75 + Apps	Adm	3.50–3.74 Apps	Adm	3.25–3.49 Apps	Adm	3.00–3.24 Apps	Adm	2.75–2.99 Apps	Adm	2.50–2.74 Apps	Adm	2.25–2.49 Apps	Adm	2.00–2.24 Apps	Adm	Below 2.00 Apps	Adm	No GPA Apps	Adm	Total Apps	Adm
175–180	0	0	2	2	0	0	0	0	0	0	0	0	0	0	0	0	0	0	0	0	2	2
170–174	0	0	0	0	1	1	3	3	0	0	0	0	0	0	0	0	0	0	0	0	4	4
165–169	9	9	11	11	16	16	10	10	7	6	2	1	1	0	0	0	0	0	0	0	56	53
160–164	44	42	61	59	61	61	44	43	30	29	11	10	5	2	2	0	0	0	1	1	259	247
155–159	67	63	138	125	164	123	109	58	74	43	33	13	13	5	5	0	0	0	7	3	610	433
150–154	69	45	114	50	151	25	142	23	72	13	51	7	19	1	4	0	1	0	8	1	631	165
145–149	20	1	38	5	47	5	73	4	38	3	19	0	15	0	8	1	0	0	3	1	261	20
140–144	4	0	9	0	14	0	33	0	24	0	14	0	12	0	4	0	1	0	4	0	119	0
135–139	0	0	0	0	2	0	14	0	9	0	15	0	5	0	3	0	1	0	2	0	51	0
130–134	0	0	0	0	1	0	4	0	4	0	4	0	1	0	1	0	1	0	0	0	16	0
125–129	0	0	0	0	0	0	0	0	1	0	4	0	1	0	0	0	1	0	1	0	8	0
120–124	0	0	0	0	0	0	0	0	1	0	0	0	0	0	0	0	0	0	0	0	1	0
Total	213	160	373	252	457	231	432	141	260	94	153	31	72	8	27	1	5	0	26	6	2018	924

Apps = Number of Applicants
Adm = Number Admitted
Reflects 99% of the total applicant pool; highest LSAT data reported.

UNIVERSITY OF MARYLAND FRANCIS KING CAREY SCHOOL OF LAW

500 West Baltimore Street
Baltimore, MD 21201-1786
Phone: 410.706.3492; Fax: 410.706.1793
E-mail: admissions@law.umaryland.edu; Website: www.law.umaryland.edu

ABA
Approved
Since
1930

The Basics

Type of school	Public
Term	Semester
Application deadline	4/1
Application fee	$70
Financial aid deadline	3/1
Can first year start other than fall?	No
Student to faculty ratio	11.7 to 1
# of housing spaces available restricted to law students	
graduate housing for which law students are eligible	425

Faculty and Administrators

	Total		Men		Women		Minorities	
	Spr	Fall	Spr	Fall	Spr	Fall	Spr	Fall
Full-time	64	61	31	31	33	30	14	16
Other full-time	1	3	0	0	1	3	0	0
Deans, librarians, & others who teach	15	13	4	3	11	10	3	3
Part-time	86	51	56	36	30	15	7	5
Total	166	128	91	70	75	58	24	24

Curriculum

	Full-Time	Part-Time
Typical first-year section size	76	73
Is there typically a "small section" of the first-year class, other than Legal Writing, taught by full-time faculty	Yes	Yes
If yes, typical size offered last year	23	24
# of classroom course titles beyond first-year curriculum	231	

# of upper division courses, excluding seminars, with an enrollment:		
Under 25	119	
25–49	25	
50–74	24	
75–99	10	
100+	0	

# of seminars	76	
# of seminar positions available	1,202	
# of seminar positions filled	799	173
# of positions available in simulation courses	721	
# of simulation positions filled	516	87
# of positions available in faculty supervised clinical courses	387	
# of faculty supervised clinical positions filled	348	22
# involved in field placements	234	35
# involved in law journals	178	14
# involved in moot court or trial competitions	74	2
# of credit hours required to graduate	85	

JD Enrollment and Ethnicity

	Men		Women		Full-Time		Part-Time		1st-Year		Total		JD Degs. Awd.
	#	%	#	%	#	%	#	%	#	%	#	%	
All Hispanics	37	7.5	49	10.6	75	10.2	11	5.0	28	10.1	86	9.0	26
Am. Ind./AK Nat.	1	0.2	1	0.2	0	0.0	2	0.9	0	0.0	2	0.2	2
Asian	43	8.7	50	10.8	72	9.8	21	9.5	31	11.2	93	9.7	31
Black/Af. Am.	34	6.9	62	13.4	63	8.6	33	14.9	24	8.7	96	10.0	30
Nat. HI/Pac. Isl.	0	0.0	1	0.2	0	0.0	1	0.5	0	0.0	1	0.1	0
2 or more races	11	2.2	14	3.0	21	2.9	4	1.8	13	4.7	25	2.6	1
Subtotal (minor.)	126	25.6	177	38.2	231	31.4	72	32.6	96	34.8	303	31.7	90
Nonres. Alien	5	1.0	6	1.3	9	1.2	2	0.9	6	2.2	11	1.2	2
White/Cauc.	352	71.4	269	58.1	478	65.0	143	64.7	170	61.6	621	65.0	202
Unknown	10	2.0	11	2.4	17	2.3	4	1.8	4	1.4	21	2.2	3
Total	493	51.6	463	48.4	735	76.9	221	23.1	276	28.9	956		297

Transfers

Transfers in	22
Transfers out	18

Tuition and Fees

	Resident	Nonresident
Full-time	$25,405	$36,684
Part-time	$19,440	$27,899
Tuition Guarantee Program	N	

Living Expenses

Estimated living expenses for singles

Living on campus	Living off campus	Living at home
$22,469	$28,139	$16,979

UNIVERSITY OF MARYLAND FRANCIS KING CAREY SCHOOL OF LAW

ABA
Approved
Since
1930

GPA and LSAT Scores

	Total	Full-Time	Part-Time
# of apps	3,994	3,504	490
# of offers	788	712	76
# of matrics	276	225	51
75% GPA	3.75	3.71	3.83
Median GPA	3.60	3.53	3.71
25% GPA	3.31	3.31	3.30
75% LSAT	163	163	162
Median LSAT	162	162	157
25% LSAT	156	156	153

Grants and Scholarships (from prior year)

	Total #	Total %	Full-Time #	Full-Time %	Part-Time #	Part-Time %
Total # of students	967		734		233	
Total # receiving grants	588	60.8	481	65.5	107	45.9
Less than 1/2 tuition	499	51.6	396	54.0	103	44.2
Half to full tuition	85	8.8	81	11.0	4	1.7
Full tuition	4	0.4	4	0.5	0	0.0
More than full tuition	0	0.0	0	0.0	0	0.0
Median grant amount			$4,000		$4,000	

Informational and Library Resources

Total amount spent on library materials	$1,468,848
Study seating capacity inside the library	509
# of full-time equivalent professional librarians	13
Hours per week library is open	105
# of open, wired connections available to students	1,296
# of networked computers available for use by students	80
Has wireless network?	Y
Requires computer?	Y

JD Attrition (from prior year)

	Academic #	Other #	Total #	Total %
1st year	3	21	24	8.1
2nd year	0	5	5	1.6
3rd year	0	1	1	0.3
4th year	0	0	0	0.0

Employment (9 months after graduation)

For up-to-date employment data, go to employmentsummary.abaquestionnaire.org on the ABA website.

Bar Passage Rates

First-time takers	276	Reporting %	73.19
Average school %	86.14	Average state %	79.96
Average pass difference	6.18		

Jurisdiction	Takers	Passers	Pass %	State %	Diff %
Maryland	202	174	86.14	79.96	6.18

UNIVERSITY OF MARYLAND FRANCIS KING CAREY SCHOOL OF LAW

500 West Baltimore Street
Baltimore, MD 21201-1786
Phone: 410.706.3492; Fax: 410.706.1793
E-mail: admissions@law.umaryland.edu; Website: www.law.umaryland.edu

Introduction

The University of Maryland Francis King Carey School of Law was established in 1816, making it one of the oldest law schools in the nation. Today, its outstanding faculty, innovative programs, and superb student body make it one of the most vibrant places to study law.

Taking advantage of its location in the Baltimore-Washington corridor, Maryland Carey Law has a wealth of opportunities for working and learning as part of the state and national legal, political, and business communities. Because of its foundational commitment to integrating theory and practice, Maryland Carey Law offers extensive clinical and experiential learning opportunities, an academically rigorous core curriculum, and specialty programs that are consistently recognized as among the very best in the country.

Maryland Carey Law's student body is highly talented, diverse, and collegial. The school's small size and low student-to-faculty ratio create a welcoming community dedicated to fully developing each student's talents. Our nationally distinctive Cardin Requirement provides that each full-time student will have a faculty-supervised experience providing free legal services to people and organizations that lack access to justice. This requirement helps instill a spirit of public service in all students—regardless of their chosen career path.

UM Carey Law students are recruited by many of the nation's most respected law firms. They assume positions of leadership as lawyers and judges, business executives and community advocates, legislators and policymakers, and other agents of social, political, and economic progress.

Maryland Carey Law is fully accredited by the ABA, is a member of the AALS, and has a chapter of the Order of the Coif.

Community of Students, Faculty, and Alumni

At UM Carey Law, entering students quickly become part of a supportive community. We are diverse in age, gender, race, academic background, ideology, and prior employment, and this diversity is reflected in our students and in our faculty and deans. Nearly 40 percent of students in the entering class come from outside of Maryland, including many from foreign countries. Our student body represents more than 130 undergraduate institutions, nearly 15 percent have prior graduate degrees, and many more have had impressive careers.

Our faculty are national leaders in a wide range of subject areas, and they are readily available to support and advise students. Smaller classes and a 12 to 1 student-to-faculty ratio enable close working relationships to develop in a professional and intellectually vibrant setting. Many resources are available to students to ease their transition to law school. Students also directly benefit from a wide network of engaged alumni who occupy positions of professional leadership throughout the state, region, and nation. By acting as mentors, volunteer judges, and adjunct faculty, alumni help connect each student's law school experience with the professional life of the surrounding legal community.

Location

Maryland Carey Law's location in the Baltimore-Washington corridor—the country's second largest market for legal employers—is one of our greatest assets. New in 2002, our facility sits just a few blocks from Baltimore's beautiful Inner Harbor and Camden Yards, and—along with the rest of the burgeoning University of Maryland campus—is playing a vital role in the city's downtown renaissance.

The law school is also a simple commute via public transportation from Capitol Hill and an easy drive to Maryland's capital in Annapolis, providing our students unique access to all levels of the federal and state government and judiciary. Students take full advantage of our proximity to Washington, DC, pursuing externships and careers with leading national law firms, public interest groups, government agencies, and other organizations of prominence.

Our proximity to the other professional schools on the UM campus allows us to offer an array of interdisciplinary courses and joint-degree programs. These offerings produce sophisticated graduates who are prepared to practice in an environment of increasing complexity.

Law School Complex and Library

The School of Law and the Thurgood Marshall Law Library occupy a modern complex opened in 2002. Our classrooms and courtrooms are fully equipped with the latest educational technology, as well as wired and wireless Internet access for student use.

The Thurgood Marshall Law Library houses a collection of about 534,000 volumes and equivalents accessible through the online catalog. A staff of 26, including 12 librarians, provides customized reference and consulting services to faculty and students. In addition to LexisNexis and Westlaw, the library offers an extensive array of legal and nonlegal web-based electronic databases. Seating in the library includes carrels, tables in attractive reading rooms, and comfortable lounge areas, all located in spaces full of natural light.

Curriculum and Specialty Programs

The rigorous core curriculum at UM Carey Law forms the basis for more specialized study through over 200 elective courses, seminars, independent studies, simulations, clinics, and externships. The first-year curriculum involves both traditional substantive courses like those at many schools, together with a small section course taught by a full-time faculty member to focus on analytical reasoning, research, and writing. A wide array of upper-level courses in key fields allow students to either sample an array of subject areas, or focus in on a particular area of practice. Research, writing, and advocacy are strong components throughout the program as well, with introductory and advanced courses to hone these critical skills. A student's analytical writing culminates in the production of an academic paper to satisfy the advanced writing requirement. Many students have gone on to publish and win writing competitions with these papers.

Maryland Carey Law is home to several nationally recognized specialty programs. These programs are a magnet for leading faculty from across the country as they provide opportunities for in-depth scholarship and teaching. Three of our specialty programs—Law and Health Care, Environmental Law, and Clinical Law—have long established national reputations for excellence. Our other specialty areas continue to grow and are on the cutting edge of key issues—Business Law, Intellectual Property Law, International and Comparative Law, and Women, Leadership, and Equality. The School is also noted for its excellence in the area of Trial Advocacy.

Regardless of what course of study they pursue, students can expect a challenging law school experience that will cultivate depth of understanding and clarity of thought—the hallmarks of the most successful lawyers.

Clinical Law Program

Through the Cardin Requirement, named after our alumnus US Senator Benjamin Cardin, each full-time day student gains hands-on legal experience by representing actual clients who would otherwise lack access to justice. This program is a hallmark of Maryland Carey Law's commitment to helping students learn to integrate theory and practice, rigorously reflect on their own practice experience, and become lifelong learners committed and capable of continuing to develop legal skills and knowledge. Each year, over 25 faculty and 250 students provide more than 110,000 hours of free legal services to those in need. They work in nearly every area of law practice.

Our legal clinic is among the best and largest in the nation. In addition to in-house clinical work, students may gain experience in public and private nonprofit externships in the Baltimore-Washington region.

Dual Degrees and Interdisciplinary Study

Today's lawyer must practice in an environment of increasing sophistication. Maryland Carey Law offers several dual-degree programs in partnership with other leading academic institutions in the region. Dual-degree programs include Business Administration, Community Planning, Criminal Justice, Government, Liberal Arts, Pharmacy, Public Policy, Public Health, Public Management, and Social Work.

Admission

The Admission Committee selects applicants who have the greatest potential for succeeding in law school studies and whose background, character, and experience will contribute to the diversity that we believe is important to the quality of legal education.

The factors we consider in the admission file evaluation process include geographic origin, cultural and language background, barriers overcome, and extracurricular pursuits such as work, leadership activities, and service or social experiences. The personal statement and letters of recommendation are the primary means for candidates to convey this information. First-year students are admitted only in the fall. The School of Law uses a rolling admission process, reviewing applications in the order in which files are completed. Applications should be filed as early as possible after September 1 of the year preceding enrollment and before April 1. Applicants are encouraged to complete the application early; applications completed later may be at a competitive disadvantage. In addition, applicants are encouraged to visit the school, but interviews are not part of the admission process.

Student Activities

The law school is home to more than 35 active and diverse student-run organizations. Students enforce the law school's honor code, participate in inter- and intraschool advocacy competitions, and volunteer in the local community and around the globe. Students can further their writing and editing expertise by participating in one of the five student-edited scholarly journals or serving as a Legal Writing Center Fellow. The Office of Student Affairs provides group and one-on-one academic advising to students at all stages of their legal education, leadership education to student leaders, and financial literacy workshops for all interested students. A newly opened state-of-the-art university Student Center provides swimming, weight lifting, cardio, and other athletic and wellness programs. University housing near Maryland Carey Law includes residences for all the campus schools, providing wonderful opportunities for students to befriend people working in other professional disciplines.

Scholarships and Need-Based Financial Assistance

The UM Carey School of Law offers a number of scholarships and traditional need-based financial aid assistance. All applicants are considered for the scholarship program based on the totality of the information available in the applicant's admission file and evidence of potential unique contributions to the academic and cocurricular programs, as well as student life. Such potential should be clearly described in the personal statement, résumé, and other admission documents. All admitted applicants **must** file the FAFSA as soon after January 1 as possible in order to be considered for scholarships or need-based financial assistance.

Career Development

Students at UM Carey Law benefit from the institution's national reputation and connections to alumni in the private and public sectors in Maryland; Washington, DC; and beyond. The Career Development Office offers students and alumni a range of professional resources to prepare them for launching their legal job search and obtaining employment.

APPLICANT PROFILE

The University of Maryland Francis King Carey School of Law's admission policy focuses on the academic potential of applicants coupled with a flexible assessment of applicants' talents, experiences, and potential to contribute to the learning of those around them. Each applicant is evaluated on the basis of all the information available in his or her file, including UGPA, LSAT score, a personal statement, letters of recommendation, résumé, advanced degrees, professional accomplishments, and other related information.

THE UNIVERSITY OF MEMPHIS—CECIL C. HUMPHREYS SCHOOL OF LAW

One North Front Street
Memphis, TN 38103-2189
Phone: 901.678.5403; Fax: 901.678.0741
E-mail: lawadmissions@memphis.edu; Website: www.memphis.edu/law

ABA Approved Since 1965

The Basics

Type of school	Public
Term	Semester
Application deadline	3/1
Application fee	$25
Financial aid deadline	5/1
Can first year start other than fall?	No
Student to faculty ratio	19.5 to 1
# of housing spaces available restricted to law students	
graduate housing for which law students are eligible	125

Faculty and Administrators

	Total		Men		Women		Minorities	
	Spr	Fall	Spr	Fall	Spr	Fall	Spr	Fall
Full-time	17	18	12	12	5	6	2	2
Other full-time	1	0	1	0	0	0	1	0
Deans, librarians, & others who teach	6	5	3	3	3	2	0	0
Part-time	33	28	22	20	11	8	5	5
Total	57	51	38	35	19	16	8	7

JD Enrollment and Ethnicity

	Men		Women		Full-Time		Part-Time		1st-Year		Total		JD Degs. Awd.
	#	%	#	%	#	%	#	%	#	%	#	%	
All Hispanics	5	2.0	2	1.1	7	1.8	0	0.0	2	1.4	7	1.7	3
Am. Ind./AK Nat.	3	1.2	0	0.0	2	0.5	1	3.7	1	0.7	3	0.7	1
Asian	6	2.4	4	2.3	8	2.0	2	7.4	3	2.1	10	2.4	0
Black/Af. Am.	19	7.7	21	12.1	23	5.8	17	63.0	14	9.7	40	9.5	5
Nat. HI/Pac. Isl.	0	0.0	0	0.0	0	0.0	0	0.0	0	0.0	0	0.0	0
2 or more races	0	0.0	0	0.0	0	0.0	0	0.0	0	0.0	0	0.0	1
Subtotal (minor.)	33	13.4	27	15.5	40	10.2	20	74.1	20	13.9	60	14.3	10
Nonres. Alien	0	0.0	0	0.0	0	0.0	0	0.0	0	0.0	0	0.0	0
White/Cauc.	214	86.6	147	84.5	354	89.8	7	25.9	124	86.1	361	85.7	117
Unknown	0	0.0	0	0.0	0	0.0	0	0.0	0	0.0	0	0.0	0
Total	247	58.7	174	41.3	394	93.6	27	6.4	144	34.2	421		127

Curriculum

	Full-Time	Part-Time
Typical first-year section size	75	0
Is there typically a "small section" of the first-year class, other than Legal Writing, taught by full-time faculty	No	No
If yes, typical size offered last year		
# of classroom course titles beyond first-year curriculum	73	

# of upper division courses, excluding seminars, with an enrollment:		
	Under 25	52
	25–49	14
	50–74	12
	75–99	5
	100+	1

# of seminars	9	
# of seminar positions available	108	
# of seminar positions filled	97	0
# of positions available in simulation courses	160	
# of simulation positions filled	152	0
# of positions available in faculty supervised clinical courses	38	
# of faculty supervised clinical positions filled	34	0
# involved in field placements	72	0
# involved in law journals	99	0
# involved in moot court or trial competitions	29	0
# of credit hours required to graduate	90	

Transfers

Transfers in	2
Transfers out	2

Tuition and Fees

	Resident	Nonresident
Full-time	$15,690	$37,562
Part-time	$13,747	$21,699
Tuition Guarantee Program	N	

Living Expenses

Estimated living expenses for singles

Living on campus	Living off campus	Living at home
$15,195	$15,195	$9,433

THE UNIVERSITY OF MEMPHIS—CECIL C. HUMPHREYS SCHOOL OF LAW

*ABA
Approved
Since
1965*

GPA and LSAT Scores

	Total	Full-Time	Part-Time
# of apps	861	861	0
# of offers	302	293	9
# of matrics	144	136	8
75% GPA	3.62	3.64	3.43
Median GPA	3.42	3.42	3.37
25% GPA	3.09	3.10	2.92
75% LSAT	157	158	150
Median LSAT	155	155	149
25% LSAT	153	153	145

Grants and Scholarships (from prior year)

	Total		Full-Time		Part-Time	
	#	%	#	%	#	%
Total # of students	432		408		24	
Total # receiving grants	133	30.8	121	29.7	12	50.0
Less than 1/2 tuition	58	13.4	47	11.5	11	45.8
Half to full tuition	61	14.1	61	15.0	0	0.0
Full tuition	8	1.9	8	2.0	0	0.0
More than full tuition	6	1.4	5	1.2	1	4.2
Median grant amount			$7,209		$2,000	

Informational and Library Resources

Total amount spent on library materials	$793,644
Study seating capacity inside the library	287
# of full-time equivalent professional librarians	3
Hours per week library is open	168
# of open, wired connections available to students	0
# of networked computers available for use by students	71
Has wireless network?	Y
Requires computer?	N

JD Attrition (from prior year)

	Academic	Other	Total	
	#	#	#	%
1st year	9	11	20	12.2
2nd year	5	0	5	3.6
3rd year	1	0	1	0.8
4th year	0	0	0	0.0

Employment (9 months after graduation)

For up-to-date employment data, go to
employmentsummary.abaquestionnaire.org on the ABA website.

Bar Passage Rates

First-time takers	124	Reporting %	96.77
Average school %	88.33	Average state %	84.24
Average pass difference	4.09		

Jurisdiction	Takers	Passers	Pass %	State %	Diff %
Tennessee	120	106	88.33	84.24	4.09

THE UNIVERSITY OF MEMPHIS—CECIL C. HUMPHREYS SCHOOL OF LAW

One North Front Street
Memphis, TN 38103-2189
Phone: 901.678.5403; Fax: 901.678.0741
E-mail: lawadmissions@memphis.edu; Website: www.memphis.edu/law

Memphis and the School of Law

Memphis is one of the South's largest, most beautiful, and most diverse cities. Memphis has one of the lowest cost-of-living rates of any major US city, and its temperate climate provides ample opportunity for year-round activities. Memphis has a rich history and an unmatched musical heritage. The School of Law brings together unique individuals with a wide variety of cultural, geographical, employment, and academic backgrounds. Many of its students come to law school immediately after finishing their undergraduate education; however, a significant number have been in the workforce or have completed advanced degrees. The diversity within the student body enriches the classroom experience for all students and enhances the overall quality of the educational program.

In 2011, the School of Law was recognized as a "best value" because Memphis is among schools that can boast a high bar exam passage rate, a strong job placement rate for graduates, and an affordable tuition. The School of Law has been cited elsewhere for "quality of life," reflecting student responses to questions about building aesthetics, sense of community, location, classroom facilities, social life, and library staff. In January 2010, the School of Law began classes in the newly renovated US Custom House and Post Office located in the heart of legal, business, and cultural districts in downtown Memphis. This beautiful state-of-the-art building offers a magnificent view of the Mississippi River and is within blocks of numerous law offices and both state and federal courthouses.

History of the School of Law

The Cecil C. Humphreys School of Law at the University of Memphis was established in response to widespread interest in developing a full-time accredited law program to serve Memphis and West Tennessee. The Cecil C. Humphreys School of Law opened in 1962 and was accredited by the American Bar Association (ABA) in 1965. The law school was named in honor of Cecil C. Humphreys, then-president of Memphis State University and an educator of great distinction. Dr. Humphreys led the group that worked with the state legislature to found the law school. The law school is an active member of the Association of American Law Schools (AALS).

Since its inception, the School of Law has graduated over 5,000 students and continues its tradition of preparing competent and ethical attorneys. Our graduates can be found throughout the United States, employed in private practice, federal and state judiciaries, corporate boardrooms, government agencies, and public service organizations.

The University of Memphis

The University of Memphis serves as a regional center for education, service, and research; and it is linked historically, intellectually, and emotionally to Memphis. It is a learner-centered metropolitan research university that enrolls over 22,000 students and is accredited by the Commission on Colleges of the Southern Association of Colleges and Schools.

Curriculum

The School of Law offers a full-time day program and a reduced-load day program. The challenging curriculum prepares our students for the practice of law. The curriculum reflects a commitment to traditional legal education, and academic emphasis is placed on fundamental lawyering skills and areas of knowledge.

Lawyering Skills, Legal Clinics, and Externships

In-house clinics in Child and Family Litigation, Civil Litigation, and Elder Law offer upper-level students training through the vehicle of faculty-supervised, live-client representations. Specially admitted to practice by the Tennessee Supreme Court, clinic students perform case-related work, participate in classroom seminars and case supervision sessions, and complete reading assignments, writing assignments, oral presentations, simulations, and exercises designed to encourage the development of lawyering skills at both practical and theoretical levels.

Students may also earn credit and hands-on training through enrollment in an externship program that combines supervised field placements in judicial, governmental, and nonprofit legal settings with a weekly, faculty-led classroom seminar designed to explore issues of professionalism, ethics, and experiential learning. Current externship placements include federal and state courts; US Attorney's Office; Office of the Federal Public Defender; Tennessee Office of the Post-Conviction Defender; Shelby County District Attorney General's Office; Shelby County Public Defender's Office; US Equal Employment Opportunity Commission (EEOC); National Labor Relations Board (NLRB); City of Memphis Law Division; Memphis-Shelby County Airport Authority; health law externships; Memphis Area Legal Services, Inc.; and the Community Legal Center.

Joint- and Dual-Degree Programs

The School of Law and the Fogelman College of Business and Economics offer a coordinated-degree program leading to both the JD and MBA degrees. The purpose of this program is to allow students to study business management and law. This joint degree enables students to complete the JD and MBA in considerably less time than would be required to complete each degree separately.

The School of Law and the Department of Political Science offer a dual degree leading to both the JD and MA degrees. Credit toward degrees in these disciplines can be earned simultaneously if admission and curricula are carefully structured. Students can complete both degrees in less time than would normally be required to complete each degree separately.

Library and Information Technology

The University of Memphis law library serves students, faculty, the legal community, and the public with reference services and access to its collection of print and electronic resources. The law library occupies five levels of the historic School of Law building and offers students many options for study—from study rooms to a three-sided glass reading room overlooking the Mississippi River. Students have access to computers in labs and open study areas. There is wireless access throughout the building.

Student Programs and Activities

The *University of Memphis Law Review* is a scholarly journal edited and staffed entirely by students. Law review members have numerous opportunities to improve their legal research, writing, and editing skills. The *Mental Health Law and Policy Journal* provides a scholarly publication dedicated to mental health law and policy issues.

The Moot Court Board is composed of 20 third-year students who are dedicated to the development of advocacy skills. In addition to intraschool competitions, the law school fields teams in national moot court, mock trial, and alternative dispute resolution competitions. The University of Memphis teams have earned national recognition for their performances in major national moot court and mock trial competitions. In 2011, a Memphis team won the Thurgood Marshall Mock Trial Competition while other teams reached the final round of major moot court competitions.

The Student Bar Association coordinates a wide variety of activities, ranging from social events to a speaker series. There are 15 active student organizations, ranging from legal fraternities to special interest and service organizations.

Admission

Applicants initially are evaluated by the Admissions Office based on a weighted combination of LSAT score and cumulative undergraduate GPA as calculated by the Law School Admission Council. Those not admitted, or denied, as a result of this evaluation will be reviewed by the Faculty Admission Committee using nonquantifiable factors such as quality of the applicant's undergraduate institution, level and rigor of coursework, letters of recommendation or evaluations, graduate work, employment during and after college, extracurricular activities, educational diversity, and state of residence. In an attempt to attract a diverse student population, the school has developed a selection process that reviews the merits of all qualified applicants but assures that admission is based on a comprehensive range of criteria demonstrated to be predictive of success in law school.

Career Services

The Career Service Office provides information about employment opportunities and career exploration, with seminars on job-search skills and roundtable discussions with practitioners. Students and graduates have access to our data management program, Symplicity, which houses job postings, resource materials, and the like. In addition to hosting a large number of firms, corporations, and public interest/governmental employers for on-campus interviewing and seminars, the School of Law is a member of several organizations that conduct annual recruiting conferences.

Employment for Memphis law graduates has remained consistently high during the last decade. Of those known graduates seeking legal employment in the graduating class of 2011, 88.8 percent were employed within nine months of graduation, as reported to NALP. The University of Memphis has graduates practicing in all 50 states and in several foreign countries.

Tennessee Institute for Pre-Law

Applicants from Tennessee as well as applicants from Crittenden County, Arkansas, and applicants from De Soto, Marshall, Tate, and Tunica counties in Mississippi are eligible to apply for the Tennessee Institute for Pre-Law (TIP) program, which facilitates law school admission for students from diverse backgrounds who do not meet traditional academic standards for admission. Participants who successfully complete the program are guaranteed admission to the law school. The TIP program is available to applicants who will have met the requirements for a bachelor's degree prior to the start of the program. The TIP program is a five-week program of classroom instruction that simulates the first-year law school curriculum.

APPLICANT PROFILE

The University of Memphis—Cecil C. Humphreys School of Law
This grid includes only applicants who earned 120–180 LSAT scores under standard administrations.

LSAT Score	3.75 +		3.50–3.74		3.25–3.49		3.00–3.24		2.75–2.99		2.50–2.74		2.25–2.49		2.00–2.24		Below 2.00		No GPA		Total	
	Apps	Adm	Apps	Adm	Apps	Adm	Apps	Adm	Apps	Adm	Apps	Adm	Apps	Adm	Apps	Adm	Apps	Adm	Apps	Adm	Apps	Adm
175–180	0	0	0	0	0	0	0	0	0	0	0	0	0	0	0	0	0	0	0	0	0	0
170–174	0	0	1	1	0	0	1	0	1	1	0	0	0	0	1	1	0	0	0	0	4	3
165–169	4	4	8	7	1	1	3	3	2	2	1	1	0	0	0	0	1	0	0	0	20	18
160–164	18	15	11	9	11	10	15	12	9	8	3	2	5	2	3	2	0	0	0	0	75	60
155–159	26	25	39	31	39	27	44	35	21	14	7	2	6	0	3	2	2	0	1	0	188	136
150–154	24	16	54	19	47	20	42	13	43	3	21	1	13	2	6	1	1	0	2	0	253	75
145–149	12	2	29	1	30	2	29	2	25	2	12	1	9	0	3	0	1	0	4	0	154	10
140–144	5	0	8	0	13	0	19	1	17	1	15	0	15	0	3	0	2	0	1	0	98	2
135–139	2	0	5	1	7	0	9	0	5	0	8	0	5	0	2	0	1	0	4	0	48	1
130–134	0	0	1	0	2	0	2	0	1	0	4	0	6	0	3	0	0	0	2	0	21	0
125–129	0	0	0	0	0	0	0	0	0	0	1	0	0	0	1	0	0	0	0	0	2	0
120–124	0	0	0	0	0	0	0	0	0	0	0	0	0	0	1	0	0	0	0	0	1	0
Total	91	62	156	69	150	60	164	66	124	31	72	7	59	4	26	6	8	0	14	0	864	305

Apps = Number of Applicants
Adm = Number Admitted
Reflects 99% of the total applicant pool; highest LSAT data reported.

MERCER UNIVERSITY—WALTER F. GEORGE SCHOOL OF LAW

Office of Admissions, 1021 Georgia Avenue
Macon, GA 31207
Phone: 478.301.2605; Fax: 478.301.2989
E-mail: martin_sv@law.mercer.edu; Website: www.law.mercer.edu

ABA
Approved
Since
1925

The Basics

Type of school	Private
Term	Semester
Application deadline	3/15
Application fee	$50
Financial aid deadline	4/1
Can first year start other than fall?	No
Student to faculty ratio	14.0 to 1
# of housing spaces available restricted to law students	
graduate housing for which law students are eligible	32

Faculty and Administrators

	Total		Men		Women		Minorities	
	Spr	Fall	Spr	Fall	Spr	Fall	Spr	Fall
Full-time	27	26	18	16	9	10	3	3
Other full-time	0	0	0	0	0	0	0	0
Deans, librarians, & others who teach	8	8	5	5	3	3	0	0
Part-time	33	21	26	18	7	3	1	1
Total	68	55	49	39	19	16	4	4

Curriculum

	Full-Time	Part-Time
Typical first-year section size	83	0
Is there typically a "small section" of the first-year class, other than Legal Writing, taught by full-time faculty	Yes	No
If yes, typical size offered last year	30	
# of classroom course titles beyond first-year curriculum	96	
# of upper division courses, excluding seminars, with an enrollment: Under 25	121	
25–49	17	
50–74	8	
75–99	4	
100+	0	
# of seminars	13	
# of seminar positions available	195	
# of seminar positions filled	138	0
# of positions available in simulation courses	864	
# of simulation positions filled	706	0
# of positions available in faculty supervised clinical courses	28	
# of faculty supervised clinical positions filled	28	0
# involved in field placements	108	0
# involved in law journals	46	0
# involved in moot court or trial competitions	68	0
# of credit hours required to graduate	91	

JD Enrollment and Ethnicity

	Men		Women		Full-Time		Part-Time		1st-Year		Total		JD Degs. Awd.
	#	%	#	%	#	%	#	%	#	%	#	%	
All Hispanics	9	3.6	1	0.5	10	2.2	0	0.0	0	0.0	10	2.2	2
Am. Ind./AK Nat.	2	0.8	4	2.0	6	1.3	0	0.0	2	1.4	6	1.3	2
Asian	15	5.9	11	5.6	26	5.8	0	0.0	7	4.7	26	5.8	4
Black/Af. Am.	11	4.3	28	14.1	39	8.6	0	0.0	11	7.4	39	8.6	14
Nat. HI/Pac. Isl.	0	0.0	0	0.0	0	0.0	0	0.0	0	0.0	0	0.0	0
2 or more races	0	0.0	0	0.0	0	0.0	0	0.0	0	0.0	0	0.0	0
Subtotal (minor.)	37	14.6	44	22.2	81	18.0	0	0.0	20	13.5	81	18.0	22
Nonres. Alien	1	0.4	0	0.0	1	0.2	0	0.0	1	0.7	1	0.2	4
White/Cauc.	183	72.3	138	69.7	321	71.2	0	0.0	100	67.6	321	71.2	96
Unknown	32	12.6	16	8.1	48	10.6	0	0.0	27	18.2	48	10.6	9
Total	253	56.1	198	43.9	451	100.0	0	0.0	148	32.8	451		131

Transfers

Transfers in	8
Transfers out	10

Tuition and Fees

	Resident	Nonresident
Full-time	$36,860	$36,860
Part-time		
Tuition Guarantee Program	N	

Living Expenses

Estimated living expenses for singles

Living on campus	Living off campus	Living at home
$18,114	$18,114	$18,114

MERCER UNIVERSITY—WALTER F. GEORGE SCHOOL OF LAW

ABA
Approved
Since
1925

GPA and LSAT Scores

	Total	Full-Time	Part-Time
# of apps	1,434	1,434	0
# of offers	634	634	0
# of matrics	149	149	0
75% GPA	3.66	3.66	0.00
Median GPA	3.40	3.40	0.00
25% GPA	3.07	3.07	0.00
75% LSAT	158	158	0
Median LSAT	155	155	0
25% LSAT	151	151	0

Grants and Scholarships (from prior year)

	Total		Full-Time		Part-Time	
	#	%	#	%	#	%
Total # of students	439		439		0	
Total # receiving grants	144	32.8	144	32.8	0	0.0
Less than 1/2 tuition	51	11.6	51	11.6	0	0.0
Half to full tuition	40	9.1	40	9.1	0	0.0
Full tuition	32	7.3	32	7.3	0	0.0
More than full tuition	21	4.8	21	4.8	0	0.0
Median grant amount			$25,000		$0	

Informational and Library Resources

Total amount spent on library materials	$795,407
Study seating capacity inside the library	416
# of full-time equivalent professional librarians	5
Hours per week library is open	68
# of open, wired connections available to students	748
# of networked computers available for use by students	33
Has wireless network?	Y
Requires computer?	Y

JD Attrition (from prior year)

	Academic	Other	Total	
	#	#	#	%
1st year	2	10	12	7.3
2nd year	1	0	1	0.7
3rd year	0	1	1	0.8
4th year	0	0	0	0.0

Employment (9 months after graduation)

For up-to-date employment data, go to
employmentsummary.abaquestionnaire.org on the ABA website.

Bar Passage Rates

First-time takers	142	Reporting %	80.99
Average school %	90.43	Average state %	83.61
Average pass difference	6.82		

Jurisdiction	Takers	Passers	Pass %	State %	Diff %
Georgia	115	104	90.43	83.61	6.82

MERCER UNIVERSITY—WALTER F. GEORGE SCHOOL OF LAW

Office of Admissions, 1021 Georgia Avenue
Macon, GA 31207
Phone: 478.301.2605; Fax: 478.301.2989
E-mail: martin_sv@law.mercer.edu; Website: www.law.mercer.edu

Introduction

The Walter F. George School of Law of Mercer University is located in Macon, Georgia, about 80 miles south of Atlanta. Founded in 1873, it is one of the oldest private law schools in the nation. Named for a distinguished alumnus who served as a United States senator for 36 years, the school became a member of AALS in 1923 and has been ABA-approved since 1925. With its distinctive Woodruff Curriculum and a total student body of roughly 440, Mercer Law School provides an educational environment that fosters in-depth learning, a candid and lively exchange of views, and a genuine sense of community and collegiality.

Admission

Mercer University's Walter F. George School of Law accepts applications between September 1 and March 15 from prospective students wishing to begin their studies in the fall semester. Applicants must have completed a bachelor's degree prior to law school enrollment. They must register with the Credential Assembly Service (CAS) and take the LSAT, preferably in the summer or fall before application is made. Applicants must submit two letters of recommendation, an application fee, and a personal statement candidly discussing their strengths and weaknesses as prospective law students.

LSAT score and undergraduate GPA figure significantly into the admission decision, but the Admissions Committee considers an array of other factors in arriving at an overall judgment of the applicant's likely contribution to the educational enterprise and his or her potential for success in the profession. Such factors as the applicant's employment history, community and military service, advanced degrees, leadership ability, personal hardships, and other relevant background information will be evaluated.

Curriculum

Mercer's Woodruff Curriculum and the atmosphere of the law school work together to provide students with a thorough intellectual foundation, strong practical skills, professional relationships, and a commitment to ethical behavior. Mercer is one of a few select schools in the country to receive the prestigious Gambrell Professionalism Award from the American Bar Association. The award cites the depth and excellence of the Woodruff Curriculum and its serious commitment to professionalism.

The Woodruff Curriculum helps students develop essential problem-solving, counseling, and trial and appellate advocacy skills. It also helps ensure that they acquire the level of understanding of law and the legal system needed to excel in any of the various forms of legal practice that they may choose to enter—law firm, legal aid office, in-house corporate counsel, government legal employment, and so forth.

All students take research and writing courses during at least four semesters of law study, and many take a research or writing course each term. Mercer is the first law school in the nation to offer a Certificate in Advanced Legal Writing, Research, and Drafting. Students are selected for the certificate program through an application process. In 2003, in recognition of Mercer's nationally known Legal Writing Program, the Legal Writing Institute selected Mercer as its host school. The Legal Writing Institute is the world's largest organization of lawyers, judges, and law professors devoted to improving legal writing.

Special Programs

Law school provides a foundation upon which lawyers build successful careers and meaningful lives. At Mercer Law, that foundation includes rigorous intellectual training anchored by nationally recognized programs in legal writing, ethics and professionalism, and public service.

The Law and Public Service Program offers students the opportunity to earn academic credit while helping to represent clients in one of the law school's clinics, such as the Habeas Project or Public Defender's Clinic, in judges' chambers through the Judicial Field Placement program, and summer externships through various agencies. Students may also be selected as fellows through the Public Interest Fellowship program. After completing the fellowship, the fellows are offered a one-time loan forgiveness grant conditional on their making a two-year commitment to a public interest employer in Georgia after graduation.

Since 1985, the National Criminal Defense College (NCDC) has held its summer Trial Practice Institute every year on the Mercer Law School campus. NCDC conducts two, two-week trial skills sessions for nearly 200 public defenders and criminal defense attorneys from across the country.

Joint JD/MBA Program

Mercer's School of Law and Mercer's School of Business and Economics offer a joint program leading to both the Juris Doctor and Master of Business Administration degrees. The applicant must be admitted separately to each school. For more information, visit our website at www.law.mercer.edu.

Business Certificate Program

Students in good standing in the Walter F. George School of Law may choose to take up to three graduate courses in the School of Business and Economics without applying for admission to the MBA program. Currently, two specific combinations of courses can be taken for a Certificate in Practice Management or a Certificate in Corporate Finance.

LLM Program

Beginning Fall of 2012, Mercer Law School will offer an LLM program in Federal Criminal Practice and Procedure. The program is designed for law school graduates seeking to prepare themselves for federal criminal practice as prosecutors, federal defenders, or private defense counsel. The program provides a solid foundation of knowledge and skills for all aspects of federal criminal practice, including substantive federal law, grand jury investigations, pretrial practice, trial advocacy, sentencing, and appellate practice. The program has been fully approved by all of the relevant accrediting bodies. Visit our website at www.law.mercer.edu/academics/llm.

Library Facilities

The Furman Smith Law Library is the center for legal information and research at the Law School. Law students have access to a rich and varied collection of print and electronic resources, and the law library's website features an extensive collection of annotated links to legal research materials. Students can access resources whether on or off campus. In the law library, students find comfortable research and study areas conducive to quiet study or to collaborative work. Carrels, tables, soft seating, "smart" study rooms, and a technology lounge are available to law students, all in a wireless environment. In addition, each first-year student receives a laptop computer to use during his or her legal education at Mercer Law School. The law library staff of 16 includes 7 professional law librarians who teach legal research courses and provide superior service to students, faculty, and the legal community.

Student Activities

At Mercer University's Walter F. George School of Law, excellence is measured by more than what happens inside the classroom. You will find a broad array of activities outside the classroom that have been designed to engage the members of our academic community and enable our students to stand out once they enter the professional world.

In Mercer's moot court and mock trial programs, students improve their written and oral advocacy, negotiation, and client counseling skills. Mercer Law's Moot Court program is among the top programs in the nation, based on our record of wins in national competitions.

The *Mercer Law Review* (the oldest continually published law review in Georgia) has been edited and published quarterly by law students since 1949.

In addition to moot court and the *Law Review*, Mercer offers its students the opportunity to participate in over two dozen student organizations where they can gain valuable leadership and relationship-building experiences.

Financial Aid

Mercer awards over $3 million in scholarship aid every year to students whose academic records, LSAT scores, and personal achievements demonstrate the potential for outstanding performance in the study of law. The priority deadline for scholarship consideration is January 1.

Two of our most prestigious scholarships are the George W. Woodruff Scholarship (full tuition plus a $5,000 stipend) and the Walter F. George Foundation Public Service Scholarship (full tuition plus a $6,000 summer community service fellowship). In order to be considered for the George W. Woodruff scholarship, you must have your admission application and scholarship application completed and received in our office no later than January 15. The Woodruff Scholarship application may be found online at www.law.mercer.edu/admissions/financialaid/scholarships. You may also apply online through LSAC's website, LSAC.org.

In addition to scholarship aid, students may qualify for student loans, and work-study is available after the first year of law school.

Career Services

Mercer Law School has an active career services office and alumni and faculty members also support students in their efforts to find satisfying employment. The office assists students in obtaining permanent, summer, and part-time employment.

Services offered include arranging on-campus interviews and off-campus interviewing consortia and providing career-planning and skill development seminars and employer outreach activities. Individual career counseling and assistance with résumé and cover-letter writing also comprise much of the work of the office. An extensive library of career resources is available for student use.

The Office of Career Services reports that 86 percent of the class of 2011 was employed or was pursuing advanced degrees within six to nine months after graduation.

APPLICANT PROFILE

Mercer University—Walter F. George School of Law
This grid includes only applicants who earned 120–180 LSAT scores under standard administrations.

LSAT Score	3.75 +		3.50–3.74		3.25–3.49		3.00–3.24		2.75–2.99		2.50–2.74		2.25–2.49		2.00–2.24		Below 2.00		No GPA		Total	
	Apps	Adm	Apps	Adm	Apps	Adm	Apps	Adm	Apps	Adm	Apps	Adm	Apps	Adm	Apps	Adm	Apps	Adm	Apps	Adm	Apps	Adm
175–180	0	0	0	0	0	0	0	0	0	0	0	0	0	0	1	1	0	0	0	0	1	1
170–174	0	0	1	1	0	0	0	0	1	1	0	0	0	0	0	0	0	0	0	0	2	2
165–169	4	4	5	5	2	2	4	4	2	2	1	1	2	2	0	0	0	0	0	0	20	20
160–164	22	22	29	29	26	26	15	14	13	13	9	9	2	2	5	2	1	0	1	1	123	118
155–159	33	33	53	52	69	61	66	62	31	28	28	21	6	4	2	0	1	0	1	0	290	261
150–154	43	35	84	65	84	42	86	27	56	12	32	2	19	3	7	1	2	0	3	2	416	189
145–149	29	15	50	13	61	7	64	3	52	0	30	0	10	0	1	0	1	0	3	1	301	39
140–144	13	0	18	1	38	0	37	0	37	0	37	0	20	0	9	0	0	0	1	0	210	1
135–139	3	0	8	0	12	0	9	0	12	0	6	0	7	0	3	0	0	0	0	0	60	0
130–134	0	0	2	0	0	0	2	0	5	0	2	0	1	0	5	0	3	0	0	0	20	0
125–129	0	0	0	0	0	0	3	0	2	0	0	0	4	0	2	0	1	0	0	0	12	0
120–124	0	0	0	0	0	0	0	0	0	0	0	0	0	0	0	0	0	0	0	0	0	0
Total	147	109	250	166	292	138	286	110	211	56	145	33	71	11	35	4	9	0	9	4	1455	631

Apps = Number of Applicants
Adm = Number Admitted
Reflects 100% of the total applicant pool; highest LSAT data reported.

UNIVERSITY OF MIAMI SCHOOL OF LAW

PO Box 248087
Coral Gables, FL 33124-8087
Phone: 305.284.2523; Fax: 305.284.3084
E-mail: admissions@law.miami.edu; Website: www.law.miami.edu

The Basics

Type of school	Private
Term	Semester
Application deadline	7/31
Application fee	$60
Financial aid deadline	3/1
Can first year start other than fall?	No
Student to faculty ratio	13.2 to 1
# of housing spaces available restricted to law students	
graduate housing for which law students are eligible	

Faculty and Administrators

	Total		Men		Women		Minorities	
	Spr	Fall	Spr	Fall	Spr	Fall	Spr	Fall
Full-time	82	82	45	45	37	37	17	18
Other full-time	0	0	0	0	0	0	0	0
Deans, librarians, & others who teach	20	21	6	5	14	16	6	6
Part-time	105	86	74	61	31	25	21	16
Total	207	189	125	111	82	78	44	40

Curriculum

	Full-Time	Part-Time
Typical first-year section size	97	0
Is there typically a "small section" of the first-year class, other than Legal Writing, taught by full-time faculty	Yes	No
If yes, typical size offered last year	49	
# of classroom course titles beyond first-year curriculum	151	

# of upper division courses, excluding seminars, with an enrollment:		
	Under 25	64
	25–49	41
	50–74	20
	75–99	13
	100+	12

# of seminars	115	
# of seminar positions available	2,505	
# of seminar positions filled	1,645	0
# of positions available in simulation courses	1,150	
# of simulation positions filled	967	0
# of positions available in faculty supervised clinical courses	182	
# of faculty supervised clinical positions filled	182	0
# involved in field placements	271	0
# involved in law journals	219	0
# involved in moot court or trial competitions	150	0
# of credit hours required to graduate	88	

JD Enrollment and Ethnicity

	Men		Women		Full-Time		Part-Time		1st-Year		Total		JD Degs. Awd.
	#	%	#	%	#	%	#	%	#	%	#	%	
All Hispanics	116	14.9	102	17.5	210	16.3	8	11.3	68	15.5	218	16.0	54
Am. Ind./AK Nat.	5	0.6	4	0.7	9	0.7	0	0.0	3	0.7	9	0.7	1
Asian	17	2.2	30	5.2	46	3.6	1	1.4	20	4.6	47	3.5	18
Black/Af. Am.	35	4.5	49	8.4	80	6.2	4	5.6	26	5.9	84	6.2	33
Nat. HI/Pac. Isl.	0	0.0	1	0.2	1	0.1	0	0.0	1	0.2	1	0.1	0
2 or more races	6	0.8	4	0.7	10	0.8	0	0.0	4	0.9	10	0.7	0
Subtotal (minor.)	179	23.0	190	32.6	356	27.6	13	18.3	122	27.9	369	27.1	106
Nonres. Alien	18	2.3	6	1.0	21	1.6	3	4.2	10	2.3	24	1.8	15
White/Cauc.	527	67.7	357	61.3	837	64.9	47	66.2	285	65.1	884	65.0	227
Unknown	55	7.1	29	5.0	76	5.9	8	11.3	21	4.8	84	6.2	37
Total	779	57.2	582	42.8	1290	94.8	71	5.2	438	32.2	1361		385

Transfers

Transfers in	9
Transfers out	33

Tuition and Fees

	Resident	Nonresident
Full-time	$39,848	$39,848
Part-time		
Tuition Guarantee Program	N	

Living Expenses

Estimated living expenses for singles

Living on campus	Living off campus	Living at home
N/A	$22,034	$10,910

UNIVERSITY OF MIAMI SCHOOL OF LAW

ABA
Approved
Since
1941

GPA and LSAT Scores

	Total	Full-Time	Part-Time
# of apps	4,670	4,670	0
# of offers	2,195	2,195	0
# of matrics	447	447	0
75% GPA	3.57	3.57	0.00
Median GPA	3.38	3.38	0.00
25% GPA	3.19	3.19	0.00
75% LSAT	160	160	0
Median LSAT	158	158	0
25% LSAT	156	156	0

Grants and Scholarships (from prior year)

	Total #	Total %	Full-Time #	Full-Time %	Part-Time #	Part-Time %
Total # of students	1,353		1,334		19	
Total # receiving grants	437	32.3	437	32.8	0	0.0
Less than 1/2 tuition	176	13.0	176	13.2	0	0.0
Half to full tuition	243	18.0	243	18.2	0	0.0
Full tuition	1	0.1	1	0.1	0	0.0
More than full tuition	17	1.3	17	1.3	0	0.0
Median grant amount			$23,000		$0	

Informational and Library Resources

Total amount spent on library materials	$2,027,875
Study seating capacity inside the library	652
# of full-time equivalent professional librarians	10
Hours per week library is open	111
# of open, wired connections available to students	26
# of networked computers available for use by students	149
Has wireless network?	Y
Requires computer?	N

JD Attrition (from prior year)

	Academic #	Other #	Total #	Total %
1st year	9	37	46	9.6
2nd year	3	4	7	1.5
3rd year	0	0	0	0.0
4th year	0	0	0	0.0

Employment (9 months after graduation)

For up-to-date employment data, go to employmentsummary.abaquestionnaire.org on the ABA website.

Bar Passage Rates

First-time takers	464	Reporting %	76.94
Average school %	84.31	Average state %	77.63
Average pass difference	6.68		

Jurisdiction	Takers	Passers	Pass %	State %	Diff %
Florida	357	301	84.31	77.63	6.68

UNIVERSITY OF MIAMI SCHOOL OF LAW

PO Box 248087
Coral Gables, FL 33124-8087
Phone: 305.284.2523; Fax: 305.284.3084
E-mail: admissions@law.miami.edu; Website: www.law.miami.edu

Introduction

The University of Miami School of Law is on the main campus of one of the largest private research universities in the United States. The surrounding South Florida region is unique and stands at the crossroads of the Americas in a dynamic area of international trade and commerce. Students attend law school in a beautiful, subtropical setting while taking advantage of the opportunities available in the surrounding legal community. Miami Law is accredited by the ABA, is a member of the AALS, and has a chapter of the prestigious scholastic society, the Order of the Coif.

Faculty

The faculty have exceptional credentials. They are graduates of the world's top universities and law schools, have completed prestigious judicial clerkships, and have significant work experience in private practice and government. They are leading scholars in their fields and are renowned for combining their scholarly distinction and real-world experience with an enthusiastic approach to teaching. Their expertise is especially strong in international and foreign law, arbitration, taxation, criminal law, securities regulation, immigration, human rights, the Internet, legal theory, evidence, and ethics.

Library

With over 645,000 volumes and volume-equivalents and a wide array of electronic resources, Miami Law's library is one of the most comprehensive resources for legal research in the Southeast. The library has liberal hours, a full-time staff of 28, and ample seating for individual and group study. The campus is wireless.

Curriculum

The school provides a solid foundation in all the traditional subjects basic to understanding and practicing the law. In addition, the school is constantly expanding its offerings to ensure they reflect the opportunities of the changing world.

Choosing from more than 250 courses, workshops, and seminars, students ordinarily complete the JD degree in three years of full-time study. Summer sessions are available. Miami's course offerings in inter-American, international, arbitration, and transnational law are outstanding. Joint JD/Master's programs are offered in medicine business administration, public health, music business, communications, and marine affairs and policy. In addition, JD/LLM degrees are offered in taxation, real property development, international law, inter-American law, transnational law, international arbitration, and ocean and coastal law. The school also offers a triple degree option where students who were undergraduate business majors can earn a JD, an MBA, and an LLM in tax or real property in four years.

Master of Laws (LLM) programs include inter-American law, international arbitration, international law, ocean and coastal law, taxation, estate planning, real property development, and transnational law for foreign lawyers. A JD degree (or equivalent degree from a foreign law school) is required for entrance into an LLM program.

Special Programs

The school has 10 clinics in Immigration, Investor Rights, Human Rights, Tenants' Rights, Federal Appellate, Children and Youth Law, Health and Elder Law, and Bankruptcy Assistance. In addition, there is the Miami Innocence Project and the Capital Defense Project.

The Center for Ethics and Public Service is an interdisciplinary project teaching the values of ethical judgment, professional responsibility, and public service and includes the Summer Public Interest Fellowship Program, the Professional Responsibility and Ethics Program (PREP), and the Historic Black Church Program.

Miami Law also conducts the nationally known STREET LAW program in which law students teach law at local high schools to empower youth through interactive education about law, democracy, and human rights while furthering professional development.

HOPE (Helping Others Through Pro Bono Efforts) is the law school's public interest resource center. This center helps students understand the array of public interest opportunities at Miami Law and provides guidance and training to law students dedicated to community service and advocacy.

Miami Law offers one of the most comprehensive and sophisticated Litigation Skills training programs in the nation, integrating trial, pretrial, litigation, and clinical experiences. Directed by a full-time faculty member, distinguished trial attorneys and judges from both state and federal courts assist with trial and pretrial courses and help supervise externship placements.

Study-abroad options consist of exchange programs in Germany, Israel, France, Brazil, Ireland, Belgium, Spain, China, and Switzerland. Through these programs, students can focus on specific interests such as international law, arbitration of international business disputes, comparative law issues in international business, foreign legal systems, and human rights. In addition, the school has an International Moot Court Program in which students take a workshop, obtain course credit, and participate in international moot court competitions, some of which are conducted in Spanish.

Other unique programs include the school's LawWithoutWalls program—a unique opportunity where students from Miami Law and from law schools around the world collaborate across countries to conduct investigative research and identify a problem in legal education or practice. Miami's Mindfulness in Law Program coordinates special wellness programs to help students achieve a better balance between work and life.

Admission

Admission is competitive. Undergraduate and graduate grade-point averages are used in the review process. While all LSAT scores are considered, the highest score is given the greatest weight. Two letters of recommendation or two evaluations (or combination thereof) are required and a personal statement is strongly encouraged. Work experience, extracurricular activities, special skills, and background are also considered. First-year students are admitted only in the fall semester. Applicants are urged to apply as early as possible after September 1. Applications received after February 3 will be considered on a space-available basis until July 31.

The Student Body and Student Life

Miami's student body is highly talented and exceptionally diverse. The school is consistently among the leaders in numbers of Hispanic, African American, and foreign students graduated from its JD program.

The school's many student activities include an active Student Bar Association, Honor Council, Moot Court Board, and more than 55 diverse student organizations that provide members with personal, academic, and career support. All encourage student leadership and involvement in pro bono activities, assist in recruiting students, and provide networking and career opportunities with alumni and other members of the legal community. The school's leadership works closely with student organizations and facilitates or cosponsors a broad array of special programs and events throughout the year. The school's organizations include the Black, Hispanic, Caribbean, South Asian, Middle Eastern, and Asian/Pacific American law student organizations; OUTLaw; Miami Law Women; Federalist Society; International Law Society; Entertainment and Sports Law Society; the Student Animal Legal Defense Fund; and many more. Miami's law journals include the *University of Miami Law Review, University of Miami Inter-American Law Review, University of Miami International and Comparative Law Review, Race and Social Justice Law Review, Business Law Review, National Security and Armed Conflict Law Review,* and *Psychology, Public Policy, and Law Review.*

Expenses and Financial Aid

Scholarship aid available through the school does not exceed the cost of tuition. Most scholarships are merit based, although need is sometimes considered. Admitted applicants are automatically considered for most scholarship awards. Applicants who wish to be considered for a merit scholarship should complete their admission files prior to January 6. Most scholarships are awarded on a rolling basis. Those admitted by February 3 are considered for the prestigious Harvey T. Reid and Soia Mentschikoff scholarships. In addition, admitted students are eligible to apply for the public interest-related Miami Scholars Program, which requires a separate application with a deadline of April 1.

The law school assists and encourages all students to apply for federal aid (loans) prior to considering private educational loans. Federal loans may be applied for by first completing the FAFSA online at www.fafsa.gov. Our Federal School Code is E00532. Any additional financial aid information can be found on our website at www.law.miami.edu/finaid.

Career Services

The Career Development Office (CDO) offers extraordinary individual career counseling to law students and alumni, with attorneys in different specialty areas providing guidance. The CDO offers a wide range of job-related programming and job fairs, networking opportunities with attorneys in varied practice areas, and access to a resource library and national job postings via the Internet. The On-Campus Interview Program attracts national and local employers, providing opportunities with law firms, government agencies, public service organizations, corporate counsel, and the judiciary.

Miami Law also has its Legal Corps Program, an ambitious postgraduate fellowship program that places recent law graduates in government agencies, public interest organizations, and judicial chambers in Florida and throughout the country and pays them $2,500 a month for six months.

APPLICANT PROFILE

University of Miami School of Law
This grid includes only applicants who earned 120–180 LSAT scores under standard administrations.

LSAT Score	GPA									
	3.75 +	3.50–3.74	3.25–3.49	3.00–3.24	2.75–2.99	2.50–2.74	2.25–2.49	2.00–2.24	Below 2.00	No GPA
175–180										
170–174										
165–169										
160–164										
155–159										
150–154										
145–149										
140–144										
135–139										
130–134										
125–129										
120–124										

■ Good Possibility   □ Possible   ▨ Unlikely

When reviewing the grid, it is important to note that admission to the school is based upon all aspects of an applicant's background, and not limited to the LSAT and undergraduate grade-point average.

THE UNIVERSITY OF MICHIGAN LAW SCHOOL

Admissions Office, 701 South State Street, Suite 2200
Ann Arbor, MI 48109-3091
Phone: 734.764.0537
E-mail: law.jd.admissions@umich.edu; Website: www.law.umich.edu

The Basics

Type of school	Public
Term	Semester
Application deadline	11/15 2/15
Application fee	$75
Financial aid deadline	
Can first year start other than fall?	Yes
Student to faculty ratio	12.8 to 1
# of housing spaces available restricted to law students	258
graduate housing for which law students are eligible	1,200

Faculty and Administrators

	Total		Men		Women		Minorities	
	Spr	Fall	Spr	Fall	Spr	Fall	Spr	Fall
Full-time	72	70	45	47	27	23	10	8
Other full-time	20	20	12	11	8	9	2	2
Deans, librarians, & others who teach	4	3	3	3	1	0	0	0
Part-time	33	35	24	25	9	10	2	2
Total	129	128	84	86	45	42	14	12

JD Enrollment and Ethnicity

	Men		Women		Full-Time		Part-Time		1st-Year		Total		JD Degs. Awd.
	#	%	#	%	#	%	#	%	#	%	#	%	
All Hispanics	23	3.7	30	5.6	53	4.6	0	0.0	23	6.4	53	4.6	18
Am. Ind./AK Nat.	4	0.7	1	0.2	5	0.4	0	0.0	1	0.3	5	0.4	1
Asian	40	6.5	69	12.9	109	9.5	0	0.0	31	8.7	109	9.5	39
Black/Af. Am.	15	2.4	18	3.4	33	2.9	0	0.0	13	3.6	33	2.9	10
Nat. HI/Pac. Isl.	0	0.0	0	0.0	0	0.0	0	0.0	0	0.0	0	0.0	0
2 or more races	23	3.7	19	3.6	42	3.7	0	0.0	13	3.6	42	3.7	16
Subtotal (minor.)	105	17.1	137	25.7	242	21.1	0	0.0	81	22.7	242	21.1	84
Nonres. Alien	15	2.4	15	2.8	30	2.6	0	0.0	8	2.2	30	2.6	7
White/Cauc.	440	71.5	335	62.7	775	67.5	0	0.0	222	62.2	775	67.5	250
Unknown	55	8.9	47	8.8	102	8.9	0	0.0	46	12.9	102	8.9	37
Total	615	53.5	534	46.5	1149	100.0	0	0.0	357	31.1	1149		378

Curriculum

	Full-Time	Part-Time
Typical first-year section size	92	0
Is there typically a "small section" of the first-year class, other than Legal Writing, taught by full-time faculty	Yes	No
If yes, typical size offered last year	46	
# of classroom course titles beyond first-year curriculum	182	

# of upper division courses, excluding seminars, with an enrollment:	Under 25	95
	25–49	54
	50–74	10
	75–99	7
	100+	9

# of seminars	61	
# of seminar positions available	846	
# of seminar positions filled	768	0
# of positions available in simulation courses	723	
# of simulation positions filled	626	0
# of positions available in faculty supervised clinical courses	345	
# of faculty supervised clinical positions filled	333	0
# involved in field placements	30	0
# involved in law journals	476	0
# involved in moot court or trial competitions	58	0
# of credit hours required to graduate	82	

Transfers

Transfers in	39
Transfers out	3

Tuition and Fees

	Resident	Nonresident
Full-time	$46,830	$49,740
Part-time		
Tuition Guarantee Program	N	

Living Expenses

Estimated living expenses for singles

Living on campus	Living off campus	Living at home
$18,130	$18,130	$7,050

THE UNIVERSITY OF MICHIGAN LAW SCHOOL

ABA
Approved
Since
1923

GPA and LSAT Scores

	Total	Full-Time	Part-Time
# of apps	5,424	5,424	0
# of offers	1,162	1,162	0
# of matrics	359	359	0
75% GPA	3.87	3.87	0.00
Median GPA	3.76	3.76	0.00
25% GPA	3.59	3.59	0.00
75% LSAT	170	170	0
Median LSAT	169	169	0
25% LSAT	167	167	0

Grants and Scholarships (from prior year)

	Total #	Total %	Full-Time #	Full-Time %	Part-Time #	Part-Time %
Total # of students	1,134		1,134		0	
Total # receiving grants	787	69.4	787	69.4	0	0.0
Less than 1/2 tuition	698	61.6	698	61.6	0	0.0
Half to full tuition	45	4.0	45	4.0	0	0.0
Full tuition	27	2.4	27	2.4	0	0.0
More than full tuition	17	1.5	17	1.5	0	0.0
Median grant amount			$15,000		$0	

Informational and Library Resources

Total amount spent on library materials	$2,823,172
Study seating capacity inside the library	854
# of full-time equivalent professional librarians	8.35
Hours per week library is open	112
# of open, wired connections available to students	399
# of networked computers available for use by students	224
Has wireless network?	Y
Requires computer?	N

JD Attrition (from prior year)

	Academic #	Other #	Total #	Total %
1st year	0	0	0	0.0
2nd year	1	4	5	1.3
3rd year	0	3	3	0.8
4th year	0	0	0	0.0

Employment (9 months after graduation)

For up-to-date employment data, go to employmentsummary.abaquestionnaire.org on the ABA website.

Bar Passage Rates

First-time takers	369	Reporting %	75.34
Average school %	93.54	Average state %	82.92
Average pass difference	10.62		

Jurisdiction	Takers	Passers	Pass %	State %	Diff %
New York	117	111	94.87	84.92	9.95
California	59	52	88.14	71.24	16.90
Illinois	57	54	94.74	89.38	5.36
Michigan	45	43	95.56	84.83	10.73

THE UNIVERSITY OF MICHIGAN LAW SCHOOL

Admissions Office, 701 South State Street, Suite 2200
Ann Arbor, MI 48109-3091
Phone: 734.764.0537
E-mail: law.jd.admissions@umich.edu; Website: www.law.umich.edu

Introduction

The University of Michigan Law School, founded in 1859, is one of the nation's finest institutions of legal education. The school's distinguished and diverse faculty, many preeminent in their fields, have a history of devotion to both scholarship and teaching. Our students come from around the globe to contribute their remarkable talents and accomplishments and make the Law School a collegial community that exudes a sense of serious purpose, academic achievement, and social commitment. Never restricted to the privileged, in 1870, Michigan—then the largest law school in the country—became the second university to confer a law degree on an African American. That same year, Michigan became the first major law school to admit a woman, and in 1871, its graduate, Sarah Killgore, became the first woman with a law degree in the nation to be admitted to the bar.

Faculty

Michigan has more than 80 full-time faculty members, with many distinguished visiting scholars further enhancing course offerings. While maintaining a long tradition of eminence in constitutional, criminal, international, and comparative law, the interdisciplinary breadth of the faculty is reflected in an extraordinary range of expertise, including classics, economics, feminist theory, history, life sciences, natural resources, philosophy, political theory, and public policy. We offer depth as well, whether measured by the number of professors who are also voting faculty members of a world-class department in another discipline, the number with PhDs in cognate disciplines, or the number who are Fellows of the American Academy of Arts and Sciences.

Physical Facilities and Library

The location of residential and academic buildings within the strikingly beautiful Gothic architecture of the William W. Cook Law Quadrangle fosters the integration of activities for both students and faculty. The new state-of-the-art South Hall academic building and a 16,000-square-foot, glass-roofed commons opened in 2011, providing additional dynamic, inspiring spaces for learning as well as social interactions.

With more than one million volumes, the Law Library's comprehensive collection covers Anglo-American, foreign, comparative, and international law, and includes legislation, court reports, and administrative material from all US jurisdictions, Great Britain, Europe, and most Asian and South American countries. In 1957, the library became the first depository of EU documents at an American university. It is also a selective depository for US government publications and extensively collects documents of international intergovernmental organizations. There is special depth in collections relating to indigenous peoples. Law students also have access to all other university libraries.

Curriculum

Recognized as preeminent in interdisciplinary legal studies, the insights and methods of many other fields are apparent throughout our broad curriculum. Formal dual-degree programs are available in 14 disciplines, while others are created ad hoc, sometimes with other institutions. Alternatively, students may count 12 credits of graduate-level work in other departments toward their JD. With the Law School located at the center of the university, it is easy for students to take advantage of these options, and about 15 percent of second- and third-year students do so.

A key component of the first year is our exceptional Legal Practice Program. This comprehensive class provides individualized instruction in legal writing, research, and oral advocacy by full-time faculty to first-year students.

Particularly renowned for international scholarship, Michigan's leadership is evident in its requirement that all students complete Transnational Law—the first top law school to so recognize the centrality of the field to modern lawyering. The Geneva Externship Program provides 20 students annually with a unique "in" to extremely competitive jobs in the public international field, while other programs, such as the South Africa Externship Program, the Program for Law and Development in Cambodia, and our AIRE Centre internships provide students with advanced training in international areas of interest.

As one of the leaders in American legal education, Michigan's curriculum is strong across the board. Students with interest in business, corporate, and securities; intellectual property; criminal; international; tax; constitutional; environmental; and public interest law should pay special attention to Michigan's extensive offerings.

Clinical Opportunities

Michigan is committed to the union of theory and practice, and our clinical practice program, with more than 30 years of experience, is unquestionably one of the nation's best. Michigan is one of only two states to allow students to appear in court as early as their second year, which means that our students have more opportunities to represent clients selected from a rich pool of cases—often in smaller jurisdictions, where a faster timetable allows students to handle many cases from beginning to end. Beyond the General Clinic, where students are involved in civil and criminal trial work, as well as immigration and refugee cases, our diverse offerings include litigation clinics in Child Advocacy Law, Juvenile Justice, Criminal Appellate Practice, and Human Trafficking, as well as our groundbreaking non-DNA Innocence Clinic; transactional clinics such as Community and Economic Development, Entrepreneurship, International Transactions, Federal Appellate Litigation Clinic, and Low Income Tax; the interdisciplinary medicolegal Pediatric Advocacy Clinic; an Environmental Law Clinic run in cooperation with the National Wildlife Federation; and a Mediation Clinic. Students can also participate in the Family Law Project, a student-run advocacy program for victims of domestic violence, as well as a variety of practicums—in fields ranging from copyright to bankruptcy—in which real cases are dissected in a classroom setting.

Admission and Student Body

Please refer to Applicant Profile for more information.

Student Activities

Approximately 450 students participate in six journals: the *Michigan Law Review*, the *Michigan Journal of Law Reform*, the *Michigan Journal of International Law*, the *Michigan Journal of Gender & Law*, the *Michigan Telecommunications and Technology Law Review*, and the *Michigan Journal of Race & Law*. Two new provisional journals in the fields of private equity and environmental law further expand options for writing and editing. Students interested in honing advocacy skills may choose to enter numerous moot court competitions. The Law School Student Senate funds more than 60 student organizations dedicated to affinity group membership and legal interests; students also participate in university groups. Our voluntary Pro Bono Pledge gives students yet one more outlet to serve the world outside the Law School with their developing legal skills; projects range from local to global in providing underrepresented individuals with valuable expertise.

Financial Aid

Our financial aid resources are substantial, and we distribute more than $3.5 million in grants annually to each entering class. Grants range in size from $5,000 to as much as full tuition plus a stipend, and average about $15,000 annually. Our resources are divided between grants made with reference to financial need, and merit awards made to outstanding candidates who are remarkable for their anticipated contribution to the Law School and the profession.

Michigan's newly redesigned and generous income-based Loan Repayment Assistance Program (LRAP) provides graduates with the flexibility to choose jobs from an unlimited range of law-related opportunities, including lower-paying public interest positions, while still maintaining a reasonable lifestyle.

Career Planning

Michigan offers unsurpassed opportunities for career prospects. Our location in the center of the country means that employers from all major markets target our graduates, and our on-campus recruiting program is consistently one of the nation's largest, even in comparison to other top schools—both in absolute numbers of employers recruiting and in relative terms of interviews per student. While the majority of our graduates go to the best and largest private-sector firms across the nation, the range of work performed by our alumni is truly extraordinary. Michigan is, for example, among the leaders in training people for the state and federal bench, as well as academia. Each year our graduates earn prestigious post-graduate fellowships, including those offered by the Skadden Foundation and Equal Justice Works. And as one of only a handful of schools regularly sending its graduates to more than 30 states and abroad, our students have confidence that their degrees will be portable wherever they choose to live. The largest number of our graduates go to New York City and Chicago, followed closely by California and Washington, DC. Our reach extends well beyond these cities, though; the most recent class sent graduates to markets ranging from Seattle to Miami, London to Madrid, and to Hanoi, to name just a few.

Our seven full-time attorney-counselors and two part-time alumni counselors have broad legal experience and advise students about the full range of professional opportunities. Both when the market is flourishing and when it contracts, Michigan's robust recruiting program and the depth of its counselors' expertise serve students exceptionally well.

Housing

Ann Arbor combines ease of living with superb cultural, athletic, and entertainment offerings. The on-campus Lawyers Club, to be renovated during the 2012–2013 academic year, houses many first-year, upper-class, and LLM students, allowing easy access to academic buildings and camaraderie of life in the Law Quad. High-quality, off-campus housing is available in a wide variety of choices. Economical university family housing is also available a short (and free) bus ride away, in northeast Ann Arbor.

APPLICANT PROFILE

We choose not to provide an applicant profile because we do not believe a grid based on undergraduate GPA and LSAT scores can accurately reflect our comprehensive admission process, which focuses on many elements in an application in order to determine an applicant's particular intellectual strengths, nonacademic achievements, and unique personal circumstances. We view our student body as one of our greatest assets, and our goal is to admit a group of students who, individually and collectively, are among the best applying to US law schools in a given year. We seek a mix of students with varying backgrounds and experiences who will respect and learn from each other. Our most general measures are an applicant's LSAT score and undergraduate GPA. As measured by those statistics, Michigan is among a handful of the most selective law schools in the country. However, each of these measures is far from perfect. Even the highest possible scores will not guarantee admission, and low scores will likewise not automatically result in a denial, as both circumstances may have significant offsetting considerations.

MICHIGAN STATE UNIVERSITY COLLEGE OF LAW

Office of Admissions and Financial Aid, 300 Law College Building
East Lansing, MI 48824-1300
Phone: 800.844.9352, 517.432.0222; Fax: 517.432.0098
E-mail: admiss@law.msu.edu; Website: www.law.msu.edu

ABA
Approved
Since
1941

The Basics

Type of school	Private
Term	Semester
Application deadline	4/30
Application fee	$60
Financial aid deadline	4/1
Can first year start other than fall?	No
Student to faculty ratio	14.0 to 1
# of housing spaces available restricted to law students	
graduate housing for which law students are eligible	1,049

Faculty and Administrators

	Total		Men		Women		Minorities	
	Spr	Fall	Spr	Fall	Spr	Fall	Spr	Fall
Full-time	46	51	23	27	23	24	7	8
Other full-time	5	4	3	2	2	2	1	0
Deans, librarians, & others who teach	19	10	8	5	11	5	2	2
Part-time	54	48	42	34	12	14	1	1
Total	124	113	76	68	48	45	11	11

JD Enrollment and Ethnicity

	Men		Women		Full-Time		Part-Time		1st-Year		Total		JD Degs. Awd.
	#	%	#	%	#	%	#	%	#	%	#	%	
All Hispanics	15	3.2	30	6.8	30	4.2	15	7.5	16	5.2	45	4.9	7
Am. Ind./AK Nat.	6	1.3	11	2.5	11	1.5	6	3.0	7	2.3	17	1.9	3
Asian	19	4.0	12	2.7	23	3.2	8	4.0	11	3.6	31	3.4	9
Black/Af. Am.	22	4.7	49	11.1	54	7.5	17	8.5	25	8.1	71	7.8	16
Nat. HI/Pac. Isl.	2	0.4	2	0.5	4	0.6	0	0.0	0	0.0	4	0.4	1
2 or more races	11	2.3	13	2.9	19	2.7	5	2.5	15	4.9	24	2.6	1
Subtotal (minor.)	75	15.9	117	26.4	141	19.7	51	25.6	74	24.0	192	21.0	37
Nonres. Alien	26	5.5	26	5.9	47	6.6	5	2.5	23	7.5	52	5.7	20
White/Cauc.	349	73.9	277	62.5	491	68.6	135	67.8	201	65.3	626	68.4	205
Unknown	22	4.7	23	5.2	37	5.2	8	4.0	10	3.2	45	4.9	20
Total	472	51.6	443	48.4	716	78.3	199	21.7	308	33.7	915		282

Curriculum

	Full-Time	Part-Time
Typical first-year section size	77	0
Is there typically a "small section" of the first-year class, other than Legal Writing, taught by full-time faculty	No	No
If yes, typical size offered last year		

# of classroom course titles beyond first-year curriculum		156
# of upper division courses, excluding seminars, with an enrollment:	Under 25	139
	25–49	33
	50–74	13
	75–99	9
	100+	1

# of seminars		96
# of seminar positions available		1,865
# of seminar positions filled	980	59
# of positions available in simulation courses		806
# of simulation positions filled	610	15
# of positions available in faculty supervised clinical courses		194
# of faculty supervised clinical positions filled	118	4
# involved in field placements	328	25
# involved in law journals	192	3
# involved in moot court or trial competitions	103	1
# of credit hours required to graduate		88

Transfers

Transfers in	52
Transfers out	13

Tuition and Fees

	Resident	Nonresident
Full-time	$35,840	$35,840
Part-time	$28,712	$28,712
Tuition Guarantee Program		N

Living Expenses

Estimated living expenses for singles

Living on campus	Living off campus	Living at home
$15,437	$15,437	$15,437

ABA Approved Since 1941

GPA and LSAT Scores

	Total	Full-Time	Part-Time
# of apps	3,732	3,551	181
# of offers	1,185	1,147	38
# of matrics	307	306	1
75% GPA	3.74	3.74	2.88
Median GPA	3.54	3.55	2.88
25% GPA	3.22	3.23	2.88
75% LSAT	160	160	156
Median LSAT	157	157	156
25% LSAT	152	152	156

Grants and Scholarships (from prior year)

	Total #	Total %	Full-Time #	Full-Time %	Part-Time #	Part-Time %
Total # of students	884		804		80	
Total # receiving grants	391	44.2	376	46.8	15	18.8
Less than 1/2 tuition	84	9.5	82	10.2	2	2.5
Half to full tuition	163	18.4	159	19.8	4	5.0
Full tuition	144	16.3	135	16.8	9	11.3
More than full tuition	0	0.0	0	0.0	0	0.0
Median grant amount			$23,591		$12,333	

Informational and Library Resources

Total amount spent on library materials	$1,190,146
Study seating capacity inside the library	455
# of full-time equivalent professional librarians	8
Hours per week library is open	109
# of open, wired connections available to students	1,059
# of networked computers available for use by students	57
Has wireless network?	Y
Requires computer?	Y

JD Attrition (from prior year)

	Academic #	Other #	Total #	Total %
1st year	8	17	25	8.6
2nd year	0	1	1	0.3
3rd year	0	1	1	0.4
4th year	0	0	0	0.0

Employment (9 months after graduation)

For up-to-date employment data, go to employmentsummary.abaquestionnaire.org on the ABA website.

Bar Passage Rates

First-time takers	295	Reporting %	70.51
Average school %	84.61	Average state %	85.52

Average pass difference −0.91

Jurisdiction	Takers	Passers	Pass %	State %	Diff %
Michigan	152	137	90.13	84.83	5.30
Illinois	31	25	80.65	89.38	−8.73
New York	25	14	56.00	84.92	−28.92

MICHIGAN STATE UNIVERSITY COLLEGE OF LAW

Office of Admissions and Financial Aid, 300 Law College Building
East Lansing, MI 48824-1300
Phone: 800.844.9352, 517.432.0222; Fax: 517.432.0098
E-mail: admiss@law.msu.edu; Website: www.law.msu.edu

Introduction

With a broad and rigorous curriculum that provides extensive opportunities for students to gain valuable practical experience, Michigan State University (MSU) College of Law successfully prepares graduates for legal employment in settings across the nation—litigation, transactional law, business and industry, alternative dispute resolution, and public interest—to mention just a few.

As a law school with a 100-plus year tradition of graduating outstanding lawyers, judges, and entrepreneurs, students at MSU Law benefit from the college's status as a private law school located in the heart of a Big 10, world-class research university. The College of Law's location in East Lansing provides students with convenient access to externships and employment with state and federal agencies and courts, and an array of law firms and corporations. MSU Law is fully accredited by the ABA and is a member of the AALS.

Academic Programs

The College of Law curriculum provides a thorough education in all principal areas of law and practice. A total of 88 credit hours is required for graduation, with 29 of these credits being prescribed by the College of Law. The College of Law teaches core legal skills, supplemented with academic concentrations, programmatic initiatives, and scholarly research and exchanges. The educational program of the college teaches and reinforces the ethical core of good lawyering, the values of professionalism and service, the art of client representation and trial advocacy, and the understanding of legal principles, private rights, and public policy.

The College of Law strives to continuously strengthen academic quality in all programs and activities of the college. The college is committed to fostering flexible opportunities for professional growth, innovation, research, and scholarship by the faculty. The faculty is committed to excellence in instruction, making significant contributions to legal research, and engaging in public service and community outreach. The staff is committed to providing necessary service, support, and creativity.

The elective and required curriculum of the College of Law integrates theory and practice, thereby helping to ensure that graduates of MSU Law are well prepared for their first professional positions and the professional responsibilities for decades to come.

Focus Areas: Law students at MSU have the opportunity to choose a focus area or certificate program when selecting elective courses. Focus areas include Alternative Dispute Resolution (ADR); Child and Family Advocacy; Corporate Law; Criminal Law; Environmental and Natural Resource Law; Family Law; Indigenous Law; Intellectual Property, Information, and Communications Law; International and Comparative Law; Public Law and Regulation; Taxation Law; and Trial Practice/Litigation.

Canadian and American Law Degree Program: MSU Law students who rank in the top half of the class may enroll in the dual-degree program with the University of Ottawa Faculty of Law, thereby earning both a US and a Canadian law degree in four years.

Study-Abroad Programs: The College of Law offers an ever-expanding list of study-abroad options, including the MSU Law Canadian program, and study-abroad programs in Croatia, England, Japan, and Poland.

Dual-Degree Options: Law students with an interest in broadening their skills set have the opportunity to pursue a dual degree with another graduate program at Michigan State University. Dual degrees are established with more than a dozen graduate programs, with the typical dual-degree student being able to earn the law degree and a master's degree in just four years.

Master of Laws (LLM) Program: An LLM is offered for international lawyers. An LLM/MJ (Master of Jurisprudence) is offered in Intellectual Property and Communications Law for domestic and international students.

Experiential Learning

MSU Law Clinics: The College of Law operates law clinics to provide students with the opportunity to apply the skills they have learned in the classroom. Students enrolled in the clinics may handle cases from start to finish, thereby gaining résumé-building experience from their clinical experiences, all while helping members of their own community. Law clinics available to MSU students include the Civil Rights Clinic, First Amendment Clinic, Housing Clinic, Immigration Clinic, Plea and Sentencing Clinic, Small Business and Nonprofit Law Clinic, Tax Clinic, and Chance at Childhood Law and Social Work Clinic.

Spring Semester in Washington, DC: The College of Law's Washington, DC, Semester Program provides the opportunity for 25 students to spend a full spring semester in our nation's capital, working 32 hours weekly for federal agencies while also enrolling in several law courses taught by MSU Law faculty. The DC program provides valuable practical experience and insights into employment with the federal government.

Externships: Externships, which are field placements that provide practical legal training under the supervision of practicing attorneys and faculty members, may be completed with a variety of legal employers—judicial, legal aid, nonprofit, and governmental. Annually, more than 200 students enroll in externships, with summer externships located throughout the US and abroad.

MSU Law Journals: *Michigan State Law Review, MSU Journal of International Law, MSU Journal of Medicine and Law,* and *Journal of Business and Securities Law.*

Trial Practice Institute: MSU Law alumnus Geoffrey N. Fieger has partnered with the College of Law to establish a premier trial practice institute, designed specifically to train law students as successful trial lawyers. Students interview at the end of their first year of law school, and selected students start the program at the beginning of their second year. The institute offers hands-on learning experiences through clinics, externships, field placements, and simulations.

Career Services

Graduates of the College of Law can be found in all regions of the country and abroad. In a typical year, graduates accept employment in 25 or more states. The most common career path of recent graduates is private practice, with graduates accepting employment with law firms of all sizes. Other recent MSU Law graduates have accepted judicial clerkships (4–8 percent), employment in business or industry (15–25 percent), governmental employment (10–15 percent), and public interest work (3–5 percent). Placement rates for new graduates consistently exceed 90 percent.

Admission

MSU Law has an admission process designed to identify individuals who have the potential to excel in their legal studies and the practice of law. The College of Law seeks to enroll students who are academically talented and who bring to the classroom a diversity of personal and professional experiences and perspectives. The College of Law's Admission Committee considers many variables in addition to the applicant's undergraduate record and score on the LSAT.

The Admission Committee encourages candidates for the Juris Doctor program to apply for admission at the earliest possible date after October 1 and prior to March 1. The Admission Office accepts applications through late spring, with a final deadline of April 30. Candidates whose applications are received prior to February 1 will be given

priority consideration for scholarship assistance. Applications for admission are reviewed on a rolling-admission basis beginning in early November and continuing through late spring. Applications generally are reviewed according to the date they are complete with all supporting materials. Admission to Michigan State University College of Law is granted for the fall term only for both the full-time and part-time programs.

Scholarship Assistance

The College of Law offers one of the most generous scholarship programs among law schools nationally, with as many as 60 full-tuition scholarships awarded to members of each incoming class. Additionally, the College of Law annually awards 50 scholarships ranging in value up to $25,000. Every applicant who is offered admission to the College of Law is considered for scholarship assistance, though grants based on financial need require an application. Law students who achieve a GPA of 3.60 or higher at the end of their first year of full-time studies at MSU Law automatically are provided a scholarship that covers one-half, three-quarters, or 100 percent of tuition.

APPLICANT PROFILE

Michigan State University College of Law
This grid includes only applicants who earned 120–180 LSAT scores under standard administrations.

LSAT Score	3.75 + Apps	3.75 + Adm	3.50–3.74 Apps	3.50–3.74 Adm	3.25–3.49 Apps	3.25–3.49 Adm	3.00–3.24 Apps	3.00–3.24 Adm	2.75–2.99 Apps	2.75–2.99 Adm	2.50–2.74 Apps	2.50–2.74 Adm	2.25–2.49 Apps	2.25–2.49 Adm	2.00–2.24 Apps	2.00–2.24 Adm	Below 2.00 Apps	Below 2.00 Adm	No GPA Apps	No GPA Adm	Total Apps	Total Adm
170–180	9	5	3	2	4	0	1	1	1	1	0	0	0	0	1	0	0	0	0	0	19	9
165–169	42	30	41	23	20	12	14	5	7	3	5	1	5	0	1	0	0	0	4	3	139	77
160–164	121	79	157	102	89	46	75	33	38	22	21	8	12	2	5	0	1	1	12	5	531	298
155–159	150	103	246	156	210	87	188	71	109	31	63	13	26	0	7	0	0	0	14	5	1013	466
150–154	117	65	210	111	235	60	228	26	110	5	69	2	25	0	16	0	3	0	19	3	1032	272
145–149	46	25	92	26	125	3	100	6	76	4	48	0	41	1	15	0	3	0	12	0	558	65
140–144	13	2	37	2	42	1	63	6	42	1	35	2	22	1	10	0	2	0	7	0	273	15
Below 140	2	0	8	0	15	0	18	0	29	0	27	0	11	0	6	0	3	0	9	1	128	1
Total	500	309	794	422	740	209	687	148	412	67	268	26	142	4	61	0	12	1	77	17	3693	1203

Apps = Number of Applicants
Adm = Number Admitted
Reflects 99% of the total applicant pool; highest LSAT data reported.

UNIVERSITY OF MINNESOTA LAW SCHOOL

290 Walter F. Mondale Hall, 229 19th Avenue South
Minneapolis, MN 55455
Phone: 612.625.3487; Fax: 612.626.1874
E-mail: jdadmissions@umn.edu; Website: www.law.umn.edu

ABA
Approved
Since
1923

The Basics

Type of school	Public
Term	Semester
Application deadline	4/1
Application fee	$75
Financial aid deadline	5/1
Can first year start other than fall?	No
Student to faculty ratio	10.8 to 1
# of housing spaces available restricted to law students	
graduate housing for which law students are eligible	

Faculty and Administrators

	Total		Men		Women		Minorities	
	Spr	Fall	Spr	Fall	Spr	Fall	Spr	Fall
Full-time	60	53	33	32	27	21	6	6
Other full-time	7	8	4	5	3	3	1	1
Deans, librarians, & others who teach	9	7	4	3	5	4	1	1
Part-time	136	102	89	62	47	40	10	3
Total	212	170	130	102	82	68	18	11

Curriculum

	Full-Time	Part-Time
Typical first-year section size	98	0
Is there typically a "small section" of the first-year class, other than Legal Writing, taught by full-time faculty	Yes	No
If yes, typical size offered last year	49	
# of classroom course titles beyond first-year curriculum	182	

# of upper division courses, excluding seminars, with an enrollment:		
	Under 25	68
	25–49	26
	50–74	10
	75–99	5
	100+	1

# of seminars	72	
# of seminar positions available	864	
# of seminar positions filled	847	0
# of positions available in simulation courses	365	
# of simulation positions filled	359	0
# of positions available in faculty supervised clinical courses	340	
# of faculty supervised clinical positions filled	332	0
# involved in field placements	145	0
# involved in law journals	174	0
# involved in moot court or trial competitions	190	0
# of credit hours required to graduate	88	

JD Enrollment and Ethnicity

	Men #	Men %	Women #	Women %	Full-Time #	Full-Time %	Part-Time #	Part-Time %	1st-Year #	1st-Year %	Total #	Total %	JD Degs. Awd.
All Hispanics	8	1.9	11	3.3	19	2.5	0	0.0	3	1.2	19	2.5	12
Am. Ind./AK Nat.	4	1.0	4	1.2	8	1.1	0	0.0	3	1.2	8	1.1	3
Asian	29	6.9	24	7.3	53	7.0	0	0.0	20	8.2	53	7.0	24
Black/Af. Am.	14	3.3	13	3.9	27	3.6	0	0.0	7	2.9	27	3.6	4
Nat. HI/Pac. Isl.	1	0.2	1	0.3	2	0.3	0	0.0	0	0.0	2	0.3	0
2 or more races	18	4.3	18	5.4	36	4.8	0	0.0	21	8.6	36	4.8	0
Subtotal (minor.)	74	17.6	71	21.5	145	19.3	0	0.0	54	22.0	145	19.3	43
Nonres. Alien	13	3.1	21	6.3	34	4.5	0	0.0	21	8.6	34	4.5	10
White/Cauc.	313	74.3	229	69.2	542	72.1	0	0.0	166	67.8	542	72.1	193
Unknown	21	5.0	10	3.0	31	4.1	0	0.0	4	1.6	31	4.1	15
Total	421	56.0	331	44.0	752	100.0	0	0.0	245	32.6	752		261

Transfers

Transfers in	31
Transfers out	9

Tuition and Fees

	Resident	Nonresident
Full-time	$34,817	$43,385
Part-time		
Tuition Guarantee Program		N

Living Expenses

Estimated living expenses for singles

Living on campus	Living off campus	Living at home
N/A	$14,244	$7,576

ABA Approved Since 1923

GPA and LSAT Scores

	Total	Full-Time	Part-Time
# of apps	3,546	3,546	0
# of offers	880	880	0
# of matrics	246	246	0
75% GPA	3.90	3.90	0.00
Median GPA	3.80	3.80	0.00
25% GPA	3.41	3.41	0.00
75% LSAT	167	167	0
Median LSAT	167	167	0
25% LSAT	157	157	0

Grants and Scholarships (from prior year)

	Total #	Total %	Full-Time #	Full-Time %	Part-Time #	Part-Time %
Total # of students	752		752		0	
Total # receiving grants	495	65.8	495	65.8	0	0.0
Less than 1/2 tuition	233	31.0	233	31.0	0	0.0
Half to full tuition	211	28.1	211	28.1	0	0.0
Full tuition	12	1.6	12	1.6	0	0.0
More than full tuition	39	5.2	39	5.2	0	0.0
Median grant amount			$15,000		$0	

Informational and Library Resources

Total amount spent on library materials	$2,144,986
Study seating capacity inside the library	773
# of full-time equivalent professional librarians	11
Hours per week library is open	81
# of open, wired connections available to students	1
# of networked computers available for use by students	80
Has wireless network?	Y
Requires computer?	Y

JD Attrition (from prior year)

	Academic #	Other #	Total #	Total %
1st year	1	14	15	5.8
2nd year	0	0	0	0.0
3rd year	0	0	0	0.0
4th year	0	0	0	0.0

Employment (9 months after graduation)

For up-to-date employment data, go to employmentsummary.abaquestionnaire.org on the ABA website.

Bar Passage Rates

First-time takers	275	Reporting %	71.27
Average school %	93.87	Average state %	91.17
Average pass difference	2.70		

Jurisdiction	Takers	Passers	Pass %	State %	Diff %
Minnesota	168	164	97.62	92.21	5.41
New York	28	20	71.43	84.92	−13.49

UNIVERSITY OF MINNESOTA LAW SCHOOL

290 Walter F. Mondale Hall, 229 19th Avenue South
Minneapolis, MN 55455
Phone: 612.625.3487; Fax: 612.626.1874
E-mail: jdadmissions@umn.edu; Website: www.law.umn.edu

Introduction

The University of Minnesota Law School, founded in 1888, is one of the country's premier law schools. Under the leadership of international scholar, Dean David Wippman, the quality of Minnesota's faculty, the academic credentials of its students, and the caliber of its library and physical facilities are the strongest in the history of the school. For over 120 years, the school's tradition of excellence and innovation in legal education has made it among the best in the nation. In keeping with its Midwestern traditions, the Law School provides a personal, collegial environment for the study of law. At the same time, the school's location in the midst of a thriving cosmopolitan area provides a variety of academic, employment, cultural, and recreational opportunities. Students have easy access to the resources of a world-class research university and to the Twin Cities of Minneapolis and St. Paul, one of the most progressive and livable metropolitan communities in the country.

Faculty

The faculty's wide-ranging expertise allows students to choose from an academically rich and innovative curriculum that integrates theory and doctrine with skills, ethics, and practice.

Faculty members are prolific and influential scholars, having published over 250 books and close to 2,500 articles. Thirty-six percent of the tenured faculty are invited members of the prestigious American Law Institute, and 68 percent of them have been honored with chair-level appointments. Members of the faculty include a chair of the United Nations Sub-Commission on the Promotion and Protection of Human Rights (the first US citizen to chair the commission since Eleanor Roosevelt), a member of the American Academy of Arts and Sciences, and a former counselor on international law for the US Department of State.

But while the faculty's scholarship has earned them national acclaim, their equally energetic passion for teaching and mentoring, along with a 10.8:1 student-to-faculty ratio, have earned them the respect and appreciation of their students.

Student Body/Admission

With 246 students in the most recent entering class, the student body is large enough to enjoy the benefits of diverse backgrounds, perspectives, and interests, while remaining small enough to foster the kind of collegial and supportive community that is a hallmark of Minnesota life.

Although the atmosphere and camaraderie reflect distinctly Minnesotan values, 35 states plus DC, 7 countries, and over 150 undergraduate institutions are represented in the current JD student body. The admissions committee looks beyond a simple evaluation of LSAT scores and undergraduate GPA to compose a class that will produce leaders in the legal profession. Many students have advanced degrees and prior work experience.

Library and Physical Facilities

The award-winning Walter F. Mondale Hall was substantially expanded in 2001. The building houses all faculty offices, eight law school research institutes, model classrooms in varying sizes, a beautiful auditorium, the law clinics, a cafeteria, the law school bookstore, student lockers, offices for student organizations and publications, a variety of lounge areas, and a computer lab. All incoming JD students are issued laptops, and wireless access is available in all student areas of the building.

Mondale Hall also houses the law library, which is the seventh largest in the United States with over one million volumes. The library offers students 24-hour access. The professional staff takes pride in the outstanding collection of materials and in the individualized service it provides to students and faculty.

Curriculum

Minnesota is implementing curriculum innovations that are designed to merge traditionally doctrinal pedagogy with clinical instruction. Beginning in the first year, students will build on basic lawyering skills, doctrinal concepts, and ethical considerations to craft professional solutions to realistic problems in the new Practice and Professionalism class. First-year students will also enjoy Minnesota's rich curriculum with the opportunity to choose an elective in their second semester. Minnesota continues to be one of only a handful of schools with three years of writing requirements and enjoys one of the smallest first-year writing section sizes, with 10 to 12 students per section. Second-year students are required to participate in a journal or competitive moot court.

Drawing on the strength of a world-class university, qualified students may pursue dual or joint degrees with a myriad of nationally ranked graduate and professional schools. Especially noteworthy is Minnesota's unique joint-degree program in law, health, and the life sciences. Students also enjoy the opportunity to specialize in various subject areas. Currently, concentrations are available in health law and bioethics, human rights, and labor and employment law.

Clinical Programs

With 24 separate clinics, Minnesota has one of the country's largest and most active clinical programs. Through the clinics, students represent real clients under the close tutelage of the clinic faculty. Over 50 percent of the student body participates in a live-client clinic prior to graduation, providing more than 18,000 hours of pro bono legal work for the Twin Cities community each year.

Special Programs

Minnesota hosts international exchange programs in Brazil, France, Germany, Ireland, Italy, the Netherlands, Spain, Sweden, and Uruguay, and a six-week Summer Study-Abroad Program in Beijing, China. These programs enable interested students to study abroad and allow students to benefit from the international perspectives students from these countries bring to the classroom.

Through the Law School Public Service Program, students are asked to perform 50 hours of pro bono legal service for low-income and disadvantaged Minnesotans. Those who complete at least 50 hours of service are recognized for their dedication with a notation on their transcript and at the graduation ceremony.

Nine major research institutes are housed in the Law School: the Human Rights Center; Institute on Race and Poverty; Corporate Institute; Consortium on Law and Values in Health, Environment, and the Life Sciences; Institute on Crime and Public Policy; Rubina Institute of Criminal Law and Criminal Justice; Institute on Law and Economics; Institute on Law and Politics; and the Institute on Law and Rationality. These institutes enrich the school's intellectual life, contribute to policy debate and formation, and provide research and employment opportunities for selected law students.

Student Activities

Minnesota hosts seven student-edited journals: *ABA Journal of Labor and Employment Law; Constitutional Commentary; Crime and Justice; Law and Inequality: A Journal of Theory and Practice; Minnesota Journal of International Law; Minnesota Journal of Law, Science, and Technology;* and *Minnesota Law Review.* Students receive academic credit for their journal work.

Students also receive credit for moot court participation. The breadth of Minnesota's moot court program is unusual, with eight programs spanning a wide variety of subject areas: Civil Rights Moot Court, Intellectual Property Moot Court, International Moot Court, Environmental Law Moot Court, Wagner Labor and Employment Law Moot Court, National Moot Court, ABA Moot Court, and Maynard Pirsig Moot Court.

Student extracurricular activities include nearly 50 separate student organizations, spanning the full spectrum of political viewpoints, social interests, and intellectual and recreational activities (not to mention a full-blown musical theater production).

Expenses and Financial Aid

In recent years, over 90 percent of the student body has received financial aid and over 70 percent of each incoming class received a scholarship of some kind. Second- and third-year students also may apply for research assistantships.

Career and Professional Development

With alumni in all 50 states and over 250 federal and state court judges nationwide, Minnesota graduates are leaders in the judiciary, government, law practice, business, and academics. Employers interview on campus, at regional interview programs sponsored by the Career Center, and at job fairs for nearly 700 offices, including law firms, corporations, and governmental agencies from around the United States. Employers nationwide regularly solicit résumés from students for job postings. Each year, 15 to 20 percent of the graduates accept prestigious judicial clerkships.

APPLICANT PROFILE

University of Minnesota Law School
This grid includes only applicants who earned 120–180 LSAT scores under standard administrations.

LSAT Score	3.75 +		3.50–3.74		3.25–3.49		3.00–3.24		2.75–2.99		2.50–2.74		2.25–2.49		2.00–2.24		Below 2.00		No GPA		Total	
	Apps	Adm	Apps	Adm	Apps	Adm	Apps	Adm	Apps	Adm	Apps	Adm	Apps	Adm	Apps	Adm	Apps	Adm	Apps	Adm	Apps	Adm
175–180	16	9	10	6	10	3	10	3	3	1	2	1	0	0	2	1	0	0	2	0	55	24
170–174	86	33	73	26	58	34	37	13	16	5	13	9	3	1	1	0	0	0	8	4	295	125
165–169	203	123	268	155	201	93	108	48	51	24	20	9	14	7	1	1	1	0	40	18	907	478
160–164	226	93	242	2	200	2	115	1	36	0	19	0	6	1	4	0	0	0	40	4	888	103
155–159	137	72	172	1	166	2	97	2	58	0	35	0	8	0	3	0	0	0	30	2	706	79
150–154	71	39	75	4	108	4	92	5	54	0	31	0	19	0	10	0	0	0	17	2	477	54
145–149	16	7	20	1	32	0	28	0	15	0	13	0	10	0	2	0	0	0	4	0	140	8
140–144	2	0	6	0	4	0	11	0	12	0	1	0	2	0	2	0	1	0	1	0	42	0
135–139	0	0	0	0	3	0	5	0	5	0	3	0	4	0	1	0	0	0	1	0	22	0
130–134	0	0	0	0	1	0	0	0	0	0	1	0	1	0	0	0	0	0	0	0	3	0
125–129	0	0	0	0	0	0	1	0	0	0	2	0	0	0	0	0	0	0	1	0	4	0
120–124	0	0	0	0	0	0	0	0	0	0	0	0	0	0	0	0	0	0	0	0	0	0
Total	757	376	866	195	783	138	504	72	250	30	140	19	67	9	26	2	2	0	144	30	3539	871

Apps = Number of Applicants
Adm = Number Admitted
Reflects 100% of the total applicant pool; highest LSAT data reported.

THE UNIVERSITY OF MISSISSIPPI SCHOOL OF LAW

Robert C. Khayat Law Center, PO Box 1848
University, MS 38677
Phone: Admission: 662.915.6910, Main: 662.915.7361; Fax: 662.915.1289
E-mail: lawmiss@olemiss.edu; Website: www.law.olemiss.edu

ABA
Approved
Since
1930

The Basics

Type of school	Public
Term	Semester
Application deadline	3/1
Application fee	$40
Financial aid deadline	3/1
Can first year start other than fall?	No
Student to faculty ratio	22.6 to 1
# of housing spaces available restricted to law students	
graduate housing for which law students are eligible	

Faculty and Administrators

	Total		Men		Women		Minorities	
	Spr	Fall	Spr	Fall	Spr	Fall	Spr	Fall
Full-time	21	17	15	13	6	4	4	3
Other full-time	6	6	4	4	2	2	1	1
Deans, librarians, & others who teach	10	8	7	5	3	3	0	0
Part-time	21	21	11	9	10	12	1	1
Total	58	52	37	31	21	21	6	5

Curriculum

		Full-Time	Part-Time
Typical first-year section size		56	0
Is there typically a "small section" of the first-year class, other than Legal Writing, taught by full-time faculty		No	No
If yes, typical size offered last year			
# of classroom course titles beyond first-year curriculum		83	
# of upper division courses, excluding seminars, with an enrollment:	Under 25	101	
	25–49	27	
	50–74	6	
	75–99	4	
	100+	0	
# of seminars		24	
# of seminar positions available		602	
# of seminar positions filled		397	0
# of positions available in simulation courses		352	
# of simulation positions filled		273	0
# of positions available in faculty supervised clinical courses		30	
# of faculty supervised clinical positions filled		60	0
# involved in field placements		117	0
# involved in law journals		80	0
# involved in moot court or trial competitions		59	0
# of credit hours required to graduate		90	

JD Enrollment and Ethnicity

	Men		Women		Full-Time		Part-Time		1st-Year		Total		JD Degs. Awd.
	#	%	#	%	#	%	#	%	#	%	#	%	
All Hispanics	11	3.8	4	1.7	15	2.8	0	0.0	6	3.4	15	2.8	2
Am. Ind./AK Nat.	3	1.0	2	0.8	5	0.9	0	0.0	2	1.1	5	0.9	3
Asian	1	0.3	5	2.1	6	1.1	0	0.0	2	1.1	6	1.1	0
Black/Af. Am.	19	6.6	43	17.8	62	11.7	0	0.0	20	11.2	62	11.7	17
Nat. HI/Pac. Isl.	0	0.0	0	0.0	0	0.0	0	0.0	0	0.0	0	0.0	0
2 or more races	1	0.3	0	0.0	1	0.2	0	0.0	1	0.6	1	0.2	1
Subtotal (minor.)	35	12.1	54	22.3	89	16.8	0	0.0	31	17.4	89	16.8	23
Nonres. Alien	0	0.0	0	0.0	0	0.0	0	0.0	0	0.0	0	0.0	0
White/Cauc.	250	86.5	186	76.9	436	82.1	0	0.0	141	79.2	436	82.1	128
Unknown	4	1.4	2	0.8	6	1.1	0	0.0	6	3.4	6	1.1	0
Total	289	54.4	242	45.6	531	100.0	0	0.0	178	33.5	531		151

Transfers

Transfers in	1
Transfers out	6

Tuition and Fees

	Resident	Nonresident
Full-time	$11,293	$24,692
Part-time		
Tuition Guarantee Program		N

Living Expenses

Estimated living expenses for singles

Living on campus	Living off campus	Living at home
$18,214	$18,214	$18,214

THE UNIVERSITY OF MISSISSIPPI SCHOOL OF LAW

*ABA
Approved
Since
1930*

GPA and LSAT Scores

	Total	Full-Time	Part-Time
# of apps	1,656	1,656	0
# of offers	534	534	0
# of matrics	180	180	0
75% GPA	3.69	3.69	0.00
Median GPA	3.49	3.49	0.00
25% GPA	3.24	3.24	0.00
75% LSAT	157	157	0
Median LSAT	155	155	0
25% LSAT	151	151	0

Grants and Scholarships (from prior year)

	Total #	Total %	Full-Time #	Full-Time %	Part-Time #	Part-Time %
Total # of students	516		516		0	
Total # receiving grants	204	39.5	204	39.5	0	0.0
Less than 1/2 tuition	89	17.2	89	17.2	0	0.0
Half to full tuition	87	16.9	87	16.9	0	0.0
Full tuition	9	1.7	9	1.7	0	0.0
More than full tuition	19	3.7	19	3.7	0	0.0
Median grant amount			$1,050		$0	

Informational and Library Resources

Total amount spent on library materials	$807,486
Study seating capacity inside the library	316
# of full-time equivalent professional librarians	6
Hours per week library is open	109
# of open, wired connections available to students	998
# of networked computers available for use by students	42
Has wireless network?	Y
Requires computer?	N

JD Attrition (from prior year)

	Academic #	Other #	Total #	Total %
1st year	2	4	6	3.0
2nd year	1	11	12	7.3
3rd year	0	1	1	0.7
4th year	0	0	0	0.0

Employment (9 months after graduation)

For up-to-date employment data, go to employmentsummary.abaquestionnaire.org on the ABA website.

Bar Passage Rates

First-time takers	170	Reporting %	74.12
Average school %	86.51	Average state %	80.53
Average pass difference	5.98		

Jurisdiction	Takers	Passers	Pass %	State %	Diff %
Mississippi	118	101	85.59	80.28	5.31
Tennessee	8	8	100.00	84.24	15.76

THE UNIVERSITY OF MISSISSIPPI SCHOOL OF LAW

Robert C. Khayat Law Center, PO Box 1848
University, MS 38677
Phone: Admission: 662.915.6910, Main: 662.915.7361; Fax: 662.915.1289
E-mail: lawmiss@olemiss.edu; Website: www.law.olemiss.edu

Introduction

In 1854, recognizing the need for formal law instruction in the state of Mississippi, the legislature established the Department of Law at the University of Mississippi. In 2011, the School of Law moved into a $50-million LEED-certified facility, the Robert C. Khayat Law Center.

Oxford, a small town of approximately 19,000 people, lies nestled in the quiet hills of North Mississippi, just 75 miles southeast of bustling Memphis, Tennessee, and 180 miles north of the state capital of Jackson.

The new building has traditional Greek Revival architecture to match the architectural style of the campus, and it is state-of-the-art in terms of instructional space.

The University of Mississippi is the fourth oldest state-supported law school in the nation. The School of Law is fully approved by the American Bar Association and is a long-standing member of the Association of American Law Schools.

Library and Physical Facilities

Designed to enhance clinical experiences for students, the Robert C. Khayat School of Law is the only LEED-certified building in the state of Mississippi. It features a student lounge and courtyard, student organizations suite, group study rooms, Career Services interview rooms, Moot Court suite, café and dining room and classrooms with advanced technology to offer an outstanding learning environment to our students. It also holds suites for our various legal clinics, the *Mississippi Law Journal*, and has a lecture theater seating 220 people.

In addition, the Grisham Law Library is planned for collaborative learning as well as quiet study and research. Occupying two floors on the building's west side, it contains a classic, light-filled reading room; group-study rooms of varying sizes that can be reserved online; a computer lab with new, fully equipped workstations and high-speed printers; and over 300 seats at open tables, generously sized carrels, and comfortable leather club chairs and sofas. The library's information resources include approximately 135,000 titles in print, electronic and other formats, and subscriptions to a wide range of online legal information systems and databases.

Admission

Admission to law school is gained by committee approval based upon an applicant's credentials. These credentials include a satisfactory LSAT score and an acceptable academic record at the undergraduate level. A bachelor's degree from an accredited school is required before an applicant can register for law school.

There are no prelaw requisites. Every applicant must take the LSAT and register with LSAC's Credential Assembly Service. An LSAT score obtained more than five years before application is not valid, and the applicant will be required to retake the test. Applications are available the September preceding admission, with the application completion deadline for both summer and fall enrollment being March 1. However, early application is encouraged. Applicants who file late risk being placed on a waiting list.

Although the LSAT and GPA are the most important factors in the admission process, other considerations are (1) grade patterns and progression; (2) quality of undergraduate institution; (3) difficulty of major field of study; (4) number of years since bachelor's degree was earned; (5) job experience; (6) social, personal, or economic circumstances that may have affected college grades or performance on the LSAT or academic record; (7) nonacademic achievements; (8) letters of recommendation; and (9) residency.

Entrance Dates

Students are given the option to enter in the summer or fall of each admission year. Because summer and fall enrollees are considered as one class, the same standards are applied in the decision-making process.

Curriculum

First-year students complete a set curriculum focused on the development of analytical skills and a foundation of substantive knowledge. Additionally, the first year features an innovative two-week January Skill Session devoted to concrete lawyering proficiencies, such as negotiation and drafting skills. Second- and third-year students select their own courses and area(s) of emphasis from among a wide range of doctrinal and practical courses, including seminars, clinics, and skills courses focused on litigation, transactions, counseling, and public service. The curriculum offers generous opportunities for students to pursue **in-depth study** in areas such as constitutional theory and civil rights, legal ethics, business and commercial transactions, banking and securities law, environmental law, taxation, health law and bioethics, bankruptcy, and family law. Students may also elect to pursue a **certificate in criminal law** with courses such as cybercrime, sentencing, white-collar crime, and international criminal law.

Clinical Programs

Civil Legal Clinic—Students provide legal services to low-income clients in public service programs focused on elder law, tax law, consumer law, child advocacy, housing law, legislation, domestic violence, family law, and business development.

Criminal Appeals Clinic—Students represent indigent clients during criminal appeals, briefing and arguing cases before the Mississippi Supreme Court and Mississippi Court of Appeals.

Prosecutorial Externship Program—Combines classroom instruction and placements with local, state, and federal agencies to prepare students for careers as prosecutors. In the externships, students represent the government in criminal matters by filing motions, making oral arguments to judges, and appearing before juries.

Mississippi Innocence Project—Students litigate wrongful conviction claims on behalf of state prisoners. Cases entail examination of forensic and DNA evidence, witness interviews, and in-depth investigation into claims of actual innocence. Students also work to on criminal justice reform efforts, such as DNA testing legislation.

Student Activities

The University of Mississippi School of Law has an active student body that participates in almost 30 student organizations. The **Law School Student Body** (LSSB) serves as the student government and includes the honor council and student liaisons to faculty committees. Other organizations include, but are not limited to the Environmental Law Society, OUTlaw, Public Interest Law Foundation, Business Law Society, and the Gorove Society of International Law.

The *Mississippi Law Journal*, serving the Mississippi Bar since 1928, operates as the primary law review of The University of Mississippi School of Law. Its scholarly publication includes general-interest articles authored by students, faculty, scholars, and practitioners focusing on both regional and national issues.

The *Mississippi Sports Law Review* is a student-run scholarly publication producing a biannual journal that addresses current legal issues that arise in collegiate and professional sports.

The **Moot Court Board** offers students the opportunity to compete interscholastically in both trial and appellate advocacy events around the country. Led by back-to-back national championships in the National Environmental Law Moot Court Competition, the Board has achieved a top-25 ranking each of the past three years for its appellate advocacy

program. Further, students also take part in national-level competitions focused on negotiations, transactions, and interviewing and counseling.

Summer-Abroad Programs

The School of Law offers an opportunity to earn up to six semester credit hours in its summer session held annually in England at Downing College, Cambridge University. Classes offered are for full academic credit and are subject to the same academic standards maintained in the domestic program.

Career Services

The Career Services Office, staffed by a director and an assistant director, helps students develop individualized career plans and provides instruction on job search and career development skills. The staff also facilitates access to employers and employment resources through programming, job listings, and on campus interviews. The law school is an active member of NALP and annually participates in the Atlanta Legal Hiring Conference, the Equal Justice Works Public Interest Career Fair, the Patent Law Interview Program, and the Southeastern Minority Job Fair.

APPLICANT PROFILE

The University of Mississippi School of Law
This grid includes only applicants who earned 120–180 LSAT scores under standard administrations.

LSAT Score	3.75 + Apps	Adm	3.50–3.74 Apps	Adm	3.25–3.49 Apps	Adm	3.00–3.24 Apps	Adm	2.75–2.99 Apps	Adm	2.50–2.74 Apps	Adm	2.25–2.49 Apps	Adm	2.00–2.24 Apps	Adm	Below 2.00 Apps	Adm	No GPA Apps	Adm	Total Apps	Adm
175–180	0	0	0	0	0	0	0	0	0	0	0	0	0	0	0	0	0	0	0	0	0	0
170–174	0	0	2	2	1	0	0	0	0	0	0	0	0	0	0	0	0	0	0	0	3	2
165–169	4	4	7	7	6	6	1	1	4	4	3	0	2	0	0	0	0	0	0	0	27	22
160–164	26	25	26	26	35	34	23	20	25	8	7	3	6	2	2	0	1	0	1	0	152	118
155–159	51	49	88	80	112	71	78	22	52	13	24	1	10	0	1	0	3	1	2	1	421	238
150–154	72	40	103	22	127	20	98	17	61	4	35	1	12	0	6	0	2	0	8	0	524	104
145–149	34	7	50	13	60	6	64	6	48	1	32	1	9	0	6	0	2	0	3	0	308	34
140–144	3	1	19	4	33	3	21	1	26	0	11	0	12	0	6	0	2	0	5	0	138	9
135–139	0	0	2	0	6	0	11	0	7	0	13	0	2	0	1	0	2	0	2	0	46	0
130–134	0	0	1	0	1	0	3	0	2	0	4	0	1	0	3	0	0	0	0	0	15	0
125–129	0	0	0	0	1	0	0	0	0	0	0	0	1	0	0	0	0	0	0	0	2	0
120–124	0	0	0	0	0	0	0	0	0	0	0	0	0	0	0	0	0	0	0	0	0	0
Total	190	126	298	154	382	140	299	67	225	30	129	6	55	2	25	0	12	1	21	1	1636	527

Apps = Number of Applicants
Adm = Number Admitted
Reflects 100% of the total applicant pool; highest LSAT data reported.

MISSISSIPPI COLLEGE SCHOOL OF LAW

151 E. Griffith Street
Jackson, MS 39201
Phone: 601.925.7152; Fax: 601.925.7166
E-mail: lawadmissions@mc.edu; Website: http://law.mc.edu

ABA
Approved
Since
1980

The Basics

Type of school	Private
Term	Semester
Application deadline	6/1
Application fee	$0
Financial aid deadline	6/1
Can first year start other than fall?	Yes
Student to faculty ratio	16.5 to 1
# of housing spaces available restricted to law students	
graduate housing for which law students are eligible	

Faculty and Administrators

	Total Spr	Total Fall	Men Spr	Men Fall	Women Spr	Women Fall	Minorities Spr	Minorities Fall
Full-time	28	26	13	13	15	13	5	3
Other full-time	0	0	0	0	0	0	0	0
Deans, librarians, & others who teach	6	6	4	4	2	2	1	1
Part-time	73	84	41	46	32	38	6	8
Total	107	116	58	63	49	53	12	12

JD Enrollment and Ethnicity

	Men #	Men %	Women #	Women %	Full-Time #	Full-Time %	Part-Time #	Part-Time %	1st-Year #	1st-Year %	Total #	Total %	JD Degs. Awd.
All Hispanics	4	1.2	3	1.3	7	1.3	0	0.0	5	2.3	7	1.2	3
Am. Ind./AK Nat.	1	0.3	2	0.9	3	0.5	0	0.0	2	0.9	3	0.5	0
Asian	3	0.9	2	0.9	5	0.9	0	0.0	3	1.4	5	0.9	2
Black/Af. Am.	20	5.8	28	12.1	46	8.3	2	9.5	16	7.4	48	8.3	12
Nat. HI/Pac. Isl.	0	0.0	0	0.0	0	0.0	0	0.0	0	0.0	0	0.0	0
2 or more races	0	0.0	0	0.0	0	0.0	0	0.0	0	0.0	0	0.0	0
Subtotal (minor.)	28	8.1	35	15.2	61	11.0	2	9.5	26	12.1	63	10.9	17
Nonres. Alien	0	0.0	0	0.0	0	0.0	0	0.0	0	0.0	0	0.0	0
White/Cauc.	303	87.8	186	80.5	470	84.7	19	90.5	169	78.6	489	84.9	147
Unknown	14	4.1	10	4.3	24	4.3	0	0.0	20	9.3	24	4.2	1
Total	345	59.9	231	40.1	555	96.4	21	3.6	215	37.3	576		165

Curriculum

	Full-Time	Part-Time
Typical first-year section size	69	1
Is there typically a "small section" of the first-year class, other than Legal Writing, taught by full-time faculty	No	No
If yes, typical size offered last year		
# of classroom course titles beyond first-year curriculum	87	
# of upper division courses, excluding seminars, with an enrollment: Under 25	87	
25–49	22	
50–74	16	
75–99	5	
100+	0	
# of seminars	14	
# of seminar positions available	285	
# of seminar positions filled	213	0
# of positions available in simulation courses	777	
# of simulation positions filled	622	1
# of positions available in faculty supervised clinical courses	52	
# of faculty supervised clinical positions filled	25	0
# involved in field placements	154	0
# involved in law journals	40	0
# involved in moot court or trial competitions	73	0
# of credit hours required to graduate	90	

Transfers

Transfers in	0
Transfers out	10

Tuition and Fees

	Resident	Nonresident
Full-time	$29,150	$29,150
Part-time		
Tuition Guarantee Program	Y	

Living Expenses

Estimated living expenses for singles

Living on campus	Living off campus	Living at home
$21,225	$21,225	$21,225

MISSISSIPPI COLLEGE SCHOOL OF LAW

ABA
Approved
Since
1980

GPA and LSAT Scores

	Total	Full-Time	Part-Time
# of apps	1,717	1,714	3
# of offers	990	987	3
# of matrics	214	212	2
75% GPA	3.44	3.44	4.00
Median GPA	3.19	3.19	3.79
25% GPA	2.78	2.78	3.79
75% LSAT	152	152	153
Median LSAT	149	149	152
25% LSAT	147	147	152

Grants and Scholarships (from prior year)

	Total #	Total %	Full-Time #	Full-Time %	Part-Time #	Part-Time %
Total # of students	547		536		11	
Total # receiving grants	164	30.0	164	30.6	0	0.0
Less than 1/2 tuition	65	11.9	65	12.1	0	0.0
Half to full tuition	39	7.1	39	7.3	0	0.0
Full tuition	41	7.5	41	7.6	0	0.0
More than full tuition	19	3.5	19	3.5	0	0.0
Median grant amount			$12,000		$0	

Informational and Library Resources

Total amount spent on library materials	$1,066,096
Study seating capacity inside the library	385
# of full-time equivalent professional librarians	5
Hours per week library is open	104
# of open, wired connections available to students	0
# of networked computers available for use by students	30
Has wireless network?	Y
Requires computer?	N

JD Attrition (from prior year)

	Academic #	Other #	Total #	Total %
1st year	5	16	21	9.8
2nd year	0	1	1	0.6
3rd year	0	0	0	0.0
4th year	0	0	0	0.0

Employment (9 months after graduation)

For up-to-date employment data, go to employmentsummary.abaquestionnaire.org on the ABA website.

Bar Passage Rates

First-time takers	163	Reporting %	82.21
Average school %	71.64	Average state %	81.29
Average pass difference	–9.65		

Jurisdiction	Takers	Passers	Pass %	State %	Diff %
Mississippi	104	74	71.15	80.28	–9.13
Tennessee	16	10	62.50	84.24	–21.74
Alabama	8	6	75.00	84.91	–9.91
Illinois	3	3	100.00	89.38	10.62
Texas	3	3	100.00	82.68	17.32

MISSISSIPPI COLLEGE SCHOOL OF LAW

151 E. Griffith Street
Jackson, MS 39201
Phone: 601.925.7152; Fax: 601.925.7166
E-mail: lawadmissions@mc.edu; Website: http://law.mc.edu

Introduction to MC Law School

Mississippi College School of Law (MC Law) is in downtown Jackson, Mississippi, and serves as a state-of-the-art legal center for the mid-South. Jackson is the state capital, boasts a metropolitan population of 480,000, and is the political, cultural, and commercial center of Mississippi. Forty-eight percent of all Mississippi attorneys work in the Jackson metro area.

MC Law's attractive campus includes an administrative building, a modern classroom building, electronic courtrooms, a nationally recognized law library, a student center, and a new Advocacy Center. A safe and convenient student parking lot adjoins the law school. Within walking distance of the law school lies the state legislature, federal and state administrative agencies, and federal and state courts.

MC Law is part of Mississippi College—a university located in nearby Clinton, Mississippi, that has a liberal arts undergraduate program, nursing school, graduate school, physician assistant school, business school, and law school. MC Law is accredited by the American Bar Association and is a member of the Association of American Law Schools, the International Association of Law Schools, and the American Society of Comparative Law. Graduates of MC Law are eligible to take the bar examination in all 50 states.

Admission Procedures

When admitting students, the Admissions Office uses a "whole-person" concept and considers undergraduate GPA, LSAT score, and personal or academic achievements and honors. Every applicant must take the LSAT and register for the Credential Assembly Service (CAS) prior to being considered for admission. There is no application fee if an online application is used. The school makes admission decisions on a rolling basis to permit early notification. Decisions are made without discrimination on the basis of race, religion, gender, orientation, age, military service, or national origin. A summer start program is available. The application deadline is June 15. When an applicant is accepted, a deposit of $250 is required to reserve a seat in the entering class. A second deposit of $250 is required at a specified date. Upon enrollment, these nonrefundable payments are credited to the applicant's tuition. Tuition is locked in so that a student pays the same tuition throughout law school with no subsequent increase. All applicants are automatically considered for merit-based scholarships that exceed $2 million.

Dynamic Learning Environment

The diversity of the student body adds to the learning environment. Over 60 percent of our students come from outside Mississippi. Many students have work experience, military service, or advanced degrees. This diversity fosters an exciting exchange of ideas inside and outside the classroom. Our students receive one-on-one attention and interaction with professors that extend beyond the classroom. The school is dedicated to maintaining a supportive learning environment. Because of our size and collegial atmosphere, students form lasting relationships with one another, collaborate on team projects, and are active in a variety of cocurricular and extracurricular activities.

Curriculum and Course Offerings

MC Law offers a broad curriculum which integrates the theoretical aspects of the law with practical, hands-on training. First-year law students are required to take fundamental courses that focus on the major doctrinal areas of law, as well as development of legal writing and research skills. MC Law offers a broad range of second- and third-year elective courses. Our curriculum emphasizes the following disciplines: litigation and dispute resolution, family law, business and tax law, bioethics and health law, international law, and advocacy. MC Law offers a Louisiana Civil Law Certificate program for those who want to practice in Louisiana or to study comparative law. The law school operates on a semester basis. Students may begin their studies in June or August. Summer and intersession terms are available to second- and third-year students who wish to accelerate or enrich their studies. An Executive Program allows students to attend on a part-time basis.

Faculty

Teaching is our strength. Our faculty members have impeccable credentials and are leaders in their fields of study. From insurance to international law and from constitutional law to ethics, our professors are regularly cited in courts, scholarly journals, and the media. MC Law is renowned for the extraordinary level of interaction between faculty and students. Because of our strategic location, federal and state judges and some of the best legal practitioners teach as adjunct professors, giving our students valuable practical training and helpful networking opportunities.

Legal Centers at MC Law

MC Law maintains legal centers to allow a subject area to be developed through course offerings, speakers, moot court teams, student organizations, externships, and cocurricular activities. MC Law supports these centers: Family and Children's Law, Bioethics and Health Law, Litigation and Dispute Resolution, Business and Tax Law, Public Service Law, and International and Comparative Law.

International and Comparative Law Center

The International and Comparative Law Center permits our students to take a global focus in their legal education. In addition to the international law-related courses the center oversees, students can participate in legal studies in Merida, Mexico; Seoul, South Korea; and Berlin, Germany. The Center coordinates a series of speakers and programs with an international theme.

Externship Skills Training Program

At MC Law, classroom theory and practical application go hand in hand. In addition to courses in legal doctrine, a wide range of instruction in the skills of modern practice is offered to second- and third-year students. Student externs work alongside practicing attorneys in government offices and public interest organizations. Depending on the particular externship, students present cases in court, interview witnesses, prepare pleadings, take depositions, negotiate with opposing parties, research legal issues, and draft court opinions. This program allows students to practice in the real world what they have learned in more traditional law school classes and gain experience prior to graduation. Students may take an externship in their home state. Many students secure employment as a result of this extern program.

Student Activities

The *Mississippi College Law Review* is a legal journal edited and published by law students who are selected on the basis of grades and the ability to do creative scholarly research and writing. Membership on the *Law Review* staff is recognized as both an honor and a unique educational experience. The law school also provides an appellate advocacy program administered by the Moot Court Board, composed of second- and third-year students. This required program provides students with instruction and practice in both brief writing and oral argument. The school's legal aid office allows students to acquire client interviewing skills and substantive practical experience while providing a valuable pro bono service.

The Law Student Bar Association is the organized student government of the law school. Other student activities include two national legal fraternity chapters, Phi Alpha Delta and Phi Delta Phi; student chapters of the Mississippi Association for Justice and the Defense Lawyers Association; the Women's Student Bar Association; the Federal Bar Association; the Black Law Students Association (BLSA); and the Environmental Law Association.

Career Services

The Career Services Office assists in job placement and career development. In addition to the traditional on-campus interviews, the law school participates in regional interviews and offers a series of workshops throughout the year. Students are encouraged to work in local or national public interest or government agencies through the MC Law/Federal Work-Study public interest program. Graduates are employed by major law firms, corporations, and government agencies throughout the United States, with a primary focus in the Southeast. Students have received clerkships with the United States Court of Appeals, United States District Courts, and the appellate and trial courts of various states. A number of graduates serve as JAG officers in the military services.

Minority Student Program

The law school offers a variety of programs to assist minority students: scholarships/stipends, student organizations, and an academic support program. Minority students are strongly encouraged to apply, and each applicant's entire record will be carefully considered. We are interested in students who have overcome challenges in life and who are the first in their family to attend law school. The BLSA chapter is an active contributor to student life and reaches out to the local community.

Library

The law library has a collection of more than 360,000 volumes and is committed to acquiring materials for both the immediate and the long-term needs of the law school. Emphasis is placed on development of the collections of statutes, legal periodicals, federal and state legislative materials, reports of federal and state appellate courts, federal administrative agency materials, specialized loose-leaf services, and microforms and treatises that support our teaching and scholarship. The library is a member of the American Association of Law Libraries. The technology division supports a Wi-Fi system and a computer help desk for students. Newly constructed study rooms and a coffee bar are available for group use.

Advocacy

MC Law sends 25 teams to regional and national trial and appellate advocacy moot court competitions. Preparation for these competitions flows from intraschool competitions in the 1L year and a required appellate advocacy course in the 2L year. These programs give MC Law students skills and confidence that serve them well in practice. MC Law's advocacy program has received national recognition and is well known in the legal community.

APPLICANT PROFILE

Mississippi College School of Law
This grid includes only applicants who earned 120–180 LSAT scores under standard administrations.

LSAT Score	GPA								
	3.75 +	3.50–3.74	3.25–3.49	3.00–3.24	2.75–2.99	2.50–2.74	2.25–2.49	2.00–2.24	Below 2.00
175–180									
170–174									
165–169									
160–164									
155–159									
150–154									
145–149									
140–144									
135–139									
130–134									
125–129									
120–124									

■ Good Possibility □ Possible ▨ Unlikely

UNIVERSITY OF MISSOURI SCHOOL OF LAW

Office of Admissions, 103 Hulston Hall
Columbia, MO 65211
Phone: 573.882.6042, toll-free: 888.MULaw4U; Fax: 573.882.9625
E-mail: mulawadmissions@missouri.edu; Website: www.law.missouri.edu

The Basics

Type of school	Public
Term	Semester
Application deadline	3/1
Application fee	$60
Financial aid deadline	3/1
Can first year start other than fall?	No
Student to faculty ratio	12.7 to 1
# of housing spaces available restricted to law students	
graduate housing for which law students are eligible	

Curriculum

	Full-Time	Part-Time
Typical first-year section size	75	0
Is there typically a "small section" of the first-year class, other than Legal Writing, taught by full-time faculty	Yes	No
If yes, typical size offered last year	35	
# of classroom course titles beyond first-year curriculum	129	
# of upper division courses, excluding seminars, with an enrollment: Under 25	101	
25–49	22	
50–74	7	
75–99	6	
100+	0	
# of seminars	2	
# of seminar positions available	42	
# of seminar positions filled	39	0
# of positions available in simulation courses	218	
# of simulation positions filled	118	0
# of positions available in faculty supervised clinical courses	47	
# of faculty supervised clinical positions filled	46	0
# involved in field placements	60	0
# involved in law journals	94	0
# involved in moot court or trial competitions	170	0
# of credit hours required to graduate	89	

Faculty and Administrators

	Total Spr	Total Fall	Men Spr	Men Fall	Women Spr	Women Fall	Minorities Spr	Minorities Fall
Full-time	28	28	19	18	9	10	3	2
Other full-time	0	0	0	0	0	0	0	0
Deans, librarians, & others who teach	9	10	6	7	3	3	3	2
Part-time	20	11	12	7	8	4	0	0
Total	57	49	37	32	20	17	6	4

JD Enrollment and Ethnicity

	Men #	Men %	Women #	Women %	Full-Time #	Full-Time %	Part-Time #	Part-Time %	1st-Year #	1st-Year %	Total #	Total %	JD Degs. Awd.
All Hispanics	6	2.2	7	4.3	13	3.1	0	0.0	4	2.8	13	3.0	5
Am. Ind./AK Nat.	0	0.0	1	0.6	1	0.2	0	0.0	1	0.7	1	0.2	1
Asian	4	1.5	5	3.1	9	2.1	0	0.0	1	0.7	9	2.1	4
Black/Af. Am.	14	5.2	17	10.5	30	7.1	1	16.7	13	9.2	31	7.2	6
Nat. HI/Pac. Isl.	0	0.0	0	0.0	0	0.0	0	0.0	0	0.0	0	0.0	0
2 or more races	10	3.7	3	1.9	12	2.8	1	16.7	6	4.3	13	3.0	2
Subtotal (minor.)	34	12.6	33	20.4	65	15.3	2	33.3	25	17.7	67	15.5	18
Nonres. Alien	0	0.0	2	1.2	2	0.5	0	0.0	0	0.0	2	0.5	1
White/Cauc.	223	82.9	123	75.9	342	80.5	4	66.7	111	78.7	346	80.3	120
Unknown	12	4.5	4	2.5	16	3.8	0	0.0	5	3.5	16	3.7	2
Total	269	62.4	162	37.6	425	98.6	6	1.4	141	32.7	431		141

Transfers

Transfers in	9
Transfers out	3

Tuition and Fees

	Resident	Nonresident
Full-time	$17,784	$34,000
Part-time		
Tuition Guarantee Program		N

Living Expenses

Estimated living expenses for singles

Living on campus	Living off campus	Living at home
$16,542	$16,542	$16,542

UNIVERSITY OF MISSOURI SCHOOL OF LAW

ABA
Approved
Since
1923

GPA and LSAT Scores

	Total	Full-Time	Part-Time
# of apps	851	851	0
# of offers	348	348	0
# of matrics	133	133	0
75% GPA	3.70	3.70	0.00
Median GPA	3.49	3.49	0.00
25% GPA	3.18	3.18	0.00
75% LSAT	161	161	0
Median LSAT	158	158	0
25% LSAT	156	156	0

Grants and Scholarships (from prior year)

	Total #	Total %	Full-Time #	Full-Time %	Part-Time #	Part-Time %
Total # of students	446		442		4	
Total # receiving grants	250	56.1	250	56.6	0	0.0
Less than 1/2 tuition	221	49.6	221	50.0	0	0.0
Half to full tuition	21	4.7	21	4.8	0	0.0
Full tuition	0	0.0	0	0.0	0	0.0
More than full tuition	8	1.8	8	1.8	0	0.0
Median grant amount			$5,000		$0	

Informational and Library Resources

Total amount spent on library materials	$827,619
Study seating capacity inside the library	502
# of full-time equivalent professional librarians	7
Hours per week library is open	73
# of open, wired connections available to students	0
# of networked computers available for use by students	56
Has wireless network?	Y
Requires computer?	N

JD Attrition (from prior year)

	Academic #	Other #	Total #	Total %
1st year	5	14	19	12.6
2nd year	0	2	2	1.3
3rd year	0	0	0	0.0
4th year	0	0	0	0.0

Employment (9 months after graduation)

For up-to-date employment data, go to employmentsummary.abaquestionnaire.org on the ABA website.

Bar Passage Rates

First-time takers	140	Reporting %	87.14
Average school %	95.08	Average state %	90.24
Average pass difference	4.84		

Jurisdiction	Takers	Passers	Pass %	State %	Diff %
Missouri	122	116	95.08	90.24	4.84

UNIVERSITY OF MISSOURI SCHOOL OF LAW

Office of Admissions, 103 Hulston Hall
Columbia, MO 65211
Phone: 573.882.6042, toll-free: 888.MULaw4U; Fax: 573.882.9625
E-mail: mulawadmissions@missouri.edu; Website: www.law.missouri.edu

Introduction

The University of Missouri School of Law (MU) is a dynamic and collegial community. Founded in 1839, MU was the first state university west of the Mississippi River. Established in 1872, the School of Law has had an enviable history of service to the state and the nation. Graduates include judges, governors, attorneys general, and legislators who serve locally and nationwide. The law school is a charter member of the Association of American Law Schools (AALS) and is fully accredited.

Located in Columbia, MU is 35 miles from Jefferson City, the state capital. The location provides law students with easy access to the legislature, the Supreme Court, and the various offices of state government. In addition to living and studying in one of America's most livable cities, students are within two hours of the cultural, athletic, and entertainment centers of St. Louis and Kansas City. Students and their families enjoy Columbia's Midwestern friendliness. It combines a small-town feel with the diversity and opportunities often found only in larger cities. Columbia truly offers something for everyone.

Faculty

At MU Law, the faculty focus is on students and is achieved through teaching, research, and service. An open-door policy for students is the norm. MU Law faculty are recognized for achievement inside and outside the classroom through teaching awards, appointments on committees and boards, and publications in national academic journals and media outlets throughout the state and nation.

Enrollment/Student Body

The law school student body is composed of students from numerous states and foreign countries. This diverse and collegial group of students provides a wealth of experience and fosters a stimulating learning environment. MU maintains a smaller incoming class size to foster greater interaction with faculty and peers.

Curriculum

The academic program leading to the JD degree traditionally consists of six semesters of study. One seven-week semester is offered each summer. To graduate, students must complete 89 semester hours, including a writing requirement and a professional perspectives requirement. Students must have a minimum average of 77.5 on a scale of 65 to 100 to graduate.

Student Experience

John K. Hulston Hall was designed with the student experience in mind. Students have many different comfortable places to study, including individual study carrels housed in the library. Due to the law school's focus on student collaboration, many lounge and meeting spaces are available. Students have 24-hour access to the building, including the law library.

Students have access to amenities located on the MU campus, including the student recreation facility, the campus library, and the newly renovated student center. The law school is part of the large university campus with NCAA Division I athletics, concert series, and diverse programming.

Special Programs: Alternative Dispute Resolution

The Center for the Study of Dispute Resolution is a unique feature of the law school and provides national leadership in this area of the law. First-year law students are exposed to an overview of dispute resolution processes. MU also offers a variety of dispute resolution courses and other educational opportunities for second- and third-year students.

One of the first programs of its kind in the country, the center houses a Master of Laws in Dispute Resolution degree program.

Dual-Degree Programs

The School of Law offers several dual-degree programs, including Business Administration, Public Affairs, Health Administration, Library Science, Human Development and Family Studies, Economics, Educational Leadership and Policy Analysis, and Personal Financial Planning. Through the world's first school of journalism, students can pursue a joint master's or doctoral degree.

The law school has established other dual-degree programs to meet individual interests. Traditionally, dual-degree students spend their first year in the School of Law. (Students must fulfill the entrance requirements of both schools.)

Certificate Programs

The law school offers a certificate in Alternative Dispute Resolution. In addition, a certificate in Journalism, the Digital Globe, or the European Union is available to law students through the Graduate School. Students can complete these certificates by concentrating a set number of elective hours in these areas.

Study-Abroad Programs

The MU School of Law offers opportunities to study abroad in South Africa, Austria, and the United Kingdom.

Since 2004, MU has conducted a summer program in Cape Town, South Africa, in cooperation with the University of the Western Cape. The program consists of three two-credit courses in different areas of comparative law and includes field trips to the Cape of Good Hope, the Stellenbosch wine region, Robben Island, and other scenic and historical locations.

In cooperation with Georgia State University, MU offers a Summer Academy in International Commercial Arbitration. Based at Johannes Kepler University in Linz, Austria, the program includes field trips to Vienna, Salzburg, Budapest, Venice, and other locations in Central and Eastern Europe.

MU is also part of the London Law Consortium. This group of six ABA-approved schools offers second- and third-year students a culturally enriching spring semester in London.

With law school approval, students can also obtain academic credit while studying in another ABA-approved law school's international program.

Clinics and Externships

MU provides students with practical experience to enhance lawyering skills and to promote awareness of ethical issues. An active externship and judicial clerkship program and five clinical programs—the Criminal Prosecution Clinic, Family Violence Clinic, Legislative Clinic, Mediation Clinic, and Innocence Clinic—have been developed to enrich student skills. Students, subject to the rules of the Supreme Court of Missouri, are able to practice law in these programs.

Student Activities

All students are eligible to participate in the writing competition for membership on the *Missouri Law Review*, the *Journal of Dispute Resolution*, or the *Journal of Environmental and Sustainability Law*. Also open to all students, the Board of Advocates sponsors a wide variety of advocacy competitions. The school has chapters of the Order of Barristers, the Student Bar Association, and two legal fraternities. In addition, MU is one of only 81 law schools with a chapter of the Order of the Coif, the national law school honor society. Other student organizations, encompassing almost every aspect of social and academic life, are also offered.

Admission

A faculty committee reviews all applications. In many cases, factors other than the GPA or LSAT score have proven to be determinative. If the LSAT is repeated, the committee will consider all scores in its evaluation.

Students are encouraged to apply early and to visit the law school. The Admissions Office can arrange for students to meet with an admission counselor, attend a class, and tour the facility.

Expenses and Financial Aid

MU offers an outstanding value. Out-of-state students can be eligible to obtain Missouri residency after their first year of law school. Financial assistance is available to students in the form of scholarships, federal loans, research assistantships, and work-study.

Career Development

The Office of Career Development serves as a liaison between students or alumni and prospective employers. Students are taught to use their analytical and advocacy skills to achieve career goals. Workshops, seminars, and individual counseling are offered to help students successfully employ their lawyering skills. Additional resources include a smart suite which allows students to interview with prospective employers, facilitates student employment, and creates the ability to record and replay mock interviews.

APPLICANT PROFILE

University of Missouri School of Law
This grid includes only applicants who earned 120–180 LSAT scores under standard administrations.

LSAT Score	GPA								
	3.75 +	3.50–3.74	3.25–3.49	3.00–3.24	2.75–2.99	2.50–2.74	2.25–2.49	2.00–2.24	Below 2.00
175–180									
170–174									
165–169									
160–164									
155–159									
150–154									
145–149									
140–144									
135–139									
130–134									
125–129									
120–124									

■ Good Possibility   □ Possible   ▨ Unlikely

This chart is to be used as a general guide only. Nonnumerical factors are strongly considered for all applicants.

UNIVERSITY OF MISSOURI—KANSAS CITY SCHOOL OF LAW

5100 Rockhill Road
Kansas City, MO 64110
Phone: 816.235.1644; Fax: 816.235.5276
E-mail: law@umkc.edu; Website: www.law.umkc.edu

The Basics

Type of school	Public
Term	Semester
Application deadline	3/1
Application fee	$60
Financial aid deadline	3/1
Can first year start other than fall?	No
Student to faculty ratio	13.3 to 1
# of housing spaces available restricted to law students	
graduate housing for which law students are eligible	500

Faculty and Administrators

	Total		Men		Women		Minorities	
	Spr	Fall	Spr	Fall	Spr	Fall	Spr	Fall
Full-time	28	31	15	20	13	11	4	2
Other full-time	4	6	3	3	1	3	0	1
Deans, librarians, & others who teach	9	9	5	5	4	4	0	0
Part-time	34	14	27	11	7	3	0	0
Total	75	60	50	39	25	21	4	3

Curriculum

		Full-Time	Part-Time
Typical first-year section size		57	0
Is there typically a "small section" of the first-year class, other than Legal Writing, taught by full-time faculty		No	No
If yes, typical size offered last year			
# of classroom course titles beyond first-year curriculum		134	
# of upper division courses, excluding seminars, with an enrollment:	Under 25	101	
	25–49	27	
	50–74	11	
	75–99	8	
	100+	0	
# of seminars		14	
# of seminar positions available		232	
# of seminar positions filled		180	0
# of positions available in simulation courses		548	
# of simulation positions filled		413	0
# of positions available in faculty supervised clinical courses		161	
# of faculty supervised clinical positions filled		99	0
# involved in field placements		113	0
# involved in law journals		127	0
# involved in moot court or trial competitions		53	0
# of credit hours required to graduate		91	

JD Enrollment and Ethnicity

	Men		Women		Full-Time		Part-Time		1st-Year		Total		JD Degs. Awd.
	#	%	#	%	#	%	#	%	#	%	#	%	
All Hispanics	10	3.3	5	3.0	12	2.7	3	10.7	3	1.9	15	3.2	6
Am. Ind./AK Nat.	2	0.7	1	0.6	3	0.7	0	0.0	2	1.3	3	0.6	2
Asian	6	2.0	7	4.2	13	3.0	0	0.0	5	3.2	13	2.8	6
Black/Af. Am.	7	2.3	13	7.8	17	3.9	3	10.7	8	5.1	20	4.3	10
Nat. HI/Pac. Isl.	0	0.0	0	0.0	0	0.0	0	0.0	0	0.0	0	0.0	0
2 or more races	1	0.3	0	0.0	1	0.2	0	0.0	1	0.6	1	0.2	0
Subtotal (minor.)	26	8.7	26	15.6	46	10.5	6	21.4	19	12.1	52	11.2	24
Nonres. Alien	3	1.0	1	0.6	3	0.7	1	3.6	2	1.3	4	0.9	4
White/Cauc.	248	82.9	133	79.6	360	82.2	21	75.0	128	81.5	381	81.8	107
Unknown	22	7.4	7	4.2	29	6.6	0	0.0	8	5.1	29	6.2	19
Total	299	64.2	167	35.8	438	94.0	28	6.0	157	33.7	466		154

Transfers

Transfers in	9
Transfers out	5

Tuition and Fees

	Resident	Nonresident
Full-time	$16,730	$31,772
Part-time	$10,199	$19,224
Tuition Guarantee Program		N

Living Expenses

Estimated living expenses for singles

Living on campus	Living off campus	Living at home
$17,354	$18,060	$11,440

UNIVERSITY OF MISSOURI—KANSAS CITY SCHOOL OF LAW

ABA
Approved
Since
1936

GPA and LSAT Scores

	Total	Full-Time	Part-Time
# of apps	892	846	46
# of offers	357	350	7
# of matrics	149	146	3
75% GPA	3.66	3.66	3.71
Median GPA	3.35	3.35	3.53
25% GPA	3.01	3.00	3.36
75% LSAT	157	157	164
Median LSAT	155	155	163
25% LSAT	153	153	159

Grants and Scholarships (from prior year)

	Total #	Total %	Full-Time #	Full-Time %	Part-Time #	Part-Time %
Total # of students	483		459		24	
Total # receiving grants	187	38.7	185	40.3	2	8.3
Less than 1/2 tuition	138	28.6	136	29.6	2	8.3
Half to full tuition	33	6.8	33	7.2	0	0.0
Full tuition	8	1.7	8	1.7	0	0.0
More than full tuition	8	1.7	8	1.7	0	0.0
Median grant amount			$7,500		$2,025	

Informational and Library Resources

Total amount spent on library materials	$820,493
Study seating capacity inside the library	399
# of full-time equivalent professional librarians	8
Hours per week library is open	100
# of open, wired connections available to students	46
# of networked computers available for use by students	55
Has wireless network?	Y
Requires computer?	N

JD Attrition (from prior year)

	Academic #	Other #	Total #	Total %
1st year	10	0	10	5.5
2nd year	1	7	8	5.2
3rd year	0	0	0	0.0
4th year	0	0	0	0.0

Employment (9 months after graduation)

For up-to-date employment data, go to employmentsummary.abaquestionnaire.org on the ABA website.

Bar Passage Rates

First-time takers	147	Reporting %	88.44
Average school %	88.46	Average state %	90.24
Average pass difference	−1.78		

Jurisdiction	Takers	Passers	Pass %	State %	Diff %
Missouri	130	115	88.46	90.24	−1.78

UNIVERSITY OF MISSOURI—KANSAS CITY SCHOOL OF LAW

5100 Rockhill Road
Kansas City, MO 64110
Phone: 816.235.1644; Fax: 816.235.5276
E-mail: law@umkc.edu; Website: www.law.umkc.edu

Introduction

The University of Missouri—Kansas City School of Law (UMKC) takes pride in being the urban public law school with the small liberal arts feel. UMKC serves and collaborates with the legal communities in two major metropolitan areas of the states of Missouri and Kansas. Students, faculty, and alumni actively lead and participate in professional activities with area bar associations, lawyers, and law firms, as well as government agencies and the judiciary.

UMKC law school graduates hold important positions in legal arenas across the country, distinguishing themselves in private practice, government service, academia, and corporate roles. UMKC is one of only six law schools to have educated both a president of the United States and a US Supreme Court justice. Many other UMKC alumni currently serve as judges at the federal, state, and local levels.

UMKC School of Law is committed to providing a high-quality legal education in a professional and supportive environment, concentrating always on the foundations of good lawyering: respect for people, knowledge, ideas, and justice. UMKC is one of the most student-friendly law schools in the country, with outstanding student-faculty interaction and alumni providing mentoring to our students through the UMKC Inns of Court program.

Founded in 1895, the school is accredited by the American Bar Association (ABA) and is a member of the Association of American Law Schools (AALS).

Faculty

Our faculty are outstanding scholars and excellent teachers who use their extensive practice experience to bring the curriculum to life. For example, Professors Tony Luppino and Bob Downs teach a Business Organizations Lab along with their doctrinal course that allows students to practice the skills they are learning. And, under the guidance of seasoned trial lawyer Rafe Foreman, Douglas Stripp Dean's Distinguished Professor and Director of Advocacy, students learn to see advocacy in action by strategizing, developing, and trying cases both for competition and actual practice. Our faculty are nationally recognized in their areas of expertise. For example, Professor Doug Linder's Famous Trials website receives seven to nine million hits per month, and Professor Bill Black speaks nationally and internationally on the financial crisis and the causes of (and potential cures for) the economic collapse. The faculty do this impressive work while taking time to know and interact with students on a regular basis.

Library and Physical Facilities

Office suites shared by faculty and students are designed to foster the exchange of ideas and to promote collegiality between faculty and students. The school has over 121,000 square feet of usable space, which includes our recently renovated Thompson Courtroom with viewing theater, the new Stoup Courtroom, and the new Tom and Vina Hyde Collaborative Instructional and Technology Library, ensuring that students learn in a technologically advanced environment.

The Leon E. Bloch Law Library combines the traditions of print media with emerging electronic media in preparing the lawyer for the future and supporting the legal community.

Curriculum

Courses are taught in a variety of formats. Many of the substantive courses include problem solving, simulations, service learning, and the development of skills components essential to the practice of law. The first-year JD program offers a yearlong intensive Introduction to Law and Lawyering Processes course. The upper-level program includes a combination of required courses, as well as a broad selection of elective courses.

All first-year sections have 60 or fewer students, and first-year legal research and writing classes have no more than 24 students each. Among the 114 upper-division courses offered each year, 84 have an enrollment of fewer than 25 students, and 19 more have an enrollment of between 25 and 49 students. A law school strategies program that includes supervised, structured study groups, a lecture series, and weekly workshops is open to all students. Additional opportunities include a weeklong summer program, which is available on a limited basis.

While the school's innovative Solo and Small Firm Initiative prepares students for general practice, those seeking more focused study can pursue one of our five emphasis areas: Litigation; Business and Entrepreneurial Law; Urban, Land Use and Environmental Law; International, Comparative, and Foreign Law; and Law in Service to Children and Families. These emphases build on our long-standing tradition of excellence in these areas and prepare students to enter the job market with specialized knowledge and skills.

A part-time day program is available for those students with family or career responsibilities who are unable to enroll on a full-time basis. Full-time students may graduate in two and one-half years by attending two summer sessions.

JD/MBA and JD/MPA Programs

The School of Law has established dual-degree programs with the Henry W. Bloch School of Business and Public Administration. The program allows students to earn a JD degree and a Master of Business Administration or Master of Public Administration degree on an accelerated basis through cross-acceptance of some credit hours. Applicants must satisfy the admission requirements of each school.

JD/LLM and Combined-Degree Programs

The School of Law has adopted combined-degree programs that allow qualified JD students to apply, with approval, up to 12 credit hours of UMKC tax or estate planning courses toward an LLM on an accelerated basis, generally requiring only one additional semester (or two summer sessions) beyond that required for the JD degree.

Student Activities

The law school's location in a metropolitan area provides many opportunities for students to engage in real-life representation of clients in clinical programs. More than 50 percent of our students take advantage of internships and clinics that include UMKC's Child and Family Services Clinic, Tax Clinic, Entrepreneurial Legal Services Clinic, and the Innocence Project Clinic. The school also offers a number of field placements. Students may also participate in our Pro Bono/Public Service Program designed to instill a sense of civic responsibility and meet the needs of those with limited means in the community.

Students obtain advanced skills development in trial and appellate advocacy through sequenced upper-level courses and competition participation. Students also participate in client counseling and negotiation competitions. UMKC teams frequently win regional and national honors in these competitions. UMKC has the best record of any law school in the country in advancing its teams to the national finals of the Negotiation Competition.

UMKC benefits from an active Student Bar Association, which represents students and plays an important role in establishing school policy. Three national legal fraternities have chapters at the school, as do Black Law Students, Hispanic Law Students, Jewish Law Students, Asian Pacific Islander Law Students, Women Law Students, and Nontraditional Law Students. Additional student organizations specialize in many areas of interest, with over 30 total student groups. Students also have the opportunity to participate in study-abroad programs that visit China, Ireland, and Oxford, England. The school provides many opportunities for development of personal relationships that will last throughout one's career.

Admission

The School of Law restricts the number of students admitted each year to achieve a favorable faculty-to-student ratio,

providing the best possible legal education for each student enrolled. Because many more people apply to the law school than there are seats available, admission is highly competitive. While substantial weight is given to the LSAT score and undergraduate GPA, the law school and its faculty believe that using factors in addition to the LSAT and GPA contribute to an intellectually stimulating and diverse environment. These factors include racial, ethnic, cultural, gender, age, or other forms of diversity; triumphs over challenges and barriers based on societal discrimination or economic disadvantage; outstanding leadership qualities; serious and sustained commitment to significant public or community service; advanced or specialized educational achievements; accomplishments or qualities indicative of potential for contributing to scholarly and creative initiatives; and potential to provide high-quality legal services to clients.

Students may be admitted with a bachelor's degree from an approved institution, or in appropriate cases, with 90 hours of acceptable academic work. Arrangements can be made to meet with students and faculty, visit a class, or tour the school.

Career Services

The Office of Career Services assists law students in exploring and defining career options. It also provides advice and assistance in résumé preparation and interviewing skills. The office sponsors a series of programs to introduce students to a variety of career opportunities. Participants in the school's Judicial Clerkship Initiative have enjoyed a high placement rate in pursuing clerkships with state and federal judges.

APPLICANT PROFILE

University of Missouri—Kansas City School of Law

LSAT Score	GPA								
	3.75 +	3.50–3.74	3.25–3.49	3.00–3.24	2.75–2.99	2.50–2.74	2.25–2.49	2.00–2.24	Below 2.00
175–180	■	■	■	■	■			▒	▒
170–174	■	■	■	■	■			▒	▒
165–169	■	■	■	■	■			▒	▒
160–164	■	■	■	■	■			▒	▒
155–159	■	■	■	■				▒	▒
150–154	■	■	■	■				▒	▒
145–149	▒	▒	▒	▒	▒	▒		▒	▒
140–144	▒	▒	▒	▒	▒	▒		▒	▒
135–139	▒	▒	▒	▒	▒	▒		▒	▒
130–134	▒	▒	▒	▒	▒	▒		▒	▒
125–129	▒	▒	▒	▒	▒	▒		▒	▒
120–124	▒	▒	▒	▒	▒	▒		▒	▒

■ Good Possibility   ☐ Possible   ▒ Unlikely

UNIVERSITY OF MONTANA SCHOOL OF LAW

32 Campus Drive
Missoula, MT 59812
Phone: 406.243.4311
E-mail: lawadmis@umontana.edu; Website: www.umt.edu/law

ABA
Approved
Since
1923

The Basics

Type of school	Public
Term	Semester
Application deadline	3/15
Application fee	$60
Financial aid deadline	3/1
Can first year start other than fall?	No
Student to faculty ratio	14.9 to 1
# of housing spaces available restricted to law students	
graduate housing for which law students are eligible	252

Faculty and Administrators

	Total		Men		Women		Minorities	
	Spr	Fall	Spr	Fall	Spr	Fall	Spr	Fall
Full-time	14	14	7	8	7	6	4	2
Other full-time	0	0	0	0	0	0	0	0
Deans, librarians, & others who teach	7	6	4	3	3	3	0	0
Part-time	16	14	11	8	5	6	0	0
Total	37	34	22	19	15	15	4	2

JD Enrollment and Ethnicity

	Men		Women		Full-Time		Part-Time		1st-Year		Total		JD Degs. Awd.
	#	%	#	%	#	%	#	%	#	%	#	%	
All Hispanics	4	2.7	3	2.9	7	2.8	0	0.0	2	2.4	7	2.8	1
Am. Ind./AK Nat.	6	4.0	2	1.9	8	3.2	0	0.0	2	2.4	8	3.2	1
Asian	0	0.0	2	1.9	2	0.8	0	0.0	0	0.0	2	0.8	0
Black/Af. Am.	1	0.7	0	0.0	1	0.4	0	0.0	0	0.0	1	0.4	0
Nat. HI/Pac. Isl.	0	0.0	0	0.0	0	0.0	0	0.0	0	0.0	0	0.0	0
2 or more races	2	1.3	7	6.8	9	3.6	0	0.0	6	7.1	9	3.6	0
Subtotal (minor.)	13	8.7	14	13.6	27	10.7	0	0.0	10	11.8	27	10.7	2
Nonres. Alien	1	0.7	1	1.0	2	0.8	0	0.0	1	1.2	2	0.8	1
White/Cauc.	135	90.6	88	85.4	223	88.5	0	0.0	74	87.1	223	88.5	77
Unknown	0	0.0	0	0.0	0	0.0	0	0.0	0	0.0	0	0.0	4
Total	149	59.1	103	40.9	252	100.0	0	0.0	85	33.7	252		84

Curriculum

	Full-Time	Part-Time
Typical first-year section size	43	0
Is there typically a "small section" of the first-year class, other than Legal Writing, taught by full-time faculty	No	No
If yes, typical size offered last year		
# of classroom course titles beyond first-year curriculum	69	

# of upper division courses, excluding seminars with an enrollment:		
	Under 25	25
	25–49	7
	50–74	0
	75–99	0
	100+	0

# of seminars	25	
# of seminar positions available	370	
# of seminar positions filled	323	0
# of positions available in simulation courses	80	
# of simulation positions filled	80	0
# of positions available in faculty supervised clinical courses	26	
# of faculty supervised clinical positions filled	16	0
# involved in field placements	73	0
# involved in law journals	48	0
# involved in moot court or trial competitions	29	0
# of credit hours required to graduate	90	

Transfers

Transfers in	6
Transfers out	5

Tuition and Fees

	Resident	Nonresident
Full-time	$11,578	$27,513
Part-time		
Tuition Guarantee Program		N

Living Expenses

Estimated living expenses for singles

Living on campus	Living off campus	Living at home
$12,840	$12,840	$5,340

ABA
Approved
Since
1923

GPA and LSAT Scores

	Total	Full-Time	Part-Time
# of apps	429	429	0
# of offers	196	196	0
# of matrics	85	85	0
75% GPA	3.62	3.62	0.00
Median GPA	3.44	3.44	0.00
25% GPA	3.23	3.23	0.00
75% LSAT	157	157	0
Median LSAT	155	155	0
25% LSAT	152	152	0

Grants and Scholarships (from prior year)

	Total #	Total %	Full-Time #	Full-Time %	Part-Time #	Part-Time %
Total # of students	256		256		0	
Total # receiving grants	84	32.8	84	32.8	0	0.0
Less than 1/2 tuition	62	24.2	62	24.2	0	0.0
Half to full tuition	18	7.0	18	7.0	0	0.0
Full tuition	0	0.0	0	0.0	0	0.0
More than full tuition	4	1.6	4	1.6	0	0.0
Median grant amount			$3,600		$0	

Informational and Library Resources

Total amount spent on library materials	$891,867
Study seating capacity inside the library	360
# of full-time equivalent professional librarians	3
Hours per week library is open	77
# of open, wired connections available to students	178
# of networked computers available for use by students	36
Has wireless network?	Y
Requires computer?	N

JD Attrition (from prior year)

	Academic #	Other #	Total #	Total %
1st year	0	1	1	1.2
2nd year	0	6	6	7.0
3rd year	0	0	0	0.0
4th year	0	0	0	0.0

Employment (9 months after graduation)

For up-to-date employment data, go to employmentsummary.abaquestionnaire.org on the ABA website.

Bar Passage Rates

First-time takers	76	Reporting %	93.42
Average school %	91.56	Average state %	92.90
Average pass difference	−1.34		

Jurisdiction	Takers	Passers	Pass %	State %	Diff %
Montana	68	62	91.18	93.45	−2.27
Alaska	3	3	100.00	80.55	19.45

UNIVERSITY OF MONTANA SCHOOL OF LAW

32 Campus Drive
Missoula, MT 59812
Phone: 406.243.4311
E-mail: lawadmis@umontana.edu; Website: www.umt.edu/law

Introduction

The University of Montana (UM) School of Law is located in Missoula on the west slopes of the Rocky Mountains. Missoula is situated halfway between Yellowstone and Glacier National Parks and is surrounded by several of the largest designated wilderness areas in the continental United States. The city is known for its outdoor opportunities and quality of life.

The School of Law was established in 1911 and serves as a legal center for the state. It has been accredited by the Association of American Law Schools (AALS) since 1914 and by the American Bar Association (ABA) since 1923. As one of the smallest law schools in the nation, the University of Montana School of Law offers students a congenial academic, intellectual, and social environment.

As the School of Law enters its second century of preparing students for the practice of law and community leadership, we have expanded and substantially renovated our building. Students now enjoy new classrooms, formal and informal study spaces, clinic and student-group offices, and community areas.

UM's Program

The University of Montana School of Law integrates theory and practice throughout its curriculum to instill entry-level practice and competence in its graduates. The School of Law's curriculum, teaching methodology, and assessment techniques are designed to address the following components of a lawyer's work: (1) knowledge of the law, (2) ability to apply legal rules to solve problems, (3) ability to use lawyering skills (e.g., negotiation and client counseling), (4) perspective on the societal role and responsibility of lawyers, and (5) sensitivity to the dynamics of social and interpersonal interaction.

The school has created three distinctive programs to acquaint first-year students with the ways lawyers think and work: (1) the Introductory Program, (2) the Lawyer Skills Program, and (3) the Law Firm Program. In the Introductory Program, students are initiated into the legal culture by surveying legal history, the American legal system, the litigation process, legal writing, and legal analysis and jurisprudence. The School of Law is one of the few to introduce first-year students to the skills involved in dispute resolution, including client counseling, legal document drafting, and oral argument. UM's program encourages students to cooperate and collaborate rather than compete as they begin to think and work as lawyers. Entering students belong to *law firms*—groups of seven students directed by upper-class students.

The school has long emphasized performance in its curriculum. The school's Legal Writing and Dispute Resolution programs represent a comprehensive approach to lawyering skills. Students master specific transactional skills such as planning an estate, drafting a contract, and creating a small business.

The upper-division clinical training program provides students with a wide range of opportunities to earn required academic credit by working on cases under the supervision of faculty and practicing attorneys in Missoula. The clinical offerings include ACLU, Associated Students of UM Legal Services, Child Support Enforcement Division, Criminal Defense, DNRC Forestry and Trust Land Management Divisions, Federal Judicial, Indian Law, Innocence Project, Land Use, Mediation, Missoula City Attorney's Office, Missoula County Attorney's Office, Montana Legal Services Association, National Wildlife Federation, Natural Resource, Office of State Public Defender, Rocky Mountain Elk Foundation, UM Legal Counsel's Office, USDA General Counsel, and US Department of Justice.

Special Programs

The School of Law offers three certificate programs: (1) Environmental and Natural Resource Law and the opportunity to participate in natural resource clinics, the *Public Land and Resources Law Review*, the Environmental Law Group, and the Environmental Law Moot Court Team; (2) Alternative Dispute Resolution and the opportunity to participate in the Mediation Clinic; and (3) American Indian Law and the opportunity to participate in the Indian Law Clinic, the Native American Law Student Association (NALSA), and the NALSA Moot Court Team.

In conjunction with the School of Law, UM's graduate school offers a certificate in Natural Resources Conflict Resolution. It is the only graduate-level certificate program in the Rocky Mountain West region specifically designed to provide students with a working knowledge of the theory and practice of collaboration, consensus building, and conflict resolution as they apply to natural resources and the environment.

The School of Law offers three joint-degree programs. Students can combine their law degrees with a Master of Science in Environmental Studies, a Master of Business Administration, or a Master of Public Administration. These programs can lead to completion of the joint degree in as little as three years. The School of Law also offers concentrations in the areas of Trial Advocacy, Business, and Tax Law.

Admission

A committee of law faculty reviews applications. Candidates must be of good moral character, have intellectual promise, and have a baccalaureate degree from an approved college or university prior to matriculation. Applicants are considered in resident or nonresident pools. The School of Law seeks a diverse student body and welcomes applications from members of groups historically underrepresented in the legal profession.

The School of Law recommends that you submit your application as soon as possible. We begin reviewing completed applications as they are submitted. Applications are not considered complete until all application materials, including the LSAC Law School Report, are received. If your file is completed by February 15, you will be notified of a decision (admit, deny, or retain for further review) by March 15. If your file is completed by March 15, you will be notified of a decision by April 15. Files completed after March 15 may be considered on a space-available basis.

The most important admission criteria are the cumulative undergraduate GPA and the LSAT score. If the LSAT is repeated, all scores will be used in evaluating the applicant. The admission committee weighs such factors as writing ability; college attended; trend in grades; quality of work in difficult courses; experience prior to application to law school, including graduate study; ability to overcome economic or other disadvantages; and change in performance after an absence from school.

The school recognizes a commitment to provide full opportunities for the study of law and entry into the legal profession of qualified members of groups (notably racial and ethnic minorities) who have been victims of discrimination.

Student Activities

All students are members of the Student Bar Association (SBA). The SBA contributes to the professional development and the social life of the student body. Other student organizations include the American Association for Justice (AAJ), ACLU, American Constitution Society, Student Animal Legal Defense Fund, Christian Legal Society, Environmental Law Group, Federalist Society, Intellectual Property Group, International Law Student Association, Military Law Society, Montana Public Interest Law Coalition, Native American Law Student Association, Outdoor Recreation Law Group, OUTlaws, Clayberg Inn of Phi Delta Phi national law fraternity, Rural Advocacy League, and Women's Law Caucus. The *Montana Law Review* and the *Public Land and Resources Law Review* afford supplementary training in analyzing legal problems precisely and presenting legal issues cogently.

The School of Law is proud of its performance in interscholastic competitions. Nearly every year, the School of Law fields teams that compete at the national level. Most recently, UM won the 2000 National Moot Court Competition championship. UM won the ATLA trial competition national championship in 1992 and the national ABA Client Counseling Competition championship in 1990. Additionally, the Environmental Law Moot Court Team, which competes at the National Environmental Law Moot Court Competition each year, won the Best Oralist Award in 2002, and competed in the final round in 2005. Likewise, the Indian Law and Jessup International Law Moot Court teams have won oralist and brief honors in their respective national and, in the case of the Jessup team, international competitions.

APPLICANT PROFILE

University of Montana School of Law

LSAT Score	GPA								
	3.75 +	3.50–3.74	3.25–3.49	3.00–3.24	2.75–2.99	2.50–2.74	2.25–2.49	2.00–2.24	Below 2.00
175–180	■	■	■	■	■	□	□	▨	▨
170–174	■	■	■	■	■	□	□	▨	▨
165–169	■	■	■	■	■	□	□	▨	▨
160–164	■	■	■	■	■	□	□	▨	▨
155–159	■	■	■	■	■	□	□	▨	▨
150–154	■	■	■	■	□	□	□	▨	▨
145–149	□	□	□	▨	▨	▨	▨	▨	▨
140–144	□	□	▨	▨	▨	▨	▨	▨	▨
135–139	▨	▨	▨	▨	▨	▨	▨	▨	▨
130–134	▨	▨	▨	▨	▨	▨	▨	▨	▨
125–129	▨	▨	▨	▨	▨	▨	▨	▨	▨
120–124	▨	▨	▨	▨	▨	▨	▨	▨	▨

■ Good Possibility   □ Possible   ▨ Unlikely

UNIVERSITY OF NEBRASKA COLLEGE OF LAW

PO Box 830902
Lincoln, NE 68583-0902
Phone: 402.472.8333; Fax: 402.472.5185
E-mail: lawadm@unl.edu; Website: http://law.unl.edu/

The Basics

Type of school	Public
Term	Semester
Application deadline	3/1
Application fee	$50
Financial aid deadline	5/1
Can first year start other than fall?	No
Student to faculty ratio	12.9 to 1
# of housing spaces available restricted to law students	
graduate housing for which law students are eligible	247

Faculty and Administrators

	Total		Men		Women		Minorities	
	Spr	Fall	Spr	Fall	Spr	Fall	Spr	Fall
Full-time	24	27	18	18	6	9	2	3
Other full-time	2	2	2	2	0	0	0	0
Deans, librarians, & others who teach	10	9	5	4	5	5	0	0
Part-time	27	28	18	17	9	11	0	0
Total	63	66	43	41	20	25	2	3

Curriculum

	Full-Time	Part-Time
Typical first-year section size	70	0
Is there typically a "small section" of the first-year class, other than Legal Writing, taught by full-time faculty	Yes	No
If yes, typical size offered last year	37	
# of classroom course titles beyond first-year curriculum	86	

# of upper division courses, excluding seminars, with an enrollment:		
	Under 25	62
	25–49	23
	50–74	10
	75–99	1
	100+	1

# of seminars	10	
# of seminar positions available	122	
# of seminar positions filled	122	0
# of positions available in simulation courses	454	
# of simulation positions filled	445	0
# of positions available in faculty supervised clinical courses	56	
# of faculty supervised clinical positions filled	55	0
# involved in field placements	25	0
# involved in law journals	31	0
# involved in moot court or trial competitions	72	0
# of credit hours required to graduate	93	

JD Enrollment and Ethnicity

	Men		Women		Full-Time		Part-Time		1st-Year		Total		JD Degs. Awd.
	#	%	#	%	#	%	#	%	#	%	#	%	
All Hispanics	7	2.9	2	1.3	9	2.3	0	0.0	4	3.1	9	2.3	2
Am. Ind./AK Nat.	2	0.8	2	1.3	4	1.0	0	0.0	1	0.8	4	1.0	1
Asian	3	1.3	2	1.3	5	1.3	0	0.0	1	0.8	5	1.3	6
Black/Af. Am.	4	1.7	2	1.3	6	1.5	0	0.0	2	1.6	6	1.5	6
Nat. HI/Pac. Isl.	0	0.0	0	0.0	0	0.0	0	0.0	0	0.0	0	0.0	0
2 or more races	0	0.0	0	0.0	0	0.0	0	0.0	0	0.0	0	0.0	0
Subtotal (minor.)	16	6.7	8	5.2	24	6.1	0	0.0	8	6.2	24	6.1	15
Nonres. Alien	2	0.8	0	0.0	2	0.5	0	0.0	0	0.0	2	0.5	0
White/Cauc.	221	92.5	146	94.8	366	93.4	1	100.0	121	93.8	367	93.4	115
Unknown	0	0.0	0	0.0	0	0.0	0	0.0	0	0.0	0	0.0	0
Total	239	60.8	154	39.2	392	99.7	1	0.3	129	32.8	393		130

Transfers

Transfers in	1
Transfers out	2

Tuition and Fees

	Resident	Nonresident
Full-time	$13,887	$29,966
Part-time		
Tuition Guarantee Program		N

Living Expenses

Estimated living expenses for singles

Living on campus	Living off campus	Living at home
$14,310	$13,858	$7,678

UNIVERSITY OF NEBRASKA COLLEGE OF LAW

*ABA
Approved
Since
1923*

GPA and LSAT Scores

	Total	Full-Time	Part-Time
# of apps	825	825	0
# of offers	400	400	0
# of matrics	128	128	0
75% GPA	3.79	3.79	0.00
Median GPA	3.51	3.51	0.00
25% GPA	3.33	3.33	0.00
75% LSAT	159	159	0
Median LSAT	157	157	0
25% LSAT	153	153	0

Grants and Scholarships (from prior year)

	Total #	Total %	Full-Time #	Full-Time %	Part-Time #	Part-Time %
Total # of students	414		412		2	
Total # receiving grants	201	48.6	201	48.8	0	0.0
Less than 1/2 tuition	102	24.6	102	24.8	0	0.0
Half to full tuition	59	14.3	59	14.3	0	0.0
Full tuition	0	0.0	0	0.0	0	0.0
More than full tuition	40	9.7	40	9.7	0	0.0
Median grant amount			$8,000		$0	

Informational and Library Resources

Total amount spent on library materials	$786,771
Study seating capacity inside the library	372
# of full-time equivalent professional librarians	6
Hours per week library is open	109
# of open, wired connections available to students	2
# of networked computers available for use by students	6
Has wireless network?	Y
Requires computer?	N

JD Attrition (from prior year)

	Academic #	Other #	Total #	Total %
1st year	5	8	13	8.9
2nd year	1	1	2	1.5
3rd year	0	0	0	0.0
4th year	0	0	0	0.0

Employment (9 months after graduation)

For up-to-date employment data, go to
employmentsummary.abaquestionnaire.org on the ABA website.

Bar Passage Rates

First-time takers	121	Reporting %	80.17
Average school %	96.90	Average state %	88.62
Average pass difference	8.28		

Jurisdiction	Takers	Passers	Pass %	State %	Diff %
Nebraska	64	64	100.00	89.83	10.17
Iowa	15	15	100.00	91.09	8.91
Colorado	13	10	76.92	82.79	-5.87
Arizona	5	5	100.00	80.74	19.26

UNIVERSITY OF NEBRASKA COLLEGE OF LAW

PO Box 830902
Lincoln, NE 68583-0902
Phone: 402.472.8333; Fax: 402.472.5185
E-mail: lawadm@unl.edu; Website: http://law.unl.edu/

Introduction

Founded in 1891, the University of Nebraska College of Law offers an excellent legal education at a reasonable cost. Large enough to offer a diverse curriculum, yet small enough to ensure that students are not lost in the crowd, Nebraska Law is a charter member of the AALS and is accredited by the ABA. It is located on the University of Nebraska's East Campus in the state's capital, Lincoln, which has a population of approximately 260,000 and offers a vibrant array of opportunities.

Curriculum

Nebraska Law's academic year runs from late August to early May. A two-day orientation before the beginning of the fall semester introduces first-year students to the college. Each incoming student is assigned a faculty advisor who can answer questions about law school, course selections, and career goals. The first-year curriculum is 18 credit hours the first semester and 15 credit hours the second semester. It includes international law, civil procedure, contracts, criminal law, legal writing, property, and torts. Courses in the second and third years are elective, with the exception of required courses in constitutional law, professional responsibility, a research seminar, and a professional skills course. The curriculum encompasses a broad range of subjects, and offers particular depth in the areas of litigation, alternative dispute resolution, taxation, environmental, employment, international, space and telecommunications, and corporate and commercial law. Students who wish to focus on a particular area of the law may pursue the Litigation Skills Program of Concentrated Study, the Intellectual Property Law Program of Concentrated Study, the Business Transactions Program of Concentrated Study, or the Solo Practitioner/Small Firm Practice Program of Concentrated Study. Students may also develop an individualized program of concentrated study in areas of law that are of particular interest.

The College of Law provides an Academic Resource Program for first-year students to assist them in developing and improving fundamental skills such as note taking, briefing cases, legal analysis, outlining, and writing examinations. The program provides weekly skills classes as well as a series of lectures and individual academic counseling.

Although completing the requirements for a JD degree normally takes three years, it is possible to graduate in two and a half years by attending summer school. The college offers no night classes and rarely accepts part-time students. Students receiving the JD degree are qualified to practice in any state upon passage of that state's bar examination.

Skills and Clinical Education

In addition to establishing a solid foundation based on legal theory, students also need to develop practical skills to effectively represent clients and function as lawyers. Nebraska Law has offered courses that help develop such skills through "learning by doing" since the early 1970s. Professional skills-development courses offered include pretrial litigation, trial advocacy, appellate advocacy, mediation, negotiations, alternative dispute resolution, client interviewing and counseling, construction law, business planning, family law, and criminal law. These classes allow second- and third-year students to develop lawyering skills in simulated settings. The College of Law also offers students the opportunity to learn practical skills by handling real cases for actual clients in a clinical setting. In the Civil Clinic, third-year students represent clients in and out of court in matters such as bankruptcy, domestic relations, immigration, and landlord-tenant disputes. Students in the Criminal Clinic prosecute misdemeanor cases in Lancaster County. As part of the Entrepreneurship Clinic, students will advise start-up businesses on basic legal issues.

Joint-Degree Programs

The college's interdisciplinary program in law and psychology is recognized as one of the finest in the nation. Nebraska Law also participates in eight other joint-degree programs and will work with students individually to design programs in disciplines not covered by a formal program. In each program, students will earn two degrees with fewer credit hours and in less time than if the degrees were pursued separately. The formal joint-degree programs include JD/MBA (Business), JD/MPA (Accounting), JD/PhD (Psychology), JD/MA (Political Science), JD/MCRP (Community and Regional Planning), JD/MA (Journalism), JD/MA (Social Gerontology), and JD/MPH (Public Health).

Library and Physical Facilities

The Schmid Law Library has a collection of about 395,000 volumes and a full complement of the latest developments in information technology. The library provides seating for 335 students and has 14 group-study rooms, each with full access to power and fast data connections, both wired and wireless, for the best access to the Internet from any place in the library. The five professional librarians and the staff strive to create a service-oriented environment for legal research and scholarship. All these attributes combine to make the Schmid Law Library not only the largest, but the most effective, efficient, and friendliest law library in the region.

In addition to the library, Nebraska Law's classrooms, Hamann Auditorium, and Welpton Courtroom feature attractive decor, adjustable chairs, laptop compatibility, and state-of-the-art technology.

Student Activities

The *Nebraska Law Review*, published by a student editorial board, publishes leading articles from well-known authorities in their fields, as well as student notes and comments. Other extracurricular academic programs include the National Moot Court Competition, Client Counseling Competition, and National Trial Competition.

Students can become involved in over 25 activities and organizations, including the Student Bar Association, Women's Law Caucus, Black Law Students Association, Nebraska Entertainment and Sports Law Association, Equal Justice Society, Federalist Society, Student Intellectual Property Law Association, Multicultural Legal Society, and two national legal fraternities.

Career Services

The College of Law operates its own Career Services Office for students seeking full-time employment or summer clerkships. The office provides students with a variety of placement-related services and also organizes on-campus interviews by private law firms, governmental agencies, corporations, and other potential employers. Students will also benefit from programs hosted by the Career Services Office on various areas of law, alternative legal careers, networking, and drafting and perfecting résumés and cover letters.

Admission

Admission decisions are made on a rolling basis. Students are required to have a bachelor's degree from an accredited institution, take the LSAT, and register with LSAC's Credential Assembly Service. In making its decisions, the Admissions Committee seeks to identify those individuals who have the ability to compete successfully in a rigorous academic environment. The major factors that the committee considers are the applicant's LSAT score and the applicant's undergraduate grade-point average. However, admission decisions are not simply a function of the numbers. The committee also takes into account any upward (or downward) trend in the applicant's academic performance over time, quality of the applicant's undergraduate institution, course of study, personal statement, work experience, graduate study, extracurricular activities, letters of recommendation, and other information supplied by the applicant.

Nebraska Law hosts a number of open houses and other campus visit programs throughout the year. Go to http://law.unl.edu/visit for more information.

APPLICANT PROFILE

The University of Nebraska College of Law has opted not to include a detailed applicant profile that isolates the undergraduate grade-point average and LSAT score for applied and admitted students. While these credentials are important, the Admissions Committee reviews all information supplied by the applicant and considers many factors beyond the LSAT score and undergraduate grade-point average in making admission decisions.

UNIVERSITY OF NEVADA, LAS VEGAS, WILLIAM S. BOYD SCHOOL OF LAW

4505 Maryland Parkway, Box 451003
Las Vegas, NV 89154-1003
Phone: 702.895.2440; Fax: 702.895.2414
E-mail: request@law.unlv.edu; Website: www.law.unlv.edu

ABA
Approved
Since
2000

The Basics

Type of school	Public
Term	Semester
Application deadline	3/15
Application fee	$50
Financial aid deadline	2/1
Can first year start other than fall?	No
Student to faculty ratio	11.9 to 1
# of housing spaces available restricted to law students	
graduate housing for which law students are eligible	60

Faculty and Administrators

	Total		Men		Women		Minorities	
	Spr	Fall	Spr	Fall	Spr	Fall	Spr	Fall
Full-time	26	32	10	11	16	21	5	7
Other full-time	0	1	0	0	0	1	0	0
Deans, librarians, & others who teach	9	9	4	4	5	5	2	1
Part-time	14	20	11	15	3	5	0	1
Total	49	62	25	30	24	32	7	9

Curriculum

	Full-Time	Part-Time
Typical first-year section size	54	32
Is there typically a "small section" of the first-year class, other than Legal Writing, taught by full-time faculty	No	No
If yes, typical size offered last year		

# of classroom course titles beyond first-year curriculum		88
# of upper division courses, excluding seminars, with an enrollment:	Under 25	84
	25–49	25
	50–74	8
	75–99	1
	100+	0
# of seminars		16
# of seminar positions available		197
# of seminar positions filled	139	15
# of positions available in simulation courses	337	
# of simulation positions filled	216	62
# of positions available in faculty supervised clinical courses	52	
# of faculty supervised clinical positions filled	52	5
# involved in field placements	142	10
# involved in law journals	58	16
# involved in moot court or trial competitions	31	3
# of credit hours required to graduate	89	

JD Enrollment and Ethnicity

	Men		Women		Full-Time		Part-Time		1st-Year		Total		JD Degs. Awd.
	#	%	#	%	#	%	#	%	#	%	#	%	
All Hispanics	23	8.6	29	14.6	36	11.1	16	11.3	14	10.2	52	11.2	12
Am. Ind./AK Nat.	3	1.1	5	2.5	6	1.9	2	1.4	2	1.5	8	1.7	4
Asian	25	9.4	25	12.6	35	10.8	15	10.6	17	12.4	50	10.8	14
Black/Af. Am.	12	4.5	14	7.0	10	3.1	16	11.3	4	2.9	26	5.6	5
Nat. HI/Pac. Isl.	1	0.4	2	1.0	2	0.6	1	0.7	2	1.5	3	0.6	0
2 or more races	0	0.0	0	0.0	0	0.0	0	0.0	0	0.0	0	0.0	0
Subtotal (minor.)	64	24.1	75	37.7	89	27.5	50	35.5	39	28.5	139	29.9	35
Nonres. Alien	0	0.0	0	0.0	0	0.0	0	0.0	0	0.0	0	0.0	1
White/Cauc.	189	71.1	114	57.3	217	67.0	86	61.0	90	65.7	303	65.2	82
Unknown	13	4.9	10	5.0	18	5.6	5	3.5	8	5.8	23	4.9	10
Total	266	57.2	199	42.8	324	69.7	141	30.3	137	29.5	465		128

Transfers

Transfers in	5
Transfers out	5

Tuition and Fees

	Resident	Nonresident
Full-time	$24,752	$35,752
Part-time	$16,126	$23,182
Tuition Guarantee Program		N

Living Expenses

Estimated living expenses for singles

Living on campus	Living off campus	Living at home
$17,610	$20,680	$11,010

UNIVERSITY OF NEVADA, LAS VEGAS, WILLIAM S. BOYD SCHOOL OF LAW

ABA
Approved
Since
2000

GPA and LSAT Scores

	Total	Full-Time	Part-Time
# of apps	1,381	1,149	232
# of offers	294	246	48
# of matrics	140	104	36
75% GPA	3.64	3.63	3.66
Median GPA	3.39	3.43	3.29
25% GPA	3.12	3.18	2.91
75% LSAT	161	162	157
Median LSAT	159	159	156
25% LSAT	157	157	153

Grants and Scholarships (from prior year)

	Total #	Total %	Full-Time #	Full-Time %	Part-Time #	Part-Time %
Total # of students	475		347		128	
Total # receiving grants	184	38.7	154	44.4	30	23.4
Less than 1/2 tuition	77	16.2	52	15.0	25	19.5
Half to full tuition	81	17.1	80	23.1	1	0.8
Full tuition	0	0.0	0	0.0	0	0.0
More than full tuition	26	5.5	22	6.3	4	3.1
Median grant amount			$16,450		$9,584	

Informational and Library Resources

Total amount spent on library materials	$1,089,675
Study seating capacity inside the library	341
# of full-time equivalent professional librarians	7
Hours per week library is open	101
# of open, wired connections available to students	345
# of networked computers available for use by students	35
Has wireless network?	Y
Requires computer?	N

JD Attrition (from prior year)

	Academic #	Other #	Total #	Total %
1st year	2	11	13	8.9
2nd year	1	1	2	1.3
3rd year	1	0	1	0.7
4th year	0	0	0	0.0

Employment (9 months after graduation)

For up-to-date employment data, go to employmentsummary.abaquestionnaire.org on the ABA website.

Bar Passage Rates

First-time takers	146	Reporting %	89.73
Average school %	71.76	Average state %	72.72
Average pass difference	−0.96		

Jurisdiction	Takers	Passers	Pass %	State %	Diff %
Nevada	131	94	71.76	72.72	−0.96

UNIVERSITY OF NEVADA, LAS VEGAS, WILLIAM S. BOYD SCHOOL OF LAW

4505 Maryland Parkway, Box 451003
Las Vegas, NV 89154-1003
Phone: 702.895.2440; Fax: 702.895.2414
E-mail: request@law.unlv.edu; Website: www.law.unlv.edu

Introduction

The William S. Boyd School of Law, the first and only public law school in Nevada history, commenced classes in fall 1998 and now has graduated over 1,500 students. Located in a unique, dynamic, and continually growing metropolitan area, BSL offers its students an evolving social climate in which to study the law and observe and participate in its application. The law school is fully accredited by the American Bar Association and is a member of the Association of American Law Schools.

Faculty

The full-time faculty consists of experienced, accomplished, and well-respected legal educators. All faculty members have excellent credentials, experience, and reputations; all are people for whom teaching and mentoring of students is very important; and all are people who are eager to serve their community through scholarship, civic involvement, and various outreach programs. The law school also taps into the wealth of talent in the local bar for adjunct faculty who teach a variety of specialized courses.

Curriculum

The Boyd School of Law offers and encourages its students to undertake a generalist curriculum. Specific course offerings are constantly reviewed and revised as societal needs, student interest, and faculty resources change. The curriculum generally emphasizes the responsibilities, skills, and values required of members of the legal profession. This emphasis comes to the fore in Lawyering Process, a three-semester required course that offers students the opportunity to examine the relationship between legal analysis and other legal skills such as research, writing, oral advocacy, and client interviewing and counseling, with significant emphasis on professionalism and ethics.

Programs of Study

The law school offers a traditional three-year, full-time JD program, as well as a four-year, part-time JD program during evening hours and a four-year, part-time JD program during day hours. Additionally, three dual-degree programs have been established: Juris Doctor/Master of Business Administration, Juris Doctor/Master of Social Work, and Juris Doctor/PhD in Education.

Community Service

A unique aspect of a Boyd education is an early focus on service learning. Under the supervision of attorneys from Legal Aid Center of Southern Nevada, Nevada Legal Services, and the law school, all first-year students participate in a community service program directing informational workshops and providing legal information to those in need on the subjects of bankruptcy, foreclosure mediation, small claims, family law, paternity custody, immigration, mediation, and guardianship. After the first year, in our Partners in Pro Bono Program, students work one-on-one with attorney

mentors on pro bono cases. These programs are intended to acquaint students with the large unmet need for legal services and to instill a lasting commitment to community service and pro bono work.

Hands-on Experience

The Thomas and Mack Legal Clinic houses the school's "law firm" and offers an integrated academic and practice-based educational experience that teaches students to be reflective practitioners and community-oriented professionals. The clinic has focused on seven specific areas: appellate litigation, education, family justice, innocence, immigration, juvenile justice, and mediation. Additionally, the law school provides an extensive externship program. Working closely with the legal community, the law school has established a year-round program offering opportunities for students to extern with the federal and state judiciary, government and public service agencies, and Nevada and US legislatures.

Saltman Center for Conflict Resolution

The Saltman Center for Conflict Resolution was established in 2003 to provide a venue for advanced study of the nature of conflict and the methods through which conflicts may be resolved. The work of the center encompasses conflicts arising out of regional, national, and international concerns, in both the public and private sectors. Recognizing that a sophisticated understanding of conflict necessarily requires insights derived from disciplines other than law, the center places particular emphasis on interdisciplinary approaches to understanding and resolving disputes. The center's faculty teach courses on mediation, negotiations, alternative dispute resolution, and arbitration as well as a clinical offering in the area of mediation.

Student Activities

The *Nevada Law Journal* is a publication devoted to scholarly research on the subject of national legal interest as well as on issues of particular interest to the Nevada legal community.

The *UNLV Gaming Law Journal* is a journal of legal scholarship published by the students and dedicated to analyzing the law and policy implications of gaming case law, legislation, administrative regulations, and important gaming legal events.

The Society of Advocates is the school's appellate and trial forensic program. The society consists of an executive board and team members who participate in interscholastic competitions. Teams compete in mock trial, client counseling, negotiation, mediation, and alternative dispute resolution competitions, as well as traditional appellate advocacy. Boyd's teams have been very successful in winning regional, national, and international competitions.

Students also participate in over 30 student organizations.

Career Services

The Department of Career Services offers personalized career counseling, employment workshops, a job opportunity board, on-campus interviewing programs, and a state-of-the-art online job-search program to assist students.

Academic Success Program

The Boyd School of Law Academic Success Program provides students a comprehensive network of presentations, activities, tutorials, and workshops designed to stimulate learning and to amplify the classroom experience. The program supplements the curriculum with opportunities to enhance learning skills and develop more efficient and effective methods of studying, comprehending, and writing. As part of this program, the student-operated Center for Academic Success and Enrichment (CASE) offers students mentoring, advising, and tutoring.

Facility

The Boyd School of Law facility includes the William S. Boyd Hall, the James E. Rogers Center for Administration and Justice, and the Thomas and Mack Moot Court Facility. Classrooms include state-of-the art technology for presentations using PowerPoint, video, and document cameras, and are equipped to facilitate videoconferencing and distance learning. Classroom, lounge, and study space offer students indoor and outdoor wireless access seating areas where they can make productive use of their time between classes.

Library

The Wiener-Rogers Law Library holds the most substantial collection of legal materials in the state of Nevada. The library is staffed by excellent, service-oriented librarians who have come from major libraries across the country. Patrons and students have access to a core collection of important material in printed and micro formats. The library offers one computer lab and provides numerous carrels for individual study, as well as group study rooms. The growing library collection now exceeds 350,000 volumes and microform volume equivalents.

Admission

The Boyd School of Law seeks to enroll an academically well-qualified, accomplished, and diverse group of individuals who will contribute to the vitality of the school's educational program, the community, and the legal profession after graduation. Applicants for admission may demonstrate qualification and accomplishment through distinguished academic records as undergraduate or graduate students, successful careers, meaningful contributions to their communities, or successful efforts to meet challenges associated with race, ethnicity, gender, economic status, or disability. Students of diverse backgrounds, attitudes, and interests contribute to the breadth and quality of the classroom and nonclassroom dialogues, which are critical elements of legal education.

APPLICANT PROFILE

The Boyd School of Law has elected not to publish an applicant profile based on LSAT score and undergraduate GPA. Those two factors, while certainly important, are not the only factors taken into consideration. The Boyd School of Law uses no form of indexing system in reaching its admission decisions. Each completed application file is reviewed in its entirety.

NEW ENGLAND LAW | BOSTON

154 Stuart Street
Boston, MA 02116
Phone: 617.422.7210; Fax: 617.422.7201
E-mail: admit@nesl.edu; Website: www.nesl.edu

ABA
Approved
Since
1969

The Basics

Type of school	Private
Term	Semester
Application deadline	3/15
Application fee	$65
Financial aid deadline	4/5
Can first year start other than fall?	No
Student to faculty ratio	23.3 to 1
# of housing spaces available restricted to law students	
graduate housing for which law students are eligible	

Faculty and Administrators

	Total		Men		Women		Minorities	
	Spr	Fall	Spr	Fall	Spr	Fall	Spr	Fall
Full-time	36	37	23	24	13	13	4	4
Other full-time	1	1	0	1	1	0	0	0
Deans, librarians, & others who teach	6	5	3	2	3	3	0	0
Part-time	74	82	43	50	31	32	5	9
Total	117	125	69	77	48	48	9	13

Curriculum

	Full-Time	Part-Time
Typical first-year section size	99	92
Is there typically a "small section" of the first-year class, other than Legal Writing, taught by full-time faculty	No	No
If yes, typical size offered last year		
# of classroom course titles beyond first-year curriculum	154	
# of upper division courses, excluding seminars, with an enrollment: Under 25	84	
25–49	58	
50–74	12	
75–99	10	
100+	4	
# of seminars	40	
# of seminar positions available	524	
# of seminar positions filled	232	155
# of positions available in simulation courses	811	
# of simulation positions filled	452	193
# of positions available in faculty supervised clinical courses	75	
# of faculty supervised clinical positions filled	69	3
# involved in field placements	233	25
# involved in law journals	78	6
# involved in moot court or trial competitions	9	2
# of credit hours required to graduate	86	

JD Enrollment and Ethnicity

	Men		Women		Full-Time		Part-Time		1st-Year		Total		JD Degs. Awd.
	#	%	#	%	#	%	#	%	#	%	#	%	
All Hispanics	16	3.2	15	2.4	23	2.8	8	2.5	13	3.4	31	2.7	4
Am. Ind./AK Nat.	0	0.0	1	0.2	0	0.0	1	0.3	1	0.3	1	0.1	0
Asian	17	3.4	24	3.8	34	4.2	7	2.1	19	5.0	41	3.6	18
Black/Af. Am.	6	1.2	13	2.0	16	2.0	3	0.9	11	2.9	19	1.7	3
Nat. HI/Pac. Isl.	0	0.0	0	0.0	0	0.0	0	0.0	0	0.0	0	0.0	0
2 or more races	10	2.0	18	2.8	18	2.2	10	3.1	10	2.6	28	2.5	0
Subtotal (minor.)	49	9.7	71	11.1	91	11.2	29	8.9	54	14.2	120	10.5	25
Nonres. Alien	3	0.6	6	0.9	8	1.0	1	0.3	2	0.5	9	0.8	2
White/Cauc.	374	74.4	462	72.4	597	73.3	239	73.3	270	71.1	836	73.3	228
Unknown	77	15.3	99	15.5	119	14.6	57	17.5	54	14.2	176	15.4	53
Total	503	44.1	638	55.9	815	71.4	326	28.6	380	33.3	1141		308

Transfers

Transfers in	2
Transfers out	33

Tuition and Fees

	Resident	Nonresident
Full-time	$40,984	$40,984
Part-time	$30,760	$30,760
Tuition Guarantee Program		N

Living Expenses

Estimated living expenses for singles

Living on campus	Living off campus	Living at home
N/A	$21,030	$13,050

ABA Approved Since 1969

GPA and LSAT Scores

	Total	Full-Time	Part-Time
# of apps	3,164	2,529	635
# of offers	2,234	1,845	389
# of matrics	385	291	94
75% GPA	3.39	3.42	3.24
Median GPA	3.15	3.19	3.02
25% GPA	2.92	2.96	2.72
75% LSAT	153	154	152
Median LSAT	151	152	149
25% LSAT	149	149	148

Grants and Scholarships (from prior year)

	Total #	Total %	Full-Time #	Full-Time %	Part-Time #	Part-Time %
Total # of students	1,132		796		336	
Total # receiving grants	650	57.4	542	68.1	108	32.1
Less than 1/2 tuition	469	41.4	417	52.4	52	15.5
Half to full tuition	120	10.6	83	10.4	37	11.0
Full tuition	61	5.4	42	5.3	19	5.7
More than full tuition	0	0.0	0	0.0	0	0.0
Median grant amount			$10,000		$12,750	

Informational and Library Resources

Total amount spent on library materials	$1,171,676
Study seating capacity inside the library	507
# of full-time equivalent professional librarians	9
Hours per week library is open	104
# of open, wired connections available to students	159
# of networked computers available for use by students	64
Has wireless network?	Y
Requires computer?	N

JD Attrition (from prior year)

	Academic #	Other #	Total #	Total %
1st year	10	73	83	21.2
2nd year	2	2	4	1.1
3rd year	2	5	7	2.2
4th year	0	2	2	2.6

Employment (9 months after graduation)

For up-to-date employment data, go to employmentsummary.abaquestionnaire.org on the ABA website.

Bar Passage Rates

First-time takers	306	Reporting %	81.37
Average school %	87.54	Average state %	88.56

Average pass difference −1.02

Jurisdiction	Takers	Passers	Pass %	State %	Diff %
Massachusetts	191	172	90.05	89.67	0.38
New York	58	46	79.31	84.92	−5.61

NEW ENGLAND LAW | BOSTON

The information on these pages was provided by the law school.

154 Stuart Street
Boston, MA 02116
Phone: 617.422.7210; Fax: 617.422.7201
E-mail: admit@nesl.edu; Website: www.nesl.edu

Introduction

New England Law | Boston offers an exceptional academic program; an engaged, welcoming community; and a menu of experiential learning opportunities that are among the most varied in the nation—all in the heart of Boston's legal community. Founded in 1908 as Portia Law School, the first law school in the nation exclusively for women, New England Law has been coeducational since 1938.

The law school officially announced the shortening of its name from New England School of Law to New England Law | Boston during its centennial celebrations in 2008. The law school is accredited by the American Bar Association (ABA) and is a member of the Association of American Law Schools (AALS).

The Faculty

The faculty offers elite academic credentials, a wealth of legal practice experience, and a strong desire to help students reach their goals. Because of the school's location in the heart of the legal community, the school's adjunct professors are drawn from a pool of outstanding practitioners, including more than a dozen judges.

Even US Supreme Court Justices have provided their points of view in the school's classrooms. The following five justices all visited the law school, gave lectures, and interacted with students: Chief Justice John G. Roberts, Jr., taught in our annual summer programs in Galway, Ireland, and in Malta. Justice Ruth Bader Ginsburg spent a day with students, as did Justice Sandra Day O'Connor (retired) during her two-day visit for the school's centennial in 2008. Justices Antonin Scalia and Anthony M. Kennedy lectured during visits to the law school, and Justice Scalia also taught in our Ireland summer program.

Academic Program

Whether it's a placement at the attorney general's office, with a district attorney, or at the EPA, among many others, the law school offers one of the most wide-ranging, experiential-learning programs in the country. Through 16 clinics, four academic centers, and multiple cocurricular activities, students gain hands-on experience with the benefit of consistent faculty supervision. Programs include a variety of judicial clerkship opportunities.

The law school is one of a handful in the country to place students regularly at a variety of international criminal tribunals—International Criminal Tribunals for the former Yugoslavia and Rwanda (The Hague, Netherlands); Special Tribunal for Lebanon (The Hague); Extraordinary Chambers in the Courts of Cambodia (Phnom Penh); and International Criminal Court (The Hague).

The law school has two nationally distributed journals, the New England Law Review and the New England Journal on Criminal and Civil Confinement. The curriculum at New England Law prepares students to practice in any jurisdiction in the United States.

Academic Centers

The Center for International Law and Policy provides students with the opportunity to move beyond the walls of the classroom, confront critical social and legal issues, and apply what they are learning to real-world problems. Recently, students have been working on the preparation of issue briefs related to the work of the United Nations Human Rights Council. Students have also provided legal research and analysis to international prosecutors on issues pending before the international tribunals, from the contours of command responsibility to the interpretation of the Genocide Convention.

The Center for Law and Social Responsibility engages students and faculty in public interest work in areas such as the environment, children and families, and wrongful convictions. Some recent projects include representing townspeople who are fighting the construction of a carbon-polluting power plant near an elementary school, and investigating potential wrongful conviction cases.

The Center for Business Law offers a wide range of challenging opportunities, with placements at organizations like NASDAQ, FINRA, and insurance giant Liberty Mutual. Two center projects have involved students working on an article on corporate governance and another on a new style business organizations casebook.

Our newest center, the Center for Public Health and Tobacco Policy (affiliated with the Center for Law and Social Responsibility) was established in 2010 with a grant from the New York State Department of Health. The center conducts legal research and provides evidence-based policy support on tobacco-related issues to New York State and its contractors. Reducing the availability of tobacco products, protecting nonsmokers from secondhand smoke, and minimizing tobacco advertising are among the efforts supported through the center's work.

Diversity

The law school's earliest alumnae broke major barriers blocking the entry of women into the legal profession. (Blanche Braxton '21, for example, was the first African American woman admitted to the Massachusetts Bar.) The school's pioneering roots are evident today as it continues to offer a quality legal education to students from a broad range of backgrounds. The school is one of only a few in the United States offering a program that provides parents with primary child-rearing responsibilities with an opportunity to pursue a legal education.

New England Law fosters a comfortable and supportive atmosphere for students of color. A cornerstone of that commitment is the Charles Hamilton Houston Enrichment Program. The program seeks to address racial bias in the legal profession and the law, promote diversity in the student body, and reduce isolation. The program combines discussion groups with guest speakers and community-building activities.

Study Options

Students may enroll in the full-time day division, the part-time day or evening divisions, or the Special Part-Time Program.

New England Law accepts foreign lawyers in an advanced placement JD program or an LLM program in Advanced Legal Studies.

Study Abroad

Students may study in summer-abroad programs in Galway, Ireland; London; Malta; Chile; or Prague; or in semester-abroad programs in Denmark, the Netherlands, Tanzania, Paris X-Nanterre, or Cambodia. An international criminal process clinic in The Hague enrolls students for a summer or semester.

Financial Aid

Our generous financial aid program consists of a combination of federal loan programs, merit scholarships, and institutional need-based grants. Federal work-study funding is also available.

Student Activities

New England Law has a Student Bar Association, which oversees more than two dozen student groups. These organizations sponsor speakers, social events, and volunteer activities during the year. Student representatives sit on most faculty committees.

Career Services

The Career Services Office (CSO) provides students with individual career counseling, job-search resources, and career programs and workshops. The office maintains an extensive resource library and an online Recruitment and Programming Center with services that include a searchable job-posting database, employer recruitment programs, an e-mail service that sends students job postings, an alumni networking and mentoring program, and postings of job-related programs sponsored by the CSO and outside organizations.

As a member of the Massachusetts Law School Consortium, New England Law participates in recruitment programs with the state's six other ABA-accredited law schools. The school is also a member of the Northeast Law School Consortium and participates in recruitment programs with eight ABA-accredited law schools in the region.

Most students take the Massachusetts Bar exam, while many take exams in New York, the District of Columbia, Florida, New Hampshire, and New Jersey.

APPLICANT PROFILE

New England Law | Boston
This grid includes only applicants who earned 120–180 LSAT scores under standard administrations.

LSAT Score	3.75 +		3.50–3.74		3.25–3.49		3.00–3.24		2.75–2.99		2.50–2.74		2.25–2.49		2.00–2.24		Below 2.00		No GPA		Total	
	Apps	Adm	Apps	Adm	Apps	Adm	Apps	Adm	Apps	Adm	Apps	Adm	Apps	Adm	Apps	Adm	Apps	Adm	Apps	Adm	Apps	Adm
175–180	0	0	0	0	1	1	0	0	0	0	0	0	0	0	0	0	0	0	0	0	1	1
170–174	0	0	1	1	0	0	0	0	0	0	2	1	0	0	0	0	0	0	0	0	3	2
165–169	4	4	5	5	8	8	9	9	1	1	2	1	4	2	0	0	0	0	0	0	33	30
160–164	19	19	19	18	40	36	33	30	22	17	11	11	9	7	4	2	1	0	2	1	160	141
155–159	55	54	102	95	127	118	124	117	83	69	51	45	23	20	6	5	2	0	3	3	576	526
150–154	73	72	181	176	211	203	259	245	184	159	109	96	39	31	10	10	7	0	10	5	1083	997
145–149	31	27	90	57	190	109	198	110	104	56	71	32	31	8	13	3	1	0	13	3	742	405
140–144	4	0	40	0	42	0	61	0	35	0	33	0	12	0	8	0	3	0	6	0	244	0
135–139	3	0	8	0	6	0	10	0	17	0	17	0	7	0	4	0	2	0	2	0	76	0
130–134	0	0	0	0	2	0	2	0	5	0	6	0	1	0	0	0	0	0	2	0	20	0
125–129	0	0	1	0	0	0	2	0	0	0	1	0	0	0	0	0	1	0	1	0	6	0
120–124	0	0	0	0	0	0	0	0	3	0	0	0	0	0	0	0	0	0	0	0	3	0
Total	189	176	447	352	627	475	698	511	454	302	303	186	126	68	45	20	19	0	39	12	2947	2102

Apps = Number of Applicants
Adm = Number Admitted
Reflects 99% of the total applicant pool; highest LSAT data reported.

UNIVERSITY OF NEW HAMPSHIRE SCHOOL OF LAW

Two White Street
Concord, NH 03301
Phone: 603.228.9217; Fax: 603.229.0425
E-mail: admissions@law.unh.edu; Website: www.law.unh.edu

ABA
Approved
Since
1974

The Basics

Type of school	Private
Term	Semester
Application deadline	4/1
Application fee	$55
Financial aid deadline	3/31
Can first year start other than fall?	No
Student to faculty ratio	15.2 to 1
# of housing spaces available restricted to law students	3
graduate housing for which law students are eligible	

Faculty and Administrators

	Total		Men		Women		Minorities	
	Spr	Fall	Spr	Fall	Spr	Fall	Spr	Fall
Full-time	24	21	13	13	11	8	1	1
Other full-time	9	14	4	4	5	10	0	0
Deans, librarians, & others who teach	9	8	5	4	4	4	1	1
Part-time	45	27	28	14	17	13	0	2
Total	87	70	50	35	37	35	2	4

Curriculum

		Full-Time	Part-Time
Typical first-year section size		72	0
Is there typically a "small section" of the first-year class, other than Legal Writing, taught by full-time faculty		Yes	No
If yes, typical size offered last year		15	
# of classroom course titles beyond first-year curriculum		102	
# of upper division courses, excluding seminars, with an enrollment:	Under 25	108	
	25–49	16	
	50–74	12	
	75–99	4	
	100+	0	
# of seminars		16	
# of seminar positions available		328	
# of seminar positions filled		198	0
# of positions available in simulation courses		1,055	
# of simulation positions filled		799	0
# of positions available in faculty supervised clinical courses		207	
# of faculty supervised clinical positions filled		159	0
# involved in field placements		132	0
# involved in law journals		44	0
# involved in moot court or trial competitions		53	0
# of credit hours required to graduate		85	

JD Enrollment and Ethnicity

	Men		Women		Full-Time		Part-Time		1st-Year		Total		JD Degs. Awd.
	#	%	#	%	#	%	#	%	#	%	#	%	
All Hispanics	11	4.6	4	2.6	14	3.6	1	50.0	4	2.9	15	3.8	7
Am. Ind./AK Nat.	0	0.0	0	0.0	0	0.0	0	0.0	0	0.0	0	0.0	1
Asian	17	7.1	18	11.6	35	8.9	0	0.0	8	5.7	35	8.9	16
Black/Af. Am.	6	2.5	11	7.1	17	4.3	0	0.0	8	5.7	17	4.3	7
Nat. HI/Pac. Isl.	0	0.0	0	0.0	0	0.0	0	0.0	0	0.0	0	0.0	0
2 or more races	6	2.5	2	1.3	8	2.0	0	0.0	2	1.4	8	2.0	3
Subtotal (minor.)	40	16.7	35	22.6	74	18.9	1	50.0	22	15.7	75	19.0	34
Nonres. Alien	5	2.1	8	5.2	13	3.3	0	0.0	0	0.0	13	3.3	6
White/Cauc.	194	81.2	111	71.6	304	77.6	1	50.0	117	83.6	305	77.4	107
Unknown	0	0.0	1	0.6	1	0.3	0	0.0	1	0.7	1	0.3	0
Total	239	60.7	155	39.3	392	99.5	2	0.5	140	35.5	394		147

Transfers

Transfers in	0
Transfers out	11

Tuition and Fees

	Resident	Nonresident
Full-time	$39,990	$39,990
Part-time		
Tuition Guarantee Program		N

Living Expenses

Estimated living expenses for singles

Living on campus	Living off campus	Living at home
$20,091	$20,091	$20,091

UNIVERSITY OF NEW HAMPSHIRE SCHOOL OF LAW

ABA
Approved
Since
1974

GPA and LSAT Scores

	Total	Full-Time	Part-Time
# of apps	1,247	1,247	0
# of offers	627	627	0
# of matrics	146	146	0
75% GPA	3.57	3.57	0.00
Median GPA	3.25	3.25	0.00
25% GPA	3.00	3.00	0.00
75% LSAT	158	158	0
Median LSAT	154	154	0
25% LSAT	151	151	0

Grants and Scholarships (from prior year)

	Total #	Total %	Full-Time #	Full-Time %	Part-Time #	Part-Time %
Total # of students	419		419		0	
Total # receiving grants	278	66.3	278	66.3	0	0.0
Less than 1/2 tuition	222	53.0	222	53.0	0	0.0
Half to full tuition	55	13.1	55	13.1	0	0.0
Full tuition	1	0.2	1	0.2	0	0.0
More than full tuition	0	0.0	0	0.0	0	0.0
Median grant amount			$10,000		$0	

Informational and Library Resources

Total amount spent on library materials	$1,025,075
Study seating capacity inside the library	306
# of full-time equivalent professional librarians	8
Hours per week library is open	105
# of open, wired connections available to students	321
# of networked computers available for use by students	52
Has wireless network?	Y
Requires computer?	N

JD Attrition (from prior year)

	Academic #	Other #	Total #	Total %
1st year	4	20	24	18.3
2nd year	0	0	0	0.0
3rd year	0	0	0	0.0
4th year	0	0	0	0.0

Employment (9 months after graduation)

For up-to-date employment data, go to employmentsummary.abaquestionnaire.org on the ABA website.

Bar Passage Rates

First-time takers	158	Reporting %	70.25
Average school %	81.98	Average state %	85.75

Average pass difference −3.77

Jurisdiction	Takers	Passers	Pass %	State %	Diff %
Massachusetts	41	34	82.93	89.67	−6.74
New Hampshire	36	29	80.56	82.09	−1.53
New York	34	28	82.35	84.92	−2.57

UNIVERSITY OF NEW HAMPSHIRE SCHOOL OF LAW

Two White Street
Concord, NH 03301
Phone: 603.228.9217; Fax: 603.229.0425
E-mail: admissions@law.unh.edu; Website: www.law.unh.edu

Introduction

The University of New Hampshire School of Law is known throughout the world as an innovative leader in legal education, providing its students with the skills to lead and serve, and to meet the emerging needs of a global society. UNH Law emphasizes individually tailored legal programs and a broad range of learning settings, including lectures and seminars, real-client clinics, independent study, and externships in law firms, courts, and private and public agencies. In addition, we promote a community spirit of caring and compassion, with a close working relationship between students and faculty. Self-reliant students who know their own strengths and objectives thrive at UNH Law and find the focus on personal pride and responsibility more motivating than fear or competition.

UNH Law, formerly known as Franklin Pierce Law Center, is one of the smallest law schools in the United States. This intimate, hands-on education is complemented by its affiliation with the University of New Hampshire, which provides the resources of a major research university. Each entering class numbers approximately 140 students, allowing for a 14:1 student-to-teacher ratio. Classes are small, especially after the first year; the majority of courses enroll 35 or fewer students.

Located in New Hampshire's capital city of Concord (45,000 population), UNH Law is ideally situated one hour from Boston, the Atlantic seacoast, the state's Lakes Region, and the White Mountains. Our excellent facilities, enhanced by the recent opening of the Franklin Pierce Center for Intellectual Property, are a short walk from the center of New Hampshire's state government.

Special Programs

- **Intellectual Property**—Housed in the new Franklin Pierce Center for Intellectual Property, UNH Law's internationally recognized intellectual property specialization (patents, licensing, technology transfer, trade secrets, trademarks, cyberlaw, and copyrights) is supported by 14 full-time faculty members, all intellectual property lawyers. Training includes learning to advise clients regarding intellectual property protection, infringement, and technology transfer. Our International Technology Transfer Institute allows students to work on innovation and technology transfer projects around the world. Students with technical backgrounds may focus on patent law, with many passing the patent bar prior to graduation. Other intellectual property areas do not require a technical background.
- **Commerce and Technology Law**—The business curriculum prepares students for traditional types of practice and brings new opportunities for students choosing to confront the legal issues involving electronic commerce. The business and e-commerce curriculum also integrates well with the intellectual property curriculum, particularly for students interested in business and legal innovations associated with the Internet.
- **Social Justice Institute**—This hands-on professional training program prepares students for public interest law in private practice, governmental service, social policy advocacy, and criminal practice. Clinic students represent clients in cases involving misdemeanor and felony defense, predatory lending, bankruptcy and consumer fraud, and unemployment compensation, as well as trademark, copyright, and small business transactions.
- **Criminal Law**—Our criminal law curriculum offers courses, individual mentoring, clinics, and externships to prepare students for careers in prosecution or defense. Criminal Practice Clinic students represent clients charged with misdemeanor and juvenile offenses at the district court level. In the Appellate Defender Program, students prepare briefs for the New Hampshire Supreme Court in criminal cases. Externship opportunities are available in prosecutorial positions at the local, state, and federal level, and in defense positions with law firms and governmental agencies.
- **International Criminal Law and Justice**—This program is designed to prepare the next generation of lawyers, peacekeepers, policy makers, and law enforcement professionals who will be confronting global issues of criminal law and justice. The program includes a one-week seminar in Washington, DC; explores legal responses to terrorism, counterfeiting, intellectual property crimes, and human trafficking; and more.

International Summer Institutes in China and Ireland

- The Intellectual Property Summer Institute at Tsinghua University in Beijing offers an overview of China's patent, copyright, and trademark laws, as well as an introduction to some of the major international instruments and institutions regulating international trade and intellectual property.
- The eLaw Summer Institute at University College Cork, Ireland, focuses on law and emerging policy of the information age.

Academic Opportunities

The Daniel Webster Scholar Honors Program is a comprehensive, practice-based program focused on making law students client-ready. Admission to the program is competitive; application is made at the end of the 1L year. Second- and third-year students complete a range of courses, demonstrate their developing professional skills and judgment, and compile a portfolio of work. Students who successfully complete the program will be certified as having passed the New Hampshire Bar examination, subject to passing character and fitness requirements.

The UNH Law Externship Program exchanges a full-credit semester in the classroom for a real-life experience working in an active legal position. Externs work with experienced attorneys and judges while under the close supervision of a faculty member.

Joint-Degree Programs and LLM

UNH Law offers three joint-degree programs: JD/Master of Laws (LLM) in Intellectual Property, JD/LLM in Commerce and Technology, and JD/LLM in International Criminal Law and Justice. Summer programs enable students to earn additional credits needed to complete joint-degree programs in three years. The three LLM degrees are designed for law graduates who wish to examine the legally sophisticated intellectual property issues that often arise in policy making and teaching.

Through the affiliation with the University of New Hampshire, UNH Law offers a dual JD/MBA degree. By spending their second year at UNH's Whittemore School of Business and Economics, students are able to earn both degrees in 3.5 years.

Student Activities

Students prepare notes and comments for *IDEA: The Intellectual Property Law Review* and for the *UNH Law Review*. Students organize and participate in a wide variety of formal organizations and informal activities and events throughout the year, including two dozen officially recognized student groups.

Career Services

The Career Services Office works with students and alumni to find the best match to meet their skills and interests in changing legal markets. The office provides extensive individual counseling and guidance; brings attorneys to campus to provide firsthand information about the practice of law; advises students of all resources through weekly publications and job boards; coordinates the efforts of faculty, staff, and student groups to provide information about opportunities to gain experience; and conducts outreach to employers. More than 70 percent of our graduates secure positions outside New Hampshire.

Faculty

UNH Law's faculty is the key to our pioneering, practice-ready legal education. Coming from a wide variety of backgrounds,

including as patent attorneys, civil liberties lawyers, federal law clerks, and corporate attorneys, they enliven the classroom with their firsthand knowledge of what lawyers need to know, and what employers are looking for. The UNH Law faculty is known for producing scholarship that addresses real-world issues, from legal ethics to intellectual property valuation.

Clinics

As a pioneer in practice-ready legal education, UNH Law has always offered a wide range of clinical opportunities for students:

- Immigration Law Clinic
- Agency Rule Writing, Advocacy, and Policy Analysis Clinic
- Mediation Clinic
- Consumer and Commercial Law Clinic
- Intellectual Property and Transaction Clinic
- Intellectual Property Amicus Clinic
- International Technology Transfer Institute Clinic
- Criminal Practice Clinic
- Appellate Defender Program
- Street Law Project

Admission

While LSAT scores and grade-point average are factors that must be considered in the decision-making process, neither alone determines admission. Every application receives a thorough and thoughtful review. The candidate's personal statement, letters of recommendation, and résumé are evaluated along with the numbers. Community service, employment during college, and other nonacademic accomplishments are given weight to the extent that they reflect initiative, social responsibility, focus, and maturity.

APPLICANT PROFILE

The University of New Hampshire School of Law seeks to admit students who will make a contribution to the law school community, to the legal profession, and to society. Admission is based on a whole-person review of each application, including academic ability and aptitude, demonstration of academic success, relevant experience

that addresses the school's mission or areas of excellence, leadership, diversity, moral character, community service, and other qualitative personal attributes. UNH Law values diverse opinions, backgrounds, and perspectives; this enrichment within the classroom and community is core to the educational experience.

THE UNIVERSITY OF NEW MEXICO SCHOOL OF LAW

MSC11-6070, 1 University of New Mexico
Albuquerque, NM 87131-0001
Phone: 505.277.2146; Fax: 505.277.9958
E-mail: admissions@law.unm.edu; Website: http://lawschool.unm.edu

ABA
Approved
Since
1948

The Basics

Type of school	Public
Term	Semester
Application deadline	2/15
Application fee	$50
Financial aid deadline	3/1
Can first year start other than fall?	No
Student to faculty ratio	10.2 to 1
# of housing spaces available restricted to law students	
graduate housing for which law students are eligible	

Faculty and Administrators

	Total		Men		Women		Minorities	
	Spr	Fall	Spr	Fall	Spr	Fall	Spr	Fall
Full-time	29	28	11	14	18	14	12	13
Other full-time	5	5	2	2	3	3	0	0
Deans, librarians, & others who teach	14	10	7	4	7	6	4	3
Part-time	49	33	28	17	21	16	8	6
Total	97	76	48	37	49	39	24	22

Curriculum

		Full-Time	Part-Time
Typical first-year section size		38	0
Is there typically a "small section" of the first-year class, other than Legal Writing, taught by full-time faculty		No	No
If yes, typical size offered last year			
# of classroom course titles beyond first-year curriculum		126	
# of upper division courses, excluding seminars, with an enrollment:	Under 25	84	
	25–49	18	
	50–74	6	
	75–99	0	
	100+	0	
# of seminars		18	
# of seminar positions available		182	
# of seminar positions filled		158	0
# of positions available in simulation courses		136	
# of simulation positions filled		124	0
# of positions available in faculty supervised clinical courses		120	
# of faculty supervised clinical positions filled		118	0
# involved in field placements		74	0
# involved in law journals		66	0
# involved in moot court or trial competitions		43	0
# of credit hours required to graduate		86	

JD Enrollment and Ethnicity

	Men		Women		Full-Time		Part-Time		1st-Year		Total		JD Degs. Awd.
	#	%	#	%	#	%	#	%	#	%	#	%	
All Hispanics	52	27.2	48	27.9	100	27.6	0	0.0	34	29.6	100	27.5	33
Am. Ind./AK Nat.	13	6.8	17	9.9	30	8.3	0	0.0	10	8.7	30	8.3	10
Asian	1	0.5	8	4.7	9	2.5	0	0.0	4	3.5	9	2.5	0
Black/Af. Am.	4	2.1	6	3.5	10	2.8	0	0.0	2	1.7	10	2.8	5
Nat. HI/Pac. Isl.	1	0.5	0	0.0	1	0.3	0	0.0	1	0.9	1	0.3	0
2 or more races	1	0.5	0	0.0	1	0.3	0	0.0	1	0.9	1	0.3	1
Subtotal (minor.)	72	37.7	79	45.9	151	41.7	0	0.0	52	45.2	151	41.6	49
Nonres. Alien	1	0.5	0	0.0	1	0.3	0	0.0	0	0.0	1	0.3	0
White/Cauc.	98	51.3	78	45.3	175	48.3	1	100.0	55	47.8	176	48.5	57
Unknown	20	10.5	15	8.7	35	9.7	0	0.0	8	7.0	35	9.6	0
Total	191	52.6	172	47.4	362	99.7	1	0.3	115	31.7	363		106

Transfers

Transfers in	4
Transfers out	0

Tuition and Fees

	Resident	Nonresident
Full-time	$14,532	$32,661
Part-time		
Tuition Guarantee Program		N

Living Expenses

Estimated living expenses for singles

Living on campus	Living off campus	Living at home
$13,968	$14,418	$8,818

THE UNIVERSITY OF NEW MEXICO SCHOOL OF LAW

ABA
Approved
Since
1948

GPA and LSAT Scores

	Total	Full-Time	Part-Time
# of apps	921	921	0
# of offers	237	237	0
# of matrics	113	113	0
75% GPA	3.69	3.69	0.00
Median GPA	3.33	3.33	0.00
25% GPA	3.05	3.05	0.00
75% LSAT	161	161	0
Median LSAT	157	157	0
25% LSAT	152	152	0

Grants and Scholarships (from prior year)

	Total #	Total %	Full-Time #	Full-Time %	Part-Time #	Part-Time %
Total # of students	351		351		0	
Total # receiving grants	109	31.1	109	31.1	0	0.0
Less than 1/2 tuition	76	21.7	76	21.7	0	0.0
Half to full tuition	15	4.3	15	4.3	0	0.0
Full tuition	5	1.4	5	1.4	0	0.0
More than full tuition	13	3.7	13	3.7	0	0.0
Median grant amount		$4,650		$0		

Informational and Library Resources

Total amount spent on library materials	$657,255
Study seating capacity inside the library	303
# of full-time equivalent professional librarians	7
Hours per week library is open	83
# of open, wired connections available to students	330
# of networked computers available for use by students	76
Has wireless network?	Y
Requires computer?	Y

JD Attrition (from prior year)

	Academic #	Other #	Total #	Total %
1st year	0	4	4	3.5
2nd year	0	0	0	0.0
3rd year	0	0	0	0.0
4th year	0	0	0	0.0

Employment (9 months after graduation)

For up-to-date employment data, go to employmentsummary.abaquestionnaire.org on the ABA website.

Bar Passage Rates

First-time takers	88	Reporting %	87.50
Average school %	88.31	Average state %	88.35
Average pass difference	−0.04		

Jurisdiction	Takers	Passers	Pass %	State %	Diff %
New Mexico	77	68	88.31	88.35	−0.04

THE UNIVERSITY OF NEW MEXICO SCHOOL OF LAW

MSC11-6070, 1 University of New Mexico
Albuquerque, NM 87131-0001
Phone: 505.277.2146; Fax: 505.277.9958
E-mail: admissions@law.unm.edu; Website: http://lawschool.unm.edu

Introduction

Located in Albuquerque, the School of Law is known for its small classes, easy student-faculty interaction, and programs in clinical law, natural resources law, and Indian law. The excellent student-to-faculty ratio, one of the best in the country, facilitates a sense of community in the educational experience. It also allows the school to offer more courses with smaller enrollments. The school is a member of the Association of American Law Schools (AALS) and is approved by the American Bar Association (ABA). The University of New Mexico is the state's flagship institution, with approximately 33,000 students on its main and branch campuses.

Curriculum

The Juris Doctor (JD) program offers a full-time day curriculum. Students normally complete the required 86 hours of law credit for the JD degree in three academic years (six semesters). A limited number of entering students may be admitted to the Flexible Time Program, which allows students to take fewer credit hours per semester and graduate in five academic years. All students must take the standard first-year curriculum, including basic courses in torts, contracts, civil procedure, property, criminal law, and constitutional law. Emphasis is also placed on the skills of advocacy: legal writing, oral argument, litigation, counseling, and negotiation. First-year classes range in size from approximately 18 to 58 students. After completion of the first-year curriculum, courses are elective except for Ethics and a clinical program. Typically, one half of the electives have fewer than 15 students. Every student must complete the advanced writing requirement.

Special Programs

Clinical Law. UNM's program in Clinical Law is regarded as one of the finest practical lawyering programs in the country and includes the Law Practice Clinic, the Business and Tax Clinic, the Community Lawyering Clinic, and the Southwest Indian Law Clinic. Students may participate in the extern placement program and elect assignment to a judge's office, the public defender's office, federal and state administrative offices, and private practitioners. The school also offers an innovative course in Criminal Law in Practice, in which students receive hands-on experience in either prosecution or defense of criminal cases at both the misdemeanor and felony levels. Unlike most other law schools, UNM requires six credit hours of clinical work for graduation. In 1970, the New Mexico Supreme Court adopted a rule permitting students to practice before state courts.

Indian Law. UNM has long been a leader in Indian law and has developed one of the most comprehensive programs in the country. The school offers students the Southwest Indian Law Clinic, the *Tribal Law Journal*, the Indian Law Certificate (ILC), scholarly research, guest lectures, seminars, and social activities. An ILC student completes the JD while enrolling in 21 hours of required and elective Indian law courses.

Natural Resources Law. UNM is widely known for its strength in the areas of natural resources and environmental law and offers a number of electives in these subjects.

Students who want to gain a more comprehensive understanding of resource problems may participate in the Natural Resources Certificate Program, which may include work on the *Natural Resources Journal*, an internationally recognized quarterly.

Business Law. UNM's Economic Development Program gives students the training they need to become well-prepared business lawyers. An enhanced curriculum includes the Business and Tax Clinic, which offers services to small businesses, start-ups, nonprofit organizations, and economic development programs. Students learn how to advise entrepreneurs on a wide range of business issues.

International Law. The school has developed a variety of programs and courses that provide opportunities for students interested in international law. Students may expand their experience through coursework at the law school and through the study-abroad and exchange programs.

- *Guanajuato Summer Law Institute*. The School of Law, in conjunction with the Universidad de Guanajuato, Southwestern University, and Texas Tech University, offers four to six weeks of summer law study in Guanajuato, Mexico. The institute features an introduction to Mexican law and international law subjects related to Latin America. The institute is ABA-approved.
- *Visiting Programs*. In conjunction with the University of New Mexico's Office of International Programs, law students can take advantage of UNM-sponsored exchange programs throughout Central and South America, Europe, Asia, and Africa.

Dual-Degree Programs

Three established dual JD and master's degree programs are offered: the JD and MPA in Public Administration, the JD and MBA, and the JD and MA in Latin American Studies. Students can also earn the JD degree and an MA, MS, or PhD in other academic fields. Students must satisfy the admission and academic requirements of both the School of Law and the graduate school.

Facilities

The School of Law, a state-of-the-art facility, is located on the northern edge of the UNM campus. The building is wireless and laptop friendly. The School of Law includes classroom and seminar rooms, all faculty offices, student organization and publication offices, a computer lab, the Clinical Program, and the law library. The School of Law is also home to the American Indian Law Center, Inc., the Utton Transboundary Resources Center, and the Institute of Public Law. Adjacent to the School of Law is the Albuquerque branch of the New Mexico Court of Appeals.

Law Library. The UNM Law Library is the largest legal research facility in New Mexico. The library offers a wide variety of electronic products, including more than 75 subscription databases. Its book and microform collection of 403,430 includes special collections in American Indian law, Mexican and Latin American law, land grant law, natural resources, and archival collections. The library's 32,443 square feet of space provides 303 seats, including 92 student carrels and 211 noncarrel seats, plus numerous areas for study, lounging, and browsing. Wireless Internet broadcasters; group study rooms equipped with audiovisual equipment; two student organization meeting rooms; photocopy, print, and scanning facilities; a microform reader/printer; the school's computer lab for student use; and a classroom for legal research instruction are found in the library. The library is also home to the Governor Bruce King Archives and Reading Room, which serves as a meeting space for special events.

Career Services. The school's smaller size allows for individualized attention in all aspects of career development and job-search methodology. Regular workshops are provided on résumé and cover letter writing, interviewing, and job-search strategies. In addition, the law school sponsors on-campus interviews, a mock interview program, and presentations on various practice opportunities.

Student Activities

Activities include the *Natural Resources Journal*, the *New Mexico Law Review*, the *Tribal Law Journal*, and several moot court and mock trial competitions. All law students are members of the University's Graduate/Professional Student Association and the Student Bar Association. Students may participate in one or more of the 30 law student organizations.

Admission and Financial Aid

Applicants must take the LSAT, register for the LSAC Credential Assembly Service, and have a bachelor's degree from an accredited university or college before registration in the fall. A five-member committee reviews applications. Substantial weight is given to the applicant's personal statement, prior work experience, extracurricular activities, letters of recommendation, and other information supplied by the applicant. Applications from New Mexico residents are given a preference. Students apply for financial aid by filing the FAFSA. Types of financial aid include loans, grants, and work-study programs. The school awards grants to students based on the Access Group's Need Access application.

Albuquerque

The Albuquerque metropolitan area has a population of approximately 750,000. Situated along the Rio Grande, the city is located at a high desert elevation of 5,000 to 7,000 feet and is surrounded by the Sandia Mountains.

From golf to skiing to hiking to fly-fishing, students have access to outdoor New Mexico. In addition, students have the opportunity to visit museums and art galleries and take in concerts and theater. The combination of multiple cultures reflected in food, music, art, architecture, and local customs heightens Albuquerque's appeal.

APPLICANT PROFILE

The University of New Mexico School of Law
This grid includes only applicants who earned 120–180 LSAT scores under standard administrations.

LSAT Score	3.75 +		3.50–3.74		3.25–3.49		3.00–3.24		2.75–2.99		2.50–2.74		2.25–2.49		2.00–2.24		Below 2.00		No GPA		Total	
	Apps	Adm	Apps	Adm	Apps	Adm	Apps	Adm	Apps	Adm	Apps	Adm	Apps	Adm	Apps	Adm	Apps	Adm	Apps	Adm	Apps	Adm
175–180	0	0	0	0	0	0	0	0	0	0	1	1	0	0	0	0	0	0	0	0	1	1
170–174	0	0	1	1	3	3	0	0	1	1	0	0	0	0	0	0	0	0	0	0	5	5
165–169	2	2	5	4	8	7	9	6	3	2	3	1	3	1	0	0	0	0	0	0	33	23
160–164	17	14	17	12	17	11	14	12	7	4	5	1	6	1	3	0	1	0	0	0	87	55
155–159	36	24	53	25	48	20	37	16	28	10	9	2	9	1	2	0	0	0	4	1	226	99
150–154	31	9	44	10	64	7	49	4	25	0	27	3	7	0	4	0	2	0	6	1	259	34
145–149	14	0	28	1	35	1	46	9	23	4	16	1	7	0	1	0	1	1	5	0	176	17
140–144	4	0	17	0	13	1	17	1	16	0	10	0	3	0	3	0	0	0	2	0	85	2
135–139	0	0	7	0	3	0	9	1	9	0	3	0	3	0	3	0	0	0	3	0	40	1
130–134	0	0	3	0	0	0	2	0	1	0	7	0	1	0	2	0	0	0	1	0	17	0
125–129	0	0	0	0	0	0	0	0	2	0	1	0	0	0	0	0	0	0	1	0	4	0
120–124	0	0	0	0	0	0	0	0	0	0	0	0	0	0	1	0	0	0	0	0	1	0
Total	104	49	175	53	191	50	183	49	115	21	82	9	39	3	19	0	4	1	22	2	934	237

Apps = Number of Applicants
Adm = Number Admitted
Reflects 99% of the total applicant pool; highest LSAT data reported.

NEW YORK LAW SCHOOL

185 West Broadway
New York, NY 10013
Phone: 212.431.2888; Fax: 212.966.1522
E-mail: admissions@nyls.edu; Website: www.nyls.edu

The Basics

Type of school	Private
Term	Semester
Application deadline	4/1
Application fee	$0
Financial aid deadline	4/1
Can first year start other than fall?	No
Student to faculty ratio	21.3 to 1
# of housing spaces available restricted to law students	99
graduate housing for which law students are eligible	99

Faculty and Administrators

	Total		Men		Women		Minorities	
	Spr	Fall	Spr	Fall	Spr	Fall	Spr	Fall
Full-time	59	70	40	49	19	21	8	11
Other full-time	5	9	2	2	3	7	0	3
Deans, librarians, & others who teach	16	15	4	4	12	11	0	0
Part-time	133	118	77	76	56	42	7	7
Total	213	212	123	131	90	81	15	21

Curriculum

	Full-Time	Part-Time
Typical first-year section size	128	121
Is there typically a "small section" of the first-year class, other than Legal Writing, taught by full-time faculty	Yes	Yes
If yes, typical size offered last year	43	20
# of classroom course titles beyond first-year curriculum	234	
# of upper division courses, excluding seminars, with an enrollment: Under 25	211	
25–49	59	
50–74	32	
75–99	15	
100+	37	
# of seminars	155	
# of seminar positions available	2,956	
# of seminar positions filled	1,867	343
# of positions available in simulation courses	2,659	
# of simulation positions filled	1,566	573
# of positions available in faculty supervised clinical courses	218	
# of faculty supervised clinical positions filled	168	8
# involved in field placements	352	27
# involved in law journals	300	44
# involved in moot court or trial competitions	113	17
# of credit hours required to graduate	86	

JD Enrollment and Ethnicity

	Men		Women		Full-Time		Part-Time		1st-Year		Total		JD Degs. Awd.
	#	%	#	%	#	%	#	%	#	%	#	%	
All Hispanics	100	11.9	132	14.3	167	12.2	65	16.3	85	16.9	232	13.1	52
Am. Ind./AK Nat.	3	0.4	1	0.1	2	0.1	2	0.5	0	0.0	4	0.2	0
Asian	29	3.4	37	4.0	47	3.4	19	4.8	44	8.7	66	3.7	39
Black/Af. Am.	41	4.9	85	9.2	79	5.8	47	11.8	34	6.7	126	7.1	36
Nat. HI/Pac. Isl.	1	0.1	0	0.0	1	0.1	0	0.0	1	0.2	1	0.1	1
2 or more races	8	1.0	11	1.2	15	1.1	4	1.0	2	0.4	19	1.1	14
Subtotal (minor.)	182	21.6	266	28.8	311	22.8	137	34.3	166	32.9	448	25.4	142
Nonres. Alien	0	0.0	0	0.0	0	0.0	0	0.0	0	0.0	0	0.0	0
White/Cauc.	565	67.1	571	61.9	911	66.7	225	56.3	307	60.9	1136	64.4	303
Unknown	95	11.3	86	9.3	143	10.5	38	9.5	31	6.2	181	10.3	70
Total	842	47.7	923	52.3	1365	77.3	400	22.7	504	28.6	1765		515

Transfers

Transfers in	14
Transfers out	54

Tuition and Fees

	Resident	Nonresident
Full-time	$47,800	$47,800
Part-time	$36,900	$36,900
Tuition Guarantee Program		Y

Living Expenses

Estimated living expenses for singles

Living on campus	Living off campus	Living at home
$23,221	$23,221	$10,372

ABA Approved Since 1954

GPA and LSAT Scores

	Total	Full-Time	Part-Time
# of apps	5,997	5,054	943
# of offers	2,604	2,294	310
# of matrics	488	375	113
75% GPA	3.44	3.45	3.39
Median GPA	3.22	3.25	3.13
25% GPA	2.98	3.01	2.93
75% LSAT	156	157	154
Median LSAT	154	154	152
25% LSAT	151	152	149

Grants and Scholarships (from prior year)

	Total		Full-Time		Part-Time	
	#	%	#	%	#	%
Total # of students	1,923		1,492		431	
Total # receiving grants	728	37.9	633	42.4	95	22.0
Less than 1/2 tuition	647	33.6	564	37.8	83	19.3
Half to full tuition	71	3.7	62	4.2	9	2.1
Full tuition	10	0.5	7	0.5	3	0.7
More than full tuition	0	0.0	0	0.0	0	0.0
Median grant amount			$10,000		$7,500	

Informational and Library Resources

Total amount spent on library materials	$1,498,131
Study seating capacity inside the library	700
# of full-time equivalent professional librarians	15
Hours per week library is open	98
# of open, wired connections available to students	0
# of networked computers available for use by students	124
Has wireless network?	Y
Requires computer?	N

JD Attrition (from prior year)

	Academic	Other	Total	
	#	#	#	%
1st year	32	56	88	13.7
2nd year	2	3	5	0.8
3rd year	1	0	1	0.2
4th year	0	0	0	0.0

Employment (9 months after graduation)

For up-to-date employment data, go to employmentsummary.abaquestionnaire.org on the ABA website.

Bar Passage Rates

First-time takers	450	Reporting %	96.22
Average school %	81.99	Average state %	84.92

Average pass difference –2.93

Jurisdiction	Takers	Passers	Pass %	State %	Diff %
New York	433	355	81.99	84.92	–2.93

NEW YORK LAW SCHOOL

185 West Broadway
New York, NY 10013
Phone: 212.431.2888; Fax: 212.966.1522
E-mail: admissions@nyls.edu; Website: www.nyls.edu

Introduction

New York Law School has developed a unique approach to legal education that it calls *The Right Program for Each Student*. It acknowledges and accommodates our students' differing expectations, ambitions, and levels of ability. New York Law School has developed several individualized programs to meet the needs of the various segments of the student body. The John Marshall Harlan Scholars Program is a rigorous academic honors program which gives students the opportunity to focus their law school studies and gain depth and substantive expertise. The Comprehensive Curriculum Program is unique to New York Law School and provides intensive support for students, helping them turn a weak start to law school into a powerful finish. A focus on collaborative learning is achieved through the project-based learning courses aimed at combining attention to legal theory and practice.

Founded in 1891, New York Law School is one of the oldest independent law schools in the country. The school is fully accredited by the American Bar Association and is a member of the Association of American Law Schools.

Location/Physical Facilities/Library

New York Law School is located in the historic TriBeCa district in Lower Manhattan. It is an extraordinary setting for the study of law and one of the city's most colorful and dynamic neighborhoods. Lower Manhattan is the site of New York's largest concentration of government agencies, courts, law firms, banks, corporate headquarters, and securities exchanges. Federal Courts, New York State Civil and Criminal Courts, Family Court, and the Court of International Trade are within a four-block radius of the Law School.

The opening of a striking new building during the 2009–2010 academic year doubled the size of the school's facilities and provided the most modern and technologically advanced law building in New York City. This new building houses a four-story library that contains more than 500,000 volumes and periodicals, individual and group study space, an auditorium, classrooms, student activity space, and a penthouse dining facility for students.

Student Life

We are committed to giving students a first-rate law school experience—in and out of the classroom. In return, we demand of them the seriousness of purpose necessary to become ethical professionals—the kind of lawyers sought by clients, law firms, government agencies, advocacy groups, and corporations.

New York Law School has a long-standing and continuing interest in enrolling students from varied backgrounds, including older students, minority students, women, career-changers, and public servants. Students range in age from 20 to 55, with the average age being 25.

Faculty

The Law School's distinguished full-time faculty is composed of productive scholars who are dedicated educators and who share a strong commitment to the school's vision and philosophy embodied in its core values: embracing innovation, fostering integrity and professionalism, and advancing justice for a diverse society. A national survey of law faculty scholarship includes them among the 50 most prolific law faculties in the country and notes the significant number of their books that are published by university presses. Leading jurists and attorneys who work in nearby offices are members of the adjunct faculty.

Curriculum and Special Programs

The required curriculum, composed of the entire first year and part of the second year, provides a foundation in legal reasoning and in areas of law that are considered indispensable building blocks of a legal education. In the second year and thereafter, students may design their programs with elective courses chosen from an extraordinarily rich array.

Elements such as legal analysis and legal writing, counseling, interviewing, negotiating, advocacy, planning, and strategizing form the core subject areas of the school's Legal Practice Program. Six clinical programs offer students the opportunity to represent real clients.

Externship and judicial internship programs permit students to do actual lawyering work in law offices.

Admission

In the admission process, a number of factors are taken into account, including the applicant's academic record and LSAT scores. The admission committee also looks for those applicants who have demonstrated leadership ability, motivation, and a sense of service and responsibility to society. Excellence in a particular field of study, progression of grades, strength of undergraduate curriculum, work and community service experience, graduate study in other disciplines, and extracurricular activities all are considered as well. Writing ability receives particular attention, and the admission committee strongly urges applicants to submit the optional writing sample.

The school seeks to enroll students who, through their diversity of backgrounds, experiences, perspectives, and ambitions, promise to enrich the law school community and, ultimately, the larger society. We do not charge an application fee.

Academic Centers

The Institute for Information Law and Policy is the home for the study of technology, intellectual property, and information law. It includes our Media Law Center and the Program on Law and Journalism. The Institute offers a certificate of mastery in law office technology and a patent bar preparation curriculum.

The Center for New York City Law focuses on governmental and legal processes in the urban setting.

The Center for International Law focuses on legal issues relating to international trade and finance.

The Justice Action Center seeks to develop students' expertise in civil rights and civil liberties law and international human rights.

The Center on Business Law and Policy focuses on business and corporate law.

The Center on Financial Services Law focuses on law in financial services, including regulatory reforms and other current issues in this global industry.

The Center for Professional Values serves as a vehicle through which to examine the role of the legal profession and alternative approaches to the practice of law.

The Center for Real Estate Studies enables students to study both the private practice and public regulation of real estate.

The Diane Abbey Law Center for Children and Families exists to ensure that children and the families who care for them receive the legal assistance they need to remain safe and secure, and to thrive.

Moot Court/Law Journals/Student Organizations

New York Law School students exhibit well-honed courtroom skills, in recent years winning outright three national moot court competitions and earning awards in many others. The school's annual Robert F. Wagner Sr. Labor and Employment Law Competition is one of the nation's largest student-run moot court competitions.

The Law School currently has three scholarly publications, edited and staffed by students, which are an integral part of the Law School's program: Law Review, Journal

of International and Comparative Law, and Journal of Human Rights.

Students have established some 35 interest organizations as well.

Expenses and Financial Aid

New York Law School has established a program of financial aid to assist students in meeting the costs of a legal education through grants, scholarships, work-study awards, and loans. Scholarships are awarded on the basis of academic merit and financial need.

Office of Professional Development

The Office of Professional Development brings together three key student services: Student Life, Career Services, and Public Interest and Community Service. This innovative structure allows us to offer students personal attention from their first day of study to help them pursue their professional goals. The Career Services Office offers a wide array of services, including individual career counseling, on-campus interview programs, career panels and workshops, alumni network and mentoring programs, online employer databases, and information on summer, full-, and part-time positions, and alternative career opportunities.

APPLICANT PROFILE

New York Law School
This grid includes only applicants who earned 120–180 LSAT scores under standard administrations.

LSAT Score	3.75 + Apps	3.75 + Adm	3.50–3.74 Apps	3.50–3.74 Adm	3.25–3.49 Apps	3.25–3.49 Adm	3.00–3.24 Apps	3.00–3.24 Adm	2.75–2.99 Apps	2.75–2.99 Adm	2.50–2.74 Apps	2.50–2.74 Adm	Below 2.50 Apps	Below 2.50 Adm	No GPA Apps	No GPA Adm	Total Apps	Total Adm
170–180	9	6	3	3	6	5	3	3	5	5	1	1	1	1	0	0	28	24
165–169	21	19	34	34	35	35	22	22	12	11	11	11	11	6	1	1	147	139
160–164	55	53	106	104	124	123	109	108	49	45	42	30	33	18	9	8	527	489
155–159	102	100	212	208	274	267	273	267	185	153	85	48	74	22	21	21	1226	1086
150–154	138	96	283	189	398	191	413	145	275	63	179	15	112	7	41	9	1839	715
145–149	66	13	162	15	278	37	302	40	202	17	109	5	84	0	29	0	1232	127
140–144	27	1	74	1	94	3	124	1	98	1	72	1	74	0	15	0	578	8
Below 140	6	0	11	0	37	0	64	0	62	0	51	0	58	0	15	0	304	0
Total	424	288	885	554	1246	661	1310	586	888	295	550	111	447	54	131	39	5881	2588

Apps = Number of Applicants
Adm = Number Admitted
Reflects 99% of the total applicant pool; highest LSAT data reported.

NEW YORK UNIVERSITY SCHOOL OF LAW

40 Washington Square South
New York, NY 10012
Phone: 212.998.6060; Fax: 212.995.4527
E-mail: law.moreinfo@nyu.edu; Website: www.law.nyu.edu

ABA
Approved
Since
1930

The Basics

Type of school	Private
Term	Semester
Application deadline	2/15
Application fee	$75
Financial aid deadline	4/15
Can first year start other than fall?	No
Student to faculty ratio	9.0 to 1
# of housing spaces available restricted to law students	810
graduate housing for which law students are eligible	

Faculty and Administrators

	Total		Men		Women		Minorities	
	Spr	Fall	Spr	Fall	Spr	Fall	Spr	Fall
Full-time	126	141	91	97	35	44	17	19
Other full-time	17	22	6	7	11	15	1	4
Deans, librarians, & others who teach	14	15	5	6	9	9	1	1
Part-time	107	72	72	51	35	21	9	5
Total	264	250	174	161	90	89	28	29

Curriculum

		Full-Time	Part-Time
Typical first-year section size		95	0
Is there typically a "small section" of the first-year class, other than Legal Writing, taught by full-time faculty		No	No
If yes, typical size offered last year			
# of classroom course titles beyond first-year curriculum		308	
# of upper division courses, excluding seminars, with an enrollment:	Under 25	159	
	25–49	69	
	50–74	43	
	75–99	16	
	100+	16	
# of seminars		145	
# of seminar positions available		3,578	
# of seminar positions filled		2,213	0
# of positions available in simulation courses		203	
# of simulation positions filled		179	0
# of positions available in faculty supervised clinical courses		212	
# of faculty supervised clinical positions filled		205	0
# involved in field placements		211	0
# involved in law journals		646	0
# involved in moot court or trial competitions		138	0
# of credit hours required to graduate		83	

JD Enrollment and Ethnicity

	Men		Women		Full-Time		Part-Time		1st-Year		Total		JD Degs. Awd.
	#	%	#	%	#	%	#	%	#	%	#	%	
All Hispanics	60	7.0	47	7.8	107	7.3	0	0.0	33	7.3	107	7.3	36
Am. Ind./AK Nat.	1	0.1	0	0.0	1	0.1	0	0.0	0	0.0	1	0.1	2
Asian	77	9.0	79	13.1	156	10.7	0	0.0	53	11.8	156	10.7	46
Black/Af. Am.	39	4.5	61	10.1	100	6.8	0	0.0	27	6.0	100	6.8	30
Nat. HI/Pac. Isl.	0	0.0	0	0.0	0	0.0	0	0.0	0	0.0	0	0.0	1
2 or more races	5	0.6	4	0.7	9	0.6	0	0.0	9	2.0	9	0.6	1
Subtotal (minor.)	182	21.2	191	31.6	373	25.5	0	0.0	122	27.1	373	25.5	116
Nonres. Alien	17	2.0	32	5.3	49	3.3	0	0.0	18	4.0	49	3.3	16
White/Cauc.	509	59.3	293	48.4	802	54.8	0	0.0	275	61.1	802	54.8	224
Unknown	151	17.6	89	14.7	240	16.4	0	0.0	35	7.8	240	16.4	110
Total	859	58.7	605	41.3	1464	100.0	0	0.0	450	30.7	1464		466

Transfers

Transfers in	56
Transfers out	1

Tuition and Fees

	Resident	Nonresident
Full-time	$50,336	$50,336
Part-time		
Tuition Guarantee Program		N

Living Expenses

Estimated living expenses for singles

Living on campus	Living off campus	Living at home
$22,754	$22,754	$22,754

NEW YORK UNIVERSITY SCHOOL OF LAW

ABA
Approved
Since
1930

GPA and LSAT Scores

	Total	Full-Time	Part-Time
# of apps	7,280	7,280	0
# of offers	1,759	1,759	0
# of matrics	450	450	0
75% GPA	3.85	3.85	0.00
Median GPA	3.71	3.71	0.00
25% GPA	3.57	3.57	0.00
75% LSAT	174	174	0
Median LSAT	172	172	0
25% LSAT	170	170	0

Grants and Scholarships (from prior year)

	Total #	Total %	Full-Time #	Full-Time %	Part-Time #	Part-Time %
Total # of students	1,431		1,431		0	
Total # receiving grants	668	46.7	668	46.7	0	0.0
Less than 1/2 tuition	522	36.5	522	36.5	0	0.0
Half to full tuition	43	3.0	43	3.0	0	0.0
Full tuition	103	7.2	103	7.2	0	0.0
More than full tuition	0	0.0	0	0.0	0	0.0
Median grant amount			$15,000		$0	

Informational and Library Resources

Total amount spent on library materials	$2,537,183
Study seating capacity inside the library	850
# of full-time equivalent professional librarians	37
Hours per week library is open	101
# of open, wired connections available to students	790
# of networked computers available for use by students	190
Has wireless network?	Y
Requires computer?	Y

JD Attrition (from prior year)

	Academic #	Other #	Total #	Total %
1st year	0	6	6	1.3
2nd year	0	5	5	1.0
3rd year	0	2	2	0.4
4th year	0	0	0	0.0

Employment (9 months after graduation)

For up-to-date employment data, go to employmentsummary.abaquestionnaire.org on the ABA website.

Bar Passage Rates

First-time takers	499	Reporting %	81.96
Average school %	96.33	Average state %	84.92
Average pass difference	11.41		

Jurisdiction	Takers	Passers	Pass %	State %	Diff %
New York	409	394	96.33	84.92	11.41

NEW YORK UNIVERSITY SCHOOL OF LAW

40 Washington Square South
New York, NY 10012
Phone: 212.998.6060; Fax: 212.995.4527
E-mail: law.moreinfo@nyu.edu; Website: www.law.nyu.edu

Introduction

Founded in 1835, New York University School of Law has a long record of academic excellence, national scholarly influence, and innovative achievements. It has long been a pacesetter in legal education, pioneering new approaches to practical-skills training and the early recognition that law has an increasingly global dimension to which all students should be exposed in the classroom. Its innovative lawyering, clinical, and advocacy programs; interdisciplinary colloquia; public interest initiatives; and law-and-business transaction courses have all served as models for others. The law school has a proud history of fairness and openness: More than 100 years ago, NYU Law became one of the first law schools to routinely admit women and other groups discriminated against by many other institutions, and it continues to offer opportunities to exceptional students from groups historically underrepresented in the profession. The school's location in the financial and cultural capital of the world provides students ready access to the very best practitioners and policy makers, including top executives in business and finance, as well as leaders of international, governmental, and public interest organizations. Through its numerous clinics, centers, and institutes, the law school provides unparalleled professional experience for students who graduate to pursue careers in government, business, and, of course, the legal profession.

Curriculum

The curriculum at NYU School of Law is designed to offer students the best possible foundation in legal theory and practice, and to empower them with the skills they need to be successful lawyers—and leaders—in the twenty-first century. Taught by top-tier faculty, the curriculum is distinguished by its depth and breadth across all traditional areas of legal study, its interdisciplinary strength, and its global perspective. The law school is committed to providing students with a sophisticated understanding of how US law interacts with—and is informed by—the regimes of other nations and the international community, and to educating lawyers who will use their degrees to become leaders of the profession and of society.

In recent years, the law school has implemented several significant innovations in the curriculum, including the addition of a first-year Administrative and Regulatory State course and a first-year elective that allows students to choose among constitutional law, corporations, international law, tax, or property. The Lawyering Program, recognized by the Carnegie Foundation as the best of its kind, complements the theoretical and doctrinal courses offered in the first year and sets the foundation for more than 32 fieldwork clinics that students can take in the upper years, including new offerings in business law, tax, and federal regulation.

Students take classes taught by faculty who are leaders in their fields—including international, environmental, and criminal law—as well as by the foremost scholars in civil procedure, torts, and administrative law and policy. NYU Law has a distinguished interdisciplinary curriculum, including its law and philosophy program and a robust law and business program. The latter offers unique transactional courses that

teach students how lawyers can add value to the strategic development, design, negotiation, and implementation of deals in law, finance, real estate, entertainment, tax, and business. Aside from these programs, students enjoy intellectual and pedagogical diversity, mixing traditional classes with a choice of courses in cutting-edge fields such as the law of democracy and law and security, as well as colloquia, clinics, independent research, journal work, study abroad, fellowships, and more.

Faculty

NYU Law's preeminent faculty are not only engaged in high-level scholarly inquiry and teaching, but can also be found contributing to the world beyond the classroom, advising international tribunals, testifying before Congress, authoring briefs in important cases, or working to protect the rights of immigrants and children. The faculty actively mentor their students, involving them in important work and helping them to develop their own scholarship. The faculty has expanded significantly in recent years, with 44 new members joining since 2002—resulting in a total growth of 30 percent. More than merely increasing the faculty's size and its diversity, these additions have expanded the breadth and depth of scholarship undertaken at the school. Recent additions have brought expertise across the curriculum as well as in interdisciplinary fields, such as empirical legal studies, legal history, law and politics, law and economics, and law and philosophy. The school also attracts leading academics as visitors, who bring fresh perspectives and further enhance the robust intellectual life of the community.

Institutes and Centers

A rich intellectual life outside the classroom is sustained by more than 25 institutes and centers, including the Brennan Center for Justice, the Hauser Global Law School Program, the Institute for International Law and Justice, the Frank J. Guarini Center on Environmental and Land Use Law, the Institute for Policy and Integrity, and the Pollack Center for Law and Business. These enterprises bring together leading faculty and professional teams of lawyers, economists, and policy experts to produce research and commentary that influence the real world of law, policy, and business. They also provide students with unique opportunities to work on sophisticated projects in the areas of national security, real estate, criminal justice, human rights, and international law, among many others.

Library and Physical Facilities

NYU School of Law's library contains one of the largest academic law collections in the world. Located in Greenwich Village, the law school's campus includes the recently renovated Vanderbilt Hall and its neighbor, Furman Hall, finished in 2004. In the fall of 2010, the law school opened a new academic facility, Wilf Hall, which, along with a newly restored townhouse at 22 Washington Square North, houses the law school's many centers and institutes. D'Agostino Hall, Mercer Residence, and two low-rise, on-campus apartment buildings provide housing for more than 800 law students.

Student Journals and Activities

There are nine student-edited publications, and additional writing opportunities are available through the Moot Court Board. There are more than 65 student organizations, including the Law Students for Human Rights, the award-winning Suspension Representation Project, and the school's student government group, the Student Bar Association.

Career Services

NYU School of Law has an extensive career services program. Career planning for first-year students includes personal career counseling, workshops on all aspects of the job search, specialty panels featuring speakers from all areas of practice, and a videotape mock interview program. Each year, more than 500 private law firms, public interest organizations, government agencies, corporations, and public accounting firms visit the law school to interview students. More than 70 percent of these employers are from outside New York.

The Public Interest Law Center provides students interested in public service with comprehensive support, including advice on courses and career opportunities. The Public Interest Summer Funding Program guarantees funding to all first- and second-year students who work in public interest positions. The Public Interest Law Center, in conjunction with other area law schools, also sponsors an annual public interest legal career fair, the largest event of its kind in the country.

Admission

The admission process is highly selective, seeking men and women of exceptional ability with diverse experiences,

APPLICANT PROFILE

NYU School of Law does not provide a profile chart because we believe that while an applicant's undergraduate record and LSAT scores are important, they are not the sole determinants for admission. No index or cut-off is used in reviewing applications. There is no particular combination of grades or scores that assures admittance or guarantees

backgrounds, and points of view. The Committee on Admissions reviews each undergraduate transcript closely, with attention to factors such as trends in the applicant's grades, class rank, the ratio of pass/fail to graded courses, the diversity and depth of coursework, and the length of time since graduation.

Other aspects of the application also influence the decision; the committee evaluates work experience and extracurricular and community activities for evidence of advancement, leadership, and the capacity for assuming responsibility. Factors other than undergraduate grades and LSAT scores may be particularly significant for applicants who have experienced educational or socioeconomic disadvantages.

Financial Aid

NYU School of Law has several scholarship programs. The flagship Root-Tilden-Kern Scholarship Program selects entering students for their intellectual potential and demonstrated commitment to public service through law. AnBryce Scholarships are awarded to outstanding students who are among the first in their immediate families to pursue a graduate degree. The Furman Academic Scholarships are given to students who show promise in becoming legal academics. Scholarships are also available in the areas of business law, international law, and Latino human rights. A limited number of other awards are also made on the basis of intellectual potential or evidence that the student will enrich the law school's educational environment. Additionally, the school provides need-based grants. Federal and private loans also provide funding. Graduates who pursue careers in public service may be eligible for postgraduation benefits through the school's generous and groundbreaking Loan Repayment Assistance Program.

rejection. The Committee on Admissions simply aims to enroll an entering class with the strongest combination of qualifications and the greatest potential to contribute to the vibrant intellectual life of the school, to the legal profession as a whole, and, more broadly, to society in general.

UNIVERSITY OF NORTH CAROLINA SCHOOL OF LAW

Campus Box 3380, 5026 Van Hecke-Wettach Hall
Chapel Hill, NC 27599-3380
Phone: 919.962.5109; Fax: 919.843.7939
E-mail: law_admissions@unc.edu; Website: www.law.unc.edu

ABA
Approved
Since
1923

The Basics

Type of school	Public
Term	Semester
Application deadline	3/1
Application fee	$75
Financial aid deadline	3/1
Can first year start other than fall?	No
Student to faculty ratio	14.7 to 1
# of housing spaces available restricted to law students	
graduate housing for which law students are eligible	126

Faculty and Administrators

	Total		Men		Women		Minorities	
	Spr	Fall	Spr	Fall	Spr	Fall	Spr	Fall
Full-time	43	44	26	26	17	18	8	6
Other full-time	0	0	0	0	0	0	0	0
Deans, librarians, & others who teach	15	15	10	9	5	6	2	2
Part-time	40	37	28	22	12	15	4	6
Total	98	96	64	57	34	39	14	14

JD Enrollment and Ethnicity

	Men		Women		Full-Time		Part-Time		1st-Year		Total		JD Degs. Awd.
	#	%	#	%	#	%	#	%	#	%	#	%	
All Hispanics	33	8.7	40	10.2	73	9.5	0	0.0	22	8.9	73	9.5	21
Am. Ind./AK Nat.	6	1.6	3	0.8	9	1.2	0	0.0	3	1.2	9	1.2	8
Asian	16	4.2	30	7.6	46	6.0	0	0.0	17	6.9	46	6.0	2
Black/Af. Am.	20	5.3	38	9.7	58	7.5	0	0.0	20	8.1	58	7.5	16
Nat. HI/Pac. Isl.	2	0.5	1	0.3	3	0.4	0	0.0	0	0.0	3	0.4	7
2 or more races	14	3.7	13	3.3	27	3.5	0	0.0	6	2.4	27	3.5	6
Subtotal (minor.)	91	24.0	125	31.8	216	28.0	0	0.0	68	27.4	216	28.0	60
Nonres. Alien	5	1.3	7	1.8	12	1.6	0	0.0	3	1.2	12	1.6	0
White/Cauc.	244	64.4	241	61.3	485	62.8	0	0.0	160	64.5	485	62.8	125
Unknown	39	10.3	20	5.1	59	7.6	0	0.0	17	6.9	59	7.6	63
Total	379	49.1	393	50.9	772	100.0	0	0.0	248	32.1	772		248

Curriculum

	Full-Time	Part-Time
Typical first-year section size	85	0
Is there typically a "small section" of the first-year class, other than Legal Writing, taught by full-time faculty	Yes	No
If yes, typical size offered last year	28	
# of classroom course titles beyond first-year curriculum	134	
# of upper division courses, excluding seminars, with an enrollment: Under 25	67	
25–49	32	
50–74	9	
75–99	7	
100+	4	
# of seminars	29	
# of seminar positions available	434	
# of seminar positions filled	355	0
# of positions available in simulation courses	1,116	
# of simulation positions filled	1,057	0
# of positions available in faculty supervised clinical courses	68	
# of faculty supervised clinical positions filled	68	0
# involved in field placements	161	0
# involved in law journals	226	0
# involved in moot court or trial competitions	73	0
# of credit hours required to graduate	86	

Transfers

Transfers in	4
Transfers out	6

Tuition and Fees

	Resident	Nonresident
Full-time	$19,012	$34,119
Part-time		
Tuition Guarantee Program	N	

Living Expenses

Estimated living expenses for singles

Living on campus	Living off campus	Living at home
$21,244	$21,244	$8,888

UNIVERSITY OF NORTH CAROLINA SCHOOL OF LAW

*ABA
Approved
Since
1923*

GPA and LSAT Scores

	Total	Full-Time	Part-Time
# of apps	2,576	2,576	0
# of offers	462	462	0
# of matrics	248	248	0
75% GPA	3.69	3.69	0.00
Median GPA	3.51	3.51	0.00
25% GPA	3.33	3.33	0.00
75% LSAT	165	165	0
Median LSAT	163	163	0
25% LSAT	161	161	0

Grants and Scholarships (from prior year)

	Total #	Total %	Full-Time #	Full-Time %	Part-Time #	Part-Time %
Total # of students	778		778		0	
Total # receiving grants	674	86.6	674	86.6	0	0.0
Less than 1/2 tuition	568	73.0	568	73.0	0	0.0
Half to full tuition	88	11.3	88	11.3	0	0.0
Full tuition	4	0.5	4	0.5	0	0.0
More than full tuition	14	1.8	14	1.8	0	0.0
Median grant amount		$1,550			$0	

Informational and Library Resources

Total amount spent on library materials	$1,847,170
Study seating capacity inside the library	520
# of full-time equivalent professional librarians	13
Hours per week library is open	109
# of open, wired connections available to students	598
# of networked computers available for use by students	98
Has wireless network?	Y
Requires computer?	N

JD Attrition (from prior year)

	Academic #	Other #	Total #	Total %
1st year	1	12	13	5.1
2nd year	0	0	0	0.0
3rd year	0	0	0	0.0
4th year	0	0	0	0.0

Employment (9 months after graduation)

For up-to-date employment data, go to employmentsummary.abaquestionnaire.org on the ABA website.

Bar Passage Rates

First-time takers	222	Reporting %	72.07
Average school %	91.25	Average state %	78.42

Average pass difference   12.83

Jurisdiction	Takers	Passers	Pass %	State %	Diff %
North Carolina	140	130	92.86	77.50	15.36
New York	20	16	80.00	84.92	–4.92

UNIVERSITY OF NORTH CAROLINA SCHOOL OF LAW

Campus Box 3380, 5026 Van Hecke-Wettach Hall
Chapel Hill, NC 27599-3380
Phone: 919.962.5109; Fax: 919.843.7939
E-mail: law_admissions@unc.edu; Website: www.law.unc.edu

Introduction

The University of North Carolina, the first state university chartered in the United States, has offered degrees in law since 1845. The School of Law has been a member of the American Association of Law Schools since 1920 and has been an approved law school since the American Bar Association began its accreditation activities in 1923. The School of Law is one of the outstanding institutions in the United States, and the University of North Carolina is recognized as being among the nation's leaders in graduate and professional education. The programs at the School of Law reflect a powerful, active commitment to the goals of teaching, scholarship, and public service. The town of Chapel Hill, a university community, is close to the Research Triangle Park, the metropolitan and industrial centers of Greensboro and Durham, and the state capital, Raleigh. The immediate area offers an attractive blend of a strong academic atmosphere in a multicultural, cosmopolitan setting.

Library and Physical Facilities

Housed on five floors within the law school, the library provides critical support to the school's academic program and to lawyers and members of the public throughout the state. Its collection, which totals over 547,000 volumes, includes court reports for American and English appellate courts, current codes and session laws for all states, and other primary legal materials. Within the library, a university computer lab provides Internet access, electronic mail, and word-processing capabilities, and it is easily accessible to law students. Additionally, students may bring their own laptop computers and connect to the university's network in many of the high-technology classrooms, library study carrels, and other areas in the building.

The School of Law aims to provide a quality legal education that will prepare students to practice successfully in any jurisdiction. The three-year Juris Doctor program begins with a first-year core curriculum designed to provide a theoretical and analytical foundation for law students. The second-year curriculum provides an important bridge between the core instruction of the first year and the culminating electives, seminars, and skills-oriented instruction of the third year. Finally, in the third year, the curriculum is designed to provide a capstone for students' legal education and begin the transition into practice.

Dual-Degree Programs/Certificate Programs

Ten formal dual JD and master's degree programs are available: JD/MPP (in conjunction with Duke University), JD/MBA, JD/MPA, JD/MPH, JD/MRP, JD/MSW, JD/MASA, JD/MAMC, JD/MSLS, or MSIS.

The Nonprofit Leadership Certificate Program prepares graduate students for leadership roles in North Carolina's rapidly growing nonprofit sector. The program provides an in-depth examination of leadership issues within human services, education, the arts, and other nonprofit organizations.

International Study Opportunities

In addition to the regularly taught courses in international business and human rights and the *International Law Journal*, students interested in international law can enhance their legal experience further with foreign study during the school year in France, the Netherlands, Mexico, England, and Scotland. Additionally, after the first year, students may also participate in the school's Summer Law Programs in Sydney, Australia; Augsburg, Germany; or Sorrento, Italy.

Centers and Initiatives

Carolina boasts nationally recognized centers in banking and financial services; civil rights; poverty, work, and opportunity; our new Center for Law, Environment, Adaptation, and Resources (CLEAR); and the Center for Law and Government. All are key areas tied to our history and the unique opportunities unfolding in North Carolina, the South, and the world. These centers and initiatives expand and enliven our curriculum, push the frontiers of teaching and research, and open new channels of scholarship for students.

Student Activities

Outside of the classroom, student organizations provide a forum for the enormous talent and energy characteristic of Carolina law students. Students can write for five prominent student publications—the *North Carolina Law Review*, the *North Carolina Journal of International Law and Commercial Regulation*, the *North Carolina Banking Institute Journal*, the *First Amendment Law Review*, and the *North Carolina Journal of Law and Technology*. The Student Bar Association sponsors a full range of professional, athletic, and social events; a speakers program; minority recruitment events; a legal research service for practicing lawyers; and participation in school governance. The Moot Court Program is student operated and fields a number of successful teams in regional, national, and international competitions. Over 50 student organizations are active in the School of Law, including the Black Law Students Association, Parents as Law Students, the Federalist Society, the Hispanic/Latino Law Students Association, the Native American Law Students Association, ACLU, Women in Law, American Constitution Society, and our nationally recognized Pro Bono Program.

Expenses and Financial Aid

Full-time tuition and fees for the 2011–2012 school year—North Carolina resident, $19,012; nonresident, $34,120. Estimated additional expenses—$21,244. Chancellors' Scholars Program scholarships are available, as well as other merit-based scholarships. Need-based assistance is awarded on the basis of FAFSA information. Students must submit parental information to FAFSA to be considered for need-based grants.

Admitted applicants are automatically considered for merit-based scholarships. Awards range from $5,000 to full tuition. Scholarship offers are made beginning in February.

Housing

There are graduate dormitories near the law school for single students; however, most students live off campus. University student family housing and private apartments are available. Information may be obtained from the University Housing Office, Carr Building CB 5500, Chapel Hill, NC 27399-5580; 919.962.5401.

Career Services Office

The Career Services Office staff assists students and alumni with summer and permanent positions. Each year, approximately 200 employers from across the nation interview at the School of Law. Of those 2010 graduates seeking employment and reporting to the Career Services Office, 95 percent had accepted employment or were in graduate school within nine months of graduation. Of those 2010 graduates who entered into legal practice, 47 percent entered private practice; 22 percent entered public sector work, including public interest; 15 percent accepted judicial clerkships; 13 percent entered business/corporate-related practice; and 2 percent entered academia. Regarding job location, 53 percent were employed in North Carolina; 9.3 percent were employed in New York, New Jersey, and Pennsylvania; 3 percent were employed in Arkansas, Louisiana, Oklahoma, and Texas; and 2 percent were employed in Alaska, California, Hawaii, Oregon, and Washington. Almost 77 percent of our students are employed in the South Atlantic region of the country, which includes Delaware; Washington, DC; Florida; Georgia; Maryland; North Carolina; South Carolina; Virginia; and West Virginia. One percent were employed in a foreign country.

APPLICANT PROFILE

University of North Carolina School of Law
This grid includes only applicants who earned 120–180 LSAT scores under standard administrations.

LSAT Score	3.75 +		3.50–3.74		3.25–3.49		3.00–3.24		2.75–2.99		2.50–2.74		2.25–2.49		2.00–2.24		Below 2.00		No GPA		Total	
	Apps	Adm	Apps	Adm	Apps	Adm	Apps	Adm	Apps	Adm	Apps	Adm	Apps	Adm	Apps	Adm	Apps	Adm	Apps	Adm	Apps	Adm
175–180	2	1	2	2	1	1	3	1	0	0	1	0	0	0	0	0	0	0	0	0	9	5
170–174	18	15	20	13	17	10	13	4	7	1	1	0	1	0	0	0	0	0	0	0	77	43
165–169	86	52	139	47	94	36	50	15	16	1	5	0	2	0	0	0	0	0	9	2	401	153
160–164	179	55	216	53	199	45	115	24	34	0	14	1	6	0	3	0	0	0	12	2	778	180
155–159	136	11	198	20	173	23	92	6	40	1	22	0	8	0	2	0	1	0	13	1	685	62
150–154	58	6	84	7	81	6	59	2	33	0	17	0	5	0	5	0	1	0	7	0	350	21
145–149	15	0	29	1	32	0	38	0	27	0	17	0	3	0	2	0	0	0	3	0	166	1
140–144	2	0	11	0	14	0	19	0	9	0	7	0	5	0	3	0	0	0	2	0	72	0
135–139	2	0	4	0	5	0	4	0	4	0	1	0	2	0	3	0	0	0	1	0	26	0
130–134	0	0	0	0	0	0	2	0	4	0	3	0	2	0	1	0	0	0	0	0	12	0
125–129	0	0	0	0	2	0	1	0	1	0	2	0	1	0	0	0	0	0	1	0	8	0
120–124	0	0	0	0	0	0	0	0	0	0	0	0	0	0	0	0	0	0	0	0	0	0
Total	498	140	703	143	618	121	396	52	175	3	90	1	35	0	19	0	2	0	48	5	2584	465

Apps = Number of Applicants
Adm = Number Admitted
Reflects 100% of the total applicant pool; highest LSAT data reported.

NORTH CAROLINA CENTRAL UNIVERSITY SCHOOL OF LAW

640 Nelson Street
Durham, NC 27707
Phone: 919.530.6333; Fax: 919.530.6030
E-mail: recruiter@nccu.edu; Website: law.nccu.edu

The Basics

Type of school	Public
Term	Semester
Application deadline	3/31
Application fee	$50
Financial aid deadline	4/15
Can first year start other than fall?	No
Student to faculty ratio	14.7 to 1
# of housing spaces available restricted to law students	
graduate housing for which law students are eligible	32

Faculty and Administrators

	Total		Men		Women		Minorities	
	Spr	Fall	Spr	Fall	Spr	Fall	Spr	Fall
Full-time	28	31	11	11	17	20	18	20
Other full-time	10	7	5	3	5	4	5	4
Deans, librarians, & others who teach	13	14	2	2	11	12	9	9
Part-time	22	25	9	11	13	14	13	13
Total	73	77	27	27	46	50	45	46

Curriculum

		Full-Time	Part-Time
Typical first-year section size		55	55
Is there typically a "small section" of the first-year class, other than Legal Writing, taught by full-time faculty		No	No
If yes, typical size offered last year			
# of classroom course titles beyond first-year curriculum		99	
# of upper division courses, excluding seminars, with an enrollment:	Under 25	92	
	25–49	28	
	50–74	12	
	75–99	7	
	100+	0	
# of seminars		35	
# of seminar positions available		667	
# of seminar positions filled		333	21
# of positions available in simulation courses		575	
# of simulation positions filled		401	49
# of positions available in faculty supervised clinical courses		362	
# of faculty supervised clinical positions filled		237	17
# involved in field placements		81	8
# involved in law journals		64	4
# involved in moot court or trial competitions		35	0
# of credit hours required to graduate		88	

JD Enrollment and Ethnicity

	Men		Women		Full-Time		Part-Time		1st-Year		Total		JD Degs. Awd.
	#	%	#	%	#	%	#	%	#	%	#	%	
All Hispanics	4	1.8	8	2.6	10	2.3	2	2.1	3	1.9	12	2.3	5
Am. Ind./AK Nat.	2	0.9	3	1.0	4	0.9	1	1.1	2	1.2	5	0.9	1
Asian	5	2.3	4	1.3	7	1.6	2	2.1	2	1.2	9	1.7	8
Black/Af. Am.	91	41.4	180	57.7	247	56.5	24	25.3	72	44.4	271	50.9	81
Nat. HI/Pac. Isl.	0	0.0	0	0.0	0	0.0	0	0.0	0	0.0	0	0.0	0
2 or more races	0	0.0	0	0.0	0	0.0	0	0.0	0	0.0	0	0.0	0
Subtotal (minor.)	102	46.4	195	62.5	268	61.3	29	30.5	79	48.8	297	55.8	95
Nonres. Alien	1	0.5	1	0.3	1	0.2	1	1.1	1	0.6	2	0.4	1
White/Cauc.	115	52.3	112	35.9	163	37.3	64	67.4	80	49.4	227	42.7	76
Unknown	2	0.9	4	1.3	5	1.1	1	1.1	2	1.2	6	1.1	6
Total	220	41.4	312	58.6	437	82.1	95	17.9	162	30.5	532		178

Transfers

Transfers in	0
Transfers out	1

Tuition and Fees

	Resident	Nonresident
Full-time	$10,415	$24,343
Part-time	$10,415	$24,343
Tuition Guarantee Program	N	

Living Expenses

Estimated living expenses for singles

Living on campus	Living off campus	Living at home
$10,172	$17,500	$9,510

NORTH CAROLINA CENTRAL UNIVERSITY SCHOOL OF LAW

*ABA
Approved
Since
1950*

GPA and LSAT Scores

	Total	Full-Time	Part-Time
# of apps	2,406	1,820	586
# of offers	445	366	79
# of matrics	166	139	27
75% GPA	3.49	3.47	3.62
Median GPA	3.20	3.19	3.33
25% GPA	2.94	2.91	3.08
75% LSAT	151	151	158
Median LSAT	148	148	151
25% LSAT	145	145	147

Grants and Scholarships (from prior year)

	Total #	Total %	Full-Time #	Full-Time %	Part-Time #	Part-Time %
Total # of students	602		491		111	
Total # receiving grants	346	57.5	336	68.4	10	9.0
Less than 1/2 tuition	183	30.4	173	35.2	10	9.0
Half to full tuition	65	10.8	65	13.2	0	0.0
Full tuition	58	9.6	58	11.8	0	0.0
More than full tuition	40	6.6	40	8.1	0	0.0
Median grant amount			$6,253		$0	

Informational and Library Resources

Total amount spent on library materials	$983,003
Study seating capacity inside the library	325
# of full-time equivalent professional librarians	9
Hours per week library is open	100
# of open, wired connections available to students	137
# of networked computers available for use by students	641
Has wireless network?	Y
Requires computer?	N

JD Attrition (from prior year)

	Academic #	Other #	Total #	Total %
1st year	26	12	38	18.5
2nd year	1	4	5	2.9
3rd year	0	3	3	1.7
4th year	0	0	0	0.0

Employment (9 months after graduation)

For up-to-date employment data, go to employmentsummary.abaquestionnaire.org on the ABA website.

Bar Passage Rates

First-time takers	175	Reporting %	78.29
Average school %	72.99	Average state %	77.50
Average pass difference	−4.51		

Jurisdiction	Takers	Passers	Pass %	State %	Diff %
North Carolina	137	100	72.99	77.50	−4.51

NORTH CAROLINA CENTRAL UNIVERSITY SCHOOL OF LAW

640 Nelson Street
Durham, NC 27707
Phone: 919.530.6333; Fax: 919.530.6030
E-mail: recruiter@nccu.edu; Website: law.nccu.edu

Introduction

The mission of the North Carolina Central University School of Law is to produce competent and socially responsible members of the legal profession. NCCU School of Law accomplishes its mission by providing a challenging and broad-based educational program that stimulates intellectual inquiry of the highest order and that fosters in each student a deep sense of professional responsibility and personal integrity. Founded in 1939 to provide an opportunity for a legal education to African Americans, the School of Law now provides this opportunity to one of the most diverse student bodies in the nation. This environment of diversity better prepares our students to effect positive change in the broader society.

The School of Law has been accredited by the North Carolina State Bar Council and the ABA since 1950. Today, NCCU School of Law remains one of the most affordable and diverse law schools in the country. The School of Law offers two programs leading to the Juris Doctor degree: a full-time day program and the oldest ABA-accredited part-time evening program between Atlanta, Georgia, and Washington, DC. The School of Law participates in an interinstitutional agreement with Duke University and the University of North Carolina at Chapel Hill that permits students to enroll in electives at any member law school without an increase in tuition.

Facilities, Library, and Technology

The Albert L. Turner Law School building is a state-of-the-art facility that provides the law school community with an attractive, comfortable, and technology-friendly environment in which to work and study. The entire building is wireless. Students are provided a laptop and software for use throughout their matriculation. All classrooms are equipped with state-of-the-art multimedia resources, including smart boards, video and teleconferencing capabilities, and lectern computers with Internet access. The School of Law has several state-of-the-art group-study rooms, a moot courtroom, and the Great Hall for gatherings.

The law library, with more than 400,000 volumes and volume equivalents, provides the resources needed to support the Juris Doctor program, the JD/MLS and JD/MBA dual-degree programs, and the legal community. The law library is a selective North Carolina and United States government depository and has a special collection in civil rights law.

Special Academic Programs

Joint-Degree Options—There are two joint-degree programs available to Day Program students. The joint-degree JD/MBA Program allows students who are interested in a career in law and business to receive both degrees in four years. The joint-degree JD/MLS Program allows students who are interested in a career in law librarianship to simultaneously pursue both degrees. Students must apply and be accepted to each program separately.

Evening Program—The Evening Program is a four-year, year-round program that offers a unique opportunity for motivated professionals to pursue a legal education while maintaining their current daytime work commitments.

Academic Support Program—The Academic Support Program is available to assist students with the rigors of law school. Through the tutorial program, workshops, one-on-one guidance, and readily available resources, all students have access to information to enable them to become effective and successful law students.

Faculty Advising Program—Each student is assigned a faculty advisor who is available to discuss questions or problems related to the School of Law experience, career choices, and personal problems that might affect academic performance. They also advise students on taking appropriate classes and monitor their progress.

Clinical Program—The award-winning Clinical Program is highly rated. It operates year-round from a state-of-the-art model law office. The program offers as many as 13 innovative clinical experiences that provide law students with the opportunity to gain practical skills in the area of law that interests them the most. It is the most comprehensive program of any law school in the state. In-house clinical professors teach skills courses and supervise clinical students who represent real clients with real legal issues.

Invest in Success Program—This bar preparation program is a joint effort with the faculty and academic support staff. Various faculty members conduct weekly substantive law reviews during the summer. The Office of Academic Support conducts workshops on various topics and works with students to improve their essay exam writing skills. Special attention is given to those students who underperformed in NC Distinctions, the School of Law's bar-prep-for-credit course.

Institutes—The law school offers special programs and certificates through our Biotechnology and Pharmaceutical Law Institute and the Dispute Resolution Institute.

Admission

Admission to the School of Law is competitive, with approximately 3,000 applicants competing for approximately 180 to 190 seats in the Day Program and 40 to 45 seats in the Evening Program. Students are admitted for the fall semester only on a rolling admission basis. Applicants are evaluated for admission based on a range of attributes, including academic achievement, performance on the LSAT, personal and professional experiences, intelligence and reasoning ability, individuality of thought and creativity, initiative and motivation, judgment and maturity, oral and written communication skills, integrity, leadership ability, and their potential contribution to the legal profession.

Because it is presumed that Evening Program students will have full-time employment, the Admissions Committee places greater weight on the quantifiable performance predictors for applicants to the Evening Program. Electronic applications for admission are accepted from October 1 through March 31 via our website at law.nccu.edu or the Law School Admission Council's website at LSAC.org.

Please note: Prospective applicants should view the School of Law website at law.nccu.edu for information regarding the School of Law.

Performance-Based Admission Program (PBAP)

As part of its commitment to the school's mission, North Carolina Central University School of Law offers prospective students opportunities to gain admission through its Performance-Based Admission Program (PBAP). The PBAP enables applicants whose numerical predictors fall below the presumptively admissible range to demonstrate their ability through a rigorous two-week, noncredit program in the spring. The Office of Admissions selects PBAP participants based on a number of factors, including, but not limited to, a history of below-average standardized test scores followed by academic achievement, work experience, a significant time lapse between the undergraduate degree and law school application, and students who come from socially disadvantaged backgrounds. Students who successfully complete PBAP are then offered admission to NCCU's School of Law Day or Evening Program.

Student Organizations

The *North Carolina Central Law Review* is devoted to a broad range of legal topics submitted by legal scholars, attorneys, and law students. Students are selected for membership based upon GPA and performance in the annual Law Review Writing Competition. The School of Law also has the student-run *Biotechnology and Pharmaceutical Law Review*. The Moot Court Board consists of upper-class students who have demonstrated exceptional ability in appellate skills. The Trial Advocacy Board consists of student teams who participate in mock jury trial competitions. The board has gained regional and national recognition for its excellence in trial advocacy. Other student organizations include the Black Law Students Association, Christian Legal Society, Environmental Law Society, Hispanic Law Student Association, Innocence Project, Native American Law Student Association, OutLaw Alliance, Public Interest Law Organization, Sports and Entertainment Law Society, Women's Caucus, and various legal fraternities.

Career Services

The Office of Career Services offers a range of career planning and development services, including career counseling, résumé workshops, interview preparation, job postings, information sessions, reputation management, and panel discussions on legal careers. Graduates find employment in law firms, corporations, state and federal government agencies, public interest organizations, the judiciary, and the military. Consistent with our school's tradition, approximately 30 percent of our graduates entered into public service—more than half of them at the state level of service. Four percent of our graduates were accepted as judicial clerks. Of those in private practice (a little more than half of the class), most are employed in smaller law firms, while 12 percent of our graduates are employed in the business sector, primarily in either a technology-based company or a biotech/pharmaceutical company. Our graduates tend to stay in state (95 percent) and the remaining 5 percent are usually employed in the Southeast region, including Washington, DC.

Financial Aid

For information about financial aid, please visit our website at law.nccu.edu/admissions/financial-assistance.

Tuition and Expenses

NCCU School of Law provides one of the most cost-effective legal educations in the country. For information on tuition, fees, and expenses, please visit our website at law.nccu.edu/admissions/expenses or contact Student Accounting at 919.530.5071.

Housing

Limited on-campus housing is available for single law students. Write the Department of Residential Life, North Carolina Central University, PO Box 19382, Durham, NC 27707, or call 919.530.6227.

APPLICANT PROFILE

North Carolina Central University School of Law
This grid includes only applicants with 120–180 LSAT scores earned under standard administrations.

LSAT Score	3.75 +		3.50–3.74		3.25–3.49		3.00–3.24		2.75–2.99		2.50–2.74		2.25–2.49		2.00–2.24		Below 2.00		No GPA		Totals	
	Apps	Adm	Apps	Adm	Apps	Adm	Apps	Adm	Apps	Adm	Apps	Adm	Apps	Adm	Apps	Adm	Apps	Adm	Apps	Adm	Apps	Adm
175–180	0	0	0	0	0	0	0	0	0	0	0	0	0	0	0	0	0	0	0	0	0	0
170–174	0	0	0	0	2	1	0	0	0	0	1	0	0	0	0	0	0	0	0	0	3	1
165–169	1	1	2	1	2	0	3	1	1	0	2	2	0	0	1	1	0	0	1	1	13	7
160–164	7	6	9	3	7	3	13	11	14	3	4	1	5	0	2	0	2	0	1	0	64	27
155–159	10	7	22	15	38	14	33	10	34	9	16	6	12	4	6	0	2	0	0	0	173	65
150–154	25	13	50	26	65	26	77	37	49	15	45	10	13	2	15	1	7	0	7	0	353	130
145–149	27	10	52	26	75	40	130	36	96	15	85	6	42	1	18	1	6	0	8	0	539	135
140–144	15	3	45	9	98	7	133	13	110	3	76	3	51	0	25	0	5	0	5	0	563	38
135–139	10	0	16	1	40	1	44	1	41	0	33	0	24	2	11	0	5	0	8	0	232	5
130–134	0	0	1	0	9	0	14	0	10	0	8	0	9	0	7	0	5	0	1	0	64	0
125–129	0	0	2	0	1	0	3	0	3	0	3	0	2	0	2	0	0	0	3	0	19	0
120–124	0	0	0	0	0	0	0	0	0	0	1	0	1	0	0	0	0	0	0	0	2	0
Total	95	40	199	81	337	92	450	109	358	45	274	28	159	9	87	3	32	0	34	1	2025	408

Apps = Number of Applicants
Adm = Number Admitted
Reflects 99% of the total applicant pool; highest LSAT data reported.

UNIVERSITY OF NORTH DAKOTA SCHOOL OF LAW

215 Centennial Drive, Stop 9003
Grand Forks, ND 58202
Phone: 701.777.2047; Fax: 701.777.3895
E-mail: admissions@law.und.edu; Website: www.law.und.edu

ABA
Approved
Since
1923

The Basics

Type of school	Public
Term	Semester
Application deadline	4/1 7/15
Application fee	$35
Financial aid deadline	4/15
Can first year start other than fall?	No
Student to faculty ratio	18.9 to 1
# of housing spaces available restricted to law students	
graduate housing for which law students are eligible	235

Faculty and Administrators

	Total		Men		Women		Minorities	
	Spr	Fall	Spr	Fall	Spr	Fall	Spr	Fall
Full-time	10	12	7	8	3	4	1	1
Other full-time	0	0	0	0	0	0	0	0
Deans, librarians, & others who teach	6	4	1	0	5	4	0	0
Part-time	11	10	7	7	4	3	0	0
Total	27	26	15	15	12	11	1	1

Curriculum

	Full-Time	Part-Time
Typical first-year section size	85	0
Is there typically a "small section" of the first-year class, other than Legal Writing, taught by full-time faculty	No	No
If yes, typical size offered last year		

# of classroom course titles beyond first-year curriculum		64
# of upper division courses, excluding seminars, with an enrollment:	Under 25	29
	25–49	16
	50–74	8
	75–99	1
	100+	0
# of seminars		6
# of seminar positions available		92
# of seminar positions filled	79	0
# of positions available in simulation courses		157
# of simulation positions filled	84	0
# of positions available in faculty supervised clinical courses		32
# of faculty supervised clinical positions filled	13	0
# involved in field placements	50	0
# involved in law journals	36	0
# involved in moot court or trial competitions	12	0
# of credit hours required to graduate		90

JD Enrollment and Ethnicity

	Men		Women		Full-Time		Part-Time		1st-Year		Total		JD Degs. Awd.
	#	%	#	%	#	%	#	%	#	%	#	%	
All Hispanics	0	0.0	0	0.0	0	0.0	0	0.0	0	0.0	0	0.0	2
Am. Ind./AK Nat.	2	1.6	6	4.8	8	3.2	0	0.0	3	3.6	8	3.2	1
Asian	1	0.8	2	1.6	3	1.2	0	0.0	1	1.2	3	1.2	0
Black/Af. Am.	1	0.8	5	4.0	6	2.4	0	0.0	4	4.8	6	2.4	2
Nat. Hl/Pac. Isl.	0	0.0	0	0.0	0	0.0	0	0.0	0	0.0	0	0.0	0
2 or more races	1	0.8	2	1.6	3	1.2	0	0.0	3	3.6	3	1.2	0
Subtotal (minor.)	5	3.9	15	12.1	20	8.0	0	0.0	11	13.1	20	8.0	5
Nonres. Alien	4	3.1	3	2.4	7	2.8	0	0.0	5	6.0	7	2.8	4
White/Cauc.	87	68.5	78	62.9	165	65.7	0	0.0	51	60.7	165	65.7	62
Unknown	31	24.4	28	22.6	59	23.5	0	0.0	16	19.0	59	23.5	10
Total	127	50.6	124	49.4	251	100.0	0	0.0	84	33.5	251		81

Transfers

Transfers in	2
Transfers out	5

Tuition and Fees

	Resident	Nonresident
Full-time	$9,895	$21,580
Part-time		
Tuition Guarantee Program	N	

Living Expenses

Estimated living expenses for singles

Living on campus	Living off campus	Living at home
$14,700	$14,700	$14,700

UNIVERSITY OF NORTH DAKOTA SCHOOL OF LAW

ABA
Approved
Since
1923

GPA and LSAT Scores

	Total	Full-Time	Part-Time
# of apps	457	457	0
# of offers	197	197	0
# of matrics	83	83	0
75% GPA	3.62	3.62	0.00
Median GPA	3.33	3.33	0.00
25% GPA	2.93	2.93	0.00
75% LSAT	154	154	0
Median LSAT	151	151	0
25% LSAT	148	148	0

Grants and Scholarships (from prior year)

	Total		Full-Time		Part-Time	
	#	%	#	%	#	%
Total # of students	256		256		0	
Total # receiving grants	80	31.3	80	31.3	0	0.0
Less than 1/2 tuition	56	21.9	56	21.9	0	0.0
Half to full tuition	15	5.9	15	5.9	0	0.0
Full tuition	7	2.7	7	2.7	0	0.0
More than full tuition	2	0.8	2	0.8	0	0.0
Median grant amount			$3,750		$0	

Informational and Library Resources

Total amount spent on library materials	$598,218
Study seating capacity inside the library	207
# of full-time equivalent professional librarians	4
Hours per week library is open	99
# of open, wired connections available to students	197
# of networked computers available for use by students	0
Has wireless network?	Y
Requires computer?	N

JD Attrition (from prior year)

	Academic	Other	Total	
	#	#	#	%
1st year	0	8	8	9.6
2nd year	0	0	0	0.0
3rd year	0	0	0	0.0
4th year	0	0	0	0.0

Employment (9 months after graduation)

For up-to-date employment data, go to
employmentsummary.abaquestionnaire.org on the ABA website.

Bar Passage Rates

First-time takers	78	Reporting %	76.92
Average school %	81.67	Average state %	83.75
Average pass difference	−2.08		

Jurisdiction	Takers	Passers	Pass %	State %	Diff %
North Dakota	60	49	81.67	83.75	−2.08

UNIVERSITY OF NORTH DAKOTA SCHOOL OF LAW

215 Centennial Drive, Stop 9003
Grand Forks, ND 58202
Phone: 701.777.2047; Fax: 701.777.3895
E-mail: admissions@law.und.edu; Website: www.law.und.edu

Introduction

Founded in 1899, the University of North Dakota (UND) School of Law blends an innovative education with creative and entrepreneurial opportunities and a spirit of community in its education of approximately 250 students. The school is a fully accredited graduate professional school awarding the JD degree. It has been a member of the AALS since 1910 and was approved by the ABA in 1923. UND Law is part of a highly respected, nationally recognized university, located in Grand Forks, North Dakota. A community of nearly 60,000, Grand Forks is in the heart of the Red River Valley on the North Dakota/Minnesota border. It offers a small-town feel with all the opportunities of an urban area and has a large legal community including county, state, and federal trial courts.

Library and Physical Facilities

The **Thormodsgard Law Library** manages a growing collection of comprehensive resources necessary for the study of law and provides a home for students. The school and library are linked everywhere with high-speed Ethernet and wireless access points. The elegant, traditionally appointed **Baker Courtroom** is used by the North Dakota Supreme Court; by tribal, federal, and district courts; and for guest lectures and trial and appellate arguments. The Computer Services office supports the web, e-mail, file sharing, database, group scheduling, servers, the in-house video system, as well as student laptops.

Curriculum

The curriculum of the School of Law covers a period of three full academic years. All the work of the first year is prescribed. Courses in the second and third years are elective, except for the course in Professional Responsibility.

Special Programs

The size of the student body is ideally suited for close professional contact with faculty, the visiting courts, legal professionals, and alumni. Students are active in the governance of the school.

UND Law offers an **American Indian Law Certificate** program and, in consultation with area tribes and Indian leaders, established the region's first **Northern Plains Indian Law Center**. The center is a clearinghouse for American Indian legal materials and provides a forum for discussing and resolving legal issues confronting Indian tribes, the states, and the federal government. It also supports tribal advocacy training programs. Among the center's programs are the Tribal Judicial Institute, the Institute for the Study of Tribal Gaming Law and Policy, the Native American Law Project, and the Tribal Environmental Law Project.

The **Clinical Education Program** provides students with the opportunity to integrate the theory and practice of Housing and Employment law in a real law office setting. Clinic students assume the role of lawyers and, in doing so, move beyond the classroom into the world of law practice. In the course of representing their clients, students gain

firsthand experience with substantive law, the many skills of lawyering, and the rules of professional ethics while earning academic credit.

A comprehensive **Externship Program** allows students an opportunity to earn academic credit while gaining practical experience in a variety of placements. Externship students receive local and state field placements throughout the academic year, as well as during the summer in the **Federal Externship Program**.

The school has an extensive **Trial Advocacy Program** in which students learn trial skills in a simulated advocacy setting under the close supervision of experienced trial lawyers. Each student in this course is responsible, with one student advocate co-counsel, for the trial of at least one full civil or criminal case during the semester. In addition, students participate in the internal Carrigan Cup trial competition as well as the external Trial Team.

The **Legislative Internship Program** provides an opportunity for selected students to serve as legislative interns at the North Dakota state capital in Bismarck during sessions of the state legislature.

Central Legal Research (CLR) provides select students with opportunities to work with attorneys and judges across North Dakota on the issues and problems faced in practice. Focusing primarily on criminal law and procedure issues, CLR students work closely with an experienced lawyer and with each other, honing their skills by writing, researching, analyzing, and discussing their individual projects. CLR students receive a full in-state tuition waiver and develop a broad writing portfolio.

Both a joint **Juris Doctor/Master of Business Administration** (JD/MBA) as well as a **Juris Doctor/Master of Public Administration** (JD/MPA) degree are offered. These joint-degree programs could be completed in four years or less.

The UND School of Law is one of approximately 80 law schools throughout the United States that have a chapter of the national legal honorary society, the **Order of the Coif**. The Order of the Coif was founded to encourage legal scholarship and advance the ethical standards of the legal profession.

UND law students may receive credit for summer law study at the **American College of Norway** in Moss. Through this specialized program, students receive a unique opportunity to study abroad and learn about the Norwegian legal system, international law, and comparative law.

Admission

The School of Law has no specific undergraduate course prerequisites and agrees with the observations in the introduction to this guide. The school admits students only in August and only for full-time study. Applications are available upon request. The policy of the faculty of the School of Law is to admit those applicants who, in the determination of the faculty, will be able to satisfactorily complete the law school program. The admission committee utilizes the following criteria to achieve this goal: (1) LSAT score; (2) undergraduate GPA; (3) past performance in an academic environment; (4) past performance in activities that would tend to predict the applicant's ability to successfully complete the law school program; and (5) other evidence relevant to predicted success and prospective professional responsibility. The total number of students admitted is, of course, limited by considerations involving space and faculty courseload.

The law school does not have a nonresident quota; however, preference is given to residents.

Students who have begun the study of law in other accredited law schools may be admitted in exceptional circumstances to advanced standing, provided they have fulfilled the requirements for admission to the University of North Dakota School of Law. Ordinarily, no transfer credit will be allowed for more than two semesters of work completed elsewhere, nor will transfer credit be given for any courses in which an unsatisfactory or failing grade has been received. Moreover, admission may be conditioned upon meeting such additional requirements as the faculty may prescribe. No student will be admitted as a transfer student with advanced standing who is not eligible to continue as a student at his or her present law school.

Student Activities

The **North Dakota Law Review** provides research and writing opportunities. Students participate in various moot court activities, with the North Dakota Supreme Court judging the moot court finals. A sampling of the organizations include the Environmental Law Society, Law Women's Caucus, Native American Law Students Association, Black Law Students Association, Public Interest Law Students Association, Student Trial Lawyers Association, and Student Bar Association. The School of Law also has chapters of the Order of the Coif, Order of the Barristers, and legal fraternities. One of the more popular activities is the Malpractice Bowl, pitting law students against medical school students in an annual flag football game.

Expenses and Financial Aid

Tuition and fees per semester for students averaging 15 credit hours in 2011–2012 are $4,947.50 for in-state residents, $6,697 for contiguous states, and $10,790 for nonresidents. The semester fees include student activity and university fees totaling $559.64 and an $800 per semester professional fee. The student activity and university fees cover payment for health services, the university center, campus publications, and drama and athletic events. The professional fee is assessed by the School of Law and is used to support and improve the law school program. Fees are subject to change without notice. Loan funds for all qualified students are available through the university Student Financial Aid Office, PO Box 8371, Grand Forks, ND 58202.

Housing

The university has a comprehensive housing system with options including family housing facilities, student apartment housing, and traditional residence halls for single students. For more detailed information, visit www.housing.und.edu.

Career Services

The Career Services Office assists students and alumni in the development of a personal career plan and provides guidance throughout the process; coordinates and sponsors a professional success program that includes speakers and workshops on a variety of topics, including legal and alternative opportunities, job search strategies, work-life balance, debt management, interviewing, and writing effective résumés and cover letters; manages an online job board and coordinates the on-campus interview program featuring public and private employers and state and federal judges yearly.

APPLICANT PROFILE

University of North Dakota School of Law
This grid includes only applicants who earned 120–180 LSAT scores under standard administrations.

LSAT Score	3.75 +		3.50–3.74		3.25–3.49		3.00–3.24		2.75–2.99		2.50–2.74		2.25–2.49		2.00–2.24		Below 2.00		No GPA		Total	
	Apps	Adm	Apps	Adm	Apps	Adm	Apps	Adm	Apps	Adm	Apps	Adm	Apps	Adm	Apps	Adm	Apps	Adm	Apps	Adm	Apps	Adm
175–180	0	0	0	0	0	0	0	0	0	0	0	0	0	0	0	0	0	0	0	0	0	0
170–174	0	0	0	0	0	0	1	0	0	0	0	0	0	0	0	0	0	0	0	0	1	0
165–169	1	1	0	0	0	0	0	0	0	0	0	0	0	0	0	0	0	0	0	0	1	1
160–164	7	7	5	5	3	3	0	0	1	0	0	0	2	2	1	0	0	0	0	0	19	17
155–159	13	11	9	6	17	14	7	6	7	5	7	5	5	3	2	0	1	0	0	0	68	50
150–154	9	8	15	11	30	19	30	12	26	16	11	1	5	3	2	0	2	0	2	2	132	72
145–149	10	8	7	3	20	6	29	10	16	4	13	2	17	4	3	0	1	0	0	0	116	37
140–144	5	2	7	2	10	1	14	4	13	3	12	1	5	0	1	0	0	0	2	2	69	15
135–139	1	0	2	0	1	0	5	0	10	1	2	0	5	0	3	0	0	0	0	0	29	1
130–134	0	0	0	0	1	0	1	0	3	0	2	0	1	0	0	0	0	0	1	1	9	1
125–129	0	0	0	0	0	0	0	0	0	0	1	0	0	0	1	0	0	0	1	0	3	0
120–124	0	0	0	0	0	0	0	0	0	0	0	0	0	0	0	0	0	0	0	0	0	0
Total	46	37	45	27	82	43	87	32	76	29	48	9	40	12	13	0	4	0	6	5	447	194

Apps = Number of Applicants
Adm = Number Admitted
Reflects 99% of the total applicant pool; highest LSAT data reported.

NORTHEASTERN UNIVERSITY SCHOOL OF LAW

400 Huntington Avenue, 101 Knowles Center
Boston, MA 02115
Phone: 617.373.2395; Fax: 617.373.8865
E-mail: lawadmissions@neu.edu; Website: www.northeastern.edu/law

ABA
Approved
Since
1969

The Basics

Type of school	Private
Term	Quarter
Application deadline	11/15 3/1 6/15
Application fee	$75
Financial aid deadline	2/15
Can first year start other than fall?	No
Student to faculty ratio	15.2 to 1
# of housing spaces available restricted to law students	46
graduate housing for which law students are eligible	

Faculty and Administrators

	Total		Men		Women		Minorities	
	Spr	Fall	Spr	Fall	Spr	Fall	Spr	Fall
Full-time	34	36	15	14	19	22	9	9
Other full-time	1	1	0	0	1	1	0	0
Deans, librarians, & others who teach	8	9	0	2	8	7	1	1
Part-time	41	45	22	25	19	20	9	8
Total	84	91	37	41	47	50	19	18

JD Enrollment and Ethnicity

	Men		Women		Full-Time		Part-Time		1st-Year		Total		JD Degs. Awd.
	#	%	#	%	#	%	#	%	#	%	#	%	
All Hispanics	26	9.5	49	12.8	75	11.4	0	0.0	35	16.1	75	11.4	20
Am. Ind./AK Nat.	0	0.0	4	1.0	4	0.6	0	0.0	0	0.0	4	0.6	3
Asian	16	5.9	45	11.7	61	9.3	0	0.0	23	10.6	61	9.3	11
Black/Af. Am.	12	4.4	55	14.4	67	10.2	0	0.0	16	7.4	67	10.2	21
Nat. HI/Pac. Isl.	0	0.0	0	0.0	0	0.0	0	0.0	0	0.0	0	0.0	0
2 or more races	9	3.3	9	2.3	18	2.7	0	0.0	9	4.1	18	2.7	0
Subtotal (minor.)	63	23.1	162	42.3	225	34.3	0	0.0	83	38.2	225	34.3	55
Nonres. Alien	1	0.4	1	0.3	2	0.3	0	0.0	1	0.5	2	0.3	0
White/Cauc.	172	63.0	169	44.1	341	52.0	0	0.0	117	53.9	341	52.0	103
Unknown	37	13.6	51	13.3	88	13.4	0	0.0	16	7.4	88	13.4	30
Total	273	41.6	383	58.4	656	100.0	0	0.0	217	33.1	656		188

Curriculum

	Full-Time	Part-Time
Typical first-year section size	70	0

	Yes	No
Is there typically a "small section" of the first-year class, other than Legal Writing, taught by full-time faculty	Yes	No
If yes, typical size offered last year	14	

# of classroom course titles beyond first-year curriculum		96
# of upper division courses, excluding seminars, with an enrollment:	Under 25	60
	25–49	30
	50–74	9
	75–99	3
	100+	1
# of seminars		14
# of seminar positions available		215
# of seminar positions filled	194	0
# of positions available in simulation courses	235	
# of simulation positions filled	237	0
# of positions available in faculty supervised clinical courses	121	
# of faculty supervised clinical positions filled	101	0
# involved in field placements	538	0
# involved in law journals	83	0
# involved in moot court or trial competitions	39	0
# of credit hours required to graduate		87

Transfers

Transfers in	9
Transfers out	2

Tuition and Fees

	Resident	Nonresident
Full-time	$42,296	
Part-time		
Tuition Guarantee Program	N	

Living Expenses

Estimated living expenses for singles

Living on campus	Living off campus	Living at home
$9,720	$19,500	$19,500

NORTHEASTERN UNIVERSITY SCHOOL OF LAW

ABA
Approved
Since
1969

GPA and LSAT Scores

	Total	Full-Time	Part-Time
# of apps	3,670	3,670	0
# of offers	1,349	1,349	0
# of matrics	217	217	0
75% GPA	3.64	3.64	0.00
Median GPA	3.48	3.48	0.00
25% GPA	3.24	3.24	0.00
75% LSAT	163	163	0
Median LSAT	162	162	0
25% LSAT	154	154	0

Grants and Scholarships (from prior year)

	Total #	Total %	Full-Time #	Full-Time %	Part-Time #	Part-Time %
Total # of students	629		629		0	
Total # receiving grants	535	85.1	535	85.1	0	0.0
Less than 1/2 tuition	513	81.6	513	81.6	0	0.0
Half to full tuition	9	1.4	9	1.4	0	0.0
Full tuition	13	2.1	13	2.1	0	0.0
More than full tuition	0	0.0	0	0.0	0	0.0
Median grant amount			$8,500		$0	

Informational and Library Resources

Total amount spent on library materials	$1,777,971
Study seating capacity inside the library	369
# of full-time equivalent professional librarians	8
Hours per week library is open	108
# of open, wired connections available to students	375
# of networked computers available for use by students	80
Has wireless network?	Y
Requires computer?	N

JD Attrition (from prior year)

	Academic #	Other #	Total #	Total %
1st year	0	5	5	2.3
2nd year	0	4	4	1.8
3rd year	0	0	0	0.0
4th year	0	0	0	0.0

Employment (9 months after graduation)

For up-to-date employment data, go to employmentsummary.abaquestionnaire.org on the ABA website.

Bar Passage Rates

First-time takers	172	Reporting %	90.70
Average school %	89.10	Average state %	89.67
Average pass difference	−0.57		

Jurisdiction	Takers	Passers	Pass %	State %	Diff %
Massachusetts	156	139	89.10	89.67	−0.57

The information on these pages was provided by the law school.

NORTHEASTERN UNIVERSITY SCHOOL OF LAW

400 Huntington Avenue, 101 Knowles Center
Boston, MA 02115
Phone: 617.373.2395; Fax: 617.373.8865
E-mail: lawadmissions@neu.edu; Website: www.northeastern.edu/law

Introduction

"Experiential" and "collaborative" are today's hot buttons in legal education. But for one school, those buttons have been hot for more than 40 years. At Northeastern University School of Law, we developed our practical learning education model in 1968. Central to it is our Cooperative Legal Education Program, which allows students to graduate with four, quarter-long, full-time jobs on their résumés. Combining classroom theory and rigorous academics with work experience, Northeastern law students receive their JD degrees in the same three-year period as students at other schools, but graduate with at least 1,500 hours of full-time work experience.

We walk the walk in terms of collaboration, too. Instead of grades, students get written evaluations from their professors and co-op employers. Without an onerous class rank, students are free to work together and take intellectual risks. The school cultivates a culture of cooperation, collaboration, and mutual respect. Our talented students, graduates, and faculty understand what it is lawyers do, how they should do it, and the difference they can make in the lives of others. Consistently recognized as one of the best public interest programs in the nation, the school's commitment to social justice extends through the curriculum, co-op program, clinics and institutes, and student group activism.

Northeastern law students are people who believe that if you don't agree with the system—change it. They're risk takers who enjoy using the law—and their careers—in both traditional and nontraditional ways. They're team players who thrive on learning together as opposed to learning at the expense of others. They're realists who believe practical experience is critical to the legal education process. And best of all, they're passionate idealists who truly believe they can change the world.

Learning Through Experience

Northeastern's **Cooperative Legal Education Program** guarantees all students four, full-time work experiences (co-ops) prior to graduation. Students alternate periods of academic study with equal periods of workplace experience during their second and third years of law school. During the first year, students follow a traditional, two-semester, full-time academic schedule. At the end of the first year, students switch to a year-round, quarter system. For the remaining two years, students alternate every three months between working full time on co-op and attending classes. By participating in four, full-time co-op placements with four different legal employers, students are provided with an extraordinary opportunity to experience the actual practice of law and to determine their career paths based on practical training.

More than 900 employers worldwide currently participate in the co-op program, representing virtually every practice area, including law firms of all sizes, trial and appellate judges in federal and state courts, public defender and legal services organizations, government agencies, corporate and union legal departments, and a variety of advocacy groups. Students work with employers in more than 40 states and countries. In recent years, students have increasingly developed their own co-ops in the United States and abroad.

Students may be paid on co-op with salaries ranging from minimal compensation for public interest employers to more than $3,100 per week for large private firms. Some students may be eligible for federal Work-Study funding; additionally, every qualified law student is guaranteed one $2,500 stipend to support an unfunded government or public interest law co-op.

Clinics and Institutes

Northeastern offers students the opportunity to engage in advocacy on behalf of individuals and community organizations often unacknowledged or underrepresented by the justice system. Together, the clinics, institutes, and special programs reflect and fulfill a commitment to social and economic justice that distinguishes Northeastern as one of the nation's foremost public interest law schools. Students can participate with faculty and staff in the work of the following outstanding research and service centers: the **Domestic Violence Institute**, the **Public Health Advocacy Institute**, the **Program on Human Rights and the Global Economy**, the **Civil Rights and Restorative Justice Project**, and the **Program on Health Policy and Law**. Northeastern also offers seven clinics: **Civil Rights and Restorative Justice, Community Business, Criminal Advocacy, Domestic Violence, Poverty Law and Practice, Prisoners' Rights**, and **Public Health**. The clinics differ from one another by substantive legal focus, advocacy experience, and the primary skills each seeks to impart. Students engage in challenging legal practice with the support of clinical faculty who provide the requisite training, close supervision, and opportunity for reflection.

Putting Public Service Into Practice

Nationally recognized as a leader in public interest law, Northeastern shares, supports, and encourages our students' passion for justice. Recently, over 90 percent of our students fulfilled our public interest law graduation requirement through a public interest co-op, and about 45 percent of our students participated in our clinics providing legal assistance to underserved communities. In addition, every first-year student participates in **Legal Skills in Social Context**, a one-of-a-kind, year-long signature course introducing the central skills of effective lawyering: legal research, objective and persuasive legal writing, client representation, critical analysis, and oral skills—all heavily grounded in the social contexts in which the law is practiced. "Law offices" of about 14 first-year students plan and execute a social justice project—an extensive real-world legal research project on behalf of a community-based or public service organization.

Student Life

The School of Law has one of the most diverse student bodies in the country. Fifty-five percent of the students in the first-year class are women, 39 percent are people of color, 11 percent identify as LGBT, and 11 percent hold advanced degrees. Our first-year students range in age from 20 to 45 and approximately 71 percent have taken one or more years after graduation from college before enrolling in law school. They come from 31 different states and over 140 various undergraduate institutions. Students are active participants in the law school community, serving on all of the school's standing committees, including the Admissions Committee. Students also run a wide variety of more than 30 organizations, ranging from the American Civil Liberties Union to the Queer Caucus to the *Northeastern University Law Journal*.

Dual-Degree Programs

Northeastern offers seven dual-degree programs. In cooperation with Tufts University School of Medicine, students may pursue a JD/MPH program. Completion of the dual-degree program takes three and a half years, rather than the average five years if the degrees were obtained sequentially. The School of Law has also partnered with Brandeis University's Heller School of Social Policy and Management to offer a JD/MA in sustainable international development. This accelerated four-year program includes combined law/international development co-ops. For students interested in environmental law, the School of Law, in conjunction with Vermont Law School, offers its law students the opportunity to earn both a JD and a master's degree in environmental law and policy (MELP) in the same three-year period it would take to earn just the JD. Dual degrees are also available from other schools and colleges at Northeastern University, including a JD/MBA, JD/MSA/MBA, JD/MS/PhD-Law and Public Policy, and JD/MA-Music Industry Leadership.

Career Services

The Office of Career Services actively assists students and graduates in their pursuit of professionally rewarding careers. Students generally find their postgraduate employment prospects to be substantially enhanced through the co-op program; on average, approximately 40 percent accept

postgraduate employment with one of their former co-op employers. Northeastern graduates are employed throughout the world in every practice area. They may be found teaching at distinguished law schools, sitting on the bench at both the state and federal levels, practicing as partners in prominent law firms, and serving as directors of legal aid and public defender programs throughout the nation. Graduates of Northeastern enter public service careers at a rate that is three times the national average. In addition, graduates have been awarded prestigious postgraduate fellowships, including those granted by Skadden, Equal Justice Works, Georgetown, and the Center for Constitutional Rights.

Financing Your Education

Northeastern is committed to providing access to all admitted students. Each year, the School of Law awards more than $1.5 million to first-year students based on a combination of need and merit. Scholarships include the Dean's Scholarship, Academic Excellence Scholarship, Public Interest Law Scholarship, Social Justice Scholarship, Peace Corps Scholarship, Teach For America Scholarship, and Designated Law Scholarship. These scholarships represent a three-year commitment, with awards guaranteed for the upper-level years as long as the student remains in good academic standing. The law school also provides co-op stipends, endowed scholarships for upper-level students, and a **Loan Deferral and Forgiveness Program** for graduates pursuing careers in public interest.

LLM

Building on our signature approach to experience-based legal education, we recently launched an LLM program designed to provide foreign law graduates with the skills and training necessary to succeed in global legal practice environments. This vibrant LLM program allows students to specialize in specific practice areas.

APPLICANT PROFILE

Northeastern University School of Law does not provide an applicant profile based solely upon LSAT scores and undergraduate GPAs. The Admissions Committee at Northeastern seeks to enroll a diverse, talented, and passionate student body that is eager to make a difference in the world. In keeping with the school's collaborative community spirit, the School of Law incorporates students, staff, and faculty in its admissions process as members of the

school's Admissions Committee. In making its decisions, the Admissions Committee considers academic criteria, including undergraduate grades and LSAT score, as well as other accomplishments, work experience, life experience, community involvement, the essays and personal statement, recommendations from individuals who know the candidate well, and any other relevant information.

NORTHERN ILLINOIS UNIVERSITY COLLEGE OF LAW

Swen Parson Hall, Room 151
DeKalb, IL 60115-2890
Phone: 815.753.8595; Fax: 815.753.5680
E-mail: lawadm@niu.edu; Website: www.niu.edu/law

ABA
Approved
Since
1978

The Basics

Type of school	Public
Term	Semester
Application deadline	4/1
Application fee	$50
Financial aid deadline	3/1
Can first year start other than fall?	No
Student to faculty ratio	17.2 to 1
# of housing spaces available restricted to law students	
graduate housing for which law students are eligible	300

Faculty and Administrators

	Total		Men		Women		Minorities	
	Spr	Fall	Spr	Fall	Spr	Fall	Spr	Fall
Full-time	13	17	6	9	7	8	7	6
Other full-time	6	3	2	1	4	2	0	0
Deans, librarians, & others who teach	9	10	6	6	3	4	1	2
Part-time	6	10	6	9	0	1	1	1
Total	34	40	20	25	14	15	9	9

Curriculum

		Full-Time	Part-Time
Typical first-year section size		55	0
Is there typically a "small section" of the first-year class, other than Legal Writing, taught by full-time faculty		No	No
If yes, typical size offered last year			
# of classroom course titles beyond first-year curriculum		60	
# of upper division courses, excluding seminars, with an enrollment:	Under 25	45	
	25–49	21	
	50–74	6	
	75–99	1	
	100+	0	
# of seminars		7	
# of seminar positions available		98	
# of seminar positions filled		66	0
# of positions available in simulation courses		156	
# of simulation positions filled		145	0
# of positions available in faculty supervised clinical courses		50	
# of faculty supervised clinical positions filled		22	0
# involved in field placements		44	0
# involved in law journals		44	0
# involved in moot court or trial competitions		30	0
# of credit hours required to graduate		90	

JD Enrollment and Ethnicity

	Men		Women		Full-Time		Part-Time		1st-Year		Total		JD Degs. Awd.
	#	%	#	%	#	%	#	%	#	%	#	%	
All Hispanics	14	7.8	9	6.3	23	7.3	0	0.0	5	4.5	23	7.2	5
Am. Ind./AK Nat.	1	0.6	0	0.0	1	0.3	0	0.0	0	0.0	1	0.3	0
Asian	5	2.8	10	7.0	15	4.8	0	0.0	5	4.5	15	4.7	4
Black/Af. Am.	15	8.4	9	6.3	23	7.3	1	16.7	11	9.9	24	7.5	3
Nat. HI/Pac. Isl.	1	0.6	0	0.0	1	0.3	0	0.0	1	0.9	1	0.3	0
2 or more races	1	0.6	1	0.7	2	0.6	0	0.0	0	0.0	2	0.6	0
Subtotal (minor.)	37	20.7	29	20.4	65	20.6	1	16.7	22	19.8	66	20.6	12
Nonres. Alien	0	0.0	0	0.0	0	0.0	0	0.0	0	0.0	0	0.0	0
White/Cauc.	132	73.7	104	73.2	231	73.3	5	83.3	84	75.7	236	73.5	74
Unknown	10	5.6	9	6.3	19	6.0	0	0.0	5	4.5	19	5.9	8
Total	179	55.8	142	44.2	315	98.1	6	1.9	111	34.6	321		94

Transfers

Transfers in	0
Transfers out	4

Tuition and Fees

	Resident	Nonresident
Full-time	$18,688	$33,311
Part-time		
Tuition Guarantee Program	N	

Living Expenses

Estimated living expenses for singles

Living on campus	Living off campus	Living at home
$17,226	$17,226	$6,016

NORTHERN ILLINOIS UNIVERSITY COLLEGE OF LAW

ABA
Approved
Since
1978

GPA and LSAT Scores

	Total	Full-Time	Part-Time
# of apps	1,058	998	60
# of offers	475	460	15
# of matrics	103	102	1
75% GPA	3.42	3.43	3.28
Median GPA	3.20	3.19	3.28
25% GPA	3.00	3.00	3.28
75% LSAT	155	155	155
Median LSAT	152	152	155
25% LSAT	150	150	155

Grants and Scholarships (from prior year)

	Total #	Total %	Full-Time #	Full-Time %	Part-Time #	Part-Time %
Total # of students	332		321		11	
Total # receiving grants	151	45.5	147	45.8	4	36.4
Less than 1/2 tuition	41	12.3	40	12.5	1	9.1
Half to full tuition	108	32.5	105	32.7	3	27.3
Full tuition	2	0.6	2	0.6	0	0.0
More than full tuition	0	0.0	0	0.0	0	0.0
Median grant amount			$6,846		$11,125	

Informational and Library Resources

Total amount spent on library materials	$865,558
Study seating capacity inside the library	228
# of full-time equivalent professional librarians	5
Hours per week library is open	98
# of open, wired connections available to students	16
# of networked computers available for use by students	32
Has wireless network?	Y
Requires computer?	N

JD Attrition (from prior year)

	Academic #	Other #	Total #	Total %
1st year	3	9	12	8.6
2nd year	0	0	0	0.0
3rd year	0	0	0	0.0
4th year	0	0	0	0.0

Employment (9 months after graduation)

For up-to-date employment data, go to employmentsummary.abaquestionnaire.org on the ABA website.

Bar Passage Rates

First-time takers	81	Reporting %	111.11
Average school %	82.22	Average state %	89.38

Average pass difference −7.16

Jurisdiction	Takers	Passers	Pass %	State %	Diff %
Illinois	90	74	82.22	89.38	−7.16

NORTHERN ILLINOIS UNIVERSITY COLLEGE OF LAW

Swen Parson Hall, Room 151
DeKalb, IL 60115-2890
Phone: 815.753.8595; Fax: 815.753.5680
E-mail: lawadm@niu.edu; Website: www.niu.edu/law

Introduction

Northern Illinois University was founded in 1895, and the College of Law was established in 1978. NIU Law seeks to prepare its graduates not only for the traditional role of lawyers but also for the myriad tasks lawyers are called upon to perform. The school has a diverse and professionally distinguished faculty dedicated to teaching and scholarship.

Our Campus

NIU Law is located in DeKalb, a community conveniently located approximately 65 miles west of Chicago and 25 miles from the suburban area on the Ronald Reagan Memorial Tollway (I-88). DeKalb is close enough to the Chicago metropolitan area to draw on its many resources, yet it retains its own college town flavor. It is a safe and affordable environment with a high quality of life.

The university's main campus is set on 755 acres of rolling country land. The lush campus features two lagoons, several museums, and a vast variety of cultural opportunities. It provides an excellent environment for the study of law.

Though on a relatively large campus with all of the associated activities and opportunities, the College of Law is a small oasis at NIU's center.

Libraries

The David C. Shapiro Memorial Law Library provides one of the best ratios of library materials to students of any American law school. The law library offers in-depth, research-level coverage of more than 32 areas of American law and study-level coverage of almost all other areas. Coverage of international, European Union, and British law is provided at study level. As a federally designated depository, the law library also receives selected government documents. In addition to its physical collection of over 262,000 volumes and volume equivalents, the library also offers access to Westlaw, LexisNexis, and a wide range of other web-based legal resources. Laptop users enjoy convenient access to these electronic resources anywhere in the law school through NIU Law's wireless network. Access to most of these resources is also available off campus. The library also features a student computer lab that offers desktop high-speed Internet access and laser printing.

Further research support is provided through Founders Memorial Library, the university's main library, which is conveniently located adjacent to NIU Law. Founders Memorial Library contains over 2 million volumes and an additional 1.3 million federal, state, and international government documents. It also subscribes to diverse collections of nonlegal web-based resources that may be accessed either on or off campus.

Enrollment/Student Body

The student body represents universities from coast to coast and reflects a broad spectrum of ethnicities, cultures, and home states. Our low student-to-faculty ratio, which is normally 15 to 1, facilitates a supportive environment with a lively exchange of ideas. NIU Law provides an atmosphere of shared goals and achievement and a genuine sense of community.

Curriculum and Clinical Experience Opportunities

NIU Law provides its students with a curriculum that will make them well-rounded legal professionals. The first-year program consists of the traditional ABA-required courses. After the first year, the only required courses are Constitutional Law II, Professional Responsibility, Introduction to Lawyering Skills, and a seminar; the remaining courses may be selected from a wide range of electives. A total of 90 credit hours are required to graduate from the College of Law. NIU Law offers an Academic Support Program to help first-year students succeed.

During the summer, electives are offered on the main campus. Also during the summer, NIU Law offers an international law program in France. During this program, students receive six hours of credit in international and comparative law.

The clinical lawyering skills programs offer students the opportunity to acquire the essential techniques needed in pretrial and trial work through structured simulations and experiences in an array of legal settings. The externship programs provide students with sound experience under the supervision of highly qualified practicing attorneys or with opportunities to be law clerks for state or federal judges. The Zeke Giorgi Legal Clinic in Rockford gives students the opportunity to apply legal theory as they represent clients and resolve disputes in a real-world setting.

Admission

NIU Law has an entering class of 110 to 115 students out of an applicant pool ranging from 1,000 to 1,500 students. NIU Law is a relatively selective institution. NIU Law grants admission on a competitive basis through an evaluation of an applicant's aptitude and professional promise. Factors of most importance to the admission committee are the applicant's undergraduate record, LSAT score, reasons for seeking admission, school or community activities and accomplishments, employment background, and ability to add diversity to the law school community and the legal profession.

Applicants must submit their applications online at the Law School Admission Council's (LSAC) website at LSAC.org. In addition to the applications, prospective students must submit personal statements, résumés, and application fees directly through LSAC.org. NIU Law requires applicants to use the LSAC Credential Assembly Service (CAS). International students who do not have a degree from a United States institution must submit all international transcripts and TOEFL scores to CAS. In order for NIU Law to receive LSAT scores, applicants need to submit official undergraduate and graduate transcripts as well as two letters of recommendation to CAS. Applicants are encouraged to submit their applications early, even if they have not taken the LSAT, due to the limited number of seats in each entering class.

Student Activities

Students are offered a wide variety of educational and professionally oriented activities. Among these are the *Northern Illinois University Law Review*, a forum for the expression of serious legal scholarship; the Trial Advocacy Society; and the Moot Court Society. Students compete in a wide selection of moot court and alternative dispute resolution competitions. Organizations range from the Asian American Law Student Organization to the Women's Law Caucus.

Expenses and Financial Aid

NIU Law offers its students small class sizes and a quality legal education at an affordable cost. For the 2011–2012 academic year, in-state tuition and fees equal $19,204, and out-of-state tuition and fees equal $34,060. Out-of-state residents may apply and qualify for in-state tuition within six months. Accordingly, few second- and third-year students are classified as out-of-state residents.

Scholarships and grants are available for students from a variety of sources. After their first year, students may qualify for research assistantships or graduate assistantships.

Information on scholarships, grants, and loans is available on our website at www.niu.edu/law. The priority deadline for the FAFSA application is March 1.

Career Opportunities

The Office of Career Opportunities has a strong track record in assisting and preparing graduates for rewarding careers through references to prospective employers and through on-campus interviews. The office assists current students in obtaining enriching summer legal employment. Due to NIU Law's small class size, personalized counseling is a reality.

Housing

Affordable housing is available both on and off campus. Handicap-accessible housing is also available. For information about on-campus housing, prospective students may telephone 815.753.9669 or visit the student housing website at www.niu.edu/housing.

Many moderately priced apartments are available close to the university. The housing budget is $10,600. Prospective students may contact off-campus housing at 815.753.9999 or visit the website at www.niu.edu/comnontrad/housing/index.shtml.

Correspondence

We encourage you to visit our law school community and our website. Check our admissions web pages for activities and programming, or call us at 815.753.8595.

APPLICANT PROFILE

Northern Illinois University College of Law

This grid includes only applicants who earned 120–180 LSAT scores under standard administrations.

LSAT Score	3.75 +		3.50–3.74		3.25–3.49		3.00–3.24		2.75–2.99		2.50–2.74		2.25–2.49		2.00–2.24		Below 2.00		No GPA		Total	
	Apps	Adm	Apps	Adm	Apps	Adm	Apps	Adm	Apps	Adm	Apps	Adm	Apps	Adm	Apps	Adm	Apps	Adm	Apps	Adm	Apps	Adm
170–180	1	1	1	1	0	0	0	0	0	0	0	0	0	0	0	0	0	0	0	0	2	2
165–169	1	1	0	0	1	1	0	0	4	4	0	0	0	0	0	0	0	0	0	0	6	6
160–164	11	10	13	13	14	12	11	11	4	3	1	1	1	1	1	0	0	0	0	0	56	51
155–159	13	13	28	25	37	36	50	46	29	21	19	9	13	4	2	0	1	0	2	1	194	155
150–154	31	29	51	38	90	67	74	54	52	20	29	2	20	5	4	0	1	0	6	1	358	216
145–149	23	10	30	7	60	17	51	9	24	0	38	1	14	0	9	0	2	0	3	1	254	45
140–144	2	1	11	1	22	0	34	0	25	0	20	0	16	0	6	0	1	0	6	0	143	2
Below 140	1	0	3	0	6	0	8	0	9	0	9	0	4	0	8	0	2	0	2	0	52	0
Total	83	65	137	85	230	133	228	120	147	48	116	13	68	10	30	0	7	0	19	3	1065	477

Apps = Number of Applicants
Adm = Number Admitted
Reflects 99% of the total applicant pool; highest LSAT data reported.

NORTHERN KENTUCKY UNIVERSITY—SALMON P. CHASE COLLEGE OF LAW

Nunn Hall, Nunn Drive
Highland Heights, KY 41099
Phone: 859.572.5490; Fax: 859.572.6081
E-mail: chaseadmissions@nku.edu; Website: http://chaselaw.nku.edu/

ABA
Approved
Since
1954

The Basics

Type of school	Public
Term	Semester
Application deadline	4/1
Application fee	$40
Financial aid deadline	3/1
Can first year start other than fall?	No
Student to faculty ratio	14.7 to 1
# of housing spaces available restricted to law students	
graduate housing for which law students are eligible	

Faculty and Administrators

	Total		Men		Women		Minorities	
	Spr	Fall	Spr	Fall	Spr	Fall	Spr	Fall
Full-time	30	27	20	17	10	10	4	4
Other full-time	1	1	1	1	0	0	0	0
Deans, librarians, & others who teach	10	9	4	4	6	5	0	0
Part-time	21	25	10	12	11	13	1	2
Total	62	62	35	34	27	28	5	6

Curriculum

	Full-Time	Part-Time
Typical first-year section size	72	67
Is there typically a "small section" of the first-year class, other than Legal Writing, taught by full-time faculty	No	No
If yes, typical size offered last year		
# of classroom course titles beyond first-year curriculum	82	
# of upper division courses, excluding seminars, with an enrollment: Under 25	60	
25–49	33	
50–74	18	
75–99	1	
100+	0	
# of seminars	4	
# of seminar positions available	94	
# of seminar positions filled	72	20
# of positions available in simulation courses	332	
# of simulation positions filled	180	128
# of positions available in faculty supervised clinical courses	40	
# of faculty supervised clinical positions filled	29	6
# involved in field placements	36	14
# involved in law journals	29	5
# involved in moot court or trial competitions	25	4
# of credit hours required to graduate	90	

JD Enrollment and Ethnicity

	Men		Women		Full-Time		Part-Time		1st-Year		Total		JD Degs. Awd.
	#	%	#	%	#	%	#	%	#	%	#	%	
All Hispanics	4	1.2	4	1.8	5	1.4	3	1.4	1	0.6	8	1.4	2
Am. Ind./AK Nat.	1	0.3	2	0.9	2	0.6	1	0.5	2	1.1	3	0.5	0
Asian	6	1.7	3	1.3	6	1.7	3	1.4	3	1.7	9	1.6	3
Black/Af. Am.	8	2.3	12	5.4	11	3.1	9	4.1	7	4.0	20	3.5	8
Nat. HI/Pac. Isl.	0	0.0	1	0.4	0	0.0	1	0.5	0	0.0	1	0.2	0
2 or more races	1	0.3	0	0.0	0	0.0	1	0.5	0	0.0	1	0.2	0
Subtotal (minor.)	20	5.8	22	9.9	24	6.8	18	8.3	13	7.3	42	7.4	13
Nonres. Alien	0	0.0	0	0.0	0	0.0	0	0.0	0	0.0	0	0.0	0
White/Cauc.	310	89.6	191	85.7	313	88.9	188	86.6	160	90.4	501	88.0	151
Unknown	16	4.6	10	4.5	15	4.3	11	5.1	4	2.3	26	4.6	17
Total	346	60.8	223	39.2	352	61.9	217	38.1	177	31.1	569		181

Transfers

Transfers in	3
Transfers out	8

Tuition and Fees

	Resident	Nonresident
Full-time	$15,886	$33,644
Part-time	$10,998	$23,292
Tuition Guarantee Program	N	

Living Expenses

Estimated living expenses for singles

Living on campus	Living off campus	Living at home
$10,412	$16,052	$16,052

NORTHERN KENTUCKY UNIVERSITY—SALMON P. CHASE COLLEGE OF LAW

ABA Approved Since 1954

GPA and LSAT Scores

	Total	Full-Time	Part-Time
# of apps	891	746	145
# of offers	463	389	74
# of matrics	178	128	50
75% GPA	3.56	3.56	3.58
Median GPA	3.35	3.39	3.13
25% GPA	3.07	3.17	2.82
75% LSAT	156	156	158
Median LSAT	154	154	153
25% LSAT	151	152	150

Grants and Scholarships (from prior year)

	Total #	Total %	Full-Time #	Full-Time %	Part-Time #	Part-Time %
Total # of students	614		375		239	
Total # receiving grants	190	30.9	174	46.4	16	6.7
Less than 1/2 tuition	38	6.2	31	8.3	7	2.9
Half to full tuition	104	16.9	99	26.4	5	2.1
Full tuition	48	7.8	44	11.7	4	1.7
More than full tuition	0	0.0	0	0.0	0	0.0
Median grant amount			$12,000		$6,000	

Informational and Library Resources

Total amount spent on library materials	$651,666
Study seating capacity inside the library	273
# of full-time equivalent professional librarians	15
Hours per week library is open	168
# of open, wired connections available to students	31
# of networked computers available for use by students	46
Has wireless network?	Y
Requires computer?	N

JD Attrition (from prior year)

	Academic #	Other #	Total #	Total %
1st year	14	14	28	14.2
2nd year	8	8	16	10.1
3rd year	3	0	3	1.5
4th year	1	0	1	1.6

Employment (9 months after graduation)

For up-to-date employment data, go to employmentsummary.abaquestionnaire.org on the ABA website.

Bar Passage Rates

First-time takers	136	Reporting %	82.35
Average school %	83.03	Average state %	83.90

Average pass difference –0.87

Jurisdiction	Takers	Passers	Pass %	State %	Diff %
Kentucky	61	47	77.05	82.03	–4.98
Ohio	51	46	90.20	86.14	4.06

NORTHERN KENTUCKY UNIVERSITY—SALMON P. CHASE COLLEGE OF LAW

Nunn Hall, Nunn Drive
Highland Heights, KY 41099
Phone: 859.572.5490; Fax: 859.572.6081
E-mail: chaseadmissions@nku.edu; Website: http://chaselaw.nku.edu/

Introduction

Founded in 1893, NKU Chase College of Law is located on the main campus of Northern Kentucky University, a metropolitan university just seven miles south of Cincinnati, Ohio. A major Midwestern center of commerce, industry, arts, and entertainment, the region supports a thriving legal and business community. Chase offers both full-time and part-time programs of study. It is accredited by the American Bar Association and is a member of the Association of American Law Schools.

Part-Time Divisions

For 119 years, NKU Chase has been providing legal education to working professionals through its part-time evening division. In addition, Chase now offers a part-time day division designed for those who work evenings or have other commitments that prevent study in the evening. In both part-time programs, classes typically meet three times per week, although students are occasionally required to attend events on other days.

Law and Informatics Institute

Law and informatics can be understood as "the rules, principles, and regulations involving the collection, classification, storage, retrieval, and dissemination of recorded knowledge." Participants in the **Law & Informatics Institute** work to study and develop the regulations and business practices that govern the creation, acquisition, aggregation, security, manipulation, and exploitation of information. Law and informatics includes the traditional fields of patent law, copyright law, trademark law, trade secret law, and the protection of publicity rights, but it also includes much more, such as data security, privacy, international trade, criminal law, and national security law. Students participate through substantive and skills-based courses, competition teams, clinical opportunities, field placements, research projects, alumni mentorships, and student organizations.

Centers for Excellence

The **Center for Excellence in Advocacy** offers students the knowledge, skills, and values they need to represent a client from the initial client interview through the appeals process. Through innovative courses and programming, students learn the practical aspects of pretrial procedures, negotiations, mediations, trial techniques, appellate advocacy, and legislation. As a result, students develop advanced litigation skills and graduate with an in-depth understanding of cutting-edge advocacy techniques. The **Transactional Law Practice Center** provides students with multiple opportunities to develop the skill sets and knowledge employed by lawyers involved in the practice of business and transactional law. Students acquire and hone critical thinking techniques and problem-solving skills. The center offers training in interviewing, negotiating, drafting, business planning, and client counseling, along with specialized law courses in related disciplines such as accounting and corporate finance.

The **Local Government Law Center** is one of the few centers nationwide devoted primarily to state and local government law, and it is the only one based in a public law school. The center promotes the development and study of government law through teaching, scholarship, and continuing education; provides technical assistance and support to local governments; and serves the public through its website, public speaking, and community outreach.

Certificates and Concentrations

Certificate programs enable students to focus their studies on particular skill sets. Students may earn a certificate signifying excellence in Advocacy or Transactional Law by completing coursework and participating in field placements and extracurricular learning opportunities. Concentration programs provide students an opportunity to "major" in a particular law subject while simultaneously obtaining a well-rounded legal education. Chase offers concentrations in Tax and in Employment and Labor Law.

Pro Bono Service Program

The Pro Bono Service Program requires students to complete 50 hours of pro bono service prior to graduation. Students select from a variety of organizations designated as approved placement sites, or they design their own pro bono projects. In addition, Chase offers several pro bono projects based at the law school. Service could include interviewing clients about legal problems, researching issues for public interest lawyers, engaging in legislative or policy analysis, teaching at-risk youth about the law, providing income tax assistance to low-income clients, or participating in legal aid clinics.

Clinics and Field Placements

Clinics: Students participating in clinics learn about the law firsthand by representing actual clients and trying real cases under the supervision of clinic directors, who are full-time faculty members and licensed attorneys. Students work alongside practitioners to gain knowledge and experience that supplements lessons learned from textbooks, while providing valuable services to clients who desperately need their help. Chase offers the

- **Children's Law Center Clinic,**
- **Constitutional Litigation Clinic,**
- **Indigent Defense Clinic,**
- **Kentucky Innocence Project**, and
- **Small Business and Nonprofit Law Clinic.**

Field Placements: An abundance of additional opportunities for study outside the classroom are also provided to allow students to develop their practical and professional skills as well as to deepen their knowledge of particular areas of law. Field placements are available in a wide variety of settings, including criminal prosecution and defense, civil family and poverty law, juvenile law, and tax law, as well as in both federal and state courts and fields specifically tailored to the individual student's interests.

Joint-Degree Programs

NKU Chase offers three joint-degree programs, two with the College of Informatics and one with the College of Business. The Juris Doctor/Master of Health Informatics program is for students who wish to practice health law with a greater understanding of regulatory compliance and data-driven health practices. The Juris Doctor/Master of Business Informatics program focuses on the study of information technology in the context of business and law. The Juris Doctor/Master of Business Administration program teaches critical management, accounting and finance, and leadership skills to enhance the student's understanding of law.

Student Activities

Competition Teams: NKU Chase offers a wide variety of national competition teams that provide students with myriad opportunities to learn-by-doing in a competitive yet collaborative environment. The competition teams are the Moot Court Team, Trial Advocacy Team, Arbitration Team, Client Counseling Team, Negotiation Team, and Transactional Lawyering Team.

Law Review: The *Northern Kentucky Law Review* is an independent journal published by NKU Chase students and includes scholarly legal writing by law professors, practitioners, jurists, and students.

Organizations: NKU Chase's many student organizations offer students a wide range of extracurricular opportunities. Through participation in these organizations, students benefit professionally and personally by learning more about specific fields of the law, networking with practitioners, hearing from guest speakers, getting to know students in other sections and class years, gaining leadership experience, and performing community service.

Scholars Program

The NKU Chase Scholars Program recognizes the achievements of outstanding students and provides financial assistance that will allow them to explore a variety of professional opportunities after graduation.

Salmon P. Chase Scholars: Full-tuition scholarship each year plus a paid research assistantship in the second or third year of study.

Henry Clay Scholars: Scholarship award amounts begin at $5,000 per year.

John Marshall Harlan Diversity Scholars: Scholarship award amounts range from $3,000 to full tuition. Diversity is defined as "the ability to enhance the multicultural and socioeconomic differences at the college of law through such characteristics as ethnicity, race, gender, age, abilities/limitations, and/or multicultural and socioeconomic background."

Career Development

The Career Development Office assists students and alumni with career planning, networking, and developing job-search skills and strategies. The office schedules fall and spring on-campus interviews; posts job notices daily; sends out e-newsletters to students; manages a student résumé database; conducts mock interviews; assists with job fair participation; and holds seminars, workshops, and networking events to prepare students for the job market. The office coordinates information sessions with attorneys, which enable students to network and learn about a wide variety of legal specialties and career options. The office also assists with the Chase Summer Public Interest Fellowship Program, which provides stipends to selected students working at public interest organizations during the summer.

Admission

NKU Chase seeks to admit applicants who have the best prospect of high-quality academic work. The Admissions Committee relies heavily on undergraduate grades and performance on the LSAT. Additional factors considered include academic performance, including course selection patterns, upward trends in grades, and post-undergraduate work completed; achievements made in another profession or vocation; community involvement and volunteerism; cultural, educational, or sociological diversity; demonstrated leadership and professionalism; employment background, including working while attending college; and letters of recommendation.

APPLICANT PROFILE

Northern Kentucky University—Salmon P. Chase College of Law
This grid includes only applicants who earned 120–180 LSAT scores under standard administrations.

LSAT Score	3.75 +		3.50–3.74		3.25–3.49		3.00–3.24		2.75–2.99		2.50–2.74		Below 2.50		No GPA		Total	
	Apps	Adm	Apps	Adm	Apps	Adm	Apps	Adm	Apps	Adm	Apps	Adm	Apps	Adm	Apps	Adm	Apps	Adm
170–180	0	0	0	0	0	0	0	0	0	0	0	0	0	0	0	0	0	0
165–169	2	2	5	5	1	1	0	0	0	0	0	0	0	0	0	0	8	8
160–164	12	12	11	10	22	22	16	16	9	8	1	1	1	0	0	0	72	69
155–159	33	29	33	31	46	43	44	40	27	21	14	11	14	4	1	0	212	179
150–154	37	33	43	36	63	47	52	22	39	11	33	9	17	5	0	0	284	163
145–149	11	3	25	10	34	6	43	6	32	3	32	3	16	0	0	0	193	31
140–144	1	0	7	0	15	1	14	0	16	1	13	1	10	0	0	0	76	3
Below 140	0	0	2	0	4	0	5	0	6	0	10	0	13	0	2	0	42	0
Total	96	79	126	92	185	120	174	84	129	44	103	25	71	9	3	0	887	453

Apps = Number of Applicants   Adm = Number Admitted   Reflects 100% of the total applicant pool; highest LSAT data reported.

NORTHWESTERN UNIVERSITY SCHOOL OF LAW

375 East Chicago Avenue
Chicago, IL 60611-3069
Phone: 312.503.3100; Fax: 312.503.0178
E-mail: admissions@law.northwestern.edu; Website: www.law.northwestern.edu

The Basics

Type of school	Private
Term	Semester
Application deadline	1/15 2/15
Application fee	$100
Financial aid deadline	3/1
Can first year start other than fall?	Yes
Student to faculty ratio	8.4 to 1
# of housing spaces available restricted to law students graduate housing for which law students are eligible	42

Faculty and Administrators

	Total		Men		Women		Minorities	
	Spr	Fall	Spr	Fall	Spr	Fall	Spr	Fall
Full-time	84	76	44	41	40	35	7	6
Other full-time	15	18	9	12	6	6	0	1
Deans, librarians, & others who teach	12	12	6	6	6	6	1	1
Part-time	78	65	59	50	19	15	10	4
Total	189	171	118	109	71	62	18	12

Curriculum

	Full-Time	Part-Time
Typical first-year section size	60	0
Is there typically a "small section" of the first-year class, other than Legal Writing, taught by full-time faculty	No	No
If yes, typical size offered last year		
# of classroom course titles beyond first-year curriculum	213	

# of upper division courses, excluding seminars, with an enrollment:		
Under 25	166	
25–49	59	
50–74	29	
75–99	0	
100+	0	

# of seminars	75	
# of seminar positions available	1,610	
# of seminar positions filled	1,233	0
# of positions available in simulation courses	1,113	
# of simulation positions filled	920	0
# of positions available in faculty supervised clinical courses	381	
# of faculty supervised clinical positions filled	351	0
# involved in field placements	272	0
# involved in law journals	413	0
# involved in moot court or trial competitions	28	0
# of credit hours required to graduate	84	

JD Enrollment and Ethnicity

	Men		Women		Full-Time		Part-Time		1st-Year		Total		JD Degs. Awd.
	#	%	#	%	#	%	#	%	#	%	#	%	
All Hispanics	29	6.8	25	6.7	54	6.7	0	0.0	23	8.7	54	6.7	23
Am. Ind./AK Nat.	0	0.0	5	1.3	5	0.6	0	0.0	0	0.0	5	0.6	1
Asian	65	15.2	78	20.9	143	17.9	0	0.0	43	16.3	143	17.9	38
Black/Af. Am.	34	7.9	25	6.7	59	7.4	0	0.0	15	5.7	59	7.4	23
Nat. HI/Pac. Isl.	0	0.0	0	0.0	0	0.0	0	0.0	0	0.0	0	0.0	1
2 or more races	14	3.3	20	5.4	34	4.2	0	0.0	12	4.5	34	4.2	0
Subtotal (minor.)	142	33.2	153	41.0	295	36.8	0	0.0	93	35.2	295	36.8	86
Nonres. Alien	23	5.4	17	4.6	40	5.0	0	0.0	10	3.8	40	5.0	0
White/Cauc.	263	61.4	203	54.4	466	58.2	0	0.0	161	61.0	466	58.2	152
Unknown	0	0.0	0	0.0	0	0.0	0	0.0	0	0.0	0	0.0	50
Total	428	53.4	373	46.6	801	100.0	0	0.0	264	33.0	801		288

Transfers

Transfers in	39
Transfers out	9

Tuition and Fees

	Resident	Nonresident
Full-time	$51,920	$51,920
Part-time		
Tuition Guarantee Program	N	

Living Expenses

Estimated living expenses for singles

Living on campus	Living off campus	Living at home
$23,500	$23,500	$23,500

NORTHWESTERN UNIVERSITY SCHOOL OF LAW

ABA Approved Since 1923

GPA and LSAT Scores

	Total	Full-Time	Part-Time
# of apps	4,548	4,548	0
# of offers	864	864	0
# of matrics	264	264	0
75% GPA	3.85	3.85	0.00
Median GPA	3.75	3.75	0.00
25% GPA	3.35	3.35	0.00
75% LSAT	171	171	0
Median LSAT	170	170	0
25% LSAT	165	165	0

Grants and Scholarships (from prior year)

	Total #	Total %	Full-Time #	Full-Time %	Part-Time #	Part-Time %
Total # of students	817		817		0	
Total # receiving grants	250	30.6	250	30.6	0	0.0
Less than 1/2 tuition	174	21.3	174	21.3	0	0.0
Half to full tuition	76	9.3	76	9.3	0	0.0
Full tuition	0	0.0	0	0.0	0	0.0
More than full tuition	0	0.0	0	0.0	0	0.0
Median grant amount			$20,000		$0	

Informational and Library Resources

Total amount spent on library materials	$863,032
Study seating capacity inside the library	609
# of full-time equivalent professional librarians	13
Hours per week library is open	96
# of open, wired connections available to students	161
# of networked computers available for use by students	104
Has wireless network?	Y
Requires computer?	Y

JD Attrition (from prior year)

	Academic #	Other #	Total #	Total %
1st year	0	16	16	5.8
2nd year	0	1	1	0.4
3rd year	0	2	2	0.7
4th year	0	0	0	0.0

Employment (9 months after graduation)

For up-to-date employment data, go to employmentsummary.abaquestionnaire.org on the ABA website.

Bar Passage Rates

First-time takers	279	Reporting %	72.04
Average school %	88.07	Average state %	86.86
Average pass difference	1.21		

Jurisdiction	Takers	Passers	Pass %	State %	Diff %
Illinois	130	125	96.15	89.38	6.77
New York	53	49	92.45	84.92	7.53
California	13	1	7.69	71.24	−63.55
New Jersey	4	1	25.00	82.34	−57.34
Pennsylvania	1	1	100.00	83.06	16.94

NORTHWESTERN UNIVERSITY SCHOOL OF LAW

375 East Chicago Avenue
Chicago, IL 60611-3069
Phone: 312.503.3100; Fax: 312.503.0178
E-mail: admissions@law.northwestern.edu; Website: www.law.northwestern.edu

Introduction

Guided by a visionary strategic plan and its recent update, "Plan 2008: Building Great Leaders for the Changing World," Northwestern University School of Law, founded in 1859, advances the understanding of law and produces graduates prepared to excel in a rapidly changing world.

Northwestern Law uniquely blends a rigorous intellectual environment with a collegial and supportive community. Our students have access to the most interdisciplinary research faculty in the nation. We also have one of the lowest student-faculty ratios (9:1), so our students enjoy an unusual amount of individual access to these scholars, even after graduation. The law school's lakefront location in the heart of downtown Chicago provides a wealth of part-time employment options for students while in school, and a spectacular setting in which to study law. Northwestern Law's proximity to courts, commerce, and public interest activities enables students to experience the practice of law, as well as its theory, in one of the most vibrant legal and business communities in the world.

Enrollment and Admission

Northwestern Law's close-knit community fosters collaborative learning, which enables students to develop outstanding leadership, team, organizational, and professional skills. We seek students with a wide variety of experience and backgrounds, and our Admissions Committee considers many factors beyond test scores and GPAs when evaluating applicants. Currently, more than 90 percent of entering JD students have at least one year of full-time work experience. Through a unique interviewing program, Northwestern Law ensures it enrolls students with strong academic credentials as well as the interpersonal skills and maturity needed to thrive in the law school community.

Faculty

Northwestern Law has a rich tradition of faculty excellence. Throughout our history, our faculty members have been engaged in major public policy debates, and that tradition is alive and well today. Northwestern Law has faculty addressing and speaking out on cutting-edge legal issues ranging from medical malpractice reform to the emergence of the constitutionality of health care reform legislation to intellectual property's transformation in a digital age, and much more.

Northwestern Law students have access to the most interdisciplinary research faculty in the nation. We have faculty working at the intersection of law and many other disciplines, including economics, psychology, philosophy, political science, sociology, and history. We have distinguished legal theorists as well as one of the strongest cohorts of empirical scholars in any law school.

Together, our faculty members combine to form what is, we believe, the most eclectic and balanced mix of legal scholars among our nation's law schools. Their diverse mix of expertise and research methodologies allows them to bring a unique perspective to both their scholarship and teaching.

Curriculum

In the rigorous first year of study, Northwestern Law provides a superior foundation in legal reasoning, analysis, and writing, as well as a thorough understanding of the structures and policies of the law. Communication, teamwork, cross-training in business, and experiential learning are also hallmarks of Northwestern Law. The law school's size enables students to have one-on-one relationships with professors, with required first-year courses taught in sections of approximately 60 students. The JD program requires 83 semester hours of credit. The broad and flexible curriculum gives upper-level students the opportunity to specialize in particular areas, to pursue advanced research in legal theory, or to pursue a range of hands-on simulation, externship, and live-client opportunities. The Owen L. Coon/James A. Rahl Senior Research Program enables third-year students to do individual research under the supervision of a professor, using library, field, and interdisciplinary research methods.

Special Degree and International Programs

A limited number of highly motivated students are enrolled in Northwestern Law's Accelerated JD program—the first such program offered by a top law school. Accelerated JD students complete the same number of credit hours as traditional three-year JD students in five semesters over the course of two calendar years.

A combined program in law and business, jointly offered with Northwestern's Kellogg School of Management, enables students to earn both a JD from the law school and an MBA degree from Kellogg after only three years of study. Students may also enroll in a highly integrated six-year JD-PhD program with the law school and one of the graduate school departments.

Northwestern Law is the only top law school in the country to offer a four-year joint-degree program leading to both a JD and an LLM in International Human Rights (JD-LLM IHR). JD-LLM IHR students receive a thorough grounding in the norms and mechanisms of international human rights law and international criminal law. A distinctive feature of the new JD-LLM IHR program is a requirement that students complete a semester-long externship with one of a number of designated international and hybrid criminal tribunals, foreign supreme courts, and international human rights organizations.

Students who wish to specialize in the study of tax law can earn an LLM in Taxation or jointly pursue a JD and an LLM in Taxation at the same time. Students educated outside the United States can earn an LLM through a nine-month program of advanced study, or an LLM degree and a certificate in business administration from Kellogg through a twelve-month program in law and business. In addition, international lawyers also have the option to earn an LLM in 15 weeks over the summer in Northwestern Law's new Accelerated Summer LLM program. Legal and business professionals abroad can earn an LLM degree from Northwestern through our Executive LLM Programs in Seoul, South Korea; Madrid, Spain; and Tel Aviv, Israel.

Clinical Programs

In Northwestern Law's comprehensive clinical program, students learn strong litigation and negotiation skills and gain direct experience with representing clients and reforming laws.

The innovative simulation-based curriculum gives students the skills they need to negotiate and communicate effectively, solve problems, prepare briefs, examine witnesses, present evidence, and argue cases.

Housing more than 20 clinics within 14 centers, the Bluhm Legal Clinic is widely recognized as the best legal clinic facility in the country. The clinic centers—Appellate Advocacy Center, Fred Bartlit Center for Trial Advocacy, Center for Criminal Defense, Center for Externships, Center for International Human Rights, Center on Negotiation and Mediation, Center on Wrongful Convictions, Center on Wrongful Convictions of Youth, Children and Family Justice Center, Civil Litigation Center, Entrepreneurship Law Center, Environmental Advocacy Center, Investor Protection Center, and the Roderick MacArthur Justice Center—are nationally recognized for their direct involvement in legal reform.

Students represent underserved clients as well as challenge the fairness of our legal institutions and propose solutions for reform. Working in teams, they assist small business owners and prepare cases in juvenile justice, immigration and asylum, and criminal matters. In addition to fine-tuning their skills as advocates, they often effect change in the law and legal institutions.

Student Activities

Northwestern Law students take an intense and energetic interest in their community and education. Six scholarly journals are available for research, writing, and editing. Students automatically belong to the Student Bar Association, which gives them a voice in curriculum and administration, and they have an opportunity to participate in more than 50 student organizations.

APPLICANT PROFILE

At Northwestern Law, emphasis on teamwork, communication, and interpersonal skills begins during the admission process, in which every applicant is urged to interview. Currently, more than 75 percent of applicants are interviewed, and college seniors must be interviewed. We also seek to enroll students with work experience, which contributes to an environment where students learn a great deal from not only faculty, but also each other.

Our students also enjoy Chicago's sophisticated yet friendly atmosphere, along with its world-class cultural, sports, and entertainment offerings. Northwestern's 20-acre Chicago campus is nestled between the shores of Lake Michigan, the energy of Michigan Avenue's Magnificent Mile, and the elegant Gold Coast residential area.

Library and Facilities

With more than a half million volumes and access to a wide range of electronic resources, the Pritzker Legal Research Center is one of the country's largest law libraries. It also provides students access to the 3.7 million volumes of the combined Northwestern University libraries.

Our modern facilities and recent additions support collaboration and interaction. Wireless technology is available throughout the law school, and recent renovations include a new 22,000-square-foot clinic center, more than 10 state-of-the-art classrooms and seminar rooms, and upgraded lighting.

Career Services

The Center for Career Strategy and Advancement proactively cultivates relationships with potential employers while assisting students in focusing their goals and developing short- and long-term career strategies. Traditionally, more than 600 national employers recruit our students. Nearly 80 percent of the recruiters are based in regions outside the Midwest.

Expenses and Financial Aid

Northwestern Law annually awards $7 million in grants and scholarships in addition to long-term, low-interest institutional loans. These resources enable the law school to cover 100 percent of a student's calculated financial need. Approximately 85 percent of our currently enrolled students receive financial aid.

NOTRE DAME LAW SCHOOL

Admissions Office, 1329 Biolchini Hall
Notre Dame, IN 46556
Phone: 574.631.6626; Fax: 574.631.5474
E-mail: lawadmit@nd.edu; Website: http://law.nd.edu

ABA
Approved
Since
1925

The Basics

Type of school	Private
Term	Semester
Application deadline	2/28
Application fee	$65
Financial aid deadline	2/15
Can first year start other than fall?	No
Student to faculty ratio	9.9 to 1
# of housing spaces available restricted to law students	
graduate housing for which law students are eligible	142

Faculty and Administrators

	Total		Men		Women		Minorities	
	Spr	Fall	Spr	Fall	Spr	Fall	Spr	Fall
Full-time	43	49	30	35	13	14	6	5
Other full-time	1	0	0	0	1	0	0	0
Deans, librarians, & others who teach	12	12	6	6	6	6	1	1
Part-time	41	47	25	29	16	18	1	2
Total	97	108	61	70	36	38	8	8

JD Enrollment and Ethnicity

	Men #	Men %	Women #	Women %	Full-Time #	Full-Time %	Part-Time #	Part-Time %	1st-Year #	1st-Year %	Total #	Total %	JD Degs. Awd.
All Hispanics	38	11.4	32	13.9	70	12.4	0	0.0	22	12.0	70	12.4	15
Am. Ind./AK Nat.	6	1.8	3	1.3	9	1.6	0	0.0	4	2.2	9	1.6	2
Asian	15	4.5	32	13.9	47	8.3	0	0.0	12	6.6	47	8.3	10
Black/Af. Am.	15	4.5	18	7.8	33	5.9	0	0.0	14	7.7	33	5.9	9
Nat. HI/Pac. Isl.	0	0.0	0	0.0	0	0.0	0	0.0	0	0.0	0	0.0	0
2 or more races	8	2.4	5	2.2	13	2.3	0	0.0	3	1.6	13	2.3	4
Subtotal (minor.)	82	24.7	90	39.0	172	30.6	0	0.0	55	30.1	172	30.6	40
Nonres. Alien	5	1.5	4	1.7	9	1.6	0	0.0	4	2.2	9	1.6	2
White/Cauc.	224	67.5	126	54.5	350	62.2	0	0.0	115	62.8	350	62.2	135
Unknown	21	6.3	11	4.8	32	5.7	0	0.0	9	4.9	32	5.7	13
Total	332	59.0	231	41.0	563	100.0	0	0.0	183	32.5	563		190

Curriculum

	Full-Time	Part-Time
Typical first-year section size	58	0
Is there typically a "small section" of the first-year class, other than Legal Writing, taught by full-time faculty	No	No
If yes, typical size offered last year		
# of classroom course titles beyond first-year curriculum	128	

# of upper division courses, excluding seminars, with an enrollment:	Under 25	91
	25–49	36
	50–74	12
	75–99	6
	100+	2

# of seminars	34	
# of seminar positions available	638	
# of seminar positions filled	453	0
# of positions available in simulation courses	171	
# of simulation positions filled	168	0
# of positions available in faculty supervised clinical courses	120	
# of faculty supervised clinical positions filled	114	0
# involved in field placements	41	0
# involved in law journals	180	0
# involved in moot court or trial competitions	97	0
# of credit hours required to graduate	90	

Transfers

Transfers in	18
Transfers out	4

Tuition and Fees

	Resident	Nonresident
Full-time	$43,335	$43,335
Part-time		
Tuition Guarantee Program	N	

Living Expenses

Estimated living expenses for singles

Living on campus	Living off campus	Living at home
$17,650	$17,650	$17,650

*ABA
Approved
Since
1925*

GPA and LSAT Scores

	Total	Full-Time	Part-Time
# of apps	3,059	3,059	0
# of offers	640	640	0
# of matrics	183	183	0
75% GPA	3.74	3.74	0.00
Median GPA	3.64	3.64	0.00
25% GPA	3.45	3.45	0.00
75% LSAT	167	167	0
Median LSAT	166	166	0
25% LSAT	162	162	0

Grants and Scholarships (from prior year)

	Total		Full-Time		Part-Time	
	#	%	#	%	#	%
Total # of students	564		564		0	
Total # receiving grants	404	71.6	404	71.6	0	0.0
Less than 1/2 tuition	361	64.0	361	64.0	0	0.0
Half to full tuition	38	6.7	38	6.7	0	0.0
Full tuition	2	0.4	2	0.4	0	0.0
More than full tuition	3	0.5	3	0.5	0	0.0
Median grant amount		$16,000		$0		

Informational and Library Resources

Total amount spent on library materials	$1,662,902
Study seating capacity inside the library	585
# of full-time equivalent professional librarians	9
Hours per week library is open	95
# of open, wired connections available to students	86
# of networked computers available for use by students	94
Has wireless network?	Y
Requires computer?	N

JD Attrition (from prior year)

	Academic	Other	Total	
	#	#	#	%
1st year	0	8	8	4.7
2nd year	0	2	2	1.0
3rd year	1	2	3	1.6
4th year	0	0	0	0.0

Employment (9 months after graduation)

For up-to-date employment data, go to
employmentsummary.abaquestionnaire.org on the ABA website.

Bar Passage Rates

First-time takers	170	Reporting %	100.00
Average school %	90.00	Average state %	82.18
Average pass difference	7.82		

Jurisdiction	Takers	Passers	Pass %	State %	Diff %
Illinois	35	35	100.00	89.38	10.62
California	28	21	75.00	71.24	3.76
New York	22	20	90.91	84.92	5.99
Indiana	13	11	84.62	80.93	3.69
Others (24)	72	66	91.67		

NOTRE DAME LAW SCHOOL

Admissions Office, 1329 Biolchini Hall
Notre Dame, IN 46556
Phone: 574.631.6626; Fax: 574.631.5474
E-mail: lawadmit@nd.edu; Website: http://law.nd.edu

Introduction

With a rich history that dates to its founding in 1869, Notre Dame Law School today enjoys a national and international reputation for preparing consummate professionals—men and women who are extraordinarily competent in their professional endeavors and who commit themselves to serve their clients and the profession effectively and honorably. Distinctive among nationally regarded law schools as a result of the school's and the university's Catholic heritage and tradition, faith and values, and community spirit, the Law School inspires students to examine their practice of law within the context of their responsibilities as members of the bar, as leaders within their respective fields, and as citizens of the world community.

Enrollment/Student Body

The student body represents the national stature and international nature of the programs of the Law School and the university. Our student body of approximately 575 students represents nearly all states and a number of foreign countries. The small size of the student body fosters a sense of community and allows significant interaction between faculty and students.

Faculty

Faculty members come to Notre Dame Law School with experience in private practice and government service, and represent a wide range of undergraduate institutions, law schools, and state bars. Members of the faculty are well regarded for their commitment to teaching, as well as their accessibility to students outside of the classroom as advisors and mentors. At the same time, these premier scholars publish in leading journals and are invited to participate in academic conferences around the world.

Library and Physical Facilities

In January 2009, the Law School moved into the Eck Hall of Law, a beautiful and spacious three-story, 85,000-square-foot building. It is connected to the existing building by a covered walkway and chapel, with a common area above. The design captures the Law School's commitment to shaping the minds, hearts, and souls of the next generation of Notre Dame lawyers. In June 2010, the equally beautiful gothic structure that has been home to the Law School since 1930, reopened after undergoing a major renovation. Biolchini Hall houses an expanded Kresge Law Library, several administrative offices, four journal offices, and additional classroom space.

The Kresge Law Library is among the top American law school research libraries. The staff is noted for its service to law school faculty, students, staff, and the larger university community.

The Law School provides significant computing support for students and other members of the law school community. Five full-time technology professionals offer assistance for both hardware and software, in addition to other computing and technology needs.

Curriculum

The JD curriculum provides a strong foundation in those areas that have proven to be fundamental to the actual practice of law in every American jurisdiction, while giving students the opportunity to tailor coursework to particular career aspirations. The law school offers programs of study in Business Law; Criminal Law; Global Law; Law, Ethics, and Public Policy; and Public Law; as well as interdisciplinary programs in Church, State, and Society; Constitutional Structure and Design; Family Law Mediation; Law and Economics; and Law and Human Development. In addition to the JD degree, the Law School confers three graduate law degrees: an LLM in International and Comparative Law, an LLM in International Human Rights, and a JSD (also in International Human Rights). The LLM in International and Comparative Law is offered exclusively at the Law School's London Law Centre.

London Programs

Notre Dame Law School recognizes that today's legal practice increasingly involves problems that the law of no one nation can resolve. Hence, JD candidates may augment their legal education by participating in study-abroad programs offered by the Law School through its London Law Centre. Second-year students who wish to immerse themselves in comparative and international law, as well as in the traditions of the American and British common-law systems, can study in the only yearlong overseas program offered by an American law school. Students who desire a shorter international-study experience and who have completed their first year of law school can spend a semester or summer in London.

Student Life

The sense of community and the quality of student life at Notre Dame have developed out of long-standing traditions that make the Notre Dame Law School experience different: admission policies that emphasize the importance of qualitative factors such as service to others; a mission that focuses on teaching, scholarship, and service in the legal and Judeo-Christian traditions; and an emphasis on forming and nurturing collegial relationships between students and faculty. The Law School is centrally located on the Notre Dame campus, and law students fully participate in athletic, cultural, religious, and social events on the campus. Law students also manage to find a comfortable balance between their studies and involvement in the Law School's four law journals and any of 30 organizations that reflect the professional and personal interests of the student body.

Expenses and Financial Aid

Notre Dame is committed to providing a legal education of the highest quality at a tuition structure that compares favorably to other nationally regarded private law schools. Additionally, law students benefit from the low cost of living in northern Indiana.

In recent years, scholarship assistance has been provided annually to approximately 60–70 percent of entering students on the basis of merit, commitment to the Law School's mission, and financial need. Scholarships are renewable for all three years of legal study if the student remains in good standing.

Housing

Many single law students choose to live on campus in graduate-student housing. Married students with children can live in the unfurnished University Village apartments. Students who wish to live off campus can find reasonably priced accommodations near the campus and can secure on-campus parking for a nominal additional charge.

Career Development

Notre Dame Law School graduates have, in recent years, found rewarding work all over the country and in a wide variety of practice areas. Employers participate in interviews exclusive to Notre Dame law students in Los Angeles; Washington, DC; and New York, as well as on campus. Employers are interested in interviewing Notre Dame law students because of the Law School's reputation for preparing extraordinarily competent lawyers. A national network of over 8,000 Law School alumni and friends assists students and graduates in finding employment opportunities across the country.

Graduates of Notre Dame Law School have been successful in terms of obtaining judicial clerkships. These highly sought-after positions provide graduates with a unique opportunity to learn firsthand about the inner workings of the judicial system, while at the same time allowing them to hone important legal skills and problem-solving abilities.

The Career Development Office (CDO) also coordinates a variety of initiatives to encourage students who wish to be employed in public interest work following graduation. These include a variety of informational programs and services, including participation in our campus-wide, nonprofit career night. The CDO also participates in public interest law career fairs across the country and is a sponsoring and coordinating school for the Midwest Public Interest Law Career Conference in Chicago. Additionally, the office coordinates a comprehensive summer stipend program that provides funding for over 100 students working in public interest positions each summer. The Law School's Loan Repayment Assistance Program (LRAP) assists eligible law school graduates who choose to work in public interest, public service, or other similar positions after graduation. The Law School seeks to help reduce the financial pressures that can discourage graduates from pursuing positions in public interest and public service employment.

Please visit our website for the most current employment information.

APPLICANT PROFILE

Each year, the Law School Admissions Committee employs a whole-person review philosophy to create a class from a large number of highly qualified applicants. We seek to enroll multidimensional students with a wide range of talents, backgrounds, experiences, accomplishments, and points of view. Academic ability, as reflected in the LSAT score and academic performance in college, are important; however, the committee considers a broad array of elements in addition to these two quantitative measures. Notre Dame Law School officials involved in the admission process are mindful of the school's objective to produce lawyers who are competent, compassionate, and committed to serving their clients with integrity. The admission process is highly selective and seeks to enroll men and women of exceptional ability. We do not provide an applicant profile grid because it would be based solely on LSAT and GPA.

NOVA SOUTHEASTERN UNIVERSITY—SHEPARD BROAD LAW CENTER

3305 College Avenue
Fort Lauderdale, FL 33314-7721
Phone: 954.262.6117; Fax: 954.262.3844
E-mail: admission@nsu.law.nova.edu; Website: www.nsulaw.nova.edu

ABA
Approved
Since
1975

The Basics

Type of school	Private
Term	Semester
Application deadline	4/1
Application fee	$53
Financial aid deadline	4/15
Can first year start other than fall?	No
Student to faculty ratio	16.0 to 1
# of housing spaces available restricted to law students	32
graduate housing for which law students are eligible	308

Faculty and Administrators

	Total		Men		Women		Minorities	
	Spr	Fall	Spr	Fall	Spr	Fall	Spr	Fall
Full-time	50	52	28	29	22	23	10	14
Other full-time	9	8	4	3	5	5	4	3
Deans, librarians, & others who teach	9	8	3	3	6	5	3	3
Part-time	37	57	29	35	8	22	9	9
Total	105	125	64	70	41	55	26	29

Curriculum

	Full-Time	Part-Time
Typical first-year section size	65	62
Is there typically a "small section" of the first-year class, other than Legal Writing, taught by full-time faculty	No	No
If yes, typical size offered last year		

# of classroom course titles beyond first-year curriculum		93
# of upper division courses, excluding seminars, with an enrollment:	Under 25	165
	25–49	43
	50–74	45
	75–99	6
	100+	0
# of seminars		20
# of seminar positions available		400
# of seminar positions filled	278	69
# of positions available in simulation courses		1,408
# of simulation positions filled	970	278
# of positions available in faculty supervised clinical courses		100
# of faculty supervised clinical positions filled	28	17
# involved in field placements	58	26
# involved in law journals	92	12
# involved in moot court or trial competitions	59	11
# of credit hours required to graduate		90

JD Enrollment and Ethnicity

	Men		Women		Full-Time		Part-Time		1st-Year		Total		JD Degs. Awd.
	#	%	#	%	#	%	#	%	#	%	#	%	
All Hispanics	99	19.6	128	23.5	164	19.2	63	32.3	80	22.9	227	21.6	57
Am. Ind./AK Nat.	2	0.4	1	0.2	0	0.0	3	1.5	1	0.3	3	0.3	3
Asian	22	4.3	27	5.0	43	5.0	6	3.1	18	5.1	49	4.7	10
Black/Af. Am.	17	3.4	43	7.9	41	4.8	19	9.7	19	5.4	60	5.7	9
Nat. HI/Pac. Isl.	2	0.4	2	0.4	3	0.4	1	0.5	0	0.0	4	0.4	7
2 or more races	1	0.2	4	0.7	3	0.4	2	1.0	3	0.9	5	0.5	0
Subtotal (minor.)	143	28.3	205	37.7	254	29.7	94	48.2	121	34.6	348	33.1	86
Nonres. Alien	0	0.0	0	0.0	0	0.0	0	0.0	0	0.0	0	0.0	1
White/Cauc.	336	66.4	300	55.1	552	64.6	84	43.1	200	57.1	636	60.6	194
Unknown	27	5.3	39	7.2	49	5.7	17	8.7	28	8.0	66	6.3	21
Total	506	48.2	544	51.8	855	81.4	195	18.6	350	33.3	1050		302

Transfers

Transfers in	8
Transfers out	55

Tuition and Fees

	Resident	Nonresident
Full-time	$33,250	$33,250
Part-time	$25,060	$25,060
Tuition Guarantee Program	N	

Living Expenses

Estimated living expenses for singles

Living on campus	Living off campus	Living at home
$18,564	$24,618	$10,929

NOVA SOUTHEASTERN UNIVERSITY—SHEPARD BROAD LAW CENTER

ABA
Approved
Since
1975

GPA and LSAT Scores

	Total	Full-Time	Part-Time
# of apps	2,298	1,930	368
# of offers	931	828	103
# of matrics	354	297	57
75% GPA	3.43	3.44	3.34
Median GPA	3.22	3.25	3.08
25% GPA	2.98	3.02	2.77
75% LSAT	152	152	151
Median LSAT	150	150	148
25% LSAT	148	148	147

Grants and Scholarships (from prior year)

	Total #	Total %	Full-Time #	Full-Time %	Part-Time #	Part-Time %
Total # of students	1,100		894		206	
Total # receiving grants	186	16.9	168	18.8	18	8.7
Less than 1/2 tuition	133	12.1	124	13.9	9	4.4
Half to full tuition	28	2.5	25	2.8	3	1.5
Full tuition	22	2.0	18	2.0	4	1.9
More than full tuition	3	0.3	1	0.1	2	1.0
Median grant amount			$10,000		$7,500	

Informational and Library Resources

Total amount spent on library materials	$1,333,509
Study seating capacity inside the library	532
# of full-time equivalent professional librarians	14
Hours per week library is open	104
# of open, wired connections available to students	4
# of networked computers available for use by students	10
Has wireless network?	Y
Requires computer?	Y

JD Attrition (from prior year)

	Academic #	Other #	Total #	Total %
1st year	66	44	110	28.0
2nd year	9	31	40	10.8
3rd year	0	1	1	0.4
4th year	1	0	1	1.9

Employment (9 months after graduation)

For up-to-date employment data, go to
employmentsummary.abaquestionnaire.org on the ABA website.

Bar Passage Rates

First-time takers	255	Reporting %	96.47
Average school %	83.33	Average state %	77.63
Average pass difference	5.70		

Jurisdiction	Takers	Passers	Pass %	State %	Diff %
Florida	246	205	83.33	77.63	5.70

NOVA SOUTHEASTERN UNIVERSITY—SHEPARD BROAD LAW CENTER

3305 College Avenue
Fort Lauderdale, FL 33314-7721
Phone: 954.262.6117; Fax: 954.262.3844
E-mail: admission@nsu.law.nova.edu; Website: www.nsulaw.nova.edu

Introduction

NSU Law Center is one of 16 graduate and professional schools of Nova Southeastern University, the largest private independent university in Florida and the sixth largest in the United States. NSU Law is accredited by the ABA and is a member of the AALS. The Law Center is located in the suburbs of Fort Lauderdale, in the heart of South Florida's fast-growing Broward, Miami-Dade, Palm Beach area. We encourage applicants to tour the campus and speak with the staff of the Admissions Office.

Curriculum and Special Academic/Professional Programs

The Law Center offers a rigorous traditional academic program in three-year day and four-year evening versions. NSU Law prides itself on preparing graduates to make a smooth transition from the classroom to the courtroom or boardroom.

Lawyering Skills and Values (LSV)—Every student completes a four-semester LSV sequence that combines traditional legal reasoning, writing, and research with an introduction to lawyer interviewing, counseling, negotiating, mediating, advocating, and other critical skills in a simulated law firm experience.

Clinical Opportunities—Clinical education is an important part of the NSU Law experience. The Law Center offers students a pioneering combination of academics and clinical experience that gives students the knowledge and skills they need to hit the ground running and launch a successful career in the highly competitive legal marketplace. Students have an opportunity to participate in numerous supervised clinical and externship experiences in the Alternative Dispute Resolution, Business Practice, Children and Families Law, Criminal Justice, Environmental and Land Use Law, International Practice, or Personal Injury Litigation clinics. During the clinical program, students are introduced to a practice specialty under the guidance of a seasoned mentor. Each clinical semester begins with intensive classes that focus on advanced substantive law and lawyering skills in the clinic specialty plus interdisciplinary topics. For the rest of the term, faculty members supervise the students' representation of clients in Law Center clinics, government agencies, nonprofit organizations, and private law offices.

International Dual-Degree Opportunities—NSU Law students have an opportunity to study both common law and civil law through our dual-degree program with the University of Barcelona. With successful completion of the program and the appropriate bar requirements, students can qualify for admission to the bar in both Spain and the United States. As lawyers, dual-degree graduates will have an opportunity to practice in the United States and Spain, and to practice transactional law in the European Union. The dual degree will also assist those wishing to practice in Latin America. Opportunities are also available in the Czech Republic and Italy.

Joint Degrees—NSU Law offers students opportunities to earn a second graduate degree in a complementary discipline and in a compressed time frame.

Internships—In addition to an award-winning pro bono service program, the Law Center operates judicial internship, mediation, street law, consumer protection, and dependency workshop programs that provide valuable real-world experiences.

Two Admission Programs

The Law Center's Admissions Committee oversees two separate programs. The Regular Admission Program combines each applicant's undergraduate grades and LSAT score according to a weighted formula based on the academic success of NSU Law students. The committee also values the applicant's personal statement, writing sample, work experience, and letters of recommendation. While no single factor is determinative, if the LSAT/UGPA combination does not demonstrate the promise of academic achievement, an applicant is unlikely to be offered regular admission.

Selected applicants who are denied regular admission will be offered the opportunity to earn admission to the Law Center by successful performance in NSU Law's unique Alternative Admissions Model Program for Legal Education (AAMPLE). In the 33 years of AAMPLE's operation, more than 1,000 students have qualified for admission. AAMPLE students who enroll in a six-week summer session and earn a C+ average in the two courses are offered admission to the Law Center. AAMPLE is presented in two formats, the traditional on-campus program and an innovative online model.

Approximately 37 percent of our applicants are offered seats through the Regular Admission Program. Another 24 percent are invited to AAMPLE. Applicants are encouraged to review the charts that follow this narrative to evaluate the likelihood of being admitted to the Law Center via the Regular Admission or AAMPLE. NSU Law's two admission programs produce a diverse student body. Recent classes were nearly evenly divided between men and women, with members of minority groups comprising approximately 38 percent of the class.

The Admissions Committee awards partial tuition scholarships on the basis of academic merit to approximately 28 percent of students admitted through the Regular Admission Program.

Faculty

NSU Law professors have a long tradition of teaching excellence. The faculty's open-door policy is enhanced by our sophisticated wireless communications system and pioneering laptop program. Limits on the size of first-year sections result in more individualized feedback. The faculty's expertise is reflected in rich classroom discussion and a wide range of scholarly publications and professional service.

Library and Physical Facilities

Nova Southeastern has been a technology pioneer for more than a decade. NSU Law Center installed the first wireless system in a law school in 1996 and was the first US law school to provide totally wireless access to all faculty, staff, and students. NSU Law leads the way in the use of technology in legal education.

The Law Library's extensive holdings include special collections in tax, criminal law, law and popular culture, admiralty, and international law. With more than 340,000 volume/volume equivalents, the Law Library provides access to primary and secondary sources of US law as well as case-finding and updating tools. The Law Library and Technology Center is designated as a United Nations depository and as a depository for US and Florida government documents.

Leo Goodwin Sr. Hall, which houses the Law Center, has two courtrooms used by students in the school's trial advocacy and moot court programs as well as by the National Institute for Trial Advocacy and state appellate court judges.

Student Activities

The Law Center is home to three significant publications: the *Nova Law Review*, the *Journal of International and Comparative Law*, and the *International Citator and Research Project*.

The Moot Court Society sponsors intramural competitions. Members of the society compete in major national events. The Association of Trial Lawyers of America and other student advocacy groups field teams in competitions around the country.

Students shape the life of the Law Center through their involvement in a wide range of service organizations and social clubs. Extremely active groups include the Asian Pacific American Law Students Association, Black Law Students Association, Jewish Law Students Association, Hispanic Law Student Association, Lambda Law Society, Student Bar Association, Florida Association for Women Lawyers, National Association for Public Interest Law, International Law Society, Native American Law Students Association, and a variety of practice specialty and sports clubs. Students also guide chapters of national legal fraternities, participate with lawyers and judges in the Inns of Court, and serve on faculty committees.

Career Services

Our Career Development Office assists students and alumni with career counseling and the employment process. In addition to facilitating on-campus interviews and résumé distributions, the director coordinates career-option seminars and interviewing workshops. The office also sponsors skill courses and assists students in finding pro bono experiences with law firms and legal agencies throughout the country.

APPLICANT PROFILE

Nova Southeastern University—Shepard Broad Law Center
Regular Admission Program

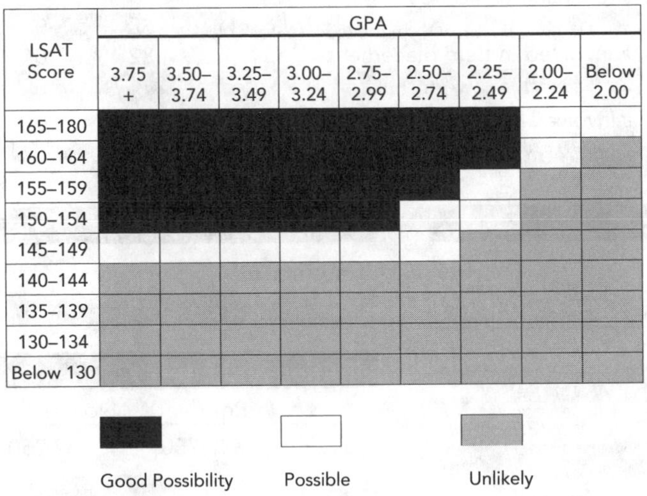
GPA
LSAT Score
3.75 +
3.50– 3.74
3.25– 3.49
3.00– 3.24
2.75– 2.99
2.50– 2.74
2.25– 2.49
2.00– 2.24
Below 2.00
165–180
160–164
155–159
150–154
145–149
140–144
135–139
130–134
Below 130
Good Possibility
Possible
Unlikely

Please use this chart as a general guide in determining admission chances for the Regular Admission Program. Nonnumerical factors are also considered during the file evaluation process.

AAMPLE
Enrolled/Successful

LSAT Score	GPA									
	3.75 +	3.50– 3.74	3.25– 3.49	3.00– 3.24	2.75– 2.99	2.50– 2.74	2.25– 2.49	2.00– 2.24	Below 2.00	Unknown GPA
150–159							3/3	2/1		
145–149	1/0	4/3	17/12	14/8	15/8	11/7	6/2	1/0		3/2
140–144	1/1	7/3	21/10	10/6	13/4	12/2	4/1			2/1
135–139		1/0	1/1			2/0				
130–134										

Please use this chart to determine the possibility of being admitted through AAMPLE (Alternative Admission Model Program for Legal Education).
The chart reflects admission data for the Summer 2011 AAMPLE combined, including both on-campus and online AAMPLE. Overall, there were 116 students enrolled in on-campus AAMPLE, with 58 successful, and 35 enrolled in online AAMPLE, 17 of whom were successful in 2011.

OHIO NORTHERN UNIVERSITY—CLAUDE W. PETTIT COLLEGE OF LAW

525 South Main Street
Ada, OH 45810
Phone: 877.452.9668, 419.772.2211; Fax: 419.772.3042
E-mail: lawadmissions@onu.edu; Website: www.law.onu.edu

ABA
Approved
Since
1948

The Basics

Type of school	Private
Term	Semester
Application deadline	
Application fee	$0
Financial aid deadline	6/1
Can first year start other than fall?	No
Student to faculty ratio	14.0 to 1
# of housing spaces available restricted to law students	52
graduate housing for which law students are eligible	52

Faculty and Administrators

	Total		Men		Women		Minorities	
	Spr	Fall	Spr	Fall	Spr	Fall	Spr	Fall
Full-time	18	19	12	13	6	6	4	4
Other full-time	1	1	1	1	0	0	0	0
Deans, librarians, & others who teach	10	9	4	4	6	5	0	0
Part-time	15	8	11	6	4	2	0	0
Total	44	37	28	24	16	13	4	4

Curriculum

	Full-Time	Part-Time
Typical first-year section size	55	0
Is there typically a "small section" of the first-year class, other than Legal Writing, taught by full-time faculty	No	No
If yes, typical size offered last year		
# of classroom course titles beyond first-year curriculum		97

# of upper division courses, excluding seminars, with an enrollment:		
	Under 25	62
	25–49	18
	50–74	8
	75–99	0
	100+	0

# of seminars		13
# of seminar positions available		156
# of seminar positions filled	97	0
# of positions available in simulation courses		541
# of simulation positions filled	372	0
# of positions available in faculty supervised clinical courses		75
# of faculty supervised clinical positions filled	30	0
# involved in field placements	82	0
# involved in law journals	41	0
# involved in moot court or trial competitions	23	0
# of credit hours required to graduate		90

JD Enrollment and Ethnicity

	Men		Women		Full-Time		Part-Time		1st-Year		Total		JD Degs. Awd.
	#	%	#	%	#	%	#	%	#	%	#	%	
All Hispanics	2	1.1	3	2.4	5	1.6	0	0.0	3	2.7	5	1.6	1
Am. Ind./AK Nat.	3	1.6	0	0.0	3	1.0	0	0.0	1	0.9	3	1.0	0
Asian	4	2.2	3	2.4	7	2.3	0	0.0	3	2.7	7	2.3	1
Black/Af. Am.	9	4.9	9	7.1	18	5.8	0	0.0	4	3.6	18	5.8	8
Nat. HI/Pac. Isl.	0	0.0	0	0.0	0	0.0	0	0.0	0	0.0	0	0.0	0
2 or more races	0	0.0	0	0.0	0	0.0	0	0.0	0	0.0	0	0.0	0
Subtotal (minor.)	18	9.7	15	11.9	33	10.6	0	0.0	11	9.9	33	10.6	10
Nonres. Alien	0	0.0	0	0.0	0	0.0	0	0.0	0	0.0	0	0.0	0
White/Cauc.	158	85.4	100	79.4	258	83.0	0	0.0	97	87.4	258	83.0	80
Unknown	9	4.9	11	8.7	20	6.4	0	0.0	3	2.7	20	6.4	7
Total	185	59.5	126	40.5	311	100.0	0	0.0	111	35.7	311		97

Transfers

Transfers in	1
Transfers out	3

Tuition and Fees

	Resident	Nonresident
Full-time	$32,750	$32,750
Part-time		
Tuition Guarantee Program		N

Living Expenses

Estimated living expenses for singles

Living on campus	Living off campus	Living at home
$16,748	$16,748	$16,748

OHIO NORTHERN UNIVERSITY—CLAUDE W. PETTIT COLLEGE OF L

ABA
Approved
Since
1948

GPA and LSAT Scores

	Total	Full-Time	Part-Time
# of apps	1,228	1,228	0
# of offers	502	502	0
# of matrics	112	112	0
75% GPA	3.66	3.66	0.00
Median GPA	3.36	3.36	0.00
25% GPA	3.03	3.03	0.00
75% LSAT	156	156	0
Median LSAT	154	154	0
25% LSAT	149	149	0

Grants and Scholarships (from prior year)

	Total		Full-Time		Part-Time	
	#	%	#	%	#	%
Total # of students	313		313		0	
Total # receiving grants	177	56.5	177	56.5	0	0.0
Less than 1/2 tuition	41	13.1	41	13.1	0	0.0
Half to full tuition	125	39.9	125	39.9	0	0.0
Full tuition	11	3.5	11	3.5	0	0.0
More than full tuition	0	0.0	0	0.0	0	0.0
Median grant amount			$23,000		$0	

Informational and Library Resources

Total amount spent on library materials	$845,433
Study seating capacity inside the library	304
# of full-time equivalent professional librarians	3
Hours per week library is open	113
# of open, wired connections available to students	307
# of networked computers available for use by students	69
Has wireless network?	Y
Requires computer?	N

JD Attrition (from prior year)

	Academic	Other	Total	
	#	#	#	%
1st year	9	7	16	13.3
2nd year	0	0	0	0.0
3rd year	0	0	0	0.0
4th year	0	0	0	0.0

Employment (9 months after graduation)

For up-to-date employment data, go to employmentsummary.abaquestionnaire.org on the ABA website.

Bar Passage Rates

First-time takers	94	Reporting %	72.34
Average school %	82.35	Average state %	85.16

Average pass difference −2.81

Jurisdiction	Takers	Passers	Pass %	State %	Diff %
Ohio	43	37	86.05	86.14	−0.09
Pennsylvania	11	8	72.73	83.06	−10.33
New York	7	6	85.71	84.92	0.79
Florida	4	2	50.00	77.63	−27.63
Illinois	3	3	100.00	89.38	10.62

OHIO NORTHERN UNIVERSITY—CLAUDE W. PETTIT COLLEGE OF LAW

525 South Main Street
Ada, OH 45810
Phone: 877.452.9668, 419.772.2211; Fax: 419.772.3042
E-mail: lawadmissions@onu.edu; Website: www.law.onu.edu

Introduction

Founded in 1885, the Ohio Northern University Pettit College of Law is the second oldest of the nine Ohio law schools. The college was accredited by the American Bar Association in 1948 and is a member of the Association of American Law Schools. Annually, the college enrolls more than 310 students from more than 40 states in its full-time Juris Doctor degree and concurrent JD/LLM and JD/MPPA programs. Dedicated to the rigorous pursuits of teaching and practicing law, the college's esteemed faculty is committed to fostering an open-door policy and a strong mentoring program to students with a passion for legal scholastic excellence. The College's goal is not only to educate, but also to ensure the development of practical skills, morals, and leadership needed to be successful in the practice of law. ONU Law is located in Ada, Ohio, with an off-campus legal clinic in Lima, Ohio.

The College and the University

The Claude W. Pettit College of Law is centered in Tilton Hall, a modern building that houses all law classes, two moot court rooms, and the Taggart Law Library.

The College of Law lies at the center of the 342-acre tree-lined campus. The university's facilities are readily available to all law students and are located only steps away from the law building. These facilities include walking and biking trails, a sports center, and the Freed Center for the Performing Arts. Law students may bowl, swim, and play handball, racquet sports, and basketball all year round in indoor and outdoor facilities. The sports center houses a wide variety of modern fitness machines and one of the best indoor tracks in the Midwest.

Student Life

Community is part of your law school experience.

Your involvement in cocurricular activities plays an important role in your law school experience. By participating in any of more than 20 different student organizations, you'll build long-lasting relationships with peers and faculty. Law student organizations are active in bringing speakers to campus, coordinating Continuing Legal Education (CLE) programs, organizing networking events, promoting philanthropy, and doing community service.

Improve your oral advocacy and brief writing skills by participating in moot court. The *Ohio Northern University Law Review*, a highly respected law journal of the College of Law, is edited and published by students three times a year.

While taking a break from studying, you'll discover the cultural side of the university. Theatre, dance, music, and other programs are hosted regularly at the acclaimed Freed Center for the Performing Arts. Permanent and provisional art collections are on display at the Elzay Gallery of Art. If sports are more your interest, you can attend a game at Dial-Roberson Stadium or participate in a number of intramural sports activities at King-Horn Sports Center. You can also watch Ohio Northern athletes compete in 21 varsity sports.

Faculty

With a 10:1 student-to-faculty ratio, our professors and staff will know you by name and interact with you on a personal level.

From the moment you arrive on campus, you will notice something different about our faculty. They are engaged in your education and truly interested in seeing you succeed. This is individualized attention you won't encounter at a larger school. Our professors have studied at some of the most prestigious schools in the United States—including Harvard, Columbia, Yale, and Duke—and practiced at some of the largest firms in the country. More than 50 percent of the faculty holds a PhD or LLM degree in addition to their JD degree.

Curriculum

Ohio Northern takes learning beyond traditional theory and brings the practice of law to life in the classroom.

During your first year, your studies will focus on the foundations of the law. The school's innovative first-year curriculum, however, will also introduce you to modern practice. During the first-year January term, practicing lawyers will demonstrate how legal theory shapes what they do in courtrooms and boardrooms. A court of appeals will actually hear cases in the law building during the term, giving you a chance to interact with the judges and lawyers. In the second and third years of study, students have the opportunity to take a wide array of electives.

CONCURRENT JD AND LLM: Our concurrent JD and LLM in Democratic Governance and Rule of Law degree is designed for students who have a passion for bringing democracy and law reform to developing countries. You will build valuable international relationships through domestic and overseas externships and by studying with the international LLM students. You will graduate in three years with both your Juris Doctor and LLM degrees.

INTERNATIONAL LLM: Our one-year International LLM in Democratic Governance and Rule of Law provides an opportunity for young lawyers from transitional democracies to study democracy and law at Ohio Northern.

CONCURRENT JD/MPPA: Students with an interest in taxation can earn both their law degree and a Masters of Professional Practice in Accounting within three calendar years. As a JD/MPPA student, you will take courses in the summer following your first year and be placed in an externship that will offer a valuable field experience in tax accounting following your second year.

CERTIFICATE PROGRAMS: The achievements of students who have focused their studies and excelled in areas of corporate law, bankruptcy and commercial law, criminal law, international law, public law and policy, civil litigation, taxation, and real property law will be recognized upon graduation with Certificates of Achievement.

Practical Skills

Get involved, apply your learning in a real-life scenario, and compete on a national stage.

CLINIC: By participating in a clinic, you can enhance your writing, analytical, and communication skills and garner valuable courtroom and client experience. Nearly 70 percent of ONU students choose to take advantage of this unique opportunity and participate in a clinic study before they graduate.

SKILLS COURSES: Each student must complete at least 10 hours of instruction in one of the many courses designated as skills courses. These classes will allow you to acquire actual skills you will be able to apply as a practicing attorney, such as drafting real estate closing documents, planning an estate, and writing a judicial opinion.

Career Services

Of those reporting (82 percent of the graduating class of 2010), and in accordance with NALP placement reporting standards, ONU has exceeded the national placement rate for the past nine years. Ninety-six percent of the class of 2010 was employed or enrolled in an LLM program within nine months of graduation.

We realize legal training is only part of the equation; your ultimate goal is to find a job. Our skilled staff in the Office of Career Services is here to help. We provide workshops and coordinate individual meetings to help you with résumé preparation, interviewing skills, professional image, and other career-development techniques. We also tap into our more than 5,000 distinguished alumni worldwide to offer networking options and further strengthen our recruiting channels across the country and around the globe.

Each year employers look to ONU for assistance in hiring law clerks, summer associates, and attorneys. Whether you want to pursue a career in private practice, government, business, or judicial clerkships, ONU will prepare you for a successful career and work with you to find the right job.

Admission and Financial Aid

Ohio Northern University is committed to a culturally and socially diverse student body. While Ohio Northern gives significant weight to the LSAT and undergraduate GPA, the Admissions Committee may consider other factors such as candidates' undergraduate programs, grade trends, completion of other graduate degrees, professional accomplishments, and

socioeconomic or cultural barriers faced by the applicant. Although letters of recommendation are not required, letters from persons who have a basis to assess the candidate's intellectual ability and potential for success in law school, such as former professors or employers, are strongly recommended.

The Summer Starter Program is an opportunity for students whose outstanding undergraduate performance indicates probable academic success in law school, despite disproportionate LSAT scores. Candidates who qualify for the program, based on their application, will be invited to interview for the program on campus.

The College of Law also provides scholarship awards for students whose undergraduate records demonstrate academic excellence. Scholarship amounts range from $5,000 to $33,000 and are renewable provided the student maintains a 3.0 cumulative GPA at the end of the first year. Additionally, substantial scholarships may be awarded to students who excel in their first year of law school. In order to foster diversity in the student body and the legal profession, the university awards grants-in-aid to eligible students. The college generally awards approximately $4 million of institutional aid annually to all three classes.

Students are encouraged to schedule a campus visit where they can sit in on a class, meet with a financial aid counselor, tour the facilities, and talk with current students. Contact lawadmissions@onu.edu to make arrangements.

Facilities and Technology

The college contains state-of-the-art facilities, including two moot courtrooms (used as both moot courtrooms and classrooms), a technology classroom, wireless capabilities throughout the building, and classrooms equipped with plasma televisions and SMART Board technology. The college recently dedicated its Alumni Moot Courtroom, which boasts the latest technology found in courthouses around the country.

The Taggart Law Library features an outstanding collection of federal, state, and international legal materials. In addition, the technology research center is available for research, training, and printing. The library is open seven days a week and provides seating for up to 304 students. The reading rooms of the library offer ideal locations for both quiet and group study.

APPLICANT PROFILE

Ohio Northern University—Claude W. Pettit College of Law
This grid includes only applicants who earned 120–180 LSAT scores under standard administrations.

LSAT Score	GPA								
	3.75 +	3.50–3.74	3.25–3.49	3.00–3.24	2.75–2.99	2.50–2.74	2.25–2.49	2.00–2.24	Below 2.00
175–180									
170–174									
165–169									
160–164									
155–159									
150–154									
145–149									
140–144									
135–139									
130–134									
125–129									
120–124									

Good Possibility   Possible   Unlikely

THE OHIO STATE UNIVERSITY MORITZ COLLEGE OF LAW

John Deaver Drinko Hall, 55 West 12th Avenue
Columbus, OH 43210-1391
Phone: 614.292.8810; Fax: 614.292.1492
E-mail: lawadmit@osu.edu; Website: http://moritzlaw.osu.edu

ABA
Approved
Since
1923

The Basics

Type of school	Public
Term	Semester
Application deadline	3/15
Application fee	$60
Financial aid deadline	2/15
Can first year start other than fall?	No
Student to faculty ratio	15.1 to 1
# of housing spaces available restricted to law students	
graduate housing for which law students are eligible	927

Faculty and Administrators

	Total		Men		Women		Minorities	
	Spr	Fall	Spr	Fall	Spr	Fall	Spr	Fall
Full-time	37	38	23	21	14	17	5	6
Other full-time	6	8	4	7	2	1	1	1
Deans, librarians, & others who teach	11	12	9	9	2	3	4	4
Part-time	25	23	14	19	11	4	4	3
Total	79	81	50	56	29	25	14	14

Curriculum

	Full-Time	Part-Time
Typical first-year section size	75	0
Is there typically a "small section" of the first-year class, other than Legal Writing, taught by full-time faculty	Yes	No
If yes, typical size offered last year	38	
# of classroom course titles beyond first-year curriculum	113	

# of upper division courses, excluding seminars, with an enrollment:		
	Under 25	64
	25–49	31
	50–74	14
	75–99	7
	100+	0

# of seminars	28	
# of seminar positions available	414	
# of seminar positions filled	367	0
# of positions available in simulation courses	192	
# of simulation positions filled	174	0
# of positions available in faculty supervised clinical courses	137	
# of faculty supervised clinical positions filled	134	0
# involved in field placements	52	0
# involved in law journals	308	0
# involved in moot court or trial competitions	43	0
# of credit hours required to graduate	88	

JD Enrollment and Ethnicity

	Men		Women		Full-Time		Part-Time		1st-Year		Total		JD Degs. Awd.
	#	%	#	%	#	%	#	%	#	%	#	%	
All Hispanics	9	2.3	19	6.5	28	4.1	0	0.0	7	3.3	28	4.1	11
Am. Ind./AK Nat.	2	0.5	6	2.0	8	1.2	0	0.0	2	0.9	8	1.2	0
Asian	21	5.4	33	11.2	54	7.9	0	0.0	21	9.8	54	7.9	16
Black/Af. Am.	27	7.0	18	6.1	45	6.6	0	0.0	15	7.0	45	6.6	15
Nat. HI/Pac. Isl.	2	0.5	0	0.0	2	0.3	0	0.0	1	0.5	2	0.3	0
2 or more races	0	0.0	0	0.0	0	0.0	0	0.0	0	0.0	0	0.0	4
Subtotal (minor.)	61	15.8	76	25.9	137	20.1	0	0.0	46	21.4	137	20.1	46
Nonres. Alien	4	1.0	5	1.7	9	1.3	0	0.0	3	1.4	9	1.3	3
White/Cauc.	291	75.4	201	68.4	492	72.4	0	0.0	160	74.4	492	72.4	182
Unknown	30	7.8	12	4.1	42	6.2	0	0.0	6	2.8	42	6.2	0
Total	386	56.8	294	43.2	680	100.0	0	0.0	215	31.6	680		231

Transfers

Transfers in	9
Transfers out	1

Tuition and Fees

	Resident	Nonresident
Full-time	$26,118	$41,068
Part-time		
Tuition Guarantee Program	N	

Living Expenses

Estimated living expenses for singles

Living on campus	Living off campus	Living at home
$20,990	$20,990	$20,990

THE OHIO STATE UNIVERSITY MORITZ COLLEGE OF LAW

ABA
Approved
Since
1923

GPA and LSAT Scores

	Total	Full-Time	Part-Time
# of apps	2,300	2,300	0
# of offers	898	898	0
# of matrics	211	211	0
75% GPA	3.81	3.81	0.00
Median GPA	3.63	3.63	0.00
25% GPA	3.45	3.45	0.00
75% LSAT	165	165	0
Median LSAT	163	163	0
25% LSAT	159	159	0

Grants and Scholarships (from prior year)

	Total #	Total %	Full-Time #	Full-Time %	Part-Time #	Part-Time %
Total # of students	693		693		0	
Total # receiving grants	547	78.9	547	78.9	0	0.0
Less than 1/2 tuition	490	70.7	490	70.7	0	0.0
Half to full tuition	41	5.9	41	5.9	0	0.0
Full tuition	4	0.6	4	0.6	0	0.0
More than full tuition	12	1.7	12	1.7	0	0.0
Median grant amount		$9,000		$0		

Informational and Library Resources

Total amount spent on library materials	$1,623,863
Study seating capacity inside the library	729
# of full-time equivalent professional librarians	8
Hours per week library is open	107
# of open, wired connections available to students	0
# of networked computers available for use by students	58
Has wireless network?	Y
Requires computer?	N

JD Attrition (from prior year)

	Academic #	Other #	Total #	Total %
1st year	0	5	5	2.2
2nd year	0	3	3	1.3
3rd year	1	1	2	0.8
4th year	0	0	0	0.0

Employment (9 months after graduation)

For up-to-date employment data, go to employmentsummary.abaquestionnaire.org on the ABA website.

Bar Passage Rates

First-time takers	202	Reporting %	79.21
Average school %	88.75	Average state %	85.96
Average pass difference	2.79		

Jurisdiction	Takers	Passers	Pass %	State %	Diff %
Ohio	136	119	87.50	86.14	1.36
New York	24	23	95.83	84.92	10.91

THE OHIO STATE UNIVERSITY MORITZ COLLEGE OF LAW

John Deaver Drinko Hall, 55 West 12th Avenue
Columbus, OH 43210-1391
Phone: 614.292.8810; Fax: 614.292.1492
E-mail: lawadmit@osu.edu; Website: http://moritzlaw.osu.edu

Introduction

Founded in 1891, the Ohio State University Moritz College of Law has played a leading role in the legal profession through countless contributions made by graduates and faculty. The administration of the College of Law is committed to advancing the quality and reputation of the college through ongoing improvements to the academic program and student services, thereby creating a learning environment that is second to none.

Ohio State's 9,600 law alumni are central to the college's national reputation. Graduates of the college include justices of the Ohio Supreme Court, governors, current and former US senators and representatives, managing partners in law firms, chief executive officers, professors, and attorneys with nonprofit organizations and public interest law firms.

The comprehensive scope of the university and its location in the state capital provide law students with access to a wealth of educational, professional, cultural, and recreational resources and opportunities. Law students are able to pursue joint degrees with one of the university's more than 100 graduate programs and also may extern with federal and state judges or find employment with one of the more than 500 law firms located in central Ohio.

Academic Program

With approximately 140 classes offered annually, Ohio State students have a rich array of courses from which to choose. The curriculum is designed to provide a strong theoretical and analytical foundation, as well as multiple opportunities for developing and honing lawyering skills.

Alternative Dispute Resolution—The College of Law is widely regarded as having one of the nation's finest programs in the area of Alternative Dispute Resolution. The program emphasizes training in an array of dispute resolution methods beyond litigation, including negotiation, mediation, and arbitration. Students with an especially strong interest may want to serve as a member or editor of the *Ohio State Journal on Dispute Resolution* or pursue a certificate in Dispute Resolution.

Clinical Opportunities—The College of Law offers an extensive selection of clinics in civil law, criminal law, children's issues, entrepreneurial business, mediation, and legislation. Students enrolled in a clinic course benefit from working with real clients, the court, or other parties while receiving intensive feedback and supervision from one of the college's 15 clinical faculty members. The fieldwork component of each clinic course is augmented by a classroom component in which topics such as lawyering skills, legal doctrine, and ethical and strategic issues are addressed.

Judicial Externship Program—Ohio State law students have the opportunity to gain firsthand insight into the judicial system through the college's Judicial Externship Program. As externs, students earn academic credit for conducting legal research and drafting legal documents for justices of the Ohio Supreme Court and for judges at the federal and county levels.

Joint Degrees—Law students who wish to gain in-depth experience in a second field of study may enroll as a combined-degree candidate in one of the established

joint-degree programs: the JD/MBA, the JD/MA in Public Policy (a program that can be completed in three years at no additional tuition cost), or the JD/MHA. Law students also are permitted to individually tailor a joint-degree program with many of the university's 100-plus master's programs and 90 PhD programs.

A Global Perspective on the Law—Students with an interest in international law may select from a menu of approximately 20 courses that have an international law or comparative law focus, including semester-long and summer study-abroad programs in Oxford, England. The College of Law awards a Certificate in International Trade and Development to students who combine their law coursework with select courses in international economics, politics, history, culture, and foreign language.

Faculty

One of the most frequently cited strengths of the College of Law is the quality of the faculty. Faculty members are consistently recognized for the experiences they bring to the classroom, the clarity of their teaching, and their accessibility to students outside of the classroom. As a group, they are highly regarded for being committed teachers who care about students. Members of the Ohio State law faculty also have earned a reputation within the profession for their expertise in specific areas of the law. Faculty are regularly cited in court and in the national media; they serve on legal reform commissions, help draft model statutes, and provide testimony before Congress.

Moritz Law Library

The Moritz Law Library provides Ohio State law students with one of the largest collections among law school libraries in the nation and access to a vast array of electronic databases. The law library and law building are completely wireless, allowing for ease of access to the web and online resources for all law students.

Extracurricular Opportunities

Learning Outside of the Classroom—Recognizing that a student's legal education rests on what occurs in the classroom as well as the intellectual interchange and professional development outside of the classroom, the College of Law strives to provide an environment that is rich with extracurricular and cocurricular opportunities. Each year, the college brings to campus more than 100 speakers to address students, law faculty, and members of the bar.

The Program on Law and Leadership seeks to increase the awareness and understanding of leadership development among lawyers as well as excite and equip students for future leadership roles both in and beyond the profession. It has multiple components: education, a speaker series, skills workshops, scholarships, career assessment, and mentoring.

Ohio State law students have the opportunity to refine their legal writing skills through participation in one of the college's five highly regarded law journals: the *Ohio State Law Journal*, the *Ohio State Journal on Dispute Resolution*, the *Ohio State Journal of Criminal Law*, the *I/S: A Journal of Law and Policy* for the *Information Society*, and the *Entrepreneurial Business Law Journal*. Students are able to refine their skills in the areas of oral advocacy and legal writing through a variety of intramural and interscholastic competitions. In recent years, Ohio State law students have competed in approximately 14 interscholastic moot court competitions, including the National Moot Court Competition, the Jessup International Law Moot Court Competition, the Frederick Douglass Moot Court Competition, the National Health Law Moot Court Competition, the Civil Rights Moot Court Competition, the Corporate Law Competition, and the Criminal Procedure Moot Court Competition.

Service to the Public—The College of Law enjoys a strong reputation for its commitment to public service as part of the educational mission of the college. Ohio State law students are encouraged to become involved in the Leadership Program or in one or more of the college's many public interest initiatives, such as the Pro Bono Research Group. To encourage Ohio State law students to accept low-paying or volunteer positions with public interest organizations during the summer, the college and the Public Interest Law Foundation annually offer several student-funded fellowships.

Placement Opportunities

Moritz College of Law students and graduates are provided with an array of career and professional development services by a staff of six full- and part-time professionals, four of whom have JDs. Students and alumni have access to an online job-posting system and a wide variety of programs, workshops, and events. All programming and counseling services are designed to teach skills and to provide a foundation for gaining legal and professional career experience. The on-campus recruiting program, which

brings over 120 employers to campus to interview students annually, is conducted through a state-of-the-art, web-based recruiting system that allows students access at all hours. Alumni and practitioners interact with students through many avenues, including a practice interview program and a mentoring program. Each year, students find employment across the country. Ohio State is a member of the National Law School Consortium, which hosts job fairs and events in a number of major legal markets nationwide. Cutting-edge technology, current resources, talented staff, and creative initiatives give Ohio State students a sound professional development foundation.

Admission and Financial Aid

The Moritz College of Law is committed to enrolling highly motivated men and women who have excelled academically and who bring to the College of Law a diversity of personal and professional backgrounds. In selecting members of each entering class, the Admissions Committee seeks to enroll individuals who represent all segments of society, as well as those who, as attorneys, will respect the profession's public service obligations.

An Ohio State legal education offers one of the best values among nationally regarded law schools. The annual cost of tuition for residents of Ohio is roughly half the tuition charged by comparably ranked private law schools. Columbus also boasts a cost of living that compares favorably to major cities across the country. Nonresidents of Ohio who relocate to the state may be reclassified as Ohio residents after residing in the state for 12 months. Each year, the College of Law awards more than $3 million in need-based and merit-based financial aid to members of the student body.

APPLICANT PROFILE

The Ohio State University Moritz College of Law
This grid includes only applicants who earned 120–180 LSAT scores under standard administrations.

LSAT Score	3.75 +		3.50–3.74		3.25–3.49		3.00–3.24		2.75–2.99		2.50–2.74		2.25–2.49		2.00–2.24		Below 2.00		No GPA		Total	
	Apps	Adm	Apps	Adm	Apps	Adm	Apps	Adm	Apps	Adm	Apps	Adm	Apps	Adm	Apps	Adm	Apps	Adm	Apps	Adm	Apps	Adm
175–180	4	4	3	3	1	1	1	1	1	0	2	0	0	0	0	0	0	0	0	0	12	9
170–174	22	22	21	21	8	7	5	4	2	0	2	1	1	0	0	0	0	0	0	0	61	55
165–169	90	85	109	105	61	56	31	20	22	3	5	0	2	0	0	0	0	0	6	5	326	274
160–164	181	158	183	127	148	78	82	28	21	2	13	0	1	0	3	0	0	0	21	7	653	400
155–159	151	59	184	38	146	24	61	4	33	1	14	0	8	0	4	0	1	0	18	0	620	126
150–154	57	11	80	11	72	5	64	2	32	0	22	0	6	0	0	0	1	0	10	0	344	29
145–149	17	2	31	1	37	2	30	0	22	0	18	0	7	0	2	0	1	0	1	0	166	5
140–144	5	0	11	0	10	0	19	0	15	0	10	0	7	0	2	0	1	0	1	0	81	0
135–139	1	0	1	0	3	0	5	0	3	0	5	0	2	0	1	0	0	0	2	0	23	0
130–134	1	0	0	0	1	0	0	0	3	0	2	0	1	0	0	0	0	0	1	0	9	0
125–129	0	0	0	0	1	0	0	0	0	0	2	0	0	0	1	0	0	0	1	0	5	0
120–124	0	0	0	0	0	0	0	0	0	0	0	0	0	0	0	0	0	0	0	0	1	0
Total	529	341	623	306	488	173	298	59	154	6	95	1	35	0	14	0	4	0	61	12	2301	898

Apps = Number of Applicants
Adm = Number Admitted
Reflects 100% of total applicant pool; highest LSAT data reported.

UNIVERSITY OF OKLAHOMA COLLEGE OF LAW

Andrew M. Coats Hall, 300 Timberdell Road
Norman, OK 73019
Phone: 405.325.4726; Fax: 405.325.0502
E-mail: admissions@law.ou.edu; Website: www.law.ou.edu

ABA
Approved
Since
1923

The Basics

Type of school	Public
Term	Semester
Application deadline	3/15
Application fee	$50
Financial aid deadline	3/1
Can first year start other than fall?	No
Student to faculty ratio	13.9 to 1
# of housing spaces available restricted to law students	
graduate housing for which law students are eligible	530

Faculty and Administrators

	Total		Men		Women		Minorities	
	Spr	Fall	Spr	Fall	Spr	Fall	Spr	Fall
Full-time	32	33	23	21	9	12	5	5
Other full-time	0	2	0	2	0	0	0	0
Deans, librarians, & others who teach	5	5	3	3	2	2	0	0
Part-time	18	15	12	11	6	4	3	2
Total	55	55	38	37	17	18	8	7

Curriculum

		Full-Time	Part-Time
Typical first-year section size		38	0
Is there typically a "small section" of the first-year class, other than Legal Writing, taught by full-time faculty		No	No
If yes, typical size offered last year			
# of classroom course titles beyond first-year curriculum		111	
# of upper division courses, excluding seminars, with an enrollment:	Under 25	54	
	25–49	38	
	50–74	13	
	75–99	3	
	100+	3	
# of seminars		18	
# of seminar positions available		288	
# of seminar positions filled		273	0
# of positions available in simulation courses		225	
# of simulation positions filled		219	0
# of positions available in faculty supervised clinical courses		55	
# of faculty supervised clinical positions filled		52	0
# involved in field placements		79	0
# involved in law journals		126	0
# involved in moot court or trial competitions		95	0
# of credit hours required to graduate		90	

JD Enrollment and Ethnicity

	Men		Women		Full-Time		Part-Time		1st-Year		Total		JD Degs. Awd.
	#	%	#	%	#	%	#	%	#	%	#	%	
All Hispanics	15	5.0	6	2.6	21	4.0	0	0.0	6	3.9	21	4.0	6
Am. Ind./AK Nat.	25	8.4	18	7.8	43	8.1	0	0.0	13	8.6	43	8.1	11
Asian	8	2.7	12	5.2	20	3.8	0	0.0	3	2.0	20	3.8	11
Black/Af. Am.	13	4.4	10	4.3	23	4.3	0	0.0	10	6.6	23	4.3	7
Nat. HI/Pac. Isl.	0	0.0	1	0.4	1	0.2	0	0.0	1	0.7	1	0.2	0
2 or more races	0	0.0	1	0.4	1	0.2	0	0.0	1	0.7	1	0.2	0
Subtotal (minor.)	61	20.5	48	20.7	109	20.6	0	0.0	34	22.4	109	20.6	35
Nonres. Alien	0	0.0	1	0.4	1	0.2	0	0.0	0	0.0	1	0.2	1
White/Cauc.	231	77.5	176	75.9	407	76.8	0	0.0	114	75.0	407	76.8	126
Unknown	6	2.0	7	3.0	13	2.5	0	0.0	4	2.6	13	2.5	1
Total	298	56.2	232	43.8	530	100.0	0	0.0	152	28.7	530		163

Transfers

Transfers in	13
Transfers out	1

Tuition and Fees

	Resident	Nonresident
Full-time	$19,051	$29,476
Part-time		
Tuition Guarantee Program		N

Living Expenses

Estimated living expenses for singles

Living on campus	Living off campus	Living at home
$18,081	$18,081	$12,437

UNIVERSITY OF OKLAHOMA COLLEGE OF LAW

ABA Approved Since 1923

GPA and LSAT Scores

	Total	Full-Time	Part-Time
# of apps	1,105	1,105	0
# of offers	347	347	0
# of matrics	153	153	0
75% GPA	3.75	3.75	0.00
Median GPA	3.48	3.48	0.00
25% GPA	3.23	3.23	0.00
75% LSAT	161	161	0
Median LSAT	158	158	0
25% LSAT	155	155	0

Grants and Scholarships (from prior year)

	Total #	Total %	Full-Time #	Full-Time %	Part-Time #	Part-Time %
Total # of students	537		537		0	
Total # receiving grants	429	79.9	429	79.9	0	0.0
Less than 1/2 tuition	342	63.7	342	63.7	0	0.0
Half to full tuition	76	14.2	76	14.2	0	0.0
Full tuition	0	0.0	0	0.0	0	0.0
More than full tuition	11	2.0	11	2.0	0	0.0
Median grant amount			$3,483		$0	

Informational and Library Resources

Total amount spent on library materials	$844,306
Study seating capacity inside the library	456
# of full-time equivalent professional librarians	7
Hours per week library is open	99
# of open, wired connections available to students	105
# of networked computers available for use by students	122
Has wireless network?	Y
Requires computer?	N

JD Attrition (from prior year)

	Academic #	Other #	Total #	Total %
1st year	1	4	5	2.9
2nd year	0	2	2	1.0
3rd year	0	2	2	1.2
4th year	0	0	0	0.0

Employment (9 months after graduation)

For up-to-date employment data, go to employmentsummary.abaquestionnaire.org on the ABA website.

Bar Passage Rates

First-time takers	174	Reporting %	77.59
Average school %	96.30	Average state %	89.02
Average pass difference	7.28		

Jurisdiction	Takers	Passers	Pass %	State %	Diff %
Oklahoma	135	130	96.30	89.02	7.28

UNIVERSITY OF OKLAHOMA COLLEGE OF LAW

Andrew M. Coats Hall, 300 Timberdell Road
Norman, OK 73019
Phone: 405.325.4726; Fax: 405.325.0502
E-mail: admissions@law.ou.edu; Website: www.law.ou.edu

Introduction

The University of Oklahoma College of Law is one of our nation's great public law schools. Founded in 1909, OU Law provides a dynamic intellectual community dedicated to teaching, learning, research, and service in the pursuit of law and justice. OU Law delivers an exemplary legal education at an accessible cost to students and is consistently recognized as a "Best Value" law school.

The OU Law campus is located just south of the university's main campus in Norman, a city of approximately 100,000 adjacent to the Oklahoma City metropolitan area. OU Law enrolls more than 500 students annually in their Juris Doctor (JD) and Master of Laws (LLM) degree programs. The entering JD class is approximately 175 students and first-year sections consist of 45 students. The John B. Turner LLM program attracts students worldwide wishing to specialize in the college's core areas: energy, natural resources, and Native American law.

OU Law is housed in beautiful Andrew M. Coats Hall, where a $19-million renovation and expansion was completed in 2002. It has the most extensive law library in Oklahoma and houses three courtrooms equipped with the latest technology for training and enrichment purposes. Throughout the past 10 years, OU Law graduates taking the bar exam averaged a 94 percent passage rate. More than 40 full-time OU Law faculty foster student success while preparing them for the practice of law and for leadership positions in the state, nation, and world.

Admission

OU Law utilizes a rolling admission process. A faculty committee meets regularly throughout the academic year to review applications. Admission to OU Law is highly competitive, and many factors are considered in the selection process. Although considerable weight is given to undergraduate grade-point average and performance on the LSAT, thoughtful attention is also given to an applicant's extracurricular activities, employment experience, graduate studies, military service, and adjustments to personal difficulties, as well as other relevant factors.

In addition to the regular fall entering class, OU Law enrolls about 20 students in a special Early Admission Program (EAP) each summer. Admission is offered to a select group of students who have demonstrated a probable capacity for success in the study and practice of law. The focus of the program is to give students a first-look at law school, help build confidence and skills necessary to succeed in law school, and provide the opportunity to earn law school credits during the summer. Students in the program typically receive five hours of credit for the summer study and then join the fall class.

International Programs

Since 1974, OU Law has held a summer program in Oxford, England, for American law students. The program affords students an opportunity to live and study in stimulating and beautiful surroundings under the guidance of American and English legal educators. The 2012 Oxford Summer Program at Brasenose College offers 12 credit hours. Classes will not meet on Fridays to provide students with time for sightseeing and travels.

Students enrolled in the International Human Rights Clinic travel abroad to compile extensive reports that are submitted to the United Nations Human Rights Council for the UN's regular review of these areas. In August 2011, students traveled to Morocco and Ecuador. Other countries visited included Uganda, Venezuela, and Suriname. Through these experiences, OU Law students learn how to become advocates for the voiceless while gaining a global perspective of the rule of law.

In addition, OU Law is currently developing a summer program for students at Renmin University of China Law School in Beijing.

Library and Physical Facilities

The OU College of Law is housed in a stunning 170,000-square-foot, state-of-the-art facility, featuring study rooms, courtrooms, classrooms, and a law library equipped with the latest technology.

The 250-seat Dick Bell Courtroom is one of the largest and most technologically advanced courtrooms in the nation and hosts live trials from the various courts in central Oklahoma. The Bell Courtroom has hosted appellate cases from both the Oklahoma Court of Criminal Appeals (including a death penalty appeal) and the US Court of Appeals for the 10th Circuit, as well as civil trials from the US District Court for the Western District of Oklahoma.

The Donald E. Pray Law Library at OU Law provides a comfortable and modern setting for studying the law and conducting legal research. The law library features the Chapman Great Reading Room, a rare books room, 2 computer labs, 50 computer workstations that provide access to several online resources, 6 group-study rooms, wireless Internet access, 425 seats, and the most comprehensive law resources collection in the state. More than 100 seats have built-in power outlets and network connections. In addition, the library includes four multimedia study rooms; each accommodates eight students and features a large LCD monitor, Blu-ray player, video camera, and DVD recorder.

Student Activities

OU Law has more than 30 student organizations to accommodate a variety of interests, including a robust competitions program and three major student-directed journals: *Oklahoma Law Review*, *American Indian Law Review*, and *Oklahoma Journal of Law and Technology*.

Since 1948, the *Oklahoma Law Review* has been published quarterly to give expression to legal scholarship nationally and to serve the profession and the public with timely discussion of important legal issues. The *American Indian Law Review*, published biannually, serves as a nationwide scholarly forum for the presentation of important developments in Native American law and affairs. The *Oklahoma Journal of Law and Technology* is a web-based collection of important articles on the various aspects of intellectual property. The student Board of Editors continually monitors and updates the articles and other material on the website.

OU Law's competitions program affords students the opportunity to participate in a wide range of extracurricular interscholastic appellate moot court, counseling and interviewing, negotiation, and trial advocacy competitions. The student Board of Advocates works closely with the students to facilitate participation in these competitions and provide intramural competitions for 1L and upper-level students.

Career Services

The Office of Professional and Career Development (OPCD) is dedicated to assisting law students explore various legal, business, and alternative career options. The OPCD provides comprehensive counseling, programming, and job-search resources for current law students and alumni. Students should contact the OPCD to receive individualized cover letter and résumé review. In addition, the OPCD hosts a fall and spring recruiting program to assist prospective employers in securing interns and associates.

OU Law student services include one-on-one career counseling; on-campus recruitment programs; "Lunch and Learn" presentations and speakers; mock interviews; internship and externship assistance; online job postings; networking events; and résumé, cover letter, and application material review. Since 2008, an average of 88 percent of OU Law graduates secured positions within nine months of graduation. Our graduates are employed in a variety of positions, including academics, business, government, military, judicial clerkships, law firms, public interest, and nonprofits.

APPLICANT PROFILE

University of Oklahoma College of Law
This grid includes only applicants who earned 120–180 LSAT scores under standard administrations.

LSAT Score	3.75 +		3.50–3.74		3.25–3.49		3.00–3.24		2.75–2.99		2.50–2.74		Below 2.50		No GPA		Total	
	Apps	Adm	Apps	Adm	Apps	Adm	Apps	Adm	Apps	Adm	Apps	Adm	Apps	Adm	Apps	Adm	Apps	Adm
170–180	3	3	2	2	1	1	3	1	0	0	0	0	0	0	0	0	9	7
165–169	15	13	15	10	10	8	5	3	6	3	3	0	0	0	0	0	54	37
160–164	40	33	41	33	37	25	31	16	7	5	8	2	7	4	1	1	172	119
155–159	53	36	75	33	77	37	57	26	34	10	20	3	10	1	3	0	329	146
150–154	40	17	57	12	65	10	48	4	35	0	18	0	11	0	5	0	279	43
145–149	12	0	40	0	27	2	35	0	13	0	11	0	6	0	3	0	147	2
140–144	2	0	7	0	8	0	16	0	13	0	14	0	8	0	2	0	70	0
Below 140	1	0	3	0	5	0	8	0	6	0	7	0	6	0	2	0	38	0
Total	166	102	240	90	230	83	203	50	114	18	81	5	48	5	16	1	1098	354

Apps = Number of Applicants
Adm = Number Admitted
Reflects 99% of the total applicant pool; highest LSAT data reported.

OKLAHOMA CITY UNIVERSITY SCHOOL OF LAW

2501 North Blackwelder Avenue
Oklahoma City, OK 73106-1493
Phone: 866.529.6281 or 405.208.5354
E-mail: lawquestions@okcu.edu; Website: http://law.okcu.edu/

ABA
Approved
Since
1960

The Basics

Type of school	Private
Term	Semester
Application deadline	8/1
Application fee	$50
Financial aid deadline	3/1
Can first year start other than fall?	No
Student to faculty ratio	17.8 to 1
# of housing spaces available restricted to law students	
graduate housing for which law students are eligible	30

Faculty and Administrators

	Total		Men		Women		Minorities	
	Spr	Fall	Spr	Fall	Spr	Fall	Spr	Fall
Full-time	28	27	16	16	12	11	4	4
Other full-time	3	4	2	2	1	2	0	1
Deans, librarians, & others who teach	5	4	3	2	2	2	1	1
Part-time	28	16	19	12	9	4	5	2
Total	64	51	40	32	24	19	10	8

Curriculum

		Full-Time	Part-Time
Typical first-year section size		75	0
Is there typically a "small section" of the first-year class, other than Legal Writing, taught by full-time faculty		No	No
If yes, typical size offered last year			
# of classroom course titles beyond first-year curriculum		135	
# of upper division courses, excluding seminars, with an enrollment:	Under 25	126	
	25–49	42	
	50–74	21	
	75–99	4	
	100+	0	
# of seminars		13	
# of seminar positions available		186	
# of seminar positions filled		163	0
# of positions available in simulation courses		408	
# of simulation positions filled		310	0
# of positions available in faculty supervised clinical courses		32	
# of faculty supervised clinical positions filled		21	0
# involved in field placements		61	0
# involved in law journals		52	0
# involved in moot court or trial competitions		21	0
# of credit hours required to graduate		90	

JD Enrollment and Ethnicity

	Men		Women		Full-Time		Part-Time		1st-Year		Total		JD Degs. Awd.
	#	%	#	%	#	%	#	%	#	%	#	%	
All Hispanics	24	6.8	9	3.6	29	5.5	4	5.1	12	5.9	33	5.5	10
Am. Ind./AK Nat.	12	3.4	17	6.8	23	4.4	6	7.7	9	4.4	29	4.8	8
Asian	9	2.5	7	2.8	15	2.8	1	1.3	5	2.5	16	2.6	5
Black/Af. Am.	13	3.7	10	4.0	20	3.8	3	3.8	8	3.9	23	3.8	6
Nat. HI/Pac. Isl.	0	0.0	0	0.0	0	0.0	0	0.0	0	0.0	0	0.0	0
2 or more races	14	4.0	11	4.4	24	4.6	1	1.3	15	7.4	25	4.1	8
Subtotal (minor.)	72	20.3	54	21.5	111	21.1	15	19.2	49	24.0	126	20.8	37
Nonres. Alien	2	0.6	4	1.6	5	0.9	1	1.3	3	1.5	6	1.0	3
White/Cauc.	280	79.1	191	76.1	410	77.8	61	78.2	151	74.0	471	77.9	138
Unknown	0	0.0	2	0.8	1	0.2	1	1.3	1	0.5	2	0.3	1
Total	354	58.5	251	41.5	527	87.1	78	12.9	204	33.7	605		179

Transfers

Transfers in	3
Transfers out	25

Tuition and Fees

	Resident	Nonresident
Full-time	$35,470	$35,470
Part-time	$23,670	$23,670
Tuition Guarantee Program	N	

Living Expenses

Estimated living expenses for singles

Living on campus	Living off campus	Living at home
$16,860	$16,860	$16,860

ABA
Approved
Since
1960

GPA and LSAT Scores

	Total	Full-Time	Part-Time
# of apps	1,204	1,116	88
# of offers	642	607	35
# of matrics	201	185	16
75% GPA	3.45	3.46	3.38
Median GPA	3.13	3.13	3.04
25% GPA	2.85	2.86	2.79
75% LSAT	154	155	151
Median LSAT	151	151	149
25% LSAT	149	149	148

Grants and Scholarships (from prior year)

	Total		Full-Time		Part-Time	
	#	%	#	%	#	%
Total # of students	636		564		72	
Total # receiving grants	271	42.6	257	45.6	14	19.4
Less than 1/2 tuition	182	28.6	172	30.5	10	13.9
Half to full tuition	71	11.2	67	11.9	4	5.6
Full tuition	3	0.5	3	0.5	0	0.0
More than full tuition	15	2.4	15	2.7	0	0.0
Median grant amount			$12,000		$5,889	

Informational and Library Resources

Total amount spent on library materials	$650,621
Study seating capacity inside the library	474
# of full-time equivalent professional librarians	8
Hours per week library is open	104
# of open, wired connections available to students	190
# of networked computers available for use by students	82
Has wireless network?	Y
Requires computer?	N

JD Attrition (from prior year)

	Academic	Other	Total	
	#	#	#	%
1st year	14	31	45	20.0
2nd year	3	2	5	2.6
3rd year	1	0	1	0.5
4th year	0	0	0	0.0

Employment (9 months after graduation)

For up-to-date employment data, go to employmentsummary.abaquestionnaire.org on the ABA website.

Bar Passage Rates

First-time takers	158	Reporting %	84.18
Average school %	81.95	Average state %	87.69

Average pass difference –5.74

Jurisdiction	Takers	Passers	Pass %	State %	Diff %
Oklahoma	105	92	87.62	89.02	–1.40
Texas	28	17	60.71	82.68	–21.97

The information on these pages was provided by the law school.

OKLAHOMA CITY UNIVERSITY SCHOOL OF LAW

2501 North Blackwelder Avenue
Oklahoma City, OK 73106-1493
Phone: 866.529.6281 or 405.208.5354
E-mail: lawquestions@okcu.edu; Website: http://law.okcu.edu/

Introduction

At Oklahoma City University School of Law (OCU LAW) we introduce students to an educational philosophy that purposefully and carefully blends the theory and practice of law in all of its forms. Located within minutes of some of Oklahoma's largest law firms, corporations, banks, city and state government agencies, the state capital, and state and federal courts, our location enables our students to gain valuable experience before graduation.

Oklahoma City, the capital of Oklahoma, boasts a metropolitan population that numbers over one million and covers 625 square miles. In the past 10 years, Oklahoma City has undergone a revitalization resulting in a new NBA team, a new AAA baseball stadium, the establishment of Bricktown as a premier historic entertainment district, a new public library, creation of a new riverfront recreation area, and increased investment in public schools. It is considered an easy, comfortable, and friendly place to live.

Faculty

The faculty at OCU LAW are committed to the intellectual and professional growth of every student. They hold law degrees from a variety of law schools, including the nation's most prestigious. Many faculty members also hold advanced degrees in law and other fields of study, and most have significant practice-based experience.

Library and Physical Facilities

Classes at OCU LAW are held in the Sarkeys Law Center. It houses two moot courtrooms and classrooms equipped with contemporary technology. The building features several common areas that foster interaction between students and faculty. The OCU LAW Library, located in the nearby historic Gold Star Memorial Building, houses a collection of over 321,561 volumes and volume equivalents and features computer labs with access to all online research databases. A wireless network is available in all law school facilities.

Scheduling Options

The School of Law offers a full-time JD program with either a traditional day or sunset (late afternoon/early evening) schedule. Our part-time program is available with sunset classes. By attending summer sessions, full-time students may complete their degree requirements (90 semester hours) in as little as two and a half years and part-time students in three and a half years.

Special Programs

In Oklahoma, students who have completed just 45 course hours are eligible for a limited license, and those who qualify may appear in court under certain circumstances. As a companion to this state licensing policy, OCU LAW has created a range of externship opportunities where academic credit can be earned in a variety of practice placement sites with field supervisors, operating under the guidance of a full-time director of externship programs.

The School of Law operates three legal centers for its students and the legal community. The Center on Alternative Dispute Resolution provides coherence and structure for the varied activities of OCU LAW in the areas of negotiation, mediation, and arbitration. The Native American Legal Resource Center focuses on Native American law and provides legal services to tribes and tribal courts, frequently through federal grants. The Center for the Study of State Constitutional Law and Government promotes scholarship and discussion on important issues relating to state government.

OCU LAW cosponsors (with Stetson University) summer international programs in Buenos Aires, Argentina; Granada, Spain; Freiberg, Germany; The Hague, the Netherlands; and Tianjin, China.

Office of Admission

OCU LAW seeks serious, motivated students who value education and demonstrate a commitment to the values and ethics of the legal profession. Many factors are considered in the evaluation of applications. Reviewers look for evidence of analytical and critical thinking, as well as reading, research, and writing skills that suggest the applicant is prepared for law school. Additionally, the committee considers factors such as work and life experience, cultural and economic background, advanced degrees, and extracurricular and community activities.

The Alternate Summer Admission Program (ASAP) offers a limited number of applicants who do not meet traditional admission requirements an opportunity to demonstrate their capacity for law study and to earn admission for the fall by attending and passing two summer classes. Any applicant not offered direct admission will automatically be considered for admission through the summer program.

OCU LAW uses a rolling admission review process and will review applications until the class is filled. Applications received by February 1, with LSAT scores on record, will receive priority consideration for admission and scholarship assistance. To be eligible for priority review, applicants should take the June, October, or December LSAT in the year prior to which they are applying.

Scholarships

Each year OCU LAW awards over $1.5 million in scholarships. New applicants are evaluated and encouraged to apply for our generous scholarships ranging from $5,000 to full-tuition awards. The Hatton W. Sumners Scholarship, for example, is a full-tuition award that includes a book and living expense stipend. The Sumners Scholarships are competitive and awarded based on academic and leadership potential demonstrated within the scholarship application and during an on-campus interview. Applications for the Sumners award are due February 1. Additional scholarship assistance is available to returning upper-division students based on academic performance.

Student Services

OCU LAW actively provides law students with opportunities to be engaged with the larger legal community. Numerous guest speakers, programs, and activities are sponsored to provide students with exposure to local, state, and national leaders; scholars; and legal professionals.

The entire staff at the law school is committed to assisting law students. The associate dean for students offers broad support to students and student organizations. Financial aid advisors provide loan and debt management counseling, and a student technology coordinator assists students with their computing needs. A very accessible professional library staff, which includes five librarians with JD degrees, aids students in the development of important research skills.

Professional and Career Development Center

The Professional and Career Development Center (PCDC) hosts a wide range of workshops and guest speakers in addition to offering personal career counseling and employer cultivation efforts. The center seeks to expose law students to various areas of the law, provide the resources needed to successfully conduct an employment search, and guide them in developing the skills, ethics, and values of a legal

professional. Details of services provided, contact information for career counselors, and a list of programs and workshops are available on the Professional and Career Development section of the OCU LAW website.

Curriculum

The School of Law offers a joint JD/MBA program and specialized certificate programs in alternative dispute resolution, public law, and business law (with concentrations in e-commerce or in financial services and commercial law). The core curriculum for every OCU LAW student includes a purposeful balance of legal theory and practical application. It provides a well-grounded foundation in the basic doctrines, functions, and ethical principles that underlie law and law practice, and is designed to produce graduates who have a breadth of understanding that enables them to become leaders in law, business, government, and civic life.

APPLICANT PROFILE

Oklahoma City University School of Law
This grid includes only applicants who earned 120–180 LSAT scores under standard administrations.

LSAT Score	GPA 3.75 +		3.50–3.74		3.25–3.49		3.00–3.24		2.75–2.99		2.50–2.74		2.25–2.49		2.00–2.24		Below 2.00		No GPA		Total	
	Apps	Adm	Apps	Adm	Apps	Adm	Apps	Adm	Apps	Adm	Apps	Adm	Apps	Adm	Apps	Adm	Apps	Adm	Apps	Adm	Apps	Adm
175–180	0	0	0	0	0	0	0	0	0	0	0	0	0	0	0	0	0	0	0	0	0	0
170–174	0	0	0	0	1	1	0	0	0	0	0	0	0	0	0	0	0	0	0	0	1	1
165–169	2	2	2	2	0	0	0	0	1	1	1	1	0	0	0	0	0	0	0	0	6	6
160–164	8	8	10	9	9	9	8	8	5	3	1	1	1	0	3	2	0	0	0	0	45	40
155–159	15	13	27	27	27	27	29	29	14	11	19	16	9	5	5	3	2	0	0	0	147	131
150–154	30	28	50	48	67	54	82	76	68	63	40	37	26	14	8	1	1	0	3	2	375	323
145–149	19	14	32	20	66	35	69	27	64	25	47	13	29	0	6	0	3	0	10	3	345	137
140–144	6	0	20	2	30	0	35	0	39	0	31	1	16	0	9	0	3	0	6	0	195	3
135–139	3	0	3	0	12	0	9	0	10	0	8	0	6	0	4	0	0	0	1	0	56	0
130–134	1	0	1	0	2	0	1	0	3	0	1	0	3	0	4	0	3	0	3	0	22	0
125–129	0	0	0	0	1	0	2	0	1	0	3	0	1	0	2	0	0	0	0	0	10	0
120–124	0	0	0	0	0	0	0	0	0	0	0	0	0	0	0	0	0	0	0	0	0	0
Total	84	65	145	108	215	126	235	140	205	103	151	69	91	19	41	6	12	0	23	5	1202	641

Apps = Number of Applicants
Adm = Number Admitted
Reflects 100% of the total applicant pool; highest LSAT data reported.

UNIVERSITY OF OREGON SCHOOL OF LAW

Office of Admissions, 1221 University of Oregon
Eugene, OR 97403-1221
Phone: 541.346.3846; Fax: 541.346.3984
E-mail: admissions@law.uoregon.edu; Website: www.law.uoregon.edu

ABA
Approved
Since
1923

ABA
AMERICAN BAR ASSOCIATION
Section of Legal Education
and Admissions to the Bar

The Basics

Type of school	Public
Term	Semester
Application deadline	3/1
Application fee	$50
Financial aid deadline	3/1
Can first year start other than fall?	No
Student to faculty ratio	14.3 to 1
# of housing spaces available restricted to law students	
graduate housing for which law students are eligible	72

Faculty and Administrators

	Total		Men		Women		Minorities	
	Spr	Fall	Spr	Fall	Spr	Fall	Spr	Fall
Full-time	29	30	16	17	13	13	7	7
Other full-time	3	2	0	0	3	2	1	1
Deans, librarians, & others who teach	3	4	1	1	2	3	0	0
Part-time	33	23	17	14	16	9	2	0
Total	68	59	34	32	34	27	10	8

Curriculum

	Full-Time	Part-Time
Typical first-year section size	61	0
Is there typically a "small section" of the first-year class, other than Legal Writing, taught by full-time faculty	No	No
If yes, typical size offered last year		
# of classroom course titles beyond first-year curriculum	113	
# of upper division courses, excluding seminars, with an enrollment: Under 25	68	
25–49	24	
50–74	11	
75–99	3	
100+	0	
# of seminars	23	
# of seminar positions available	454	
# of seminar positions filled	325	0
# of positions available in simulation courses	559	
# of simulation positions filled	419	0
# of positions available in faculty supervised clinical courses	214	
# of faculty supervised clinical positions filled	152	0
# involved in field placements	78	0
# involved in law journals	117	0
# involved in moot court or trial competitions	24	0
# of credit hours required to graduate	85	

JD Enrollment and Ethnicity

	Men		Women		Full-Time		Part-Time		1st-Year		Total		JD Degs. Awd.
	#	%	#	%	#	%	#	%	#	%	#	%	
All Hispanics	8	2.8	4	1.8	12	2.4	0	0.0	3	1.6	12	2.4	9
Am. Ind./AK Nat.	2	0.7	2	0.9	4	0.8	0	0.0	1	0.5	4	0.8	4
Asian	13	4.6	16	7.1	29	5.7	0	0.0	11	6.0	29	5.7	16
Black/Af. Am.	13	4.6	1	0.4	14	2.8	0	0.0	5	2.7	14	2.8	6
Nat. HI/Pac. Isl.	1	0.4	1	0.4	2	0.4	0	0.0	1	0.5	2	0.4	0
2 or more races	9	3.2	7	3.1	16	3.2	0	0.0	9	4.9	16	3.2	2
Subtotal (minor.)	46	16.4	31	13.8	77	15.2	0	0.0	30	16.4	77	15.2	37
Nonres. Alien	2	0.7	3	1.3	5	1.0	0	0.0	3	1.6	5	1.0	0
White/Cauc.	224	79.7	180	80.4	404	80.0	0	0.0	145	79.2	404	80.0	129
Unknown	9	3.2	10	4.5	19	3.8	0	0.0	5	2.7	19	3.8	8
Total	281	55.6	224	44.4	505	100.0	0	0.0	183	36.2	505		174

Transfers

Transfers in	4
Transfers out	7

Tuition and Fees

	Resident	Nonresident
Full-time	$26,061	$32,505
Part-time		
Tuition Guarantee Program	N	

Living Expenses

Estimated living expenses for singles

Living on campus	Living off campus	Living at home
$14,460	$14,460	$6,882

UNIVERSITY OF OREGON SCHOOL OF LAW

ABA Approved Since 1923

GPA and LSAT Scores

	Total	Full-Time	Part-Time
# of apps	2,178	2,178	0
# of offers	887	887	0
# of matrics	183	183	0
75% GPA	3.60	3.60	0.00
Median GPA	3.39	3.39	0.00
25% GPA	3.17	3.17	0.00
75% LSAT	160	160	0
Median LSAT	159	159	0
25% LSAT	157	157	0

Grants and Scholarships (from prior year)

	Total #	Total %	Full-Time #	Full-Time %	Part-Time #	Part-Time %
Total # of students	526		526		0	
Total # receiving grants	349	66.3	349	66.3	0	0.0
Less than 1/2 tuition	328	62.4	328	62.4	0	0.0
Half to full tuition	17	3.2	17	3.2	0	0.0
Full tuition	0	0.0	0	0.0	0	0.0
More than full tuition	4	0.8	4	0.8	0	0.0
Median grant amount		$5,000		$0		

Informational and Library Resources

Total amount spent on library materials	$707,094
Study seating capacity inside the library	329
# of full-time equivalent professional librarians	8
Hours per week library is open	107
# of open, wired connections available to students	1,354
# of networked computers available for use by students	38
Has wireless network?	Y
Requires computer?	Y

JD Attrition (from prior year)

	Academic #	Other #	Total #	Total %
1st year	1	15	16	9.1
2nd year	1	4	5	2.9
3rd year	0	0	0	0.0
4th year	0	0	0	0.0

Employment (9 months after graduation)

For up-to-date employment data, go to employmentsummary.abaquestionnaire.org on the ABA website.

Bar Passage Rates

First-time takers	172	Reporting %	97.67
Average school %	75.01	Average state %	75.11

Average pass difference –0.10

Jurisdiction	Takers	Passers	Pass %	State %	Diff %
Oregon	112	82	73.21	75.22	–2.01
California	17	11	64.71	71.24	–6.53
Washington	17	11	64.71	71.22	–6.51
Nevada	7	7	100.00	72.72	27.28
Others (6)	15	15	100.00		

UNIVERSITY OF OREGON SCHOOL OF LAW

Office of Admissions, 1221 University of Oregon
Eugene, OR 97403-1221
Phone: 541.346.3846; Fax: 541.346.3984
E-mail: admissions@law.uoregon.edu; Website: www.law.uoregon.edu

In Brief

The University of Oregon School of Law is Oregon's only public law school. In 1923, Oregon Law became one of the first law schools to be approved by the American Bar Association. It is the only law school in the state with membership in the Order of the Coif and one of only two in the Pacific Northwest that is an integral part of a large, comprehensive AAU-ranked research university. Oregon Law is housed in the William W. Knight Law Center on the university's historic 295-acre campus in Eugene, the state's second largest city. The award-winning Knight Law Center, which includes the John E. Jaqua Law Library, is home to the Doctor of Jurisprudence (JD) program, the Oregon LLM in Environmental and Natural Resources Law, and the Master's in Conflict and Dispute Resolution, an interdisciplinary program of the University of Oregon Graduate School. The Green Business Initiative (GBI) and the Portland Externships programs are law school initiatives based at the University of Oregon in downtown Portland. Oregon Law offers program options that support a broad range of professional interests, and our class size (ranging between 150 and 180) is just right to provide individualized attention.

Our Students and Faculty

Oregon Law is a small, tight-knit community of interesting multifaceted students who are smart, friendly, and energetic. Among the characteristics that distinguish the first-year class: 64 percent are residents of states other than Oregon; (with 28 states represented); 95 colleges and universities are represented; 10 percent were college athletes; 70 percent majored in something other than political science; 48 percent come with volunteer or paid experience in the legal profession; 35 percent speak more than one language, and they visited, worked, or studied in 60 different countries; 15 percent of the students are the first in their family to graduate from college.

Perhaps, most significantly, 81 percent were engaged in public interest or public service employment or activities prior to entering Oregon Law. That passion and dedication flourishes at Oregon Law. In 2010 and 2012, the University of Oregon School of Law was recognized nationally for its public interest program.

Full-time faculty form the core of a respected community of scholars and teachers at Oregon Law. Engaged nationally on important issues in their fields, innovative in the classroom, and passionate about the law, the accomplishments of the faculty earned Oregon Law membership in the academy's honorary scholastic society, the Order of the Coif. A select group of adjunct faculty, who are practicing members of the bar, also contribute to broadening the professional network of our students. Finally, our Law Library faculty oversee vast information resources that support the work of both faculty and students.

Curriculum

- Oregon Law offers a diverse curriculum that supports a wide variety of career goals and interests. All students at Oregon Law are engaged in full-time study.
- **Centers and Programs** fuel much of the academic energy at Oregon Law. These include the Appropriate Dispute Resolution Center; Business Law; Family, Child Advocacy, and Elder Law; Environmental and Natural Resources Law Program; Center for Law and Entrepreneurship; Legal Research and Writing (LRW) Program; Ocean and Coastal Law Center; Oregon Child Advocacy Project; Oregon Office for Community Dispute Resolution; Public Service Initiatives that include the Pro Bono Program and Public Interest-Public Service (PIPS) Program; and the Wayne Morse Center for Law and Politics. Oregon Law's Environmental and Natural Resources Law, Appropriate Dispute Resolution, and Legal Research and Writing programs are consistently recognized on a national level.
- Oregon Law offers **eight concurrent JD/master's degree programs.** A concurrent degree enables law students to earn a master's degree through another program at the University of Oregon, requiring only one additional year of study. Students apply separately to the master's program of their choice. The concurrent degree programs at the university are Business and Law with the Lundquist College of Business (JD/MBA), Conflict and Dispute Resolution and Law (JD/MA or MS), Environmental Studies and Law with the Environmental Studies Program (JD/MA or MS), International Studies and Law with the Department of International Studies (JD/MA or MS), Communication and Society and Law with the School of Journalism and Communication (JD/MA or MS), Community & Regional Planning Graduate Program and Law (JD/MCRP), or Master of Public Administration and Law (JD/MPA) with the Department of Planning, Public Policy, and Management. An Oregon Law student also can earn a concurrent master's degree in Water Resources Policy and Management (JD/MS) through the Water Resources Graduate Program at Oregon State University in Corvallis.
- About one-third of Oregon Law students choose to concentrate their legal studies in a specialized area. Following a prescribed set of electives, students can earn a **"statement of completion"** in one of 12 areas. These include business law, criminal law, dispute resolution, environmental and natural resources law, estate planning, intellectual property law, international law, law and entrepreneurship, ocean and coastal law, public interest and public service law, Green Business law, and tax law.
- More than 80 percent of Oregon Law students graduate with "real world" experience, completing at least one for-credit **clinic** or **externship** as part of their legal training, giving them practical skills and experience before they enter the workforce. Externships are available locally, in Portland, or throughout the Northwest region. There is opportunity to propose your own externship as well. The addition of **1L Fellowships** gives incoming first-year students the chance to work closely with faculty and gain practical experience from day one.
- A semester-long **foreign exchange program** with the University of Adelaide School of Law, situated in South Australia's capital, is another program option for students, particularly those focusing on international law. Many international study programs sponsored by other ABA law schools also are open to Oregon Law students for degree credit.
- The Oregon **LLM** in Environmental and Natural Resources Law is an advanced law degree program offered at Oregon Law. The cohort that participates in this one-year program

is a small and select group of US law school graduates and international lawyers seeking more specialized training in environmental and natural resources law.

Admission Decisions

Oregon Law receives applications from many more qualified applicants than there are seats in the class. The fact that the first-year class is small makes the admission process competitive. Our admissions committee reads each applicant's file in a comprehensive and holistic way. To ensure fair consideration of a breadth of applicants, our admissions committee is comprised of faculty, both senior and new; program administrators; a law student; and admission officers. The committee is charged with determining if an applicant is prepared to succeed academically in law school. Both the LSAT and GPA, as well as other non-numeral factors, are considered. The committee also assesses to what extent an applicant's interests and goals match those reflected in the Oregon Law curriculum and community. The Oregon Law application process asks that you earnestly and fully respond to a wide range of questions, you provide us with a résumé of your professional experiences and accomplishments, and provide two letters of recommendation and/or evaluations. No specific LSAT score, GPA, or combination of test score and grades ensure admission. While Oregon is a public law school, we welcome applications from nonresidents. (In Fall 2011, 64 percent of the 1L class were residents of states other than Oregon.) Both residents and nonresidents are considered equally for scholarships at the time of admission. Scholarship renewal rates are high, ensuring that a student will be able to rely on this support for three years.

Student Life

Students come to Eugene, Oregon, from all over the country. In this city of 150,000, (metropolitan area of 350,000), life is relaxed and interactions are less formal. Rent is low compared to other West Coast cites. As the home of a Pac 12, Division I university, the city's designation as "Track Town, USA," and the setting equidistant from the Pacific Coast and Cascade Mountains, law students are drawn to the considerable outdoor activity in Eugene. And while many graduates work in major urban centers, the choice to go to law school in a more manageable and friendly setting is a common theme among Oregon Law alumni and students. However, the diversions of a busy metropolis, additional externships, and an extensive network of Oregon Law alumni are easily accessible to students in Portland, just two hours north of Eugene.

There are about 40 active student organizations promoting events throughout the year. Among them is Land, Air, Water (LAW), which annually hosts PIELC, the oldest and largest public interest environmental law conference in the world. There is an active women law students group, five multicultural organizations, and an LGBTQ organization. The School of Law supports three student-run publications: *Oregon Law Review*, *Journal of Environmental Law and Litigation,* and the *Oregon Review of International Law.* There are numerous public interest fundraisers and community outreach and mentoring programs in which to participate. Students also serve on numerous committees of the law school, including faculty hiring, dean's advisory, diversity, and others. Oregon Law alumni also participate with students in many public interest fundraising and community outreach events, as well as networking events throughout the year.

Careers

The Center for Career Planning and Professional Development provides comprehensive and personalized career counseling to law students. The Center capitalizes on its relationships with a network of more than 5,500 Oregon Law alumni, the larger UO alumni network, and a collegial, supportive legal community. An associate director of public service initiatives helps develop public interest externship opportunities, works on fundraising initiatives for our Loan Repayment Assistance Program (LRAP), and works in conjunction with the Center to assist public interest students in their job searches. More than half of the most recent graduating class chose to remain in Oregon, but alumni work on Wall Street, in Oregon, in DC, throughout the West, and across the globe. Graduates have risen to prominent positions, particularly in Portland and Washington state and in the judiciary. For 12 of the last 13 years, Oregon graduates have passed the Oregon state bar examination at rates that have exceeded or equaled the state average.

APPLICANT PROFILE

University of Oregon School of Law

LSAT Score	GPA								
	3.75 +	3.50–3.74	3.25–3.49	3.00–3.24	2.75–2.99	2.50–2.74	2.25–2.49	2.00–2.24	Below 2.00
175–180									
170–174									
165–169									
160–164									
155–159									
150–154									
145–149									
140–144									
135–139									
130–134									
125–129									
120–124									

■ Good Possibility   □ Possible   ▨ Unlikely

PACE UNIVERSITY SCHOOL OF LAW

78 North Broadway
White Plains, NY 10603
Phone: 914.422.4210; Fax: 914.989.8714
E-mail: admissions@law.pace.edu; Website: www.law.pace.edu

ABA
Approved
Since
1978

The Basics

Type of school	Private
Term	Semester
Application deadline	11/15 3/1
Application fee	$65
Financial aid deadline	2/15
Can first year start other than fall?	Yes
Student to faculty ratio	12.7 to 1
# of housing spaces available restricted to law students	
graduate housing for which law students are eligible	110

Faculty and Administrators

	Total		Men		Women		Minorities	
	Spr	Fall	Spr	Fall	Spr	Fall	Spr	Fall
Full-time	47	48	30	28	17	20	5	3
Other full-time	1	0	1	0	0	0	0	0
Deans, librarians, & others who teach	8	7	2	2	6	5	0	1
Part-time	36	48	24	30	12	18	1	2
Total	92	103	57	60	35	43	6	6

Curriculum

	Full-Time	Part-Time
Typical first-year section size	55	35
Is there typically a "small section" of the first-year class, other than Legal Writing, taught by full-time faculty	No	No
If yes, typical size offered last year		
# of classroom course titles beyond first-year curriculum	162	
# of upper division courses, excluding seminars, with an enrollment: Under 25	167	
25–49	49	
50–74	9	
75–99	4	
100+	0	
# of seminars	32	
# of seminar positions available	480	
# of seminar positions filled	351	109
# of positions available in simulation courses	432	
# of simulation positions filled	305	123
# of positions available in faculty supervised clinical courses	104	
# of faculty supervised clinical positions filled	73	25
# involved in field placements	214	39
# involved in law journals	93	23
# involved in moot court or trial competitions	46	19
# of credit hours required to graduate	88	

JD Enrollment and Ethnicity

	Men		Women		Full-Time		Part-Time		1st-Year		Total		JD Degs. Awd.
	#	%	#	%	#	%	#	%	#	%	#	%	
All Hispanics	14	4.2	26	5.9	30	4.7	10	7.6	13	6.1	40	5.2	11
Am. Ind./AK Nat.	0	0.0	3	0.7	3	0.5	0	0.0	3	1.4	3	0.4	0
Asian	20	6.0	36	8.1	49	7.6	7	5.3	15	7.1	56	7.2	18
Black/Af. Am.	6	1.8	21	4.7	22	3.4	5	3.8	5	2.4	27	3.5	6
Nat. HI/Pac. Isl.	0	0.0	0	0.0	0	0.0	0	0.0	0	0.0	0	0.0	0
2 or more races	12	3.6	14	3.2	23	3.6	3	2.3	3	1.4	26	3.4	0
Subtotal (minor.)	52	15.7	100	22.5	127	19.7	25	18.9	39	18.4	152	19.6	35
Nonres. Alien	1	0.3	4	0.9	5	0.8	0	0.0	3	1.4	5	0.6	1
White/Cauc.	248	74.7	305	68.7	465	72.2	88	66.7	152	71.7	553	71.3	177
Unknown	31	9.3	35	7.9	47	7.3	19	14.4	18	8.5	66	8.5	8
Total	332	42.8	444	57.2	644	83.0	132	17.0	212	27.3	776		221

Transfers

Transfers in	7
Transfers out	19

Tuition and Fees

	Resident	Nonresident
Full-time	$40,978	$40,978
Part-time	$30,746	$30,746
Tuition Guarantee Program		N

Living Expenses

Estimated living expenses for singles

Living on campus	Living off campus	Living at home
$20,096	$22,002	$7,706

PACE UNIVERSITY SCHOOL OF LAW

*ABA
Approved
Since
1978*

GPA and LSAT Scores

	Total	Full-Time	Part-Time
# of apps	2,735	2,439	296
# of offers	1,101	1,042	59
# of matrics	242	226	16
75% GPA	3.65	3.65	3.57
Median GPA	3.42	3.42	3.28
25% GPA	3.12	3.12	3.05
75% LSAT	156	156	155
Median LSAT	154	154	151
25% LSAT	151	151	149

Grants and Scholarships (from prior year)

	Total		Full-Time		Part-Time	
	#	%	#	%	#	%
Total # of students	788		614		174	
Total # receiving grants	437	55.5	347	56.5	90	51.7
Less than 1/2 tuition	296	37.6	237	38.6	59	33.9
Half to full tuition	115	14.6	86	14.0	29	16.7
Full tuition	24	3.0	22	3.6	2	1.1
More than full tuition	2	0.3	2	0.3	0	0.0
Median grant amount			$17,000		$12,000	

Informational and Library Resources

Total amount spent on library materials	$1,304,269
Study seating capacity inside the library	545
# of full-time equivalent professional librarians	10
Hours per week library is open	101
# of open, wired connections available to students	320
# of networked computers available for use by students	77
Has wireless network?	Y
Requires computer?	N

JD Attrition (from prior year)

	Academic	Other	Total	
	#	#	#	%
1st year	3	25	28	10.5
2nd year	6	3	9	3.4
3rd year	1	3	4	2.0
4th year	0	1	1	1.8

Employment (9 months after graduation)

For up-to-date employment data, go to employmentsummary.abaquestionnaire.org on the ABA website.

Bar Passage Rates

First-time takers	218	Reporting %	95.41
Average school %	75.48	Average state %	84.92
Average pass difference	−9.44		

Jurisdiction	Takers	Passers	Pass %	State %	Diff %
New York	208	157	75.48	84.92	−9.44

PACE UNIVERSITY SCHOOL OF LAW

78 North Broadway
White Plains, NY 10603
Phone: 914.422.4210; Fax: 914.989.8714
E-mail: admissions@law.pace.edu; Website: www.law.pace.edu

A Well-Rounded Legal Education

Pace Law School is a national law school, recognized for its high-quality environmental law program. Students can explore a wide range of curricular offerings or pursue one of 16 areas of study. Pace Law School also offers a variety of clinics, centers, externships, and simulation courses for hands-on practical experience. White Plains, New York, home to Pace Law, is also home to federal and state court houses, numerous law firms, corporations, public interest organizations, and government entities and is just 20 miles north of the heart—and pulse—of New York City.

Founded in 1976, Pace Law benefits from its network of more than 7,000 alumni throughout the world. Pace Law offers full-time and part-time day programs with the opportunity to pursue a Master of Laws in Environmental Law (including the nation's first Climate Change track and the Land Use Sustainability track); a Master of Laws in Comparative Legal Studies; and a Doctor of Laws in Environmental Law. The school is part of Pace University, a comprehensive, independent, and diversified university with campuses in New York City and Westchester County.

A Varied Curriculum

The JD program provides students with the fundamental skills necessary for the practice of law nationally, and the flexibility to shape their elective coursework based on particular career goals. The curriculum is based on the concept that rigorous standards and high-quality teaching can coexist with an atmosphere congenial to learning and enjoyment. Students can obtain certificates in Environmental Law and in International Law by completing a sequence of courses with a specified GPA in the applicable area. Pace Law offers the opportunity to pursue joint degrees in the JD/MBA and JD/MPA programs, as well as the JD/MEM with Yale's School of Forestry and Environmental Studies, the JD/MS in Environmental Policy with Bard College, and the JD/MA in Women's History with Sarah Lawrence College. Graduate law degrees, an LLM in Comparative Legal Studies or Environmental Law and an SJD in Environmental Law, attract attorneys from around the world. Pace Law JD candidates taking 12 credits of environmental law may earn LLM degrees in one additional semester.

The majority of elective classes have fewer than 25 students, which enables close faculty-student relationships. The range of scholarship reflects a faculty of diverse interests, and the curriculum offers courses in traditional areas of legal study, legal theory, and specialized studies. Areas of study include constitutional law, commercial law, corporate law, civil litigation and dispute resolution, criminal law and criminal procedure, evidence, family law, intellectual property, real estate law, women's justice, and land use law. Faculty scholarship also covers such specialized areas as the Americans with Disabilities Act, children's legal representation, environmental and toxic torts, equal pay, hazardous waste, health-care fraud, international commercial law, land use, legal and ethical issues in health care, nonprofit organizations, prosecutorial and judicial ethics, racially motivated violence, securities fraud, and white-collar crime.

Renowned Centers and Programs

Pace Law School offers many clinics, simulation courses, and externships through a myriad of on-campus centers, institutes, and lawyering skills programs.

Students can represent the underserved through the Family Court Externship with the Pace Women's Justice Center, preserve individual liberties through our John Jay Legal Services Immigration Justice Clinic, or work side by side with assistant district attorneys through a prosecution externship preparing and prosecuting criminal cases.

In the popular and growing field of environmental law, students work on conservation and development matters through the Land Use Law Center; help nation-states develop climate change policies through the country's only United Nations Environmental Diplomacy Externship; extern with a federal agency in Washington, DC; and help accelerate the world's transition to clean, efficient, and renewable energy alternatives through the Pace Energy and Climate Center.

Pace Law's international programs allow students to spend a summer abroad with one of the United Nations War Crimes Tribunals, or intern locally with law firms and corporate legal departments handling international trade matters. Students may also spend the spring semester abroad through the Pace London Law Program.

Judicial externship programs allow students to hone their writing skills in a mentoring program with a faculty member and in the chambers of a state or United States district or circuit federal court judge.

Whatever your interests, Pace Law has the facilities and resources to help you pursue them.

Modern Library and Physical Facilities

The Pace Law Library is housed in an airy, modern facility. The law library contains an extensive collection of law and law-related publications, provides access to materials in other libraries in metropolitan New York and throughout the United States, and subscribes to national online research systems such as LexisNexis, Westlaw, HeinOnline, and BNA's Law School Professional Information Center. Pace Law students have free access to these databases from computer terminals distributed throughout the law library as well as in the student lounge, and from their home computers. A wireless network is available in the law library, classroom buildings, and throughout the campus. The library was recently renovated and features attractive, comfortable spaces in which students can study individually or in groups.

Financial Aid

A comprehensive aid program has been developed to include scholarships, need-based grants, employment, loans, and a loan-forgiveness program for graduates who choose a public interest career. Over $1.6 million has been allocated for first-year students. These funds may be available on the basis of financial need and academic merit.

Supportive Career Development Services

The Center for Career and Professional Development and the Public Interest Law Center (jointly the "Center") offer a number of services to students and alumni, including one-on-one counseling and résumé review; panels and programs regarding the many areas of legal practice; specific job, internship, and fellowship opportunities; a winter career fair; and on-campus interview and résumé-collection programs. The Center publishes dozens of online career guides that provide an overview of practice specialties and related legal employment markets, descriptions of the various types of legal employers, and specific legal-recruiting information. The Center also provides sample résumés and cover letters and other resources. The staff actively solicits and identifies employment opportunities through an on-campus career fair, targeted mailings, and other outreach activities.

Student Activities

Pace Law publishes three law reviews, the *Pace Law Review*, the *Pace Environmental Law Review*, and the *Pace International Law Review*. Students also work on the *Journal of Court Innovations*, a joint journal created by Pace Law and the New York State Judicial Institute; *GreenLaw*, an online blog published by the Pace Law Center for Environmental

Legal Studies; and the *Pace IP, Sports and Entertainment Law Forum*, an online publication dedicated to the discussion of emerging legal issues in the intellectual property, sports and entertainment law fields. Students compete in interscholastic moot court competitions; host the largest environmental moot court competition in the country (the National Environmental Law Moot Court Competition); and participate in the Pace-founded Willem C. Vis International Commercial Arbitration Moot, the first and largest international commercial arbitration moot court competition of its kind, in Vienna, Austria. Pace Law also sponsors 27 active student organizations, focusing on professional interests, diversity, politics, and social action.

Admission/Visits to Campus

Pace Law School seeks students with demonstrated potential to meaningfully contribute to the diversity of the law school community and legal profession. Full-time students may apply to enter in September or January. The January-entry program allows students to complete the degree through an accelerated two-and-a-half-year program.

Pace Law hosts several open-house programs that include tours; discussions with faculty, administrators, and students; and information regarding the admission process, financial aid, placement, and campus life. For a complete list of our on-campus events, visit our website at www.law.pace.edu.

APPLICANT PROFILE

Pace University School of Law
This grid includes only applicants who earned 120–180 LSAT scores under standard administrations.

LSAT Score	GPA																				
	3.75 +		3.50–3.74		3.25–3.49		3.00–3.24		2.75–2.99		2.50–2.74		2.25–2.49		2.00–2.24		Below 2.00		No GPA		Total	
	Apps	Adm	Apps	Adm	Apps	Adm	Apps	Adm	Apps	Adm	Apps	Adm	Apps	Adm	Apps	Adm	Apps	Adm	Apps	Adm	Apps	Adm
175–180	1	1	0	0	0	0	0	0	0	0	0	0	0	0	0	0	0	0	0	0	1	1
170–174	3	3	4	3	2	2	1	1	3	3	2	2	1	0	0	0	0	0	0	0	16	14
165–169	7	7	14	13	11	8	7	5	3	0	1	1	6	2	1	0	0	0	1	0	51	36
160–164	34	30	46	41	53	46	35	32	15	10	17	11	11	3	1	1	0	0	3	2	215	176
155–159	53	44	108	92	122	97	136	112	79	60	29	22	17	9	6	1	0	0	7	5	557	442
150–154	76	59	156	102	179	82	169	33	112	17	50	4	26	0	10	0	4	0	11	2	793	299
145–149	36	12	81	30	141	14	119	4	91	1	46	0	22	0	9	0	1	0	10	0	556	61
140–144	15	1	46	0	42	0	55	0	45	0	30	0	14	0	9	0	3	0	3	0	262	1
135–139	5	0	5	0	14	0	20	0	22	0	17	0	14	0	2	0	1	0	4	0	104	0
130–134	0	0	1	0	3	0	8	0	3	0	12	0	2	0	4	0	0	0	4	0	37	0
125–129	0	0	1	0	1	0	0	0	6	0	0	0	0	0	3	0	1	0	1	0	13	0
120–124	0	0	0	0	0	0	1	0	3	0	1	0	0	0	0	0	0	0	0	0	5	0
Total	230	157	462	281	568	249	551	187	382	91	205	40	113	14	45	2	10	0	44	9	2610	1030

Apps = Number of Applicants
Adm = Number Admitted
Reflects 99% of the total applicant pool; highest LSAT data reported.

UNIVERSITY OF THE PACIFIC, MCGEORGE SCHOOL OF LAW

3200 Fifth Avenue
Sacramento, CA 95817
Phone: 916.739.7105; Fax: 916.739.7301
E-mail: mcgeorge@pacific.edu; Website: www.mcgeorge.edu

ABA
Approved
Since
1969

The Basics

Type of school	Private
Term	Semester
Application deadline	5/1
Application fee	$50
Financial aid deadline	
Can first year start other than fall?	No
Student to faculty ratio	15.0 to 1
# of housing spaces available restricted to law students	167
graduate housing for which law students are eligible	167

Faculty and Administrators

	Total Spr	Total Fall	Men Spr	Men Fall	Women Spr	Women Fall	Minorities Spr	Minorities Fall
Full-time	46	49	27	28	19	21	7	9
Other full-time	0	0	0	0	0	0	0	0
Deans, librarians, & others who teach	11	11	5	4	6	7	0	0
Part-time	57	45	38	31	19	14	9	4
Total	114	105	70	63	44	42	16	13

JD Enrollment and Ethnicity

	Men #	Men %	Women #	Women %	Full-Time #	Full-Time %	Part-Time #	Part-Time %	1st-Year #	1st-Year %	Total #	Total %	JD Degs. Awd.
All Hispanics	32	6.7	31	7.2	46	7.0	17	6.7	18	7.9	63	6.9	23
Am. Ind./AK Nat.	7	1.5	12	2.8	16	2.5	3	1.2	8	3.5	19	2.1	5
Asian	73	15.2	77	18.0	114	17.5	36	14.1	38	16.7	150	16.5	33
Black/Af. Am.	10	2.1	8	1.9	9	1.4	9	3.5	5	2.2	18	2.0	12
Nat. HI/Pac. Isl.	0	0.0	0	0.0	0	0.0	0	0.0	0	0.0	0	0.0	0
2 or more races	0	0.0	0	0.0	0	0.0	0	0.0	0	0.0	0	0.0	0
Subtotal (minor.)	122	25.4	128	29.9	185	28.3	65	25.5	69	30.3	250	27.5	73
Nonres. Alien	8	1.7	5	1.2	9	1.4	4	1.6	4	1.8	13	1.4	0
White/Cauc.	350	72.9	295	68.9	459	70.3	186	72.9	155	68.0	645	71.0	230
Unknown	0	0.0	0	0.0	0	0.0	0	0.0	0	0.0	0	0.0	0
Total	480	52.9	428	47.1	653	71.9	255	28.1	228	25.1	908		303

Curriculum

	Full-Time	Part-Time
Typical first-year section size	95	50
Is there typically a "small section" of the first-year class, other than Legal Writing, taught by full-time faculty	Yes	No
If yes, typical size offered last year	50	
# of classroom course titles beyond first-year curriculum	168	
# of upper division courses, excluding seminars, with an enrollment: Under 25	129	
25–49	41	
50–74	19	
75–99	28	
100+	3	
# of seminars	22	
# of seminar positions available	394	
# of seminar positions filled	249	72
# of positions available in simulation courses	493	
# of simulation positions filled	320	117
# of positions available in faculty supervised clinical courses	230	
# of faculty supervised clinical positions filled	144	47
# involved in field placements	231	87
# involved in law journals	85	19
# involved in moot court or trial competitions	31	12
# of credit hours required to graduate	88	

Transfers

Transfers in	15
Transfers out	24

Tuition and Fees

	Resident	Nonresident
Full-time	$41,393	
Part-time	$27,533	
Tuition Guarantee Program	N	

Living Expenses

Estimated living expenses for singles

Living on campus	Living off campus	Living at home
$21,014	$21,014	$21,014

UNIVERSITY OF THE PACIFIC, MCGEORGE SCHOOL OF LAW

ABA
Approved
Since
1969

GPA and LSAT Scores

	Total	Full-Time	Part-Time
# of apps	3,555	3,282	273
# of offers	1,396	1,318	78
# of matrics	225	176	49
75% GPA	3.57	3.56	3.63
Median GPA	3.40	3.41	3.38
25% GPA	3.09	3.11	3.01
75% LSAT	160	160	158
Median LSAT	158	158	156
25% LSAT	155	155	152

Grants and Scholarships (from prior year)

	Total		Full-Time		Part-Time	
	#	%	#	%	#	%
Total # of students	1,026		724		302	
Total # receiving grants	670	65.3	511	70.6	159	52.6
Less than 1/2 tuition	578	56.3	437	60.4	141	46.7
Half to full tuition	78	7.6	63	8.7	15	5.0
Full tuition	8	0.8	6	0.8	2	0.7
More than full tuition	6	0.6	5	0.7	1	0.3
Median grant amount			$11,320		$5,000	

Informational and Library Resources

Total amount spent on library materials	$1,576,752
Study seating capacity inside the library	590
# of full-time equivalent professional librarians	8
Hours per week library is open	108
# of open, wired connections available to students	275
# of networked computers available for use by students	61
Has wireless network?	Y
Requires computer?	N

JD Attrition (from prior year)

	Academic	Other	Total	
	#	#	#	%
1st year	15	12	27	7.9
2nd year	1	27	28	9.6
3rd year	1	4	5	1.7
4th year	0	1	1	1.1

Employment (9 months after graduation)

For up-to-date employment data, go to
employmentsummary.abaquestionnaire.org on the ABA website.

Bar Passage Rates

First-time takers	298	Reporting %	95.97
Average school %	69.58	Average state %	71.24
Average pass difference	−1.66		

Jurisdiction	Takers	Passers	Pass %	State %	Diff %
California	286	199	69.58	71.24	−1.66

UNIVERSITY OF THE PACIFIC, MCGEORGE SCHOOL OF LAW

3200 Fifth Avenue
Sacramento, CA 95817
Phone: 916.739.7105; Fax: 916.739.7301
E-mail: mcgeorge@pacific.edu; Website: www.mcgeorge.edu

Overview

The University of the Pacific, McGeorge School of Law is in Sacramento, California, capital of the nation's most populous state and one of the world's leading economies. The school is a member of the AALS, is accredited by the ABA, and has a chapter of the Order of the Coif.

Day- and evening-division programs provide the flexibility to earn a JD degree in three, four, or five years of study. More than 1,000 students pursue a JD, LLM, or JSD on Pacific McGeorge's unique 13-acre, law-school-only campus. The school's reputation for educating well-prepared, practice-ready lawyers grows from the vitality of students and faculty working together. The diversity of the student body is reflected in the 150 or more colleges and universities that students attended as undergraduates, the 50 or more major fields, the range in years from age 20 to over 60, and the gender and ethnic diversity represented annually by the growing number of students from a wide range of ethnic and cultural heritages.

Library and Physical Facilities

Pacific McGeorge's students study on a campus designed exclusively for legal education that includes class and seminar rooms; student center; technologically equipped trial courtroom; lecture hall; clinical legal education center; law library and computer center; administrative, faculty, and student services offices; recreational facilities; and student apartments.

The new Legal Studies Center is a comprehensive legal research facility that contains over 500,000 volumes. The Center includes a new state-of-the-art student study area, computer lab, group study rooms, and wireless Internet capabilities. Pacific McGeorge librarians are experts in legal research methodology and assist students in using the Center's electronic and traditional resources.

Curriculum

Pacific McGeorge offers more than 100 advanced elective course offerings, ranging from comprehensive courses in traditional areas such as business, constitutional law, criminal justice, and family and juvenile law, to a wide variety of courses in specialty areas such as environmental (both US and international), entertainment, labor, intellectual property, mass media, banking, and elder law. Certificate and concentration curricula are offered for those with specific career interests.

Clinical Experience: Pacific McGeorge believes that clinical education—working in a practice setting while guided by a faculty mentor—is a key part of the law school experience. On-campus clinics include Administrative Adjudication, Parole Representation, Victim's Rights, Bankruptcy, Immigration, Appellate Advocacy, Elder and Health Law, Mediation, and Federal Defender Clinic. Off campus, the internship program makes available more than 125 placements.

Certificate Programs

- **Advocacy:** Advocacy is an integral part of the law, including representing clients in civil and criminal litigation, at administrative hearings, or applying alternative dispute-resolution techniques to negotiate business matters or to avoid litigation. The Advocacy certificate especially prepares those interested in pursuing courtroom advocacy. Additionally, a one-year LLM in Experiential Law Teaching empowers international and domestic lawyers and law professors to implement advocacy principles in their practices and classrooms.
- **International Legal Studies:** Law and accounting firms, government agencies, and corporations require lawyers savvy in international law. The International Legal Studies curriculum balances public international law and private international law. Study-abroad opportunities include a Summer Institute in Salzburg, Austria, as well as opportunities to pursue an LLM in Transnational Business Practice, or an LLM or JSD in International Water Resources Law.
- **Public Law & Policy:** The Public Law & Policy certificate prepares students for private or public service careers in government. Students benefit from hands-on experience and develop networking contacts with governmental entities. Graduates practice as consultants, lobbyists, in-house counsel, or in staff and policy positions with legislative branches, executive departments, or administrative agencies. A one- or two-year LLM program in Public Law & Policy is also available.

Concentrations

- **Business Law:** The demands and complexities of a global economy require a strong basis in business law. The Business Law concentration prepares students to pursue general business law practice or specialized law practice in entertainment law, employment law, banking law, real estate law, and more.
- **Criminal Justice:** The Criminal Justice concentration offers wide-ranging electives, including sentencing and postconviction remedies, white-collar crime, capital punishment, criminal pretrial litigation, evidence courses, juvenile law, family violence, and problems in criminal justice. Internship and specialization opportunities provide hands-on training.
- **Environmental Law:** Local, national, and international laws govern myriad aspects of environmental law and vary from an extremely specific to a very broad focus. The Environmental Law concentration provides the foundation necessary to pursue careers working in environmental issues or environmental law.
- **Intellectual Property:** The diverse Intellectual Property concentration prepares graduates to practice in areas such as the entertainment industry, music and theater law, intellectual property litigation, sports, trademark and domain-name law, patent and biotechnology law, and computer and Internet law.
- **Tax:** The Tax concentration offers a specialized curriculum and a variety of elective tax courses to prepare graduates to work as tax, business, or estate planning specialists.

Student Activities

Over 40 professional, social, and academic student organizations at Pacific McGeorge represent the breadth of interests and diversity of the student community. Student staffs manage, edit, and write for the *McGeorge Law Review* and the *Pacific McGeorge Global Business and Development Law Journal*. Pacific McGeorge competition teams compete with notable success in a wide range of trial, appellate, counseling, and dispute-resolution competitions on the regional and national levels.

Admission and Financial Aid

Admission is competitive. Prelegal education includes at least a bachelor's degree or senior standing from an accredited college or university. An applicant's undergraduate record and LSAT results are important factors in the decision process. When there are multiple LSAT scores, the highest may be accorded significant weight. Other factors considered are grade patterns or trends, employment and career accomplishments, graduate work, and extracurricular or community activities. Ethnic, cultural, and experiential backgrounds that contribute to student-body diversity are valued. Strong merit- and need-based financial aid programs provide scholarship awards and grants to entering and advanced students. A knowledgeable financial aid staff provides counseling to assist students in minimizing student loan indebtedness.

Housing

Pacific McGeorge has 150 on-campus apartments, furnished and unfurnished, including one- and two-bedroom units, studios, and townhouses. Early application is advised. The school's full-time housing coordinator also assists in locating off-campus accommodations that are readily available in Sacramento.

Career Services

The Pacific McGeorge Career Development Office (CDO) provides comprehensive career search assistance for permanent, part-time, and summer employment. The CDO staff is available to help students identify their interests, introduce them to the vast array of career development and employment opportunity resources, and assist with career decision making. The CDO focuses on career counseling, individualized review and critique of résumés and cover letters, and job search strategy development.

Pacific McGeorge faculty and alumni play a major role in our programs, sharing their experience and offering advice to students seeking career opportunities in their fields of expertise. Alumni participate in a Day in the Life Speakers Series, the Alumni Mentor Program, and mock interviews. In addition, the CDO hosts employer on-campus interviews for students and maintains up-to-date listings of specific employment opportunities, as well as an extensive library of resource materials.

APPLICANT PROFILE

University of the Pacific, McGeorge School of Law
This grid includes only applicants who earned 120–180 LSAT scores under standard administrations.

LSAT Score	GPA																				
	3.75 +		3.50–3.74		3.25–3.49		3.00–3.24		2.75–2.99		2.50–2.74		2.25–2.49		2.00–2.24		Below 2.00		No GPA		Total	
	Apps	Adm	Apps	Adm	Apps	Adm	Apps	Adm	Apps	Adm	Apps	Adm	Apps	Adm	Apps	Adm	Apps	Adm	Apps	Adm	Apps	Adm
175–180	0	0	0	0	1	1	0	0	0	0	1	0	0	0	0	0	0	0	0	0	2	1
170–174	2	2	5	5	4	4	5	5	3	3	0	0	0	0	0	0	0	0	0	0	19	19
165–169	29	28	34	34	28	28	25	25	23	15	15	3	2	1	1	0	0	0	1	1	158	135
160–164	67	65	101	100	102	98	111	108	60	46	29	17	15	3	6	2	3	0	1	1	495	440
155–159	109	104	245	243	224	159	181	76	111	33	67	14	19	2	9	0	1	0	9	4	975	635
150–154	102	31	188	78	214	35	198	8	125	1	61	0	27	0	9	0	4	0	10	0	938	153
145–149	26	2	88	4	117	1	123	0	80	0	53	1	33	0	14	0	0	0	7	0	541	8
140–144	9	0	32	0	45	0	54	0	38	0	34	0	23	0	3	0	1	0	7	0	246	0
135–139	10	0	13	0	14	0	23	0	20	0	14	0	20	0	4	0	1	0	4	0	123	0
130–134	1	0	5	0	2	0	5	0	5	0	5	0	2	0	1	0	0	0	6	0	32	0
125–129	0	0	0	0	0	0	1	0	1	0	1	0	2	0	1	0	0	0	0	0	6	0
120–124	0	0	0	0	0	0	0	0	0	0	0	0	0	0	0	0	0	0	0	0	0	0
Total	355	232	711	464	751	326	726	222	466	98	280	35	143	6	48	2	10	0	45	6	3535	1391

Apps = Number of Applicants
Adm = Number Admitted
Reflects 99% of the total applicant pool; highest LSAT data reported.

UNIVERSITY OF PENNSYLVANIA LAW SCHOOL

3501 Samson Street
Philadelphia, PA 19104-6204
Phone: 215.898.7400; Fax: 215.898.9606
E-mail: admissions@law.upenn.edu; Website: www.law.upenn.edu

ABA
Approved
Since
1923

The Basics

Type of school	Private
Term	Semester
Application deadline	3/1
Application fee	$80
Financial aid deadline	3/1
Can first year start other than fall?	No
Student to faculty ratio	10.4 to 1
# of housing spaces available restricted to law students	
graduate housing for which law students are eligible	999

Faculty and Administrators

	Total		Men		Women		Minorities	
	Spr	Fall	Spr	Fall	Spr	Fall	Spr	Fall
Full-time	65	62	48	47	17	15	6	8
Other full-time	7	7	0	0	7	7	2	2
Deans, librarians, & others who teach	6	1	3	1	3	0	0	0
Part-time	52	45	43	33	9	12	7	4
Total	130	115	94	81	36	34	15	14

Curriculum

	Full-Time	Part-Time
Typical first-year section size	85	0
Is there typically a "small section" of the first-year class, other than Legal Writing, taught by full-time faculty	Yes	No
If yes, typical size offered last year	42	
# of classroom course titles beyond first-year curriculum	169	

# of upper division courses, excluding seminars, with an enrollment:		
	Under 25	82
	25–49	29
	50–74	13
	75–99	6
	100+	6

# of seminars	66	
# of seminar positions available	924	
# of seminar positions filled	793	0
# of positions available in simulation courses	629	
# of simulation positions filled	558	0
# of positions available in faculty supervised clinical courses	142	
# of faculty supervised clinical positions filled	139	0
# involved in field placements	32	0
# involved in law journals	377	0
# involved in moot court or trial competitions	128	0
# of credit hours required to graduate	89	

JD Enrollment and Ethnicity

	Men		Women		Full-Time		Part-Time		1st-Year		Total		JD Degs. Awd.
	#	%	#	%	#	%	#	%	#	%	#	%	
All Hispanics	15	3.5	17	4.5	32	4.0	0	0.0	15	5.7	32	4.0	12
Am. Ind./AK Nat.	1	0.2	0	0.0	1	0.1	0	0.0	1	0.4	1	0.1	0
Asian	52	12.3	66	17.3	118	14.7	0	0.0	40	15.2	118	14.6	35
Black/Af. Am.	26	6.1	33	8.6	59	7.3	0	0.0	19	7.2	59	7.3	20
Nat. HI/Pac. Isl.	1	0.2	0	0.0	1	0.1	0	0.0	1	0.4	1	0.1	0
2 or more races	14	3.3	21	5.5	35	4.3	0	0.0	8	3.0	35	4.3	14
Subtotal (minor.)	109	25.7	137	35.9	246	30.6	0	0.0	84	31.8	246	30.5	81
Nonres. Alien	14	3.3	16	4.2	30	3.7	0	0.0	8	3.0	30	3.7	5
White/Cauc.	274	64.6	202	52.9	475	59.0	1	100.0	144	54.5	476	59.1	187
Unknown	27	6.4	27	7.1	54	6.7	0	0.0	28	10.6	54	6.7	0
Total	424	52.6	382	47.4	805	99.9	1	0.1	264	32.8	806		273

Transfers

Transfers in	25
Transfers out	4

Tuition and Fees

	Resident	Nonresident
Full-time	$50,718	$50,718
Part-time		
Tuition Guarantee Program	N	

Living Expenses

Estimated living expenses for singles

Living on campus	Living off campus	Living at home
$20,542	$20,542	$10,050

ABA
Approved
Since
1923

GPA and LSAT Scores

	Total	Full-Time	Part-Time
# of apps	4,952	4,952	0
# of offers	863	863	0
# of matrics	266	266	0
75% GPA	3.93	3.93	0.00
Median GPA	3.86	3.86	0.00
25% GPA	3.58	3.58	0.00
75% LSAT	171	171	0
Median LSAT	170	170	0
25% LSAT	166	166	0

Grants and Scholarships (from prior year)

	Total #	Total %	Full-Time #	Full-Time %	Part-Time #	Part-Time %
Total # of students	803		802		1	
Total # receiving grants	351	43.7	351	43.8	0	0.0
Less than 1/2 tuition	278	34.6	278	34.7	0	0.0
Half to full tuition	56	7.0	56	7.0	0	0.0
Full tuition	17	2.1	17	2.1	0	0.0
More than full tuition	0	0.0	0	0.0	0	0.0
Median grant amount			$15,000		$0	

Informational and Library Resources

Total amount spent on library materials	$1,496,959
Study seating capacity inside the library	551
# of full-time equivalent professional librarians	12
Hours per week library is open	115
# of open, wired connections available to students	33
# of networked computers available for use by students	159
Has wireless network?	Y
Requires computer?	N

JD Attrition (from prior year)

	Academic #	Other #	Total #	Total %
1st year	0	6	6	2.4
2nd year	0	5	5	1.8
3rd year	0	1	1	0.4
4th year	0	0	0	0.0

Employment (9 months after graduation)

For up-to-date employment data, go to employmentsummary.abaquestionnaire.org on the ABA website.

Bar Passage Rates

First-time takers	273	Reporting %	79.49
Average school %	94.46	Average state %	82.46
Average pass difference	12.00		

Jurisdiction	Takers	Passers	Pass %	State %	Diff %
New York	140	136	97.14	84.92	12.22
Pennsylvania	44	41	93.18	83.06	10.12
California	33	28	84.85	71.24	13.61

UNIVERSITY OF PENNSYLVANIA LAW SCHOOL

3501 Samson Street
Philadelphia, PA 19104-6204
Phone: 215.898.7400; Fax: 215.898.9606
E-mail: admissions@law.upenn.edu; Website: www.law.upenn.edu

Introduction

The hallmarks of the Penn Law experience are a cross-disciplinary, globally focused legal education and a vibrant and collegial community that prepares graduates to navigate an increasingly complex world as leaders and influential decision makers. Penn Law, one of the nation's leading law schools, is part of the University of Pennsylvania, one of the world's preeminent research universities. Our faculty collaborate with renowned scholars across Penn and throughout the world. Students enrich their legal educations with study in other disciplines via courses and clinics, certificate programs, joint-degree programs, and public interest projects.

As part of the rigors of legal studies at Penn and unique among top law schools, our students truly own their educational experiences, actively contributing to a collaborative and supportive environment where they learn to solve problems while developing critical professional skills. By taking risks in the classroom, students learn to challenge their thinking; working effectively with colleagues on- and off-campus, they learn about management, leadership, and networking; and by investing in the full life of Penn Law, they discover their strengths and hone their talents.

Faculty

Penn Law faculty are unparalleled in the depth and breadth of their intellectual interests, the quality of their scholarship, and their teaching excellence. More than 70 percent of faculty members hold advanced degrees in addition to the JD and close to 50 percent hold secondary appointments or an affiliation within the University. Research institutes, centers, and programs foster innovation and attract leading scholars and practitioners from around the globe to address major legal questions and problems in such areas as business, environment, international and comparative studies, health, intellectual property, regulation, and technology.

The Law School enjoys a low student-to-faculty ratio, and faculty employ an open-door policy and encourage students to join in their research endeavors.

Physical Facilities and Library

Penn Law's four, fully connected buildings surrounding a courtyard are central to our educational mission of collaboration between students, faculty, and staff. Golkin Hall, featuring a state-of-the-art courtroom, auditorium, office space, and classrooms, opened in 2012.

Biddle Law Library, premier among law libraries, is a modern complex with expansive areas, group study rooms, computer labs, and places for quiet study. Librarians teach legal research courses and work closely with students and faculty.

Curriculum

Penn Law's cross-disciplinary curriculum is unrivaled among the leading law schools, providing future lawyers with insights and skills in the various fields in which their clients operate. Students may take classes and earn certificates or joint/dual degrees throughout Penn. The 1L curriculum includes foundational courses plus two electives and legal writing and research instruction individually and in small-group courses. Upper-level students choose electives ranging from standards, such as corporations and evidence, to introductory courses in specialized areas of the law and seminars in emerging fields. As part of their JD degree, students may supplement their legal education with up to four courses at Penn's esteemed graduate and professional schools.

We also offer the Master of Laws (LLM), Master of Comparative Law (LLCM), and Doctor of Juridical Science (SJD).

Joint-Degree, Certificate, and Clinical Programs

Penn's three-year JD/MBA (Wharton) is the country's first fully integrated, three-year program offered on one campus by elite law and business schools. Penn offers accelerated, three-year JD/master's degrees in Education, Environmental Studies, Public Health, Public Administration, Social Policy, Bioethics, Criminology, International Studies, and Islamic Studies. Other degree programs include City and Regional Planning, Islamic Studies, and Social Work. Additionally, Penn offers joint JD/PhD degrees in American Legal History, Philosophy, and Psychology. We also offer dual master's degrees in Finance and Law with Sciences Po in Paris and a JD/LLM with Hong Kong University.

Students can also earn certificates in Business and Public Policy, Environmental Policy or Science, Cross-Sector Innovation, Gender and Sexuality Studies, Global Human Rights, East Asian Studies, Middle East and Islamic Studies, Nonprofit Management, and other ad hoc programs.

Our clinical programs are designed to help students build strong relationships with a diverse array of actual clients and develop essential lawyering skills in a real-world professional setting. Penn Law's clinics include opportunities in litigation, business transactions, child advocacy, mediation, legislation, and interdisciplinary practice, as well as international, appellate, and intellectual property and technology law.

International Engagement

Penn Law's curriculum is infused with global analysis at all levels. Through our many international program offerings, students have access to world-class faculty and globally recognized visiting scholars, joint degrees and certificates, overseas fellowship and internship opportunities, the Transnational Legal Clinic, and the Global Research Seminar, an intensive international course where students and faculty investigate contemporary legal challenges, culminating in meetings with experts and stakeholders during an overseas research trip.

The study-abroad program offers opportunities in Tokyo, Hamburg, Beijing, Tel Aviv, Barcelona, Paris, and Hong Kong. This wide array of opportunities allows students to apply what they learn in the classroom to real-world settings abroad.

Public Service

Penn has a long-standing commitment to public service. All students participate in our ABA award-winning pro bono program, gaining practical experience and professional skills while implementing solutions to complex societal problems; thus benefiting underserved causes, communities, and government agencies. The Toll Public Interest Center is dedicated to ensuring that all students graduate with valuable pro bono experience and a commitment to service wherever their legal careers take them. The Center offers strong mentoring to public interest students and oversees two dozen student initiatives as well as the Toll Public Interest Scholars Program.

We are at the forefront of support for public service careers with scholarships, guaranteed summer funding, and generously funded loan forgiveness and fellowships for post-graduate work.

Student Body Profile and Activities

Our JD students come from 40 states, 20 countries, and more than 200 undergraduate institutions, creating one of the nation's most diverse student bodies. About 11 percent of students hold advanced degrees and, on average, 65 percent have taken time off before law school. The diversity of the community, including 100 LLMs from around the globe, creates a dynamic and engaging classroom environment. Over 90 student groups provide countless opportunities for students to work and socialize together. Activities cover a wide spectrum of academic interest areas, identity groups, political affiliations, sports, journals, moot court and mock trial programs, and service organizations.

The *University of Pennsylvania Law Review* is the nation's oldest law review and among the most distinguished. Penn Law's tradition of exceptional journal scholarship also includes the *Journal of Business Law*, *Journal of Constitutional Law*, *East Asia Law Review*, *Journal of International Law*, and *Journal of Law and Social Change*.

Penn Law's nationally recognized moot court program is fed by great student interest in appellate advocacy. Our many mock trial teams travel and compete successfully throughout the country and overseas.

Admission

The demand for a Penn Law education has risen dramatically. In 2010–2011, close to 5,000 applicants sought admission to the JD program.

The Law School evaluates each application holistically. While academic excellence is of primary importance, we take all factors into consideration and do not apply numeric LSAT or GPA cutoffs. Instead, each file is read by members of the Admissions Committee; letters of recommendation, examples of written expression, and a résumé are also considered to develop a full picture of each applicant.

We begin processing applications on September 1. Applications received by November 15, and completed by December 1, will be considered for our early decision (binding) program; these applicants receive a decision by the end of December. The regular admission deadline is March 1. Our program is limited to fall semester, full-time students.

First-year students who have achieved excellent records in a full-time law school program may apply as transfer students by July 1 following their first year. Transfer decisions are made on a rolling basis, beginning in mid-June.

Housing

Students enjoy a green university campus combined with an exciting and affordable urban experience minutes from downtown Philadelphia, one of the nation's most historic and liveliest cities. Students select from a wide range of on- and off-campus living arrangements.

Expenses and Financial Aid

Penn Law is committed to making the benefits of a legal education accessible and affordable for all students. We maintain a substantial need-based grant and loan aid program, offering approximately 80 percent of the student body financial assistance. Penn Law guarantees summer funding for public service-related work and offers generous loan forgiveness and repayment programs for graduates who pursue public interest careers. We also consider all admittees for merit-based scholarships.

Career Services

Our Career Planning and Professionalism office exposes students to a vast array of legal employers, nationally and internationally, as well as to Penn alumni worldwide, and provides students with a wealth of resources and programs to assist students in determining their professional goals and preparing for rewarding careers.

Penn Law's Center on Professionalism offers students programming to develop critical complementary skills and expand students' knowledge of the competencies needed for leadership in the profession.

Penn Law graduates enjoy fulfilling and rewarding careers in every arena of practice, business, and advocacy. In recent years, graduates began their careers in private practice (70–75 percent), judicial clerkships (15–20 percent), government or public interest (4–8 percent), academia (1–2 percent), and business and industry (3–4 percent).

APPLICANT PROFILE

Penn Law has chosen not to include an applicant profile because LSAT and GPA figures alone do not capture the qualities that make our students so dynamic. We value our students' diverse backgrounds, rich life experiences, leadership, community service, professional accomplishments, advanced degrees and coursework, motivation, initiative, and exemplary writing skills. While admission to Penn Law requires an excellent academic record, the Admissions Committee approaches each application holistically and takes all of these factors into consideration.

THE PENNSYLVANIA STATE UNIVERSITY, DICKINSON SCHOOL OF LAW

Lewis Katz Building, University Park, PA 16802-1017; Phone: 814.867.1251; Fax: 814.867.0405
333 West South Street, Carlisle, PA 17013-2899; Phone: 717.240.5207; Fax: 717.241.3503
E-mail: admissions@law.psu.edu; Website: www.law.psu.edu; Phone: 800.840.1122

ABA Approved Since 1931

The Basics

Type of school	Public
Term	Semester
Application deadline	3/15
Application fee	$60
Financial aid deadline	3/1
Can first year start other than fall?	No
Student to faculty ratio	9.2 to 1
# of housing spaces available restricted to law students	
graduate housing for which law students are eligible	424

Faculty and Administrators

	Total		Men		Women		Minorities	
	Spr	Fall	Spr	Fall	Spr	Fall	Spr	Fall
Full-time	54	53	31	30	23	23	7	6
Other full-time	3	2	3	2	0	0	1	1
Deans, librarians, & others who teach	16	15	7	6	9	9	2	2
Part-time	26	17	18	10	8	7	1	1
Total	99	87	59	48	40	39	11	10

Curriculum

	Full-Time	Part-Time
Typical first-year section size	40	0
Is there typically a "small section" of the first-year class, other than Legal Writing, taught by full-time faculty	No	No
If yes, typical size offered last year		
# of classroom course titles beyond first-year curriculum	123	
# of upper division courses, excluding seminars, with an enrollment: Under 25	203	
25–49	23	
50–74	11	
75–99	1	
100+	0	
# of seminars	24	
# of seminar positions available	430	
# of seminar positions filled	249	0
# of positions available in simulation courses	871	
# of simulation positions filled	566	2
# of positions available in faculty supervised clinical courses	124	
# of faculty supervised clinical positions filled	100	0
# involved in field placements	92	0
# involved in law journals	84	0
# involved in moot court or trial competitions	32	0
# of credit hours required to graduate	88	

JD Enrollment and Ethnicity

	Men		Women		Full-Time		Part-Time		1st-Year		Total		JD Degs. Awd.
	#	%	#	%	#	%	#	%	#	%	#	%	
All Hispanics	5	1.5	1	0.4	6	1.0	0	0.0	1	0.5	6	1.0	12
Am. Ind./AK Nat.	0	0.0	1	0.4	1	0.2	0	0.0	1	0.5	1	0.2	0
Asian	10	3.0	20	7.6	30	5.0	0	0.0	2	1.1	30	5.0	3
Black/Af. Am.	12	3.6	21	8.0	33	5.5	0	0.0	18	9.7	33	5.5	8
Nat. HI/Pac. Isl.	0	0.0	0	0.0	0	0.0	0	0.0	0	0.0	0	0.0	0
2 or more races	5	1.5	8	3.1	13	2.2	0	0.0	4	2.2	13	2.2	3
Subtotal (minor.)	32	9.6	51	19.5	83	13.9	0	0.0	26	14.0	83	13.9	26
Nonres. Alien	9	2.7	11	4.2	20	3.4	0	0.0	10	5.4	20	3.4	2
White/Cauc.	285	85.3	191	72.9	476	79.9	0	0.0	146	78.5	476	79.9	134
Unknown	8	2.4	9	3.4	17	2.9	0	0.0	4	2.2	17	2.9	13
Total	334	56.0	262	44.0	596	100.0	0	0.0	186	31.2	596		175

Transfers

Transfers in	5
Transfers out	20

Tuition and Fees

	Resident	Nonresident
Full-time	$38,614	$38,614
Part-time		
Tuition Guarantee Program	N	

Living Expenses

Estimated living expenses for singles

Living on campus	Living off campus	Living at home
$23,056	$23,056	$23,056

THE PENNSYLVANIA STATE UNIVERSITY, DICKINSON SCHOOL OF LAW

ABA
Approved
Since
1931

GPA and LSAT Scores

	Total	Full-Time	Part-Time
# of apps	4,820	4,820	0
# of offers	1,466	1,466	0
# of matrics	185	185	0
75% GPA	3.77	3.77	0.00
Median GPA	3.55	3.55	0.00
25% GPA	3.31	3.31	0.00
75% LSAT	161	161	0
Median LSAT	159	159	0
25% LSAT	156	156	0

Grants and Scholarships (from prior year)

	Total		Full-Time		Part-Time	
	#	%	#	%	#	%
Total # of students	618		617		1	
Total # receiving grants	364	58.9	364	59.0	0	0.0
Less than 1/2 tuition	271	43.9	271	43.9	0	0.0
Half to full tuition	92	14.9	92	14.9	0	0.0
Full tuition	1	0.2	1	0.2	0	0.0
More than full tuition	0	0.0	0	0.0	0	0.0
Median grant amount			$10,000		$0	

Informational and Library Resources

Total amount spent on library materials	$1,459,868
Study seating capacity inside the library	395
# of full-time equivalent professional librarians	8
Hours per week library is open	96
# of open, wired connections available to students	0
# of networked computers available for use by students	123
Has wireless network?	Y
Requires computer?	N

JD Attrition (from prior year)

	Academic	Other	Total	
	#	#	#	%
1st year	3	28	31	13.6
2nd year	1	1	2	1.0
3rd year	0	0	0	0.0
4th year	0	0	0	0.0

Employment (9 months after graduation)

For up-to-date employment data, go to employmentsummary.abaquestionnaire.org on the ABA website.

Bar Passage Rates

First-time takers	207	Reporting %	100.00
Average school %	76.80	Average state %	82.33

Average pass difference   –5.53

Jurisdiction	Takers	Passers	Pass %	State %	Diff %
Pennsylvania	113	94	83.19	83.06	0.13
New York	25	21	84.00	84.92	–0.92
New Jersey	14	3	21.43	82.34	–60.91
California	10	4	40.00	71.24	–31.24
Others (17)	45	37	82.22		

THE PENNSYLVANIA STATE UNIVERSITY, DICKINSON SCHOOL OF LAW

Lewis Katz Building, University Park, PA 16802-1017; Phone: 814.867.1251; Fax: 814.867.0405
333 West South Street, Carlisle, PA 17013-2899; Phone: 717.240.5207; Fax: 717.241.3503
E-mail: admissions@law.psu.edu; Website: www.law.psu.edu; Phone: 800.840.1122

Introduction

Founded in 1834, Penn State Law is the oldest law school in Pennsylvania and the fifth oldest in the nation. The law school embraces the university's mission to improve the lives of the people of Pennsylvania, the nation, and the world through legal teaching, scholarship, and service. Over the past few years, Penn State University has invested more than $150 million in distinguished faculty appointments, new signature facilities, and exciting new clinics.

Our law school is an engaged, diverse, and multidisciplinary intellectual community that challenges students to research, think, and act like lawyers. Through an intensive and comprehensive program of study that includes both classroom-based and experiential learning, our students are prepared to practice law at the highest level in an increasingly global world. As part of a world-class research university, Penn State Law students have access to extensive academic and programmatic resources to enhance their learning experience. Courses are offered at Penn State's University Park campus in State College, Pennsylvania, and at the law school's historic home in Carlisle, Pennsylvania.

Faculty

Penn State's faculty includes one of the nation's leading scholars of corporate mergers and acquisitions, the world's preeminent scholar of DNA evidence and issues of statistics in law, the world's preeminent expert on Russian law, leading scholars of commercial arbitration, renowned scholars of antitrust and law and economics, former law clerks to United States Supreme Court Justices, a leading scholar of international banking and finance, the first legal counsel to the African Union, the legal counsel to the Greek Presidency of the European Union, and other active and influential teachers and scholars.

Our faculty scholars value academic rigor and are committed to sharing their knowledge, engaging students, and sustaining an intense and comprehensive legal program. They encourage students to participate in vigorous in-class discussion and provide abundant opportunities for thoughtful discourse and research outside of the classroom.

Curriculum

Our curriculum is designed to produce leaders and lawyers with high professional and ethical standards and the ability to navigate legal, policy, and social developments in all areas of human endeavor. After completing required first-year coursework, students can explore professional and intellectual interests by choosing elective courses in a variety of areas, including criminal law, trial advocacy, government and politics, and science and intellectual property. Experiential learning programs, including clinics, externships, moot court teams, concentrated research opportunities, and law journals enhance the curriculum by providing opportunities for students to distinguish themselves and explore their strengths.

Academic Programs and Activities

Experiential Learning: The law school's curriculum features a wide range of experiential learning opportunities, including semester-long government agency externships in Washington, DC, and clinics that focus on child advocacy, immigrants' rights, appellate civil rights litigation, rural economic development, international sustainable development, disability law, and family law. Clinical professors include the former deputy director of the Lawyers' Committee for Civil Rights Under Law and the former deputy director of the National Immigration Forum.

Centers: Students can pursue focused scholarship through academic centers that include the Center for the Study of Mergers and Acquisitions; Institute for Sports Law, Policy, and Research; Institute of Arbitration Law and Practice; Center for Government Law and Public Policy Studies; Center on Children and the Law; and Agricultural Law Resource and Reference Center.

Joint Degrees: Students can pursue joint-degree programs and other forms of multidisciplinary study with other graduate departments within the university, including the School of International Affairs, Smeal College of Business, College of Education, and College of Agricultural Sciences.

Public Interest: In addition to our clinics, students can explore service-oriented careers through field placements with legal services, public defenders, and nonprofit public interest offices. Our Miller Center for Public Interest Advocacy works with a network of attorneys to enable students to participate in pro bono cases.

International Programs

As citizens of a global society, we provide a rich international curriculum with opportunities for immersion in international cultures and legal systems. Our integration with Penn State's School of International Affairs enriches the intellectual life of our law school and particularly our curriculum, which offers opportunities for international interactions and cross-border, interdisciplinary studies. Law students may take International Affairs electives and learn from a faculty of former diplomats, national leaders, and government analysts, as well as scholars of international economics, agricultural development, and business.

Many of our law faculty have exceptional depth in international issues, enabling the law school to offer advanced coursework in comparative and international commercial law, constitutional law, corporate law, and humanitarian law, among other areas. We have student exchange programs with the University of Cape Town in South Africa, the University of Maastricht Faculty of Law in the Netherlands, and Yeditepe University in Turkey, as well as an externship at the International Court of Justice. In partnership with leading universities worldwide, Penn State Law has produced *The World on Trial*, a public television series focused on international human rights issues. The law school also offers one of the oldest and most prestigious master of laws programs for foreign-trained lawyers, whose presence at the law school enrich the diversity of our educational experience.

Physical Facilities, Technology, and Library

The university has invested more than $120 million in new and renovated facilities for the law school in Carlisle and University Park. Our buildings reflect the serious academic nature of the study of law, with state-of-the-art libraries, classrooms, and gathering spaces that enhance opportunities for learning, spontaneous discussion, and passionate debate.

Our facilities are reciprocally designed and equipped with sophisticated and high definition audiovisual technologies that provide our students with access to technology, allow for the real-time delivery of classes and programs between Carlisle and University Park, and enable us to conduct courses and other collaborative projects with schools and institutions worldwide. In addition to electronic courtrooms, our facilities feature class and seminar rooms equipped with integrated high-definition video, personal video systems to complement the teaching experience, and advanced recording technologies. Consistent with Penn State's commitment to sustainability and "green" design, the law school buildings achieved Leadership in Energy and Environmental Design (LEED) certification requirements and encourage efficient energy use.

With holdings of more than a half-million volumes and access to a wealth of electronic resources, the Penn State Law Library fully supports the research and study activities of students, faculty, and members of the bar. Additionally, legal and interdisciplinary research is greatly enhanced through access to the vast print and electronic collections held by other university libraries.

Our building initiatives, combined with an additional several million dollars annually for faculty and program development, represent one of the largest investments ever made in an American law school.

Student Activities

Law students may pursue activities in legal scholarship, trial advocacy, and public service to refine their legal skills and develop their leadership styles. Law students edit and publish three journals: the *Penn State Law Review*, the *Penn State Journal of Law and International Affairs*, and the *Yearbook on*

Arbitration and Mediation. Second- and third-year students can also pursue valuable trial experience by engaging in moot court team competitions at both the regional and national levels. Our vibrant student body supports more than 40 active student groups that organize social events, serve the underrepresented, host speakers, and establish professional networks. Law students are also welcome to participate in the hundreds of organizations, events, and activities available at Penn State's flagship University Park campus.

Career Services

Dedicated to keeping in touch with a profession that is both fast-paced and nuanced, our Career Planning and Development Office offers a dynamic menu of programs and high-quality individual counseling sessions and programming to assist students in identifying and achieving their career goals. Our career services professionals maintain contact with employers across the country, resulting in two formal, on-campus interview programs and the posting of more than 1,500 positions annually. Students can participate in more than 20 job fairs, including one in the District of Columbia, two exclusively devoted to public interest, several minority job fairs, and one exclusively devoted to patent law.

Admission and Financial Aid

You can apply online at www.law.psu.edu. Admitted students may choose to attend first-year classes in University Park or Carlisle, Pennsylvania.

The Financial Aid Office works with accepted students to obtain the funding necessary to finance their education. All admitted students are considered for scholarship opportunities.

APPLICANT PROFILE

The Pennsylvania State University, Dickinson School of Law
This grid includes only applicants who earned 120–180 LSAT scores under standard administrations.

LSAT Score	GPA																	
	3.75 +		3.50–3.74		3.25–3.49		3.00–3.24		2.75–2.99		2.50–2.74		Below 2.50		No GPA		Total	
	Apps	Adm	Apps	Adm	Apps	Adm	Apps	Adm	Apps	Adm	Apps	Adm	Apps	Adm	Apps	Adm	Apps	Adm
170–180	12	10	5	5	5	3	8	6	2	1	5	2	2	0	0	0	39	27
165–169	51	49	53	48	43	34	38	32	21	10	17	5	15	2	8	8	246	188
160–164	142	132	201	184	210	170	163	124	81	28	51	9	30	4	25	20	903	671
155–159	223	164	407	176	425	81	290	33	153	6	61	2	51	0	40	5	1650	467
150–154	139	40	230	29	281	28	242	18	163	3	74	0	58	0	30	0	1217	118
145–149	37	0	68	0	75	0	94	0	72	0	41	0	31	0	13	0	431	0
140–144	7	0	33	0	39	0	48	0	38	0	29	0	21	0	4	0	219	0
Below 140	6	0	4	0	22	0	24	0	29	0	20	0	17	0	4	0	126	0
Total	617	395	1001	442	1100	316	907	213	559	48	298	18	225	6	124	33	4831	1471

Apps = Number of Applicants
Adm = Number Admitted
Reflects 100% of the total applicant pool; highest LSAT data reported.

PEPPERDINE UNIVERSITY SCHOOL OF LAW

24255 Pacific Coast Highway
Malibu, CA 90263
Phone: 310.506.4611; Fax: 310.506.7668
E-mail: lawadmis@pepperdine.edu; Website: http://law.pepperdine.edu

ABA
Approved
Since
1972

The Basics

Type of school	Private
Term	Semester
Application deadline	2/1 4/1
Application fee	$60
Financial aid deadline	4/1
Can first year start other than fall?	No
Student to faculty ratio	14.3 to 1
# of housing spaces available restricted to law students	
graduate housing for which law students are eligible	251

Faculty and Administrators

	Total		Men		Women		Minorities	
	Spr	Fall	Spr	Fall	Spr	Fall	Spr	Fall
Full-time	38	35	26	24	12	11	6	5
Other full-time	1	1	1	1	0	0	0	0
Deans, librarians, & others who teach	10	8	5	3	5	5	0	0
Part-time	57	59	42	48	15	11	2	2
Total	106	103	74	76	32	27	8	7

Curriculum

	Full-Time	Part-Time
Typical first-year section size	68	0
Is there typically a "small section" of the first-year class, other than Legal Writing, taught by full-time faculty	No	No
If yes, typical size offered last year		
# of classroom course titles beyond first-year curriculum	149	
# of upper division courses, excluding seminars, with an enrollment: Under 25	133	
25–49	40	
50–74	14	
75–99	6	
100+	5	
# of seminars	40	
# of seminar positions available	864	
# of seminar positions filled	542	0
# of positions available in simulation courses	2,029	
# of simulation positions filled	1,647	0
# of positions available in faculty supervised clinical courses	111	
# of faculty supervised clinical positions filled	86	0
# involved in field placements	179	0
# involved in law journals	219	0
# involved in moot court or trial competitions	116	0
# of credit hours required to graduate	88	

JD Enrollment and Ethnicity

	Men		Women		Full-Time		Part-Time		1st-Year		Total		JD Degs. Awd.
	#	%	#	%	#	%	#	%	#	%	#	%	
All Hispanics	16	5.1	23	7.2	39	6.2	0	0.0	12	6.0	39	6.2	9
Am. Ind./AK Nat.	0	0.0	0	0.0	0	0.0	0	0.0	0	0.0	0	0.0	1
Asian	25	8.0	23	7.2	48	7.6	0	0.0	15	7.5	48	7.6	16
Black/Af. Am.	4	1.3	16	5.0	20	3.2	0	0.0	11	5.5	20	3.2	14
Nat. HI/Pac. Isl.	0	0.0	0	0.0	0	0.0	0	0.0	0	0.0	0	0.0	0
2 or more races	11	3.5	17	5.3	28	4.5	0	0.0	12	6.0	28	4.5	0
Subtotal (minor.)	56	18.0	79	24.8	135	21.5	0	0.0	50	24.9	135	21.5	40
Nonres. Alien	4	1.3	9	2.8	13	2.1	0	0.0	6	3.0	13	2.1	0
White/Cauc.	192	61.7	177	55.7	369	58.7	0	0.0	115	57.2	369	58.7	139
Unknown	59	19.0	53	16.7	112	17.8	0	0.0	30	14.9	112	17.8	50
Total	311	49.4	318	50.6	629	100.0	0	0.0	201	32.0	629		229

Transfers

Transfers in	16
Transfers out	8

Tuition and Fees

	Resident	Nonresident
Full-time	$42,840	$42,840
Part-time		
Tuition Guarantee Program	N	

Living Expenses

Estimated living expenses for singles

Living on campus	Living off campus	Living at home
$25,476	$25,476	$25,476

PEPPERDINE UNIVERSITY SCHOOL OF LAW

*ABA
Approved
Since
1972*

GPA and LSAT Scores

	Total	Full-Time	Part-Time
# of apps	3,192	3,192	0
# of offers	1,078	1,078	0
# of matrics	202	202	0
75% GPA	3.78	3.78	0.00
Median GPA	3.63	3.63	0.00
25% GPA	3.33	3.33	0.00
75% LSAT	165	165	0
Median LSAT	163	163	0
25% LSAT	158	158	0

Grants and Scholarships (from prior year)

	Total #	Total %	Full-Time #	Full-Time %	Part-Time #	Part-Time %
Total # of students	667		667		0	
Total # receiving grants	470	70.5	470	70.5	0	0.0
Less than 1/2 tuition	360	54.0	360	54.0	0	0.0
Half to full tuition	91	13.6	91	13.6	0	0.0
Full tuition	0	0.0	0	0.0	0	0.0
More than full tuition	19	2.8	19	2.8	0	0.0
Median grant amount			$15,000		$0	

Informational and Library Resources

Total amount spent on library materials	$983,733
Study seating capacity inside the library	461
# of full-time equivalent professional librarians	10
Hours per week library is open	106
# of open, wired connections available to students	80
# of networked computers available for use by students	34
Has wireless network?	Y
Requires computer?	N

JD Attrition (from prior year)

	Academic #	Other #	Total #	Total %
1st year	7	13	20	9.0
2nd year	0	0	0	0.0
3rd year	0	0	0	0.0
4th year	0	0	0	0.0

Employment (9 months after graduation)

For up-to-date employment data, go to
employmentsummary.abaquestionnaire.org on the ABA website.

Bar Passage Rates

First-time takers	202	Reporting %	89.60
Average school %	87.29	Average state %	71.24
Average pass difference	16.05		

Jurisdiction	Takers	Passers	Pass %	State %	Diff %
California	181	158	87.29	71.24	16.05

PEPPERDINE UNIVERSITY SCHOOL OF LAW

24255 Pacific Coast Highway
Malibu, CA 90263
Phone: 310.506.4611; Fax: 310.506.7668
E-mail: lawadmis@pepperdine.edu; Website: http://law.pepperdine.edu

Introduction

Pepperdine School of Law is located in Malibu, California, just 30 miles from downtown Los Angeles, making it a conducive environment for the intense study of law. Malibu offers an almost rural setting, yet it is an integral part of greater Los Angeles, providing access to one of the largest legal communities in the world. Pepperdine is a Christian university committed to the highest standards of academic excellence and Christian values, where students are strengthened for lives of purpose, service, and leadership.

Student Body

Pepperdine students bring a broad spectrum of backgrounds. They share a strong desire to attain high levels of achievement in academics, their personal lives, and their careers. Students come to Pepperdine from diverse socioeconomic, cultural, and religious backgrounds for the emphasis on integrity, service, and justice with a desire to become trusted leaders.

Faculty

Although the faculty have distinguished themselves through scholarly research and writing as well as leadership positions in prestigious legal organizations, the faculty's primary mission is to teach—to help students see the structure of legal thought and to be available as professional examples of a multifaceted profession. They demonstrate to their students that lawyers should be people-oriented individuals with strong moral character, capable of guiding their clients toward what is just and honorable as well as what is legally permissible.

Library and Physical Facilities

The School of Law occupies the Odell McConnell Law Center, located on the university's 830-acre campus overlooking the Pacific Ocean. The Jerene Appleby Harnish Library is the focal point of the school, housing a collection of over 400,000 volumes and volume equivalents. Students enjoy access to a multitude of leading online legal research services. Wireless network access is available throughout the Law Center. The facility contains two high-tech courtrooms, as well as lecture halls, seminar rooms, a bookstore, student dining area, and lounges.

Curriculum

Pepperdine offers a three-year, full-time JD program; four-year, full-time JD/MBA and JD/MPP dual-degree programs; a five-year, full-time JD/MDiv dual-degree program; a concurrent JD/MDR-degree program; and an LLM in Dispute Resolution. A student enrolled full time in a summer session can accelerate graduation by one semester. The required core courses are complemented by an extensive selection of elective courses.

The Palmer Center for Entrepreneurship and the Law

Unique in the nation, the Palmer Center prepares students for the modern hybrid role of lawyer, business consultant, financial strategist, and venture capitalist, and equips them with credentials and options in the field of entrepreneurship. Through carefully tailored coursework, the Palmer Center integrates multifaceted law and business disciplines into a distinctive and dynamic certificate program that supplements and complements the traditional JD degree.

Straus Institute for Dispute Resolution

The Straus Institute is the most comprehensive program of its type in the nation. Students studying in the field of dispute resolution can complete a special certificate program as part of their Juris Doctor degree or a Master's in Dispute Resolution. The LLM in Dispute Resolution began January 2003.

Nootbaar Institute on Law, Religion, and Ethics

The Nootbaar Institute was created to explore the nexus between these three disciplines, with particular emphasis on religion and the practice of law. While affirming Pepperdine's Christian identity, the institute draws from the largest possible pool of religious voices, seeking dialogue and common ground with other faith traditions.

Global Justice Program

The Global Justice Program partners with a global network of foreign judicial systems, human rights agencies, development organizations, and international universities. The partnerships provide the framework for a variety of initiatives, including juvenile justice, judicial reform, antihuman trafficking efforts, and human rights advocacy. Through these initiatives, students and faculty collaborate to seek justice and create a lasting impact in some of the world's most vulnerable places. Under the umbrella of the Herbert and Elinor Nootbaar Institute for Law, Religion, and Ethics, the Global Justice Program is growing rapidly in response to student interest and demand from global partners.

Clinical Education

Clinical law programs provide students with the opportunity to refine their skills under the supervision of faculty, lawyers, and judges. The majority of clinical law opportunities are with district attorneys, public defenders, and state and federal court judges. There are a number of programs offering experience in corporate and securities law, tax law, juvenile law, family law, labor law, consumer protection, environmental law, and trade regulation. Placements are also available within the film, television, and music industries.

Career Development Office

The Career Development Office (CDO) assists students as they navigate their transition from student to professional. Experienced staff is available for individual appointments to discuss job-search strategies, résumé-writing and interviewing skills, networking opportunities, and other aspects of career counseling. In addition, throughout the academic year, the CDO offers workshops and programs designed to illuminate the job-search process. The CDO frequently hosts guest speakers, providing students with the opportunity to talk directly with professionals currently working in specific areas of interest. Each fall and spring, employers visit Pepperdine to interview interested law students for full-time summer and postgraduate positions.

Public Interest Opportunities

Pepperdine has partnered with the Los Angeles Union Rescue Mission to develop the Pepperdine/Union Rescue Mission Legal Aid Clinic. Located in downtown Los Angeles, the mission provides emergency food and shelter, health services, recovery programs, education, job training, and counseling within a Christian context. Students volunteer at the mission, where they meet with residents regarding legal concerns. The Pepperdine/Union Rescue Mission Family Law Clinic helps clients resolve issues such as child custody and support. The Special Education Advocacy Clinic gives students an opportunity to gain valuable experience advocating for children with disabilities. The Asylum Clinic provides law student representation to indigent and near-indigent foreign-born individuals who seek to legalize their status in the United States based on their fear of religious and other persecution abroad. The clinic provides students real-world experience in immigration law and litigation, and also provides advocacy for persons of faith as well as other vulnerable persons.

London Program

Students have the opportunity to study law in London at Pepperdine's university-owned facility in the museum district of South Kensington. While in London, students may serve as externs in clinical placements.

Exchange Programs

Students have the opportunity to participate in exchange programs with the University of Copenhagen in Denmark and the University of Augsburg in Germany. Classes are taught in English in both programs.

Student Activities

Pepperdine has earned a national reputation for excellence in appellate advocacy and trial advocacy competitions. Editorial and staff positions are awarded for the *Pepperdine Law*

Review, Pepperdine Dispute Resolution Law Journal, National Association of Administrative Law Judges Journal, and the *Journal of Business, Entrepreneurship, and the Law.*

Wm. Matthew Byrne Jr. Judicial Clerkship Institute

Each year, Pepperdine University School of Law brings law students from across the country to its campus for the Wm. Matthew Byrne Jr. Judicial Clerkship Institute (Byrne JCI). Through the Byrne JCI, students who have been accepted into federal judicial clerkship positions have the opportunity to gain distinctive, comprehensive training by federal judges.

Admission

Admission is based on the applicant's academic record, LSAT score, and a written personal statement, as well as a response to the university's mission statement and other information that reflects outstanding academic and professional promise. Applications are also evaluated on the basis of employment experience, extracurricular activities, community involvement, commitment to high standards of morality and ethics, maturity, initiative, and motivation. The admission process is guided by the view that a student body that reflects diversity provides a superior educational environment. Admission decisions may be based on consideration of factors that include racial and ethnic origin, unique work or service experience, a history of overcoming disadvantage, or unusual life experiences. First-year students are admitted only in the fall.

Expenses and Financial Aid

Pepperdine's active financial aid program provides over 85 percent of the student body with some type of assistance. Scholarships are available to students with outstanding academic credentials and to those with demonstrated financial need. The deadline for completed applications for financial aid is April 1 of the entering year.

Housing

The George Page Residential Complex is located directly across the street from the Law Center. The 72-unit complex houses graduate students in four-bedroom apartments. The Admission Office also provides an extensive housing referral service.

APPLICANT PROFILE

Pepperdine University School of Law
This grid includes only applicants who earned 120–180 LSAT scores under standard administrations.

LSAT Score	3.75 +		3.50–3.74		3.25–3.49		3.00–3.24		2.75–2.99		2.50–2.74		Below 2.50		No GPA		Total	
	Apps	Adm	Apps	Adm	Apps	Adm	Apps	Adm	Apps	Adm	Apps	Adm	Apps	Adm	Apps	Adm	Apps	Adm
175–180	2	2	1	1	1	1	0	0	0	0	2	1	1	0	0	0	7	5
170–174	24	21	18	15	14	13	13	12	3	1	3	0	3	1	0	0	78	63
165–169	119	110	112	101	77	69	51	46	30	14	14	2	5	0	5	3	413	345
160–164	156	148	238	172	202	81	120	43	53	9	22	2	24	1	14	1	829	457
155–159	151	82	253	64	194	9	141	9	72	3	36	2	21	0	9	0	877	169
150–154	64	7	83	4	114	3	110	4	51	1	35	0	32	0	5	0	494	19
Below 150	27	1	71	5	84	0	118	1	92	0	66	0	41	0	10	0	509	7
Total	543	371	776	362	686	176	553	115	301	28	178	7	127	2	43	4	3207	1065

Apps = Number of Applicants
Adm = Number Admitted
Reflects 100% of the total applicant pool; highest LSAT data reported.

PHOENIX SCHOOL OF LAW

One North Central Avenue
Phoenix, AZ 85004
Phone: 602.682.6800; Fax: 602.682.6999
E-mail: admissions@phoenixlaw.edu; Website: www.phoenixlaw.edu

The Basics

Type of school	Private
Term	Semester
Application deadline	
Application fee	$50
Financial aid deadline	
Can first year start other than fall?	Yes
Student to faculty ratio	18.3 to 1
# of housing spaces available restricted to law students	
graduate housing for which law students are eligible	

Faculty and Administrators

	Total		Men		Women		Minorities	
	Spr	Fall	Spr	Fall	Spr	Fall	Spr	Fall
Full-time	29	32	11	13	18	19	9	12
Other full-time	1	3	0	1	1	2	0	0
Deans, librarians, & others who teach	4	2	1	0	3	2	3	2
Part-time	26	29	20	16	6	13	5	7
Total	60	66	32	30	28	36	17	21

Curriculum

		Full-Time	Part-Time
Typical first-year section size		62	58
Is there typically a "small section" of the first-year class, other than Legal Writing, taught by full-time faculty		No	No
If yes, typical size offered last year			
# of classroom course titles beyond first-year curriculum		60	
# of upper division courses, excluding seminars, with an enrollment:	Under 25	95	
	25–49	30	
	50–74	15	
	75–99	0	
	100+	0	
# of seminars		5	
# of seminar positions available		100	
# of seminar positions filled		46	31
# of positions available in simulation courses		200	
# of simulation positions filled		88	44
# of positions available in faculty supervised clinical courses		180	
# of faculty supervised clinical positions filled		65	8
# involved in field placements		127	14
# involved in law journals		45	20
# involved in moot court or trial competitions		8	3
# of credit hours required to graduate		87	

JD Enrollment and Ethnicity

	Men		Women		Full-Time		Part-Time		1st-Year		Total		JD Degs. Awd.
	#	%	#	%	#	%	#	%	#	%	#	%	
All Hispanics	67	13.1	70	15.3	108	15.5	29	10.7	87	16.5	137	14.1	17
Am. Ind./AK Nat.	5	1.0	6	1.3	10	1.4	1	0.4	6	1.1	11	1.1	1
Asian	19	3.7	30	6.6	38	5.5	11	4.0	22	4.2	49	5.1	8
Black/Af. Am.	26	5.1	44	9.6	48	6.9	22	8.1	45	8.6	70	7.2	6
Nat. HI/Pac. Isl.	2	0.4	1	0.2	2	0.3	1	0.4	3	0.6	3	0.3	0
2 or more races	9	1.8	9	2.0	14	2.0	4	1.5	13	2.5	18	1.9	0
Subtotal (minor.)	128	25.0	160	34.9	220	31.6	68	25.0	176	33.5	288	29.7	32
Nonres. Alien	2	0.4	6	1.3	7	1.0	1	0.4	3	0.6	8	0.8	0
White/Cauc.	340	66.5	266	58.1	426	61.1	180	66.2	323	61.4	606	62.5	84
Unknown	41	8.0	26	5.7	44	6.3	23	8.5	24	4.6	67	6.9	15
Total	511	52.7	458	47.3	697	71.9	272	28.1	526	54.3	969		131

Transfers

Transfers in	11
Transfers out	31

Tuition and Fees

	Resident	Nonresident
Full-time	$37,764	
Part-time	$30,540	
Tuition Guarantee Program		N

Living Expenses

Estimated living expenses for singles

Living on campus	Living off campus	Living at home
N/A	$26,100	N/A

ABA Approved Since 2007

GPA and LSAT Scores

	Total	Full-Time	Part-Time
# of apps	2,299	2,039	260
# of offers	1,677	1,512	165
# of matrics	450	371	79
75% GPA	3.32	3.32	3.39
Median GPA	3.05	3.04	3.09
25% GPA	2.70	2.70	2.53
75% LSAT	151	151	152
Median LSAT	148	148	148
25% LSAT	146	146	146

Grants and Scholarships (from prior year)

	Total #	Total %	Full-Time #	Full-Time %	Part-Time #	Part-Time %
Total # of students	724		514		210	
Total # receiving grants	411	56.8	312	60.7	99	47.1
Less than 1/2 tuition	390	53.9	296	57.6	94	44.8
Half to full tuition	19	2.6	15	2.9	4	1.9
Full tuition	0	0.0	0	0.0	0	0.0
More than full tuition	2	0.3	1	0.2	1	0.5
Median grant amount			$7,000		$5,500	

Informational and Library Resources

Total amount spent on library materials	$839,351
Study seating capacity inside the library	212
# of full-time equivalent professional librarians	7
Hours per week library is open	107
# of open, wired connections available to students	0
# of networked computers available for use by students	19
Has wireless network?	Y
Requires computer?	Y

JD Attrition (from prior year)

	Academic #	Other #	Total #	Total %
1st year	22	34	56	11.8
2nd year	7	5	12	8.8
3rd year	0	1	1	1.0
4th year	0	0	0	0.0

Employment (9 months after graduation)

For up-to-date employment data, go to employmentsummary.abaquestionnaire.org on the ABA website.

Bar Passage Rates

First-time takers	68	Reporting %	100.00
Average school %	76.46	Average state %	80.51

Average pass difference –4.05

Jurisdiction	Takers	Passers	Pass %	State %	Diff %
Arizona	60	47	78.33	80.74	–2.41
California	3	0	0.00	71.24	–71.24
Michigan	1	1	100.00	84.83	15.17
New Jersey	1	1	100.00	82.34	17.66
Others (3)	3	3	100.00		

PHOENIX SCHOOL OF LAW

One North Central Avenue
Phoenix, AZ 85004
Phone: 602.682.6800; Fax: 602.682.6999
E-mail: admissions@phoenixlaw.edu; Website: www.phoenixlaw.edu

Introduction to Phoenix School of Law

At Phoenix School of Law, our overarching commitment is to our students. Our faculty, staff, students, and alumni are passionate about our three-part mission:

(1) An educational experience that is student-outcome centered.

Our faculty, staff, students, and alumni share a responsibility to help students develop the values, skills, and knowledge required of legal professionals. Recognizing the rigors of a legal education, every member of the PhoenixLaw community contributes to our intellectually demanding, supportive, multicultural learning environment. PhoenixLaw also fosters a culture of humility, transparency, dignity, fairness, and respect.

(2) Outcome-driven programs and experiences that yield professionally prepared graduates.

In addition to the traditional emphasis on doctrine, critical thinking, and writing skills, at PhoenixLaw we impart real-world experience. By focusing on the practical skills and methodologies of law practice, combined with the faculty and staff's accountability for market-leading student outcomes, we prepare our students to be effective lawyers and give them a head start in legal practice.

(3) A commitment to serving underserved communities and student populations.

This premise has a broad spectrum, and begins with the location of PhoenixLaw in a community that historically has been underserved by legal education. It continues by immersing PhoenixLaw students in a culture that encourages service to individuals and groups that have historically been underserved by the legal profession. We impart to our students the understanding that the ability to interact effectively with persons of diverse backgrounds and experiences is a significant skill necessary for their success.

PhoenixLaw is a community of accomplished students, notable alumni, distinguished faculty, and experienced staff. We provide an exceptional law school education and experience to our students, setting ourselves apart on the basis of our outcomes and our culture. We welcome you to join our dynamic community.

Full- and Part-Time Programs

At Phoenix School of Law, students have the flexibility of three program options to pursue their legal education: full-time day, part-time day, and part-time evening. Full-time faculty members teach all program options. Additionally, all of our students benefit from our adjunct professors who share their practical knowledge based on their firsthand experiences as law practitioners in the Phoenix metro area. In addition to the fall, spring, and optional summer semester, Phoenix School of Law offers students the opportunity to take elective courses during three, one-week intersessions.

Admission

Phoenix School of Law admits students after a careful and thorough application evaluation. Highly qualified applicants typically are admitted first. Admission decisions may include attention to factors that enhance the educational experience of the entire student body. The Admissions Committee weighs all characteristics bearing upon the ability of an applicant to study law successfully. Undergraduate grades and majors, the difficulty of the undergraduate field of study, LSAT scores, personal statements, and letters of recommendation are important. Additionally, Phoenix School of Law evaluates other criteria, such as work and life experiences, accomplishments, graduate study and degrees, the LSAT writing sample, and other factors that may provide meaningful insight into the applicant's potential to succeed in law school.

Curriculum

The faculty and administration at the Phoenix School of Law believe that students must be exposed to traditional theory, practical skills, and ethical instruction in a variety of different ways that extend beyond the classroom in order to create law graduates who are professionally prepared. At PhoenixLaw, there are several main areas of focus for experiential learning:

Infusion of Skills and Values: Since the School of Law's inception, faculty members have taken a coordinated approach to teaching key skills and values as part of their courses. PhoenixLaw faculty members have assumed responsibility for teaching 17 specific skills throughout the core curriculum.

General Practice Skills: As a requirement for graduation, all students must satisfactorily complete a capstone course—the General Practice Skills (GPS) course. The course's objective is to infuse skills and values essential to the practice of law in the final year course curriculum. The course is taught by adjunct professors who are all practicing attorneys in the local legal community.

Clinical and Externship Programs: The goals of these programs include teaching practice-ready professional skills and values, promoting pro bono service to underserved segments of the community, and providing students with opportunities to engage in small group/collaborative work, while exposing students to the rich tapestry of legal service opportunities. An additional goal is that through the clinical and externship experience, each student will demonstrate improved skills of learning from practice and will have developed a strong commitment to the value of lifelong learning in the practice of law. The PhoenixLaw Clinics include the Mediation Clinic, Veterans Tax Clinic, Veterans Legal Assistance Clinic, Human Rights and Immigration Clinic, American Indian Law Clinic, Juvenile Defense Clinic, and the Municipal Prosecution Clinic.

Faculty

The faculty at the Phoenix School of Law are an extraordinary and diverse staff of professors who are dedicated to providing every student with academic support and mentorship. Educated at some of the best law schools around the nation, they have a wide range of special interests and have worked in large private firms, government agencies, public interest organizations, and as judicial clerks. Our faculty also includes several retired judges. The PhoenixLaw faculty is actively involved in scholarship and public service, but their first priority is teaching our students.

Mentoring Programs

Upon starting classes at PhoenixLaw, each student is assigned a faculty mentor. This mentor helps guide the student through his or her law school experience and develop a professional relationship that extends beyond the classroom and to the student's career. Mentors act as advisors, assisting the student in understanding and applying policies and procedures, accessing information, and pursuing appropriate avenues to obtain information and approvals. Mentoring is also provided via various student organizations, where 2L and 3L students assist the 1Ls by guiding them through their first year of law school.

Critical Legal Skills and Bar Exam Preparation

Helping students to succeed in law school is the goal of PhoenixLaw's Critical Legal Skills (CLS) program. The CLS staff provides classes and workshops, as well as small-group and individual academic support counseling to assist students in:
- adjusting to a rigorous legal learning environment;
- developing time management and stress management skills to meet the personal tasks and academic demands of law school;
- identifying individualized learning style preferences to enhance efficiency and effectiveness in academics and practice;
- developing the necessary study skills, classroom preparation, and exam preparation tools to succeed in law school;
- maximizing effective writing, analytical, oratory, and legal reasoning skills;
- passing the bar examination by offering a comprehensive bar strategies course to ensure that students understand the bar review and exam process.

Career Services

PhoenixLaw's Center for Professional Development (CPD) is a full-service career counseling and resource center, committed to assisting each student in identifying, developing, and attaining his or her individual career goals. Students meet with a member of the CPD staff in their first year to discuss unique career-planning goals and to develop effective job-search strategies. Individual counseling sessions are supplemented by career-planning workshops and programs, including résumé and cover letter workshops, interview skills workshops, networking skills workshops, career panels, and mock interview programs, to name a few.

CPD offers a comprehensive recruitment program that brings students together with employers and provides them with opportunities to gain practical experience. Each semester CPD hosts employers for on-campus interviews, performs résumé collections, and distributes weekly job postings. The variety of recruitment opportunities for employers has resulted in the placement of PhoenixLaw graduates in large and regional private firms, judicial clerkships, government agencies, public interest groups, and the business sector.

Library and Information Technology

The Phoenix School of Law Library subscribes to several electronic databases and provides workshops and training throughout the year to supplement research skills that students learn in their legal writing courses and other classes. The law library is continuously expanding its collection, including multiple formats, such as electronic, print, and audio, to best accommodate each student's learning style and maximize results.

PhoenixLaw employs the latest technology to make learning more effective for our students. From state-of-the-art classrooms, intranet, and wireless technology, to smart boards and podcasting, our Information Technology Department is continually implementing new ways to enhance the learning experience.

APPLICANT PROFILE

Phoenix School of Law

LSAT Score	GPA									
	3.75 +	3.50–3.74	3.25–3.49	3.00–3.24	2.75–2.99	2.50–2.74	2.25–2.49	2.00–2.24	Below 2.00	No GPA
175–180	■	■	■	■	■	■	■	□	▨	▨
170–174	■	■	■	■	■	■	■	□	▨	▨
165–169	■	■	■	■	■	■	■	□	▨	▨
160–164	■	■	■	■	■	■	■	□	▨	▨
157–159	■	■	■	■	■	■	□	▨	▨	▨
154–156	■	■	■	■	■	■	□	▨	▨	▨
150–153	■	■	■	■	■	□	▨	▨	▨	▨
145–149	□	□	□	□	□	□	▨	▨	▨	▨
140–144	▨	▨	▨	▨	▨	▨	▨	▨	▨	▨
135–139	▨	▨	▨	▨	▨	▨	▨	▨	▨	▨
130–134	▨	▨	▨	▨	▨	▨	▨	▨	▨	▨
125–129	▨	▨	▨	▨	▨	▨	▨	▨	▨	▨
120–124	▨	▨	▨	▨	▨	▨	▨	▨	▨	▨

■ Good Possibility □ Possible ▨ Unlikely

The information contained in this chart should be used as an estimated guide as to the likelihood of admission. The Admissions Committee engages in a holistic review of all information submitted by candidates for admission. LSAT and UGPA are not the sole determinants for admission.

UNIVERSITY OF PITTSBURGH SCHOOL OF LAW

3900 Forbes Avenue, Barco Law Building
Pittsburgh, PA 15260
Phone: 412.648.1413; Fax: 412.648.1318
E-mail: admitlaw@pitt.edu; Website: www.law.pitt.edu

*ABA
Approved
Since
1923*

The Basics

Type of school	Public
Term	Semester
Application deadline	3/1
Application fee	$55
Financial aid deadline	3/1
Can first year start other than fall?	No
Student to faculty ratio	14.0 to 1
# of housing spaces available restricted to law students	
graduate housing for which law students are eligible	

Faculty and Administrators

	Total		Men		Women		Minorities	
	Spr	Fall	Spr	Fall	Spr	Fall	Spr	Fall
Full-time	44	40	24	22	20	18	4	5
Other full-time	3	4	3	3	0	1	0	0
Deans, librarians, & others who teach	11	11	4	4	7	7	0	0
Part-time	61	52	46	37	15	15	4	3
Total	119	107	77	66	42	41	8	8

Curriculum

		Full-Time	Part-Time
Typical first-year section size		87	0
Is there typically a "small section" of the first-year class, other than Legal Writing, taught by full-time faculty		No	No
If yes, typical size offered last year			
# of classroom course titles beyond first-year curriculum		200	
# of upper division courses, excluding seminars, with an enrollment:	Under 25	122	
	25–49	28	
	50–74	14	
	75–99	8	
	100+	3	
# of seminars		22	
# of seminar positions available		287	
# of seminar positions filled		235	0
# of positions available in simulation courses		264	
# of simulation positions filled		209	0
# of positions available in faculty supervised clinical courses		188	
# of faculty supervised clinical positions filled		179	0
# involved in field placements		205	0
# involved in law journals		190	0
# involved in moot court or trial competitions		112	0
# of credit hours required to graduate		88	

JD Enrollment and Ethnicity

	Men		Women		Full-Time		Part-Time		1st-Year		Total		JD Degs. Awd.
	#	%	#	%	#	%	#	%	#	%	#	%	
All Hispanics	6	1.5	10	3.4	16	2.3	0	0.0	6	2.7	16	2.3	8
Am. Ind./AK Nat.	0	0.0	1	0.3	1	0.1	0	0.0	1	0.4	1	0.1	1
Asian	11	2.7	14	4.8	25	3.6	0	0.0	2	0.9	25	3.6	20
Black/Af. Am.	27	6.6	31	10.7	58	8.3	0	0.0	22	9.7	58	8.3	14
Nat. HI/Pac. Isl.	0	0.0	0	0.0	0	0.0	0	0.0	0	0.0	0	0.0	0
2 or more races	0	0.0	3	1.0	3	0.4	0	0.0	2	0.9	3	0.4	0
Subtotal (minor.)	44	10.7	59	20.3	103	14.7	0	0.0	33	14.6	103	14.7	43
Nonres. Alien	0	0.0	0	0.0	0	0.0	0	0.0	0	0.0	0	0.0	0
White/Cauc.	247	60.2	156	53.6	403	57.5	0	0.0	117	51.8	403	57.5	166
Unknown	119	29.0	76	26.1	195	27.8	0	0.0	76	33.6	195	27.8	45
Total	410	58.5	291	41.5	701	100.0	0	0.0	226	32.2	701		254

Transfers

Transfers in	10
Transfers out	10

Tuition and Fees

	Resident	Nonresident
Full-time	$28,734	$35,508
Part-time		
Tuition Guarantee Program	N	

Living Expenses

Estimated living expenses for singles

Living on campus	Living off campus	Living at home
$16,960	$16,960	$16,960

UNIVERSITY OF PITTSBURGH SCHOOL OF LAW

*ABA
Approved
Since
1923*

GPA and LSAT Scores

	Total	Full-Time	Part-Time
# of apps	2,379	2,379	0
# of offers	868	868	0
# of matrics	230	230	0
75% GPA	3.66	3.66	0.00
Median GPA	3.45	3.45	0.00
25% GPA	3.14	3.14	0.00
75% LSAT	161	161	0
Median LSAT	159	159	0
25% LSAT	157	157	0

Grants and Scholarships (from prior year)

	Total #	Total %	Full-Time #	Full-Time %	Part-Time #	Part-Time %
Total # of students	739		739		0	
Total # receiving grants	396	53.6	396	53.6	0	0.0
Less than 1/2 tuition	280	37.9	280	37.9	0	0.0
Half to full tuition	109	14.7	109	14.7	0	0.0
Full tuition	4	0.5	4	0.5	0	0.0
More than full tuition	3	0.4	3	0.4	0	0.0
Median grant amount			$12,000		$0	

Informational and Library Resources

Total amount spent on library materials	$946,596
Study seating capacity inside the library	425
# of full-time equivalent professional librarians	16
Hours per week library is open	101
# of open, wired connections available to students	140
# of networked computers available for use by students	57
Has wireless network?	Y
Requires computer?	N

JD Attrition (from prior year)

	Academic #	Other #	Total #	Total %
1st year	0	10	10	3.9
2nd year	2	0	2	0.9
3rd year	0	0	0	0.0
4th year	0	0	0	0.0

Employment (9 months after graduation)

For up-to-date employment data, go to
employmentsummary.abaquestionnaire.org on the ABA website.

Bar Passage Rates

First-time takers	199	Reporting %	81.91
Average school %	86.50	Average state %	83.06
Average pass difference	3.44		

Jurisdiction	Takers	Passers	Pass %	State %	Diff %
Pennsylvania	163	141	86.50	83.06	3.44

UNIVERSITY OF PITTSBURGH SCHOOL OF LAW

3900 Forbes Avenue, Barco Law Building
Pittsburgh, PA 15260
Phone: 412.648.1413; Fax: 412.648.1318
E-mail: admitlaw@pitt.edu; Website: www.law.pitt.edu

Introduction

The University of Pittsburgh School of Law (Pitt Law), founded in 1895, is a leader in legal education. It features a broad and varied curriculum, an internationally accomplished faculty, state-of-the-art physical facilities, and a talented and diverse student body hailing from all over the globe. Pitt Law is located in its own six-story building on campus in Oakland, the cultural and educational center of Pittsburgh. State and federal courts, major corporate headquarters, and hundreds of law firms are located nearby in downtown Pittsburgh, only minutes from campus. The dynamic Oakland area is home to four colleges and universities; the world-renowned, multihospital University of Pittsburgh Medical Center; numerous scientific and high-tech offices and research centers; museums; art galleries; coffee houses; and libraries. The Pitt campus abuts a beautiful 429-acre city park. Desirable and affordable residential areas are situated nearby and all mass transit in the city is free to Pitt students.

Faculty

Without question, one of the most invigorating aspects of attending Pitt Law is the faculty. Students have the opportunity to work with and alongside some of the finest legal scholars in the world. While Pitt Law's faculty are known nationally and internationally for their legal scholarship, Pitt Law students appreciate how accessible and committed to teaching they are.

Library and Physical Facilities

The Barco Law Library is an attractive, 450,000-volume, open-stack research facility housed on three floors of the School of Law building. Classrooms with state-of-the-art technology are located on the first and ground floors of the School of Law building.

In spring 2011, construction was completed on the student lounge, which provides a multipurpose space for students to study, socialize, and relax between classes. The new space offers a Starbucks coffee shop with "grab-n-go" food items, ample seating, a new student organization office suite that offers both collaborative and private work environments, new student lockers to better accommodate books and personal items, comfortable couches and chairs that promote student gathering, soft lighting, and increased electrical access for laptop use. This newly built-out space is adjacent to the Teplitz Memorial Courtroom where moot court sessions are held.

Curricular and Special Programs

Unlike the harsh, competitive stereotype of law school, Pitt Law fosters a spirit of personal achievement and collaboration. The courses are challenging and the standards are high, but students find the professors are encouraging and motivating. Rather than a culture that thrives on creating stress, Pitt Law offers an educational atmosphere of creativity, openness, growth, and excellence.

- *Clinical Programs*—Academics and reality meet head-on in our legal clinics. Pitt Law students have the opportunity to obtain hands-on experience in several clinical programs, including a Tax Clinic; an Environmental Law Clinic; a Civil Practice Clinic with a focus on either Health Law or Elder Law; a Family Law Clinic; a Securities and Arbitration Clinic; and an Immigration Law Clinic. With a supervising attorney, students do it all: pretrial preparation, negotiation, litigation, and counseling real-life clients about real-life legal concerns.
- *Programs of Specialized Study*—One way to prepare for law practice in an increasingly complex society is to develop specialized expertise. Pitt Law students may seize that advantage through participation in diverse programs of specialized study that permit students to focus their studies in high-demand areas of practice. Pitt Law has such programs in the areas of civil litigation; environmental law, science, and policy; health law; international and comparative law; and intellectual property and technology law.
- *Joint-Degree Programs*—Prompted by the recognized value of attorneys who work effectively across disciplines, we offer several joint-degree programs that provide rigorous, integrated training, effectively merging law and a number of allied fields. They include the JD/MBA with both Pitt and Carnegie Mellon University; the JD/MPH with our Graduate School of Public Health; the JD/MPA, JD/MPIA, and JD/MID with our Graduate School of Public and International Affairs; the JD/MA (Bioethics); the JD/MSW (Social Work); and the JD/MSPPM and JD/MAM with the Heinz College at Carnegie Mellon University.
- *Semester in DC*—Pitt Law students can spend a semester working for a nonprofit or government agency in Washington, DC, while earning a full semester's worth of academic credit. The DC Externship Program allows students to combine supervised field work with a government or nonprofit employer, a related academic seminar, and the option of earning additional credit by pursuing an independent study related to the externship. Members of the Pitt Law alumni network are eager to serve as mentors to Pitt Law students, and many DC area employers are interested in receiving externship applications from Pitt Law students.
- *Innovation Practice Institute (IPI)*—Pitt Law is uniquely situated amid some of the world's leading innovators in fields ranging from regenerative medicine to robotics, to entertainment technology, to alternative energy and green building. Taking advantage of this environment, IPI gives Pitt Law students the opportunity to immerse themselves in experiential, cross-disciplinary, project-based learning to develop the skills and confidence to participate as professionals in the innovation culture and economy.

Center for International Legal Education (CILE)

In today's world, legal problems regularly involve many nations and many sets of laws. Today's global lawyer understands the political, cultural, and social influences on the legal systems of other countries and uses that knowledge for the benefit of his or her clients. CILE faculty prepare Pitt Law students for successful futures in tomorrow's world. Students study the workings of foreign legal systems and explore the wide array of issues facing practicing attorneys in the global marketplace. The center also coordinates international programs at Pitt with the University Center for

International Studies and affiliated area studies programs, and it supervises a number of specialized language classes, such as French for Lawyers, Spanish for Lawyers, German for Lawyers, and Chinese for Lawyers.

Student Activities

The *University of Pittsburgh Law Review*, the *Journal of Law and Commerce*, and the *Journal of Technology Law and Policy* are among the journals published by law students. More than 30 law student organizations thrive at Pitt Law, reflecting the diverse social and intellectual interests and experiences of our students. They include the Asian Law Students Association, the Black Law Students Association, the Environmental Law Council, the Federalist Society, the Hispanic Law Society, the Jewish Law Students Association, the Lesbian-Gay Rights Organization (OUTLAW), the Pitt Law Women's Association, and the Pitt Legal Income Sharing Foundation, among others.

Career Services

The Career Services Office (CSO) provides year-round assistance to Pitt Law students and graduates. The office serves as a clearinghouse for information on summer, part-time, and permanent work with law firms, corporations, accounting firms, government agencies, judges, and other legal employers. It also helps students develop practical job-search strategies, helps demystify the dynamics of the legal job market, offers strategies for finding the perfect job in that market, and offers information and counseling regarding nontraditional careers utilizing professional skills gained in law school. The CSO works closely with Pitt Law's Alumni Office to create opportunities for students to connect with our large network of alumni.

Admission and Financial Aid

Pitt Law has a highly competitive admission process and decision-making is based upon several factors; the GPA and LSAT scores serve as the most important of those. When evaluating an undergraduate degree, the admission committee pays careful attention to the strength of the major field of study, looking specifically for a prospective student to have shown evidence of discipline and the ability to handle a rigorous and demanding program. The same assessment is made of graduate and professional work. A required personal statement provides a view into the nonacademic world of the applicant. This is critical to Pitt Law's ability to enroll a diverse class—students with various backgrounds and a range of experiences. Similarly, letters of recommendation and résumés provide a broader view of the applicant's accomplishments. Applicants are reviewed on a rolling notification basis. Pitt Law assists accepted students in securing the financial resources needed to cover the cost of their legal education. Approximately half of the student body receives merit or need-based scholarships. Pitt Law also offers a Public Interest Scholarship and numerous named scholarships. All students admitted to Pitt Law are automatically considered for scholarships and notifications of awards are included in their acceptance letters.

The City of Pittsburgh

Today Pittsburgh is spectacular—a thriving business center and a high-tech hotbed rated America's most livable city in 2011! Our campus is at the center of it all. We are a stroll away from wonderfully diverse neighborhoods, acres of parks, scores of restaurants and shops, three major league sports arenas, movies, museums, galleries, dance clubs, coffee houses, and riverside cafés, and that's just the short list. A quick commute on your bike takes you to the nucleus of the law and business community in downtown Pittsburgh. You'll also find the heart of the cultural district downtown, offering world-class theater, opera, symphony, ballet, and dance. For a law student, Pittsburgh is a lot more than a livable city—it's a context for building a strong career. There is no finer preparation for law than learning in a setting that gives you a wealth of opportunity to put theory into practice. Pittsburgh is the global headquarters for Fortune 500 corporations, home to one of the nation's largest medical centers, a hub of public policy interest, and host to more than 2,500 high technology companies—all served by a robust and sophisticated practicing bar. Pitt Law's location near the heart of the legal community makes practitioners accessible as mentors in the classroom and models in the field and permits many students to get real legal experience while still in school.

APPLICANT PROFILE

University of Pittsburgh School of Law
This grid includes only applicants who earned 120–180 LSAT scores under standard administrations.

LSAT Score	GPA															
	3.75 +		3.50–3.74		3.25–3.49		3.00–3.24		2.75–2.99		2.50–2.74		Below 2.50		No GPA		Total	
	Apps	Adm	Apps	Adm	Apps	Adm	Apps	Adm	Apps	Adm	Apps	Adm	Apps	Adm	Apps	Adm	Apps	Adm
170–180	11	9	7	4	6	5	7	5	3	2	4	2	5	0	1	1	44	28
165–169	53	40	52	36	38	22	16	3	15	4	10	5	5	1	5	2	194	113
160–164	104	82	145	115	120	93	99	56	45	27	27	14	12	4	17	9	569	400
155–159	112	55	227	101	198	68	109	27	55	12	21	4	11	0	17	3	750	270
150–154	58	8	87	7	118	13	113	12	40	7	24	2	21	0	7	0	468	49
145–149	20	1	30	3	30	0	37	1	39	1	18	0	16	0	6	0	196	6
140–144	1	0	12	0	20	1	21	0	18	0	13	0	9	0	3	0	97	1
Below 140	4	0	3	0	6	0	10	0	9	0	5	0	8	0	2	0	47	0
Total	363	195	563	266	536	202	412	104	224	53	122	27	87	5	58	15	2365	867

Apps = Number of Applicants
Adm = Number Admitted
Reflects 99% of the total applicant pool; highest LSAT data reported.

PONTIFICAL CATHOLIC UNIVERSITY OF PUERTO RICO SCHOOL OF LAW

2250 Avenida Las Americas, Suite 633
Ponce, PR 00717-9997
Phone: 787.841.2000, exts. 1836, 1837; Fax: 787.841.4620
E-mail: derecho@email.pucpr.edu; Website: www.pucpr.edu/derecho

ABA
Approved
Since
1967

The Basics

Type of school	Private
Term	Semester
Application deadline	4/15 9/30
Application fee	
Financial aid deadline	2/1 7/2
Can first year start other than fall?	Yes
Student to faculty ratio	31.9 to 1
# of housing spaces available restricted to law students	
graduate housing for which law students are eligible	

Faculty and Administrators

	Total		Men		Women		Minorities	
	Spr	Fall	Spr	Fall	Spr	Fall	Spr	Fall
Full-time	17	21	12	14	5	7	17	21
Other full-time	5	5	4	4	1	1	5	5
Deans, librarians, & others who teach	7	7	4	4	3	3	7	7
Part-time	28	25	17	19	11	6	28	25
Total	57	58	37	41	20	17	57	58

Curriculum

		Full-Time	Part-Time
Typical first-year section size		46	46
Is there typically a "small section" of the first-year class, other than Legal Writing, taught by full-time faculty		No	No
If yes, typical size offered last year			
# of classroom course titles beyond first-year curriculum		97	
# of upper division courses, excluding seminars, with an enrollment:	Under 25	59	
	25–49	68	
	50–74	30	
	75–99	1	
	100+	0	
# of seminars		16	
# of seminar positions available		384	
# of seminar positions filled		72	230
# of positions available in simulation courses		333	
# of simulation positions filled		118	142
# of positions available in faculty supervised clinical courses		7	
# of faculty supervised clinical positions filled		6	1
# involved in field placements		90	1
# involved in law journals		59	10
# involved in moot court or trial competitions		0	0
# of credit hours required to graduate		94	

JD Enrollment and Ethnicity

	Men		Women		Full-Time		Part-Time		1st-Year		Total		JD Degs. Awd.
	#	%	#	%	#	%	#	%	#	%	#	%	
All Hispanics	421	100.0	429	100.0	607	100.0	243	100.0	301	100.0	850	100.0	196
Am. Ind./AK Nat.	0	0.0	0	0.0	0	0.0	0	0.0	0	0.0	0	0.0	0
Asian	0	0.0	0	0.0	0	0.0	0	0.0	0	0.0	0	0.0	0
Black/Af. Am.	0	0.0	0	0.0	0	0.0	0	0.0	0	0.0	0	0.0	0
Nat. HI/Pac. Isl.	0	0.0	0	0.0	0	0.0	0	0.0	0	0.0	0	0.0	0
2 or more races	0	0.0	0	0.0	0	0.0	0	0.0	0	0.0	0	0.0	0
Subtotal (minor.)	421	100.0	429	100.0	607	100.0	243	100.0	301	100.0	850	100.0	196
Nonres. Alien	0	0.0	0	0.0	0	0.0	0	0.0	0	0.0	0	0.0	0
White/Cauc.	0	0.0	0	0.0	0	0.0	0	0.0	0	0.0	0	0.0	0
Unknown	0	0.0	0	0.0	0	0.0	0	0.0	0	0.0	0	0.0	0
Total	421	49.5	429	50.5	607	71.4	243	28.6	301	35.4	850		196

Transfers

Transfers in	15
Transfers out	36

Tuition and Fees

	Resident	Nonresident
Full-time	$14,446	
Part-time	$11,006	
Tuition Guarantee Program		N

Living Expenses

Estimated living expenses for singles

Living on campus	Living off campus	Living at home
$25,375	$30,189	$23,849

PONTIFICAL CATHOLIC UNIVERSITY OF PUERTO RICO SCHOOL OF LAW

ABA
Approved
Since
1967

GPA and LSAT Scores

	Total	Full-Time	Part-Time
# of apps	576	406	170
# of offers	374	260	114
# of matrics	304	208	96
75% GPA	3.57	3.57	3.54
Median GPA	3.25	3.25	3.26
25% GPA	2.97	2.99	2.89
75% LSAT	138	138	139
Median LSAT	135	136	134
25% LSAT	132	129	131

Grants and Scholarships (from prior year)

	Total #	Total %	Full-Time #	Full-Time %	Part-Time #	Part-Time %
Total # of students	834		535		299	
Total # receiving grants	86	10.3	56	10.5	30	10.0
Less than 1/2 tuition	61	7.3	44	8.2	17	5.7
Half to full tuition	15	1.8	6	1.1	9	3.0
Full tuition	10	1.2	6	1.1	4	1.3
More than full tuition	0	0.0	0	0.0	0	0.0
Median grant amount			$3,000		$3,000	

Informational and Library Resources

Total amount spent on library materials	$680,020
Study seating capacity inside the library	308
# of full-time equivalent professional librarians	4
Hours per week library is open	98
# of open, wired connections available to students	102
# of networked computers available for use by students	30
Has wireless network?	Y
Requires computer?	N

JD Attrition (from prior year)

	Academic #	Other #	Total #	Total %
1st year	16	42	58	21.4
2nd year	0	8	8	3.4
3rd year	1	3	4	2.0
4th year	2	0	2	4.0

Employment (9 months after graduation)

For up-to-date employment data, go to employmentsummary.abaquestionnaire.org on the ABA website.

Bar Passage Rates

First-time takers	156	Reporting %	100.00
Average school %	39.74	Average state %	51.61

Average pass difference −11.87

Jurisdiction	Takers	Passers	Pass %	State %	Diff %
Puerto Rico	156	62	39.74	51.61	−11.87

PONTIFICAL CATHOLIC UNIVERSITY OF PUERTO RICO SCHOOL OF LAW

2250 Avenida Las Americas, Suite 633
Ponce, PR 00717-9997
Phone: 787.841.2000, exts. 1836, 1837; Fax: 787.841.4620
E-mail: derecho@email.pucpr.edu; Website: www.pucpr.edu/derecho

Introduction

The School of Law of the Pontifical Catholic University of Puerto Rico was founded in 1961. It is located within the main campus of the Pontifical Catholic University of Puerto Rico, on the southern part of the island in the historical city of Ponce, one of the most beautiful places in Puerto Rico.

The primary objective of the Pontifical Catholic University School of Law is the formation of lawyers imbued with a deep love and concern for their Catholic faith and imbedded in the redeeming truths of Christian philosophy and ethics. The law school of the Pontifical Catholic University of Puerto Rico hopes to contribute to upholding the high ethical, cultural, and literary accomplishments of the Puerto Rican bar, which historically represents a tradition of moral austerity, intellectual achievement, and professional competence.

Library and Physical Facilities

The School of Law occupies the Spellman Building. Its location on the campus of Pontifical Catholic University of Puerto Rico enables students to study related academic disciplines, to participate in the intellectual life, and to enjoy many other facilities of the university.

Among the materials in the library is a comprehensive and growing collection of legal treatises, tests, monographs, and periodicals, including the most important and recent publications in civil, common, and comparative law. Modern audiovisual equipment and computerized services are also available. The library is an authorized depository for United Nations documents as well as for United States government documents. In addition, it offers the services of the Westlaw and LexisNexis systems, which permit computer-assisted legal research.

Curriculum

The required subjects are:
- Administrative Law
- Advanced Legal Analysis
- Civil Procedure
- Constitutional Law
- Contracts
- Corporations
- Criminal Procedure
- Evidence
- Family Law
- Federal Jurisdiction
- Fundamentals of Research, Analysis, and Writing
- Intermediate Research, Analysis, and Writing
- Introduction to Law
- Legal Aid Clinic
- Legal Ethics and Professional Responsibility
- Mercantile Law
- Mortgages
- Notarial Law
- Obligations
- Penal Law
- Property Law
- Successions and Donations
- Theology
- Torts
- Trial Practice
- Workshop Bar Preparation

The basic program covers three years in the day division or four years in the evening division.

The school curriculum includes a clinical program for third-year students. Pursuant to a rule approved by the Supreme Court of the Commonwealth of Puerto Rico in 1974, students practice trial advocacy under the supervision of law school professors in the Courts of First Instance and in administrative agencies.

The Pontifical Catholic University of Puerto Rico also offers a combined JD/MBA degree. For the combined degree, students are required to complete 85 credit hours at the School of Law (79 required credits and 6 elective credits), plus 9 credit hours in electives completed at the Graduate Program of the School of Business Administration, for a total of 94 credit hours. In addition, the students must complete 34 credit hours at the School of Business Administration (31 required credits and 3 electives) and an additional 9 approved elective credits in JD, for a total of 43 credits, plus 4 hours of Theology.

Admission

Application for admission is open to men and women of good character who have received a bachelor's degree from a qualified institution and have obtained a 2.5 grade-point average.

The required forms for application for admission and all other information may be obtained from the registrar of the law school and should be filed with all supporting documents before April 15. The School of Law admits beginning students in August and January for both the full-time and part-time programs.

Applicants are required to take both the LSAT and the Examen de Admisión a Estudios de Posgrado (EXADEP) (formerly PAEG).

Test scores are not the only factor considered. Besides the objective factors, there are many intangible and personal considerations, such as strong motivation, disadvantaged circumstances, evidence of improving performance, and relevant work experience. A personal interview of the applicant by a committee is essential before a decision is made. Applicants of both sexes and from all religious, racial, social, and ethnic backgrounds are encouraged to apply.

All courses are offered only in Spanish. Consequently, students are required to be proficient in Spanish.

Student Activities

The law review, *Revista de Derecho Puertorriqueño*, is devoted to scholarly analysis and discussion of development of the law. It publishes student notes, comments, and surveys, as well as articles of outstanding quality submitted by attorneys, judges, and other members of the legal profession. The school has a student council, a chapter of the National Association of Law Students of Puerto Rico, and an Association for Women's Rights. Local chapters of Phi Alpha Delta international law fraternity, the Delta Theta Phi law fraternity, and the Law Student Division of the ABA are also active and well organized in the law school.

Housing

Students live either in university residences or private housing. Inquiries concerning housing facilities should be addressed to the Housing Office, Pontifical Catholic University of Puerto Rico, 2250 Avenida Las Americas, Suite 545, Ponce, PR 00717-9997.

Expenses and Financial Aid

There is a deferred plan for students who have financial difficulties at the time of registration. The university has made available for law students several full-tuition scholarships to be awarded on the basis of scholastic excellence. The university also has an office for student loans and other types of financial services.

Applicant Profile Not Available

UNIVERSITY OF PUERTO RICO SCHOOL OF LAW

PO Box 23349, UPR Station
San Juan, PR 00931-3349
Phone: 787.999.9553; Fax: 787.999.9564
E-mail: admisiones@law.upr.edu; Website: www.law.upr.edu

ABA
Approved
Since
1945

The Basics

Type of school	Public
Term	Semester
Application deadline	2/15
Application fee	$20
Financial aid deadline	5/15
Can first year start other than fall?	No
Student to faculty ratio	22.9 to 1
# of housing spaces available restricted to law students	18
graduate housing for which law students are eligible	18

Faculty and Administrators

	Total		Men		Women		Minorities	
	Spr	Fall	Spr	Fall	Spr	Fall	Spr	Fall
Full-time	24	23	17	18	7	5	23	22
Other full-time	12	4	8	3	4	1	9	4
Deans, librarians, & others who teach	8	3	4	1	4	2	8	3
Part-time	52	58	34	38	18	20	52	58
Total	96	88	63	60	33	28	92	87

Curriculum

	Full-Time	Part-Time
Typical first-year section size	70	42
Is there typically a "small section" of the first-year class, other than Legal Writing, taught by full-time faculty	No	No
If yes, typical size offered last year		
# of classroom course titles beyond first-year curriculum	108	
# of upper division courses, excluding seminars, with an enrollment: Under 25	122	
25–49	48	
50–74	20	
75–99	13	
100+	3	
# of seminars	49	
# of seminar positions available	735	
# of seminar positions filled	158	85
# of positions available in simulation courses	0	
# of simulation positions filled	128	38
# of positions available in faculty supervised clinical courses	445	
# of faculty supervised clinical positions filled	212	113
# involved in field placements	44	8
# involved in law journals	49	7
# involved in moot court or trial competitions	11	1
# of credit hours required to graduate	92	

JD Enrollment and Ethnicity

	Men		Women		Full-Time		Part-Time		1st-Year		Total		JD Degs. Awd.
	#	%	#	%	#	%	#	%	#	%	#	%	
All Hispanics	307	100.0	401	100.0	523	100.0	185	100.0	372	100.0	708	100.0	226
Am. Ind./AK Nat.	0	0.0	0	0.0	0	0.0	0	0.0	0	0.0	0	0.0	0
Asian	0	0.0	0	0.0	0	0.0	0	0.0	0	0.0	0	0.0	0
Black/Af. Am.	0	0.0	0	0.0	0	0.0	0	0.0	0	0.0	0	0.0	0
Nat. HI/Pac. Isl.	0	0.0	0	0.0	0	0.0	0	0.0	0	0.0	0	0.0	0
2 or more races	0	0.0	0	0.0	0	0.0	0	0.0	0	0.0	0	0.0	0
Subtotal (minor.)	307	100.0	401	100.0	523	100.0	185	100.0	372	100.0	708	100.0	226
Nonres. Alien	0	0.0	0	0.0	0	0.0	0	0.0	0	0.0	0	0.0	8
White/Cauc.	0	0.0	0	0.0	0	0.0	0	0.0	0	0.0	0	0.0	0
Unknown	0	0.0	0	0.0	0	0.0	0	0.0	0	0.0	0	0.0	0
Total	307	43.4	401	56.6	523	73.9	185	26.1	372	52.5	708		234

Transfers

Transfers in	11
Transfers out	0

Tuition and Fees

	Resident	Nonresident
Full-time	$7,771	$9,673
Part-time	$6,451	$11,973
Tuition Guarantee Program		Y

Living Expenses

Estimated living expenses for singles

Living on campus	Living off campus	Living at home
$10,895	$15,155	$10,455

UNIVERSITY OF PUERTO RICO SCHOOL OF LAW

*ABA
Approved
Since
1945*

GPA and LSAT Scores

	Total	Full-Time	Part-Time
# of apps	551	377	174
# of offers	200	149	51
# of matrics	194	145	49
75% GPA	3.84	3.83	3.85
Median GPA	3.59	3.59	3.58
25% GPA	3.36	3.38	3.32
75% LSAT	151	151	149
Median LSAT	146	146	146
25% LSAT	143	143	142

Grants and Scholarships (from prior year)

	Total #	Total %	Full-Time #	Full-Time %	Part-Time #	Part-Time %
Total # of students	737		545		192	
Total # receiving grants	0	0.0	0	0.0	0	0.0
Less than 1/2 tuition	0	0.0	0	0.0	0	0.0
Half to full tuition	0	0.0	0	0.0	0	0.0
Full tuition	0	0.0	0	0.0	0	0.0
More than full tuition	0	0.0	0	0.0	0	0.0
Median grant amount			$0		$0	

Informational and Library Resources

Total amount spent on library materials	$1,072,881
Study seating capacity inside the library	437
# of full-time equivalent professional librarians	8
Hours per week library is open	112
# of open, wired connections available to students	170
# of networked computers available for use by students	49
Has wireless network?	Y
Requires computer?	N

JD Attrition (from prior year)

	Academic #	Other #	Total #	Total %
1st year	5	12	17	4.5
2nd year	3	1	4	2.9
3rd year	1	1	2	1.0
4th year	0	0	0	0.0

Employment (9 months after graduation)

For up-to-date employment data, go to employmentsummary.abaquestionnaire.org on the ABA website.

Bar Passage Rates

First-time takers	129	Reporting %	167.44
Average school %	62.96	Average state %	51.61

Average pass difference 11.35

Jurisdiction	Takers	Passers	Pass %	State %	Diff %
Puerto Rico	216	136	62.96	51.61	11.35

UNIVERSITY OF PUERTO RICO SCHOOL OF LAW

PO Box 23349, UPR Station
San Juan, PR 00931-3349
Phone: 787.999.9553; Fax: 787.999.9564
E-mail: admisiones@law.upr.edu; Website: www.law.upr.edu

Introduction

The University of Puerto Rico School of Law was founded in 1913 at its present site on the University Campus at Río Piedras, within the metropolitan area of San Juan in the heart of the Caribbean. The University of Puerto Rico is accredited by the Middle States Colleges Association. The School of Law has been accredited by the American Bar Association since 1945 and by the Association of American Law Schools since 1948. It is also accredited by the Council on Higher Education and the Puerto Rico Supreme Court.

Academic and Special Programs

The Academic Program: The guiding principle behind our academic program is to increase and diversify the learning and development experiences of our students. That is the reason why half of our study program is elective. Our students can take courses ranging from theoretical to practical, to issues pertaining to civil rights, technology, feminism, business, international relations, and comparative law. In addition, our students, as part of their program, have to participate in a clinical program.

The study program consists of 92 credit hours. The majority of the courses are taught in Spanish.
Degree Offered: Juris Doctor
Joint-Degree Programs:
- Dual Juris Doctor and Law Degree Program (Licenciatura en Derecho) with the University of Barcelona, Spain
- Juris Doctor and Master of Business Administration with the University of Puerto Rico Graduate School of Business Administration
- Juris Doctor and Doctor of Medicine with the University of Puerto Rico School of Medicine
- Juris Doctor and Master of Public Policy with the Humphrey School of Public Affairs at the University of Minnesota
Graduate: LLM for Latin American and Caribbean lawyers
Special Programs: The School of Law has student exchange programs with the University of Arizona James E. Rogers College of Law, the University of Connecticut School of Law, the University of Palermo in Argentina, the University of Chile Law School, the University of Ottawa Faculty of Law in Canada, and the University of Amberes in Belgium. Under these programs, students register at their home institution, but will take a full courseload at the host institution. The credits and grades earned during a single semester will be awarded by the home institution according to the standard procedure of the home law school. Students also have a chance to participate in a summer law program at the University of Barcelona, Spain. Also, the school has a winter exchange program with the University of Ottawa Faculty of Law in Canada, through which students can earn four credits studying Law and Technology or Law, Technology, and Feminism for one week in Canada and two weeks in Puerto Rico.

Clinical Program

In March 1974, the Puerto Rico Supreme Court approved rules for the local courts to allow students to practice law and participate in judicial proceedings. The US District Court followed suit in 1991. Our curriculum requires that students in their last year of study complete a two-semester clinical program. The clinical program stands as clear testimony of our school's commitment to community service. The Legal Aid Clinic handles over 1,300 cases per year, offering assistance to those in need of legal aid. Our clinic offers our students the opportunity to practice law in a wide range of areas in an environment resembling the facilities of a modern, medium-sized law firm.
- Cyber Law
- Community Economic Development
- Criminal Law (federal and state)
- Family Law
- Mediation
- Gay and Lesbian Rights
- Civil Rights
- Environmental Law
- Employment Law
- Civil Cases (in general)
- Juvenile Law
- Health Rights for Women Inmates

Admission

In order to be admitted to the University of Puerto Rico School of Law, applicants must take two aptitude tests: the Law School Admission Test (LSAT) and the Examen de Admisión a Estudios de Posgrado (EXADEP). The tests must be taken no later than February of the year of application. Applicants must also have a bachelor's degree from an accredited institution before enrolling.

The entering class is selected by converting the LSAT, the EXADEP, and the GPA into the student's admission index and making offers of admission to those with the 200 highest admission indexes. However, 7 percent of the new class is chosen from those with 201–260 indexes based on a complete profile of the applicant, taking into consideration his or her ability to study law, his or her past accomplishments, and his or her disadvantages in receiving a postsecondary education.

Applicants who cannot take the required aptitude tests because of disability are considered individually by the admission committee. The University of Puerto Rico does not discriminate against students on the basis of race, color, religion, gender, age, marital status, national origin, or disability.

Expenses and Financial Aid

Resident law students pay tuition and fees amounting to $127 per credit each semester. Nonresident students who are US citizens pay the same amount that would be required from Puerto Rican students if they were to study in the state from which the nonresidents come, thus establishing a reciprocity principle. Nonresident students who are not US citizens pay additional tuition and fees amounting approximately to $2,327.50 for eight or more credits for each semester.

All financial aid for the University of Puerto Rico School of Law is administered by the school's Office of Financial Aid. Each student is considered on his or her own merit and need. Awards are made only after an applicant has been admitted.

Alumni

Our student body is made up of graduates from public and private universities in Puerto Rico and the states, as well as foreign institutions. They come from a wide range of academic backgrounds and social experiences, providing a unique atmosphere in the classroom and outside. Our alumni are leaders in the legal field and in the public arena serving as governors, US ambassadors, partners in major law firms, Puerto Rico Supreme Court Justices, attorneys general, presidents of the University of Puerto Rico, and chief executive officers in the banking industry.

Library and Physical Facilities

The School of Law's library is the largest law library in the Caribbean. Its collection encompasses both the Romano-Germanic civil law and Anglo-American common law traditions. Also, our library has been designated as a European Documentation Center by the European Union and a selective depository for US government documents. Our school is equipped with state-of-the-art technology, smart classrooms, courtroom-classrooms, and wireless connections for the students.

APPLICANT PROFILE

University of Puerto Rico School of Law
This grid includes only applicants who earned 120–180 LSAT scores under standard administrations.

LSAT Score	3.75 +		3.50–3.74		3.25–3.49		3.00–3.24		2.75–2.99		2.50–2.74		2.25–2.49		2.00–2.24		Below 2.00		No GPA		Total	
	Apps	Adm	Apps	Adm	Apps	Adm	Apps	Adm	Apps	Adm	Apps	Adm	Apps	Adm	Apps	Adm	Apps	Adm	Apps	Adm	Apps	Adm
175–180	0	0	0	0	0	0	0	0	0	0	0	0	0	0	0	0	0	0	0	0	0	0
170–174	0	0	0	0	0	0	0	0	0	0	0	0	0	0	0	0	0	0	0	0	0	0
165–169	1	1	0	0	0	0	1	1	0	0	0	0	0	0	0	0	0	0	0	0	2	2
160–164	0	0	1	1	1	1	3	2	0	0	2	2	0	0	0	0	0	0	0	0	7	6
155–159	8	8	0	0	4	4	1	1	4	4	0	0	0	0	1	1	0	0	1	0	19	18
150–154	9	9	9	8	3	3	8	8	6	6	3	2	0	0	1	1	0	0	0	0	39	37
145–149	19	19	18	16	11	10	14	8	9	5	5	1	3	0	3	0	0	0	1	0	83	59
140–144	24	23	33	24	33	16	25	5	14	2	12	0	2	0	1	0	1	0	3	0	148	70
135–139	26	15	15	4	13	1	15	0	10	0	4	0	7	0	2	0	0	0	7	0	99	20
130–134	12	3	5	0	11	1	8	0	9	0	9	0	0	0	0	0	0	0	7	0	61	4
125–129	4	1	5	0	3	0	2	0	3	0	0	0	0	0	2	0	0	0	2	0	21	1
120–124	0	0	0	0	1	0	3	0	1	0	0	0	1	0	0	0	0	0	3	0	9	0
Total	103	79	86	53	80	36	80	25	56	17	35	5	13	0	10	2	1	0	24	0	488	217

Apps = Number of Applicants
Adm = Number Admitted
Reflects 99% of the total applicant pool; highest LSAT data reported.

QUINNIPIAC UNIVERSITY SCHOOL OF LAW

275 Mount Carmel Avenue
Hamden, CT 06518
Phone: 203.582.3400; Fax: 203.582.3339
E-mail: ladm@quinnipiac.edu; Website: http://law.quinnipiac.edu

ABA
Approved
Since
1992

The Basics

Type of school	Private
Term	Semester
Application deadline	3/1
Application fee	$65
Financial aid deadline	
Can first year start other than fall?	No
Student to faculty ratio	12.6 to 1
# of housing spaces available restricted to law students	
graduate housing for which law students are eligible	

Faculty and Administrators

	Total		Men		Women		Minorities	
	Spr	Fall	Spr	Fall	Spr	Fall	Spr	Fall
Full-time	26	29	17	17	9	12	2	2
Other full-time	7	6	5	4	2	2	2	0
Deans, librarians, & others who teach	3	3	2	2	1	1	0	0
Part-time	43	34	28	26	15	8	0	0
Total	79	72	52	49	27	23	4	2

Curriculum

	Full-Time	Part-Time
Typical first-year section size	61	40
Is there typically a "small section" of the first-year class, other than Legal Writing, taught by full-time faculty	No	No
If yes, typical size offered last year		
# of classroom course titles beyond first-year curriculum		107
# of upper division courses, excluding seminars, with an enrollment: Under 25		82
25–49		23
50–74		7
75–99		1
100+		0
# of seminars		6
# of seminar positions available		84
# of seminar positions filled	58	5
# of positions available in simulation courses		264
# of simulation positions filled	39	181
# of positions available in faculty supervised clinical courses		76
# of faculty supervised clinical positions filled	49	22
# involved in field placements	79	0
# involved in law journals	50	10
# involved in moot court or trial competitions	48	5
# of credit hours required to graduate		86

JD Enrollment and Ethnicity

	Men		Women		Full-Time		Part-Time		1st-Year		Total		JD Degs. Awd.
	#	%	#	%	#	%	#	%	#	%	#	%	
All Hispanics	8	3.5	12	5.7	14	3.9	6	7.3	4	3.3	20	4.6	4
Am. Ind./AK Nat.	0	0.0	2	0.9	2	0.6	0	0.0	1	0.8	2	0.5	1
Asian	8	3.5	15	7.1	21	5.9	2	2.4	4	3.3	23	5.3	7
Black/Af. Am.	4	1.8	4	1.9	5	1.4	3	3.7	3	2.5	8	1.8	7
Nat. HI/Pac. Isl.	0	0.0	0	0.0	0	0.0	0	0.0	0	0.0	0	0.0	0
2 or more races	2	0.9	4	1.9	5	1.4	1	1.2	3	2.5	6	1.4	0
Subtotal (minor.)	22	9.7	37	17.5	47	13.2	12	14.6	15	12.4	59	13.5	19
Nonres. Alien	0	0.0	1	0.5	1	0.3	0	0.0	1	0.8	1	0.2	0
White/Cauc.	179	78.9	154	73.0	269	75.6	64	78.0	78	64.5	333	76.0	107
Unknown	26	11.5	19	9.0	39	11.0	6	7.3	26	21.5	45	10.3	8
Total	227	51.8	211	48.2	356	81.3	82	18.7	121	27.6	438		134

Transfers

Transfers in	4
Transfers out	6

Tuition and Fees

	Resident	Nonresident
Full-time	$45,050	$45,050
Part-time	$31,780	$31,780
Tuition Guarantee Program	N	

Living Expenses

Estimated living expenses for singles

Living on campus	Living off campus	Living at home
N/A	$19,874	$13,746

QUINNIPIAC UNIVERSITY SCHOOL OF LAW

*ABA
Approved
Since
1992*

GPA and LSAT Scores

	Total	Full-Time	Part-Time
# of apps	2,037	1,858	179
# of offers	959	905	54
# of matrics	123	104	19
75% GPA	3.54	3.55	3.52
Median GPA	3.33	3.29	3.38
25% GPA	3.09	3.08	3.22
75% LSAT	158	158	154
Median LSAT	156	157	153
25% LSAT	154	154	150

Grants and Scholarships (from prior year)

	Total #	Total %	Full-Time #	Full-Time %	Part-Time #	Part-Time %
Total # of students	467		340		127	
Total # receiving grants	311	66.6	261	76.8	50	39.4
Less than 1/2 tuition	206	44.1	156	45.9	50	39.4
Half to full tuition	82	17.6	82	24.1	0	0.0
Full tuition	23	4.9	23	6.8	0	0.0
More than full tuition	0	0.0	0	0.0	0	0.0
Median grant amount			$20,000		$5,000	

Informational and Library Resources

Total amount spent on library materials	$957,464
Study seating capacity inside the library	350
# of full-time equivalent professional librarians	5
Hours per week library is open	93
# of open, wired connections available to students	0
# of networked computers available for use by students	107
Has wireless network?	Y
Requires computer?	N

JD Attrition (from prior year)

	Academic #	Other #	Total #	Total %
1st year	5	8	13	8.0
2nd year	0	1	1	0.7
3rd year	0	2	2	1.7
4th year	0	0	0	0.0

Employment (9 months after graduation)

For up-to-date employment data, go to employmentsummary.abaquestionnaire.org on the ABA website.

Bar Passage Rates

First-time takers	108	Reporting %	71.30
Average school %	88.31	Average state %	84.76
Average pass difference	3.55		

Jurisdiction	Takers	Passers	Pass %	State %	Diff %
Connecticut	77	68	88.31	84.76	3.55

QUINNIPIAC UNIVERSITY SCHOOL OF LAW

275 Mount Carmel Avenue
Hamden, CT 06518
Phone: 203.582.3400; Fax: 203.582.3339
E-mail: ladm@quinnipiac.edu; Website: http://law.quinnipiac.edu

Introduction

Excellent law schools share many common traits—faculty renowned for their scholarship and commitment to teaching; academically rigorous courses; loyal, successful alumni; and motivated, focused students. All of these are essential components of Quinnipiac Law's identity. However, what sets Quinnipiac apart is its personal, student-centered approach to the law school experience. Contributing to this identity is a favorable 13:1 student-to-faculty ratio, the extraordinary accessibility of the faculty, and an environment that both challenges and supports its students as they prepare for careers in law.

Nestled among the hills, woods, and waterways of Connecticut on one of the most beautiful campuses in New England, yet just 75 miles from New York City, Quinnipiac's setting and location are ideal. The beautiful, state-of-the-art law center opened in 1995. Wireless computer access throughout provides students with a modern, relaxed, and safe environment for study.

Faculty

Our faculty's academic credentials span the nation's leading institutions from Harvard, Yale, and Berkeley to Chicago, Michigan, and Columbia. They combine excellence in scholarship and teaching with exceptional accessibility. The care with which faculty members demonstrate their interest in each student's progress and success is a distinguishing characteristic of Quinnipiac Law. Most faculty have an open-door policy and generously share their expertise, insight, and time. The low student-to-faculty ratio (13:1) allows students to work closely with faculty, and this translates into a different kind of law school experience.

Library and Physical Facilities

The 50,000-square-foot law library is at the center of the School of Law complex. With a collection of more than 450,000 volumes, it also provides comprehensive access to numerous electronic resources and databases such as LexisNexis, Westlaw/Dialog, JSTOR, and other web-based services. Its interlibrary loan network makes it possible to obtain materials from any library in the world. The beautiful facility features spacious public areas, numerous reading rooms, and individual study carrels, providing a comfortable and relaxing environment for research and study.

Curriculum

The law school is fully approved by the ABA and is a member of AALS. Full-time day and part-time evening programs are offered beginning each fall. The academic program is designed to prepare students to be generalists or specialists. The program provides a dynamic blend of traditional classroom instruction and extensive practical learning opportunities.

Students who wish to focus on a specific area of study may choose from six different concentrations—**Civil Advocacy and Dispute Resolution**, **Criminal Law and Advocacy**, **Family Law**, **Health Law**, **Intellectual Property**, and **Tax**. About one-third of our students choose a focus in one of the above concentrations. However, one may develop an informal concentration in a variety of other fields with the advice and assistance of a faculty member.

The law school also offers a joint JD/MBA degree (with a health care management track) and a summer study-abroad program with Trinity College in Dublin, Ireland.

Special Programs

Quinnipiac is recognized as having one of the premier clinical and externship programs in the country, and students often cite their experiences in these programs as one of the highlights of their law school career. Every student is guaranteed participation in at least one of these practical learning opportunities that allow students to bridge the gap between theory and practice. A total of 15 clinical and externship programs are available to students.

The six clinical programs include **Civil**, **Tax**, **Advanced**, **Evening** (for part-time students), **Defense Appellate**, and **Prosecution Appellate**. The **Civil Clinic** typically deals with the following types of cases or issues: education, employment, health, housing, family and children, immigration, law reform, and poverty. The nine externship programs are **Corporate Counsel**, **Criminal Justice**, **Family and Juvenile Law**, **Judicial**, **Legal Services**, **Legislative**, **Mediation**, **Public Interest**, and **Field Placement II**.

Quinnipiac has established two centers in specialized fields of law—the **Center for Health Law and Policy** and the **Center on Dispute Resolution**—both of which draw on the considerable academic strengths and resources within the law school community.

Admission

Admission is competitive and based upon a variety of factors: undergraduate academic record, LSAT scores, personal statement, letters of recommendation, résumé, and other evidence such as advanced degrees, life and work experience, and extracurricular activities. Applications are welcomed from students of color, nontraditional students, and all students who add to the diversity of the student body. A rolling admission system is employed; however, the priority application deadline for admission and scholarship consideration is March 1. *Candidates for the full-tuition Dean's Fellows awards must apply by February 1.*

Student Activities

Quinnipiac students often comment about the strong sense of community that permeates the law school. That sense of community is enhanced by the numerous and varied opportunities for students to participate in cocurricular activities, including a dynamic Student Bar Association, more than 25 different student organizations, a thriving Moot Court Society, a Mock Trial team, an active *Quinnipiac Law Review*, and two student journals—the *Health Law Journal* and the *Probate Law Journal*.

Expenses and Financial Aid

Approximately 90 percent of the student body receives some form of financial assistance. Every applicant is considered for merit-based scholarships that range from $3,000 to full tuition per year. March 1 is the application deadline for most merit awards. However, candidates for the full-tuition Dean's Fellows scholarships must submit applications by February 1. Total institutional scholarships and grants for the 2011–2012 academic year totaled approximately $5.3 million.

Housing

Campus housing for graduate and professional students is not available. However, there is ample, affordable housing available near the campus and throughout New Haven county. The School of Law Admissions Office maintains a housing website and roommate locator online for its admitted students and also provides personal assistance in securing off-campus accommodations.

Career Services

The Office of Career Services provides students and graduates with the expert guidance necessary to make informed career decisions. It offers substantial support through individual counseling and workshops on topics such as writing résumés and interviewing techniques.

The office coordinates on- and off-campus recruitment programs. Students interview with employers for a variety of summer internships and permanent jobs in the private and public sector.

Over the past six years, more than 90 percent of our graduates have been employed within nine months of graduation. The graduating class of 2010 had a 90 percent placement rate and found employment as follows: 35 percent entered private practice, 17 percent took positions in business and industry, 24 percent chose government service work, 9 percent received judicial clerkships, 9 percent went into public interest law, and 2 percent were studying for advanced degrees. The remainder went into other fields of employment.

APPLICANT PROFILE

Quinnipiac University School of Law
This grid includes only applicants who earned 120–180 LSAT scores under standard administrations.

LSAT Score	3.75 +		3.50–3.74		3.25–3.49		3.00–3.24		2.75–2.99		2.50–2.74		Below 2.50		No GPA		Total	
	Apps	Adm	Apps	Adm	Apps	Adm	Apps	Adm	Apps	Adm	Apps	Adm	Apps	Adm	Apps	Adm	Apps	Adm
170–180	3	3	1	1	5	5	2	2	0	0	0	0	1	0	0	0	12	11
165–169	14	14	15	15	18	17	11	11	5	5	8	8	2	2	1	1	74	73
160–164	46	46	65	63	66	62	44	43	22	22	14	12	10	5	0	0	267	253
155–159	75	75	119	109	141	130	102	92	69	41	35	12	26	3	4	3	571	465
150–154	62	30	124	44	131	35	177	22	101	6	52	1	30	0	6	0	683	138
145–149	21	3	30	2	55	5	60	4	34	1	23	0	21	0	5	0	249	15
140–144	7	0	20	0	18	0	29	0	11	0	11	0	13	0	0	0	109	0
Below 140	5	0	4	0	11	0	11	0	12	0	7	0	9	0	2	0	61	0
Total	233	171	378	234	445	254	436	174	254	75	150	33	112	10	18	4	2026	955

Apps = Number of Applicants
Adm = Number Admitted
Reflects 99% of the total applicant pool; highest LSAT data reported.

REGENT UNIVERSITY SCHOOL OF LAW

1000 Regent University Drive, RH239
Virginia Beach, VA 23464
Phone: 757.352.4584; Fax: 757.352.4139
E-mail: lawschool@regent.edu; Website: www.regent.edu/law

ABA
Approved
Since
1989

The Basics

Type of school	Private
Term	Semester
Application deadline	6/1
Application fee	$50
Financial aid deadline	6/1
Can first year start other than fall?	No
Student to faculty ratio	15.4 to 1
# of housing spaces available restricted to law students	
graduate housing for which law students are eligible	860

Faculty and Administrators

	Total		Men		Women		Minorities	
	Spr	Fall	Spr	Fall	Spr	Fall	Spr	Fall
Full-time	22	23	15	16	7	7	4	5
Other full-time	3	2	2	1	1	1	1	0
Deans, librarians, & others who teach	9	9	6	6	3	3	1	1
Part-time	21	21	17	15	4	6	1	2
Total	55	55	40	38	15	17	7	8

Curriculum

	Full-Time	Part-Time
Typical first-year section size	80	80
Is there typically a "small section" of the first-year class, other than Legal Writing, taught by full-time faculty	Yes	Yes
If yes, typical size offered last year	40	40
# of classroom course titles beyond first-year curriculum	69	

# of upper division courses, excluding seminars, with an enrollment:		
	Under 25	86
	25–49	14
	50–74	17
	75–99	3
	100+	1

	Full-Time	Part-Time
# of seminars	6	
# of seminar positions available	85	
# of seminar positions filled	45	2
# of positions available in simulation courses	486	
# of simulation positions filled	315	13
# of positions available in faculty supervised clinical courses	56	
# of faculty supervised clinical positions filled	23	2
# involved in field placements	79	4
# involved in law journals	61	1
# involved in moot court or trial competitions	51	0
# of credit hours required to graduate	90	

JD Enrollment and Ethnicity

	Men		Women		Full-Time		Part-Time		1st-Year		Total		JD Degs. Awd.
	#	%	#	%	#	%	#	%	#	%	#	%	
All Hispanics	7	3.0	8	3.9	15	3.6	0	0.0	4	2.6	15	3.5	3
Am. Ind./AK Nat.	4	1.7	3	1.5	7	1.7	0	0.0	1	0.6	7	1.6	3
Asian	7	3.0	14	6.9	21	5.1	0	0.0	4	2.6	21	4.8	11
Black/Af. Am.	9	3.9	9	4.4	15	3.6	3	15.0	7	4.5	18	4.1	7
Nat. HI/Pac. Isl.	0	0.0	0	0.0	0	0.0	0	0.0	0	0.0	0	0.0	0
2 or more races	4	1.7	5	2.5	9	2.2	0	0.0	9	5.8	9	2.1	0
Subtotal (minor.)	31	13.4	39	19.2	67	16.2	3	15.0	25	16.2	70	16.1	24
Nonres. Alien	1	0.4	0	0.0	1	0.2	0	0.0	1	0.6	1	0.2	0
White/Cauc.	188	81.4	158	77.8	330	79.7	16	80.0	119	77.3	346	79.7	91
Unknown	11	4.8	6	3.0	16	3.9	1	5.0	9	5.8	17	3.9	4
Total	231	53.2	203	46.8	414	95.4	20	4.6	154	35.5	434		119

Transfers

Transfers in	4
Transfers out	6

Tuition and Fees

	Resident	Nonresident
Full-time	$32,780	$32,780
Part-time	$26,420	$26,420
Tuition Guarantee Program		N

Living Expenses

Estimated living expenses for singles

Living on campus	Living off campus	Living at home
$20,570	$20,570	$20,570

REGENT UNIVERSITY SCHOOL OF LAW

ABA Approved Since 1989

GPA and LSAT Scores

	Total	Full-Time	Part-Time
# of apps	1,180	1,135	45
# of offers	445	435	10
# of matrics	154	148	6
75% GPA	3.60	3.62	3.15
Median GPA	3.28	3.29	2.97
25% GPA	2.96	2.99	2.92
75% LSAT	158	158	151
Median LSAT	153	153	149
25% LSAT	150	150	147

Grants and Scholarships (from prior year)

	Total		Full-Time		Part-Time	
	#	%	#	%	#	%
Total # of students	428		409		19	
Total # receiving grants	374	87.4	360	88.0	14	73.7
Less than 1/2 tuition	295	68.9	282	68.9	13	68.4
Half to full tuition	58	13.6	57	13.9	1	5.3
Full tuition	21	4.9	21	5.1	0	0.0
More than full tuition	0	0.0	0	0.0	0	0.0
Median grant amount			$5,000		$4,000	

Informational and Library Resources

Total amount spent on library materials	$696,258
Study seating capacity inside the library	324
# of full-time equivalent professional librarians	5
Hours per week library is open	109
# of open, wired connections available to students	218
# of networked computers available for use by students	61
Has wireless network?	Y
Requires computer?	N

JD Attrition (from prior year)

	Academic	Other	Total	
	#	#	#	%
1st year	15	13	28	16.7
2nd year	0	3	3	2.3
3rd year	0	0	0	0.0
4th year	0	0	0	0.0

Employment (9 months after graduation)

For up-to-date employment data, go to employmentsummary.abaquestionnaire.org on the ABA website.

Bar Passage Rates

First-time takers	113	Reporting %	83.19
Average school %	86.17	Average state %	80.58
Average pass difference	5.59		

Jurisdiction	Takers	Passers	Pass %	State %	Diff %
Virginia	46	40	86.96	78.15	8.81
Pennsylvania	7	6	85.71	83.06	2.65
Texas	7	5	71.43	82.68	−11.25
Maryland	6	5	83.33	79.96	3.37
New York	6	5	83.33	84.92	−1.59

REGENT UNIVERSITY SCHOOL OF LAW

1000 Regent University Drive, RH239
Virginia Beach, VA 23464
Phone: 757.352.4584; Fax: 757.352.4139
E-mail: lawschool@regent.edu; Website: www.regent.edu/law

Introduction

Regent Law offers an ABA-approved and nationally recognized rigorous academic experience in the context of a Christian worldview. Its 2700-plus alumni, which include Virginia Governor Bob McDonnell '89, exemplify Regent Law's motto—"Law is more than a profession. It's a calling."—by providing excellent and principled legal counsel. The law school is composed of approximately 420 students and is situated on a stately, Georgian-style campus in Virginia Beach, Virginia, minutes from the Atlantic Ocean, less than a two-hour drive from Richmond, and less than four hours from Washington, DC.

Rigorous Academics and Christian Worldview

With an internationally recognized faculty and robust advocacy skills training program, Regent Law is academically excellent and competitive with law schools nationwide. While affirming the faith of individual students, the school embraces a Christian worldview, encouraging students to see law as a vocation, or "calling." Regent's worldview provides a platform for developing the highest ethical standards in its students; it also helps make Regent a diverse and richly supportive academic community.

Academic Program/Legal Skills

Regent's Center for Advocacy Skills develops practical lawyering skills through clinical practice, including a civil litigation clinic, a robust legal research and writing curriculum, a partnership with the American Center for Law and Justice (the nation's foremost public interest law firm defending religious liberties), extensive externship opportunities, and highly successful student Moot Court, Negotiation, and Trial Advocacy teams. Recent national team awards include the 2010 NBLSA International Negotiation Championship; 2009 National Pretrial Competition (with Best Brief and Best Oralist awards); 2008 and 2009 Spong Moot Court Championships; and ABA National Negotiation and National Moot Court titles in 2007 and 2006, respectively.

Center for Global Justice, Human Rights, and the Rule of Law

Regent's Center for Global Justice is a comprehensive response to the plight of the enslaved, oppressed, and trafficked worldwide. Through programming including funded international summer internships, a unique global justice curriculum, and an annual symposium, the Center for Global Justice equips students with the tools they need to be advocates for the oppressed around the world. See regent.edu/globaljustice for more information.

Full- and Part-Time Programs

The School of Law offers full- and part-time 90-semester-hour Juris Doctor programs, in-residence only. Students in the full-time program normally complete their degrees in three years; part-time students complete their degrees in four to five years.

Admission and the Bar

The goal of our admissions committee is to enroll men and women who demonstrate academic promise, strong motivation, and a commitment to the school's mission as a Christ-centered institution. The committee recognizes that this means more than simply enrolling those with the highest credentials. It also includes seeking to admit men and women who take seriously the critical roles they will assume as counselors, conciliators, and followers of Christ. Committee members evaluate each candidate's college-level academic performance, career accomplishments, skills relevant to the practice of law, writing skills as evidenced in the personal statement, and results of the LSAT. Additionally, two letters of recommendation are required to support the application for admission. Admission decisions are made on a rolling basis typically within two to three weeks from the time the application becomes complete.

Academic Assistance

Regent Law is on the cutting edge of legal pedagogy in offering academic assistance to its students. Regent employs two faculty members, a director and associate director of academic success, who oversee the three components of the school's Academic Success Program. First, the school invites selected first-year students to attend a two-week program as a condition for admission into the school. The program helps students develop excellent law school study skills and introduces them to selected areas of the law in small sections taught by members of the full-time faculty. Second, the school offers study skills workshops during the spring and fall semesters. Third, the associate director meets one-on-one with students to provide individualized counseling on how to improve their study strategies. The second and third components are available to all students. Student feedback on the school's Academic Success Program has been very positive.

The Law Library

Immediately adjacent to the School of Law and occupying the entire third floor of the library building, the newly renovated law library features 140 carrels in secluded study areas, as well as areas for group interaction, with both LAN and WiFi connections throughout for accessing essential legal research databases. With holdings of over 401,000 volumes and equivalents, the library's collection strengths are constitutional law and history, legal history, jurisprudence, law and faith, philosophy of law, international human rights, and family law.

International Law and International Study Opportunities

The School of Law has established the *Regent Journal of International Law* and has a very active International Law Society. The *Journal* is jointly edited by students from Regent University School of Law, making it a truly international publication. International study opportunities include a summer program in Strasbourg, France, focusing on international law and human rights; a summer program in Israel focusing on issues of international law and the State of Israel and providing a hermeneutical comparison of Biblical and Qur'anic law, and opportunities to study at Handong International Law School in South Korea; at Shantou University, China; and in Barcelona and Madrid, Spain.

Housing

Regent Law students may choose from Regent Village (on campus) and a variety of off-campus housing options. Regent Village offers convenient and quality housing in a safe, friendly atmosphere within a five-minute shuttle ride of the law school. Regent Village options include one-, two-, and three-bedroom apartments. Housing applications are accepted from admitted candidates only. Rates are comparable to or less than similar apartment complexes in the vicinity.

Financial Aid

The School of Law is committed to helping students finance their legal education by awarding over $3.7 million in scholarships and grants, ranging from $500 to full tuition. In recent years, over 80 percent of law students received aid in the form of Regent scholarships and grants. Typically, admitted

candidates with LSAT scores greater than or equal to 160, UGPAs greater than or equal to 3.0, and personal goals evidencing a calling toward Christian leadership and service have been awarded academic merit scholarships ranging from 80 to 100 percent of tuition costs. Other scholarships are awarded on the basis of academic promise and other factors indicative of potential for law school success. Regent also provides grant assistance for qualified students who are called to serve minority communities upon graduation. Students not awarded financial assistance the first year of law school may qualify for assistance in future years based on academic performance. Regent provides a student loan repayment assistance program (LRAP) for qualified graduates practicing in the area of public interest law. A variety of loan options, including Stafford and Graduate PLUS, are available to meet the tuition and living expenses related to law school.

Campus Visitations

The campus visitation event schedule can be seen at www.regent.edu/lawvisitation. The Office of Admissions encourages prospective student visits. To RSVP for campus visitations or to arrange a visit to the law school, please e-mail lawschool@regent.edu or telephone 757.352.4584.

APPLICANT PROFILE

Regent University School of Law
This grid includes only applicants who earned 120–180 LSAT scores under standard administrations.

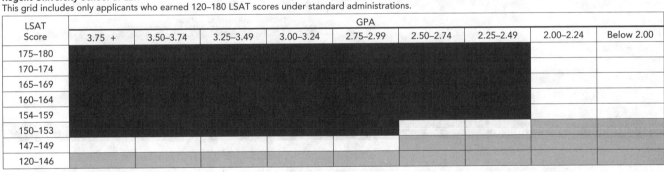

LSAT Score	GPA								
	3.75 +	3.50–3.74	3.25–3.49	3.00–3.24	2.75–2.99	2.50–2.74	2.25–2.49	2.00–2.24	Below 2.00
175–180									
170–174									
165–169									
160–164									
154–159									
150–153									
147–149									
120–146									

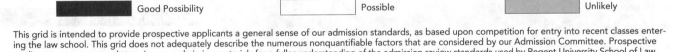

Good Possibility   Possible   Unlikely

This grid is intended to provide prospective applicants a general sense of our admission standards, as based upon competition for entry into recent classes entering the law school. This grid does not adequately describe the numerous nonquantifiable factors that are considered by our Admission Committee. Prospective applicants are encouraged to review our admission materials for a fuller understanding of the admission review standards used by Regent University School of Law.

UNIVERSITY OF RICHMOND SCHOOL OF LAW

28 Westhampton Way
University of Richmond, VA 23173
Phone: 804.289.8189; Fax: 804.287.6516
E-mail: lawadmissions@richmond.edu; Website: http://law.richmond.edu

ABA
Approved
Since
1928

The Basics

Type of school	Private
Term	Semester
Application deadline	2/15 4/15
Application fee	$50
Financial aid deadline	3/1
Can first year start other than fall?	Yes
Student to faculty ratio	12.4 to 1
# of housing spaces available restricted to law students	8
graduate housing for which law students are eligible	8

Faculty and Administrators

	Total		Men		Women		Minorities	
	Spr	Fall	Spr	Fall	Spr	Fall	Spr	Fall
Full-time	28	32	19	21	9	11	2	3
Other full-time	3	3	0	0	3	3	0	0
Deans, librarians, & others who teach	9	9	4	3	5	6	0	0
Part-time	62	53	36	31	26	22	0	3
Total	102	97	59	55	43	42	2	6

JD Enrollment and Ethnicity

	Men		Women		Full-Time		Part-Time		1st-Year		Total		JD Degs. Awd.
	#	%	#	%	#	%	#	%	#	%	#	%	
All Hispanics	4	1.6	0	0.0	4	0.9	0	0.0	2	1.3	4	0.9	1
Am. Ind./AK Nat.	1	0.4	2	1.0	3	0.7	0	0.0	0	0.0	3	0.7	2
Asian	13	5.3	16	7.7	29	6.4	0	0.0	9	5.9	29	6.4	4
Black/Af. Am.	20	8.1	18	8.7	37	8.2	1	50.0	12	7.8	38	8.4	16
Nat. HI/Pac. Isl.	1	0.4	1	0.5	2	0.4	0	0.0	0	0.0	2	0.4	0
2 or more races	0	0.0	0	0.0	0	0.0	0	0.0	0	0.0	0	0.0	0
Subtotal (minor.)	39	15.9	37	17.8	75	16.6	1	50.0	23	15.0	76	16.7	23
Nonres. Alien	8	3.3	6	2.9	14	3.1	0	0.0	1	0.7	14	3.1	1
White/Cauc.	188	76.4	160	76.9	347	76.8	1	50.0	113	73.9	348	76.7	142
Unknown	11	4.5	5	2.4	16	3.5	0	0.0	16	10.5	16	3.5	0
Total	246	54.2	208	45.8	452	99.6	2	0.4	153	33.7	454		166

Curriculum

	Full-Time	Part-Time
Typical first-year section size	51	0
Is there typically a "small section" of the first-year class, other than Legal Writing, taught by full-time faculty	No	No
If yes, typical size offered last year		
# of classroom course titles beyond first-year curriculum	101	

# of upper division courses, excluding seminars, with an enrollment:	Under 25	97
	25–49	19
	50–74	8
	75–99	5
	100+	0

# of seminars	16	
# of seminar positions available	256	
# of seminar positions filled	177	0
# of positions available in simulation courses	531	
# of simulation positions filled	431	0
# of positions available in faculty supervised clinical courses	53	
# of faculty supervised clinical positions filled	47	0
# involved in field placements	88	0
# involved in law journals	150	0
# involved in moot court or trial competitions	57	0
# of credit hours required to graduate	86	

Transfers

Transfers in	20
Transfers out	10

Tuition and Fees

	Resident	Nonresident
Full-time	$35,430	$35,430
Part-time		
Tuition Guarantee Program		N

Living Expenses

Estimated living expenses for singles

Living on campus	Living off campus	Living at home
$14,570	$15,780	$6,480

UNIVERSITY OF RICHMOND SCHOOL OF LAW

ABA
Approved
Since
1928

GPA and LSAT Scores

	Total	Full-Time	Part-Time
# of apps	2,371	2,371	0
# of offers	563	563	0
# of matrics	154	154	0
75% GPA	3.66	3.66	0.00
Median GPA	3.50	3.50	0.00
25% GPA	3.13	3.13	0.00
75% LSAT	164	164	0
Median LSAT	162	162	0
25% LSAT	158	158	0

Grants and Scholarships (from prior year)

	Total #	Total %	Full-Time #	Full-Time %	Part-Time #	Part-Time %
Total # of students	460		452		8	
Total # receiving grants	259	56.3	259	57.3	0	0.0
Less than 1/2 tuition	214	46.5	214	47.3	0	0.0
Half to full tuition	43	9.3	43	9.5	0	0.0
Full tuition	0	0.0	0	0.0	0	0.0
More than full tuition	2	0.4	2	0.4	0	0.0
Median grant amount			$10,000		$0	

Informational and Library Resources

Total amount spent on library materials	$1,522,295
Study seating capacity inside the library	675
# of full-time equivalent professional librarians	8
Hours per week library is open	106
# of open, wired connections available to students	695
# of networked computers available for use by students	48
Has wireless network?	Y
Requires computer?	Y

JD Attrition (from prior year)

	Academic #	Other #	Total #	Total %
1st year	1	11	12	8.2
2nd year	0	0	0	0.0
3rd year	0	0	0	0.0
4th year	0	0	0	0.0

Employment (9 months after graduation)

For up-to-date employment data, go to
employmentsummary.abaquestionnaire.org on the ABA website.

Bar Passage Rates

First-time takers	156	Reporting %	85.90
Average school %	82.09	Average state %	78.15
Average pass difference	3.94		

Jurisdiction	Takers	Passers	Pass %	State %	Diff %
Virginia	134	110	82.09	78.15	3.94

UNIVERSITY OF RICHMOND SCHOOL OF LAW

28 Westhampton Way
University of Richmond, VA 23173
Phone: 804.289.8189; Fax: 804.287.6516
E-mail: lawadmissions@richmond.edu; Website: http://law.richmond.edu

Introduction

The University of Richmond School of Law, founded in 1870, enjoys an established reputation for preparing its graduates for legal careers. Accredited by the ABA and a member of the AALS, its graduates are qualified to seek admission to the bar in all 50 states and the District of Columbia.

Situated on the university's 350-acre suburban campus, the school is only a 15-minute drive from downtown Richmond and its thriving legal community. In addition to being home to a number of international law firms, Richmond is the capital of the Commonwealth of Virginia, with numerous state and federal offices, and is the seat of both the Supreme Court of Virginia and the US Court of Appeals for the Fourth Circuit.

Library and Physical Facilities

The law school, located in a collegiate, gothic-style building, includes a moot courtroom that is the site of many classes, events, and mock trials, and where a panel of federal judges from the Fourth Circuit hears oral arguments once a year. The building has both wired and wireless connections, with almost 900 wired network connections. Every student has an individual study carrel, bearing his/her name, which functions as a personal office in the law library. The library offers a comprehensive collection of both electronic and print resources.

Curriculum

Courses in contracts, torts, criminal law, civil procedure, property, constitutional law, and legislation and regulation comprise the first-year curriculum. Required upper-level courses include professional responsibility and a third-year writing seminar. Elective courses in a variety of areas are available. In addition, all students complete a comprehensive, two-year program in legal reasoning, writing, research, and fundamental lawyering skills and values.

Academic Success Program and Bar Passage

Richmond Law has a comprehensive Academic Success Program geared toward assisting students to achieve at their highest possible academic level. The program also supports students in preparing for the bar exam, in whatever jurisdiction they choose to take it. Richmond Law consistently has one of the highest bar passage rates among first-time test takers in the Commonwealth of Virginia.

Special Programs

Several dual-degree programs allow students to earn the JD degree as well as a master's degree in a related discipline. Dual-degree programs are available in business administration, health administration, social work, urban studies and planning, and public administration, as well as others.

The law school operates the Children's Law Center through which students may participate in the Children's Defense Clinic, the Education Rights Clinic, the Jeanette Lipman Family Law Clinic, and the Advanced Children's Law Clinic.

Exciting clinical placements are arranged for academic credit in various legal arenas, including civil, criminal, judicial, legislative, corporate, and nonprofit placements. Students receive credit while obtaining valuable work experience in courts, law offices, corporations, and government and public interest agencies.

The Intellectual Property Institute has developed a curriculum to enable students to obtain a Certificate of Concentration in Intellectual Property Law. Students may also participate in the Intellectual Property and Transactional Law Clinic, through which they can represent for-profit and nonprofit organizations, business start-ups, artists, authors, and inventors.

The National Center for Family Law fosters research, scholarship, reports, conferences, symposia, legislative testimony, and other public participation and discourse on issues related to Family Law. Students may earn a Certificate of Concentration in Family Law.

The Robert R. Merhige Jr. Center for Environmental Studies engages in research, instruction, and public outreach on energy and environmental issues in the Mid-Atlantic region and beyond. The center hosts conferences, symposia, and speakers on pressing environmental issues, generating dialogue for policy solutions.

The Institute for Actual Innocence (IAI) works to identify, investigate, and exonerate wrongfully convicted individuals in the Commonwealth of Virginia. Students, with hands-on involvement by faculty and practicing lawyers, conduct reinvestigations of cases where credible evidence of actual innocence is present. Students learn the subtleties and pitfalls involved in interviewing witnesses, inmates, and other parties central to criminal cases. They learn to analyze a criminal trial or appellate record for new evidentiary perspectives. The IAI offers an environment for students to express their problem-solving, interpersonal, and analytical skills.

UR Downtown, a satellite campus in the heart of the city of Richmond, serves as a hub of community-based service, learning, research, and collaboration with nonprofit and government partners. UR Downtown aims to address pressing community needs through a combination of pro bono legal services provided by law students and attorneys, and community-based research and services provided by undergraduates and faculty.

International Programs

Richmond Law offers an extremely popular summer program at Emmanuel College in Cambridge, England, and an exchange program with the University of Paris, as well as with more than 20 universities worldwide, 9 of which have acclaimed law programs.

Student Activities

A student board publishes the *University of Richmond Law Review* on a quarterly basis. The *Richmond Journal of Law and Technology*, the first student-edited scholarly journal in the world to be published exclusively in electronic form, went online April 10, 1995. The *Richmond Journal of Law and the Public Interest* is a second online journal published by our students as an interdisciplinary journal dedicated to current and often controversial issues affecting the public. The *Richmond Journal of Global Law and Business* provides scholarly and practical insight into major legal and business issues affecting our global economy.

Richmond's moot court activities allow students to test their research, brief-writing, trial, negotiation, and appellate advocacy skills. Beginning in their 1L year, students participate in intraschool tournaments that lead to membership on the Moot Court Board, the Trial Advocacy Board (TAB), and the Client Counseling and Negotiation Board (CCNB). Moot Court, TAB, and CCNB teams represent the law school in regional, national, and international competitions.

Admission

Applications are reviewed as they become complete. All decisions are released by March 31. The admission committee considers the UGPA and LSAT as two important items, although extracurricular and community service activities and employment experience, among other factors, are also of interest. The law school provides an equal educational opportunity without regard to race, color, national origin, sex, disability, or religion.

We encourage class visits and, in keeping with our very personal approach to admission, we also encourage you to take advantage of meeting with a law student. Law students are available to give tours seven days a week and may be reached at LSAR@richmond.edu.

Expenses and Financial Aid

Institutional aid in the form of grants and scholarships is available on the basis of need and merit. Financial Aid decisions are often made based on submission of the FAFSA, and we recommend filing this form by February 25 to get the fullest consideration of all available aid. Parental income is not evaluated in determining financial aid for students who are considered independent by the law school. All applicants are considered for merit scholarships; a separate application form is not required. Merit awards are based on undergraduate academic achievement and aptitude for the study of law.

John Marshall Scholars Program—The law school's most prestigious awards offer $10,000 annual stipends in addition to $20,000 merit scholarships, as well as other honors, and are renewable annually if criteria are met. If invited to compete for the John Marshall Scholarship, a separate application must be submitted. Committee consideration for these scholarships is based solely on merit and personal attributes. John Marshall Scholars participate in a specially designed John Marshall Scholar seminar—a unique educational opportunity taught by a justice of the Supreme Court of Virginia.

Housing

Limited on-campus housing is available on a first-come, first-served basis. Richmond offers an abundance of good, affordable housing in proximity to the law school. For information on housing, contact the Admissions Office.

Career Services

The Career Services Office (CSO) works closely with law students and alumni by helping to align their interests and talents with a desired career path, and assisting them with developing the skills and knowledge necessary to conduct successful job searches. The CSO conducts a comprehensive, on-campus interview program that includes law firms and government and public interest employers, and it participates in a number of national job fairs. It also maintains an extensive employment database and organizes regular informational programs and networking opportunities.

Richmond is home to Fortune 500 companies, the Virginia General Assembly, international law firms, major nonprofit organizations, and more types of courts than any city in the U.S. outside of Washington, DC, or Boston, which affords students a myriad of opportunities for externships and part-time employment while in their second and third years of study.

APPLICANT PROFILE

University of Richmond School of Law
This grid includes only applicants who earned 120–180 LSAT scores under standard administrations.

LSAT Score	3.75 +		3.50–3.74		3.25–3.49		3.00–3.24		2.75–2.99		2.50–2.74		2.25–2.49		2.00–2.24		Below 2.00		No GPA		Total	
	Apps	Adm	Apps	Adm	Apps	Adm	Apps	Adm	Apps	Adm	Apps	Adm	Apps	Adm	Apps	Adm	Apps	Adm	Apps	Adm	Apps	Adm
175–180	0	0	1	0	2	1	1	0	1	1	2	0	0	0	0	0	0	0	0	0	7	2
170–174	4	1	3	1	6	4	7	3	3	0	3	2	1	1	0	0	0	0	0	0	27	12
165–169	22	18	34	22	39	28	33	16	17	7	6	5	5	1	1	1	0	0	3	2	160	100
160–164	69	65	116	107	119	59	98	46	38	16	17	6	15	1	6	4	0	0	5	2	483	306
155–159	75	26	131	53	171	7	99	4	72	5	32	1	13	0	9	0	2	1	5	0	609	97
150–154	48	8	103	13	104	8	116	6	80	3	49	1	19	0	9	2	3	0	7	0	538	41
145–149	19	0	36	0	44	0	73	0	49	0	27	0	11	0	5	0	1	0	3	0	268	0
140–144	6	0	16	0	28	0	25	0	30	0	29	0	14	0	8	0	3	0	5	0	164	0
135–139	2	0	5	0	8	0	11	0	12	0	7	0	6	0	4	0	2	0	2	0	59	0
130–134	0	0	0	0	4	0	7	0	2	0	5	0	2	0	5	0	2	0	1	0	28	0
125–129	1	0	1	0	0	0	1	0	0	0	1	0	1	0	0	0	0	0	0	0	5	0
120–124	0	0	0	0	0	0	0	0	0	0	0	0	0	0	0	0	0	0	0	0	0	0
Total	246	118	446	196	525	107	471	75	304	32	178	15	87	3	47	7	13	1	31	4	2348	558

Apps = Number of Applicants
Adm = Number Admitted
Reflects 99% of the total applicant pool; highest LSAT data reported.

ROGER WILLIAMS UNIVERSITY SCHOOL OF LAW

Ten Metacom Avenue
Bristol, RI 02809-5171
Phone: 401.254.4555 or 800.633.2727; Fax: 401.254.4516
E-mail: admissions@rwu.edu; Website: http://law.rwu.edu

ABA
Approved
Since
1995

The Basics

Type of school	Private
Term	Semester
Application deadline	3/15
Application fee	$60
Financial aid deadline	2/15
Can first year start other than fall?	No
Student to faculty ratio	17.0 to 1
# of housing spaces available restricted to law students	
graduate housing for which law students are eligible	72

Faculty and Administrators

	Total		Men		Women		Minorities	
	Spr	Fall	Spr	Fall	Spr	Fall	Spr	Fall
Full-time	26	27	12	13	14	14	3	3
Other full-time	0	2	0	1	0	1	0	1
Deans, librarians, & others who teach	6	7	3	3	3	4	0	1
Part-time	35	34	21	26	14	8	2	2
Total	67	70	36	43	31	27	5	7

Curriculum

	Full-Time	Part-Time
Typical first-year section size	66	0
Is there typically a "small section" of the first-year class, other than Legal Writing, taught by full-time faculty	No	No
If yes, typical size offered last year		
# of classroom course titles beyond first-year curriculum	100	

# of upper division courses, excluding seminars, with an enrollment:		
	Under 25	52
	25–49	17
	50–74	7
	75–99	4
	100+	0

# of seminars	35	
# of seminar positions available	651	
# of seminar positions filled	466	0
# of positions available in simulation courses	160	
# of simulation positions filled	139	0
# of positions available in faculty supervised clinical courses	67	
# of faculty supervised clinical positions filled	67	0
# involved in field placements	71	0
# involved in law journals	55	0
# involved in moot court or trial competitions	32	0
# of credit hours required to graduate	90	

JD Enrollment and Ethnicity

	Men		Women		Full-Time		Part-Time		1st-Year		Total		JD Degs. Awd.
	#	%	#	%	#	%	#	%	#	%	#	%	
All Hispanics	17	6.1	20	7.2	37	6.7	0	0.0	19	9.8	37	6.7	7
Am. Ind./AK Nat.	2	0.7	0	0.0	2	0.4	0	0.0	1	0.5	2	0.4	0
Asian	5	1.8	9	3.2	14	2.5	0	0.0	4	2.1	14	2.5	2
Black/Af. Am.	8	2.9	9	3.2	17	3.1	0	0.0	10	5.2	17	3.1	5
Nat. HI/Pac. Isl.	0	0.0	0	0.0	0	0.0	0	0.0	0	0.0	0	0.0	0
2 or more races	3	1.1	5	1.8	8	1.4	0	0.0	7	3.6	8	1.4	0
Subtotal (minor.)	35	12.6	43	15.5	78	14.1	0	0.0	41	21.2	78	14.1	14
Nonres. Alien	2	0.7	3	1.1	5	0.9	0	0.0	3	1.6	5	0.9	1
White/Cauc.	208	75.1	208	74.8	416	75.0	0	0.0	133	68.9	416	75.0	126
Unknown	32	11.6	24	8.6	56	10.1	0	0.0	16	8.3	56	10.1	17
Total	277	49.9	278	50.1	555	100.0	0	0.0	193	34.8	555		158

Transfers

Transfers in	5
Transfers out	11

Tuition and Fees

	Resident	Nonresident
Full-time	$39,550	$39,550
Part-time		
Tuition Guarantee Program	N	

Living Expenses

Estimated living expenses for singles

Living on campus	Living off campus	Living at home
$22,582	$22,582	$22,582

ABA
Approved
Since
1995

GPA and LSAT Scores

	Total	Full-Time	Part-Time
# of apps	1,388	1,388	0
# of offers	922	922	0
# of matrics	194	194	0
75% GPA	3.55	3.55	0.00
Median GPA	3.30	3.30	0.00
25% GPA	3.07	3.07	0.00
75% LSAT	155	155	0
Median LSAT	151	151	0
25% LSAT	149	149	0

Grants and Scholarships (from prior year)

	Total #	Total %	Full-Time #	Full-Time %	Part-Time #	Part-Time %
Total # of students	540		540		0	
Total # receiving grants	270	50.0	270	50.0	0	0.0
Less than 1/2 tuition	180	33.3	180	33.3	0	0.0
Half to full tuition	34	6.3	34	6.3	0	0.0
Full tuition	53	9.8	53	9.8	0	0.0
More than full tuition	3	0.6	3	0.6	0	0.0
Median grant amount			$13,500		$0	

Informational and Library Resources

Total amount spent on library materials	$839,295
Study seating capacity inside the library	403
# of full-time equivalent professional librarians	6
Hours per week library is open	110
# of open, wired connections available to students	112
# of networked computers available for use by students	36
Has wireless network?	Y
Requires computer?	N

JD Attrition (from prior year)

	Academic #	Other #	Total #	Total %
1st year	10	16	26	12.7
2nd year	0	0	0	0.0
3rd year	0	0	0	0.0
4th year	0	0	0	0.0

Employment (9 months after graduation)

For up-to-date employment data, go to employmentsummary.abaquestionnaire.org on the ABA website.

Bar Passage Rates

First-time takers	169	Reporting %	110.00
Average school %	83.10	Average state %	84.47
Average pass difference	−1.37		

Jurisdiction	Takers	Passers	Pass %	State %	Diff %
Massachusetts	109	98	89.91	89.67	0.24
Rhode Island	77	55	71.43	76.95	−5.52
New York	27	24	88.89	84.92	3.97

ROGER WILLIAMS UNIVERSITY SCHOOL OF LAW

Ten Metacom Avenue
Bristol, RI 02809-5171
Phone: 401.254.4555 or 800.633.2727; Fax: 401.254.4516
E-mail: admissions@rwu.edu; Website: http://law.rwu.edu

Introduction

Roger Williams University School of Law offers a world-class faculty, a strong and diverse student body, and an extraordinarily close and symbiotic relationship with the local bench and bar. The faculty hail from the nation's top law schools, boasting an impressive academic productivity, while bringing a wealth of hands-on experience—regional, national, and international—in virtually every area of the law to the student-teacher experience. Students reap the benefits of this dynamic through high bar-pass rates and diverse professional placements. By attending Rhode Island's only law school, they gain unparalleled access to the state's most sought-after judicial internships and the undivided attention of a state bar that functions in many ways as a de facto extension of a fast-growing alumni base. Students are regularly exposed to top legal minds. Leading members of the state and federal bench and bar teach here as adjuncts. Nationally known legal experts lecture at the law school, both as permanent faculty and distinguished guests. Each year, the Rhode Island Supreme Court hears final arguments in our internal moot court competition. RWU Law offers a rigorous and competitive legal education in a warm, open, and supportive environment.

Location

Located in picturesque Bristol, Rhode Island, on the banks of Mount Hope Bay, RWU Law offers idyllic walking trails and easy waterfront access. Bristol is a classic New England village, complete with tree-lined streets, a town green, and waterfront parks—as well as gourmet restaurants that stand alongside lively pubs and whimsical shops. In the summer, local waterways come alive with swimmers and boaters, while thousands throng to the town's famous Independence Day parade, established in 1785. A half hour north is Providence, a city of artistic and intellectual ambiance, bustling with theaters, museums, art galleries, antique shops, bookstores, and a mélange of ethnic neighborhoods, restaurants, and cultural events. Providence is also the seat of Rhode Island's legal culture, with the beautiful Frank Licht Judicial Complex anchoring the divide between the busy downtown and the bohemian atmosphere of College Hill, home to Brown University and the Rhode Island School of Design.

Library and Physical Facilities

Our Law Library is dedicated to providing the best possible resources for legal research. With a collection of more than 300,000 volumes and an ever-expanding menu of nearly 4,000 serial subscriptions, the Law Library houses one of the region's finest collections of printed legal materials, while also providing access to numerous online services and free Internet sources. Its 35,000-square-foot facility includes 16 private group-study rooms, several of them A/V equipped, and scores of computer workstations with ample wireless and wired network connections. In addition to its director, the Law Library offers five highly qualified law librarians and six support staff members to assist and advance the pedagogical and research needs of students and faculty. RWU Law offers an attractive learning environment, with plenty of comfortable sofas, chairs, and tables, and many quiet study nooks sprinkled through the law school building. In addition to the Law School Bistro, law students can grab a meal at the RWU Dining Commons, a new facility offering dining options for every taste and appetite, with a focus on organic and locally grown foods. Many law students also enjoy working out in RWU's state-of-the-art Recreation Center, featuring a fully equipped gym, squash courts, yoga and relaxation classes, basketball courts, and an indoor swimming pool.

Curriculum

The curriculum integrates intellectual theory, case analysis, and practical lawyering skills. The fundamental building blocks of effective lawyering constitute the first- and second-year curriculum. Students learn the skills of traditional legal analysis and the ability to elicit and convey information that every lawyer must master. The Legal Methods program and other required courses prepare students to become problem solvers; to comprehend, analyze, and synthesize complex material; and to communicate their positions effectively. In the latter years of their education, students gain expertise in legal specialties through clustering elective courses in particular fields of interest.

Joint-Degree Programs

Roger Williams University offers both a JD/Master of Science in Criminal Justice and a JD/Master of Science in Historic Preservation. The Criminal Justice program is designed to prepare graduates to formulate system policy and serve effectively as administrators to United States justice system agencies. The Historic Preservation program prepares graduates to understand the extensive legal and regulatory mechanisms used to protect cultural and historic resources. The School of Law also offers two joint-degree programs in conjunction with the University of Rhode Island. The JD/Master of Marine Affairs program is geared toward students interested in maritime, admiralty, and environmental law. The JD/Master of Science in Labor Relations and Human Resources program is designed for students interested in issues relating to employment and labor relations.

Special Programs

Marine Affairs Institute—The institute is recognized as a distinguished focal point for the exploration of legal, economic, and policy issues raised by the development of the oceans and coastal zone. Students take elective courses in traditional admiralty law and practice, pollution and environmental regulation, coastal zoning, fisheries, and the international law of the sea.

Feinstein Institute—The school believes that lawyers should serve the communities that support them. Introducing students to volunteerism and public service as part of their legal education, therefore, sets the stage for a lifetime of commitment. Thus, students are required to complete 50 hours of community service.

Honors Program

The Honors Program is a three-year program of seminars, clinics, and externships. Scholarships of $20,000 to full tuition are awarded to students selected for the Honors Program.

The Admissions Committee selects students, evaluating them on their academic records, LSAT scores, and recommendations.

Practical Experience

The School of Law operates a Criminal Defense Clinic and an Immigration Clinic in Providence. These clinics provide a service to the community by helping indigent clients and, at the same time, provide an excellent opportunity for students to represent clients before courts and agencies under the supervision of a faculty member. The School of Law also operates a Mediation Clinic in Bristol. As the only law school in Rhode Island, externship opportunities abound. Students may engage in a semester-long supervised clerkship in a judge's chamber or in a public interest or governmental law office for academic credit.

Study Abroad

The London Program on Comparative Advocacy internship combines classroom learning at the Inner Temple (one of the four Inns of Court) with a unique opportunity for students to be trained in English common law trial techniques with a barrister or judge. The School of Law also offers programs in Tianjin, China; Buenos Aires, Argentina; and The Hague, Netherlands through a partnership with Stetson University College of Law.

Admission

Admission is competitive and is based on the undergraduate grade-point average (UGPA) and the Law School Admission Test (LSAT) score, as well as other indicators of probable success in the study of law, such as graduate degree, work experience, undergraduate extracurricular activities, and community service. Applicants must register with LSAC's Credential Assembly Service. A personal statement and the $60 fee must accompany all applications. One letter of recommendation is required.

Financial Aid

Merit-based scholarships of up to full tuition are available; no separate application is required. Federal and state governmental agencies, as well as private lenders, offer students loans at comparative rates and flexible repayment terms. Students must file the Free Application for Federal Student Aid (FAFSA) to be considered for federal loans.

Student Activities

Law Review—Membership on the *Roger Williams University Law Review* is considered one of the most valuable and prestigious student activities available. The *Law Review* is staffed and primarily administered by students who are selected based upon superior academic achievement and writing ability.

Moot Court Board—The Moot Court Board is composed of students possessing superior appellate advocacy and writing ability. This prestigious organization sponsors speakers and programs on appellate advocacy, an intraschool competition, and moot court teams.

Extracurricular Activities—Student organizations include, but are not limited to, the Multicultural Law Students Association, Women's Law Association, the Alliance (LGBT), Black Law Students Association, Latino Law Students Association, Asian Pacific American Law Students Association, Older Wiser Law Students, Maritime Law Society, Sports and Entertainment Law Society, International Law Society, Association for Public Interest Law, and Association of Trial Lawyers of America.

Career Services

The Office of Career Services is dedicated to serving the needs of law students, alumni, and the legal community. The office features a welcoming suite for career research, on-campus interviews, and mock interviews. All of these tools help to prepare students to take advantage of the versatility of the Juris Doctor degree.

APPLICANT PROFILE

Roger Williams University School of Law

LSAT Score	GPA								
	3.75 +	3.50–3.74	3.25–3.49	3.00–3.24	2.75–2.99	2.50–2.74	2.25–2.49	2.00–2.24	Below 2.00
175–180									
170–174									
165–169									
160–164									
155–159									
150–154									
145–149									
140–144									
135–139									
130–134									
125–129									
120–124									

■ Good Possibility   □ Possible   ▨ Unlikely

This chart is to be used as a general guide only. Nonnumerical factors are strongly considered for all applicants.

RUTGERS—THE STATE UNIVERSITY OF NEW JERSEY—SCHOOL OF LAW—CAMDEN

217 North Fifth Street
Camden, NJ 08102
Phone: 856.225.6102 or 800.466.7561; Fax: 856.969.7903
E-mail: admissions@camlaw.rutgers.edu; Website: www.camlaw.rutgers.edu

ABA
Approved
Since
1950

The Basics

Type of school	Public
Term	Semester
Application deadline	4/15 6/1
Application fee	$65
Financial aid deadline	7/15
Can first year start other than fall?	Yes
Student to faculty ratio	13.0 to 1
# of housing spaces available restricted to law students	
graduate housing for which law students are eligible	223

Faculty and Administrators

	Total		Men		Women		Minorities	
	Spr	Fall	Spr	Fall	Spr	Fall	Spr	Fall
Full-time	53	45	33	27	20	18	5	4
Other full-time	4	4	1	1	3	3	1	1
Deans, librarians, & others who teach	13	13	6	6	7	7	1	1
Part-time	55	42	38	25	17	17	3	0
Total	125	104	78	59	47	45	10	6

Curriculum

		Full-Time	Part-Time
Typical first-year section size		63	27
Is there typically a "small section" of the first-year class, other than Legal Writing, taught by full-time faculty		No	No
If yes, typical size offered last year			
# of classroom course titles beyond first-year curriculum		179	
# of upper division courses, excluding seminars, with an enrollment:	Under 25	150	
	25–49	29	
	50–74	20	
	75–99	2	
	100+	0	
# of seminars		42	
# of seminar positions available		681	
# of seminar positions filled		431	65
# of positions available in simulation courses		777	
# of simulation positions filled		554	90
# of positions available in faculty supervised clinical courses		208	
# of faculty supervised clinical positions filled		163	21
# involved in field placements		153	13
# involved in law journals		153	10
# involved in moot court or trial competitions		25	1
# of credit hours required to graduate		84	

JD Enrollment and Ethnicity

	Men		Women		Full-Time		Part-Time		1st-Year		Total		JD Degs. Awd.
	#	%	#	%	#	%	#	%	#	%	#	%	
All Hispanics	38	6.9	22	7.1	43	6.6	17	7.8	30	8.8	60	6.9	7
Am. Ind./AK Nat.	1	0.2	0	0.0	1	0.2	0	0.0	0	0.0	1	0.1	0
Asian	40	7.2	16	5.1	46	7.1	10	4.6	22	6.5	56	6.5	30
Black/Af. Am.	21	3.8	28	9.0	33	5.1	16	7.3	19	5.6	49	5.7	13
Nat. HI/Pac. Isl.	0	0.0	1	0.3	1	0.2	0	0.0	1	0.3	1	0.1	0
2 or more races	5	0.9	4	1.3	6	0.9	3	1.4	6	1.8	9	1.0	0
Subtotal (minor.)	105	19.0	71	22.8	130	20.1	46	21.1	78	23.0	176	20.3	50
Nonres. Alien	3	0.5	1	0.3	4	0.6	0	0.0	2	0.6	4	0.5	3
White/Cauc.	420	75.9	218	69.9	470	72.6	168	77.1	253	74.6	638	73.8	175
Unknown	25	4.5	22	7.1	43	6.6	4	1.8	6	1.8	47	5.4	15
Total	553	63.9	312	36.1	647	74.8	218	25.2	339	39.2	865		243

Transfers

Transfers in	36
Transfers out	16

Tuition and Fees

	Resident	Nonresident
Full-time	$24,094	$35,358
Part-time	$19,695	$29,075
Tuition Guarantee Program	N	

Living Expenses

Estimated living expenses for singles

Living on campus	Living off campus	Living at home
$16,084	$21,594	$8,314

RUTGERS—THE STATE UNIVERSITY OF NEW JERSEY—SCHOOL OF LAW—CAMDEN

ABA
Approved
Since
1950

GPA and LSAT Scores

	Total	Full-Time	Part-Time
# of apps	1,663	1,663	0
# of offers	649	649	0
# of matrics	282	137	145
75% GPA	3.62	3.70	3.65
Median GPA	3.32	3.40	3.24
25% GPA	3.00	3.00	3.00
75% LSAT	161	161	161
Median LSAT	159	161	159
25% LSAT	156	158	155

Grants and Scholarships (from prior year)

	Total		Full-Time		Part-Time	
	#	%	#	%	#	%
Total # of students	789		573		216	
Total # receiving grants	223	28.3	205	35.8	18	8.3
Less than 1/2 tuition	193	24.5	177	30.9	16	7.4
Half to full tuition	30	3.8	28	4.9	2	0.9
Full tuition	0	0.0	0	0.0	0	0.0
More than full tuition	0	0.0	0	0.0	0	0.0
Median grant amount			$5,000		$5,000	

Informational and Library Resources

Total amount spent on library materials	$752,826
Study seating capacity inside the library	396
# of full-time equivalent professional librarians	5
Hours per week library is open	103
# of open, wired connections available to students	130
# of networked computers available for use by students	43
Has wireless network?	Y
Requires computer?	Y

JD Attrition (from prior year)

	Academic	Other	Total	
	#	#	#	%
1st year	3	26	29	10.8
2nd year	2	1	3	1.1
3rd year	2	0	2	0.9
4th year	0	0	0	0.0

Employment (9 months after graduation)

For up-to-date employment data, go to employmentsummary.abaquestionnaire.org on the ABA website.

Bar Passage Rates

First-time takers	279	Reporting %	88.53
Average school %	81.38	Average state %	82.34
Average pass difference	−0.96		

Jurisdiction	Takers	Passers	Pass %	State %	Diff %
New Jersey	247	201	81.38	82.34	−0.96

RUTGERS—THE STATE UNIVERSITY OF NEW JERSEY—SCHOOL OF LAW—CAMDEN

217 North Fifth Street
Camden, NJ 08102
Phone: 856.225.6102 or 800.466.7561; Fax: 856.969.7903
E-mail: admissions@camlaw.rutgers.edu; Website: www.camlaw.rutgers.edu

Introduction

Chartered in 1766 by George III of Great Britain as the Queen's College, Rutgers—The State University of New Jersey is one of the oldest and largest state higher educational systems in the nation. The law school at the Camden campus is proud to continue this national reputation of excellence. With more than 100 faculty and staff members, the law school is a leading center of legal education. Noted for excellence in scholarship and rigor in training of new lawyers, the law school faculty is internationally recognized in fields as diverse as international law, health law, family and women's rights law, state constitutional law, and legal history.

Located at the base of the Benjamin Franklin Bridge, just minutes from the Liberty Bell and Independence Hall in Philadelphia, the law school is in one of the nation's largest legal markets. With its thriving, 40-acre, tree-lined urban campus in Camden, New Jersey, Rutgers is a handsome blend of converted Victorian buildings and newly constructed facilities. The Susquehanna Bank Center at the Waterfront, an indoor/outdoor concert venue; the Adventure Aquarium; the USS Battleship New Jersey; the new law and graduate apartments across the street from the law school; the River LINE rail system; and Campbell's Field (the minor league baseball stadium), just a few blocks from the law school, are centerpieces for the ongoing development of Camden's waterfront. Camden, which is the county seat, has federal and local courts adjacent to the law school. A member of the Association of American Law Schools, the school is included on the list of approved schools of the American Bar Association.

Faculty

Faculty scholarship has been cited by numerous courts, including the United States Supreme Court, and faculty members have authored numerous casebooks and significant legal works. Faculty members have testified before Congress and serve as consultants and reporters for the American Bar Association, the American Law Institute, and several federal and state commissions, and act as counsel in important public interest litigation.

Library and Physical Facilities

The law school opened the doors to its new law building in 2008. A 2,300 square-foot courtroom and lobby with the new addition of 53,000 square feet almost doubles the size of the existing law building. The $40-million construction project has created state-of-the art classrooms, renovated two 100- to 150-seat lecture theaters and multiple seminar rooms, and expanded space for student organizations and social life at the law school. A magnificent two-story glass bridge and art display houses a student lounge and Law Café and welcomes visitors crossing the Benjamin Franklin Bridge from Philadelphia into New Jersey. A selective federal repository, the law library, with more than 500,000 bibliographic units, is one of the largest in the state. In addition to having access to traditional materials, students are trained on a number of computerized research systems, including a myriad of databases available on the Internet.

Curriculum and Special Programs

The first-year curriculum includes the traditional core legal courses and our highly nationally ranked yearlong course in research, writing, and analysis. Central to the curriculum is the lawyering program that engages students in simulated lawyering activities and practical applications of the law. Upper-class students can typically choose from more than 100 exciting elective courses each year, including electronic commerce, intellectual property, media policy, children's law, and international human rights.

An outstanding Externship Program offers third-year students the opportunity to work with federal and state judges, public agencies, and public interest organizations. Other students participate in the Civil Practice Clinic and pro bono programs at the law school. Live client experiences include the Domestic Violence Project, the Pro Bono Bankruptcy Project, the Immigration Project, the Mediation Project, and the Elder Law Clinic, or representing clients in connection with the LEAP Charter School. Each of these programs constitutes a comprehensive initiative that reflects the law school's commitment to public service.

Students may pursue their legal studies in the full-time day program or the part-time program, available day or evening. Both programs are subject to the same rigorous admission and academic standards.

Joint-Degree Programs

Eight formal joint JD and master's or doctoral degree programs are available with the University of Medicine and Dentistry, Graduate School of Business, Bloustein School of Planning and Public Policy, School of Social Work, and Graduate School—Camden, including the JD/MD, JD/DO, JD/MPA, JD/MBA, JD/MPH, JD/MPAP, JD/MSW, and JD/MCRP. Upon approval of the faculty, students may also pursue self-designed joint-degree programs within Rutgers University or with other graduate institutions.

Admission

Although admission is highly competitive, the Committee on Admissions does consider each applicant's file individually, and special qualities may occasionally overcome lower numbers. Important factors to the committee include LSAT score, undergraduate and graduate grade-point average, undergraduate and graduate institutions, work experience, and letters of recommendation. Typically, half of the full-time entering class scores in the top quartile on the LSAT (160 or higher) with a median GPA of 3.4. The entering class size each fall is about 225 full- and part-time day and 45 part-time evening students. The law school draws from 34 states and 3 foreign countries. More than 250 colleges and universities are represented in the student body. Decisions are made on a rolling basis beginning in early December. The law school has rolling admission and will consider candidates who take the February or June LSAT. However, early applicants have an enhanced opportunity for admission. Applicants may also apply for advanced standing as transfer students but are only eligible upon completion of one year of law study. Students may request an application from the law school or apply online at www.camlaw.rutgers.edu/. For full details on admission statistics and criteria, please see our website.

Housing

In 2012, a state-of-the-art, 12-story housing facility opened for graduate students providing comfortable apartment living with a touch of luxury. More information is online at housing.camden.rutgers.edu/330Microsite. First-year admitted students are invited to utilize the law school's housing webpage and to attend the Dean's Law and Housing Day in the spring.

Financial Aid

In the 2010–2011 academic year, over $22 million was distributed to law students through fellowships, grants, loans, and employment. The average financial aid package was approximately $29,064, with 96 percent of the student body receiving some form of assistance. The William D. Ford Federal Direct Loan Program, the largest financial aid program, provided more than $20.2 million to our law students in the last academic year. For fall consideration, the FAFSA should be submitted by March 1. Merit-based scholarships are also available for outstanding academic performance.

Career Services

The Office of Career Planning and Professional Development helps students and alumni develop and achieve their career goals through an holistic approach that includes individual counseling sessions; professional development programs designed to assist students in cultivating professional skills and obtaining summer, school year, and post-graduation employment; networking events; mentor programs; mock interview programs; access to various job fairs including one in the District of Columbia and two exclusively devoted to

public interest/public service jobs; and an on-campus interview program.

In 2010, the Office of Career Planning and Professional Development implemented a Professional Development Certificate Program to supplement the subject-based legal analysis from classroom learning with the professional development skills needed in order to succeed in the practice of law. The program helps to prepare students for practice, fosters a culture of professionalism, and encourages continuing professional development. The program is modeled on continuing legal education programs in which practicing lawyers choose from a menu of options in order to satisfy their CLE obligations. Past programs include Public Speaking for Lawyers, Networking for a Summer or Post-Grad Job, Business Development for Law Students, Starting your Own Practice, and panel discussions on various practice areas and settings.

Employment data on the class of 2011 can be found at https://camlaw.rutgers.edu/sites/default/files/charts.pdf.

Student Activities

Among the numerous student organizations are the Latino Law Students Association, Asian/Pacific American Law Students Association, Association for Public Interest Law, Black Law Students Association, Christian Legal Society, Community Outreach Group, Cyberlaw, Environmental Law Students Association, Francis Deak International Law Society, OUTLAW Student Bar Association, Health Law Society, Italian-American Law Students Organization, Jewish Law Students Association, Law Journal (publishes the *Rutgers Law Journal*), *Journal of Law and Public Policy*, *Rutgers Journal of Law and Religion*, Phi Alpha Delta law fraternity, Pro Bono/Public Interest Steering Committee, and the Women's Law Caucus.

APPLICANT PROFILE

Rutgers—The State University of New Jersey—School of Law—Camden
This grid includes only applicants who earned 120–180 LSAT scores under standard administrations.

LSAT Score	GPA								
	3.75 +	3.50–3.74	3.25–3.49	3.00–3.24	2.75–2.99	2.50–2.74	2.25–2.49	2.00–2.24	Below 2.00
175–180									
170–174									
165–169									
160–164									
155–159									
150–154									
145–149									
140–144									
135–139									
130–134									
125–129									
120–124									

Good Possibility   Possible   Unlikely

RUTGERS UNIVERSITY SCHOOL OF LAW—NEWARK

Center for Law and Justice, 123 Washington Street
Newark, NJ 07102
Phone: 973.353.5554; Fax: 973.353.3459
E-mail: lawinfo@andromeda.rutgers.edu; Website: www.law.newark.rutgers.edu

ABA Approved Since 1941

The Basics

Type of school	Public
Term	Semester
Application deadline	3/15
Application fee	$65
Financial aid deadline	3/15
Can first year start other than fall?	No
Student to faculty ratio	17.0 to 1
# of housing spaces available restricted to law students graduate housing for which law students are eligible	110

Faculty and Administrators

	Total		Men		Women		Minorities	
	Spr	Fall	Spr	Fall	Spr	Fall	Spr	Fall
Full-time	36	34	22	21	14	13	11	10
Other full-time	1	1	0	0	1	1	0	0
Deans, librarians, & others who teach	14	12	9	9	5	3	4	5
Part-time	44	39	32	27	12	12	4	2
Total	95	86	63	57	32	29	19	17

Curriculum

		Full-Time	Part-Time
Typical first-year section size		60	54
Is there typically a "small section" of the first-year class, other than Legal Writing, taught by full-time faculty		Yes	Yes
If yes, typical size offered last year		29	27
# of classroom course titles beyond first-year curriculum		126	
# of upper division courses, excluding seminars, with an enrollment:	Under 25	84	
	25–49	32	
	50–74	13	
	75–99	5	
	100+	4	
# of seminars		32	
# of seminar positions available		640	
# of seminar positions filled		349	50
# of positions available in simulation courses		500	
# of simulation positions filled		259	94
# of positions available in faculty supervised clinical courses		213	
# of faculty supervised clinical positions filled		166	34
# involved in field placements		107	12
# involved in law journals		182	18
# involved in moot court or trial competitions		42	0
# of credit hours required to graduate		84	

JD Enrollment and Ethnicity

	Men #	Men %	Women #	Women %	Full-Time #	Full-Time %	Part-Time #	Part-Time %	1st-Year #	1st-Year %	Total #	Total %	JD Degs. Awd.
All Hispanics	46	10.3	44	12.5	63	10.8	27	12.6	29	12.7	90	11.3	22
Am. Ind./AK Nat.	3	0.7	0	0.0	3	0.5	0	0.0	2	0.9	3	0.4	2
Asian	52	11.6	45	12.8	65	11.1	32	14.9	24	10.5	97	12.1	28
Black/Af. Am.	58	12.9	64	18.2	87	14.9	35	16.3	31	13.6	122	15.3	34
Nat. Hl/Pac. Isl.	0	0.0	1	0.3	0	0.0	1	0.5	1	0.4	1	0.1	0
2 or more races	5	1.1	6	1.7	8	1.4	3	1.4	5	2.2	11	1.4	0
Subtotal (minor.)	164	36.6	160	45.5	226	38.6	98	45.6	92	40.4	324	40.5	86
Nonres. Alien	2	0.4	7	2.0	7	1.2	2	0.9	4	1.8	9	1.1	7
White/Cauc.	282	62.9	185	52.6	352	60.2	115	53.5	132	57.9	467	58.4	154
Unknown	0	0.0	0	0.0	0	0.0	0	0.0	0	0.0	0	0.0	0
Total	448	56.0	352	44.0	585	73.1	215	26.9	228	28.5	800		247

Transfers

Transfers in	22
Transfers out	8

Tuition and Fees

	Resident	Nonresident
Full-time	$25,385	$37,117
Part-time	$16,558	$24,382
Tuition Guarantee Program	N	

Living Expenses

Estimated living expenses for singles

Living on campus	Living off campus	Living at home
$16,675	$22,185	$8,905

ABA
Approved
Since
1941

GPA and LSAT Scores

	Total	Full-Time	Part-Time
# of apps	2,797	2,218	579
# of offers	799	697	102
# of matrics	224	174	50
75% GPA	3.59	3.61	3.39
Median GPA	3.36	3.43	3.04
25% GPA	3.06	3.17	2.74
75% LSAT	160	160	159
Median LSAT	158	158	157
25% LSAT	155	155	155

Grants and Scholarships (from prior year)

	Total #	Total %	Full-Time #	Full-Time %	Part-Time #	Part-Time %
Total # of students	839		610		229	
Total # receiving grants	287	34.2	253	41.5	34	14.8
Less than 1/2 tuition	240	28.6	212	34.8	28	12.2
Half to full tuition	33	3.9	28	4.6	5	2.2
Full tuition	7	0.8	7	1.1	0	0.0
More than full tuition	7	0.8	6	1.0	1	0.4
Median grant amount			$6,000		$5,000	

Informational and Library Resources

Total amount spent on library materials	$756,811
Study seating capacity inside the library	532
# of full-time equivalent professional librarians	18
Hours per week library is open	95
# of open, wired connections available to students	570
# of networked computers available for use by students	180
Has wireless network?	Y
Requires computer?	Y

JD Attrition (from prior year)

	Academic #	Other #	Total #	Total %
1st year	1	26	27	9.6
2nd year	0	7	7	2.8
3rd year	0	3	3	1.2
4th year	0	0	0	0.0

Employment (9 months after graduation)

For up-to-date employment data, go to
employmentsummary.abaquestionnaire.org on the ABA website.

Bar Passage Rates

First-time takers	256	Reporting %	85.16
Average school %	83.49	Average state %	82.34
Average pass difference	1.15		

Jurisdiction	Takers	Passers	Pass %	State %	Diff %
New Jersey	218	182	83.49	82.34	1.15

RUTGERS UNIVERSITY SCHOOL OF LAW—NEWARK

Center for Law and Justice, 123 Washington Street
Newark, NJ 07102
Phone: 973.353.5554; Fax: 973.353.3459
E-mail: lawinfo@andromeda.rutgers.edu; Website: www.law.newark.rutgers.edu

Introduction

Rutgers University School of Law—Newark has been a pioneer in legal education for more than 100 years. Few law schools can match our contributions to the advancement of legal theory and practice, the diversity of our faculty and student body, the accomplishments of our public interest programs, and our reputation for outstanding academic quality and a progressive tradition. Our law professors are prominent scholars and experts in established and emerging areas of law who challenge students in an intense yet supportive environment. Our students come to us from around the world, bringing wide-ranging backgrounds and perspectives that enrich discourse in the classroom and throughout the law school community. Our clinical program offers invaluable hands-on instruction by noted litigators and teachers and the opportunity to provide service to the underserved. Our dual-degree program with several academic disciplines within the university and with the state's medical school enables students to add an interdisciplinary perspective to their study of law. The law school is located in the heart of New Jersey's largest city, which is home to leading law firms, courts, government agencies, major cultural institutions, Fortune 100 companies, entrepreneurial ventures, and public interest groups that offer numerous learning, internship, and volunteer opportunities.

The Center for Law and Justice

The law school is housed in the Center for Law and Justice, one of the finest law school buildings in the country. Highlights include a light-filled library with more than 790,000 volumes and electronic volume-equivalents and five computer labs; lecture rooms with excellent acoustics, sight lines, and power lines at every seat; an attractive courtroom complex where the Appellate Division of the Superior Court regularly hears cases; and numerous lounge and study areas. Wireless Internet access is available throughout the building and in all classrooms. The Center opens onto a pedestrian plaza and a garden terrace—favorite gathering spots for students and faculty.

Faculty

The faculty contribute to every aspect of the law school experience. Faculty members examine, shape, and resolve new and developing issues of law. Particular concentrations of academic strength lie in the fields of criminal law, constitutional law, intellectual property, legal history, and international law, with notable expertise as well in family law, race and the law, and labor and employment law. Faculty engage students through teaching styles that range from traditional Socratic method to interactive problem-solving. The faculty is diverse, ensuring the kind of intellectual inquiry that provides a rich foundation for a career in law.

Curriculum

The rigorous curriculum ensures the development of professional skills and values within a theoretical framework that promotes intellectual growth and a commitment to justice.

First-year students learn the essential conceptual, analytical, and research methods to be effective lawyers in complex environments. Upper-level students build on those skills through our extensive curriculum of over 200 class, clinic, and seminar options. The faculty review the curriculum regularly to ensure that the offerings prepare students for a rapidly changing legal environment.

An accredited semester of study abroad sends students to Leiden University in the Netherlands for an intensive program in international law, European Union law, comparative law, legal history, and law and international economics. The Rutgers Division of Global Affairs, located in our building, also serves as a nexus for students interested in the international dimension.

Joint-degree programs are available with the Rutgers Graduate Schools of Business, Planning and Public Policy, Criminal Justice, and Social Work, as well as with the University of Medicine and Dentistry of New Jersey. Students are encouraged to take advantage of the rich curriculum offerings throughout the university through cross-disciplinary registration. The Foreign Lawyer Program permits persons with foreign law degrees to earn a JD in two years.

Centers, institutes, and programs integrate faculty scholarship and activity, student interests and participation, and outreach to the larger university, legal, and other communities. As one example, the Center for Law, Science, and Technology supports faculty and student interest in intellectual property law, as well as in the intersection of law and science more generally. Among other activities, the Center holds an annual conference on patent law involving leaders from the judiciary, practice, industry, and the academic community.

Clinics and Public Service

The clinical program provides students with hands-on legal experience in real cases involving underrepresented clients, communities, or causes. Guided by talented and accomplished faculty with expertise in litigation, legislation, mediation, or transactional practice, our eight clinics are noted for their diversity, breadth, and comprehensiveness of experiences, as well as for their involvement in cases and projects of social and community impact. Clinical students provide corporate, transactional, and intellectual property legal services to nonprofits and start-up, for-profit businesses; litigate important constitutional and international human rights issues; provide representation to low-income children and their families; represent immigrants seeking various forms of relief from removal; assist low-income clients on tax matters; and participate in a wide range of community education and advocacy efforts. Other opportunities include pro bono work, internships, fellowships, and summer placements. The Loan Repayment Assistance Program assists graduates pursuing careers in public service.

Students and Student Life

Rutgers enrolls students of extraordinary academic and professional promise who enrich the community with their intellectual strength and significant life and work experience.

Many students have earned advanced degrees while others provide a global perspective to the classroom.

Diversity of views enlivens the classroom and creates an inclusive environment. Our Minority Student Program reflects the faculty's long-standing commitment to preserve the diversity of the law school and to advance diversity in the legal profession. Student-run organizations reflect myriad interests, political positions, and backgrounds, from the Women's Law Forum to the Entertainment and Sports Law Society. Student publications include the *Rutgers Law Review*, *Rutgers Computer and Technology Law Journal*, *Women's Rights Law Reporter*, *Rutgers Race and the Law Review*, and the online *Rutgers Law Record*.

Admission

The faculty believe that diverse perspectives and backgrounds are essential to a complete understanding of the law and its relation to contemporary society. The law school seeks and attracts a talented student body with a breadth of experience and provides unparalleled opportunities for those who have been historically excluded from the legal profession.

The Admissions Committee considers a broad range of factors, including, but not limited to, educational and employment experiences, community service, LSAT score, UGPA, race, ethnicity, socioeconomic background, and extraordinary family circumstances. Every applicant can choose to compete for admission with primary emphasis placed on numerical indicators (LSAT score and UGPA) or nonnumerical indicators (experiences and accomplishments).

In each entering class, 35–40 percent of our students are people of color. All regions of the country and more than two dozen foreign countries are represented.

Housing

On-campus graduate housing is located in close proximity to the law school. The recent addition of a new residence hall has increased the availability of on-campus housing for law students. Nearby suburban communities offer a variety of housing options. Public transportation is widely available.

Career Development

The Office of Career Services provides traditional and innovative services and programs, helping students and graduates develop career goals and conduct successful job searches. Individual counseling, skills training programs, panels, workshops, networking events, and on- and off-campus interview programs that attract many of the nation's leading law firms are just a few of the services offered. The office also works closely with prospective employers to maximize recruitment opportunities.

APPLICANT PROFILE

Rutgers University School of Law—Newark

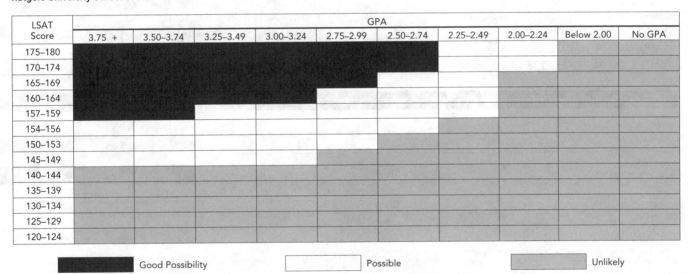

LSAT Score	GPA									
	3.75 +	3.50–3.74	3.25–3.49	3.00–3.24	2.75–2.99	2.50–2.74	2.25–2.49	2.00–2.24	Below 2.00	No GPA
175–180										
170–174										
165–169										
160–164										
157–159										
154–156										
150–153										
145–149										
140–144										
135–139										
130–134										
125–129										
120–124										

Good Possibility   Possible   Unlikely

The information contained in this grid should be used as an approximate gauge as to the likelihood of admission. The Admissions Committee gives considerable weight to individual accomplishments and other nonnumerical factors in the admissions process. LSAT and UGPA are not the sole determinants for admission.

ST. JOHN'S UNIVERSITY SCHOOL OF LAW

8000 Utopia Parkway
Queens, NY 11439
Phone: 718.990.6474; Fax: 718.990.2526
E-mail: lawinfo@stjohns.edu; Website: www.law.stjohns.edu

ABA
Approved
Since
1937

The Basics

Type of school	Private
Term	Semester
Application deadline	4/1
Application fee	$60
Financial aid deadline	4/1
Can first year start other than fall?	No
Student to faculty ratio	15.4 to 1
# of housing spaces available restricted to law students	69
graduate housing for which law students are eligible	

Faculty and Administrators

	Total		Men		Women		Minorities	
	Spr	Fall	Spr	Fall	Spr	Fall	Spr	Fall
Full-time	44	52	25	26	19	26	9	10
Other full-time	3	4	0	1	3	3	0	0
Deans, librarians, & others who teach	9	10	6	7	3	3	0	0
Part-time	88	65	72	46	16	19	9	3
Total	144	131	103	80	41	51	18	13

Curriculum

		Full-Time	Part-Time
Typical first-year section size		92	56
Is there typically a "small section" of the first-year class, other than Legal Writing, taught by full-time faculty		No	No
If yes, typical size offered last year			
# of classroom course titles beyond first-year curriculum		244	
# of upper division courses, excluding seminars, with an enrollment:	Under 25	148	
	25–49	41	
	50–74	11	
	75–99	14	
	100+	0	
# of seminars		30	
# of seminar positions available		541	
# of seminar positions filled		321	27
# of positions available in simulation courses		1,169	
# of simulation positions filled		712	125
# of positions available in faculty supervised clinical courses		215	
# of faculty supervised clinical positions filled		202	13
# involved in field placements		190	32
# involved in law journals		280	14
# involved in moot court or trial competitions		140	8
# of credit hours required to graduate		86	

Transfers

Transfers in	2
Transfers out	2

JD Enrollment and Ethnicity

	Men		Women		Full-Time		Part-Time		1st-Year		Total		JD Degs. Awd.
	#	%	#	%	#	%	#	%	#	%	#	%	
All Hispanics	42	7.8	49	12.3	72	9.1	19	12.8	33	11.2	91	9.7	19
Am. Ind./AK Nat.	0	0.0	0	0.0	0	0.0	0	0.0	0	0.0	0	0.0	0
Asian	35	6.5	37	9.3	60	7.6	12	8.1	25	8.5	72	7.7	25
Black/Af. Am.	18	3.4	24	6.0	26	3.3	16	10.8	12	4.1	42	4.5	18
Nat. HI/Pac. Isl.	0	0.0	0	0.0	0	0.0	0	0.0	0	0.0	0	0.0	2
2 or more races	13	2.4	11	2.8	22	2.8	2	1.4	7	2.4	24	2.6	6
Subtotal (minor.)	108	20.1	121	30.3	180	22.9	49	33.1	77	26.1	229	24.5	70
Nonres. Alien	9	1.7	3	0.8	12	1.5	0	0.0	5	1.7	12	1.3	6
White/Cauc.	413	77.1	263	65.9	579	73.6	97	65.5	206	69.8	676	72.3	195
Unknown	6	1.1	12	3.0	16	2.0	2	1.4	7	2.4	18	1.9	6
Total	536	57.3	399	42.7	787	84.2	148	15.8	295	31.6	935		277

Tuition and Fees

	Resident	Nonresident
Full-time	$46,450	$46,450
Part-time	$34,840	$34,840
Tuition Guarantee Program	N	

Living Expenses

Estimated living expenses for singles

Living on campus	Living off campus	Living at home
$23,816	$23,091	$9,880

ST. JOHN'S UNIVERSITY SCHOOL OF LAW

ABA
Approved
Since
1937

GPA and LSAT Scores

	Total	Full-Time	Part-Time
# of apps	4,057	3,429	628
# of offers	1,639	1,496	143
# of matrics	293	242	51
75% GPA	3.69	3.68	3.75
Median GPA	3.49	3.48	3.53
25% GPA	3.18	3.16	3.30
75% LSAT	162	162	157
Median LSAT	160	160	154
25% LSAT	154	154	150

Grants and Scholarships (from prior year)

	Total		Full-Time		Part-Time	
	#	%	#	%	#	%
Total # of students	940		764		176	
Total # receiving grants	381	40.5	359	47.0	22	12.5
Less than 1/2 tuition	117	12.4	108	14.1	9	5.1
Half to full tuition	123	13.1	117	15.3	6	3.4
Full tuition	138	14.7	132	17.3	6	3.4
More than full tuition	3	0.3	2	0.3	1	0.6
Median grant amount			$30,000		$20,000	

Informational and Library Resources

Total amount spent on library materials	$1,506,215
Study seating capacity inside the library	596
# of full-time equivalent professional librarians	9
Hours per week library is open	100
# of open, wired connections available to students	0
# of networked computers available for use by students	91
Has wireless network?	Y
Requires computer?	N

JD Attrition (from prior year)

	Academic	Other	Total	
	#	#	#	%
1st year	6	5	11	3.2
2nd year	2	4	6	2.0
3rd year	0	1	1	0.4
4th year	0	0	0	0.0

Employment (9 months after graduation)

For up-to-date employment data, go to employmentsummary.abaquestionnaire.org on the ABA website.

Bar Passage Rates

First-time takers	299	Reporting %	92.31
Average school %	85.87	Average state %	84.92
Average pass difference	0.95		

Jurisdiction	Takers	Passers	Pass %	State %	Diff %
New York	276	237	85.87	84.92	0.95

ST. JOHN'S UNIVERSITY SCHOOL OF LAW

8000 Utopia Parkway
Queens, NY 11439
Phone: 718.990.6474; Fax: 718.990.2526
E-mail: lawinfo@stjohns.edu; Website: www.law.stjohns.edu

Introduction

St. John's University School of Law is a forceful presence and an integral part of the New York metropolitan area. It imparts to its students training and competency in the basic skills and techniques of the legal profession, a grasp of the history and the system of common law, and a familiarity with important statutes and decisions in federal and state jurisdictions.

St. John's School of Law is approved by the ABA and is a member of the AALS.

Physical Facilities and Library

The showpiece of the law school building is its beautiful law library, which incorporates the most recent advances in law library science and technology. It contains a computer laboratory and several study rooms for student conferences. The library occupies approximately 50,000 square feet on five of the eight building levels. It has been designated a depository library for US government and UN documents.

The School of Law has recently completed a major renovation of its moot court, producing a beautiful, state-of-the-art facility that incorporates technologies that further the teaching and research missions of St. John's. In addition, the School of Law has completed renovations of first-year classrooms, clinic offices, the professional skills center, the writing center, and the faculty library.

New York City

The School of Law is located on the Queens Campus of St. John's University. Situated on almost 100 rolling acres in a residential area, the campus boasts a spectacular view of the Manhattan skyline. The campus is easily accessible to Manhattan and all of New York City, and the location provides opportunities and access to the world's largest law firms, businesses, government agencies, and courts.

Clinical and Externship Programs

Elective clinical programs and externships are available to second- and third-year students.

Externships: Civil, Criminal Justice, Judicial, Special Education, Judicial/Matrimonial Alternative Dispute Resolution (ADR), Street Law.

Clinics: Elder Law; Child Advocacy; Securities Arbitration; Refugee and Immigrant Rights; Prosecution; Immigrant Tenant Advocacy; Bread and Life: Immigration; Criminal Defense; Bankruptcy Advocacy; Economic Justice; Domestic Violence Litigation; Consumer Protection; and Family Law Mediation.

Vincentian Scholarship Program

The mission statement of St. John's University School of Law calls for the law school "to provide a superior legal education for a diverse population of students with special awareness for economic fairness and equal opportunity, consistent with and in fulfillment of the Vincentian tradition and mission." In furtherance of this Vincentian tradition and mission, the School of Law provides five full-tuition Vincentian scholarships each year in its ongoing effort to achieve a diverse student body.

Student Activities

Publications—*St. John's Law Review/St. Thomas More Institute for Research, Journal of Catholic Legal Studies, Journal of Civil Rights and Economic Development, New York International Law Review, American Bankruptcy Institute Law Review, N.Y. Litigator,* and *N.Y. Real Property Law Journal.*

Mock Trial and Appellate Activities—Moot Court Honor Society, Frank S. Polestino Trial Advocacy Institute.

Specialized Legal Activities—Student Bar Association, Admiralty Law Society, Women's Law Association, Bankruptcy Law Society, Environmental Law Club, International Law Society, Intellectual Property, Labor and Employment Club, Real Property Club, Black Law Students Association, South Asian Law Students Association, Asian Pacific American Law Students Association, Latino American Law Students Association, and Entertainment, Arts, and Sports Law Society. The school also maintains chapters in two legal societies, Phi Delta Phi and Phi Alpha Delta.

Special Diversity Admission Program

The School of Law sponsors a program for individuals who have faced the challenges of discrimination, chronic financial hardship, or other social, educational, or physical disadvantages to such an extent that their undergraduate performance or LSAT score would not otherwise warrant unconditional acceptance into the entering class. This Summer Institute Program consists of a substantive course taught and graded according to the same qualitative standard applied to all first-year courses, as well as a legal writing course. The program enables individuals whose LSAT scores and GPAs are not reliable predictors of their success to demonstrate their ability to succeed in the study of law.

Centers

Hugh L. Carey Center for Dispute Resolution, Ronald H. Brown Center for Civil Rights and Economic Development, Center for Bankruptcy Studies, Center for International and Comparative Law, Center for Labor and Employment Law, Center for Law and Religion, Writing Center, Center for Professional Skills, and Public Interest Law Center.

Academic Support

The Writing Center is a place where students can brainstorm about ideas, practice writing exam essays, edit scholarly pieces, submit papers to writing competitions, find publication sources for articles, polish briefs and memoranda for use as writing samples, practice proper citation form, hone grammar skills, or get help with any general writing problems. The Writing Center was recently renovated, is located on the first floor of the law school building, and is staffed by some of the law school's best writers.

Career Development

The Career Development Office provides an array of services, including résumé and cover letter critiquing, mock interview coaching, job and judicial clerkship postings, newsletters, lists of prospective employers, interview programs, and career education panels. Recent graduates have obtained employment in many areas of the legal profession. The placement rate at nine months after graduation for all graduates of the class of 2011 was 84.8 percent. When full-time degree-seekers and graduates not seeking employment are removed from the denominator, and graduates with deferred start dates are added to the numerator and denominator, the placement rate for the Class of 2011 was 88.7 percent.

Alumni of the law school are currently practicing throughout the United States and its territories. Many have achieved positions of prominence in executive and legislative branches of the government, as members of the judiciary, and in both private and corporate practice. Two recent governors of New York, a congressman for New York, a recent governor of the US Virgin Islands, and a former governor of California were graduates of St. John's School of Law.

Financial Aid and Housing

The School of Law provides extensive financial scholarship aid to students annually. There are university housing facilities, and many students find other suitable living accommodations in the vicinity of the university. In addition, the Admission Office coordinates a housing network for students.

Summer Study-Abroad Programs

Each summer, St. John's University offers study-abroad programs as a way to enjoy the experience of learning in a different setting. Students have the pleasure of learning and gaining credits toward graduation in Rome and Paris. Courses in International or Comparative Law are traditionally offered in a four-week program (for up to six credits for each program). US and international law students are allowed to apply. They also have the opportunity to visit top Italian and French legal institutions and develop networking connections for future reference. Limited externships are available after each program.

LLM Programs

LLM in Bankruptcy—St. John's has the nation's first master's program in bankruptcy. It is designed to meet an important and special educational need in the field of bankruptcy law. Matriculating students will be required to complete 30 credits, including the preparation and defense of a major thesis on a current significant bankruptcy topic. Students may matriculate on a full- or part-time basis.

LLM in US Legal Studies—St. John's offers an LLM program tailored exclusively for international law school graduates. The program is one year in residence and requires the completion of 24 credits. Students may enroll on a full- or part-time basis.

Beginning in Fall 2012, St. John's will introduce two new LLM programs, an LLM in International and Comparative Sports Law and an LLM in Transnational Legal Practice.

APPLICANT PROFILE

St. John's University School of Law

LSAT Score	GPA								
	3.75 +	3.50–3.74	3.25–3.49	3.00–3.24	2.75–2.99	2.50–2.74	2.25–2.49	2.00–2.24	Below 2.00
175–180									
170–174									
165–169									
160–164									
155–159									
150–154									
145–149									
140–144									
135–139									
130–134									
125–129									
120–124									

■ Good Possibility   □ Possible   ▨ Unlikely

Average LSAT data reported.

SAINT LOUIS UNIVERSITY SCHOOL OF LAW

3700 Lindell Boulevard
St. Louis, MO 63108
Phone: 314.977.2800; Fax: 314.977.1464
E-mail: admissions@law.slu.edu; Website: http://law.slu.edu

ABA
Approved
Since
1924

The Basics

Type of school	Private
Term	Semester
Application deadline	3/1
Application fee	$55
Financial aid deadline	3/1
Can first year start other than fall?	No
Student to faculty ratio	13.7 to 1
# of housing spaces available restricted to law students	
graduate housing for which law students are eligible	

Faculty and Administrators

	Total Spr	Total Fall	Men Spr	Men Fall	Women Spr	Women Fall	Minorities Spr	Minorities Fall
Full-time	51	55	28	32	23	23	6	8
Other full-time	13	10	1	1	12	9	1	0
Deans, librarians, & others who teach	15	16	5	5	10	11	1	1
Part-time	54	47	34	29	20	18	3	4
Total	133	128	68	67	65	61	11	13

Curriculum

	Full-Time	Part-Time
Typical first-year section size	87	35
Is there typically a "small section" of the first-year class, other than Legal Writing, taught by full-time faculty	Yes	Yes
If yes, typical size offered last year	26	35
# of classroom course titles beyond first-year curriculum	155	
# of upper division courses, excluding seminars, with an enrollment: Under 25	268	
25–49	55	
50–74	17	
75–99	8	
100+	2	
# of seminars	37	
# of seminar positions available	474	
# of seminar positions filled	295	54
# of positions available in simulation courses	1,352	
# of simulation positions filled	937	165
# of positions available in faculty supervised clinical courses	146	
# of faculty supervised clinical positions filled	111	35
# involved in field placements	116	17
# involved in law journals	113	6
# involved in moot court or trial competitions	41	5
# of credit hours required to graduate	91	

JD Enrollment and Ethnicity

	Men #	Men %	Women #	Women %	Full-Time #	Full-Time %	Part-Time #	Part-Time %	1st-Year #	1st-Year %	Total #	Total %	JD Degs. Awd.
All Hispanics	14	2.7	18	4.3	30	3.7	2	1.6	11	3.7	32	3.4	9
Am. Ind./AK Nat.	1	0.2	1	0.2	2	0.2	0	0.0	0	0.0	2	0.2	2
Asian	10	2.0	23	5.5	29	3.6	4	3.2	10	3.4	33	3.5	9
Black/Af. Am.	13	2.5	32	7.6	36	4.5	9	7.3	15	5.1	45	4.8	19
Nat. HI/Pac. Isl.	1	0.2	0	0.0	1	0.1	0	0.0	0	0.0	1	0.1	0
2 or more races	12	2.4	12	2.9	23	2.9	1	0.8	9	3.1	24	2.6	5
Subtotal (minor.)	51	10.0	86	20.5	121	15.0	16	12.9	45	15.3	137	14.7	44
Nonres. Alien	2	0.4	3	0.7	4	0.5	1	0.8	0	0.0	5	0.5	0
White/Cauc.	451	88.4	324	77.1	668	82.9	107	86.3	240	81.6	775	83.3	223
Unknown	6	1.2	7	1.7	13	1.6	0	0.0	9	3.1	13	1.4	5
Total	510	54.8	420	45.2	806	86.7	124	13.3	294	31.6	930		272

Transfers

Transfers in	9
Transfers out	17

Tuition and Fees

	Resident	Nonresident
Full-time	$36,175	$36,175
Part-time	$26,325	$26,325
Tuition Guarantee Program	N	

Living Expenses

Estimated living expenses for singles

Living on campus	Living off campus	Living at home
$23,456	$23,456	$23,456

SAINT LOUIS UNIVERSITY SCHOOL OF LAW

ABA
Approved
Since
1924

GPA and LSAT Scores

	Total	Full-Time	Part-Time
# of apps	2,040	1,738	302
# of offers	1,116	1,023	93
# of matrics	295	268	27
75% GPA	3.58	3.61	3.49
Median GPA	3.39	3.39	3.29
25% GPA	3.13	3.14	2.90
75% LSAT	158	158	156
Median LSAT	154	154	153
25% LSAT	151	151	149

Grants and Scholarships (from prior year)

	Total		Full-Time		Part-Time	
	#	%	#	%	#	%
Total # of students	938		800		138	
Total # receiving grants	360	38.4	330	41.3	30	21.7
Less than 1/2 tuition	258	27.5	230	28.8	28	20.3
Half to full tuition	70	7.5	70	8.8	0	0.0
Full tuition	32	3.4	30	3.8	2	1.4
More than full tuition	0	0.0	0	0.0	0	0.0
Median grant amount			$17,515		$6,590	

Informational and Library Resources

Total amount spent on library materials	$891,846
Study seating capacity inside the library	502
# of full-time equivalent professional librarians	10
Hours per week library is open	103
# of open, wired connections available to students	601
# of networked computers available for use by students	65
Has wireless network?	Y
Requires computer?	N

JD Attrition (from prior year)

	Academic	Other	Total	
	#	#	#	%
1st year	4	14	18	5.5
2nd year	1	25	26	8.5
3rd year	1	0	1	0.4
4th year	0	1	1	2.8

Employment (9 months after graduation)

For up-to-date employment data, go to
employmentsummary.abaquestionnaire.org on the ABA website.

Bar Passage Rates

First-time takers	286	Reporting %	84.27
Average school %	91.70	Average state %	90.08
Average pass difference	1.62		

Jurisdiction	Takers	Passers	Pass %	State %	Diff %
Missouri	196	182	92.86	90.24	2.62
Illinois	45	39	86.67	89.38	−2.71

SAINT LOUIS UNIVERSITY SCHOOL OF LAW

3700 Lindell Boulevard
St. Louis, MO 63108
Phone: 314.977.2800; Fax: 314.977.1464
E-mail: admissions@law.slu.edu; Website: http://law.slu.edu

Introduction

The mission of Saint Louis University School of Law (SLU LAW) is to advance the understanding and development of law, and prepare students to achieve professional success and personal satisfaction through leadership and service to others. The school is guided by the Jesuit tradition of academic excellence, freedom of inquiry, and respect for individual differences.

Located in the growing midtown neighborhood just west of downtown St. Louis, SLU LAW is perfectly positioned to provide students with unparalleled exposure to the legal world. St. Louis boasts an impressive list of law firms, corporate offices, and governmental agencies, in addition to local, state, and federal courthouses throughout the city and surrounding counties. Our urban setting provides countless opportunities for students to foster their professional development through internships, clerkships, and the SLU LAW Legal Clinics.

With an accomplished, accessible faculty and a diverse curriculum, SLU LAW provides a challenging yet collegial environment designed to foster success for dedicated students. Whatever the interest—health, corporate and finance, criminal, international, intellectual property, tax, securities, real estate, labor and employment, or litigation—SLU LAW can help students achieve their desired career goals.

First-year, full-time law students will be assigned to two small sections of classes ranging between 20–35 students depending on the class. This allows for individualized instruction and focused student interaction and, most importantly, builds a sense of support and community among classmates. The remaining classes are formed by combining different small sections to allow students to get to know others in their entering class.

For those who work full time and are unable to attend classes during the day, SLU LAW offers a challenging **Part-Time Program**—the only program of its kind in the state of Missouri. Through this program, students can earn their law degree in four years with summer attendance or five years without summer attendance.

Special Academic Programs

Centers for Excellence—SLU LAW features one of the premier health law studies programs in the nation, along with specialized centers in employment law, the interdisciplinary study of law, and international and comparative law.

- The **Center for Health Law Studies** boasts a nationally recognized faculty, an unparalleled curriculum, an opportunity for students to spend a semester in Washington, DC, working for a federal agency, and some of the country's finest health law publications.
- The **Wefel Center for Employment Law** specializes in issues of labor disputes, benefits, hiring and discharging, and arbitration.
- The **Center for International and Comparative Law** offers a specialized program of study in areas such as public international law, international criminal law, and international corporate law. Students receive instruction from faculty who have experienced and studied foreign legal systems.
- The **Center for the Interdisciplinary Study of Law** advances legal theory and promotes interdisciplinary legal scholarship by facilitating the integration of insights from other academic disciplines with law and policy research.

Concentrations—In addition to the concentration programs through our Centers for Excellence, the School of Law offers concentrations in the following areas: Business Transactional Law; Civil Litigation Skills; Criminal Litigation Skills; Taxation; Urban Development, Land Use, and Environmental Law; and Intellectual Property.

Study Abroad and Exchange Programs—Through the Center for International and Comparative Law, students can study law at Saint Louis University's campus in **Madrid, Spain**, earning up to six credit hours of comparative law with foreign and American professors who have extensive experience in the fields of foreign and American criminal law, civil law, and global human rights. SLU LAW also has study abroad opportunities in the following locations: Bern, Switzerland; Cork, Ireland; Paris or Orleans, France; Germany; and Southeast Asia.

Dual-Degree Programs—The School of Law offers intensive dual-degree programs in cooperation with Saint Louis University's graduate schools, including the Schools of Business, Public Health, and Public Policy. Candidates in a dual-degree program must complete the first-year law curriculum before beginning the dual-degree program. The dual-degree programs available are JD/MBA, JD/Master of Accounting, JD/MHA, JD/MA in Public Administration, JD/MA in Urban Affairs, JD/MPH, JD/MPH in Health Policy, JD/MSW, JD/MA in Sociology and Criminal Justice, and JD/PhD in Health Care Ethics.

Public Service

SLU LAW has a strong commitment to public service and a faculty pro bono director. Starting with orientation and continuing throughout the year, SLU LAW students participate in public service events and projects. Some of our programs include Make a Difference Day—Homeward Bound, Habitat for Humanity, Court Appointed Special Advocates, Stand Down for Homeless Veterans, and the Tax Assistance Program. Through the SLU LAW Legal Clinics, our students give 39,000 hours of free legal time annually to the surrounding community.

Professional Skills Training

Students participate in courses that focus on lawyering skills through simulated client situations or live client representation under the supervision of a faculty member. **Legal Clinics** allow students to represent clients in a variety of settings, from court appearances to appeals to real estate matters. Students in the judicial clerkship programs clerk for area judges. Externships allow students to work in outside placements ranging from government agencies to large health care systems. Simulated professional skills experiences include the **Trial Advocacy Program**, **Moot Court**, and **Appellate Advocacy Program**, as well as multiple drafting courses. Drafting courses are offered in a variety of specialized areas such as intellectual property, health law, real estate, and secured transactions. Courses such as Client Counseling and Negotiations provide students with the tools necessary for skillful client interaction and the art of effective negotiation in client representation. Many of the competitions and cocurricular activities also allow students to apply legal theory to simulated client representation.

Cocurricular Activities

SLU LAW allows students to perfect their writing and editing skills by working on one of **three law journals**—*Saint Louis University Law Journal, Saint Louis University Public Law Review*, and the *Journal of Health Law and Policy*. Qualifying students are invited to write and edit the collections of scholarly work submitted by lawyers and law professors across the world. A broad spectrum of student competitions at the local, regional, and national levels allows students to further their skills. **Moot Court Competitions** hone a student's skills in the appellate phase of litigation, including research, analysis, writing, and oral argument before judges. SLU LAW students regularly compete in the National Health Law Moot Court Competition, the ABA Moot Court Competition, the Frederick Douglass Moot Court Competition, the Jessup Moot Court Competition (International Law), the Intellectual Property Moot Court Competition, and the National Environmental Law Moot Court Competition. This year, SLU LAW was one of only 16 law schools invited to participate in the 2012 Andrews Kurth Moot Court National Championship, and our Black Law Students Association Moot Court Team placed first in the nation at the Frederick Douglas Moot Court Competition. Numerous **Trial Advocacy Competitions** allow SLU LAW students to practice the skills necessary for trying cases before a jury. Each year students participate in the Texas Young Lawyers Association Trial Advocacy Competition, the ABA Employment Law Trial Advocacy Competition, and the Thurgood Marshall Mock Trial Competition. Other competitions include the ABA's Client Counseling and Negotiations competitions.

Financial Aid/Scholarships

The Saint Louis University School of Law awards a substantial number of merit-based scholarships to a select group of highly qualified admitted students, including 10 full-tuition scholarships through the 1843 Scholars program. The school has a variety of ways to help students meet their financial goals. Admitted students may contact the School of Law's Financial Aid Coordinator at fin_aid@law.slu.edu for assistance with financial aid.

Library

The Omer Poos Law Library serves as the center for legal and interdisciplinary research. SLU LAW's databases allow students to access a wide variety of legal materials at any time from anywhere. The library provides a state-of-the-art research environment with access to scores of electronic resources and a collection of over 600,000 volumes. Research librarians hold both law and library science degrees and are available during the day and evening to assist students with research. The SLU LAW library faculty and staff take pride in providing personal attention and service to students.

Career Services

The Career Services Office, staffed by licensed attorneys, assists students in identifying their career goals and preparing themselves to be marketable to employers. Students with differing backgrounds and career goals benefit from the personalized assistance that the office provides. Across the nation, SLU LAW alumni work at large and small firms, excel as CEOs and in-house counsel, and serve in national, state, and local government organizations.

APPLICANT PROFILE

Saint Louis University School of Law
This grid includes only applicants who earned 120–180 LSAT scores under standard administrations.

LSAT Score	3.75 +		3.50–3.74		3.25–3.49		3.00–3.24		2.75–2.99		2.50–2.74		2.25–2.49		2.00–2.24		Below 2.00		No GPA		Total	
	Apps	Adm	Apps	Adm	Apps	Adm	Apps	Adm	Apps	Adm	Apps	Adm	Apps	Adm	Apps	Adm	Apps	Adm	Apps	Adm	Apps	Adm
175–180	1	1	0	0	0	0	0	0	0	0	1	1	0	0	0	0	0	0	0	0	2	2
170–174	3	3	1	1	5	5	2	2	2	1	0	0	1	1	0	0	0	0	0	0	14	13
165–169	18	17	22	22	14	13	10	9	4	4	1	1	1	1	0	0	0	0	1	0	71	67
160–164	53	49	69	67	53	53	31	30	18	15	6	4	5	3	3	1	0	0	4	2	242	224
155–159	81	79	113	104	114	98	82	64	56	36	20	9	9	4	6	2	0	0	3	2	484	398
150–154	72	47	98	63	133	87	109	58	65	23	41	4	14	0	9	0	0	0	10	1	551	283
145–149	21	12	37	22	62	18	53	20	49	0	29	0	19	0	8	0	1	0	9	0	288	72
140–144	5	0	14	3	19	1	17	0	20	1	12	0	13	1	8	0	2	0	2	0	112	6
135–139	0	0	2	0	5	0	6	0	10	0	7	0	4	0	1	0	1	0	2	0	38	0
130–134	0	0	0	0	1	0	3	0	4	0	7	0	1	0	1	0	1	0	1	0	19	0
125–129	0	0	1	0	2	0	0	0	1	0	3	0	2	0	0	0	0	0	1	0	10	0
120–124	0	0	0	0	0	0	0	0	0	0	0	0	0	0	0	0	0	0	0	0	0	0
Total	254	208	357	282	408	275	313	183	229	80	127	19	69	10	36	3	5	0	33	5	1831	1065

Apps = Number of Applicants
Adm = Number Admitted
Reflects 99% of the total applicant pool; highest LSAT data reported.

ST. MARY'S UNIVERSITY SCHOOL OF LAW

One Camino Santa Maria
San Antonio, TX 78228-8601
Phone: 210.436.3523; Toll-free: 866.639.5831; Fax: 210.431.4202
E-mail: lawadmissions@stmarytx.edu; Website: www.stmarytx.edu/law

ABA
Approved
Since
1948

The Basics

Type of school	Private
Term	Semester
Application deadline	3/1
Application fee	$55
Financial aid deadline	3/31
Can first year start other than fall?	No
Student to faculty ratio	22.3 to 1
# of housing spaces available restricted to law students	
graduate housing for which law students are eligible	108

Faculty and Administrators

	Total		Men		Women		Minorities	
	Spr	Fall	Spr	Fall	Spr	Fall	Spr	Fall
Full-time	30	31	18	20	12	11	5	4
Other full-time	5	7	1	1	4	6	1	2
Deans, librarians, & others who teach	12	11	8	7	4	4	5	5
Part-time	55	57	29	38	26	19	8	9
Total	102	106	56	66	46	40	19	20

Curriculum

	Full-Time	Part-Time
Typical first-year section size	85	52
Is there typically a "small section" of the first-year class, other than Legal Writing, taught by full-time faculty	No	No
If yes, typical size offered last year		
# of classroom course titles beyond first-year curriculum	110	
# of upper division courses, excluding seminars, with an enrollment: Under 25	48	
25–49	28	
50–74	16	
75–99	18	
100+	0	
# of seminars	8	
# of seminar positions available	121	
# of seminar positions filled	106	11
# of positions available in simulation courses	229	
# of simulation positions filled	199	26
# of positions available in faculty supervised clinical courses	72	
# of faculty supervised clinical positions filled	58	14
# involved in field placements	28	3
# involved in law journals	83	3
# involved in moot court or trial competitions	90	4
# of credit hours required to graduate	90	

JD Enrollment and Ethnicity

	Men		Women		Full-Time		Part-Time		1st-Year		Total		JD Degs. Awd.
	#	%	#	%	#	%	#	%	#	%	#	%	
All Hispanics	143	27.9	96	24.8	168	25.3	71	30.2	75	24.7	239	26.6	63
Am. Ind./AK Nat.	3	0.6	3	0.8	4	0.6	2	0.9	1	0.3	6	0.7	2
Asian	15	2.9	13	3.4	21	3.2	7	3.0	9	3.0	28	3.1	12
Black/Af. Am.	13	2.5	22	5.7	21	3.2	14	6.0	15	4.9	35	3.9	13
Nat. HI/Pac. Isl.	0	0.0	1	0.3	1	0.2	0	0.0	1	0.3	1	0.1	0
2 or more races	2	0.4	1	0.3	1	0.2	2	0.9	3	1.0	3	0.3	0
Subtotal (minor.)	176	34.4	136	35.1	216	32.5	96	40.9	104	34.2	312	34.7	90
Nonres. Alien	0	0.0	0	0.0	0	0.0	0	0.0	0	0.0	0	0.0	0
White/Cauc.	336	65.6	251	64.9	448	67.5	139	59.1	200	65.8	587	65.3	174
Unknown	0	0.0	0	0.0	0	0.0	0	0.0	0	0.0	0	0.0	0
Total	512	57.0	387	43.0	664	73.9	235	26.1	304	33.8	899		264

Transfers

Transfers in	4
Transfers out	5

Tuition and Fees

	Resident	Nonresident
Full-time	$29,406	$29,406
Part-time	$17,610	$17,610
Tuition Guarantee Program		N

Living Expenses

Estimated living expenses for singles

Living on campus	Living off campus	Living at home
$15,424	$15,424	$15,424

ST. MARY'S UNIVERSITY SCHOOL OF LAW

ABA Approved Since 1948

GPA and LSAT Scores

	Total	Full-Time	Part-Time
# of apps	1,604	1,389	215
# of offers	724	654	70
# of matrics	255	212	43
75% GPA	3.42	3.43	3.32
Median GPA	3.08	3.11	2.90
25% GPA	2.79	2.82	2.67
75% LSAT	156	156	154
Median LSAT	154	154	152
25% LSAT	151	152	151

Grants and Scholarships (from prior year)

	Total		Full-Time		Part-Time	
	#	%	#	%	#	%
Total # of students	828		675		153	
Total # receiving grants	299	36.1	201	29.8	98	64.1
Less than 1/2 tuition	296	35.7	198	29.3	98	64.1
Half to full tuition	1	0.1	1	0.1	0	0.0
Full tuition	0	0.0	0	0.0	0	0.0
More than full tuition	2	0.2	2	0.3	0	0.0
Median grant amount			$2,010		$1,240	

Informational and Library Resources

Total amount spent on library materials	$1,042,815
Study seating capacity inside the library	513
# of full-time equivalent professional librarians	6
Hours per week library is open	108
# of open, wired connections available to students	562
# of networked computers available for use by students	89
Has wireless network?	Y
Requires computer?	N

JD Attrition (from prior year)

	Academic	Other	Total	
	#	#	#	%
1st year	14	21	35	9.7
2nd year	2	10	12	4.4
3rd year	0	4	4	1.6
4th year	0	0	0	0.0

Employment (9 months after graduation)

For up-to-date employment data, go to employmentsummary.abaquestionnaire.org on the ABA website.

Bar Passage Rates

First-time takers	245	Reporting %	92.65
Average school %	79.74	Average state %	82.68

Average pass difference –2.94

Jurisdiction	Takers	Passers	Pass %	State %	Diff %
Texas	227	181	79.74	82.68	–2.94

ST. MARY'S UNIVERSITY SCHOOL OF LAW

One Camino Santa Maria
San Antonio, TX 78228-8601
Phone: 210.436.3523; Toll-free: 866.639.5831; Fax: 210.431.4202
E-mail: lawadmissions@stmarytx.edu; Website: www.stmarytx.edu/law

Introduction

St. Mary's University School of Law was founded in 1927 as part of the oldest and largest Catholic university in the Southwest. St. Mary's is located in the beautiful, unique, and legendary city of San Antonio. San Antonio combines a diverse blend of historic sites, natural beauty, charming vistas, and urban amenities. With its culturally rich population and environment, San Antonio is the perfect backdrop for the mission and goals of the School of Law. Enriched by the spirit of the Society of Mary (Marianists), the school imparts to its students the knowledge and attributes of mind and character essential to public service. St. Mary's is vigilant of the need to preserve a tradition of excellence in legal education with the development of new programs and methodologies for the changing world, and now offers a **part-time evening program** in addition to its traditional full-time day program.

Library and Physical Facilities

The Sarita Kenedy East Law Library is the largest legal information center in San Antonio and the surrounding area. The library is housed in a spacious, bright, and beautiful building. There is ample study-table seating and large private study carrels. Small conference rooms accommodate groups for discussion and collaboration. A federal depository library, the collection consists of print, microfilm, and multimedia items totaling over 400,000 volumes (or equivalent), which cover a wide range of subjects, including US federal and state laws, and foreign, comparative, and international law. The collection and resources are cataloged and searchable through an automated library information system. The library subscribes to LexisNexis, Westlaw, Loislaw, HeinOnline, LLMC-Digital, the Center for Computer-Assisted Legal Instruction (CALI), the Index to Legal Periodicals Full Text, Congressional Universe, AccessUN, the United Nations Treaty Series, and other information databases. Computers and Internet access, both wired and wireless, are available and supported throughout the library facilities. The library is staffed with eight degreed librarians and about eight paraprofessionals who provide friendly, quality service.

The Law Classroom Building contains four amphitheater-style classrooms with electronically retractable walls and a newly renovated and technologically advanced modern courtroom at its center. Electrical outlets and data ports are located at each student's seat, and the public lounges provide wireless access.

The School of Law's four primary buildings are located around an oak-shaded quadrangle, forming a central gathering spot. The Alumni Athletic and Convocation Center offers 135,000 square feet of wellness and fitness options. The center provides for ceremonial facilities as well as athletic endeavors.

Curriculum

Required full-time, first-year courses are Constitutional Law, Contracts, Criminal Law, Legal Research and Writing, Civil Procedure, Property, and Torts. All students must also take the required courses of Professional Responsibility, Evidence, and Texas Civil Procedure (only required of those planning to take the Texas bar examination), as well as a specified number of courses from a menu-style core curriculum. Students must also complete a research paper.

Clinical Legal Education

The Clinical Program at St. Mary's offers three clinical classes: Civil Justice, Criminal Justice, and Immigration/Human Rights. The clinics teach substantive law, lawyering skills, and responsibilities through the supervised representation of low-income clients and the development of community-based projects. The Civil Justice Clinic represents persons who are homeless; victims of violent crimes; persons who are undocumented, primarily in family law; social security claims; consumer issues; and tax controversies. The Criminal Justice Clinic accepts representation of individuals of any age in misdemeanor and low felony cases as well as some innocence claims. Immigration/Human Rights students represent indigent foreign nationals and refugees in Immigration Court and assist clients with applications for asylum, T and U (trafficking and violent crime victim) visas, and benefits under the Violence Against Women Act.

International Law

The **St. Mary's Institute on World Legal Problems** is conducted at the University of Innsbruck in Austria during July and August. The program is designed to provide law students with a broader understanding of global issues and the role law can play in their peaceful resolution.

Seven justices of the United States Supreme Court have participated in the program as distinguished visiting jurists—former Chief Justice William H. Rehnquist; current Chief Justice John G. Roberts, Jr.; Justice Antonin Scalia; Justice Samuel A. Alito, Jr.; Justice Ruth Bader Ginsburg; former Justice Sandra Day O'Connor; and former Justice John Paul Stevens. The program draws students and faculty from all parts of the United States and abroad. It has included students from at least 100 American law schools as well as from Austria, Hungary, China, and Russia. More than 40 visiting professors from law schools in the United States and several foreign countries have also participated.

The Innsbruck Institute is part of the law school's program in international and comparative law.

The **St. Mary's University School of Law Institute on Chinese Law and Business** is a new program of legal studies that prepares law students for the challenges of representing clients doing business with Chinese partners. This summer program is conducted with the cooperation of Beihang University in Beijing.

St. Mary's houses a **Center for Terrorism Law**, a nonpartisan, nonprofit institution dedicated to the study of legal issues associated with terrorism, with particular emphasis on cyberspace and information assurance technologies.

Judicial Internships

St. Mary's students may participate in a wide range of pregraduation judicial internships with outstanding state and federal courts. Students work under the supervision of a judge or staff attorney, performing legal research and writing projects that often include the drafting of orders that will be used to decide pending cases, the composition of jury instructions, the researching of evidentiary questions, or attendance at settlement conferences.

Admission Standards

St. Mary's goal is to create an intellectually stimulating student body composed of persons with diverse backgrounds who share a desire for academic excellence and accomplishment in the practice of law. In addition to academic ability, St. Mary's seeks evidence of qualities such as leadership ability, maturity, community organization skills, knowledge of other languages and cultures, a history of overcoming disadvantage, public interest accomplishments, or success in a previous career. A faculty committee reviews all applications. No one is automatically rejected. All files are read.

Student Activities

St. Mary's has over 30 active student organizations. Student organizations are a key part of the collegial environment of the law school.

St. Mary's has two law reviews—the *St. Mary's Law Journal* and *The Scholar: St. Mary's Law Review on Minority Issues*. The reviews offer students excellent opportunities to develop advanced legal research and writing skills. The *Law Journal* has been cited as a persuasive authority in hundreds of court decisions.

St. Mary's students are active in moot court and mock trial competitions. During the spring semester, first-year students participate in a school-wide moot court competition. Second- and third-year students can compete in on-campus tournaments and in St. Mary's External Advocacy Program

(EAP). St. Mary's EAP students travel throughout the US to attend the ABA National Moot Court, National Mock Trial, ATLA Mock Trial, and negotiation competitions.

Career Services

The role of the Office of Career Services is to assist law students and graduates with their career searches by informing them of career options and job-search strategies and connecting them with potential employers. Career Services does so by sponsoring programs and job fairs designed to educate, facilitate, and connect students with potential employers during and after law school.

One-on-one confidential strategy sessions with the assistant dean provide a unique opportunity for students to develop a personal plan to assess and meet their career goals. The office maintains a job bank and a résumé bank. The Student Resource Center offers an extensive and up-to-date library of career resources and directories of attorneys, as well as computer terminals with Internet resources, to help students direct and begin their careers in legal and nontraditional positions. Students have extensive opportunities to interact with alumni, who assist with career programming and networking events throughout the year.

For the students in the class of 2010 who reported employment status, 86 percent are employed, with almost all of them working in the legal field.

LLM Degrees

St. Mary's offers both an LLM Degree in American Legal Studies and another in International Comparative Law.

APPLICANT PROFILE

St. Mary's University School of Law
This grid includes only applicants who earned 120–180 LSAT scores under standard administrations.

LSAT Score	3.75 +		3.50–3.74		3.25–3.49		3.00–3.24		2.75–2.99		2.50–2.74		2.25–2.49		2.00–2.24		Below 2.00		No GPA		Total	
	Apps	Adm	Apps	Adm	Apps	Adm	Apps	Adm	Apps	Adm	Apps	Adm	Apps	Adm	Apps	Adm	Apps	Adm	Apps	Adm	Apps	Adm
175–180	0	0	0	0	0	0	0	0	0	0	0	0	0	0	0	0	0	0	0	0	0	0
170–174	0	0	0	0	1	1	2	2	0	0	0	0	0	0	0	0	0	0	0	0	3	3
165–169	0	0	5	5	3	3	6	6	0	0	4	4	3	3	2	2	0	0	0	0	23	23
160–164	20	20	15	15	12	12	17	17	12	12	13	12	4	4	6	6	0	0	1	0	100	98
155–159	21	20	54	52	61	61	53	51	50	50	27	26	12	10	6	4	1	1	3	3	288	278
150–154	35	30	65	51	98	71	106	71	96	41	58	25	37	9	5	2	6	2	8	3	514	305
145–149	21	2	39	3	66	0	67	4	67	3	44	0	26	1	8	0	2	0	7	0	347	13
140–144	8	0	26	0	31	1	43	0	38	2	34	1	18	0	8	0	1	0	10	0	217	4
135–139	0	0	2	0	11	0	11	0	18	0	11	0	3	0	5	0	1	0	3	0	65	0
130–134	0	0	2	0	2	0	6	0	5	0	2	0	3	0	2	0	2	0	1	0	25	0
125–129	0	0	0	0	0	0	2	0	2	0	1	0	0	0	2	0	0	0	0	0	7	0
120–124	0	0	0	0	0	0	0	0	0	0	0	0	0	0	0	0	0	0	0	0	0	0
Total	105	72	208	126	285	149	313	151	288	108	194	68	106	27	44	14	13	3	33	6	1589	724

Apps = Number of Applicants
Adm = Number Admitted
Reflects 99% of the total applicant pool; highest LSAT data reported.

UNIVERSITY OF ST. THOMAS SCHOOL OF LAW—MINNEAPOLIS

1000 LaSalle Avenue
Minneapolis, MN 55403
Phone: 651.962.4895
E-mail: lawschool@stthomas.edu; Website: www.stthomas.edu/law

ABA
Approved
Since
2003

The Basics

Type of school	Private
Term	Semester
Application deadline	7/1
Application fee	$0
Financial aid deadline	7/1
Can first year start other than fall?	No
Student to faculty ratio	13.6 to 1
# of housing spaces available restricted to law students	
graduate housing for which law students are eligible	

Faculty and Administrators

	Total		Men		Women		Minorities	
	Spr	Fall	Spr	Fall	Spr	Fall	Spr	Fall
Full-time	28	30	17	19	11	11	6	5
Other full-time	0	0	0	0	0	0	0	0
Deans, librarians, & others who teach	11	12	5	5	6	7	1	1
Part-time	81	64	51	45	30	19	7	7
Total	120	106	73	69	47	37	14	13

Curriculum

	Full-Time	Part-Time
Typical first-year section size	85	0
Is there typically a "small section" of the first-year class, other than Legal Writing, taught by full-time faculty	Yes	No
If yes, typical size offered last year	43	
# of classroom course titles beyond first-year curriculum		91

# of upper division courses, excluding seminars, with an enrollment:	Under 25	123
	25–49	21
	50–74	7
	75–99	6
	100+	0

# of seminars		15
# of seminar positions available		234
# of seminar positions filled	171	0
# of positions available in simulation courses		452
# of simulation positions filled	419	0
# of positions available in faculty supervised clinical courses		83
# of faculty supervised clinical positions filled	77	0
# involved in field placements	637	0
# involved in law journals	38	0
# involved in moot court or trial competitions	29	0
# of credit hours required to graduate		88

JD Enrollment and Ethnicity

	Men #	Men %	Women #	Women %	Full-Time #	Full-Time %	Part-Time #	Part-Time %	1st-Year #	1st-Year %	Total #	Total %	JD Degs. Awd.
All Hispanics	7	2.6	11	5.3	18	3.7	0	0.0	11	6.5	18	3.7	4
Am. Ind./AK Nat.	4	1.5	0	0.0	4	0.8	0	0.0	2	1.2	4	0.8	0
Asian	11	4.0	15	7.2	26	5.4	0	0.0	5	3.0	26	5.4	5
Black/Af. Am.	6	2.2	6	2.9	12	2.5	0	0.0	3	1.8	12	2.5	4
Nat. HI/Pac. Isl.	0	0.0	1	0.5	1	0.2	0	0.0	1	0.6	1	0.2	0
2 or more races	2	0.7	4	1.9	6	1.2	0	0.0	2	1.2	6	1.2	0
Subtotal (minor.)	30	10.9	37	17.7	67	13.9	0	0.0	24	14.2	67	13.9	13
Nonres. Alien	1	0.4	0	0.0	1	0.2	0	0.0	1	0.6	1	0.2	0
White/Cauc.	215	78.5	150	71.8	363	75.5	2	100.0	124	73.4	365	75.6	108
Unknown	28	10.2	22	10.5	50	10.4	0	0.0	20	11.8	50	10.4	13
Total	274	56.7	209	43.3	481	99.6	2	0.4	169	35.0	483		134

Transfers

Transfers in	3
Transfers out	11

Tuition and Fees

	Resident	Nonresident
Full-time	$34,898	$34,898
Part-time		
Tuition Guarantee Program		N

Living Expenses

Estimated living expenses for singles

Living on campus	Living off campus	Living at home
N/A	$18,890	$18,890

UNIVERSITY OF ST. THOMAS SCHOOL OF LAW—MINNEAPOLIS

ABA
Approved
Since
2003

GPA and LSAT Scores

	Total	Full-Time	Part-Time
# of apps	1,283	1,283	0
# of offers	711	711	0
# of matrics	171	171	0
75% GPA	3.54	3.54	0.00
Median GPA	3.30	3.30	0.00
25% GPA	3.07	3.07	0.00
75% LSAT	161	161	0
Median LSAT	156	156	0
25% LSAT	153	153	0

Grants and Scholarships (from prior year)

	Total #	Total %	Full-Time #	Full-Time %	Part-Time #	Part-Time %
Total # of students	475		475		0	
Total # receiving grants	277	58.3	277	58.3	0	0.0
Less than 1/2 tuition	91	19.2	91	19.2	0	0.0
Half to full tuition	71	14.9	71	14.9	0	0.0
Full tuition	115	24.2	115	24.2	0	0.0
More than full tuition	0	0.0	0	0.0	0	0.0
Median grant amount			$25,000		$0	

Informational and Library Resources

Total amount spent on library materials	$832,625
Study seating capacity inside the library	379
# of full-time equivalent professional librarians	5
Hours per week library is open	83
# of open, wired connections available to students	640
# of networked computers available for use by students	80
Has wireless network?	Y
Requires computer?	N

JD Attrition (from prior year)

	Academic #	Other #	Total #	Total %
1st year	0	2	2	1.2
2nd year	1	15	16	9.6
3rd year	0	0	0	0.0
4th year	0	0	0	0.0

Employment (9 months after graduation)

For up-to-date employment data, go to
employmentsummary.abaquestionnaire.org on the ABA website.

Bar Passage Rates

First-time takers	153	Reporting %	86.27
Average school %	90.16	Average state %	91.08

Average pass difference   −0.92

Jurisdiction	Takers	Passers	Pass %	State %	Diff %
Minnesota	113	100	88.50	92.21	−3.71
Wisconsin	9	9	100.00	92.93	7.07
California	5	5	100.00	71.24	28.76
Colorado	3	3	100.00	82.79	17.21
Arizona	2	2	100.00	80.74	19.26

UNIVERSITY OF ST. THOMAS SCHOOL OF LAW—MINNEAPOLIS

1000 LaSalle Avenue
Minneapolis, MN 55403
Phone: 651.962.4895
E-mail: lawschool@stthomas.edu; Website: www.stthomas.edu/law

Introduction

The University of St. Thomas School of Law has a mission, inspired by its Catholic identity, to help students integrate faith and reason in the search for truth through a focus on morality and social justice. The close-knit community, drawn together by this unique mission, shares a distinctive vision of what law and the legal profession can be. The School of Law attracts students from across the country who want to be servant leaders and who understand their responsibility to serve their clients, the community, and those who are most in need of, and least able to pay for, legal assistance.

Curriculum

The School of Law curriculum includes more than 85 elective courses, 14 required courses, and 4 joint degrees. But numbers don't tell the whole story. We have deliberately designed our curriculum not only to ensure that our students have the doctrinal knowledge and practical skills necessary for legal practice, but also that they are equipped with the relationship skills that are increasingly essential to professional success. With the distinctive Foundations of Justice course, along with a variety of practicum courses, clinics, externships, and other opportunities for experiential learning, St. Thomas puts relationships at the center of legal education. This is evidenced most powerfully by our award-winning mentor externship that matches each student with an experienced lawyer or judge for each year of law school. In addition to introducing students to a variety of lawyering tasks, mentors help their students prepare to face the intellectual, ethical, and moral challenges of professional life.

Students can also pursue one of four joint-degree programs, including Business Administration (JD/MBA), Catholic Studies (JD/MA), Public Policy (JD/MA), and Social Work (JD/MSW).

Special Programs

At the Interprofessional Center for Counseling and Legal Services (IPC), law students work side by side with students from graduate programs in social work and professional psychology. The IPC is among the first clinical programs in the country to forge an equal partnership among the three disciplines. The IPC gives students experience working with actual clients on active cases.

The Holloran Center for Ethical Leadership unites leaders from a range of professions who work together to pursue practical solutions and create effective tools in confronting the challenge of creating ethical leaders. The center hosts an annual national professionalism conference, business and law roundtables on ethical governance, and Trusted Advisor Seminars with recognized leaders from the Twin Cities.

The Terrence J. Murphy Institute for Catholic Thought, Law and Public Policy is a collaboration between the Center for Catholic Studies and the School of Law. The institute explores the various interactions between law and Catholic thought on topics ranging from workers' rights, to criminal law, to marriage and family.

The Area

The University of St. Thomas School of Law is located in downtown Minneapolis, the regional center for business and culture. Minneapolis and the nearby capital city of St. Paul make up the core of the Twin Cities metropolitan area—a metro area of more than 3.5 million residents. The Twin Cities are home to a vibrant business community that features 20 of Fortune 500's largest US corporations. The Twin Cities are also home to a lively legal community that has embraced the School of Law through the mentor externship and summer employment opportunities.

The seemingly limitless recreational opportunities and distinctive beauty of the region add immeasurably to the quality of life. The Twin Cities metropolitan area boasts 949 lakes and many parks, giving outdoor enthusiasts plenty of options from which to choose.

Admission

The School of Law seeks to identify students who show the potential to distinguish themselves academically and to integrate faith and values into their professional character and identity.

The Admissions Committee reviews applications with the goal of understanding the strengths, skills, and unique perspectives of each applicant. The committee examines quantitative criteria such as LSAT scores and undergraduate transcripts, but it also focuses on qualitative factors, such as writing skills, leadership experience, motivation, public service orientation, and commitment to our mission of exploring the integration of faith and reason. Thus a student's personal statement, letters of recommendation, and similar information play an important role in assisting the committee in determining whether the student and the School of Law are a good fit.

Faculty

At St. Thomas, you will be taught, shaped, and challenged by professors who are leading experts in their fields, and who will push you to be more than technically competent; they will encourage you to go deeper into the law, to understand a field in a way that equips you to provide stellar client service, to aspire to meaningful professional leadership, and to chart paths of possible societal engagement and reform. Our professors take their research seriously because they take their teaching seriously. They are excelling on both fronts, receiving national recognition for scholarly impact and overall quality. Further, our relatively small student body, coupled with the faculty's commitment to building a supportive community, means that your interactions with professors usually will not be confined to the classroom. Our professors are approachable, engaging, and dedicated to the well-being of our students.

Enrollment/Student Body

The student body is diverse. In the fall 2011 entering class, students represented 27 states and 90 undergraduate institutions. While many students come to the School of Law directly from undergraduate institutions, a significant number have earned postgraduate degrees or have work experience.

Library and Physical Facilities

The School of Law occupies a beautiful building of over 150,000 square feet in downtown Minneapolis near the federal courthouse and major law firms and businesses. The building has several defining features that make it "quite simply breathtaking," as described by an ABA site-evaluation team. These include the dramatic four-story Schulze Grand Atrium, used for lectures, conferences, and social gatherings; the Frey Moot Courtroom, which provides a striking setting in which to learn lawyering skills or hear moot court arguments; and the beautiful Chapel of St. Thomas More.

Modern technology enhances the classrooms, library, group study areas, moot courtroom, and private offices. A computer lab and a computer training center accommodate student research needs.

The library, with its ample seating, 12 group study rooms, and 3 AV viewing rooms, provides an attractive, functional environment for group or individual study. The library's strong electronic collection provides convenient access to many resources from both on and off campus.

Financial Aid

St. Thomas is committed to making high-quality legal education available to students by offering scholarships, grants, employment, and loans. The School of Law administers two scholarship programs that acknowledge applicants who have outstanding academic records and who contribute to our diversity or are particularly likely to contribute to the school's mission. All incoming students are automatically considered for scholarship awards. Admitted applicants who participate in select service programs are also eligible for a Dean's Service Scholarship.

The UST Loan Repayment Assistance Program (UST-LRAP) provides up to $6,000 in annual assistance for up to 10 years for qualifying applicants. In general, graduates with financial need who undertake public service jobs benefiting the poor and underserved will be eligible to receive assistance with repaying loans for law school tuition.

Career Services

Alumni and students work with federal and state judges; international, national, and local public interest organizations; corporations; banks; the government; and law firms of all sizes.

The Office of Career and Professional Development (CPD) provides a wide variety of services to our students and alumni, including one-to-one career counseling, mock interviews, workshops on job skills, and insights into the job market. CPD does significant networking outreach to employers and assists students in their own networking activities. It also offers a strong online job center for students to search job postings from around the country and significant online resources for students on a variety of career and professional development topics.

Student Activities

The University of St. Thomas School of Law has nearly 50 student groups, including Federalist and American Constitutional Societies; Black, Latino, Asian, and Women Law Student groups; as well as several faith-based student organizations and groups formed around practice area interests. The School of Law Sports and Recreation Club organizes participation in athletic leagues for several sports. An active, collaborative Student Government enhances UST's high quality of life.

The *University of St. Thomas Law Journal* gives students the opportunity to contribute to the development of legal scholarship and further hone their research, analytical, and writing abilities. The Board of Advocates oversees interscholastic competitions in moot court, trial advocacy, client counseling, and negotiation.

All students are required to perform 50 hours of community service work, exploring a variety of ways in which their interests, skills, and talents can best serve the public. The student-led Public Service Board administers the School of Law's public service requirement and maintains and distributes information about public service opportunities.

APPLICANT PROFILE

University of St. Thomas School of Law—Minneapolis
This grid includes only applicants who earned 120–180 LSAT scores under standard administrations.

LSAT Score	3.75 +		3.50–3.74		3.25–3.49		3.00–3.24		2.75–2.99		2.50–2.74		2.25–2.49		2.00–2.24		Below 2.00		No GPA		Total	
	Apps	Adm	Apps	Adm	Apps	Adm	Apps	Adm	Apps	Adm	Apps	Adm	Apps	Adm	Apps	Adm	Apps	Adm	Apps	Adm	Apps	Adm
175–180	0	0	1	1	0	0	0	0	0	0	0	0	0	0	0	0	0	0	0	0	1	1
170–174	1	1	1	1	1	1	3	3	1	1	0	0	0	0	0	0	0	0	0	0	7	7
165–169	10	10	10	10	8	8	2	2	3	3	1	1	0	0	0	0	0	0	1	1	35	35
160–164	35	35	30	29	30	29	18	17	9	7	8	8	5	4	3	2	0	0	1	1	139	132
155–159	38	36	56	51	65	61	48	45	27	26	27	22	12	10	7	5	1	0	4	4	285	260
150–154	31	29	45	36	78	67	77	41	52	20	42	13	17	6	7	2	1	0	7	2	357	216
145–149	12	4	37	12	58	12	47	5	28	1	16	1	16	0	6	0	1	0	8	1	229	36
140–144	4	1	8	2	22	0	23	0	22	2	15	0	7	0	3	0	2	0	5	0	111	5
135–139	1	0	3	0	9	1	8	0	12	0	12	0	5	0	3	0	1	0	7	0	61	1
130–134	0	0	1	0	1	0	2	0	3	0	7	0	2	0	2	0	2	0	1	0	21	0
125–129	0	0	0	0	0	0	3	0	0	0	3	0	0	0	5	0	0	0	3	0	14	0
120–124	0	0	0	0	0	0	0	0	0	0	0	0	0	0	1	0	0	0	0	0	1	0
Total	132	116	192	142	272	179	231	113	157	60	131	45	64	20	37	9	8	0	37	9	1261	693

Apps = Number of Applicants
Adm = Number Admitted
Reflects 99% of the total applicant pool; highest LSAT data reported.

ST. THOMAS UNIVERSITY SCHOOL OF LAW

16401 NW 37th Avenue
Miami Gardens, FL 33054
Phone: 800.245.4569, 305.623.2310; Fax: 305.623.2357
E-mail: admitme@stu.edu; Website: www.stu.edu/lawschool

ABA
Approved
Since
1988

The Basics

Type of school	Private
Term	Semester
Application deadline	5/1
Application fee	$60
Financial aid deadline	5/31
Can first year start other than fall?	No
Student to faculty ratio	16.1 to 1
# of housing spaces available restricted to law students	
graduate housing for which law students are eligible	100

Faculty and Administrators

	Total		Men		Women		Minorities	
	Spr	Fall	Spr	Fall	Spr	Fall	Spr	Fall
Full-time	35	37	19	21	16	16	7	9
Other full-time	2	2	2	2	0	0	0	0
Deans, librarians, & others who teach	7	7	4	4	3	3	3	3
Part-time	42	34	32	25	10	9	10	9
Total	86	80	57	52	29	28	20	21

Curriculum

	Full-Time	Part-Time
Typical first-year section size	68	0
Is there typically a "small section" of the first-year class, other than Legal Writing, taught by full-time faculty	No	No
If yes, typical size offered last year		
# of classroom course titles beyond first-year curriculum	116	
# of upper division courses, excluding seminars, with an enrollment: Under 25	145	
25–49	41	
50–74	22	
75–99	1	
100+	0	
# of seminars	17	
# of seminar positions available	272	
# of seminar positions filled	199	0
# of positions available in simulation courses	385	
# of simulation positions filled	311	0
# of positions available in faculty supervised clinical courses	26	
# of faculty supervised clinical positions filled	26	0
# involved in field placements	135	0
# involved in law journals	123	0
# involved in moot court or trial competitions	72	0
# of credit hours required to graduate	90	

JD Enrollment and Ethnicity

	Men		Women		Full-Time		Part-Time		1st-Year		Total		JD Degs. Awd.
	#	%	#	%	#	%	#	%	#	%	#	%	
All Hispanics	105	28.8	163	46.0	268	37.3	0	0.0	96	37.9	268	37.3	84
Am. Ind./AK Nat.	4	1.1	2	0.6	6	0.8	0	0.0	4	1.6	6	0.8	1
Asian	9	2.5	12	3.4	21	2.9	0	0.0	7	2.8	21	2.9	3
Black/Af. Am.	16	4.4	30	8.5	46	6.4	0	0.0	19	7.5	46	6.4	17
Nat. HI/Pac. Isl.	0	0.0	0	0.0	0	0.0	0	0.0	0	0.0	0	0.0	0
2 or more races	17	4.7	15	4.2	32	4.5	0	0.0	10	4.0	32	4.5	9
Subtotal (minor.)	151	41.4	222	62.7	373	51.9	0	0.0	136	53.8	373	51.9	114
Nonres. Alien	3	0.8	6	1.7	9	1.3	0	0.0	3	1.2	9	1.3	5
White/Cauc.	211	57.8	126	35.6	337	46.9	0	0.0	114	45.1	337	46.9	102
Unknown	0	0.0	0	0.0	0	0.0	0	0.0	0	0.0	0	0.0	0
Total	365	50.8	354	49.2	719	100.0	0	0.0	253	35.2	719		221

Transfers

Transfers in	4
Transfers out	12

Tuition and Fees

	Resident	Nonresident
Full-time	$34,618	$34,618
Part-time		
Tuition Guarantee Program	N	

Living Expenses

Estimated living expenses for singles

Living on campus	Living off campus	Living at home
$24,210	$22,904	$11,539

ST. THOMAS UNIVERSITY SCHOOL OF LAW

ABA Approved Since 1988

GPA and LSAT Scores

	Total	Full-Time	Part-Time
# of apps	2,040	2,040	0
# of offers	938	938	0
# of matrics	251	251	0
75% GPA	3.32	3.32	0.00
Median GPA	3.03	3.03	0.00
25% GPA	2.66	2.66	0.00
75% LSAT	153	153	0
Median LSAT	150	150	0
25% LSAT	148	148	0

Grants and Scholarships (from prior year)

	Total		Full-Time		Part-Time	
	#	%	#	%	#	%
Total # of students	733		733		0	
Total # receiving grants	310	42.3	310	42.3	0	0.0
Less than 1/2 tuition	221	30.2	221	30.2	0	0.0
Half to full tuition	87	11.9	87	11.9	0	0.0
Full tuition	2	0.3	2	0.3	0	0.0
More than full tuition	0	0.0	0	0.0	0	0.0
Median grant amount			$14,000		$0	

Informational and Library Resources

Total amount spent on library materials	$675,516
Study seating capacity inside the library	500
# of full-time equivalent professional librarians	6
Hours per week library is open	106
# of open, wired connections available to students	70
# of networked computers available for use by students	29
Has wireless network?	Y
Requires computer?	N

JD Attrition (from prior year)

	Academic	Other	Total	
	#	#	#	%
1st year	29	24	53	19.4
2nd year	8	1	9	3.9
3rd year	0	1	1	0.4
4th year	0	0	0	0.0

Employment (9 months after graduation)

For up-to-date employment data, go to employmentsummary.abaquestionnaire.org on the ABA website.

Bar Passage Rates

First-time takers	184	Reporting %	85.33
Average school %	74.52	Average state %	77.63
Average pass difference	–3.11		

Jurisdiction	Takers	Passers	Pass %	State %	Diff %
Florida	157	117	74.52	77.63	–3.11

ST. THOMAS UNIVERSITY SCHOOL OF LAW

16401 NW 37th Avenue
Miami Gardens, FL 33054
Phone: 800.245.4569, 305.623.2310; Fax: 305.623.2357
E-mail: admitme@stu.edu; Website: www.stu.edu/lawschool

Introduction

St. Thomas University School of Law, fully accredited by the American Bar Association and the prestigious Association of American Law Schools, was founded in 1984 and is one of the most culturally diverse and technologically advanced law schools in the country. St. Thomas emphasizes professional ethics throughout its programs, provides intensive academic support on an individual and small-group basis, and offers a broad curriculum, including an array of clinical experiences.

St. Thomas University is located on a 140-acre campus several miles northwest of Miami. Fifteen miles southeast, in downtown Miami, stands the federal courthouse, the location of the United States District Court for the Southern District of Florida. State trial and appellate courts are several blocks away. Approximately 20 miles to the north of the law school is the city of Ft. Lauderdale, another venue for state and appellate courts.

Library and Physical Facilities

The Alex A. Hanna Law Library at St. Thomas University School of Law furnishes students with an online catalog to assist them in locating both digital content and traditional materials. The Library meets the needs of students in the twenty-first century by providing them with a wide array of online databases to assist with their research and allow them to pursue their interests in scholarship. Moreover, the library has a large microform collection to provide added depth of resources. A wireless network enables students, through their laptops or one of 20 library workstations, to access digital information resources from anywhere on campus. Students may also access most of the databases from home through the school's proxy server. Professional reference staff provides instruction in performing online and traditional research. Reference services are also available to assist students in the evenings and on weekends.

Clinical Legal Education Programs

St. Thomas University School of Law requires six credits of professional skills courses to graduate. Students are eligible to participate in any of the law school's 10 clinical offerings in an effort to meet that requirement.

Bankruptcy Clinic—The Bankruptcy Clinic offers a comprehensive set of legal services focused on assisting and empowering low-income individuals in their interaction with the bankruptcy system.

Family Court Clinic—This clinic allows third-year students an opportunity to represent clients in both Family Court and the Domestic Violence Court. The Family Court Clinic is a two-semester, two-track, four-credits-per-semester course. The family division track allows students to learn about family law matters, including the dissolution of marriage, paternity, custody, and adoption cases. In the domestic violence division, students are given the opportunity to provide in-court representation to victims of domestic violence in civil permanent injunction hearings.

Appellate Litigation Clinic—This is a year-long clinical program open to third-year students that provides experience in handling criminal cases in state appellate courts. Each student will have primary responsibility for at least two cases from inception through record preparation, all relevant motions, and the writing of briefs and oral arguments. The program also features a weekly seminar in the appellate process.

Immigration Clinic—Third-year law students will represent asylum seekers, battered spouses and children who have fled their native country, and other noncitizens seeking immigration relief in Immigration Court before the Board of Immigration Appeals and the Department of Homeland Security (formerly the INS).

Judicial Internship—Judicial internships provide an opportunity for students to hear arguments, discuss cases with judges, and apply research and writing skills to real facts. Interns will work closely with supervising staff attorneys and judges.

Tax Clinic—The Tax Clinic, offered to second- and third-year students, is one of the components of the law school's skills training program. The student represents clients before the Internal Revenue Service (IRS), the District Counsel, and the United States Tax Court. In addition, the student is expected to attend conferences with the IRS, job fairs in the community, and Tax Court sessions.

Civil Practice Clinic—This course can be taken full time or part time in one semester and is available to second- and third-year students. Those students whose placement requires they be a Certified Legal Intern must be in their third year. Typical placements include Legal Aid, City Attorney, County Attorney, Attorney General, or other public sector agencies handling civil matters.

Criminal Practice Clinic—This course can be taken full time or part time in one semester and is only available to incoming third-year students. Typical placements include the offices of the State Attorney, US Attorney, and Public Defender. The externship also contains a classroom component in which students discuss their cases and review relevant law.

Students learn through a combination of actual trial practice and classroom work. Under the supervision of an assistant state attorney, the students engage in plea bargain negotiations and try cases.

Placement in the Public Defender's office provides students with the opportunity to defend indigent adults and minors charged with felonies and misdemeanor crimes.

Elder Law Clinic—This course covers the growing legal needs of the elderly. Students will work with the Probate Division of the Circuit Court and members of the Elder Law Bar on case management issues and strategies to deal with a continually aging population.

Florida Supreme Court—For one semester, the intern will function as a law clerk to an individual justice or as a central staff law clerk working for all of the justices.

Graduate-Degree Programs

The **LLM Program in Intercultural Human Rights** offers in-depth instruction on a critical issue of our time: the protection of human dignity across political, cultural, and religious lines. The faculty of global distinction includes top-level United Nations experts, outstanding scholars, judges, and practitioners in the field. This program of global renown has attracted students from over 65 countries since its inception in 2001. A one-year 24-credit program, it offers mostly one-week compact courses in intercultural human rights. It features human rights law and complaint procedures; international law; humanitarian law;

human rights and terrorism; issues of refugees, women, and children; indigenous peoples; religion; criminal law; and international trade, taught by eminent faculty from the United Nations and prominent centers of scholarship.

The **JSD Program in Intercultural Human Rights** provides a premier opportunity for human rights scholars to make a lasting contribution to this dynamic and action-oriented field. The JSD degree is conferred upon successful completion of a dissertation in the field, the passing of the rigorosum, and proof of publication of the dissertation.

Special Programs

- **Summer-in-Spain Program**—Law students have the opportunity to take six credits at the Royal College University Escorial María Cristina, a part of the University of Madrid. The program is designed to prepare participants for practicing law in the globalized twenty-first century.
- **Summer Conditional Program**—Applicants who may not have strong academic credentials, but nonetheless possess the abilities necessary to succeed in a rigorous program of legal study, may be invited to participate in a summer conditional program. Students who successfully complete the summer conditional program are offered admission to the fall entering class. This program is usually offered each year but, under special circumstances, may not be available.
- **Joint-Degree Programs**—The law school offers four joint-degree programs in cooperation with other graduate divisions of the university. A JD/MBA in Accounting couples lawyering skills with those traditionally in great demand in the corporate, tax, and accounting worlds. The joint JD/MBA in International Business opens the burgeoning field of international transactional law to the new attorney. The JD/MS in Marriage and Family Counseling, one of the only programs of its kind in the country, fills a serious need in the family lawyer's repertory of skills. A joint JD/MS in Sports Administration prepares participants for a diverse set of positions in the world of sports.
- **Academic Support Program**—The law school is committed to the success of its students and offers a comprehensive support system, including Dean's Fellows, tutors, practice examinations, lectures, a director for academic support, and a program to assist graduates with the bar examination.

Career Services

The Office of Career Services is dedicated to assisting students in identifying and attaining their professional goals. It offers a range of traditional and innovative services, including a career services resource center, on-campus interviews with major law firms and government agencies, and speakers drawn from various areas of legal practice.

Student Activities

The *St. Thomas Law Review* is a student-operated scholarly journal, publishing articles submitted by law faculty and members of the bench and bar nationwide. Membership is determined on the basis of academic excellence and demonstrated writing ability.

The Student Bar Association sponsors various social and educational programs for the student body and otherwise represents student interests. In the student-run Moot Court Program, teams of student advocates compete in interscholastic tournaments across the country, preparing written briefs and presenting oral arguments in simulated appellate cases presided over by members of the bench and bar. Numerous student organizations are active on campus.

Housing

Law students can reserve on-campus housing at the University Inn or Villanova Hall, which offer private rooms with private baths and a choice of meal plans.

For law students desiring to live off campus, numerous apartment complexes are located within minutes of the law school.

APPLICANT PROFILE

St. Thomas University School of Law
This grid includes only applicants who earned 120–180 LSAT scores under standard administrations.

LSAT Score	GPA 3.75 +		3.50–3.74		3.25–3.49		3.00–3.24		2.75–2.99		2.50–2.74		2.25–2.49		2.00–2.24		Below 2.00		No GPA		Total	
	Apps	Adm	Apps	Adm	Apps	Adm	Apps	Adm	Apps	Adm	Apps	Adm	Apps	Adm	Apps	Adm	Apps	Adm	Apps	Adm	Apps	Adm
175–180	0	0	0	0	0	0	0	0	0	0	0	0	0	0	0	0	0	0	0	0	0	0
170–174	0	0	0	0	0	0	0	0	0	0	0	0	0	0	0	0	0	0	0	0	0	0
165–169	2	1	2	2	1	1	2	2	1	1	1	1	1	1	0	0	0	0	0	0	10	9
160–164	4	4	5	3	3	3	4	4	7	6	2	2	2	2	3	2	1	1	0	0	31	27
155–159	11	10	19	18	25	24	31	30	23	21	22	20	16	14	7	5	1	0	0	0	155	142
150–154	23	22	43	42	82	77	95	91	81	71	65	61	40	35	18	13	7	2	3	3	457	417
145–149	29	25	62	46	124	67	167	85	124	52	113	33	71	10	23	2	7	1	13	7	733	328
140–144	10	0	40	1	73	1	93	2	81	0	74	2	49	0	20	0	3	0	10	1	453	7
135–139	1	0	8	0	24	0	20	0	33	0	26	0	18	0	6	0	4	0	6	2	146	2
130–134	0	0	0	0	3	0	7	0	7	0	12	0	8	0	5	0	3	0	8	1	53	1
125–129	0	0	0	0	1	0	3	0	1	0	6	0	0	0	2	0	2	0	3	0	18	0
120–124	0	0	0	0	0	0	1	0	1	0	2	0	0	0	1	0	0	0	1	0	6	0
Total	80	62	179	112	336	173	423	214	359	151	323	119	205	62	85	22	28	4	44	14	2062	933

Apps = Number of Applicants
Adm = Number Admitted
Reflects 99% of the total applicant pool; highest LSAT data reported.

SAMFORD UNIVERSITY, CUMBERLAND SCHOOL OF LAW

800 Lakeshore Drive
Birmingham, AL 35229
Phone: 800.888.7213; Fax: 205.726.2057
E-mail: lawadm@samford.edu; Website: www.cumberland.samford.edu

ABA
Approved
Since
1949

The Basics

Type of school	Private
Term	Semester
Application deadline	2/28
Application fee	$50
Financial aid deadline	3/1
Can first year start other than fall?	No
Student to faculty ratio	18.0 to 1
# of housing spaces available restricted to law students	
graduate housing for which law students are eligible	

Faculty and Administrators

	Total		Men		Women		Minorities	
	Spr	Fall	Spr	Fall	Spr	Fall	Spr	Fall
Full-time	22	23	16	17	6	6	4	4
Other full-time	0	0	0	0	0	0	0	0
Deans, librarians, & others who teach	5	5	3	3	2	2	2	2
Part-time	32	25	24	16	8	9	1	2
Total	59	53	43	36	16	17	7	8

Curriculum

		Full-Time	Part-Time
Typical first-year section size		54	0
Is there typically a "small section" of the first-year class, other than Legal Writing, taught by full-time faculty		No	No
If yes, typical size offered last year			
# of classroom course titles beyond first-year curriculum		112	
# of upper division courses, excluding seminars, with an enrollment:	Under 25	75	
	25–49	37	
	50–74	16	
	75–99	0	
	100+	0	
# of seminars		17	
# of seminar positions available		226	
# of seminar positions filled		176	0
# of positions available in simulation courses		466	
# of simulation positions filled		397	0
# of positions available in faculty supervised clinical courses		0	
# of faculty supervised clinical positions filled		0	0
# involved in field placements		49	0
# involved in law journals		91	0
# involved in moot court or trial competitions		46	0
# of credit hours required to graduate		90	

JD Enrollment and Ethnicity

	Men		Women		Full-Time		Part-Time		1st-Year		Total		JD Degs. Awd.
	#	%	#	%	#	%	#	%	#	%	#	%	
All Hispanics	4	1.4	7	3.4	11	2.2	0	0.0	3	1.9	11	2.2	1
Am. Ind./AK Nat.	1	0.4	2	1.0	3	0.6	0	0.0	0	0.0	3	0.6	2
Asian	7	2.5	4	2.0	11	2.2	0	0.0	6	3.7	11	2.2	0
Black/Af. Am.	7	2.5	19	9.3	26	5.3	0	0.0	6	3.7	26	5.3	9
Nat. HI/Pac. Isl.	0	0.0	1	0.5	1	0.2	0	0.0	0	0.0	1	0.2	0
2 or more races	7	2.5	7	3.4	14	2.9	0	0.0	2	1.2	14	2.9	0
Subtotal (minor.)	26	9.2	40	19.5	66	13.5	0	0.0	17	10.6	66	13.5	12
Nonres. Alien	0	0.0	5	2.4	5	1.0	0	0.0	5	3.1	5	1.0	0
White/Cauc.	243	85.6	151	73.7	394	80.6	0	0.0	134	83.2	394	80.6	114
Unknown	15	5.3	9	4.4	24	4.9	0	0.0	5	3.1	24	4.9	22
Total	284	58.1	205	41.9	489	100.0	0	0.0	161	32.9	489		148

Transfers

Transfers in	7
Transfers out	14

Tuition and Fees

	Resident	Nonresident
Full-time	$34,848	$34,848
Part-time	$20,714	$20,714
Tuition Guarantee Program		N

Living Expenses

Estimated living expenses for singles

Living on campus	Living off campus	Living at home
N/A	$21,902	$21,902

SAMFORD UNIVERSITY, CUMBERLAND SCHOOL OF LAW

ABA Approved Since 1949

GPA and LSAT Scores

	Total	Full-Time	Part-Time
# of apps	1,405	1,405	0
# of offers	588	588	0
# of matrics	152	152	0
75% GPA	3.53	3.53	0.00
Median GPA	3.29	3.29	0.00
25% GPA	2.97	2.97	0.00
75% LSAT	157	157	0
Median LSAT	155	155	0
25% LSAT	152	152	0

Grants and Scholarships (from prior year)

	Total #	Total %	Full-Time #	Full-Time %	Part-Time #	Part-Time %
Total # of students	491		491		0	
Total # receiving grants	174	35.4	174	35.4	0	0.0
Less than 1/2 tuition	88	17.9	88	17.9	0	0.0
Half to full tuition	48	9.8	48	9.8	0	0.0
Full tuition	31	6.3	31	6.3	0	0.0
More than full tuition	7	1.4	7	1.4	0	0.0
Median grant amount			$18,000		$0	

Informational and Library Resources

Total amount spent on library materials	$882,769
Study seating capacity inside the library	474
# of full-time equivalent professional librarians	7
Hours per week library is open	105
# of open, wired connections available to students	200
# of networked computers available for use by students	71
Has wireless network?	Y
Requires computer?	N

JD Attrition (from prior year)

	Academic #	Other #	Total #	Total %
1st year	1	3	4	2.4
2nd year	2	14	16	9.2
3rd year	0	0	0	0.0
4th year	0	0	0	0.0

Employment (9 months after graduation)

For up-to-date employment data, go to employmentsummary.abaquestionnaire.org on the ABA website.

Bar Passage Rates

First-time takers	148	Reporting %	79.05
Average school %	94.02	Average state %	84.91
Average pass difference	9.11		

Jurisdiction	Takers	Passers	Pass %	State %	Diff %
Alabama	117	110	94.02	84.91	9.11

SAMFORD UNIVERSITY, CUMBERLAND SCHOOL OF LAW

800 Lakeshore Drive
Birmingham, AL 35229
Phone: 800.888.7213; Fax: 205.726.2057
E-mail: lawadm@samford.edu; Website: www.cumberland.samford.edu

Introduction

Cumberland School of Law, established in 1847 as a part of Cumberland University in Lebanon, Tennessee, is one of the oldest law schools in the country. The law school was acquired by Samford University in 1961. Today, Samford University is the largest privately supported and fully accredited institution of higher learning in Alabama. Samford's beautiful 300-acre campus is located in a suburban area of Birmingham, the state's largest industrial, business, and cultural center. Cumberland School of Law has been a member of the Association of American Law Schools (AALS) since 1952 and has been accredited by the American Bar Association (ABA) since 1949.

Advocacy and Skills Training

Samford's emphasis on teaching students the art and science of courtroom advocacy begins with the first-year curriculum. Lawyering and Legal Reasoning is a six-credit, two-semester course that provides students with hands-on, practical instruction in prelitigation skills, such as client interviewing, counseling, memorandum preparation, and negotiation; pretrial skills, including summary judgment motions and making compelling oral arguments; and appellate litigation skills. This intensive course prepares students to work effectively in their first summer clerkships, where they are expected to research cases and write briefs.

The state-of-the-art Advanced Trial Advocacy Courtroom provides students with access to the modern technology found in most courtrooms across the country. In the law school's Advanced Trial Advocacy course, 12 upper-level students learn how to reproduce evidence with three-dimensional digital presenters, video, and DVD reenactments. By mastering this technology and completing the hands-on training in the Advanced Trial Advocacy course, students will be equipped for success in any courtroom.

Samford has an exceptional record of recent trial advocacy competition victories. In the 2010–2011 academic year alone, the law school earned 12 top 10 placements at national and regional law school advocacy competitions. It won the 2008 American Association for Justice National Championship (finishing as a runner-up in 2009) and both the ABA and Association of Trial Lawyers of America national championships (including several national second- and third-place awards). To date, Samford has also won 40 regional championships and the coveted American College of Trial Lawyers' Emil Gumpert Award for Excellence in Teaching Trial Advocacy. The law school also offers a Certificate in Trial Advocacy to recognize students' achievements. Samford law students have the chance to earn class credit and professional experience working for Birmingham's major law firms, judges' offices, and corporate legal departments. The clinical curriculum offers second- and third-year students judicial and corporate externships, as well as externships in the offices of the IRS, US Attorney, and organizations that serve underrepresented or economically disadvantaged groups. In addition, the Alabama Third-Year Practice Rule gives third-year students a chance to practice law under the supervision of a licensed attorney.

Library and Physical Facilities

The Lucille Stewart Beeson Law Library, a free-standing Georgian structure, is visually stunning, as well as superbly functional. The building's design is intended to make all facilities easily accessible to students with disabilities. All 474 study carrels and 13 conference rooms are wired for data transmission. In addition, law students have full access to the university's four campus libraries, as well as six computer labs. Wireless Internet access is available here and in many areas around campus.

Center for Biotechnology, Law, and Ethics (CBLE)

As one of the first of its kind in the United States, the CBLE is dedicated to furthering practical training in the legal disciplines critical to biotechnology. Samford's unique program builds on a base of intellectual property, health care, environmental, tort, and natural resources law. The CBLE highlights issues related to the medical, pharmaceutical, and agricultural sectors, and offers students research opportunities. In addition, the CBLE hosts an annual symposium during which experts from around the world speak on such topics.

Center for Community Mediation and Public Interest Law Project (CCMC)

The CCMC emphasizes a commitment to public service, an important attribute of the education received at Samford. The CCMC provides free and confidential mediation services to the Birmingham community. Students completing the Mediator Practice course are eligible to volunteer as mediators. The mission of the Public Interest Law Project is to promote, encourage, and complete community service and legal public interest projects in the Birmingham community. Each year, the law school partners with the Alabama State Bar to hold a number of legal clinics throughout the state to help senior citizens and the underprivileged.

Joint-Degree Programs

To broaden their perspective and prepare them for careers in special fields, Samford law students may pursue eight different joint-degree programs: JD/Master of Accountancy, JD/Master of Business Administration, JD/Master of Public Health, JD/Master of Public Administration, JD/Master of Divinity, JD/MA in Theological Studies, JD/MS in Environmental Management, and JD/MS in Bioethics. Some of these joint-degree programs can be completed in three years.

Admission

The law school seeks a diverse student body that will make a contribution to the law school and the legal profession. To that end, every applicant's file is thoroughly reviewed for admission. In addition to the LSAT and GPA, difficulty of major, personal challenges overcome, graduate work completed, scholarly achievements, and volunteer and work experience are also considered. Applications are evaluated on a rolling basis, so it is important to apply early.

Applications for fall admission are accepted from September 1 to February 28.

Transfer students are accepted for fall semester. Once a transfer student is admitted, the Associate Dean for Academic Affairs will confirm the number of law school credit hours that will transfer to Samford University's Cumberland School of Law. In most instances, all credit hours for regular first-year law courses earned at an ABA-approved law school with a grade of C or better will transfer, up to a maximum of 40 credit hours.

Visiting students are accepted for summer, fall, and spring semesters.

Please visit this webpage for more information on these applications—http://cumberland.samford.edu/application.

Flex-Time Option

The law school's flex-time option allows students a maximum of five years to complete their studies. Flex students are required to take a minimum of eight credit hours each semester. Flex students attend classes during the day and pay an hourly tuition rate.

Scholarships

Generous merit-based scholarship assistance is awarded to Samford's entering and current law students annually. In addition, numerous other scholarships are provided to those students who distinguish themselves academically, make outstanding contributions through leadership in the law school, or demonstrate financial need.

Student Activities

The Student Bar Association functions as the first professional organization of a law student's career. In addition to the more than two dozen outstanding organizations, students may also be invited to join one of three national legal fraternities and be inducted into two honorary societies, Order of the Barrister and Curia Honoris. Student-run publications include *Cumberland Law Review* and *American Journal of Trial Advocacy*.

International Law

Samford conducts an ABA-approved international summer program that is offered at Sidney Sussex College, Cambridge, England. There is also a cooperative arrangement between Samford University and NALSAR University of Law in Hyderabad, India. The graduate degree of Master of Comparative Law is offered to international law school graduates. Each year, two Samford law graduates are awarded full-tuition scholarships for studies toward an LLM degree at Norwich Law School in England.

Career Development

The Office of Career Development provides the training, resources, and guidance to enable Samford law students and alumni to make well-informed career choices, secure employment as quickly and efficiently as possible, and forge rewarding careers. To help students and graduates achieve these goals, the office provides career counseling, résumé editing, practice interviews, on-campus interview programs, job fairs, job listings, instructional handouts, a resource library, and extensive educational programming. In addition to educational programs on résumé drafting, interviewing skills, networking, and job searching, Career Development also presents a "Lunch with a Lawyer" series, in which practitioners and other legal professionals come to the law school to discuss the practical aspects of their work in a variety of traditional and nontraditional legal jobs. All programs are taught by the attorneys on the Career Development staff, Samford law alumni, and others.

APPLICANT PROFILE

Samford University, Cumberland School of Law

LSAT Score	GPA								
	3.75 +	3.50–3.74	3.25–3.49	3.00–3.24	2.75–2.99	2.50–2.74	2.25–2.49	2.00–2.24	Below 2.00
175–180	■	■	■	■	■	□	▨	▨	▨
170–174	■	■	■	■	■	□	▨	▨	▨
165–169	■	■	■	■	■	□	▨	▨	▨
160–164	■	■	■	■	■	□	▨	▨	▨
155–159	■	■	■	■	■	□	▨	▨	▨
150–154	□	□	□	□	▨	▨	▨	▨	▨
145–149	▨	▨	▨	▨	▨	▨	▨	▨	▨
140–144	▨	▨	▨	▨	▨	▨	▨	▨	▨
135–139	▨	▨	▨	▨	▨	▨	▨	▨	▨
130–134	▨	▨	▨	▨	▨	▨	▨	▨	▨
125–129	▨	▨	▨	▨	▨	▨	▨	▨	▨
120–124	▨	▨	▨	▨	▨	▨	▨	▨	▨

■ Good Possibility   □ Possible   ▨ Unlikely

UNIVERSITY OF SAN DIEGO SCHOOL OF LAW

Warren Hall Room 203, 5998 Alcalá Park
San Diego, CA 92110-2492
Phone: 619.260.4528; Fax: 619.260.2218
E-mail: jdinfo@sandiego.edu; Website: www.law.sandiego.edu

ABA
Approved
Since
1961

The Basics

Type of school	Private
Term	Semester
Application deadline	2/1
Application fee	$50
Financial aid deadline	3/1
Can first year start other than fall?	No
Student to faculty ratio	14.0 to 1
# of housing spaces available restricted to law students graduate housing for which law students are eligible	45

Faculty and Administrators

	Total		Men		Women		Minorities	
	Spr	Fall	Spr	Fall	Spr	Fall	Spr	Fall
Full-time	53	55	40	41	13	14	3	4
Other full-time	9	8	1	2	8	6	1	1
Deans, librarians, & others who teach	8	8	4	4	4	4	2	2
Part-time	54	56	42	40	12	16	7	7
Total	124	127	87	87	37	40	13	14

Curriculum

	Full-Time	Part-Time
Typical first-year section size	75	35
Is there typically a "small section" of the first-year class, other than Legal Writing, taught by full-time faculty	No	No
If yes, typical size offered last year		
# of classroom course titles beyond first-year curriculum	145	
# of upper division courses, excluding seminars, with an enrollment: Under 25	208	
25–49	46	
50–74	15	
75–99	15	
100+	4	
# of seminars	27	
# of seminar positions available	450	
# of seminar positions filled	244	91
# of positions available in simulation courses	865	
# of simulation positions filled	421	153
# of positions available in faculty supervised clinical courses	247	
# of faculty supervised clinical positions filled	196	39
# involved in field placements	278	33
# involved in law journals	176	29
# involved in moot court or trial competitions	40	12
# of credit hours required to graduate	86	

JD Enrollment and Ethnicity

	Men		Women		Full-Time		Part-Time		1st-Year		Total		JD Degs. Awd.
	#	%	#	%	#	%	#	%	#	%	#	%	
All Hispanics	48	9.6	59	12.2	91	10.8	16	11.3	35	11.8	107	10.9	29
Am. Ind./AK Nat.	0	0.0	3	0.6	3	0.4	0	0.0	2	0.7	3	0.3	2
Asian	62	12.4	93	19.2	128	15.2	27	19.0	47	15.9	155	15.8	49
Black/Af. Am.	5	1.0	10	2.1	13	1.5	2	1.4	5	1.7	15	1.5	3
Nat. HI/Pac. Isl.	0	0.0	2	0.4	1	0.1	1	0.7	0	0.0	2	0.2	0
2 or more races	19	3.8	28	5.8	43	5.1	4	2.8	15	5.1	47	4.8	9
Subtotal (minor.)	134	26.9	195	40.3	279	33.2	50	35.2	104	35.1	329	33.5	92
Nonres. Alien	1	0.2	4	0.8	4	0.5	1	0.7	3	1.0	5	0.5	3
White/Cauc.	337	67.7	263	54.3	514	61.2	86	60.6	168	56.8	600	61.1	213
Unknown	26	5.2	22	4.5	43	5.1	5	3.5	21	7.1	48	4.9	10
Total	498	50.7	484	49.3	840	85.5	142	14.5	296	30.1	982		318

Transfers

Transfers in	35
Transfers out	15

Tuition and Fees

	Resident	Nonresident
Full-time	$42,754	$42,754
Part-time	$30,874	$30,874
Tuition Guarantee Program		N

Living Expenses

Estimated living expenses for singles

Living on campus	Living off campus	Living at home
$22,451	$22,451	$12,364

ABA
Approved
Since
1961

GPA and LSAT Scores

	Total	Full-Time	Part-Time
# of apps	4,289	4,009	280
# of offers	1,626	1,554	72
# of matrics	300	273	27
75% GPA	3.59	3.60	3.48
Median GPA	3.43	3.44	3.31
25% GPA	3.24	3.24	3.07
75% LSAT	162	162	162
Median LSAT	160	160	159
25% LSAT	158	158	156

Grants and Scholarships (from prior year)

	Total		Full-Time		Part-Time	
	#	%	#	%	#	%
Total # of students	1,007		831		176	
Total # receiving grants	458	45.5	381	45.8	77	43.8
Less than 1/2 tuition	182	18.1	140	16.8	42	23.9
Half to full tuition	233	23.1	207	24.9	26	14.8
Full tuition	26	2.6	17	2.0	9	5.1
More than full tuition	17	1.7	17	2.0	0	0.0
Median grant amount			$22,000		$13,050	

Informational and Library Resources

Total amount spent on library materials	$1,453,751
Study seating capacity inside the library	602
# of full-time equivalent professional librarians	9
Hours per week library is open	112
# of open, wired connections available to students	240
# of networked computers available for use by students	63
Has wireless network?	Y
Requires computer?	N

JD Attrition (from prior year)

	Academic	Other	Total	
	#	#	#	%
1st year	4	29	33	10.2
2nd year	0	2	2	0.6
3rd year	0	2	2	0.6
4th year	0	0	0	0.0

Employment (9 months after graduation)

For up-to-date employment data, go to employmentsummary.abaquestionnaire.org on the ABA website.

Bar Passage Rates

First-time takers	305	Reporting %	100.00
Average school %	67.56	Average state %	72.16
Average pass difference	−4.60		

Jurisdiction	Takers	Passers	Pass %	State %	Diff %
California	280	182	65.00	71.24	−6.24
New York	5	4	80.00	84.92	−4.92
Illinois	4	4	100.00	89.38	10.62
Washington	3	3	100.00	71.22	28.78
Others (9)	13	13	100.00		

UNIVERSITY OF SAN DIEGO SCHOOL OF LAW

Warren Hall Room 203, 5998 Alcalá Park
San Diego, CA 92110-2492
Phone: 619.260.4528; Fax: 619.260.2218
E-mail: jdinfo@sandiego.edu; Website: www.law.sandiego.edu

Introduction

As one of the most selective law schools in the country, the University of San Diego (USD) School of Law is a leading center of academic excellence. The school's internationally regarded faculty of scholars and expert practitioners create a demanding, yet welcoming, environment that emphasizes individualized legal education. The school is also known as a leader in creating programs and courses to prepare future lawyers to practice in a rapidly changing world marked by globalization and dramatic advancements in technology. Founded in 1954, the law school is part of the University of San Diego, a private, nonprofit, independent Roman Catholic university. The university is located on a 182-acre campus overlooking Mission Bay and the Pacific Ocean, featuring Spanish Renaissance architecture and well-maintained, garden-like grounds.

Admission

USD School of Law strives to draw talented students from all regions of the country and from different ethnic and social backgrounds. The university is committed to advancing academic excellence, expanding legal and professional knowledge, creating a diverse and inclusive community, and preparing leaders dedicated to ethical conduct and compassionate service.

Accreditation and Membership

Accredited—American Bar Association (ABA), Committee of Bar Examiners—State of California.
Membership—Association of American Law Schools (AALS), Order of the Coif.

Legal Research Center (LRC)

The Pardee Legal Research Center offers a full range of traditional printed and state-of-the-art electronic services. Computer legal research systems include those of BNA, CCH, HeinOnline, LegalTrac, LexisNexis, and Westlaw. Among all law libraries at ABA-accredited schools, USD is in the top one-third in collection size with over three quarters of a million in print and electronic titles.

Special Programs

Summer Law Study Abroad—USD School of Law, in cooperation with foreign universities, conducts summer law study programs overseas. The programs introduce American law students to foreign law and legal institutions and provide intensive study during four- to five-week sessions. Classes abroad sensitize students to the cultural differences that influence effective international dealing and expose students to the perspectives of foreign experts.
Clinical Education Program—This program is recognized as one of the most extensive and successful in the nation, including client-based clinics and placement clinics as well as an externship/internship program. In the legal clinics, which close about 620 cases each year, students represent low-income clients in nine areas of law under the supervision of a clinical professor who is a licensed attorney specializing in that area.

Research and Advocacy Institutes—Recently, the school launched two new research institutes: the Center for Corporate and Securities Law and the Center for Intellectual Property Law and Markets. Launched in 2010, the Technology Entrepreneurship Law Clinic provides students with hands-on legal experience by serving local technology start-ups. USD also houses the Center for Public Interest Law, Children's Advocacy Institute, Institute for Law and Philosophy, Center for the Study of Constitutional Originalism, Energy Policy Initiatives Center, and Center for Education Policy and Law.

Concurrent Degrees—Students desiring to concentrate in business or international relations may concurrently pursue the JD/MBA, JD/International MBA, or JD/MA in International Relations.

Legal Writing and Research—Students receive extensive training in a variety of legal skills, including first-year legal writing and research, interviewing, counseling, discovery, trial advocacy, and alternative dispute resolution.

Oral Advocacy—USD's National Moot Court and National Mock Trial teams consistently rank among the finest teams in the nation. Students participate in the Duberstein Moot Court Competition, focusing on appellate brief writing and oral arguments about a pressing issue facing the Bankruptcy Bar. A select few students are given the opportunity to brief and argue appeals through the Ninth Circuit Appellate Clinic.

Campus Highlights

The law school buildings sit directly across from the Student Life Pavilion, a 62,000-square-foot expansion of the Hahn University Center (UC), the nexus of the USD campus. The UC offers 134,000 square feet of office space for student organizations and multiuse areas, including a bakery, deli, grill, mini-grocery store, pizza parlor, and the university's main dining hall.

Student Activities

With more than 40 different groups available, student organizations not only serve the various interests of our students but also develop a sense of community among their members. The active groups promote leadership, conduct orientation programs, provide study assistance, represent group concerns, sponsor speaker programs, and promote community relations. The school's four law journals, the *San Diego International Law Journal*, the *Journal of Contemporary Legal Issues*, the *San Diego Law Review*, and the *San Diego Journal of Climate and Energy Law*, each offer opportunities to be on the inside of developing legal scholarship.

Financial Aid

The School of Law is committed to providing all possible financial assistance to eligible students whose personal resources are insufficient to meet their educational expenses. Sources of financial aid include over 450 need/merit, merit, and diversity-based scholarships; federal plans, such as work-study programs; the Perkins, Direct, and Graduate PLUS federal loan programs; and institutional loans. Private loan programs are also available to assist law students with supplemental financing.

Career Services

USD Law's Career Services office is committed to supporting all students in achieving their diverse career objectives. Throughout their law school years, students are offered opportunities to explore career options with private law firms, government agencies, and public interest organizations, and to obtain internships, fellowships, and clerkships with federal and state courts nationwide. Traditionally, more than 200 interviewers each year interview USD students on and off campus as part of an extensive recruiting process.

USD's law graduates practice in 50 states, the District of Columbia, and at least 50 foreign countries. For the graduating class of 2010, within nine months of graduation, approximately 85.5 percent were employed or enrolled in a full-time degree program. For the class of 2011, approximately 46.5 percent accepted positions with law firms and 14.4 percent began their careers in public service, including local, state, and federal government; federal courts; and public interest agencies. Others pursued careers in a range of business and corporate positions. The median salary for graduates in private practice was $87,231. The median salary for graduates working in the public sectors was $60,666.

Housing

The USD Department of Residential Life and the School of Law Office of Admissions assist in providing information and resources in locating on- and off-campus accommodations.

APPLICANT PROFILE

University of San Diego School of Law
(Note: This chart is to be used as a general guide only. Nonnumerical factors are also considered.)

LSAT Score	GPA								
	3.75 +	3.50–3.74	3.25–3.49	3.00–3.24	2.75–2.99	2.50–2.74	2.25–2.49	2.00–2.24	Below 2.00
175–180	■	■	■	■	■	■	□		
170–174	■	■	■	■	■	■	□		
165–169	■	■	■	■	■	□			
160–164	■	■	■	■	■	□			
155–159	■	■							
150–154									
145–149									
140–144									
135–139									
130–134									
125–129									
120–124									

■ Good Possibility   □ Possible   ▓ Unlikely

UNIVERSITY OF SAN FRANCISCO SCHOOL OF LAW

USF School of Law, 2130 Fulton Street
San Francisco, CA 94117-1080
Phone: 415.422.6586; Fax: 415.422.5442
E-mail: lawadmissions@usfca.edu; Website: www.usfca.edu/law

*ABA
Approved
Since
1935*

The Basics

Type of school	Private
Term	Semester
Application deadline	2/1
Application fee	$60
Financial aid deadline	2/15
Can first year start other than fall?	No
Student to faculty ratio	14.8 to 1
# of housing spaces available restricted to law students	
graduate housing for which law students are eligible	25

Faculty and Administrators

	Total		Men		Women		Minorities	
	Spr	Fall	Spr	Fall	Spr	Fall	Spr	Fall
Full-time	38	38	20	19	18	19	13	13
Other full-time	0	0	0	0	0	0	0	0
Deans, librarians, & others who teach	8	7	4	4	4	3	2	1
Part-time	39	40	30	31	9	9	5	4
Total	85	85	54	54	31	31	20	18

Curriculum

	Full-Time	Part-Time
Typical first-year section size	96	63
Is there typically a "small section" of the first-year class, other than Legal Writing, taught by full-time faculty	No	No
If yes, typical size offered last year		
# of classroom course titles beyond first-year curriculum	104	
# of upper division courses, excluding seminars, with an enrollment: Under 25	85	
25–49	36	
50–74	11	
75–99	6	
100+	0	
# of seminars	18	
# of seminar positions available	360	
# of seminar positions filled	295	15
# of positions available in simulation courses	320	
# of simulation positions filled	281	34
# of positions available in faculty supervised clinical courses	144	
# of faculty supervised clinical positions filled	95	9
# involved in field placements	121	6
# involved in law journals	138	6
# involved in moot court or trial competitions	110	4
# of credit hours required to graduate	86	

JD Enrollment and Ethnicity

	Men		Women		Full-Time		Part-Time		1st-Year		Total		JD Degs. Awd.
	#	%	#	%	#	%	#	%	#	%	#	%	
All Hispanics	45	13.9	43	11.1	70	12.0	18	13.8	29	11.8	88	12.4	25
Am. Ind./AK Nat.	3	0.9	2	0.5	2	0.3	3	2.3	2	0.8	5	0.7	3
Asian	34	10.5	58	14.9	75	12.9	17	13.1	34	13.8	92	12.9	24
Black/Af. Am.	24	7.4	31	8.0	36	6.2	19	14.6	24	9.8	55	7.7	13
Nat. HI/Pac. Isl.	1	0.3	1	0.3	2	0.3	0	0.0	0	0.0	2	0.3	0
2 or more races	20	6.2	21	5.4	34	5.8	7	5.4	16	6.5	41	5.8	17
Subtotal (minor.)	127	39.3	156	40.1	219	37.6	64	49.2	105	42.7	283	39.7	82
Nonres. Alien	0	0.0	0	0.0	0	0.0	0	0.0	0	0.0	0	0.0	0
White/Cauc.	162	50.2	201	51.7	305	52.4	58	44.6	123	50.0	363	51.0	129
Unknown	34	10.5	32	8.2	58	10.0	8	6.2	18	7.3	66	9.3	25
Total	323	45.4	389	54.6	582	81.7	130	18.3	246	34.6	712		236

Transfers

Transfers in	6
Transfers out	20

Tuition and Fees

	Resident	Nonresident
Full-time	$40,544	$40,544
Part-time	$28,945	$28,945
Tuition Guarantee Program		N

Living Expenses

Estimated living expenses for singles

Living on campus	Living off campus	Living at home
$21,824	$20,660	$10,060

UNIVERSITY OF SAN FRANCISCO SCHOOL OF LAW

ABA
Approved
Since
1935

GPA and LSAT Scores

	Total	Full-Time	Part-Time
# of apps	4,215	3,719	496
# of offers	1,603	1,467	136
# of matrics	246	189	57
75% GPA	3.57	3.60	3.38
Median GPA	3.40	3.49	3.20
25% GPA	3.08	3.17	2.88
75% LSAT	159	160	158
Median LSAT	157	158	156
25% LSAT	155	155	153

Grants and Scholarships (from prior year)

	Total #	Total %	Full-Time #	Full-Time %	Part-Time #	Part-Time %
Total # of students	739		589		150	
Total # receiving grants	254	34.4	206	35.0	48	32.0
Less than 1/2 tuition	168	22.7	133	22.6	35	23.3
Half to full tuition	86	11.6	73	12.4	13	8.7
Full tuition	0	0.0	0	0.0	0	0.0
More than full tuition	0	0.0	0	0.0	0	0.0
Median grant amount			$10,000		$6,750	

Informational and Library Resources

Total amount spent on library materials	$1,646,472
Study seating capacity inside the library	428
# of full-time equivalent professional librarians	7
Hours per week library is open	98
# of open, wired connections available to students	1,030
# of networked computers available for use by students	75
Has wireless network?	Y
Requires computer?	N

JD Attrition (from prior year)

	Academic #	Other #	Total #	Total %
1st year	18	38	56	22.3
2nd year	2	5	7	2.9
3rd year	2	3	5	2.4
4th year	0	0	0	0.0

Employment (9 months after graduation)

For up-to-date employment data, go to employmentsummary.abaquestionnaire.org on the ABA website.

Bar Passage Rates

First-time takers	207	Reporting %	70.05
Average school %	85.52	Average state %	71.24
Average pass difference	14.28		

Jurisdiction	Takers	Passers	Pass %	State %	Diff %
California	145	124	85.52	71.24	14.28

UNIVERSITY OF SAN FRANCISCO SCHOOL OF LAW

USF School of Law, 2130 Fulton Street
San Francisco, CA 94117-1080
Phone: 415.422.6586; Fax: 415.422.5442
E-mail: lawadmissions@usfca.edu; Website: www.usfca.edu/law

Introduction

Founded in 1912, the University of San Francisco (USF) School of Law has a tradition of educating effective lawyers who graduate with the professional skills and theoretical foundation necessary to succeed in the legal profession.

The San Francisco Bay Area is an extension of the campus and plays a vital role in the educational experience. The school is located on a hilltop campus overlooking Golden Gate Park, the Pacific Ocean, and downtown San Francisco. It is minutes away from the Civic Center, home to federal, state, and local government agencies, as well as federal and state courts, including the California Supreme Court. The city and its surrounding communities provide exceptional learning, practice, and service placements to complement the academic program. Students represent clients in law school clinics, extern in major national and international law firms, clerk for judges, and work for public interest organizations.

The USF School of Law is fully accredited by the American Bar Association and is a member of the Association of American Law Schools.

Commitment to Justice

The USF School of Law offers a rigorous education with a global perspective in a diverse, supportive community. Our graduates are skilled, ethical professionals prepared for any legal career, with a commitment to social justice as their enduring foundation. Our inclusive Jesuit mission integrates humanity and ethical conduct into the practice of law. Evidence of this mission in action includes our extensive list of programs dedicated to serving communities throughout the United States and around the globe and our unique curriculum focused on ethics and professional responsibility.

Degree Programs

The USF School of Law offers full- and part-time Juris Doctor (JD) programs that empower students to develop their analytical abilities, master legal writing and research skills, acquire a firm foundation of basic law, explore an array of specialties, and refine their professional legal skills in practical settings. The full-time program requires three years of study, while the part-time program can be completed in four years. Students in the part-time program may accelerate their studies and complete the degree in seven semesters or they may convert to the full-time program after the first year and graduate in three years. In conjunction with the USF School of Management, the law school offers a four-year, full-time concurrent JD/MBA degree program. The law school also offers a Master of Laws (LLM) in International Transactions and Comparative Law for foreign lawyers and an LLM in Intellectual Property and Technology Law for foreign and US lawyers.

Inspiring Facilities

The USF School of Law is housed in the Koret Law Center and comprises Kendrick Hall, where classrooms and faculty offices are located, and the Dorraine Zief Law Library. Kendrick Hall, built in the 1960s and recently renovated, features a rotunda skylight, spiral stairways, and circular configurations that enhance natural light and offer informal gathering spaces for students and faculty. Students prepare for trial practice in a state-of-the-art, 70-seat moot courtroom. Administrative offices are located in Kendrick Hall to provide easy access to services and staff. Office space for student organizations and clinical programs, a student lounge, and a café are found here as well.

Linked to Kendrick Hall by a soaring glass atrium, the Dorraine Zief Law Library, which opened in 2000, is a modern, technologically advanced study environment. It houses an extensive collection and connects to countless online resources. The library also features individual and group study rooms equipped with audiovisual equipment, computer classrooms, and research rooms.

As part of a larger campus community, USF law students benefit from the amenities and facilities of a major urban university, including the outstanding recreational and fitness facilities of USF's award-winning Koret Health and Recreation Center. The university's 55-acre campus also features a main library, bookstore, student center, and dining facilities.

Educating Legal Professionals

The core curriculum, concentrated in the first three semesters of the full-time and part-time programs, includes courses essential to a solid understanding of dominant legal concepts. The core curriculum is complemented by a rich offering of courses and programs providing almost unlimited opportunities for specialized study and practical experience. Elective courses, which full-time students may pursue in their first year, are constantly updated to reflect changes in the law, to meet the pace of technological change, and to match student interest.

JD certificate programs and elective clusters offer concentrated study for students who wish to pursue particular career objectives or develop specialized skills. Notable among these are courses in international and comparative law, public interest law, advocacy and alternative dispute resolution, business law, and intellectual property and cyberspace law.

There are also vast opportunities to hone practical skills in one of our many externship programs or by handling real cases under the supervision of a professor in a USF law clinic, such as the Child Advocacy Clinic, Criminal and Juvenile Justice Law Clinic, Employment Law Clinic, Frank C. Newman International Human Rights Law Clinic, Internet and Intellectual Property Justice Clinic, Investor Justice Clinic, and Mediation Clinic. Our Civil and Criminal Law Externship Program matches students with private law firms, district attorneys, public defenders, or one of our other 220 preapproved employers throughout the city and region, while the Judicial Externship Program facilitates student placements in a variety of courthouses.

International Programs

Our extensive menu of international programs provides exceptional opportunities to study and extern abroad. Traditional study abroad and exchange programs are offered in China, the Czech Republic, Ireland, Luxemburg, and

Mexico, and externship and service opportunities are offered in India, Vietnam, Haiti, Cambodia, Argentina, and the Philippines, among other countries. USF's innovative Frank C. Newman International Human Rights Law Clinic affords many students the opportunity to personally present their research and policy proposals to the United Nations Commission on Human Rights in Geneva or the Commission on the Status of Women in New York. The Center for Law and Global Justice acquaints students with differing legal traditions and provides opportunities for international externships and service learning. The center is a resource for international programming and courses, and creates opportunities for students to conduct research on critical human rights issues.

Student Activities

Much of a USF law student's education takes place outside the classroom. Students expand their scholarship interests by writing, editing, and publishing several law journals, including the *USF Law Review*, *USF Maritime Law Journal*, and *Intellectual Property Law Bulletin*. Opportunities to hone advocacy and leadership skills abound. Students participate in the annual Advocate of the Year Competition, compete in interschool moot court and trial advocacy competitions, and also take part in countless externship and clinical opportunities. All students attending the law school are members of the Student Bar Association (SBA), which gives students a voice in school policy and works with more than 35 student organizations that reflect the diversity and varied interests of students. The USF Public Interest Law Foundation's annual gala auction raises funds for students working in unpaid summer internships in the public interest and public sector and is one example of the many student-sponsored events held each year.

Frequent panels, guest speakers, special programs, and symposia provide students with regular opportunities for intellectual interchange with faculty, alumni, members of the bench and bar, and visiting dignitaries. Examples of recent symposia include Clean Technology and the Law: The Legal Infrastructure for Promoting the Development and

Dissemination of Clean Technologies; Litigation, Settlement and the Public Interest: Fluid Recovery and Cy Pres Relief; The Emerging Role of Intellectual Property Protection in the (Digital) Cloud; The Future of Same-Sex Marriage; and the award-winning California Water Law symposium Who Controls the Water? Reforming California Water Law Governance in the Age of Scarcity.

The Law Student Pro Bono Project and the Law In Motion Service Program offer opportunities for service, sponsoring a variety of legal and nonlegal community outreach and pro bono projects.

Distinguished Teachers and Scholars

USF School of Law professors bring to the classroom the highest educational credentials, substantial practical experience, and an underlying dedication to teaching, scholarship, and service. They are respected authors, researchers, and legal theorists who write books, casebooks, practice guides, law review articles, and book reviews. Faculty members have achieved numerous scholastic accomplishments—graduating from elite law schools, earning honors, and serving as editors of prestigious law journals. Almost all have substantial practical experience and continue to be involved in service to the community and the profession. Their zeal for teaching comes to life in the classroom, in clinics, and in informal conversations with students. They create an intellectually challenging but supportive atmosphere in which each student thrives.

The full-time faculty is complemented by approximately 60 adjunct professors, including federal and state court judges, attorneys from public agencies, and other distinguished members of the bar in private practice. Our location in the dynamic San Francisco Bay Area legal community allows the law school to expand its curriculum with specialized courses and provides students access to a wealth of practical expertise.

APPLICANT PROFILE

University of San Francisco School of Law
This grid includes only applicants who earned 120–180 LSAT scores under standard administrations.

LSAT Score	3.75 +		3.50–3.74		3.25–3.49		3.00–3.24		2.75–2.99		2.50–2.74		2.25–2.49		2.00–2.24		Below 2.00		No GPA		Total	
	Apps	Adm	Apps	Adm	Apps	Adm	Apps	Adm	Apps	Adm	Apps	Adm	Apps	Adm	Apps	Adm	Apps	Adm	Apps	Adm	Apps	Adm
175–180	0	0	1	1	1	1	1	1	0	0	1	1	0	0	1	0	0	0	0	0	5	4
170–174	8	8	8	8	10	10	3	3	4	3	7	4	4	1	0	0	0	0	0	0	44	37
165–169	24	23	57	57	40	38	38	35	29	18	16	8	2	0	2	0	0	0	4	3	212	182
160–164	76	76	164	159	174	160	146	128	71	38	39	19	22	11	7	1	2	0	13	9	714	601
155–159	108	93	263	227	329	127	267	82	154	30	72	13	31	5	10	0	1	0	14	5	1249	582
150–154	93	43	176	83	239	22	232	13	153	7	89	3	42	0	16	0	3	0	24	0	1067	171
145–149	28	3	79	7	128	2	123	6	94	3	51	0	43	0	11	0	1	0	11	0	569	21
140–144	2	0	18	1	31	0	64	0	39	0	36	0	15	0	8	0	1	0	5	0	219	1
135–139	1	0	5	0	5	0	11	0	19	0	14	0	9	0	6	0	4	0	4	0	78	0
130–134	0	0	2	0	4	0	3	0	1	0	8	0	4	0	6	0	0	0	6	0	34	0
125–129	0	0	1	0	0	0	1	0	0	0	2	0	1	0	1	0	0	0	0	0	6	0
120–124	0	0	0	0	0	0	0	0	0	0	0	0	0	0	0	0	0	0	0	0	0	0
Total	340	246	774	543	961	360	889	268	564	99	335	48	173	17	68	1	12	0	81	17	4197	1599

Apps = Number of Applicants
Adm = Number Admitted
Reflects 99% of the total applicant pool; highest LSAT data reported.

SANTA CLARA UNIVERSITY SCHOOL OF LAW

500 El Camino Real
Santa Clara, CA 95053
Phone: 408.554.5048; Fax: 408.554.7897
E-mail: LawAdmissions@scu.edu; Website: http://law.scu.edu

ABA
Approved
Since
1937

The Basics

Type of school	Private
Term	Semester
Application deadline	2/1
Application fee	$75
Financial aid deadline	3/1
Can first year start other than fall?	No
Student to faculty ratio	11.9 to 1
# of housing spaces available restricted to law students	
graduate housing for which law students are eligible	68

Faculty and Administrators

	Total		Men		Women		Minorities	
	Spr	Fall	Spr	Fall	Spr	Fall	Spr	Fall
Full-time	64	61	34	30	30	31	12	11
Other full-time	4	2	2	1	2	1	1	1
Deans, librarians, & others who teach	12	11	5	5	7	6	2	2
Part-time	43	39	21	21	22	18	7	6
Total	123	113	62	57	61	56	22	20

Curriculum

	Full-Time	Part-Time
Typical first-year section size	76	78
Is there typically a "small section" of the first-year class, other than Legal Writing, taught by full-time faculty	Yes	Yes
If yes, typical size offered last year	39	39
# of classroom course titles beyond first-year curriculum	170	

# of upper division courses, excluding seminars, with an enrollment:	Under 25	131
	25–49	49
	50–74	19
	75–99	17
	100+	1

# of seminars	102	
# of seminar positions available	1,879	
# of seminar positions filled	1,530	0
# of positions available in simulation courses	329	
# of simulation positions filled	301	0
# of positions available in faculty supervised clinical courses	266	
# of faculty supervised clinical positions filled	238	0
# involved in field placements	382	0
# involved in law journals	104	0
# involved in moot court or trial competitions	42	0
# of credit hours required to graduate	86	

JD Enrollment and Ethnicity

	Men		Women		Full-Time		Part-Time		1st-Year		Total		JD Degs. Awd.
	#	%	#	%	#	%	#	%	#	%	#	%	
All Hispanics	48	9.4	38	8.3	73	9.9	13	5.7	36	12.3	86	8.9	26
Am. Ind./AK Nat.	5	1.0	2	0.4	6	0.8	1	0.4	0	0.0	7	0.7	2
Asian	117	23.0	123	26.9	162	22.0	78	34.1	58	19.8	240	24.8	70
Black/Af. Am.	11	2.2	9	2.0	17	2.3	3	1.3	6	2.0	20	2.1	10
Nat. Hl/Pac. Isl.	3	0.6	3	0.7	3	0.4	3	1.3	2	0.7	6	0.6	0
2 or more races	10	2.0	15	3.3	21	2.8	4	1.7	10	3.4	25	2.6	1
Subtotal (minor.)	194	38.1	190	41.5	282	38.2	102	44.5	112	38.2	384	39.7	109
Nonres. Alien	17	3.3	26	5.7	33	4.5	10	4.4	10	3.4	43	4.4	11
White/Cauc.	298	58.5	239	52.2	421	57.0	116	50.7	169	57.7	537	55.5	176
Unknown	0	0.0	3	0.7	2	0.3	1	0.4	2	0.7	3	0.3	0
Total	509	52.6	458	47.4	738	76.3	229	23.7	293	30.3	967		296

Transfers

Transfers in	22
Transfers out	9

Tuition and Fees

	Resident	Nonresident
Full-time	$41,790	$41,790
Part-time	$29,254	$29,254
Tuition Guarantee Program		N

Living Expenses

Estimated living expenses for singles

Living on campus	Living off campus	Living at home
$21,956	$21,956	$21,956

SANTA CLARA UNIVERSITY SCHOOL OF LAW

ABA
Approved
Since
1937

GPA and LSAT Scores

	Total	Full-Time	Part-Time
# of apps	3,689	3,360	329
# of offers	1,338	1,210	128
# of matrics	287	215	72
75% GPA	3.47	3.48	3.43
Median GPA	3.24	3.25	3.22
25% GPA	3.02	3.07	2.73
75% LSAT	161	162	160
Median LSAT	160	160	157
25% LSAT	157	158	157

Grants and Scholarships (from prior year)

	Total #	Total %	Full-Time #	Full-Time %	Part-Time #	Part-Time %
Total # of students	983		749		234	
Total # receiving grants	452	46.0	355	47.4	97	41.5
Less than 1/2 tuition	399	40.6	322	43.0	77	32.9
Half to full tuition	32	3.3	20	2.7	12	5.1
Full tuition	21	2.1	13	1.7	8	3.4
More than full tuition	0	0.0	0	0.0	0	0.0
Median grant amount			$10,000		$8,000	

Informational and Library Resources

Total amount spent on library materials	$1,474,229
Study seating capacity inside the library	504
# of full-time equivalent professional librarians	9
Hours per week library is open	106
# of open, wired connections available to students	933
# of networked computers available for use by students	62
Has wireless network?	Y
Requires computer?	N

JD Attrition (from prior year)

	Academic #	Other #	Total #	Total %
1st year	19	32	51	15.6
2nd year	0	3	3	1.0
3rd year	0	0	0	0.0
4th year	0	0	0	0.0

Employment (9 months after graduation)

For up-to-date employment data, go to
employmentsummary.abaquestionnaire.org on the ABA website.

Bar Passage Rates

First-time takers	322	Reporting %	88.82
Average school %	70.28	Average state %	71.24
Average pass difference	−0.96		

Jurisdiction	Takers	Passers	Pass %	State %	Diff %
California	286	201	70.28	71.24	−0.96

SANTA CLARA UNIVERSITY SCHOOL OF LAW

500 El Camino Real
Santa Clara, CA 95053
Phone: 408.554.5048; Fax: 408.554.7897
E-mail: LawAdmissions@scu.edu; Website: http://law.scu.edu

Introduction

Santa Clara Law, just 40 miles south of San Francisco, is located on the lush, historic, 105-acre campus of Santa Clara University, California's oldest operating institution of higher learning. The university was founded by the Jesuits in 1851 on the site of the Mission Santa Clara de Asis, one of California's original 21 missions. Established in 1911, Santa Clara Law has fostered an exceptional academic program based on the Jesuit tradition for more than 100 years. Approved by the ABA, Santa Clara Law is a member of the Order of the Coif and the AALS.

Santa Clara Law students are committed to excellence, ethics, and social justice. The school strives to prepare its students to serve as lawyers who lead in any field, and offers students ample opportunities to apply their skills in internships, clinics, field placements, and community involvement.

Location

Santa Clara Law is located in the heart of Silicon Valley, one of the most vibrant and exciting economies in the world, and home to leading national and international law firms as well as companies such as Google, Apple, eBay, Intel, and Yahoo!

Our location enhances the curriculum, including the nationally acclaimed high-tech and intellectual property program, which features experienced Silicon Valley executives and attorneys who share their experience in courses, workshops, and lectures. In addition, students benefit from the location through internship and job opportunities, lectures, and networking events.

The San Francisco Bay Area is one of the most beautiful regions in the US, and the Mediterranean climate boasts sun more than 300 days a year. North of Santa Clara are the world-class cities of Berkeley, Oakland, and San Francisco. Southwest are the coastal towns of Santa Cruz, Monterey, Carmel, and Big Sur.

Diversity

Santa Clara Law is one of the most diverse law schools in the country, and the school offers an array of programs that encourage and support diversity. Santa Clara Law students learn with students from all 50 states and numerous foreign countries, and they are taught by a diverse and talented group of faculty members who are committed to an inclusive learning experience. Forty-one percent of applicants for fall 2011 were from outside California, and the 2011 entering class included 41 percent minorities and 48 percent women.

Library and Physical Facilities

Towering palm trees, spacious lawns, and vibrant flower gardens surround the Heafey Law Library. A traditional moot courtroom provides the setting for advocacy training and activities of the Edwin A. Heafey Jr. Center for Trial and Appellate Advocacy. Other facilities include the Bergin Hall faculty office building and Bannan Hall, where our law career services, Academic Success Program, and many other programs are located. Students also have access to the full array of campus facilities, including computer labs, the Cowell Student Health Center, Benson Memorial Center, and the Pat Malley Fitness Center, which includes a well-equipped weight room, fitness classes, an outdoor pool, locker rooms with steam rooms and saunas, and courts for basketball, volleyball, and racquetball.

Curriculum

Santa Clara Law offers full- and part-time programs (with day and evening classes), extensive diversity outreach programs, and an Academic Success Program. More than 200 courses are available, and 86 semester units are required to graduate. The degrees available include JD, JD/MBA, JD/MSIS, LLM in International Law, LLM in US Law for Foreign Attorneys, and LLM in Intellectual Property. An academic orientation introduces first-year students to the study of law. The first-year curriculum is prescribed.

The JD/MBA and the JD/MSIS combined-degree programs are a powerful union of Santa Clara's nationally recognized School of Law and Leavey School of Business. Students earn both degrees in a full-time program lasting three and one-half to four years.

International Law Certificate

The International Law Program sponsors summer law study programs in more locations than any other American law school, including programs in: Munich, Germany; Strasbourg, France; Geneva, Switzerland; Oxford, England; Hong Kong; Singapore; Shanghai, China; The Hague, the Netherlands; Istanbul, Turkey; San Jose, Costa Rica; Tokyo, Japan; Vienna; Budapest; Sydney, Australia; and Seoul, Korea. Nearly all programs offer internships with law offices, corporations, or groups particularly suited to allow students on-site observation and participation in areas of international law. Students may earn a certificate in International Law.

Computer and High-Technology Law Certificate

With its central Silicon Valley location, **Santa Clara Law is one of the top places in the country to study intellectual property and high-tech law** for good reasons. Students learn from a dozen full-time faculty members with expertise in every aspect of intellectual property (IP) and high-tech law plus two dozen part-time faculty members working in IP and high-tech law at leading Silicon Valley firms and companies. Students have unparalleled internship opportunities with leading high-tech companies and law firms. The IP and high-tech curriculum is one of the largest in the country, and students can create a highly personalized course of study, including a certificate in High-Tech Law or International High-Tech Law.

Public Interest and Social Justice Law Certificate

The Santa Clara Law community has a true commitment to social justice, and students serve the poor and the marginalized in many ways while in law school, including work for the Center for Social Justice and Public Service, which offers an array of resources for students who want to focus on this area during their legal education and in practice. Santa Clara Law takes seriously the charge of graduating lawyers who lead with a commitment to a more humane and just world, and many students choose to earn a certificate in Public Interest.

Clinical Programs

Santa Clara Law students can participate in a wide variety of clinical and field experiences. The Katharine and George Alexander Community Law Center houses four clinics, including Immigration, Low Income Taxpayer, Workers' Rights, and Consumer clinics. Students participate in all phases of a case from the initial client interview through the trial. Northern California Innocence Project students work with legal staff to evaluate claims of factual innocence. Students work with prisoners, crime and evidence labs, law enforcement, defense attorneys, and prosecutors to help exonerate the wrongfully convicted. Students may also work as judges' clerks in appellate courts, including the California Supreme Court, or trial courts, including the United States District Court or county superior courts.

Student Activities

Santa Clara Law has 35 student groups, including an extensive array of minority student organizations and national and international moot court teams. The school's quarterly, *Santa Clara Law Review*, is published by a student editorial board. The *Computer and High Technology Law Journal* provides a practical resource for the high-tech industry and

legal community. The *Journal of International Law* is a respected, peer-reviewed scholarly journal. Through the Student Bar Association and student-faculty committees, students participate in the decision processes of the school.

Admission

A faculty committee reviews all applications. No one is automatically accepted or rejected. When the LSAT is repeated, the highest score received is used.

Santa Clara Law has a policy for special admission, and applicants may request special consideration because of race, disadvantaged background, or other factors.

Applicants are encouraged to visit Santa Clara Law. Arrangements can be made through the Admissions Office to tour the campus, attend a class, or meet with an admission counselor.

Career Services

Law Career Services offers several workshops, presentations, and services to help students launch a career. These include on-campus interviewing, job fairs, mock interviews, diversity receptions, and speed networking. Each year, a number of law firms, companies, and public and government agencies interview on campus or request résumés from our students. A high percentage of our graduates are employed within nine months of graduation in positions throughout the United States.

APPLICANT PROFILE

Santa Clara University School of Law
This grid includes only applicants who earned 120–180 LSAT scores under standard administrations.

LSAT Score	3.75 + Apps	3.75 + Adm	3.50–3.74 Apps	3.50–3.74 Adm	3.25–3.49 Apps	3.25–3.49 Adm	3.00–3.24 Apps	3.00–3.24 Adm	2.75–2.99 Apps	2.75–2.99 Adm	2.50–2.74 Apps	2.50–2.74 Adm	2.25–2.49 Apps	2.25–2.49 Adm	2.00–2.24 Apps	2.00–2.24 Adm	Below 2.00 Apps	Below 2.00 Adm	No GPA Apps	No GPA Adm	Total Apps	Total Adm
175–180	4	4	3	3	2	2	2	1	1	1	2	1	0	0	1	1	0	0	0	0	15	13
170–174	17	15	21	21	16	13	11	9	8	6	4	4	3	3	0	0	0	0	2	2	82	73
165–169	51	51	73	66	71	66	66	61	45	37	23	12	9	2	3	1	0	0	11	8	352	304
160–164	110	89	201	153	190	140	167	128	59	32	36	19	24	11	4	1	1	0	13	5	805	578
155–159	116	50	255	103	293	97	240	56	114	16	51	11	20	2	7	1	0	0	24	12	1120	348
150–154	68	2	138	2	185	7	181	5	100	1	55	1	18	0	4	0	3	0	14	0	766	18
145–149	18	0	52	0	73	0	60	0	60	0	35	0	24	0	6	0	1	0	11	0	340	0
140–144	2	0	14	0	25	0	35	0	25	0	18	0	14	0	3	0	0	0	4	0	140	0
135–139	3	0	4	0	6	0	9	0	8	0	7	0	6	0	2	0	0	0	3	0	48	0
130–134	0	0	2	0	4	0	3	0	1	0	6	0	5	0	3	0	0	0	3	0	27	0
125–129	0	0	1	0	0	0	0	0	0	0	1	0	1	0	1	0	0	0	0	0	4	0
120–124	0	0	0	0	0	0	0	0	0	0	0	0	0	0	0	0	0	0	0	0	0	0
Total	389	211	764	348	865	325	774	260	421	93	238	48	124	18	34	4	5	0	85	27	3699	1334

Apps = Number of Applicants
Adm = Number Admitted
Reflects 99% of the total applicant pool; highest LSAT data reported.

SEATTLE UNIVERSITY SCHOOL OF LAW

901 12th Avenue, Sullivan Hall
Seattle, WA 98122-1090
Phone: 206.398.4200; Fax: 206.398.4058
E-mail: lawadmis@seattleu.edu; Website: www.law.seattleu.edu

ABA
Approved
Since
1994

The Basics

Type of school	Private
Term	Semester
Application deadline	3/1
Application fee	$60
Financial aid deadline	
Can first year start other than fall?	Yes
Student to faculty ratio	12.3 to 1
# of housing spaces available restricted to law students	
graduate housing for which law students are eligible	

Faculty and Administrators

	Total		Men		Women		Minorities	
	Spr	Fall	Spr	Fall	Spr	Fall	Spr	Fall
Full-time	63	61	34	32	29	29	17	18
Other full-time	3	4	3	2	0	2	2	2
Deans, librarians, & others who teach	11	3	5	3	6	0	3	1
Part-time	66	49	50	35	16	14	9	2
Total	143	117	92	72	51	45	31	23

JD Enrollment and Ethnicity

	Men		Women		Full-Time		Part-Time		1st-Year		Total		JD Degs. Awd.
	#	%	#	%	#	%	#	%	#	%	#	%	
All Hispanics	22	4.5	37	7.3	46	5.7	13	6.6	20	6.3	59	5.9	18
Am. Ind./AK Nat.	1	0.2	10	2.0	10	1.2	1	0.5	1	0.3	11	1.1	0
Asian	45	9.1	52	10.2	75	9.3	22	11.2	41	12.9	97	9.7	40
Black/Af. Am.	15	3.0	15	2.9	23	2.9	7	3.6	9	2.8	30	3.0	11
Nat. HI/Pac. Isl.	2	0.4	4	0.8	3	0.4	3	1.5	0	0.0	6	0.6	12
2 or more races	24	4.9	23	4.5	39	4.8	8	4.1	21	6.6	47	4.7	11
Subtotal (minor.)	109	22.2	141	27.6	196	24.3	54	27.6	92	29.0	250	25.0	92
Nonres. Alien	5	1.0	4	0.8	8	1.0	1	0.5	1	0.3	9	0.9	3
White/Cauc.	352	71.5	349	68.4	565	70.1	136	69.4	209	65.9	701	70.0	208
Unknown	26	5.3	16	3.1	37	4.6	5	2.6	15	4.7	42	4.2	11
Total	492	49.1	510	50.9	806	80.4	196	19.6	317	31.6	1002		314

Curriculum

		Full-Time	Part-Time
Typical first-year section size		85	56
Is there typically a "small section" of the first-year class, other than Legal Writing, taught by full-time faculty		No	No
If yes, typical size offered last year			
# of classroom course titles beyond first-year curriculum		178	
# of upper division courses, excluding seminars, with an enrollment:	Under 25	129	
	25–49	42	
	50–74	20	
	75–99	9	
	100+	1	
# of seminars		58	
# of seminar positions available		1,150	
# of seminar positions filled		686	66
# of positions available in simulation courses		616	
# of simulation positions filled		383	77
# of positions available in faculty supervised clinical courses		104	
# of faculty supervised clinical positions filled		91	12
# involved in field placements		168	9
# involved in law journals		120	11
# involved in moot court or trial competitions		34	0
# of credit hours required to graduate		90	

Transfers

Transfers in	23
Transfers out	20

Tuition and Fees

	Resident	Nonresident
Full-time	$39,282	$39,282
Part-time	$32,725	$32,725
Tuition Guarantee Program		N

Living Expenses

Estimated living expenses for singles

Living on campus	Living off campus	Living at home
$17,997	$17,997	$9,969

SEATTLE UNIVERSITY SCHOOL OF LAW

ABA
Approved
Since
1994

GPA and LSAT Scores

	Total	Full-Time	Part-Time
# of apps	2,226	2,034	192
# of offers	1,031	947	84
# of matrics	322	263	59
75% GPA	3.52	3.52	3.44
Median GPA	3.32	3.33	3.22
25% GPA	3.10	3.12	2.90
75% LSAT	159	160	158
Median LSAT	157	157	156
25% LSAT	154	155	153

Grants and Scholarships (from prior year)

	Total #	Total %	Full-Time #	Full-Time %	Part-Time #	Part-Time %
Total # of students	1,011		808		203	
Total # receiving grants	520	51.4	464	57.4	56	27.6
Less than 1/2 tuition	493	48.8	441	54.6	52	25.6
Half to full tuition	17	1.7	13	1.6	4	2.0
Full tuition	10	1.0	10	1.2	0	0.0
More than full tuition	0	0.0	0	0.0	0	0.0
Median grant amount			$10,000		$9,500	

Informational and Library Resources

Total amount spent on library materials	$1,218,902
Study seating capacity inside the library	429
# of full-time equivalent professional librarians	9
Hours per week library is open	119
# of open, wired connections available to students	2,500
# of networked computers available for use by students	16
Has wireless network?	Y
Requires computer?	Y

JD Attrition (from prior year)

	Academic #	Other #	Total #	Total %
1st year	1	32	33	10.3
2nd year	0	6	6	1.9
3rd year	0	3	3	0.9
4th year	0	0	0	0.0

Employment (9 months after graduation)

For up-to-date employment data, go to employmentsummary.abaquestionnaire.org on the ABA website.

Bar Passage Rates

First-time takers	306	Reporting %	93.79
Average school %	77.70	Average state %	71.22
Average pass difference	6.48		

Jurisdiction	Takers	Passers	Pass %	State %	Diff %
Washington	287	223	77.70	71.22	6.48

SEATTLE UNIVERSITY SCHOOL OF LAW

901 12th Avenue, Sullivan Hall
Seattle, WA 98122-1090
Phone: 206.398.4200; Fax: 206.398.4058
E-mail: lawadmis@seattleu.edu; Website: www.law.seattleu.edu

Introduction

Seattle University School of Law is the most diverse law school in the Pacific Northwest, dedicated to the twin goals of academic excellence and education for justice.

The School of Law is home to leading academic programs, including one of the country's top-ranked legal writing programs and the Ronald A. Peterson Law Clinic, as well as distinguished centers and institutes. These programs, and a superb faculty, support the law school's mission to educate outstanding lawyers to be leaders for a just and humane world.

The school enrolls just over 1,000 students representing more than 200 undergraduate schools and drawn from the top third of the national law school applicant pool. We serve an impressive body of students, whose diversity encompasses age, life experience, and cultural heritage. The law school is recognized nationally for its diverse faculty and welcoming environment. It is the only Washington law school with a part-time program geared to meet the needs of working professionals.

The law school is accredited by the ABA and holds membership in the AALS. Students may pursue a Juris Doctor or one of many joint degrees.

Location

Located in the heart of dynamic Seattle, the law school is a vital part of the community. It is located on the beautiful urban campus of Seattle University in the lively Capitol Hill neighborhood just steps from downtown Seattle. The area offers a mix of exciting, professional, cultural, and recreational opportunities.

One of the most beautiful and livable cities in the United States, Seattle is a legal, business, technological, and cultural hub that provides law students access to summer and school-year employment with major players in the economy, multinational law firms, and public agencies.

Sullivan Hall, home to the law school, is an award-winning, state-of-the-art facility with the latest technology throughout its impressive library, classrooms, courtroom, and study and activity areas. The School of Law Annex is a modern building less than a block from Sullivan Hall, which was built to accommodate the growing law school. It houses the clinical and externship programs, student journals, and additional classrooms.

Focus-Area and First-Year Curriculum

Our innovative first-year studies are rigorous, emphasizing sound legal analytical skills while allowing students to choose an elective course in the second semester. Our focus-area curriculum allows students to select a primary area of interest and supports that with enrollment in a prescribed range of courses. Students may focus their upper-division legal studies in one of 14 substantive areas, including Civil Advocacy, Criminal Practice, Environmental Law, Health Law, Labor and Employment, or Real Estate Law.

Faculty

Seattle University School of Law is home to an outstanding faculty of committed teacher-scholars. Our professors do not choose between scholarship and teaching, but rather are experts in their fields who are drawn to share their knowledge with students.

A primary mission that drives the academic program is the faculty's desire to prepare students to practice the law with competence, honor, and commitment to public service. Our talented faculty members teach students to analyze problems and construct policy arguments, as well as train them to write and speak with clarity and precision.

The teaching is both demanding and humane. It blends legal theory, doctrinal analysis, and comprehensive practical-skills training. Reflecting the Jesuit tradition of open inquiry, social responsibility, and concern for personal growth, the law school values freedom of conscience, thought, and speech.

Since 2000, law school faculty members have authored or coauthored more than 117 books, 130 book chapters, and more than 900 articles that have appeared in prestigious law reviews and specialized journals. Articles by our faculty are among the most read on Social Sciences Research Network (SSRN).

Academic Enrichment Programs

Access to Justice Institute (ATJI)—The mission of ATJI is to inspire all law students toward a lifelong commitment to equal justice. The institute connects students to public interest opportunities that fulfill unmet legal needs, facilitates advocacy and legal skills training, hosts social justice forums and events, counsels students in public interest career exploration, and collaborates with local, state, and national efforts to promote equal justice.

Center for Law and Equality—The Fred T. Korematsu Center for Law and Equality aims to advance social justice by fostering critical thinking about discrimination in US society and through targeted advocacy to promote equality and freedom. The center's work is divided into three units: research, advocacy, and education projects.

International Initiatives—Seattle University School of Law is a leader in global legal education and has expanded its international reach to offer students and faculty a greater world view. Among the many compelling programs are the International and Comparative Law Program opportunities for international internships and externships.

Adolf A. Berle Jr. Center on Corporations, Law and Society—The Berle Center facilitates the study of the constantly evolving American and global economic system; the ongoing struggle for power between and among corporations, governments, individuals, and society; and the role of law in mediating and shaping the nature of our economic relations and institutions.

Admission and Financial Aid

In admission decisions, the law school places equal emphasis on three factors: (1) LSAT performance; (2) the undergraduate academic record; and (3) personal achievements, especially talents or factors that contribute to our law school community in special and significant ways.

We also admit a limited group of applicants annually through our **Access Admission Program**, which addresses those cases in which traditional admission criteria are inadequate predictors of success in law school and in the practice of law. Members of historically disadvantaged, underrepresented, or physically challenged groups are among those individuals considered for this program (limited to no more than 10 percent of the entering class).

The law school's **Scholarship Program** is among the most ambitious in the region, awarding over $3 million per year to approximately 350 students. Its objectives are twofold: to offer to all students—regardless of economic or social background—the advantages of a private legal education, and to recognize and reward—regardless of financial need—the achievements and outstanding potential of the most highly qualified students in the applicant pool. Upon admission, all entering students are automatically considered for scholarships. The School of Law offers a **Loan Repayment Assistance Program** to support graduates who choose full-time public interest legal careers as licensed attorneys doing law-related, public interest work. It offers two annual full-tuition **Scholars for Justice Awards** to outstanding students committed to social justice work and a full-tuition **Native American Scholarship** to an enrolled member of a federally recognized tribe.

APPLICANT PROFILE

Seattle University School of Law
This grid includes only applicants who earned 120–180 LSAT scores under standard administrations.

LSAT Score	GPA								
	3.75 +	3.50–3.74	3.25–3.49	3.00–3.24	2.75–2.99	2.50–2.74	2.25–2.49	2.00–2.24	Below 2.00
175–180									
170–174									
165–169									
160–164									
155–159									
150–154									
145–149									
140–144									
135–139									
130–134									
125–129									
120–124									

■ Good Possibility   □ Possible   ▨ Unlikely

This chart is to be used as a general guide only. Nonnumerical factors are strongly considered for all applicants.

SETON HALL UNIVERSITY SCHOOL OF LAW

Office of Admissions, One Newark Center
Newark, NJ 07102-5210
Phone: 888.415.7271, 973.642.8747; Fax: 973.642.8876
E-mail: admitme@shu.edu; Website: http://law.shu.edu

ABA
Approved
Since
1951

The Basics

Type of school	Private
Term	Semester
Application deadline	4/1
Application fee	$65
Financial aid deadline	4/1
Can first year start other than fall?	No
Student to faculty ratio	14.6 to 1
# of housing spaces available restricted to law students	
graduate housing for which law students are eligible	

Faculty and Administrators

	Total		Men		Women		Minorities	
	Spr	Fall	Spr	Fall	Spr	Fall	Spr	Fall
Full-time	52	49	29	29	23	20	9	10
Other full-time	5	6	3	4	2	2	0	0
Deans, librarians, & others who teach	16	16	3	3	13	13	2	2
Part-time	101	79	64	48	37	31	9	8
Total	174	150	99	84	75	66	20	20

Curriculum

	Full-Time	Part-Time
Typical first-year section size	65	50
Is there typically a "small section" of the first-year class, other than Legal Writing, taught by full-time faculty	No	No
If yes, typical size offered last year		
# of classroom course titles beyond first-year curriculum	156	

# of upper division courses, excluding seminars, with an enrollment:	Under 25	191
	25–49	57
	50–74	19
	75–99	3
	100+	1

# of seminars	31	
# of seminar positions available	496	
# of seminar positions filled	255	132
# of positions available in simulation courses	1,505	
# of simulation positions filled	885	354
# of positions available in faculty supervised clinical courses	132	
# of faculty supervised clinical positions filled	118	12
# involved in field placements	157	39
# involved in law journals	150	14
# involved in moot court or trial competitions	55	16
# of credit hours required to graduate	88	

JD Enrollment and Ethnicity

	Men		Women		Full-Time		Part-Time		1st-Year		Total		JD Degs. Awd.
	#	%	#	%	#	%	#	%	#	%	#	%	
All Hispanics	33	6.2	35	7.8	33	4.9	35	11.3	19	7.0	68	6.9	9
Am. Ind./AK Nat.	3	0.6	0	0.0	2	0.3	1	0.3	1	0.4	3	0.3	0
Asian	36	6.8	38	8.4	42	6.2	32	10.3	16	5.9	74	7.5	21
Black/Af. Am.	16	3.0	23	5.1	16	2.4	23	7.4	12	4.4	39	4.0	6
Nat. HI/Pac. Isl.	0	0.0	0	0.0	0	0.0	0	0.0	0	0.0	0	0.0	0
2 or more races	2	0.4	5	1.1	2	0.3	5	1.6	2	0.7	7	0.7	5
Subtotal (minor.)	90	16.9	101	22.4	95	14.1	96	31.0	50	18.4	191	19.4	41
Nonres. Alien	6	1.1	4	0.9	5	0.7	5	1.6	1	0.4	10	1.0	3
White/Cauc.	437	82.0	345	76.7	573	85.1	209	67.4	221	81.3	782	79.6	249
Unknown	0	0.0	0	0.0	0	0.0	0	0.0	0	0.0	0	0.0	0
Total	533	54.2	450	45.8	673	68.5	310	31.5	272	27.7	983		293

Transfers

Transfers in	16
Transfers out	14

Tuition and Fees

	Resident	Nonresident
Full-time	$46,840	$46,840
Part-time	$35,340	$35,340
Tuition Guarantee Program	N	

Living Expenses

Estimated living expenses for singles

Living on campus	Living off campus	Living at home
N/A	$22,752	$12,357

SETON HALL UNIVERSITY SCHOOL OF LAW

ABA Approved Since 1951

GPA and LSAT Scores

	Total	Full-Time	Part-Time
# of apps	3,439	2,779	660
# of offers	1,664	1,494	170
# of matrics	266	203	63
75% GPA	3.66	3.67	3.56
Median GPA	3.50	3.52	3.23
25% GPA	3.22	3.31	2.96
75% LSAT	161	162	155
Median LSAT	159	160	152
25% LSAT	155	157	149

Grants and Scholarships (from prior year)

	Total #	Total %	Full-Time #	Full-Time %	Part-Time #	Part-Time %
Total # of students	1,053		704		349	
Total # receiving grants	485	46.1	398	56.5	87	24.9
Less than 1/2 tuition	227	21.6	168	23.9	59	16.9
Half to full tuition	220	20.9	192	27.3	28	8.0
Full tuition	38	3.6	38	5.4	0	0.0
More than full tuition	0	0.0	0	0.0	0	0.0
Median grant amount			$25,000		$10,000	

Informational and Library Resources

Total amount spent on library materials	$1,266,249
Study seating capacity inside the library	603
# of full-time equivalent professional librarians	8
Hours per week library is open	81
# of open, wired connections available to students	10
# of networked computers available for use by students	154
Has wireless network?	Y
Requires computer?	Y

JD Attrition (from prior year)

	Academic #	Other #	Total #	Total %
1st year	21	15	36	10.0
2nd year	10	2	12	4.0
3rd year	0	0	0	0.0
4th year	0	0	0	0.0

Employment (9 months after graduation)

For up-to-date employment data, go to employmentsummary.abaquestionnaire.org on the ABA website.

Bar Passage Rates

First-time takers	310	Reporting %	93.87
Average school %	91.41	Average state %	82.34
Average pass difference	9.07		

Jurisdiction	Takers	Passers	Pass %	State %	Diff %
New Jersey	291	266	91.41	82.34	9.07

SETON HALL UNIVERSITY SCHOOL OF LAW

Office of Admissions, One Newark Center
Newark, NJ 07102-5210
Phone: 888.415.7271, 973.642.8747; Fax: 973.642.8876
E-mail: admitme@shu.edu; Website: http://law.shu.edu

Introduction

Founded in 1951, Seton Hall University School of Law is the only private law school in the state of New Jersey. While it values its Catholic identity, the law school is a pluralistic community representing a diversity of racial, cultural, religious, and socioeconomic backgrounds. The school is consistently recognized for its outstanding teaching and high level of student satisfaction.

One Newark Center, Our Home

Rich in history and culture, Newark is a city to explore. Whatever your interest, you'll find it here—the performing and visual arts, sports, great food, and captivating architecture are within easy reach. The law school is a block from Newark's Penn Station, from which a 20-minute train ride takes students to Manhattan and the world's largest law firms. Students can walk to Newark's major law firms, government agencies, and the federal and state courthouses. Housing options are extensive. Students enjoy living in nearby historic buildings and, with its expansive network of train lines, Newark is within easy reach of New York City, Hoboken, Jersey City, and many suburban communities. The law school's open, welcoming design is a reflection of the faculty and administration's commitment to students. Offices, classrooms, moot courtrooms, and the library are interconnected by balconies overlooking a striking five-story, glass-encased atrium. The entire law school complex is saturated with Wi-Fi Internet connectivity, including access to wireless printing. The building has unusually large student space, including newly renovated student journal and organization offices, lounges, meeting rooms, a chapel, and a cafeteria. The Peter W. Rodino Jr. Law Library is located on three floors and accommodates 600 students and 100 terminals for student use. The Law Library's collection contains more than 425,000 volumes covering a wide array of law and law-related subjects. Health Law and Intellectual Property Law are areas of particular strength. The Rodino Library is a depository for US government documents and for New Jersey state documents.

Curriculum

The JD requires 88 credits to graduate and may be completed as a full-time or a part-time program. The school offers both a day and an evening program following a semester calendar. The program emphasizes humanistic principles and encourages their synthesis with knowledge of the law and professional responsibility. The law school is committed to in-depth training in legal writing and research.

In addition to the core required courses, more than 200 courses are offered in a wide range of areas grouped as follows: Constitutional Law, Corporate Law, Criminal Law and Procedure, Health and Drug Law, Intellectual Property and Entertainment Law, International Legal Studies, Labor and Employment Law, Personal and Family Law, Property and Estates Law, Public Interest, and Taxation. Externships, journals, and pro bono and moot court programs are also included in the school's offerings.

Master of Laws (LLM) and a Master of Science in Jurisprudence (MSJ) are also offered in the areas of health, science, and technology law.

Public Interest

Seton Hall School of Law is committed to public interest and clinical education. Through the Seton Hall Law Center for Social Justice, students are provided with one of the most comprehensive clinical and pro bono programs offered by any New York area law school. The school's clinics presently represent more than 3,000 disadvantaged and underrepresented clients each year in a wide range of litigation such as civil litigation, family law, impact litigation, immigration and human rights, immigrant workers rights, juvenile justice, and civil rights and constitutional litigation. Clinical projects include International Human Rights/Rule of Law and Urban Revitalization. The Center for Social Justice provides services in the public's interest while training and mentoring future attorneys whose careers will be dedicated in whole or in part to public interest work. Students can take part in various programs geared toward public interest beginning as early as their first year, including clinical programs, externships, and pro bono assignments. Scholarship and other financial assistance are available through the Distinguished Public Interest Scholarship, Summer Public Interest Law Fellowship, and Public Interest Loan Repayment Assistance Program.

Special Programs

Internships—The law school offers judicial internships with justices of the New Jersey Supreme Court, judges of the New Jersey Appellate Division, Chancery and Law Courts, the Third Circuit Court of Appeals, the US District Courts, and the US Bankruptcy Courts. There are myriad internship programs with nonprofit and government agencies.

Externships—Externship offerings include environmental law; health law; entertainment law; international organizations, the European Court of Justice or Court of First Instance; the Federal Public Defender; Securities and Exchange Commission; New York Stock Exchange; Internal Revenue Service; National Labor Relations Board; and US Attorney's Office.

Concentrations—The law school offers concentrations in Health Law and Intellectual Property Law that allow students to study a specialized curriculum developed by faculty in consultation with attorneys and government officials working in the field. The breadth and depth of both curricula is unparalleled. In addition to coursework, students have the opportunity to participate in externships and take part in frequent symposia and colloquia.

Joint-Degree Programs—JD/MBA—a four-year program with Seton Hall University Stillman School of Business; **JD/MADIR**—a four-year program with Seton Hall University Whitehead School of Diplomacy and International Relations; **JD/MD**—a six-year program with the Robert Wood Johnson Medical School of the University of Medicine and Dentistry of New Jersey; **MSJ/MD**—a five-year program with the Robert Wood Johnson Medical School of the University of Medicine and Dentistry of New Jersey.

Journals—The law school offers students an opportunity to advance legal scholarship through four student journals—the *Seton Hall Law Review*, *Seton Hall Legislative Journal*, *Circuit Review*, and the *Journal of Sports and Entertainment Law*.

International Study—The law school offers two summer study-abroad programs in the Middle East: in Egypt at the American University in Cairo and in Jordan at the University of Jordan in Amman. Additionally, a summer program in Leuven, Belgium, and Geneva, Switzerland, focusing on intellectual property is offered. Seton Hall's Zanzibar program is the only ABA-approved winter-intersession program focusing on modern-day slavery and human trafficking. And, a winter-intersession program in Chamonix, France, focuses on international human rights.

LLM and MSJ Degrees—Seton Hall offers LLM degrees in Health Law and Intellectual Property. Seton Hall also offers a Master of Science in Jurisprudence (MSJ) degree in Health Law, Science, and Technology, which provides professionals with a solid foundation in the legal aspects of health care and intellectual property regulation. Such a concentrated exposure to health law issues can be vital to medical directors, regulatory and contract compliance officers, risk and case managers, employee benefits personnel, lobbyists, and pharmaceutical employees. Full- and part-time programs are available for both the LLM and MSJ degrees.

Moot Court Program—Students represent the law school in the National Moot Court competition as well as in 10 interschool competitions focusing on specific areas of law.

LEO Institute—The Monsignor Thomas Fahy Legal Education Opportunities Institute provides an intense summer classroom experience for educationally disadvantaged students. Applicants from disadvantaged groups, regardless of race, religion, age, sex, sexual orientation, or national origin, may wish to inquire about this program.

Student Activities

There are more than 35 student organizations at Seton Hall Law, representing various personal and professional interests. The Student Bar Association (SBA) and other student organizations sponsor a variety of practical, social, and educational events. The SBA plays a major role in orientation, coordinates the first-year mentoring program, and sponsors a holiday party each November in Newark and a Barristers' Ball in the spring. Organizations sponsor career seminars focused on different areas of the law, host symposiums and panel discussions that focus on current legal and societal issues, and plan annual banquets and networking receptions during the year.

Committed to Your Success

At Seton Hall you will find a school committed to your success. The majority of our students participate in hands-on clinical training or externships, and 94 percent of our students are employed within nine months of graduation. Seton Hall Law maintains a proactive Career Services Office staffed by full-time counselors who assist students in defining their career objectives and goals and establishing contact with employers. Each fall and spring, law firms, accounting firms, and public interest and governmental employers conduct interviews through the school's On-Campus Interview Program. Alumni are practicing nationwide.

APPLICANT PROFILE

Seton Hall University School of Law
This grid includes only applicants who earned 120–180 LSAT scores under standard administrations.

LSAT Score	GPA 3.75 +		3.50–3.74		3.25–3.49		3.00–3.24		2.75–2.99		2.50–2.74		Below 2.50		No GPA		Total	
	Apps	Adm	Apps	Adm	Apps	Adm	Apps	Adm	Apps	Adm	Apps	Adm	Apps	Adm	Apps	Adm	Apps	Adm
170–180	14	14	9	8	6	6	6	5	5	5	3	3	0	0	0	0	43	41
165–169	33	30	58	57	38	37	24	23	18	13	18	13	11	4	1	1	201	178
160–164	134	130	213	210	174	166	159	145	69	35	49	13	32	8	6	5	836	712
155–159	124	115	291	239	232	151	173	72	70	15	38	7	25	5	15	6	968	610
150–154	58	21	126	25	170	24	156	16	99	6	53	6	36	1	19	1	717	100
145–149	20	2	56	4	97	7	88	5	66	3	35	1	38	3	17	0	417	25
140–144	14	0	32	1	42	0	43	0	32	0	24	0	27	0	4	1	218	2
Below 140	2	0	6	0	15	0	27	0	21	0	21	0	26	0	2	0	120	0
Total	399	312	791	544	774	391	676	266	380	77	241	43	195	21	64	14	3520	1668

Apps = Number of Applicants
Adm = Number Admitted
Reflects 99% of the total applicant pool; highest LSAT data reported.

SMU DEDMAN SCHOOL OF LAW

Office of Admissions, PO Box 750110
Dallas, TX 75275-0110
Phone: 214.768.2550, 888.768.5291; Fax: 214.768.2549
E-mail: lawadmit@smu.edu; Website: www.law.smu.edu

ABA
Approved
Since
1927

The Basics

Type of school	Private
Term	Semester
Application deadline	11/1 2/15
Application fee	$75
Financial aid deadline	11/2 2/15
Can first year start other than fall?	No
Student to faculty ratio	16.5 to 1
# of housing spaces available restricted to law students	
graduate housing for which law students are eligible	

Faculty and Administrators

	Total		Men		Women		Minorities	
	Spr	Fall	Spr	Fall	Spr	Fall	Spr	Fall
Full-time	39	38	24	22	15	16	9	8
Other full-time	5	3	1	2	4	1	0	0
Deans, librarians, & others who teach	9	9	6	6	3	3	0	0
Part-time	58	56	47	47	11	9	2	2
Total	111	106	78	77	33	29	11	10

Curriculum

		Full-Time	Part-Time
Typical first-year section size		90	75
Is there typically a "small section" of the first-year class, other than Legal Writing, taught by full-time faculty		No	No
If yes, typical size offered last year			
# of classroom course titles beyond first-year curriculum		120	
# of upper division courses, excluding seminars, with an enrollment:	Under 25	115	
	25–49	61	
	50–74	10	
	75–99	41	
	100+	2	
# of seminars		23	
# of seminar positions available		445	
# of seminar positions filled		240	103
# of positions available in simulation courses		894	
# of simulation positions filled		508	108
# of positions available in faculty supervised clinical courses		126	
# of faculty supervised clinical positions filled		104	45
# involved in field placements		42	33
# involved in law journals		191	61
# involved in moot court or trial competitions		51	7
# of credit hours required to graduate		87	

JD Enrollment and Ethnicity

	Men		Women		Full-Time		Part-Time		1st-Year		Total		JD Degs. Awd.
	#	%	#	%	#	%	#	%	#	%	#	%	
All Hispanics	37	7.7	40	10.3	56	10.4	21	6.4	15	6.5	77	8.9	21
Am. Ind./AK Nat.	10	2.1	2	0.5	5	0.9	7	2.1	0	0.0	12	1.4	5
Asian	33	6.9	35	9.0	35	6.5	33	10.1	18	7.8	68	7.9	18
Black/Af. Am.	19	4.0	24	6.2	25	4.6	18	5.5	9	3.9	43	5.0	14
Nat. HI/Pac. Isl.	0	0.0	1	0.3	1	0.2	0	0.0	1	0.4	1	0.1	0
2 or more races	5	1.0	5	1.3	8	1.5	2	0.6	5	2.2	10	1.2	1
Subtotal (minor.)	104	21.7	107	27.6	130	24.1	81	24.8	48	20.7	211	24.4	59
Nonres. Alien	4	0.8	0	0.0	3	0.6	1	0.3	2	0.9	4	0.5	1
White/Cauc.	344	71.8	260	67.2	386	71.5	218	66.9	179	77.2	604	69.7	210
Unknown	27	5.6	20	5.2	21	3.9	26	8.0	3	1.3	47	5.4	2
Total	479	55.3	387	44.7	540	62.4	326	37.6	232	26.8	866		272

Transfers

Transfers in	21
Transfers out	2

Tuition and Fees

	Resident	Nonresident
Full-time	$42,057	$42,057
Part-time	$31,543	$31,543
Tuition Guarantee Program	N	

Living Expenses

Estimated living expenses for singles

Living on campus	Living off campus	Living at home
$20,238	$20,238	$20,238

*ABA
Approved
Since
1927*

GPA and LSAT Scores

	Total	Full-Time	Part-Time
# of apps	2,809	2,146	663
# of offers	578	463	115
# of matrics	232	157	75
75% GPA	3.81	3.84	3.74
Median GPA	3.67	3.72	3.57
25% GPA	3.31	3.34	3.16
75% LSAT	165	166	162
Median LSAT	163	165	160
25% LSAT	157	158	152

Grants and Scholarships (from prior year)

	Total #	Total %	Full-Time #	Full-Time %	Part-Time #	Part-Time %
Total # of students	887		549		338	
Total # receiving grants	584	65.8	415	75.6	169	50.0
Less than 1/2 tuition	364	41.0	204	37.2	160	47.3
Half to full tuition	192	21.6	183	33.3	9	2.7
Full tuition	9	1.0	9	1.6	0	0.0
More than full tuition	19	2.1	19	3.5	0	0.0
Median grant amount			$20,200		$7,000	

Informational and Library Resources

Total amount spent on library materials	$1,430,660
Study seating capacity inside the library	787
# of full-time equivalent professional librarians	6
Hours per week library is open	104
# of open, wired connections available to students	0
# of networked computers available for use by students	106
Has wireless network?	Y
Requires computer?	N

JD Attrition (from prior year)

	Academic #	Other #	Total #	Total %
1st year	0	0	0	0.0
2nd year	4	10	14	5.2
3rd year	1	4	5	1.8
4th year	1	0	1	1.2

Employment (9 months after graduation)

For up-to-date employment data, go to
employmentsummary.abaquestionnaire.org on the ABA website.

Bar Passage Rates

First-time takers	248	Reporting %	93.15
Average school %	82.68	Average state %	82.68

Average pass difference

Jurisdiction	Takers	Passers	Pass %	State %	Diff %
Texas	231	191	82.68	82.68	0.00

SMU DEDMAN SCHOOL OF LAW

Office of Admissions, PO Box 750110
Dallas, TX 75275-0110
Phone: 214.768.2550, 888.768.5291; Fax: 214.768.2549
E-mail: lawadmit@smu.edu; Website: www.law.smu.edu

Introduction

Founded in 1925, SMU Dedman School of Law is located on a magnificent tree-lined campus in a beautiful residential neighborhood just five miles north of downtown Dallas. SMU offers an intimate learning community within a vibrant urban center.

With a relatively small entering class size, an outstanding teaching faculty, and distinguished guest lecturers, SMU offers a scholarly community with fantastic opportunities both inside and outside the classroom. SMU also has a well-rounded, diverse student body from approximately 200 colleges and universities, 30 states, and 20 countries.

Law School Campus

SMU offers a beautiful setting in which to pursue legal studies. The Law School Quadrangle, a six-acre, self-contained corner of the campus, offers students convenient access to all law school facilities. The larger SMU campus offers students a variety of housing options, a childcare facility, a health center, and a new fitness/wellness center.

SMU recently completed a multimillion-dollar renovation of all of the law school classrooms. A four-story parking garage with 500 spaces is available exclusively for law student parking, and a new dining hall opened in 2005.

Curriculum

SMU offers seven degree programs: JD (full-time day or part-time evening), JD/MBA, JD/MA in Economics, LLM (General), LLM (Taxation), LLM (for foreign attorneys), and SJD.

Students find a sophisticated curriculum that complements SMU's wide breadth of class offerings with extensive depth of focus. The JD curriculum is designed to achieve the goal of producing lawyers who are capable and responsible professionals through its emphasis on providing substantive knowledge, ethical and moral training, and practical skills to serve clients in local, national, and global communities.

Each JD student must complete 87 credit hours. Thirty-one of these hours comprise the mandatory first-year curriculum. After the first year, students must complete a course in professional responsibility, two upper-level writing courses (including an edited writing seminar in which an extensive scholarly, expository writing project is reviewed and critiqued by the professor), Constitutional Law II, and a practical skills course.

SMU offers many small classes in which students will get to know their classmates and professors. Each entering class is divided into three sections (two full-time day and one part-time evening) of approximately 90 students each. Each semester, first-year students are assigned to a legal research, writing, and advocacy class of approximately 25 students. Over one-half of SMU's upper-division courses have fewer than 25 students, and approximately three-quarters have fewer than 50 students.

SMU's rich upper-division curricular offerings, with over 165 upper-division courses per year, provide students with a wide range of courses and the freedom to tailor a program of study that furthers their professional and personal goals. With traditional strengths in business, litigation, tax, and international law, the curriculum extends to many areas, including intellectual property, health care, environmental, and family law.

SMU's LLM programs are intended to enhance careers in the private practice of law, teaching, and public service by providing the opportunity for students who already have their basic law degree to increase their understanding of legal theory and policies. The LLM program for foreign attorneys is the largest graduate program, enrolling approximately 40 students from about 20 countries each year. SMU has over 1,400 international alumni from over 70 countries, including many who hold significant positions in major international corporations, in the highest courts of their nations, and in other key government and private entities.

Student Activities and Law Reviews

Students are able to enhance their legal education by participating in numerous programs and conferences sponsored by various faculty and student groups and centers. Selected law students serve on five major journals for which they receive academic credit. Law students are able to expand their legal education experience by participating in over 20 moot court, trial advocacy, client counseling, and negotiation competitions held at the local, regional, national, and international level, and by becoming active members in over 30 student organizations.

Externships and Clinics

Externships offer students the opportunity to work at a government agency for up to two hours of course credit. Popular externships include those with the US Attorney, the SEC, and the EPA.

Clinics offer students an opportunity to engage in the practice of law for up to six hours of course credit. Currently SMU has six clinical opportunities: civil litigation, criminal defense, federal taxation, small business, consumer law, and child advocacy.

Public Service

All students are required to perform 30 hours of public service before graduating. This model public service program not only allows the student to learn in a hands-on setting, but also provides an early exposure to pro bono practice, which is integral to the US legal system. SMU professors voluntarily hold themselves to this same requirement.

Overseas Study

SMU offers students an opportunity to study law for six weeks at University College at Oxford University in England.

Career Services and Bar Passage

SMU provides students with job placement assistance throughout their legal careers. The Career Services Office helps students develop their job search and career development skills, and partners with students in locating summer and permanent job opportunities.

SMU graduates fare very well in the legal market. Within nine months of graduation, approximately 95 percent of the class of 2010 was employed. They had an average starting salary of over $103,000 in the private sector and an average starting salary of over $92,000 overall.

In July 2011, 86.96 percent of SMU first-time test takers passed the Texas bar exam. The statewide pass rate was approximately 82.3 percent.

Admission

SMU looks for excellent, well-rounded students with strong academic backgrounds, life experiences, and perspectives that will enrich its educational community. Each application is considered in its entirety: LSAT score, undergraduate performance, graduate studies, work experience, activities, personal statement, and letters of recommendation are all read and evaluated. Applications can be downloaded from the web.

Scholarships

SMU provides approximately 50 percent of its entering class with scholarship assistance. SMU law scholarships, including several full-tuition Hutchison scholarships, are awarded on the basis of the admission application, including the applicant's answer to an optional question. In addition, two private foundations, the Hatton W. Sumners Foundation and the Dallas Bar Foundation, fund and select five to nine additional full-tuition scholarships per entering class. Both foundations require a separate scholarship application, available from the SMU Admissions Office's website. The Sarah T. Hughes Scholarships, sponsored by the Dallas Bar Foundation, are awarded to outstanding minority applicants. The Sumners Scholars are selected from a competitive pool of applicants with strong academics and extracurricular activities. Both foundations require that the SMU application, the respective scholarship application, and all supporting documents be submitted by February 15.

APPLICANT PROFILE

SMU Dedman School of Law
This grid includes only applicants who earned 120–180 LSAT scores under standard administrations.

LSAT Score	GPA																									
	3.75 +		3.50–3.74		3.25–3.49		3.00–3.24		2.75–2.99		2.50–2.74		2.25–2.49		2.00–2.24		Below 2.00		No GPA		Total	
	Apps	Adm	Apps	Adm	Apps	Adm	Apps	Adm	Apps	Adm	Apps	Adm	Apps	Adm	Apps	Adm	Apps	Adm	Apps	Adm	Apps	Adm
175–180	1	1	0	0	3	3	2	1	1	1	3	3	0	0	1	0	0	0	0	0	11	9
170–174	24	23	13	12	11	9	20	11	3	2	0	0	3	0	0	0	0	0	0	0	74	57
165–169	53	49	87	76	77	54	43	30	16	8	10	6	3	2	1	1	0	0	5	4	295	230
160–164	104	69	132	19	124	16	81	15	32	6	19	4	8	5	3	1	0	0	9	3	512	138
155–159	95	47	161	21	145	4	98	1	64	1	30	3	15	0	4	0	1	0	13	2	626	79
150–154	49	29	78	22	121	5	101	1	61	2	34	0	15	0	6	0	3	0	13	1	481	60
145–149	18	11	55	5	50	0	49	1	33	0	23	1	13	0	6	0	2	0	17	3	266	21
140–144	5	0	17	0	21	0	28	1	18	0	15	0	8	0	8	0	0	0	9	2	129	3
135–139	2	0	3	0	2	0	8	0	10	0	4	0	1	0	2	0	1	0	2	1	35	1
130–134	0	0	1	0	0	0	3	0	2	0	6	0	5	0	0	0	1	0	5	0	23	0
125–129	0	0	0	0	1	0	2	0	0	0	1	0	0	0	0	0	0	0	0	0	4	0
120–124	0	0	0	0	0	0	0	0	0	0	2	0	0	0	0	0	0	0	0	0	2	0
Total	351	229	547	155	555	91	435	61	240	20	147	17	71	7	31	2	8	0	73	16	2458	598

Apps = Number of Applicants
Adm = Number Admitted
Reflects 92% of the total applicant pool; highest LSAT data reported.

UNIVERSITY OF SOUTH CAROLINA SCHOOL OF LAW

701 Main Street
Columbia, SC 29208
Phone: 803.777.6605; Fax: 803.777.2847
E-mail: usclaw@law.sc.edu; Website: www.law.sc.edu

ABA
Approved
Since
1925

The Basics

Type of school	Public
Term	Semester
Application deadline	3/1
Application fee	$60
Financial aid deadline	3/1
Can first year start other than fall?	No
Student to faculty ratio	16.4 to 1
# of housing spaces available restricted to law students	
graduate housing for which law students are eligible	429

Faculty and Administrators

	Total		Men		Women		Minorities	
	Spr	Fall	Spr	Fall	Spr	Fall	Spr	Fall
Full-time	35	33	21	21	14	12	4	3
Other full-time	2	1	2	1	0	0	0	0
Deans, librarians, & others who teach	11	12	5	4	6	8	0	1
Part-time	18	20	14	16	4	4	0	2
Total	66	66	42	42	24	24	4	6

Curriculum

	Full-Time	Part-Time
Typical first-year section size	71	0
Is there typically a "small section" of the first-year class, other than Legal Writing, taught by full-time faculty	No	No
If yes, typical size offered last year		

# of classroom course titles beyond first-year curriculum		108
# of upper division courses, excluding seminars, with an enrollment:	Under 25	55
	25–49	30
	50–74	23
	75–99	13
	100+	0
# of seminars		18
# of seminar positions available		318

	Full-Time	Part-Time
# of seminar positions filled	302	0
# of positions available in simulation courses	524	
# of simulation positions filled	442	0
# of positions available in faculty supervised clinical courses	71	
# of faculty supervised clinical positions filled	65	0
# involved in field placements	28	0
# involved in law journals	173	0
# involved in moot court or trial competitions	45	0
# of credit hours required to graduate	90	

JD Enrollment and Ethnicity

	Men		Women		Full-Time		Part-Time		1st-Year		Total		JD Degs. Awd.
	#	%	#	%	#	%	#	%	#	%	#	%	
All Hispanics	10	2.6	4	1.5	14	2.1	0	0.0	4	1.9	14	2.1	9
Am. Ind./AK Nat.	0	0.0	4	1.5	4	0.6	0	0.0	0	0.0	4	0.6	0
Asian	5	1.3	6	2.2	11	1.7	0	0.0	4	1.9	11	1.7	5
Black/Af. Am.	16	4.1	37	13.5	53	8.0	0	0.0	24	11.3	53	8.0	14
Nat. HI/Pac. Isl.	0	0.0	0	0.0	0	0.0	0	0.0	0	0.0	0	0.0	0
2 or more races	11	2.8	8	2.9	19	2.9	0	0.0	9	4.2	19	2.9	3
Subtotal (minor.)	42	10.7	59	21.5	101	15.2	0	0.0	41	19.2	101	15.2	31
Nonres. Alien	2	0.5	0	0.0	2	0.3	0	0.0	2	0.9	2	0.3	0
White/Cauc.	346	88.3	214	78.1	559	84.1	1	100.0	168	78.9	560	84.1	188
Unknown	2	0.5	1	0.4	3	0.5	0	0.0	2	0.9	3	0.5	3
Total	392	58.9	274	41.1	665	99.8	1	0.2	213	32.0	666		222

Transfers

Transfers in	9
Transfers out	5

Tuition and Fees

	Resident	Nonresident
Full-time	$21,026	$42,072
Part-time		
Tuition Guarantee Program	N	

Living Expenses

Estimated living expenses for singles

Living on campus	Living off campus	Living at home
$16,849	$16,849	$8,780

UNIVERSITY OF SOUTH CAROLINA SCHOOL OF LAW

*ABA
Approved
Since
1925*

GPA and LSAT Scores

	Total	Full-Time	Part-Time
# of apps	1,986	1,986	0
# of offers	725	725	0
# of matrics	213	213	0
75% GPA	3.63	3.63	0.00
Median GPA	3.35	3.35	0.00
25% GPA	3.08	3.08	0.00
75% LSAT	160	160	0
Median LSAT	158	158	0
25% LSAT	155	155	0

Grants and Scholarships (from prior year)

	Total		Full-Time		Part-Time	
	#	%	#	%	#	%
Total # of students	682		681		1	
Total # receiving grants	407	59.7	407	59.8	0	0.0
Less than 1/2 tuition	371	54.4	371	54.5	0	0.0
Half to full tuition	31	4.5	31	4.6	0	0.0
Full tuition	3	0.4	3	0.4	0	0.0
More than full tuition	2	0.3	2	0.3	0	0.0
Median grant amount			$18,676		$0	

Informational and Library Resources

Total amount spent on library materials	$1,121,508
Study seating capacity inside the library	523
# of full-time equivalent professional librarians	9
Hours per week library is open	99
# of open, wired connections available to students	42
# of networked computers available for use by students	42
Has wireless network?	Y
Requires computer?	Y

JD Attrition (from prior year)

	Academic	Other	Total	
	#	#	#	%
1st year	2	9	11	4.6
2nd year	1	7	8	3.6
3rd year	0	0	0	0.0
4th year	0	0	0	0.0

Employment (9 months after graduation)

For up-to-date employment data, go to employmentsummary.abaquestionnaire.org on the ABA website.

Bar Passage Rates

First-time takers	193	Reporting %	77.20
Average school %	86.58	Average state %	79.69
Average pass difference	6.89		

Jurisdiction	Takers	Passers	Pass %	State %	Diff %
South Carolina	149	129	86.58	79.69	6.89

The information on these pages was provided by the law school.

UNIVERSITY OF SOUTH CAROLINA SCHOOL OF LAW

701 Main Street
Columbia, SC 29208
Phone: 803.777.6605; Fax: 803.777.2847
E-mail: usclaw@law.sc.edu; Website: www.law.sc.edu

Introduction

The University of South Carolina School of Law, established in 1867, is located in Columbia, South Carolina. With a metropolitan population approaching 700,000, Columbia combines the advantages of a progressive, growing area with the pace of a smaller city. The School of Law is located two blocks from the state capitol building. As the seat of state government, Columbia is home to the South Carolina Supreme Court, Court of Appeals, federal district and bankruptcy courts, South Carolina criminal and civil courts, and courts of special jurisdiction. As part of a major research university, law students can take advantage of rich interdisciplinary opportunities and a lively social and athletic scene. Columbia residents enjoy easy access to the mountains and the beautiful South Carolina low country and coastal region. The School of Law is accredited by the American Bar Association and has been a member of the Association of American Law Schools since 1924.

Library and Academic Programs

Since its founding, the School of Law has provided outstanding preparation for law students. The curriculum combines traditional teaching methods and courses with modern, state-of-the-art instruction. The School of Law houses a major research library with a collection of more than 500,000 volumes and extensive computer-assisted research capabilities, including LexisNexis, Westlaw, Loislaw, HeinOnline, BNA, SSRN, and the online catalog. The library also includes the South Carolina Legal History Collection. Law students and faculty have access to the collection of the main university library, the Thomas Cooper Library. A highly skilled staff of librarians provides assistance and instruction in research and reference techniques. The library is open approximately 100 hours per week and for extended hours during the examination period. The computer lab and an electronic learning facility are also located within the library. Individual closed study carrels are available for assignment to students, and larger study rooms and open carrels are also available. A wireless computer network is available throughout the building and the law center.

The School of Law offers a full-time-only day program leading to the Juris Doctor degree. In order to earn the JD, a student must successfully complete 90 semester hours of coursework. In each semester, a student must register for a minimum of 12 credit hours. The School of Law offers one seven-week summer session each year.

In addition to all first-year courses, students are required to take Criminal Procedure, Professional Responsibility, a professional skills course, and a perspective course, and to satisfy an upper-level writing requirement. The School of Law offers advanced courses that allow detailed study in corporate and commercial law, tax and estate planning, environmental law, family law, international law, and litigation. The peer-assistance tutoring program provides academic support to first-year students, and numerous resources are available to assist students in succeeding academically.

Dual-Degree Programs

The School of Law, in cooperation with other graduate programs at USC, currently offers dual JD and master's degrees in the following: International Business Administration, Human Resources, Accountancy, Economics, Public Administration, Criminology and Criminal Justice, Social Work, Earth and Environmental Resources Management, Mass Communication, and Health Services Policy and Management. The USC School of Law and Vermont Law School offer a dual degree in environmental law and policy, in which students may earn a JD from USC and a Master of Environmental Law and Policy degree from Vermont Law School in only three years.

Clinics, Public Service, and Special Programs

The School of Law recognizes that experiential learning in the area of professional skills is essential to a well-rounded legal education. Under special court rule, third-year law students in South Carolina may represent clients and appear in court when enrolled in a clinical legal education course. The clinical education program offers courses designed to develop critical lawyering skills. The program offers training in trial advocacy, interviewing, counseling, negotiation, alternative dispute resolution, and legal drafting. Clinics include criminal practice, veterans' rights, bankruptcy, federal litigation, and nonprofit organizations. Externships are available in children's law and foreign practice.

The Pro Bono Program, one of the longest operating programs of its type, has an outstanding national and local reputation. Under the leadership of a full-time director and a student board, the program offers students opportunities to work with a wide range of public interest organizations, including CASA, Volunteer Lawyers for the Arts, the Homeless Legal Clinic, juvenile arbitration, the Greater Columbia Literacy Project, Project Ayuda, the Legal Justice Center, the public defenders' office, the South Carolina Department of Consumer Affairs, the South Carolina Office of Indigent Defense, and volunteer income tax assistance, among others.

The Law School's Children's Law Center provides training to professionals who work with children in the juvenile and family courts. The Nelson Mullins Riley and Scarborough Center on Professionalism at the Law School provides a professionalism series for first-year students and is a national leader in the development of mentoring programs to assist in the transition from law school to law practice. The National Advocacy Center and the National College of District Attorneys are located on the USC campus. The Advocacy Center, operated by the US Department of Justice, provides intensive training to approximately 15,000 federal prosecutors and attorneys from across the country. The National College of District Attorneys provides training to nearly 2,000 prosecutors.

Admission

The School of Law seeks to enroll qualified students who will enhance and embrace the school's rigorous educational environment and, as graduates, make positive societal contributions to South Carolina, the region, and the nation.

In making decisions, the Faculty Committee on Admissions employs a holistic approach, taking into account all information available about each candidate. No single factor is conclusive. While undergraduate grades and the Law School Admission Test (LSAT) are important, the committee's decision is also influenced by other factors, including the applicant's personal statement, graduate study, military service, leadership and community service, employment or other life experience, residency, letters of recommendation, and potential for contribution to a diverse educational environment.

Scholarships and Financial Aid

While many students depend on federal and private student loans to help finance their legal education, the School of Law does offer scholarship assistance based both on merit and on financial need. Merit-based scholarships may range from $500 to full tuition. Awards are made on a rolling basis, typically beginning in March of each year. Candidates who want priority consideration for merit-based scholarships should make sure that the completed application and all supporting materials are received in the Office of Admissions no later than February 1. There is no separate application for merit-based scholarships. Applicants who wish to be considered for need-based scholarships or loans should submit the FAFSA.

Office of Career Services

The Office of Career Services serves as a liaison between students and legal employers and offers services to equip students with the skills and information necessary for a successful employment search. The Office of Career Services uses Symplicity. Services available include individual counseling, résumé writing and interviewing seminars, on-campus interviews, and participation in job fairs. The School of Law regularly participates in the Southeastern Law Placement Consortium in Atlanta; the Mid-Atlantic Legal Recruiting Conference in Washington, DC; the Southeastern Minority Job Fair; the Patent Law Interview Program in Chicago; the Southeastern Legal Hiring Conference; and the National Public Interest Career Fair.

Student Activities

The School of Law publishes the *South Carolina Law Review*; the *ABA Real Property, Trust and Estate Law Journal*; the *Southeastern Environmental Law Journal*; the *Journal of Law and Education*; and the *South Carolina Journal of International Law and Business*. Moot court and mock trial teams are sponsored in national, international, ABA, and various other competitions. Students who have obtained high academic achievement are eligible for membership in the Order of the Coif, a national legal honorary society, and the Order of the Wig and Robe, a local scholastic organization founded in 1935. The Peer Mentoring Program pairs each first-year student with an upper-class student to help with the transition to law school. Student organizations include the Student Bar Association; Black Law Students Association; Women in Law; SALSA, the Hispanic Law Students Association; APALSA, the Asian Pacific Law Students Association; Christian Legal Society; Environmental Law Society; Children's Advocacy Law Society; Federalist Society; Health Law Society; Intellectual Property Law Society; James L. Petigru Public Interest Law Society; Just Democracy; International Law Society; OutLaw; Sports and Entertainment Law Society; Law School Democrats; Law School Republicans; national law fraternities Phi Alpha Delta and Phi Delta Phi; Service Members and Veterans in Law; and the American Constitution Society, among others.

APPLICANT PROFILE

University of South Carolina School of Law
This grid includes only applicants who earned 120–180 LSAT scores under standard administrations.

LSAT Score	3.75 +		3.50–3.74		3.25–3.49		3.00–3.24		2.75–2.99		2.50–2.74		2.25–2.49		2.00–2.24		Below 2.00		No GPA		Total	
	Apps	Adm	Apps	Adm	Apps	Adm	Apps	Adm	Apps	Adm	Apps	Adm	Apps	Adm	Apps	Adm	Apps	Adm	Apps	Adm	Apps	Adm
170–180	3	3	3	3	4	4	1	1	3	3	0	0	0	0	0	0	0	0	0	0	14	14
165–169	14	13	31	31	16	12	17	17	10	8	3	2	1	1	0	0	0	0	0	0	92	84
160–164	57	57	71	68	81	77	63	62	23	19	22	19	5	4	6	3	1	0	5	3	334	312
155–159	82	58	117	72	149	64	122	35	63	17	32	7	13	3	6	2	0	0	3	1	587	259
150–154	54	9	96	13	123	13	110	11	56	3	33	0	13	1	4	0	1	0	6	1	496	51
145–149	34	7	38	3	47	3	71	5	36	0	28	1	7	0	4	1	1	0	4	0	270	20
140–144	3	0	10	1	30	0	19	0	21	0	11	0	12	0	5	0	0	0	0	0	111	1
Below 140	3	0	8	0	7	0	15	0	7	0	11	0	9	0	1	0	0	0	2	0	63	0
Total	250	147	374	191	457	173	418	131	219	50	140	29	60	9	26	6	3	0	20	5	1967	741

Apps = Number of Applicants
Adm = Number Admitted
Reflects 99% of the total applicant pool; highest LSAT data reported.

THE UNIVERSITY OF SOUTH DAKOTA SCHOOL OF LAW

414 E. Clark
Vermillion, SD 57069-2390
Phone: 605.677.5443; Fax: 605.677.5417
E-mail: law@usd.edu; Website: www.usd.edu/law

ABA
Approved
Since
1923

The Basics

Type of school	Public
Term	Semester
Application deadline	3/1
Application fee	$35
Financial aid deadline	3/15
Can first year start other than fall?	No
Student to faculty ratio	32.8 to 1
# of housing spaces available restricted to law students graduate housing for which law students are eligible	188

Faculty and Administrators

	Total		Men		Women		Minorities	
	Spr	Fall	Spr	Fall	Spr	Fall	Spr	Fall
Full-time	10	1	8	1	2	0	0	0
Other full-time	1	0	1	0	0	0	0	0
Deans, librarians, & others who teach	2	0	2	0	0	0	0	0
Part-time	7	8	3	5	4	3	0	1
Total	20	9	14	6	6	3	0	1

Curriculum

	Full-Time	Part-Time
Typical first-year section size	74	0
Is there typically a "small section" of the first-year class, other than Legal Writing, taught by full-time faculty	Yes	No
If yes, typical size offered last year	37	
# of classroom course titles beyond first-year curriculum	47	

# of upper division courses, excluding seminars, with an enrollment:		
Under 25	34	
25–49	9	
50–74	4	
75–99	3	
100+	0	

# of seminars	0	
# of seminar positions available	0	
# of seminar positions filled	0	0
# of positions available in simulation courses	146	
# of simulation positions filled	139	0
# of positions available in faculty supervised clinical courses	0	
# of faculty supervised clinical positions filled	0	0
# involved in field placements	10	0
# involved in law journals	28	0
# involved in moot court or trial competitions	30	0
# of credit hours required to graduate	90	

JD Enrollment and Ethnicity

	Men		Women		Full-Time		Part-Time		1st-Year		Total		JD Degs. Awd.
	#	%	#	%	#	%	#	%	#	%	#	%	
All Hispanics	1	0.8	2	1.9	3	1.3	0	0.0	1	1.1	3	1.3	1
Am. Ind./AK Nat.	3	2.3	3	2.9	6	2.5	0	0.0	1	1.1	6	2.5	2
Asian	2	1.5	1	1.0	3	1.3	0	0.0	2	2.3	3	1.3	0
Black/Af. Am.	2	1.5	1	1.0	3	1.3	0	0.0	0	0.0	3	1.3	3
Nat. HI/Pac. Isl.	0	0.0	0	0.0	0	0.0	0	0.0	0	0.0	0	0.0	0
2 or more races	2	1.5	2	1.9	4	1.7	0	0.0	1	1.1	4	1.7	0
Subtotal (minor.)	10	7.5	9	8.7	19	8.1	0	0.0	5	5.7	19	8.0	6
Nonres. Alien	0	0.0	0	0.0	0	0.0	0	0.0	0	0.0	0	0.0	0
White/Cauc.	123	92.5	95	91.3	217	91.9	1	100.0	84	95.5	218	92.0	49
Unknown	0	0.0	0	0.0	0	0.0	0	0.0	0	0.0	0	0.0	0
Total	133	56.1	104	43.9	236	99.6	1	0.4	88	37.1	237		55

Transfers

Transfers in	2
Transfers out	1

Tuition and Fees

	Resident	Nonresident
Full-time	$12,340	$24,306
Part-time	$6,107	$12,090
Tuition Guarantee Program		N

Living Expenses

Estimated living expenses for singles

Living on campus	Living off campus	Living at home
$11,459	$13,900	N/A

THE UNIVERSITY OF SOUTH DAKOTA SCHOOL OF LAW

ABA Approved Since 1923

GPA and LSAT Scores

	Total	Full-Time	Part-Time
# of apps	400	400	0
# of offers	236	236	0
# of matrics	90	90	0
75% GPA	3.53	3.53	0.00
Median GPA	3.27	3.27	0.00
25% GPA	3.05	3.05	0.00
75% LSAT	148	148	0
Median LSAT	150	150	0
25% LSAT	152	152	0

Grants and Scholarships (from prior year)

	Total		Full-Time		Part-Time	
	#	%	#	%	#	%
Total # of students	205		203		2	
Total # receiving grants	0	0.0	0	0.0	0	0.0
Less than 1/2 tuition	0	0.0	0	0.0	0	0.0
Half to full tuition	0	0.0	0	0.0	0	0.0
Full tuition	0	0.0	0	0.0	0	0.0
More than full tuition	0	0.0	0	0.0	0	0.0
Median grant amount			$0		$0	

Informational and Library Resources

Total amount spent on library materials	$559,551
Study seating capacity inside the library	248
# of full-time equivalent professional librarians	3
Hours per week library is open	168
# of open, wired connections available to students	268
# of networked computers available for use by students	37
Has wireless network?	Y
Requires computer?	N

JD Attrition (from prior year)

	Academic	Other	Total	
	#	#	#	%
1st year	0	4	4	5.3
2nd year	0	0	0	0.0
3rd year	0	0	0	0.0
4th year	0	0	0	0.0

Employment (9 months after graduation)

For up-to-date employment data, go to employmentsummary.abaquestionnaire.org on the ABA website.

Bar Passage Rates

First-time takers	63	Reporting %	88.89
Average school %	98.21	Average state %	97.93
Average pass difference	0.28		

Jurisdiction	Takers	Passers	Pass %	State %	Diff %
South Dakota	50	49	98.00	98.75	–0.75
Iowa	6	6	100.00	91.09	8.91

THE UNIVERSITY OF SOUTH DAKOTA SCHOOL OF LAW

414 E. Clark
Vermillion, SD 57069-2390
Phone: 605.677.5443; Fax: 605.677.5417
E-mail: law@usd.edu; Website: www.usd.edu/law

Introduction

The University of South Dakota School of Law (USD Law), located on the University of South Dakota campus in Vermillion, is noted for its contributions in training distinguished leaders for the bench, the bar, and the lawmaking bodies of the state and region. Established in 1901, USD Law is approved by the ABA and is a member of the AALS. The law school offers a strong American Indian Law Program, and is among the top best-value law schools in the nation. The city of Vermillion, with a population of about 11,000 and located in the southeastern corner of South Dakota along the Missouri National Recreational River, provides a small-town atmosphere. The professional community setting at USD Law provides students with opportunities for individual attention by professors. USD Law offers an extraordinary experience in legal education at a remarkably reasonable tuition rate for both residents and nonresidents. Eighty percent of upper-level courses had 28 or fewer students enrolled in fall 2011.

Library and Physical Facilities

The three-level McKusick Law Library is equipped to meet the research needs of students, faculty, and members of the bar. Students, staff, and faculty have access to the law school facility seven days a week, 24 hours a day through swipe-card access. It is South Dakota's largest and most complete law library, providing essential research services to the courts, legislature, government agencies, lawyers, private citizens, and students conducting interdisciplinary research. The book and microform collections include court reports, statutes, and other legal authorities.

The School of Law building was completed in 1981 and features a balconied courtroom in the middle of the building as the architectural focal point. The courtroom is fully equipped with state-of-the-art videoconferencing technologies and has an adjoining audiovisual control room and judges' chambers. The building also contains two large classrooms; two smaller classrooms; a seminar room; a computer laboratory; a student lounge, locker, and lunch area; and suites of offices for faculty, administration, and student organizations. The law school building is equipped for both wired and wireless network connectivity. The student organization suites contain study carrels for member use. The law library has 231 study seats, including 162 carrels assigned to members of the student body.

Curriculum

Ninety semester credits are required for the JD degree. The first-year curriculum is required of all students. In the second and third years, electives are available in addition to required courses. During the summer, an externship program is offered for six credit hours. Externs learn by doing under the close supervision of an attorney and the externship director. Skills training is also provided to second- and third-year students in the trial techniques course, negotiations, and other courses, each of which utilizes to the fullest extent the technological capabilities of the law school.

Special Programs

- Joint-Degree Programs—There are nine programs with other graduate departments, with master's degrees available in professional accountancy, business administration, history, English, psychology, education administration, political science, public administration, and administrative studies. Qualifying students may transfer nine hours of approved interdisciplinary coursework for JD credit and can complete both programs in three years and receive maximum credit.
- Interdisciplinary Study—For upper-division students not in a joint-degree program, up to six graduate credits in other university divisions may be taken and applied toward the hours required for the JD degree. This allows a law student to broaden the educational experience by the pursuit of new disciplines.
- The USD School of Law and Vermont Law School offer a dual degree in environmental law. Students earn a JD from USD and a Master of Environmental Law and Policy (MELP) from Vermont Law School.
- Areas of Curricular Emphases—The American Indian Law Program provides students with the knowledge, skills, and experiences necessary to meet the challenges and opportunities in working with sovereign tribes and native people. A nationally recognized professor directs a unique and extensive curriculum with a concentration in the study of American Indian law. Nine American Indian reservations are located within the borders of South Dakota. The law school hosts the longest running biennial Indian Law Symposium in the United States, supports the Native American Law Student Association (twice named national chapter of the year), and works closely on the USD campus with the American Indian Studies Department and the Institute of American Indian Studies.

Admission Options

- Flex-Time Program—This program permits certain well-qualified students to take less than the normal load of credits each semester and obtain a JD in five years instead of three. The program admits a limited number of students who could not attend law school on a full-time basis. The law school does not offer evening or weekend courses.
- Accelerated Admission—An applicant may apply for accelerated admission and be admitted to and enroll in law school without final completion of the requirements for the applicant's undergraduate degree. The undergraduate degree must be attained by the applicant prior to graduation from law school.
- Law Honors Scholars Program—High school seniors who are accepted as USD undergraduate Honors Scholars may apply for and receive provisional (automatic) admission to the law school upon successful completion of their undergraduate degree in four years with a 3.5 GPA, fulfillment of the University Honors Program requirements, and completion of the LSAT for statistical purposes only.
- Law Screening Program—Applicants who are not regularly admitted may be invited to participate in the Law Screening Program. The summer program consists of two courses offered in five weeks of lectures and finals during

the sixth week. Participants are admitted or denied admission on the basis of their performance on final exams, which are graded anonymously.

Student Activities

The *South Dakota Law Review* publishes articles by legal scholars, lawyers, jurists, and students three times a year. Other cocurricular activities include a Moot Court Board, Alternative Dispute Resolution Board, and Trial Advocacy teams. Boards successfully compete at the intramural, regional, and national levels. The school is active in the Law Student Division of the ABA. Other organizations include Student Bar Association, Women in Law, Black Law Students Association, Christian Legal Society, Law School Democrats, Federalist Society, Delta Theta Phi, Phi Alpha Delta, Phi Delta Phi, Trial Advocacy Group, Veterans Legal Assistance Group, and the Native American Law Student Association (NALSA) USD chapter, which has been represented nationally and hosted the national NALSA Moot Court Tournament in spring 2010.

SD Supreme Court—Each spring, USD Law hosts the three-day March term of the Supreme Court of South Dakota, which provides an extraordinary opportunity for law and undergraduate students, faculty, and the public to observe oral arguments before the state's highest appeals court. The law school also works closely with Access to Justice, the pro bono office of the State Bar of South Dakota.

Pro Bono Opportunities—The Law School provides substantial pro bono experiences for students assisting people with their legal needs by working closely with Access to Justice and AmeriCorps, the South Dakota Bar's pro bono office, as well as an Elder Law Program, R.D. Hurd Volunteer Society, area legal services offices, South Dakota Innocence Project, Equal Justice Works, Volunteer Income Tax Assistance (VITA) program, the Domestic Violence Legal Program, and Law School Defenders Society.

Career Services

The placement opportunities for third-year law students are excellent in South Dakota, the surrounding areas, and throughout the United States. Approximately 29 percent of the graduates are placed in judicial clerkships, and 21 percent are employed outside South Dakota. The law school has an active program to place first- and second-year students in summer internship programs with law firms.

APPLICANT PROFILE

The University of South Dakota School of Law

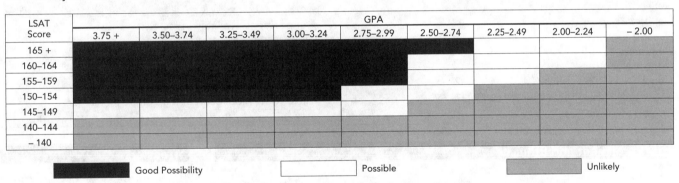

USD School of Law considers many factors beyond LSAT score and GPA. This chart should be used only as a general rule.

For fall 2011:

Applicants:	400	
Completed applications:	400	
Standard full-time admits:	223	
Accepted from Law Screening or PLSI:	13	
Total admitted:	236	
Matriculated full-time:	90	

Stats for the 223 standard admits:	LSAT	GPA
75th—	156	3.59
Median:	152	3.31
25th—	150	3.05

SOUTH TEXAS COLLEGE OF LAW

1303 San Jacinto Street
Houston, TX 77002-7006
Phone: 713.659.8040; Fax: 713.646.2906
E-mail: admissions@stcl.edu; Website: www.stcl.edu

ABA
Approved
Since
1959

The Basics

Type of school	Private	
Term	Semester	
Application deadline	2/15	10/1
Application fee	$55	
Financial aid deadline	5/1	10/1
Can first year start other than fall?	Yes	
Student to faculty ratio	22.6 to 1	
# of housing spaces available restricted to law students		
graduate housing for which law students are eligible		

Faculty and Administrators

	Total		Men		Women		Minorities	
	Spr	Fall	Spr	Fall	Spr	Fall	Spr	Fall
Full-time	42	44	27	29	15	15	4	7
Other full-time	0	0	0	0	0	0	0	0
Deans, librarians, & others who teach	6	6	4	4	2	2	1	1
Part-time	39	41	27	28	12	13	3	6
Total	87	91	58	61	29	30	8	14

Curriculum

	Full-Time	Part-Time
Typical first-year section size	100	70
Is there typically a "small section" of the first-year class, other than Legal Writing, taught by full-time faculty	No	No
If yes, typical size offered last year		
# of classroom course titles beyond first-year curriculum	144	

# of upper division courses, excluding seminars, with an enrollment:		
Under 25	135	
25–49	58	
50–74	17	
75–99	22	
100+	1	

# of seminars	20	
# of seminar positions available	394	
# of seminar positions filled	224	92
# of positions available in simulation courses	426	
# of simulation positions filled	298	102
# of positions available in faculty supervised clinical courses	238	
# of faculty supervised clinical positions filled	122	30
# involved in field placements	109	51
# involved in law journals	253	55
# involved in moot court or trial competitions	76	9
# of credit hours required to graduate	90	

JD Enrollment and Ethnicity

	Men #	Men %	Women #	Women %	Full-Time #	Full-Time %	Part-Time #	Part-Time %	1st-Year #	1st-Year %	Total #	Total %	JD Degs. Awd.
All Hispanics	101	14.8	95	16.3	151	15.2	45	16.6	89	14.5	196	15.5	38
Am. Ind./AK Nat.	1	0.1	4	0.7	4	0.4	1	0.4	2	0.3	5	0.4	4
Asian	50	7.3	61	10.5	81	8.1	30	11.1	50	8.2	111	8.8	31
Black/Af. Am.	15	2.2	33	5.7	29	2.9	19	7.0	24	3.9	48	3.8	12
Nat. HI/Pac. Isl.	1	0.1	1	0.2	1	0.1	1	0.4	1	0.2	2	0.2	2
2 or more races	23	3.4	12	2.1	28	2.8	7	2.6	12	2.0	35	2.8	7
Subtotal (minor.)	191	27.9	206	35.3	294	29.5	103	38.0	178	29.0	397	31.3	94
Nonres. Alien	1	0.1	2	0.3	3	0.3	0	0.0	2	0.3	3	0.2	2
White/Cauc.	492	71.9	375	64.3	699	70.2	168	62.0	433	70.6	867	68.4	303
Unknown	0	0.0	0	0.0	0	0.0	0	0.0	0	0.0	0	0.0	0
Total	684	54.0	583	46.0	996	78.6	271	21.4	613	48.4	1267		399

Transfers

Transfers in	14
Transfers out	10

Tuition and Fees

	Resident	Nonresident
Full-time	$26,850	$26,850
Part-time	$18,100	$18,100
Tuition Guarantee Program	N	

Living Expenses

Estimated living expenses for singles

Living on campus	Living off campus	Living at home
N/A	$21,150	$21,150

ABA
Approved
Since
1959

GPA and LSAT Scores

	Total	Full-Time	Part-Time
# of apps	2,307	1,972	335
# of offers	1,021	896	125
# of matrics	424	358	66
75% GPA	3.48	3.49	3.42
Median GPA	3.24	3.23	3.26
25% GPA	2.92	2.92	2.92
75% LSAT	157	157	153
Median LSAT	154	154	151
25% LSAT	152	152	149

Grants and Scholarships (from prior year)

	Total #	Total %	Full-Time #	Full-Time %	Part-Time #	Part-Time %
Total # of students	1,305		1,009		296	
Total # receiving grants	463	35.5	399	39.5	64	21.6
Less than 1/2 tuition	434	33.3	373	37.0	61	20.6
Half to full tuition	26	2.0	25	2.5	1	0.3
Full tuition	0	0.0	0	0.0	0	0.0
More than full tuition	3	0.2	1	0.1	2	0.7
Median grant amount			$4,200		$1,350	

Informational and Library Resources

Total amount spent on library materials	$1,929,296
Study seating capacity inside the library	895
# of full-time equivalent professional librarians	10
Hours per week library is open	106
# of open, wired connections available to students	1,380
# of networked computers available for use by students	105
Has wireless network?	Y
Requires computer?	N

JD Attrition (from prior year)

	Academic #	Other #	Total #	Total %
1st year	24	16	40	5.9
2nd year	8	2	10	3.3
3rd year	3	1	4	1.3
4th year	0	1	1	3.7

Employment (9 months after graduation)

For up-to-date employment data, go to
employmentsummary.abaquestionnaire.org on the ABA website.

Bar Passage Rates

First-time takers	373	Reporting %	97.59
Average school %	86.81	Average state %	82.68
Average pass difference	4.13		

Jurisdiction	Takers	Passers	Pass %	State %	Diff %
Texas	364	316	86.81	82.68	4.13

The information on these pages was provided by the law school.

SOUTH TEXAS COLLEGE OF LAW

1303 San Jacinto Street
Houston, TX 77002-7006
Phone: 713.659.8040; Fax: 713.646.2906
E-mail: admissions@stcl.edu; Website: www.stcl.edu

Introduction

South Texas College of Law, situated at the very core of Houston's vibrant downtown legal and financial centers, is a private, nonprofit, independent law school founded in 1923. South Texas is the oldest law school in Houston and one of the largest in the nation. Accredited by the American Bar Association and also a member of the AALS, South Texas offers full- and part-time programs leading to the Doctor of Jurisprudence degree.

Admission

South Texas enrolls full-time (day) and part-time (evening) students. Full- and part-time students are admitted to South Texas in the fall semester, while only full-time students are admitted in the spring. Admission application deadlines are February 15 for fall consideration and October 1 for spring. Early application is encouraged. All applicants must have a baccalaureate degree from an accredited college or university of approved standing. In addition, applicants must register with LSAC's Credential Assembly Service and take the LSAT no later than the February administration for Fall consideration and no later than the October administration for spring.

Admission is based primarily on proven academic and intellectual ability, measured largely by the LSAT and the quality of undergraduate education. Capacity for leadership, dedication to community or public service, hardships overcome, excellence in a particular field, motivation, graduate study, work experience, career achievement, extracurricular activities, and character are also factors taken into consideration.

Students are chosen not only for their potential for academic success, but also for their ability to enhance the overall diversity of the class. South Texas makes every effort to achieve broad diversity in terms of background, geography, undergraduate institutions represented, ethnic origin, and race.

Curriculum

The curriculum at South Texas combines traditional classroom instruction with a broad range of innovative simulated and clinical courses. The college offers a class scheduling system whereby students may select convenient class times rather than have to choose between day and evening divisions. To accommodate part-time working students, a complete curriculum of classes is scheduled after 5:30 PM, with a few classes also scheduled on Saturdays.

For students interested in the increased globalization of law, South Texas offers a variety of study-abroad programs throughout the year. Two ABA-approved cooperative exchange programs allow students to study for a semester in the Netherlands or Denmark. Summer programs are offered in Malta, Turkey, Ireland, England, Chile, and the Czech Republic.

JD/MBA Cooperative Program

Through a special cooperative program, students in the JD program at South Texas College of Law are eligible to apply for admission to the MBA program at Mays Business School, Texas A&M University. Upon acceptance into the MBA program, students are granted a leave of absence after their second year of law studies to attain their MBA and then return to South Texas to complete their JD degree.

Special Programs

Development of strong legal and advocacy skills is important at South Texas, as evidenced by its four Centers of Excellence and its skills and clinical programs.

Since 1980, the **Advocacy Program** has outperformed all other law school teams in the nation by winning an array of state, regional, and national championship victories. The **Frank Evans Center for Conflict Resolution** allows students to learn from and interact with practicing attorneys who specialize in mediation and arbitration. The **Corporate Compliance Center** involves students who are interested in working as in-house counsel, corporate counsel, outside counsel, and business lawyers. The center explores issues such as how companies promote policies and procedures that ensure legal and ethical behavior and how companies detect and deter wrongdoing. The **Transactional Practice Center** is designed to teach students the fundamental elements of completing a business transaction such as purchasing or developing real estate, buying or selling a corporation, or creating a partnership.

South Texas offers an array of **on-site clinics** in which students hone their legal skills and develop their professional identities while working for real clients on actual cases under the direct supervision of faculty and staff. The wide range of cases addressed in these direct representation clinics includes refugee and asylum law, domestic violence, claims of actual innocence and wrongful conviction, family law, estate planning, guardianship, and probate. Clinical students appear before administrative agencies, as well as state and federal trial and appellate courts.

Second- and third-year South Texas students take full advantage of the law school's downtown Houston location and enroll in **academic internships** that place them in the real world of lawyering, including state and federal trial and appellate court chambers, prosecutors' and defenders' offices, public interest legal service providers, and state and federal government agencies. International internship opportunities include work with defense and victims' counsel in The Hague international tribunals and with the United Nations High Commission on Refugees in Malta.

Both the academic internships and direct representation clinics complement the **Pro Bono Honors Program**, a cocurricular project that encourages, recognizes, and supports student volunteer legal service during their final two years of law school study.

Academic Assistance and Counseling. Students are encouraged to participate in the varied programs and services offered, which are designed to help them reach their full academic potential.

The **Langdell Scholar Program**, conducted by course-proficient upper level students, continues to benefit students in mastering the framework of legal analysis, while garnering a proficiency in effective outlining, study skills, and exam-taking techniques. Students attend these valuable sessions voluntarily or are selected into the program based on their LSAT performance and undergraduate GPA.

Student Activities

Students at South Texas have the opportunity to become members of approximately 40 active student organizations representing a wide range of interests.

Scholarly Publications

South Texas College of Law students participate in journals on the basis of outstanding scholarship and writing ability. Our students edit and publish a variety of scholarly publications, including the *South Texas Law Review, Currents: International Trade Law Journal,* and the *Corporate Counsel Review*; and coedit the *Construction Law Journal* and *Texas Business Journal* in conjunction with each journal's respective state bar section.

Library and Physical Facilities

South Texas ensures that students have access to, and are trained with, state-of-the-art tools now used in the legal profession. The T. Gerald Treece Courtroom houses a nine-seat judges' bench and boasts the very latest courtroom technology available to trial attorneys. The courtroom is heavily used by the school's nationally recognized advocacy program for practice and competitions. It is also available to the members of Houston's legal community, including the judiciary.

The Fred Parks Law Library supports a diverse legal collection, with over a half million volumes and over 61,000 titles, for the scholarly research and academic needs of the student body, faculty, and legal community. The library also houses a Special Collections Department showcased in The Jesse Jones Reading Room where an impressive catalog of seminal works in legal history, English common law, Spanish and Mexican law, and Texas legal history are available by appointment. The library encompasses more than 72,000 square feet. Each of the 895 seats in the six-story facility is wired for data and power and is Internet accessible through wireless connectivity. The building is crowned with a

conference center and rooftop terrace, which is a perfect place for students to congregate and to hold special campus events.

Financial Assistance

South Texas offers an extensive financial aid program that includes scholarships; grants; federal, state, and private loans; and the opportunity to earn funds through the Federal Work-Study Program. Our financial aid program measures the ability of students to pay tuition, fees, and living expenses, then awards aid (federal, state, and institutional) to all who apply and qualify for assistance. Incoming students are automatically considered for merit scholarships based on their undergraduate grade point average and LSAT score. Continuing students are eligible for both merit- and need-based scholarships. For additional information, please contact the Office of Scholarships and Financial Aid for eligibility and documentation requirements at 713.646.1820. You may also browse the financial aid webpage at www.stcl.edu/fao/.

Career Services

In light of today's competitive job market, the Career Resources Center (CRC) continues to provide South Texas students and graduates with a full range of services to assist in their employment search, while at the same time being responsive to the changes in hiring trends and patterns. The office serves as a counseling and resource center for students seeking employment on either a full- or part-time basis and assists graduates pursuing permanent employment. In addition to on-campus recruiting, the CRC also offers an array of professional development programs and career panels designed to assist students in their job-search preparation and networking. The objective of the CRC staff is to aid students in exploring career options, while helping them build valuable job-search skills utilizing their strengths and abilities. By taking advantage of the many programs and services offered by the CRC, students are better equipped to maximize their career-planning opportunities.

APPLICANT PROFILE

South Texas College of Law
This grid includes only applicants who earned 120–180 LSAT scores under standard administrations.

LSAT Score	3.75 +		3.50–3.74		3.25–3.49		3.00–3.24		2.75–2.99		2.50–2.74		2.25–2.49		2.00–2.24		Below 2.00		No GPA		Total	
	Apps	Adm	Apps	Adm	Apps	Adm	Apps	Adm	Apps	Adm	Apps	Adm	Apps	Adm	Apps	Adm	Apps	Adm	Apps	Adm	Apps	Adm
170–180	1	0	0	0	3	2	1	1	0	0	0	0	1	1	0	0	0	0	0	0	6	4
165–169	4	4	5	5	8	8	10	9	6	6	3	3	2	2	1	1	0	0	0	0	39	38
160–164	10	10	30	29	31	30	23	21	16	15	10	9	4	3	6	4	0	0	0	0	130	121
155–159	36	35	58	58	87	85	83	78	74	65	29	21	20	7	3	1	2	0	1	0	393	350
150–154	39	24	81	61	124	92	133	90	107	50	52	9	28	2	11	0	8	0	14	8	597	336
145–149	27	13	48	18	93	12	97	4	93	4	56	2	34	1	9	1	5	0	15	1	477	56
140–144	5	0	31	2	43	2	54	0	43	0	33	0	26	0	13	0	0	0	14	0	262	4
Below 140	2	0	7	0	12	0	23	0	21	0	25	0	17	0	7	0	3	0	3	0	120	0
Total	124	86	260	173	401	231	424	203	360	140	208	44	132	16	50	7	18	0	47	9	2024	909

Apps = Number of Applicants
Adm = Number Admitted
Reflects 100% of the total applicant pool; highest LSAT data reported.

UNIVERSITY OF SOUTHERN CALIFORNIA, GOULD SCHOOL OF LAW

699 Exposition Boulevard
Los Angeles, CA 90089-0074
Phone: 213.740.2523; Fax: 213.740.4570
E-mail: admissions@law.usc.edu; Website: http://lawweb.usc.edu/

ABA
Approved
Since
1924

The Basics

Type of school	Private
Term	Semester
Application deadline	2/1
Application fee	$75
Financial aid deadline	3/1
Can first year start other than fall?	No
Student to faculty ratio	12.5 to 1
# of housing spaces available restricted to law students	
graduate housing for which law students are eligible	46

Faculty and Administrators

	Total		Men		Women		Minorities	
	Spr	Fall	Spr	Fall	Spr	Fall	Spr	Fall
Full-time	41	45	26	30	15	15	6	5
Other full-time	2	2	0	0	2	2	0	0
Deans, librarians, & others who teach	16	16	6	6	10	10	4	4
Part-time	82	56	60	32	22	24	9	7
Total	141	119	92	68	49	51	19	16

Curriculum

		Full-Time	Part-Time
Typical first-year section size		70	0
Is there typically a "small section" of the first-year class, other than Legal Writing, taught by full-time faculty		Yes	No
If yes, typical size offered last year		35	
# of classroom course titles beyond first-year curriculum		113	
# of upper division courses, excluding seminars, with an enrollment:	Under 25	82	
	25–49	23	
	50–74	10	
	75–99	5	
	100+	10	
# of seminars		31	
# of seminar positions available		516	
# of seminar positions filled		265	0
# of positions available in simulation courses		504	
# of simulation positions filled		403	0
# of positions available in faculty supervised clinical courses		88	
# of faculty supervised clinical positions filled		87	0
# involved in field placements		132	0
# involved in law journals		164	0
# involved in moot court or trial competitions		55	0
# of credit hours required to graduate		88	

JD Enrollment and Ethnicity

	Men		Women		Full-Time		Part-Time		1st-Year		Total		JD Degs. Awd.
	#	%	#	%	#	%	#	%	#	%	#	%	
All Hispanics	38	11.4	31	9.8	69	10.6	0	0.0	32	16.2	69	10.6	29
Am. Ind./AK Nat.	2	0.6	0	0.0	2	0.3	0	0.0	0	0.0	2	0.3	1
Asian	54	16.2	68	21.6	122	18.8	0	0.0	27	13.7	122	18.8	43
Black/Af. Am.	18	5.4	24	7.6	42	6.5	0	0.0	10	5.1	42	6.5	15
Nat. HI/Pac. Isl.	0	0.0	1	0.3	1	0.2	0	0.0	1	0.5	1	0.2	0
2 or more races	6	1.8	16	5.1	22	3.4	0	0.0	10	5.1	22	3.4	3
Subtotal (minor.)	118	35.4	140	44.4	258	39.8	0	0.0	80	40.6	258	39.8	91
Nonres. Alien	5	1.5	8	2.5	13	2.0	0	0.0	3	1.5	13	2.0	3
White/Cauc.	169	50.8	137	43.5	306	47.2	0	0.0	97	49.2	306	47.2	93
Unknown	41	12.3	30	9.5	71	11.0	0	0.0	17	8.6	71	11.0	20
Total	333	51.4	315	48.6	648	100.0	0	0.0	197	30.4	648		207

Transfers

Transfers in	24
Transfers out	4

Tuition and Fees

	Resident	Nonresident
Full-time	$50,591	$50,591
Part-time		
Tuition Guarantee Program		N

Living Expenses

Estimated living expenses for singles

Living on campus	Living off campus	Living at home
$21,915	$21,915	$11,115

UNIVERSITY OF SOUTHERN CALIFORNIA, GOULD SCHOOL OF LAW

ABA
Approved
Since
1924

GPA and LSAT Scores

	Total	Full-Time	Part-Time
# of apps	5,987	5,987	0
# of offers	1,528	1,528	0
# of matrics	199	199	0
75% GPA	3.77	3.77	0.00
Median GPA	3.69	3.69	0.00
25% GPA	3.54	3.54	0.00
75% LSAT	167	167	0
Median LSAT	167	167	0
25% LSAT	165	165	0

Grants and Scholarships (from prior year)

	Total #	Total %	Full-Time #	Full-Time %	Part-Time #	Part-Time %
Total # of students	651		651		0	
Total # receiving grants	368	56.5	368	56.5	0	0.0
Less than 1/2 tuition	316	48.5	316	48.5	0	0.0
Half to full tuition	42	6.5	42	6.5	0	0.0
Full tuition	6	0.9	6	0.9	0	0.0
More than full tuition	4	0.6	4	0.6	0	0.0
Median grant amount			$15,000		$0	

Informational and Library Resources

Total amount spent on library materials	$1,153,596
Study seating capacity inside the library	230
# of full-time equivalent professional librarians	9
Hours per week library is open	100
# of open, wired connections available to students	42
# of networked computers available for use by students	110
Has wireless network?	Y
Requires computer?	N

JD Attrition (from prior year)

	Academic #	Other #	Total #	Total %
1st year	0	0	0	0.0
2nd year	0	9	9	4.1
3rd year	0	0	0	0.0
4th year	0	0	0	0.0

Employment (9 months after graduation)

For up-to-date employment data, go to employmentsummary.abaquestionnaire.org on the ABA website.

Bar Passage Rates

First-time takers	195	Reporting %	89.23
Average school %	90.23	Average state %	71.24
Average pass difference	18.99		

Jurisdiction	Takers	Passers	Pass %	State %	Diff %
California	174	157	90.23	71.24	18.99

UNIVERSITY OF SOUTHERN CALIFORNIA, GOULD SCHOOL OF LAW

699 Exposition Boulevard
Los Angeles, CA 90089-0074
Phone: 213.740.2523; Fax: 213.740.4570
E-mail: admissions@law.usc.edu; Website: http://lawweb.usc.edu/

Introduction

The University of Southern California, Gould School of Law is a private, highly selective national law school with over a 105-year history and a reputation for academic excellence. Under the leadership of a stellar, energetic faculty, the school's rigorous, interdisciplinary program focuses on the law as an expression of social values and an instrument for implementing social goals. USC is known for its diverse student body, its leadership in clinical education, and its tight-knit alumni network composed of national leaders in the legal profession, business, and the public sector. With 200 entering students in each class, the school is small, informal, and collegial.

USC Law School is located on the beautiful 226-acre main campus of the University of Southern California, just south of downtown Los Angeles and in the heart of the city's exciting Arts and Entertainment Corridor, LA Live. The campus offers a lush, parklike atmosphere within a bustling urban setting. A dynamic laboratory for legal training, Los Angeles, the second largest legal market in the US, is a center of state, national, and international commerce and government. The law school is housed in a five-level facility that provides a superb setting for professional training and sophisticated legal research.

Curriculum

USC's curriculum is comprehensive, uniquely interdisciplinary, and designed to challenge. Courses provide a solid foundation in all substantive areas of law as well as extensive opportunities to explore specializations in traditional and emerging fields. Many faculty members have expertise in both law and other disciplines, such as economics, communication, public policy, medicine, history, psychology, and philosophy. The first-year curriculum consists of courses that examine the foundation of the legal system. The second and third years of study allow students to pursue individual interests in areas such as international law, intellectual property, entertainment law, corporations and business-government relationships, taxation, bioethics, and civil rights and liberties.

Special Programs

Dual Degrees: The law school offers 15 dual-degree programs in coordination with USC graduate and professional schools and the California Institute of Technology. These programs enable qualified students to earn a law degree and a master's degree in the following fields: Business Administration, Business Taxation, Economics, Communications Management, Gerontology, International Relations, Philosophy, Political Science, Public Administration, Public Policy, Real Estate Development, and Social Work. A JD/PharmD program and a JD/PhD program in Social Science with the California Institute of Technology are also offered.

Certificate Programs: The law school offers two certificate programs in Business Law and Entertainment Law.

Legal Clinics: The nationally recognized Post-Conviction Justice Project, the Small Business Clinic, the Mediation Clinic, and the Immigration Clinic enable students to gain valuable advocacy and lawyering skills by representing real clients under faculty supervision. Students in the Intellectual Property and Technology Law Clinic review technology contracts, engage in patent evaluation and application, assist with litigation, and perform film clearance work. Students in the International Human Rights Clinic work on projects and cases both locally and internationally that confront the most pressing human rights concerns of our day.

Public Service Programs: The Office of Public Service provides comprehensive opportunities and coordination for all external service learning and community service. These opportunities include more than 70 clinical field placements, allowing students to earn academic credit while engaging in service learning at government and public interest agencies and with federal and state judges, as well as pro bono and community service in the surrounding Los Angeles neighborhoods.

International Programs: USC offers students several opportunities to study abroad. Students can participate in the law school's semester abroad exchange program with the University of Hong Kong, Bocconi University (Italy), University Jean Moulin Lyon (France), and Bond University (Australia). Moreover, students may participate in programs offered around the world by other ABA-approved law schools.

Research Centers: Law students participate in the scholarly activities of several interdisciplinary research centers: the Pacific Center for Health Policy and Ethics; Saks Institute for Mental Health Law, Policy, and Ethics; the Center in Law, Economics, and Organization; the USC-Caltech Center for the Study of Law and Politics; the Center for Law, History, and Culture; and the Center for Law and Philosophy.

Continuing Legal Education: Students help coordinate the law school's practice-oriented programs and serve as research assistants for the Institute on Entertainment Law and Business, Institute on Taxation, Institute on Trusts and Estates, Real Estate Law and Business Conference, Corporate Counsel Institute, and Intellectual Property Institute.

Student Activities and Cocurricular Programs

Academic life is exciting and fast-paced, and students are often engaged in numerous scholarly pursuits and cocurricular programs. The *Southern California Law Review* has one of the largest circulations in the country. Students also publish the *Southern California Interdisciplinary Law Journal* and the *Southern California Review of Law and Social Justice*. The Moot Court Honors Program sends participants to national and state competitions.

Public service activities abound. The Public Interest Law Foundation is one of the largest in the country, providing summer grants for public service employment as well as the Irmas Fellowship for public interest law, which awards a year's salary to a third-year student committed to postgraduate work in public interest.

The diversity of USC Law School's student population is reflected in nearly 40 political, religious, social, cultural, and ethnic organizations. Our students play an active and valued role in the day-to-day operation of the law school, including service on faculty committees. Students are given a wide range of opportunities to create and implement ideas for activities and are encouraged to pursue their interests by forming new student organizations or planning social or academic events. Asian, African American, Muslim, Middle

Eastern, Jewish, and Latino law students are represented by associations. Other student organizations include the Student Bar Association, international and entertainment law societies, Art Law Society, Women's Law Association, OUTLaw, Legal Aid Alternative Breaks Project, Christian Legal Society, Public Interest Law Foundation, Health Law and Bioethics Society, Business Law Society, Corporate Law Society, Intellectual Property and Technology Law Society, Street Law, Sports Law, Trial Lawyers, and chapters of the ACLU and the Federalist Society.

Professional Careers

USC graduates accept job offers in all regions of the country, with New York and Washington, DC, being the most popular placement locations outside the West Coast. A number of graduates begin their professional careers as judicial law clerks to federal and state judges. Each year, several hundred private firms, government agencies, public interest organizations, and corporations from throughout the country come to USC to recruit students for summer and permanent employment. An off-campus recruiting program helps coordinate interviews with East Coast employers. The school's enthusiastic network of alumni is a valuable tool in the job-search process. The Alumni Mentor Lunch provides first-year students with the opportunity to meet graduates who practice in the student's field of interest, and other programs bring alumni from a range of fields to campus to discuss career opportunities. Overall placement statistics are consistently strong; historically, more than 91 percent of each graduating class finds employment within nine months of graduation. Average starting salaries are among the highest in the nation.

Housing

Graduate law housing is available in an apartment-style residence located within easy walking distance of the law school for a limited number of incoming students. The two-bedroom apartments are fully furnished. A roommate referral service is available to help incoming students arrange shared housing in various Los Angeles neighborhoods.

Admission and Financial Aid

Admission decisions are made on the basis of the student's academic record, LSAT score and writing sample, personal statement, letters of recommendation, résumé, extracurricular activities, and other information in the file. The Admissions Committee gives primary consideration to outstanding academic and professional promise and to qualities that will enhance the diversity of the student body or enrich the law school educational environment. Two letters of recommendation are required; applicants are strongly urged to submit at least one academic recommendation letter. The law school operates on a semester basis and admits only full-time students. USC is committed to helping students successfully finance their legal education. In addition to various loan programs, the law school offers substantial scholarship awards to a large percentage of the incoming class. Most scholarships are based on merit as evidenced by strong academic credentials and test scores. In addition, the school offers a Loan Repayment Assistance Program, which assists graduates who accept employment with governmental agencies and public interest organizations that traditionally offer lower pay than private firms.

APPLICANT PROFILE

University of Southern California, Gould School of Law
This grid includes only applicants who earned 120–180 LSAT scores under standard administrations.

LSAT Score	3.75 +		3.50–3.74		3.25–3.49		3.00–3.24		2.75–2.99		2.50–2.74		2.25–2.49		2.00–2.24		Below 2.00		No GPA		Total	
	Apps	Adm	Apps	Adm	Apps	Adm	Apps	Adm	Apps	Adm	Apps	Adm	Apps	Adm	Apps	Adm	Apps	Adm	Apps	Adm	Apps	Adm
175–180	34	30	41	33	20	7	14	4	2	0	4	1	0	0	1	0	0	0	0	0	116	75
170–174	268	245	280	184	118	32	54	3	21	0	11	0	2	0	0	0	0	0	12	4	766	468
165–169	633	446	669	300	307	31	145	3	41	2	20	0	7	0	0	0	1	0	46	1	1869	783
160–164	358	67	429	46	302	33	153	13	52	1	26	1	12	0	2	0	0	0	44	0	1378	161
155–159	159	9	234	12	213	9	124	1	49	0	29	0	10	0	5	0	0	0	17	0	840	31
150–154	67	1	101	1	119	1	101	0	52	0	34	0	12	0	4	0	1	0	17	0	508	3
145–149	23	0	39	0	60	0	60	0	41	0	20	0	11	0	6	0	1	0	8	0	269	0
140–144	2	0	21	0	23	0	33	0	27	0	21	0	7	0	0	0	0	0	5	0	139	0
135–139	2	0	7	0	7	0	9	0	11	0	9	0	6	0	2	0	1	0	2	0	56	0
130–134	1	0	2	0	4	0	2	0	2	0	6	0	2	0	1	0	0	0	1	0	21	0
125–129	0	0	2	0	0	0	0	0	1	0	1	0	2	0	1	0	0	0	1	0	8	0
120–124	0	0	0	0	0	0	1	0	0	0	1	0	0	0	0	0	0	0	0	0	2	0
Total	1547	798	1825	576	1173	113	696	24	299	3	182	2	71	0	22	0	4	0	153	5	5972	1521

Apps = Number of Applicants
Adm = Number Admitted
Reflects 99% of the total applicant pool; highest LSAT data reported.

SOUTHERN ILLINOIS UNIVERSITY SCHOOL OF LAW

Office of Admissions, 1150 Douglas Drive, Mailcode 6804
Carbondale, IL 62901
Phone: 800.739.9187 or 618.453.8858; Fax: 618.453.8921
E-mail: lawadmit@siu.edu; Website: www.law.siu.edu

ABA
Approved
Since
1974

The Basics

Type of school	Public
Term	Semester
Application deadline	4/1
Application fee	
Financial aid deadline	4/1
Can first year start other than fall?	No
Student to faculty ratio	13.0 to 1
# of housing spaces available restricted to law students	
graduate housing for which law students are eligible	360

Faculty and Administrators

	Total		Men		Women		Minorities	
	Spr	Fall	Spr	Fall	Spr	Fall	Spr	Fall
Full-time	23	24	9	10	14	14	3	4
Other full-time	0	2	0	1	0	1	0	0
Deans, librarians, & others who teach	8	8	5	5	3	3	1	2
Part-time	14	8	9	4	5	4	1	1
Total	45	42	23	20	22	22	5	7

Curriculum

	Full-Time	Part-Time
Typical first-year section size	72	0
Is there typically a "small section" of the first-year class, other than Legal Writing, taught by full-time faculty	No	No
If yes, typical size offered last year		
# of classroom course titles beyond first-year curriculum	72	

# of upper division courses, excluding seminars, with an enrollment:		
	Under 25	86
	25–49	18
	50–74	12
	75–99	1
	100+	0

# of seminars	8	
# of seminar positions available	96	
# of seminar positions filled	60	0
# of positions available in simulation courses	595	
# of simulation positions filled	344	0
# of positions available in faculty supervised clinical courses	52	
# of faculty supervised clinical positions filled	38	0
# involved in field placements	105	0
# involved in law journals	65	0
# involved in moot court or trial competitions	35	0
# of credit hours required to graduate	90	

JD Enrollment and Ethnicity

	Men		Women		Full-Time		Part-Time		1st-Year		Total		JD Degs. Awd.
	#	%	#	%	#	%	#	%	#	%	#	%	
All Hispanics	3	1.3	2	1.4	5	1.3	0	0.0	1	0.8	5	1.3	2
Am. Ind./AK Nat.	2	0.9	2	1.4	4	1.1	0	0.0	0	0.0	4	1.1	0
Asian	8	3.4	3	2.1	11	2.9	0	0.0	2	1.7	11	2.9	4
Black/Af. Am.	3	1.3	2	1.4	5	1.3	0	0.0	1	0.8	5	1.3	4
Nat. HI/Pac. Isl.	1	0.4	0	0.0	1	0.3	0	0.0	0	0.0	1	0.3	0
2 or more races	0	0.0	0	0.0	0	0.0	0	0.0	0	0.0	0	0.0	0
Subtotal (minor.)	17	7.3	9	6.3	26	7.0	0	0.0	4	3.4	26	6.9	10
Nonres. Alien	0	0.0	0	0.0	0	0.0	0	0.0	0	0.0	0	0.0	0
White/Cauc.	198	84.6	122	85.9	317	85.0	3	100.0	103	87.3	320	85.1	96
Unknown	19	8.1	11	7.7	30	8.0	0	0.0	11	9.3	30	8.0	5
Total	234	62.2	142	37.8	373	99.2	3	0.8	118	31.4	376		111

Transfers

Transfers in	1
Transfers out	6

Tuition and Fees

	Resident	Nonresident
Full-time	$15,994	$36,154
Part-time		
Tuition Guarantee Program		N

Living Expenses

Estimated living expenses for singles

Living on campus	Living off campus	Living at home
$14,546	$14,546	$14,546

SOUTHERN ILLINOIS UNIVERSITY SCHOOL OF LAW

ABA Approved Since 1974

GPA and LSAT Scores

	Total	Full-Time	Part-Time
# of apps	699	699	0
# of offers	353	353	0
# of matrics	120	120	0
75% GPA	3.62	3.62	0.00
Median GPA	3.30	3.30	0.00
25% GPA	2.96	2.96	0.00
75% LSAT	156	156	0
Median LSAT	153	153	0
25% LSAT	151	151	0

Grants and Scholarships (from prior year)

	Total #	Total %	Full-Time #	Full-Time %	Part-Time #	Part-Time %
Total # of students	382		380		2	
Total # receiving grants	155	40.6	155	40.8	0	0.0
Less than 1/2 tuition	97	25.4	97	25.5	0	0.0
Half to full tuition	39	10.2	39	10.3	0	0.0
Full tuition	14	3.7	14	3.7	0	0.0
More than full tuition	5	1.3	5	1.3	0	0.0
Median grant amount			$5,000		$0	

Informational and Library Resources

Total amount spent on library materials	$869,632
Study seating capacity inside the library	349
# of full-time equivalent professional librarians	5
Hours per week library is open	78
# of open, wired connections available to students	12
# of networked computers available for use by students	53
Has wireless network?	Y
Requires computer?	N

JD Attrition (from prior year)

	Academic #	Other #	Total #	Total %
1st year	3	10	13	9.0
2nd year	0	0	0	0.0
3rd year	0	0	0	0.0
4th year	0	0	0	0.0

Employment (9 months after graduation)

For up-to-date employment data, go to employmentsummary.abaquestionnaire.org on the ABA website.

Bar Passage Rates

First-time takers	129	Reporting %	85.27
Average school %	75.45	Average state %	89.47

Average pass difference –14.02

Jurisdiction	Takers	Passers	Pass %	State %	Diff %
Illinois	98	73	74.49	89.38	–14.89
Missouri	12	10	83.33	90.24	–6.91

The information on these pages was provided by the law school.

SOUTHERN ILLINOIS UNIVERSITY SCHOOL OF LAW

Office of Admissions, 1150 Douglas Drive, Mailcode 6804
Carbondale, IL 62901
Phone: 800.739.9187 or 618.453.8858; Fax: 618.453.8921
E-mail: lawadmit@siu.edu; Website: www.law.siu.edu

Introduction

Southern Illinois University School of Law is an outstanding, small public law school that provides an optimal mix of theoretical and experiential educational opportunities in a student-centered environment. SIU School of Law emphasizes **excellence in academics**. Students learn from faculty members who are nationally recognized in their fields and are engaged with the legal community on local, state, national, and international levels.

Students at SIU School of Law receive a strong grounding in legal theory and **excellent training in professional skills development**. In addition to a nationally recognized Lawyering Skills Program and an award-winning professionalism program, the SIU School of Law provides skills training through clinical and externship programs, a semester-in-practice program, moot court, pro bono opportunities, and a wide variety of extracurricular activities.

Law students at SIU receive a **rigorous legal education in a supportive environment**. Students benefit from individualized attention from professors and administrators who genuinely care about their success. In addition to a 13:1 student-to-faculty ratio, SIU School of Law has an excellent student support system that includes an Academic Success Program and bar exam preparation support.

SIU School of Law prepares **practice-ready graduates** for a changing legal profession in a global environment.

Campus

The School of Law is located on the campus of Southern Illinois University Carbondale, a 143-year-old university with a tradition of excellence as well as a diverse, multicultural student body of approximately 20,000. Carbondale, a community of 27,000 people, is one of the most scenic areas of Illinois. National forests, state parks, historic sites, campgrounds, theaters, festivals, and cultural events make Carbondale's quality of life among the highest in small cities in Illinois.

Curriculum

All students have a uniform first-year curriculum. A broad range of courses are offered in the second and third years.

SIU School of Law is at the forefront of legal education in providing a strong **Writing Across the Curriculum** program. Our students acquire strong legal writing skills by practicing those skills in every course in the law school and receiving substantial constructive critiques of their work throughout the three-year curriculum.

An innovative and **nationally recognized first-year Lawyering Skills Program** gives students a solid foundation in basic lawyering skills, including legal research and writing, oral advocacy, client interviewing and counseling, and negotiation. In addition, the school has a strong health law curriculum and is the site for the National Health Law Moot Court Competition as well as a Center for Health Law and Policy.

After three years of intensive education in **theory and skills**, graduates are prepared to not only pass the bar, but also to begin their careers with confidence in the skills they have learned and practiced while in law school.

A Master of Legal Studies (MLS) program and Master of Laws (LLM) program are also available.

Dual Degrees

Recognizing the increasing complexity of the law, the SIU School of Law has partnered with the SIUC Graduate School and the SIU School of Medicine to offer a variety of concurrent JD/Master's degree programs. Current partnerships include: accountancy, business administration, education, electrical and computer engineering, public administration, and social work. A six-year program offered in cooperation with the School of Medicine permits students to concurrently obtain JD and MD degrees.

Professional Skills Training

Clinical programs enable senior law students to represent clients under the supervision of licensed attorneys. The Civil Practice/Elder Clinic provides direct legal assistance to persons 60 years of age and older in the 13 southernmost counties of Illinois. Students may participate in the Public Interest or Judicial Externship Program and obtain academic credit while working at nonprofit, local, state, or federal legal or judicial offices. The Domestic Violence Clinic provides legal assistance to victims of domestic violence. The Juvenile Justice Clinic provides legal services to minors as guardians ad litem.

The **semester-in-practice** program allows second- and third-year students the opportunity to spend a semester living and working in different locations. The **Law and Government** Program, located in the Illinois state capital of Springfield, focuses on state and local government. The **Criminal Trial Practice** Program, with locations in southeast Missouri and Chicago, provides hands-on experience with the Public Defender or State's Attorney's Offices. The **Health Law and Policy** Program offers students the opportunity to engage with state and not-for-profit entities in the health care field in Springfield, Illinois.

SIU School of Law provides a comprehensive **trial and appellate moot court** program with teams that have successfully competed in the McGee National Civil Rights Moot Court, ABA Moot Court, and Darras Disability Law Moot Court competitions, among others. In addition, SIU School of Law holds an annual intramural Appellate Moot Court Competition.

All entering law students are assigned to a study group and an upper-level law student tutor as part of the **Academic Success** program and participate in the **Professionalism and the Law** class. Both programs give students additional tools and skills necessary in the legal profession. The Professionalism class grew out of the SIU School of Law Professional Development program, which was awarded the coveted E. Smythe Gambrell Award from the American Bar Association. The law school was recognized for its design and implementation of a model professionalism program for law students.

Special Programs

SIU School of Law sponsors two annual lecture series: the Hiram H. Lesar Distinguished Lecture Series and the Dr. Arthur Grayson Distinguished Lecture Series. In addition, SIU

School of Law cosponsors an annual health law symposium, the SIU/SIH Health Policy Institute, that attracts health law policy experts from across the country.

SIU School of Law has partnered with the University of Missouri—Kansas City to offer students a four-week, study-abroad program in Ireland. The program allows students to receive six elective credit hours and the chance to study at some of Ireland's preeminent institutions.

Library and Physical Facilities

SIU School of Law's primary facility is the Lesar Law Building, housing the classrooms, courtroom, auditorium, faculty offices, and law library. Because the number of activities and services has expanded since the main building was completed in 1981, the clinics are located directly across from the main building, creating an informal law school campus within the broader university grounds. All together, the facilities offer over 100,000 square feet of space.

Law students enjoy 24-hour access to the law library, which has ample study space. In addition to a rich print and microform collection, the law library has evolved to meet the changing nature of legal research and user expectations by providing wireless access to a wide array of electronic legal materials. Law students also have virtual as well as physical access to the university's Morris Library, which houses a major research collection and is located within walking distance of the law school. The law librarians, who hold both law and library science degrees, are committed to teaching law students the fundamentals of legal research formally, by coteaching the Lawyering Skills first-year course, and informally, through their interactions at the reference desk.

Student Activities

SIU School of Law publishes the *Southern Illinois University Law Journal*, which provides editorial and writing experience for a number of upper-class students. Students with a particular interest in health law have the opportunity to write and edit for the *Journal of Legal Medicine*. As mentioned previously, the school provides a comprehensive trial and appellate moot court program as well as an annual intramural Appellate Moot Court Competition.

All students belong to the **Student Bar Association (SBA)**. The SBA serves as a channel of communication between students and faculty. In addition to providing services to its members, the SBA schedules lectures and coordinates two major social events annually, including Barristers Ball and Chili Trivia. Students can also participate in a wide variety of other student organizations depending on their specific interests. Students play an active role in law school governance, serving on most faculty committees.

Career Services

SIU School of Law graduates find employment nationwide, with **alumni in 48 states and several international countries**, including Austria, Belgium, Canada, Hong Kong, Japan, Puerto Rico, Ukraine, and the Virgin Islands. The Office of Career Services provides services for both enrolled students and alumni, including individual career counseling, on-campus interviews, career workshops, and more. Students have the opportunity to participate in a variety of regional and national job fairs and career conferences. The Career Library contains diverse career materials, including national and international directories, judicial clerkship information, and government and public interest job information.

Expenses, Scholarships, and Financial Aid

SIU School of Law offers **competitive scholarships** ranging from $4,000 to full tuition. Scholarships are awarded to incoming students who demonstrate a high aptitude for the study of law. Financial support from the State of Illinois combined with a generous program of scholarships for both incoming and current students allow graduates of the SIU School of Law to enjoy an **average debt load that is below the national law school average**. Students can qualify for the in-state resident tuition rate after they have been an Illinois resident for six consecutive months. Student loans and work-study opportunities are administered by the university's Financial Aid Office. Information concerning in-state resident applications, loans, and financial aid procedures may be obtained from the Office of Admissions.

APPLICANT PROFILE

Southern Illinois University School of Law
This grid includes only applicants who earned 120–180 LSAT scores under standard administrations.

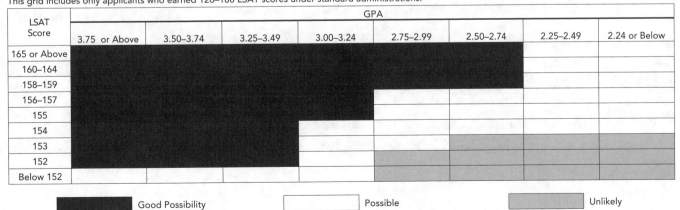

LSAT Score	GPA							
	3.75 or Above	3.50–3.74	3.25–3.49	3.00–3.24	2.75–2.99	2.50–2.74	2.25–2.49	2.24 or Below
165 or Above								
160–164								
158–159								
156–157								
155								
154								
153								
152								
Below 152								

■ Good Possibility ☐ Possible ▨ Unlikely

This grid reflects the highest LSAT score of the applicant.

SOUTHERN UNIVERSITY LAW CENTER

Admission Office, PO Box 9294
Baton Rouge, LA 70813
Phone: 225.771.4976 or 800.537.1135; Fax: 225.771.2121
E-mail: admission@sulc.edu; Website: www.sulc.edu

ABA
Approved
Since
1953

The Basics

Type of school	Public
Term	Semester
Application deadline	2/28 5/1
Application fee	$25
Financial aid deadline	4/15
Can first year start other than fall?	No
Student to faculty ratio	14.0 to 1
# of housing spaces available restricted to law students	
graduate housing for which law students are eligible	5

Faculty and Administrators

	Total		Men		Women		Minorities	
	Spr	Fall	Spr	Fall	Spr	Fall	Spr	Fall
Full-time	36	39	17	17	19	22	23	26
Other full-time	0	0	0	0	0	0	0	0
Deans, librarians, & others who teach	5	5	4	4	1	1	5	5
Part-time	19	30	14	16	5	14	7	19
Total	60	74	35	37	25	37	35	50

JD Enrollment and Ethnicity

	Men		Women		Full-Time		Part-Time		1st-Year		Total		JD Degs. Awd.
	#	%	#	%	#	%	#	%	#	%	#	%	
All Hispanics	36	10.6	38	9.7	14	2.9	60	24.2	33	12.8	74	10.2	1
Am. Ind./AK Nat.	0	0.0	1	0.3	0	0.0	1	0.4	1	0.4	1	0.1	0
Asian	3	0.9	1	0.3	2	0.4	2	0.8	1	0.4	4	0.5	2
Black/Af. Am.	158	46.6	236	60.5	279	58.0	115	46.4	140	54.3	394	54.0	95
Nat. HI/Pac. Isl.	1	0.3	0	0.0	1	0.2	0	0.0	0	0.0	1	0.1	0
2 or more races	0	0.0	0	0.0	0	0.0	0	0.0	0	0.0	0	0.0	0
Subtotal (minor.)	198	58.4	276	70.8	296	61.5	178	71.8	175	67.8	474	65.0	98
Nonres. Alien	0	0.0	0	0.0	0	0.0	0	0.0	0	0.0	0	0.0	0
White/Cauc.	137	40.4	110	28.2	181	37.6	66	26.6	77	29.8	247	33.9	53
Unknown	4	1.2	4	1.0	4	0.8	4	1.6	6	2.3	8	1.1	0
Total	339	46.5	390	53.5	481	66.0	248	34.0	258	35.4	729		151

Curriculum

	Full-Time	Part-Time
Typical first-year section size	57	88
Is there typically a "small section" of the first-year class, other than Legal Writing, taught by full-time faculty	No	No
If yes, typical size offered last year		
# of classroom course titles beyond first-year curriculum	64	
# of upper division courses, excluding seminars, with an enrollment: Under 25	27	
25–49	14	
50–74	22	
75–99	1	
100+	0	
# of seminars	9	
# of seminar positions available	93	
# of seminar positions filled	81	12
# of positions available in simulation courses	335	
# of simulation positions filled	193	50
# of positions available in faculty supervised clinical courses	179	
# of faculty supervised clinical positions filled	97	34
# involved in field placements	29	0
# involved in law journals	40	7
# involved in moot court or trial competitions	11	0
# of credit hours required to graduate	96	

Transfers

Transfers in	0
Transfers out	5

Tuition and Fees

	Resident	Nonresident
Full-time	$10,014	$16,614
Part-time	$6,744	$13,344
Tuition Guarantee Program		N

Living Expenses

Estimated living expenses for singles

Living on campus	Living off campus	Living at home
$18,922	$18,922	$18,922

*ABA
Approved
Since
1953*

GPA and LSAT Scores

	Total	Full-Time	Part-Time
# of apps	1,049	738	311
# of offers	403	270	133
# of matrics	258	152	106
75% GPA	3.11	3.21	3.06
Median GPA	2.85	2.91	2.79
25% GPA	2.50	2.59	2.48
75% LSAT	148	149	146
Median LSAT	145	146	144
25% LSAT	142	143	142

Grants and Scholarships (from prior year)

	Total #	Total %	Full-Time #	Full-Time %	Part-Time #	Part-Time %
Total # of students	721		486		235	
Total # receiving grants	148	20.5	148	30.5	0	0.0
Less than 1/2 tuition	0	0.0	0	0.0	0	0.0
Half to full tuition	131	18.2	131	27.0	0	0.0
Full tuition	0	0.0	0	0.0	0	0.0
More than full tuition	17	2.4	17	3.5	0	0.0
Median grant amount			$2,077		$0	

Informational and Library Resources

Total amount spent on library materials	$864,254
Study seating capacity inside the library	285
# of full-time equivalent professional librarians	3
Hours per week library is open	99
# of open, wired connections available to students	535
# of networked computers available for use by students	58
Has wireless network?	Y
Requires computer?	N

JD Attrition (from prior year)

	Academic #	Other #	Total #	Total %
1st year	54	5	59	18.4
2nd year	0	0	0	0.0
3rd year	1	6	7	3.3
4th year	0	0	0	0.0

Employment (9 months after graduation)

For up-to-date employment data, go to employmentsummary.abaquestionnaire.org on the ABA website.

Bar Passage Rates

First-time takers	113	Reporting %	75.22
Average school %	58.82	Average state %	66.26
Average pass difference	−7.44		

Jurisdiction	Takers	Passers	Pass %	State %	Diff %
Louisiana	85	50	58.82	66.26	−7.44

SOUTHERN UNIVERSITY LAW CENTER

Admission Office, PO Box 9294
Baton Rouge, LA 70813
Phone: 225.771.4976 or 800.537.1135; Fax: 225.771.2121
E-mail: admission@sulc.edu; Website: www.sulc.edu

Introduction

In September 1947, the Southern University school of law was officially opened, and it was redesignated as a law center in 1985. Accredited by the American Bar Association, the Supreme Court of Louisiana, and the Southern Association of Colleges and Secondary Schools, the Law Center maintains a high standard of professional education. It is fully approved by the Veterans Administration for the training of eligible veterans. The Southern University Law Center adheres to the principle of equal opportunity without regard to ethnicity, gender, creed, national origin, age, disability, or marital status.

The Law Center is located in Baton Rouge, the capital of Louisiana. With a population of over 600,000, this seat of state government includes state agencies and courts. As a hub of legal activity, Baton Rouge offers law students many opportunities to participate in state government through interaction with the legislature, state agencies, and private law firms.

Library

The law library contains more than 450,000 volumes, 1,000,000 microfiche, 40,000 rolls of microfilm, and 800 law reviews. The library offers research assistance and reference services to students, faculty, and the public. Its collection adequately supports the curriculum and conforms to the standards of the American Bar Association. Both federal and Louisiana state governments have designated Southern University Law Center Library as an official depository for government documents. A complete collection of Louisiana legal materials, including continuing legal education materials of the Louisiana Bar Association, is provided in the library. Although library acquisitions reflect the civil law tradition of Louisiana, sufficient materials for research in the common law and a substantial number of basic legal reference works are available. Media equipment in the library includes copying machines for printed materials and microform.

The library occupies a 30,000-square-foot area, which includes computer and multimedia law learning labs. Cooperative arrangements with the Louisiana State University Law Center Library provide access to one of the largest Anglo-American and civil law resource collections in the southern region. Interlibrary loans from other libraries can be made through the Southern University Law Library.

Curriculum

The program of study is designed to give students a comprehensive knowledge of both the civil law and the common law. While emphasis is given to the substantive and procedural law of Louisiana with its French and Spanish origins, Anglo-American law is strongly integrated into the curriculum. Fundamental differences in method and approach, and the results reached in the two systems, are analyzed.

The civil law system of Louisiana offers the law student a unique educational opportunity. The program of instruction examines the historical background of the Anglo-American setting. Students are trained in the art of advocacy, legal research, and the sources and social purposes of legal principles. Techniques to discipline the students' minds in legal reasoning are an integral part of the educational objectives of the Law Center. Students are instructed in the ethics of the legal profession and the professional responsibility of the lawyer to society.

The Juris Doctor (JD) degree is offered at the Southern University Law Center through a full-time and a part-time day/evening program. The JD program has a three-year curriculum requiring 96 hours of academic credits. The part-time program requires enrollment in at least eight credit hours each semester and can be completed in four years. A JD and Master of Public Administration (JD/MPA) joint degree is also offered by the Law Center and the Southern University Nelson Mandela School of Public Policy and Urban Affairs. The JD/MPA joint-degree program requires 123 hours of academic credit and can be completed in four years.

Admission

The Law Center does not prescribe any prelegal courses, but strongly recommends a foundation in such courses as English, speech, political science, history, economics, psychology, logic, mathematics, analytical courses, and science.

Students beginning the study of law are admitted only in the fall semester. Applicants are advised to take the LSAT prior to the February test date of the expected year of enrollment. Under no circumstances will a score received on a test administered more than three years prior to the anticipated date of acceptance be considered. All applications for admission are reviewed by a special committee. Many variables are taken into consideration for admission, including, but not limited to, the undergraduate grade-point average and the LSAT. Work experience and past pursuits are also reviewed.

Completed application forms, in addition to two letters of recommendation and one copy of an official transcript showing degree earned, should be filed with the admission office during the fall semester prior to the year in which admission is sought.

Student Activities

Third-year law students are eligible to enroll in the Clinical Education Program, which allows students to handle cases under the direct supervision of a full-time faculty member of the Law Center.

The *Southern University Law Review* is a scholarly periodical published under the auspices of the Southern University Law Center. Editorial administration and managerial responsibilities are handled by the student members of the *Law Review* staff with guidance from a faculty advisor. Students who complete the first year with at least 29 credit hours and are ranked in the top 7 percent of their class at the end of the spring semester shall be offered membership. Students who complete the first year with at least 29 credit hours and a cumulative undergraduate grade-point average of 3.0 may participate in the "write-on" competition.

Law Review membership provides eligible students with a wealth of experience in legal research and writing.

The Student Bar Association (SBA), an affiliate of the American Law Student Association, is a self-governing organization that receives the full cooperation of the Law Center faculty. Any student in good standing enrolled at the Law Center is eligible for membership.

The purpose of the Student Bar Association is to promote the general welfare of the Law Center, encourage high scholarship among its members, and cultivate rapport and cooperation among the students, faculty, and members of the legal profession.

Housing

Limited dormitory accommodations are available for law students. All students desiring to live in campus housing are required to submit an application to the Housing Office, in addition to a security deposit of $50. Applications should be made to the Director of Housing, Southern University, as early as possible.

Other Student Organizations

Other student organizations include the Moot Court Board; Law Student Division, ABA; Black Law Students Association; Delta Theta Phi Law Fraternity, International; Phi Alpha Delta Law Fraternity, International; Women in Law; Environmental Law Society; Sports and Entertainment Legal Association; Louisiana Trial Lawyers Association; Christians at Law Society; International Law Students Association; Southern Student Association of Criminal Defense Lawyers; Public Interest Law Society; Phi Delta Phi International Legal Fraternity; Business Entrepreneurship Leadership Association; and the Thurgood Marshall Club.

Career Services

The Office of Career Counseling and Development assists students and alumni in obtaining meaningful employment opportunities. Information on part-time employment before graduation is available through this office. The office maintains a resource center directed toward résumé and cover letter writing, interview skills, and legal career opportunities. The Law Center is a member of the National Association for Legal Career Professionals (formerly National Association for Law Placement) and subscribes to its standards for promoting career planning and development activities.

Applicant Profile Not Available

SOUTHWESTERN LAW SCHOOL

3050 Wilshire Boulevard
Los Angeles, CA 90010-1106
Phone: 213.738.6834; Fax: 213.383.1688
E-mail: admissions@swlaw.edu; Website: www.swlaw.edu

ABA
Approved
Since
1970

The Basics

Type of school	Private
Term	Semester
Application deadline	4/1
Application fee	$60
Financial aid deadline	6/1
Can first year start other than fall?	No
Student to faculty ratio	14.3 to 1
# of housing spaces available restricted to law students	
graduate housing for which law students are eligible	

Faculty and Administrators

	Total		Men		Women		Minorities	
	Spr	Fall	Spr	Fall	Spr	Fall	Spr	Fall
Full-time	56	56	30	31	26	25	14	13
Other full-time	4	4	2	2	2	2	1	1
Deans, librarians, & others who teach	10	10	4	4	6	6	1	1
Part-time	49	29	32	23	17	6	10	5
Total	119	99	68	60	51	39	26	20

Curriculum

		Full-Time	Part-Time
Typical first-year section size		83	86
Is there typically a "small section" of the first-year class, other than Legal Writing, taught by full-time faculty		No	No
If yes, typical size offered last year			
# of classroom course titles beyond first-year curriculum		172	
# of upper division courses, excluding seminars, with an enrollment:	Under 25	164	
	25–49	45	
	50–74	25	
	75–99	13	
	100+	0	
# of seminars		22	
# of seminar positions available		416	
# of seminar positions filled		216	67
# of positions available in simulation courses		1,241	
# of simulation positions filled		726	262
# of positions available in faculty supervised clinical courses		99	
# of faculty supervised clinical positions filled		72	18
# involved in field placements		302	34
# involved in law journals		90	17
# involved in moot court or trial competitions		79	25
# of credit hours required to graduate		87	

JD Enrollment and Ethnicity

	Men		Women		Full-Time		Part-Time		1st-Year		Total		JD Degs. Awd.
	#	%	#	%	#	%	#	%	#	%	#	%	
All Hispanics	67	12.2	97	17.0	94	12.7	70	18.3	63	15.9	164	14.6	36
Am. Ind./AK Nat.	3	0.5	2	0.4	3	0.4	2	0.5	1	0.3	5	0.4	2
Asian	54	9.8	90	15.8	104	14.1	40	10.4	52	13.1	144	12.8	38
Black/Af. Am.	28	5.1	25	4.4	22	3.0	31	8.1	12	3.0	53	4.7	25
Nat. HI/Pac. Isl.	2	0.4	2	0.4	1	0.1	3	0.8	2	0.5	4	0.4	1
2 or more races	13	2.4	16	2.8	23	3.1	6	1.6	13	3.3	29	2.6	4
Subtotal (minor.)	167	30.3	232	40.7	247	33.5	152	39.7	143	36.1	399	35.6	106
Nonres. Alien	6	1.1	2	0.4	8	1.1	0	0.0	6	1.5	8	0.7	3
White/Cauc.	325	59.0	291	51.1	417	56.5	199	52.0	225	56.8	616	55.0	132
Unknown	53	9.6	45	7.9	66	8.9	32	8.4	22	5.6	98	8.7	55
Total	551	49.2	570	50.8	738	65.8	383	34.2	396	35.3	1121		296

Transfers

Transfers in	6
Transfers out	19

Tuition and Fees

	Resident	Nonresident
Full-time	$42,200	$42,200
Part-time	$28,200	$28,200
Tuition Guarantee Program		N

Living Expenses

Estimated living expenses for singles

Living on campus	Living off campus	Living at home
N/A	$26,819	$13,094

SOUTHWESTERN LAW SCHOOL

*ABA
Approved
Since
1970*

GPA and LSAT Scores

	Total	Full-Time	Part-Time
# of apps	3,383	2,879	504
# of offers	1,207	1,019	188
# of matrics	404	285	119
75% GPA	3.48	3.50	3.37
Median GPA	3.29	3.34	3.16
25% GPA	3.04	3.10	2.95
75% LSAT	157	157	154
Median LSAT	154	155	152
25% LSAT	152	153	150

Grants and Scholarships (from prior year)

	Total		Full-Time		Part-Time	
	#	%	#	%	#	%
Total # of students	1,095		741		354	
Total # receiving grants	373	34.1	284	38.3	89	25.1
Less than 1/2 tuition	143	13.1	96	13.0	47	13.3
Half to full tuition	145	13.2	120	16.2	25	7.1
Full tuition	49	4.5	48	6.5	1	0.3
More than full tuition	36	3.3	20	2.7	16	4.5
Median grant amount			$16,861		$10,800	

Informational and Library Resources

Total amount spent on library materials	$1,628,327
Study seating capacity inside the library	610
# of full-time equivalent professional librarians	9
Hours per week library is open	108
# of open, wired connections available to students	326
# of networked computers available for use by students	142
Has wireless network?	Y
Requires computer?	N

JD Attrition (from prior year)

	Academic	Other	Total	
	#	#	#	%
1st year	25	20	45	11.1
2nd year	7	19	26	8.3
3rd year	0	2	2	0.6
4th year	0	0	0	0.0

Employment (9 months after graduation)

For up-to-date employment data, go to employmentsummary.abaquestionnaire.org on the ABA website.

Bar Passage Rates

First-time takers	288	Reporting %	97.22
Average school %	58.57	Average state %	71.24

Average pass difference −12.67

Jurisdiction	Takers	Passers	Pass %	State %	Diff %
California	280	164	58.57	71.24	−12.67

The information on these pages was provided by the law school.

SOUTHWESTERN LAW SCHOOL

3050 Wilshire Boulevard
Los Angeles, CA 90010-1106
Phone: 213.738.6834; Fax: 213.383.1688
E-mail: admissions@swlaw.edu; Website: www.swlaw.edu

More Than 100 Years of Innovative Legal Education

With a long-standing emphasis on diversity, public service, innovative programs, and a mid-city campus featuring a world-renowned Art Deco landmark, Southwestern Law School reflects the vibrancy of Los Angeles and provides an ideal setting for law study. Founded more than 100 years ago as an independent, nonprofit, nonsectarian institution, Southwestern is fully approved by the ABA and is a member of the AALS. It is the only law school to offer four JD courses of study that differ in scheduling and instructional approach, including traditional full- and part-time programs, as well as a unique two-year accelerated curriculum. Concurrent three- and four-year JD/MBA programs are also available. Since the early 1900s, Southwestern's 15,000 alumni have included prominent public officials—from members of Congress to mayors, and over 400 judges—as well as founders of major law firms and general counsels of multinational corporations. The law school has strong ties to the legal, business, and civic sectors, and its Biederman Entertainment and Media Law Institute is closely linked to the entertainment industry in Hollywood and internationally.

Diverse and Talented Student Body

There is a strong sense of community among the students who come to Southwestern from virtually every state and a dozen foreign countries, and represent over 250 undergraduate institutions. About two-thirds have prior work experience or have already completed advanced degrees in diverse disciplines from accounting to urban planning. In the most recent entering class, women and men are equally represented, while minorities make up 37 percent and students report fluency in over 20 foreign languages. The average age is 26, with a range from 21 to over 50 years old.

Distinguished Faculty

Southwestern's faculty focus on enhancing the classroom experience and providing personal attention to each student. The full-time faculty include internationally recognized experts in alternative dispute resolution, antitrust, civil rights, criminal justice, entertainment and media, environmental, ethics, human rights, intellectual property, international, technology, and trial advocacy, among other areas of the law. The adjunct faculty of distinguished judges and attorneys are known for their expertise in specialized practices and enjoy sharing their real-world knowledge with students in stimulating elective courses.

Award-Winning Campus Facilities

Southwestern has created a welcoming student-centered oasis within a campus that encompasses nearly two city blocks in the heart of Los Angeles. The $29-million campus expansion, completed in 2004, includes the restoration and adaptation of the world-renowned historic Bullocks Wilshire building and provides award-winning facilities featuring state-of-the-art multimedia technology in the classrooms, courtrooms, and clinics; wireless Internet access; spacious dining facilities and student lounges in restored historic areas;

large terraces with panoramic city views; tranquil student commons and promenade plazas; and a 10,000-square-foot, spa-quality fitness center. Southwestern's Taylor Law Library is the second largest academic law library facility in California, and the Dixon Courtroom and Advocacy Center is one of the most technologically sophisticated centers of its kind. The law school's new on-campus student housing complex is currently under construction and scheduled to open in Fall 2013.

Two-, Three-, and Four-Year JD Programs

Southwestern's four JD programs include a three-year, full-time day program; a four-year, part-time evening program; PLEAS—a four-year, part-time day program for students with child- or elder-care responsibilities; and SCALE—an accelerated two-year, full-time program featuring small classes, practical skills training, and real-world experience. Southwestern has also established exciting new partnerships with the Drucker Graduate School of Management of Claremont Graduate University to offer a JD/MBA and JD/MA in Management, and with the Pardee RAND Graduate School to offer a unique Certificate Program in Public Policy. LLM programs are offered in individualized law studies and in entertainment and media law.

Comprehensive Curriculum

Recognized by the Carnegie Foundation for innovation, Southwestern's cutting-edge, first-year curriculum provides a unique opportunity for students to choose one of three tracks in their legal research and writing course—appellate, negotiation, or trial advocacy—and to take an elective as early as their second semester. Recent upper-division enhancements include a January intersession, capstone courses, and special "mini-term" courses taught by international legal experts. The required traditional curriculum includes 17 courses, while more than 250 elective courses; 150 externship placements; practicum programs in Appellate Litigation, Immigration Appeals, and Entertainment; and three clinical programs allow students to design a broad-based legal education or emphasize an area of law. Southwestern's location, faculty expertise, alumni presence in the profession, and history have enabled the law school to develop a reputation as a leader, particularly in entertainment and media law, international law, criminal law, and trial advocacy/litigation. Southwestern sponsors summer law programs in Argentina, Canada, England, and Mexico. A wide array of academic support programs and individualized counseling is provided by the Dean of Students and Diversity Affairs, the Director of Academic Support and Bar-Related Programs, and the Writing Center to ensure student success.

Entertainment and Media Law Institute

Southwestern was the first law school to establish a center focused on entertainment and media law. The internationally recognized Biederman Entertainment and Media Law Institute features the largest contingent of full-time entertainment and media law faculty of any law school, and benefits from an extensive network of alumni and adjunct faculty who hold prominent positions in these industries. The institute sponsors more than 60 courses and 60 externship placements, the Biederman Scholars program, a special law firm practicum, a scholarly journal, and summer programs in Los Angeles and London, in addition to lectures and symposia with industry leaders. Southwestern also established the first LLM program in Entertainment and Media Law, offered on campus and online.

Student Activities

Southwestern's interscholastic Moot Court Honors Program, Negotiation Honors Program, Trial Advocacy Honors Program, and client counseling teams consistently earn top awards in competitions around the country. Students demonstrate their outstanding research, writing, and editing skills through service on the *Southwestern Law Review* and the *Southwestern Journal of International Law*, as well as the *Journal of International Media and Entertainment Law* published in conjunction with the ABA Forums on Communications Law and the Entertainment and Sports Industries. The Student Bar Association sponsors award-winning student welfare and community outreach programs and oversees over 50 student organizations, including three legal fraternities; minority, cultural, political, and religious groups; and societies focused on specific areas of law.

Public Interest Opportunities

Southwestern encourages, recognizes, and rewards students' public interest involvement through its Public Service Policy and a variety of programs: the Children's Rights, Immigration Law, and Street Law clinics; special scholarship funds; the Public Interest Service Award; the Silbert Public Interest Fellowship Program; Public Interest Summer Grants for students working with public service agencies; extensive student volunteer work with local schools and community organizations; and a large selection of externships. During the annual Public Interest Law Week, the entire law school community rallies to raise awareness and funds supporting public interest activities.

Career Services and Alumni Network

The Career Services Office offers individualized career counseling and coordinates a full calendar of workshops, networking events, mock interviews, and panel presentations, as well as the Alumni Resource Network to help students prepare for and secure legal employment. The office sponsors intensive on- and off-campus interview programs and provides web-based access to extensive job listings and on-campus interview opportunities through Symplicity. Although the majority of Southwestern graduates choose to practice in California, alumni can be found in 47 states and 17 foreign countries.

Admission Criteria

Admission to Southwestern is highly selective, with an average acceptance rate over the past five years of 32 percent. While emphasis is placed on undergraduate GPA and LSAT scores earned within the past three years, community involvement, work experience, motivation, recommendations, and diversity are also major factors. Transfer applications are considered from students who have successfully completed at least one year at another ABA-approved law school.

Financial Aid/Scholarships

About 90 percent of Southwestern's students receive some form of financial aid that may include scholarships, grants, loans, and work-study funds. Among the more than 80 institutional scholarship funds is the Wildman/Schumacher Scholarship Program, which provides up to full-tuition renewable scholarships to members of the first-year entering class who demonstrate exceptional academic and leadership potential.

APPLICANT PROFILE

Southwestern Law School
This grid includes only applicants who earned 120–180 LSAT scores under standard administrations.

LSAT Score	GPA 3.75 +	3.50–3.74	3.25–3.49	3.00–3.24	2.75–2.99	2.50–2.74	2.25–2.49	2.00–2.24	Below 2.00
175–180	Good Possibility	Good Possibility	Good Possibility	Good Possibility	Good Possibility	Possible	Possible	Possible	Unlikely
170–174	Good Possibility	Good Possibility	Good Possibility	Good Possibility	Good Possibility	Possible	Possible	Possible	Unlikely
165–169	Good Possibility	Good Possibility	Good Possibility	Good Possibility	Good Possibility	Possible	Possible	Unlikely	Unlikely
160–164	Good Possibility	Good Possibility	Good Possibility	Good Possibility	Good Possibility	Possible	Possible	Unlikely	Unlikely
155–159	Good Possibility	Good Possibility	Good Possibility	Good Possibility	Possible	Possible	Unlikely	Unlikely	Unlikely
150–154	Good Possibility	Good Possibility	Good Possibility	Good Possibility	Possible	Unlikely	Unlikely	Unlikely	Unlikely
145–149	Unlikely	Unlikely	Unlikely	Unlikely	Unlikely	Unlikely	Unlikely	Unlikely	Unlikely
140–144	Unlikely	Unlikely	Unlikely	Unlikely	Unlikely	Unlikely	Unlikely	Unlikely	Unlikely
135–139	Unlikely	Unlikely	Unlikely	Unlikely	Unlikely	Unlikely	Unlikely	Unlikely	Unlikely
130–134	Unlikely	Unlikely	Unlikely	Unlikely	Unlikely	Unlikely	Unlikely	Unlikely	Unlikely
125–129	Unlikely	Unlikely	Unlikely	Unlikely	Unlikely	Unlikely	Unlikely	Unlikely	Unlikely
120–124	Unlikely	Unlikely	Unlikely	Unlikely	Unlikely	Unlikely	Unlikely	Unlikely	Unlikely

Legend: ■ Good Possibility □ Possible ▨ Unlikely

STANFORD UNIVERSITY LAW SCHOOL

Office of Admissions, 559 Nathan Abbott Way
Stanford, CA 94305-8610
Phone: 650.723.4985; Fax: 650.723.0838
E-mail: Admissions@law.stanford.edu; Website: www.law.stanford.edu

ABA
Approved
Since
1923

The Basics

Type of school	Private
Term	Quarter
Application deadline	2/1
Application fee	$100
Financial aid deadline	3/15
Can first year start other than fall?	No
Student to faculty ratio	7.8 to 1
# of housing spaces available restricted to law students	
graduate housing for which law students are eligible	636

Faculty and Administrators

	Total		Men		Women		Minorities	
	Spr	Fall	Spr	Fall	Spr	Fall	Spr	Fall
Full-time	62	59	40	39	22	20	10	8
Other full-time	8	6	1	2	7	4	2	2
Deans, librarians, & others who teach	16	16	10	10	6	6	3	2
Part-time	66	28	43	21	23	7	8	3
Total	152	109	94	72	58	37	23	15

Curriculum

	Full-Time	Part-Time
Typical first-year section size	60	0
Is there typically a "small section" of the first-year class, other than Legal Writing, taught by full-time faculty	Yes	No
If yes, typical size offered last year	30	
# of classroom course titles beyond first-year curriculum	223	

# of upper division courses, excluding seminars, with an enrollment:	Under 25	127
	25–49	29
	50–74	15
	75–99	4
	100+	3

	Full-Time	Part-Time
# of seminars	88	
# of seminar positions available	1,458	
# of seminar positions filled	935	0
# of positions available in simulation courses	459	
# of simulation positions filled	401	0
# of positions available in faculty supervised clinical courses	288	
# of faculty supervised clinical positions filled	232	0
# involved in field placements	61	0
# involved in law journals	399	0
# involved in moot court or trial competitions	38	0
# of credit hours required to graduate	111	

JD Enrollment and Ethnicity

	Men		Women		Full-Time		Part-Time		1st-Year		Total		JD Degs. Awd.
	#	%	#	%	#	%	#	%	#	%	#	%	
All Hispanics	39	11.9	34	13.9	73	12.8	0	0.0	28	15.6	73	12.8	20
Am. Ind./AK Nat.	1	0.3	0	0.0	1	0.2	0	0.0	0	0.0	1	0.2	1
Asian	27	8.3	31	12.7	58	10.2	0	0.0	23	12.8	58	10.2	19
Black/Af. Am.	17	5.2	25	10.2	42	7.4	0	0.0	15	8.3	42	7.4	13
Nat. HI/Pac. Isl.	0	0.0	0	0.0	0	0.0	0	0.0	0	0.0	0	0.0	0
2 or more races	20	6.1	20	8.2	40	7.0	0	0.0	13	7.2	40	7.0	20
Subtotal (minor.)	104	31.8	110	45.1	214	37.5	0	0.0	79	43.9	214	37.5	73
Nonres. Alien	5	1.5	6	2.5	11	1.9	0	0.0	4	2.2	11	1.9	3
White/Cauc.	200	61.2	120	49.2	320	56.0	0	0.0	83	46.1	320	56.0	116
Unknown	18	5.5	8	3.3	26	4.6	0	0.0	14	7.8	26	4.6	1
Total	327	57.3	244	42.7	571	100.0	0	0.0	180	31.5	571		193

Transfers

Transfers in	15
Transfers out	1

Tuition and Fees

	Resident	Nonresident
Full-time	$49,179	$49,179
Part-time		
Tuition Guarantee Program	N	

Living Expenses

Estimated living expenses for singles

Living on campus	Living off campus	Living at home
$25,803	$27,279	N/A

STANFORD UNIVERSITY LAW SCHOOL

*ABA
Approved
Since
1923*

GPA and LSAT Scores

	Total	Full-Time	Part-Time
# of apps	3,783	3,783	0
# of offers	372	372	0
# of matrics	180	180	0
75% GPA	3.93	3.93	0.00
Median GPA	3.85	3.85	0.00
25% GPA	3.72	3.72	0.00
75% LSAT	172	172	0
Median LSAT	170	170	0
25% LSAT	167	167	0

Grants and Scholarships (from prior year)

	Total #	Total %	Full-Time #	Full-Time %	Part-Time #	Part-Time %
Total # of students	571		571		0	
Total # receiving grants	352	61.6	352	61.6	0	0.0
Less than 1/2 tuition	152	26.6	152	26.6	0	0.0
Half to full tuition	189	33.1	189	33.1	0	0.0
Full tuition	6	1.1	6	1.1	0	0.0
More than full tuition	5	0.9	5	0.9	0	0.0
Median grant amount			$26,027		$0	

Informational and Library Resources

Total amount spent on library materials	$968,896
Study seating capacity inside the library	508
# of full-time equivalent professional librarians	10
Hours per week library is open	103
# of open, wired connections available to students	90
# of networked computers available for use by students	66
Has wireless network?	Y
Requires computer?	Y

JD Attrition (from prior year)

	Academic #	Other #	Total #	Total %
1st year	0	1	1	0.6
2nd year	0	4	4	2.1
3rd year	0	1	1	0.5
4th year	0	0	0	0.0

Employment (9 months after graduation)

For up-to-date employment data, go to employmentsummary.abaquestionnaire.org on the ABA website.

Bar Passage Rates

First-time takers	152	Reporting %	97.37
Average school %	98.66	Average state %	76.05
Average pass difference	22.61		

Jurisdiction	Takers	Passers	Pass %	State %	Diff %
California	96	94	97.92	71.24	26.68
New York	52	52	100.00	84.92	15.08

STANFORD UNIVERSITY LAW SCHOOL

Office of Admissions, 559 Nathan Abbott Way
Stanford, CA 94305-8610
Phone: 650.723.4985; Fax: 650.723.0838
E-mail: Admissions@law.stanford.edu; Website: www.law.stanford.edu

Introduction

Stanford Law School is part of one of the world's leading research institutions, providing plentiful opportunities for interdisciplinary cooperation. Stanford University is a private university located in the heart of Silicon Valley, just 35 miles south of San Francisco. The university's 8,180 acres stretch between the foothills of the Santa Cruz Mountains and the cities of Palo Alto and Menlo Park in a part of the country that offers an ideal Mediterranean climate of dry, warm summers and wet, but temperate winters.

Current enrollment at the university is more than 15,000 students, of whom more than 8,000 are graduate students. The law school is small, with 571 JD students, 60 LLM and JSM students, and approximately 70 faculty members including clinical faculty, senior lecturers, and emeriti. The school has teaching and research ties with schools and departments across campus. Law School courses are taught in 16 multimedia classrooms with full wireless Internet connectivity.

Stanford Law School offers a unique combination of the classic and cutting edge in legal education. The school is preparing its students for a rich and varied professional life in an era of great excitement and rapid change—much of it generated by the remarkable innovations in information technology pioneered in Silicon Valley—and for careers in an increasingly global community.

Faculty

Stanford Law School's faculty is distinguished not only for its scholarship, but also for its commitment to teaching and curricular innovation. The school's unusually low student-to-faculty ratio of 7.8 to 1 creates an intimate, collegial environment that fosters students' intellectual and professional development both in and out of the classroom. Students have many opportunities to work closely with faculty members as research assistants on scholarly projects, and the faculty encourages interested students to develop their own scholarship for future academic careers. The relationships formed between Stanford Law faculty and students often last a lifetime.

Instruction at Stanford Law takes place primarily in small classes and seminars and through individually directed research. It also takes place via a diverse range of legal clinics, which offer students experience with real cases and clients and personalized feedback.

The faculty is continually engaged in developing new teaching methods to complement curricular innovations. Case studies, similar to those of business schools, challenge students to consider the interaction of legal and nonlegal factors involved in a given situation. Numerous interdisciplinary opportunities allow faculty and students from the law school and other parts of the university, joined by practitioners and policymakers, to engage in applied research.

Library and Physical Facilities

Housed within Crown Quadrangle is the Robert Crown Law Library, which holds an excellent collection of print materials and a vast collection of online resources. Popular with the law students are the library's spacious reading rooms. An entire floor of the library, with its comfortable reading room and technology-enabled meeting rooms and classroom, is available 24 hours a day, 7 days a week. The friendly and service-minded staff members are dedicated to helping students, faculty, and staff with all their research needs.

Special Programs

Joint-Degree Programs—Stanford Law School has dramatically expanded its joint-degree programs, leveraging the highly rated graduate schools and academic programs across Stanford University. To facilitate interdisciplinary study and scholarship, and simplify the pursuit of joint degrees, Stanford Law has adapted the law school calendar to be compatible with that of the wider university. The school offers more than 20 formal joint-degree programs in such areas as Bioengineering; Business; Computer Science; Economics; Education; Electrical Engineering; Environment and Resources; Health Research and Policy; History; International, Comparative and Area Studies; International Policy Studies; Management Science and Engineering; Medicine; Philosophy; Political Science; Psychology; Public Policy; and Sociology. Joint-degree programs are also offered with Princeton's Woodrow Wilson School of Public and International Affairs and with Johns Hopkins' School of Advanced International Studies. For students with specialized career aspirations, opportunities to customize a joint degree are limitless.

Programs and Centers—Stanford Law School's 20-plus innovative academic programs and centers give students the opportunity for concentrated study and close interaction with faculty. Students may engage in graduate-level research and policy-oriented study through centers and programs such as the Stanford Constitutional Law Center; Stanford Criminal Justice Center; Environmental and Natural Resources Law and Policy Program; Stanford Center on International Conflict and Negotiation; Rule of Law Program; Stanford Program in International and Comparative Law; Arthur and Toni Rembe Rock Center for Corporate Governance; John M. Olin Program in Law and Economics; Stanford Program in Law, Science & Technology; Center for E-Commerce; Center for Internet and Society; Center for Law and the Biosciences; Transatlantic Technology Law Forum; CodeX: Stanford Center for Legal Informatics; Stanford Center on the Legal Profession; Martin Daniel Gould Center for Conflict Resolution; Gould Negotiation and Mediation Program; and John and Terry Levin Center for Public Service and Public Interest Law.

Team-Taught Courses and Concentration—Stanford Law now offers 13 team-oriented, problem-solving courses, many of which are cotaught by law school faculty and faculty from Stanford's other top-rated schools and departments. Classes are open to students from a variety of disciplines.

Clinical Program—Stanford Law is a leader in the development of clinical teaching and has expanded its clinical program to include 10 clinics that offer students the opportunity to undertake, under the close supervision of experienced practitioners, the roles and responsibilities of practicing lawyers. Students engage in witness examination, depositions, discovery, negotiations, drafting pleadings and memos, oral arguments, and analysis of tactical and ethical problems. Clinics include the Criminal Defense Clinic, Criminal Prosecution Clinic, IP and Innovation Clinic,

Environmental Law Clinic, Immigrants' Rights Clinic, International Human Rights and Conflict Resolution Clinic, Organizations and Transactions Clinic, Stanford Community Law Clinic, Supreme Court Litigation Clinic, and Youth and Education Law Project.

Housing

Stanford provides a variety of housing options for law students. Students may choose from furnished single rooms to four-bedroom apartments equipped with full kitchens. A new residence built specifically for law students and other graduate students from around campus—and adjacent to the law school—intensifies the interdisciplinary learning experience. The university also lists off-campus housing opportunities. More information about housing is available at the Housing Assignment Services website: www.stanford.edu/dept/hds/has/.

Student Activities

More than 50 student organizations plus nine journals and a film documentary project enrich the law school experience. Opportunities for scholarly work are provided through the *Stanford Law Review* and journals focused on civil rights and civil liberties; international law; law, business, and finance; law and policy; technology law; environmental law; animal law and policy; and law, science, and policy. Advocacy skills are developed in moot court and mock trial.

Students who are female, Asian, African American, Latino, Native American, Christian, or LGBT will all find groups that share their particular concerns. Other organizations focus on environmental law, international law, law and technology, and public interest law. Local affiliates of the Federalist Society, the American Constitution Society, and the National Lawyers Guild are present.

Expenses and Financial Aid

Estimated expenses are as follows: for 2011–2012, full-time tuition is $47,460, with additional expenses including housing estimated at $27,522 for single students living on campus and $28,998 for single students living off campus. Scholarships are awarded on the basis of financial need. The purpose of financial aid is to assist students who would otherwise be unable to pursue a legal education at Stanford. Approximately 80 percent of the student body receives tuition fellowship or loan assistance.

The school also offers funding to students who dedicate a law school summer to qualified public service work. And for graduates who take low-paying public interest jobs and have substantial educational debt, the school has an excellent loan repayment assistance program—the Miles and Nancy Rubin Loan Repayment Assistance Program.

Career Services

The Office of Career Services, together with the John and Terry Levin Center for Public Service and Public Interest Law, provides assistance and guidance to students in every facet of their job search. Resources on both legal and nonlaw options; education, including substantive programming; and ongoing counseling help students to identify and achieve their career goals. In addition, the office's On-Campus Interviewing Programs each spring and fall collectively bring to campus approximately 250 employers recruiting for over 500 offices worldwide.

A survey of students graduating in the class of 2010 shows the following employment patterns: law firm associates, 57 percent; judicial clerks, 32 percent; business (legal and nonlegal), 2 percent; public interest, government, or law teaching, 9 percent.

APPLICANT PROFILE

Our admission process takes into consideration many factors besides the undergraduate GPA and LSAT score. A statistical grid, as is typically provided here, only takes into consideration these two factors. We have chosen not to provide applicants with such a grid because our admission process would not be accurately portrayed.

STETSON UNIVERSITY COLLEGE OF LAW

1401 61st Street South
Gulfport, FL 33707
Phone: 727.562.7802; Fax: 727.343.0136
E-mail: lawadmit@law.stetson.edu; Website: www.law.stetson.edu

ABA
Approved
Since
1930

The Basics

Type of school	Private
Term	Semester
Application deadline	4/15
Application fee	$55
Financial aid deadline	8/1
Can first year start other than fall?	No
Student to faculty ratio	14.1 to 1
# of housing spaces available restricted to law students	212
graduate housing for which law students are eligible	

Faculty and Administrators

	Total		Men		Women		Minorities	
	Spr	Fall	Spr	Fall	Spr	Fall	Spr	Fall
Full-time	54	58	28	30	26	28	8	9
Other full-time	3	1	3	1	0	0	0	0
Deans, librarians, & others who teach	5	4	2	2	3	2	0	0
Part-time	52	70	36	52	16	18	2	8
Total	114	133	69	85	45	48	10	17

JD Enrollment and Ethnicity

	Men		Women		Full-Time		Part-Time		1st-Year		Total		JD Degs. Awd.
	#	%	#	%	#	%	#	%	#	%	#	%	
All Hispanics	62	11.4	62	11.6	101	11.8	23	10.2	52	14.9	124	11.5	17
Am. Ind./AK Nat.	4	0.7	10	1.9	10	1.2	4	1.8	8	2.3	14	1.3	5
Asian	15	2.8	14	2.6	21	2.5	8	3.6	13	3.7	29	2.7	11
Black/Af. Am.	21	3.9	41	7.6	57	6.7	5	2.2	17	4.9	62	5.7	25
Nat. HI/Pac. Isl.	0	0.0	1	0.2	0	0.0	1	0.4	0	0.0	1	0.1	0
2 or more races	0	0.0	0	0.0	0	0.0	0	0.0	0	0.0	0	0.0	0
Subtotal (minor.)	102	18.8	128	23.9	189	22.1	41	18.2	90	25.8	230	21.3	58
Nonres. Alien	6	1.1	6	1.1	12	1.4	0	0.0	3	0.9	12	1.1	0
White/Cauc.	390	71.7	366	68.3	587	68.7	169	75.1	233	66.8	756	70.0	236
Unknown	46	8.5	36	6.7	67	7.8	15	6.7	23	6.6	82	7.6	28
Total	544	50.4	536	49.6	855	79.2	225	20.8	349	32.3	1080		322

Curriculum

	Full-Time	Part-Time
Typical first-year section size	70	70
Is there typically a "small section" of the first-year class, other than Legal Writing, taught by full-time faculty	No	No
If yes, typical size offered last year		
# of classroom course titles beyond first-year curriculum	302	

# of upper division courses, excluding seminars, with an enrollment:		
	Under 25	276
	25–49	57
	50–74	18
	75–99	3
	100+	2

# of seminars	27	
# of seminar positions available	488	
# of seminar positions filled	286	49
# of positions available in simulation courses	1,321	
# of simulation positions filled	863	170
# of positions available in faculty supervised clinical courses	212	
# of faculty supervised clinical positions filled	99	8
# involved in field placements	289	27
# involved in law journals	69	10
# involved in moot court or trial competitions	83	6
# of credit hours required to graduate	88	

Transfers

Transfers in	16
Transfers out	15

Tuition and Fees

	Resident	Nonresident
Full-time	$35,466	$35,466
Part-time	$24,582	$24,582
Tuition Guarantee Program	N	

Living Expenses

Estimated living expenses for singles

Living on campus	Living off campus	Living at home
$21,860	$21,860	$21,860

STETSON UNIVERSITY COLLEGE OF LAW

*ABA
Approved
Since
1930*

GPA and LSAT Scores

	Total	Full-Time	Part-Time
# of apps	3,192	2,814	378
# of offers	1,210	1,095	115
# of matrics	344	277	67
75% GPA	3.57	3.58	3.52
Median GPA	3.34	3.36	3.26
25% GPA	3.11	3.13	2.98
75% LSAT	157	158	157
Median LSAT	155	155	154
25% LSAT	153	153	152

Grants and Scholarships (from prior year)

	Total		Full-Time		Part-Time	
	#	%	#	%	#	%
Total # of students	1,081		867		214	
Total # receiving grants	303	28.0	273	31.5	30	14.0
Less than 1/2 tuition	96	8.9	86	9.9	10	4.7
Half to full tuition	79	7.3	69	8.0	10	4.7
Full tuition	72	6.7	65	7.5	7	3.3
More than full tuition	56	5.2	53	6.1	3	1.4
Median grant amount			$8,395		$5,700	

Informational and Library Resources

Total amount spent on library materials	$1,605,666
Study seating capacity inside the library	863
# of full-time equivalent professional librarians	9
Hours per week library is open	93
# of open, wired connections available to students	1,595
# of networked computers available for use by students	117
Has wireless network?	Y
Requires computer?	Y

JD Attrition (from prior year)

	Academic	Other	Total	
	#	#	#	%
1st year	7	12	19	5.3
2nd year	1	23	24	6.3
3rd year	0	0	0	0.0
4th year	0	0	0	0.0

Employment (9 months after graduation)

For up-to-date employment data, go to
employmentsummary.abaquestionnaire.org on the ABA website.

Bar Passage Rates

First-time takers	291	Reporting %	100.00
Average school %	75.94	Average state %	77.63

Average pass difference −1.69

Jurisdiction	Takers	Passers	Pass %	State %	Diff %
Florida	291	221	75.94	77.63	−1.69

STETSON UNIVERSITY COLLEGE OF LAW

1401 61st Street South
Gulfport, FL 33707
Phone: 727.562.7802; Fax: 727.343.0136
E-mail: lawadmit@law.stetson.edu; Website: www.law.stetson.edu

Introduction

Founded in 1900, Stetson University College of Law is Florida's first law school. The law school's main campus is in Gulfport, a suburb of St. Petersburg, and was originally built as a resort complex with magnificent Mediterranean Revival architecture. A satellite campus in downtown Tampa hosts some classes in our part-time and full-time JD programs and houses the Tampa branch of Florida's Second District Court of Appeal. Stetson is fully accredited by the American Bar Association and has been an Association of American Law Schools member since 1931. The college is an equal opportunity educational institution. For additional information, visit www.law.stetson.edu.

Dolly and Homer Hand Law Library and Physical Facilities

Stetson's amazing facilities boast seven courtrooms—including the nation's first elder-friendly courtroom—and modern classrooms designed to enhance the learning experience. The Student Center features organizational offices, interviewing rooms, a gym, a pool, and nearby athletic fields. The Hand Law Library in Gulfport and the satellite library in Tampa form one of the Southeast's most advanced research and communications technology centers. Housing more than 420,000 volumes and providing 48 group-study rooms, this library system offers 24/7 swipe card access, wireless access to many online databases, and outstanding legal reference assistance with nine professional librarians on staff. There is a laptop requirement for all students.

Admission

Last year, Stetson received 3,217 applications, offered admission to 1,210 applicants, and enrolled 344 first-year students: 277 full time and 67 part time. The 2011 entering class included 25 percent minority students and 44.5 percent women; 113 undergraduate institutions, 30 states, and 3 countries were represented within the group of new students. These numbers represent the fall full-time and part-time 2011 entering classes. We no longer offer a spring JD start date. The student body consists of approximately 842 full-time and 225 part-time JD students, 19 students in the International Law LLM program (from 13 countries), and 36 Elder Law LLM students (online program). Our students, faculty, and staff work together toward one common goal: preparing our students to be the best lawyers and leaders possible.

Faculty

The intellectual exchange among students and faculty continues, both inside and outside the classroom. The 63 full-time professors are engaged in projects that bring Stetson regional, national, and international prominence, but make teaching and working with students their top priority. Each semester, the full-time faculty is supplemented by approximately 54 practicing attorneys and judges who serve as adjunct professors in specialized areas.

Curriculum

A balanced curriculum blends fundamental courses, practical training, and a diverse range of electives. Stetson is a pioneer and a national leader in advocacy and clinical training.

Stetson's academic success programs include advising, an academic orientation, bar exam preparation led by a full-time director of bar preparation services, a for-credit Multistate Strategies course, courses that fuse academic and critical thinking skills with substantive content, and skills workshops designed to help students realize their academic potential. All JD students must complete a pro bono graduation requirement, and first-year students participate in the Professionalism Series.

Clinics and Internships: Stetson offers upper-level students a wide variety of opportunities to work closely with attorneys and judges, and, in some cases, actually represent clients and try cases under the supervision of an attorney. Clinics and internships are available in the areas of bankruptcy, child advocacy, elder law, civil poverty, consumer protection, environmental law, labor and employment law, family law, government and administrative law, federal and state litigation, corporate law, intellectual property, immigration, criminal prosecution and federal and state defense, military justice and veterans law, as well as a variety of judicial internships at the federal and state levels, including opportunities with state supreme courts in Florida and Georgia.

Certificates of Concentration: Students may apply to a certificate program in advocacy, elder law, environmental law, or international law. Students focus their elective credits, receive mentoring, and volunteer pro bono service in their chosen concentration.

Advocacy: Stetson is recognized as one of the best law schools for advocacy. Stetson's teams routinely win international, national, regional, and state mock trial, moot court, and alternative dispute resolution competitions.

Academic Journals: The *Stetson Law Review* publishes three issues each year. Stetson also publishes the *Journal of International Aging Law and Policy* in cooperation with AARP and the *Journal of International Wildlife Law and Policy*.

Honors Program: Full-time students who rank in the top 15 percent of their entering class after their first or second semester and part-time students who rank in the top 15 percent of their entering class after their first or second year are invited to interview for a spot in the Honors Program, which features a special colloquium and seminar. Honors Program students also are invited to attend faculty colloquia and other special events.

Expenses and Financial Aid

Full-time tuition for 2011–2012 (fall/spring) was $35,146, and part-time tuition for 2011–2012 (fall/spring/summer) was $30,577. Partial- and full-tuition scholarships are offered on a competitive basis. Additional scholarships are offered for continuing students. There is no financial aid deadline. Stetson offers a public service scholarship for third-year students and is a proud participant in the Department of Veterans Affairs Yellow Ribbon Program.

Special Programs

In addition to the traditional full-time program, Stetson offers a part-time evening JD program that allows students to earn a law degree in four years (including summers); part-time students must take classes at both the Gulfport and Tampa campuses. Qualified international attorneys may receive advanced standing to complete the JD program in two years. Stetson offers dual-degree programs for the JD/MBA, JD/MD, JD/MPH, and JD/Grado en Derecho (Spanish law degree). Stetson offers one- and two-semester exchange programs in France, Mexico, and Spain. Students may also study abroad in Argentina, China, England, the Netherlands, Spain, Switzerland, and the Cayman Islands. A rotating one-week travel experience is also offered; the 2012 trip is to Rome. A semester-abroad program in London is offered each fall. Stetson has Centers for Excellence in Advocacy, Elder Law, Higher Education Law and Policy, and International Law, as well as law and policy institutes for Biodiversity Law and Caribbean Law. Students may participate in a civil rights travel experience in the summer.

High-Profile Speakers and Conferences: Past speakers include US Supreme Court Justices Antonin Scalia and Clarence Thomas, Florida Supreme Court Justices, former US Attorney General Janet Reno, Innocence Project founder Barry Scheck, civil rights icon Congressman John Lewis, and Kenneth Feinberg. Students are encouraged to attend the numerous seminars and conferences sponsored by Stetson for practicing attorneys, judges, and other professionals.

Residential Life

Stetson offers a variety of housing opportunities on and near campus, including 49 dorm rooms, some of which are designated for special-needs students. The university also owns 43 single-family homes and a 32-unit apartment complex, all located within a few blocks of the campus. A waiting list is maintained for these spaces. The Office of Residential Life also maintains a roommates-wanted list and a general listing of other rental opportunities in the local area, although these rentals are not formally affiliated with Stetson.

Career Development

Stetson's commitment to empowering students and alumni to achieve their individual goals is reflected in its strong career development program. The Office of Career Development presents useful and practical career tools and services to help students launch the career they want, through individual and group coaching, programming on career strategy and planning, research, document preparation and publishing, communication and outreach, decision-making, and mentoring. Among the office's signature offerings are the ToolKit, a specially-designed career curriculum kicked off with full-day orientation and interactive walk-through, and the Solo Practice Institute and Network—a 3-day program with 12 months of subsequent monthly offerings offering solo Stetson alumni the foundational skills and mentors they will need to succeed. Alumni are located in 48 states, DC, 2 US territories, and 22 countries.

Office of Student Life

The Office of Student Life offers student activities that support Stetson's academic mission and enrich the law school experience, such as cultural programs, experiential education trips, pro bono service opportunities, and monthly leadership luncheons. Stetson has more than 45 diverse and active student organizations. The Student Bar Association is the umbrella organization under which all others are coordinated. The Stetson Chapter of the American Bar Association (ABA) Law Student Division has been recognized regionally and nationally as one of the largest and best, and the Student Leadership Development Program was awarded the ABA's prestigious E. Smythe Gambrell Professionalism Award for excellence in professionalism programming. A strong Office of Student Life presence on campus allows students many opportunities to hone their leadership and communication skills, network socially with their peers and legal professionals, and grow interpersonally as strong future members of the legal profession.

APPLICANT PROFILE

Stetson University College of Law
This grid includes only applicants who earned 120–180 LSAT scores under standard administrations.

LSAT Score	3.75 +		3.50–3.74		3.25–3.49		3.00–3.24		2.75–2.99		2.50–2.74		2.25–2.49		2.00–2.24		Below 2.00		No GPA		Total	
	Apps	Adm	Apps	Adm	Apps	Adm	Apps	Adm	Apps	Adm	Apps	Adm	Apps	Adm	Apps	Adm	Apps	Adm	Apps	Adm	Apps	Adm
175–180	0	0	0	0	0	0	0	0	0	0	0	0	0	0	0	0	0	0	0	0	0	0
170–174	1	1	0	0	1	1	0	0	0	0	0	0	0	0	0	0	0	0	0	0	2	2
165–169	12	11	12	12	14	13	7	7	4	4	5	4	5	2	1	0	1	1	3	3	64	57
160–164	42	42	65	63	57	56	48	47	19	18	20	12	13	10	3	1	1	0	1	1	269	250
155–159	94	93	124	122	147	139	124	100	83	54	52	17	22	7	10	0	0	0	6	6	662	538
150–154	77	55	158	103	192	91	185	49	126	19	67	5	36	2	17	0	2	0	9	5	869	329
145–149	46	7	88	6	134	9	161	3	112	1	70	0	37	0	16	0	3	0	12	0	679	26
140–144	16	0	43	1	67	0	87	1	90	0	52	0	34	0	15	0	4	0	7	0	415	2
135–139	3	0	9	0	27	0	23	0	37	0	27	0	19	0	5	0	2	0	8	0	160	0
130–134	1	0	6	0	5	0	14	0	10	0	7	0	7	0	2	0	1	0	6	0	59	0
125–129	2	0	0	0	1	0	2	0	0	0	2	0	2	0	2	0	1	0	0	0	12	0
120–124	0	0	0	0	0	0	0	0	1	0	0	0	0	0	0	0	0	0	1	0	2	0
Total	294	209	505	307	645	309	651	207	482	96	302	38	175	21	71	1	15	1	53	15	3193	1204

Apps = Number of Applicants   Adm = Number Admitted   Reflects 99% of the total applicant pool; highest LSAT data reported.

SUFFOLK UNIVERSITY LAW SCHOOL

David J. Sargent Hall, 120 Tremont Street
Boston, MA 02108-4977
Phone: 617.573.8144; Fax: 617.523.1367
E-mail: lawadm@suffolk.edu; Website: www.law.suffolk.edu

ABA
Approved
Since
1953

The Basics

Type of school	Private
Term	
Application deadline	3/1
Application fee	$60
Financial aid deadline	3/1
Can first year start other than fall?	No
Student to faculty ratio	17.0 to 1
# of housing spaces available restricted to law students	
graduate housing for which law students are eligible	

Faculty and Administrators

	Total		Men		Women		Minorities	
	Spr	Fall	Spr	Fall	Spr	Fall	Spr	Fall
Full-time	75	70	46	41	29	29	12	11
Other full-time	5	6	1	1	4	5	0	0
Deans, librarians, & others who teach	16	15	9	9	7	6	1	1
Part-time	73	59	55	44	18	15	3	2
Total	169	150	111	95	58	55	16	14

Curriculum

	Full-Time	Part-Time
Typical first-year section size	90	90
Is there typically a "small section" of the first-year class, other than Legal Writing, taught by full-time faculty	Yes	No
If yes, typical size offered last year	45	
# of classroom course titles beyond 1st year curriculum	0	

# of upper division courses, excluding seminars, with an enrollment:		
Under 25	168	
25–49	76	
50–74	31	
75–99	6	
100+	16	

# of seminars	58	
# of seminar positions available	1,027	
# of seminar positions filled	649	273
# of positions available in simulation courses	1,135	
# of simulation positions filled	725	246
# of positions available in faculty supervised clinical courses	109	
# of faculty supervised clinical positions filled	90	19
# involved in field placements	113	18
# involved in law journals	139	23
# involved in moot court or trial competitions	135	22
# of credit hours required to graduate	84	

JD Enrollment and Ethnicity

	Men		Women		Full-Time		Part-Time		1st-Year		Total		JD Degs. Awd.
	#	%	#	%	#	%	#	%	#	%	#	%	
All Hispanics	23	2.6	41	5.2	49	4.5	15	2.6	33	6.2	64	3.8	12
Am. Ind./AK Nat.	2	0.2	4	0.5	5	0.5	1	0.2	3	0.6	6	0.4	1
Asian	48	5.4	80	10.1	92	8.4	36	6.2	43	8.1	128	7.6	46
Black/Af. Am.	17	1.9	30	3.8	35	3.2	12	2.1	18	3.4	47	2.8	12
Nat. HI/Pac. Isl.	1	0.1	0	0.0	1	0.1	0	0.0	0	0.0	1	0.1	0
2 or more races	33	3.7	21	2.7	38	3.5	16	2.8	22	4.1	54	3.2	12
Subtotal (minor.)	124	13.9	176	22.3	220	20.0	80	13.8	119	22.3	300	17.8	83
Nonres. Alien	16	1.8	21	2.7	24	2.2	13	2.2	16	3.0	37	2.2	14
White/Cauc.	733	82.4	578	73.1	837	76.0	474	81.7	399	74.7	1311	78.0	379
Unknown	17	1.9	16	2.0	20	1.8	13	2.2	0	0.0	33	2.0	19
Total	890	52.9	791	47.1	1101	65.5	580	34.5	534	31.8	1681		495

Transfers

Transfers in	23
Transfers out	19

Tuition and Fees

	Resident	Nonresident
Full-time	$42,660	$42,660
Part-time	$31,994	$31,994
Tuition Guarantee Program	N	

Living Expenses

Estimated living expenses for singles

Living on campus	Living off campus	Living at home
N/A	$21,414	$14,798

SUFFOLK UNIVERSITY LAW SCHOOL

ABA Approved Since 1953

GPA and LSAT Scores

	Total	Full-Time	Part-Time
# of apps	2,934	2,391	543
# of offers	2,038	1,673	365
# of matrics	538	360	178
75% GPA	3.49	3.47	3.55
Median GPA	3.26	3.26	3.26
25% GPA	2.94	2.92	2.97
75% LSAT	157	157	155
Median LSAT	154	155	152
25% LSAT	151	152	150

Grants and Scholarships (from prior year)

	Total #	Total %	Full-Time #	Full-Time %	Part-Time #	Part-Time %
Total # of students	1,681		1,090		591	
Total # receiving grants	727	43.2	569	52.2	158	26.7
Less than 1/2 tuition	549	32.7	409	37.5	140	23.7
Half to full tuition	137	8.1	122	11.2	15	2.5
Full tuition	35	2.1	33	3.0	2	0.3
More than full tuition	6	0.4	5	0.5	1	0.2
Median grant amount			$15,000		$6,500	

Informational and Library Resources

Total amount spent on library materials	$2,107,720
Study seating capacity inside the library	880
# of full-time equivalent professional librarians	15
Hours per week library is open	103
# of open, wired connections available to students	3,750
# of networked computers available for use by students	280
Has wireless network?	Y
Requires computer?	N

JD Attrition (from prior year)

	Academic #	Other #	Total #	Total %
1st year	8	21	29	5.5
2nd year	0	2	2	0.4
3rd year	0	0	0	0.0
4th year	1	0	1	0.8

Employment (9 months after graduation)

For up-to-date employment data, go to employmentsummary.abaquestionnaire.org on the ABA website.

Bar Passage Rates

First-time takers	496	Reporting %	77.82
Average school %	92.75	Average state %	89.67
Average pass difference	3.08		

Jurisdiction	Takers	Passers	Pass %	State %	Diff %
Massachusetts	386	358	92.75	89.67	3.08

SUFFOLK UNIVERSITY LAW SCHOOL

David J. Sargent Hall, 120 Tremont Street
Boston, MA 02108-4977
Phone: 617.573.8144; Fax: 617.523.1367
E-mail: lawadm@suffolk.edu; Website: www.law.suffolk.edu

Introduction

Suffolk University Law School has produced some of the nation's most distinguished legal professionals. Suffolk Law's curriculum combines a strong academic foundation with expertise in an array of specialty areas, and a nationally known faculty provides superior preparation for practice. Through clinical, internship, and public service opportunities, students earn credit while experiencing how the law works in the real world. Suffolk Law is an unmatched place to launch a successful career in the law.

Technology and Physical Facilities

Every seat in Sargent Hall's classrooms, library, and common areas has direct access to a high-speed network. Sargent Hall is wireless accessible throughout and all classrooms contain multimedia capabilities. A central media control room provides the ability to conduct videoconferencing and webcasting from any of the Law School's classrooms.

Concentrations and Joint-Degree Programs

Students may enroll in one of six concentrations: Business Law and Financial Services, Civil Litigation, Health and Biomedical Law, Intellectual Property (which includes a specialization in Patent Law), International Law, or Labor and Employment Law. Suffolk Law offers five, four-year, joint-degree programs that combine a Juris Doctor with a Master of Business Administration, Public Administration, International Economics, Finance, or Criminal Justice, as well as a three-year JD/MBA program.

Clinical and Internship Programs

Students are encouraged to enroll in one of our clinical programs. Suffolk Law's clinics include the Battered Women's Advocacy Program, Child Advocacy, Education Advocacy, Evening Landlord-Tenant, Family Advocacy, Health Law, Housing, Immigration, Indian Law and Indigenous Peoples, Investor Advocacy, Juvenile Internship Program, Juvenile Justice Center, Suffolk Defenders, and Suffolk Prosecutors. Additionally, students can participate in the Civil and Judicial Internship Program, interning in a variety of legal settings, including state and federal courts; federal, state, and local government agencies; legal aid organizations; public defenders' offices; and private law firms and companies.

Foreign and Graduate Programs

Suffolk Law, in conjunction with the University of Lund, offers a summer study-abroad program in Lund, Sweden. The program combines the strengths of our international law curriculum with the expertise offered by the University of Lund law faculty and the Swedish Bar and Judiciary.
Suffolk Law has an exclusive agreement with the Center for International Legal Studies (CILS) in Salzburg, Austria, to offer internships to US law students and externships to graduates with law degrees. International internships are available to JD students, and international externships are offered to LLM students and other postgraduates with law degrees.

Internships are available at law firms, businesses, and nonprofit organizations in almost every country of the world.
Suffolk Law offers two LLM degree programs. One is in Global Law and Technology, which offers specializations in Intellectual Property and Information Technology Law, Biotechnology and Health Law, International Law and Business, and US Law and Legal Methods. The second program is a General LLM, where students are able to custom design a program to best suit their own career goals. Students can choose from over 200 advanced elective courses, which are offered every year. Full-time and part-time schedules are offered. Enrollment begins in September or in January.

Academic Support Programs

The goal of the Academic Support Program (ASP) is to help students make the most of their abilities. To accomplish this goal, the faculty conducts weekly classes on such diverse topics as legal analysis and writing, course outlining, and time management. These optional classes are open to all first-year students. In addition, ASP professors are always available to meet with individual or small groups of students in order to address specific questions or issues. The ASP also has a lending library containing study aids and material on substantive legal topics. Additionally, the ASP library contains exercises on grammar, legal writing, and analysis. All students are encouraged to stop by and take advantage of these resources.

Scholarships and Loans

Suffolk Law participates in student financial aid programs to assist students in financing the cost of their legal education. Both need-based and merit-based aid is available. Financial aid awards (scholarships, grants, loans, and employment awards) are made to assist students in financing educational costs when their personal and family resources may not be sufficient. Merit-based scholarships are awarded by the law school's Admissions Committee at the time a candidate is admitted. These awards are made to students based on outstanding academic achievement.
In addition to the need-based grant and merit-based scholarship programs, Suffolk Law offers Sargent Scholarships ranging from $20,000 to full tuition to entering students with significant financial need and exceptional academic strength. All admitted students who apply for need-based financial aid are considered for an award.
Suffolk Law also has a Loan Repayment Assistance Program for students who, upon graduation, pursue low-income, public service, law-related employment.

Student Activities, Publications, and Opportunities

Students have a number of opportunities to develop legal skills outside of the classroom through participation in the *Suffolk University Law Review*, the *Suffolk Transnational Law Review*, the *Journal of High Technology Law* (www.jhtl.org), and the *Suffolk Journal of Health and Biomedical Law*. Students may also participate in the Moot Court Board (which also publishes the *Suffolk Journal of Trial and Appellate Advocacy*) as well as on moot court competition teams such as the National Trial Competition Team, ATLA Trial Team, Constitutional Law Team, Information Technology and Privacy Law Team, Intellectual Property Law Team, Jessup International Law Team, National Invitational Trial Tournament of Champions, and National Moot Court Team. Students can also join securities law student organizations and have the opportunity to participate in the governance of the Student Bar Association.

Career Development Office

Suffolk University Law School is committed to preparing students to serve diverse clients and communities. Suffolk Law graduates can be found in private practice; corporations; public interest organizations; the military; the executive, judicial, and legislative branches of government; and in rewarding careers outside the legal realm. The Career Development Office coordinates on- and off-campus recruitment programs and résumé collections throughout the academic year, and also maintains an extensive online job database, a resource library, and employment websites. Job searching support begins with a comprehensive career-based curriculum provided to first-year students and extends throughout students' time at the Law School and throughout graduates' professional careers. The Career Development Office offers one-on-one career counseling and coaching, résumé and cover letter critiques, mock interviews, and innovative programs, panels, workshops, and information sessions. Professional staff conduct employer visits and related job cultivation nationwide. The Career Development Office prides itself on connecting with students through personalized outreach and cutting-edge technology and makes sure all students are supported in their job searches and career development endeavors.

Peer Mentoring Program

This program helps nontraditional students transition to the law school environment. Suffolk University Law School defines nontraditional students as those who have been historically excluded or marginalized from the legal profession/law school community based on any of the following factors, including but not limited to race, ethnicity, socioeconomic status, or sexual orientation/identity.

This is a two week program that begins in the summer prior to the beginning of fall classes. Participating students attend classes on case briefing, outlining, stress management, and time management as well as programs with various affinity organizations, professors, and alumni. Additionally, students receive an upper-class mentor who will also assist in the students' transition to the law school community. Monthly brown bag lunches will take place throughout the academic year that will provide a continued and broader community of support for first-year students.

Rappaport Center for Law and Public Service

The Rappaport Center for Law and Public Service was established in 2006, with the generous support of the Phyllis and Jerome Lyle Rappaport Foundation. Leveraging Suffolk Law School's ideal downtown location and rich tradition of public service, the Rappaport Center brings together elected officials, senior policymakers, community advocates, private sector leaders, faculty, and students to engage in dialogue about important public policy issues. The center also provides career advising to students interested in public service, administers the law school's pro bono program, and is home to the highly competitive Rappaport Fellowship Program in Law and Public Policy. For more information about the Rappaport Center, please visit www.rappaportcenter.org.

APPLICANT PROFILE

Suffolk University Law School

LSAT Score	GPA								
	3.75 +	3.50–3.74	3.25–3.49	3.00–3.24	2.75–2.99	2.50–2.74	2.25–2.49	2.00–2.24	Below 2.00
175–180									
170–174									
165–169									
160–164									
155–159									
150–154									
145–149									
140–144									
135–139									
130–134									
125–129									
120–124									

Good Possibility   Possible   Unlikely

SUNY BUFFALO LAW SCHOOL

309 John Lord O'Brian Hall
Buffalo, NY 14260
Phone: 716.645.2907; Fax: 716.645.6676
E-mail: law-admissions@buffalo.edu; Website: www.law.buffalo.edu

The Basics

Type of school	Public
Term	Semester
Application deadline	3/1
Application fee	$75
Financial aid deadline	3/1
Can first year start other than fall?	No
Student to faculty ratio	12.5 to 1
# of housing spaces available restricted to law students	124
graduate housing for which law students are eligible	674

Curriculum

	Full-Time	Part-Time
Typical first-year section size	60	0
Is there typically a "small section" of the first-year class, other than Legal Writing, taught by full-time faculty	No	No
If yes, typical size offered last year		
# of classroom course titles beyond first-year curriculum	195	

# of upper division courses, excluding seminars, with an enrollment:		
Under 25	152	
25–49	43	
50–74	15	
75–99	2	
100+	1	

# of seminars	45	
# of seminar positions available	732	
# of seminar positions filled	496	0
# of positions available in simulation courses	1,928	
# of simulation positions filled	1,494	0
# of positions available in faculty supervised clinical courses	149	
# of faculty supervised clinical positions filled	114	0
# involved in field placements	166	0
# involved in law journals	323	0
# involved in moot court or trial competitions	86	0
# of credit hours required to graduate	90	

Faculty and Administrators

	Total		Men		Women		Minorities	
	Spr	Fall	Spr	Fall	Spr	Fall	Spr	Fall
Full-time	42	45	22	25	20	20	7	3
Other full-time	7	9	3	3	4	6	0	0
Deans, librarians, & others who teach	9	3	4	2	5	1	1	1
Part-time	72	36	45	25	27	11	7	4
Total	130	93	74	55	56	38	15	8

Transfers

Transfers in	24
Transfers out	11

Tuition and Fees

	Resident	Nonresident
Full-time	$20,718	$33,718
Part-time		
Tuition Guarantee Program	N	

JD Enrollment and Ethnicity

	Men		Women		Full-Time		Part-Time		1st-Year		Total		JD Degs. Awd.
	#	%	#	%	#	%	#	%	#	%	#	%	
All Hispanics	8	2.3	10	3.4	18	2.8	0	0.0	5	2.8	18	2.8	11
Am. Ind./AK Nat.	0	0.0	4	1.3	4	0.6	0	0.0	0	0.0	4	0.6	1
Asian	15	4.4	9	3.0	24	3.8	0	0.0	8	4.5	24	3.7	14
Black/Af. Am.	10	2.9	20	6.7	30	4.7	0	0.0	5	2.8	30	4.7	6
Nat. HI/Pac. Isl.	0	0.0	0	0.0	0	0.0	0	0.0	0	0.0	0	0.0	0
2 or more races	7	2.0	10	3.4	16	2.5	1	25.0	7	4.0	17	2.7	0
Subtotal (minor.)	40	11.7	53	17.8	92	14.4	1	25.0	25	14.2	93	14.5	32
Nonres. Alien	7	2.0	15	5.0	22	3.5	0	0.0	8	4.5	22	3.4	10
White/Cauc.	270	78.7	220	73.8	487	76.5	3	75.0	127	72.2	490	76.4	186
Unknown	26	7.6	10	3.4	36	5.7	0	0.0	16	9.1	36	5.6	16
Total	343	53.5	298	46.5	637	99.4	4	0.6	176	27.5	641		244

Living Expenses

Estimated living expenses for singles

Living on campus	Living off campus	Living at home
$20,274	$20,274	$20,274

SUNY BUFFALO LAW SCHOOL

*ABA
Approved
Since
1936*

GPA and LSAT Scores

	Total	Full-Time	Part-Time
# of apps	1,507	1,507	0
# of offers	583	583	0
# of matrics	175	175	0
75% GPA	3.70	3.70	0.00
Median GPA	3.57	3.57	0.00
25% GPA	3.36	3.36	0.00
75% LSAT	158	158	0
Median LSAT	157	157	0
25% LSAT	154	154	0

Grants and Scholarships (from prior year)

	Total		Full-Time		Part-Time	
	#	%	#	%	#	%
Total # of students	701		693		8	
Total # receiving grants	297	42.4	297	42.9	0	0.0
Less than 1/2 tuition	271	38.7	271	39.1	0	0.0
Half to full tuition	0	0.0	0	0.0	0	0.0
Full tuition	22	3.1	22	3.2	0	0.0
More than full tuition	4	0.6	4	0.6	0	0.0
Median grant amount			$5,000		$0	

Informational and Library Resources

Total amount spent on library materials	$1,157,081
Study seating capacity inside the library	590
# of full-time equivalent professional librarians	17.3
Hours per week library is open	104
# of open, wired connections available to students	25
# of networked computers available for use by students	48
Has wireless network?	Y
Requires computer?	N

JD Attrition (from prior year)

	Academic	Other	Total	
	#	#	#	%
1st year	0	0	0	0.0
2nd year	0	13	13	5.6
3rd year	1	0	1	0.4
4th year	0	0	0	0.0

Employment (9 months after graduation)

For up-to-date employment data, go to
employmentsummary.abaquestionnaire.org on the ABA website.

Bar Passage Rates

First-time takers	250	Reporting %	95.60
Average school %	83.68	Average state %	84.92
Average pass difference	−1.24		

Jurisdiction	Takers	Passers	Pass %	State %	Diff %
New York	239	200	83.68	84.92	−1.24

SUNY BUFFALO LAW SCHOOL

309 John Lord O'Brian Hall
Buffalo, NY 14260
Phone: 716.645.2907; Fax: 716.645.6676
E-mail: law-admissions@buffalo.edu; Website: www.law.buffalo.edu

New York State's Law School

SUNY Buffalo Law School is the only law school in the State University of New York system. Since 1887, our law school has prepared lawyers to practice in New York City; Washington, DC; and other major cities across the country and around the world. The University at Buffalo campus provides its 30,000 students access to vast resources in world-class undergraduate and graduate fields of study that include medicine, engineering, pharmaceutical sciences, and business management. Each year, we graduate over 200 well-educated and diverse lawyers who are ready to practice law in fields such as corporate law, tax law, public service, criminal law, and intellectual property.

Located in Amherst, New York—a suburb of Buffalo—the Law School has a small-school feel with all the advantages of a large university, including access to other professional and graduate departments, Division I sports, a fine arts center, a concert hall, and numerous other academic, social, and cultural opportunities. The greater Buffalo area offers a wide variety of social and cultural activities such as downhill skiing, water sports, professional sports, a world-class symphony orchestra, professional theaters, nightlife, and access to Canada, all within minutes of the Law School. You can live comfortably, not to mention affordably, in Buffalo, the second largest city in New York.

Library and Physical Facilities

The Law School is housed in John Lord O'Brian Hall, a seven-story building that includes a state-of-the-art courtroom that provides students with an opportunity to watch judges and lawyers in action. The library is the core of the Law School, occupying six of the seven floors, including a law-student-only reading room with space for 84 students.

Like the Law School, the law library is committed to providing students with exceptional research and writing instructors. This enables first-year law students to gain one-on-one instruction in various research methods.

In January 2011, the Law School unveiled a newly renovated student lounge and classrooms. The Law School has also added state-of-the-art technology to enhance faculty teaching and student learning.

Curriculum

The Law School provides a flexible curriculum that affords students a broad range of curricular options, practical coursework, and special programs. Our curriculum emphasizes the study of law as well as the practical application of law to prepare our students to practice their profession upon graduation. The Law School offers a large number of interdisciplinary courses in a variety of programs and concentrations that include Family Law, Finance Transactions, Labor and Employment Law, Environmental Law, Civil Litigation, Criminal Law, International Law, and Intellectual Property.

Instruction is offered in two semesters from early September to May, including a January bridge term and a summer session from mid-May to mid-July. Six full-time

semesters or five full-time semesters plus two summer sessions are required for graduation.

Beyond the first year, students are required to complete 60 semester credit hours, including at least one seminar and three professional skills courses. The upper-division program is wholly elective.

The Law School also offers the LLM degree in Criminal Law and a general LLM for international and domestic students. For international students, there are special courses designed to introduce them to American law and to prepare them for the New York State Bar exam. All students benefit from our small-group personalized approach that allows them to design their own curriculum.

Dual-Degree Programs—The State University of New York at Buffalo is New York State's largest campus in its university system. The campus includes nationally recognized schools of Pharmacy and Pharmaceutical Sciences, Medicine and Biomedical Sciences, and Engineering and Applied Sciences. Access to these and many other graduate and professional schools within the campus offer unparalleled access to dual-degree programs, which permit students to earn credit toward a master's or PhD degree jointly with the JD. In recent years, the most active dual-degree programs have been with management, political science, philosophy, public health, legal information management and analysis, social work, sociology, and economics.

Legal Skills

The SUNY Buffalo Law School's Legal Skills Initiative is the cornerstone of the school's curriculum. The initiative focuses on developing and producing practice-ready lawyers who are able to meet the challenges of the legal profession. A key component of the initiative is the Legal Analysis, Writing, and Research (LAWR) program. The three semesters of required LAWR coursework allow every student to receive the necessary training in these skills broken into manageable segments.

Another integral part of the Legal Skills Initiative is the Trial Technique Program, which includes our Buffalo-Niagara Trial Tournament, Trial Teams, and Trial Technique classes. Each year, SUNY Buffalo Law hosts the Buffalo-Niagara Trial Tournament, which draws over 125 students from over 30 law schools around the nation. In recent years Buffalo Law's Trial Team has won more awards than any other school at the American Bar Association regional competition. Our Trial Technique classes culminate each semester with a mock trial in a downtown Buffalo courtroom.

Special Programs

Clinical Programs—Skills training in the clinical program is coordinated with substantive law courses to give students a theoretical understanding of practical issues. Students serve clients and conduct research and fieldwork in areas such as economic development, affordable housing, mediation, family violence, elder law, and environmental and development law.

New York City Program in Finance and Law—Provides SUNY Buffalo law students with an introduction to New York City's financial markets and a gateway to its highly competitive financial-sector job market. Each year, approximately 25 students are selected to participate in this unique program, which is located in New York City.

Externships

Each semester over 50 law school students are placed in supervised externships and another 20 or more students are placed in judicial clerkships. Externships and judicial clerkships provide law students with unique legal and public service experience as they work in a variety of government and nonprofit organizations, and get credit for doing so. Students learn how to work with a client and address the client's specific needs and goals—something that's difficult to teach in a classroom.

Our students help judges, attorneys, and legislators with pressing legal questions that arise in ongoing cases, in the development of public policy or legislation, and in response to citizen inquiries or problems.

Law School Culture and Student Activities

SUNY Buffalo Law School students experience a relaxed, friendly, and collaborative atmosphere. There are ample extracurricular activities. The Student Bar Association, an elected representative body, oversees all law school student organizations. Our Moot Court Board sponsors mock appellate practice competitions. The *Opinion* is the student newspaper, the *Buffalo Law Review* is a professional journal edited by students, and there are specialty journals in environmental law, affordable housing and community development law, intellectual property, criminal law, human rights law, and social policy concerning women.

Admission

Each year the SUNY Buffalo Law School enrolls about 200 first-year students. All first-year students start in the fall semester. Transfer and visiting students can start in either the fall or spring semesters. Our application priority deadline is March 1. The LSAT and LSAC Credential Assembly Service are required.

Although we have a limited number of seats for each incoming class, we do consider qualitative factors in addition to the traditional quantitative factors (GPA and LSAT). These factors include, but are not limited to, academic achievement, personal statements, character traits, writing ability, recommendations, and work experience. If an application reveals that the applicant has been educationally, socially, economically, or otherwise disadvantaged, the Admissions Committee will review the application for signs of achievement that should lead to success in law school.

Expenses and Financial Aid

SUNY Buffalo is able to offer state-subsidized tuition to New York residents and a reasonable out-of-state tuition charge. In-state tuition; out-of-state tuition; estimated additional expenses—$22,000. (Tuition and living expenses are subject to change without notice.)

This results in overall educational expenses that are less than half the cost of many law schools. Dean's tuition waivers and scholarships are available to students demonstrating high academic achievement, and state aid is offered on a need basis to qualified students. Additional alumni-sponsored scholarships are offered to second- and third-year students.

Career Services

The ultimate goal of nearly every law student is establishing his or her career upon graduation. Ninety-six percent of the SUNY Buffalo Law School graduates find positions or enter advanced degree programs within months of their graduation. Our Career Services Office (CSO) provides job-search and résumé services for third-year and LLM students, and helps first- and second-year students conduct their summer job searches. As products of New York State's Law School, many SUNY Buffalo graduates find employment in New York City and Buffalo; however, many of our graduates also find positions in other regions of the country.

For more information about career services, contact the office: telephone, 716.645.2056; fax, 716.645.7336; e-mail, law-careers@buffalo.edu.

APPLICANT PROFILE

SUNY Buffalo Law School
This grid includes only applicants who earned 120–180 LSAT scores under standard administrations.

LSAT Score	GPA															
	3.75 +		3.50–3.74		3.25–3.49		3.00–3.24		2.75–2.99		2.50–2.74		Below 2.50		No GPA		Total	
	Apps	Adm	Apps	Adm	Apps	Adm	Apps	Adm	Apps	Adm	Apps	Adm	Apps	Adm	Apps	Adm	Apps	Adm
170–180	4	4	1	1	1	1	3	3	1	0	0	0	1	1	1	1	12	11
165–169	19	19	26	25	7	7	8	8	3	3	5	2	3	1	0	0	71	65
160–164	50	50	51	49	43	41	24	23	21	17	5	5	11	4	2	1	207	190
155–159	54	48	71	57	102	54	71	35	37	13	18	4	13	2	9	6	375	219
150–154	46	26	92	36	95	20	90	9	64	3	27	1	25	0	10	0	449	95
145–149	12	4	43	10	53	1	54	1	54	1	20	0	23	0	6	0	265	17
140–144	7	0	24	1	22	0	26	0	24	0	19	0	20	0	4	0	146	1
Below 140	3	0	7	0	12	0	12	0	14	0	13	0	17	0	5	0	83	0
Total	195	151	315	179	335	124	288	79	218	37	107	12	113	8	37	8	1608	598

Apps = Number of Applicants   Adm = Number Admitted   Reflects 99% of the total applicant pool; highest LSAT data reported.

SYRACUSE UNIVERSITY COLLEGE OF LAW

Office of Admissions and Financial Aid, Suite 340
Syracuse, NY 13244-1030
Phone: 315.443.1962; Fax: 315.443.9568
E-mail: admissions@law.syr.edu; Website: www.law.syr.edu

ABA
Approved
Since
1923

The Basics

Type of school	Private
Term	Semester
Application deadline	4/1
Application fee	$75
Financial aid deadline	2/15
Can first year start other than fall?	No
Student to faculty ratio	12.9 to 1
# of housing spaces available restricted to law students	
graduate housing for which law students are eligible	

Faculty and Administrators

	Total		Men		Women		Minorities	
	Spr	Fall	Spr	Fall	Spr	Fall	Spr	Fall
Full-time	41	41	27	27	14	14	7	6
Other full-time	15	13	6	5	9	8	4	3
Deans, librarians, & others who teach	7	6	3	2	4	4	1	1
Part-time	24	23	20	16	4	7	0	0
Total	87	83	56	50	31	33	12	10

Curriculum

		Full-Time	Part-Time
Typical first-year section size		65	0
Is there typically a "small section" of the first-year class, other than Legal Writing, taught by full-time faculty		Yes	No
If yes, typical size offered last year		45	
# of classroom course titles beyond first-year curriculum		113	
# of upper division courses, excluding seminars, with an enrollment:	Under 25	115	
	25–49	26	
	50–74	10	
	75–99	2	
	100+	0	
# of seminars		16	
# of seminar positions available		190	
# of seminar positions filled		156	0
# of positions available in simulation courses		548	
# of simulation positions filled		429	0
# of positions available in faculty supervised clinical courses		142	
# of faculty supervised clinical positions filled		139	0
# involved in field placements		123	0
# involved in law journals		101	0
# involved in moot court or trial competitions		51	0
# of credit hours required to graduate		87	

JD Enrollment and Ethnicity

	Men		Women		Full-Time		Part-Time		1st-Year		Total		JD Degs. Awd.
	#	%	#	%	#	%	#	%	#	%	#	%	
All Hispanics	12	3.2	9	3.3	20	3.1	1	20.0	7	2.8	21	3.3	14
Am. Ind./AK Nat.	2	0.5	1	0.4	3	0.5	0	0.0	2	0.8	3	0.5	0
Asian	24	6.5	25	9.1	47	7.3	2	40.0	17	6.7	49	7.6	25
Black/Af. Am.	9	2.4	9	3.3	18	2.8	0	0.0	8	3.2	18	2.8	8
Nat. HI/Pac. Isl.	0	0.0	1	0.4	1	0.2	0	0.0	0	0.0	1	0.2	0
2 or more races	17	4.6	12	4.4	29	4.5	0	0.0	15	5.9	29	4.5	35
Subtotal (minor.)	64	17.3	57	20.7	118	18.4	3	60.0	49	19.4	121	18.8	82
Nonres. Alien	12	3.2	6	2.2	18	2.8	0	0.0	12	4.7	18	2.8	7
White/Cauc.	271	73.2	197	71.6	467	73.0	1	20.0	183	72.3	468	72.6	60
Unknown	23	6.2	15	5.5	37	5.8	1	20.0	8	3.2	38	5.9	43
Total	370	57.4	275	42.6	640	99.2	5	0.8	253	39.2	645		192

Transfers

Transfers in	3
Transfers out	17

Tuition and Fees

	Resident	Nonresident
Full-time	$45,647	$45,647
Part-time		
Tuition Guarantee Program		N

Living Expenses

Estimated living expenses for singles

Living on campus	Living off campus	Living at home
$19,353	$19,353	$19,353

SYRACUSE UNIVERSITY COLLEGE OF LAW

*ABA
Approved
Since
1923*

GPA and LSAT Scores

	Total	Full-Time	Part-Time
# of apps	2,484	2,484	0
# of offers	1,190	1,190	0
# of matrics	255	255	0
75% GPA	3.56	3.56	0.00
Median GPA	3.36	3.36	0.00
25% GPA	3.10	3.10	0.00
75% LSAT	157	157	0
Median LSAT	155	155	0
25% LSAT	153	153	0

Grants and Scholarships (from prior year)

	Total		Full-Time		Part-Time	
	#	%	#	%	#	%
Total # of students	638		635		3	
Total # receiving grants	454	71.2	454	71.5	0	0.0
Less than 1/2 tuition	346	54.2	346	54.5	0	0.0
Half to full tuition	86	13.5	86	13.5	0	0.0
Full tuition	10	1.6	10	1.6	0	0.0
More than full tuition	12	1.9	12	1.9	0	0.0
Median grant amount			$8,400		$0	

Informational and Library Resources

Total amount spent on library materials	$1,409,997
Study seating capacity inside the library	396
# of full-time equivalent professional librarians	10
Hours per week library is open	106
# of open, wired connections available to students	19
# of networked computers available for use by students	76
Has wireless network?	Y
Requires computer?	Y

JD Attrition (from prior year)

	Academic	Other	Total	
	#	#	#	%
1st year	14	21	35	13.9
2nd year	1	21	22	11.4
3rd year	0	7	7	3.6
4th year	0	0	0	0.0

Employment (9 months after graduation)

For up-to-date employment data, go to employmentsummary.abaquestionnaire.org on the ABA website.

Bar Passage Rates

First-time takers	190	Reporting %	100.00
Average school %	70.54	Average state %	83.05
Average pass difference	−12.51		

Jurisdiction	Takers	Passers	Pass %	State %	Diff %
New York	125	88	70.40	84.92	−14.52
California	18	6	33.33	71.24	−37.91
Maryland	10	7	70.00	79.96	−9.96
Illinois	4	2	50.00	89.38	−39.38
Others (13)*	33	31	93.94		

SYRACUSE UNIVERSITY COLLEGE OF LAW

Office of Admissions and Financial Aid, Suite 340
Syracuse, NY 13244-1030
Phone: 315.443.1962; Fax: 315.443.9568
E-mail: admissions@law.syr.edu; Website: www.law.syr.edu

Introduction

Syracuse University College of Law was established in 1895. The College of Law is a charter member of the AALS and is fully approved by the ABA. Embedded in a dynamic teaching and research university, the College of Law is one of the oldest of the 11 schools and colleges comprising Syracuse University. The College of Law complex is located on the 200-acre SU main campus overlooking scenic Central New York and the city of Syracuse.

Curriculum

Syracuse University College of Law's mission is guided by the philosophy that the best way to educate lawyers to practice in today's world is to engage them in a process of interdisciplinary learning while teaching them to apply what they learn in the classroom to real legal issues, problems, and clients. Beginning in the first year and continuing throughout the curriculum, students are exposed to educational settings that integrate opportunities to acquire a better understanding of legal theory and doctrine, develop professional skills, and gain exposure to the values and ethics of the legal profession. As a result, Syracuse students are better prepared for the practice of law.

Interdisciplinary Learning Opportunities

- **Disability Law and Policy Program**—Students may pursue a joint degree in law and disability studies and certificate programs in disability law and policy. Coursework, internships, and the Disability Rights Clinic push the boundaries of a traditional legal education and engage students in hands-on learning for the public good.
- **Institute for National Security and Counterterrorism (INSCT)**—The institute, a joint enterprise of the College of Law and the Maxwell School of Citizenship and Public Affairs, is dedicated to interdisciplinary teaching, research, and public service focused on important national and global problems of security and terrorism. INSCT students pursuing professional and doctoral degrees engage in advanced coursework toward specialty certificates in security and terrorism studies. The institute's research portfolio is broad and deep, ranging from faculty-supervised student working papers and research reports, to significant articles and books for academic journals and presses, to sponsorship of major workshops and conferences designed to further a research agenda in security or terrorism. While all INSCT research advances knowledge in the field, many projects are conducted on behalf of, or in consultation with, agencies, municipalities, and other public entities, thus providing direct public service.
- **Technology Commercialization Law Program**—The program is a course concentration within the law curriculum that provides an interdisciplinary and applied approach to the study of commercial development of new technologies. The program combines classroom courses, case study problem-solving, negotiation and drafting exercises, and applied research projects.
- **Family Law and Social Policy Center**—The center prepares students for a career in family law by engaging them in interdisciplinary research, providing them with applied learning experiences, and connecting them with the community to provide services that benefit families and children. The center offers opportunities that blend interdisciplinary theory and practice in the field of family law in challenging and rewarding ways. These combined experiences allow students to emerge from the program with the professional skills and experiences necessary to launch successful and satisfying careers in family law.
- **Center for Global Law and Practice**—The center provides students with specialized foreign, comparative, and international courses as well as cocurricular offerings. Students are exposed to the myriad ways in which the process of globalization increasingly impacts trade and commerce; the environment; national, regional, and local governments; individual rights and welfare; and even the legal profession itself. A summer-abroad program is offered in London.
- **Center for Indigenous Law, Governance, and Citizenship**—The center is a research-based law and policy institute focused on indigenous nations, their development, and their interaction with the US and Canadian governments.
- **Institute for the Study of the Judiciary, Politics, and the Media (IJPM)**—The institute is a collaborative effort between Syracuse University's College of Law, Maxwell School of Citizenship and Public Affairs, and the S. I. Newhouse School of Public Communications. The institute is devoted to the study of issues at the intersection of law, politics, and the media. The institute sponsors lectures, conferences, and symposia designed to foster discussion and debate among legal scholars, sitting judges, and working journalists.
- **Center on Property, Citizenship, and Social Entrepreneurism**—The center brings together experts from a variety of fields and institutions to discuss and explore issues related to modern real estate transactions and finance; community development and housing; global property law systems; and access to ownership for inclusion of the elderly, the poor, and persons with disabilities.
- **Burton Blatt Institute (BBI) Centers of Innovation on Disability**—Through research and scholarship in action, the institute will advance the civic, economic, and social participation of persons with disabilities in a global society. The institute seeks to create a collaborative environment—with entrepreneurial innovation and best business practices—to foster public-private dialogue, and create the capacity to transform policy, systems, and people through inclusive education, the workforce, and communities.

Other Opportunities for Specialization

- **Clinical Programs**—Legal concepts learned in the classroom come to life for students who participate in the in-house clinics and externship program. Students work with lawyers in law offices, becoming immersed in the actual practice of law through their work on real cases affecting real clients. Students provide much-needed legal services to our community, as many of our clients are unable to afford private counsel. Diverse clinical opportunities at the College of Law include the Criminal Defense Law Clinic, the Community Development Law Clinic, the Children's Rights and Family Law Clinic, the Disability Rights Clinic, the Elder Law Clinic, the Low Income Taxpayer Law Clinic, and the Securities Arbitration Clinic/Consumer Law Clinic. In addition, the externship program provides opportunities for students to work in government offices, judges' chambers, university-based programs, and public interest organizations.

- **Joint-Degree Programs**—Students who desire a greater degree of specialization may select from a number of joint-degree opportunities. Formal joint-degree programs exist in public administration, international relations, business administration or accounting, communications, environmental law, education (disability studies), social work, and engineering. Joint degrees may also be designed to fit special career objectives.
- **Advocacy Skills**—Syracuse Law is recognized for its exceptional advocacy programs. Students are actively involved, and have been highly successful, in national and regional moot court competitions. Syracuse students participate in intraschool programs throughout the year in trial and appellate competitions covering a wide variety of areas.

Library

The law library's four spacious levels within the College of Law complex house more than 473,000 volumes in print and microform; 2,200 serials; and extensive audio, video, and electronic holdings—all accessible through the university-wide online library catalog. On the main floor, the circulation and reference desks offer conveniently located services and research support in close proximity to the Electronic Research Center. The library adds approximately 2,500 new titles to its catalog each year, including a growing number of licensed electronic databases.

Admission

History reveals that undergraduate grades and LSAT scores are reliable measures, in most cases, for predicting probable success in law study. Thus, an index combining grades and test scores becomes a factor in most admission decisions. However, recognizing that numerical indicators are not always the best predictors of success in law school—even when considered in combination with other factors—the college admits a limited number of students each year through its Legal Education Opportunity (LEO) Program. The program's dual objectives are to recruit and admit persons who may have been deprived of equal education opportunities for reasons of race, gender, poverty, or other factors beyond their control; and to recruit and admit persons with unusual accomplishments, backgrounds, and experiences that suggest traditional admission criteria may be inadequate predictors of likely success in law study.

Financial Aid

The college is committed to assisting students in financing their legal education through a comprehensive financial aid program. Awards are made from a variety of sources, including merit-based scholarships; need-based tuition grants; and from federal sources, including the work-study program and the Perkins and Direct Loan programs.

Professional and Career Development

The Office of Professional and Career Development provides a full range of career-oriented services to students, including a broad mix of innovative and traditional support. Programming is designed to prepare students for leadership, service, and professionalism, while developing their ability to deal with lifelong career planning. The Professional and Career Development staff work one-on-one with students assisting them in crafting job search strategies that focus on their interests and capitalize on their strengths.

APPLICANT PROFILE

Syracuse University College of Law
This grid includes only applicants who earned 120–180 LSAT scores under standard administrations.

LSAT Score	3.75 +		3.50–3.74		3.25–3.49		3.00–3.24		2.75–2.99		2.50–2.74		2.25–2.49		2.00–2.24		Below 2.00		No GPA		Total	
	Apps	Adm	Apps	Adm	Apps	Adm	Apps	Adm	Apps	Adm	Apps	Adm	Apps	Adm	Apps	Adm	Apps	Adm	Apps	Adm	Apps	Adm
170–180	1	1	0	0	0	0	1	1	0	0	1	1	1	0	0	0	0	0	0	0	4	3
165–169	5	5	14	13	8	7	14	14	3	3	7	4	2	0	0	0	0	0	2	1	55	47
160–164	29	29	50	49	40	39	31	31	27	22	17	6	9	0	6	0	0	0	5	3	214	179
155–159	58	56	144	140	171	163	146	136	82	59	38	11	13	0	10	0	0	0	17	5	679	570
150–154	76	53	164	105	212	119	193	80	131	28	63	2	22	1	6	0	3	0	18	3	888	391
145–149	24	0	70	4	95	2	95	1	66	1	41	0	19	0	11	0	0	0	10	0	431	8
120–144	6	0	30	1	37	0	41	0	36	0	32	0	14	0	5	0	4	0	4	0	209	1
Total	199	144	472	312	563	330	521	263	345	113	199	24	80	1	38	0	7	0	56	12	2480	1199

Apps = Number of Applicants
Adm = Number Admitted
Reflects 99% of the total applicant pool; highest LSAT data reported.

TEMPLE UNIVERSITY—JAMES E. BEASLEY SCHOOL OF LAW

1719 North Broad Street
Philadelphia, PA 19122
Phone: 800.560.1428; Fax: 215.204.9319
E-mail: lawadmis@temple.edu; Website: www.law.temple.edu

The Basics

Type of school	Public
Term	Semester
Application deadline	3/1
Application fee	$60
Financial aid deadline	3/1
Can first year start other than fall?	No
Student to faculty ratio	12.2 to 1
# of housing spaces available restricted to law students	
graduate housing for which law students are eligible	

Faculty and Administrators

	Total		Men		Women		Minorities	
	Spr	Fall	Spr	Fall	Spr	Fall	Spr	Fall
Full-time	60	58	35	34	25	24	15	13
Other full-time	0	0	0	0	0	0	0	0
Deans, librarians, & others who teach	11	12	5	5	6	7	2	2
Part-time	124	103	82	61	42	42	18	14
Total	195	173	122	100	73	73	35	29

Curriculum

	Full-Time	Part-Time
Typical first-year section size	60	60
Is there typically a "small section" of the first-year class, other than Legal Writing, taught by full-time faculty	No	No
If yes, typical size offered last year		

# of classroom course titles beyond first-year curriculum		191
# of upper division courses, excluding seminars, with an enrollment:	Under 25	208
	25–49	61
	50–74	13
	75–99	8
	100+	2
# of seminars		51
# of seminar positions available		768

	Full-Time	Part-Time
# of seminar positions filled	523	113
# of positions available in simulation courses	1,150	
# of simulation positions filled	761	142
# of positions available in faculty supervised clinical courses	74	
# of faculty supervised clinical positions filled	59	7
# involved in field placements	257	5
# involved in law journals	145	11
# involved in moot court or trial competitions	36	1
# of credit hours required to graduate	88	

JD Enrollment and Ethnicity

	Men		Women		Full-Time		Part-Time		1st-Year		Total		JD Degs. Awd.
	#	%	#	%	#	%	#	%	#	%	#	%	
All Hispanics	36	7.0	41	10.6	68	9.4	9	5.0	29	10.7	77	8.5	17
Am. Ind./AK Nat.	6	1.2	3	0.8	8	1.1	1	0.6	2	0.7	9	1.0	2
Asian	32	6.2	41	10.6	64	8.9	9	5.0	25	9.3	73	8.1	31
Black/Af. Am.	29	5.6	39	10.1	58	8.0	10	5.6	20	7.4	68	7.5	21
Nat. HI/Pac. Isl.	0	0.0	0	0.0	0	0.0	0	0.0	0	0.0	0	0.0	0
2 or more races	6	1.2	7	1.8	13	1.8	0	0.0	6	2.2	13	1.4	0
Subtotal (minor.)	109	21.2	131	33.9	211	29.2	29	16.1	82	30.4	240	26.6	71
Nonres. Alien	5	1.0	4	1.0	8	1.1	1	0.6	3	1.1	9	1.0	0
White/Cauc.	396	76.9	246	63.6	498	69.0	144	80.0	180	66.7	642	71.2	242
Unknown	5	1.0	6	1.6	5	0.7	6	3.3	5	1.9	11	1.2	6
Total	515	57.1	387	42.9	722	80.0	180	20.0	270	29.9	902		319

Transfers

Transfers in	3
Transfers out	7

Tuition and Fees

	Resident	Nonresident
Full-time	$19,788	$32,718
Part-time	$15,958	$26,308
Tuition Guarantee Program	N	

Living Expenses

Estimated living expenses for singles

Living on campus	Living off campus	Living at home
$20,684	$20,684	$15,118

TEMPLE UNIVERSITY—JAMES E. BEASLEY SCHOOL OF LAW

ABA
Approved
Since
1933

GPA and LSAT Scores

	Total	Full-Time	Part-Time
# of apps	4,144	3,739	405
# of offers	1,574	1,465	109
# of matrics	270	215	55
75% GPA	3.56	3.54	3.62
Median GPA	3.39	3.39	3.39
25% GPA	3.16	3.16	3.16
75% LSAT	163	163	160
Median LSAT	160	161	158
25% LSAT	158	158	157

Grants and Scholarships (from prior year)

	Total		Full-Time		Part-Time	
	#	%	#	%	#	%
Total # of students	983		797		186	
Total # receiving grants	454	46.2	423	53.1	31	16.7
Less than 1/2 tuition	354	36.0	326	40.9	28	15.1
Half to full tuition	16	1.6	16	2.0	0	0.0
Full tuition	84	8.5	81	10.2	3	1.6
More than full tuition	0	0.0	0	0.0	0	0.0
Median grant amount			$7,500		$3,750	

Informational and Library Resources

Total amount spent on library materials	$1,397,333
Study seating capacity inside the library	664
# of full-time equivalent professional librarians	13
Hours per week library is open	96
# of open, wired connections available to students	394
# of networked computers available for use by students	118
Has wireless network?	Y
Requires computer?	N

JD Attrition (from prior year)

	Academic	Other	Total	
	#	#	#	%
1st year	1	6	7	2.1
2nd year	1	8	9	3.1
3rd year	0	0	0	0.0
4th year	0	0	0	0.0

Employment (9 months after graduation)

For up-to-date employment data, go to employmentsummary.abaquestionnaire.org on the ABA website.

Bar Passage Rates

First-time takers	311	Reporting %	76.85
Average school %	92.05	Average state %	83.06
Average pass difference	8.99		

Jurisdiction	Takers	Passers	Pass %	State %	Diff %
Pennsylvania	239	220	92.05	83.06	8.99

TEMPLE UNIVERSITY—James E. BEASLEY SCHOOL OF LAW

1719 North Broad Street
Philadelphia, PA 19122
Phone: 800.560.1428; Fax: 215.204.9319
E-mail: lawadmis@temple.edu; Website: www.law.temple.edu

Introduction

Temple Law School is recognized both nationally and internationally as a leader in legal education. We offer both day and evening programs, and students may enroll on either a full- or part-time basis. Our innovative student-centered curriculum integrates both critical thinking and practical legal skills and has been developed in response to new realities and new challenges, such as globalization, technology, and interdisciplinary studies. Our students, faculty, and alumni are shaping the law at every level and are making an impact in Philadelphia, the United States, and around the world.

Located in the heart of a thriving, urban university, the law school complex consists of three recently renovated buildings designed to provide students with a state-of-the-art educational environment. Students at Temple build lawyering skills both in the classroom and in the law firms, courts, public service agencies, and financial institutions of Philadelphia, a major legal, commercial, and cultural center.

Temple students are bright, dynamic, and diverse. They come from a variety of backgrounds and disciplines. Many have traveled and lived in other countries, and their real-life experiences vitalize classroom discussion. A recent entering class hailed from 136 colleges and universities, and from 31 states and foreign countries. Ten percent had earned advanced degrees, and nearly 75 percent had at least one year of work experience before entering law school.

The faculty is an extraordinary group who are recognized throughout the world as legal experts, scholars, and policy makers. Their breadth of experience in virtually every area of practice brings a rich and distinctive quality to classroom discussions. While their accomplishments are many, it is the faculty's commitment to teaching that many students note as their greatest achievement.

The Study of Law at Temple

Trial skills enhance every lawyer's abilities in areas that intersect all aspects of practice, and Temple students benefit from one of the most advanced **trial advocacy** programs in the nation. Experienced faculty, innovative teaching methods, and extensive clinical offerings set Temple's program above the rest. The trial advocacy curriculum includes the innovative Integrated Program, which combines the teaching of trial advocacy, evidence, and civil procedure in a year-long course. Future litigators may also earn a Certificate in Trial Advocacy and Litigation by completing a robust list of advocacy courses and engaging in live client clinical experiences. Temple's reputation in trial advocacy programs is enhanced by our record in law school trial competitions, having won an unparalleled 21 consecutive National Trial Competition regional championships, 5 national championships, and 15 invitational tournaments.

Temple students have access to an extensive array of programs to prepare them to practice law in an increasingly global society. Temple's strength in **international law** includes opportunities for summer study in Rome, Italy, as well as a semester-abroad program in Tokyo, Japan, and exchange programs with law schools in China, Ireland, Israel, the Netherlands, Germany, India, Puerto Rico, and Switzerland. Additionally, Temple offers a Master of Laws program for international students holding foreign law degrees and has many active student organizations, such as an international law journal, the International Law Society, and the Jessup International Law Moot Court team. Temple's strong reputation in international law has been enhanced by the JD/LLM in Transnational Law for American law students; an LLM program in Beijing, China, in which Chinese lawyers study American law; and the creation of the Institute for International Law and Public Policy. Students may also design individualized study-abroad options at law schools around the world.

Temple is a pioneer in **intellectual property and technology law**, preparing students to learn and succeed in the virtual world. Temple has expanded the boundaries of traditional intellectual property law by integrating bodies of law that focus on the rapid expansion of the Internet, electronic commerce, biotechnologies, and other newly emerging legal issues. With faculty members who are experts in the field, and through hands-on activities outside the classroom, such as writing for a journal specializing in technology law or participating on the Intellectual Property Law Moot Court team, students learn how to meet the challenges of practicing law in a world without borders.

Temple offers superior training in **business and tax law**, including a creative program that combines the teaching of professional responsibility, substantive law courses, and business skills, such as interviewing, negotiating, and drafting. Prospective business lawyers can also pursue a JD/LLM in Taxation or, in conjunction with the Fox School of Business and Management, pursue a dual JD/MBA degree, or earn a Certificate in Business Law.

Temple's **health care law** curriculum explores the legal profession's role in the health care industry and prepares students to practice in the wide range of substantive areas that comprise health care law. In 2009, the Center for Health Law, Policy and Practice was created and, through a grant from the Robert Wood Johnson Foundation, Temple became home to the National Program Office of the foundation's Public Health Law Research Program. Students can further prepare to meet the challenges of this dynamic field by pursuing a dual JD/MPH degree.

Public service is a Temple tradition. The Office of Public Interest Programs is the focal point for public interest activities at the law school. Students provide legal services in the Philadelphia area through the extensive clinical program, the Temple Legal Aid Office, and various volunteer and community outreach programs. Public interest careers are supported by the Student Public Interest Network, which provides grants for summer internships; the Public Interest Scholars Program, which provides scholarships to entering students with a demonstrated commitment to public service; and the Barrack Public Interest Fellowships, a loan repayment assistance program for graduates in public interest jobs.

The curriculum is anchored by the first-year **legal research and writing program**. Instruction in law schools is founded on the notion of teaching each student to think like an attorney. Temple's legal research and writing program is a year-long course of study that teaches the basics of writing and speaking like a lawyer. Students learn basic legal research techniques and the fundamentals of legal writing. It is one of the most intensive and advanced programs of its kind in the country and is rated as one of the best in the nation.

Student Activities

Students are an integral part of policy making and governance at the law school. The Student Bar Association is the governing organization that oversees the more than 30 student groups that flourish at Temple, including the Black Law Students Association, the Latino Law Students Association, the Asian/Pacific Islander American Law Student Association, the Women's Law Caucus, and OUTLaw. Student publications include the *Temple Law Review;* the *Temple Journal of Science, Technology, and Environmental Law;* the *Temple International and Comparative Law Journal;* and the *Temple Political and Civil Rights Law Review*. Students who excel in advocacy may participate in the National Trial Team or the Moot Court Honor Society.

Career Planning

Temple students are poised and ready to succeed in every sector of the legal job market, having acquired unique practical training that other schools do not offer. As graduates, they carry a strong reputation for being able to hit the ground running, confident and prepared to practice law in the field of their choice. The Career Planning Office assists students with the development of strategies for securing employment and provides the resources necessary to supplement each student's individualized job search. Through the school's online career planning manager, students can search job postings,

participate in various recruiting programs, and apply for jobs. In addition, one-on-one career counseling is available, and workshops and programs are offered to assist students in sharpening their job-search skills, including résumé writing, networking, and interviewing. Temple alumni are working in all 50 states and around the world and in a variety of legal fields.

Admission and Financial Aid

Temple's highly competitive admission process is designed to look at the whole person. The faculty Admissions Committee carefully evaluates each application and is committed to admitting the very best from a pool of talented applicants. In keeping with Temple's commitment to diversity and its mission of offering opportunities to students who might otherwise be precluded from pursuing a high-quality legal education, the committee may consider an application under Sp.A.C.E., its discretionary admission process. Through this process, the committee carefully selects applicants who have outstanding performance records and exceptional aptitudes for the study and practice of law that are not necessarily reflected by grades and LSAT scores alone.

The financial aid program supports the admission process with a combination of loans and both need- and merit-based scholarships, including the Beasley Scholars program, Conwell Law Scholarships, Law Faculty Scholarships, the Rubin-Presser Public Interest Scholars program, and First Year Scholar Awards.

APPLICANT PROFILE

Temple University—James E. Beasley School of Law
This grid includes only applicants who earned 120–180 LSAT scores under standard administrations.

LSAT Score	GPA																					
	3.75 +		3.50–3.74		3.25–3.49		3.00–3.24		2.75–2.99		2.50–2.74		2.25–2.49		2.00–2.24		Below 2.00		No GPA		Total	
	Apps	Adm	Apps	Adm	Apps	Adm	Apps	Adm	Apps	Adm	Apps	Adm	Apps	Adm	Apps	Adm	Apps	Adm	Apps	Adm	Apps	Adm
170–180	28	26	24	24	13	13	12	10	3	3	6	4	1	1	2	2	0	0	2	1	91	84
165–169	69	67	92	89	90	86	69	63	19	13	19	8	8	4	1	0	0	0	4	3	371	333
160–164	172	149	292	260	269	219	213	159	74	42	25	12	23	12	3	1	0	0	15	6	1086	860
155–159	135	47	249	73	271	72	208	56	109	22	51	4	14	1	6	1	0	0	13	1	1056	277
150–154	80	4	138	10	184	10	193	5	89	1	43	0	23	0	5	0	2	0	11	0	768	30
145–149	34	1	66	1	76	0	98	1	68	0	47	0	21	0	10	0	1	0	14	0	435	3
140–144	6	0	24	0	46	0	52	0	29	0	26	0	13	0	7	0	4	0	2	0	209	0
Below 140	2	0	8	0	23	0	33	0	20	0	37	0	9	0	14	0	2	0	3	0	151	0
Total	526	294	893	457	972	400	878	294	411	81	254	28	112	18	48	4	9	0	64	11	4167	1587

Apps = Number of Applicants
Adm = Number Admitted
Reflects 99% of the total applicant pool; highest LSAT data reported.

UNIVERSITY OF TENNESSEE COLLEGE OF LAW

Admissions Office, 1505 W. Cumberland Avenue, Suite 161
Knoxville, TN 37996-1810
Phone: 865.974.4131; Fax: 865.974.1572
E-mail: lawadmit@utk.edu; Website: www.law.utk.edu

ABA
Approved
Since
1925

The Basics

Type of school	Public
Term	Semester
Application deadline	2/15
Application fee	$15
Financial aid deadline	3/1
Can first year start other than fall?	No
Student to faculty ratio	14.5 to 1
# of housing spaces available restricted to law students	
graduate housing for which law students are eligible	

Faculty and Administrators

	Total		Men		Women		Minorities	
	Spr	Fall	Spr	Fall	Spr	Fall	Spr	Fall
Full-time	28	27	19	17	9	10	3	3
Other full-time	3	3	0	1	3	2	0	0
Deans, librarians, & others who teach	15	15	5	6	10	9	1	1
Part-time	37	36	22	21	15	15	0	0
Total	83	81	46	45	37	36	4	4

Curriculum

	Full-Time	Part-Time
Typical first-year section size	55	0
Is there typically a "small section" of the first-year class, other than Legal Writing, taught by full-time faculty	Yes	No
If yes, typical size offered last year	16	

# of classroom course titles beyond first-year curriculum		90	
# of upper division courses, excluding seminars, with an enrollment:	Under 25	90	
	25–49	30	
	50–74	14	
	75–99	0	
	100+	0	
# of seminars		21	
# of seminar positions available		348	
# of seminar positions filled	299		0
# of positions available in simulation courses		784	
# of simulation positions filled	637		0
# of positions available in faculty supervised clinical courses		155	
# of faculty supervised clinical positions filled	155		0
# involved in field placements	60		0
# involved in law journals	224		0
# involved in moot court or trial competitions	45		0
# of credit hours required to graduate		89	

JD Enrollment and Ethnicity

	Men		Women		Full-Time		Part-Time		1st-Year		Total		JD Degs. Awd.
	#	%	#	%	#	%	#	%	#	%	#	%	
All Hispanics	16	5.8	14	6.6	30	6.2	0	0.0	12	7.5	30	6.2	8
Am. Ind./AK Nat.	1	0.4	1	0.5	2	0.4	0	0.0	1	0.6	2	0.4	1
Asian	6	2.2	14	6.6	20	4.1	0	0.0	3	1.9	20	4.1	7
Black/Af. Am.	18	6.5	31	14.6	49	10.1	0	0.0	18	11.3	49	10.1	23
Nat. HI/Pac. Isl.	1	0.4	0	0.0	1	0.2	0	0.0	1	0.6	1	0.2	0
2 or more races	14	5.1	5	2.4	19	3.9	0	0.0	11	6.9	19	3.9	5
Subtotal (minor.)	56	20.4	65	30.7	121	24.9	0	0.0	46	28.9	121	24.8	44
Nonres. Alien	1	0.4	1	0.5	2	0.4	0	0.0	0	0.0	2	0.4	1
White/Cauc.	215	78.2	145	68.4	359	73.9	1	100.0	111	69.8	360	73.9	97
Unknown	3	1.1	1	0.5	4	0.8	0	0.0	2	1.3	4	0.8	5
Total	275	56.5	212	43.5	486	99.8	1	0.2	159	32.6	487		147

Transfers

Transfers in	7
Transfers out	3

Tuition and Fees

	Resident	Nonresident
Full-time	$16,456	$35,200
Part-time		
Tuition Guarantee Program	N	

Living Expenses

Estimated living expenses for singles

Living on campus	Living off campus	Living at home
$18,594	$18,594	$12,914

UNIVERSITY OF TENNESSEE COLLEGE OF LAW

ABA
Approved
Since
1925

GPA and LSAT Scores

	Total	Full-Time	Part-Time
# of apps	1,277	1,277	0
# of offers	435	435	0
# of matrics	160	160	0
75% GPA	3.75	3.75	0.00
Median GPA	3.53	3.53	0.00
25% GPA	3.24	3.24	0.00
75% LSAT	162	162	0
Median LSAT	160	160	0
25% LSAT	156	156	0

Grants and Scholarships (from prior year)

	Total		Full-Time		Part-Time	
	#	%	#	%	#	%
Total # of students	482		482		0	
Total # receiving grants	299	62.0	299	62.0	0	0.0
Less than 1/2 tuition	228	47.3	228	47.3	0	0.0
Half to full tuition	58	12.0	58	12.0	0	0.0
Full tuition	1	0.2	1	0.2	0	0.0
More than full tuition	12	2.5	12	2.5	0	0.0
Median grant amount		$5,000			$0	

Informational and Library Resources

Total amount spent on library materials	$977,611
Study seating capacity inside the library	415
# of full-time equivalent professional librarians	7
Hours per week library is open	96
# of open, wired connections available to students	94
# of networked computers available for use by students	94
Has wireless network?	Y
Requires computer?	N

JD Attrition (from prior year)

	Academic	Other	Total	
	#	#	#	%
1st year	1	7	8	4.7
2nd year	2	0	2	1.3
3rd year	0	0	0	0.0
4th year	0	0	0	0.0

Employment (9 months after graduation)

For up-to-date employment data, go to employmentsummary.abaquestionnaire.org on the ABA website.

Bar Passage Rates

First-time takers	159	Reporting %	79.87
Average school %	89.76	Average state %	84.24
Average pass difference	5.52		

Jurisdiction	Takers	Passers	Pass %	State %	Diff %
Tennessee	127	114	89.76	84.24	5.52

UNIVERSITY OF TENNESSEE COLLEGE OF LAW

Admissions Office, 1505 W. Cumberland Avenue, Suite 161
Knoxville, TN 37996-1810
Phone: 865.974.4131; Fax: 865.974.1572
E-mail: lawadmit@utk.edu; Website: www.law.utk.edu

Introduction

For more than a century, the University of Tennessee College of Law has offered a strong combination of practical and theoretical legal training. Established in 1890, the College of Law is a charter member of the AALS and is ABA approved.

Enrollment/Student Body

The College of Law enrolls a small, selective, and diverse class each August. The 2011 entering class was composed of 160 students, of which 42 percent were women, 58 percent were men, and 29 percent were students of color. Entering students were graduates of 75 colleges and universities across the nation and around the world, and were residents of 16 states. Although many members of each entering class are pursuing a law degree directly from undergraduate school, a number of law students have advanced degrees and have had careers in fields as diverse as engineering, teaching, medicine, journalism, and business. In the 2011–2012 academic year, the student population of the College of Law is 486, of which 25 percent are students of color.

Faculty

The quality of our faculty is evidenced by their legal training at some of the finest law schools in the United States, the significance of their scholarly writings, their activity in professional associations, and their involvement with public service. Current students at UT tell potential candidates for admission that they find the faculty to be excellent teachers—accessible and caring.

College of Law, Library, and Physical Facilities

The law center at the University of Tennessee—a melding of the old with the new—is an exceptional setting for education in the twenty-first century. The 110,000-square-foot facility was completed in 1997 and is located on Cumberland Avenue, just across from the University Center, in the heart of the campus. The law center includes the Joel A. Katz Law Library, dedicated to a distinguished corporate and entertainment lawyer and alumnus.

Location

The College of Law is located on the main campus of the University of Tennessee. Knoxville is the largest city in eastern Tennessee and the third largest in the state. More than 28,000 students attend UTK. Knoxville has the natural advantage of being located in the foothills of the Great Smoky Mountains, making hiking, biking, golf, and fishing popular and accessible activities. Knoxville is close to major legal markets in the Southeast, including Atlanta, Nashville, Birmingham, and Charlotte.

Curriculum

First-year students begin law school with a week-long introductory period in which a series of minicourses introduce students to the study of law. Second- and third-year students may choose from over 90 elective courses. Two dual-degree programs are offered—the JD/MBA and the JD/MPA (Master of Public Administration).

The College of Law offers two optional concentrations for students. The **James L. Clayton Center for Entrepreneurial Law** offers integrated upper-division courses that expose students to facets of law that affect business deals and provide hands-on experience in negotiating and documenting transactions with insight into the needs and concerns of the business community. A **Business Clinic** is offered for students seeking practical experience working with business clients.

The **Center for Advocacy and Dispute Resolution** allows interested students to focus their second- and third-year experience toward a career in advocacy (commonly known as litigation or trial practice) with an expanded emphasis on alternative forms of dispute resolution. UT was recognized by the American College of Trial Lawyers for the 1996 Emil Gumpert Award for Excellence in Teaching Trial Advocacy.

The **Charles H. Miller Legal Clinic** is the site for UT's clinical programs. Established in 1947, this is one of the oldest continually operating clinical programs in the United States and is nationally recognized for excellence in teaching. UT also offers a Mediation Clinic, in which students work in teams to mediate real civil and misdemeanor cases in the lower courts. Other clinical programs currently focus on business, domestic violence, and environmental issues.

UT offers three **Externships**—judicial, prosecutorial, and public defender. The Prosecutorial Externship program enables students to prosecute real cases on behalf of the state under the supervision of experienced district attorneys in Knox County.

Student Activities and Programs

Students can choose from a variety of student programs, activities, publications, and organizations. A complete listing is available on our website.

Participation in UT's Moot Court program enables students to compete in intracollege and national competitions. A UT team placed second in the 2011 National Moot Court Competition and reached the "Sweet Sixteen" in 2012. In 2010, Tennessee fielded the national championship team in the Giles Sutherland Rich Memorial intellectual property moot court competition and placed first in the Region VII National Moot Court Competition. UT won three Jerome Prince Evidence Moot Court national championships and was the first team in the history of that competition to win back-to-back titles in 2000 and 2001.

The *Tennessee Law Review* offers participants an excellent opportunity to conduct legal research and produce writings of a scholarly and practical nature. *Transactions* provides an opportunity for students to write about topical issues and legal developments of interest to the business bar. Students participating in the *Tennessee Journal of Law and Policy* analyze the latest developments in law and public decision making. The Student Bar Association and various other student organizations offer numerous programs, services, and special events. The national honor society, Order of the Coif, and two leading professional fraternities, Phi Delta Phi and Phi Alpha Delta, have local chapters here.

UT Pro Bono is a student-directed, community service organization. Working with local attorneys and legal aid organizations, UT Pro Bono serves as a resource by providing law students for research, educational, and investigatory assistance. UT's Mentoring Program matches students with alumni who share common practice goals for structured experiences.

Admission

The College of Law strives to craft a class of diverse individuals, whose life experiences will enrich the law school community. Admission to the College of Law is competitive. The Admissions Committee places substantial emphasis on traditional indicators of performance—UGPA and LSAT score. The committee also considers factors such as improvement in undergraduate grades and graduate school performance, strength of undergraduate institution and major course of study, extracurricular activities, community service, and employment and professional experience. Also considered are circumstances that may have affected an applicant's grades or LSAT score; economic, social, or cultural background; and success in overcoming social or economic disadvantage. Applicants are required to submit two letters of recommendation and write a personal statement and an essay.

The College of Law recognizes its obligation to ensure legal education to qualified applicants who are members of historically underrepresented groups in the legal profession and encourages applications from such students.

Successful completion of the CLEO Summer Institute may also be considered by the Admissions Committee.

Expenses, Financial Aid, and Housing

The College of Law offers a number of scholarships for entering students. Scholarships may be based on academic credentials (LSAT score and UGPA), records of leadership and community service, or other factors as established by the scholarship donor. Candidates for admission should complete the FAFSA as soon as possible after the first of the year to be considered for scholarships in which financial need is a factor. Candidates for admission will automatically be considered for all scholarships for which they are eligible. Please check our website for more information and application guidelines. Campus apartment housing is open to law students. Knoxville also offers ample private apartment housing at a reasonable cost within walking distance or a short drive from the law school.

Career Center

Recruiting and hiring practices in the legal job market suggest that making career decisions should be an ongoing, developmental process that begins in the first year of law school and continues through and after graduation. UT students acquire the skills and knowledge necessary to research, select, and seek the right career path for them and gain necessary information about the professional areas in which a law degree can be used.

The staff of the Bettye B. Lewis Career Center offers a comprehensive menu of services for employers who seek to recruit Tennessee students through formal and informal recruitment methods, off-campus job fairs, and recruiting consortia. First-year students are introduced to career development and job-search strategies through individual counseling and small group resource training sessions called the 1L Career Integration Program. Students are coached in the development of individual job-search strategy plans throughout their law school careers.

These efforts have contributed to a consistently high employment rate for UT graduates that is well above the national average. Most graduates choose to stay in the southeastern United States, but graduates accept positions across the country. For detailed information about recent employment outcomes for Tennessee Law graduates, please see the College of Law website at www.law.utk.edu or contact the Career Center at lawcareer@utk.edu.

APPLICANT PROFILE

University of Tennessee College of Law
This grid includes only applicants who earned 120–180 LSAT scores under standard administrations.

LSAT Score	GPA 3.75 +		3.50–3.74		3.25–3.49		3.00–3.24		2.75–2.99		2.50–2.74		2.25–2.49		2.00–2.24		Below 2.00		No GPA		Total	
	Apps	Adm	Apps	Adm	Apps	Adm	Apps	Adm	Apps	Adm	Apps	Adm	Apps	Adm	Apps	Adm	Apps	Adm	Apps	Adm	Apps	Adm
175–180	1	1	0	0	0	0	2	2	0	0	0	0	0	0	0	0	0	0	0	0	3	3
170–174	2	2	2	2	1	1	1	1	3	2	0	0	0	0	0	0	0	0	0	0	9	8
165–169	17	17	26	26	12	10	7	6	9	8	5	5	3	1	0	0	0	0	1	1	80	74
160–164	61	60	68	60	72	53	35	22	17	11	9	3	5	1	1	0	0	0	4	2	272	212
155–159	78	41	112	25	87	14	68	10	28	1	7	1	7	0	4	1	2	0	6	1	399	94
150–154	37	7	61	5	52	7	38	7	29	1	12	0	11	1	0	0	1	0	5	0	246	28
145–149	16	4	29	7	23	3	38	2	19	2	13	1	3	0	2	0	1	0	3	0	147	19
140–144	3	1	11	2	11	0	15	0	9	0	10	0	9	0	3	0	2	0	1	0	74	3
135–139	1	1	2	0	5	0	3	0	6	0	4	0	4	0	1	0	1	0	4	0	31	1
130–134	0	0	0	0	1	0	1	0	1	0	1	0	0	0	4	0	0	0	1	0	9	0
125–129	0	0	1	0	0	0	0	0	0	0	1	0	0	0	1	0	0	0	1	0	4	0
120–124	0	0	0	0	0	0	0	0	0	0	0	0	0	0	0	0	0	0	0	0	0	0
Total	216	134	312	127	264	88	208	50	121	25	62	10	42	3	16	1	7	0	26	4	1274	442

Apps = Number of Applicants
Adm = Number Admitted
Reflects 99% of the total applicant pool; highest LSAT data reported.

THE UNIVERSITY OF TEXAS SCHOOL OF LAW

727 East Dean Keeton Street
Austin, TX 78705
Phone: 512.232.1200; Fax: 512.471.2765
E-mail: admissions@law.utexas.edu; Website: www.utexas.edu/law/

ABA
Approved
Since
1923

The Basics

Type of school	Public
Term	Semester
Application deadline	11/1 2/1
Application fee	$70
Financial aid deadline	3/15
Can first year start other than fall?	No
Student to faculty ratio	10.8 to 1
# of housing spaces available restricted to law students	
graduate housing for which law students are eligible	

Faculty and Administrators

	Total		Men		Women		Minorities	
	Spr	Fall	Spr	Fall	Spr	Fall	Spr	Fall
Full-time	91	83	55	50	36	33	10	8
Other full-time	2	2	1	1	1	1	0	0
Deans, librarians, & others who teach	4	2	1	1	3	1	0	0
Part-time	74	62	51	44	23	18	8	10
Total	171	149	108	96	63	53	18	18

JD Enrollment and Ethnicity

	Men		Women		Full-Time		Part-Time		1st-Year		Total		JD Degs. Awd.
	#	%	#	%	#	%	#	%	#	%	#	%	
All Hispanics	89	14.5	82	15.7	171	15.1	0	0.0	50	13.3	171	15.1	58
Am. Ind./AK Nat.	1	0.2	3	0.6	4	0.4	0	0.0	2	0.5	4	0.4	3
Asian	28	4.6	31	6.0	59	5.2	0	0.0	19	5.1	59	5.2	22
Black/Af. Am.	24	3.9	30	5.8	54	4.8	0	0.0	17	4.5	54	4.8	19
Nat. HI/Pac. Isl.	1	0.2	0	0.0	1	0.1	0	0.0	0	0.0	1	0.1	0
2 or more races	15	2.4	13	2.5	28	2.5	0	0.0	16	4.3	28	2.5	1
Subtotal (minor.)	158	25.7	159	30.5	317	27.9	0	0.0	104	27.7	317	27.9	103
Nonres. Alien	11	1.8	10	1.9	21	1.8	0	0.0	13	3.5	21	1.8	4
White/Cauc.	381	62.0	308	59.1	689	60.7	0	0.0	223	59.5	689	60.7	246
Unknown	65	10.6	44	8.4	109	9.6	0	0.0	35	9.3	109	9.6	29
Total	615	54.1	521	45.9	1136	100.0	0	0.0	375	33.0	1136		382

Curriculum

	Full-Time	Part-Time
Typical first-year section size	99	0
Is there typically a "small section" of the first-year class, other than Legal Writing, taught by full-time faculty	Yes	No
If yes, typical size offered last year	24	

# of classroom course titles beyond first-year curriculum		184
# of upper division courses, excluding seminars, with an enrollment:	Under 25	231
	25–49	44
	50–74	12
	75–99	6
	100+	9
# of seminars		66
# of seminar positions available		828
# of seminar positions filled	687	0
# of positions available in simulation courses	426	
# of simulation positions filled	334	0
# of positions available in faculty supervised clinical courses	294	
# of faculty supervised clinical positions filled	239	0
# involved in field placements	262	0
# involved in law journals	612	0
# involved in moot court or trial competitions	86	0
# of credit hours required to graduate		86

Transfers

Transfers in	6
Transfers out	6

Tuition and Fees

	Resident	Nonresident
Full-time	$30,243	$46,028
Part-time		
Tuition Guarantee Program	N	

Living Expenses

Estimated living expenses for singles

Living on campus	Living off campus	Living at home
$15,702	$15,702	$7,388

THE UNIVERSITY OF TEXAS SCHOOL OF LAW

ABA Approved Since 1923

GPA and LSAT Scores

	Total	Full-Time	Part-Time
# of apps	4,759	4,759	0
# of offers	1,303	1,303	0
# of matrics	370	370	0
75% GPA	3.80	3.80	0.00
Median GPA	3.69	3.69	0.00
25% GPA	3.56	3.56	0.00
75% LSAT	170	170	0
Median LSAT	167	167	0
25% LSAT	165	165	0

Grants and Scholarships (from prior year)

	Total #	Total %	Full-Time #	Full-Time %	Part-Time #	Part-Time %
Total # of students	1,154		1,154		0	
Total # receiving grants	1007	87.3	1007	87.3	0	0.0
Less than 1/2 tuition	853	73.9	853	73.9	0	0.0
Half to full tuition	124	10.7	124	10.7	0	0.0
Full tuition	10	0.9	10	0.9	0	0.0
More than full tuition	20	1.7	20	1.7	0	0.0
Median grant amount		$8,500			$0	

Informational and Library Resources

Total amount spent on library materials	$1,450,323
Study seating capacity inside the library	806
# of full-time equivalent professional librarians	10
Hours per week library is open	107
# of open, wired connections available to students	257
# of networked computers available for use by students	115
Has wireless network?	Y
Requires computer?	N

JD Attrition (from prior year)

	Academic #	Other #	Total #	Total %
1st year	2	4	6	1.5
2nd year	0	8	8	2.2
3rd year	0	5	5	1.3
4th year	0	0	0	0.0

Employment (9 months after graduation)

For up-to-date employment data, go to employmentsummary.abaquestionnaire.org on the ABA website.

Bar Passage Rates

First-time takers	360	Reporting %	86.94
Average school %	92.97	Average state %	82.91
Average pass difference	10.06		

Jurisdiction	Takers	Passers	Pass %	State %	Diff %
Texas	281	260	92.53	82.68	9.85
New York	32	31	96.88	84.92	11.96

THE UNIVERSITY OF TEXAS SCHOOL OF LAW

727 East Dean Keeton Street
Austin, TX 78705
Phone: 512.232.1200; Fax: 512.471.2765
E-mail: admissions@law.utexas.edu; Website: www.utexas.edu/law/

Introduction

The School of Law is located at The University of Texas at Austin. This location in the heart of the capital city provides ready access to the state legislature, the Supreme Court of Texas, the federal trial and appellate court, the offices of state and federal agencies, and the libraries and other main campus facilities. Recognized for its distinguished faculty and rich academic program, the law school has been a member of the AALS since 1907, was approved by the ABA in 1923, and is fully accredited.

Situated on the banks of the Colorado River, Austin is an eclectic city noted for its politics, scholars, rolling hills, film industry, and live music and restaurant scene. The University of Texas plays an important role in this metropolitan area of over one million people, and many entertainment and cultural activities cater to the student population.

Library and Physical Facilities

The Tarlton Law Library in the Joseph D. Jamail Center for Legal Research is one of the leading academic law libraries in the United States and one of the finest legal research centers in the Southwest. The library serves an academic community of over 1,100 full-time law students and 100 faculty members. In addition to the library's large print collection of over one million volumes, students also have access to databases, e-books, and electronic journals.

In 2010, the newly constructed Susman Academic Center was dedicated as part of the extensive renovation of the Tarlton Library. The fifth and sixth floors of the library were transformed into the Academic Center, which houses 54 faculty offices; 38 additional offices illuminated with natural light via skylights; 2 large, high-tech equipped meeting rooms, each of which can be flexibly subdivided into 2 or 3 separate areas; an expansive commons area with a two-story atrium; 2 faculty research areas; 6 additional conference rooms; and 4 seminar classrooms. The Susman Academic Center expands the Law School's available office and public spaces, and creates attractive, light-filled spaces for faculty and students to work and collaborate.

Faculty

The University of Texas School of Law has long had one of the most outstanding faculties in the nation, both in terms of scholarly distinction of the faculty members and their success in the classroom. More than one-third of the faculty is elected to the American Law Institute, one of the highest percentage memberships in the nation. Texas is also one of nine schools with four faculty elected to the American Academy of Arts and Sciences, the nation's most prestigious learned society. The law school has consistently hired the best and brightest young scholars, including eight former clerks for justices of the United States Supreme Court.

Texas enjoys a leadership position in many areas of legal study. The breadth and depth of offerings in several areas—constitutional law, environmental law, wills and estates, admiralty and maritime law, torts and product liability, labor law, jurisprudence, and philosophy—is matched by few schools in the country. With one of the largest faculties in the country, Texas is able to offer students coverage of all fields of law and exposure to truly diverse scholarly perspectives on legal questions.

Special Programs

The school offers clinical education courses for credit in such fields as actual innocence, capital punishment, children's rights, community development, criminal defense, domestic violence, environmental, housing, immigration, juvenile justice, legislative lawyering, mediation, mental health, national security, Supreme Court, and transnational worker rights. Internships are available to qualified students with the Texas Supreme Court, the Texas Court of Criminal Appeals, and the Third Court of Appeals. A limited number of internships are available for credit in the public service area. The law school also has an extensive trial-advocacy program boasting several national championships. There are a number of joint-degree programs—JD/MPAff; JD/MBA; JD/Master of Arts in Latin American Studies; JD/Master of Arts in Middle Eastern Studies; JD/Master of Arts in Russian, East European, and Eurasian Studies; JD/Master of Science in Community and Regional Planning; JD/Master of Global Policy Studies; JD/Master of Science in Social Work; and JD/Master of Science in Information Studies—in addition to several combined programs with a PhD.

Enrollment/Student Body

As a public institution of higher education, the School of Law's nonresident enrollment is limited by the Texas Legislature to 35 percent. We currently have over 143 undergraduate institutions and 34 states represented in our student body. Please refer to the statistical information for details regarding the competitiveness of our student body.

Curriculum

All first-year students are required to take a full courseload, averaging 15 hours per week, in contracts, property, torts, civil procedure, criminal law, constitutional law, brief writing and oral advocacy, and legal research and writing. After the first year, the only required courses are professional responsibility, advanced constitutional law, a writing and research seminar, and a skills class. A student may design his or her course of study from an array of course offerings in many fields of law. These offerings include interdisciplinary and advanced public and private law courses.

Student-Edited Journals

The School of Law offers many student-administered, cocurricular activities that enhance the law students' regular studies. Student-edited journals include the *American Journal of Criminal Law*; *Texas Environmental Law Journal*; *Texas Hispanic Journal of Law and Policy*; *Texas Intellectual Property Law Journal*; *Texas International Law Journal*; *Texas Journal of Oil, Gas, and Energy Law*; *Texas Journal of Women and the Law*; *Texas Journal on Civil Liberties and Civil Rights*; *Texas Law Review*; *Texas Review of Entertainment and*

Sports Law; Texas Review of Law and Politics; and *The Review of Litigation.*

Admission

Admission to the JD program at UT Law is competitive. For the entering class of 2011, approximately 4,759 applicants competed for 375 available seats. As a general rule, there are no presumptive numbers. Every application completed and submitted is reviewed in its entirety. Each applicant must take the LSAT and have earned a baccalaureate degree from an accredited college or university with a minimum grade-point average of 2.2 as calculated by the Law School Admission Council (LSAC), or have completed the equivalent of six semesters and expect to graduate during the current academic year. Each candidate must complete all application forms and fulfill all mandatory attachments as described in the application.

Financial Aid

A limited number of scholarships are available for first-year students on the basis of merit and financial need. The prestigious Townes-Rice Scholarship is offered to eight outstanding law students with full tuition and fees plus a $5,000 stipend for all three years of law school. The law school also offers an Equal Justice Scholarship for an entering student interested in a career in public interest. Scholarships and research assistantships are available for second- and third-year students. The law school administers several short-term and long-term loan funds for students with financial need, and the university offers substantial federally funded loan programs.

Housing

Approximately 95 percent of all law students live off campus. The Division of Housing and Food Services (PO Box 7666, University Station, Austin, TX 78713; telephone: 512.471.3136) has information regarding on-campus living. Other sources of information are classified ads in the student newspaper, the *Daily Texan*; apartment management services; rental agencies; and current students.

Career Services

Each year, nearly 500 employers participate in career services programs and recruit our students for summer and full-time positions through on-campus interviews, recruit-by-mail opportunities, and off-campus job fairs. Nearly 60 percent of on-campus employers are from outside the state of Texas.

APPLICANT PROFILE

The University of Texas School of Law
This grid includes only applicants who earned 120–180 LSAT scores under standard administrations.

LSAT Score	3.75 +		3.50–3.74		3.25–3.49		3.00–3.24		2.75–2.99		2.50–2.74		2.25–2.49		2.00–2.24		Below 2.00		No GPA		Total	
	Apps	Adm	Apps	Adm	Apps	Adm	Apps	Adm	Apps	Adm	Apps	Adm	Apps	Adm	Apps	Adm	Apps	Adm	Apps	Adm	Apps	Adm
175–180	31	31	24	21	22	12	14	1	2	0	4	0	0	0	1	0	0	0	1	1	99	66
170–174	253	243	191	155	102	30	57	6	16	0	6	0	2	0	1	0	0	0	8	5	636	439
165–169	437	332	470	239	254	22	120	3	35	0	6	0	10	0	2	0	1	0	41	18	1376	614
160–164	347	69	350	54	230	16	121	4	34	1	22	0	10	0	5	0	0	0	33	2	1152	146
155–159	151	17	191	8	154	6	91	0	55	0	18	0	10	1	5	0	1	0	17	0	693	32
150–154	70	2	93	0	106	2	69	0	44	0	21	0	9	0	2	0	0	0	8	0	422	4
145–149	22	0	51	1	42	0	39	0	23	0	15	0	15	0	1	0	1	0	6	0	215	1
140–144	5	0	14	0	20	0	27	0	15	0	13	0	7	0	2	0	3	0	7	0	113	0
135–139	2	0	4	0	6	0	5	0	6	0	0	0	3	0	0	0	2	0	2	0	30	0
130–134	1	0	1	0	0	0	2	0	1	0	1	0	1	0	0	0	0	0	1	0	8	0
125–129	0	0	0	0	0	0	0	0	0	0	2	0	0	0	0	0	0	0	0	0	2	0
120–124	0	0	0	0	0	0	0	0	0	0	0	0	0	0	0	0	0	0	0	0	0	0
Total	1319	694	1389	478	936	88	545	14	231	1	108	0	67	1	19	0	8	0	124	26	4746	1302

Apps = Number of Applicants
Adm = Number Admitted
Reflects 100% of the total applicant pool; highest LSAT data reported.

TEXAS SOUTHERN UNIVERSITY—THURGOOD MARSHALL SCHOOL OF LAW

Office of Admissions, 3100 Cleburne
Houston, TX 77004
Phone: 713.313.7114 or 713.313.7115; Fax: 713.313.7297
E-mail: erene@tmslaw.tsu.edu; Website: www.tsulaw.edu

ABA
Approved
Since
1949

The Basics

Type of school	Public
Term	Semester
Application deadline	4/1
Application fee	$55
Financial aid deadline	4/15
Can first year start other than fall?	No
Student to faculty ratio	14.4 to 1
# of housing spaces available restricted to law students	
graduate housing for which law students are eligible	

Faculty and Administrators

	Total		Men		Women		Minorities	
	Spr	Fall	Spr	Fall	Spr	Fall	Spr	Fall
Full-time	32	33	13	12	19	21	24	28
Other full-time	0	0	0	0	0	0	0	0
Deans, librarians, & others who teach	11	14	7	9	4	5	9	11
Part-time	20	8	16	5	4	3	16	5
Total	63	55	36	26	27	29	49	44

Curriculum

	Full-Time	Part-Time
Typical first-year section size	55	0
Is there typically a "small section" of the first-year class, other than Legal Writing, taught by full-time faculty	No	No
If yes, typical size offered last year		
# of classroom course titles beyond first-year curriculum	75	

# of upper division courses, excluding seminars, with an enrollment:	Under 25	64
	25–49	34
	50–74	22
	75–99	0
	100+	1

# of seminars	26	
# of seminar positions available	650	
# of seminar positions filled	427	0
# of positions available in simulation courses	200	
# of simulation positions filled	179	0
# of positions available in faculty supervised clinical courses	237	
# of faculty supervised clinical positions filled	237	0
# involved in field placements	71	0
# involved in law journals	12	0
# involved in moot court or trial competitions	16	0
# of credit hours required to graduate	90	

JD Enrollment and Ethnicity

	Men #	Men %	Women #	Women %	Full-Time #	Full-Time %	Part-Time #	Part-Time %	1st-Year #	1st-Year %	Total #	Total %	JD Degs. Awd.
All Hispanics	93	33.6	69	23.3	162	28.3	0	0.0	59	27.1	162	28.3	39
Am. Ind./AK Nat.	1	0.4	2	0.7	3	0.5	0	0.0	1	0.5	3	0.5	1
Asian	25	9.0	19	6.4	44	7.7	0	0.0	15	6.9	44	7.7	8
Black/Af. Am.	101	36.5	161	54.4	262	45.7	0	0.0	108	49.5	262	45.7	86
Nat. HI/Pac. Isl.	0	0.0	0	0.0	0	0.0	0	0.0	0	0.0	0	0.0	0
2 or more races	0	0.0	0	0.0	0	0.0	0	0.0	0	0.0	0	0.0	1
Subtotal (minor.)	220	79.4	251	84.8	471	82.2	0	0.0	183	83.9	471	82.2	135
Nonres. Alien	2	0.7	0	0.0	2	0.3	0	0.0	1	0.5	2	0.3	3
White/Cauc.	55	19.9	45	15.2	100	17.5	0	0.0	34	15.6	100	17.5	23
Unknown	0	0.0	0	0.0	0	0.0	0	0.0	0	0.0	0	0.0	0
Total	277	48.3	296	51.7	573	100.0	0	0.0	218	38.0	573		161

Transfers

Transfers in	1
Transfers out	4

Tuition and Fees

	Resident	Nonresident
Full-time	$16,262	$21,212
Part-time		
Tuition Guarantee Program	N	

Living Expenses

Estimated living expenses for singles

Living on campus	Living off campus	Living at home
N/A	$18,918	$18,918

TEXAS SOUTHERN UNIVERSITY—THURGOOD MARSHALL SCHOOL OF LAW

ABA Approved Since 1949

GPA and LSAT Scores

	Total	Full-Time	Part-Time
# of apps	1,911	1,911	0
# of offers	677	677	0
# of matrics	219	219	0
75% GPA	3.37	3.37	0.00
Median GPA	3.07	3.07	0.00
25% GPA	2.76	2.76	0.00
75% LSAT	149	149	0
Median LSAT	147	147	0
25% LSAT	144	144	0

Grants and Scholarships (from prior year)

	Total #	Total %	Full-Time #	Full-Time %	Part-Time #	Part-Time %
Total # of students	571		571		0	
Total # receiving grants	298	52.2	298	52.2	0	0.0
Less than 1/2 tuition	214	37.5	214	37.5	0	0.0
Half to full tuition	30	5.3	30	5.3	0	0.0
Full tuition	54	9.5	54	9.5	0	0.0
More than full tuition	0	0.0	0	0.0	0	0.0
Median grant amount			$8,174		$0	

Informational and Library Resources

Total amount spent on library materials	$946,276
Study seating capacity inside the library	378
# of full-time equivalent professional librarians	15
Hours per week library is open	108
# of open, wired connections available to students	955
# of networked computers available for use by students	99
Has wireless network?	Y
Requires computer?	N

JD Attrition (from prior year)

	Academic #	Other #	Total #	Total %
1st year	30	0	30	14.2
2nd year	2	4	6	3.2
3rd year	0	0	0	0.0
4th year	0	0	0	0.0

Employment (9 months after graduation)

For up-to-date employment data, go to employmentsummary.abaquestionnaire.org on the ABA website.

Bar Passage Rates

First-time takers	147	Reporting %	87.07
Average school %	72.66	Average state %	82.68

Average pass difference –10.02

Jurisdiction	Takers	Passers	Pass %	State %	Diff %
Texas	128	93	72.66	82.68	–10.02

TEXAS SOUTHERN UNIVERSITY—THURGOOD MARSHALL SCHOOL OF LAW

Office of Admissions, 3100 Cleburne
Houston, TX 77004
Phone: 713.313.7114 or 713.313.7115; Fax: 713.313.7297
E-mail: erene@tmslaw.tsu.edu; Website: www.tsulaw.edu

Enrollment/Student Body

A majority of the students are from Texas, but all parts of the country are represented at Texas Southern University—Thurgood Marshall School of Law. Approximately 49 percent of the students are black, 23 percent Chicano, 17 percent Caucasian, and 6 percent Asian and Native American. The median age range is between 26 and 36 years.

Introduction

The Thurgood Marshall School of Law, a state institution founded in 1947, seeks to provide a legal education and an opportunity to students from a wide range of backgrounds, including those who otherwise would not have an opportunity for legal training. The law school is accredited by the ABA. The student body is very diverse both ethnically and culturally. The law school is housed in a tri-level structure that is located just outside of downtown Houston. Near-campus housing is available in the form of modern apartments for single and married students. The school makes extensive use of legal facilities in Houston through its clinical programs.

Library and Physical Facilities

Students receive individual or group orientation and intensive training in the use of the library. The law school has undergone approximately $16 million in renovations, expanding the available space from 103,000 to 108,000 square feet.

Texas Southern University's Thurgood Marshall School of Law Library has received recognition as one of the best libraries in the nation by the *National Jurist* in their March 2010 issue. The law library was noted particularly for its resources, service, and space. It provides a variety of study spaces, including four new group study rooms, a dedicated writing lab, and over 100 carrels.

In June of 2011, the law library joined the short list of law schools that acquired Encore Synergy, a technologically advanced library system that allows users the ability to quickly find what they need by providing discovery tools. In addition, the library was one of four law libraries that purchased Sierra Services Platform from Innovative Interfaces, which will allow total customized ILS functionality.

Curriculum

Upon entry to the School of Law, all students in the first-year class are required to attend a week-long orientation program. Attention is given to examinations, briefing cases, outlining, and an overview of law school life and expectations.

The law school offers a three-year, full-time JD program. The minimum courseload is 12 hours per semester. Required courses for the first year include Lawyering Process I and II, Civil Procedure, Property, Contracts, Torts, and Criminal Law. Second-year students must take Constitutional Law, Evidence, Criminal Procedure, Trial Simulation, Business Associations, Commercial Law, Professional Responsibility, and Wills and Trusts. Second- or third-year students are required to take Federal Jurisdiction and Procedure, a seminar/independent research project, and Basic Federal Taxation. Third-year

students are required to take Consumer Rights and Texas Practice. The remaining hours required to complete the degree may be selected from a number of areas of interest.

The law school operates a full-time, in-house clinic in which students work under the supervision of faculty and adjunct faculty members. Internships are available with the Harris County District Attorney's Office, the Federal Magistrates, the Gulf Coast Legal Foundation, the US Bankruptcy Court, the Harris County Attorney's Office, the Internal Revenue Service, and the US District Court. The school operates a number of clinics, including advanced skills, basic skills, civil and criminal externships, environmental justice, family law, and housing law. A judicial externship with state and federal judges is available to academically outstanding third-year students.

Admission

The admission decision is based primarily on the applicant's motivation and intellectual capacity as demonstrated by his or her undergraduate records and his or her aptitude for the study of law as measured by the LSAT. Leadership ability, prior community service, work experience, the student's background, extracurricular activities, and graduate study in another discipline are all considered.

No particular undergraduate major is preferred; however, the school looks for applicants with broad backgrounds in the social sciences, natural sciences, humanities, and business sciences. Newly admitted students must send two seat deposits ($150 upon due date and $100 in June), which are refundable upon matriculation. The law school's student body represents one of the most culturally and ethnically diverse student bodies in the country. Transfer applications are accepted. Students seeking a transfer must submit a transcript and letter from the dean of his/her former law school stating that he or she is in good standing. All newly admitted students must submit an official transcript from the baccalaureate degree-granting institution as well as all law schools attended. No application will be evaluated by the admission committee until the LSAC Credential Assembly Service law school report has been received.

In order to ensure complete review, applications must be received by the Office of Admissions no later than April 1, although earlier submission is encouraged. Entering students are admitted only in August (fall semester). Students are notified of acceptance after the admission committee has reviewed the complete file. Admission decisions are made on a rolling basis.

Thurgood Marshall School of Law at Texas Southern University is located in the third largest city in the United States. Each fall semester, the School of Law matriculates approximately 210 students into its full-time program. The law school only has a full-time program.

TMSL has been committed to diversity throughout its history, which has been documented in periodicals and national magazines.

Thurgood Marshall School of Law at Texas Southern University embraces equal opportunity for all qualified persons without regard to race, color, religion, sexual orientation, national origin, age, disability, marital status, or veteran's status in the admission to, participation in, or employment in the programs and activities that the university operates.

Student Activities

Numerous law school organizations are active on campus. A student board edits the *Thurgood Marshall Law Review*. Moot court competitions are held in trial and appellate work, labor law, and client counseling.

Expenses and Financial Aid

About 90 percent of the students receive some form of aid. The law school administers its own competitive scholarship program. Scholarships may range up to full tuition. Between 10 and 15 percent of the students hold assistantships. The aid application deadline is April 1.

The scholarship program makes several awards (approximately 60) each year. The awards have enabled out-of-state residents to qualify for resident tuition rates. In addition, a number of law students qualify for the federal work-study programs. An applicant in need of other financial assistance should make arrangements for financial aid through the law school financial aid counselor by either calling 713.313.7243 or e-mailing kepercival@tmslaw.tsu.edu.

Student Affairs

The Office of Student Affairs provides assistance for all TMSL law students. We assist with fostering the transition from undergraduate school to law school, coordinating the registration process, overseeing activities of more than 20 student organizations, overseeing the administration of the LSSSE survey, disseminating information about registering for bar examinations for all states, and assisting students as needed in other law school related activities.

Our office begins interacting with current law students at Orientation and ends with Graduation. During a student's matriculation into the law school, our office conducts registration for classes prior to the beginning of each semester, maintains records of academic history, honors awarded, and any academic or professional activities that affect the status of a law student.

The Office of Student Affairs assists law students in other areas such as academic counseling, wellness and fitness counseling, and students with disabilities counseling. If our office is unable to solve inquiries from students, we assist in directing them to the proper office, department, or agency that will assist them.

Career Services

The Career Services Office (CSO) prepares students for employment by introducing them to various traditional and non-traditional legal career options. The CSO provides extensive guidance in interviewing skills, resume building, cover letters, and networking tools. It presents employment opportunities through numerous resources that include: on-campus interview programs, off-campus recruitment events, job fairs and access to legal job sources that regularly announce available positions. Graduates of Thurgood Marshall School of Law are employed throughout the country. Most enter private practice and federal or state government; others work in large corporations, small businesses, public interest organizations, the judiciary, and the various military JAG Corps. The CSO also conducts a substantial national employer outreach effort yearly to encourage legal employers throughout the country to recruit students from Thurgood Marshall School of Law. The CSO assists all students individually with their job search regardless of class rank or GPA, and the staff has a genuine interest and several years of experience guiding students through their self-directed job search.

APPLICANT PROFILE

Texas Southern University—Thurgood Marshall School of Law
This grid includes only applicants who earned 120–180 LSAT scores under standard administrations.

LSAT Score	3.75 +		3.50–3.74		3.25–3.49		3.00–3.24		2.75–2.99		2.50–2.74		2.25–2.49		2.00–2.24		Below 2.00		No GPA		Total	
	Apps	Adm	Apps	Adm	Apps	Adm	Apps	Adm	Apps	Adm	Apps	Adm	Apps	Adm	Apps	Adm	Apps	Adm	Apps	Adm	Apps	Adm
175–180	0	0	0	0	0	0	0	0	0	0	0	0	0	0	0	0	0	0	0	0	0	0
170–174	0	0	0	0	0	0	1	1	0	0	0	0	0	0	0	0	0	0	0	0	1	1
165–169	0	0	0	0	2	2	4	4	0	0	1	1	0	0	0	0	0	0	0	0	7	7
160–164	1	1	4	4	4	3	2	2	1	1	4	4	1	0	1	1	0	0	0	0	18	16
155–159	8	6	11	10	21	19	12	12	18	12	10	8	9	6	4	3	2	0	0	0	95	76
150–154	9	8	28	27	43	35	53	41	53	42	50	32	35	19	19	3	8	2	5	3	303	212
145–149	21	19	34	32	79	59	96	65	99	48	96	21	59	4	22	2	7	0	19	7	532	257
140–144	9	7	41	28	79	27	109	22	116	4	98	3	64	2	45	1	14	0	22	2	597	96
135–139	6	2	16	4	22	1	38	0	46	1	50	0	33	0	15	1	7	1	6	0	239	10
130–134	1	1	2	0	7	0	14	0	10	0	13	0	14	0	6	0	5	0	4	0	76	1
125–129	0	0	0	0	2	0	4	0	3	0	2	0	5	0	3	0	0	0	0	0	19	0
120–124	0	0	0	0	0	0	0	0	0	0	0	0	1	0	0	0	0	0	0	0	1	0
Total	55	44	136	105	259	146	333	147	346	108	324	69	221	31	115	11	43	3	56	12	1888	676

Apps = Number of Applicants
Adm = Number Admitted
Reflects 99% of the total applicant pool; highest LSAT data reported.

TEXAS TECH UNIVERSITY SCHOOL OF LAW

1802 Hartford Avenue
Lubbock, TX 79409
Phone: 806.742.3990; Fax: 806.742.4617
E-mail: admissions.law@ttu.edu; Website: www.law.ttu.edu

ABA
Approved
Since
1969

The Basics

Type of school	Public
Term	Semester
Application deadline	11/1 2/1
Application fee	$50
Financial aid deadline	4/15
Can first year start other than fall?	No
Student to faculty ratio	17.4 to 1
# of housing spaces available restricted to law students	
graduate housing for which law students are eligible	700

Faculty and Administrators

	Total		Men		Women		Minorities	
	Spr	Fall	Spr	Fall	Spr	Fall	Spr	Fall
Full-time	33	32	21	22	12	10	6	6
Other full-time	2	1	0	0	2	1	0	0
Deans, librarians, & others who teach	13	14	5	5	8	9	4	4
Part-time	12	10	10	7	2	3	2	2
Total	60	57	36	34	24	23	12	12

Curriculum

	Full-Time	Part-Time
Typical first-year section size	63	0
Is there typically a "small section" of the first-year class, other than Legal Writing, taught by full-time faculty	No	No
If yes, typical size offered last year		

		Full-Time	Part-Time
# of classroom course titles beyond first-year curriculum		97	
# of upper division courses, excluding seminars, with an enrollment:	Under 25	51	
	25–49	26	
	50–74	14	
	75–99	4	
	100+	5	
# of seminars		30	
# of seminar positions available		590	
# of seminar positions filled		460	0
# of positions available in simulation courses		120	
# of simulation positions filled		109	0
# of positions available in faculty supervised clinical courses		152	
# of faculty supervised clinical positions filled	152		0
# involved in field placements	115		0
# involved in law journals	156		0
# involved in moot court or trial competitions	61		0
# of credit hours required to graduate		90	

JD Enrollment and Ethnicity

	Men #	Men %	Women #	Women %	Full-Time #	Full-Time %	Part-Time #	Part-Time %	1st-Year #	1st-Year %	Total #	Total %	JD Degs. Awd.
All Hispanics	63	16.1	55	18.4	118	17.1	0	0.0	46	19.5	118	17.1	27
Am. Ind./AK Nat.	2	0.5	2	0.7	4	0.6	0	0.0	1	0.4	4	0.6	2
Asian	19	4.9	20	6.7	39	5.7	0	0.0	22	9.3	39	5.7	9
Black/Af. Am.	5	1.3	12	4.0	17	2.5	0	0.0	6	2.5	17	2.5	8
Nat. HI/Pac. Isl.	0	0.0	0	0.0	0	0.0	0	0.0	0	0.0	0	0.0	0
2 or more races	0	0.0	0	0.0	0	0.0	0	0.0	0	0.0	0	0.0	1
Subtotal (minor.)	89	22.8	89	29.8	178	25.8	0	0.0	75	31.8	178	25.8	47
Nonres. Alien	7	1.8	2	0.7	9	1.3	0	0.0	1	0.4	9	1.3	1
White/Cauc.	295	75.4	208	69.6	503	72.9	0	0.0	160	67.8	503	72.9	151
Unknown	0	0.0	0	0.0	0	0.0	0	0.0	0	0.0	0	0.0	0
Total	391	56.7	299	43.3	690	100.0	0	0.0	236	34.2	690		199

Transfers

Transfers in	9
Transfers out	2

Tuition and Fees

	Resident	Nonresident
Full-time	$22,190	$30,680
Part-time		
Tuition Guarantee Program	N	

Living Expenses

Estimated living expenses for singles

Living on campus	Living off campus	Living at home
$14,372	$14,372	$14,372

TEXAS TECH UNIVERSITY SCHOOL OF LAW

*ABA
Approved
Since
1969*

GPA and LSAT Scores

	Total	Full-Time	Part-Time
# of apps	1,420	1,420	0
# of offers	661	661	0
# of matrics	236	236	0
75% GPA	3.66	3.66	0.00
Median GPA	3.49	3.49	0.00
25% GPA	3.25	3.25	0.00
75% LSAT	158	158	0
Median LSAT	155	155	0
25% LSAT	152	152	0

Grants and Scholarships (from prior year)

	Total #	Total %	Full-Time #	Full-Time %	Part-Time #	Part-Time %
Total # of students	671		671		0	
Total # receiving grants	432	64.4	432	64.4	0	0.0
Less than 1/2 tuition	261	38.9	261	38.9	0	0.0
Half to full tuition	102	15.2	102	15.2	0	0.0
Full tuition	54	8.0	54	8.0	0	0.0
More than full tuition	15	2.2	15	2.2	0	0.0
Median grant amount			$5,384		$0	

Informational and Library Resources

Total amount spent on library materials	$1,043,594
Study seating capacity inside the library	540
# of full-time equivalent professional librarians	8
Hours per week library is open	168
# of open, wired connections available to students	1,123
# of networked computers available for use by students	101
Has wireless network?	Y
Requires computer?	N

JD Attrition (from prior year)

	Academic #	Other #	Total #	Total %
1st year	6	11	17	6.8
2nd year	0	1	1	0.4
3rd year	1	0	1	0.5
4th year	0	0	0	0.0

Employment (9 months after graduation)

For up-to-date employment data, go to
employmentsummary.abaquestionnaire.org on the ABA website.

Bar Passage Rates

First-time takers	215	Reporting %	91.16
Average school %	87.24	Average state %	82.68
Average pass difference	4.56		

Jurisdiction	Takers	Passers	Pass %	State %	Diff %
Texas	196	171	87.24	82.68	4.56

TEXAS TECH UNIVERSITY SCHOOL OF LAW

1802 Hartford Avenue
Lubbock, TX 79409
Phone: 806.742.3990; Fax: 806.742.4617
E-mail: admissions.law@ttu.edu; Website: www.law.ttu.edu

Introduction

Founded in 1967, we are located in Lubbock, Texas, on the main campus of Texas Tech University. We are accredited by the ABA and the Supreme Court of Texas, and we are a member of the selective Association of American Law Schools. In 1974, a chapter of the Order of the Coif was established, a distinction accorded to only one-third of American law schools. Our faculty embraces an open-door policy, enabling students to engage in continuing dialogue beyond formal class hours. We have a long and proud tradition of graduating practice-ready lawyers, with bar passage and employment rates consistently among the highest in the state.

Library and Physical Facilities

Our library is designed to meet the needs of a contemporary legal education. The law library supports the research and academic needs of the students and faculty with superb computer resources and wireless Internet access, complementing a substantial collection of printed materials. All students have 24/7 access to the library and assigned library carrels that serve as small office-like work spaces. All classrooms are equipped with multimedia technology. The 34,000-square-foot Lanier Professional Development Center houses the Office of Academic Success Programs, the Career Services Center, a state-of-the-art courtroom designed to support technology-driven advocacy training, and ample space for student meetings.

Programs of Study

We offer several opportunities to pursue knowledge and experience beyond the law program through our dual-degree programs. Those programs are JD/MBA, JD/MPA, JD/MD, JD/MS in Agriculture and Applied Economics, JD/MS in Accounting (Taxation), JD/Master of Environmental Toxicology, JD/Master of Biotechnology, JD/MS in Crop Science, JD/MS in Soil Science, JD/MS in Horticultural and Turfgrass Sciences, JD/MS in Entomology, JD/MS in Engineering, and JD/MS in Personal Financial Planning. We also offer certificate programs in Business Law, Health Law, and Law and Science with specializations in IP Law, Environmental Law, Biodefense Law, Energy Law, and Water Law.

Curriculum

The program of study equips students to practice law as advocates, counselors, or judges, and we recognize that legal education is also a stepping-stone to careers in government, politics, or business. The required curriculum provides a broad-based legal education. Elective courses afford students the opportunity to create an area of concentration, ranging from business law to emerging areas like health law, natural resources law, and national security law. Our nationally recognized first-year legal research and writing program, Legal Practice, runs the entire first year and provides a strong foundation by including skills beyond research and writing—for example, drafting, negotiation, and client interviewing. The School of Law offers an Academic Success program to assist students in developing the skills to succeed in the study and practice of law.

Legal Publication and Research Opportunities

Texas Tech has several publications that allow students to hone their research and writing skills. The *Texas Tech Law Review* publishes articles written by students and leading jurists, practitioners, and academics.

The State Bar of Texas selected Tech Law to publish the *Texas Tech Administrative Law Journal*. The *Estate Planning and Community Property Law Journal* is the only legal journal committed to community property law, and only the second in the nation devoted to estate planning. The *Texas Bank Lawyer* publishes articles about banking and commercial law.

The school is home to the Center for Water Law and Policy, the Center for Military Law and Policy, and the Center for Biodefense Law and Policy, which all provide research and scholarship opportunities.

Admission

We admit applicants from a wide range of backgrounds and experiences. While an applicant's LSAT and GPA figure significantly in the admission process, we also consider other factors, including extracurricular activities, public service, previous employment, and leadership qualities. A bachelor's degree from an accredited college or university is required.

We review applications on a rolling basis beginning early November. The application deadline for our early decision program is November 1. The deadline for regular decision applicants is February 1. Some students may be selected for acceptance through our Summer Entry Program.

Applications received after February 1 will be accepted but not reviewed until decisions have been made on all timely applications.

Clinical Program

With seven live-client clinics, our clinical program provides third-year students with the opportunity to represent clients and participate in real cases guided by full-time, tenure-track faculty. The Civil Practice Clinic handles a wide range of civil matters. The Criminal Defense and Capital Punishment Clinics provide a unique opportunity for law students to represent clients in state and federal criminal courts. Tax Clinic students represent taxpayers in disputes with the IRS. With the Innocence Project, students investigate claims of actual innocence made by state and federal prisoners. The Family Law and Housing Clinic takes cases concerning those issues from Legal Aid of Northwest Texas. Our newest clinic, the Caprock Regional Criminal Defense Clinic, serves a 16-county region by providing representation to indigent clients in misdemeanor and juvenile cases.

Second-year students also have the opportunity to participate in our Alternative Dispute Resolution and Health Care and Bioethics Mediation clinics, which focus on resolving legal issues without litigation.

Advocacy Program

The Texas Tech School of Law advocacy program produces champions. We are proud of our multiple national and regional championships in the country's toughest advocacy competitions, including back-to-back National Moot Court Competition championships (the nation's oldest and most prestigious competition) in 2011 and 2012, the 2010 National Entertainment Law Moot Court national championship, three straight national championships at the National Latino/a Law Student Association Moot Court Competition, and the 2010 International Negotiation Competition championship. Students also gain advocacy experience in simulated practice settings through numerous intramural competitions. The Lanier Center for Professional Development houses a courtroom featuring state-of-the-art technology, as well as several practice rooms used by students to develop the skills needed to practice in the courtrooms of the future.

Student Activities

The Student Bar Association is the focal point for many student activities. The school has approximately 50 student organizations covering a wide variety of topics and interests. This includes groups such as the Black Law Students Association, Environmental Law Society, Federalist Society, Lambda, and the Student Public Interest Initiative.

Study-Abroad Programs

Texas Tech is a consortium partner in the Summer Law Institute, a cooperative teaching program with the historic University of Guanajuato, Mexico. The Summer Law Institute offers an introduction to Mexican law, international law, and legal subjects of interest to both US and Mexican lawyers, such as NAFTA.

Students are also offered legal study for credit through cooperative programs with the University of Lyon in France; La Trobe University in Melbourne, Australia; University of Copenhagen in Denmark; and Vytautas Magnus University School of Law in Kaunas, Lithuania, as well as opportunities to create their own study-abroad programs for credit.

Financial Aid and Scholarships

The School of Law offers numerous scholarships to entering students. Competitive scholarships are awarded to many nonresident applicants, making them eligible for in-state tuition. Additional scholarships are available for second- and third-year students.

Grants and educational loan funds are available for students who qualify. Please visit www.law.ttu.edu/prospective/financialaid/ for more information.

APPLICANT PROFILE

Texas Tech University School of Law
This grid includes only applicants who earned 120–180 LSAT scores under standard administrations.

LSAT Score	3.75 +		3.50–3.74		3.25–3.49		3.00–3.24		2.75–2.99		2.50–2.74		Below 2.50		No GPA		Total	
	Apps	Adm	Apps	Adm	Apps	Adm	Apps	Adm	Apps	Adm	Apps	Adm	Apps	Adm	Apps	Adm	Apps	Adm
170–180	4	3	1	1	2	2	1	0	1	0	0	0	0	0	0	0	9	6
165–169	4	4	11	10	10	9	8	8	8	6	1	1	2	2	0	0	44	40
160–164	27	25	29	28	34	29	29	27	12	9	12	7	7	3	1	0	151	128
155–159	40	39	92	89	86	80	69	52	47	15	26	3	12	4	1	0	373	282
150–154	52	44	81	56	104	37	95	19	64	2	32	1	24	1	7	2	459	162
145–149	23	10	52	20	56	8	56	0	36	0	10	0	18	0	5	0	256	38
140–144	4	0	24	1	19	1	22	0	17	0	15	0	13	0	2	0	116	2
Below 140	3	0	6	0	9	0	12	0	8	0	7	0	9	0	0	0	54	0
Total	157	125	296	205	320	166	292	106	193	32	103	12	85	10	16	2	1462	658

Apps = Number of Applicants
Adm = Number Admitted
Reflects 99% of the total applicant pool; highest LSAT data reported.

TEXAS WESLEYAN UNIVERSITY SCHOOL OF LAW

1515 Commerce Street, Office of Admissions
Fort Worth, TX 76102
Phone: 817.212.4040, 800.733.9529, ext. 4040; Fax: 817.212.4141
E-mail: lawadmissions@law.txwes.edu; Website: www.law.txwes.edu

ABA
Approved
Since
1994

The Basics

Type of school	Private
Term	Semester
Application deadline	3/31
Application fee	$55
Financial aid deadline	
Can first year start other than fall?	No
Student to faculty ratio	19.4 to 1
# of housing spaces available restricted to law students	
graduate housing for which law students are eligible	

Faculty and Administrators

	Total		Men		Women		Minorities	
	Spr	Fall	Spr	Fall	Spr	Fall	Spr	Fall
Full-time	23	31	13	16	10	15	2	7
Other full-time	5	1	4	1	1	0	1	0
Deans, librarians, & others who teach	7	7	5	5	2	2	3	3
Part-time	26	22	16	11	10	11	2	1
Total	61	61	38	33	23	28	8	11

Curriculum

	Full-Time	Part-Time
Typical first-year section size	72	52
Is there typically a "small section" of the first-year class, other than Legal Writing, taught by full-time faculty	No	No
If yes, typical size offered last year		
# of classroom course titles beyond first-year curriculum	114	
# of upper division courses, excluding seminars, with an enrollment: Under 25	116	
25–49	36	
50–74	12	
75–99	9	
100+	1	
# of seminars	16	
# of seminar positions available	260	
# of seminar positions filled	145	55
# of positions available in simulation courses	289	
# of simulation positions filled	180	34
# of positions available in faculty supervised clinical courses	75	
# of faculty supervised clinical positions filled	39	22
# involved in field placements	61	17
# involved in law journals	70	20
# involved in moot court or trial competitions	44	11
# of credit hours required to graduate	90	

JD Enrollment and Ethnicity

	Men		Women		Full-Time		Part-Time		1st-Year		Total		JD Degs. Awd.
	#	%	#	%	#	%	#	%	#	%	#	%	
All Hispanics	40	10.1	29	8.7	38	8.8	31	10.4	37	9.2	69	9.5	17
Am. Ind./AK Nat.	4	1.0	2	0.6	2	0.5	4	1.3	3	0.7	6	0.8	1
Asian	14	3.5	19	5.7	19	4.4	14	4.7	13	3.2	33	4.5	17
Black/Af. Am.	12	3.0	21	6.3	9	2.1	24	8.0	18	4.5	33	4.5	14
Nat. HI/Pac. Isl.	0	0.0	1	0.3	0	0.0	1	0.3	1	0.2	1	0.1	0
2 or more races	11	2.8	7	2.1	11	2.6	7	2.3	14	3.5	18	2.5	0
Subtotal (minor.)	81	20.4	79	23.7	79	18.3	81	27.1	86	21.4	160	21.9	49
Nonres. Alien	0	0.0	0	0.0	0	0.0	0	0.0	0	0.0	0	0.0	0
White/Cauc.	310	78.1	242	72.7	342	79.4	210	70.2	305	75.9	552	75.6	166
Unknown	6	1.5	12	3.6	10	2.3	8	2.7	11	2.7	18	2.5	12
Total	397	54.4	333	45.6	431	59.0	299	41.0	402	55.1	730		227

Transfers

Transfers in	5
Transfers out	14

Tuition and Fees

	Resident	Nonresident
Full-time	$28,790	$28,790
Part-time	$20,390	$20,390
Tuition Guarantee Program	N	

Living Expenses

Estimated living expenses for singles

Living on campus	Living off campus	Living at home
$15,858	$15,858	$15,858

TEXAS WESLEYAN UNIVERSITY SCHOOL OF LAW

ABA Approved Since 1994

GPA and LSAT Scores

	Total	Full-Time	Part-Time
# of apps	1,823	1,506	317
# of offers	764	649	115
# of matrics	236	164	72
75% GPA	3.48	3.51	3.44
Median GPA	3.22	3.21	3.23
25% GPA	2.94	2.95	2.88
75% LSAT	155	156	154
Median LSAT	153	153	152
25% LSAT	151	151	150

Grants and Scholarships (from prior year)

	Total #	Total %	Full-Time #	Full-Time %	Part-Time #	Part-Time %
Total # of students	764		487		277	
Total # receiving grants	268	35.1	191	39.2	77	27.8
Less than 1/2 tuition	189	24.7	131	26.9	58	20.9
Half to full tuition	62	8.1	48	9.9	14	5.1
Full tuition	17	2.2	12	2.5	5	1.8
More than full tuition	0	0.0	0	0.0	0	0.0
Median grant amount			$7,500		$6,250	

Informational and Library Resources

Total amount spent on library materials	$1,668,547
Study seating capacity inside the library	383
# of full-time equivalent professional librarians	7
Hours per week library is open	104
# of open, wired connections available to students	59
# of networked computers available for use by students	74
Has wireless network?	Y
Requires computer?	N

JD Attrition (from prior year)

	Academic #	Other #	Total #	Total %
1st year	18	30	48	11.7
2nd year	0	1	1	0.6
3rd year	0	0	0	0.0
4th year	0	0	0	0.0

Employment (9 months after graduation)

For up-to-date employment data, go to employmentsummary.abaquestionnaire.org on the ABA website.

Bar Passage Rates

First-time takers	240	Reporting %	97.92
Average school %	77.02	Average state %	82.68
Average pass difference	−5.66		

Jurisdiction	Takers	Passers	Pass %	State %	Diff %
Texas	235	181	77.02	82.68	−5.66

TEXAS WESLEYAN UNIVERSITY SCHOOL OF LAW

1515 Commerce Street, Office of Admissions
Fort Worth, TX 76102
Phone: 817.212.4040, 800.733.9529, ext. 4040; Fax: 817.212.4141
E-mail: lawadmissions@law.txwes.edu; Website: www.law.txwes.edu

Introduction

Established in 1989, the law school became part of Texas Wesleyan University in 1992 with a mission to provide excellence in legal education. The program emphasizes service to our diverse student body, our profession, and our community through outstanding teaching and scholarship, the development of innovative academic programs, and a commitment to public service, as well as by promoting the highest ethical standards in the practice of law. The law school is fully approved by the ABA and offers both full-time and part-time programs leading to the Juris Doctor degree. The law school is located in downtown Fort Worth, Texas, in close proximity to the legal and judicial communities. The Fort Worth/Dallas Metroplex, with approximately 5.8 million residents, has rapidly grown to become one of the largest and most diverse metropolitan areas in the country, offering a relatively low cost of living, a growing economy, and extensive opportunities for professional advancement.

Student Body

Texas Wesleyan Law is committed to educating students of diverse backgrounds, varied life experiences, and differing educational perspectives. In its short but dynamic 20-year history, Texas Wesleyan School of Law has provided excellence in legal education to traditional full-time students as well as to accomplished nontraditional part-time students. The increasing rise in the quality of students is a reflection of our continued emphasis on service to a diverse student body, the profession, and the community.

Faculty

Texas Wesleyan Law has a highly qualified, energetic, accessible faculty. The members of the faculty hold degrees from the top law schools across the country and have diverse professional backgrounds and experience. They have served in a variety of high-level governmental positions, in the judiciary and state legislatures, and in law firms. Faculty members are talented and active scholars that have published numerous books and articles. The student-to-faculty ratio ensures that students have the attention they need, both inside and outside of the classroom.

Library and Physical Facilities

The law school boasts first-rate facilities, including spacious classrooms, well-designed courtrooms, an in-house law clinic, and an impressive library. Texas Wesleyan's law library contains more than 250,000 volumes and equivalents. The law library's mission is to support the educational, instructional, curricular, and research needs of the faculty, students, and staff. In addition to its law book collection, the law library subscribes to major online electronic legal information services, including LexisNexis, Westlaw, and legal research Internet sites. Complementing the library's book and electronic sources, an extensive collection of US Congressional documents, including full transcripts of all congressional hearings since 1970, is available on microfiche. The law library has 8 full-time librarians and a staff of 14 and is open 112 hours per week, 89 of which have reference services available.

Curriculum

Ninety (90) hours of academic course credit are required for completion of the Juris Doctor degree. Students may choose between full-time day, part-time day, or part-time evening courseloads. The part-time program and Texas Wesleyan's flexible scheduling make it possible for those with continuing business and family responsibilities to meet their obligations while obtaining a legal education. The law school offers over 115 courses divided among traditional law courses and advanced courses that provide training in a variety of specialized law areas. Students are required to complete a minimum of 30 hours of pro bono legal service and 3 credit hours of professional oral skills learning before graduation.

Skills Training

To help students develop necessary practical lawyering skills, Texas Wesleyan has developed a series of courses in its Juris Doctor curriculum—each called a practicum—in some substantive areas as well as in particular skills areas. The law school also offers a variety of externships with trial and appellate courts, government agencies, nonprofit organizations, and law firms. For academic credit, students perform legal tasks and apply their academic studies to real client cases, gaining valuable insight into the operation of legal institutions. Texas Wesleyan also has an in-house legal clinic that functions as an actual law office where students represent indigent clients in court under the direction of a faculty supervisor. All skills programs are coordinated by a full-time professor.

The law school also prides itself on its ability to help students apply lessons learned in the classroom to real-world legal problems through the Equal Justice Program, a mandatory 30-hour community-related pro bono requirement that must be completed by every student before graduation. Students can fulfill this requirement in many ways, such as by volunteering with a public service agency or with a private attorney doing pro bono work. In addition, the school is committed to serving the community through a variety of programs, such as National Adoption Day, Street Law, and High School Law Day, in which students can gain legal experience while helping to address community legal needs.

Finally, the law school has added a new three-hour professional skills requirement. The requirement is intended to further enhance theoretical learning and reinforce practical lawyering skills. This requirement can be satisfied by completing coursework or participating in competitions that emphasize a student's oral skills. Examples of programming that will meet this requirement include Trial Advocacy, Mediation, Clinics, and moot court or mock trial competitions.

Student Life

Texas Wesleyan Law's student organizations provide a broad spectrum of opportunities for student involvement. Our enthusiastic law students engage in competitions and leadership activities at the state, regional, and national levels.

Students have won numerous competitions in negotiations, mock trial, and recently, the national moot court championships in entertainment law and information technology and privacy law. Through membership in law student organizations, participants reap the benefits of professional contacts, social activities, and exposure to legal specialties. Our student organizations provide opportunities for students to engage in professional bar associations, legal specialties, networking opportunities, and public service projects. In addition, the *Texas Wesleyan Law Review* encourages legal scholarship on issues of interest to academicians, practitioners, and law students. The *Law Review* is published by student editors with a faculty advisor. Participation is limited to those who meet academic requirements and those who are selected through a writing competition.

Career Services

The Texas Wesleyan University School of Law Office of Career Services assists students, graduates, and employers in their mutual efforts to link those seeking legal positions with those providing legal employment opportunities. The Office of Career Services also supports students in securing part-time or temporary employment while attending law school. A range of services, such as one-on-one career counseling, résumé and cover letter review, career seminars, on-campus interviews, off-campus job fairs, and an online job bank are available to students and graduates. The Office of Career Services also provides numerous online and hard-copy career resources in the career planning library. The school is a member of NALP, the Association for Legal Career Professionals.

Expenses and Financial Aid

Texas Wesleyan Law offers a highly competitive and low private tuition cost. Tuition and general costs vary by courseload. For 2011–2012, annual tuition for full-time students was $28,000; for part-time students, $19,600. Fees were an additional $395 per semester. The law school works with individual students to provide the best financial aid package the student is eligible to receive. The financial aid package may include several types of assistance for financing a law school education, including scholarships, grants, employment opportunities, and loan programs. A majority of law students receive some form of financial assistance.

Admission

To be considered for admission, an applicant to Texas Wesleyan School of Law must hold a baccalaureate degree from a regionally accredited college or university prior to matriculation. A Law School Admission Test (LSAT) score is also required. The law school offers full- and part-time programs, and new students are admitted only in the fall. The final deadline for applying is March 31; however, the School of Law reviews applications and awards scholarships on a rolling basis, so applicants are encouraged to apply early.

The admission committee will endeavor to determine the academic and professional promise of each applicant. Accordingly, the admission committee evaluates all factors relevant to an applicant's potential to be successful in meeting the academic standards of the Juris Doctor program, as well as his or her potential for success on the bar examination and in other professional endeavors. Traditional criteria, such as undergraduate academic achievement, LSAT performance, graduate studies, work experience, life experience, activities, honors, the personal statement, recommendation letters, and other experiences, are used in the admission evaluation process.

APPLICANT PROFILE

Texas Wesleyan University School of Law
This grid includes only applicants who earned 120–180 LSAT scores under standard administrations.

LSAT Score	GPA 3.75 + Apps	Adm	3.50–3.74 Apps	Adm	3.25–3.49 Apps	Adm	3.00–3.24 Apps	Adm	2.75–2.99 Apps	Adm	2.50–2.74 Apps	Adm	Below 2.50 Apps	Adm	No GPA Apps	Adm	Total Apps	Adm
170–180	2	1	1	1	1	1	4	4	0	0	0	0	0	0	0	0	8	7
165–169	2	2	6	6	2	1	6	6	0	0	1	0	2	0	0	0	19	15
160–164	21	18	14	13	17	14	19	16	11	8	11	2	9	2	1	0	103	73
155–159	19	17	59	54	74	66	63	45	55	42	32	11	27	4	3	1	332	240
150–154	47	41	76	65	126	89	130	90	98	61	70	22	53	5	5	2	605	375
145–149	34	5	49	14	81	14	100	15	75	7	45	0	45	0	9	0	438	55
140–144	10	0	28	0	34	1	49	1	51	0	35	0	50	0	8	0	265	2
Below 140	4	0	10	0	9	0	30	0	25	0	27	0	32	0	5	0	142	0
Total	139	84	243	153	344	186	401	177	315	118	221	35	218	11	31	3	1912	767

Apps = Number of Applicants
Adm = Number Admitted
Reflects 99% of the total applicant pool; highest LSAT data reported.

THE THOMAS M. COOLEY LAW SCHOOL

PO Box 13038, 300 S. Capitol Avenue, Lansing, MI 48901
9445 Camden Field Parkway, Riverview, FL 33578
Phone: 517.371.5140, ext. 2244; Fax: 517.334.5718
E-mail: admissions@cooley.edu; Website: www.cooley.edu

*ABA
Approved
Since
1975*

The Basics

Type of school	Private		
Term	Semester		
Application deadline	9/1	1/1	5/1
Application fee	$0		
Financial aid deadline	9/1	1/1	5/1
Can first year start other than fall?	Yes		
Student to faculty ratio	22.4 to 1		
# of housing spaces available restricted to law students			
graduate housing for which law students are eligible	20		

Faculty and Administrators

	Total		Men		Women		Minorities	
	Spr	Fall	Spr	Fall	Spr	Fall	Spr	Fall
Full-time	97	102	57	61	40	41	13	13
Other full-time	3	2	2	1	1	1	0	0
Deans, librarians, & others who teach	25	26	8	8	17	18	5	6
Part-time	186	185	121	118	65	67	26	20
Total	311	315	188	188	123	127	44	39

Curriculum

	Full-Time	Part-Time
Typical first-year section size	50	50
Is there typically a "small section" of the first-year class, other than Legal Writing, taught by full-time faculty	No	No
If yes, typical size offered last year		
# of classroom course titles beyond first-year curriculum	268	
# of upper division courses, excluding seminars, with an enrollment: Under 25	488	
25–49	152	
50–74	109	
75–99	81	
100+	15	
# of seminars	488	
# of seminar positions available	9,014	
# of seminar positions filled	1,192	4,681
# of positions available in simulation courses	5,578	
# of simulation positions filled	751	2,948
# of positions available in faculty supervised clinical courses	574	
# of faculty supervised clinical positions filled	74	290
# involved in field placements	171	671
# involved in law journals	99	391
# involved in moot court or trial competitions	17	68
# of credit hours required to graduate	90	

JD Enrollment and Ethnicity

	Men		Women		Full-Time		Part-Time		1st-Year		Total		JD Degs. Awd.
	#	%	#	%	#	%	#	%	#	%	#	%	
All Hispanics	87	4.7	116	6.6	42	5.7	161	5.6	98	6.0	203	5.6	62
Am. Ind./AK Nat.	12	0.6	7	0.4	4	0.5	15	0.5	8	0.5	19	0.5	4
Asian	86	4.6	87	4.9	35	4.7	138	4.8	81	4.9	173	4.8	52
Black/Af. Am.	182	9.8	345	19.5	82	11.1	445	15.4	276	16.8	527	14.5	105
Nat. Hl/Pac. Isl.	2	0.1	7	0.4	3	0.4	6	0.2	8	0.5	9	0.2	2
2 or more races	43	2.3	52	2.9	21	2.8	74	2.6	56	3.4	95	2.6	15
Subtotal (minor.)	412	22.2	614	34.7	187	25.4	839	29.0	527	32.0	1026	28.3	240
Nonres. Alien	103	5.5	111	6.3	57	7.7	157	5.4	114	6.9	214	5.9	43
White/Cauc.	1283	69.0	1005	56.8	472	64.0	1816	62.8	972	59.0	2288	63.1	689
Unknown	62	3.3	38	2.1	21	2.8	79	2.7	34	2.1	100	2.8	27
Total	1860	51.3	1768	48.7	737	20.3	2891	79.7	1647	45.4	3628		999

Transfers

Transfers in	11
Transfers out	227

Tuition and Fees

	Resident	Nonresident
Full-time	$34,340	$34,340
Part-time	$22,090	$22,090
Tuition Guarantee Program	N	

Living Expenses

Estimated living expenses for singles

Living on campus	Living off campus	Living at home
$14,686	$14,686	$14,686

THE THOMAS M. COOLEY LAW SCHOOL

ABA
Approved
Since
1975

GPA and LSAT Scores

	Total	Full-Time	Part-Time
# of apps	4,032	3,433	599
# of offers	3,230	2,795	435
# of matrics	1,161	188	973
75% GPA	3.35	3.42	3.35
Median GPA	3.02	3.07	2.99
25% GPA	2.61	2.74	2.59
75% LSAT	151	154	149
Median LSAT	146	150	145
25% LSAT	143	145	142

Grants and Scholarships (from prior year)

	Total #	Total %	Full-Time #	Full-Time %	Part-Time #	Part-Time %
Total # of students	3,931		691		3240	
Total # receiving grants	2163	55.0	585	84.7	1578	48.7
Less than 1/2 tuition	1333	33.9	355	51.4	978	30.2
Half to full tuition	684	17.4	189	27.4	495	15.3
Full tuition	146	3.7	41	5.9	105	3.2
More than full tuition	0	0.0	0	0.0	0	0.0
Median grant amount			$9,017		$6,558	

Informational and Library Resources

Total amount spent on library materials	$3,564,758
Study seating capacity inside the library	1,647
# of full-time equivalent professional librarians	28
Hours per week library is open	122
# of open, wired connections available to students	48
# of networked computers available for use by students	253
Has wireless network?	Y
Requires computer?	N

JD Attrition (from prior year)

	Academic #	Other #	Total #	Total %
1st year	124	211	335	16.3
2nd year	33	87	120	12.1
3rd year	8	3	11	1.3
4th year	0	0	0	0.0

Employment (9 months after graduation)

For up-to-date employment data, go to employmentsummary.abaquestionnaire.org on the ABA website.

Bar Passage Rates

First-time takers	851	Reporting %	71.92
Average school %	74.35	Average state %	84.53

Average pass difference −10.18

Jurisdiction	Takers	Passers	Pass %	State %	Diff %
Michigan	336	284	84.52	84.83	−0.31
Illinois	86	61	70.93	89.38	−18.45
New York	85	53	62.35	84.92	−22.57
California	40	11	27.50	71.24	−43.74
Others (2)	65	46	70.77		

The information on these pages was provided by the law school.

THE THOMAS M. COOLEY LAW SCHOOL

PO Box 13038, 300 S. Capitol Avenue, Lansing, MI 48901
9445 Camden Field Parkway, Riverview, FL 33578
Phone: 517.371.5140, ext. 2244; Fax: 517.334.5718
E-mail: admissions@cooley.edu; Website: www.cooley.edu

President's Welcome

The Thomas M. Cooley Law School has earned the reputation for providing graduates with the practical skills necessary for a seamless transition from academia to the real world. Cooley's emphasis on sound academic knowledge, practice skills, and professionalism prepares our graduates for roles of leadership. Cooley was established to provide an opportunity to those who share the dream of becoming a lawyer. Our stated mission is to provide access to the legal profession.

Choosing a law school is a daunting task, particularly with so much misinformation, subjectivity, and bias confronting the potential law student. When you are researching law schools, please look at the three essential attributes of every successful law school—high-quality people, an excellent legal education program, and first-class facilities. These attributes are what should guide your law school selection.

Cooley pioneered practice-based legal education, and has provided law students with the knowledge, skills, and ethics needed for successful practice since 1972. You are invited to learn more about why the people of Cooley are its greatest asset, how our program is a model of modern legal education theory and practice, and how Cooley's facilities are unmatched in size, scope, functionality, and beauty.

People—Our Greatest Asset

Cooley is the largest law school in the nation with the largest full-time faculty in the country, nearly all of whom are former practicing lawyers or judges. Their highest priority is helping students become competent lawyers, and they are accessible and supportive of student activities.

A Global Community—Our students come from all 50 states, we lead all law schools in minority enrollment and foreign national students, and our graduates are found in every state and in numerous foreign countries. Our size and diversity allow our students to practice legal skills as they would in the real world—as a global community.

Knowledge, Skills, and Ethics

Broad Knowledge and Practical Curriculum—Cooley's 90-credit-hour curriculum provides all students with the substantive knowledge, legal skills, and ethics needed for bar examinations, law practice, and further graduate study. Students complete 63 hours of required substantive and skills-based courses, and have the option of focusing their electives in one of ten practice area concentrations.

Practical Skills and Clinics—Students build legal skills through simulation courses. Competitions in client counseling, negotiation, pretrial, trial, and appellate skills allow outstanding students to gain recognition on national teams competing against others across the country. Practice skills are woven into substantive courses throughout the curriculum. Cooley's expansive clinical programs immerse students in hands-on learning. Students can choose from one of Cooley's ten clinics or from more than 2,700 externship sites around the globe.

World Leader in Plain English Writing—Recognized as a world leader in training students in the use of plain language,

Cooley has the preeminent research and writing program and an innovative curriculum.

Lifelong Ethics—Beginning with the application process, Cooley fosters a culture of professionalism. At each step of the law school journey, students are challenged to adopt professionalism as a way of life.

Facilities—Unmatched in Size and Beauty

Four Campus Locations in Michigan: Ann Arbor, Auburn Hills, Grand Rapids, and Lansing, and one in Tampa Bay, Florida—Cooley's five distinct campuses are unmatched in size and functionality. Each campus has a full complement of faculty, staff, libraries, and services. Our buildings and technology meet the academic and research needs of today's legal community. High-tech courtrooms and classrooms are equipped with the latest technology to enhance the educational experience. Cooley's library facilities are among the nation's largest and finest. The 700,000+ volume collection includes research materials from all 50 states as well as federal and international materials.

Accessible, Affordable Legal Education

The Juris Doctor curriculum is offered at each of Cooley's locations. Cooley operates a rolling admissions process with the option of starting classes in January, May, or September. Students can study full or part time. They can complete the JD degree in two to five years by choosing from flexible scheduling options. Classes are offered mornings, afternoons, evenings, and on weekends.

Cooley uses a straightforward, objective formula to determine eligibility (UGPA x 15 + Highest LSAT = Admission Index). Admission to Cooley is also contingent on meeting character and fitness standards. There is no application fee.

Scholarships—Thanks in part to a generous scholarship program, Cooley is among the nation's most affordable independent law schools. Prospective students can determine the scholarship amount before applying. Students can earn up to 100 percent of tuition in two ways:

1. Admission Index levels:

Index	Honors Scholarship
215+	100%
210–214	75%
205–209	50%
195–204	25%

2. Student's highest LSAT score:

LSAT	Honors Scholarship
163+	100%
158–162	75%
153–157	50%
149–152	25%

Michigan and Florida residents may qualify for resident and LSAT Honors Scholarships. Qualified **Canadian students** may be eligible to attend Cooley at a reduced cost. **Transfer students** are eligible for scholarships. Students retain their scholarships throughout their enrollment as long as they are not subject to sanctions under the Honor Code Disciplinary Procedures. Nonscholarship financial aid is available. Please refer to www.cooley.edu for the most current information.

Expenses—Tuition: $1,225 per credit hour in 2011–2012. **Fees:** $20 per term. See Cooley's online tuition calculator to compare tuition costs.

An Active, Engaged Academic Community

Scholarly Community, Scholarly Publications—Cooley faculty have experience in practice, a focus on teaching, and an interest in scholarship. Cooley's *Thomas M. Cooley Law Review* provides students opportunities to edit and publish traditional in-depth legal scholarship. The student editors of the *Journal of Practical and Clinical Law* work with lawyers and professors to address common concerns of lawyers and judges. Cooley's newest publications, the *Art and Museum Law Journal* and the *Journal of Ethics and Responsibility,* expand scholarship opportunities. **Symposia** bring together scholars from around the world to discuss timely topics. **Centers** in Ethics and Responsibility, Forensic Science and the Law, and Indian Law foster discussion and research. **Collaborations** with major research institutions open opportunities for dual-degree programs, including Juris Doctor/Master of Public Administration, Juris Doctor/Master of Social Work, and Juris Doctor/Master of Business Administration programs with Oakland University and Western Michigan University. **Service**—Cooley strives to foster the highest caliber of relationships with surrounding communities. The Cooley Volunteer Corps matches organizations with students seeking substantive volunteer experiences. All students are members of the Student Bar Association, and there are more than 50 clubs and organizations in which students can become involved.

Commitment to Academic Success

Students receive support and enrichment at the Academic Resource Center (ARC). The staff provide ongoing assistance though Introduction to Law class, seminars, one-on-one coaching, and other programs to help students refine

skills critical to a successful legal career. Cooley provides students with institutional support to prepare them for state bar examinations, including practice bar exams, prebar courses, and individual counseling. Computer-assisted legal instruction, assistance for students requiring disability accommodations, and other support services are all free to students.

A Culture of Professionalism

National Professionalism Award—Cooley was awarded the American Bar Association's *E. Smythe Gambrell Professionalism Award* for its innovative Professionalism Plan. Professional development combines classroom experience, volunteering, public service, pro bono work, clinical experience, employment, and mentoring. **Faculty and Career and Professional Development** staff assist students in developing professionalism portfolios that prepare them for their chosen careers. Students can take advantage of résumé review services, mock interview programs, online job bulletins, and workshops.

Graduate and International Studies

LLM—Cooley offers graduate law degrees in Tax, Intellectual Property, Corporate Law and Finance, Insurance Law, US Law for Foreign Lawyers, and Self-Directed Legal Studies. Dual JD/LLM degree programs are available. LLM tuition in 2011–2012 is $631 per credit hour.

International Studies—Cooley students study law around the world. Each January, Cooley's 13-week program in Australia beckons students "down under." In the summer, Cooley invites students to Toronto, Canada. Cooley cooperates with other law schools to provide students with options extending around the globe.

APPLICANT PROFILE

Typically, schools include a statistical table showing the likelihood of admission to their program. Cooley instead uses a straightforward, fair, objective, and transparent formula to

determine eligibility for admission. Please visit our website at www.cooley.edu for the several ways to qualify for admission.

THOMAS JEFFERSON SCHOOL OF LAW

1155 Island Avenue
San Diego, CA 92101
Phone: 619.297.9700; 800.956.5070; Fax: 619.961.1300
E-mail: admissions@tjsl.edu; Website: www.tjsl.edu

ABA Approved Since 1996

The Basics

Type of school	Private
Term	Semester
Application deadline	11/1 3/1
Application fee	$50
Financial aid deadline	5/1
Can first year start other than fall?	Yes
Student to faculty ratio	19.3 to 1
# of housing spaces available restricted to law students	172
graduate housing for which law students are eligible	

Faculty and Administrators

	Total		Men		Women		Minorities	
	Spr	Fall	Spr	Fall	Spr	Fall	Spr	Fall
Full-time	40	39	20	21	20	18	8	8
Other full-time	3	3	0	0	3	3	2	1
Deans, librarians, & others who teach	7	8	6	6	1	2	0	0
Part-time	25	28	18	20	7	8	2	0
Total	75	78	44	47	31	31	12	9

Curriculum

	Full-Time	Part-Time
Typical first-year section size	75	75
Is there typically a "small section" of the first-year class, other than Legal Writing, taught by full-time faculty	No	No
If yes, typical size offered last year		
# of classroom course titles beyond first-year curriculum	102	

# of upper division courses, excluding seminars, with an enrollment:		
	Under 25	60
	25–49	25
	50–74	23
	75–99	2
	100+	1

# of seminars	17	
# of seminar positions available	340	
# of seminar positions filled	109	85
# of positions available in simulation courses	695	
# of simulation positions filled	236	278
# of positions available in faculty supervised clinical courses	24	
# of faculty supervised clinical positions filled	19	5
# involved in field placements	285	86
# involved in law journals	65	21
# involved in moot court or trial competitions	61	26
# of credit hours required to graduate	88	

JD Enrollment and Ethnicity

	Men		Women		Full-Time		Part-Time		1st-Year		Total		JD Degs. Awd.
	#	%	#	%	#	%	#	%	#	%	#	%	
All Hispanics	78	13.0	72	15.5	96	12.6	54	17.6	69	19.8	150	14.1	41
Am. Ind./AK Nat.	6	1.0	5	1.1	7	0.9	4	1.3	4	1.1	11	1.0	1
Asian	11	1.8	29	6.2	28	3.7	12	3.9	27	7.8	40	3.8	0
Black/Af. Am.	31	5.2	32	6.9	44	5.8	19	6.2	21	6.0	63	5.9	14
Nat. HI/Pac. Isl.	48	8.0	41	8.8	59	7.8	30	9.8	4	1.1	89	8.3	23
2 or more races	0	0.0	0	0.0	0	0.0	0	0.0	0	0.0	0	0.0	0
Subtotal (minor.)	174	29.0	179	38.4	234	30.8	119	38.8	125	35.9	353	33.1	79
Nonres. Alien	9	1.5	6	1.3	15	2.0	0	0.0	4	1.1	15	1.4	1
White/Cauc.	417	69.5	281	60.3	510	67.2	188	61.2	219	62.9	698	65.5	155
Unknown	0	0.0	0	0.0	0	0.0	0	0.0	0	0.0	0	0.0	0
Total	600	56.3	466	43.7	759	71.2	307	28.8	348	32.6	1066		235

Transfers

Transfers in	3
Transfers out	43

Tuition and Fees

	Resident	Nonresident
Full-time	$41,000	$41,000
Part-time	$30,000	$30,000
Tuition Guarantee Program	N	

Living Expenses

Estimated living expenses for singles

Living on campus	Living off campus	Living at home
$26,530	$26,530	$14,250

THOMAS JEFFERSON SCHOOL OF LAW

*ABA
Approved
Since
1996*

GPA and LSAT Scores

	Total	Full-Time	Part-Time
# of apps	2,697	2,321	376
# of offers	1,478	1,280	198
# of matrics	440	338	102
75% GPA	3.26	3.25	3.30
Median GPA	3.01	3.00	3.02
25% GPA	2.76	2.77	2.74
75% LSAT	153	153	150
Median LSAT	151	151	148
25% LSAT	148	149	146

Grants and Scholarships (from prior year)

	Total #	Total %	Full-Time #	Full-Time %	Part-Time #	Part-Time %
Total # of students	966		687		279	
Total # receiving grants	454	47.0	329	47.9	125	44.8
Less than 1/2 tuition	344	35.6	266	38.7	78	28.0
Half to full tuition	108	11.2	63	9.2	45	16.1
Full tuition	1	0.1	0	0.0	1	0.4
More than full tuition	1	0.1	0	0.0	1	0.4
Median grant amount			$14,000		$12,000	

Informational and Library Resources

Total amount spent on library materials	$1,011,418
Study seating capacity inside the library	372
# of full-time equivalent professional librarians	10
Hours per week library is open	119
# of open, wired connections available to students	0
# of networked computers available for use by students	25
Has wireless network?	Y
Requires computer?	Y

JD Attrition (from prior year)

	Academic #	Other #	Total #	Total %
1st year	32	67	99	28.0
2nd year	8	7	15	4.4
3rd year	1	0	1	0.6
4th year	0	0	0	0.0

Employment (9 months after graduation)

For up-to-date employment data, go to employmentsummary.abaquestionnaire.org on the ABA website.

Bar Passage Rates

First-time takers	212	Reporting %	100.00
Average school %	54.70	Average state %	72.91
Average pass difference	−18.21		

Jurisdiction	Takers	Passers	Pass %	State %	Diff %
California	177	99	55.93	71.24	−15.31
New York	8	5	62.50	84.92	−22.42
Arizona	5	2	40.00	80.74	−40.74
New Jersey	5	1	20.00	82.34	−62.34
Nevada	2	0	00.00	72.72	−72.72

THOMAS JEFFERSON SCHOOL OF LAW

1155 Island Avenue
San Diego, CA 92101
Phone: 619.297.9700; 800.956.5070; Fax: 619.961.1300
E-mail: admissions@tjsl.edu; Website: www.tjsl.edu

Welcome

Thomas Jefferson School of Law (TJSL) is a private, nonprofit, and independent law school. Accredited by the ABA and a member of AALS, the law school emphasizes an individualized approach to learning by integrating the cognitive sciences and learning theory into its curriculum.

The flexible curriculum allows students to begin their studies in either August or January. Also, students can pursue a law degree in a full- or part-time (day or evening) program and accelerate graduation by attending classes in the summer. This multitrack approach, traceable to the school's roots as a longtime supporter of military personnel and working adults, gives students the option of pursuing a law degree full or part time while continuing their employment.

Admission

Thomas Jefferson utilizes a rolling admission process under which applicants are considered when their applications are complete. While there is no deadline for the fall or spring term, applications are accepted through July for the fall term and through December for the spring term. However, due to the large applicant pool, early applications are encouraged. The Admissions Committee functions with a holistic approach, which includes considering the applicant's LSAT score, undergraduate record, extracurricular activities, work ethic and experience, and demonstrated ability to overcome adversity. Decisions are made and sent out on a rolling basis.

New Campus Opened Spring 2011

The law school recently moved into a new eight-story, high-rise building in Downtown San Diego. The law school expects to earn Gold Level certification from the Leadership in Energy and Environmental Design (LEED) Green Building Rating System of the US Green Building Council. The $70-million campus features a state-of-the-art library, in-house legal clinics, and a café. The location places students within walking distance from many law firms, major businesses, and the state and federal courts. Student housing is available within one block of the law school.

Vibrant and Diverse Student Community

The mission of the Thomas Jefferson School of Law is to provide an outstanding legal education for a nationally based, diverse student body in a collegial and supportive environment. The law school lives up to that mission in every way. The TJSL campus truly reflects its commitment to diversity: the student body is gender-balanced, 20 percent of the students are the first in their family to attend law school, students of color consistently represent between 30–35 percent of the student body, many students are openly GLBT, at least 20 percent are multilingual, and they represent more than 23 countries.

San Diego—America's Finest City

San Diego is uniquely situated and has major advantages for the study of law, professional development, and personal fulfillment. Its mild Mediterranean climate promises nearly 265 days of sunshine annually and moderate temperatures throughout the year. As the border city to Tijuana, Mexico, and just 120 miles south of Los Angeles, San Diego is a training ground for everything from international law to entertainment law. Also, as the second largest city in California and the eighth largest city in the United States, it is a vibrant social and economic center.

Internationally Renowned Faculty

TJSL is proud to have a first-rate faculty consisting of distinguished practitioners and scholars. Our professors have structured business transactions at both the international and the domestic levels and have litigated before the World Court at The Hague, the US Supreme Court, and federal and state trial and appellate courts. Their clients have ranged from the largest multinational corporations to the most impoverished members of society.

All 44 members of our faculty pride themselves on providing quality instruction and being accessible to students outside the classroom. First-year students are assigned faculty advisors, but all members of the faculty emphasize being available to students outside of class.

Cutting-Edge Legal Skills Programs

Our academic resources consist of a writing lab, student organization-led study sessions, and individual feedback from professors. However, the anchor of our academic resources is the highly effective academic success program, the **SUMMIT Series**, which is a part of the first-year curriculum and continues until preparation for the bar exam. The series brings scientific principles in psychology, neuroscience, and cognitive science to the study of law and equips students with a personal and succinct methodology for acquiring the fundamental skills to succeed in law school and on the bar exam. Our **Bar Secrets** course is a continuation of these principles and is a proven means of preparing for the California bar exam.

Progressive and Practical Curriculum

The academic program at Thomas Jefferson School of Law has been carefully designed to ensure a balanced and comprehensive curriculum that will prepare students to practice in any area of the law. During their first semester, entering students have the opportunity, in all their courses, to receive feedback from the faculty on their written legal analytical skills in order to enhance their understanding of the course material and hone their performance prior to final exams.

Academic Centers. A growing faculty has allowed the school to acquire special strengths in the areas of law that most reflect our changing world; that is, those relating to technological change, globalization, and the transformation of our social order. To provide an institutional framework for the study of these embryonic areas of law, the school has established four Academic Centers: (1) the **Center for Law and Intellectual Property** prepares students for careers related to high technology and communications; (2) the **Center for Global Legal Studies** prepares students for the transborder aspects of contemporary legal practice and offers a wide variety of courses in international law; (3) the **Center for Law and Social Justice** prepares students for practice geared toward the preservation of the values of liberty and equality in an ever-changing world; and (4) the **Center for Sports Law and Policy** prepares students for engagement with and employment in the growing sports industry.

The Externship Program. Rated as one of the top law schools in the United States for externships, TJSL offers a large number of courses that train students in professional skills, supplemented by a variety of field-placement programs. Our externship coordinator works with students to place them in an endless number and type of for-credit legal positions. Past placements consist of public legal agencies, private law firms, corporations, and sports teams. Students may earn up to 10 credits from externship placements.

JD/MBA Program

In eight semesters, students can earn a Juris Doctor degree from Thomas Jefferson School of Law and a Master of Business Administration degree from San Diego State University (SDSU). The objective of the concurrent degree program is to prepare students who are competent in both law and business for career opportunities in areas where the two fields converge.

Applicants must adhere to the application process for each institution, including taking both the LSAT for law school admission and GMAT for business school admission. The curricular sequence requires students to attend their first two semesters as a full-time student at TJSL. Students take classes at both campuses the following semesters.

International Law Programs

Thomas Jefferson School of Law offers three LLM (Master of Laws) programs and a JSD (Scientiae Juridicae Doctor) via residence, web and videoconferencing, and a combination thereof. Two of the LLMs—International Trade and Investment and International Tax and Financial Services—create practice-ready graduates set to engage with globally oriented firms and clients. The third LLM is for foreign law graduates to obtain a working knowledge of the US legal system, and obtain eligibility for certain state bar exams. The JSD is the interchangeable equivalent to a PhD in the social sciences, requiring a publicly defended, substantial dissertation and postgraduate coursework.

Student Activities

Thomas Jefferson School of Law has more than 30 student organizations that provide a source of mutual support for various groups of students, including the Student Bar Association, Black Law Students Association, Student Veterans of America, and the Criminal Law Society. Student organizations are also formed as a result of heightened student interest in substantive areas of law practice, such as the International Law Society, the Entertainment and Sports Law Societies, and the Public Interest Law Foundation.

These organizations promote leadership within the community, as well as programming on various areas of the law. Student leaders serve as members of law school committees and provide a student voice to decision making. Student managed and edited publications include the *Thomas Jefferson Law Review* and the *iPlog*, which focuses on intellectual property. Cocurricular programs include the Moot Court, Mock Trial, and Alternative Dispute Resolution teams.

A Focus on Career Development

Currently staffed by four diverse lawyers, the Career Services team members work closely with the Externship Office to provide individual counseling to every student. Starting in the first semester, the staff works to develop a personal relationship with each student to assess interests and preferences, and develop strategies for securing internships. From there, the staff continues to engage and work closely with each student in every phase of the student's law school career, from developing a legal résumé and cover letter to helping the student negotiate a salary for the first postgraduate legal position. With an active on-campus recruiting program, the Career Services Office uses cutting-edge technology to assist students with securing internships and postgraduate positions. This includes providing every student with access to Symplicity, a comprehensive, web-based legal recruiting tool through which a student applies for internships and postgraduate legal positions. Communication with students about job postings and career-related topics is done through the school's website and with the help of most social media outlets including Twitter and Facebook.

Financial Aid and Scholarships

TJSL commits more than $5 million annually in scholarship assistance. Over 40 percent of first-year students receive awards that range from $4,000 to full-tuition scholarships. Offering both need- and merit-based scholarships, TJSL uses its funds for both recruitment as well as retention. Initial awards are based on information accessible through the application. Applicants who have significant financial need and would like to be considered for financial aid may submit a separate request for scholarship consideration. All scholarship recipients receive a detailed offer letter containing the terms of the award and any criteria for renewal.

The law school also makes awards from all available federal sources, including the work-study program, Direct Loan programs, Perkins Loans, and Veterans benefits under the Post 9/11 GI Bill. Approximately 95 percent of the student body receives some form of federal assistance. Applicants should submit the FAFSA at www.fafsa.gov. Our school code is 013780.

Applicant Profile Not Available

THE UNIVERSITY OF TOLEDO COLLEGE OF LAW

2801 West Bancroft Street, MS 507
Toledo, OH 43606-3390
Phone: 419.530.4131; Fax: 419.530.4345
E-mail: law.admissions@utoledo.edu; Website: law.utoledo.edu

ABA
Approved
Since
1939

The Basics

Type of school	Public
Term	Semester
Application deadline	8/1
Application fee	$0
Financial aid deadline	4/1
Can first year start other than fall?	No
Student to faculty ratio	13.2 to 1
# of housing spaces available restricted to law students	
graduate housing for which law students are eligible	

Faculty and Administrators

	Total		Men		Women		Minorities	
	Spr	Fall	Spr	Fall	Spr	Fall	Spr	Fall
Full-time	23	28	14	16	9	12	3	3
Other full-time	0	0	0	0	0	0	0	0
Deans, librarians, & others who teach	4	4	2	2	2	2	0	0
Part-time	23	17	15	12	8	5	0	0
Total	50	49	31	30	19	19	3	3

Curriculum

		Full-Time	Part-Time
Typical first-year section size		53	36
Is there typically a "small section" of the first-year class, other than Legal Writing, taught by full-time faculty		No	No
If yes, typical size offered last year			
# of classroom course titles beyond first-year curriculum		87	
# of upper division courses, excluding seminars, with an enrollment:	Under 25	82	
	25–49	30	
	50–74	8	
	75–99	1	
	100+	0	
# of seminars		5	
# of seminar positions available		67	
# of seminar positions filled		53	3
# of positions available in simulation courses		426	
# of simulation positions filled		184	43
# of positions available in faculty supervised clinical courses		90	
# of faculty supervised clinical positions filled		44	5
# involved in field placements		83	9
# involved in law journals		46	1
# involved in moot court or trial competitions		44	5
# of credit hours required to graduate		89	

JD Enrollment and Ethnicity

	Men		Women		Full-Time		Part-Time		1st-Year		Total		JD Degs. Awd.
	#	%	#	%	#	%	#	%	#	%	#	%	
All Hispanics	7	2.7	7	4.0	11	3.1	3	3.8	3	1.9	14	3.2	2
Am. Ind./AK Nat.	1	0.4	2	1.1	2	0.6	1	1.3	2	1.3	3	0.7	0
Asian	6	2.3	5	2.9	9	2.5	2	2.5	3	1.9	11	2.5	5
Black/Af. Am.	11	4.2	5	2.9	13	3.6	3	3.8	3	1.9	16	3.7	3
Nat. HI/Pac. Isl.	0	0.0	0	0.0	0	0.0	0	0.0	0	0.0	0	0.0	0
2 or more races	0	0.0	0	0.0	0	0.0	0	0.0	0	0.0	0	0.0	0
Subtotal (minor.)	25	9.5	19	10.9	35	9.8	9	11.3	11	7.1	44	10.1	10
Nonres. Alien	4	1.5	2	1.1	5	1.4	1	1.3	1	0.6	6	1.4	3
White/Cauc.	170	64.9	121	69.1	238	66.7	53	66.3	93	60.4	291	66.6	64
Unknown	63	24.0	33	18.9	79	22.1	17	21.3	49	31.8	96	22.0	38
Total	262	60.0	175	40.0	357	81.7	80	18.3	154	35.2	437		115

Transfers

Transfers in	3
Transfers out	22

Tuition and Fees

	Resident	Nonresident
Full-time	$20,742	$31,846
Part-time	$15,569	$23,897
Tuition Guarantee Program		N

Living Expenses

Estimated living expenses for singles

Living on campus	Living off campus	Living at home
$15,078	$17,726	$8,533

THE UNIVERSITY OF TOLEDO COLLEGE OF LAW

ABA
Approved
Since
1939

GPA and LSAT Scores

	Total	Full-Time	Part-Time
# of apps	1,440	1,301	139
# of offers	626	578	48
# of matrics	136	118	18
75% GPA	3.57	3.57	3.49
Median GPA	3.33	3.35	3.25
25% GPA	3.05	3.05	3.12
75% LSAT	155	155	156
Median LSAT	153	153	153
25% LSAT	150	151	150

Grants and Scholarships (from prior year)

	Total		Full-Time		Part-Time	
	#	%	#	%	#	%
Total # of students	460		365		95	
Total # receiving grants	185	40.2	166	45.5	19	20.0
Less than 1/2 tuition	35	7.6	30	8.2	5	5.3
Half to full tuition	66	14.3	62	17.0	4	4.2
Full tuition	76	16.5	66	18.1	10	10.5
More than full tuition	8	1.7	8	2.2	0	0.0
Median grant amount			$13,819		$8,535	

Informational and Library Resources

Total amount spent on library materials	$474,833
Study seating capacity inside the library	486
# of full-time equivalent professional librarians	4
Hours per week library is open	109
# of open, wired connections available to students	34
# of networked computers available for use by students	23
Has wireless network?	Y
Requires computer?	N

JD Attrition (from prior year)

	Academic	Other	Total	
	#	#	#	%
1st year	6	33	39	20.6
2nd year	0	9	9	6.0
3rd year	0	2	2	2.1
4th year	0	2	2	7.7

Employment (9 months after graduation)

For up-to-date employment data, go to employmentsummary.abaquestionnaire.org on the ABA website.

Bar Passage Rates

First-time takers	139	Reporting %	92.09
Average school %	84.38	Average state %	85.79
Average pass difference	−1.41		

Jurisdiction	Takers	Passers	Pass %	State %	Diff %
Ohio	94	79	84.04	86.14	−2.10
Michigan	34	29	85.29	84.83	0.46

THE UNIVERSITY OF TOLEDO COLLEGE OF LAW

2801 West Bancroft Street, MS 507
Toledo, OH 43606-3390
Phone: 419.530.4131; Fax: 419.530.4345
E-mail: law.admissions@utoledo.edu; Website: law.utoledo.edu

Introduction

The University of Toledo is a state university of more than 23,000 students, conveniently located on the western edge of Toledo, in one of the city's nicest residential areas. The city of Toledo offers both the cultural amenities of a big city and the affordable cost of living and close-knit feel of a small town.

The College of Law, located on the main campus of the University of Toledo, is accredited by the ABA and is a member of the AALS and the League of Ohio Law Schools. We have been training lawyers since 1906 and, in 1984, were awarded a chapter of the Order of the Coif.

Toledo Law is a vibrant community of outstanding faculty, students, and alumni who are making a difference across the country and around the world. We offer a rich and engaged classroom experience guided by faculty members who are leaders in their fields and a wide range of programs designed to help you develop and sharpen the practical skills you will need. From your first day on campus, you will be part of a close-knit community committed to your success.

Enrollment/Student Body

Total enrollment in the College of Law is around 450 students. The Fall 2011 entering class consisted of 137 students.

The diverse student body at Toledo Law is engaged in learning and service. Over the last several years, our students have come to us from over 130 undergraduate institutions in 13 states, 3 US territories, and 7 foreign countries.

Students come from a variety of backgrounds. Many come straight from college, while others have worked for years. This diversity exposes students to an interesting, stimulating, and creative atmosphere where insights and ideas flourish. Our diversity is reflected in student groups and activities, representing a broad spectrum of social, political, ethnic, and religious perspectives.

Faculty

The faculty of Toledo Law is distinctive. Our faculty makes students and learning their top priority. They have open-door policies, participate in student events, and make every student's future a personal concern. With a student/faculty ratio of 13:1, students at Toledo Law get the personal attention they deserve.

In addition to being outstanding teachers, they are outstanding scholars, and many have earned national acclaim. The faculty includes graduates of top law schools, Fulbright scholars, members of the prestigious American Law Institute, and accomplished lawyers with years of private practice and public interest experience.

Library and Physical Facilities

The spacious, newly renovated Law Center includes tiered classrooms, a striking student lounge, a state-of-the-art moot courtroom, and an amphitheater-style auditorium. The entire building offers next-generation wireless access and all classrooms include Smart Board technology.

Occupying four levels within the Law Center, the library contains group study rooms and a modern computer lab available for use by law students. Students are trained in the use of two vast electronic law libraries—LexisNexis and Westlaw.

Curriculum

Toledo Law requires the successful completion of 89 semester hours for graduation. The curriculum in the first year of the full-time program and the first two years of the part-time program consists of required courses. An extensive upper-level curriculum covers traditional as well as cutting-edge subjects, and incorporates development of professional legal skills and values.

Our academic success program provides teaching assistants for students in all basic required courses and offers tutors for any student who requests academic support.

Special Programs

Certificates of Concentration: Students can graduate with certificates of concentration in criminal, environmental, intellectual property, international, and labor/employment law.

Joint-Degree Programs: Toledo Law has joint-degree programs leading to a Master of Science in Engineering, a Master of Business Administration, a Master of Public Administration, or a Master of Arts in Criminal Justice. Students may also design individual joint-degree programs.

Legal Clinics: A pioneer in clinical legal education, Toledo Law provides an atmosphere for learning basic lawyering techniques and allows students the opportunity to further sharpen their skills in live client settings. Under close supervision, students appear in court in both civil and criminal cases. The clinical program is an important component of the overall educational experience for upper-level students. The wide array of clinical offerings enables students to gain practical legal experience before graduation. Toledo Law offers a Civil Practice Clinic, a Criminal Law Practice Program, a Dispute Resolution Clinic, a Domestic Violence and Juvenile Law Clinic, and a Public Service Externship Clinic.

Speaker Series, Symposia, and National Conferences: Toledo Law hosts a top-notch speaker series and multiple symposia and conferences. For example, Toledo Law hosts an annual Great Lakes Water Conference to address legal and policy issues critical to the Great Lakes. Entering its second decade, the conference has become a high-profile international forum for addressing some of the most important environmental issues of our time.

Student Activities

The *University of Toledo Law Review* is published four times a year by student members who are selected on the basis of academic performance and a writing competition.

Training and practice in brief writing and oral argument beyond the required appellate advocacy course are obtained through the Moot Court Program and Trial Advocacy Team, in the Charles Fornoff Intramural Moot Court Competition, and in several national and regional competitions.

The Student Bar Association, American Constitution Society, Black Law Students Association, Business Law Association, Criminal Justice Society, Environmental Law

Society, Family and Juvenile Law Society, Federalist Society, Health Law Association, Intellectual Property Law Society, International Law Society, Labor and Employment Law Association, OUTLaw (LGBT), Public Interest Law Association, Sports Law Association, and Women Law Students Association are among many active organizations.

Admission

Applicants must have received a bachelor's degree from an accredited college or university before the first day of law classes. We do not require any particular prelaw curriculum. We recommend that students take courses involving analysis, writing, and quantitative skills.

Admission decisions are the responsibility of the Admissions Committee. The committee begins to review applications in October for admission to the next fall's entering class. Applications are reviewed and decisions are made on a continuing basis.

The Admissions Committee considers undergraduate grades and transcript, LSAT scores, recommendations, professional experience, postgraduate educational experience, extracurricular activities, community service and involvement, and a personal statement.

Prospective students are encouraged to visit the law school, talk to our students and faculty, and sit in on a class. Appointments can be made through the Law Admissions Office.

Financial Aid

Toledo Law strives to provide a quality legal education at an affordable cost. The College of Law awards scholarships totaling in excess of $1.5 million each year, and all admitted students are considered for scholarship awards without separate application.

The goal of the financial aid program is to ensure that graduates have the greatest freedom to choose their careers without constraints from financial obligations.

Residents of Monroe County, Michigan, are treated as Ohio residents for tuition purposes. All remaining non-Ohio residents are charged an out-of-state surcharge to attend the University of Toledo. However, Toledo Law will cover this surcharge with an out-of-state tuition award for qualified residents of the following six Michigan counties: Hillsdale, Lenawee, Macomb, Oakland, Washtenaw, and Wayne.

In and Around Toledo

Toledo is one of the four largest metropolitan areas in Ohio and within 60 miles of Detroit and Ann Arbor, Michigan. Toledo offers both the cultural amenities of a big city and the affordable cost of living and close-knit feel of a small town. With a symphony, a ballet, a world-class art museum, a hands-on science museum, professional sports teams, and one of the region's best zoos, there is plenty to do and see.

Toledo also provides prime access to legal opportunities. The City of Toledo is home to local, state, and federal courts, and the Toledo Bar Association, which offers membership to law students, is a great resource for connecting to the local legal community.

Professional Development/Career Services

Toledo Law places top priority on providing comprehensive career planning and professional development for its students and graduates. The Office of Professional Development/Law Career Services assists students through workshops and counseling, and brings members of the local bar association and alumni from around the country together to support students in every aspect of professional growth and development.

As a result of both on- and off-campus interviews, second- and third-year students accept summer law clerk and attorney positions in all major cities of Ohio and Michigan, as well as locations throughout the United States. Graduates are successfully practicing in major law firms, government offices, the judiciary, and in public interest positions in nearly every state. Graduates also can be found in Asia, Europe, and Africa.

Toledo Law alumni are a valuable resource for current students as they pursue employment opportunities nationwide.

APPLICANT PROFILE

The University of Toledo College of Law
This grid includes only applicants who earned 120–180 LSAT scores under standard administrations.

LSAT Score	GPA								
	3.75 +	3.50–3.74	3.25–3.49	3.00–3.24	2.75–2.99	2.50–2.74	2.25–2.49	2.00–2.24	Below 2.00
175–180									
170–174									
165–169									
160–164									
155–159									
150–154									
145–149									
140–144									
135–139									
130–134									
125–129									
120–124									

■ Good Possibility   ☐ Possible   ▨ Unlikely

TOURO COLLEGE—JACOB D. FUCHSBERG LAW CENTER

225 Eastview Drive
Central Islip, NY 11722
Phone: 631.761.7010; Fax: 631.761.7019
E-mail: admissions@tourolaw.edu; Website: www.tourolaw.edu

ABA Approved Since 1983

The Basics

Type of school	Private
Term	Semester
Application deadline	7/15
Application fee	$60
Financial aid deadline	5/12
Can first year start other than fall?	No
Student to faculty ratio	16.5 to 1
# of housing spaces available restricted to law students	
graduate housing for which law students are eligible	

Faculty and Administrators

	Total Spr	Total Fall	Men Spr	Men Fall	Women Spr	Women Fall	Minorities Spr	Minorities Fall
Full-time	35	36	20	21	15	15	3	2
Other full-time	3	4	2	2	1	2	0	0
Deans, librarians, & others who teach	8	9	1	1	7	8	1	2
Part-time	35	35	27	25	8	10	5	5
Total	81	84	50	49	31	35	9	9

Curriculum

	Full-Time	Part-Time
Typical first-year section size	70	59
Is there typically a "small section" of the first-year class, other than Legal Writing, taught by full-time faculty	No	No
If yes, typical size offered last year		
# of classroom course titles beyond first-year curriculum	101	
# of upper division courses, excluding seminars, with an enrollment: Under 25	126	
25–49	30	
50–74	20	
75–99	1	
100+	3	
# of seminars	9	
# of seminar positions available	180	
# of seminar positions filled	104	29
# of positions available in simulation courses	612	
# of simulation positions filled	296	154
# of positions available in faculty supervised clinical courses	140	
# of faculty supervised clinical positions filled	100	23
# involved in field placements	142	23
# involved in law journals	36	11
# involved in moot court or trial competitions	28	10
# of credit hours required to graduate	88	

JD Enrollment and Ethnicity

	Men #	Men %	Women #	Women %	Full-Time #	Full-Time %	Part-Time #	Part-Time %	1st-Year #	1st-Year %	Total #	Total %	JD Degs. Awd.
All Hispanics	32	7.4	42	11.3	59	10.2	15	6.7	34	12.8	74	9.2	16
Am. Ind./AK Nat.	1	0.2	1	0.3	2	0.3	0	0.0	1	0.4	2	0.2	0
Asian	26	6.0	24	6.4	32	5.5	18	8.0	13	4.9	50	6.2	14
Black/Af. Am.	26	6.0	61	16.4	52	9.0	35	15.6	25	9.4	87	10.8	12
Nat. HI/Pac. Isl.	0	0.0	1	0.3	1	0.2	0	0.0	1	0.4	1	0.1	0
2 or more races	0	0.0	0	0.0	0	0.0	0	0.0	0	0.0	0	0.0	0
Subtotal (minor.)	85	19.7	129	34.6	146	25.2	68	30.2	74	27.8	214	26.6	42
Nonres. Alien	4	0.9	4	1.1	8	1.4	0	0.0	4	1.5	8	1.0	7
White/Cauc.	319	73.8	225	60.3	402	69.3	142	63.1	177	66.5	544	67.6	163
Unknown	24	5.6	15	4.0	24	4.1	15	6.7	11	4.1	39	4.8	8
Total	432	53.7	373	46.3	580	72.0	225	28.0	266	33.0	805		220

Transfers

Transfers in	23
Transfers out	51

Tuition and Fees

	Resident	Nonresident
Full-time	$41,890	$41,890
Part-time	$31,400	$31,400
Tuition Guarantee Program	N	

Living Expenses

Estimated living expenses for singles

Living on campus	Living off campus	Living at home
$24,635	$24,635	$11,086

TOURO COLLEGE—JACOB D. FUCHSBERG LAW CENTER

ABA Approved Since 1983

GPA and LSAT Scores

	Total	Full-Time	Part-Time
# of apps	1,652	1,340	313
# of offers	851	706	145
# of matrics	260	195	65
75% GPA	3.42	3.40	3.47
Median GPA	3.18	3.17	3.19
25% GPA	2.91	2.93	2.88
75% LSAT	153	153	153
Median LSAT	151	151	149
25% LSAT	148	149	147

Grants and Scholarships (from prior year)

	Total		Full-Time		Part-Time	
	#	%	#	%	#	%
Total # of students	828		601		227	
Total # receiving grants	414	50.0	332	55.2	82	36.1
Less than 1/2 tuition	382	46.1	309	51.4	73	32.2
Half to full tuition	28	3.4	22	3.7	6	2.6
Full tuition	4	0.5	1	0.2	3	1.3
More than full tuition	0	0.0	0	0.0	0	0.0
Median grant amount			$8,400		$6,900	

Informational and Library Resources

Total amount spent on library materials	$1,325,828
Study seating capacity inside the library	476
# of full-time equivalent professional librarians	12.5
Hours per week library is open	83
# of open, wired connections available to students	0
# of networked computers available for use by students	48
Has wireless network?	Y
Requires computer?	N

JD Attrition (from prior year)

	Academic	Other	Total	
	#	#	#	%
1st year	14	55	69	23.8
2nd year	2	7	9	3.5
3rd year	0	0	0	0.0
4th year	0	0	0	0.0

Employment (9 months after graduation)

For up-to-date employment data, go to employmentsummary.abaquestionnaire.org on the ABA website.

Bar Passage Rates

First-time takers	249	Reporting %	72.29
Average school %	71.11	Average state %	84.92

Average pass difference −13.81

Jurisdiction	Takers	Passers	Pass %	State %	Diff %
New York	180	128	71.11	84.92	−13.81

TOURO COLLEGE—JACOB D. FUCHSBERG LAW CENTER

225 Eastview Drive
Central Islip, NY 11722
Phone: 631.761.7010; Fax: 631.761.7019
E-mail: admissions@tourolaw.edu; Website: www.tourolaw.edu

Premier Building and Location

Established in 1980, Touro Law Center is fully accredited by the American Bar Association and is a member of the Association of American Law Schools. The Law Center occupies a dynamic 185,000-square-foot, state-of-the-art building in Central Islip on the south shore of Long Island. Touro Law is at the center of what is arguably the nation's first integrated "law campus," comprising a United States courthouse and federal building and a New York State court center, with supreme, family, and district courts.

Located about one hour by car or train east of New York City on Long Island, Central Islip boasts a wide variety of affordable housing options. Students may also use the Office of Admissions' Housing Information Network, which provides current listings of accommodations, as well as information regarding car pools and shared living arrangements. On-campus parking is free of charge.

New Curriculum: Courtrooms as Classrooms

Touro is a leader in bridging the gap between law school and legal practice, between the classroom and the courtroom. Taking advantage of its unique location as part of a law campus, adjacent to and working with both a federal courthouse and a state courthouse, Touro Law offers an innovative Collaborative Court Program that enables students to experience the workings of the judicial system from the very first days of their legal education. Beginning in their first semester, students are exposed to true legal practice through simulations in both litigation and nonlitigation settings and through faculty-supervised small-group visits to courts in session, court-related agencies, and court administration. In an effort to facilitate experiential learning, Touro Law invites students not only to observe live proceedings, but also to discuss with the participants (judges, attorneys, and sometimes the parties themselves) their perspectives on law in action.

Practice Modules: A central feature of the upper-level curriculum is the linkage of substantive law with practice modules in Business Organizations, Criminal Procedure, Family Law, Trusts and Estates, and International Sales Law and Arbitration. Using the rules they have learned in the classroom, students solve practical problems, such as helping investors select an appropriate business entity, drawing up a criminal indictment, structuring a marital separation agreement, or drafting a will that satisfies an individual's personal and financial interests.

Clinics: Touro Law offers seven in-house clinics where clients bring real cases to law students working in on-campus offices: Advanced Bankruptcy, Civil Rights Litigation, Elder Law, Family Law, Mortgage Foreclosure and Bankruptcy, Not-for-Profit Corporation Law, and Veterans' and Servicemembers' Rights. Some clinics are arranged to accommodate the scheduling needs of part-time evening students.

Field Placement Externships: There are six field placement externship areas in which students work off campus: Advanced Criminal Prosecution (Suffolk County District Court); Business and Technology Law (Internet and high-tech companies, corporate law departments, and law firms); Civil

Practice (law firms, corporations, and private and public agencies); Criminal Law (district attorneys' and legal aid/public defenders' offices); Judicial Clerkship (state and federal judges' chambers); and the US Attorney's Office Externship (Eastern District of New York). In addition, students can elect to gain experiences through a variety of independent externships.

Public Advocacy Center (PAC) and Public Service Projects: In a unique concept, Touro Law's William Randolph Hearst Public Advocacy Center (PAC) houses 15 independent public interest agencies at the law school where students can gain practical experience in Immigration Law, Housing Law, Employment Law, Rights of Children, Education Law, Constitutional Law, Poverty Law, Disability Law, and Not-for-Profit Law. The center is also the focal point for student pro bono activities, including the Student Disaster Relief Network, Street Law, Foreclosure Project, Domestic Violence Project, unemployment representation, and a tax assistance program. Students can work for academic credit, for financial compensation, or on a pro bono basis for these agencies. Touro also provides a broad selection of externship placements in public interest organizations.

Institutes: Touro Law hosts the Institute for Business, Law, and Technology; the Jewish Law Institute; and the Institute for Holocaust Law and International Human Rights.

Summer Programs: In addition to the Law Center's on-site summer program, which features special programs on New York law, there are opportunities for work and study abroad in Croatia, Germany, India, Israel, and Vietnam. Touro Law also offers summer internships in law firms, courts, and government offices in Europe and Israel.

Students and Faculty

The Law Center's students, coming from diverse backgrounds and experiences, represent more than 101 undergraduate institutions and a broad mix of majors. Women make up 46 percent of the total enrollment; minorities, 27 percent.

Touro Law is proud to offer two honor societies: the *Touro Law Review* and the Moot Court Board. There are also almost 40 student organizations devoted to specialized professional and social concerns.

Of Touro Law's 50 full-time faculty members, many have advanced degrees in other disciplines, including medicine, philosophy, business, and finance. Almost all have extensive practice backgrounds, ranging from the judicial bench, major law firms, and criminal prosecution and defense to government agencies and public interest organizations.

The faculty shares one common characteristic: accessibility to students. Every entering student is assigned a faculty advisor, matched by background or interest area, for discussions on any aspect of the law school experience, including study strategy, course selection, and career goals. With an open-door policy and a student-to-faculty ratio of 16:1, everyone reaps the benefits of a personal and dynamic educational experience.

Academic Programs

Juris Doctor (JD): Touro Law offers a three-year full-time JD degree program as well as a four-year, part-time day program. Touro also offers four-year and five-year part-time evening programs. Students wishing to accelerate their academic progress toward graduation may attend summer sessions.

Dual Degrees: The JD may be combined with a Master of Business Administration (MBA), a Master of Public Administration (MPA) in Health Care, or a Master of Social Work (MSW), allowing students to complete the two degrees with significant time and cost savings.

Master of Laws (LLM): The Law Center also offers a 24-credit general LLM, full time or part time, and a 27-credit LLM in US Legal Studies (for foreign law graduates), full time or part time.

Academic Support and Enrichment

The Law Center provides a unique program of outside-the-classroom assistance. Teaching assistants (TAs) review material covered in class and conduct small group sessions on effective study methods and test-taking techniques. The Writing Center offers students an opportunity for intensive, individual work to develop their professional writing skills. Assistance is available in all facets of writing—from reviewing the basics to polishing an article for publication. In addition, the Legal Education Access Program (LEAP) enhances the experience of students of color through a four-week summer program for new students and mentoring during the academic year.

The Touro Law Center Honors Program offers approximately 20 to 25 exceptional students per class year an enriched, comprehensive law school experience. Students in the Honors Program will participate in enhanced academic, experiential, and social opportunities as part of a community of student scholars.

Career Services

The Career Services Office offers students and graduates valuable hands-on assistance in their search for part-time,

full-time, and summer employment. Graduates work in national, regional, and local law firms as well as federal, state, and local government agencies; not-for-profit organizations; and in the legal departments of corporations and municipalities.

Admission and Financial Aid

Touro Law Center does not provide an applicant profile grid for its entering class because such data fails to reflect the complexity of the selection process.

At no point on a purely objective scale is an applicant assured of a particular decision. Among the most important criteria are the LSAT score and UGPA. However, evaluation is based on a variety of factors that may be indicative of potential for success—college major and course selection, graduate study, work experience, community involvement, and character.

In order to finance law school, Touro provides access to federal loans and work study, New York State loan and assistance programs, and need-based Touro Grants.

Scholarships

Most students receive some form of financial aid, and about 65 percent of entering students receive scholarships. Institutional aid is available to entering students (based on LSAT/UGPA) and to continuing law students (based on law school academic performance). Assistance includes dean's fellowships (full-tuition remission), merit scholarships (up to 90 percent tuition remission), and incentive awards (up to $9,000 per year). In addition, the Law Center offers stipends for public interest law fellowships, judicial clerkships, and federal work-study placements during the summer.

APPLICANT PROFILE

Please refer to the section on Admission and Financial Aid.

TULANE UNIVERSITY LAW SCHOOL

John Giffen Weinmann Hall, 6329 Freret Street
New Orleans, LA 70118
Phone: 504.865.5930; Fax: 504.865.6710
E-mail: admissions@law.tulane.edu; Website: www.law.tulane.edu

ABA
Approved
Since
1925

The Basics

Type of school	Private
Term	Semester
Application deadline	4/15
Application fee	$60
Financial aid deadline	2/15
Can first year start other than fall?	No
Student to faculty ratio	14.1 to 1
# of housing spaces available restricted to law students	
graduate housing for which law students are eligible	166

Faculty and Administrators

	Total		Men		Women		Minorities	
	Spr	Fall	Spr	Fall	Spr	Fall	Spr	Fall
Full-time	47	43	30	27	17	16	4	5
Other full-time	9	9	2	3	7	6	0	0
Deans, librarians, & others who teach	5	4	2	2	3	2	0	0
Part-time	50	30	44	26	6	4	2	1
Total	111	86	78	58	33	28	6	6

JD Enrollment and Ethnicity

	Men		Women		Full-Time		Part-Time		1st-Year		Total		JD Degs. Awd.
	#	%	#	%	#	%	#	%	#	%	#	%	
All Hispanics	22	5.5	16	4.3	38	4.9	0	0.0	10	3.9	38	4.9	13
Am. Ind./AK Nat.	1	0.2	4	1.1	5	0.6	0	0.0	1	0.4	5	0.6	3
Asian	7	1.7	3	0.8	10	1.3	0	0.0	2	0.8	10	1.3	8
Black/Af. Am.	22	5.5	26	7.0	48	6.2	0	0.0	13	5.0	48	6.2	20
Nat. HI/Pac. Isl.	2	0.5	5	1.3	7	0.9	0	0.0	2	0.8	7	0.9	0
2 or more races	2	0.5	5	1.3	7	0.9	0	0.0	0	0.0	7	0.9	0
Subtotal (minor.)	56	13.9	59	15.9	115	14.8	0	0.0	28	10.9	115	14.8	44
Nonres. Alien	4	1.0	8	2.2	12	1.5	0	0.0	3	1.2	12	1.5	5
White/Cauc.	300	74.4	274	73.7	574	74.1	0	0.0	181	70.2	574	74.1	172
Unknown	43	10.7	31	8.3	74	9.5	0	0.0	46	17.8	74	9.5	20
Total	403	52.0	372	48.0	775	100.0	0	0.0	258	33.3	775		241

Curriculum

	Full-Time	Part-Time
Typical first-year section size	81	0
Is there typically a "small section" of the first-year class, other than Legal Writing, taught by full-time faculty	No	No
If yes, typical size offered last year		
# of classroom course titles beyond first-year curriculum	203	
# of upper division courses, excluding seminars, with an enrollment: Under 25	87	
25–49	63	
50–74	17	
75–99	6	
100+	4	
# of seminars	28	
# of seminar positions available	527	
# of seminar positions filled	443	0
# of positions available in simulation courses	483	
# of simulation positions filled	389	0
# of positions available in faculty supervised clinical courses	118	
# of faculty supervised clinical positions filled	112	0
# involved in field placements	52	0
# involved in law journals	259	0
# involved in moot court or trial competitions	89	0
# of credit hours required to graduate	88	

Transfers

Transfers in	0
Transfers out	13

Tuition and Fees

	Resident	Nonresident
Full-time	$43,684	$43,684
Part-time		
Tuition Guarantee Program		N

Living Expenses

Estimated living expenses for singles

Living on campus	Living off campus	Living at home
$20,450	$20,450	$10,180

*ABA
Approved
Since
1925*

GPA and LSAT Scores

	Total	Full-Time	Part-Time
# of apps	2,780	2,780	0
# of offers	1,050	1,050	0
# of matrics	259	259	0
75% GPA	3.68	3.68	0.00
Median GPA	3.53	3.53	0.00
25% GPA	3.31	3.31	0.00
75% LSAT	163	163	0
Median LSAT	161	161	0
25% LSAT	158	158	0

Grants and Scholarships (from prior year)

	Total		Full-Time		Part-Time	
	#	%	#	%	#	%
Total # of students	770		769		1	
Total # receiving grants	498	64.7	498	64.8	0	0.0
Less than 1/2 tuition	326	42.3	326	42.4	0	0.0
Half to full tuition	172	22.3	172	22.4	0	0.0
Full tuition	0	0.0	0	0.0	0	0.0
More than full tuition	0	0.0	0	0.0	0	0.0
Median grant amount			$20,000		$0	

Informational and Library Resources

Total amount spent on library materials	$1,090,107
Study seating capacity inside the library	520
# of full-time equivalent professional librarians	8
Hours per week library is open	113
# of open, wired connections available to students	293
# of networked computers available for use by students	97
Has wireless network?	Y
Requires computer?	N

JD Attrition (from prior year)

	Academic	Other	Total	
	#	#	#	%
1st year	0	10	10	3.9
2nd year	2	20	22	8.0
3rd year	2	0	2	0.8
4th year	0	0	0	0.0

Employment (9 months after graduation)

For up-to-date employment data, go to employmentsummary.abaquestionnaire.org on the ABA website.

Bar Passage Rates

First-time takers	255	Reporting %	80.00
Average school %	78.92	Average state %	73.18
Average pass difference	5.74		

Jurisdiction	Takers	Passers	Pass %	State %	Diff %
Louisiana	122	91	74.59	66.26	8.33
Texas	54	46	85.19	82.68	2.51
New York	28	24	85.71	84.92	0.79

TULANE UNIVERSITY LAW SCHOOL

The information on these pages was provided by the law school.

John Giffen Weinmann Hall, 6329 Freret Street
New Orleans, LA 70118
Phone: 504.865.5930; Fax: 504.865.6710
E-mail: admissions@law.tulane.edu; Website: www.law.tulane.edu

Introduction

The opportunity to attend law school in New Orleans, perhaps the most dynamic city in the United States today, can transform an ordinary law school experience into an extraordinary one. Tulane Law School, established in 1847, is among the oldest law schools in the United States. The Law School is located on the main university campus in uptown New Orleans, in a picturesque neighborhood of residences, both large and small, as well as restaurants, bookstores, and other commercial establishments.

New Orleans

New Orleans offers extensive legal resources, including the US Court of Appeals for the Fifth Circuit, US District Court, the Louisiana Supreme Court, and all of the lower state civil, criminal, and specialized courts. Within the legal community, students have the opportunity to work with both prosecutors and public defenders, in the private sector, the public sector, and in the public interest. Life outside of the law is rich, too. New Orleans is justly renowned for its music and its food. In addition to numerous events at Tulane University, students enjoy the advantages of city life and the richness of New Orleans culture. Concerts, festivals, and innumerable citywide events take place throughout the year.

Facilities

The Law School is housed in the 160,000-square-foot John Giffen Weinmann Hall. Designed to integrate classrooms, other student spaces, faculty offices, and a library containing both national and international collections, the building is centrally located on Tulane University's campus. Immediately adjacent to Weinmann Hall is the Law School's Career Development Office. Within minutes of the Law School building are the university's Howard-Tilton Memorial Library, housing over one million volumes; the Lavin-Bernick Center for Student Life; university dining facilities; the university bookstore; the Reily Student Recreation Center; the Freeman School of Business; the Newcomb Art Gallery; and various auditoriums and performance venues.

The Academic Program

The Law School curriculum offers a full range of common law and federal subjects. In addition, Tulane offers electives in civil law, with the result that students have the opportunity to pursue comparative education in the world's two major legal systems. The breadth and depth of the curriculum permit students to survey a broad range of subject areas or to concentrate in one or more. The background, enthusiasm, and scholarship of the internationally known faculty further enrich the educational experience.

Six semesters in residence, completion of 88 credits with at least a C average, fulfillment of an upper-level writing requirement, and a 30-hour pro bono obligation are required for graduation from the JD degree program. The first-year curriculum comprises eight required courses, including Legal Research and Writing.

After the first year, all courses are elective, except for the required Legal Profession course. All first-year and many upper-level courses are taught in multiple sections to allow for smaller classes. The upper-level curriculum includes introductory as well as advanced courses in a broad range of subject areas, including international and comparative law, business and corporate law, environmental law, maritime law, criminal law, intellectual property, taxation, and litigation and procedure, among others.

At the graduate level, the Law School offers a general LLM program and an SJD program, as well as specialized LLM programs in Admiralty, Energy and Environmental Law, American Business Law, American Law, and International and Comparative Law.

Special Programs

The school offers optional concentration programs that allow JD students to receive one certificate of completion of successful studies in (a) European Legal Studies, (b) Environmental Law, (c) Maritime Law, (d) Sports Law, (e) Civil Law, or (f) International and Comparative Law. Tulane's Eason-Weinmann Center for Comparative Law, the Payson Center for International Development, the Maritime Law Center, and the Institute for Water Law and Policy add depth to the curriculum and interesting opportunities for students. Tulane also offers strong curricula in intellectual property law and constitutional law, as well as business, corporate, and commercial law.

Tulane conducts an annual summer school in New Orleans and offers summer-study programs abroad in England, the Netherlands, Italy, Germany, Greece, and Brazil. Semester-long exchange programs with select law schools in Argentina, Australia, China, Denmark, France, Germany, Hong Kong, Italy, the Netherlands, and Spain are also offered.

The school was the first in the country to require that each student complete 30 hours of legal pro bono work prior to graduation.

Clinical and Skills Programs

The school offers live-client clinical programs in civil litigation, criminal defense, juvenile litigation, domestic violence, environmental law, and legislative and administrative advocacy. In addition, there is a trial advocacy course and a negotiation and mediation advocacy course. Third-year students may participate in year-long externships with federal and state judges, with a variety of public interest organizations, or with certain government agencies. Students may receive credit for summer externships throughout the world. A week-long intersession "boot camp" is offered each January, with separate tracks for civil litigation, criminal pre-trial, and transactional practice.

Joint-Degree Programs

Joint-degree programs are offered in conjunction with Tulane's Freeman School of Business (JD/MBA and JD/MACCT), School of Public Health and Tropical Medicine (JD/MHA and JD/MPH), and School of Social Work

(JD/MSW). The JD/MS in International Development is offered in cooperation with the Law School's Payson Center for International Development, and the JD/MA in Latin American Studies is offered in cooperation with the Stone Center for Latin American Studies. Proposals for programs in cooperation with other Tulane academic departments are considered on an ad hoc basis.

Admission and Financial Aid

Our admission process is based on a complete review of all of the information in each candidate's file. This naturally includes the LSAT score and the undergraduate academic record. In the case of multiple LSAT scores, the school sees all scores but will give more weight to the highest score based on the candidate's explanation. Tulane looks closely at subjective factors such as grade trends, courseload, undergraduate school, nonacademic activities, the student's background and experience, barriers overcome, the personal statement, and optional letters of recommendation or evaluations. The Law School processes applications for admission beginning September 1 and announces decisions beginning December 1. All candidates receive consideration for merit-based scholarship awards. Need-based and credit-based loans require submission of the FAFSA. A loan repayment assistance program is available to graduates working full time in eligible public interest employment.

Student Life

Journals published or edited at Tulane Law School include the Tulane Law Review, Tulane Maritime Law Journal, Tulane Environmental Law Journal, Law and Sexuality, Tulane European and Civil Law Forum, Tulane Journal of International and Comparative Law, Tulane Journal of Technology and Intellectual Property, and Sports Lawyers Journal. An active moot court program holds trial and appellate competitions

within the school and fields teams for a variety of interschool competitions, including alternative dispute resolution methods. The Law School has a chapter of the Order of the Coif.

The Student Bar Association functions as the student government and recommends students for appointment to faculty committees. Over 40 student organizations exist at Tulane, including the International Law Society, Black Law Students Association, La Alianza del Derecho, Asian-Pacific-American Law Students Association, Business Law Society, and Sports Law Society, among others. The Tulane Public Interest Law Foundation raises funds, matched by the Law School, to support as many as 30 students each summer in public interest fellowships with a variety of organizations. The Environmental Law Society hosts a major "science and the public interest" conference each spring.

Most students live in a variety of off-campus neighborhoods throughout the New Orleans metropolitan area, often within walking or biking distance of the Law School.

Career Services

The Law School Career Development Office assists both students and alumni in their job searches. Each student is assigned a career counselor as a first-year student and thereafter has access to a full range of career counseling services from the entire staff as well as to programs on job-search skills and practice areas. A large career services library is available, including extensive online resources. Tulane organizes both on- and off-campus interview programs for its students. Career development staff members also engage in employer outreach activities on a national basis. The office takes a proactive stance in assisting students with their job searches, with the result that Tulane graduates find law-related employment throughout the United States.

APPLICANT PROFILE

Tulane University Law School
This grid includes only applicants who earned 120–180 LSAT scores under standard administrations.

LSAT Score	GPA								
	3.75 +	3.50–3.74	3.25–3.49	3.00–3.24	2.75–2.99	2.50–2.74	2.25–2.49	2.00–2.24	Below 2.00
175–180	■	■	■	■					▩
170–174	■	■	■	■					
165–169	■	■	■	■				▩	
160–164	■	■	■					▩	
155–159	■						▩	▩	
150–154					▩	▩	▩	▩	
145–149			▩	▩	▩	▩	▩	▩	
140–144	▩	▩	▩	▩	▩	▩	▩	▩	
135–139	▩	▩	▩	▩	▩	▩	▩	▩	
130–134	▩	▩	▩	▩	▩	▩	▩	▩	
125–129	▩	▩	▩	▩	▩	▩	▩	▩	
120–124	▩	▩	▩	▩	▩	▩	▩	▩	

■ Good Possibility   ☐ Possible   ▩ Unlikely

THE UNIVERSITY OF TULSA COLLEGE OF LAW

3120 East Fourth Place
Tulsa, OK 74104-3189
Phone: 918.631.2406; Fax: 918.631.3630
E-mail: lawadmissions@utulsa.edu; Website: www.utulsa.edu/law/admissions/

ABA Approved Since 1950

The Basics

Type of school	Private
Term	Semester
Application deadline	2/1 7/31
Application fee	$30
Financial aid deadline	3/1
Can first year start other than fall?	No
Student to faculty ratio	11.2 to 1
# of housing spaces available restricted to law students	
graduate housing for which law students are eligible	256

Faculty and Administrators

	Total		Men		Women		Minorities	
	Spr	Fall	Spr	Fall	Spr	Fall	Spr	Fall
Full-time	27	26	15	15	12	11	4	4
Other full-time	0	1	0	1	0	0	0	0
Deans, librarians, & others who teach	4	4	2	2	2	2	0	0
Part-time	24	17	16	14	8	3	1	1
Total	55	48	33	32	22	16	5	5

Curriculum

	Full-Time	Part-Time
Typical first-year section size	37	0
Is there typically a "small section" of the first-year class, other than Legal Writing, taught by full-time faculty	No	No
If yes, typical size offered last year		
# of classroom course titles beyond first-year curriculum	125	
# of upper division courses, excluding seminars, with an enrollment: Under 25	62	
25–49	24	
50–74	7	
75–99	0	
100+	9	
# of seminars	9	
# of seminar positions available	134	
# of seminar positions filled	99	0
# of positions available in simulation courses	394	
# of simulation positions filled	257	0
# of positions available in faculty supervised clinical courses	20	
# of faculty supervised clinical positions filled	19	0
# involved in field placements	140	0
# involved in law journals	148	0
# involved in moot court or trial competitions	29	0
# of credit hours required to graduate	88	

JD Enrollment and Ethnicity

	Men #	Men %	Women #	Women %	Full-Time #	Full-Time %	Part-Time #	Part-Time %	1st-Year #	1st-Year %	Total #	Total %	JD Degs. Awd.
All Hispanics	5	2.3	5	3.6	10	3.1	0	0.0	1	0.9	10	2.8	4
Am. Ind./AK Nat.	21	9.5	19	13.7	32	9.9	8	20.5	12	10.3	40	11.1	8
Asian	3	1.4	2	1.4	4	1.2	1	2.6	1	0.9	5	1.4	3
Black/Af. Am.	5	2.3	6	4.3	9	2.8	2	5.1	5	4.3	11	3.0	2
Nat. HI/Pac. Isl.	0	0.0	0	0.0	0	0.0	0	0.0	0	0.0	0	0.0	0
2 or more races	6	2.7	8	5.8	14	4.3	0	0.0	7	6.0	14	3.9	0
Subtotal (minor.)	40	18.0	40	28.8	69	21.4	11	28.2	26	22.4	80	22.2	17
Nonres. Alien	2	0.9	0	0.0	2	0.6	0	0.0	1	0.9	2	0.6	1
White/Cauc.	164	73.9	90	64.7	228	70.8	26	66.7	87	75.0	254	70.4	86
Unknown	16	7.2	9	6.5	23	7.1	2	5.1	2	1.7	25	6.9	16
Total	222	61.5	139	38.5	322	89.2	39	10.8	116	32.1	361		120

Transfers

Transfers in	2
Transfers out	9

Tuition and Fees

	Resident	Nonresident
Full-time	$32,056	
Part-time	$17,565	
Tuition Guarantee Program		N

Living Expenses

Estimated living expenses for singles

Living on campus	Living off campus	Living at home
$16,536	$20,110	$9,268

THE UNIVERSITY OF TULSA COLLEGE OF LAW

ABA Approved Since 1950

GPA and LSAT Scores

	Total	Full-Time	Part-Time
# of apps	1,466	1,466	0
# of offers	582	582	0
# of matrics	108	108	0
75% GPA	3.58	3.58	0.00
Median GPA	3.32	3.32	0.00
25% GPA	3.06	3.06	0.00
75% LSAT	157	157	0
Median LSAT	155	155	0
25% LSAT	152	152	0

Grants and Scholarships (from prior year)

	Total		Full-Time		Part-Time	
	#	%	#	%	#	%
Total # of students	406		368		38	
Total # receiving grants	220	54.2	220	59.8	0	0.0
Less than 1/2 tuition	103	25.4	103	28.0	0	0.0
Half to full tuition	97	23.9	97	26.4	0	0.0
Full tuition	14	3.4	14	3.8	0	0.0
More than full tuition	6	1.5	6	1.6	0	0.0
Median grant amount			$16,000		$0	

Informational and Library Resources

Total amount spent on library materials	$865,347
Study seating capacity inside the library	693
# of full-time equivalent professional librarians	8
Hours per week library is open	107
# of open, wired connections available to students	88
# of networked computers available for use by students	95
Has wireless network?	Y
Requires computer?	N

JD Attrition (from prior year)

	Academic	Other	Total	
	#	#	#	%
1st year	7	5	12	8.4
2nd year	1	15	16	11.1
3rd year	1	0	1	0.8
4th year	0	0	0	0.0

Employment (9 months after graduation)

For up-to-date employment data, go to employmentsummary.abaquestionnaire.org on the ABA website.

Bar Passage Rates

First-time takers	131	Reporting %	71.76
Average school %	89.36	Average state %	89.02
Average pass difference	0.34		

Jurisdiction	Takers	Passers	Pass %	State %	Diff %
Oklahoma	94	84	89.36	89.02	0.34

THE UNIVERSITY OF TULSA COLLEGE OF LAW

3120 East Fourth Place
Tulsa, OK 74104-3189
Phone: 918.631.2406; Fax: 918.631.3630
E-mail: lawadmissions@utulsa.edu; Website: www.utulsa.edu/law/admissions/

Introduction

Legal education at the University of Tulsa offers a world of new energy and infinite possibilities. Our law school family proves daily that it is possible for friendliness, challenge, respect, and excellence to coexist in law school. Housed in the newly renovated and technologically advanced John Rogers Hall on the University of Tulsa campus, and fully accredited by the ABA, the law school presents a forum for the study and exploration of legal issues enhanced by professors with exemplary credentials. With an 11.2:1 student-to-faculty ratio, a true open-door policy invites students to expand their legal education from the classroom through one-on-one accessibility and interaction with the TU Law faculty. We also honor student talent with scholarships ranging from partial to full tuition. Approximately 67 percent of an entering class receives merit- or need-based assistance. Coming from many locales and backgrounds, our student body is a rich fabric of diversity that expands the learning experience of every student. Beautiful, culturally diverse, and extraordinarily friendly, the city of Tulsa offers our students award-winning ballet, national touring concerts, world-class museums, gorgeous parks, and vibrant neighborhood shopping areas. Tulsa also boasts an internationally recognized, burgeoning environment for high-tech industry and commerce.

Curriculum and Specialization

Full-time and reduced schedule options, as well as summer classes, are available. Students may choose either general legal study, which covers a broad expanse of expertise, or a specific concentration. Certificates offered include Sustainable Energy and Natural Resources Law, Native American Law, Comparative and International Law, and Health Law.

Summer- and semester-abroad programs offer students the opportunity to experience different cultures on three overseas continents. The summer-abroad programs include Dublin (Ireland), Tianjin (China), and Buenos Aires (Argentina). Students also have the opportunity for a fall semester of study in London.

Students at Tulsa have a great variety of career choices available to them, which are enhanced by the opportunity for interdisciplinary study. The following joint-degree programs are available: JD/MBA, JD/MA in Anthropology, JD/MA in History, JD/MA in Industrial/Organizational Psychology, JD/MA in English, JD/MS in Computer Science, JD/MS in Biological Sciences, JD/MA in Clinical Psychology, JD/MS in Geosciences, JD/MS in Finance, and JD/MS in Taxation.

Practical Experience

Tulsa law students gain first-hand training beyond the classroom. The Boesche Legal Clinic offers the Immigrant Rights Project in which law students have the opportunity to represent clients in important immigration proceedings under the supervision of an expert clinical education professor.

Students may earn academic credit through legal and judicial externships. Legal externs work in a law firm, business, nonprofit organization, or government entity under the supervision of highly skilled attorneys pursuant to academic plans they negotiate with their supervising attorneys and the College of Law. Judicial externs work in federal and state courts under the supervision of a judge or a lawyer who is a court clerk or a court administrator.

The College of Law also offers nonacademic practical experiences. The Legal Internship Program enables a student to represent clients in criminal and civil cases, subject to rules authorized by the Oklahoma Supreme Court. The Pro Bono Program allows students to assist with cases going to trial, assist with civil legal matters, participate in interviewing clients and witnesses, and perform research.

A Federal Criminal Defense Practicum is offered by the Honorable Claire V. Eagan, Judge of the United States District Court for the Northern District of Oklahoma, and other dedicated professionals within the Northern District's criminal justice system. Students are guided through every step of a federal criminal case.

Professors

Knowledge and experience, matched by a passion for teaching, typify the character of the professors at the University of Tulsa. Recognized nationally and internationally for their expertise, Tulsa professors are always accessible to their students. Specializations and strong experiential expertise in areas as diverse as international trade, energy regulation, family and juvenile law, sports law, Native American tribal jurisdiction, trial advocacy, and bioethics confirm the rich learning experience available to Tulsa law students. The ability to develop strong relationships with professors will strengthen Tulsa students' law school experiences and their future legal practice in remarkable ways.

Library and Physical Facilities

Cited by the *National Jurist* as one of the top libraries in the US, the impressive Mabee Legal Information Center (MLIC) is an ideal locale for collaborating, preparing for class or exams, working on journal scholarship, conducting extensive research, conferring with reference librarians, or preparing for a moot court competition. Over 50 computers are available for use through the information center, including several laptops that are available for check out. Student staffing offices for the Board of Advocates, the *Tulsa Law Review*, and the *Energy Law Journal* provide generous working space for these important enterprises at the College of Law. Specialized classrooms include a technology training center and the Alternative Dispute Resolution Center where negotiation exercises are possible within a variety of simulation configurations. The Utsey Family Native American Law Center and the Frank M. Rowell, Jr., Comparative and International Law Center offer inviting forums for study, research, and the exchange of ideas, with impressive artwork providing a showcase for these two disciplines. The John F. Hicks and John Rogers Archives Room was opened to preserve the rich history of the college and to provide the means to collect important documents, photographs, and artifacts for the many significant achievements of the College of Law now and in the future.

If quiet study is for you, the two main reading rooms offer quiet, inviting, wide-open spaces with natural lighting. With over 600 seats available and six miles of shelving space, there is plenty of space for students, alumni, and books.

Professional librarians, most with law degrees, are ready to help with legal research in the 400,000-volume collection. An impressive array of electronic resources is accessible to students on-site or from home. McFarlin Library, the main campus library, provides students and faculty with direct access to print and electronic library holdings of more than three million items.

The College of Law has 802.11n wireless access available throughout the building. Classrooms are equipped with a full array of technology, including dual wide-screen HD projectors/screens, computers, VGA and HDMI connectivity, wireless microphones, and built-in classroom capture and recording capabilities.

The Boesche Legal Clinic and the modern Price-Turpen model courtroom bring the same state-of-the-art capacities to the study and training for trial and appellate advocacy. These are outstanding facilities in which the best in preparation is available for Tulsa law students as they prepare for future legal practice and train for many regional and national moot court competitions.

Office of Professional Development

Students at TU enjoy a full-service Professional Development Office (PDO) offering support and resources for students' respective professional aspirations. PDO counselors are attorneys with wide-ranging practice experience in local and regional markets. Students participate in professionalism programs as a requisite to graduation, including a first-semester seminar on the legal profession taught by the dean. These programs cover topics such as setting professional goals, managing the stresses of legal practice, and legal market trends. TU Law's placement rate of over 92 percent in 2010 and 90 percent in 2011 is in part due to a strong focus on professional development, mentoring, and networking opportunities. These percentages compete with or exceed the respective national annual placement rates reported by law schools.

Housing

Law students at Tulsa may choose to live on or off campus. On-campus housing includes well-maintained and modern apartments built exclusively for law and graduate students. Located within an easy walking distance from the law school, each apartment unit includes computer connections and large, spacious floor plans. With a very attractive low cost of living, the city of Tulsa offers a great variety of affordable housing opportunities. Information about housing may be obtained by calling 918.631.5249 or by contacting the Office of Law Admissions at 918.631.2406.

APPLICANT PROFILE

The University of Tulsa College of Law
This chart is to be used as a guide only. Nonnumerical factors are strongly considered for all applicants.

LSAT Score	3.75 +	3.50–3.74	3.25–3.49	3.00–3.24	2.75–2.99	2.50–2.74	2.25–2.49	Below 2.25	Totals
175–180	0	0	0	1	0	0	0	0	1
170–174	1	0	1	0	1	0	0	0	3
165–169	6	10	2	0	1	1	0	0	20
160–164	17	11	17	11	6	1	3	3	69
155–159	38	44	58	46	20	19	10	4	239
150–154	36	62	62	33	18	3	0	0	214
145–149	7	16	5	2	3	1	0	0	34
140–144	0	1	1	0	0	0	0	0	2
Below 140	0	0	0	0	0	0	0	0	0
Total	105	144	146	93	49	25	13	7	582

UNIVERSITY OF UTAH S.J. QUINNEY COLLEGE OF LAW

332 South 1400 East, Room 101
Salt Lake City, UT 84112-0730
Phone: 801.581.6833; Fax: 801.820.9154
E-mail: admissions@law.utah.edu; Website: www.law.utah.edu

ABA
Approved
Since
1927

The Basics

Type of school	Public
Term	Semester
Application deadline	2/15
Application fee	$60
Financial aid deadline	4/1
Can first year start other than fall?	No
Student to faculty ratio	9.4 to 1
# of housing spaces available restricted to law students	4
graduate housing for which law students are eligible	286

Faculty and Administrators

	Total		Men		Women		Minorities	
	Spr	Fall	Spr	Fall	Spr	Fall	Spr	Fall
Full-time	36	37	24	26	12	11	6	7
Other full-time	0	0	0	0	0	0	0	0
Deans, librarians, & others who teach	9	8	5	4	4	4	0	0
Part-time	27	10	21	7	6	3	0	0
Total	72	55	50	37	22	18	6	7

Curriculum

	Full-Time	Part-Time
Typical first-year section size	42	0
Is there typically a "small section" of the first-year class, other than Legal Writing, taught by full-time faculty	Yes	No
If yes, typical size offered last year	20	
# of classroom course titles beyond first-year curriculum	121	

# of upper division courses, excluding seminars, with an enrollment:		
	Under 25	78
	25–49	21
	50–74	7
	75–99	2
	100+	0

# of seminars	13	
# of seminar positions available	156	
# of seminar positions filled	107	0
# of positions available in simulation courses	763	
# of simulation positions filled	441	0
# of positions available in faculty supervised clinical courses	0	
# of faculty supervised clinical positions filled	0	0
# involved in field placements	330	0
# involved in law journals	103	0
# involved in moot court or trial competitions	32	0
# of credit hours required to graduate	88	

JD Enrollment and Ethnicity

	Men		Women		Full-Time		Part-Time		1st-Year		Total		JD Degs. Awd.
	#	%	#	%	#	%	#	%	#	%	#	%	
All Hispanics	8	3.5	11	6.6	19	4.8	0	0.0	3	2.6	19	4.8	8
Am. Ind./AK Nat.	2	0.9	1	0.6	3	0.8	0	0.0	1	0.9	3	0.8	2
Asian	7	3.0	9	5.4	16	4.0	0	0.0	4	3.5	16	4.0	5
Black/Af. Am.	1	0.4	3	1.8	4	1.0	0	0.0	1	0.9	4	1.0	1
Nat. HI/Pac. Isl.	0	0.0	0	0.0	0	0.0	0	0.0	0	0.0	0	0.0	2
2 or more races	0	0.0	0	0.0	0	0.0	0	0.0	0	0.0	0	0.0	0
Subtotal (minor.)	18	7.8	24	14.4	42	10.6	0	0.0	9	7.9	42	10.6	18
Nonres. Alien	1	0.4	2	1.2	3	0.8	0	0.0	2	1.8	3	0.8	0
White/Cauc.	201	87.0	132	79.0	333	83.7	0	0.0	100	87.7	333	83.7	100
Unknown	11	4.8	9	5.4	20	5.0	0	0.0	3	2.6	20	5.0	16
Total	231	58.0	167	42.0	398	100.0	0	0.0	114	28.6	398		134

Transfers

Transfers in	24
Transfers out	2

Tuition and Fees

	Resident	Nonresident
Full-time	$20,760	$39,410
Part-time		
Tuition Guarantee Program		N

Living Expenses

Estimated living expenses for singles

Living on campus	Living off campus	Living at home
$20,802	$20,802	$12,462

UNIVERSITY OF UTAH S.J. QUINNEY COLLEGE OF LAW

ABA
Approved
Since
1927

GPA and LSAT Scores

	Total	Full-Time	Part-Time
# of apps	1,230	1,230	0
# of offers	378	378	0
# of matrics	114	114	0
75% GPA	3.72	3.72	0.00
Median GPA	3.54	3.54	0.00
25% GPA	3.41	3.41	0.00
75% LSAT	163	163	0
Median LSAT	161	161	0
25% LSAT	157	157	0

Grants and Scholarships (from prior year)

	Total #	Total %	Full-Time #	Full-Time %	Part-Time #	Part-Time %
Total # of students	402		402		0	
Total # receiving grants	205	51.0	205	51.0	0	0.0
Less than 1/2 tuition	129	32.1	129	32.1	0	0.0
Half to full tuition	72	17.9	72	17.9	0	0.0
Full tuition	1	0.2	1	0.2	0	0.0
More than full tuition	3	0.7	3	0.7	0	0.0
Median grant amount			$6,044		$0	

Informational and Library Resources

Total amount spent on library materials	$792,107
Study seating capacity inside the library	665
# of full-time equivalent professional librarians	7
Hours per week library is open	79
# of open, wired connections available to students	250
# of networked computers available for use by students	49
Has wireless network?	Y
Requires computer?	Y

JD Attrition (from prior year)

	Academic #	Other #	Total #	Total %
1st year	0	4	4	3.3
2nd year	0	0	0	0.0
3rd year	0	0	0	0.0
4th year	0	0	0	0.0

Employment (9 months after graduation)

For up-to-date employment data, go to
employmentsummary.abaquestionnaire.org on the ABA website.

Bar Passage Rates

First-time takers	117	Reporting %	82.91
Average school %	85.57	Average state %	89.35

Average pass difference −3.78

Jurisdiction	Takers	Passers	Pass %	State %	Diff %
Utah	97	83	85.57	89.35	−3.78

UNIVERSITY OF UTAH S.J. QUINNEY COLLEGE OF LAW

332 South 1400 East, Room 101
Salt Lake City, UT 84112-0730
Phone: 801.581.6833; Fax: 801.820.9154
E-mail: admissions@law.utah.edu; Website: www.law.utah.edu

Introduction

Established in 1913, the University of Utah S.J. Quinney College of Law is nationally recognized for its outstanding academic reputation, stellar faculty, intimate learning environment, innovative curriculum, excellent faculty-to-student ratio, and stunning location. The College of Law is a vibrant learning community with both well-established expertise and exciting new projects on the critical issues of our time: climate change, conflict and security, health justice, the new frontier of family law, technology commercialization, conservation, addiction, innocence, victims' rights, global mediation, and many others. We have also launched four innovative, crosscutting initiatives in leadership, cross-disciplinary training, smart technology, and global legal education. These creative intellectual investments have generated astounding results for each class of 115–125 entering students.

Among the students, there is a prevailing sense of community fostered by an open and service-oriented faculty and administration. The law school is less than a 10-minute drive or light rail ride from downtown Salt Lake City—the seat of federal, state, and local governmental bodies. Salt Lake City is the economic center of the region and is regularly voted one of America's most livable cities. This location provides ample professional opportunities for our students, as well as superb outdoor recreational access and a strong cultural scene.

Library and Physical Facilities

The S.J. Quinney Law Library and the law building are wireless environments. First-year students are provided with their own study hall furnished with group-study tables and carrels. Advanced students are provided carrels that also have wireless network access in the adjacent Quinney law library—a modern, spacious facility with the latest technological equipment and library research services.

The library holds more than 345,000 volumes of law and law-related material and serves as a depository for US government documents. CD-ROM and web-based databases provide access to primary legal materials, journal indexes, directories, and other law-related information. There is a computer lab with 31 workstations located in the library. Eight librarians (six with law degrees) teach the research component of the Legal Methods course.

Curriculum

The Quinney law school's innovative academic programs blend theory and practice skills that prepare graduates to tackle the major questions of our time and practice law in any jurisdiction. The curriculum is designed to allow more efficient and rational sequencing of legal education that responds to the evolving legal, social, and ethical needs of our society.

The entering students are first offered an intensive four-day Introduction to Law course before they begin the required first-year curriculum. The first-year doctrinal courses include a small section in which enrollment is limited to no more than 25 students. Second-year students select from a variety of foundational courses. In the third year, students may take year-long intensive courses that provide the opportunity for in-depth study, research, and a practicum in a focused area of law.

Additionally, outside the formal classroom, clinical and cocurricular opportunities ensure that students learn the most critical professional and intellectual lessons in simulated competitions and real-world settings. We have several award-winning moot court teams, three first-rate journals, and a series of new projects working on the major issues of our time. These include the Global Justice Project, the Family Law Project, the Biolaw Project, the New Economy Project, and the Innovation Project. Through our think tanks, projects, clinics (over 300 placements each year), and award-winning pro bono initiative (with 325 placements each semester), our students contributed over 40,000 hours of public service in just one year.

Special Programs

The Wallace Stegner Center for Land, Resources, and the Environment provides opportunities for students to engage in academic courses and related law activities focusing on public lands, environmental and natural resources law, and energy law. A Certificate in Environmental and Natural Resources Law is awarded to students who complete a sequence of approved courses with a specified GPA. The law school also offers an LLM degree in natural resources and environmental law.

The clinical programs offer both live and simulated opportunities for students to assume the lawyering role. In the Civil Clinic and the Criminal Clinic, students represent clients, investigate cases, and appear in court. In the Judicial Clinic, students act as clerks to judges, researching issues and drafting opinions in pending cases. The Judicial Extern Program allows students to spend a semester away from school working as full-time clerks for certain courts. Other clinical opportunities are available in our Environmental, Health Law, Legislative, and Mediation clinics.

The Utah Criminal Justice Center is an interdisciplinary partnership between the University of Utah and state government.

The Pro Bono Initiative is a voluntary program offered to emphasize the centrality of public service to the legal profession. The College of Law encourages students to perform at least 50 hours of law-related volunteer work during their time in law school. The Pro Bono Initiative facilitates this opportunity by providing students with a broad spectrum of developed volunteer placements.

Through the London Law Consortium, students engage in the law school's study-abroad program during the spring semester.

The College of Law maintains four formal joint-degree programs. Students may earn joint degrees in the areas of business (JD/MBA), public administration (JD/MPA), public policy (JD/MPP), or social work (JD/MSW).

The Academic Support Program provides structured assistance to students whose backgrounds and experiences before law school suggest a need for such assistance. Students request to participate in the program after admission to the College of Law.

Admission Standards

No applicant is accepted or rejected without members of the Admission Committee having first fully considered the entire application. The personal statement should expand on the applicant's biographic and academic background and motivations for seeking a legal education. The College of Law makes a special effort to attract students from diverse cultural, educational, economic, ethnic, racial, and nontraditional backgrounds. Each applicant is evaluated for the contribution that person can make to the student body or the legal profession, in addition to evidence of demonstrated high academic ability.

Student Activities

The *Utah Law Review*, the *Journal of Law and Family Studies*, and the *Utah Environmental Law Review* are professional journals edited and published by students. The *Utah Law Review* selects staff members on the basis of academic achievement and a writing competition. The other journals select staff members based on a writing competition.

Student organizations include the Student Bar Association, Women's Law Caucus, Natural Resources Law Forum, Minority Law Caucus, International Law Society, Business Law Society, Federalist Society, OUTLaws, Public Interest Law Organization, Phi Delta Phi, Jackie Chiles Law Society, J. Reuben Clark Law Society, Sports Law Club, Student Intellectual Property Law Association, SJQ Veteran's Association, Utah Student Association of Criminal Defense Lawyers, and Student Litigation Society.

Financial Aid

The College of Law provides an effective financial aid program that includes generous scholarships. The University of Utah participates in Federal Perkins, Stafford, and Graduate PLUS loan programs. More information on these student loan programs is available at www.law.utah.edu/admissions/financial-aid/. Merit scholarships are awarded to selected candidates based on the information contained in their application materials. Need-based scholarships are awarded to students based on information provided through the Free Application for Federal Student Aid and a separate application provided to all admitted candidates. The law school also has a Loan Forgiveness Program for qualified graduates who practice in the public sector or the public interest field.

Career Services

College of Law students and graduates have access to one of the most attentive and dedicated legal career services programs in the US. The office, known as the Professional Development Office (PDO), transmits information to prospective employers, both on and off campus, and coordinates the on-campus interview process. The PDO also conducts personal career counseling and assists students with the development of their résumés and other material used in the employment search. The PDO maintains a resource library and sponsors numerous seminars throughout the year.

APPLICANT PROFILE

University of Utah S.J. Quinney College of Law
This grid includes only applicants who earned 120–180 LSAT scores under standard administrations.

LSAT Score	3.75 +		3.50–3.74		3.25–3.49		3.00–3.24		2.75–2.99		2.50–2.74		2.25–2.49		2.00–2.24		Below 2.00		No GPA		Total	
	Apps	Adm	Apps	Adm	Apps	Adm	Apps	Adm	Apps	Adm	Apps	Adm	Apps	Adm	Apps	Adm	Apps	Adm	Apps	Adm	Apps	Adm
175–180	2	2	1	1	1	1	0	0	0	0	0	0	0	0	0	0	0	0	0	0	4	4
170–174	6	6	9	8	5	5	5	3	1	1	2	1	2	0	0	0	0	0	0	0	30	24
165–169	30	26	36	30	21	16	12	7	9	4	4	2	3	1	1	0	0	0	3	1	119	87
160–164	60	54	92	61	72	35	24	4	16	1	6	1	3	1	1	0	0	0	7	2	281	159
155–159	70	26	124	34	105	14	41	5	20	0	5	0	8	0	2	1	0	0	7	2	382	82
150–154	27	2	41	8	68	7	46	2	25	0	14	1	4	0	2	0	0	0	4	0	231	20
145–149	12	0	18	0	33	2	23	0	14	0	8	0	4	0	0	0	3	1	4	1	119	4
140–144	2	0	11	1	11	0	12	0	12	0	3	0	2	0	2	0	0	0	3	0	58	1
135–139	2	0	2	0	1	0	2	0	4	0	4	0	2	0	0	0	0	0	2	0	19	0
130–134	0	0	0	0	1	0	1	0	1	0	3	0	1	0	0	0	0	0	1	0	8	0
125–129	0	0	0	0	0	0	0	0	0	0	1	0	0	0	0	0	0	0	0	0	1	0
120–124	0	0	0	0	0	0	0	0	0	0	0	0	0	0	0	0	0	0	0	0	0	0
Total	211	116	334	143	318	80	166	21	102	6	50	5	29	2	8	1	3	1	31	6	1252	381

Apps = Number of Applicants
Adm = Number Admitted
Reflects 100% of the total applicant pool; highest LSAT data reported.

VALPARAISO UNIVERSITY LAW SCHOOL

656 S. Greenwich Street, Wesemann Hall
Valparaiso, IN 46383-4945
Phone: 219.465.7821; Fax: 219.465.7975
E-mail: law.admissions@valpo.edu; Website: www.valpo.edu/law/

ABA
Approved
Since
1929

The Basics

Type of school	Private
Term	Semester
Application deadline	6/1
Application fee	$60
Financial aid deadline	3/1
Can first year start other than fall?	No
Student to faculty ratio	15.6 to 1
# of housing spaces available restricted to law students	
graduate housing for which law students are eligible	

Faculty and Administrators

	Total		Men		Women		Minorities	
	Spr	Fall	Spr	Fall	Spr	Fall	Spr	Fall
Full-time	31	27	21	18	10	9	5	5
Other full-time	3	2	3	2	0	0	1	0
Deans, librarians, & others who teach	9	9	4	4	5	5	0	0
Part-time	31	27	19	14	12	13	2	1
Total	74	65	47	38	27	27	8	6

Curriculum

	Full-Time	Part-Time
Typical first-year section size	84	0
Is there typically a "small section" of the first-year class, other than Legal Writing, taught by full-time faculty	No	No
If yes, typical size offered last year		
# of classroom course titles beyond first-year curriculum	104	
# of upper division courses, excluding seminars, with an enrollment: Under 25	76	
25–49	33	
50–74	11	
75–99	3	
100+	2	
# of seminars	13	
# of seminar positions available	192	
# of seminar positions filled	181	4
# of positions available in simulation courses	761	
# of simulation positions filled	469	19
# of positions available in faculty supervised clinical courses	134	
# of faculty supervised clinical positions filled	128	0
# involved in field placements	170	5
# involved in law journals	47	1
# involved in moot court or trial competitions	170	0
# of credit hours required to graduate	90	

JD Enrollment and Ethnicity

	Men		Women		Full-Time		Part-Time		1st-Year		Total		JD Degs. Awd.
	#	%	#	%	#	%	#	%	#	%	#	%	
All Hispanics	31	10.1	19	7.3	50	9.2	0	0.0	22	10.1	50	8.8	8
Am. Ind./AK Nat.	3	1.0	2	0.8	4	0.7	1	4.0	2	0.9	5	0.9	2
Asian	17	5.5	10	3.9	21	3.9	6	24.0	14	6.5	27	4.8	3
Black/Af. Am.	25	8.1	40	15.4	61	11.3	4	16.0	30	13.8	65	11.5	13
Nat. HI/Pac. Isl.	3	1.0	0	0.0	3	0.6	0	0.0	0	0.0	3	0.5	0
2 or more races	5	1.6	8	3.1	12	2.2	1	4.0	7	3.2	13	2.3	0
Subtotal (minor.)	84	27.4	79	30.5	151	27.9	12	48.0	75	34.6	163	28.8	26
Nonres. Alien	2	0.7	2	0.8	4	0.7	0	0.0	4	1.8	4	0.7	4
White/Cauc.	215	70.0	173	66.8	376	69.5	12	48.0	134	61.8	388	68.6	149
Unknown	6	2.0	5	1.9	10	1.8	1	4.0	4	1.8	11	1.9	1
Total	307	54.2	259	45.8	541	95.6	25	4.4	217	38.3	566		180

Transfers

Transfers in	1
Transfers out	28

Tuition and Fees

	Resident	Nonresident
Full-time	$38,086	$38,086
Part-time	$23,790	$23,790
Tuition Guarantee Program		N

Living Expenses

Estimated living expenses for singles

Living on campus	Living off campus	Living at home
N/A	$12,760	$6,260

VALPARAISO UNIVERSITY LAW SCHOOL

*ABA
Approved
Since
1929*

GPA and LSAT Scores

	Total	Full-Time	Part-Time
# of apps	1,391	1,313	78
# of offers	990	953	37
# of matrics	218	210	8
75% GPA	3.46	3.48	3.29
Median GPA	3.19	3.19	2.96
25% GPA	2.95	2.96	2.59
75% LSAT	151	152	148
Median LSAT	149	149	148
25% LSAT	147	147	147

Grants and Scholarships (from prior year)

	Total #	Total %	Full-Time #	Full-Time %	Part-Time #	Part-Time %
Total # of students	566		531		35	
Total # receiving grants	149	26.3	147	27.7	2	5.7
Less than 1/2 tuition	28	4.9	26	4.9	2	5.7
Half to full tuition	76	13.4	76	14.3	0	0.0
Full tuition	36	6.4	36	6.8	0	0.0
More than full tuition	9	1.6	9	1.7	0	0.0
Median grant amount		$17,990		$0		

Informational and Library Resources

Total amount spent on library materials	$981,043
Study seating capacity inside the library	397
# of full-time equivalent professional librarians	5
Hours per week library is open	112
# of open, wired connections available to students	43
# of networked computers available for use by students	45
Has wireless network?	Y
Requires computer?	N

JD Attrition (from prior year)

	Academic #	Other #	Total #	Total %
1st year	5	33	38	18.4
2nd year	0	3	3	1.8
3rd year	0	2	2	1.1
4th year	0	0	0	0.0

Employment (9 months after graduation)

For up-to-date employment data, go to
employmentsummary.abaquestionnaire.org on the ABA website.

Bar Passage Rates

First-time takers	160	Reporting %	99.38
Average school %	83.06	Average state %	83.50

Average pass difference –0.44

Jurisdiction	Takers	Passers	Pass %	State %	Diff %
Indiana	74	58	78.38	80.93	–2.55
Illinois	42	36	85.71	89.38	–3.67
Michigan	4	4	100.00	84.83	15.17
Texas	4	4	100.00	82.68	17.32
Others (17)	35	30	85.71		

VALPARAISO UNIVERSITY LAW SCHOOL

656 S. Greenwich Street, Wesemann Hall
Valparaiso, IN 46383-4945
Phone: 219.465.7821; Fax: 219.465.7975
E-mail: law.admissions@valpo.edu; Website: www.valpo.edu/law/

Introduction

The Law School at Valparaiso University was founded in 1879. Throughout its 133-year history, Valparaiso Law has been a community dedicated to delivering a strong program in both legal theory and experiential education, and recruiting students who are **committed to service**. Our graduates are not just solid lawyers, but great people; not just influential leaders, but ones who use their influence for the highest service and the greater good.

Hiring partners at law firms continue to rank research and writing skills as the most important skill set for a new lawyer. Many law schools require only one year of legal writing. Valparaiso Law offers **exceptional legal research and writing** by requiring three years of writing and one year of research coursework.

Valparaiso Law students have the opportunity to practice their research and writing skills through participation in our clinic and externship programs and in fulfilling pro bono service requirements. These and other experiential education programs teach the **hands-on practice of law**—and do it really well. As a result, our students leave the Law School with the legal training they need to go out into the world, serve clients, and serve larger purposes.

Valparaiso University Law School's **Lawyering Skills Center** provides a genuine law firm environment for the teaching and learning of critical legal skills. Its custom-designed spaces support the Law School's skills curricula and house the 45-year-old Law Clinic. At the Center, students have the opportunity to learn about and practice appellate advocacy, dispute resolution, moot court, mock trial, client counseling, negotiation, arbitration, pretrial, and trial skills. The eight live clinics also offer students the opportunity to practice law so that, upon graduation, Valparaiso Law students can make an immediate contribution to their employers.

Curriculum and Experiential Education

The Law School provides a comprehensive and intensive study of the foundations of law, an introduction to the substantive areas of law, and an opportunity for advanced study in specific areas. The curriculum provides a grounding in legal analysis, legal writing and research, practical skills training, perspectives on the law, and ethics. The curriculum focuses on six key areas: **general practice**, **business law**, **public interest representation**, **property**, **litigation**, and **taxation**. To learn more, visit www.valpo.edu/law/current-students/curriculum.

Upon completing the required foundational first-year curriculum, students are given the opportunity to explore various avenues of study. In the summer prior to and during the second year, students begin pursuing externships and also take elective courses. By the third year, most required courses have been completed and students select courses for general legal competency and in their areas of interest, and engage in externships, internships, and the Law Clinic.

Students are expected to gain experience in the law profession by participating in externships that award course credit. They also earn academic credit by participating in one of the eight live-client law clinics as 3Ls. Students are encouraged to work as interns, both paid and unpaid,

and to enhance their legal skills as they fulfill their 40-hour commitment of pro bono legal service.

Degree Programs

We offer the JD degree as a three-year full-time day, a five-year part-time day, or a two and one-half-year accelerated day program. In addition, students may elect to complete both a JD and a master's degree in four years of full-time study. The Law School also offers an LLM program for international students who have already obtained a law degree from their native countries.

Special Programs

Clinic Program—Students receive a special license to practice law from the Indiana Supreme Court and participate in all stages of legal practice in one of the following areas: civil, criminal, domestic violence, juvenile, mediation, sports law, tax, and wrongful conviction. Each year, Clinic students handle over 700 cases for underserved community members.

Externships—The Law School offers over 85 externships at 125 different sites in the Valparaiso area, Chicago, Indianapolis, and other locations throughout the United States.

International Summer Programs—Valparaiso Law offers a comparative law program in London and Cambridge, England, and a program in international human rights in Chile and Argentina.

Honors Program—First-year students are selected for this unique learning community based on academic performance and demonstrated leadership.

The Summer Public Interest Stipend Program—Supports students who choose to work without pay in a public sector internship in the United States or at an international site.

The Loan Repayment Assistance Program offers financial assistance to graduates who incur education loan debts and choose to go into public service employment.

Bar Preparation Program—Includes a bar preparation course (offered every semester), individual counseling, and elective courses that cover state-specific materials. Our bar passage rate averaged 83 percent over 21 states in 2010.

Academic Success Program—The Academic Success Program assists students with the transition to law school via a 10-day summer program prior to law school entry and an 8-session workshop program held during the fall semester.

Career Planning

Our service mission is to assist all students and graduates in planning career paths, preparing for the job market, and identifying and creating professional opportunities. We work closely with employers, including our 5,000 alumni, in developing career-related networks for our law students. In the last five years, an average of 82 percent of our graduates were employed within nine months of graduation. About half were employed in law firms and the other half in judicial clerkships, government, public interest work, business, and academia.

Faculty

Fulbright scholars, clerks to federal appellate and state supreme court judges, government servants: our professors bring practical experience in public and private sectors to their teaching. Their scholarship spans a wide range of legal theory. Visit www.valpo.edu/law/faculty.

Library and Physical Facilities

The Valparaiso Law Library is the largest legal research facility in northwest Indiana. The library provides study space and access to legal electronic and print resources. The Law School occupies two buildings: Wesemann Hall houses classrooms, the law library, courtrooms, a jury room, a new café and outdoor patio, and administration and faculty offices; Heritage Hall houses the Lawyering Skills Center and the Valparaiso Law Clinic.

Student Activities

The *Valparaiso University Law Review* is a scholarly journal published three times a year. Because of Valparaiso's emphasis on research and writing, membership for the *Law Review* is based on academic achievement as well as excellence in legal writing. Students interested in enhancing their advocacy skills participate on the Trial Advocacy team, in the Moot Court and International Moot Court Societies, on the Client Counseling team, and in other skills-specific competition groups. Student competition teams receive Law School support to participate in national and international contests.

Valparaiso Law has 25 active student organizations that are academic, service, and culturally focused and represent a wide cross section of society. Visit www.valpo.edu/law/current-students/student-organizations.

ICLEO Program

Valparaiso Law participates in and strongly supports the Indiana CLEO program, which provides financial and counseling assistance the summer before and while in law school to those selected as Fellows. Each year, an average of 7 to 10 incoming Valparaiso Law students are chosen as ICLEO Fellows. For more information, see www.valpo.edu/law/prospective-students/p-icleo-grant-program.

Student Body Profile

Our student body is composed of individuals committed to fostering a culture of respect, integrity, and inclusiveness. We actively recruit students of all races, ethnicities, ages, socioeconomic statuses, abilities, national origins, sexual identities, religions, and veteran statuses. Our total JD student body is composed of 29 percent racial and ethnic groups underrepresented in the law; 54 percent males, 46 percent females; and 33 percent age 25 and older.

Expenses and Financial Aid

The Law School is committed to helping students meet the cost of attendance. Approximately one third of all JD students receive scholarship assistance. Ninety-five percent of all law students receive assistance through federal loans, including the Grad PLUS loan program.

Location and Community

Valparaiso University Law School maintains strong ties to Valparaiso, a small city of 30,000 in northwest Indiana, located 60 miles from downtown Chicago. The larger Valparaiso community offers the best of Midwestern livability: close proximity to nature in the nearby beaches and parks along Lake Michigan; a vibrant local arts scene; a variety of shopping and dining experiences; and quiet, safe, and relatively inexpensive housing. We encourage you to visit our website at www.valpo.edu/law/admissions/index.php and visit the Law School. Tours can be arranged through the Office of Admissions. Visitors are hosted by an assistant director, sit in on a class, and meet with students and faculty.

APPLICANT PROFILE

Admission to Valparaiso Law is competitive. The selection process involves a holistic application review by a faculty Admissions Committee that considers motivation, professionalism, maturity, and service to others, as well as academic achievement.

VANDERBILT UNIVERSITY LAW SCHOOL

131 21st Avenue South
Nashville, TN 37203
Phone: 615.322.6452; Fax: 615.322.1531
E-mail: admissions@law.vanderbilt.edu; Website: www.law.vanderbilt.edu

*ABA
Approved
Since
1925*

AMERICAN BAR ASSOCIATION
Section of Legal Education
and Admissions to the Bar

The Basics

Type of school	Private
Term	Semester
Application deadline	3/15 2/15
Application fee	$50
Financial aid deadline	2/15
Can first year start other than fall?	No
Student to faculty ratio	13.4 to 1
# of housing spaces available	
restricted to law students	20
graduate housing for which law students are eligible	40

Faculty and Administrators

	Total		Men		Women		Minorities	
	Spr	Fall	Spr	Fall	Spr	Fall	Spr	Fall
Full-time	32	41	21	26	11	15	5	8
Other full-time	0	0	0	0	0	0	0	0
Deans, librarians, & others who teach	11	11	5	5	6	6	0	0
Part-time	53	34	38	23	15	11	1	3
Total	96	86	64	54	32	32	6	11

Curriculum

	Full-Time	Part-Time
Typical first-year section size	96	0
Is there typically a "small section" of the first-year class, other than Legal Writing, taught by full-time faculty	Yes	No
If yes, typical size offered last year	48	
# of classroom course titles beyond first-year curriculum	141	

# of upper division courses, excluding seminars, with an enrollment:		
Under 25	89	
25–49	27	
50–74	13	
75–99	3	
100+	4	

# of seminars	16	
# of seminar positions available	285	
# of seminar positions filled	219	0
# of positions available in simulation courses	702	
# of simulation positions filled	647	0
# of positions available in faculty supervised clinical courses	80	
# of faculty supervised clinical positions filled	77	0
# involved in field placements	146	0
# involved in law journals	183	0
# involved in moot court or trial competitions	11	0
# of credit hours required to graduate	88	

JD Enrollment and Ethnicity

	Men		Women		Full-Time		Part-Time		1st-Year		Total		JD Degs. Awd.
	#	%	#	%	#	%	#	%	#	%	#	%	
All Hispanics	12	3.8	13	4.9	25	4.3	0	0.0	5	2.6	25	4.3	10
Am. Ind./AK Nat.	1	0.3	0	0.0	1	0.2	0	0.0	0	0.0	1	0.2	1
Asian	15	4.7	11	4.1	26	4.4	0	0.0	9	4.7	26	4.4	7
Black/Af. Am.	12	3.8	35	13.1	47	8.0	0	0.0	16	8.3	47	8.0	22
Nat. HI/Pac. Isl.	0	0.0	0	0.0	0	0.0	0	0.0	0	0.0	0	0.0	0
2 or more races	6	1.9	9	3.4	15	2.6	0	0.0	10	5.2	15	2.6	0
Subtotal (minor.)	46	14.4	68	25.5	114	19.5	0	0.0	40	20.7	114	19.5	40
Nonres. Alien	13	4.1	11	4.1	24	4.1	0	0.0	6	3.1	24	4.1	7
White/Cauc.	204	63.9	160	59.9	364	62.1	0	0.0	105	54.4	364	62.1	132
Unknown	56	17.6	28	10.5	84	14.3	0	0.0	42	21.8	84	14.3	19
Total	319	54.4	267	45.6	586	100.0	0	0.0	193	32.9	586		198

Transfers

Transfers in	13
Transfers out	4

Tuition and Fees

	Resident	Nonresident
Full-time	$46,148	$46,148
Part-time		
Tuition Guarantee Program	N	

Living Expenses

Estimated living expenses for singles

Living on campus	Living off campus	Living at home
$22,516	$22,516	$22,516

VANDERBILT UNIVERSITY LAW SCHOOL

ABA Approved Since 1925

GPA and LSAT Scores

	Total	Full-Time	Part-Time
# of apps	3,987	3,987	0
# of offers	1,054	1,054	0
# of matrics	193	193	0
75% GPA	3.84	3.84	0.00
Median GPA	3.73	3.73	0.00
25% GPA	3.48	3.48	0.00
75% LSAT	170	170	0
Median LSAT	169	169	0
25% LSAT	165	165	0

Grants and Scholarships (from prior year)

	Total		Full-Time		Part-Time	
	#	%	#	%	#	%
Total # of students	586		586		0	
Total # receiving grants	434	74.1	434	74.1	0	0.0
Less than 1/2 tuition	281	48.0	281	48.0	0	0.0
Half to full tuition	132	22.5	132	22.5	0	0.0
Full tuition	2	0.3	2	0.3	0	0.0
More than full tuition	19	3.2	19	3.2	0	0.0
Median grant amount			$20,000		$0	

Informational and Library Resources

Total amount spent on library materials	$1,615,807
Study seating capacity inside the library	261
# of full-time equivalent professional librarians	5
Hours per week library is open	111
# of open, wired connections available to students	270
# of networked computers available for use by students	50
Has wireless network?	Y
Requires computer?	N

JD Attrition (from prior year)

	Academic	Other	Total	
	#	#	#	%
1st year	0	5	5	2.6
2nd year	0	2	2	1.0
3rd year	0	2	2	1.0
4th year	0	0	0	0.0

Employment (9 months after graduation)

For up-to-date employment data, go to employmentsummary.abaquestionnaire.org on the ABA website.

Bar Passage Rates

First-time takers	190	Reporting %		70.00
Average school %	93.23	Average state %		82.37
Average pass difference	10.86			

Jurisdiction	Takers	Passers	Pass %	State %	Diff %
New York	43	39	90.70	84.92	5.78
Tennessee	33	33	100.00	84.24	15.76
California	18	14	77.78	71.24	6.54
Florida	16	16	100.00	77.63	22.37
Others (2)	23	22	95.65		

VANDERBILT UNIVERSITY LAW SCHOOL

131 21st Avenue South
Nashville, TN 37203
Phone: 615.322.6452; Fax: 615.322.1531
E-mail: admissions@law.vanderbilt.edu; Website: www.law.vanderbilt.edu

Welcome to a New Way of Thinking

Among the nation's leading law schools, Vanderbilt is recognized for its distinguished faculty, its talented students from across the nation and abroad, and its rigorous curriculum with an array of joint-degree, specialized, and interdisciplinary programs. Building on this tradition of excellence, Vanderbilt has established itself as a leader in designing programs that connect outstanding theoretical training to real-world experiences relevant to twenty-first century law practice. A legal education that links the best scholarly research to effective lawyering provides immediate advantages to Vanderbilt graduates.

With about 195 students in each entering JD class, Vanderbilt fosters a tradition of challenging intellectual inquiry in an atmosphere of mutual respect. This small-school sense of collegiality combined with a distinguished and accessible faculty creates an exceptional environment to prepare for leadership in private practice, public service, business, or government. With state-of-the-art facilities situated on a beautiful and vibrant university campus in a sophisticated and livable city, Vanderbilt offers a first-rate legal education in a setting that promotes a great quality of life.

A Distinguished and Accessible Faculty

The central experience of a Vanderbilt legal education is working closely with leading experts in an array of fields, including corporate and business law, constitutional law, litigation, criminal law, negotiation, international law, law and economics, law and human behavior, dispute resolution, and intellectual property. Widely respected for their scholarly impact, professors draw on their cutting-edge research to create engaging educational experiences that not only train students "to think like lawyers," but also to use their training effectively in practice. Faculty members take an open-door, student-centered approach, extending their availability to students well beyond class times.

A Rigorous and Relevant Curriculum

An outstanding foundational curriculum reinforced by experiential and interdisciplinary approaches to advanced training are the hallmarks of a Vanderbilt legal education. The first-year curriculum provides an intellectual framework on which to build a legal education tailored to individual needs and interests in the second and third years. Entering students begin their studies with "Life of the Law," a course designed to distill the core ideas on which legal education is based, providing tools and information helpful to mastering law school. First-year sections of 65 students study torts, contracts, criminal law, civil procedure, property, and the regulatory state. Legal writing and a spring semester elective course round out the first-year curriculum.

Upper-level courses are almost entirely elective, allowing students to choose from a broad curriculum, combining courses, seminars, clinics, externships, independent studies, and Vanderbilt courses outside the law school. Students may also participate in programs that focus on particular areas of law. The Law and Business Program is designed to produce lawyers who understand the complex corporate finance and regulatory environments that corporate managers face. The Cecil D. Branstetter Litigation and Dispute Resolution Program is directed at connecting scholarly research on litigation and court systems to practice-based skills and strategies used to settle disputes. The International Legal Studies Program offers a unique International Law Practice Lab in which students undertake specific projects for real-world clients such as the Iraqi Special Tribunal and the International Criminal Court. The Environmental Law Program offers an extensive curriculum and a range of research and experiential opportunities. The Intellectual Property Program coordinates with noted practitioners to provide fellowships and externship opportunities to students interested in studying technology, intellectual property, entertainment, and innovation law. Vanderbilt also offers programs in criminal justice, law and government, and social justice.

International Study, Special Programs, Clinics, and Joint Degrees

Vanderbilt-in-Venice allows students to study abroad in the rich cultural center of Venice, Italy. Taught by Vanderbilt Law and University of Venice faculty, courses cover topics in international law with intensive classwork augmented by outside experiences. The six-week program concludes in early July, allowing students to work or intern during the remainder of the summer.

Vanderbilt's PhD in Law and Economics provides the next generation of training in this field: a combination of professional and academic degrees that train scholars for academic positions, law practice, policy making, and public interest work. Students either have a JD upon entry to the PhD program, or obtain a PhD and JD concurrently at Vanderbilt. The JD/PhD in Neuroscience Program is associated with the MacArthur Foundation Research Network on Law and Neuroscience at Vanderbilt University, which addresses a focused set of problems in criminal justice and challenging issues arising at the intersection of the two disciplines.

Joint-degree programs make it possible to combine the JD with an MBA, MD, MDiv, MTS, MPP, MA, or PhD in conjunction with the university's various graduate and professional schools. The law school also offers an LLM program for international lawyers and the LLM/MA in Latin American Studies.

Students earn academic credit while serving the public in real practice settings through the Law School's clinical programs. Clinical offerings include international law, appellate litigation, civil practice, criminal practice, community and economic development, domestic violence, intellectual property and the arts, and individualized semester externships. Students also can gain valuable experience in nonprofits, government agencies, and other organizations around the world through robust externship and stipend opportunities.

Law School Building and Library

The Law School facilities are among the best designed in the nation, featuring a central open courtyard with adjacent café, comfortable lounges, and abundant natural light. Situated on a park-like campus that is designated a national arboretum, the building is designed for twenty-first century legal studies and research with wireless connectivity, state-of-the-art classrooms and trial courtroom, and on-site and remote access to a host of electronic resources. The law library provides a variety of study spaces, including two reading rooms and nearly 200 carrels. The service-oriented library staff oversees a collection of over 605,000 volumes and more than 250 electronic databases, and all other Vanderbilt libraries, containing more than 3.3 million volumes, are also available to law students.

Student Life, Journals, and Law School Environs

One of the reasons that students choose Vanderbilt is the congenial, collaborative atmosphere on campus. Spirited competition in an atmosphere of mutual respect creates a rare combination of intellectual vibrancy with a strong sense of community. A busy schedule of visiting speakers, symposia, and conferences is augmented by the activities of more than 50 student organizations. Four student publications provide opportunities to strengthen legal research and writing skills—*Vanderbilt Law Review*, *Vanderbilt Journal of Entertainment and Technology Law*, *Vanderbilt Journal of Transnational Law*, and *Environmental Law and Policy Annual Review* in conjunction with the Environmental Law Institute (ELI) in Washington, DC.

Vanderbilt is an internationally recognized university with strong partnerships among its 10 schools, neighboring institutions, and the Nashville community. In the natural beauty of Tennessee, Vanderbilt's hometown has emerged as a vibrant and progressive city that offers numerous professional opportunities, wide-ranging cultural and recreational options, and a great quality of life. Among the nation's most livable cities, Nashville is the state capital with a metropolitan area population of 1.6 million, and Vanderbilt is ideally situated in this major center for legal activity, allowing students an array of opportunities in law firms, state and federal courts and government, public agencies, nonprofits, and corporations.

Career Services

Vanderbilt offers comprehensive resources to help students explore career options and to guide graduates to careers across the United States and abroad. Legal employers across the nation come to campus to recruit students for summer and permanent employment and solicit students' résumés throughout the year. For the JD classes of 2006 through 2010, 18 percent of graduates took employment in Tennessee, while 82 percent fanned out broadly over 41 other states, DC, and abroad with the largest numbers in New York (10.5 percent); Washington, DC (8.6 percent); Atlanta (7.6 percent); Chicago (5.7 percent); Texas (5.7 percent); and California (5.5 percent). About 15 percent of graduating students have obtained judicial clerkships each year, the great majority with federal judges. In all, the Law School's alumni network covers 49 states; Washington, DC; 3 US territories; and 27 foreign nations.

Scholarships and Loan Repayment Assistance

Vanderbilt provides generous financial assistance through need- and merit-based scholarships. All admitted applicants are considered for merit scholarships, and several Law Scholar Merit Awards of full tuition plus stipend are given each year through a supplemental application process. Vanderbilt's Loan Repayment Assistance Program provides financial support to graduates who choose low-paying public service employment upon graduation.

APPLICANT PROFILE

Admission to Vanderbilt is competitive, and the selection process reflects our belief that the quality of the educational environment at the Law School benefits from considering a range of information about each prospective student that is far broader than GPA and LSAT. Each file is reviewed in its entirety for indicators of academic excellence, intellectual curiosity, hard work, interest in others' welfare, obstacles overcome, professionalism, and other characteristics of successful law students. We believe that talented students with a mix of backgrounds, perspectives, and goals promote a vibrant and beneficial educational environment and that full-file review in the admission process is central to that objective. We do not provide a two-factor applicant profile grid to describe a multifactor selection process in which decisions are based on experienced judgment applied to individual cases.

VERMONT LAW SCHOOL

168 Chelsea Street, PO Box 96
South Royalton, VT 05068
Phone: 888.277.5985 (toll-free) or 802.831.1239; Fax: 802.831.1174
E-mail: admiss@vermontlaw.edu; Website: www.vermontlaw.edu

ABA
Approved
Since
1975

The Basics

Type of school	Private
Term	Semester
Application deadline	3/1
Application fee	$60
Financial aid deadline	3/15
Can first year start other than fall?	No
Student to faculty ratio	16.9 to 1
# of housing spaces available restricted to law students	
graduate housing for which law students are eligible	

Faculty and Administrators

	Total		Men		Women		Minorities	
	Spr	Fall	Spr	Fall	Spr	Fall	Spr	Fall
Full-time	28	29	13	13	15	16	2	3
Other full-time	12	14	6	7	6	7	1	1
Deans, librarians, & others who teach	28	29	10	10	18	19	6	6
Part-time	27	19	18	10	9	9	0	1
Total	95	91	47	40	48	51	9	11

Curriculum

	Full-Time	Part-Time
Typical first-year section size	75	0
Is there typically a "small section" of the first-year class, other than Legal Writing, taught by full-time faculty	Yes	No
If yes, typical size offered last year	36	
# of classroom course titles beyond first-year curriculum	132	
# of upper division courses, excluding seminars, with an enrollment: Under 25	100	
25–49	61	
50–74	11	
75–99	3	
100+	0	
# of seminars	35	
# of seminar positions available	555	
# of seminar positions filled	395	0
# of positions available in simulation courses	674	
# of simulation positions filled	496	0
# of positions available in faculty supervised clinical courses	110	
# of faculty supervised clinical positions filled	77	0
# involved in field placements	188	0
# involved in law journals	123	0
# involved in moot court or trial competitions	35	0
# of credit hours required to graduate	87	

JD Enrollment and Ethnicity

	Men		Women		Full-Time		Part-Time		1st-Year		Total		JD Degs. Awd.
	#	%	#	%	#	%	#	%	#	%	#	%	
All Hispanics	9	3.2	6	2.1	15	2.7	0	0.0	7	4.5	15	2.7	4
Am. Ind./AK Nat.	2	0.7	3	1.1	5	0.9	0	0.0	3	1.9	5	0.9	0
Asian	9	3.2	10	3.5	19	3.4	0	0.0	6	3.9	19	3.4	7
Black/Af. Am.	4	1.4	8	2.8	12	2.1	0	0.0	1	0.6	12	2.1	2
Nat. HI/Pac. Isl.	0	0.0	0	0.0	0	0.0	0	0.0	0	0.0	0	0.0	0
2 or more races	3	1.1	4	1.4	7	1.2	0	0.0	2	1.3	7	1.2	4
Subtotal (minor.)	27	9.5	31	11.0	58	10.2	0	0.0	19	12.3	58	10.2	17
Nonres. Alien	0	0.0	0	0.0	0	0.0	0	0.0	0	0.0	0	0.0	4
White/Cauc.	227	79.9	215	76.2	442	78.1	0	0.0	119	77.3	442	78.1	138
Unknown	30	10.6	36	12.8	66	11.7	0	0.0	16	10.4	66	11.7	16
Total	284	50.2	282	49.8	566	100.0	0	0.0	154	27.2	566		175

Transfers

Transfers in	4
Transfers out	4

Tuition and Fees

	Resident	Nonresident
Full-time	$43,993	$43,993
Part-time		
Tuition Guarantee Program	N	

Living Expenses

Estimated living expenses for singles

Living on campus	Living off campus	Living at home
N/A	$20,146	N/A

VERMONT LAW SCHOOL

ABA Approved Since 1975

GPA and LSAT Scores

	Total	Full-Time	Part-Time
# of apps	1,020	1,020	0
# of offers	704	704	0
# of matrics	151	151	0
75% GPA	3.54	3.54	0.00
Median GPA	3.26	3.26	0.00
25% GPA	3.00	3.00	0.00
75% LSAT	159	159	0
Median LSAT	154	154	0
25% LSAT	151	151	0

Grants and Scholarships (from prior year)

	Total		Full-Time		Part-Time	
	#	%	#	%	#	%
Total # of students	607		607		0	
Total # receiving grants	404	66.6	404	66.6	0	0.0
Less than 1/2 tuition	255	42.0	255	42.0	0	0.0
Half to full tuition	129	21.3	129	21.3	0	0.0
Full tuition	20	3.3	20	3.3	0	0.0
More than full tuition	0	0.0	0	0.0	0	0.0
Median grant amount			$15,675		$0	

Informational and Library Resources

Total amount spent on library materials	$1,000,234
Study seating capacity inside the library	358
# of full-time equivalent professional librarians	6
Hours per week library is open	110
# of open, wired connections available to students	110
# of networked computers available for use by students	105
Has wireless network?	Y
Requires computer?	N

JD Attrition (from prior year)

	Academic	Other	Total	
	#	#	#	%
1st year	4	11	15	6.9
2nd year	0	0	0	0.0
3rd year	1	1	2	1.1
4th year	0	0	0	0.0

Employment (9 months after graduation)

For up-to-date employment data, go to employmentsummary.abaquestionnaire.org on the ABA website.

Bar Passage Rates

First-time takers	159	Reporting %	71.70
Average school %	79.82	Average state %	85.37

Average pass difference −5.55

Jurisdiction	Takers	Passers	Pass %	State %	Diff %
New York	29	24	82.76	84.92	−2.16
Vermont	26	23	88.46	89.02	−0.56
Massachusetts	24	20	83.33	89.67	−6.34
New Hampshire	12	10	83.33	82.09	1.24
Others (3)	23	14	60.87		

VERMONT LAW SCHOOL

168 Chelsea Street, PO Box 96
South Royalton, VT 05068
Phone: 888.277.5985 (toll-free) or 802.831.1239; Fax: 802.831.1174
E-mail: admiss@vermontlaw.edu; Website: www.vermontlaw.edu

Introduction

Vermont Law School (VLS) operates from the belief that lawyers and legal scholars should advocate for the common good and help protect the natural world, and that legal education in service to those objectives should be both rigorous and practical. The school's legal scholars, practitioners, and staff guide and prepare students to impact fields affecting the public interest, public policy, and social justice. Graduates work for nonprofit organizations, private firms, government agencies, and educational institutions.

As an international leader in environmental law, VLS is active in broadening the array of social justice, energy policy, and climate crisis issues to be addressed by legal scholarship and in legal education. The school features distinctive programs in international law and dual JD/master's degree programs in business administration, environmental management, environmental policy, philosophy, and other fields.

Vermont Law School also works with advocacy organizations, domestic and international governments, and other educational institutions that share its commitment to make substantial, positive change in their communities and countries. The experiential education VLS provides prepares its graduates to engage in the critical issues of our time.

Faculty

The stimulating environment at Vermont Law School has attracted scholars and practitioners of national and international renown. In their teaching, VLS faculty strike a balance between scholarship and application, between rigorous research and a realistic approach to problem solving. They understand the nuanced analytic and political abilities needed in advocacy work, while also recognizing the portfolio of core skills graduates will need in their first jobs and throughout their legal careers.

As legal experts, VLS faculty are frequently sought out by national and international law firms, educational institutions, government agencies, and advocacy organizations. VLS faculty members regularly work on important cases in environmental law, international and comparative law, human rights, national security law, business law, and constitutional law, providing frequent opportunities for students to engage in related independent study and research projects. Because of the school's size and focus on teaching, close relationships between students and faculty tend to last a lifetime.

Curriculum and Experiential Programs

The fundamentals of law are rigorously addressed in the required general curriculum, in addition to which VLS students can customize their educations to build skill sets in practice areas on the leading edge of the law and social change.

At VLS, in-depth scholarship is balanced with experiential opportunities that highlight what lawyers are actually called upon to do in the field. VLS students are able to take advantage of many clinics and experiential programs that provide hands-on training and involve students in real cases and legal issues. These include:

- The **Semester in Practice** program, which matches self-directed students with mentors, who are legal professionals in a range of fields, for independent projects.
- The **South Royalton Legal Clinic**, which serves low-income area residents who need assistance in matters involving family law, housing, welfare and unemployment, health care, immigration, Social Security, children's rights, consumer protection, bankruptcy, contracts, wills, and civil rights. Guided by experienced attorneys, students represent clients in state court, federal court, and administrative hearings.
- The **Environmental and Natural Resource Law Clinic**, which is where qualified students work alongside legal experts to advance environmental protection goals while developing their research, advocacy, and litigation skills.
- The **Legislative Clinic**, which takes advantage of VLS's proximity to the state capital through internships with the Vermont General Assembly.
- The **Mediation Clinic**, which trains students to mediate civil disputes in Vermont Superior Court, Small Claims Court, and the Environmental Court. Students also mediate conflicts in which the parties choose to avoid court or postpone filing a court action until attempting mediation.
- **Judicial externships**, which are programs structured to provide students with both academic background on judicial issues and hands-on experience working in judges' chambers.
- **JD, MELP (Master of Environmental Law and Policy)**, and **LLM internships** in which students gain real-world experience in general and environmental law and policy in a wide variety of settings both locally and worldwide.
- The **General Practice Program (GPP)**, which simulates a professional law firm with professors as partners overseeing student associates who are expected to perform a range of legal activities and handle client cases. The GPP received the 2007 E. Smythe Gambrell Professionalism Award from the American Bar Association.

Joint- and Dual-Degrees and Specialized Program Offerings

In addition to the general JD program, VLS offers:
- A unique, one-year master's degree in environmental law and policy and specialized programs in land use, energy, climate change, and international environmental law.
- Dual JD/master's degree programs in business administration, environmental management, environmental policy, philosophy, and other fields through partnerships with Yale, Dartmouth, Northeastern, Cambridge, Cergy-Pontoise, Seville, Thunderbird School of Global Management, University of South Carolina, University of South Dakota, and the University of Vermont.
- Semester exchange programs with five US law schools as well as Cergy-Pontoise, McGill, Renmin (China), and Trento.
- The largest number of, and most extensive, environmental law courses in the country, taught by some of the top scholars in the field.
- Extensive summer programs that attract legal, energy, industry, and environmental experts from around the country and the world who teach courses and lead seminars on a range of pressing topics.

Student Community

Recent VLS students have come from every state and from countries including China, Guam, Brazil, Canada, Italy, Japan, Russia, and Spain. The undergraduate institutions they attended span the geographic spectrum of the country and range in size and type from Yale to the University of Colorado to Western Washington University. In a typical year, the entering class will represent over 40 states and at least 150 undergraduate institutions. Men and women are equally represented in both the student and faculty populations. And while some students come to VLS soon after graduating from college, others have spent years in a wide variety of professions, including engineering, teaching, lobbying, corporate management, and nonprofit programming. This important mix of backgrounds allows VLS to enjoy a diversity of perspectives on campus and in the classroom.

VLS's size and emphasis on collaboration foster an environment where students are valued for the contributions they make and the initiative they take within the VLS community. Whether through independent collaboration with faculty, engagement with one of the many active student organizations, or participation with the Student Government Association, students help shape academic and cocurricular coursework and campus policies.

Admission

Successful candidates demonstrate substantial academic ability and motivation and will bring diverse perspectives and interests, as well as strong talents, to the community. The two admission criteria that are weighed most heavily are academic records and two required personal essays. In addition, the school responds favorably to candidates who have been active in their communities and engaged with student organizations or professional endeavors. VLS is committed to supporting individuals traditionally underrepresented in the legal profession. Applications are reviewed on a rolling basis, beginning on the first of December.

Tuition and Financial Aid

At Vermont Law School, a combination of merit scholarships, loans, tuition grants, and work-study opportunities are employed to address the financial needs of law school candidates. On average, 90 percent of the student body receives some form of financial assistance, and approximately 40 percent of enrolling students receive VLS merit- or need-based aid. In addition to counseling students on loan repayment strategies—including the new federal income-based loan repayment and loan forgiveness program—VLS offers a Loan Repayment Assistance Program, which is designed to support graduates pursuing public interest careers in repaying educational debts.

Career Services

In addition to the network of staff, peers, and faculty advocates who serve as ready resources to every VLS student and graduate, the Office of Career Services operates as a clearinghouse for information on professional and experiential opportunities for students throughout their law school years. The office provides tools for résumé and interview preparation, assists students in researching and applying for internships and summer jobs, and helps them explore a range of postgraduate placements. The office also provides a three-year guide to finding a job, including a searchable online directory of alumni, an online job posting site, and comprehensive guides to career planning and judicial clerkships.

APPLICANT PROFILE

Vermont Law School
This grid includes only applicants who earned 120–180 LSAT scores under standard administrations.

LSAT Score	3.75 +		3.50–3.74		3.25–3.49		3.00–3.24		2.75–2.99		2.50–2.74		Below 2.50		No GPA		Total	
	Apps	Adm	Apps	Adm	Apps	Adm	Apps	Adm	Apps	Adm	Apps	Adm	Apps	Adm	Apps	Adm	Apps	Adm
170–180	5	5	1	1	1	1	0	0	2	2	1	1	0	0	0	0	10	10
165–169	10	9	20	20	8	8	7	7	4	3	0	0	5	2	0	0	54	49
160–164	16	16	32	32	27	26	22	22	12	8	6	5	4	2	2	2	121	113
155–159	34	33	43	42	61	60	45	44	37	32	16	12	13	4	3	3	252	230
150–154	24	24	39	39	51	50	69	64	45	32	20	10	19	0	6	3	273	222
145–149	11	7	21	16	41	22	34	14	25	8	21	4	13	0	2	0	168	71
140–144	5	0	17	1	23	0	17	4	10	0	13	0	6	0	1	0	92	5
Below 140	3	0	2	0	3	0	8	1	8	0	6	0	14	0	1	0	45	1
Total	108	94	175	151	215	167	202	156	143	85	83	32	74	8	15	8	1015	701

Apps = Number of Applicants
Adm = Number Admitted
Reflects 98% of the total applicant pool; highest LSAT data reported.

VILLANOVA UNIVERSITY SCHOOL OF LAW

299 North Spring Mill Road
Villanova, PA 19085
Phone: 610.519.7010; Fax: 610.519.6291
E-mail: admissions@law.villanova.edu; Website: www.law.villanova.edu

ABA
Approved
Since
1954

The Basics

Type of school	Private
Term	Semester
Application deadline	4/12
Application fee	$75
Financial aid deadline	
Can first year start other than fall?	No
Student to faculty ratio	19.3 to 1
# of housing spaces available restricted to law students	
graduate housing for which law students are eligible	

Faculty and Administrators

	Total		Men		Women		Minorities	
	Spr	Fall	Spr	Fall	Spr	Fall	Spr	Fall
Full-time	32	32	20	19	12	13	5	4
Other full-time	8	8	2	2	6	6	0	0
Deans, librarians, & others who teach	17	12	7	5	10	7	2	2
Part-time	67	50	50	38	17	12	8	6
Total	124	102	79	64	45	38	15	12

Curriculum

		Full-Time	Part-Time
Typical first-year section size		79	0
Is there typically a "small section" of the first-year class, other than Legal Writing, taught by full-time faculty		Yes	No
If yes, typical size offered last year		41	
# of classroom course titles beyond first-year curriculum		118	
# of upper division courses, excluding seminars, with an enrollment:	Under 25	103	
	25–49	24	
	50–74	12	
	75–99	17	
	100+	2	
# of seminars		16	
# of seminar positions available		236	
# of seminar positions filled		219	0
# of positions available in simulation courses		745	
# of simulation positions filled		679	0
# of positions available in faculty supervised clinical courses		109	
# of faculty supervised clinical positions filled	109	0
# involved in field placements	212	0
# involved in law journals	124	0
# involved in moot court or trial competitions	43	0
# of credit hours required to graduate		88	

JD Enrollment and Ethnicity

	Men		Women		Full-Time		Part-Time		1st-Year		Total		JD Degs. Awd.
	#	%	#	%	#	%	#	%	#	%	#	%	
All Hispanics	28	7.1	26	7.9	54	7.4	0	0.0	8	3.7	54	7.4	14
Am. Ind./AK Nat.	1	0.3	1	0.3	2	0.3	0	0.0	2	0.9	2	0.3	2
Asian	16	4.1	26	7.9	42	5.8	0	0.0	10	4.6	42	5.8	19
Black/Af. Am.	10	2.5	9	2.7	19	2.6	0	0.0	6	2.8	19	2.6	3
Nat. HI/Pac. Isl.	0	0.0	0	0.0	0	0.0	0	0.0	0	0.0	0	0.0	0
2 or more races	8	2.0	5	1.5	13	1.8	0	0.0	1	0.5	13	1.8	2
Subtotal (minor.)	63	15.9	67	20.3	130	17.9	0	0.0	27	12.5	130	17.9	40
Nonres. Alien	2	0.5	1	0.3	3	0.4	0	0.0	0	0.0	3	0.4	2
White/Cauc.	312	79.0	249	75.5	561	77.4	0	0.0	172	79.6	561	77.4	212
Unknown	18	4.6	13	3.9	31	4.3	0	0.0	17	7.9	31	4.3	0
Total	395	54.5	330	45.5	725	100.0	0	0.0	216	29.8	725		254

Transfers

Transfers in	20
Transfers out	17

Tuition and Fees

	Resident	Nonresident
Full-time	$37,780	$37,780
Part-time		
Tuition Guarantee Program		N

Living Expenses

Estimated living expenses for singles

Living on campus	Living off campus	Living at home
N/A	$22,607	$11,357

*ABA
Approved
Since
1954*

GPA and LSAT Scores

	Total	Full-Time	Part-Time
# of apps	3,014	3,014	0
# of offers	1,475	1,475	0
# of matrics	218	218	0
75% GPA	3.69	3.69	0.00
Median GPA	3.57	3.57	0.00
25% GPA	3.36	3.36	0.00
75% LSAT	161	161	0
Median LSAT	160	160	0
25% LSAT	157	157	0

Grants and Scholarships (from prior year)

	Total #	Total %	Full-Time #	Full-Time %	Part-Time #	Part-Time %
Total # of students	765		765		0	
Total # receiving grants	266	34.8	266	34.8	0	0.0
Less than 1/2 tuition	129	16.9	129	16.9	0	0.0
Half to full tuition	103	13.5	103	13.5	0	0.0
Full tuition	33	4.3	33	4.3	0	0.0
More than full tuition	1	0.1	1	0.1	0	0.0
Median grant amount			$20,000		$0	

Informational and Library Resources

Total amount spent on library materials	$1,124,142
Study seating capacity inside the library	453
# of full-time equivalent professional librarians	9
Hours per week library is open	168
# of open, wired connections available to students	434
# of networked computers available for use by students	60
Has wireless network?	Y
Requires computer?	N

JD Attrition (from prior year)

	Academic #	Other #	Total #	Total %
1st year	2	18	20	7.9
2nd year	1	0	1	0.4
3rd year	0	0	0	0.0
4th year	0	0	0	0.0

Employment (9 months after graduation)

For up-to-date employment data, go to
employmentsummary.abaquestionnaire.org on the ABA website.

Bar Passage Rates

First-time takers	228	Reporting %	85.53
Average school %	89.24	Average state %	83.41
Average pass difference	5.83		

Jurisdiction	Takers	Passers	Pass %	State %	Diff %
Pennsylvania	159	143	89.94	83.06	6.88
New York	36	31	86.11	84.92	1.19

The information on these pages was provided by the law school.

VILLANOVA UNIVERSITY SCHOOL OF LAW

299 North Spring Mill Road
Villanova, PA 19085
Phone: 610.519.7010; Fax: 610.519.6291
E-mail: admissions@law.villanova.edu; Website: www.law.villanova.edu

Introduction

Today, as never before, there is a need for law schools to teach far more than the letter of the law. They must give future lawyers a sense of the importance of their role in the larger society, and they must prepare lawyers to work in an environment of burgeoning technology with issues of global importance.

With its Catholic roots, Villanova offers a legal education designed to teach the rules of law and their application; to demonstrate how lawyers analyze legal issues and express arguments and conclusions; to inculcate the skills of the counselor, advocate, and decision maker; and to explore the ethical and moral dimensions of law practice and professional conduct. The school is also providing leadership in information technology, public interest, taxation, and international law, among other fields.

Few law schools are located in a more beautiful and tranquil environment. Adjacent to the university campus is Philadelphia's Main Line. The school is at the approximate midpoint of East Coast legal centers in New York and Washington, DC, and only 20 minutes by commuter rail from the center of Philadelphia.

Opened in 1953, the school is approved by the American Bar Association and is a member of the Association of American Law Schools. Students are graduates of well over 100 colleges and universities; many have significant work experience outside of the law. The atmosphere of the school is noted for its collegiality.

Faculty

While Villanova faculty members are recognized nationally and internationally for their legal scholarship and for their contributions to the study and practice of law, they are also deeply committed to teaching. The student-to-faculty ratio is 17 to 1.

Library and Physical Facilities

The spectacular new building opened its doors in July 2009, providing almost twice as much usable space as the law school's former home.

A soaring commons anchors the main floor and provides a breathtaking public space and comfortable, casual seating for students, faculty, and staff. Bright, spacious classrooms are tailored to the size and nature of the classes being taught and are equipped with state-of-the-art technology. The stunning Ceremonial Courtroom provides an inspiring venue for trial and advocacy events. Faculty offices are located adjacent to the classrooms to ensure that the give and take of the classroom continues after class.

The building's hallmark is its student-centeredness. The most beautiful, comfortable, and spacious places are the student areas. For example, the library reading rooms are elegantly appointed and bathed in natural light by their three floor-to-ceiling window walls. The student lounge overlooks the quad on the first floor, again boasting floor-to-ceiling windows. The dining room and the coffee bar emphasize our commitment to the importance of quality of life for students who are working long hours.

The library in the new building occupies almost an entire wing and anchors one of the main entrances. Highly functional, beautifully appointed, and equipped with the latest technology, the library's open spaces, glass walls, and high ceilings draw users.

Joint JD/MBA Program

Offered in collaboration with Villanova's top-ranked School of Business, the joint JD/MBA program is designed to provide careful integration of the two disciplines and to allow students to earn both degrees in far less time than it would take to obtain them separately. Students in this program typically begin their MBA studies after the first year of law school and often finish both degrees in three to four years.

Joint JD/LLM in International Studies

Joint programs offered with the University of Edinburgh, Scotland; Leiden University, the Netherlands; the University of London; the University of Singapore; and the City University of Hong Kong allow students to earn both a JD and an international LLM in three years. Students spend the first two years at Villanova, completing their JD courses. They then study abroad during the third year, completing the LLM. Each school accepts credits from the other, allowing students who qualify for this highly selective program to finish both degrees in the time it would normally take to finish the JD.

Joint JD/LLM in Taxation and LLM in Taxation

Students in the JD/LLM in Taxation program earn both the JD and the graduate law degree in taxation in less time and at a reduced cost than earning the degrees separately. Beginning in their second year of law school, JD students enroll in a series of tax courses that, taken together, qualify for both degrees. Following the award of the JD degree, a student can complete the remaining LLM requirements in one additional academic semester.

The interdisciplinary LLM program is conducted under the auspices of the School of Law and the Villanova School of Business. The program enriches the tax curriculum available to JD candidates, who are able to enroll in LLM courses.

Joint JD/MPA Program

The JD/MPA (Master of Public Administration) program is offered in collaboration with Villanova's College of Liberal Arts and Sciences, and is designed for law students who wish to earn both degrees in far less time than it would take to obtain them separately. Students in this program typically begin their MPA studies after the first year of law school and often finish both degrees in three to four years.

Special Programs

Beyond the skills of written and oral expression developed in the first-year writing program and the required upper-level moot court program, drafting, and seminar courses, Villanova students acquire the fundamental skills of the practicing lawyer—including counseling, negotiation, advocacy, mediation, dispute resolution, conciliation, and mature judgment. Hands-on clinical opportunities allow students to apply classroom experiences to real-world client representation, often while performing public service. Clinical programs include Federal Tax; Civil Justice; Asylum, Refugee, and Emigrant Services; and Farmworkers Legal Aid.

Student Activities

The *Villanova Law Review* is a scholarly journal prepared and edited by law students. Members are selected on the basis of academic rank or through an open writing competition.

The *Villanova Environmental Law Journal* publishes both student and outside articles dealing with environmental issues. Students are selected for membership by an open writing competition.

The *Villanova Sports and Entertainment Law Journal* contains articles prepared by practitioners and professors in sports and entertainment law as well as by students. Membership is earned by selection through an open writing competition.

Each year, second- and third-year students have the opportunity to practice lawyering skills through the Client Interviewing and Counseling Competition, the Reimel Moot Court Competition, and several outside moot court competitions.

Student organizations include the Asian and Pacific American Law Students Association, Black Law Students Association, Corporate Law Society, Criminal Law Society, Environmental and Energy Law Society, Health Law Society, Intellectual Property Society, International Law Society, Jewish Law Students Association, Hispanic American Law Students Association, Justinian Society, OUTLaw, Phi Delta Phi, Pro Bono Society, St. Thomas More Society, Sports and Entertainment Law Society, Student Animal Legal Defense Fund, Tax Law Society, and Women's Law Caucus.

Career Strategy and Advancement

The mission of the Office of Career Strategy and Advancement is to partner with our students to provide career planning, career education, recruitment programs, and individual counseling to assist students in the achievement of their career goals and objectives. Distinctive features and programs include three attorney-advisors, including a public service/pro bono specialist; a career specialist dedicated to working with our alumni; an open-door policy, including open house events and a daily "on call" advisor for walk-ins and "quick questions"; small group workshops; dozens of career workshops and panel programs on topics ranging from interviews, résumés, and networking, to public interest careers, judicial clerkships, and a multitude of practice specialty areas; a mentoring program designed to match students with alumni for "real-world" advice; recruitment programs throughout the year, including an array of employers in private practice (large and small firms), government, nonprofits, the judiciary, and corporations; special recruitment programs designed to enhance diversity in the profession; job fairs targeting unique geographic or practice preferences; and job-search coaching for new graduates on the job market. The office also coordinates pro bono programs, such as "Lawyering Together" and other projects, that provide students with the opportunity to serve the disadvantaged while developing skills and positive relationships with practicing attorneys.

APPLICANT PROFILE

Villanova has chosen not to provide prospective students with an admission profile based on individual undergraduate GPAs and LSAT scores. The Admissions Committee seeks to create a diverse community by adhering to a comprehensive evaluation of a candidate's file that includes academic performance as well as professional promise. Each candidate's background, interests, accomplishments, and goals are considered before a decision is made.

UNIVERSITY OF VIRGINIA SCHOOL OF LAW

Office of Admissions, 580 Massie Road
Charlottesville, VA 22903-1738
Phone: 434.924.7351; Fax: 434.982.2128
E-mail: lawadmit@virginia.edu; Website: www.law.virginia.edu

ABA
Approved
Since
1923

The Basics

Type of school	Public
Term	Semester
Application deadline	3/1
Application fee	$80
Financial aid deadline	2/17
Can first year start other than fall?	No
Student to faculty ratio	11.1 to 1
# of housing spaces available restricted to law students	
graduate housing for which law students are eligible	779

Faculty and Administrators

	Total		Men		Women		Minorities	
	Spr	Fall	Spr	Fall	Spr	Fall	Spr	Fall
Full-time	80	85	60	63	20	22	8	9
Other full-time	1	1	0	0	1	1	1	1
Deans, librarians, & others who teach	6	7	4	4	2	3	1	1
Part-time	110	92	88	77	22	15	3	2
Total	197	185	152	144	45	41	13	13

Curriculum

	Full-Time	Part-Time
Typical first-year section size	68	0
Is there typically a "small section" of the first-year class, other than Legal Writing, taught by full-time faculty	Yes	No
If yes, typical size offered last year	31	
# of classroom course titles beyond first-year curriculum	259	

# of upper division courses, excluding seminars, with an enrollment:		
	Under 25	145
	25–49	44
	50–74	26
	75–99	13
	100+	5

	Full-Time	Part-Time
# of seminars	91	
# of seminar positions available	1,459	
# of seminar positions filled	1,112	0
# of positions available in simulation courses	926	
# of simulation positions filled	824	0
# of positions available in faculty supervised clinical courses	96	
# of faculty supervised clinical positions filled	91	0
# involved in field placements	159	0
# involved in law journals	650	0
# involved in moot court or trial competitions	86	0
# of credit hours required to graduate	86	

JD Enrollment and Ethnicity

	Men		Women		Full-Time		Part-Time		1st-Year		Total		JD Degs. Awd.
	#	%	#	%	#	%	#	%	#	%	#	%	
All Hispanics	28	4.6	25	5.1	53	4.8	0	0.0	13	3.6	53	4.8	16
Am. Ind./AK Nat.	3	0.5	2	0.4	5	0.5	0	0.0	0	0.0	5	0.5	4
Asian	58	9.6	62	12.7	120	11.0	0	0.0	36	9.9	120	11.0	20
Black/Af. Am.	36	6.0	41	8.4	77	7.0	0	0.0	27	7.5	77	7.0	18
Nat. HI/Pac. Isl.	0	0.0	0	0.0	0	0.0	0	0.0	0	0.0	0	0.0	0
2 or more races	13	2.2	15	3.1	28	2.6	0	0.0	12	3.3	28	2.6	0
Subtotal (minor.)	138	22.8	145	29.7	283	25.9	0	0.0	88	24.3	283	25.9	58
Nonres. Alien	2	0.3	5	1.0	7	0.6	0	0.0	0	0.0	7	0.6	4
White/Cauc.	404	66.9	296	60.5	700	64.0	0	0.0	231	63.8	700	64.0	231
Unknown	60	9.9	43	8.8	103	9.4	0	0.0	43	11.9	103	9.4	85
Total	604	55.3	489	44.7	1093	100.0	0	0.0	362	33.1	1093		378

Transfers

Transfers in	12
Transfers out	1

Tuition and Fees

	Resident	Nonresident
Full-time	$44,600	$49,600
Part-time		
Tuition Guarantee Program		N

Living Expenses

Estimated living expenses for singles

Living on campus	Living off campus	Living at home
$20,800	$20,800	$20,800

UNIVERSITY OF VIRGINIA SCHOOL OF LAW

ABA Approved Since 1923

GPA and LSAT Scores

	Total	Full-Time	Part-Time
# of apps	7,379	7,379	0
# of offers	688	688	0
# of matrics	357	357	0
75% GPA	3.94	3.94	0.00
Median GPA	3.86	3.86	0.00
25% GPA	3.49	3.49	0.00
75% LSAT	171	171	0
Median LSAT	170	170	0
25% LSAT	165	165	0

Grants and Scholarships (from prior year)

	Total		Full-Time		Part-Time	
	#	%	#	%	#	%
Total # of students	1,106		1,105		1	
Total # receiving grants	500	45.2	500	45.2	0	0.0
Less than 1/2 tuition	349	31.6	349	31.6	0	0.0
Half to full tuition	109	9.9	109	9.9	0	0.0
Full tuition	38	3.4	38	3.4	0	0.0
More than full tuition	4	0.4	4	0.4	0	0.0
Median grant amount			$18,000		$0	

Informational and Library Resources

Total amount spent on library materials	$1,379,692
Study seating capacity inside the library	809
# of full-time equivalent professional librarians	14
Hours per week library is open	112
# of open, wired connections available to students	78
# of networked computers available for use by students	34
Has wireless network?	Y
Requires computer?	Y

JD Attrition (from prior year)

	Academic	Other	Total	
	#	#	#	%
1st year	0	4	4	1.1
2nd year	0	5	5	1.4
3rd year	1	0	1	0.3
4th year	0	0	0	0.0

Employment (9 months after graduation)

For up-to-date employment data, go to employmentsummary.abaquestionnaire.org on the ABA website.

Bar Passage Rates

First-time takers	311	Reporting %	100.00
Average school %	94.85	Average state %	81.08
Average pass difference	13.77		

Jurisdiction	Takers	Passers	Pass %	State %	Diff %
Virginia	112	102	91.07	78.15	12.92
New York	99	96	96.97	84.92	12.05
California	26	25	96.15	71.24	24.91
Texas	24	24	100.00	82.68	17.32
Others (16)	50	48	96.00		

UNIVERSITY OF VIRGINIA SCHOOL OF LAW

Office of Admissions, 580 Massie Road
Charlottesville, VA 22903-1738
Phone: 434.924.7351; Fax: 434.982.2128
E-mail: lawadmit@virginia.edu; Website: www.law.virginia.edu

Introduction

Founded by Thomas Jefferson in 1819, the University of
Virginia School of Law is a world-renowned training ground
for distinguished lawyers and public servants. Located in
Charlottesville, Virginia, just two hours southwest of
Washington, DC, the Law School offers students a unique
environment in which to study law.

Considered one of the top law schools in the nation,
Virginia has educated generations of lawyers, instilling in
them a commitment to leadership, integrity, and community
service. The Law School is justly famous for its collegial
environment that bonds students and faculty, and student
satisfaction is consistently cited as among the highest in
American law schools. At Virginia, law students share their
experiences in a cooperative spirit, both in and out of the
classroom, and build a network that lasts well beyond their
three years here.

Curriculum and Degrees

Virginia offers more than 200 courses and seminars each year,
including 20 clinics and other opportunities for hands-on
training. Students pursuing interdisciplinary ideas benefit from
an environment where nearly half of all law faculty hold
advanced degrees in fields such as psychology, economics,
philosophy, history, medicine, and theology. Each first-year
student takes one small-section class of 30 students during the
first semester, which helps bond classmates from the start.

Virginia's curriculum is enhanced by several academic
programs, including those in international law, human rights,
law and public service, criminal law, environmental law, legal
and constitutional history, race and law, intellectual property,
health law, and immigration law. The Program in Law and
Business offers students courses that integrate business and
legal analysis in the law school classroom. Foundational
courses in accounting and finance allow students in the
program to take more advanced instruction in real-life
corporate law problems.

Students may enroll in several dual-degree programs. The
JD/MBA program is a four-year program in conjunction with
the Darden School of Business. Other dual-degree programs
include a JD/MA in English, government, foreign affairs,
history, or philosophy; a JD/MS in accounting; a JD/MUEP
(urban and environmental planning); a JD/MPP (public policy);
and a JD/MPH (public health). In addition, students may
combine a law degree from Virginia with the MPA (public
affairs) from Princeton; MALD (law and diplomacy) from the
Fletcher School at Tufts; or the MA in international relations
and international economics from Johns Hopkins.

Facilities

The Law School is located in an expansive and attractive
setting that fosters learning and personal growth. The library,
with more than 870,000 volumes and volume equivalents, is
one of the largest law libraries in the country. Virginia offers
numerous study spaces, offices for student organizations and
journals, and a large dining facility.

Admission

Each year, many highly qualified college graduates apply for
the necessarily limited number of places in the first-year class.
Our admission process aims to select from the applicant pool
an entering class of students who will contribute to this
academic community during their three years of residency
and, ultimately, to society and the legal profession. To that
end, we consider many factors. These include not only
intellectual aptitude and academic achievement, but also
individual accomplishments and experiences—such as
dedication or a constructive response to adversity—that
predict success, as well as geographic, racial, ethnic,
economic, and ideological diversity.

Rigid standards based simply on a combination of an LSAT
score and cumulative undergraduate grade-point average
cannot be the only criteria for selecting an entering class. We
assess each applicant as an individual. This assessment takes
into account not only LSAT scores and undergraduate grades,
but also the strength of an applicant's undergraduate or
graduate curriculum, trends in grades, the maturing effect of
experiences since college, the nature and quality of any work
experience, significant achievement in extracurricular
activities in college, service in the military, contributions to
campus or community through service and leadership, and
personal qualities displayed. An applicant's experiences
surmounting economic, social, or educational difficulties with
grace and courage, demonstrating the capacity to grow in
response to challenge, and showing compassion for the
welfare of others can play a role in the admission decision.

If the University of Virginia is your first choice for law
school, you may apply under the Binding Expedited Decision
option. Expedited Decision applicants commit to enrolling if
admitted and must withdraw all applications to other law
schools once notified of admission to Virginia. Expedited
Decision applicants will receive a decision within 15 days of
the date on which their applications become complete.

While individual interviews are not a part of the admission
process, prospective students are encouraged to visit the
School of Law. When classes are in session, student-led tours
are available and classes are open to visitors. On most Friday
afternoons throughout the summer and during the school
year, the school also holds admission information sessions
and student life panels for prospective students. Check our
website at www.law.virginia.edu/admissions for details.

Financial Aid

The Law School helps students finance their legal education
through a variety of resources, including scholarships,
federally sponsored loan programs, and private-sector
educational loans. While the primary responsibility for
financing a legal education rests with students and their
families, the Financial Aid Office works with students to
identify sources of financial support and develop realistic
budgets to meet their educational and professional goals.

Career Services

After law school, Virginia graduates join the nation's leading
law firms, clerk for federal and state courts, and serve in and

even establish nationally recognized public interest organizations. Our alumni are leaders in their fields: Virginia has a high number of graduates who are law firm chairpersons and managing partners, and are well represented as chief legal officers at top US companies. Virginia Law is consistently among the top law schools in the number of graduates hired by leading law firms. We have graduates at each of the American Lawyer top 100 firms.

Virginia Law has ranked third in placing clerks at the US Supreme Court since 2005. Currently, Virginia Law has four Supreme Court clerks. Graduates have been awarded Skadden, Equal Justice Works, and Independence Foundation Fellowships, which are among the nation's most prestigious public service grants.

Public Service

Virginia upholds Thomas Jefferson's conviction that lawyers have a special obligation to serve the public interest. We are committed to nurturing the civic virtues that support his ideal of public responsibility: integrity, civility, and service. The Law School offers hundreds of thousands of dollars in fellowships to students pursuing public service careers, and its loan forgiveness program removes the burden of debt repayment from students who choose lower-paying public service careers, making virtually any career a practical possibility.

The Virginia Loan Forgiveness Program helps repay the loans of graduates who earn less than $75,000 annually in public service positions.

The Mortimer Caplin Public Service Center provides individual counseling and sponsors events focused on educating students about working in the public sector.

The Pro Bono Project is a voluntary program encouraging all students to complete at least 75 hours of pro bono service during their three years of law school. Opportunities are available locally and nationwide. The center also organizes pro bono projects that focus on areas such as child advocacy, immigration law, and veterans' disability claims.

Each year the Law School provides more than $350,000 to students working in public service over the summer. Virginia Law also offers numerous post-graduate public service fellowships.

Student Life

Ten academic journals and 70 student organizations—from social clubs to groups dedicated to the community's legal needs—ensure that students explore the world outside law school and expand their legal experiences while leading well-rounded lives.

Charlottesville is a picturesque and thriving greater metropolitan area of more than 201,000. Area restaurants are featured in publications such as *Gourmet* magazine and the *New York Times*. Theater, opera, and music are community fixtures; each year the city hosts the nationally acclaimed Virginia Film Festival and gathers literary luminaries for the Virginia Festival of the Book. Students enjoy going to sporting events and concerts in one of the country's finest college arenas.

APPLICANT PROFILE

The University of Virginia School of Law has elected not to provide an applicant profile based only on GPA and LSAT, as these numbers cannot be the sole criteria for selecting an entering class. Each applicant is assessed as an individual, taking into account not only LSAT scores and undergraduate grades, but also the strength of an applicant's undergraduate or graduate curriculum, trends in grades, the maturing effect of experiences since college, the nature and quality of any work experience, significant achievement in extracurricular activities, service in the military, contributions to campus or community through service and leadership, and personal qualities.

WAKE FOREST UNIVERSITY SCHOOL OF LAW

Box 7206
Winston-Salem, NC 27109
Phone: 336.758.5437; Fax: 336.758.3930
E-mail: admissions@law.wfu.edu; Website: www.law.wfu.edu

ABA
Approved
Since
1936

The Basics

Type of school	Private
Term	Semester
Application deadline	3/15
Application fee	$60
Financial aid deadline	5/1
Can first year start other than fall?	No
Student to faculty ratio	9.6 to 1
# of housing spaces available restricted to law students	
graduate housing for which law students are eligible	

Faculty and Administrators

	Total		Men		Women		Minorities	
	Spr	Fall	Spr	Fall	Spr	Fall	Spr	Fall
Full-time	43	41	26	26	17	15	5	7
Other full-time	4	7	1	3	3	4	1	1
Deans, librarians, & others who teach	8	7	2	1	6	6	2	2
Part-time	17	17	12	13	5	4	0	0
Total	72	72	41	43	31	29	8	10

Curriculum

	Full-Time	Part-Time
Typical first-year section size	42	0
Is there typically a "small section" of the first-year class, other than Legal Writing, taught by full-time faculty	No	No
If yes, typical size offered last year		

# of classroom course titles beyond first-year curriculum		108

# of upper division courses, excluding seminars, with an enrollment:	Under 25	77
	25–49	30
	50–74	11
	75–99	1
	100+	0

# of seminars		38
# of seminar positions available		594
# of seminar positions filled	448	0
# of positions available in simulation courses		432
# of simulation positions filled	413	0
# of positions available in faculty supervised clinical courses		145
# of faculty supervised clinical positions filled	135	0
# involved in field placements	28	0
# involved in law journals	175	0
# involved in moot court or trial competitions	75	0
# of credit hours required to graduate		90

JD Enrollment and Ethnicity

	Men		Women		Full-Time		Part-Time		1st-Year		Total		JD Degs. Awd.
	#	%	#	%	#	%	#	%	#	%	#	%	
All Hispanics	14	4.8	16	7.5	30	6.2	0	0.0	16	8.7	30	5.9	4
Am. Ind./AK Nat.	5	1.7	3	1.4	8	1.6	0	0.0	0	0.0	8	1.6	0
Asian	5	1.7	9	4.2	13	2.7	1	5.3	7	3.8	14	2.8	6
Black/Af. Am.	20	6.8	26	12.2	46	9.4	0	0.0	24	13.0	46	9.1	9
Nat. HI/Pac. Isl.	1	0.3	0	0.0	1	0.2	0	0.0	1	0.5	1	0.2	0
2 or more races	4	1.4	2	0.9	6	1.2	0	0.0	6	3.3	6	1.2	0
Subtotal (minor.)	49	16.7	56	26.3	104	21.4	1	5.3	54	29.3	105	20.8	19
Nonres. Alien	1	0.3	0	0.0	1	0.2	0	0.0	0	0.0	1	0.2	2
White/Cauc.	207	70.6	140	65.7	330	67.8	17	89.5	117	63.6	347	68.6	130
Unknown	36	12.3	17	8.0	52	10.7	1	5.3	13	7.1	53	10.5	8
Total	293	57.9	213	42.1	487	96.2	19	3.8	184	36.4	506		159

Transfers

Transfers in	8
Transfers out	6

Tuition and Fees

	Resident	Nonresident
Full-time	$38,756	
Part-time		
Tuition Guarantee Program	N	

Living Expenses

Estimated living expenses for singles

Living on campus	Living off campus	Living at home
N/A	$20,705	N/A

*ABA
Approved
Since
1936*

GPA and LSAT Scores

	Total	Full-Time	Part-Time
# of apps	2,632	2,632	0
# of offers	948	948	0
# of matrics	185	185	0
75% GPA	3.76	3.76	0.00
Median GPA	3.57	3.57	0.00
25% GPA	3.20	3.20	0.00
75% LSAT	164	164	0
Median LSAT	163	163	0
25% LSAT	160	160	0

Grants and Scholarships (from prior year)

	Total		Full-Time		Part-Time	
	#	%	#	%	#	%
Total # of students	487		487		0	
Total # receiving grants	231	47.4	231	47.4	0	0.0
Less than 1/2 tuition	110	22.6	110	22.6	0	0.0
Half to full tuition	90	18.5	90	18.5	0	0.0
Full tuition	24	4.9	24	4.9	0	0.0
More than full tuition	7	1.4	7	1.4	0	0.0
Median grant amount			$18,257		$0	

Informational and Library Resources

Total amount spent on library materials	$892,633
Study seating capacity inside the library	523
# of full-time equivalent professional librarians	7
Hours per week library is open	103
# of open, wired connections available to students	0
# of networked computers available for use by students	24
Has wireless network?	0
Requires computer?	Y

JD Attrition (from prior year)

	Academic	Other	Total	
	#	#	#	%
1st year	0	7	7	4.2
2nd year	2	7	9	5.7
3rd year	0	2	2	1.2
4th year	0	0	0	0.0

Employment (9 months after graduation)

For up-to-date employment data, go to
employmentsummary.abaquestionnaire.org on the ABA website.

Bar Passage Rates

First-time takers	167	Reporting %	81.44
Average school %	86.77	Average state %	79.21
Average pass difference	7.56		

Jurisdiction	Takers	Passers	Pass %	State %	Diff %
North Carolina	87	74	85.06	77.50	7.56
New York	18	15	83.33	84.92	–1.59
South Carolina	10	10	100.00	79.69	20.31
New Jersey	8	7	87.50	82.34	5.16
Others (3)	13	12	92.31		

WAKE FOREST UNIVERSITY SCHOOL OF LAW

Box 7206
Winston-Salem, NC 27109
Phone: 336.758.5437; Fax: 336.758.3930
E-mail: admissions@law.wfu.edu; Website: www.law.wfu.edu

Introduction

Wake Forest University School of Law, established in 1894, is located in Winston-Salem, a culturally rich mid-sized city in the Piedmont Triad area of North Carolina. The law school is conveniently located on the beautiful 135-acre campus of Wake Forest University. It is a member of the AALS and is ABA approved. Current students come from 32 states, 1 foreign country, and 96 undergraduate institutions. Wake Forest is nationally recognized as one of the nation's "best value" law schools.

Wake Forest offers students a solid and personalized legal education. Class sizes are smaller than at virtually any other law school in the nation, with approximately 40 students in each first-year section and 20 students in first-year legal writing sections. With a student-faculty ratio of 10:1, you get more than just an open-door policy. Our faculty will call you by name, invite you to their homes, join you for lunch, and encourage your involvement in research and community service. Because giving back to the community is paramount to your growth as a person and a lawyer, the heart of our approach is to help you become fine citizen lawyers.

Admission and Financial Aid

First-year students are admitted only in the fall semester for full-time study. Applicants must have a bachelor's degree from an accredited college or university. Other requirements include the application, dean's certification before matriculation, two academic recommendations, LSAT and LSAC Credential Assembly Service, and application fee of $60. The application deadline is March 15. Completed files are individually reviewed to select a diverse group of students who are likely to succeed in law school and contribute to the legal profession. The LSAT and undergraduate GPA, as well as a number of subjective factors, are considered. This includes personal talents, work experience, community service, leadership potential, graduate study, and a history of overcoming social or economic hardship—indicating intellectual capacity, character, motivation, and maturity. For multiple LSAT scores, the higher test score will be used. Early application is encouraged as scholarship offers begin in late January. The applicant's file must be complete for consideration.

A $300 nonrefundable deposit is due by April 15, and a tuition deposit must be paid by June 15. (Both fees are applicable toward tuition.) Personal interviews are not required; however, all applicants are encouraged to visit the law school. Transfer students meeting the admission requirements are accepted on a space-available basis after the successful completion of one year at an AALS- or ABA-approved law school. Merit, need-based, and diversity scholarships are available. The FAFSA is recommended by April 1.

Clinical and Externship Programs

Wake Forest University School of Law is committed to helping you practice what you learn. Through several outstanding programs—some curricular, some extracurricular, and some cocurricular—our students work, argue, research, write, and practice, often while helping citizens in need. Our approach tightly integrates study, practice, and experience, and it develops great lawyers.

In the Litigation Clinic, students are placed in offices such as the US attorney, the district attorney, the public defender, legal aid, the National Labor Relations Board, private law firms, and corporate counsel. In addition to receiving classroom instruction and skills training in interviewing, counseling, negotiation, and discovery, students represent clients under the supervision of an experienced attorney. Each student will be placed in concurrent civil and criminal assignments.

The Elder Law Clinic represents low- to moderate-income clients over the age of 60. Located at the Wake Forest Baptist Medical Center, the clinic features a classroom component that is jointly taught by members of the law and medical school faculties. Students draft essential documents, such as wills and powers of attorney, and handle administrative representation and state court litigation with a clinic professor/attorney.

The Community Law and Business Clinic provides a legal resource for low-income entrepreneurs and nonprofit organizations working to improve the quality of life in low-wealth communities. Students assist in various stages of the business development process and gain experience in a transactional practice setting.

The Innocence and Justice Clinic allows law students to work with defense attorneys, prosecutors, and law enforcement officers to identify cases with prisoners who might qualify for DNA testing to demonstrate their innocence.

The Appellate Advocacy Clinic represents low-income clients in all sorts of appeals, both civil and criminal, and in a variety of appellate courts, including the Fourth Circuit and Seventh Circuit. Working in pairs, students handle an actual appeal from start to finish, with advice and assistance from their professor, who is counsel of record. Students also travel to Washington, DC, to observe arguments at the United States Supreme Court.

The Child Advocacy Clinic allows students to represent children in three settings: deciding custody in high-conflict cases, deciding custody in civil domestic violence actions, and representing children of indigent parents in issues involving the public schools.

The Wake Forest School of Law Program in Washington provides students with the opportunity to spend a semester in practice in the most diverse and vibrant legal environment in the world. The program includes both an externship component and a programmatic initiative that includes conferences, roundtables, symposia, and lectures.

Joint-Degree Programs

The law school currently offers the following joint degrees: JD/MBA program with the School of Business, a JD/MA in Religion, a JD/MDiv with the Divinity School, and a JD/MA in Bioethics with the Graduate School of Arts and Sciences. Admission and scholarship decisions are made independently at each school. The law school also offers an LLM in American Law for graduates of international law schools. A separate LLM application is required and may be obtained at http://law.wfu.edu/llm or by writing the director of the LLM program.

International Study Opportunities

Students in good standing may participate in a four-week program offered each summer at the Worrell House, the university's residential center near Regent's Park in London, England; at Casa Artom on the Grand Canal in Venice, Italy; and at the University of Vienna in Vienna, Austria. Students participating in this program can earn up to six hours of academic credit. US Supreme Court Justice Ruth Bader Ginsberg has guest lectured as part of several Wake Forest summer programs.

Library and Physical Facilities

The law school is located in the Worrell Professional Center, which contains classrooms, faculty and administrative offices, and the Professional Center Library. The 200-seat auditorium also functions as a courtroom. The law school frequently hosts oral arguments for the North Carolina Court of Appeals and the Court of Appeals for the Fourth Circuit. The Worrell Professional Center, including the library, is accessible to students 24 hours a day, 365 days a year.

Wake Forest prepares students to embrace the rapidly changing technological environment of the legal profession. Classrooms feature multimedia theaters allowing technology to augment classroom teaching. Many professors routinely use course websites and WebEx to distribute essential course information and supplement class discussions.

Each student is required to have a laptop. The law school wireless network gives students instant access to e-mail, essential legal research systems, the Internet, and a variety of other resources. A university-wide network allows students to register for courses, receive grades, obtain transcripts, and interact with university offices.

Student Activities

Students have a wide variety of extracurricular activities to choose from to supplement their education. There are three academic journals: the *Wake Forest Law Review*, the *Journal of Business and Intellectual Property Law*, and the *Journal of Law and Policy*. Each year students participate in the Walker and Stanley moot court competitions, and those who are invited to join the Moot Court Board compete against students from around the country in moot court competitions featuring a variety of legal issues. For students interested in trial advocacy, the 1L Trial Bar and Zeliff competitions give them a chance to practice their oral advocacy skills.

In addition to more than 30 student organizations, there are many pro bono opportunities. The Wake Forest Pro Bono Project aims to provide assistance to attorneys who provide high quality legal services, at no fee or at a substantially reduced fee, to individuals in need and to create a lifelong commitment to pro bono work among Wake Forest students.

Career Services

The Office of Career and Professional Development aggressively seeks opportunities for students in both summer and permanent legal positions. Knowledgeable staff members, including three former practicing attorneys, personally counsel students to assist them in developing solid career portfolios. The office also conducts workshops in résumé preparation, interviewing, and career planning. Faculty and staff expand career opportunities by visiting law firms, corporations, and agencies throughout the country to acquaint them with the exceptional Wake Forest program. A large number of employers interview students on campus each year or request that résumés be forwarded by the Office of Career and Professional Development. Wake Forest law graduates are located in all 50 states and more than 40 countries and territories.

APPLICANT PROFILE

Wake Forest University School of Law
This grid includes only applicants who earned 120–180 LSAT scores under standard administrations.

LSAT Score	3.75 +		3.50–3.74		3.25–3.49		3.00–3.24		2.75–2.99		2.50–2.74		2.25–2.49		2.00–2.24		Below 2.00		No GPA		Total	
	Apps	Adm	Apps	Adm	Apps	Adm	Apps	Adm	Apps	Adm	Apps	Adm	Apps	Adm	Apps	Adm	Apps	Adm	Apps	Adm	Apps	Adm
175–180	1	0	2	2	0	0	3	3	1	1	1	1	0	0	0	0	0	0	0	0	8	7
170–174	16	15	19	18	23	21	14	9	5	3	4	1	3	2	0	0	0	0	0	0	84	69
165–169	64	61	127	115	85	80	62	52	37	21	17	7	5	3	0	0	3	0	13	11	413	350
160–164	173	164	250	131	230	51	162	36	45	7	23	3	9	1	5	0	0	0	21	2	918	395
155–159	114	22	182	22	155	15	93	8	39	7	11	0	4	0	4	1	2	0	8	0	612	75
150–154	51	3	70	12	67	8	57	10	23	5	16	0	9	0	3	0	0	0	4	0	300	38
145–149	19	5	35	2	23	4	47	0	16	0	14	0	4	0	3	0	0	0	4	0	165	11
140–144	8	0	11	0	9	0	18	0	9	0	10	0	5	0	5	0	1	0	1	0	77	0
135–139	4	0	3	0	3	0	8	0	7	0	4	0	3	0	0	0	0	0	0	0	32	0
130–134	0	0	0	0	0	0	1	0	3	0	2	0	2	0	1	0	0	0	1	0	10	0
125–129	0	0	0	0	0	0	1	0	0	0	2	0	0	0	0	0	0	0	1	0	4	0
120–124	0	0	0	0	0	0	0	0	0	0	0	0	0	0	0	0	0	0	0	0	0	0
Total	450	270	699	302	595	179	466	118	185	44	104	12	44	6	21	1	6	0	53	13	2623	945

Apps = Number of Applicants
Adm = Number Admitted
Reflects 100% of the total applicant pool; highest LSAT data reported.

WASHBURN UNIVERSITY SCHOOL OF LAW

1700 SW College Avenue
Topeka, KS 66621-0001
Phone: 800.WASHLAW or 800.927.4529; Fax: 785.670.1120
E-mail: admissions@washburnlaw.edu; Website: http://washburnlaw.edu

ABA
Approved
Since
1923

The Basics

Type of school	Public
Term	Semester
Application deadline	4/1 11/1
Application fee	$40
Financial aid deadline	7/1
Can first year start other than fall?	Yes
Student to faculty ratio	11.9 to 1
# of housing spaces available restricted to law students	
graduate housing for which law students are eligible	192

Faculty and Administrators

	Total		Men		Women		Minorities	
	Spr	Fall	Spr	Fall	Spr	Fall	Spr	Fall
Full-time	30	30	18	18	12	12	6	6
Other full-time	1	1	1	1	0	0	0	0
Deans, librarians, & others who teach	6	5	6	4	0	1	1	1
Part-time	26	29	15	17	11	12	0	0
Total	63	65	40	40	23	25	7	7

Curriculum

	Full-Time	Part-Time
Typical first-year section size	80	0
Is there typically a "small section" of the first-year class, other than Legal Writing, taught by full-time faculty	Yes	No
If yes, typical size offered last year	32	
# of classroom course titles beyond first-year curriculum	98	

# of upper division courses, excluding seminars, with an enrollment:		
	Under 25	56
	25–49	27
	50–74	11
	75–99	4
	100+	0

# of seminars	31	
# of seminar positions available	501	
# of seminar positions filled	389	0
# of positions available in simulation courses	602	
# of simulation positions filled	428	0
# of positions available in faculty supervised clinical courses	80	
# of faculty supervised clinical positions filled	73	0
# involved in field placements	113	0
# involved in law journals	61	0
# involved in moot court or trial competitions	49	0
# of credit hours required to graduate	90	

JD Enrollment and Ethnicity

	Men		Women		Full-Time		Part-Time		1st-Year		Total		JD Degs. Awd.
	#	%	#	%	#	%	#	%	#	%	#	%	
All Hispanics	10	3.9	7	4.5	17	4.1	0	0.0	9	7.4	17	4.1	8
Am. Ind./AK Nat.	5	2.0	7	4.5	12	2.9	0	0.0	3	2.5	12	2.9	1
Asian	5	2.0	5	3.2	10	2.4	0	0.0	7	5.7	10	2.4	5
Black/Af. Am.	12	4.7	5	3.2	17	4.1	0	0.0	7	5.7	17	4.1	4
Nat. HI/Pac. Isl.	1	0.4	0	0.0	1	0.2	0	0.0	1	0.8	1	0.2	0
2 or more races	0	0.0	0	0.0	0	0.0	0	0.0	0	0.0	0	0.0	0
Subtotal (minor.)	33	12.9	24	15.3	57	13.8	0	0.0	27	22.1	57	13.8	18
Nonres. Alien	2	0.8	6	3.8	8	1.9	0	0.0	2	1.6	8	1.9	1
White/Cauc.	211	82.4	125	79.6	336	81.4	0	0.0	89	73.0	336	81.4	121
Unknown	10	3.9	2	1.3	12	2.9	0	0.0	4	3.3	12	2.9	2
Total	256	62.0	157	38.0	413	100.0	0	0.0	122	29.5	413		142

Transfers

Transfers in	6
Transfers out	6

Tuition and Fees

	Resident	Nonresident
Full-time	$17,290	$26,950
Part-time		
Tuition Guarantee Program	N	

Living Expenses

Estimated living expenses for singles

Living on campus	Living off campus	Living at home
$16,952	$16,952	$16,952

ABA Approved Since 1923

GPA and LSAT Scores

	Total	Full-Time	Part-Time
# of apps	883	883	0
# of offers	352	352	0
# of matrics	124	124	0
75% GPA	3.61	3.61	0.00
Median GPA	3.20	3.20	0.00
25% GPA	2.86	2.86	0.00
75% LSAT	158	158	0
Median LSAT	155	155	0
25% LSAT	152	152	0

Grants and Scholarships (from prior year)

	Total #	Total %	Full-Time #	Full-Time %	Part-Time #	Part-Time %
Total # of students	454		454		0	
Total # receiving grants	209	46.0	209	46.0	0	0.0
Less than 1/2 tuition	75	16.5	75	16.5	0	0.0
Half to full tuition	76	16.7	76	16.7	0	0.0
Full tuition	0	0.0	0	0.0	0	0.0
More than full tuition	58	12.8	58	12.8	0	0.0
Median grant amount			$14,000		$0	

Informational and Library Resources

Total amount spent on library materials	$1,360,652
Study seating capacity inside the library	397
# of full-time equivalent professional librarians	9
Hours per week library is open	101
# of open, wired connections available to students	28
# of networked computers available for use by students	51
Has wireless network?	Y
Requires computer?	N

JD Attrition (from prior year)

	Academic #	Other #	Total #	Total %
1st year	8	17	25	15.2
2nd year	0	2	2	1.4
3rd year	0	0	0	0.0
4th year	0	0	0	0.0

Employment (9 months after graduation)

For up-to-date employment data, go to employmentsummary.abaquestionnaire.org on the ABA website.

Bar Passage Rates

First-time takers	143	Reporting %	72.03
Average school %	89.32	Average state %	90.03

Average pass difference –0.71

Jurisdiction	Takers	Passers	Pass %	State %	Diff %
Kansas	90	80	88.89	90.00	–1.11
Missouri	13	12	92.31	90.24	2.07

WASHBURN UNIVERSITY SCHOOL OF LAW

1700 SW College Avenue
Topeka, KS 66621-0001
Phone: 800.WASHLAW or 800.927.4529; Fax: 785.670.1120
E-mail: admissions@washburnlaw.edu; Website: http://washburnlaw.edu

Introduction

Washburn University School of Law was founded in 1903, became a member of the AALS in 1905, and appeared on the initial list of ABA-approved schools in 1923. The essence of Washburn Law is the commitment of the law school community at every level—from the dean's office to facilities staff—to the success of our students. In addition, the law school endeavors to impart to its students the value of treating others with respect, dignity, and a sense of caring. Its network of more than 7,000 alumni located in all 50 states and internationally includes nationally recognized lawyers, state and federal judges, politicians, journalists, and senior executives of Fortune 500 companies.

Curriculum

All entering students participate in the law school's Ex-L program, which begins during an elaborate and rigorous "first week" program designed to teach students the learning strategies they need to succeed in law school. Ex-L includes a structured study-group program in which groups of four to six students meet twice per week to apply cooperative learning strategies to their law school experience under the supervision of carefully trained and supervised upper-division students. Second- and third-year students satisfy advanced writing and oral presentation requirements and take one or more classes from a group of Perspectives on Law courses, and one or more classes from a group of Skills courses.

Centers for Excellence

Four Centers for Excellence complement Washburn's tradition of excellence in teaching. Students may add an element of concentration by participating in one of the school's eight certificate programs, most of which are administered through the centers.

Business and Transactional Law Center—The center provides students with additional educational opportunities in business law while developing the essential skills of transactional lawyers. The hands-on involvement of alumni actively engaged in business and transactional law also allows the center to accomplish a major subsidiary goal: making the law school experience more realistic and relevant, by providing additional opportunities to bridge the gap between theory and practice.

Center for Excellence in Advocacy—The center trains law students in the persuasive and skilled use of advocacy techniques. Students hone their advocacy skills in Washburn's live-client Law Clinic and in a variety of advocacy skills courses. The center coordinates student participation in trial advocacy, negotiation, and client counseling; sponsors national and regional advocacy conferences; and hosts a practitioner in residence each year.

Center for Law and Government—Washburn Law is ideally situated to offer law students unique and varied opportunities to learn about lawmaking, judicial decision making, administrative law, and the regulatory process, given its proximity to the state capitol, the state judicial center, the federal courthouse, and state agencies. As its primary focus, the center provides superior legal education to prepare

highly qualified public servants for a broad range of careers associated with local, state, and federal government.

Children and Family Law Center—Washburn houses the American Bar Association's *Family Law Quarterly*. Students working in the center have the opportunity to take a range of courses related to children and families and to participate in the Washburn Law Clinic representing clients in divorce, children in need of care, and other family law cases.

Certificate Programs

Washburn Law offers certificates of specialization in Advocacy, Business and Transactional Law, Estate Planning, Family Law, International and Comparative Law, Law and Government, Natural Resources Law, and Tax Law. The certificate programs allow students to fully develop their legal interests in these fields. Students who earn certificates graduate with a highly developed working knowledge of the practice area.

Law Clinic

In 1970, Washburn Law Clinic was one of the nation's first in-house clinics. From its inception, faculty members teaching in the clinic have been on a tenure track, placing our clinic at the forefront of legal education. Faculty-supervised students provide a full range of legal services to live clients in six clinics—Children and Family Law Clinic, Criminal Defense Clinic, Tribal and State Court Practice Clinic, Civil Litigation Clinic, Criminal Appellate Advocacy Clinic, and Small Business and Nonprofit Transactional Law Clinic.

International Programs

Currently, Washburn expands students' understandings of different legal systems through its summer program at the University of the West Indies, in Barbados, and its semester-long program at Maastricht University, in the Netherlands.

Externships

Washburn Law's externship program allows students to earn course credit through placement in legal settings outside the law school. Students can experience the practice of law in a wide variety of settings tailored to their specific interests and needs. Students are closely supervised by an attorney and by the externship director.

Accelerated-Degree Option

This option allows students to complete law school in two years by taking courses during both summers.

Facilities and Technology

For 25 years, the Washburn Law Library has been at the top of all law school libraries for new titles added, its extensive collection, and its innovative use of technology. WashLaw has been a premier legal research portal since its creation in the early 1990s, and it is nationally acclaimed as a comprehensive source for legal information on the Internet. Students have wireless access throughout the building. Classrooms include enhanced audio, video, and computer technologies. The state-of-the-art Robinson Courtroom and Bianchino Technology Center offers students the opportunity to practice their skills in a high-tech environment.

Admission

While an applicant's LSAT score and GPA are significant factors, there is no bright-line cutoff. The Admissions Committee uses the highest LSAT score for multiple-test takers. It carefully considers other factors, including a determination of whether the individual would be an asset for the class as a whole based on characteristics such as gender, ethnicity, geographic diversity, international experience, and undergraduate institution.

Student Activities

More than 30 active student organizations, including Black, Hispanic, Asian, and Native American law student associations, accommodate the wide and diverse interests students bring to the law school and add to the cultural and intellectual life of the law school community.

Students may be selected to serve on the board of editors of the Washburn Law Journal or the student editorial board of the ABA's peer-reviewed Family Law Quarterly, which has been located at Washburn since 1992, enhancing the Children and Family Law Center.

Expenses and Financial Aid

Scholarships are awarded based on academic performance. Contribution to diversity is also considered in making scholarship awards. Resident status for tuition purposes can be established with a primary Kansas residence after six months. Topeka is one of the most affordable housing markets in the country. Most students live in the residential areas surrounding the campus.

Professional Development

The Professional Development Office offers programs that emphasize assessment of career goals, exploration of varied applications of a legal education, and support for the transition into the professional marketplace. The office makes available extensive resources regarding local, regional, national, and international legal employment in the public and private sectors, graduate and foreign study, and judicial clerkships.

Washburn Law graduates enjoy great success in seeking employment. Washburn Law alumni reside in every state in the nation, the District of Columbia, and internationally.

Writing Program

During the past several years, Washburn Law has made a major commitment of resources to its Legal Analysis, Research, and Writing program, resulting in national recognition. All first-year students must complete six hours of graded legal analysis, research, and writing. An upper-level writing project is also required. The class sizes are small and are taught by tenure-track professors dedicated to legal writing as their chosen profession.

Spring Start Program

Students may start law school in January through the Spring Start Program, which provides an alternative for those who do not want to wait for the traditional fall start.

Pro Bono Program

Students are encouraged to embrace their future professional obligation to provide legal services to individuals of limited means. Through the Washburn Law Pro Bono Program, they may participate in a pro bono initiative that rewards pro bono work with recognition at graduation.

APPLICANT PROFILE

Washburn University School of Law
This grid includes only applicants who earned 120–180 LSAT scores under standard administrations.

LSAT Score	GPA 3.75 +		3.50–3.74		3.25–3.49		3.00–3.24		2.75–2.99		2.50–2.74		Below 2.50		No GPA		Total	
	Apps	Adm	Apps	Adm	Apps	Adm	Apps	Adm	Apps	Adm	Apps	Adm	Apps	Adm	Apps	Adm	Apps	Adm
170–180	0	0	0	0	0	0	1	1	1	1	0	0	0	0	0	0	2	2
165–169	2	2	1	1	0	0	1	1	0	0	3	3	0	0	0	0	7	7
160–164	8	8	5	5	6	6	4	3	3	3	3	3	3	3	0	0	32	31
155–159	22	19	17	17	29	28	27	26	18	15	10	9	18	12	1	1	142	127
150–154	26	20	31	22	45	20	49	22	38	19	25	9	23	4	2	1	239	117
145–149	11	2	33	5	31	9	42	8	42	7	24	2	22	1	6	0	211	34
140–144	1	0	11	2	18	0	21	0	18	0	8	0	10	0	6	0	93	2
Below 140	2	0	6	0	9	0	9	0	7	0	5	0	5	0	8	0	51	0
Total	72	51	104	52	138	63	154	61	127	45	78	26	81	20	23	2	777	320

Apps = Number of Applicants
Adm = Number Admitted
Reflects 100% of the total applicant pool; highest LSAT data reported.

UNIVERSITY OF WASHINGTON SCHOOL OF LAW

William H. Gates Hall, Box 353020
Seattle, WA 98195-3020
Phone: 206.543.4078; Fax: 206.685.4201
E-mail: lawadm@u.washington.edu; Website: www.law.washington.edu

ABA
Approved
Since
1924

The Basics

Type of school	Public
Term	Quarter
Application deadline	2/15
Application fee	$60
Financial aid deadline	2/28
Can first year start other than fall?	No
Student to faculty ratio	9.0 to 1
# of housing spaces available restricted to law students	
graduate housing for which law students are eligible	500

Faculty and Administrators

	Total		Men		Women		Minorities	
	Spr	Fall	Spr	Fall	Spr	Fall	Spr	Fall
Full-time	49	51	28	28	21	23	12	12
Other full-time	6	5	3	1	3	4	2	1
Deans, librarians, & others who teach	5	5	1	1	4	4	0	0
Part-time	102	49	68	32	34	17	10	4
Total	162	110	100	62	62	48	24	17

Curriculum

	Full-Time	Part-Time
Typical first-year section size	52	0
Is there typically a "small section" of the first-year class, other than Legal Writing, taught by full-time faculty	Yes	No
If yes, typical size offered last year	26	
# of classroom course titles beyond first-year curriculum	181	

# of upper division courses, excluding seminars, with an enrollment:	Under 25	99
	25–49	53
	50–74	19
	75–99	3
	100+	0

# of seminars	61	
# of seminar positions available	915	
# of seminar positions filled	752	0
# of positions available in simulation courses	488	
# of simulation positions filled	488	0
# of positions available in faculty supervised clinical courses	167	
# of faculty supervised clinical positions filled	152	0
# involved in field placements	169	0
# involved in law journals	133	0
# involved in moot court or trial competitions	46	0
# of credit hours required to graduate	135	

JD Enrollment and Ethnicity

	Men		Women		Full-Time		Part-Time		1st-Year		Total		JD Degs. Awd.
	#	%	#	%	#	%	#	%	#	%	#	%	
All Hispanics	21	7.1	14	5.6	35	6.4	0	0.0	18	9.9	35	6.4	6
Am. Ind./AK Nat.	5	1.7	7	2.8	12	2.2	0	0.0	4	2.2	12	2.2	6
Asian	27	9.2	29	11.6	56	10.3	0	0.0	20	11.0	56	10.3	18
Black/Af. Am.	5	1.7	4	1.6	9	1.7	0	0.0	6	3.3	9	1.7	3
Nat. HI/Pac. Isl.	2	0.7	1	0.4	3	0.6	0	0.0	1	0.5	3	0.6	0
2 or more races	0	0.0	0	0.0	0	0.0	0	0.0	0	0.0	0	0.0	8
Subtotal (minor.)	60	20.3	55	22.0	115	21.1	0	0.0	49	26.9	115	21.1	41
Nonres. Alien	7	2.4	7	2.8	14	2.6	0	0.0	4	2.2	14	2.6	8
White/Cauc.	214	72.5	182	72.8	396	72.7	0	0.0	119	65.4	396	72.7	128
Unknown	14	4.7	6	2.4	20	3.7	0	0.0	10	5.5	20	3.7	6
Total	295	54.1	250	45.9	545	100.0	0	0.0	182	33.4	545		183

Transfers

Transfers in	12
Transfers out	4

Tuition and Fees

	Resident	Nonresident
Full-time	$26,380	$40,450
Part-time		
Tuition Guarantee Program	N	

Living Expenses

Estimated living expenses for singles

Living on campus	Living off campus	Living at home
$18,573	$18,573	$8,184

UNIVERSITY OF WASHINGTON SCHOOL OF LAW

*ABA
Approved
Since
1924*

GPA and LSAT Scores

	Total	Full-Time	Part-Time
# of apps	2,656	2,656	0
# of offers	586	586	0
# of matrics	182	182	0
75% GPA	3.82	3.82	0.00
Median GPA	3.67	3.67	0.00
25% GPA	3.44	3.44	0.00
75% LSAT	166	166	0
Median LSAT	164	164	0
25% LSAT	161	161	0

Grants and Scholarships (from prior year)

	Total #	Total %	Full-Time #	Full-Time %	Part-Time #	Part-Time %
Total # of students	550		550		0	
Total # receiving grants	241	43.8	241	43.8	0	0.0
Less than 1/2 tuition	183	33.3	183	33.3	0	0.0
Half to full tuition	30	5.5	30	5.5	0	0.0
Full tuition	0	0.0	0	0.0	0	0.0
More than full tuition	28	5.1	28	5.1	0	0.0
Median grant amount			$6,000		$0	

Informational and Library Resources

Total amount spent on library materials	$1,341,952
Study seating capacity inside the library	414
# of full-time equivalent professional librarians	11.5
Hours per week library is open	89
# of open, wired connections available to students	0
# of networked computers available for use by students	48
Has wireless network?	Y
Requires computer?	N

JD Attrition (from prior year)

	Academic #	Other #	Total #	Total %
1st year	0	4	4	2.2
2nd year	0	0	0	0.0
3rd year	0	0	0	0.0
4th year	0	0	0	0.0

Employment (9 months after graduation)

For up-to-date employment data, go to employmentsummary.abaquestionnaire.org on the ABA website.

Bar Passage Rates

First-time takers	176	Reporting %	93.75
Average school %	82.42	Average state %	71.22
Average pass difference	11.20		

Jurisdiction	Takers	Passers	Pass %	State %	Diff %
Washington	165	136	82.42	71.22	11.20

UNIVERSITY OF WASHINGTON SCHOOL OF LAW

William H. Gates Hall, Box 353020
Seattle, WA 98195-3020
Phone: 206.543.4078; Fax: 206.685.4201
E-mail: lawadm@u.washington.edu; Website: www.law.washington.edu

Introduction

Founded in 1899, the University of Washington School of Law is one of the nation's top public law schools and one of the world's most respected centers for interdisciplinary legal studies. It offers the unmatched assets of a major research university located in Seattle, a thriving city that is one of the world's leading economic and cultural hubs. The School of Law has 67 full-time faculty members and 545 JD students. With the favorable student-to-faculty ratio, classes are generally small, with frequent opportunities for student-teacher contact. Each first-year student attends at least one class of 30 students or fewer in addition to a small section of Legal Analysis, Research, and Writing.

Guided by what is relevant in the 21st century, the School of Law provides students with the skills that give them a competitive edge in the changing legal profession and an awareness of their ethical and public service responsibilities. The law school prepares them to be Leaders for the Global Common Good through inspired teaching, scholarly discovery, ethical advocacy, and generous public service. The school is a member of the AALS, approved by the ABA, and holds a chapter of the Order of the Coif.

Curriculum

The first-year curriculum is prescribed. In the second and third years, all courses are elective except for an advanced writing requirement, a skills course requirement, and a course in professional responsibility. In addition to traditional courses and seminars, advanced students may participate in courses in Trial and Advocacy or one of 12 clinics—Innocence Project Northwest, Bankruptcy Client Representation Project, Mediation, Children and Youth Advocacy, Legislative Advocacy, Workers' Rights, Street Law, Tribal Court Public Defense, Immigration Law, Technology Law and Public Policy, Entrepreneurial Law, or Federal Tax. Students must also perform 60 hours of public service legal work.

Students are encouraged to rely on their initiative and to develop their own powers of perception. Classroom discussion, in which students participate fully, is one means used to assist this development. Independent research projects, either in the context of a seminar or through individualized study under faculty supervision, are also emphasized. Although it is a state law school, Washington's state law is not emphasized unduly. Graduates of the school are prepared to practice law anywhere in the United States or internationally.

Special Programs

Concentration tracks are available in Asian Law, Dispute Resolution, Environmental Law, Health Law, Intellectual Property, International and Comparative Law, and Public Service Law. Advanced degree programs include Asian Law, Global Business Law, Health Law, Intellectual Property Law and Policy, and Taxation (LLM programs), as well as a PhD in Asian and Comparative Law.

Scholarly centers and projects include the Asian Law Center; Barer Institute for Law and Global Human Services; Center for Advanced Study and Research on Intellectual Property (CASRIP); Center for Law in Science and Global Health; Center for Public Service Law; Global Health and Justice Project; Law, Business and Entrepreneurship Program; Law, Technology and Arts; Native American Law Center; Summer Institute in Transnational Law and Practice; Three Degrees Project on climate justice; and the Visiting Scholars Program.

JD students may take courses in any of the LLM programs during their second and third years of study. Additionally, JD students may enroll in graduate-level courses from other disciplines offered at the UW and may count a limited number of those credits toward their JD degree. Students may pursue the JD concurrently with any graduate degree program to which they have been admitted. The UW also offers a highly regarded Master's degree in Law Librarianship.

Admission Standards

When selecting its entering class, the law school does not make all of its admission decisions based on predicted academic performance. Other factors include individual achievement, experiences, and diverse backgrounds, such as geographic, racial, ethnic, economic, and/or ideological diversity.

Gates Public Service Law Scholars Program

Five Gates Public Service Law (PSL) Scholars are selected annually from among the first-year students admitted to the UW School of Law JD program. Each Gates PSL Scholar award covers tuition, books, other normal fees, costs of room and board, and incidental expenses. Acceptance of a Gates PSL scholarship represents a commitment on the part of each recipient to work in public service for at least five years following graduation. More information about the program, including the application it requires, may be found at www.law.washington.edu/GatesScholar.

Student Life

The *Washington Law Review*, *Pacific Rim Law and Policy Journal*, *Washington Journal of Environmental Law and Policy*, and the *Washington Journal of Law, Technology & Arts* are edited and published by students. In addition to these four academic journals, there are over 50 active student organizations, societies, forums, clubs, and community service projects.

The law school is located in Seattle, Washington, a haven for both city dwellers and outdoor enthusiasts. Renowned for its coffee shops, farmers' markets, mountain and water views, and vibrant arts scene, the city provides countless opportunities for both personal and professional growth. Some of the most prominent businesses in the area include Boeing, Microsoft, Nordstrom, Starbucks, Nintendo, Expedia, Costco, Amazon, and REI. Seattle is also an innovative center for medical, biomedical, and biotechnology research and is a living laboratory for natural resource and environmental protection efforts.

Career Services

The Center for Professional and Leadership Development (CPLD) provides professional development coaching, recruiting opportunities, electronic job-search tools, and special events to students to help them advance their careers. Relationships matter in the practice of the law, and many of the events and activities are planned to create and promote new relationships among attorneys, alumni, and UW School of Law students.

Campus Visits

The law school invites prospective students to visit a large-section, first-year class. The schedule can be found at www.law.washington.edu/admissions/Visit.

William H. Gates Hall

The law school moved into its $80-million facility in September 2003. The building is named for William H. Gates Sr., a 1950 graduate of the UW School of Law and father of the Microsoft cofounder. Gates Hall provides wired and wireless network connections, high-speed network printing, access to media resources for group projects, trial advocacy and class presentations, and smart-podium technology that supports audio and video podcasting. Multifunctional classrooms create a stimulating learning environment. The Marian Gould Gallagher Law Library, which houses the largest public legal collection in the Pacific Northwest, is an invaluable resource for students and practitioners alike.

APPLICANT PROFILE

University of Washington School of Law
This grid includes only applicants who earned 120–180 LSAT scores under standard administrations.

LSAT Score	GPA 3.75 +		3.50–3.74		3.25–3.49		3.00–3.24		2.75–2.99		2.50–2.74		2.25–2.49		2.00–2.24		Below 2.00		No GPA		Total	
	Apps	Adm	Apps	Adm	Apps	Adm	Apps	Adm	Apps	Adm	Apps	Adm	Apps	Adm	Apps	Adm	Apps	Adm	Apps	Adm	Apps	Adm
175–180	3	3	7	6	4	2	5	2	2	0	3	0	0	0	0	0	0	0	0	0	24	13
170–174	49	34	56	40	38	19	18	2	8	1	4	0	0	0	0	0	0	0	1	0	174	96
165–169	149	98	192	93	102	34	57	15	25	1	10	0	4	0	1	0	0	0	16	11	556	252
160–164	209	84	290	60	180	17	107	14	25	0	15	1	5	0	4	0	0	0	39	5	874	181
155–159	118	15	169	12	128	1	72	2	35	1	7	0	2	0	3	0	0	0	20	0	554	31
150–154	43	4	58	4	67	1	59	0	25	0	19	0	5	0	1	0	0	0	8	0	285	9
145–149	8	0	22	0	21	0	24	0	8	0	6	0	4	0	2	0	0	0	8	0	103	0
140–144	0	0	7	0	10	0	14	0	9	0	7	0	5	0	0	0	1	0	1	0	54	0
135–139	0	0	1	0	2	0	6	0	3	0	1	0	2	0	1	0	0	0	0	0	16	0
130–134	0	0	0	0	1	0	0	0	1	0	2	0	0	0	1	0	1	0	2	0	8	0
125–129	0	0	0	0	0	0	1	0	0	0	0	0	0	0	0	0	0	0	0	0	1	0
120–124	0	0	0	0	0	0	0	0	0	0	0	0	0	0	0	0	0	0	0	0	0	0
Total	579	238	802	215	553	74	362	35	142	3	74	1	27	0	13	0	2	0	95	16	2649	582

Apps = Number of Applicants
Adm = Number Admitted
Reflects 100% of the total applicant pool; highest LSAT data reported.

WASHINGTON AND LEE UNIVERSITY SCHOOL OF LAW

Office of Admissions, Sydney Lewis Hall
Lexington, VA 24450
Phone: 540.458.8503; Fax: 540.458.8586
E-mail: LawAdm@wlu.edu; Website: www.law.wlu.edu

*ABA
Approved
Since
1923*

The Basics

Type of school	Private
Term	Semester
Application deadline	3/1
Application fee	$0
Financial aid deadline	2/15
Can first year start other than fall?	No
Student to faculty ratio	9.5 to 1
# of housing spaces available	
restricted to law students	56
graduate housing for which law students are eligible	56

Faculty and Administrators

	Total		Men		Women		Minorities	
	Spr	Fall	Spr	Fall	Spr	Fall	Spr	Fall
Full-time	35	35	27	23	8	12	3	2
Other full-time	0	0	0	0	0	0	0	0
Deans, librarians, & others who teach	5	5	3	3	2	2	0	0
Part-time	25	25	22	21	3	4	1	1
Total	65	65	52	47	13	18	4	3

Curriculum

		Full-Time	Part-Time
Typical first-year section size		65	0
Is there typically a "small section" of the first-year class, other than Legal Writing, taught by full-time faculty		Yes	No
If yes, typical size offered last year		24	
# of classroom course titles beyond first-year curriculum		83	
# of upper division courses, excluding seminars, with an enrollment:	Under 25	79	
	25–49	8	
	50–74	10	
	75–99	5	
	100+	0	
# of seminars		17	
# of seminar positions available		210	
# of seminar positions filled		144	0
# of positions available in simulation courses		402	
# of simulation positions filled		336	0
# of positions available in faculty supervised clinical courses		45	
# of faculty supervised clinical positions filled		45	0
# involved in field placements		98	0
# involved in law journals		115	0
# involved in moot court or trial competitions		131	0
# of credit hours required to graduate		85	

JD Enrollment and Ethnicity

	Men		Women		Full-Time		Part-Time		1st-Year		Total		JD Degs. Awd.
	#	%	#	%	#	%	#	%	#	%	#	%	
All Hispanics	2	0.9	8	4.4	10	2.5	0	0.0	3	2.5	10	2.5	5
Am. Ind./AK Nat.	0	0.0	0	0.0	0	0.0	0	0.0	0	0.0	0	0.0	1
Asian	4	1.9	8	4.4	12	3.0	0	0.0	4	3.3	12	3.0	6
Black/Af. Am.	12	5.6	15	8.3	27	6.8	0	0.0	7	5.8	27	6.8	7
Nat. HI/Pac. Isl.	0	0.0	0	0.0	0	0.0	0	0.0	0	0.0	0	0.0	2
2 or more races	3	1.4	3	1.7	6	1.5	0	0.0	3	2.5	6	1.5	4
Subtotal (minor.)	21	9.8	34	18.8	55	13.9	0	0.0	17	14.2	55	13.9	25
Nonres. Alien	2	0.9	2	1.1	4	1.0	0	0.0	0	0.0	4	1.0	3
White/Cauc.	178	83.2	142	78.5	320	81.0	0	0.0	100	83.3	320	81.0	95
Unknown	13	6.1	3	1.7	16	4.1	0	0.0	3	2.5	16	4.1	7
Total	214	54.2	181	45.8	395	100.0	0	0.0	120	30.4	395		130

Transfers

Transfers in	22
Transfers out	15

Tuition and Fees

	Resident	Nonresident
Full-time	$41,947	
Part-time		
Tuition Guarantee Program		N

Living Expenses

Estimated living expenses for singles

Living on campus	Living off campus	Living at home
$20,138	$20,138	$3,525

WASHINGTON AND LEE UNIVERSITY SCHOOL OF LAW

ABA Approved Since 1923

GPA and LSAT Scores

	Total	Full-Time	Part-Time
# of apps	3,972	3,972	0
# of offers	964	964	0
# of matrics	121	121	0
75% GPA	3.80	3.80	0.00
Median GPA	3.65	3.65	0.00
25% GPA	3.50	3.50	0.00
75% LSAT	165	165	0
Median LSAT	164	164	0
25% LSAT	159	159	0

Grants and Scholarships (from prior year)

	Total #	Total %	Full-Time #	Full-Time %	Part-Time #	Part-Time %
Total # of students	407		407		0	
Total # receiving grants	261	64.1	261	64.1	0	0.0
Less than 1/2 tuition	153	37.6	153	37.6	0	0.0
Half to full tuition	87	21.4	87	21.4	0	0.0
Full tuition	20	4.9	20	4.9	0	0.0
More than full tuition	1	0.2	1	0.2	0	0.0
Median grant amount		$15,800			$0	

Informational and Library Resources

Total amount spent on library materials	$693,104
Study seating capacity inside the library	530
# of full-time equivalent professional librarians	5
Hours per week library is open	168
# of open, wired connections available to students	340
# of networked computers available for use by students	96
Has wireless network?	Y
Requires computer?	N

JD Attrition (from prior year)

	Academic #	Other #	Total #	Total %
1st year	0	3	3	2.1
2nd year	0	19	19	14.2
3rd year	0	1	1	0.8
4th year	0	0	0	0.0

Employment (9 months after graduation)

For up-to-date employment data, go to employmentsummary.abaquestionnaire.org on the ABA website.

Bar Passage Rates

First-time takers	118	Reporting %	72.88
Average school %	80.24	Average state %	79.93
Average pass difference	0.31		

Jurisdiction	Takers	Passers	Pass %	State %	Diff %
Virginia	43	31	72.09	78.15	–6.06
New York	24	24	100.00	84.92	15.08
California	7	6	85.71	71.24	14.47
Texas	6	5	83.33	82.68	0.65
Maryland	6	3	50.00	79.96	–29.96

WASHINGTON AND LEE UNIVERSITY SCHOOL OF LAW

Office of Admissions, Sydney Lewis Hall
Lexington, VA 24450
Phone: 540.458.8503; Fax: 540.458.8586
E-mail: LawAdm@wlu.edu; Website: www.law.wlu.edu

Introduction

Washington and Lee University School of Law, founded in 1849, is located in Lexington, Virginia, a three-hour interstate highway drive from Washington, DC. The School of Law is fully accredited by the ABA and is a member of the AALS. Washington and Lee is known for providing its students with an academically rigorous and professionally challenging legal education in an environment characterized by a commitment to students, small classes, a very low student-to-faculty ratio, and a collegial community. The law school is among the nation's smallest law schools with approximately 400 total students. Members of the 2011–12 student body hail from 37 states, 5 foreign countries, and 203 different undergraduate institutions.

W&L Law offers an innovative curriculum in which students are engaged in distinct yet complimentary ways over the course of their three years in law school. Students encounter a linear sequence of learning experiences rooted in the basic assumption that each year of law school should build upon the lessons of its predecessor but also present new and different challenges. The third year is entirely experiential with students learning the law through a considered blend of real and simulated client-based practice experiences.

The Honor System

The W&L community is governed by an Honor System that is the foundation for academic and student life at the university. The Honor System is an integral part of a professional education that fosters a sensitivity to the ethical imperatives of the legal profession. The Honor System means that the library is always open; students feel comfortable leaving bags, computers, books, and any number of other valuables unattended; exams are unproctored; the exam schedule for upper-level students is flexible; and professors are free to give take-home examinations.

Curriculum

All first-year classes are required. During their first year of law school, students encounter a broad and diverse selection of foundational subjects, setting a solid base for their course of upper-level study. In their second year, students augment several required classes with elective courses. The third year blends classic academic and professional values with a view toward deliberately preparing students for the transition to law practice, and integrates cognitive learning, practical skills, and development of professional identity.

Each semester of the third year begins with intensive preparatory instruction. This two-week course is followed by elective offerings in the full range of traditional subject matter, as well as clinical or extern experiences. In realistic settings that simulate actual client experiences, students exercise professional judgment, work in teams, solve problems, counsel clients, negotiate solutions, and serve as advocates and counselors—the full complement of professional skills required to apply legal theory and legal doctrines to real-world issues and serve clients ethically and honorably within the highest traditions of the profession. In addition, a semester-long course on the legal profession is

also required. Students can expect rigorous intellectual content, intense evaluation, thoughtful guidance, and meaningful feedback. For additional details about the third-year curriculum, visit www.law.wlu.edu/thirdyear.

Offerings in corporate and business law, international law, health law, and civil and criminal litigation are particularly strong. A wide variety of clinical programs and externships provide opportunities for hands-on experience as part of the academic program. Clinics include the Virginia Capital Case Clearinghouse, established to assist attorneys representing clients charged with or convicted of capital crimes; the Black Lung Legal Clinic, in which students represent coal miners seeking disability benefits under federal law; the Community Legal Practice Center, which provides a range of legal services to qualified area residents; the Tax Clinic, in which students represent low-income taxpayers in controversies with the Internal Revenue Service; the Public Prosecutors Program, in which students assist federal and state prosecutors with investigations, trial preparation, pretrial and trial practice, and appeals; the Criminal Justice Clinic, in which students defend area residents accused of misdemeanors; the Citizenship and Immigration program, through which students focus on resolving legal disputes related to immigration and naturalization; the Judicial Externship Program, through which students act as law clerks to trial, appellate, juvenile and domestic relations, and federal bankruptcy judges; the General Externship Program, through which students may pursue individual placements; and various Transnational offerings in which students work on live legal issues in Liberia, Cambodia, the European Court of Human Rights, and the International Criminal Tribunal for Former Yugoslavia.

Special Programs

JD/MHA. With Virginia Commonwealth University (VCU) in Richmond, W&L Law offers a program through which students can receive a JD and a Master in Health Administration on an accelerated basis. Dual-degree candidates must be accepted for the program by both VCU and W&L; a portion of the degree requirements are taken on the campus of each university.

LLM in United States Law. W&L Law offers a one-year program in United States law to attorneys who hold a foreign law degree.

Student Activities

Students have four journal opportunities: the *Washington and Lee Law Review*, a quarterly journal for scholarly discussion of legal issues; the *Journal of Civil Rights and Social Justice*, focusing on legal issues having an impact on racial and ethnic minorities; the *Journal of Energy, Climate, and the Environment*, devoted to environmental and natural resources issues and state and federal environmental legislation and regulation; and the *German Law Journal*, an online journal that publishes commentary and scholarship in the fields of German, European, and international law. For more information about extracurricular writing opportunities at W&L Law, please see www.law.wlu.edu/journals. A variety of moot court and advocacy competitions allow upper-level students to hone advocacy, counseling, negotiation, and trial skills. All second- and third-year students may participate in the moot court competitions.

W&L Law students have established over 50 student groups, including the Black Law Students Association, Asian Pacific American Law Students Association, Women Law Students Organization, OUTLaw, Jewish Law Students Association, Christian Legal Society, Law Families, Federalist Society, American Constitution Society, National Lawyers Guild, and chapters of three national professional fraternities. For a complete listing of organizations, please see law.wlu.edu/directory/studentorgs.asp.

Admission and Financial Aid

W&L Law actively seeks a diverse student body whose members are of different racial, ethnic, economic, and geographic backgrounds. The admission process is highly individualized. Students are not ranked by any numerical index, nor is there an assigned weight given to any objective or subjective factor presented in the application.

The Admissions Committee considers not only the cumulative undergraduate grade-point average, but also trends in grades, the rigor of an applicant's academic program, the quality of the school attended, the LSAT score, extracurricular activities, community service, evidence of leadership, graduate study, work experience, assessments of recommenders, and any information presented in the applicant's personal statement. Admission officers will interview applicants upon request. Applicants are encouraged to visit the school to sit in on classes, tour the facility, and talk with students and faculty. A generous scholarship endowment allows W&L Law to assist a large percentage of its students with merit-based scholarship awards.

Career Planning and Professional Development

W&L Law graduates practice in every state and throughout the world. More than 70 percent of recent graduates practice outside Virginia. The three counseling professionals in the Office of Career Planning and Professional Development (OCP) hold JD degrees and work with each student individually to develop a unique career plan. OCP provides instruction in résumé and cover letter writing, networking, and other career development skills. It also provides programming on a wide variety of practice specialties and settings, and acts as a liaison between students and legal employers. Law students interview with prospective employers on campus, at a satellite location in Charlottesville, and at programs throughout the United States. An active and committed alumni network assists students with contacts in every state and a variety of practice areas.

Law Library and Physical Facilities

Sydney Lewis Hall, home of the School of Law, was built in 1976 and expanded in 1991 with the addition of the Lewis F. Powell Jr. Archives, which house the Supreme Court and professional papers of retired Supreme Court Justice Powell, a graduate of the university's college and law school. Wireless Internet access is available throughout the building. Every classroom has been renovated within the past 10 years and is equipped with state-of-the-art technology; the moot courtroom was completely renovated in 2006. The building, including the law library, is open 24 hours a day, 365 days a year.

APPLICANT PROFILE

Washington and Lee University School of Law
This grid includes only applicants who earned 120–180 LSAT scores under standard administrations.

LSAT Score	3.75 +		3.50–3.74		3.25–3.49		3.00–3.24		2.75–2.99		2.50–2.74		2.25–2.49		2.00–2.24		Below 2.00		No GPA		Total	
	Apps	Adm	Apps	Adm	Apps	Adm	Apps	Adm	Apps	Adm	Apps	Adm	Apps	Adm	Apps	Adm	Apps	Adm	Apps	Adm	Apps	Adm
175–180	3	3	1	1	4	3	3	1	3	0	3	0	0	0	1	0	0	0	0	0	18	8
170–174	42	41	33	27	21	17	22	13	12	4	5	0	4	1	0	0	0	0	3	1	142	104
165–169	151	142	225	200	167	95	90	37	38	3	14	2	9	3	0	0	2	0	14	3	710	485
160–164	265	157	349	72	282	11	176	10	42	0	23	2	8	0	3	0	0	0	36	0	1184	252
155–159	145	41	257	16	246	9	143	7	48	1	19	0	6	0	2	0	0	0	14	0	880	74
150–154	78	14	137	15	146	10	124	2	42	3	21	0	13	0	5	0	2	0	11	0	579	44
145–149	19	0	35	0	53	0	57	0	36	0	20	0	5	0	2	0	1	0	6	0	234	0
140–144	5	0	20	0	28	0	26	0	22	0	17	0	10	0	6	0	2	0	3	0	139	0
135–139	2	0	7	0	8	0	9	0	13	0	7	0	5	0	1	0	1	0	1	0	54	0
130–134	1	0	1	0	1	0	3	0	2	0	4	0	1	0	3	0	1	0	1	0	18	0
125–129	0	0	0	0	0	0	1	0	0	0	1	0	0	0	0	0	0	0	0	0	2	0
120–124	0	0	0	0	0	0	0	0	0	0	0	0	0	0	0	0	0	0	0	0	0	0
Total	711	398	1065	331	956	145	654	70	258	11	134	4	61	4	23	0	9	0	89	4	3960	967

Apps = Number of Applicants
Adm = Number Admitted
Reflects 100% of the total applicant pool; highest LSAT data reported.

WASHINGTON UNIVERSITY SCHOOL OF LAW

Campus Box 1120, One Brookings Drive
St. Louis, MO 63130-4899
Phone: 314.935.4525; Fax: 314.935.8778
E-mail: admiss@wulaw.wustl.edu; Website: http://law.wustl.edu

ABA
Approved
Since
1923

The Basics

Type of school	Private
Term	Semester
Application deadline	3/1
Application fee	$70
Financial aid deadline	3/1
Can first year start other than fall?	No
Student to faculty ratio	11.0 to 1
# of housing spaces available restricted to law students	
graduate housing for which law students are eligible	970

Faculty and Administrators

	Total		Men		Women		Minorities	
	Spr	Fall	Spr	Fall	Spr	Fall	Spr	Fall
Full-time	63	67	30	33	33	34	6	10
Other full-time	0	0	0	0	0	0	0	0
Deans, librarians, & others who teach	14	14	7	7	7	7	1	1
Part-time	84	77	68	56	16	21	7	8
Total	161	158	105	96	56	62	14	19

Curriculum

		Full-Time	Part-Time
Typical first-year section size		99	0
Is there typically a "small section" of the first-year class, other than Legal Writing, taught by full-time faculty		Yes	No
If yes, typical size offered last year		51	
# of classroom course titles beyond first-year curriculum		162	
# of upper division courses, excluding seminars, with an enrollment:	Under 25	118	
	25–49	45	
	50–74	25	
	75–99	9	
	100+	1	
# of seminars		30	
# of seminar positions available		503	
# of seminar positions filled		435	0
# of positions available in simulation courses		1,346	
# of simulation positions filled		1,237	0
# of positions available in faculty supervised clinical courses		119	
# of faculty supervised clinical positions filled		118	0
# involved in field placements		175	0
# involved in law journals		341	0
# involved in moot court or trial competitions		61	0
# of credit hours required to graduate		86	

JD Enrollment and Ethnicity

	Men		Women		Full-Time		Part-Time		1st-Year		Total		JD Degs. Awd.
	#	%	#	%	#	%	#	%	#	%	#	%	
All Hispanics	6	1.2	13	3.8	19	2.2	0	0.0	6	2.5	19	2.2	4
Am. Ind./AK Nat.	2	0.4	1	0.3	3	0.4	0	0.0	1	0.4	3	0.4	4
Asian	43	8.5	37	10.8	77	9.1	3	75.0	20	8.2	80	9.4	36
Black/Af. Am.	48	9.5	44	12.8	92	10.9	0	0.0	16	6.6	92	10.8	35
Nat. Hl/Pac. Isl.	0	0.0	0	0.0	0	0.0	0	0.0	0	0.0	0	0.0	0
2 or more races	20	3.9	9	2.6	29	3.4	0	0.0	11	4.5	29	3.4	3
Subtotal (minor.)	119	23.5	104	30.2	220	26.0	3	75.0	54	22.2	223	26.2	82
Nonres. Alien	32	6.3	42	12.2	73	8.6	1	25.0	11	4.5	74	8.7	27
White/Cauc.	303	59.8	176	51.2	479	56.6	0	0.0	169	69.5	479	56.3	163
Unknown	53	10.5	22	6.4	75	8.9	0	0.0	9	3.7	75	8.8	51
Total	507	59.6	344	40.4	847	99.5	4	0.5	243	28.6	851		323

Transfers

Transfers in	42
Transfers out	16

Tuition and Fees

	Resident	Nonresident
Full-time	$46,042	$46,042
Part-time		
Tuition Guarantee Program		N

Living Expenses

Estimated living expenses for singles

Living on campus	Living off campus	Living at home
N/A	$21,925	N/A

WASHINGTON UNIVERSITY SCHOOL OF LAW

ABA Approved Since 1923

GPA and LSAT Scores

	Total	Full-Time	Part-Time
# of apps	3,847	3,847	0
# of offers	979	979	0
# of matrics	243	243	0
75% GPA	3.80	3.80	0.00
Median GPA	3.66	3.66	0.00
25% GPA	3.22	3.22	0.00
75% LSAT	169	169	0
Median LSAT	168	168	0
25% LSAT	162	162	0

Grants and Scholarships (from prior year)

	Total #	Total %	Full-Time #	Full-Time %	Part-Time #	Part-Time %
Total # of students	900		893		7	
Total # receiving grants	620	68.9	620	69.4	0	0.0
Less than 1/2 tuition	328	36.4	328	36.7	0	0.0
Half to full tuition	275	30.6	275	30.8	0	0.0
Full tuition	7	0.8	7	0.8	0	0.0
More than full tuition	10	1.1	10	1.1	0	0.0
Median grant amount			$20,000		$0	

Informational and Library Resources

Total amount spent on library materials	$1,156,046
Study seating capacity inside the library	486
# of full-time equivalent professional librarians	8
Hours per week library is open	120
# of open, wired connections available to students	814
# of networked computers available for use by students	69
Has wireless network?	Y
Requires computer?	N

JD Attrition (from prior year)

	Academic #	Other #	Total #	Total %
1st year	0	23	23	8.3
2nd year	0	3	3	1.0
3rd year	0	1	1	0.3
4th year	0	0	0	0.0

Employment (9 months after graduation)

For up-to-date employment data, go to employmentsummary.abaquestionnaire.org on the ABA website.

Bar Passage Rates

First-time takers	264	Reporting %	81.82
Average school %	89.35	Average state %	85.72
Average pass difference	3.63		

Jurisdiction	Takers	Passers	Pass %	State %	Diff %
Missouri	72	68	94.44	90.24	4.20
New York	49	40	81.63	84.92	-3.29
Illinois	33	32	96.97	89.38	7.59
California	24	16	66.67	71.24	-4.57
Others (4)	38	37	97.37		

WASHINGTON UNIVERSITY SCHOOL OF LAW

Campus Box 1120, One Brookings Drive
St. Louis, MO 63130-4899
Phone: 314.935.4525; Fax: 314.935.8778
E-mail: admiss@wulaw.wustl.edu; Website: http://law.wustl.edu

Introduction

Washington University School of Law offers its students an outstanding legal education in an intellectually challenging and collegial environment. Our faculty members are recognized for their excellent teaching and scholarship, and they are highly accessible to our students. The School of Law curriculum blends traditional theory with opportunities to participate in a wide variety of lawyering skills courses and cocurricular activities that encourage the development of practical skills and interdisciplinary learning.

Curriculum

Washington University School of Law offers a broad-based curriculum that highlights applied lawyering skills. A three-year, full-time course of study leads to the JD degree. All first-year students have half their courses in small sections of 45 students or less. These small classes increase the opportunities for participation in class discussions and individualized teacher-student contact. Second- and third-year students choose their own classes and can tailor them to fit their own particular interests. Students may also opt to enroll in courses from other graduate programs at the university and apply up to six credit hours toward the JD requirements. In addition, our Center for Interdisciplinary Studies, the Whitney R. Harris World Law Institute, and other school-sponsored conferences and symposia expose our students to a wide range of nationally and internationally renowned legal scholars.

Library and Physical Facilities

The law school is situated in state-of-the-art facilities, Anheuser-Busch and Seigle Halls. Both buildings provide well-functioning, vibrant spaces that enhance the law school's sense of community and collaboration. Although the buildings appear traditional, the latest computing and multimedia technologies are incorporated in their design. Cutting-edge information technology provides students with quick access to the Internet where they can register for courses, view grades, order transcripts, access their e-mail, and enhance their legal research capabilities. Wireless connections and digital signage are available throughout. The law library is the focal point for much of the intellectual activity at the law school. It has a collection of over 675,000 volumes and provides access to a rich collection of online databases. The library has particularly strong collections in the areas of international law, environmental law, land use planning, urban law, tax law, Chinese law, and Japanese law.

Clinical Opportunities

The School of Law's exceptional Clinical Education Program provides law students with opportunities to learn professional skills and values by working with clients, attorneys, judges, and legislators under the close supervision of experienced and expert faculty. While offering a diverse array of experiences for students, the program also benefits the larger community—locally, nationally, and internationally. The program includes the Appellate, Civil Justice, Civil Rights and Community Justice, Criminal Justice, Intellectual Property and Nonprofit Organizations, and Interdisciplinary Environmental Clinics. Lawyering and field placement courses include such placements as federal public defenders' offices; United States Attorneys' offices; local, national, and international courts; and legal services organizations. The Congressional and Administrative Law Externship offers students the opportunity to spend a semester working in Washington, DC, for a member of the United States Congress, a congressional committee, or a federal administrative agency. The New York City Regulatory and Business Externship provides the opportunity to work under the direction of attorneys in a variety of nonprofit, government, and in-house counsel offices having an emphasis on business associations and regulation. Washington University has also established an academic partnership with the Brookings Institution in Washington, DC. This affiliation provides research collaborations, internships for students, faculty exchanges, and other mutually beneficial projects in which students may be involved.

Special-Degree Programs

Washington University complements its outstanding JD program with many different joint-degree opportunities. In addition to our formal joint-degree programs, students may design their own joint degrees, combining law and another course of study that leads to a master's degree. Joint degrees offered include a JD/MBA, JD/MSW, and JD/MA in East Asian Studies. The School of Law offers LLM programs in Intellectual Property and Technology Law, Taxation, and US Law for International Students. A combined JD/LLM in Taxation may be completed in six or seven semesters. The law school also offers a unique Trans-Atlantic Law Program in conjunction with several European partner schools, including Utrecht University School of Law in the Netherlands. As part of this program, Washington University students will spend five semesters at the Washington University School of Law, then three semesters at a law school in Europe. At the conclusion, each student will receive a JD from Washington University and an LLM from one of the partner schools.

Study-Abroad Opportunities

The School of Law offers our students the opportunity to study abroad for a semester and provides international law students with the chance to study at our law school. Our students take regular courses at leading international institutions, studying under the legal scholars of the country. Washington University has exchange or study-abroad agreements in place with each of the following law schools: Utrecht University in the Netherlands, University of Pretoria in South Africa, Universidade Catolica Portuguesa in Portugal, Fudan University in China, National University of Singapore, University of KwaZulu-Natal in South Africa, Korea University, National Taiwan University, Queen's University Belfast in Northern Ireland, University of Trento in Italy, and Hong Kong University. The law school also offers the Summer Institute for Global Justice, a six-week, intensive course in Utrecht, the Netherlands, focusing on international and comparative law and the Trans-Atlantic Law Program with Utrecht University.

Student Activities

The School of Law publishes four student-edited law review periodicals: *Washington University Law Review*, *Washington University Journal of Law and Policy*, *Washington University Global Studies Law Review*, and *Washington University Jurisprudence Review*. The Trial and Advocacy Program includes a very active moot court program, mock trial competitions, and competitions in negotiation and client counseling. Students are actively involved in over 40 student organizations, including the Women's Law Caucus, Student Bar Association, Black Law Students Association, Latin American Law Students Association, Asian Pacific American Law Students Association, and OUTLAW (gay and lesbian alliance). Students also participate in a number of volunteer public service projects through student organizations or the school's Public Service Project program.

Public Interest

The School of Law has a long-standing commitment to public service and lawyering in the public interest. In addition to the extensive clinical education program, public interest law is supported in a number of different ways: the Webster Society Scholarship provides full tuition for three years and an annual stipend to entering JD students with exemplary academic credentials and an established commitment to public service; summer stipends provide funding for students who work in summer internships in public interest law; the Mel Brown Family Loan Repayment Assistance Program (LRAP) assists graduates beginning their careers in public service positions; the assistant dean of student services coordinates the law school's many public service projects; the director of career services and public interest assists students interested in pursuing careers in the public sector; and the popular Public Interest Law and Policy Speakers Series is offered.

Career Services

Our Career Services Office (CSO) is committed to matching students with outstanding employment opportunities from around the country. The priority is to connect students to the jobs they desire and employers with the students they seek. In addition to hosting extensive fall on-campus and off-campus recruiting programs, the CSO offers a wide range of services throughout the year, including workshops, a mock interview program, and other programming activities. The CSO offers programs on networking and skill development, clerkships, fellowships, researching employers, and a variety of informational sessions on different practice areas. Our graduates move on to many different locations to practice: the class of 2010 relocated to more than 30 different states, the District of Columbia, and several foreign countries. Summer employment is equally diverse. Typically 30 or more states are represented, as well as summer internships in Africa and Asia.

Housing

Students find that the cost of living in St. Louis is much less than in other large metropolitan areas. There is a wide range of affordable housing available near the School of Law. The admission office hosts two "housing days" each summer to assist students in locating housing.

Scholarship and Financial Aid

The school offers merit- and merit/need-based scholarships. Most student aid is in the form of government and privately sponsored loans. Over half the students receive some scholarship assistance; two-thirds receive loans. (Virtually all of those receiving scholarships also receive loans.) The school also offers loan repayment assistance for students who choose qualifying public interest law jobs upon graduation.

APPLICANT PROFILE

Washington University School of Law
This grid includes only applicants who earned 120–180 LSAT scores under standard administrations.

LSAT Score	GPA								
	3.75 +	3.50–3.74	3.25–3.49	3.00–3.24	2.75–2.99	2.50–2.74	2.25–2.49	2.00–2.24	Below 2.00
175–180									
170–174									
165–169									
160–164									
155–159									
150–154									
145–149									
140–144									
135–139									
130–134									
125–129									
120–124									

■ Good Possibility   □ Possible   ▨ Unlikely

WAYNE STATE UNIVERSITY LAW SCHOOL

Admissions Office, 471 West Palmer
Detroit, MI 48202
Phone: 313.577.3937; Fax: 313.993.8129
E-mail: lawinquire@wayne.edu; Website: www.law.wayne.edu

ABA
Approved
Since
1937

The Basics

Type of school	Public
Term	Semester
Application deadline	3/15
Application fee	$50
Financial aid deadline	3/1
Can first year start other than fall?	No
Student to faculty ratio	13.3 to 1
# of housing spaces available restricted to law students	
graduate housing for which law students are eligible	660

Faculty and Administrators

	Total		Men		Women		Minorities	
	Spr	Fall	Spr	Fall	Spr	Fall	Spr	Fall
Full-time	34	34	22	23	12	11	3	3
Other full-time	5	4	0	0	5	4	1	1
Deans, librarians, & others who teach	4	4	3	3	1	1	1	0
Part-time	27	24	21	18	6	6	1	2
Total	70	66	46	44	24	22	6	6

Curriculum

		Full-Time	Part-Time
Typical first-year section size		78	34
Is there typically a "small section" of the first-year class, other than Legal Writing, taught by full-time faculty		Yes	No
If yes, typical size offered last year		26	
# of classroom course titles beyond first-year curriculum		80	
# of upper division courses, excluding seminars, with an enrollment:	Under 25	61	
	25–49	22	
	50–74	9	
	75–99	2	
	100+	2	
# of seminars		17	
# of seminar positions available		316	
# of seminar positions filled		214	25
# of positions available in simulation courses		357	
# of simulation positions filled		234	43
# of positions available in faculty supervised clinical courses		120	
# of faculty supervised clinical positions filled		77	5
# involved in field placements		106	13
# involved in law journals		93	6
# involved in moot court or trial competitions		106	7
# of credit hours required to graduate		86	

Transfers

Transfers in	5
Transfers out	11

Tuition and Fees

	Resident	Nonresident
Full-time	$26,118	$28,548
Part-time	$14,116	$15,412
Tuition Guarantee Program	N	

Living Expenses

Estimated living expenses for singles

Living on campus	Living off campus	Living at home
$22,570	$22,570	$12,445

JD Enrollment and Ethnicity

	Men		Women		Full-Time		Part-Time		1st-Year		Total		JD Degs. Awd.
	#	%	#	%	#	%	#	%	#	%	#	%	
All Hispanics	9	2.7	8	3.3	14	3.0	3	2.8	5	2.8	17	3.0	4
Am. Ind./AK Nat.	2	0.6	1	0.4	3	0.6	0	0.0	0	0.0	3	0.5	2
Asian	19	5.8	19	7.9	33	7.1	5	4.6	11	6.1	38	6.7	8
Black/Af. Am.	16	4.8	18	7.5	12	2.6	22	20.4	10	5.5	34	6.0	17
Nat. HI/Pac. Isl.	0	0.0	0	0.0	0	0.0	0	0.0	0	0.0	0	0.0	0
2 or more races	0	0.0	0	0.0	0	0.0	0	0.0	0	0.0	0	0.0	0
Subtotal (minor.)	46	13.9	46	19.2	62	13.4	30	27.8	26	14.4	92	16.1	31
Nonres. Alien	7	2.1	7	2.9	14	3.0	0	0.0	3	1.7	14	2.5	7
White/Cauc.	250	75.8	174	72.5	355	76.8	69	63.9	149	82.3	424	74.4	138
Unknown	27	8.2	13	5.4	31	6.7	9	8.3	0	0.0	40	7.0	27
Total	330	57.9	240	42.1	462	81.1	108	18.9	181	31.8	570		203

WAYNE STATE UNIVERSITY LAW SCHOOL

ABA
Approved
Since
1937

GPA and LSAT Scores

	Total	Full-Time	Part-Time
# of apps	1,087	991	96
# of offers	511	481	30
# of matrics	181	164	17
75% GPA	3.65	3.65	3.64
Median GPA	3.39	3.40	3.36
25% GPA	3.11	3.12	3.10
75% LSAT	159	160	159
Median LSAT	157	157	154
25% LSAT	155	155	152

Grants and Scholarships (from prior year)

	Total #	Total %	Full-Time #	Full-Time %	Part-Time #	Part-Time %
Total # of students	612		482		130	
Total # receiving grants	260	42.5	233	48.3	27	20.8
Less than 1/2 tuition	111	18.1	107	22.2	4	3.1
Half to full tuition	60	9.8	52	10.8	8	6.2
Full tuition	38	6.2	28	5.8	10	7.7
More than full tuition	51	8.3	46	9.5	5	3.8
Median grant amount			$12,436		$10,000	

Informational and Library Resources

Total amount spent on library materials	$1,621,824
Study seating capacity inside the library	382
# of full-time equivalent professional librarians	6
Hours per week library is open	97
# of open, wired connections available to students	216
# of networked computers available for use by students	24
Has wireless network?	Y
Requires computer?	N

JD Attrition (from prior year)

	Academic #	Other #	Total #	Total %
1st year	0	15	15	7.8
2nd year	1	6	7	4.0
3rd year	0	2	2	1.0
4th year	0	1	1	2.6

Employment (9 months after graduation)

For up-to-date employment data, go to
employmentsummary.abaquestionnaire.org on the ABA website.

Bar Passage Rates

First-time takers	136	Reporting %	92.65
Average school %	90.48	Average state %	84.83
Average pass difference	5.65		

Jurisdiction	Takers	Passers	Pass %	State %	Diff %
Michigan	126	114	90.48	84.83	5.65

WAYNE STATE UNIVERSITY LAW SCHOOL

Admissions Office, 471 West Palmer
Detroit, MI 48202
Phone: 313.577.3937; Fax: 313.993.8129
E-mail: lawinquire@wayne.edu; Website: www.law.wayne.edu

Introduction

Wayne State University Law School, founded in 1927, is the only public law school in Detroit, Michigan. Located in the heart of Detroit's historic cultural center, Wayne Law offers a unique urban experience. Detroit's vibrant legal market—including government offices, state and federal courts, multinational corporations, unions, and major law firms—provides students with a wide range of opportunities for employment and internships. Our students are bright, mature, conscientious, and altruistic. They come from unique backgrounds and professions, some having previously served as doctors, musicians, actors, engineers, and law enforcement officers before pursuing the law. Wayne Law also offers a network of more than 11,000 living alumni, including established leaders of the legal community, practicing throughout the nation and in more than a dozen foreign countries. Our expert faculty's nationally and internationally recognized scholarship adds depth to our students' understanding of legal theory, doctrine, and practice. Wayne Law students, faculty, and alumni are deeply engaged in the community and profession.

The Law School's Setting and Facilities

The Law School is a flagship unit of Wayne State University, a major metropolitan research university located in the heart of Midtown about four miles from downtown Detroit. Within blocks of the Law School are the Detroit Public Library, the Detroit Institute of Arts, the Charles H. Wright Museum of African American History, the Detroit Science Center, and other cultural attractions. The City of Detroit shares an international border with Windsor, Ontario, and offers access to Michigan's largest concentration of law firms and state and federal courts. In October 2011, Wayne Law proudly celebrated the grand opening of the Damon J. Keith Center for Civil Rights. The Damon J. Keith Center for Civil Rights will advance learning; attract talented faculty, students, and lecturers; enhance programming; and promote civil rights in one of the most culturally rich and diverse cities in the United States. The Keith Center will have active programs of legal studies and will promote community engagement.

The Arthur Neef Law Library

The Arthur Neef Law Library is the second largest academic law library in Michigan and houses one of the nation's largest legal collections. With over 620,000 volumes, it serves as a major center of legal research in the Detroit and Michigan legal communities and is a designated federal government depository.

The majority of the study space in the recently renovated law library makes use of natural light. The Law School, including the library, is served by a wireless network. In addition, many library study spaces are equipped with communication ports and electrical outlets for the convenient use of notebook computers.

The law library also houses a computer laboratory featuring personal computers available for the exclusive use of Wayne State law students.

Clinical and Internship Programs

Wayne State University Law School offers its students a broad range of opportunities for practical legal training through its client clinics and its internship programs. The Law School operates six clinics: a Criminal Appellate Practice Clinic, a Disability Law Clinic, a Transnational Environmental Law Clinic, a Free Legal Aid Clinic, an Immigration and Asylum Clinic, and a Small Business Enterprises and Nonprofit Corporations Clinic. These clinical offerings give students a chance to take first-chair responsibility in a choice of settings while serving the needs of Detroit's urban community. Students also have the chance to serve as interns for state and federal judges, public prosecutors, the State Appellate Defender's Office, and many nonprofit organizations.

Joint-Degree Programs

Students may pursue joint-degree programs in one of five different areas: business administration, dispute resolution, history, political science, and economics. Joint-degree students must be admitted separately to the Law School and to the appropriate master's degree program at the university. Each joint-degree program requires a student to spend his or her first year taking exclusively law courses, followed by two and a half to three years of concurrent studies.

Intellectual Property Law Institute

Intellectual property (IP) law and related fields, such as the emerging area of electronic commerce, are among the strengths of the Wayne State law faculty. The Law School offers a tremendous variety of courses and seminars on IP-related subjects. Wayne State law students may take courses at the University of Detroit Mercy and the University of Windsor, just across the river in Canada, through the Intellectual Property Law Institute (IPLI). IPLI, which was created in 1987 as a cooperative effort of these three law schools, offers a rich curriculum for IP-focused students, including courses and seminars in patent, copyright, trademark, computer and related technology, communications and media, and entertainment law.

Program for International Legal Studies

International law cuts across all aspects of a Wayne State legal education. Fully one-third of Wayne Law's tenured and tenure-track faculty teaches and writes on international subjects. Those faculty members enjoy worldwide reputations as innovative and prolific scholars. Students can take classes on a remarkable range of international topics, from international commercial transactions to international environmental law, to the use of military force, and the protection of human rights. Study-abroad programs give students a firsthand view of other nations' legal systems and their approaches to legal education. The Law School also boasts a broad array of internationally oriented student organizations, including a highly successful Jessup International Law Moot Court Competition team.

Student Activities

Student-Edited Law Journals—Wayne State University Law School publishes two student-edited law journals. The *Wayne Law Review*, a scholarly legal journal with a nationwide circulation, has been published since 1954 by upper-class law students selected on the basis of superior academic achievement and writing ability. The *Journal of Law in Society* publishes articles drawn from an annual spring symposium on topics such as affirmative action, environmental justice, reparations for slavery, school vouchers, and gentrification. Both journals offer an opportunity for students to enhance their research and writing skills, and further their knowledge of the law, while earning law school course credit.

Moot Court—Founded in 1949, Wayne State University's Moot Court program, which helps students hone their written and oral advocacy skills, has evolved into one of the most competitive appellate advocacy programs in the country. Wayne State Moot Court teams compete in many national moot court competitions and have won many competitions, including the National Moot Court Championship in 2003.

Student Trial Advocacy Program—The Student Trial Advocacy Program (STAP) complements Wayne State's extensive offering of skills courses by providing students with instruction and experience in the techniques of trial litigation. Wayne State STAP members have successfully competed in trial advocacy competitions across the country.

Student Organizations—More than 30 student organizations add greatly to the quality of life at the Law School by sponsoring speakers and debates on topics of current interest or in specialized areas of law, jointly sponsoring outreach events for the needy, volunteering their time to public service, and collaborating to produce programs with area practitioners.

Scholarships

Wayne State University Law School is committed to attracting and retaining highly credentialed students while maintaining economic accessibility to legal education and the legal profession. We offer substantial scholarships, and award over $2.8 million in WSU and privately endowed scholarships and grants to students. The Dean's Scholars program awards 50 percent, 75 percent, and 100 percent tuition scholarships to the top students of each incoming class. These awards are renewable yearly if students maintain a GPA above an established minimum. We also offer one-year awards to incoming students and provide scholarships for continuing students based on first-year performance. More than 70 additional scholarships are awarded each year at Honors Convocation based on academic merit, future career plans, or participation in law-related activities.

Housing

As a Wayne Law student, you can live on campus either in the University Towers Apartments, the Chatsworth Apartments, or in the Towers Residential Suites. The top floors of the high-rise tower are reserved for graduate students; the majority of the rooms are suite style and there are also studio rooms available. Within the building are a café-style dining hall, a mini bookstore, and multiple fitness rooms. The Towers feature free Internet access, cable connections, multiple social and study lounges, laundry rooms, and a 24-hour staffed reception area. Students interested in living off campus have many affordable options in the metropolitan Detroit area.

Career Services

Our Career Services Office provides Wayne Law students and alumni with tools, resources, and expertise needed to identify the ideal career path, launch a successful job search, and develop a fulfilling career in, around, or outside of the law. Three professional career counselors help students navigate job searches and offer guidance on balancing the demands of finding a job while in law school. Each of our counselors has a JD, has practiced law, and specializes in counseling students interested in working in government, law firms, courts, corporations, and public interest organizations, as well as those pursuing alternative careers.

APPLICANT PROFILE

Wayne State University Law School
This grid includes only applicants who earned 120–180 LSAT scores under standard administrations.

LSAT Score	GPA 3.75 + Apps	Adm	3.50–3.74 Apps	Adm	3.25–3.49 Apps	Adm	3.00–3.24 Apps	Adm	2.75–2.99 Apps	Adm	2.50–2.74 Apps	Adm	2.25–2.49 Apps	Adm	2.00–2.24 Apps	Adm	Below 2.00 Apps	Adm	No GPA Apps	Adm	Total Apps	Adm
175–180	0	0	0	0	0	0	0	0	0	0	0	0	0	0	0	0	0	0	0	0	0	0
170–174	4	4	1	1	3	3	1	1	0	0	0	0	0	0	0	0	0	0	0	0	9	9
165–169	10	10	21	20	11	11	6	6	3	3	1	1	4	2	0	0	0	0	0	0	56	53
160–164	24	24	20	18	24	24	14	14	9	9	9	7	0	0	2	2	0	0	1	1	103	99
155–159	30	28	57	54	63	59	49	46	23	18	17	11	2	2	2	1	0	0	2	2	245	221
150–154	25	20	52	38	54	23	57	9	33	4	20	0	12	0	10	0	1	0	4	1	268	95
145–149	12	3	32	6	46	5	45	2	30	2	17	2	16	0	9	0	0	0	2	0	209	20
140–144	5	3	18	4	18	1	20	0	16	0	16	1	10	0	4	0	4	0	6	1	117	10
135–139	1	0	5	0	6	0	9	0	17	0	16	0	3	0	1	0	1	0	6	0	65	0
130–134	0	0	1	0	5	0	2	0	4	0	8	0	6	0	3	0	0	0	1	0	30	0
125–129	0	0	0	0	0	0	1	0	2	0	3	0	1	0	3	0	0	0	0	0	10	0
120–124	0	0	0	0	0	0	0	0	0	0	0	0	1	0	2	0	0	0	1	0	4	0
Total	111	92	207	141	230	126	204	78	137	36	107	22	55	4	36	3	6	0	23	5	1116	507

Apps = Number of Applicants
Adm = Number Admitted
Reflects 99% of the total applicant pool; highest LSAT data reported.

WEST VIRGINIA UNIVERSITY COLLEGE OF LAW

101 Law Center Drive, PO Box 6130
Morgantown, WV 26506-6130
Phone: 304.293.5301; Fax: 304.293.8102
E-mail: wvulaw.admissions@mail.wvu.edu; Website: http://law.wvu.edu/

*ABA
Approved
Since
1923*

The Basics

Type of school	Public
Term	Semester
Application deadline	3/1
Application fee	$50
Financial aid deadline	3/1
Can first year start other than fall?	No
Student to faculty ratio	10.6 to 1
# of housing spaces available restricted to law students	
graduate housing for which law students are eligible	5

Faculty and Administrators

	Total		Men		Women		Minorities	
	Spr	Fall	Spr	Fall	Spr	Fall	Spr	Fall
Full-time	32	34	20	24	12	10	5	6
Other full-time	3	0	2	0	1	0	0	0
Deans, librarians, & others who teach	3	3	1	1	2	2	0	0
Part-time	24	25	13	15	11	10	0	0
Total	62	62	36	40	26	22	5	6

Curriculum

	Full-Time	Part-Time
Typical first-year section size	67	67
Is there typically a "small section" of the first-year class, other than Legal Writing, taught by full-time faculty	Yes	Yes
If yes, typical size offered last year	45	45
# of classroom course titles beyond first-year curriculum	91	

# of upper division courses, excluding seminars, with an enrollment:		
	Under 25	70
	25–49	23
	50–74	12
	75–99	0
	100+	1

# of seminars	20	
# of seminar positions available	300	
# of seminar positions filled	166	0
# of positions available in simulation courses	455	
# of simulation positions filled	395	0
# of positions available in faculty supervised clinical courses	64	
# of faculty supervised clinical positions filled	57	0
# involved in field placements	29	0
# involved in law journals	42	0
# involved in moot court or trial competitions	44	0
# of credit hours required to graduate	91	

JD Enrollment and Ethnicity

	Men		Women		Full-Time		Part-Time		1st-Year		Total		JD Degs. Awd.
	#	%	#	%	#	%	#	%	#	%	#	%	
All Hispanics	4	1.5	5	3.4	9	2.2	0	0.0	7	5.0	9	2.2	0
Am. Ind./AK Nat.	1	0.4	2	1.3	3	0.7	0	0.0	0	0.0	3	0.7	0
Asian	4	1.5	3	2.0	7	1.7	0	0.0	4	2.9	7	1.7	1
Black/Af. Am.	9	3.3	11	7.4	20	4.9	0	0.0	6	4.3	20	4.8	10
Nat. HI/Pac. Isl.	1	0.4	0	0.0	1	0.2	0	0.0	0	0.0	1	0.2	0
2 or more races	2	0.7	4	2.7	6	1.5	0	0.0	6	4.3	6	1.4	0
Subtotal (minor.)	21	7.8	25	16.8	46	11.2	0	0.0	23	16.5	46	11.0	12
Nonres. Alien	1	0.4	0	0.0	1	0.2	0	0.0	1	0.7	1	0.2	0
White/Cauc.	245	91.1	123	82.6	361	87.8	7	100.0	113	81.3	368	88.0	113
Unknown	2	0.7	1	0.7	3	0.7	0	0.0	2	1.4	3	0.7	0
Total	269	64.4	149	35.6	411	98.3	7	1.7	139	33.3	418		125

Transfers

Transfers in	3
Transfers out	4

Tuition and Fees

	Resident	Nonresident
Full-time	$16,423	$31,367
Part-time		
Tuition Guarantee Program	N	

Living Expenses

Estimated living expenses for singles

Living on campus	Living off campus	Living at home
$14,831	$14,831	$14,831

WEST VIRGINIA UNIVERSITY COLLEGE OF LAW

ABA
Approved
Since
1923

GPA and LSAT Scores

	Total	Full-Time	Part-Time
# of apps	1,107	1,107	0
# of offers	506	506	0
# of matrics	141	141	0
75% GPA	3.70	3.70	0.00
Median GPA	3.41	3.41	0.00
25% GPA	3.15	3.15	0.00
75% LSAT	157	157	0
Median LSAT	154	154	0
25% LSAT	152	152	0

Grants and Scholarships (from prior year)

	Total #	Total %	Full-Time #	Full-Time %	Part-Time #	Part-Time %
Total # of students	416		410		6	
Total # receiving grants	148	35.6	148	36.1	0	0.0
Less than 1/2 tuition	81	19.5	81	19.8	0	0.0
Half to full tuition	21	5.0	21	5.1	0	0.0
Full tuition	30	7.2	30	7.3	0	0.0
More than full tuition	16	3.8	16	3.9	0	0.0
Median grant amount			$5,813		$0	

Informational and Library Resources

Total amount spent on library materials	$939,304
Study seating capacity inside the library	388
# of full-time equivalent professional librarians	3
Hours per week library is open	103
# of open, wired connections available to students	140
# of networked computers available for use by students	69
Has wireless network?	Y
Requires computer?	N

JD Attrition (from prior year)

	Academic #	Other #	Total #	Total %
1st year	0	8	8	5.9
2nd year	1	1	2	1.4
3rd year	1	1	2	1.5
4th year	0	0	0	0.0

Employment (9 months after graduation)

For up-to-date employment data, go to employmentsummary.abaquestionnaire.org on the ABA website.

Bar Passage Rates

First-time takers	129	Reporting %	79.84
Average school %	72.82	Average state %	76.44

Average pass difference −3.62

Jurisdiction	Takers	Passers	Pass %	State %	Diff %
West Virginia	103	75	72.82	76.44	−3.62

WEST VIRGINIA UNIVERSITY COLLEGE OF LAW

101 Law Center Drive, PO Box 6130
Morgantown, WV 26506-6130
Phone: 304.293.5301; Fax: 304.293.8102
E-mail: wvulaw.admissions@mail.wvu.edu; Website: http://law.wvu.edu/

Introduction

The College of Law, established in 1878, is the oldest professional school at West Virginia University. The university is located in Morgantown, West Virginia. Within a 500-mile radius of Morgantown is half of the population of the United States and one-third of the population of Canada. The College of Law has been a member of the AALS since 1914 and was fully accredited by the ABA in 1923. The college has had a chapter of the Order of the Coif since 1925.

Library and Physical Facilities

The College of Law facility measures 131,966 square feet and provides a spacious learning community for law students. The law center is home to six classrooms, two courtrooms, a distance learning center, financial aid, career services, and a law bookstore and café. Ample parking at the law center is available by permit for all law students.

The George R. Farmer Jr. Law Library, a three-story, 32,476-square-foot facility with 40,386 feet of shelving space, is home to the largest law library in the state of West Virginia. The law library is comprehensive in scope with a collection of over 300,000 volumes and equivalents. As part of a sustainable strategy, the library replaced its 42 computers with virtual desktops that significantly reduce power consumption and facilitate more efficient IT maintenance. This system also enhances network security and includes an additional 17 virtual desktops in the library's Carlin Computer Lab.

The Student Recreation Center is a $34-million, 177,000-square-foot facility complete with two swimming pools and a massive 50-foot climbing wall that stretches up through the center of the three-story building. The center also houses a wellness center, a resource library, a study area, a food-service operation, a small classroom, a meeting/conference room, and socialization areas.

Admission

The College of Law admits first-year students only in the first (fall) semester. No specific prelaw curriculum is required for admission. The college subscribes to the suggestions in this book pertaining to prelaw study and stresses the value of college courses that require extensive analytic skills and writing assignments.

Students are admitted to the College of Law on the basis of previous academic performance, scores on the Law School Admission Test, personal statements, letters of recommendation, and other factors that bear upon the potential professional qualifications of the applicant as determined by the College of Law.

Applications are accepted beginning September 1 of each year for the class to begin their studies the following August. The required seat deposit amount for residents is $200 and $400 for nonresidents, which is credited toward tuition and fees for the fall semester.

Expenses and Financial Aid

Although WVU's reasonable tuition and fees are an excellent value, the College of Law recognizes that many students may not be able to afford the full cost of a legal education without financial assistance. Limited funds in the form of tuition waivers, scholarships, and college work-study are available each year through the university. Even if the student has not been accepted to the College of Law, he or she should apply for financial aid by March 1. The Free Application for Federal Student Aid (FAFSA) must be completed in order to receive any financial assistance, including all need-based scholarships. Students must complete the FAFSA each year in order to be considered for financial aid.

More information may be obtained by contacting Eric Meadows, Financial Aid Counselor, PO Box 6130, Morgantown, WV 26506-6130; phone: 304.293.5302; e-mail: eric.meadows@mail.wvu.edu.

Housing

The majority of our students live off campus in private housing. The university's Office of Student Life assists students by providing information about off-campus housing options. You may contact them at 304.293.5611 or visit their website at www.studentlife.wvu.edu.

Student Activities

West Virginia University College of Law has over 30 student organizations. The Student Bar Association is the student government of the school. The *West Virginia Law Review* (http://wvlawreview.wvu.edu) is the fourth oldest student-governed law review in the nation, and selects members on the basis of performance during their first year in law school and on performance in a writing competition. A competitive Moot Court Program is conducted at the law school, including the National Energy and Sustainability Moot Court Competition.

Career Services

The Meredith Career Services Center provides career counseling, professional development workshops, interview programs, and job-search strategy sessions as part of a comprehensive career services program. Our graduates work in diverse settings throughout the United States and abroad, including law firms, courts, government agencies, public service organizations, corporations, and colleges and universities. The goals of the Career Services office are to educate students about possible careers in the law, encourage them to identify and set career goals, and assist them in achieving those goals. Please visit http://law.wvu.edu/career_services for more information.

Opportunities for Minority Students

The College of Law is committed to maintaining a diverse student body by welcoming students who are members of groups traditionally underrepresented in the legal profession. The Meredith Career Services Center assists minority students with securing summer employment through a Minority Clerkship Program. The College of Law also participates in the Southeast Minority Job Fair in Atlanta, a regional job fair that brings together employers and minority students.

Student organizations, such as the Black Law Students Association, provide additional opportunities for minority students.

Curriculum

Subject to modification, 91 hours are required for graduation. The 31-hour, first-year curriculum is specified. The second- and third-year programs offer a number of course options and possibilities for concentration.

Students have the option, after being admitted, to request enrollment in the part-time program that offers daytime courses congruently with the full-time program. There is not a separate nighttime track.

Educational Centers

The **Center for Energy and Sustainable Development** is an energy and environmental public policy and research organization at the College of Law. The Center focuses on promoting practices that will balance the continuing demand for energy resources—and the associated economic benefits—alongside the need to reduce the environmental impacts of developing the earth's natural resources. The Center's activities will focus on training the next generation of energy and environmental attorneys, the sustainable practices in the development of energy resources and land use policies, the development of clean energy resources, and the role of utilities in pursuing clean energy objectives.

The **Center for Law and Public Service** promotes public service at the College of Law by providing opportunities for students to engage in public interest law, fostering dialogue about current legal services and policy issues, and encouraging students to become leaders who seek creative solutions toward achieving equal access to justice in society. The Center provides multiple avenues for student public service opportunities, including the Public Service Externship program, the Pro Bono program, and, in conjunction with the West Virginia Fund for the Public Interest and the Public Interest Advocates, the summer and postgraduate fellowship programs.

Clinic Programs

Hands-on training is a key component of our Advanced Lawyering curriculum. Clinical experience prepares students for the practical challenges of legal practice and hones the skills they need to best serve their clients, the profession, and society.

Clinic programs offered include:

- **Civil Clinic**—provides eligible individuals with legal services focused on family law, social security and supplemental security income, and consumer debt relief.
- **The Child, Family, and Health Advocacy Clinic**—offers legal assistance in collaboration with physicians from the WVU Robert C. Byrd Health Sciences Center.
- **Entrepreneurship Law Clinic**—offers start-up companies, small businesses, nonprofits, and individuals legal services in areas of counseling for a product plan or business organization, licensing, employee and contractor agreements, intellectual property, financing and venture capital, planning and negotiation, dispute resolution, and generalized assistance in business formation, planning, and strategy.
- **Human Rights and Immigration Clinic**—provides legal assistance and representation to foreign citizens across the region who are facing deportation, asylum, and other immigration proceedings.
- **Land Use and Sustainability Clinic**—provides transactional legal assistance to protect and enhance water quality and promote sustainable land use practices.
- **Tax Clinic**—offers legal services to taxpayers residing in West Virginia who need to resolve a tax controversy with the Internal Revenue Service.

APPLICANT PROFILE

West Virginia University College of Law
This grid includes only applicants who earned 120–180 LSAT scores under standard administrations.

LSAT Score	3.75 +		3.50–3.74		3.25–3.49		3.00–3.24		2.75–2.99		2.50–2.74		2.25–2.49		2.00–2.24		Below 2.00		No GPA		Total	
	Apps	Adm	Apps	Adm	Apps	Adm	Apps	Adm	Apps	Adm	Apps	Adm	Apps	Adm	Apps	Adm	Apps	Adm	Apps	Adm	Apps	Adm
175–180	0	0	0	0	0	0	0	0	0	0	0	0	0	0	0	0	0	0	0	0	0	0
170–174	1	1	0	0	1	1	0	0	0	0	0	0	0	0	0	0	0	0	0	0	2	2
165–169	6	6	5	3	2	2	1	1	4	3	1	1	0	0	0	0	1	0	0	0	20	16
160–164	16	15	13	11	5	4	11	10	11	9	5	4	1	1	2	2	0	0	0	0	64	56
155–159	35	32	54	48	59	56	46	39	27	19	16	10	7	3	4	0	1	0	3	1	252	208
150–154	49	43	94	64	84	47	77	21	50	11	23	6	11	4	8	1	3	0	9	2	408	199
145–149	30	5	59	6	49	2	51	2	34	2	27	0	9	0	0	0	1	0	2	0	262	17
140–144	10	0	11	0	20	0	13	0	23	0	12	0	7	0	4	0	0	0	4	0	104	0
135–139	1	0	2	0	8	0	3	0	7	0	3	0	2	0	0	0	1	0	2	0	29	0
130–134	0	0	0	0	1	0	1	0	1	0	1	0	2	0	1	0	0	0	0	0	7	0
125–129	0	0	0	0	0	0	0	0	0	0	1	0	1	0	2	0	0	0	1	0	5	0
120–124	0	0	0	0	0	0	0	0	0	0	0	0	0	0	0	0	0	0	0	0	0	0
Total	148	102	238	132	229	112	203	73	157	44	89	21	40	8	21	3	7	0	21	3	1153	498

Apps = Number of Applicants
Adm = Number Admitted
Reflects 100% of the total applicant pool; highest LSAT data reported.

WESTERN NEW ENGLAND UNIVERSITY SCHOOL OF LAW

Office of Admissions, 1215 Wilbraham Road
Springfield, MA 01119-2684
Phone: 800.782.6665, 413.782.1406; Fax: 413.796.2067
E-mail: admissions@law.wne.edu; Website: www.law.wne.edu

ABA
Approved
Since
1974

The Basics

Type of school	Private
Term	Semester
Application deadline	3/15
Application fee	
Financial aid deadline	4/15
Can first year start other than fall?	No
Student to faculty ratio	13.8 to 1
# of housing spaces available restricted to law students	65
graduate housing for which law students are eligible	

Faculty and Administrators

	Total		Men		Women		Minorities	
	Spr	Fall	Spr	Fall	Spr	Fall	Spr	Fall
Full-time	26	27	12	12	14	15	4	5
Other full-time	1	1	1	1	0	0	0	0
Deans, librarians, & others who teach	7	6	4	4	3	2	0	0
Part-time	24	19	21	17	3	2	1	0
Total	58	53	38	34	20	19	5	5

Curriculum

	Full-Time	Part-Time
Typical first-year section size	47	19
Is there typically a "small section" of the first-year class, other than Legal Writing, taught by full-time faculty	No	No
If yes, typical size offered last year		
# of classroom course titles beyond first-year curriculum	137	
# of upper division courses, excluding seminars, with an enrollment: Under 25	80	
25–49	36	
50–74	7	
75–99	2	
100+	0	
# of seminars	12	
# of seminar positions available	216	
# of seminar positions filled	127	37
# of positions available in simulation courses	214	
# of simulation positions filled	86	22
# of positions available in faculty supervised clinical courses	88	
# of faculty supervised clinical positions filled	57	7
# involved in field placements	72	5
# involved in law journals	39	10
# involved in moot court or trial competitions	49	9
# of credit hours required to graduate	88	

JD Enrollment and Ethnicity

	Men		Women		Full-Time		Part-Time		1st-Year		Total		JD Degs. Awd.
	#	%	#	%	#	%	#	%	#	%	#	%	
All Hispanics	9	4.3	3	1.3	9	2.8	3	2.5	3	2.8	12	2.7	9
Am. Ind./AK Nat.	1	0.5	6	2.6	4	1.3	3	2.5	3	2.8	7	1.6	0
Asian	8	3.8	9	3.9	16	5.0	1	0.8	1	0.9	17	3.9	8
Black/Af. Am.	4	1.9	11	4.8	12	3.8	3	2.5	7	6.5	15	3.4	4
Nat. HI/Pac. Isl.	0	0.0	0	0.0	0	0.0	0	0.0	0	0.0	0	0.0	0
2 or more races	0	0.0	0	0.0	0	0.0	0	0.0	0	0.0	0	0.0	0
Subtotal (minor.)	22	10.6	29	12.6	41	12.8	10	8.4	14	13.1	51	11.6	21
Nonres. Alien	0	0.0	1	0.4	1	0.3	0	0.0	0	0.0	1	0.2	0
White/Cauc.	171	82.2	187	81.0	264	82.5	94	79.0	92	86.0	358	81.5	102
Unknown	15	7.2	14	6.1	14	4.4	15	12.6	2	1.9	29	6.6	31
Total	208	47.4	231	52.6	320	72.9	119	27.1	107	24.4	439		154

Transfers

Transfers in	2
Transfers out	22

Tuition and Fees

	Resident	Nonresident
Full-time	$38,240	$38,240
Part-time	$28,294	$28,294
Tuition Guarantee Program	N	

Living Expenses

Estimated living expenses for singles

Living on campus	Living off campus	Living at home
$18,461	$18,461	$7,623

WESTERN NEW ENGLAND UNIVERSITY SCHOOL OF LAW

ABA Approved Since 1974

GPA and LSAT Scores

	Total	Full-Time	Part-Time
# of apps	1,170	996	174
# of offers	590	530	60
# of matrics	106	84	22
75% GPA	3.42	3.48	3.37
Median GPA	3.17	3.18	3.10
25% GPA	2.85	2.92	2.77
75% LSAT	156	156	154
Median LSAT	153	153	152
25% LSAT	151	151	150

Grants and Scholarships (from prior year)

	Total #	Total %	Full-Time #	Full-Time %	Part-Time #	Part-Time %
Total # of students	525		387		138	
Total # receiving grants	334	63.6	284	73.4	50	36.2
Less than 1/2 tuition	215	41.0	170	43.9	45	32.6
Half to full tuition	111	21.1	107	27.6	4	2.9
Full tuition	7	1.3	6	1.6	1	0.7
More than full tuition	1	0.2	1	0.3	0	0.0
Median grant amount			$15,000		$6,000	

Informational and Library Resources

Total amount spent on library materials	$1,160,191
Study seating capacity inside the library	468
# of full-time equivalent professional librarians	7
Hours per week library is open	103
# of open, wired connections available to students	9
# of networked computers available for use by students	49
Has wireless network?	Y
Requires computer?	N

JD Attrition (from prior year)

	Academic #	Other #	Total #	Total %
1st year	7	34	41	24.1
2nd year	0	0	0	0.0
3rd year	0	0	0	0.0
4th year	0	0	0	0.0

Employment (9 months after graduation)

For up-to-date employment data, go to employmentsummary.abaquestionnaire.org on the ABA website.

Bar Passage Rates

First-time takers	164	Reporting %	74.39
Average school %	66.39	Average state %	88.02

Average pass difference −21.63

Jurisdiction	Takers	Passers	Pass %	State %	Diff %
Massachusetts	81	58	71.60	89.67	−18.07
Connecticut	41	23	56.10	84.76	−28.66

WESTERN NEW ENGLAND UNIVERSITY SCHOOL OF LAW

Office of Admissions, 1215 Wilbraham Road
Springfield, MA 01119-2684
Phone: 800.782.6665, 413.782.1406; Fax: 413.796.2067
E-mail: admissions@law.wne.edu; Website: www.law.wne.edu

Introduction

For more than three-quarters of a century, Western New England University School of Law has been preparing men and women to succeed in the legal profession. Fully accredited by the ABA and a member of the AALS, our 7,000 alumni live and work in all 50 states and many foreign countries. They include judges, attorneys practicing in small and large firms, and lawyers for corporations, businesses, nonprofit organizations, and all levels of government. We are located in the heart of the beautiful and vibrant Pioneer Valley on a suburban campus, 90 miles from Boston and 150 miles from New York City.

Western New England University School of Law offers both full-time and part-time programs, each providing a strong, well-rounded curriculum that will enable you to succeed in your career. A distinctive feature of our law school is our personalized, student-centered approach to legal education and professional development. Our first-year section size, purposely among the smallest in the country, promotes effective learning in a challenging but collegial and supportive setting. Our accessible and dedicated faculty create a learning environment that helps every student succeed and reach his or her full potential. It is a wonderful place to begin your legal career.

Admission and Scholarships

Every application is read by members of the Admissions Committee. All facets of the application are carefully considered, including race, gender, language, and educational, social, and economic obstacles overcome in the applicant's pursuit of higher education. We seek candidates with well-developed writing ability and analytical skills who will contribute to classroom discussions and the law school community.

Each year partial-tuition scholarships are awarded to applicants whose credentials and backgrounds suggest they are likely to enrich the life of the School of Law. Partial-tuition scholarships may be awarded on the basis of academic merit or an applicant's area of interest. Partial scholarships are available for applicants who demonstrate potential for success and who have overcome cultural, economic, societal, physical, or educational obstacles. All admitted applicants receive automatic scholarship consideration. Typically, at least 50 percent of the entering class receives scholarship assistance.

In addition, several students are awarded full-tuition Oliver Wendell Holmes Jr. Scholarships. The Holmes Scholars usually score in the top 20 percent of the LSAT nationally and finish very near the top of their undergraduate classes. Holmes Scholars receive full-tuition scholarships, with an additional $3,500 research stipend.

The School of Law also offers six Public Interest Scholarships to full-time students, ranging from $16,000 to full tuition, with an additional $3,500 summer stipend. Public Interest Scholars take special public interest courses, have regular meetings with public interest practitioners to discuss current issues in public interest practice, and are mentored in their public interest careers by faculty and members of the Public Interest Advisory Board. The $3,500 stipend supports the required public interest summer internship. The Public Interest Scholars program provides an exceptional opportunity to offset the cost of law school while preparing for a career in public interest lawyering. Additionally, applicants may also apply for scholarships associated with our Center for Gender and Sexuality Studies, Legislative Institute, or the Center for Innovation and Entrepreneurship. Please visit our website for more information.

Faculty

The 14:1 student-to-faculty ratio, the strong commitment to student learning, and the outstanding credentials of the 38 faculty members provide an outstanding learning environment dedicated to your professional success. The faculty have been educated at many of the nation's most prestigious law schools, and all have practiced law prior to joining our faculty. They all share a love of teaching and take pride in their ability to engage students in rigorous law study in a collaborative, collegial environment. They are productive scholars who are consistently praised by our students for their accessibility.

Curriculum

All required courses, both day and evening, are taught by full-time faculty members. Some upper-level courses are taught through classroom discussions of judicial decisions and statutes. Others are taught through simulations in which students perform the roles of lawyers in lifelike situations and through clinics in which students represent actual clients. Part-time day and evening programs are also available.

Our broad-based curriculum allows students the opportunity to focus their legal studies in many different areas of the law, including tax, public interest, and corporate law. To assist students in preparing for their careers, and selecting among electives, the School of Law offers seven concentrations (Business Law, Criminal Law, Estate Planning, International and Comparative Law, Public Interest Law, Gender and Sexuality Law, and Real Estate Law), along with several specializations. For a full list, please reference our website.

We also offer four joint-degree programs:

- JD/MBA (Master of Business Administration) with Western New England University
- JD/MSA (Master of Accounting) with Western New England University
- JD/MSW (Master of Social Work) with Springfield College
- JD/MRP (Master of Regional Planning) with the University of Massachusetts at Amherst

The Law School offers two Master of Laws (LLM) programs:

- Estate Planning and Elder Law
- Closely Held Businesses

Please visit our website for more information.

Experiential Learning: Clinics, Simulations, and Externships

Clinics and simulation courses are integral components of the curriculum at Western New England University School of Law. Each type of course offers an opportunity to put theory into practice, thereby enhancing advocacy skills and enriching the understanding of core course materials. Students also apply their legal skills through externships.

Clinics provide an opportunity for upper-class students to represent clients with actual legal problems. Currently, the School of Law offers six different clinics in which students can gain valuable lawyering skills, such as legal writing, interviewing, and negotiating. The following clinical opportunities are offered:

- Criminal Law Clinic—students prosecute cases for the Hampden County District Attorney's Office.
- Legal Services Clinic—students work in the office of Western Massachusetts Legal Services, Inc.
- Consumer Law Clinic—students work in the City of Springfield's Consumer Protection Program.
- Real Property Practicum—students work with practitioners in the real estate area.
- Small Business Clinic—students help start-up businesses at the Scibelli Enterprise Center's business incubator.
- International Human Rights Clinic—students work collaboratively with organizations to advance human rights across borders.

Simulation courses allow students to represent hypothetical clients with challenging legal problems drawn from the experiences of practicing lawyers. Students perform research, prepare legal documents, and negotiate with and argue against role-playing students and faculty.

Externships enable students to work with judges or alongside attorneys in public interest organizations or government agencies. Externs are called upon to perform research and prepare legal documents. Externships allow students to refine their lawyering skills and provide interaction with professionals who can offer advice and career insights. Students receive two or three hours of academic credit for one nonpaying externship.

Western New England University School of Law students compete in many trial, appellate, and negotiation competitions, honing their research, writing, and advocacy skills, and gaining valuable experience. Our teams have won national championships in 2009, 2008, 2006, 2004, and 2001, and numerous regional titles.

Library, Facilities, and the Area

The recently renovated S. Prestley Blake Law Center has a spacious law library, excellent classrooms, and comfortable student study and social space. With a collection of over 375,000 volumes, the Law Library also provides comprehensive access to numerous electronic resources. The School of Law's robust wireless network facilitates research and communication.

The Law Center is located in a residential section of Springfield, on Western New England University's 215-acre campus, with ample, free parking for all students. Springfield is a small city, located in the Pioneer Valley, with a wide array of recreational, social, and cultural attractions. There is a range of affordable off-campus housing options, as well as some on-campus housing options.

Attending the only law school in western Massachusetts, students have access to a host of externship and clinical opportunities throughout the Massachusetts/Connecticut/New York region, including state and federal courts, the attorney generals of several states, district attorney and state's attorney offices, public defender offices, public interest organizations, and small, medium, and large firms.

Student Activities

Western New England University School of Law students enjoy a strong sense of community and support, strengthened and nurtured by numerous and varied student organizations and cocurricular activities. The Student Bar Association plays a leading role, with elected officers and appointed members to faculty/student committees. There are many other active student organizations, including the Multi-Cultural Law Students Association, the Women's Law Association, OUTlaw, and a variety of groups formed around interests in particular areas of law and practice, including the Health Law Association, the Family Law Association, the Criminal Law Society, and the Real Estate Guild. There is also a productive *Western New England Law Review*, many active moot court teams, and a student newspaper, *Lex Brevis*.

APPLICANT PROFILE

Western New England University School of Law
This grid includes only applicants who earned 120–180 LSAT scores under standard administrations.

LSAT Score	GPA																					
	3.75 +		3.50–3.74		3.25–3.49		3.00–3.24		2.75–2.99		2.50–2.74		2.25–2.49		2.00–2.24		Below 2.00		No GPA		Total	
	Apps	Adm	Apps	Adm	Apps	Adm	Apps	Adm	Apps	Adm	Apps	Adm	Apps	Adm	Apps	Adm	Apps	Adm	Apps	Adm	Apps	Adm
175–180	0	0	0	0	1	1	0	0	0	0	0	0	0	0	0	0	0	0	0	0	1	1
170–174	2	2	0	0	0	0	0	0	0	0	1	1	0	0	0	0	0	0	0	0	3	3
165–169	4	3	3	3	4	3	1	1	0	0	1	1	3	3	1	1	0	0	0	0	17	15
160–164	10	10	5	4	5	5	11	11	7	7	3	3	2	1	1	1	0	0	0	0	44	42
155–159	15	15	27	25	20	20	47	45	21	20	13	13	5	3	2	2	0	0	3	2	153	145
150–154	28	27	57	53	62	59	82	76	58	47	37	30	24	13	6	3	3	0	5	1	362	309
145–149	15	10	44	22	73	22	82	10	55	8	26	0	23	0	8	0	1	0	8	1	335	73
140–144	6	0	24	0	26	0	31	0	26	0	21	0	5	0	6	0	2	0	1	0	148	0
135–139	2	0	9	0	8	0	8	0	10	0	12	0	5	0	3	0	2	0	3	0	62	0
130–134	0	0	0	0	0	0	5	0	3	0	3	0	2	0	1	0	2	0	1	0	17	0
125–129	1	0	0	0	0	0	1	0	0	0	1	0	1	0	0	0	1	0	1	0	6	0
120–124	0	0	0	0	0	0	0	0	1	0	1	0	0	0	0	0	0	0	0	0	2	0
Total	83	67	169	107	199	110	268	143	181	82	119	48	70	20	28	7	11	0	22	4	1150	588

Apps = Number of Applicants   Adm = Number Admitted   Reflects 99% of the total applicant pool; highest LSAT data reported.

WESTERN STATE COLLEGE OF LAW

1111 North State College Boulevard
Fullerton, CA 92831
Phone: 800.WSU.4LAW, 714.459.1101; Fax: 714.441.1748
E-mail: adm@wsulaw.edu; Website: www.wsulaw.edu

ABA
Approved
Since
2005

The Basics

Type of school	Private
Term	Semester
Application deadline	7/1
Application fee	$60
Financial aid deadline	3/2 10/15
Can first year start other than fall?	No
Student to faculty ratio	22.9 to 1
# of housing spaces available restricted to law students	
graduate housing for which law students are eligible	

Faculty and Administrators

	Total		Men		Women		Minorities	
	Spr	Fall	Spr	Fall	Spr	Fall	Spr	Fall
Full-time	13	17	11	12	2	5	2	4
Other full-time	5	6	1	1	4	5	2	3
Deans, librarians, & others who teach	6	6	2	2	4	4	2	2
Part-time	15	16	11	11	4	5	3	1
Total	39	45	25	26	14	19	9	10

Curriculum

	Full-Time	Part-Time
Typical first-year section size	56	34
Is there typically a "small section" of the first-year class, other than Legal Writing, taught by full-time faculty	No	No
If yes, typical size offered last year		
# of classroom course titles beyond first-year curriculum	50	
# of upper division courses, excluding seminars, with an enrollment: Under 25	63	
25–49	26	
50–74	6	
75–99	0	
100+	0	
# of seminars	8	
# of seminar positions available	200	
# of seminar positions filled	86	25
# of positions available in simulation courses	393	
# of simulation positions filled	160	112
# of positions available in faculty supervised clinical courses	20	
# of faculty supervised clinical positions filled	8	3
# involved in field placements	46	18
# involved in law journals	27	13
# involved in moot court or trial competitions	11	6
# of credit hours required to graduate	88	

JD Enrollment and Ethnicity

	Men		Women		Full-Time		Part-Time		1st-Year		Total		JD Degs. Awd.
	#	%	#	%	#	%	#	%	#	%	#	%	
All Hispanics	40	14.9	43	17.7	60	16.0	23	17.0	43	18.5	83	16.2	8
Am. Ind./AK Nat.	1	0.4	4	1.6	4	1.1	1	0.7	1	0.4	5	1.0	0
Asian	41	15.3	41	16.9	63	16.8	19	14.1	40	17.2	82	16.0	11
Black/Af. Am.	9	3.4	16	6.6	13	3.5	12	8.9	9	3.9	25	4.9	2
Nat. HI/Pac. Isl.	1	0.4	1	0.4	1	0.3	1	0.7	0	0.0	2	0.4	1
2 or more races	5	1.9	1	0.4	3	0.8	3	2.2	0	0.0	6	1.2	4
Subtotal (minor.)	97	36.2	106	43.6	144	38.3	59	43.7	93	39.9	203	39.7	26
Nonres. Alien	7	2.6	5	2.1	12	3.2	0	0.0	6	2.6	12	2.3	1
White/Cauc.	158	59.0	125	51.4	209	55.6	74	54.8	128	54.9	283	55.4	61
Unknown	6	2.2	7	2.9	11	2.9	2	1.5	6	2.6	13	2.5	4
Total	268	52.4	243	47.6	376	73.6	135	26.4	233	45.6	511		92

Transfers

Transfers in	11
Transfers out	16

Tuition and Fees

	Resident	Nonresident
Full-time	$37,284	$37,284
Part-time	$25,030	$25,030
Tuition Guarantee Program	N	

Living Expenses

Estimated living expenses for singles

Living on campus	Living off campus	Living at home
N/A	$24,832	$18,555

WESTERN STATE COLLEGE OF LAW

ABA
Approved
Since
2005

GPA and LSAT Scores

	Total	Full-Time	Part-Time
# of apps	1,882	1,501	381
# of offers	1,068	913	155
# of matrics	237	191	46
75% GPA	3.33	3.35	3.24
Median GPA	3.09	3.09	3.14
25% GPA	2.89	2.88	2.94
75% LSAT	155	154	156
Median LSAT	151	151	150
25% LSAT	149	149	149

Grants and Scholarships (from prior year)

	Total #	Total %	Full-Time #	Full-Time %	Part-Time #	Part-Time %
Total # of students	468		318		150	
Total # receiving grants	223	47.6	152	47.8	71	47.3
Less than 1/2 tuition	125	26.7	87	27.4	38	25.3
Half to full tuition	55	11.8	34	10.7	21	14.0
Full tuition	41	8.8	30	9.4	11	7.3
More than full tuition	2	0.4	1	0.3	1	0.7
Median grant amount			$12,000		$8,250	

Informational and Library Resources

Total amount spent on library materials	$859,654
Study seating capacity inside the library	351
# of full-time equivalent professional librarians	7
Hours per week library is open	114
# of open, wired connections available to students	40
# of networked computers available for use by students	25
Has wireless network?	Y
Requires computer?	N

JD Attrition (from prior year)

	Academic #	Other #	Total #	Total %
1st year	59	24	83	34.9
2nd year	14	2	16	15.1
3rd year	2	0	2	2.0
4th year	0	0	0	0.0

Employment (9 months after graduation)

For up-to-date employment data, go to employmentsummary.abaquestionnaire.org on the ABA website.

Bar Passage Rates

First-time takers	77	Reporting %	96.10
Average school %	81.07	Average state %	72.38
Average pass difference	8.69		

Jurisdiction	Takers	Passers	Pass %	State %	Diff %
California	64	51	79.69	71.24	8.45
Nevada	2	2	100.00	72.72	27.28
Pennsylvania	2	2	100.00	83.06	16.94
Connecticut	1	1	100.00	84.76	15.24
Others (5)	5	4	80.00		

WESTERN STATE COLLEGE OF LAW

1111 North State College Boulevard
Fullerton, CA 92831
Phone: 800.WSU.4LAW, 714.459.1101; Fax: 714.441.1748
E-mail: adm@wsulaw.edu; Website: www.wsulaw.edu

Introduction

Western State College of Law (WSCL), founded in 1966, is the oldest law school in Orange County, Southern California. Our 11,000 graduates have distinguished themselves as jurists, lawmakers, district attorneys, public defenders, and civil practitioners; they constitute a strong alumni network that mentors and enables an enviable job placement record for WSCL graduates. Located in the college town of Fullerton, in the heart of the vibrant economy and healthy legal market of Orange County, the WSCL campus is about 30 miles south of Los Angeles and 100 miles north of San Diego. It is within commuting distance of the greater Los Angeles/Orange County metropolitan areas, the fast-growing Inland Empire, and the Southland's beach cities and high technology, finance, and business centers. A private law school of fewer than 500 students, WSCL offers small class sizes, personal interaction with faculty, and an extraordinary, supportive learning environment. Repeatedly cited as one of the most ethnically diverse law school student bodies in the country, WSCL is also known for giving students practical hands-on lawyering experience along with a strong academic foundation.

Faculty

WSCL prides itself on a faculty of excellent professors whose first priority is teaching and student success. Most bring extensive real-world legal experience to the classroom in addition to their strong academic and teaching credentials. The full-time faculty is supplemented by an outstanding adjunct faculty of practicing attorneys and judges. With a student-to-faculty ratio below 20 to 1, and a highly accessible faculty, students benefit from individualized attention and mentoring.

Curriculum and Special Programs

WSCL offers a full-time program that is normally completed in three academic years and part-time day or evening programs that take four full years to complete. Students may start in any of the programs in the fall. WSCL also offers a January-start, part-time evening program; students in good standing may transition to full time in the fall. The Business Law Center and Criminal Law Practice Center programs give students the option to focus their electives to earn a Certificate in Business Law or Criminal Law with a notation on their transcript indicating their special study emphasis.

In addition to required and elective coursework, the centers also bring distinguished speakers to campus, arrange student visits to criminal justice facilities or business venues, and provide connections to practitioners, including internship and externship opportunities and career networking. The on-site Immigration Legal Clinic provides students with hands-on skills training while responding to the pressing needs of immigrants in Orange County. Students represent immigrants who cannot otherwise afford legal representation before Citizenship and Immigration Services and in Immigration Court. Each student, along with a partner, serves as the client's primary representative. Under faculty supervision, they interview the clients, investigate and gather facts,

research the relevant law, draft briefs and affidavits, file applications for relief and supporting documentation, and represent clients in immigration interviews and in court.

In the externship program, students receive placement in courts or in the offices of district attorneys, public defenders, practicing attorneys, corporate legal departments, or public interest organizations where they gain hands-on experience and earn academic credit.

Student Body and Organizations

WSCL has a diverse student body of about 500 students, with an entering class of approximately 200 students. Minority enrollment constitutes over 40 percent of the total, with an even enrollment of men and women. The fall 2011 class entered from 98 different undergraduate institutions, and about 20 percent came from 21 different states outside California. About 15 active student-led organizations enrich and complement the academic program with their cocurricular educational, networking, philanthropic, and social activities for students. These include the Student Bar Association, Asian Pacific American Law Student Association, Black Law Student Association, Latino Student Bar Association, Christian Legal Society, Business Law Association, J. Reuben Clark Society, Entertainment Sports Law Society, Gay and Lesbian Organization, Criminal Law Association, and Trial Lawyers Association. Students who qualify for the law review and moot court team gain high-visibility legal writing and competitive advocacy experience.

Library and Physical Facilities

The library has more than 175,000 on-site volumes as well as access to electronic resources on campus and remotely. Students may use the library's 20 computers, including 25 located in a large computer classroom, or the wireless network. The library has 19 study rooms, a Student Learning Center, Quiet Reading Room, and open reading areas for group or individual study. The library maintains long hours to service the needs of our students. Our librarians provide extensive reference services and training in legal research, online research, and software.

WSCL's campus is located in the heart of Fullerton's university district and consists of a four-story main building and the three-level library, with on-site parking. Most areas of both buildings are covered by Wi-Fi. The main building contains classrooms, the modern Frank and Marleen Darras Moot Court Room, an administrative suite, faculty offices, a student lounge, and a café.

Admission

All applicants are assigned to an admission advisor who assists in the admission process, may conduct a personal or telephone informational interview, and arranges for visits to the campus and contact with professors, students, or alumni. Each applicant's entire file is reviewed; admission decisions are made by a faculty committee. A bachelor's degree is required for admission. A personal statement and two letters of recommendation are required, and a résumé is encouraged. Details of the applicant's undergraduate record and LSAT score, writing ability, and maturing life and work experiences are key indicators of potential for success in law school. When there are multiple LSAT scores, the highest, most recent score may be accorded significant weight.

Admission is on a rolling basis, but application by April 1 for fall, and October 1 for spring, is highly encouraged.

Scholarships and Financial Aid

WSCL offers generous merit-based scholarships, and in the 2011 entering class, over 40 percent of new students received scholarships. No separate application is required. Admitted students are automatically considered for merit scholarships based on academic predictors (undergraduate track record and LSAT score). After the first year, law students are eligible to compete for merit scholarships, provided they rank within the top 30 percent of their class. A full range of loan programs is available to complement students' financial needs, including Stafford loans, Perkins loans, and private loans. All students receiving scholarship funds or loans should plan to file the FAFSA and a preliminary financial aid application.

Career Services and Placement

With a 46-year history in Southern California and an influential alumni network of more than 11,000 graduates, WSCL has a strong placement track record and the connections to assist students in their job searches. The May 2011 class found employment as follows: 61 percent in private practice, 22

percent in business and industry, 6 percent in academia, 4 percent in government, 3 percent in public service, and 3 percent in government/other.

The active Career Services Office arranges on-campus interviews, career-related workshops, speaker panels, networking events, and individual counseling to help educate students about the many possible areas of practice and how to secure employment. The office serves as a liaison with legal employers, both public and private. It solicits job listings from alumni and local practitioners and assists students with permanent and summer employment. The Career Resource Center provides students with reference materials and counseling on résumé writing, job-search techniques, and study-abroad programs. Convenient online job- and résumé-posting services are provided by WSCL to facilitate employment searches by students and alumni. WSCL alumni mentor students and recent graduates. Additionally, alumni assist with on-campus career fairs, mock interviews, and networking events.

Contact Us

We encourage you to visit our website, speak to an admission advisor, and arrange to visit WSCL in person so that you can sit in on a class and meet with students, alumni, and professors. Experience the personal attention and support, great learning environment, and dedication to student success that set Western State apart.

APPLICANT PROFILE

Western State College of Law
This grid includes only applicants who earned 120–180 LSAT scores under standard administrations.

LSAT Score	GPA																							
	3.75 +		3.50–3.74		3.25–3.49		3.00–3.24		2.75–2.99		2.50–2.74		2.25–2.49		2.00–2.24		Below 2.00		No GPA		Total	
	Apps	Adm	Apps	Adm	Apps	Adm	Apps	Adm	Apps	Adm	Apps	Adm	Apps	Adm	Apps	Adm	Apps	Adm	Apps	Adm	Apps	Adm
175–180	0	0	0	0	0	0	0	0	0	0	0	0	0	0	0	0	0	0	0	0	0	0
170–174	0	0	1	1	0	0	0	0	0	0	0	0	0	0	0	0	0	0	0	0	1	1
165–169	0	0	1	1	1	1	3	3	3	3	0	0	0	0	1	1	0	0	0	0	9	9
160–164	3	3	5	4	10	10	13	13	9	8	13	11	4	4	3	3	2	0	2	1	64	57
155–159	14	14	26	26	57	53	51	44	49	43	32	24	16	11	11	2	3	0	1	1	260	218
150–154	26	25	61	58	100	93	130	119	102	94	62	48	37	14	15	2	5	0	9	6	547	459
145–149	14	14	47	34	113	85	118	74	102	35	72	13	35	3	14	2	2	0	12	4	529	264
140–144	4	0	16	1	23	0	40	0	43	0	41	0	25	0	6	0	1	0	2	0	201	1
135–139	4	0	5	0	7	0	12	0	10	0	15	0	8	0	6	0	0	0	2	0	69	0
130–134	1	0	1	0	2	0	1	0	2	0	3	0	2	0	1	0	0	0	1	0	14	0
125–129	0	0	0	0	0	0	0	0	3	0	0	0	1	0	1	0	0	0	0	0	5	0
120–124	0	0	0	0	0	0	0	0	0	0	2	0	0	0	0	0	0	0	0	0	2	0
Total	66	56	163	125	313	242	368	253	323	183	240	96	128	32	58	10	13	0	29	12	1701	1009

Apps = Number of Applicants
Adm = Number Admitted
Reflects 99% of the total applicant pool; highest LSAT data reported.

WHITTIER LAW SCHOOL

3333 Harbor Boulevard
Costa Mesa, CA 92626
Phone: 714.444.4141 ext. 123; Fax: 714.444.0250
E-mail: info@law.whittier.edu; Website: www.law.whittier.edu

ABA
Approved
Since
1978

The Basics

Type of school	Private
Term	Semester
Application deadline	8/1
Application fee	$60
Financial aid deadline	5/1
Can first year start other than fall?	No
Student to faculty ratio	18.9 to 1
# of housing spaces available restricted to law students	
graduate housing for which law students are eligible	

Faculty and Administrators

	Total		Men		Women		Minorities	
	Spr	Fall	Spr	Fall	Spr	Fall	Spr	Fall
Full-time	25	29	10	14	15	15	1	3
Other full-time	2	4	0	1	2	3	0	0
Deans, librarians, & others who teach	8	8	3	2	5	6	1	1
Part-time	16	13	11	7	5	6	5	3
Total	51	54	24	24	27	30	7	7

JD Enrollment and Ethnicity

	Men		Women		Full-Time		Part-Time		1st-Year		Total		JD Degs. Awd.
	#	%	#	%	#	%	#	%	#	%	#	%	
All Hispanics	58	16.0	65	19.3	99	17.6	24	17.6	57	20.8	123	17.6	19
Am. Ind./AK Nat.	3	0.8	3	0.9	6	1.1	0	0.0	1	0.4	6	0.9	0
Asian	73	20.1	67	19.9	120	21.3	20	14.7	55	20.1	140	20.0	24
Black/Af. Am.	11	3.0	12	3.6	15	2.7	8	5.9	9	3.3	23	3.3	4
Nat. HI/Pac. Isl.	0	0.0	0	0.0	0	0.0	0	0.0	0	0.0	0	0.0	0
2 or more races	0	0.0	0	0.0	0	0.0	0	0.0	0	0.0	0	0.0	0
Subtotal (minor.)	145	39.9	147	43.6	240	42.6	52	38.2	122	44.5	292	41.7	47
Nonres. Alien	0	0.0	0	0.0	0	0.0	0	0.0	0	0.0	0	0.0	0
White/Cauc.	203	55.9	175	51.9	302	53.5	76	55.9	123	44.9	378	54.0	76
Unknown	15	4.1	15	4.5	22	3.9	8	5.9	29	10.6	30	4.3	0
Total	363	51.9	337	48.1	564	80.6	136	19.4	274	39.1	700		123

Curriculum

	Full-Time	Part-Time
Typical first-year section size	82	41
Is there typically a "small section" of the first-year class, other than Legal Writing, taught by full-time faculty	No	No
If yes, typical size offered last year		

# of classroom course titles beyond first-year curriculum		108
# of upper division courses, excluding seminars, with an enrollment:	Under 25	77
	25–49	35
	50–74	7
	75–99	2
	100+	3

# of seminars		16
# of seminar positions available		318
# of seminar positions filled	144	33
# of positions available in simulation courses		986
# of simulation positions filled	433	100
# of positions available in faculty supervised clinical courses		120
# of faculty supervised clinical positions filled	42	10
# involved in field placements	158	30
# involved in law journals	105	14
# involved in moot court or trial competitions	45	10
# of credit hours required to graduate		87

Transfers

Transfers in	20
Transfers out	32

Tuition and Fees

	Resident	Nonresident
Full-time	$39,140	$39,140
Part-time	$26,110	$26,110
Tuition Guarantee Program		N

Living Expenses

Estimated living expenses for singles

Living on campus	Living off campus	Living at home
N/A	$25,412	$25,412

ABA Approved Since 1978

GPA and LSAT Scores

	Total	Full-Time	Part-Time
# of apps	2,245	1,947	298
# of offers	1,244	1,103	141
# of matrics	274	222	52
75% GPA	3.21	3.22	3.06
Median GPA	2.95	2.99	2.74
25% GPA	2.66	2.69	2.58
75% LSAT	154	154	155
Median LSAT	152	152	152
25% LSAT	149	149	150

Grants and Scholarships (from prior year)

	Total #	Total %	Full-Time #	Full-Time %	Part-Time #	Part-Time %
Total # of students	642		475		167	
Total # receiving grants	308	48.0	244	51.4	64	38.3
Less than 1/2 tuition	234	36.4	188	39.6	46	27.5
Half to full tuition	55	8.6	41	8.6	14	8.4
Full tuition	11	1.7	10	2.1	1	0.6
More than full tuition	8	1.2	5	1.1	3	1.8
Median grant amount			$9,000		$6,500	

Informational and Library Resources

Total amount spent on library materials	$893,244
Study seating capacity inside the library	386
# of full-time equivalent professional librarians	7
Hours per week library is open	102
# of open, wired connections available to students	209
# of networked computers available for use by students	103
Has wireless network?	Y
Requires computer?	Y

JD Attrition (from prior year)

	Academic #	Other #	Total #	Total %
1st year	60	33	93	31.0
2nd year	26	2	28	14.1
3rd year	11	0	11	9.6
4th year	2	0	2	7.4

Employment (9 months after graduation)

For up-to-date employment data, go to employmentsummary.abaquestionnaire.org on the ABA website.

Bar Passage Rates

First-time takers	144	Reporting %	89.58
Average school %	52.73	Average state %	71.56

Average pass difference   −18.83

Jurisdiction	Takers	Passers	Pass %	State %	Diff %
California	124	63	50.81	71.24	−20.43
Nevada	2	2	100.00	72.72	27.28
Hawaii	1	1	100.00	77.04	22.96
Minnesota	1	1	100.00	92.21	7.79
Pennsylvania	1	1	100.00	83.06	16.94

WHITTIER LAW SCHOOL

3333 Harbor Boulevard
Costa Mesa, CA 92626
Phone: 714.444.4141 ext. 123; Fax: 714.444.0250
E-mail: info@law.whittier.edu; Website: www.law.whittier.edu

Introduction

Located in sunny Orange County, California, Whittier Law School provides a practical legal education with school-wide support for each individual student while emphasizing experiential learning. Students have significant interaction with engaged, dynamic professors in small classes and receive extensive instruction in legal writing from full-time faculty to prepare them for actual work as attorneys. The Law School prides itself on programs in academic success and bar preparation to give students the skills they need to succeed. With valuable externship opportunities and active career placement, we position students for future careers.

Midway between Los Angeles and San Diego, California, Whittier Law School is less than 10 miles from Newport Beach and other notable beaches. Over 150 law firms exist within a five-mile radius of campus, providing rich opportunities for externships and interaction with the Law School. The immediate area is also known as a world-class destination for shopping and tourism, with nearby attractions such as Huntington Beach, Crystal Cove, and Disneyland.

Part-Time Programs

In addition to the traditional three-year, full-time program, the JD can also be completed in four years, including two summer sessions, in the flexible day program. Standards for admission and retention are identical for all students, and the full-time faculty serve both programs.

Admission and Scholarships

In addition to the LSAT score and undergraduate GPA, factors such as undergraduate school, major, graduate work, work experience, and personal accomplishments are considered. Whittier Law School awards numerous tuition scholarships annually, and automatically considers all applicants for merit-based scholarships.

Special Programs

Center for Children's Rights—The center enrolls up to 20 students yearly who receive fellowships and summer stipends to prepare for careers in children's rights. Fellows participate in special classes, colloquiums, symposiums, and externships. The center also sponsors the National Juvenile Law Moot Court Competition and the *Whittier Journal of Child and Family Advocacy.*

Center for Intellectual Property Law—In addition to offering a number of fellowships, the cornerstones of this center are the IP Certificate Program, symposia, externships, and the Distinguished Speaker Series. Student groups, including the Intellectual Property Society and the Entertainment and Sports Law Society, hold numerous events.

Center for International and Comparative Law (CICL)—The center offers students the opportunity to specialize in global issues through fellowships, a certificate program, colloquia series, and symposia. In addition, Whittier Law School offers six ABA-approved study-abroad programs that expose students to a wide variety of cultures.

Clinics—Whittier Law School has two clinics: the Children's Advocacy Clinic and the Special Education Clinic. Students put their classroom learning to work representing actual clients and begin to develop a professional and ethical identity. In addition to learning practical lawyering skills such as interviewing, counseling, negotiation, fact investigation, legal drafting, and oral advocacy, students work closely with clinical faculty who help them grow from their experience.

Summer-Abroad Programs—The Law School offers six summer study-abroad programs approved by the ABA. Students from around the country can choose to study at the prestigious Bar-Ilan University in Tel Aviv, Israel; the University of Cantabria in Santander, Spain; the University of Toulouse in Toulouse, France; the University of Nanjing in Nanjing, China; Ibero-American University in Mexico City, Mexico; or the University of Barcelona in Barcelona, Spain.

Institute of Student and Graduate Academic Support—From the first day of orientation until the last day of the bar examination, Whittier Law School's unique academic-support program helps students excel in their law school studies and pass the bar exam. Full-time professors work individually with students, provide counseling and workshops, and administer a nationally recognized bar-preparation program. Whittier Law School prides itself on providing excellent school-wide student support.

Institute of Legal Writing and Professional Skills—Whittier's Legal Writing program is one of the finest, with an extensive three-year required program where students receive individualized attention and guidance. The program trains students in the practical, useful skills lawyers need to write and research. In addition, in the second year, students can choose litigation or a transactional track to begin focusing their skills. This program is one of the reasons why Whittier Law School students graduate more prepared to practice.

Concentrations in business and criminal law are also offered.

Library and Physical Facilities

Conveniently located off a major freeway, the spacious, 15-acre Whittier Law School campus is solely used by law students, so there is plentiful parking and access to facilities. With a cafeteria on campus and ample space both indoors and outside, students can take advantage of the weather to study and meet. The Law School is composed of four buildings that are completely accessible to people with disabilities, and includes one of the largest academic, law research libraries in the region. Three student computer labs support a variety of software to aid students with computer-assisted instruction, online legal research, and Internet access. Numerous conference rooms are available for group study. The entire facility is equipped with wireless Internet access.

Student Activities

Students at Whittier are involved in many organizations and activities; this is a campus where students actively engage in school life.

For over 30 years, the *Whittier Law Review* has been publishing articles of legal scholarship, giving students the opportunity to develop analytical, editing, writing, and legal research skills. In addition, the *Whittier Journal of Child and Family Advocacy*, a student-run scholarly publication focusing on topics related to juvenile and family law, is one of the few journals of its kind in the nation.

Members of the Moot Court Honors Board and the Trial Advocacy Honors Board utilize written and oral advocacy skills to represent the Law School in regional and national trial and appellate advocacy competitions.

In addition to an active Student Bar Association, over 30 student organizations represent various ethnic groups and legal specialties.

Externships and Career Services

In keeping with our emphasis on practical skills, Whittier Law School assists students and alumni in obtaining clerkships, externships, internships, and attorney and nonattorney positions. The Law School offers a variety of externships with trial and appellate judges, governmental agencies, private firms, corporate legal departments, and public interest organizations. The Career Development Office assists in résumé-building exercises, career goal identification, and career-planning strategies. Additional services include on-campus interviews, a mentor program, panels on career-related topics, a comprehensive library of career resources, and a mock interview program.

APPLICANT PROFILE

Whittier Law School
This grid includes only applicants who earned 120–180 LSAT scores under standard administrations.

LSAT Score	3.75 +		3.50–3.74		3.25–3.49		3.00–3.24		2.75–2.99		2.50–2.74		2.25–2.49		2.00–2.24		Below 2.00		No GPA		Total	
	Apps	Adm	Apps	Adm	Apps	Adm	Apps	Adm	Apps	Adm	Apps	Adm	Apps	Adm	Apps	Adm	Apps	Adm	Apps	Adm	Apps	Adm
175–180	0	0	0	0	0	0	0	0	0	0	0	0	0	0	0	0	0	0	0	0	0	0
170–174	0	0	2	1	0	0	0	0	0	0	0	0	0	0	0	0	0	0	0	0	2	1
165–169	0	0	0	0	4	3	6	6	3	3	3	3	0	0	1	1	0	0	0	0	17	16
160–164	6	6	12	11	19	17	19	18	17	15	16	16	8	6	6	5	1	1	0	0	104	95
155–159	22	22	34	32	63	60	77	73	60	55	51	47	15	14	8	6	3	2	1	1	334	312
150–154	25	23	82	73	147	138	155	142	136	102	95	60	37	26	20	12	5	1	8	4	710	581
145–149	18	9	73	36	116	45	131	34	111	25	93	14	35	2	26	3	2	0	12	2	617	170
140–144	2	0	18	1	25	1	64	1	65	1	42	2	25	0	12	0	3	0	2	0	258	6
135–139	3	0	6	0	7	0	9	0	17	0	14	0	13	0	5	0	1	0	2	0	77	0
130–134	0	0	1	0	0	0	4	0	4	0	8	0	4	0	4	0	1	0	2	0	28	0
125–129	0	0	0	0	0	0	0	0	2	0	0	0	3	0	1	0	0	0	0	0	6	0
120–124	0	0	0	0	0	0	0	0	0	0	0	0	0	0	0	0	0	0	0	0	0	0
Total	76	60	228	154	381	264	465	274	415	201	322	142	140	48	83	27	16	4	27	7	2153	1181

Apps = Number of Applicants
Adm = Number Admitted
Reflects 99% of the total applicant pool; highest LSAT data reported.

WIDENER UNIVERSITY SCHOOL OF LAW

4601 Concord Pike, PO Box 7474
Wilmington, DE 19803-0474
Phone: 302.477.2703; Fax: 302.477.2224
E-mail: lawadmissions@widener.edu; Website: http://law.widener.edu

The Basics

Type of school	Private
Term	Semester
Application deadline	5/15
Application fee	$60
Financial aid deadline	4/1
Can first year start other than fall?	No
Student to faculty ratio	14.2 to 1
# of housing spaces available restricted to law students	185
graduate housing for which law students are eligible	185

Faculty and Administrators

	Total		Men		Women		Minorities	
	Spr	Fall	Spr	Fall	Spr	Fall	Spr	Fall
Full-time	47	51	25	28	22	23	9	9
Other full-time	4	4	0	0	4	4	0	0
Deans, librarians, & others who teach	8	10	2	4	6	6	1	2
Part-time	55	43	41	29	14	14	3	4
Total	114	108	68	61	46	47	13	15

JD Enrollment and Ethnicity

	Men		Women		Full-Time		Part-Time		1st-Year		Total		JD Degs. Awd.
	#	%	#	%	#	%	#	%	#	%	#	%	
All Hispanics	19	3.6	9	2.2	20	3.1	8	2.6	13	4.1	28	3.0	6
Am. Ind./AK Nat.	0	0.0	3	0.7	3	0.5	0	0.0	3	0.9	3	0.3	1
Asian	22	4.2	23	5.5	37	5.8	8	2.6	14	4.4	45	4.8	11
Black/Af. Am.	23	4.3	45	10.8	49	7.7	19	6.2	26	8.1	68	7.2	14
Nat. Hi/Pac. Isl.	1	0.2	0	0.0	1	0.2	0	0.0	1	0.3	1	0.1	0
2 or more races	3	0.6	7	1.7	7	1.1	3	1.0	4	1.3	10	1.1	2
Subtotal (minor.)	68	12.8	87	20.9	117	18.3	38	12.3	61	19.1	155	16.4	34
Nonres. Alien	1	0.2	1	0.2	2	0.3	0	0.0	2	0.6	2	0.2	0
White/Cauc.	445	84.0	323	77.5	506	79.2	262	85.1	250	78.1	768	81.1	205
Unknown	16	3.0	6	1.4	14	2.2	8	2.6	7	2.2	22	2.3	13
Total	530	56.0	417	44.0	639	67.5	308	32.5	320	33.8	947		252

Curriculum

	Full-Time	Part-Time
Typical first-year section size	68	53
Is there typically a "small section" of the first-year class, other than Legal Writing, taught by full-time faculty	Yes	Yes
If yes, typical size offered last year	59	36
# of classroom course titles beyond first-year curriculum	138	

# of upper division courses, excluding seminars, with an enrollment:		
Under 25	156	
25–49	37	
50–74	29	
75–99	1	
100+	0	

	Full-Time	Part-Time
# of seminars	25	
# of seminar positions available	375	
# of seminar positions filled	149	100
# of positions available in simulation courses	600	
# of simulation positions filled	216	120
# of positions available in faculty supervised clinical courses	93	
# of faculty supervised clinical positions filled	52	20
# involved in field placements	60	19
# involved in law journals	72	21
# involved in moot court or trial competitions	63	40
# of credit hours required to graduate	88	

Transfers

Transfers in	2
Transfers out	40

Tuition and Fees

	Resident	Nonresident
Full-time	$36,450	$36,450
Part-time	$26,754	$26,754
Tuition Guarantee Program	N	

Living Expenses

Estimated living expenses for singles

Living on campus	Living off campus	Living at home
$17,504	$17,504	$12,644

*ABA
Approved
Since
1975*

GPA and LSAT Scores

	Total	Full-Time	Part-Time
# of apps	1,864	1,735	458
# of offers	1,173	967	206
# of matrics	313	227	86
75% GPA	3.43	3.40	3.40
Median GPA	3.12	3.14	3.03
25% GPA	2.81	2.81	2.67
75% LSAT	153	154	153
Median LSAT	152	152	150
25% LSAT	149	150	148

Grants and Scholarships (from prior year)

	Total		Full-Time		Part-Time	
	#	%	#	%	#	%
Total # of students	999		647		352	
Total # receiving grants	276	27.6	214	33.1	62	17.6
Less than 1/2 tuition	204	20.4	157	24.3	47	13.4
Half to full tuition	50	5.0	37	5.7	13	3.7
Full tuition	18	1.8	17	2.6	1	0.3
More than full tuition	4	0.4	3	0.5	1	0.3
Median grant amount			$2,975		$7,347	

Informational and Library Resources

Total amount spent on library materials	$1,059,146
Study seating capacity inside the library	426
# of full-time equivalent professional librarians	9
Hours per week library is open	107
# of open, wired connections available to students	75
# of networked computers available for use by students	141
Has wireless network?	Y
Requires computer?	N

JD Attrition (from prior year)

	Academic	Other	Total	
	#	#	#	%
1st year	34	57	91	23.5
2nd year	6	3	9	3.2
3rd year	2	0	2	0.8
4th year	0	0	0	0.0

Employment (9 months after graduation)

For up-to-date employment data, go to
employmentsummary.abaquestionnaire.org on the ABA website.

Bar Passage Rates

First-time takers	229	Reporting %	81.22
Average school %	88.17	Average state %	83.06
Average pass difference	5.11		

Jurisdiction	Takers	Passers	Pass %	State %	Diff %
Pennsylvania	186	164	88.17	83.06	5.11

WIDENER UNIVERSITY SCHOOL OF LAW

3800 Vartan Way, PO Box 69380
Harrisburg, PA 17106-9380
Phone: 717.541.3903; Fax: 717.541.3999
E-mail: lawadmissions@widener.edu; Website: http://law.widener.edu

The Basics

Type of school	Private
Term	Semester
Application deadline	5/12
Application fee	$60
Financial aid deadline	4/1
Can first year start other than fall?	No
Student to faculty ratio	14.0 to 1
# of housing spaces available restricted to law students	
graduate housing for which law students are eligible	

Faculty and Administrators

	Total		Men		Women		Minorities	
	Spr	Fall	Spr	Fall	Spr	Fall	Spr	Fall
Full-time	24	23	14	13	10	10	4	1
Other full-time	1	2	0	0	1	2	0	1
Deans, librarians, & others who teach	7	7	2	2	5	5	2	2
Part-time	21	22	14	13	7	9	0	0
Total	53	54	30	28	23	26	6	4

Curriculum

		Full-Time	Part-Time
Typical first-year section size		66	28
Is there typically a "small section" of the first-year class, other than Legal Writing, taught by full-time faculty		No	No
If yes, typical size offered last year			
# of classroom course titles beyond first-year curriculum		76	
# of upper division courses, excluding seminars, with an enrollment:	Under 25	136	
	25–49	24	
	50–74	10	
	75–99	1	
	100+	1	
# of seminars		12	
# of seminar positions available		202	
# of seminar positions filled		104	35
# of positions available in simulation courses		236	
# of simulation positions filled		179	57
# of positions available in faculty supervised clinical courses		53	
# of faculty supervised clinical positions filled		41	12
# involved in field placements		23	10
# involved in law journals		29	7
# involved in moot court or trial competitions		17	6
# of credit hours required to graduate		88	

JD Enrollment and Ethnicity

	Men		Women		Full-Time		Part-Time		1st-Year		Total		JD Degs. Awd.
	#	%	#	%	#	%	#	%	#	%	#	%	
All Hispanics	8	3.8	14	6.8	19	5.7	3	3.6	12	7.9	22	5.3	4
Am. Ind./AK Nat.	1	0.5	1	0.5	1	0.3	1	1.2	1	0.7	2	0.5	0
Asian	5	2.3	11	5.3	15	4.5	1	1.2	3	2.0	16	3.8	3
Black/Af. Am.	4	1.9	9	4.4	9	2.7	4	4.8	8	5.3	13	3.1	4
Nat. HI/Pac. Isl.	0	0.0	1	0.5	1	0.3	0	0.0	1	0.7	1	0.2	0
2 or more races	3	1.4	1	0.5	4	1.2	0	0.0	1	0.7	4	1.0	1
Subtotal (minor.)	21	9.9	37	18.0	49	14.6	9	10.8	26	17.1	58	13.8	12
Nonres. Alien	0	0.0	0	0.0	0	0.0	0	0.0	0	0.0	0	0.0	0
White/Cauc.	184	86.4	167	81.1	281	83.6	70	84.3	121	79.6	351	83.8	110
Unknown	8	3.8	2	1.0	6	1.8	4	4.8	5	3.3	10	2.4	2
Total	213	50.8	206	49.2	336	80.2	83	19.8	152	36.3	419		124

Transfers

Transfers in	1
Transfers out	17

Tuition and Fees

	Resident	Nonresident
Full-time	$36,450	$36,450
Part-time	$26,754	$26,754
Tuition Guarantee Program	N	

Living Expenses

Estimated living expenses for singles

Living on campus	Living off campus	Living at home
$17,504	$17,504	$12,644

WIDENER UNIVERSITY SCHOOL OF LAW

ABA
Approved
Since
1994

GPA and LSAT Scores

	Total	Full-Time	Part-Time
# of apps	1,386	1,186	200
# of offers	747	658	89
# of matrics	155	130	25
75% GPA	3.46	3.44	3.81
Median GPA	3.15	3.15	3.28
25% GPA	2.85	2.86	2.99
75% LSAT	152	152	152
Median LSAT	149	149	150
25% LSAT	148	148	148

Grants and Scholarships (from prior year)

	Total #	Total %	Full-Time #	Full-Time %	Part-Time #	Part-Time %
Total # of students	453		350		103	
Total # receiving grants	156	34.4	129	36.9	27	26.2
Less than 1/2 tuition	119	26.3	100	28.6	19	18.4
Half to full tuition	28	6.2	20	5.7	8	7.8
Full tuition	6	1.3	6	1.7	0	0.0
More than full tuition	3	0.7	3	0.9	0	0.0
Median grant amount			$2,000		$7,336	

Informational and Library Resources

Total amount spent on library materials	$688,317
Study seating capacity inside the library	335
# of full-time equivalent professional librarians	5
Hours per week library is open	105
# of open, wired connections available to students	10
# of networked computers available for use by students	68
Has wireless network?	Y
Requires computer?	N

JD Attrition (from prior year)

	Academic #	Other #	Total #	Total %
1st year	23	32	55	30.9
2nd year	4	0	4	3.1
3rd year	1	1	2	1.6
4th year	0	0	0	0.0

Employment (9 months after graduation)

For up-to-date employment data, go to employmentsummary.abaquestionnaire.org on the ABA website.

Bar Passage Rates

First-time takers	97	Reporting %	88.66
Average school %	88.37	Average state %	83.06
Average pass difference	5.31		

Jurisdiction	Takers	Passers	Pass %	State %	Diff %
Pennsylvania	86	76	88.37	83.06	5.31

WIDENER UNIVERSITY SCHOOL OF LAW

4601 Concord Pike, PO Box 7474, Wilmington, DE 19803-0474; Phone: 302.477.2703; Fax: 302.477.2224
3800 Vartan Way, PO Box 69380, Harrisburg, PA 17106-9380; Phone: 717.541.3903; Fax: 717.541.3999
E-mail: lawadmissions@widener.edu; Website: http://law.widener.edu

Introduction

Widener University School of Law is unique among American law schools. Widener has two campuses—one in Wilmington, Delaware, the corporate and banking center of the United States, and the other in Harrisburg, Pennsylvania, the state capital and a major center of government and commerce. Each campus offers a comprehensive curriculum of basic and advanced courses complemented by one of the most extensive clinical and skills programs in the country. The Harrisburg campus features a unique admission and academic cooperative program with the Pennsylvania State System of Higher Education.

The rich curriculum is taught by a faculty committed to personal attention and individual counseling so that all students will be encouraged to fulfill their potential. The full-time faculty is supplemented by a distinguished group of adjuncts, including two justices of the Delaware Supreme Court, two justices of the Pennsylvania Supreme Court, US Vice President Joseph Biden, and numerous lower court judges from Pennsylvania, Delaware, and New Jersey. The school is a member of the AALS and is accredited by the ABA.

Library and Physical Facilities

The Legal Information Center houses one of the most significant legal collections in the region. The combined collections of the Delaware and Harrisburg campuses exceed 200,000 volumes. The library is a selective depository for United States government documents.

The attractive 34-acre Delaware campus is located in the heart of the beautiful Brandywine River Valley. The law building houses the Legal Information Center, state-of-the-art computer facilities, faculty offices, clinics, traditional and technologically enhanced classrooms, and three moot courtrooms. The scenic 19-acre Harrisburg campus is located in a contemporary complex within minutes of the state capital.

Special Programs and Institutes

Widener is a leader in developing a coordinated lawyering skills program. The program includes clinical practice, externship placements, and comprehensive simulations.

Clinics are designed to permit students to represent actual clients under the supervision of the clinic director before courts and administrative boards. Widener operates Environmental Law, Criminal Defense, Delaware Civil, Harrisburg Civil, and Veterans Affairs clinics. A large number of supervised externships permit students to work as lawyers-in-training with state and county government agencies and nonprofit corporations. An extensive judicial externship program places students with state and federal courts at both the trial and appellate levels in Washington, DC; Delaware; Maryland; New Jersey; Pennsylvania; and Virginia. Additional public interest service opportunities are also available.

The Public Interest Resource Center on the Delaware campus and the Public Interest Initiative on the Harrisburg campus cultivate pro bono volunteer opportunities for students in public interest agencies and government offices throughout Delaware, Pennsylvania, and New Jersey; offer counseling and guidance to students who seek careers in public interest law; and recognize students and faculty for exceptional contributions to public service.

Widener offers certificate programs for specialized study in health law, law and government, business organizations law, advocacy and technology, criminal law, and environmental law. The Health Law Institute on the Delaware campus provides research, policy analysis, and specialty education for those seeking a career in the area of health law. The Law and Government Institute on the Harrisburg campus provides hands-on experience with the operation and structure of government as well as practice before government agencies. The Institute of Delaware Corporate and Business Law on the Delaware campus provides a fundamental knowledge of business law through the Business Organizations Law concentration, which serves as a predicate to advanced practice in business and corporate law. The Taishoff Advocacy, Technology, and Public Service Institute on the Delaware campus provides the extensive litigation skills that are essential to being a competent, professionally responsible trial advocate. The Advocacy Program on the Harrisburg campus offers specialized courses and practice opportunities, leading to a certificate, for students interested in a career in litigation. The Environmental Law Center on both campuses harnesses the expertise of seven nationally and internationally recognized environmental law faculty members to provide students with extensive opportunities to engage in environmental law through coursework, externships, and training skills. Additionally, both campuses offer a seven-day Intensive Trial Advocacy Program supervised by outstanding local trial lawyers and judges.

Widener offers five joint-degree programs. The JD/MBA is offered in conjunction with the university's School of Business Administration. The JD/PsyD is offered in conjunction with the university's Institute for Graduate Clinical Psychology. The JD/MPH is offered in conjunction with Thomas Jefferson University. The JD/MSLS is offered in conjunction with Clarion University of Pennsylvania. The JD/MMP is offered in conjunction with the University of Delaware.

Study-Abroad Opportunities

Widener students have the opportunity to study international and comparative law while living abroad. Widener offers study-abroad programs in Nairobi, Kenya; Lausanne, Switzerland; Sydney, Australia; Venice, Italy; and Chongqing, China.

Student Activities

Selected Delaware students publish the *Delaware Journal of Corporate Law* and the *Widener Law Review*. Selected Harrisburg students publish the *Widener Law Journal*. Delaware and Harrisburg students may also be eligible to participate in our online journal, the *Widener Journal of Law, Economics and Race*. Students on both campuses compete in regional and national interschool moot court and trial competitions. Student organizations provide opportunities for intrascholastic and interscholastic competitions, public service, and association with others who share the same interests.

Admission

While there are no fixed admission criteria, great weight is given to the applicant's LSAT score and undergraduate grade-point average. The Admissions Committee carefully considers an applicant's personal statement. Graduate degrees, writing samples, extracurricular activities, and community and professional service may enhance the application. The law school encourages those with diverse backgrounds to apply.

Applications for admission must be received by May 15. Admission decisions are made on a rolling basis, and applicants are encouraged to apply early.

The admission process is paperless. All applications and supporting documents must be submitted electronically via law.widener.edu or LSAC.org. All communications to applicants, including admission decisions, are provided through the applicant's account in Widener's admissions web portal at law.widener.edu/admissions.

Each summer, Widener conducts the Trial Admissions Program (TAP) for a small number of carefully selected applicants who show potential for success in law school despite a relatively low score on the LSAT or a lower undergraduate grade-point average. TAP is a conditional admittance program. Participants who successfully complete the six-week program are offered admission to the fall entering class.

Financial Aid

The Financial Aid Office is committed to assisting students throughout the financial aid process. In addition to merit-based scholarships offered at the time of admission to well-qualified applicants based upon their overall application, Widener Law awards a substantial amount of merit-based scholarships and the opportunity to borrow through our low-interest-rate Institutional Loan Program to students who academically excel in their first year of law school. Widener Law participates in all federal financial aid programs, including Federal Work-Study and the Federal Direct Loan Programs.

Career Development

The Career Development Office is strongly committed to helping students obtain the positions that best suit their individual needs and ambitions.

Widener's employment statistics are evidence of its success in helping graduates find a niche in the contemporary job market. Widener alumni have become judges in Delaware, New Jersey, New York, and Pennsylvania; members of the legislature; partners in major regional law firms; hospital administrators; and legal educators.

APPLICANT PROFILE

Widener University School of Law
This grid includes only applicants who earned 120–180 LSAT scores under standard administrations.

LSAT Score	3.75 +		3.50–3.74		3.25–3.49		3.00–3.24		2.75–2.99		2.50–2.74		2.25–2.49		2.00–2.24		Below 2.00		No GPA		Total	
	Apps	Adm	Apps	Adm	Apps	Adm	Apps	Adm	Apps	Adm	Apps	Adm	Apps	Adm	Apps	Adm	Apps	Adm	Apps	Adm	Apps	Adm
175–180	0	0	0	0	0	0	0	0	0	0	0	0	0	0	0	0	0	0	0	0	0	0
170–174	0	0	0	0	0	0	1	1	0	0	1	1	0	0	0	0	0	0	0	0	2	2
165–169	1	0	3	3	3	3	5	5	1	1	1	1	0	0	0	0	0	0	1	1	15	14
160–164	15	13	23	20	18	18	20	20	10	7	9	9	2	1	5	5	1	1	1	0	104	94
155–159	46	43	62	59	78	76	59	54	35	33	37	34	13	12	9	8	2	2	6	2	347	323
150–154	59	58	118	113	127	120	166	153	109	96	69	59	52	44	21	14	4	3	6	1	731	661
145–149	44	23	75	34	130	60	196	72	158	55	99	32	63	21	28	5	7	2	23	3	823	307
140–144	15	1	45	6	72	2	92	3	102	2	63	1	36	0	14	0	3	0	14	0	456	15
135–139	6	0	14	0	27	0	21	0	26	0	24	0	17	0	15	0	4	0	8	0	162	0
130–134	0	0	2	0	5	0	7	0	10	0	5	0	8	0	6	0	1	0	4	0	48	0
125–129	0	0	0	0	3	0	3	0	3	0	5	0	0	0	3	0	2	0	2	1	21	1
120–124	0	0	0	0	0	0	1	0	1	0	3	0	1	0	1	0	0	0	1	0	8	0
Total	186	138	342	235	463	279	571	308	455	194	316	137	192	78	102	32	24	8	66	8	2717	1417

Apps = Number of Applicants
Adm = Number Admitted
Reflects 98% of the total applicant pool; highest LSAT data reported.

The grid includes applicants admitted based upon successful completion of our Trial Admissions Program, rather than upon their LSAT score and undergraduate grade-point average. Additionally, nonnumerical factors are considered for all applicants.

WILLAMETTE UNIVERSITY COLLEGE OF LAW

Truman Wesley Collins Legal Center, 245 Winter Street SE
Salem, OR 97301
Phone: 503.370.6282; Fax: 503.370.6087
E-mail: law-admission@willamette.edu; Website: www.willamette.edu/wucl

ABA
Approved
Since
1938

The Basics

Type of school	Private
Term	Semester
Application deadline	3/1
Application fee	$50
Financial aid deadline	6/1
Can first year start other than fall?	No
Student to faculty ratio	12.9 to 1
# of housing spaces available restricted to law students graduate housing for which law students are eligible	26

Faculty and Administrators

	Total		Men		Women		Minorities	
	Spr	Fall	Spr	Fall	Spr	Fall	Spr	Fall
Full-time	27	25	18	17	9	8	5	4
Other full-time	4	4	2	2	2	2	1	1
Deans, librarians, & others who teach	6	6	4	4	2	2	0	0
Part-time	19	14	15	13	4	1	1	1
Total	56	49	39	36	17	13	7	6

Curriculum

	Full-Time	Part-Time
Typical first-year section size	80	0
Is there typically a "small section" of the first-year class, other than Legal Writing, taught by full-time faculty	Yes	No
If yes, typical size offered last year	46	
# of classroom course titles beyond first-year curriculum	109	

# of upper division courses, excluding seminars, with an enrollment:	Under 25	54
	25–49	13
	50–74	9
	75–99	3
	100+	1

# of seminars	24	
# of seminar positions available	333	
# of seminar positions filled	272	0
# of positions available in simulation courses	297	
# of simulation positions filled	267	0
# of positions available in faculty supervised clinical courses	82	
# of faculty supervised clinical positions filled	60	0
# involved in field placements	31	0
# involved in law journals	65	0
# involved in moot court or trial competitions	129	0
# of credit hours required to graduate	90	

JD Enrollment and Ethnicity

	Men		Women		Full-Time		Part-Time		1st-Year		Total		JD Degs. Awd.
	#	%	#	%	#	%	#	%	#	%	#	%	
All Hispanics	15	6.4	8	4.7	23	5.7	0	0.0	11	7.6	23	5.7	10
Am. Ind./AK Nat.	3	1.3	5	2.9	8	2.0	0	0.0	4	2.8	8	2.0	3
Asian	12	5.1	15	8.7	27	6.7	0	0.0	8	5.5	27	6.7	8
Black/Af. Am.	1	0.4	1	0.6	2	0.5	0	0.0	0	0.0	2	0.5	5
Nat. HI/Pac. Isl.	0	0.0	0	0.0	0	0.0	0	0.0	0	0.0	0	0.0	0
2 or more races	0	0.0	0	0.0	0	0.0	0	0.0	0	0.0	0	0.0	0
Subtotal (minor.)	31	13.2	29	16.9	60	14.8	0	0.0	23	15.9	60	14.8	26
Nonres. Alien	6	2.6	3	1.7	9	2.2	0	0.0	3	2.1	9	2.2	0
White/Cauc.	185	79.1	128	74.4	312	77.0	1	100.0	110	75.9	313	77.1	104
Unknown	12	5.1	12	7.0	24	5.9	0	0.0	9	6.2	24	5.9	0
Total	234	57.6	172	42.4	405	99.8	1	0.2	145	35.7	406		130

Transfers

Transfers in	4
Transfers out	15

Tuition and Fees

	Resident	Nonresident
Full-time	$32,540	$32,540
Part-time		
Tuition Guarantee Program	N	

Living Expenses

Estimated living expenses for singles

Living on campus	Living off campus	Living at home
$16,740	$16,740	$16,740

ABA
Approved
Since
1938

GPA and LSAT Scores

	Total	Full-Time	Part-Time
# of apps	1,092	1,092	0
# of offers	538	538	0
# of matrics	141	141	0
75% GPA	3.42	3.42	0.00
Median GPA	3.15	3.15	0.00
25% GPA	2.86	2.86	0.00
75% LSAT	157	157	0
Median LSAT	155	155	0
25% LSAT	152	152	0

Grants and Scholarships (from prior year)

	Total #	Total %	Full-Time #	Full-Time %	Part-Time #	Part-Time %
Total # of students	429		424		5	
Total # receiving grants	268	62.5	268	63.2	0	0.0
Less than 1/2 tuition	198	46.2	198	46.7	0	0.0
Half to full tuition	70	16.3	70	16.5	0	0.0
Full tuition	0	0.0	0	0.0	0	0.0
More than full tuition	0	0.0	0	0.0	0	0.0
Median grant amount			$11,000		$0	

Informational and Library Resources

Total amount spent on library materials	$641,597
Study seating capacity inside the library	498
# of full-time equivalent professional librarians	3
Hours per week library is open	168
# of open, wired connections available to students	113
# of networked computers available for use by students	32
Has wireless network?	Y
Requires computer?	N

JD Attrition (from prior year)

	Academic #	Other #	Total #	Total %
1st year	12	24	36	22.2
2nd year	3	5	8	6.0
3rd year	2	0	2	1.5
4th year	0	0	0	0.0

Employment (9 months after graduation)

For up-to-date employment data, go to
employmentsummary.abaquestionnaire.org on the ABA website.

Bar Passage Rates

First-time takers	133	Reporting %	79.70
Average school %	70.75	Average state %	74.47

Average pass difference −3.72

Jurisdiction	Takers	Passers	Pass %	State %	Diff %
Oregon	86	65	75.58	75.22	0.36
Washington	20	10	50.00	71.22	−21.22

WILLAMETTE UNIVERSITY COLLEGE OF LAW

Truman Wesley Collins Legal Center, 245 Winter Street SE
Salem, OR 97301
Phone: 503.370.6282; Fax: 503.370.6087
E-mail: law-admission@willamette.edu; Website: www.willamette.edu/wucl

Faculty

A law school faculty serves as both the brain and heart of the institution. Willamette's diverse law faculty includes some of the most respected legal minds in the country, including former federal judicial clerks, officers of the American Society of Comparative Law, First Amendment specialists, and Fulbright scholars, as well as two former justices of the Oregon Supreme Court and the current chief justice.

These scholars and master teachers are nationally recognized for their research, publications, and contributions to the law, particularly in the areas of constitutional law, commercial and business law, international and comparative law, environmental law, and dispute resolution. Yet it is their authentic, deep dedication—both as educators and as mentors—that distinguishes them from others.

Introduction

Established in 1883, Willamette University College of Law offers a learning environment that is distinctive among law schools. Located across the street from the state capitol complex and the Oregon Supreme Court, the college is situated in the epicenter of state law, government, and business.

The College of Law emphasizes small enrollment, excellence in teaching, and a high level of faculty-student interaction. We also boast a student-to-faculty ratio of 15:1. Our select enrollment of fewer than 430 students creates an intellectual intimacy unmatched by most law schools in the United States. As a community, we are committed to the advancement of knowledge through research and scholarship, to diversity, and to public service. Willamette law students should expect to be challenged, to defend their opinions, to think and rethink their ideas, and to leave with a heightened respect for themselves and confidence in what they can achieve.

Academic Programs

Willamette offers a traditional three-year, full-time Doctor of Jurisprudence program (JD), as well as a part-time day program. Both programs require the completion of 90 credit hours for graduation.

The College of Law also offers a four-year, joint-degree program that leads to the JD and MBA for Business, Government, and Not-for-Profit Management. Managed in concert with Willamette's Atkinson Graduate School of Management, the joint-degree program saves students one additional year of study. Students must apply separately for admission to each degree program and may begin the program either in the College of Law or in the Atkinson School. Students may apply prior to matriculating to Willamette or while in their first year of either the JD or MBA program.

Willamette's nationally recognized certificate programs further solidify the strong educational foundation provided at the College of Law. These specialized programs prepare students for exceptional legal careers and further distinguish them from other law school graduates. The five certificate programs are International and Comparative Law, Business

Law, Law and Government, Dispute Resolution, and Sustainability Law.

Willamette's College of Law also offers the LLM in Transnational Law and Dispute Resolution*, both advanced degrees available to those who have completed the JD at an ABA-accredited American law school or its equivalent from a foreign law school.

*Subject to formal acquiescence by the ABA.

Facility

The College of Law is housed in the award-winning Truman Wesley Collins Legal Center on the beautifully landscaped 80-acre campus of the university. The school offers all the cutting-edge amenities a student would expect from a top law school. Bright, modern classrooms provide comfortable, professional environments for learning and include a state-of-the-art wireless network.

The J.W. Long Law Library anchors the north end of the Collins Legal Center. Its many databases and more than 300,000 print volumes and microform volume equivalents include state and federal primary law sources, as well as the leading treatises, periodicals, and other secondary sources. Through a library consortium, an online shared catalog gives Willamette students access to a remarkably vast array of resources. The library, a selective federal government depository, houses special collections in public international law, tax law, and labor law. Both the Collins Legal Center and the law library are accessible to law students 24 hours a day, 7 days a week.

International Study Programs

Willamette's College of Law students have the opportunity to deepen their international experience by participating in study-abroad programs in Germany, Ecuador, and China. The summer China program acquaints students with Chinese law and Pacific Rim legal issues. It is based in Shanghai at the East China University of Political Science and Law. The Ecuador program provides students with an intensive semester immersion in the fundamentals of a civil law system and Latin American legal institutions. Students take courses at the Pontifical Catholic University of Ecuador in Quito. Proficiency in Spanish is required. The semester-long Germany program is held at the Bucerius Law School in Hamburg, the first private institution for legal study in Germany.

Academic Centers and Other Resources

The Clinical Law Program at Willamette University provides students with hands-on, professional experience in the actual practice of law. The Clinical Law Program comprises six advanced legal education courses, including specialized clinics in business law, trusts and estates, sustainability law, child and family advocacy, law and government, and international human rights. Clients are primarily nonprofit corporations and people of modest economic means.

The nationally recognized Center for Dispute Resolution produces research on conflict theory and problem solving. The center teaches the theory and practice of negotiation, mediation, arbitration, and other methods of resolving disputes. It also administers the Certificate Program in Dispute Resolution.

The Willamette Center for Law and Government provides an impartial forum for the study, discussion, and improvement of government and public policy. It also administers the Certificate Program in Law and Government.

The Oregon Law Commission, which is housed at Willamette's College of Law, was established by legislative statute to provide academic and practical support for ongoing law revision, reform, and improvement. The commission is led by a member of the College of Law faculty.

The Externship Program immerses students in the fast-paced work of the practicing lawyer. Students participate in legal work in many different contexts, under the constraints of a real-life practice in the wider legal community. The program provides an experiential learning environment that helps students develop their skills and values as novice lawyers.

Admission

Applicants are urged to apply in the fall prior to the year they intend to enter the law school. Willamette enrolls a diverse first-year law class with a wide range of goals, experiences, and cultural, ethnic, and social backgrounds, and that show evidence of previous academic success. Applications are reviewed closely, and in their entirety, to ensure an informed and fair decision. Although March 1 is the priority deadline for applications, students begin receiving admission decisions from Willamette in January.

Scholarships

The fiscal stability of Willamette University enables the College of Law to offer a strong program of financial aid to its students. Generous merit-based scholarships reward applicants whose accomplishments suggest continuing success in law school. Scholarships are renewable with a 2.90 cumulative-law GPA. Every student is automatically considered for a scholarship when the application for admission is initially reviewed. All

applicants to the College of Law should also complete and submit the Free Application for Federal Student Aid (FAFSA) prior to March 1. Federal and private loan monies also may be available.

Career Services

The Career and Professional Development Center (CPDC) provides comprehensive programs and individual coaching to assist law students and alumni in achieving their career goals. The CPDC oversees several professional development programs for students, including externships, pro bono honors, and attorney-student mentor match, as well as the traditional on-campus interviewing and job-search skills workshops.

Location

Willamette University is situated in the heart of Salem, Oregon's capital. Salem is home to a large, active legal community that readily employs and actively mentors Willamette law students. With 150,000 residents, Salem is neither a small college town nor a big city. This historic riverfront city offers all the amenities of a larger city, but has successfully maintained its hometown charm. A welcoming and affordable city, Salem boasts a vibrant downtown area, beautiful city parks, an innovative children's museum, a popular community theater, great pubs and cafés, fine dining, numerous coffeehouses and microbreweries, and a wide range of small boutiques and department stores.

Salem is surrounded by award-winning vineyards and orchards that support countless wine and food festivals. The city is only a short drive from numerous beautiful state parks that provide wilderness hiking, fishing, camping, and winter sports. The desert is a little farther east, and Oregon's spectacular coast is an hour's drive to the west. Metropolitan Portland is just 45 minutes to the north, offering easy access to national sporting events and premier music and art venues.

APPLICANT PROFILE

Willamette University College of Law
This grid includes only applicants with 120–180 LSAT scores earned under standard administrations.

LSAT Score	3.75 +		3.50–3.74		3.25–3.49		3.00–3.24		2.75–2.99		2.50–2.74		2.25–2.49		2.00–2.24		Below 2.00		No GPA		Total	
	Apps	Adm	Apps	Adm	Apps	Adm	Apps	Adm	Apps	Adm	Apps	Adm	Apps	Adm	Apps	Adm	Apps	Adm	Apps	Adm	Apps	Adm
175–180	0	0	0	0	0	0	1	1	0	0	0	0	0	0	0	0	0	0	0	0	1	1
170–174	0	0	2	2	0	0	0	0	1	1	1	1	1	1	0	0	0	0	0	0	6	5
165–169	4	4	4	4	6	6	4	4	4	3	3	2	0	0	0	0	0	0	0	0	25	23
160–164	15	14	40	40	24	22	22	19	14	11	6	4	5	2	2	0	0	0	3	3	131	115
155–159	28	26	65	58	75	70	58	47	39	29	19	12	10	4	4	4	1	1	3	3	302	254
150–154	18	9	58	26	79	36	78	37	47	17	35	7	12	3	4	2	0	0	4	1	335	138
145–149	3	0	38	0	46	0	34	0	33	0	14	1	7	0	2	0	0	0	0	0	177	1
140–144	4	0	8	0	10	0	18	0	11	0	10	0	9	0	1	0	0	0	2	0	73	0
135–139	0	0	2	0	3	0	5	0	5	0	1	0	4	0	3	0	0	0	0	0	23	0
130–134	1	0	1	0	2	0	2	0	3	0	4	0	0	0	0	0	1	0	2	0	16	0
125–129	0	0	0	0	0	0	0	0	0	0	1	0	0	0	1	0	0	0	0	0	2	0
120–124	0	0	0	0	0	0	0	0	0	0	0	0	0	0	0	0	0	0	0	0	0	0
Total	73	53	218	130	245	134	222	108	157	61	94	27	48	10	18	6	2	1	14	7	1091	537

Apps = Number of Applicants
Adm = Number Admitted
Reflects 100% of the total applicant pool; highest LSAT data reported.

WILLIAM & MARY LAW SCHOOL

613 South Henry Street
Williamsburg, VA 23185
Phone: 757.221.3785; Fax: 757.221.3261
E-mail: lawadm@wm.edu; Website: http://law.wm.edu

ABA
Approved
Since
1932

The Basics

Type of school	Public
Term	Semester
Application deadline	3/1
Application fee	$50
Financial aid deadline	2/15
Can first year start other than fall?	No
Student to faculty ratio	13.8 to 1
# of housing spaces available restricted to law students graduate housing for which law students are eligible	117

Faculty and Administrators

	Total Spr	Total Fall	Men Spr	Men Fall	Women Spr	Women Fall	Minorities Spr	Minorities Fall
Full-time	37	39	22	25	15	14	6	4
Other full-time	0	0	0	0	0	0	0	0
Deans, librarians, & others who teach	11	11	8	7	3	4	0	0
Part-time	59	49	40	37	19	12	3	4
Total	107	99	70	69	37	30	9	8

JD Enrollment and Ethnicity

	Men #	Men %	Women #	Women %	Full-Time #	Full-Time %	Part-Time #	Part-Time %	1st-Year #	1st-Year %	Total #	Total %	JD Degs. Awd.
All Hispanics	7	2.2	8	2.5	15	2.4	0	0.0	9	4.1	15	2.4	2
Am. Ind./AK Nat.	0	0.0	1	0.3	1	0.2	0	0.0	0	0.0	1	0.2	0
Asian	12	3.8	14	4.4	26	4.1	0	0.0	8	3.7	26	4.1	6
Black/Af. Am.	34	10.7	37	11.6	71	11.1	0	0.0	17	7.8	71	11.1	26
Nat. HI/Pac. Isl.	0	0.0	0	0.0	0	0.0	0	0.0	0	0.0	0	0.0	0
2 or more races	2	0.6	10	3.1	12	1.9	0	0.0	6	2.8	12	1.9	0
Subtotal (minor.)	55	17.4	70	21.9	125	19.6	0	0.0	40	18.4	125	19.6	34
Nonres. Alien	2	0.6	3	0.9	5	0.8	0	0.0	2	0.9	5	0.8	0
White/Cauc.	211	66.6	208	65.0	419	65.8	0	0.0	143	65.9	419	65.8	139
Unknown	49	15.5	39	12.2	88	13.8	0	0.0	32	14.7	88	13.8	31
Total	317	49.8	320	50.2	637	100.0	0	0.0	217	34.1	637		204

Curriculum

	Full-Time	Part-Time
Typical first-year section size	75	0
Is there typically a "small section" of the first-year class, other than Legal Writing, taught by full-time faculty	Yes	No
If yes, typical size offered last year	16	
# of classroom course titles beyond first-year curriculum	128	

# of upper division courses, excluding seminars, with an enrollment:		
Under 25	114	
25–49	41	
50–74	10	
75–99	2	
100+	2	

# of seminars	35	
# of seminar positions available	548	
# of seminar positions filled	468	0
# of positions available in simulation courses	639	
# of simulation positions filled	569	0
# of positions available in faculty supervised clinical courses	46	
# of faculty supervised clinical positions filled	43	0
# involved in field placements	169	0
# involved in law journals	322	0
# involved in moot court or trial competitions	161	0
# of credit hours required to graduate	86	

Transfers

Transfers in	11
Transfers out	3

Tuition and Fees

	Resident	Nonresident
Full-time	$26,200	$36,200
Part-time		
Tuition Guarantee Program	N	

Living Expenses

Estimated living expenses for singles

Living on campus	Living off campus	Living at home
$15,800	$15,800	$15,800

WILLIAM & MARY LAW SCHOOL

ABA Approved Since 1932

GPA and LSAT Scores

	Total	Full-Time	Part-Time
# of apps	5,937	5,937	0
# of offers	1,306	1,306	0
# of matrics	217	217	0
75% GPA	3.82	3.82	0.00
Median GPA	3.73	3.73	0.00
25% GPA	3.46	3.46	0.00
75% LSAT	167	167	0
Median LSAT	165	165	0
25% LSAT	161	161	0

Grants and Scholarships (from prior year)

	Total #	Total %	Full-Time #	Full-Time %	Part-Time #	Part-Time %
Total # of students	628		628		0	
Total # receiving grants	237	37.7	237	37.7	0	0.0
Less than 1/2 tuition	229	36.5	229	36.5	0	0.0
Half to full tuition	8	1.3	8	1.3	0	0.0
Full tuition	0	0.0	0	0.0	0	0.0
More than full tuition	0	0.0	0	0.0	0	0.0
Median grant amount			$8,000		$0	

Informational and Library Resources

Total amount spent on library materials	$1,001,558
Study seating capacity inside the library	568
# of full-time equivalent professional librarians	8
Hours per week library is open	168
# of open, wired connections available to students	41
# of networked computers available for use by students	0
Has wireless network?	Y
Requires computer?	N

JD Attrition (from prior year)

	Academic #	Other #	Total #	Total %
1st year	0	1	1	0.5
2nd year	0	8	8	3.8
3rd year	0	1	1	0.5
4th year	0	0	0	0.0

Employment (9 months after graduation)

For up-to-date employment data, go to employmentsummary.abaquestionnaire.org on the ABA website.

Bar Passage Rates

First-time takers	207	Reporting %	96.62	
Average school %	93.50	Average state %	79.65	
Average pass difference	13.85			

Jurisdiction	Takers	Passers	Pass %	State %	Diff %
Virginia	120	110	91.67	78.15	13.52
New York	13	11	84.62	84.92	−0.30
New Jersey	10	10	100.00	82.34	17.66
Pennsylvania	9	9	100.00	83.06	16.94
Others (12)	48	47	97.92		

WILLIAM & MARY LAW SCHOOL

613 South Henry Street
Williamsburg, VA 23185
Phone: 757.221.3785; Fax: 757.221.3261
E-mail: lawadm@wm.edu; Website: http://law.wm.edu

Introduction

Established in 1779 at the request of Thomas Jefferson, William & Mary Law School is the nation's oldest law school and one of its most intellectually rigorous. William & Mary combines rich historic roots, a strong national reputation, and a wealth of programs at a cost rated to be "a very good buy." William & Mary Law School advances not only its students' intellectual development, but also provides programs and training that will enable its students to use the law for the betterment of society. Many assume William & Mary is a private school, but it is not. The Law School is small enough to form a cohesive community where people know one another by name, but it is large enough to offer a wide range of programs and learning opportunities in both traditional and cutting-edge legal disciplines.

Members of the 2011–2012 student body earned undergraduate degrees from 279 colleges and universities and represent 45 states; Washington, DC; and 8 other countries. The Law School is located a few blocks from Colonial Williamsburg and within short driving distance of the metropolitan areas of Washington, DC; Richmond; and Norfolk. Visits are encouraged and may include student tours, class observations, and individual meetings with an admission dean.

Curriculum

The required first-year curriculum includes constitutional law, contracts, torts, civil procedure, property, criminal law, and legal skills. William & Mary's innovative Legal Skills program utilizes simulated law offices and client representation to teach the skills necessary for the practice of law. The Legal Skills program features a dedicated cadre of legal writing instructors who hone students' research and writing skills, and distinguished practitioners who teach students the core skills needed to become superior lawyers. The rigorous first-year Legal Skills program is augmented in the second year by a skills-track course in civil litigation, criminal litigation, and transactional work.

To earn a Juris Doctor degree, students must successfully complete 86 credit hours through full-time study, all required courses, and a significant paper of publishable quality. Students may choose yearly from more than 100 upper-level courses covering a broad range of contemporary and traditional areas of law. The Law School offers seven clinical programs (domestic violence, elder law, federal tax, legal aid, Innocence Project, special education advocacy, and veterans benefits). Students also may earn academic credit by externing with judges, prosecutors, public defenders, law firms, government agencies, legislators, civil legal service providers, corporations, and private nonprofit organizations.

Joint-Degree Programs

William & Mary offers three joint-degree programs: JD/MBA, JD/MPP, and JD/MA in American Studies. The JD/MBA and the JD/MPP combine traditional five-year programs into four years of study. Students may complete the JD/MA in either three or four years.

International Programs and Study-Abroad Opportunities

William & Mary offers a summer session in Madrid, Spain, where students can earn up to six credits in a five-week program. William & Mary professors and prominent Spanish professors and practitioners teach the courses in English. JD students may also study abroad during their third academic year in Beijing, China; Vienna, Austria; Madrid, Spain; Auckland, New Zealand; Tokyo, Japan; Luxembourg; and Hong Kong.

Additionally, the Law School offers an LLM in the American legal system for students with law degrees from outside the United States. The LLM students take courses with JD students and enrich the classroom experience with the inclusion of their unique legal traditions.

William & Mary is privileged to have an impressive core group of professors who specialize in international law as well as two robust international law programs. The Human Security Law Center offers students the opportunity to learn about the interplay between national defense and the protection of civil rights, while the Program in Comparative Legal Studies and Post-Conflict Peacebuilding serves as a focal point for research and study on comparative legal practices and the mechanisms used to reestablish justice after war and internal strife.

Special Programs and Facilities

The McGlothlin Courtroom at the Law School is the nation's most technologically advanced trial and appellate chamber. The courtroom is designed to permit trials with multiple remote appearances and web-based evidence, and it offers students hands-on training in the use of state-of-the-art courtroom technology. The Courtroom has a wide variety of features, including all available major court record systems, evidence presentation technologies, assistive and foreign language interpretation technologies, and critical infrastructure technologies. The Law School also features the Center for Legal and Court Technology, which puts the latest technology to the test in laboratory trials conducted by students in the McGlothlin Courtroom. The Center for Legal and Court Technology aims to improve the administration of justice through the use of technology.

Through the acclaimed Institute of Bill of Rights Law, the Law School has become one of the preeminent institutions studying the Constitution's Bill of Rights. The Institute sponsors lectures, symposia, and publications through which nationally known scholars explore important constitutional issues.

The Law School's Property Rights Project facilitates the exchange of ideas between scholars and practitioners by encouraging scholarship on the role of property rights in society. This year's Property Rights Conference was held in Beijing, China, and it brought together distinguished property scholars in both the United States and China.

Other important programs at the Law School include the Election Law Program, which provides assistance to judges who are called upon to resolve difficult election law disputes, and the George Wythe Society of Citizen Lawyers, a program focusing on constructive citizenship.

The Loan Repayment Assistance Program provides up to $5,000 in loan forgiveness annually for a maximum of three years to selected graduates working full time for civil legal service organizations, public defenders or prosecutors, government agencies, or other 501(c)(3) organizations with a public service mission.

Student Activities

Scholars and practitioners frequently cite articles from our five student-managed academic journals, the flagship *William & Mary Law Review*, the *William & Mary Bill of Rights Journal*, the *William & Mary Business Law Review*, the *William & Mary Environmental Law and Policy Review*, and the *William & Mary Journal of Women and the Law*.

The Law School has a highly successful Moot Court Program and National Trial Team, each team winning numerous competitions in recent years. William & Mary's Moot Court team, which competes domestically and overseas, won six tournaments last year and is currently among one of the most accomplished moot court teams in the country. The National Trial Team and Alternative Dispute Resolution Team also regularly win competitions. Additionally, William & Mary students frequently win national legal writing competitions.

As impressive as they are, law reviews and competitive teams constitute only a portion of William and Mary's vibrant student life. More than 40 student organizations reflect the diverse interests of the student body. For more information about William & Mary's student organizations, visit the Student Life section of the website.

Career Services

The Office of Career Services (OCS) is dedicated to helping students and graduates secure meaningful employment. The mission statement of the Office of Career Services charges the Office with advancing the following goals:

- partner with students and alumni to help them explore career options, learn about and obtain employment opportunities, further long-term professional development, and achieve career satisfaction;
- maintain comprehensive career and professional development resources to prepare students and alumni to be competitive candidates;
- foster professionalism, ethics, and integrity in the career-development and job-search process so students will continue to demonstrate those traits as citizen-lawyers; and
- cultivate constructive, mutually beneficial relationships with employers.

To accomplish these priorities, each student is assigned a designated career advisor. OCS also organizes dozens of workshops, programs, and guest speakers annually; arranges on-campus, Skype, and videoconference interviews and off-campus interview programs; provides access to a proprietary database of employment opportunities; and helps students develop professional relationships with alumni, practitioners, and judges.

To assist students working in government and public service internships, the Law School offers a robust summer fellowship program. For summer of 2012, the Law School awarded fellowships to 105 students to work in 17 states, the District of Columbia, Argentina, Azerbaijan, Cambodia, China, Nepal, and South Africa.

APPLICANT PROFILE

William & Mary Law School
This grid includes only applicants who earned 120–180 LSAT scores under standard administrations.

LSAT Score	GPA 3.75 + Apps	Adm	3.50–3.74 Apps	Adm	3.25–3.49 Apps	Adm	3.00–3.24 Apps	Adm	2.75–2.99 Apps	Adm	2.50–2.74 Apps	Adm	2.25–2.49 Apps	Adm	2.00–2.24 Apps	Adm	Below 2.00 Apps	Adm	No GPA Apps	Adm	Total Apps	Adm
175–180	7	7	8	6	7	5	9	5	5	1	3	0	0	0	4	0	0	0	1	1	44	25
170–174	99	97	85	72	73	42	45	9	25	3	9	0	7	0	0	0	0	0	12	2	355	225
165–169	358	335	483	279	311	91	168	21	75	4	34	4	20	1	3	0	2	0	46	6	1500	741
160–164	575	158	713	52	521	14	328	14	103	3	66	3	19	0	12	0	0	0	65	1	2402	245
155–159	167	25	222	12	170	6	102	4	47	0	25	0	9	0	6	1	1	0	16	0	765	48
150–154	64	10	104	3	101	3	82	2	57	1	20	0	6	0	7	0	2	0	12	0	455	19
145–149	27	1	37	0	45	0	43	0	35	0	24	1	8	0	2	0	1	0	4	0	226	2
140–144	8	0	16	0	28	0	23	0	14	0	5	0	4	0	6	0	2	0	4	0	110	0
135–139	2	0	7	0	6	0	7	0	8	0	4	0	4	0	2	0	0	0	3	0	43	0
130–134	0	0	0	0	2	0	4	0	2	0	5	0	1	0	1	0	0	0	0	0	15	0
125–129	0	0	0	0	1	0	0	0	0	0	0	0	1	0	0	0	0	0	0	0	2	0
120–124	0	0	0	0	0	0	0	0	0	0	0	0	0	0	0	0	0	0	0	0	0	0
Total	1307	633	1675	424	1265	161	811	55	371	12	195	8	79	1	43	1	8	0	163	10	5917	1305

Apps = Number of Applicants
Adm = Number Admitted
Reflects 99% of the total applicant pool; highest LSAT data reported.

WILLIAM MITCHELL COLLEGE OF LAW

Office of Admissions, 875 Summit Avenue
St. Paul, MN 55105
Phone: 651.290.6476; Toll-free: 888.WMCL.LAW; Fax: 651.290.7535
E-mail: admissions@wmitchell.edu; Website: www.wmitchell.edu

ABA
Approved
Since
1938

The Basics

Type of school	Private
Term	Semester
Application deadline	5/1
Application fee	$0
Financial aid deadline	4/15
Can first year start other than fall?	No
Student to faculty ratio	19.2 to 1
# of housing spaces available restricted to law students	
graduate housing for which law students are eligible	

Faculty and Administrators

	Total Spr	Total Fall	Men Spr	Men Fall	Women Spr	Women Fall	Minorities Spr	Minorities Fall
Full-time	35	39	17	21	18	18	5	6
Other full-time	2	2	1	1	1	1	0	0
Deans, librarians, & others who teach	11	11	4	4	7	7	1	1
Part-time	230	212	119	116	111	96	25	29
Total	278	264	141	142	137	122	31	36

Curriculum

	Full-Time	Part-Time
Typical first-year section size	80	70
Is there typically a "small section" of the first-year class, other than Legal Writing, taught by full-time faculty	No	No
If yes, typical size offered last year		
# of classroom course titles beyond first-year curriculum	126	
# of upper division courses, excluding seminars, with an enrollment: Under 25	80	
25–49	36	
50–74	10	
75–99	6	
100+	0	
# of seminars	86	
# of seminar positions available	1,793	
# of seminar positions filled	653	608
# of positions available in simulation courses	1,915	
# of simulation positions filled	988	474
# of positions available in faculty supervised clinical courses	565	
# of faculty supervised clinical positions filled	215	178
# involved in field placements	156	94
# involved in law journals	109	62
# involved in moot court or trial competitions	81	60
# of credit hours required to graduate	86	

JD Enrollment and Ethnicity

	Men #	Men %	Women #	Women %	Full-Time #	Full-Time %	Part-Time #	Part-Time %	1st-Year #	1st-Year %	Total #	Total %	JD Degs. Awd.
All Hispanics	13	2.5	15	3.1	18	2.6	10	3.3	8	2.6	28	2.8	1
Am. Ind./AK Nat.	4	0.8	3	0.6	4	0.6	3	1.0	3	1.0	7	0.7	7
Asian	16	3.1	21	4.3	25	3.6	12	3.9	17	5.5	37	3.7	9
Black/Af. Am.	8	1.6	15	3.1	17	2.4	6	2.0	9	2.9	23	2.3	10
Nat. HI/Pac. Isl.	4	0.8	14	2.9	11	1.6	7	2.3	0	0.0	18	1.8	0
2 or more races	5	1.0	13	2.7	16	2.3	2	0.7	12	3.9	18	1.8	1
Subtotal (minor.)	50	9.7	81	16.6	91	13.0	40	13.1	49	16.0	131	13.0	28
Nonres. Alien	4	0.8	5	1.0	6	0.9	3	1.0	5	1.6	9	0.9	2
White/Cauc.	384	74.6	341	69.7	503	72.1	222	72.5	225	73.3	725	72.2	196
Unknown	77	15.0	62	12.7	98	14.0	41	13.4	28	9.1	139	13.8	54
Total	515	51.3	489	48.7	698	69.5	306	30.5	307	30.6	1004		280

Transfers

Transfers in	7
Transfers out	14

Tuition and Fees

	Resident	Nonresident
Full-time	$35,710	$35,710
Part-time	$25,840	$25,840
Tuition Guarantee Program	N	

Living Expenses

Estimated living expenses for singles

Living on campus	Living off campus	Living at home
N/A	$18,074	N/A

WILLIAM MITCHELL COLLEGE OF LAW

ABA
Approved
Since
1938

GPA and LSAT Scores

	Total	Full-Time	Part-Time
# of apps	1,536	1,196	340
# of offers	935	834	101
# of matrics	309	260	49
75% GPA	3.62	3.62	3.53
Median GPA	3.39	3.41	3.20
25% GPA	3.16	3.21	2.92
75% LSAT	159	159	158
Median LSAT	155	155	152
25% LSAT	150	151	148

Grants and Scholarships (from prior year)

	Total		Full-Time		Part-Time	
	#	%	#	%	#	%
Total # of students	1,013		667		346	
Total # receiving grants	461	45.5	349	52.3	112	32.4
Less than 1/2 tuition	161	15.9	104	15.6	57	16.5
Half to full tuition	264	26.1	225	33.7	39	11.3
Full tuition	36	3.6	20	3.0	16	4.6
More than full tuition	0	0.0	0	0.0	0	0.0
Median grant amount			$21,970		$11,994	

Informational and Library Resources

Total amount spent on library materials	$1,080,341
Study seating capacity inside the library	689
# of full-time equivalent professional librarians	8
Hours per week library is open	109
# of open, wired connections available to students	80
# of networked computers available for use by students	70
Has wireless network?	Y
Requires computer?	N

JD Attrition (from prior year)

	Academic	Other	Total	
	#	#	#	%
1st year	8	26	34	9.6
2nd year	0	5	5	1.8
3rd year	0	0	0	0.0
4th year	0	0	0	0.0

Employment (9 months after graduation)

For up-to-date employment data, go to employmentsummary.abaquestionnaire.org on the ABA website.

Bar Passage Rates

First-time takers	289	Reporting %	87.54
Average school %	91.30	Average state %	92.21
Average pass difference	−0.91		

Jurisdiction	Takers	Passers	Pass %	State %	Diff %
Minnesota	253	231	91.30	92.21	−0.91

The information on these pages was provided by the law school.

WILLIAM MITCHELL COLLEGE OF LAW

Office of Admissions, 875 Summit Avenue
St. Paul, MN 55105
Phone: 651.290.6476; Toll-free: 888.WMCL.LAW; Fax: 651.290.7535
E-mail: admissions@wmitchell.edu; Website: www.wmitchell.edu

Introduction

William Mitchell College of Law, founded in 1900, is an independent, private law school in St. Paul, Minnesota. Named for one of the state's most respected judges, William Mitchell has pioneered a legal education that integrates practical skills with legal theory. William Mitchell welcomes both traditional and nontraditional law students from all walks of life, and students have an option of attending on a full- or part-time basis. William Mitchell College of Law's clinical, legal writing, and trial advocacy programs are nationally recognized. The college has produced many distinguished leaders at the bench and bar and in the business and civic arenas, among them the 15th Chief Justice of the United States, Warren E. Burger, and the first woman to serve on the Minnesota Supreme Court, Rosalie E. Wahl. The largest law school in Minnesota, William Mitchell has approximately 1,000 students, 41 full-time faculty members, and more than 11,000 alumni. William Mitchell has more alumni serving in the Minnesota judiciary than any other law school.

The college is accredited by the ABA, is a member of the AALS, and is approved by the US Department of Veterans Affairs.

Faculty

From day one, William Mitchell faculty members treat students as future colleagues. Faculty members are known for their teaching, scholarship, and practice. Faculty members have served on the bench, worked in the region's top law firms, and have had careers in public service, government, and corporations. William Mitchell professors have written many of the books used by law school professors and legal practitioners throughout the country. Faculty briefs and research have been accessed thousands of times by legal scholars, and professors are regularly quoted by national and international media. Many professors are exploring new ground on issues such as cyber law, intellectual property, national security, elder law, family law, and food safety. Adjunct professors, who practice at 18 of the top 25 law firms in the state, bring real-world practice to the classroom and connection to the practice of law.

Academics

William Mitchell students graduate with the practical wisdom to put the law to work. For 111 years, William Mitchell has pioneered a legal education that integrates practical skills with legal theory. William Mitchell requires students to take practical skills courses, including clinics, practicum, legal writing and research, and advocacy. In fact, William Mitchell was one of the first schools to develop a clinical program more than 30 years ago. Our clinical, legal writing, and trial advocacy programs are consistently highly rated on a national level.

In addition to more than 200 law school courses, William Mitchell has several programs designed to help law students transition to lawyers. Keystone courses, generally taken in the final year of law school, address real-world challenges, build on previous courses, and enable students to produce substantial, concrete manifestations of their learning. The Fellows Program links exceptional students with a faculty member whose research and activities are changing the law itself. Students receive specialized training beyond the regular curriculum and have access to a range of special intellectual opportunities and networking events. And, Pathways to the Profession of Law is an innovative web application that helps law students customize their course schedules, integrate their learning, and build experiences toward legal practice.

To focus faculty scholarship, spur collaboration between legal education and the profession, and continue its tradition of innovative teaching, William Mitchell has developed academic centers in critical areas of the legal profession, including the Intellectual Property Institute, Center for Negotiation and Justice, Center for Elder Justice and Policy, Rosalie Wahl Legal Practice Center, Public Health Law Center, National Security Forum, Center for Law and Business, and Indian Law Program.

Enrollment Options

William Mitchell was started as a night law school by working attorneys more than a century ago to provide legal training for people of modest means. If not for the part-time, evening tradition at William Mitchell, many successful lawyers practicing today would not have been able to pursue their law school dreams. William Mitchell is the only law school in the region with an evening option, allowing students to continue to work to help pay for school, gain work experience, and balance family life. After the first year, students have the option to switch between full- and part-time enrollment as often as each semester to accommodate work schedules and family life. Regardless of enrollment status, students achieve the same high-quality education. Advanced and elective classes are typically offered in the evening, so part-time and full-time students take classes together and have equal access to full-time and adjunct faculty. Although classes meet at set times, William Mitchell offers you enough flexibility to build your law school schedule around a clerkship, continue in your current career track or day job, or take care of other responsibilities.

Library and Physical Facilities

The Minneapolis-St. Paul region is home to more than 20 Fortune 500 companies and is frequently cited as one of the top 10 places to live and work in the United States. William Mitchell's campus is located in St. Paul, the state capital, along historic and elegant Summit Avenue. The campus is a short walk to lively Grand Avenue, with restaurants and shopping, and many students find housing in the neighborhood.

The physical design of the campus as a whole mirrors the William Mitchell philosophy that practical skills are inseparable from legal doctrine. Our Rosalie Wahl Legal Practice Center, home to our top-rated clinical and skills programs, is located in the same building as classrooms and faculty offices. The campus is also equipped with technologically advanced moot courtrooms, computer labs, seminar rooms, a student lounge and cafeteria, and offices for student organizations.

The Warren E. Burger Library's extensive in-house and online collection, customer service-oriented staff, and welcoming design make it the preferred choice for alumni, legal professionals, and faculty. Nearly all of our professional librarians have JD degrees, in addition to master's of library and information science degrees. Several have law practice experience. Our librarians help plan research strategies, locate and use legal and nonlegal resources, do computer-assisted research, and find items that are not available at William Mitchell. You'll also find our librarians in the classroom. Extended reference desk hours reflect our commitment to the needs of our students, faculty, and alumni.

Public Service Opportunities

William Mitchell's heritage is rooted in public service. Students volunteer more than 6,000 hours of supervised pro bono service each year to our partner, the Minnesota Justice Foundation, which matches interested law students with volunteer opportunities. Students also perform approximately 14,000 hours of pro bono service annually through our for-credit clinical program.

Special Programs

In addition to organizing and hosting **Mitchell in London** each year, William Mitchell is a member of the Consortium for Innovative Legal Education, a consortium of four independent law schools, which provides students with the opportunity to enroll in 10 summer and semester study-abroad programs, as well as the opportunity to study as visiting students at any of the participating schools. The **Academic Achievement Program** is designed to help students work up to their potential by teaching the skills required to solve problems effectively. Individual academic advising and Academic Achievement Workshops are available throughout the year for all students. The workshops include study strategies, time and stress management, critical reading, case briefing, legal analysis, outlining, and exam taking. William Mitchell also offers an LLM program for foreign law graduates. The yearlong program introduces students from around the world to the legal system of the United States.

Student Body

William Mitchell attracts students with a diversity of life and work experiences. That's what we call the "Mitchell Mix." Our students have all kinds of educational, professional, and cultural backgrounds. For example, students range in age from as young as 19 to over 60 and include recent college grads and students who bring professional work experience. Twenty-seven of our entering class hold graduate degrees, and more than 16 percent are people of color. Our student body represents 29 states and 19 foreign countries. Students can participate in more than 30 student organizations, including the Student Bar Association and the *William Mitchell Law Review*.

Career Development

William Mitchell's brand of legal education has earned the school a reputation for graduating lawyers who are prepared to practice. That's why 91.3 percent of the class of 2010 was employed within nine months of graduation. Career development is woven into each year of a student's legal education, helping students polish presentation, networking, and interviewing skills. Our alumni network of more than 11,000 offers students extensive opportunities to gather advice, meet attorneys, and learn about job opportunities both during school and upon graduation.

Scholarships/Financial Aid

Financial aid is available from William Mitchell in the form of merit-based scholarships, federal and alternative loans, and federal work-study. Approximately 90 percent of all William Mitchell students receive some type of financial aid.

APPLICANT PROFILE

William Mitchell College of Law
This grid includes only applicants who earned 120–180 LSAT scores under standard administrations.

LSAT Score	GPA 3.75+		3.50–3.74		3.25–3.49		3.00–3.24		2.75–2.99		2.50–2.74		2.25–2.49		2.00–2.24		Below 2.00		No GPA		Total	
	Apps	Adm	Apps	Adm	Apps	Adm	Apps	Adm	Apps	Adm	Apps	Adm	Apps	Adm	Apps	Adm	Apps	Adm	Apps	Adm	Apps	Adm
175–180	0	0	1	1	0	0	0	0	0	0	0	0	0	0	0	0	0	0	0	0	1	1
170–174	3	3	4	4	2	2	0	0	2	2	0	0	0	0	0	0	0	0	0	0	11	11
165–169	15	15	20	19	10	10	5	5	3	3	1	1	0	0	0	0	0	0	3	2	57	55
160–164	36	35	46	45	38	38	17	17	14	14	8	8	4	3	1	0	0	0	0	0	164	160
155–159	37	35	56	51	78	78	50	47	26	24	14	13	5	3	7	4	0	0	1	1	274	256
150–154	38	36	56	53	99	81	92	72	35	24	36	15	7	4	7	2	1	0	12	10	383	297
145–149	10	10	51	46	62	34	54	24	33	5	21	1	15	1	8	1	2	0	11	7	267	129
140–144	7	4	17	14	15	7	20	4	17	3	10	0	6	0	0	0	3	0	2	0	97	32
135–139	2	0	6	2	6	0	8	0	9	0	9	0	2	0	2	0	0	0	4	0	48	2
130–134	0	0	1	0	1	0	4	0	0	0	2	0	2	0	0	0	0	0	1	0	11	0
125–129	0	0	0	0	1	0	2	0	0	0	1	0	0	0	1	0	0	0	1	0	6	0
120–124	0	0	0	0	0	0	0	0	0	0	0	0	0	0	0	0	1	0	1	0	2	0
Total	148	138	258	235	312	250	252	169	139	75	102	38	41	11	27	7	6	0	36	20	1321	943

Apps = Number of Applicants
Adm = Number Admitted
Reflects 99% of the total applicant pool; highest LSAT data reported.

UNIVERSITY OF WISCONSIN LAW SCHOOL

975 Bascom Mall
Madison, WI 53706
Phone: 608.262.5914; Fax: 608.263.3190
E-mail: admissions@law.wisc.edu; Website: www.law.wisc.edu

ABA
Approved
Since
1923

The Basics

Type of school	Public
Term	Semester
Application deadline	3/1
Application fee	$56
Financial aid deadline	3/1
Can first year start other than fall?	No
Student to faculty ratio	11.3 to 1
# of housing spaces available restricted to law students	
graduate housing for which law students are eligible	870

Faculty and Administrators

	Total		Men		Women		Minorities	
	Spr	Fall	Spr	Fall	Spr	Fall	Spr	Fall
Full-time	54	57	28	31	26	26	12	10
Other full-time	12	11	3	4	9	7	1	1
Deans, librarians, & others who teach	6	5	4	3	2	2	0	0
Part-time	145	70	79	37	66	33	7	5
Total	217	143	114	75	103	68	20	16

Curriculum

	Full-Time	Part-Time
Typical first-year section size	52	0
Is there typically a "small section" of the first-year class, other than Legal Writing, taught by full-time faculty	Yes	No
If yes, typical size offered last year	20	

# of classroom course titles beyond first-year curriculum		178
# of upper division courses, excluding seminars, with an enrollment:	Under 25	154
	25–49	37
	50–74	15
	75–99	6
	100+	4
# of seminars		88
# of seminar positions available		1,289

	Full-Time	Part-Time
# of seminar positions filled	995	0
# of positions available in simulation courses	818	
# of simulation positions filled	694	0
# of positions available in faculty supervised clinical courses	443	
# of faculty supervised clinical positions filled	420	0
# involved in field placements	256	0
# involved in law journals	176	0
# involved in moot court or trial competitions	171	0
# of credit hours required to graduate	90	

JD Enrollment and Ethnicity

	Men		Women		Full-Time		Part-Time		1st-Year		Total		JD Degs. Awd.
	#	%	#	%	#	%	#	%	#	%	#	%	
All Hispanics	32	7.2	25	7.2	52	7.0	5	11.4	16	6.4	57	7.2	12
Am. Ind./AK Nat.	11	2.5	3	0.9	14	1.9	0	0.0	5	2.0	14	1.8	9
Asian	19	4.3	21	6.1	36	4.8	4	9.1	9	3.6	40	5.1	14
Black/Af. Am.	18	4.0	33	9.5	48	6.4	3	6.8	12	4.8	51	6.4	16
Nat. HI/Pac. Isl.	2	0.4	0	0.0	2	0.3	0	0.0	2	0.8	2	0.3	0
2 or more races	6	1.3	5	1.4	11	1.5	0	0.0	5	2.0	11	1.4	0
Subtotal (minor.)	88	19.8	87	25.1	163	21.8	12	27.3	49	19.5	175	22.1	51
Nonres. Alien	13	2.9	15	4.3	28	3.7	0	0.0	13	5.2	28	3.5	5
White/Cauc.	316	71.0	236	68.0	522	69.8	30	68.2	177	70.5	552	69.7	191
Unknown	28	6.3	9	2.6	35	4.7	2	4.5	12	4.8	37	4.7	7
Total	445	56.2	347	43.8	748	94.4	44	5.6	251	31.7	792		254

Transfers

Transfers in	24
Transfers out	8

Tuition and Fees

	Resident	Nonresident
Full-time	$19,683	$38,811
Part-time*	$1,645	$3,239
Tuition Guarantee Program		N

Living Expenses

Estimated living expenses for singles

Living on campus	Living off campus	Living at home
$18,030	$18,030	$10,000

*Part-time tuition and fees per credit.

UNIVERSITY OF WISCONSIN LAW SCHOOL

ABA
Approved
Since
1923

GPA and LSAT Scores

	Total	Full-Time	Part-Time
# of apps	2,864	2,864	0
# of offers	755	755	0
# of matrics	242	242	0
75% GPA	3.78	3.78	3.78
Median GPA	3.67	3.67	3.67
25% GPA	3.34	3.34	3.34
75% LSAT	165	165	165
Median LSAT	163	163	163
25% LSAT	158	158	158

Grants and Scholarships (from prior year)

	Total		Full-Time		Part-Time	
	#	%	#	%	#	%
Total # of students	804		755		49	
Total # receiving grants	319	39.7	319	42.3	0	0.0
Less than 1/2 tuition	190	23.6	190	25.2	0	0.0
Half to full tuition	99	12.3	99	13.1	0	0.0
Full tuition	6	0.7	6	0.8	0	0.0
More than full tuition	24	3.0	24	3.2	0	0.0
Median grant amount			$10,000		$0	

Informational and Library Resources

Total amount spent on library materials	$1,227,614
Study seating capacity inside the library	613
# of full-time equivalent professional librarians	11
Hours per week library is open	104
# of open, wired connections available to students	526
# of networked computers available for use by students	74
Has wireless network?	Y
Requires computer?	Y

JD Attrition (from prior year)

	Academic	Other	Total	
	#	#	#	%
1st year	2	14	16	6.1
2nd year	0	1	1	0.4
3rd year	0	0	0	0.0
4th year	0	0	0	0.0

Employment (9 months after graduation)

For up-to-date employment data, go to employmentsummary.abaquestionnaire.org on the ABA website.

Bar Passage Rates

First-time takers	254	Reporting %	100.00
Average school %	99.21	Average state %	92.93
Average pass difference	6.28		

Jurisdiction	Takers	Passers	Pass %	State %	Diff %
Wisconsin	254	252	99.21	92.93	6.28

UNIVERSITY OF WISCONSIN LAW SCHOOL

975 Bascom Mall
Madison, WI 53706
Phone: 608.262.5914; Fax: 608.263.3190
E-mail: admissions@law.wisc.edu; Website: www.law.wisc.edu

A Preeminent Law School, A World-Class University, A Beautiful City

The UW Law School is one of the most intellectually exciting law schools in the country, attracting students from around the world. These students represent a variety of backgrounds, ages, interests, races, nationalities, and life experiences, encouraging a robust exchange of ideas.

Top applicants are drawn to the UW Law School because of its tradition of excellence, its beautiful setting in the heart of one of the world's leading research universities, and its *law-in-action* philosophy, an approach that differentiates it from other law schools.

The UW Law School is located in Madison, an affordable city strategically and conveniently situated in the middle of a triangle formed by Chicago, Minneapolis, and Milwaukee. As the state capital, Madison is home to many courts and state and federal government agencies—all within walking distance of the Law School.

A Commitment to Diversity and Community

A major indicator of the strength of any law school is its student body. The fall 2011 entering class of 242 students represents 30 states and 107 undergraduate institutions. Annually, approximately 43 percent of our students are from outside of Wisconsin, between 40 and 50 percent are women, and more than 25 percent are students of color. The UW Law School's admission policies enhance the diversity, vigor, social awareness, and academic ability of the student body. There is a special feeling of community in the school and an informal, supportive atmosphere, reflecting a strong commitment by faculty and administrators to student learning, morale, and well-being.

The Faculty: Leading Scholars and Outstanding Teachers

The UW Law School's nationally recognized faculty come from a wide range of backgrounds and offer students strong role models and a variety of experiences. They are leading scholars who are also actively involved in the law. They advise on stem cell issues, represent clients on death row, work with congressional staffers to draft legislation, and provide legal advice to poor farmers in the South. They are interesting lawyers doing interesting things, but first and foremost, they are excellent teachers who are committed to their students. A superb clinical faculty and an experienced adjunct faculty provide additional teaching resources and bring practical experience into the classroom.

The Curriculum: Law in Action

Students at the UW Law School have many opportunities to experience law-in-action. An extensive curriculum places an emphasis on the dynamics of the law (how the law relates to social change and to society as a whole) while at the same time emphasizing skill development, particularly legal analysis and writing. The first-year small-section program teaches the fundamentals of legal analysis and reasoning in a supportive setting. Two of a student's first-year classes—a substantive law class and a legal research and writing class—are small sections consisting of 25 or fewer students. These small sections allow students to receive individual feedback, organize study groups, and form lasting friendships.

In the second and third year of law school, there is time both to explore the curriculum and develop the lawyering skills needed to practice. The UW Law School is a national law school that prepares future lawyers to work wherever they choose. Students select courses from an extraordinary breadth and depth of offerings, affording them the opportunity to explore cutting-edge legal issues in the classroom and/or to apply their knowledge in one of the many clinical programs.

Dual-Degree Programs

Renowned for its interdisciplinary approach, the UW Law School offers many opportunities for students to combine the study of law with a graduate degree in another subject. There are many existing dual-degree programs. If one of the existing programs does not meet a student's academic needs, the Law School will help create an individualized curriculum.

Clinical and Skills Training: Hands-on Learning

The UW Law School strongly believes that practical experience is an essential part of legal education. With one of the largest clinical programs in the country, the UW Law School offers a wide variety of hands-on lawyering experiences with real clients and excellent supervision. From representing low-income clients, to teaming up with medical students as advocates for newly diagnosed cancer patients, or assisting inmates in state and federal prisons, these experiences are invaluable opportunities. Judicial internships, externships, and our innovative lawyering skills program provide additional hands-on learning experiences.

Going Global: International Law and Study Abroad

Ten professors devote their scholarship and teaching primarily to international or comparative law, and many others integrate analysis of foreign legal developments into their domestic law courses. The Law School hosts international students and professors, bringing diverse international perspectives to the classroom, and the university has one of the largest groups of international students in the country. Students can also study with one of the ten foreign law faculties with which the Law School has exchange agreements or participate in foreign study programs of other US law schools. Additional international opportunities are available through the Law School's East Asian Legal Studies Center, established to formalize and increase the Law School's interaction in East and Southeast Asia.

Student Activities

More than 30 organizations provide outstanding opportunities for students to pursue their talents and interests. Several moot court competitions at the UW Law School enable students to gain experience with brief writing and oral advocacy, and three student journals—*Wisconsin Law Review, Wisconsin International Law Journal,* and *Wisconsin Journal of Law, Gender, and Society*—give students an opportunity to gain invaluable training in legal research and writing.

Career Opportunities

Leading law firms, government agencies, businesses, and public interest organizations seek to hire UW Law School graduates. A broad range of legal employers from many major cities participate in the on-campus interview program. The Law School also participates in off-campus job fairs each year in cities such as New York; Washington, DC; Chicago; and Minneapolis. Our students receive assistance from many of our more than 12,000 alumni throughout the country, and our graduates typically accept jobs in more than 20 different states.

APPLICANT PROFILE

Admission to the University of Wisconsin Law School is competitive. The most recent entering class had a median LSAT score of 163 and a median GPA of 3.67. The Law School does not provide a profile chart because its admission decisions involve many factors that are not represented by undergraduate GPA and LSAT scores. While candidates with higher grades and scores tend to be admitted at higher rates, GPA and LSAT scores alone are not necessarily good predictors of admission decisions on individual applications.

UNIVERSITY OF WYOMING COLLEGE OF LAW

Dept. 3035, 1000 E. University Avenue
Laramie, WY 82071
Phone: 307.766.6416; Fax: 307.766.6417
E-mail: lawadmis@uwyo.edu; Website: www.uwyo.edu/law

ABA
Approved
Since
1923

The Basics

Type of school	Public
Term	Semester
Application deadline	12/1 3/1
Application fee	$50
Financial aid deadline	3/1
Can first year start other than fall?	No
Student to faculty ratio	11.4 to 1
# of housing spaces available restricted to law students	
graduate housing for which law students are eligible	226

Faculty and Administrators

	Total Spr	Total Fall	Men Spr	Men Fall	Women Spr	Women Fall	Minorities Spr	Minorities Fall
Full-time	17	17	12	12	5	5	2	2
Other full-time	1	0	1	0	0	0	0	0
Deans, librarians, & others who teach	5	5	2	2	3	3	2	2
Part-time	13	10	9	6	4	4	0	0
Total	36	32	24	20	12	12	4	4

JD Enrollment and Ethnicity

	Men #	Men %	Women #	Women %	Full-Time #	Full-Time %	Part-Time #	Part-Time %	1st-Year #	1st-Year %	Total #	Total %	JD Degs. Awd.
All Hispanics	5	4.2	5	4.7	10	4.4	0	0.0	5	7.2	10	4.4	2
Am. Ind./AK Nat.	1	0.8	1	0.9	2	0.9	0	0.0	1	1.4	2	0.9	0
Asian	1	0.8	2	1.9	3	1.3	0	0.0	2	2.9	3	1.3	2
Black/Af. Am.	2	1.7	1	0.9	3	1.3	0	0.0	2	2.9	3	1.3	0
Nat. HI/Pac. Isl.	0	0.0	2	1.9	2	0.9	0	0.0	0	0.0	2	0.9	0
2 or more races	4	3.4	2	1.9	6	2.7	0	0.0	5	7.2	6	2.7	0
Subtotal (minor.)	13	10.9	13	12.1	26	11.5	0	0.0	15	21.7	26	11.5	4
Nonres. Alien	3	2.5	0	0.0	3	1.3	0	0.0	0	0.0	3	1.3	1
White/Cauc.	85	71.4	85	79.4	170	75.2	0	0.0	48	69.6	170	75.2	45
Unknown	18	15.1	9	8.4	27	11.9	0	0.0	6	8.7	27	11.9	23
Total	119	52.7	107	47.3	226	100.0	0	0.0	69	30.5	226		73

Curriculum

	Full-Time	Part-Time
Typical first-year section size	75	0
Is there typically a "small section" of the first-year class, other than Legal Writing, taught by full-time faculty	No	No
If yes, typical size offered last year		
# of classroom course titles beyond first-year curriculum	64	

# of upper division courses, excluding seminars, with an enrollment:		
Under 25	33	
25–49	8	
50–74	4	
75–99	0	
100+	0	

# of seminars	4	
# of seminar positions available	40	
# of seminar positions filled	30	0
# of positions available in simulation courses	188	
# of simulation positions filled	164	0
# of positions available in faculty supervised clinical courses	64	
# of faculty supervised clinical positions filled	52	0
# involved in field placements	61	0
# involved in law journals	14	0
# involved in moot court or trial competitions	24	0
# of credit hours required to graduate	89	

Transfers

Transfers in	5
Transfers out	3

Tuition and Fees

	Resident	Nonresident
Full-time	$13,203	$25,533
Part-time		
Tuition Guarantee Program	N	

Living Expenses

Estimated living expenses for singles

Living on campus	Living off campus	Living at home
$15,127	$15,127	$7,161

*ABA
Approved
Since
1923*

GPA and LSAT Scores

	Total	Full-Time	Part-Time
# of apps	540	540	0
# of offers	243	243	0
# of matrics	69	69	0
75% GPA	3.60	3.60	0.00
Median GPA	3.38	3.38	0.00
25% GPA	3.13	3.13	0.00
75% LSAT	157	157	0
Median LSAT	153	153	0
25% LSAT	150	150	0

Grants and Scholarships (from prior year)

	Total		Full-Time		Part-Time	
	#	%	#	%	#	%
Total # of students	231		231		0	
Total # receiving grants	148	64.1	148	64.1	0	0.0
Less than 1/2 tuition	119	51.5	119	51.5	0	0.0
Half to full tuition	20	8.7	20	8.7	0	0.0
Full tuition	0	0.0	0	0.0	0	0.0
More than full tuition	9	3.9	9	3.9	0	0.0
Median grant amount			$3,000		$0	

Informational and Library Resources

Total amount spent on library materials	$710,240
Study seating capacity inside the library	262
# of full-time equivalent professional librarians	3
Hours per week library is open	95
# of open, wired connections available to students	462
# of networked computers available for use by students	56
Has wireless network?	Y
Requires computer?	N

JD Attrition (from prior year)

	Academic	Other	Total	
	#	#	#	%
1st year	0	0	0	0.0
2nd year	0	5	5	6.6
3rd year	0	0	0	0.0
4th year	0	0	0	0.0

Employment (9 months after graduation)

For up-to-date employment data, go to
employmentsummary.abaquestionnaire.org on the ABA website.

Bar Passage Rates

First-time takers	59	Reporting %	83.05
Average school %	87.76	Average state %	79.24
Average pass difference	8.52		

Jurisdiction	Takers	Passers	Pass %	State %	Diff %
Colorado	26	22	84.62	82.79	1.83
Wyoming	23	21	91.30	75.22	16.08

UNIVERSITY OF WYOMING COLLEGE OF LAW

The information on these pages was provided by the law school.

Dept. 3035, 1000 E. University Avenue
Laramie, WY 82071
Phone: 307.766.6416; Fax: 307.766.6417
E-mail: lawadmis@uwyo.edu; Website: www.uwyo.edu/law

Introduction

The University of Wyoming College of Law, founded in 1920, is ABA accredited and a member of the AALS. An excellent faculty of 17 full-time and 19 part-time professors and highly qualified lecturers instructs a student body of approximately 230. The limited size of the student body and the favorable student-to-faculty ratio (10.6 to 1), create an atmosphere of friendliness and informality. Students enjoy a degree of access to faculty rarely found at larger institutions. UW Law provides a high quality, affordable legal education and is considered one of the best value schools in the nation. The College of Law is located in Laramie on the campus of the University of Wyoming, the only four-year institution of higher learning in Wyoming. The university has a student body of 13,000. Laramie is a town of 30,000 located in southeastern Wyoming at an altitude of 7,200 feet on the high plains between two mountain ranges. UW Law's proximity to the mountains provides a variety of recreational activities, including skiing, backpacking, rock climbing, hiking, mountain biking, camping, fishing, and hunting. Laramie is just two hours north of Denver, Colorado, and 45 minutes from Cheyenne—Wyoming's state capital.

Faculty

The faculty has a proven record of excellence in teaching, research, and scholarship. Particular areas of strength include environmental and natural resource law, water law, constitutional law, and international, business, and transactional law. Faculty members are actively engaged in public service and university functions. Because of our small student body, the University of Wyoming College of Law faculty has instructional and research opportunities often not available in larger institutions. Students regularly converse with their professors both inside and outside the classroom, establishing lifelong professional connections.

Curriculum

The 1L year consists of foundational subjects, including Contracts, Property, Torts, Civil Procedure, Constitutional Law, Legal Research and Writing, Criminal Law, Appellate Advocacy, and Introduction to Law. During the 2L year, students take two required courses (Evidence and Professional Responsibility) and electives of their choice. The 3L year is comprised entirely of elective and seminar courses tailored toward an area of law, including business, civil litigation, criminal, energy, environment and natural resources, general practice, government, international, public interest, real estate, and social justice. Practical legal training is available through four clinical programs, an international human rights practicum, and a rural law center. Numerous externship opportunities are available including state and federal courts, Wyoming Supreme Court, Shoshone and Arapaho Tribal Court, the US Attorney's Office, Wyoming Attorney General, state and federal public defender, FBI, JAG, municipal and government agencies, and other nonprofit entities, including the Innocence Project, ACLU, Biodiversity Conservation Alliance, and Access to Justice.

Clinics, externships, internships, and faculty research projects are available each term.

Special Programs

Students may obtain practical experience and academic credit in four clinical programs: (1) Defender Aid—students brief and argue criminal appeals for indigent persons, and assist penitentiary inmates in post-conviction cases; (2) Prosecution Assistance—students work with prosecuting attorneys in criminal cases; (3) Legal Services—students provide legal assistance to economically disadvantaged persons; and (4) Domestic Violence—students address legal issues of domestic violence victims. Students also can participate in an International Human Rights Practicum addressing immigration, asylum, and other human rights issues and an Estate Planning Practicum in which estate planning matters for qualifying individuals are addressed. All clinical programs and practicums operate under faculty supervision. Under Wyoming state law, students in the clinics can brief and argue cases before the Wyoming Supreme Court, an opportunity that is rare—if not unique—among law schools. Students also regularly appear in state court hearings and represent clients in a variety of venues and proceedings. Students have the opportunity to practice in a summer trial institute taught by experts in the field of trial advocacy.

The college offers three joint degrees: JD/MA in Environment and Natural Resources, JD/MPA, and JD/MBA. The College of Law has had a strong program in environment and natural resources for many years. Courses are offered in environmental law, oil and gas, mining law, public lands, water rights, and energy/climate. UW Law has strengths in trial and appellate practice, business planning, transactional law, estate planning, corporate and commercial law, administrative law, consumer law, American Indian law, family/domestic law, and international law.

UW Law and Kyung Hee University in Seoul, Korea, are partners in a Memorandum of Agreement which provides opportunities for UW students to study in Korea, to aid in international trade negotiations, and to assist South Korea as it implements the American jury trial system.

Admission Standards

UW Law seeks candidates whose intellectual abilities and proven academic skills make it likely that they will successfully complete our academic program and use their legal education productively. We favor candidates with potential for leadership in their chosen professions. Our students are expected to be committed to hard work, honesty, integrity, and community service commensurate with the privilege of membership in the legal profession. We seek to admit candidates whose diverse backgrounds, experiences, knowledge, and perspectives will enliven and enrich the learning experiences of fellow students, faculty, and the rest of the academic community.

The College of Law admits 75 to 80 students each fall. The college begins accepting applications on October 1 for the class entering the following August. An early admission program is available for those who apply before December 1. The entering class is selected from applications completed by

March 1. Applicants should register with LSAC's Credential Assembly Service and request official undergraduate transcripts by mid-January and take the LSAT no later than February.

Applicants must have an undergraduate degree from an accredited institution prior to matriculation. Admission is based on applicant's undergraduate records, LSAT scores, personal statement, and other criteria relevant to success in the study and practice of law. Applicants must submit two letters of recommendation. UW Law does not discriminate on the basis of race, color, religion, sex, national origin, disability, age, veteran status, sexual orientation, or political beliefs.

Student Activities

The College of Law publishes the student-edited *Wyoming Law Review* twice annually. Other organizations include Potter Law Club (student government), three law fraternities, Students for Equal Justice, Intellectual Property Club, International Law Students, Natural Resources Law Forum, Women's Law Forum, J. Reuben Clark Society, Minority Student Law Association, and the Wyoming Student Trial Lawyers. Students participate in the National Moot Court, National Environmental Law Moot Court, National Client Counseling, and the ATLA National Student Trial Advocacy. The college has two honorary societies: Order of the Coif and Excellence in Advocacy.

Career Services

About 85 percent of graduates remain in the Rocky Mountain region, but UW Law has alumni around the globe. The curriculum is broad in scope, providing a core foundation of legal knowledge applicable in a wide range of legal and geographic areas.

UW Law graduates practice primarily in small private firms or are employed by federal, state, local, and tribal governments. Students are also employed in the public interest sector, in judicial clerkships, and in the growing area of business and industry.

As with other aspects of UW Law, the small size of the student body permits Career Services to provide students with personal attention not available at larger institutions. Students receive one-on-one career counseling and job-search assistance for permanent or summer employment. Career Services also provides insightful career panels, interview experience, and résumé/cover letter workshops. A network of loyal alumni hire, often exclusively, at the College of Law. Fall and spring on-campus interviews also provide many firms and students with a chance to interview one another. An online posting system allows organizations to announce legal jobs across the country to UW students. Career services online and library resources are available to all students.

Financial Aid

About $1 million in scholarships are available, and approximately half of students receive some financial aid. Scholarship awards are based on merit, need, and special circumstance. Students should file the FAFSA prior to March 1. Scholarship applications are submitted to the College of Law. Student loans and other financial resources are administered through the UW Student Financial Aid Office.

Facilities

UW Law is composed of large classrooms, courtrooms, seminar/study rooms, and individual student lockers and study carrels. The spacious on-site library has 350,000 volumes and multiple electronic databases. Wi-Fi and the newest instructional technologies are available throughout the building. Two state-of-the-art courtroom/classrooms, a jury room, and seminar rooms were completed in 2009. The building provides a positive learning environment and is conveniently located.

APPLICANT PROFILE

University of Wyoming College of Law
This grid includes only applicants who earned 120–180 LSAT scores under standard administrations.

LSAT Score	3.75 +		3.50–3.74		3.25–3.49		3.00–3.24		2.75–2.99		2.50–2.74		2.25–2.49		2.00–2.24		Below 2.00		No GPA		Total	
	Apps	Adm	Apps	Adm	Apps	Adm	Apps	Adm	Apps	Adm	Apps	Adm	Apps	Adm	Apps	Adm	Apps	Adm	Apps	Adm	Apps	Adm
175–180	0	0	0	0	0	0	0	0	0	0	0	0	0	0	0	0	0	0	0	0	0	0
170–174	0	0	1	1	1	1	0	0	0	0	0	0	0	0	0	0	0	0	0	0	2	2
165–169	4	4	4	3	1	1	3	1	1	1	1	1	0	0	0	0	0	0	0	0	14	11
160–164	10	9	5	4	9	7	5	4	1	1	3	0	2	0	1	1	0	0	0	0	36	26
155–159	9	9	26	18	32	27	25	17	13	4	10	4	2	1	1	0	2	0	2	2	122	82
150–154	16	9	25	17	43	25	37	13	31	8	16	2	12	2	6	1	1	0	4	3	191	80
145–149	6	4	21	5	22	7	29	6	14	1	13	0	5	0	0	0	0	0	2	2	112	25
140–144	4	0	2	0	8	0	10	0	4	0	3	0	1	0	2	0	0	0	2	2	36	2
135–139	0	0	0	0	0	0	2	0	2	0	2	0	3	0	0	0	0	0	1	0	10	0
130–134	0	0	0	0	0	0	0	0	1	0	2	0	1	0	0	0	0	0	1	0	5	0
125–129	0	0	0	0	0	0	0	0	0	0	0	0	0	0	2	0	0	0	0	0	2	0
120–124	0	0	0	0	0	0	0	0	0	0	0	0	0	0	0	0	0	0	0	0	0	0
Total	49	35	84	48	116	68	111	41	67	15	50	7	26	3	12	2	3	0	12	9	530	228

Apps = Number of Applicants
Adm = Number Admitted
Reflects 99% of the total applicant pool; highest LSAT data reported.

YALE LAW SCHOOL

PO Box 208215
New Haven, CT 06520-8215
Phone: 203.432.4995
E-mail: admissions.law@yale.edu; Website: www.law.yale.edu

ABA
Approved
Since
1923

The Basics

Type of school	Private
Term	Semester
Application deadline	2/15
Application fee	
Financial aid deadline	3/15
Can first year start other than fall?	No
Student to faculty ratio	8.5 to 1
# of housing spaces available restricted to law students	
graduate housing for which law students are eligible	

Curriculum

	Full-Time	Part-Time
Typical first-year section size	70	0
Is there typically a "small section" of the first-year class, other than Legal Writing, taught by full-time faculty	Yes	No
If yes, typical size offered last year	16	
# of classroom course titles beyond first-year curriculum	178	

# of upper division courses, excluding seminars, with an enrollment:		
	Under 25	50
	25–49	18
	50–74	12
	75–99	7
	100+	3

# of seminars	88	
# of seminar positions available	1,056	
# of seminar positions filled	961	0
# of positions available in simulation courses	90	
# of simulation positions filled	71	0
# of positions available in faculty supervised clinical courses	710	
# of faculty supervised clinical positions filled	708	0
# involved in field placements	46	0
# involved in law journals	415	0
# involved in moot court or trial competitions	116	0
# of credit hours required to graduate	83	

Faculty and Administrators

	Total		Men		Women		Minorities	
	Spr	Fall	Spr	Fall	Spr	Fall	Spr	Fall
Full-time	64	61	49	47	15	14	7	9
Other full-time	10	9	6	6	4	3	0	0
Deans, librarians, & others who teach	16	15	8	9	8	6	4	2
Part-time	65	59	47	45	18	14	2	4
Total	155	144	110	107	45	37	13	15

JD Enrollment and Ethnicity

	Men		Women		Full-Time		Part-Time		1st-Year		Total		JD Degs. Awd.
	#	%	#	%	#	%	#	%	#	%	#	%	
All Hispanics	26	8.0	25	7.9	51	8.0	0	0.0	17	8.3	51	8.0	13
Am. Ind./AK Nat.	1	0.3	0	0.0	1	0.2	0	0.0	0	0.0	1	0.2	0
Asian	28	8.7	59	18.7	87	13.6	0	0.0	29	14.1	87	13.6	29
Black/Af. Am.	11	3.4	27	8.6	38	6.0	0	0.0	13	6.3	38	6.0	23
Nat. HI/Pac. Isl.	0	0.0	0	0.0	0	0.0	0	0.0	0	0.0	0	0.0	0
2 or more races	10	3.1	16	5.1	26	4.1	0	0.0	10	4.9	26	4.1	1
Subtotal (minor.)	76	23.5	127	40.3	203	31.8	0	0.0	69	33.5	203	31.8	66
Nonres. Alien	25	7.7	12	3.8	37	5.8	0	0.0	13	6.3	37	5.8	8
White/Cauc.	212	65.6	169	53.7	381	59.7	0	0.0	117	56.8	381	59.7	130
Unknown	10	3.1	7	2.2	17	2.7	0	0.0	7	3.4	17	2.7	11
Total	323	50.6	315	49.4	638	100.0	0	0.0	206	32.3	638		215

Transfers

Transfers in	8
Transfers out	0

Tuition and Fees

	Resident	Nonresident
Full-time	$52,525	$52,525
Part-time		
Tuition Guarantee Program	N	

Living Expenses

Estimated living expenses for singles

Living on campus	Living off campus	Living at home
$20,150	$20,150	$20,150

YALE LAW SCHOOL

*ABA
Approved
Since
1923*

GPA and LSAT Scores

	Total	Full-Time	Part-Time
# of apps	3,173	3,173	0
# of offers	252	252	0
# of matrics	205	205	0
75% GPA	3.96	3.96	0.00
Median GPA	3.90	3.90	0.00
25% GPA	3.83	3.83	0.00
75% LSAT	177	177	0
Median LSAT	173	173	0
25% LSAT	170	170	0

Grants and Scholarships (from prior year)

	Total		Full-Time		Part-Time	
	#	%	#	%	#	%
Total # of students	629		629		0	
Total # receiving grants	367	58.3	367	58.3	0	0.0
Less than 1/2 tuition	198	31.5	198	31.5	0	0.0
Half to full tuition	168	26.7	168	26.7	0	0.0
Full tuition	0	0.0	0	0.0	0	0.0
More than full tuition	1	0.2	1	0.2	0	0.0
Median grant amount			$23,650		$0	

Informational and Library Resources

Total amount spent on library materials	$2,604,315
Study seating capacity inside the library	441
# of full-time equivalent professional librarians	19
Hours per week library is open	104
# of open, wired connections available to students	1,009
# of networked computers available for use by students	101
Has wireless network?	Y
Requires computer?	N

JD Attrition (from prior year)

	Academic	Other	Total	
	#	#	#	%
1st year	0	1	1	0.5
2nd year	0	1	1	0.4
3rd year	0	0	0	0.0
4th year	0	0	0	0.0

Employment (9 months after graduation)

For up-to-date employment data, go to employmentsummary.abaquestionnaire.org on the ABA website.

Bar Passage Rates

First-time takers	179	Reporting %	70.39
Average school %	97.62	Average state %	82.31
Average pass difference	15.31		

Jurisdiction	Takers	Passers	Pass %	State %	Diff %
New York	102	99	97.06	84.92	12.14
California	24	24	100.00	71.24	28.76

YALE LAW SCHOOL

PO Box 208215
New Haven, CT 06520-8215
Phone: 203.432.4995
E-mail: admissions.law@yale.edu; Website: www.law.yale.edu

Introduction

Yale Law School is an extraordinary community in which to study law. Standing at the intersection of the worlds of thought and action, Yale seeks not only to promote an intellectual understanding of the law, but also to sustain the moral commitments that justice requires.

Extensive student-faculty interactions and institutional flexibility are hallmarks of the Yale Law School experience. Students enjoy countless opportunities for research and writing with professors. Our unmatched faculty-to-student ratio allows us to offer a wide range of courses and small classes, with an average class size of approximately 20 students.

The school is also part of one of the world's great research universities. Yale University is home to an abundance of intellectual, cultural, social, and athletic activities, all of which are accessible to Yale law students.

Students

The vitality of Yale Law School depends as much on the knowledge, experience, and interests of the students as it does on the faculty, the library, or the alumni. The school selects its entering class from applicants with the highest academic qualifications. Within this exceptional group, Yale seeks a diversity of backgrounds, experiences, and interests. This diversity is reflected in the many thriving student organizations and student-run journals found at the school.

Faculty

The faculty at Yale Law School is as broad-ranging in its interests and expertise as it is distinguished. It includes prominent scholars of economics, philosophy, and the social sciences as well as leading specialists in every area of law. More than 60 full-time professors are joined each year by visiting lecturers, adjunct professors from other parts of the university, and practicing lawyers. Additionally, dozens of guest lecturers from around the world—ranging from Madeleine Albright to Al Franken—help to make Yale Law School a vibrant intellectual community.

Facilities and Housing

The Sterling Law Building occupies one city block in the heart of Yale University and downtown New Haven. The recently renovated building was modeled on the English Inns of Court, with classrooms, a dining hall, faculty offices, and the law library surrounding three pleasant courtyards. All classrooms are Internet accessible, and a wireless network is available throughout the Law School. A day care center is located on site.

Yale campus housing is available, but most students live off campus, close to the Law School. Within a 10-minute walk of the school, students can find housing options ranging from high-rise apartments downtown to Victorian houses in quiet residential neighborhoods.

Curriculum and Grading

The Yale Law School curriculum is very flexible. Students are able to shape their own course of study to satisfy their unique intellectual interests and goals. In the fall semester, all first-year students take classes in constitutional law, contracts, procedure, and torts. One of these classes is a small group of about 16 students, which includes instruction in legal research and writing. After the first term, students may select any classes they wish, including independent studies, clinics, and courses outside the Law School. Two major writing projects and courses in criminal law and professional responsibility are required for graduation.

In order to allow students to concentrate on learning, rather than on GPAs, Yale Law School does not use grades in the traditional sense. During the fall of the first year, all classes are credit/fail. In subsequent terms, grades are honors, pass, low pass, and fail, with credit/fail options available. Yale Law School does not calculate class rankings.

Joint Degrees, Special Programs, and Clinical Opportunities

Yale Law School sees the study of law as interrelated with other intellectual disciplines and with practical experience. The Law School allows a number of joint degrees with other schools and departments at Yale, including JD/MBAs, JD/PhDs, and JD/MDs. Joint degrees with other universities and opportunities for intensive semester experiences outside the Law School are available.

Yale Law School also offers a number of clinical opportunities to all students beginning in the first year. For example, students gain real-world experience participating in the Lowenstein International Human Rights Clinic, Supreme Court Clinic, Environmental Protection Clinic, and the Community Development Financial Institutions Clinic. Other clinics, including advocacy for children, immigrants, and tenants provide opportunities for Yale law students to work on behalf of clients who cannot afford private attorneys.

Transfer Students and Other Degrees

Students who have completed two semesters of study at another ABA-approved law school may apply to transfer to Yale Law School. Transfer students must complete at least two years of work at Yale Law School.

In addition to the JD, Yale Law School offers an LLM degree for foreign lawyers who are interested in teaching law. The Master of Studies in Law (MSL) is a one-year program designed for mid-career professionals and journalists who desire an intensive introduction to the law. Yale also offers a JSD program for the school's LLM students.

Financial Aid and Loan Forgiveness

Financial aid is awarded solely on the basis of need, and admission decisions are made independent of financial aid decisions. Approximately 80 percent of the student body receives some form of financial aid. A financial aid award may consist of a portion in grant and a portion in loan; typically, the higher the total financial need, the higher the proportion of grant.

In addition to financial aid during law school, Yale has one of the most generous loan forgiveness programs in the country: the Career Options Assistance Program (COAP). COAP provides grants to help repay the educational loans of graduates who take relatively low-paying jobs. Unlike many loan forgiveness programs, Yale's COAP includes not only law school loans, but some undergraduate loans as well. Last year, COAP covered over $3 million worth of loan payments for over 300 graduates.

Career Development

Yale Law School graduates occupy leadership positions in a tremendous range of endeavors. The Law School's Career Development Office helps students explore the unparalleled diversity of opportunities available to them. Most students work for public interest organizations, private firms, or government entities during summer breaks. After graduation, roughly half of each class obtain judicial clerkships. Others work for law firms or corporations, while still others take advantage of public service fellowships available to Yale Law School graduates. In addition, many graduates pursue careers in academia.

The Admission Process

Yale Law School considers every application for admission in its entirety and no index or numerical cutoffs are used in the admission process. No single element in an application is decisive; the totality of available information about the applicant is taken into account. A personal statement and a 250-word essay on a subject of the applicant's choice are required. Applicants are encouraged to bring aspects of their personal background or other special characteristics to the attention of the admission committee. Two letters of recommendation are required; additional letters are also welcome.

Each application file is first reviewed by the dean of admissions. A group of the most highly rated files is then considered by faculty. Each faculty member rates applications on the basis of the faculty member's unique criteria; the weight given to various factors is within each reader's discretion.

The Law School issues decisions on a rolling basis, but most of its decisions are made by the middle of April. Unlike traditional rolling admissions processes, an applicant's chances of admission remain constant throughout the cycle. Use of the wait list varies from year to year, and the list is not ranked until offers are made.

APPLICANT PROFILE

Yale Law School

Undergraduate GPA	Below 155		155–159		160–164		165–169		170–174		175–180		Total	
	Apps	Adm	Apps	Adm	Apps	Adm	Apps	Adm	Apps	Adm	Apps	Adm	Apps	Adm
3.75 +	70	0	70	2	141	6	356	26	615	129	256	107	1508	270
3.50–3.74	92	0	68	1	121	4	187	6	223	10	83	9	774	30
3.25–3.49	90	0	50	0	70	0	79	0	76	0	28	0	393	0
3.00–3.24	67	0	37	0	25	0	35	0	20	0	6	0	190	0
Below 3.00	103	0	23	0	9	0	22	0	10	0	2	0	169	0
No GPA	37	0	13	0	19	0	30	2	20	1	5	0	124	3
Total	459	0	261	3	385	10	709	34	964	140	380	116	3158	303

Totals reflect 99% of applicant pool.
Apps = Number of Applicants
Adm = Number Admitted

Law School Attendance Figures, Fall 2011

		Full-time	Part-time	Total
First Year	Total	41,821	6,876	48,697
	Women	19,422	3,376	22,798
Second Year	Total	42,692	5,082	47,774
	Women	19,680	2,373	22,053
Third Year	Total	40,916	5,097	46,013
	Women	19,206	2,416	21,622
Fourth Year	Total		3,804	3,804
	Women		1,789	1,789
JD Total	Total	125,429	20,859	146,288
	Women	58,308	9,954	68,262
Post-JD	Total	5,798	2,362	8,160
	Women	2,852	1,131	3,983
Other	Total	1,269	741	2,010
	Women	670	501	1,171
Grand Total	Total	132,496	23,962	156,458
	Women	61,830	11,586	73,416

Professional Degrees Conferred, 2011

		Full-time	Part-time	Total
JD/LLB	Total	39,597	4,898	44,495
	Women	18,701	2,342	21,043
LLM	Total	4,939	1,028	5,967
	Women	2,374	490	2,864
MCL/MCJ	Total	10	5	15
	Women	6	4	10
SJD/JSD	Total	83	8	91
	Women	33	1	34
Other	Total	241	162	403
	Women	141	115	256
Total	Total	44,893	6,111	51,004
	Women	21,272	2,958	24,230

Teachers in Law Schools, 2011–2012

	Women	Minorities	Total
Full-time	3,318	1,424	8,281
Part-time	2,694	838	8,407
Deans & Administrators	2,517	873	4,091
Librarians	1,144	297	1,769

New aggregate categories for reporting racial/ethnicity data were adopted in 2011 in accordance with the final guidance issued by the US Department of Education. These categories are Hispanic, but if not Hispanic, then Black or African American, American Indian or Alaska Native, Asian, Native Hawaiian or Other Pacific Islander, and Two or More Races. To view the statistical charts for 1988–2010 using the former categories, go to ambar.org/LegalEdStatistics. New statistical charts have been created to reflect the new categories beginning with the 2010–2011 information. For more information, see *Federal Register*, Volume 72 (October 19, 2007) "Final Guidance on Maintaining, Collecting, and Reporting Racial and Ethnic Data to the US Department of Education," pp. 59266–59279; and The Race and Ethnicity Information Center of the Department of Education's Integrated Postsecondary Education Data System: nces.ed.gov/ipeds.

Aggregate Categories

	Academic Year	Number of Schools Reporting*	First Year	Second Year	Third Year	Fourth Year	Total
All Hispanic Enrollment	2011–12	201	3,982	3,599	3,150	296	11,027
	2010–11	200	3,962	3,231	3,005	256	10,454
Black/African American Enrollment	2011–12	201	3,763	3,267	3,120	302	10,452
	2010–11	200	3,857	3,194	3,024	277	10,352
American Indian/Alaska Native Enrollment	2011–12	201	392	362	380	31	1,165
	2010–11	200	440	381	359	28	1,208
Asian Enrollment	2011–12	201	3,390	3,321	3,258	246	10,215
	2010–11	200	3,636	3,271	3,246	262	10,415
Native Hawaiian or Other Pacific Islander Enrollment	2011–12	201	119	203	146	24	492
	2010–11	200	235	205	112	16	568
Two or More Races Enrollment	2011–12	201	1,133	897	448	30	2,508
	2010–11	200	1,061	432	521	34	2,048

Total Minority Enrollment

Academic Year	Number of Schools Reporting*	First Year	Second Year	Third Year	Fourth Year	Total
2011–12	201	12,779	11,649	10,502	929	35,859
2010–11	200	13,191	10,714	10,267	873	35,045
2009–10	197	11,840	10,227	9,629	809	32,505
2008–09	197	11,320	10,028	9,311	709	31,368
2007–08	194	10,992	9,639	9,203	764	30,598
2006–07	191	10,898	9,539	9,371	749	30,557
2005–06	190	10,462	9,644	9,061	818	29,985
2004–05	188	10,694	9,280	8,766	749	29,489
2003–04	187	10,468	9,144	8,062	721	28,318
2002–03	187	10,224	8,326	7,898	721	27,169
2001–02	184	9,557	8,172	7,785	743	26,257
2000–01	183	9,335	8,052	7,690	676	25,753
1999–00	182	9,079	7,876	7,547	751	25,253
1998–99	181	9,076	7,635	7,761	794	25,266
1997–98	178	8,493	7,740	7,705	747	24,685
1996–97	179	8,722	8,009	7,869	679	25,279
1995–96	178	9,119	8,402	7,411	622	25,554
1994–95	177	9,249	7,633	7,124	605	24,611
1993–94	176	8,595	7,244	6,409	551	22,799
1992–93	176	8,070	6,682	6,032	482	21,266
1991–92	176	7,575	6,155	5,255	425	19,410
1990–91	175	6,933	5,325	4,676	396	17,330
1989–90	175	6,172	4,890	4,264	394	15,720

Legal Education Statistics, 1984–2011

Academic Year	Number of Schools	Total LSAT Administrations	Applicants	First-year Enrollment	Total JD Enrollment	Total[1] Overall Enrollment	JD or LLB Awarded
2011–12	201	155,050	78,500	48,697	144,288	156,458	44,495
2010–11	200	171,500	87,900	52,448	147,525	157,298	44,258
2009–10	200	171,514	86,576	51,646	145,239	154,539	44,004
2008–09	200	151,398	83,371	49,414	142,922	152,033	43,588
2007–08	198	142,331	84,021	49,082	141,719	150,031	43,518
2006–07	195	140,048	88,662	48,937	141,031	148,698	43,920
2005–06	191	137,444	95,760	48,132	140,298	148,273	42,673
2004–05	188	145,258	100,604	48,239	140,376	148,169	40,023
2003–04	187	147,617	99,504	48,867	137,676	145,088	38,874
2002–03	186	148,014	90,853	48,433	132,885	140,612	38,605
2001–02	184	134,251	77,235	45,070	127,610	135,091	37,909
2000–01	183	109,030	74,550	43,518	125,173	132,464	38,157
1999–00	182	107,153	74,380	43,152	125,184	132,276	39,071
1998–99	181	104,236	71,726	42,804	125,627	131,833	39,455
1997–98	178[2]	103,991	72,340	42,186	125,886	131,801	40,114
1996–97	179	105,315	76,687	43,245	125,623	134,949	39,920
1995–96	178	114,756	84,305	43,676	129,397	135,595	39,271
1994–95	177	128,553	89,633	44,298	128,989	134,784	39,710
1993–94	176	132,028	91,892	43,644	127,802	133,339	40,213
1992–93	176	140,054	97,719	42,793	128,212	133,783	39,425
1991–92	176	145,567	99,377	44,050	129,580	135,157	38,800
1990–91	175	152,685	92,958	44,104	127,261	132,433	36,385
1989–90	175	138,865	87,288	43,826	124,471	129,698	35,520
1988–89	174	137,088	78,930	42,860	120,694	125,870	35,701
1987–88	175	115,988	68,804	41,055	117,997	123,198	35,478
1986–87	175	101,235	65,168	40,195	117,813	132,277	36,121
1985–86	175	91,848	60,338	40,796	118,700	124,092	36,829
1984–85	174	95,563	63,801	40,747	119,847	125,698	36,687

Note: Enrollment is in American Bar Association-approved law schools as of October 1, 2011. The LSAT year begins in June and ends in February of the following year. JD or LLB degrees are those awarded by approved schools for the academic year ending in the first year stated. Total new admissions to the bar include those admitted by office study, diploma privilege, and examination and study at an unapproved law school. The great bulk of those admitted graduated from approved schools.

[1] Total overall enrollment includes post-JD and other.
[2] The District of Columbia School of Law is not included in this figure.

Please note that it is the position of the Council of the ABA Section of Legal Education and Admissions to the Bar that no graduate degree in law is or should be a substitute for the first professional degree in law (JD) and should not serve as the same basis for bar admission purposes as the JD degree. The Council of the Section is licensed to accredit JD programs; it is not licensed to accredit post-JD and non-JD programs. For additional information about post-JD and non-JD programs, visit the Section's website at americanbar.org/legaled.

For specific information about the programs listed below, you should contact the schools directly. In addition, if you have not obtained a JD from an ABA-approved law school, you may wish to contact the bar admission authorities in the state(s) in which you intend to practice for more information on whether graduation from a post-JD or non-JD program will qualify you to take the bar examination in that state.

The information contained in Appendix B was collected in fall 2011. Neither the ABA nor LSAC conducts an audit to verify the accuracy of the information submitted by the respective institutions.

GRADUATE DEGREES DEFINED

While an individual law school's degree may differ slightly by name to similar programs elsewhere, most degrees offered through law schools fall into three general categories:

1) Academic master's degrees for nonlawyers, such as:
   - MS — Master of Science or Master of Studies
   - MPS — Master of Professional Studies

2) Post-JD law degrees for practicing lawyers and foreign lawyers seeking to practice in the US, such as:
   - LLM — Master of Laws
   - JM — Juris Master
   - MCL — Master of Comparative Law
   - MJ — Master of Jurisprudence
   - MLS — Master of Legal Studies

3) Research and academic-based doctorate level degrees, such as:
   - JSD — Doctor of Jurisprudence
   - SJD — Doctor of Juridical Science
   - DCL — Doctor of Comparative Law

For questions regarding specific degree descriptions, contact the school directly.

POST-JD AND NON-JD PROGRAMS BY LAW SCHOOL

Akron
Intellectual Property, LLM

Alabama
Comparative Law, LLM
General, LLM
Taxation, LLM

Albany
Advanced Legal Studies, LLM; MS
Government Administration and Regulations, LLM
Health Law, LLM
Intellectual Property, LLM
International Law, LLM

American
Advocacy, LLM
General, SJD
International Legal Studies, LLM
Law and Government, LLM

Arizona
Indigenous People's Law & Policy, LLM; SJD
International Trade Law, LLM; SJD

Arizona State
Advanced Legal Studies, LLM
Biotechnology and Genomics, LLM
General, LLM
Tribal Policy, Law and Government, LLM

Arkansas (Fayetteville)
Agriculture and Food Law, LLM

Atlanta's John Marshall
Employment Law, LLM

Baltimore
Law of the US, LLM
Taxation, LLM

Boston
American Law (for international lawyers), LLM
Banking and Financial Law, LLM
Intellectual Property, LLM
International Business, LLM
Taxation, LLM

Boston College
General, LLM

Brigham Young
American Law (for international lawyers), LLM

Brooklyn
American Law (for international lawyers), LLM

Buffalo
Criminal Law, LLM
General, LLM

California-Berkeley
General, JSD; LLM

California-Davis
US Legal System, LLM

California-Hastings
General, MS
US Law (for international lawyers), LLM

California-Los Angeles
As Approved, LLM; SJD
Business Law, LLM
Entertainment and Media Law/Policy, LLM
Juridical Studies, SJD

California Western
Comparative Law (for international lawyers), LLM; MCL
Health Law, MAS
Trial Advocacy (specializing in federal criminal law), LLM

Capital
Business, LLM
Business and Taxation, LLM
Taxation, LLM; MT

Cardozo
Comparative Legal Thought, LLM
Dispute Resolution and Advocacy, LLM
General, LLM
Intellectual Property, LLM

Case Western
Intellectual Property, LLM
International Business Law, LLM
International Criminal Law, LLM
US and Global Legal Studies, LLM

Catholic
Communications Law, LLM
National Security Law, LLM

Chapman
General, LLM
Prosecutorial Science, LLM
Taxation, LLM

Chicago
General, DCL; JSD; LLM; MCL

Chicago-Kent
Family Law, LLM
Financial Services Law, LLM
International and Transnational Law, LLM
International Intellectual Property, LLM
Science of Law, LLM
Taxation, LLM

Cincinnati
US Legal System, LLM

Cleveland State
General, LLM

Colorado
General, LLM

Columbia
General, JSD; LLM

Connecticut
Insurance Law, LLM
US Legal Studies (for international lawyers), LLM

Cornell
General, JSD; LLM

Creighton
Government Organization and Leadership, MS

Dayton
Intellectual Property and Technology, LLM; MSL

Denver
American and Comparative Law (for international lawyers), LLM
Natural Resources, LLM; MRLS
Taxation, LLM

DePaul
Health Law, LLM
Intellectual Property, LLM
International Law, LLM
Taxation, LLM

District of Columbia
General, LLM

Drake
General, LLM; MJ
Health Law, LLM; MJ
Intellectual Property, LLM; MJ

Duke
Entrepreneurship and Law, LLM
Juridical Studies, LLM
Research, SJD
US Law (for international lawyers), LLM; SJD

Duquesne
American Law (for international lawyers), LLM

Emory
General, LLM; SJD
Litigation, LLM
Taxation, LLM

Florida
Comparative Law, LLM
Environmental and Land Use Law, LLM
International Taxation, LLM
Taxation, LLM; SJD

Florida Coastal
US Law (for international lawyers), LLM

Florida International
General (for international lawyers), LLM

Florida State
American Law (for international lawyers), LLM
Environmental Law and Policy, LLM

Fordham
Banking, LLM
General, LLM; JSD
Intellectual Property and Information Technology, LLM
International Business and Trade Law, LLM
International Law and Justice, LLM
US and Comparative Law, LLM

George Mason
Intellectual Property, LLM
Law and Economics, LLM

George Washington
Business and Finance, LLM
Environmental Law, LLM
General, LLM; SJD
Government and Procurement Law, LLM
Government Procurement and Environmental Law, LLM
Intellectual Property, LLM
International and Comparative Law, LLM
International Environmental Law, LLM
Litigation and Dispute Resolution, LLM
National Security and Foreign Relations, LLM

Georgetown
As Approved, SJD
General, LLM; MSL
Global Health Law, LLM
International Business and Economic Law, LLM
International Legal Studies, LLM
National Security Law, LLM
Securities and Financial Regulation, LLM
Taxation, LLM

Georgia
General, LLM

Golden Gate
Environmental Law, LLM
Intellectual Property, LLM
International Legal Studies, LLM; SJD
Taxation, LLM
US Legal Studies (for international lawyers), LLM

Hamline
General (for international lawyers), LLM

Harvard
General, LLM; SJD

Hawaii
General (for international lawyers), LLM

Hofstra
American Legal Studies, LLM
Family Law, LLM
International Law, LLM

Houston
Energy, Environment, and Natural Resources, LLM
Foreign Scholars Program, LLM
Health Law, LLM
Intellectual Property and Information Law, LLM
International Law, LLM
Taxation, LLM

Howard
International Law (for international lawyers), LLM

Illinois
General, JSD; LLM

Indiana-Bloomington
As Approved, LLM; PhD
Comparative Law, MCL
Research, SJD

Indiana-Indianapolis
American Law (for international lawyers), LLM
General, SJD

Inter American
Litigation and Dispute Resolution, LLM

Iowa
International and Comparative Law, LLM

John Marshall (Chicago)
Comparative Legal Studies, LLM
Employee Benefits, LLM; MS
Estate Planning, LLM
Global Legal Studies, LLM; MS
Information Technology Law, LLM; MS

Intellectual Property, LLM; MS
International Business and Trade Law, LLM
Real Estate, LLM
Taxation, LLM; MS
Trial Advocacy, LLM

Judge Advocate General's School
Military Law, LLM

Kansas
Elder Law, LLM
General, SJD

Lewis & Clark
Environmental/Natural Resources, LLM

Louisiana State
As Approved, LLM; DCL

Loyola-Chicago
Appellate Advocacy, LLM
Business Law, LLM; MJ
Child and Family Law, LLM; MJ
Health Law and Policy, LLM; MJ; SJD
Rule of Law, LLM
Taxation, LLM

Loyola Marymount
American and International Legal Practice, LLM
General, LLM
Taxation, LLM

Loyola-New Orleans
US Law, LLM

Marquette
Sports Law (for international lawyers), LLM

Maryland
General, LLM

Miami
Comparative Law, LLM
Estate Planning, LLM
Inter-American Law, LLM
International Law, LLM
Ocean and Coastal Law, LLM
Real Property, Land Development and Finance, LLM
Taxation, LLM

Michigan
As Approved, LLM; MCL; SJD
International Tax, LLM

Michigan State
American Legal System (for international lawyers), LLM
Global Food Law, LLM; MJ
Intellectual Property and Communications, LLM; MJ

Minnesota
American Law (for international lawyers), LLM

Mississippi College
American Legal Studies (for international lawyers), LLM

Missouri
Dispute Resolution, LLM

Missouri-Kansas City
Estate Planning, LLM
General, LLM
Taxation, LLM
Urban Affairs, LLM

Nebraska
Online Executive Program in Space, Cyber and
Telecommunications, LLM
Space and Telecommunications, LLM

New England
US Law (for international lawyers), LLM

New Hampshire
Commerce and Technology, LLM
Intellectual Property, Commerce and Technology Law, LLM
International Criminal Law and Justice, LLM; MAS

New York Law
American Business Law, LLM
Financial Services, LLM
Mental Disability Law, MS
Real Estate Law, LLM
Taxation, LLM

New York Univ
Corporate Law, LLM
Environmental Law, LLM
General, LLM
Global Business, LLM
International Business Regulation, Litigation & Arbitration, LLM
International Legal Studies, LLM
International Taxation, LLM
Labor and Employment Law, LLM
Legal Theory, LLM
Taxation, LLM

North Carolina
US Law (for international lawyers), LLM

Northeastern
General, LLM

Northwestern
As Approved, LLM; MSL; SJD
General, LLM
Taxation, LLM

Notre Dame
International and Comparative Law, LLM
International Human Rights, LLM; SJD

Nova Southeastern
Education Law, MSL
Employment Law, MSL
Health Law, MSL

Ohio Northern
Democratic Governance and Rule of Law, LLM

Ohio State
General, LLM; MSL

Oklahoma
Energy, National Resources and Indigenous Peoples, LLM
Oregon
Conflict and Dispute Resolution, MA
Environmental and Natural Resources Law, LLM

Pace
Comparative Law (for international lawyers), LLM
Environmental Law, LLM; SJD
Real Estate Law, LLM

Pacific, McGeorge
Experiential Law Teaching, LLM
International Water Resources Law, JSD; LLM
Public Law and Policy, LLM
Transnational Business Practice, LLM
US Law and Policy (for international lawyers), LLM
US Law and Policy (public law and policy), LLM

Pennsylvania
As Approved, LLM; MCL; SJD

Pennsylvania State
Comparative Law, LLM

Pepperdine
Dispute Resolution, LLM; MDR

Pittsburgh
As Approved, JSD
General, LLM

Puerto Rico
International Law, LLM

Quinnipiac
Health Law, LLM

Regent
American Legal Studies (for international lawyers), LLM

St. John's
Bankruptcy Law, LLM
US Law (for international lawyers), LLM

Saint Louis
American Law (for international lawyers), LLM
Health Law, LLM

St. Mary's
American Legal Studies (for international lawyers), LLM
International and Comparative Law, LLM

St. Thomas (Florida)
Environmental Sustainability, LLM
Intercultural Human Rights, JSD; LLM

Samford
Business and Corporate Law, LLM
Comparative Law, LLM
General, LLM
International Law, LLM
Law, Religion, and Culture, LLM; SJD
Taxation, LLM

San Diego
Advanced Legal Studies, MS
Business and Corporate Law, LLM
Comparative Law (for international lawyers), LLM
General, LLM
International Law, LLM
Taxation, LLM

San Francisco
Intellectual Property and Technology Law, LLM
International Transactions and Comparative Law (for international lawyers), LLM

Santa Clara
Intellectual Property Law, LLM
International and Comparative Law, LLM
US Law (for international lawyers), LLM

Seattle
American Legal Studies, LLM

Seton Hall
Health Law, LLM
Intellectual Property, LLM

SMU Dedman
Comparative and International Law, LLM
General, LLM; SJD
Taxation, LLM

Southern California
Comparative Law, MCL
General (for international lawyers), LLM
Taxation, LLM

Southern Illinois
General, LLM; MLS
Health Law, LLM; MLS

Southwestern
Entertainment and Media Law, LLM
General, LLM

Stanford
As Approved, JSD; JSM; MLS
Corporate Governance and Practice, LLM
International Economic Law, Business & Policy, LLM
Law, Science and Technology, LLM

Stetson
Elder Law, LLM
International Law, LLM

Suffolk
General, JSD; LLM
Global Law and Technology, LLM
US and Global Business Law (for international lawyers), LLM

Syracuse
General (for international lawyers), LLM

Temple
American Law (for international lawyers), LLM
General, LLM
Juridical Science, SJD
Taxation, LLM
Transnational Law, LLM
Trial Advocacy, LLM

Texas
General, LLM

Texas Tech
US Legal Studies, LLM

Thomas M. Cooley
Corporate Law and Finance, LLM
General, LLM
Insurance Law, LLM
Intellectual Property, LLM
Taxation, LLM
US Legal Studies (for international lawyers), LLM

Thomas Jefferson
American Legal Studies, LLM
General, JSD
International Taxation and Financial Services, JSD; JSM; LLM; MJS
International Trade and Financial Services, LLM

Toledo
General, MSL

Touro
American Legal Studies (for international lawyers), LLM
General, LLM

Tulane
Admiralty, LLM
American Business Law, LLM
Comparative Law, MCL
Comparative Law and Latin American Studies, MCL
Energy and Environment, LLM
General, LLM; PhD; SJD
International and Comparative Law, LLM

Tulsa
American Indian and Indigenous Law, LLM; MJ
American Law (for international lawyers), LLM

Utah
Environmental and Natural Resources, LLM

Valparaiso
General, LLM

Vanderbilt
As Approved, LLM

Vermont
American Legal Studies, LLM
Environmental Law and Policy, LLM; MELP; MSEL

Villanova
Taxation, LLM

Virginia
General, LLM; SJD

Wake Forest
American Law (for international lawyers), LLM
General, SJD

Washington
Asian and Comparative Law, LLM; PhD
Health Law, LLM
Intellectual Property and Policy Law, LLM
Sustainable International Development, LLM
Taxation, LLM

Washington and Lee
US Law, LLM

Washington University
Intellectual Property and Technology Law, LLM
Juridical Studies, MJS
Research, JSD
Taxation, LLM
US Law (for international lawyers), LLM

Wayne State
Corporate and Finance, LLM
Labor Law, LLM
Taxation, LLM

Western New England
Estate Planning and Elder Law, LLM

Whittier
US Legal Studies (for international lawyers), LLM

Widener
Corporate and Business Law, DL; MJ; SJD
Corporate Law and Finance, LLM
Health Law, DL; LLM; MJ; SJD

Willamette
Transnational Law, LLM

William & Mary
American Legal System (for international lawyers), LLM

William Mitchell
General (for international lawyers), LLM

Wisconsin
As Approved, LLM; MLI; SJD
Legal Institutions, LLM

Yale
General, JSD; LLM; MSL

POST-JD AND NON-JD PROGRAMS BY CATEGORY

Admiralty/Marine Affairs/Ocean and Coastal
Miami, LLM
Tulane, LLM

Advanced Legal Studies
Albany, LLM; MS
Arizona State, MLS
San Diego, MS

Agriculture and Food Law
Arkansas (Fayetteville), LLM

American Law
Boston, LLM
Brigham Young, LLM
Brooklyn, LLM

Denver, LLM
Duquesne, LLM
Florida State, LLM
Indiana-Indianapolis, LLM
Minnesota, LLM
Saint Louis, LLM
Temple, LLM
Tulsa, LLM
Wake Forest, LLM

American Legal Studies
Hofstra, LLM
Mississippi College, LLM
Regent, LLM
St. Mary's, LLM
Seattle, LLM
Texas Tech, LLM
Thomas Jefferson, LLM
Touro, LLM
Vermont, LLM

American Legal System
Cincinnati, LLM
Michigan State, LLM
William & Mary, LLM

Animal Law
Lewis & Clark, LLM

Appellate Advocacy
Loyola-Chicago, LLM

As Approved
California-Los Angeles, LLM; SJD
Georgetown, SJD
Indiana-Bloomington, LLM; PhD
Louisiana State, LLM; DCL
Michigan, LLM; MCL; SJD
Northwestern, LLM; MSL; SJD
Pennsylvania, LLM; MCL; SJD
Pittsburgh, JSD
Stanford, JSD; JSM; MLS
Vanderbilt, LLM
Wisconsin, LLM; MLI; SJD

Asian and Comparative Law
Washington, LLM; PhD

Banking and Finance Law
Boston, LLM
Fordham, LLM
Thomas M. Cooley, LLM
Wayne State, LLM
Widener, LLM

Bankruptcy Law
St. John's, LLM

Biotechnology and Genomics
Arizona State, LLM

Business Law
California-Los Angeles, LLM
Capital, LLM
George Washington, LLM
Loyola-Chicago, LLM; MJ
New York Law, LLM
Samford, LLM
San Diego, LLM

Suffolk, LLM
Tulane, LLM
Widener, DL; MJ; SJD

Child and Family Law
Chicago-Kent, LLM
Hofstra, LLM
Loyola-Chicago, LLM; MJ

Commerce and Technology
New Hampshire, LLM

Communications Law
Catholic, LLM
Michigan State, LLM; MJ

Comparative Law/Comparative Legal Studies/Comparative Legal Thought
Alabama, LLM
California Western, LLM; MCL
Cardozo, LLM
Denver, LLM
Florida, LLM
Fordham, LLM
George Washington, LLM
Indiana-Bloomington, MCL
Iowa, LLM
John Marshall (Chicago), LLM
Miami, LLM
Notre Dame, LLM
Pace, LLM
Pennsylvania State, LLM
St. Mary's, LLM
Samford, LLM
San Diego, LLM
San Francisco, LLM
Santa Clara, LLM
SMU Dedman, LLM
Southern California, MCL
Tulane, MCL

Corporate Law/Corporate Governance
New York Univ, LLM
Samford, LLM
San Diego, LLM
Stanford, LLM
Thomas M. Cooley, LLM
Wayne State, LLM
Widener, DL; LLM; MJ; SJD

Criminal Law
Buffalo, LLM
Case Western, LLM
New Hampshire (international criminal law), LLM; MAS

Democratic Governance
Ohio Northern, LLM

Dispute Resolution
Cardozo, LLM
George Washington, LLM
John Marshall (Chicago), LLM
Missouri, LLM
Oregon, MA
Pepperdine, LLM; MDR

Economic Law
George Mason, LLM
Georgetown, LLM
Stanford, LLM

Education Law
Nova Southeastern, MSL

Elder Law
Kansas, LLM
Stetson, LLM
Western New England, LLM

Employee Benefits
John Marshall (Chicago), LLM; MS

Energy/Environment/Natural Resources
Denver, LLM; MRLS
Florida, LLM
Florida State, LLM
George Washington, LLM
Golden Gate, LLM
Houston, LLM
Lewis & Clark, LLM
New York Univ, LLM
Oklahoma, LLM
Oregon, LLM
Pace, LLM; SJD
Pacific, McGeorge, JSD; LLM
St. Thomas (Florida), LLM
Tulane, LLM
Utah, LLM
Vermont, LLM; MELP; MSEL

Entertainment and Media Law
California-Los Angeles, LLM
Southwestern, LLM

Entrepreneurship and Law
Duke, LLM

Estate Planning
John Marshall (Chicago), LLM
Miami, LLM
Missouri-Kansas City, LLM
Western New England, LLM

Experiential Law Teaching
Pacific, McGeorge, LLM

Financial Services Law
Chicago-Kent, LLM
New York Law, LLM
Thomas Jefferson, JSD; JSM; LLM

Foreign Scholars Program
Houston, LLM

General
Alabama, LLM
American, SJD
Boston College, LLM
Buffalo, LLM
California-Berkeley, JSD; LLM
California-Hastings, MS
Cardozo, LLM
Chapman, LLM
Chicago, DCL; JSD; LLM; MCL
Cleveland State, LLM

Colorado, LLM
Columbia, JSD; LLM
Cornell, JSD; LLM
District of Columbia, LLM
Drake, LLM; MJ
Emory, LLM; SJD
Florida International, LLM
Fordham, JSD; LLM
George Washington, LLM; SJD
Georgetown, LLM; MSL
Georgia, LLM
Hamline, LLM
Harvard, LLM; SJD
Hawaii, LLM
Illinois, JSD; LLM
Indiana-Indianapolis, SJD
Kansas, SJD
Loyola Marymount, LLM
Maryland, LLM
Missouri-Kansas City, LLM
New York Univ, LLM
Northeastern, LLM
Northwestern, LLM
Ohio State, LLM; MSL
Pittsburgh, LLM
Samford, LLM
San Diego, LLM
SMU Dedman, LLM; SJD
Southern California, LLM
Southern Illinois, LLM; MLS
Southwestern, LLM
Suffolk, JSD; LLM
Syracuse, LLM
Temple, LLM
Texas, LLM
Thomas M. Cooley, LLM
Thomas Jefferson, JSD
Toledo, MSL
Touro, LLM
Tulane, LLM; PhD; SJD
Valparaiso, LLM
Virginia, LLM; SJD
Wake Forest, SJD
William Mitchell, LLM
Yale, JSD; LLM; MSL

Global Food Law
Michigan State, LLM; MJ

Global Legal Studies
Case Western, LLM
John Marshall (Chicago), LLM; MS

Government/Public Policy/Law and Government
Albany, LLM
American, LLM
Creighton, MS
George Washington, LLM
Pacific, McGeorge, LLM

Health Law
Albany, LLM
California Western, MAS
DePaul, LLM
Drake, LLM; MJ
Georgetown, LLM
Houston, LLM
Loyola-Chicago, LLM; MJ; SJD
Nova Southeastern, MSL

Quinnipiac, LLM
Saint Louis, LLM
Seton Hall, LLM
Southern Illinois, LLM; MLS
Washington, LLM
Widener, DL; LLM; MJ; SJD

Human Rights
Notre Dame, LLM; SJD
St. Thomas (Florida), JSD; LLM

Indigenous Law
Arizona, LLM; SJD
Oklahoma, LLM
Tulsa, LLM

Information Technology
Fordham, LLM
John Marshall (Chicago), LLM; MS

Insurance Law
Connecticut, LLM
Thomas M. Cooley, LLM

Intellectual Property
Akron, LLM
Albany, LLM
Boston, LLM
Cardozo, LLM
Case Western, LLM
Chicago-Kent, LLM
Dayton, LLM; MSL
DePaul, LLM
Drake, LLM; MJ
Fordham, LLM
George Mason, LLM
George Washington, LLM
Golden Gate, LLM
Houston, LLM
John Marshall (Chicago), LLM; MS
Michigan State, LLM; MJ
New Hampshire, LLM
San Francisco, LLM
Santa Clara, LLM
Seton Hall, LLM
Thomas M. Cooley, LLM
Washington, LLM
Washington University, LLM

Inter-American Law
Miami, LLM

International Business and Trade Law/Economic Law
Arizona, LLM; SJD
Boston, LLM
Case Western, LLM
Fordham, LLM
Georgetown, LLM
John Marshall (Chicago), LLM
New York Univ, LLM
Pacific, McGeorge, LLM
San Francisco, LLM
Stanford, LLM
Suffolk, LLM
Thomas Jefferson, LLM

International Law/International Legal Studies/Comparative Law/Transnational Law
Albany, LLM
American, LLM
Case Western, LLM
Chicago-Kent, LLM
DePaul, LLM
Fordham, LLM
George Washington, LLM
Georgetown, LLM
Golden Gate, LLM; SJD
Hofstra, LLM
Houston, LLM
Howard, LLM
Iowa, LLM
John Marshall (Chicago), LLM
Loyola Marymount, LLM
Miami, LLM
New York Univ, LLM
Notre Dame, LLM
Puerto Rico, LLM
St. Mary's, LLM
Samford, LLM
San Diego, LLM
San Francisco, LLM
Santa Clara, LLM
SMU Dedman, LLM
Stetson, LLM
Temple, LLM
Tulane, LLM
Willamette, LLM

International Taxation
Florida, LLM
Michigan, LLM
New York Univ, LLM
Thomas Jefferson, JSD; JSM; LLM

Juridical Studies
California-Los Angeles, SJD
Duke, LLM
Temple, SJD
Washington University, MJS

Labor and Employment Law
Atlanta's John Marshall, LLM
New York Univ, LLM
Nova Southeastern, MSL
Wayne State, LLM

Latin American Studies/Comparative Law
Tulane, MCL

Legal Institutions
Wisconsin, LLM

Legal Theory
New York Univ, LLM

Litigation/Trial Advocacy
American, LLM
California Western, LLM
Emory, LLM
George Washington, LLM
Inter American, LLM
John Marshall (Chicago), LLM
Temple, LLM

Mental Disability Law
New York Law, MS

Military Law
Judge Advocate General's School, LLM

National Security Law
Catholic, LLM
George Washington, LLM
Georgetown, LLM

Prosecutorial Science
Chapman, LLM

Real Estate/Land Development
John Marshall (Chicago), LLM
Miami, LLM
New York Law, LLM
Pace, LLM

Religion and Culture
Samford, LLM; SJD

Research
Duke, SJD
Indiana-Bloomington, SJD
Washington University, JSD

Rule of Law
Loyola-Chicago, LLM

Science and Technology
Stanford, LLM

Science of Law
Chicago-Kent, LLM

Securities and Financial Regulation
Georgetown, LLM

Space and Telecommunications
Nebraska, LLM

Sports Law
Marquette (for international lawyers), LLM

Sustainable International Development
Washington, LLM

Taxation
Alabama, LLM
Baltimore, LLM
Boston, LLM
Capital, LLM; MT
Chapman, LLM
Chicago-Kent, LLM
Denver, LLM
DePaul, LLM
Emory, LLM
Florida, LLM; SJD
Georgetown, LLM
Golden Gate, LLM
Houston, LLM
John Marshall (Chicago), LLM; MS
Loyola-Chicago, LLM
Loyola Marymount, LLM
Miami, LLM
Missouri-Kansas City, LLM
New York Law, LLM

New York Univ, LLM
Northwestern, LLM
Samford, LLM
San Diego, LLM
SMU Dedman, LLM
Southern California, LLM
Temple, LLM
Thomas M. Cooley, LLM
Villanova, LLM
Washington, LLM
Washington University, LLM
Wayne State, LLM

Tribal Policy, Law, and Government
Arizona State, LLM

Urban Affairs/Urban Studies
Missouri-Kansas City, LLM

US Law/US Legal System
Baltimore, LLM
California-Davis, LLM
California-Hastings, LLM
Cincinnati, LLM
Connecticut, LLM
Duke, LLM; SJD
Florida Coastal, LLM
Fordham, LLM
Golden Gate, LLM
Loyola-New Orleans, LLM
New England, LLM
North Carolina, LLM
St. John's, LLM
Santa Clara, LLM
Texas Tech, LLM
Thomas M. Cooley, LLM
Washington and Lee, LLM
Washington University, LLM
Whittier, LLM

A NOTE TO GRADUATES OF LAW SCHOOLS LOCATED OUTSIDE THE UNITED STATES

Degrees Other Than a JD and Bar Admission

In order to obtain a license to practice law in the United States, all candidates must apply for bar admission through a state board of bar examiners. Although this board is ordinarily an agency of the highest court in the jurisdiction, occasionally the board is connected to the state's bar association. The criteria for eligibility to take the bar examination or to otherwise qualify for bar admission are set by each state, not by the ABA or the Council of the Section of Legal Education and Admissions to the Bar.

In order to sit for the bar examination, most states require an applicant to hold a Juris Doctor (JD) degree from a law school that meets established educational standards. A JD earned at an ABA-approved law school meets the educational requirements in every jurisdiction in the United States. For those individuals who have not earned a JD degree from an ABA-approved law school, bar admission authorities have developed varying requirements and criteria to ascertain if such individuals meet the minimum educational requirements for bar admission. In most jurisdictions, individuals who lack such a JD will find that they do not satisfy the minimum educational requirements for bar admission and are ineligible to take the bar exam. In some of the remaining states, graduates of foreign law schools will find that additional schooling such as an LLM is required, and a few others recognize with regularity the sufficiency of a specific foreign legal education. A number offer an alternative licensure mechanism known as a Foreign Legal Consultant, which is a limited license to practice. And finally, some jurisdictions will allow individuals to be eligible for admission without examination under certain conditions if they have been admitted to the bar in another US jurisdiction.

In the past few years, there has been a large increase in the number of graduates from schools located outside the United States enrolled in advanced degree programs (such as the LLM). Upon graduating, many of these individuals return to their home country without seeking or obtaining bar licensure in the United States. However, an increasing number of these individuals seek to be admitted to a state bar.

Unlike the JD degree bestowed by an ABA-approved law school, which carries the indicia that the holder of that degree has completed a course of study imparting standards entitling him or her to engage in the practice of law, advanced degree programs at ABA-approved law schools are not regulated and thus, are not "approved." As a result, such degrees vary in content and rigor. In other words, the American Bar Association does NOT accredit degrees of any kind other than the JD.

It is the position of the Council of the Section of Legal Education and Admissions to the Bar of the American Bar Association that no graduate degree in law (LLM, MCL, SJD, etc.) is or should be a substitute for the first professional degree in law (JD), and that no graduate degree should substitute for the JD in order to meet the legal education requirements for admission to the bar.

As a result of the variance in state bar admission rules, the ABA strongly encourages individuals to contact the state board of bar examiners in the state(s) in which they are interested in being admitted to ascertain its requirements to sit for the bar examination. Contact information for all the state board of bar examiners is available from the National Conference of Bar Examiners at www.ncbex.org and in the *Comprehensive Guide to Bar Admission Requirements*, which is available at the website above or through the ABA Service Center at 800.285.2221, Product Code: 529008712ED.

You may have questions concerning a variety of issues while you are applying to law school, once you are in law school, and even after you have your degree.

The following organizations may provide you with the answers you need.

American Association of Law Libraries (AALL)

The American Association of Law Libraries exists to provide leadership in the field of legal information, to foster the professional growth of law librarians, to develop the profession of law librarianship, and to enhance the value of law libraries to the legal community and to the public. AALL members come from all sizes and types of libraries: the Library of Congress, legislative libraries, academic law libraries, law firm libraries, bar association libraries, county law libraries, court libraries, and law libraries in business and industry. The association publishes a quarterly journal (*Law Library Journal*), a monthly magazine (*AALL Spectrum*), and an annual directory, which includes a listing of minority law librarians.

For more information, contact:

American Association of Law Libraries
105 W. Adams Street, Suite 3300
Chicago, IL 60603
Phone: 312.939.4764
www.aallnet.org

American Bar Association (ABA)

With nearly 400,000 members, including more than 40,000 law student members, the American Bar Association is the largest voluntary professional membership organization in the world. As the national voice of the legal profession, the ABA works to improve the administration of justice; promotes programs that assist lawyers and judges in their work; accredits law schools; promotes competence, ethical conduct, and professionalism; provides continuing legal education; and works to build public understanding around the world of the importance of the rule of law.

The ABA's Section of Legal Education and Admissions to the Bar advances effective legal education to serve society, the legal profession, law students, and legal academia, helping legal education through a wide range of resources and activities. To assure effective legal education, the Section provides a fair and efficient law school accreditation system. The Council and the Accreditation Committee of the Section are identified by the US Department of Education as the nationally recognized accrediting agency for professional schools of law.

The ABA Commission on Disability Rights (CDR) provides a wide range of resources for students with disabilities interested in pursuing a career, as well as for law students with disabilities. CDR has a mentorship program that pairs prospective and current law students with disabilities with lawyers with disabilities. The commission also lists career opportunities for students with disabilities. CDR's directory of bar information for applicants with disabilities (BIAD) provides information from state, territorial, and federal jurisdictions that grant licenses to practice law regarding accommodations as well as character and fitness inquiries that relate to disabilities. This information and more can be found on the commission's website: www.americanbar.org/disabilityrights.

The ABA may be contacted for information on the accreditation of law schools and the role of lawyers in the legal profession:

American Bar Association
Section of Legal Education and Admissions to the Bar
321 North Clark Street
Chicago, IL 60654-7598
Phone: 312.988.6738
www.americanbar.org/legaled

Association of American Law Schools (AALS)

The AALS is a nonprofit educational association of 176 law schools representing over 10,000 law faculty in the United States. The purpose of the association is "the improvement of the legal profession through legal education." This goal is furthered in a number of ways, including professional development programs for law professors and administrators, and a membership process that is designed to further the core values of the association. The AALS core values relate to the importance of faculty governance; scholarship, academic freedom, and diversity of viewpoints; a rigorous academic program built upon strong teaching; diversity and nondiscrimination; and the selection of students based upon intellectual ability and personal potential for success.

The AALS serves as the academic society for law teachers with an Annual Meeting that constitutes the largest gathering of law faculty in the world. The AALS is legal education's principal representative to the federal government and to other national higher education organizations and learned societies. The AALS also encourages collaboration with law professors on a global level, and has provided seed funding and continuing staff support for the International Association of Law Schools, an independent organization created with the help and encouragement of the AALS.

The AALS may be contacted for specific information about the role of legal education in the profession:

Association of American Law Schools
1201 Connecticut Avenue, NW
Suite 800
Washington, DC 20036-2717
Phone: 202.296.8851
www.aals.org

HEATH Resource Center

The HEATH Resource Center at the National Youth Transitions Center is an online clearinghouse dissemination center that presents new transition resources to assist youth with disabilities in reaching their full potential through postsecondary education and training. The HSC Foundation has partnered with The George Washington University to expand the content of the HEATH Resource Center and to designate it as the official site, The HSC Foundation's National Youth Transitions Center. The partnership's mission is to gather, develop, and disseminate information in the form of resource papers, fact sheets, directories, newsletters, and website materials to help people with disabilities reach their full potential through postsecondary education and training. Questions can be submitted to askheath@gwu.edu. Publications and resources are free to access and download. HEATH offers RSS subscriptions as well as Facebook and Twitter feeds.

For more information:

HEATH Resource Center at the National Youth
    Transitions Center
2134 G Street, N.W.
Washington, DC 20052-0001
www.heath.gwu.edu
Phone service not available.

Law School Admission Council

The Law School Admission Council (LSAC) is a nonprofit corporation that provides unique, state-of-the-art products and services to ease the admission process for law schools and their applicants worldwide. More than 200 law schools in the United States, Canada, and Australia are members of the Council and benefit from LSAC's services. All law schools approved by the American Bar Association are LSAC members, as are Canadian law schools recognized by a provincial or territorial law society or government agency. Many nonmember law schools also take advantage of LSAC's services. For all users, LSAC strives to provide the highest quality of products, services, and customer service.

Founded in 1947, the Council is best known for administering the Law School Admission Test (LSAT), with over 150,000 tests administered annually at testing centers worldwide. LSAC also processes academic credentials for an average of 85,000 law school applicants annually, provides essential software and information for admission offices and applicants, conducts educational conferences for law school professionals and prelaw advisors, sponsors and publishes research, funds diversity and other outreach grant programs, and publishes LSAT preparation books and law school guides, among many other services.

LSAC does not engage in assessing an applicant's chances for admission to any law school; all admission decisions are made by individual law schools.

For more information on the LSAT, the Credential Assembly Service, and law school admission, contact:

Law School Admission Council
662 Penn Street
PO Box 2000
Newtown PA 18940-0998
Phone: 215.968.1001
LSAC.org

For information on minority opportunities in law, contact:

Law School Admission Council
Diversity Initiatives
662 Penn Street
Newtown PA 18940-0040
Phone: 215.968.1338
LSAC.org

NALP—The Association for Legal Career Professionals

NALP is a professional association of law schools and legal employers dedicated to continuously improving career counseling and planning, recruitment and retention, and the professional development of law students, lawyers, and its members. NALP's vision is to drive innovation and collaboration in the legal profession through lifelong education and career development. NALP's mission is to connect its members by providing vision, expertise, research, and education; to cultivate fair and ethical practices; and to advocate for diversity and inclusion in the legal profession.

NALP offers information and resources related to law careers through its website and online bookstore at www.nalp.org. In addition, NALP publishes an online directory of legal employers and their hiring criteria at www.nalpdirectory.com and also an online directory of Canadian legal employers at www.nalpcanada.com. It also offers an extensive database of public opportunities for law students and lawyers through www.pslawnet.org (PSLaw Net, NALP's public service law network).

NALP is not an employment agency and does not offer placement or career counseling services. NALP believes that each law school offers unique programs and opportunities and, like the American Bar Association and the Law School Admission Council, does not rank law schools or career services offices. The NALP Directory of Law Schools, which summarizes information relevant to recruiters, is published online at www.nalplawschoolsonline.org.

For further information, contact:

NALP
1220 19th Street, NW
Suite 401
Washington, DC 20036-2405
Phone: 202.835.1001
www.nalp.org

APPENDIX D: CANADIAN LSAC-MEMBER LAW SCHOOLS

University of Alberta Faculty of Law
Admissions Office, Room 128
Edmonton, Alberta
CANADA T6G 2H5

University of British Columbia Faculty of Law
1822 East Mall
Vancouver, British Columbia
CANADA V6T 1Z1

University of Calgary Faculty of Law
Murray Fraser Hall
Calgary, Alberta
CANADA T2N 1N4

Dalhousie University Schulich School of Law
6061 University Avenue
Halifax, Nova Scotia
CANADA B3H 4H9

University of Manitoba Faculty of Law
303 Robson Hall, 224 Dysart Road
Winnipeg, Manitoba
CANADA R3T 2N2

McGill University Faculty of Law
3644 Peel Street
Montreal, Quebec
CANADA H3A 1W9

University of New Brunswick Faculty of Law
PO Box 44271
Fredericton, New Brunswick
CANADA E3B 6C2

Osgoode Hall Law School, York University
4700 Keele Street
Toronto, Ontario
CANADA M3J 1P3

University of Ottawa Faculty of Law
57 Louis Pasteur
Ottawa, Ontario
CANADA K1N 6N5

Queen's University Faculty of Law
Admissions Office, Room 200
Macdonald Hall
128 Union Street
Kingston, Ontario
CANADA K7L 3N6

University of Saskatchewan College of Law
Admissions Committee
15 Campus Drive
Saskatoon, Saskatchewan
CANADA S7N 5A6

Thompson Rivers University
Faculty of Law, HL 250
2nd Floor in the House of Learning
900 McGill Road
Kamloops, British Columbia
CANADA V2C 0C8

University of Toronto Faculty of Law
78 Queen's Park
Toronto, Ontario
CANADA M5S 2C5

University of Victoria Faculty of Law
PO Box 2400, STN CSC
Victoria, British Columbia
CANADA V8W 3H7

Western University, Canada
Josephine-Spencer Niblett Building
London, Ontario
CANADA N6A 3K7

University of Windsor Faculty of Law
401 Sunset Avenue
Windsor, Ontario
CANADA N9B 3P4

Publications Available from the ABA's Section of Legal Education & Admissions to the Bar

THE OFFICIAL GUIDE TO ABA-APPROVED LAW SCHOOLS, 2013 EDITION

A comprehensive guide to all ABA-approved law schools as well as legal education statistics, LLM programs, and the law school accreditation process.

Product Code: 529008513ED, Price: $26

2011–2012 ABA STANDARDS AND RULES OF PROCEDURE FOR APPROVAL OF LAW SCHOOLS

The current criteria that law schools must meet to obtain or retain ABA approval and to establish foreign study programs.

Product Code: 529008411ED, Price: $15

COMPREHENSIVE GUIDE TO BAR ADMISSION REQUIREMENTS, 2012 EDITION

Published annually in conjunction with the National Conference of Bar Examiners, the Guide sets out the rules and practices of all US jurisdictions for admission to the bar and on motion.

Product Code: 529008712ED, Price: $15

BEST PRACTICES REPORT ON THE USE OF ADJUNCT FACULTY

Published in 2011, the report presents current practice across legal academia in the hiring, retention, training, and supervision of adjunct faculty.

Product Code: 5290102, Price: $24.95

ADJUNCT FACULTY HANDBOOK

The Handbook covers a variety of topics on working with adjunct faculty including administration, orientation, and means of communication with adjunct faculty.

Available for free download at www.americanbar.org/legaled

SOURCEBOOK ON LEGAL WRITING PROGRAMS

The Sourcebook is a primary reference for faculty who design, direct, and teach in legal writing programs.

Product Code: 529009106ED, Price: $19

LEGAL EDUCATION AND PROFESSIONAL DEVELOPMENT: AN EDUCATIONAL CONTINUUM ("MACCRATE REPORT")

A comprehensive analysis of the role of law schools and the practicing bar in developing lawyering skills and values with recommendations for long-term change.

Product Code: 5290052, Price: $10

2010–2011 ANNUAL REPORT OF THE CONSULTANT ON LEGAL EDUCATION TO THE ABA

An overview of the events and activities of the Section of Legal Education and Admissions to the Bar during the previous association year.

Product Code: 52900891011, Price: $10

A SURVEY OF LAW SCHOOL CURRICULA— 2002–2010

This survey continues in the tradition of the 2002 Survey. It is a comprehensive empirical review of significant aspects of current law school curricula, but additionally, the 2010 Survey employs baseline results from the 2002 Survey to track curricular trends and changes since 2002.

Product Code: 5290104, Price: $49.95

A Survey of Law School Curricula: 1992–2002 is available as a free download on the Publications page of the Section's website: www.ambar.org/legaled.

LAW SCHOOL FORUMS 2012
ADMISSION ADVICE
STRAIGHT FROM THE EXPERTS

If you're considering law school, come to a Law School Forum. Admission is free.

At the forums you can ...

- talk with representatives of LSAC-member law schools from across the United States, Canada, and Australia;

- attend workshops, including financing a legal education, the law school application process, a panel discussion on being a lawyer, forum insider tips, and an LSAT overview;

- attend a panel presentation for diverse applicants;

- obtain admission materials, catalogs, and financial aid information;

- review LSAC publications and LSAT preparation materials; and

- visit the prelaw advisors' table if you want general advice about the law school admission process.

To register, view workshop schedules, and get more information about the forums, visit LSAC.org/lawschoolforums.

Law School Admission Council
PO Box 40, Newtown PA 18940-0040
P: 215.968.1001

Chicago, IL
Saturday, July 14, 2012
Palmer House Hilton

Bay Area, CA
Saturday, July 21, 2012
Oakland Marriott City Center

Atlanta, GA
Saturday, September 8, 2012
Atlanta Marriott Marquis

Miami, FL
Saturday, September 15, 2012
Hyatt Regency Miami

Houston, TX
Saturday, September 29, 2012
JW Marriott Houston

New York, NY
Friday, October 12, 2012
Saturday, October 13, 2012
Hilton New York

Canada (Toronto, ON)
Friday, October 26, 2012
Fairmont Royal York

Los Angeles, CA
Saturday, November 10, 2012
Millennium Biltmore Hotel

Boston, MA
Saturday, November 17, 2012
Renaissance Boston Waterfront